RESEARCH HANDBOOK ON LAW AND MARXISM

RESEARCH HANDBOOKS IN LEGAL THEORY

Research Handbooks in Legal Theory are designed to provide original and sophisticated discussions from an international and expert range of contributors. The volumes in this important series cover key topics within the field as well as major schools of thought, and also explore the application of legal theory to different areas of law. Comprising specially commissioned chapters from leading academics each *Research Handbook* brings together cutting-edge ideas and thought-provoking contributions and is written with a wide readership in mind. Equally useful as reference tools or high-level introductions to specific topics, issues, methods and debates, these *Research Handbooks* will be an essential resource for academic researchers and postgraduate students.

Titles in this series include:

Research Handbook on Feminist Jurisprudence
Edited by Robin West and Cynthia Grant Bowman

Research Handbook on Critical Legal Theory
Edited by Emilios Christodoulidis, Ruth Dukes and Marco Goldoni

Research Handbook on Natural Law Theory
Edited by Jonathan Crowe and Constance Youngwon Lee

Research Handbook on Private Law Theory
Edited by Hanoch Dagan and Benjamin C. Zipursky

Research Handbook on Modern Legal Realism
Edited by Shauhin Talesh, Elizabeth Mertz and Heinz Klug

Research Handbook on Law and Emotion
Edited by Susan A. Bandes, Jody Lyneé Madeira, Kathryn D. Temple and Emily Kidd White

Research Handbook on Law and Marxism
Edited by Paul O'Connell and Umut Özsu

Research Handbook on Law and Marxism

Edited by

Paul O'Connell

Reader in Law, School of Law, SOAS University of London, UK

Umut Özsu

Associate Professor of Law and Legal Studies, Department of Law and Legal Studies, Carleton University, Canada

RESEARCH HANDBOOKS IN LEGAL THEORY

Cheltenham, UK • Northampton, MA, USA

Published by
Edward Elgar Publishing Limited
The Lypiatts
15 Lansdown Road
Cheltenham
Glos GL50 2JA
UK

Edward Elgar Publishing, Inc.
William Pratt House
9 Dewey Court
Northampton
Massachusetts 01060
USA

A catalogue record for this book
is available from the British Library

Library of Congress Control Number: 2021947691

This book is available electronically in the **Elgar**online
Law subject collection
http://dx.doi.org/10.4337/9781788119863

ISBN 978 1 78811 985 6 (cased)
ISBN 978 1 78811 986 3 (eBook)

Printed and bound by CPI Group (UK) Ltd, Croydon, CR0 4YY

Contents

Contributors

Max Ajl, Postdoctoral Researcher, Department of Social Sciences, Rural Sociology Group, Wageningen University & Research

Rémi Bachand, Professor of Law, Université du Québec à Montréal

Miriam Bak McKenna, Lecturer in Law, Lund University

Clyde W Barrow, Professor of Political Science, University of Texas Rio Grande Valley

Enzo Bello, Associate Professor, Universidade Federal Fluminense, Rio de Janeiro

Bill Bowring, Professor of Law, Birkbeck, University of London

Honor Brabazon, Assistant Professor of Sociology and Legal Studies, St. Jerome's University in the University of Waterloo

Gustavo Capela, PhD Candidate in Anthropology, University of California, Berkeley

Cosmin Sebastian Cercel, Associate Professor of Law, University of Nottingham

BS Chimni, Distinguished Professor of International Law, OP Jindal Global University

Pablo Ciocchini, Lecturer in Criminology, University of Liverpool

Natalia Delgado, Lecturer in Law, University of Southampton

Matthew Dimick, Professor of Law, University of Buffalo

Radha D'Souza, Reader in Law, University of Westminster

Michael Head, Professor of Law, Western Sydney University

Nate Holdren, Associate Professor of Law, Politics, and Society, Drake University

Rob Hunter, Independent Scholar, PhD in Politics, Princeton University

Talina Hürzeler, Independent Scholar, LLB, University of New South Wales

Bob Jessop, Emeritus Professor of Sociology, University of Lancaster

Rene José Keller, Independent Scholar, PhD in Law, Universidade do Estado do Rio de Janeiro, and PhD in Social Work, Pontifícia Universidade Católica do Rio Grande do Sul

Rafael Khachaturian, Lecturer in Critical Writing, University of Pennsylvania

Stéfanie Khoury, Independent Scholar, PhD in Sociology of Law, Università degli Studi di Milano and Universidad del País Vasco

Dimitrios Kivotidis, Lecturer in Law, University of East London

Daniel McLoughlin, Senior Lecturer in Law, Society, and Criminology, University of New South Wales

Eva Nanopoulos, Senior Lecturer in Law, Queen Mary, University of London

August H Nimtz, Professor of Political Science and African American and African Studies, University of Minnesota

Paul O'Connell, Reader in Law, SOAS, University of London

Chris O'Kane, Assistant Professor of Political Science, University of Texas Rio Grande Valley

Umut Özsu, Associate Professor of Law and Legal Studies, Carleton University, Canada

Rebecca Schein, Associate Professor of Interdisciplinary Studies, Carleton University

Igor Shoikhedbrod, Assistant Professor of Political Science and Law, Justice, and Society, Dalhousie University

Nimer Sultany, Reader in Law, SOAS, University of London

Christine Sypnowich, Professor of Philosophy, Queen's University

Ahmed White, Professor of Law, University of Colorado at Boulder

1. Introduction to the *Research Handbook on Law and Marxism*

Paul O'Connell and Umut Özsu

Not long ago the world was divided, however tenuously and fractiously, between states that claimed to uphold Marx's ideas and states that opposed them openly and vehemently. With the demolition of the Berlin Wall, the dissolution of the Soviet Union, and the proliferation of grandiose declarations about the supposedly self-evident 'failure of the Marxist project',[1] Marx and Marxism were thought to have been interred once and for all. Yet as triumphalism about 'globalisation'—and the various 'counter-globalisation' movements it generated, in 'global North' and 'global South' alike—gave way to a period of recurring and pronounced capitalist crises, beginning with the 2007–9 'Great Recession', Marx's work gained greater currency, with increasing numbers of people studying the original texts, often for the first time. Far from being dead and buried, the demise of 'actually existing socialism' in eastern Europe—coupled with rising socio-economic inequality, planetary ecological degradation, new wars of imperialist aggression, and an international financial architecture that engenders sovereign defaults and currency crises by the minute—actually provided much of the spark needed to liberate Marxist thought and practice from many an inherited and ossified form. Just as 'a thousand Marxisms' emerged through the concrete struggles of workers, peasants, and activists, from Bolivia to Nepal,[2] work that engages directly with Marxist modes of critical analysis was produced across an extraordinarily wide range of scholarly disciplines.

This large-scale resurgence of interest in Marx and Marxism—a development paralleled by a similar resurgence of interest in other forms of radical politics, most notably anarchism—should come as no surprise. Inasmuch as social relations continue to be structured around the drive to produce and accumulate surplus value (and its appropriation by some at the expense of the many who labour to produce it), systematic critique of the capitalist mode of production remains unavoidable. After all, if Marxism is, as Terry Eagleton has put it, 'the most searching, rigorous, comprehensive' critique of capitalism yet undertaken, then 'as long as capitalism is still in business, Marxism must be as well'[3]—a view echoed by Daniel Bensaïd when he notes that so 'long as capital continues to dominate social relations, Marx's theory will retain its currency'.[4] In some quarters, it remains fashionable—and often politically or professionally rewarding—to claim that Marx and Marxism are mechanical and teleological, that Marxist analytical tools (e.g., surplus value, the value form, the capital relation, class struggle, ideology, materialist analysis of history, modes and relations of production) are irre-

---

[1]   Francis Fukuyama, *The End of History and the Last Man* (Free Press 1992) 293.

[2]   André Tosel, 'The Development of Marxism: From the End of Marxism-Leninism to a Thousand Marxisms—France–Italy, 1975–2005' in Jacques Bidet and Stathis Kouvelakis (eds), *Critical Companion to Contemporary Marxism* (Brill 2008) 39, 42.

[3]   Terry Eagleton, *Why Marx Was Right* (Yale University Press 2011) 2.

[4]   Daniel Bensaïd, *Marx For Our Times: Adventures and Misadventures of a Critique* (first published 1995, Gregory Elliot tr, Verso 2002) 1.

deemably Eurocentric, or even that a direct line can and should be drawn from *The Communist Manifesto* to Stalin's forced labour camps or Brezhnev's hyper-bureaucratic 'real socialism'. To the extent that relevant Marxist sources are marshalled in defence of such claims, they nearly always reflect exaggerated or plainly erroneous readings of the texts in question. The ongoing revival of interest in Marx and Marxism has already done much to undermine these caricatures, redirecting attention to the writings of Marx and those who have sought to build upon them.

It is often said that Marx never developed an integrated theory of the state, and that his observations about law and rights are fragmentary and scattered across a large number of writings. Such assessments are not unjustified; Marx's work, published and unpublished, offers no general theory of these topics on par with his critique of classical political economy. Yet Marx engaged closely with questions of law, rights, and the state, and he did so frequently, intensively, and with remarkable acuity. From a range of texts, many of which are discussed in this handbook, one need only consider Marx's early critique of Hegel's philosophy of law;[5] his argument about the fundamental insufficiency of civil and political rights in 'On the Jewish Question';[6] his spirited interventions in German debates about the customary rights of peasants to forage for wood;[7] his incisive class analysis of capitalist states and constitutional orders in 'The Eighteenth Brumaire of Louis Bonaparte' and 'The Civil War in France';[8] his lengthy and nuanced discussion of the Factory Acts in mid-nineteenth century Britain in chapters ten and fifteen of the first volume of *Capital*;[9] the central role of law in the account of 'primitive accumulation' and colonial capitalism he provides in this same book's eighth and final part;[10] and his trenchant critique of 'fair distribution' and social-democratic electoral strategy in 'The Critique of the Gotha Programme'.[11] Countless attempts have been made to develop specifically Marxist accounts of law on the basis of these and other textual sources, from Evgeny Pashukanis' 'commodity-form theory'[12] to debates about the 'relative autonomy' of law[13] to

[5]   See e.g., Karl Marx, 'Contribution to the Critique of Hegel's Philosophy of Law' [1843] in Karl Marx and Frederick Engels, *Collected Works*, vol 3 (Lawrence & Wishart 1975) 3.
[6]   Karl Marx, 'On the Jewish Question' [1844] in Karl Marx and Frederick Engels, *Collected Works*, vol 3 (Lawrence & Wishart 1975) 146.
[7]   Karl Marx, 'Proceedings of the Sixth Rhine Province Assembly. Third Article—Debates on the Law on Thefts of Wood' [1842] in Karl Marx and Frederick Engels, *Collected Works*, vol 1 (Lawrence & Wishart 1975) 224.
[8]   Karl Marx, 'The Eighteenth Brumaire of Louis Bonaparte' [1852] in Karl Marx and Frederick Engels, *Collected Works*, vol 11 (Lawrence & Wishart 1979) 99; Karl Marx, 'The Civil War in France: Address of the General Council of the International Working Men's Association' [1871] in Karl Marx and Frederick Engels, *Collected Works*, vol 22 (Lawrence & Wishart 1986) 307.
[9]   Karl Marx, *Capital: A Critique of Political Economy*, vol 1 (first published 1867, Ben Fowkes tr, Penguin 1990) chs 10, 15.
[10]   Marx, *Capital*, vol 1, chs 26–33.
[11]   Karl Marx, 'Critique of the Gotha Programme' [1875] in Karl Marx and Frederick Engels, *Collected Works*, vol 24 (Lawrence & Wishart 1989) 75.
[12]   Evgeny Pashukanis, 'The General Theory of Law and Marxism' [1924] in Evgeny Pashukanis, *Pashukanis: Selected Writings on Marxism and Law* (Piers Beirne and Robert Sharlet eds, Peter B Maggs tr, Academic Press 1980), 37.
[13]   Louis Althusser et al, *Reading* Capital*: The Complete Edition* (first published 1965, Ben Brewster and David Fernbach trs, Verso 2016); Nicos Poulantzas, *State, Power, Socialism* (Patrick Camiller tr, New Left Books 1978).

qualified defence of certain aspects of the liberal legal tradition.[14] Such approaches continue to influence a large number of contemporary debates on Marxist approaches to law, rights, and the state.

This handbook showcases and contributes to the development of these approaches. It is divided into three parts. Part I, consisting of ten chapters, offers new and critical interpretations of Marx and several key thinkers in the Marxist tradition. Clyde W Barrow opens this part of the handbook by exploring the role of legal and illegal tactics in Marx's work, and Marxist theory more generally. Daniel McLouglin and Talina Hürzeler follow with a discussion of Marx's analysis of class struggles around the Factory Acts in *Capital*. August H Nimtz reflects upon Marx's understanding of the relationship between capitalism and liberal democracy, while Cosmin Sebastian Cercel tackles Marx's important and often misunderstood statements on dictatorship. The handbook then turns to later figures in the Marxist tradition. Michael Head examines Lenin's views on law, before and after the October Revolution, as well as early Soviet debates about legality and legal change. Bill Bowring, for his part, discusses the thread of thinking on collective self-determination in Marx, Engels, and Lenin. Matthew Dimick explains and critically analyses Pashukanis' 'commodity-form theory' of law; Pablo Ciocchini and Stéfanie Khoury do the same for Antonio Gramsci's insights on the hegemonic role of law. Bob Jessop and Rafael Khachaturian conclude the handbook's first part with a pair of chapters on Nicos Poulantzas' theory of the capitalist state.

Part II also comprises ten chapters, each discussing a specific form of contemporary Marxist analysis of law. Rob Hunter and Nimer Sultany demonstrate the significance of Marxist analysis for questions of constitutional theory; Hunter theorises the constitutionalism of the capitalist state while Sultany examines Marx's engagement with constitutional issues. Nate Holdren's chapter concerns the continued importance of EP Thompson's views on law and moral economies. Chris O'Kane's chapter introduces a variety of different Frankfurt School critiques of the state. Miriam Bak McKenna provides an overview of social reproduction theory and other forms of Marxist feminism, drawing upon the work of Tithi Bhattacharya, Silvia Federici, Lise Vogel, and many others. Ahmed White undertakes a Marxist critique of labour law, and BS Chimni examines debates about law and development. Radha D'Souza and Rémi Bachand both focus on international law; D'Souza considers neocolonialism and international law, grappling with questions of competing disciplinary frameworks, while Bachand outlines the core elements of a Marxist account of the political economy of international law, partly via 'Social Structure of Accumulation Theory' and the 'École de la régulation'. Eva Nanopoulos concludes the handbook's middle section with an analysis of the class politics enshrined in the legal architecture of the European Union.

Finally, Part III, consisting of nine chapters, offers a series of studies in emergent fields of inquiry informed by Marxist critical tools and theories. Rebecca Schein leads things off with a discussion of changing modes of temporality under capitalism, particularly in light of increased reliance upon precarious 'gig-work'. Max Ajl cuts through current debates about 'green new deal' proposals, analysing the role of anti-imperialist and Indigenous peoples' struggles during the climate crisis. Enzo Bello, Gustavo Capela, and Rene José Keller rely on Louis Althusser and narrative analysis in their detailed case study of 'Operation Car Wash', a complex criminal investigation in Brazil that yields broader insights into bribery and corrup-

---

[14]   EP Thompson, *Whigs and Hunters: The Origin of the Black Act* (Pantheon Books 1975).

tion in contemporary capitalist states. Paul O'Connell then turns the discussion to the question of the relation between law and social change, arguing for a Marxist approach to law, rights, and the state that combines both critical and constructive elements to bolster movements for social change. Honor Brabazon broaches the same constellation of questions, contending that social change under neoliberal conditions requires social practices and forms of thought that go beyond traditional distinctions between 'reform' and 'revolution'. Igor Shoikhedbrod also writes about neoliberal social relations, but does so with a view to articulating a Marxist theory of law and the state that overcomes conventional formalist and instrumentalist approaches. Christine Sypnowich draws from the work of GA Cohen and revisits Cold War-era debates about socialism and the 'rule of law'. Natalia Delgado and Dimitrios Kivotidis bring the handbook to a close with a pair of chapters that explore some of the specifically methodological complexities of Marxist theories of law and the state.

In sum, this handbook demonstrates the subtlety and complexity of André Tosel's 'thousand Marxisms', and the richness of the Marxist tradition for informing critical engagement with law, rights, and state. Beyond the four corners of this handbook are a host of important debates about 'what may appropriately be called a legitimate Marxist interpretation' of the world today.[15] Those are worthwhile debates, and they are taken up by some of our contributors. But the chapters assembled here testify first and foremost to the diversity, multi-facetedness, and astonishing analytical power of Marxist critical tools. These tools are as indispensable as they have always been to understanding the role of law, rights, and the state in capitalist societies.

---

[15]   Tosel, 'Development of Marxism', 44.

PART I

MARX AND THE MARXIST TRADITION

2. Legal and illegal political tactics in Marxist political theory

Clyde W Barrow

INTRODUCTION

This chapter reviews the panoply of political tactics that were practiced or advocated by Marx, Engels, and their successors in order to draw two important distinctions that have often led to confusion in past debates about the use of legal and illegal political tactics. First, illegal tactics are not synonymous with violent tactics. In fact, most non-violent political tactics used by the working class have been deemed illegal by the state much of the time. Second, many political tactics considered legal today became legal because they were practiced when the tactics were illegal. Thus, the chapter argues that the tactical question of legality and illegality is histor-ically a constantly shifting line that cannot be defined *a priori* as a theoretical position. The question of legality and illegality therefore has always been a purely pragmatic decision about what tactics are most likely to achieve a specific strategic end at any particular point in time. Yet, by falsely elevating the problem of tactics to a theoretical level, Marxist political theory has been fractured into liberal democratic, democratic socialist, and revolutionary communist positions that now confront each other as mutually exclusive positions. On the other hand, Marx and Engels never saw these tactical positions as mutually exclusive theoretical options, but viewed them as complementary forms of political action along a spectrum of options, where tactical deployment was largely contingent on the state of the class struggle in particular times and places. Thus, Marx and Engels advocated and practiced both legal and illegal tactics during their lifetimes, including the use of physical force and violence to achieve the strategic goals of a socialist society.

THE QUESTION OF TACTICS

Most dictionaries define a tactic as 'an action or strategy carefully planned to achieve a spe-cific end'.[1] In the context of politics, Lenin defined tactics as a party's 'political conduct, or the character, the direction and methods of its political activity'.[2] The concept of tactics always refers to a course of action that is carefully planned for the purpose of reaching a clearly

---

[1] See e.g., OUP Lexico, 'Tactic', https://en.oxforddictionaries.com/definition/tactic accessed 7 April 2021. Cf Robert Knox, 'Strategy and Tactics' (2012) 21 *Finnish Yearbook of International Law* 193 (arguing that most Marxists fail to distinguish adequately between strategy (i.e., long-term goals) and tactics (i.e., immediate actions)). For a similar analysis see Paul Blackledge, 'On Strategy and Tactics: Marxism and Electoral Politics' (2019) 83 *Science & Society* 355.

[2] VI Lenin, 'Two Tactics of Social-Democracy in the Democratic Revolution' [1905] in VI Lenin, *Collected Works*, vol 9 (Progress Publishers 1962) 15, 22. See also VI Lenin, 'Letters on Tactics' [1917] in VI Lenin, *Collected Works*, vol 24 (Progress Publishers 1964) 42.

defined goal or strategic end. In Marxian political theory, the long-term strategic goal of political tactics was defined in *The Communist Manifesto* as the 'formation of the proletariat into a class, overthrow of the bourgeois supremacy, conquest of political power by the proletariat'.[3] The organisation of the proletariat as a class generates the political power necessary to overthrow the capitalist class and its state (democracy) and to establish itself as the ruling class (socialism) for the purpose of abolishing all classes (communism).

Marx and Engels argue that 'the first step in the revolution by the working class is to raise the proletariat to the position of ruling class, to win the battle of democracy'.[4] This principle was embraced by every important Marxist political theorist of the twentieth century. Eduard Bernstein, the originator of evolutionary socialism, argued that 'democracy is a condition of socialism' and he even claimed that 'there is actually no really liberal thought which does not also belong to the element of the ideas of socialism'.[5] Karl Kautsky, an authoritative proponent of orthodox Marxism after the death of Marx and Engels, concurred that '[s]ocialism without democracy is unthinkable'.[6] Similarly, Rosa Luxemburg, a founder of the German Communist Party, declared that 'without general elections, without unrestricted freedom of the press and assembly, without a free struggle of opinion, life dies out in every public institution'.[7] Even Lenin, a key leader of the 1917 Russian Revolution, endorsed a tactical resolution adopted by the 34th congress of the Russian Social Democratic Labour Party, which proclaimed 'the direct interests of the proletariat and the interests of its struggle for the final aims of socialism require the fullest possible measure of political liberty and, consequently, the replacement of the autocratic form of government by a democratic republic'.[8] There is near-universal consensus within the tradition of Marxist political theory that political (bourgeois) democracy is a prerequisite or condition of socialism. Thus, the crux of the debate about tactics is whether it is possible to enact a peaceful and lawful transition to socialism once liberal democracy is achieved or whether liberal democracy itself confines political action within the structural limits of capitalist society, thereby thwarting the final objective of the socialist movement.[9]

---

[3] Karl Marx and Frederick Engels, 'Manifesto of the Communist Party' [1848] in Karl Marx and Frederick Engels, *Collected Works*, vol 6 (Lawrence & Wishart 1976) 477, 498.

[4] Marx and Engels, 'Manifesto of the Communist Party', 504. See August H Nimtz, Jr, *Marx and Engels: Their Contribution to the Democratic Breakthrough* (State University of New York Press 2000).

[5] Eduard Bernstein, *Evolutionary Socialism* (first published 1899, Schocken 1961) 151, 166. See also Manfred B Steger, *The Quest for Evolutionary Socialism: Eduard Bernstein and Social Democracy* (CUP 1997) 140.

[6] Karl Kautsky, *The Dictatorship of the Proletariat* (first published 1918, University of Michigan Press 1964). See also Jukka Gronow, *On the Formation of Marxism: Karl Kautsky's Theory of Capitalism, the Marxism of the Second International, and Karl Marx's Critique of Political Economy* (Brill 2016) ch 12.

[7] Rosa Luxemburg, *The Russian Revolution, and Leninism or Marxism?* (first published 1918, University of Michigan Press 1961) 71. For a critical analysis of Luxemburg's theory of democracy, see also Eric D Weitz, 'Rosa Luxemburg Belongs to Us! German Communism and the Luxemburg Legacy' (1994) 27 *Central European History* 27.

[8] Lenin, 'Two Tactics of Social-Democracy', 23. See also August H Nimtz, *Lenin's Electoral Strategy from Marx and Engels Through the Revolution of 1905* (Palgrave Macmillan 2014); August H Nimtz, *Lenin's Electoral Strategy from 1907 to the October Revolution of 1917: The Ballot, the Streets— or Both* (Palgrave Macmillan 2014).

[9] Tom Bottomore concurs that 'the question of whether extensive violence would have to be used to effect a socialist transformation is a perennial one ... and has long been one of the principle issues

This question arises in the second phase of a working class revolution which, according to Marx and Engels, is to use the power and rights obtained in the struggle for democracy to achieve socialism. In *The Communist Manifesto,* Marx and Engels declared that '[t]he proletariat will use its political supremacy to wrest, by degrees, all capital from the bourgeoisie, to centralise all instruments of production in the hands of the State, *i.e.,* of the proletariat organised as the ruling class; and to increase the total of productive forces as rapidly as possible'.[10] Marx and Engels went on to concretise these general demands in a ten-point minimum program, which included a heavily graduated progressive income tax, abolition of the right of inheritance, abolition of child labour, free public schools for all children, the creation of a national bank to direct monetary policy and capital investment, the nationalisation of key transportation and communications industries, and public investment in new state and co-operative enterprises to facilitate full employment.[11] Karl Kautsky would later build on these demands to argue that socialism and democracy are not distinguished by the one being the means and the other the end, but rather 'both are means to the same end', which is 'the abolition of every kind of exploitation and oppression, be it directed against a class, a party, a sex, or a race'.[12]

In *The Communist Manifesto*, Marx and Engels anticipated a violent and apocalyptic upheaval by the working class, and '[t]hey openly declare that their ends can be attained only by the forcible overthrow of all existing social conditions'.[13] However, by 1872, Marx acknowledged 'that the institutions, customs, and traditions in different countries must be taken into account', and he suggested that in countries like the United States, England, and Holland it was possible that workers 'may achieve their aims by peaceful means'.[14] Thus, since the death of Marx and Engels, Marxist political theorists have debated the question of whether a transition to socialism can be achieved by purely legal and parliamentary means or whether the transition to socialism requires the use of illegal or even violent tactics.

In his seminal essay 'Legality and Illegality', Georg Lukács had the benefit of being able to survey the entire previous century-long debate on political tactics, including recent experiences with the rise of the German Social Democrats (1890s), the Russian Revolutions (1905

---

dividing that tradition'. Tom Bottomore (ed), *A Dictionary of Marxist Thought* (Harvard University Press 1983) 514.

[10]   Marx and Engels, 'Manifesto of the Communist Party', 504.

[11]   Marx and Engels, 'Manifesto of the Communist Party', 505. These demands were soon expanded to include universal male suffrage (at age 21), salaries for members of Parliament so that workers could serve in office, universal arming of the people, free legal services, the abolition of consumption taxes, nationalisation of all roads, railway, and passenger steamship lines, and the complete separation of church and state, including the abolition of state payments for the salaries of clergy. See Karl Marx and Frederick Engels, 'Demands of the Communist Party in Germany' [1848] in Karl Marx and Frederick Engels, *Collected Works*, vol 7 (Lawrence & Wishart 1977) 3. This document was published as a leaflet at the end of March 1848 in Paris. It was subsequently reproduced in a number of German newspapers in early April 1848.

[12]   Kautsky, *Dictatorship of the Proletariat*, 4, 5.

[13]   Marx and Engels, 'Manifesto of the Communist Party', 519.

[14]   Karl Marx, 'On the Hague Congress [A Correspondent's Report on a Speech Made at a Meeting in Amsterdam on September 8 1972]' in Karl Marx and Frederick Engels, *Collected Works*, vol 23 (Lawrence & Wishart 1988) 254. What is generally omitted from this passage is that Marx continues: 'That being true we must also admit that in most countries on the Continent, it is force that must be the lever of our revolutions; it is force which will have to be resorted to for a time in order to establish the rule of the workers.'

and 1917), the Belgian general strike (1913), and the Spartacist uprising in Germany (1919). By this point political movements influenced by Marxist theory had splintered into social democratic, socialist, communist, and syndicalist organisations based largely on disputes over tactics. However, Lukács argued that it was a mistake to reify tactics by freezing them into fixed analytical categories such as legal and illegal, because 'the mere fact of the legality or illegality of one part of the workers' movement is so dependent on "accidents" of history that to analyse it is not always to guarantee a clarification of theory'.[15] Lukács pointed out that 'the law and its calculable consequences are of no greater (if also of no smaller) importance than any other external fact of life with which it is necessary to reckon when deciding upon any definite course of action'. Consequently, every consideration of legality or illegality is always reduced in practice 'to *a mere question of tactics*, even to a question to be resolved on the spur of the moment, one for which it is scarcely possible to lay down general rules as decisions have to be taken on the basis of *immediate expediencies*'.[16]

LEGALITY AND POPULAR SOVEREIGNTY

Marx and Engels' thoughts about the tactical limits of bourgeois legality are perhaps best captured in their speeches and writings from 1849 and 1850, following the suppression of the 1848 revolutions in Germany, France, Belgium, Austria, and Italy. The culmination of their tactical thinking in the aftermath of these revolutions structured much of their thinking about political tactics in subsequent decades.[17] In early April 1848, Marx and Engels left Paris for Cologne, where Marx chaired the central committee of the Communist League. Marx also joined the Cologne Democratic Society, which was an alliance of revolutionary workers, petit-bourgeois artisans, and radical intellectuals who called for a democratic republic based on universal suffrage. Marx's main goal in returning to Germany during the climax of the revolution was to establish a newspaper, which he called the *Neue Rheinische Zeitung* and subtitled 'Organ of Democracy'. The newspaper began publication on 1 June 1848, just as the revolution took a proletarian and socialist turn in France and the German bourgeoisie recoiled at the prospect that its own republican revolution might take a similar turn.[18]

When the forces of reaction defeated the revolutionaries in France, Germany, Austria, and Italy, the Prussian King Friedrich Wilhelm IV sought to institutionalise this defeat by asking the reactionary General Brandenburg (on 2 November 1848) to form a new government to replace the democratically elected Frankfurt parliament.[19] Marx responded by calling on the

---

[15]   Georg Lukács, 'Legality and Illegality' [1920] in Georg Lukács, *History and Class Consciousness: Studies in Marxist Dialectics* (first published 1923, Rodney Livingstone tr, MIT Press 1972) 256, 256.

[16]   Lukács, 'Legality and Illegality', 263–64 (original emphases).

[17]   Much of this thinking can be found in the pages of the *Neue Rheinische Zeitung*; see Karl Marx and Frederick Engels, *Articles from the Neue Rheinische Zeitung, 1848–1849* (Progress Publishers 1972).

[18]   PN Fedoseyev et al, *Karl Marx: A Biography* (Progress Publishers 1973) 20–21; David McLellan, *Karl Marx: A Biography* (4th edn, Palgrave Macmillan 2006) 156–90.

[19]   The Frankfurt Parliament, or National Assembly, was Germany's first elected parliament convened from 18 May 1848 to 31 May 1849. It came into existence as part of the March Revolution and after considerable debate it produced the republican Frankfurt Constitution. The Frankfurt Constitution largely fulfilled liberal and nationalist aspirations by proclaiming a German Empire based on the principles of parliamentary democracy to replace the German Confederation. The parliament proposed

revolutionary National Assembly to arrest the king's ministers as '*traitors to the sovereignty of the people*', and argued that it 'should have *proscribed* and *outlawed* all officials who obey orders other than those of the Assembly'. In addition, Marx proposed that all Germans '*should refuse to pay taxes*' to the now illegitimate Prussian monarchy. Marx not only called for a tax strike in his newspaper, but personally lobbied left-wing deputies in the National Assembly to support such a measure. He even wrote that it is 'the *duty of the Rhine Province to hasten to the assistance of the Berlin National Assembly with men and weapons*', as he knew that the Prussian king would not accept his overthrow peacefully.[20]

At Marx's request, the Cologne Democratic Society (12 November 1848) also urged soldiers in the Cologne army garrison to mutiny and not allow themselves to be used as tools of political reaction against their fellow citizens. In a special supplement of the *Neue Rheinische Zeitung* (15 November 1848), Marx even called for a meeting of the Cologne *Landwehr* (civic militia), which met and demanded that the National Assembly 'call on the *Landwehr* to rise up as it did in 1813 and destroy the internal enemy as it then destroyed the external enemy'.[21] On the same day, the National Assembly adopted a no-payment-of-taxes resolution, which led Marx to call for forcible resistance to the collection of taxes.[22] Marx immediately penned a resolution that was endorsed by the Cologne Democratic District Committee. It called for (1) forcible resistance to the collection of taxes all over the country by every possible means; (2) the organisation of armed volunteer detachments to beat back the reactionary forces; and (3) the establishment of safety committees to confront government authorities who refused to abide by the National Assembly's no-taxes decision.[23]

As a result of his 'No More Tax Payments!' appeals in the *Neue Rheinische Zeitung*, Marx was summoned by the Cologne Procurator-General, but he was not arrested when it became apparent that a large crowd had gathered at the courthouse with the intent of freeing him by force. Marx continued to press his appeal in the *Neue Rheinische Zeitung*. But on 5 December 1848 the king dissolved the National Assembly, and announced a new Prussian constitution that brought an end to the German democratic revolution. The Cologne authorities took this opportunity to harass Marx, Engels, and other editors of the *Neue Rheinische Zeitung*, with a tidal wave of lawsuits aimed at shutting it down and sending its editors to jail.

---

a constitutional monarchy to be headed by a hereditary emperor, but the Prussian King Frederick William IV refused to accept the office of emperor. See Frank Eyck, *The Frankfurt Parliament, 1848–1849* (St. Martin's Press 1968).

[20]   Karl Marx, 'Counter-Revolution in Berlin' [1848] in Karl Marx and Frederick Engels, *Collected Works*, vol 8 (Lawrence & Wishart 1977) 15, 19 (original emphases).

[21]   Marx quoted in Fedoseyev et al, *Karl Marx*, 190. The Prussian *Landwehr* was established by a royal edict on 17 March 1813 to aid in defending Germany against Napoleon's army. The *Landwehr* consisted of all men between the ages of 18 and 45, who were physically able to bear arms and were not serving in the regular army. After the 1815 peace settlement, the *Landwehr* became part of the Prussian army.

[22]   Karl Marx, 'Impeachment of the Government' [1848] in Karl Marx and Frederick Engels, *Collected Works*, vol 8 (Lawrence & Wishart 1977) 25, 25–26 ('The National Assembly has declared that refusal to pay taxes is justified in law'). Karl Marx, 'Appeal' [1848] in Karl Marx and Frederick Engels, *Collected Works*, vol 8 (Lawrence & Wishart 1977) 41, 41 ('Since the Prussian National Assembly itself has ruled that taxes are not to be paid their forcible collection must be resisted everywhere and in every way').

[23]   Fedoseyev et al, *Karl Marx*, 191. See also Marx, 'Appeal', 41 ('*In order to repulse the enemy a people's militia* must be organised everywhere' (original emphasis)).

The first case to go to trial did so on 7 February 1849, and concerned an article published on 5 July 1848. The editors were accused of contempt of the Cologne Procurator-General and libel of the police. Marx was determined to beat his opponents on their own ground with their own weapons by turning the bourgeois legal system inside out. He gave a concluding speech after his attorney presented the legal case to the jury, declaring that if he were convicted, 'you abolish freedom of the press … whereas you have recognised this freedom by a Constitution and won it by a revolution'.[24] He finished his speech by stating that 'the first duty of the press now is *to undermine all the foundations of the existing political state of affairs*'.[25] Marx and his colleagues were found not guilty.

However, on the following day, Marx was arraigned in court on a charge of inciting revolt with his appeals for a tax strike. In a lengthy response, he explicitly rejected the idea that a revolution could be judged or restricted by the 'framework of legality'. He asked how 'was the idea conceived to allow the United Diet, the representative of the old society, to dictate laws to the new society which asserted its rights through the revolution?' It was '[a]llegedly in order to maintain the *legal basis*' of society.[26] However, Marx countered that:

[s]ociety is not founded upon the law; that is a legal fiction. On the contrary, the law must be founded upon society … which arises from the material mode of production prevailing at the given time … You cannot make the old laws the foundation of the new social development … They [the existing laws] were engendered by the old conditions of society and must perish with them. They are bound to change with the changing conditions of life. To maintain the old laws in face of the new needs and demands of social development is essentially the same as hypocritically upholding out-of-date particular interests in face of the up-to-date general interests. *This maintenance of the legal basis* aims at asserting such particular interests as if they were the *predominant* interests when they are *no longer dominant*; it aims at imposing on society laws which have been condemned by the conditions of life in this society … [I]t seeks to misuse political power in order forcibly to place the interests of a minority above the interests of the majority.[27]

In other words, a social revolution must by definition undertake the destruction of the old legal superstructure, which serves to facilitate the reproduction of a passing mode of production and thereby the political dominance of a declining ruling class.[28] Marx argues in this context that it was the king and his ministers who had strayed from legality by resorting to force against the sovereignty of the people, as represented by the National Assembly. By refusing to pay taxes that supported the army and the police, the people, *who are the sovereign*, had

---

[24]   Karl Marx, 'The First Trial of the *Neue Rheinische Zeitung* [Speech by Karl Marx]' [1849] in Karl Marx and Frederick Engels, *Collected Works*, vol 8 (Lawrence & Wishart 1977) 304, 313.

[25]   Marx, 'First Trial of the *Neue Rheinische Zeitung*', 317 (original emphasis).

[26]   Karl Marx, 'The Trial of the Rhenish District Committee of Democrats [Speech by Karl Marx]' [1849] in Karl Marx and Frederick Engels, *Collected Works*, vol 8 (Lawrence & Wishart 1977) 323, 327 (original emphasis).

[27]   Marx, 'Trial of the Rhenish District Committee of Democrats', 327–28 (original emphases). See Eugene Kamenka, *The Ethical Foundations of Marxism* (2nd edn, Routledge & Kegan Paul 1972) ch 10.

[28]   Kautsky observes that a *social* revolution, such as the transition from capitalism to socialism, is more than a *political* revolution, whether achieved through parliamentary means or violent insurrection. Kautsky defines a social revolution 'as a more or less rapid transformation of the foundations of the juridical and political superstructure of society arising from a change in its economic foundations'. Karl Kautsky, *The Social Revolution* (first published 1902, AM and May Wood Simons tr, Charles H Kerr 1916) 6.

engaged in a legitimate act of self-defence against a lawless government that was violating their sovereignty.

In effect, Marx was deploying Max Weber's definition of the state as an organisation that seeks 'to monopolize the legitimate use of physical force as a means of domination within a territory'.[29] However, for Marx, the key term that precedes a government's use of physical force is that it must be a 'legitimate use', and it is the people as originators of the state that decides what is a legitimate and an illegitimate use of force.[30] A state may exercise its monopoly over physical force illegitimately and at that point it is the state that is illegal—not the people who resist it. It is not up to the government, which acts as an instrument of the state (or the people), to decide the legitimacy of its own acts. Rather, it falls to the people who constitute the state to decide collectively when government—as its instrument—uses force illegitimately. Marx and his associates on the Democratic District Committee were again acquitted of the charges against them.

NOT BY PARLIAMENTARISM ALONE AND BY FORCE IF NECESSARY

After the Prussian state expelled Marx from Germany, he eventually made his way to London, where he reconstituted the central committee of the Communist League, which he thought had been insufficiently prepared for the 1848 Revolution. The German communists had been active mainly at the local level at a time when the revolutionary crisis was unfolding on a national scale. Thus, in March 1850, Marx and Engels delivered an 'Address of the Central Authority to the League', which laid out a strategy for 'Revolution in Permanence'.[31]

Marx praised the League's members for energetically taking part 'in the movement in all places, that in the press, on the barricades, and on the battlefields, they stood in the front ranks of the only decidedly revolutionary class, the proletariat'. However, Marx emphasised that the first and primary task of communists was 'to establish an independent secret and public organisation of the workers' party alongside the official democrats and make each community the central point and nucleus of workers' associations in which the attitude and interests of the proletariat will be discussed independently of bourgeois influences'.[32] Marx reiterated that the first stage of a proletarian revolution would be a democratic revolution led by the bourgeoisie and with mass support from the urban petit bourgeoisie and the rural peasantry—all of whom are fundamentally attached to the institution of private property and who view the primary role of the state as the protection of private property. These social forces were all united in their opposition to feudal economic restrictions, royal absolutism, and high taxes, but they were also united in their commitment to the right to private property and free markets, that is, capitalism.

---

[29] Max Weber, 'Politics as a Vocation' [1919] in HH Gerth and C Wright Mills (eds), *From Max Weber: Essays in Sociology* (HH Gerth and C Wright Mills tr, OUP 1946) 77, 82–83.

[30] William Connelly (ed), *Legitimacy and the State* (Basil Blackwell 1984).

[31] Karl Marx and Frederick Engels, 'Address of the Central Authority to the League, March 1850' [1850] in Karl Marx and Frederick Engels, *Collected Works*, vol 10 (Lawrence & Wishart 1978) 277. See also Richard B Day and Daniel Gaido (eds), *Witnesses to Permanent Revolution: The Documentary Record* (Haymarket 2009).

[32] Marx and Engels, 'Address of the Central Authority to the League', 282.

Thus, the democratic revolution would initially facilitate the development of capitalism and with it the growth and development of the proletariat. However, this meant that the rising proletariat would initially operate politically within the legal framework of bourgeois democracy and within an economic system structured by private property and markets. This situation generated the question of what is to be done politically within the legal framework of bourgeois democracy and capitalism. First, Marx insisted that in every electoral district an independent workers' candidate should be:

> put up alongside the bourgeois-democratic candidates, that they are as far as possible members of the League [i.e., communists], and that their election is promoted by all possible means. Even where there is no prospect whatever of their being elected, the workers must put up their own candidates in order to preserve their independence, to count their forces and to lay before the public their revolutionary attitude and party standpoint.[33]

On this point, Marx was adamant that communists 'must not allow themselves to be bribed by such arguments of the democrats as, for example, that by so doing they are splitting the democratic party and giving the reactionaries the possibility of victory. The ultimate purpose of all such phrases is to dupe the proletariat'.[34] The purpose of electoral participation in a bourgeois democracy was not necessarily to win elections, but to use this legal platform to publicly disseminate the socialist program and to expose the petit bourgeois democrats' commitment to the interests of capitalism above the interests of the working class. Marx's position was that if communists patiently held firm to their party line, in time objective conditions—sparked by an economic crisis and fuelled by the continual waffling and betrayal of workers by the petit-bourgeois democratic party—would drive the working class towards the independent workers' party at critical historical conjunctures.[35]

Absent a revolutionary conjuncture, Marx proposed that communist delegates elected to national assemblies should work to:

> [c]ompel the democrats to interfere in as many spheres as possible of the hitherto existing social order, to disturb its regular course and to compromise themselves as well as to concentrate the utmost possible productive forces, means of transport, factories, railways, etc., in the hands of the state.

Marx went on to suggest that workers' elected deputies 'must carry to the extreme the proposals of the democrats, who in any case will not act in a revolutionary but in a merely reformist manner, and transform them into direct attacks upon private property'.[36] Thus, Marx insisted that:

> if the petty bourgeois propose purchase of the railways and factories, the workers must demand that these railways and factories should be simply confiscated by the state without compensation as

---

[33]   Marx and Engels, 'Address of the Central Authority to the League', 284.

[34]   Marx and Engels, 'Address of the Central Authority to the League', 284.

[35]   While opposing opportunism (i.e., compromising with the bourgeois democratic party), Marx also emphasised that the workers' party should not engage in political adventurism by acting prematurely and without the active support of the masses. Thus, he reiterated a principle set out in *The Communist Manifesto* that communists were opposed to plots and conspiracies, which aside from always failing, provide a pretext for government authorities to arrest workers and to suppress their organisations.

[36]   Marx and Engels, 'Address of the Central Authority to the League', 286.

being the property of reactionaries. If the democrats propose proportional taxation, the workers must demand progressive taxation; if the democrats themselves put forward a moderately progressive taxation, the workers must insist on a taxation with rates that rise so steeply that big capital will be ruined by it; if the democrats demand the regulation of state debts, the workers must demand state bankruptcy.[37]

However, Marx was clear that it would only be possible to oppose the 'treachery' of petty bourgeois democrats, if 'from the first hour of victory' the workers were 'armed and organised'.[38] As in Germany in 1848, Marx called for an 'armed proletariat' that would serve as the military wing of a dual power structure, which could challenge the capitalist state from the outside even as its elected deputies challenged it from the inside. Marx called for 'the arming of the whole proletariat with rifles, muskets, cannon, and munitions', and he concluded that 'workers must try to organise themselves independently as a proletarian guard with commanders elected by themselves and with a general staff of their own choosing'. Marx went on to argue that 'arms and ammunition must not be surrendered on any pretext; any attempt at disarming must be frustrated, if necessary by force'. Importantly, Marx warned that armed proletarians must never put themselves at the command of the established state authority, but instead become the military wing 'of the revolutionary community councils which the workers will have managed to get adopted' during a revolutionary crisis. In this manner, the communists and the working class can enforce 'conditions as difficult and compromising as possible' upon bourgeois democrats.[39]

Importantly, even as late as 1874, Marx was convinced that:

> as long as the other classes, above all the capitalist class, still exist, and as long as the proletariat is still fighting against it (for when the proletariat obtains control of the government its enemies and the old organisation of society will not yet have disappeared), it must use *forcible* means, that is to say, governmental means; as long as it remains a class itself, and the economic conditions which give rise to the class struggle and the existence of classes have not vanished they must be removed or transformed by force, and the process of transforming them must be accelerated by force.[40]

Furthermore, instead of opposing the 'so-called excesses' of revolutionary movements, Marx defended acts of 'popular revenge against hated individuals or public buildings that are associated only with hateful recollections'. He even proposed that 'such instances must not only be tolerated but the leadership of them taken in hand'. In this respect, Marx contended that the entire duration of bourgeois democracy will be a 'Revolution in Permanence'.[41] Even where workers win universal suffrage, communists will have to continue exerting both internal and external pressure on state officials by demanding 'guarantees for the workers', and '[i]f nec-

---

[37]   Marx and Engels, 'Address of the Central Authority to the League', 286.

[38]   Marx and Engels, 'Address of the Central Authority to the League', 283.

[39]   Marx and Engels, 'Address of the Central Authority to the League', 283. Mao Tse-tung similarly argues that 'political power grows out of the barrel of a gun … According to the Marxist theory of the state, the army is the chief component of state power. Whoever wants to seize and retain state power must have a strong army.' Mao Tse-tung, 'Problems of War and Strategy (November 1938)' in Mao Tse-tung, *Selected Works*, vol 2 (Foreign Languages Press 1965) 225.

[40]   Karl Marx, 'Notes on Bakunin's Book *Statehood and Anarchy*' [1874–75] in Karl Marx and Frederick Engels, *Collected Works*, vol 24 (Lawrence & Wishart 1989) 485, 517 (original emphasis).

[41]   Marx and Engels, 'Address of the Central Authority to the League', 287.

essary they must wring these guarantees by force'.[42] While some commentators dismiss such statements as the legacy of a young Marx, he was still making the same point shortly before his death. For example, in an 1880 letter to Henry Mayers Hyndman about the British Reform Bills, the ten-hour working day, and other labour reforms, Marx cautions against putting too much faith in purely parliamentary tactics by reminding Hyndman that '[e]very pacific concession' of the English ruling classes 'has been wrung from them by "pressure from without"'.[43]

Later Marxists, such as Kautsky, Luxemburg, and Georges Sorel expanded the concept of pressure from without to include non-violent forms of collective action, including the political strike, the general strike, and the mass strike respectively.[44] While these tactics of collective action were peaceful in intent, Kautsky points out that whether such tactics are peaceful or violent depends primarily upon the response by the ruling class and the state. Kautsky also suggests that 'it cannot to-day be foreseen how democracy in the various States will influence the forms which the conquest of political power by the proletariat will take, and how far it will avert the use of violent methods from both sides and promote the use of peaceful means'. However, he is certain that 'in cases where the proletariat of a democratic State attains to power, one must reckon with attempts of the ruling classes to nullify by violence the realisation of democracy by the rising class'.[45] Moreover, even if the working class was to conquer political power through purely peaceful and parliamentary (legal) means, Kautsky observes that it is naïve not to recognise that 'every juridical and political measure is a force measure which is carried through by the force of the State', even when adopted by parliamentary means.[46] Legality is always rendered enforceable by the threat of force and state violence.

THE PROHIBITION ON INDIVIDUAL TERRORISM

Marx and Engels never rejected illegal tactics, nor even the necessity of violence, but they did consistently voice their opposition to secret plots and conspiracies to overthrow governments by small minorities. Marx and Engels associated secret plots and conspiracies with

---

[42]   Marx and Engels, 'Address of the Central Authority to the League', 283. Lenin likewise recognised that a bourgeois democratic revolution 'will not weaken but strengthen the domination of the bourgeoisie which at a certain juncture will inevitably go to any length to take away from the Russian proletariat as many of the gains of the revolutionary period as possible'. Lenin, 'Two Tactics of Social-Democracy', 23–24.

[43]   Karl Marx, 'Marx to Henry Mayers Hyndman, in London, 8 December 1880' in Karl Marx and Frederick Engels, *Collected Works,* vol 46 (Lawrence & Wishart 1992) 49, 49. Georges Sorel makes a similar point: 'The history of England affords more than one example of a Government giving way when numerous demonstrations against its proposals took place, even though it was strong enough to repel by force any attack on existing institutions. It seems to be an admitted principle of Parliamentary Government that the majority cannot persist in pursuing schemes which give rise to popular demonstrations of too serious a kind.'

Georges Sorel, *Reflections on Violence* (first published 1906, TE Hulme and J Roth tr, Macmillan 1972) 153.

[44]   Kautsky, *Social Revolution*, 85–90; Sorel, *Reflections on Violence*; Rosa Luxemburg, *The Mass Strike: The Political Party and the Trade Unions, and the Junius Pamphlet* (first published 1906, Harper 1971).

[45]   Kautsky, *Dictatorship of the Proletariat*, 8. See Massimo Salvadori, *Karl Kautsky and the Socialist Revolution, 1880–1938* (New Left Books 1979) 100–14.

[46]   Kautsky, *Social Revolution,* 7.

the ill-conceived political adventurism of small minorities (e.g., Blanquism, Bakuninism) and with individual acts of violence and terrorism. The tactical philosophy of 'propaganda by the deed', including uncontrolled riots and individual acts of political violence, was first articulated by some of Bakunin's Italian followers in the 1870s.[47] The theoretical basis of these tactics was the claim that terroristic attacks on government officials and public buildings, bank robberies, and kidnapping or assassinating wealthy capitalists would reveal the vulnerability of the existing system to the masses, and thereby encourage them to revolt against it. For example, William E Trautman, a founder of the Industrial Workers of the World, argued that any direct action that undermines the power of the capitalist class is:

> socially useful and beneficial, no matter whether they are 'direct actions' of individuals, or of combinations of workers ... The Russian individualist who uses explosives, responsible only to himself as an individual, may be abhorred by many, but still his action must be judged by the results he aims to achieve. If ultimately, after a long series of such violent and destructive direct actions they result in the removal of agencies of suppression and oppression his direct action is socially useful.[48]

In fact, from 1870 until 1920, anarchists in a number of countries, including Russia, Austria, Italy, and the United States, carried out a series of assassinations and bombings. Despite the claim that capitalists and government officials were the targets of terrorist violence, innocent bystanders were frequently killed or maimed in these attacks.[49] Thus, contrary to expectations, the masses failed to react positively to terrorist acts and were usually repelled by them, while giving government officials a pretext to clamp down on the entire left.

The failure of these tactics was the crux of the matter for Marx and Engels, who repeatedly voiced their opposition to secret conspiracies and individual acts of terrorism as 'more or less doomed to failure'.[50] This position was echoed by August Bebel,[51] Trotsky,[52] and Lenin, who

---

[47]   See Alexander Berkman, 'Propaganda by the Deed' in Marshall S Shatz (ed), *The Essential Works of Anarchism* (Bantam Books 1971) 356; Marie Fleming, 'Propaganda by the Deed: Terrorism and Anarchist Theory in Late Nineteenth Century Europe' (1980) 4 *Terrorism* 1. Sam Dolgoff argues that Bakunin himself did not advocate 'indiscriminate violence against persons. To the contrary, he opposed regicide and repeatedly stressed that destruction must be directed not against persons but against institutions'. Sam Dolgoff, 'Introduction' in Sam Dolgoff (ed), *Bakunin on Anarchy: Selected Works by the Activist-Founder of World Anarchism* (Alfred A Knopf 1972) 3, 13.

[48]   William E Trautmann, 'Direct Action and Sabotage' [1912] in Salvatore Salerno (ed), *Direct Action and Sabotage: Three Classic IWW Pamphlets of the 1910s* (Charles H Kerr 1997) 11–12.

[49]   See Berkman, 'Propaganda by the Deed'.

[50]   Karl Marx, 'Marx to Engels, in Manchester, 14 December 1867' in Karl Marx and Frederick Engels, *Collected Works*, vol 42 (Lawrence & Wishart 1987) 501, 501; Frederick Engels, 'Engels to August Bebel, in Berlin, 15 February 1886' in Karl Marx and Frederick Engels, *Collected Works*, vol 47 (Lawrence & Wishart 1995) 406, 408.

[51]   August Bebel, *Assassinations and Socialism* (New York Labor News Co 1898).

[52]   Trotsky points out that 'the anarchist prophets of "the propaganda of the deed" can argue all they want about the elevating and stimulating influence of terrorist acts on the masses. Theoretical considerations and political experience prove otherwise'. Leon Trotsky, *Against Individual Terrorism* (first published 1911, Pathfinder Press 1974) 7. Some years later, however, he suggested that 'under conditions of civil war, the assassination of individual oppressors ceases to be an act of individual terror ... Thus, even in the sharpest question—murder of man by man—moral absolutes prove futile'. Leon Trotsky, 'Their Morals and Ours' (1938) 4 *The New International* 173.

found it 'difficult to imagine an argument that more thoroughly disproves itself' than terrorist claims about the 'excitative significance' of terror in motivating revolutionary movements.[53]

INVENTORY AND TYPOLOGY OF POLITICAL TACTICS

In the course of their theoretical and political writings, Marx and Engels participated in, advocated, or denounced a long list of political tactics that included both legal and illegal tactics, as well as violent and non-violent tactics.[54] Some of these tactics could be initiated and performed by a single individual, such as voting or assassination, while others required organisation and collective action, such as publishing a radical newspaper or deploying a proletarian militia. Table 1.1 below provides an inventory of these political tactics—albeit one that is not complete or exhaustive—and it organises them into a typology based on whether the tactics are individualistic or collective and violent or non-violent. This typology seems to capture more or less accurately the main tactical dividing lines that differentiate liberal democracy (box 1), democratic socialism (box 2), revolutionary communism (box 3), and anarchism (box 4).

In important respects, the typology captures the actual historical development of Marxism from liberal democracy to democratic socialism and then to revolutionary communism, while rejecting anarchism. But at the same time it also fails to capture the fact that the status and use of tactics are historically contingent on place and time, and that tactics can change from illegal to legal status and vice versa; the legal status of tactics is not fixed, but fluid across time and space. Thus, the typology assumes that one is acting politically within a mature liberal republic with universal suffrage and constitutionally protected civil liberties, such as freedoms of speech, press, and assembly. In other forms of the capitalist state, however, merely voicing an opinion, publishing a newspaper, or organising a political party could all be illegal even though they are peaceful forms of political action. The fact that a tactic is non-violent tells us nothing about its legal status, because at various times and places, or under various political circumstances, any non-violent tactic can be declared illegal by the state.

Thus, a first caveat is that every one of the tactics listed in Table 1.1 *could be illegal* so the question of whether a tactic is violent or non-violent often has no bearing on its legality, because its legality will be a question of the extent to which a tactic is perceived by the ruling class and governing authorities as posing a threat to the existing capitalist system. Even in a liberal democracy, the voicing of certain views (e.g., draft resistance) or belonging to certain types of organisations (e.g., criminal syndicalism) may be illegal even though they are peaceful forms of political action. Furthermore, peaceful mass demonstrations are routinely declared unlawful assemblies and speech can be deemed an incitement to violence almost purely at the discretion of the police. As Marx frequently pointed out, government officials in a liberal democracy will react forcefully and even violently against peaceful tactics that threaten the stability of the existing capitalist order under the pretext of maintaining law and order.

---

[53]   VI Lenin, 'What is to Be Done? Burning Questions of Our Movement' [1902] in VI Lenin, *Collected Works*, vol 5 (Lawrence & Wishart 1960) 347, 419–20.

[54]   I prefer 'non-violent tactics' to 'peaceful tactics' because many non-violent tactics, such as mass demonstrations, can be quite disruptive of the peace and are designed precisely for this purpose. Hence, they can often result in orders from the police to disperse or in mass arrests of participants.

Table 2.1   *Typology of political tactics*

	Individual Action	Collective Action
Non-Violent	**Liberal Democracy 1**	**Democratic Socialism 2**
	Lawsuits and Jury Nullification	Workers' Educational Societies
	Lobbying	Newspapers and Journals
	Voting	Organise Independent Workers' Party
	Writing/Sedition	Political Strike
	Religious Blasphemy and Heresy	General Strike
	Consumer Boycott	Mass Strike
	Stand for Elective Office	Promotion of Army Mutiny/Desertion
	Tax Strike	
	Draft Resistance	
Violent	**Anarchism 4**	**Revolutionary Communism 3**
	Vandalism	Arms Purchases
	Industrial Sabotage	Destruction of Public Monuments
	Threats and Thuggery	Freeing of Political Prisoners
	Theft, Robbery, and Looting	Reprisal Against Hated Individuals
	Arson	Deployment of Proletarian Battalions
	Assassination	Mass Insurrection (Revolution)
	Bombings	

It is important to recognise that even liberal constitutional republics like the United States have a long history of criminalising political tactics such as speech and assembly, if they are deemed threats to the existing political regime. In the United States, the 1798 Sedition Act criminalised 'false statements' that were critical of the federal government or its elected federal officials.[55] The 1917 Espionage Act prohibited interference with military operations or recruitment (draft resistance and its advocacy), or the support of US enemies during officially declared wars. In 1919 the US Supreme Court unanimously ruled in *Schenck v United States* that the Espionage Act did not violate the freedom of speech of individuals convicted under its provisions.[56] This includes the conviction of the United States' first Socialist Congressman Victor L Berger, Socialist Party presidential candidate Eugene V Debs, the anarchists Emma Goldman and Alexander Berkman, and Pentagon Papers whistleblower Daniel Ellsberg, among others.[57]

The 1918 Sedition Act amended the Espionage Act by criminalising speech and expression that involves 'disloyal, profane, scurrilous, or abusive language' about the US government, the US flag, or its armed forces, or that causes others to view the US government or its institutions with contempt.[58] The Sedition Act was repealed on 13 December 1920, but by this time thirty-five states had adopted criminal syndicalism laws that made it illegal to advocate in

---

[55]   John Chester Miller, *Crisis in Freedom: The Alien and Sedition Acts* (Little, Brown, & Co 1951); Geoffrey R Stone, *Perilous Times: Free Speech in Wartime from the Sedition Act of 1798 to the War Terrorism* (WW Norton & Co 2004).

[56]   *Schenck v US* (1919) 249 US 47.

[57]   Stephen M Kohn, *American Political Prisoners: Prosecutions Under the Espionage and Seditions Acts* (Praeger 1994); Mitchell Newton-Matza, *The Espionage and Seditions Acts: World War I and the Image of Civil Liberties* (Routledge 2017).

[58]   Mitchell Newton-Matza, *The Espionage and Sedition Acts*.

speech or writing essentially any doctrine that advocates fundamental political, industrial, and social change, including anarchism, socialism, Bolshevism, communism, syndicalism, communism, or any revolutionary overthrow of the US government.[59] A crisis in the state, such as the rise of a powerful socialist movement (or even Jeffersonian democracy in the United States), can also lead to illegal tactics becoming legal (e.g., expiration of the Anti-Socialist Laws in Germany or the repeal of the Sedition Act in the United States), primarily because the ruling class is forced to make concessions to insurgent movements to preserve the system as a whole. At the same time, a crisis in the state can also lead to legal tactics becoming illegal, because the ruling class decides to suppress even peaceful political opponents and insurgent movements with force and violence.

A second caveat to the typology of political tactics in Table 1.1 is that those in boxes 1 to 3 are not mutually exclusive forms of political action except insofar as liberal democrats largely reject those in boxes 2 and 3, and their refusal to move beyond these tactics ensures that political action cannot move beyond the structural limitations of capitalism. Democratic socialists largely reject the political tactics in box 3, and all of the first three categories of political actors reject the tactics in box 4. However, revolutionary communists do not exclude any of the tactics in boxes 1 and 2, but may pursue all of them (boxes 1 through 3) depending on political circumstances.[60] Lenin described this cluster of tactics as 'Revolutionary Parliamentarism'.[61] As discussed earlier, category 4 is excluded from the list of Marxist political tactics partly on theoretical grounds (individualism), but primarily because historical experience documents the failure of these tactics and the likelihood that their use results in even greater repression of socialist movements.

CONCLUSION

This chapter concludes by reiterating two important distinctions that have often led to confusion in past debates on the question of legal and illegal tactics in Marxian political theory. First, illegal tactics are not a synonym for violent tactics. In fact, many peaceful tactics are illegal depending on the time, place, and manner of their deployment. For example, writing and publishing tracts critical of an established state or government official is peaceful, but it has been illegal even in liberal democracies such as the United States. Similarly, merely organising or joining a socialist party can be illegal. Conversely, armed self-defence (e.g., civilian militias) are potentially violent but not necessarily illegal, particularly in political jurisdictions that today allow the open carry of weapons and have 'stand your ground' laws for self-defence.[62]

---

[59]   Elbridge Foster Dowell, 'A History of Criminal Syndicalism Legislation in the United States' in *Studies in Historical and Political Science* (Johns Hopkins Press 1939); FG Franklin, 'Anti-Syndicalist Legislation' (1920) 14 *American Political Science Review* 291.
[60]   See e.g., Nimtz, *Lenin's Electoral Strategy from 1907 to the October Revolution of 1917*.
[61]   Nimtz, *Lenin's Electoral Strategy from 1907 to the October Revolution of 1917*, 176.
[62]   In the United States, 'open carry' is the act of publicly carrying a firearm on one's person in plain sight. In 2018 31 states allow the open carrying of a handgun without any license or permit, although in some cases the gun must be unloaded. Another 15 states require some form of license or permit in order to openly carry a handgun. See e.g., Giffords Law Center, 'Open Carry', https://lawcenter.giffords.org/gun-laws/policy-areas/guns-in-public/open-carry/ accessed 7 April 2021. A 'stand your ground' law establishes a right by which a person may defend one's self or others against threats or perceived threats,

Thus, the question of legality must be divorced from the separate and distinct question whether to adopt non-violent tactics as opposed to violent tactics, because illegality and violence are not identical, while the latter, as Walter Benjamin points out, is largely a moral question as opposed to a political question.[63] With regard to the latter, Eugene Kamenka argues that Marx rejected moralism, abstract rights, and normative law, because as the 'social distribution of functions, classes and movements changes, the "accepted" moral principles, constitutional rights and legal systems will also change'.[64]

Second, as has been documented in this chapter, many political tactics that are legal today became legal because they were practiced when they were illegal, such as strikes, mass demonstrations, and a critical free press. Legal tactics become legal because they are used illegally to the point that they can no longer be repressed by the state.[65] Thus, as Lukács argues, the question of legality is historically a constantly shifting line that cannot be defined *a priori* or from a purely theoretical position. It is therefore a purely pragmatic question of which tactics are most likely to achieve a specific end at a particular point in time.[66] Falsely elevating the question of tactics to a theoretical level has led to the division of Marxist political theory into liberal democratic, democratic socialist, and revolutionary communist theoretical traditions, which since the late nineteenth century have confronted each other as mutually exclusive theoretical and party positions. However, Marx and Engels never saw these positions as mutually exclusive, but as complementary forms of political action depending upon conjunctures and circumstances.

---

even to the point of applying lethal force, regardless of whether safely retreating from the situation might have been possible. In 2018 22 states had stand-your-ground laws. See e.g., National Conference of State Legislatures, 'Self Defense and "Stand Your Ground"', http://www.ncsl.org/research/civil-and-criminal -justice/self-defense-and-stand-your-ground.aspx accessed 7 April 2021.

[63]   Benjamin observes that 'a cause, however effective, becomes violent, in the precise sense of the word, only when it bears on moral issues ... The question would remain open whether violence, as a principle, could be a moral means even to a just end.' Walter Benjamin, 'Critique of Violence' [1921] in Walter Benjamin, *Reflections: Essays, Aphorisms, Autobiographical Writings* (Edmund Jephcott tr, Schocken 1986) 277, 277. From a historical perspective, the participants in all revolutions are considered illegal and immoral by the ruling powers until such time as they become the ruling power. Only a few Marxist theorists have even broached questions concerning the ethics of violence. See Sorel, *Reflections on Violence*, ch 6; Frantz Fanon, *The Wretched of the Earth* (first published 1961, Richard Philcox tr, Grove Press 1963) ch 1; Dayan Jayatilleka, *Fidel's Ethics of Violence: The Moral Dimension of the Political Thought of Fidel Castro* (Pluto Press 2007).

[64]   Kamenka, *Ethical Foundations*, 106.

[65]   For example, strikes by workers do not occur because they are legal. They are now legal because workers persistently went on strike even when it was illegal and constantly raised the stakes of such confrontations, to the point that it was more advantageous and efficient for the state to regulate unions and strikes than to outlaw them.

[66]   Lenin argues that the criterion of practice is 'the basis of the materialist theory of knowledge ... The standpoint of life, of practice, should be first and fundamental in the theory of knowledge.' VI Lenin, 'Materialism and Empirio-Criticism: Critical Comments on a Reactionary Philosophy' [1909] in VI Lenin, *Collected Works*, vol 14 (Progress Publishers 1962) 17, 138, 142.

3. Marx on the Factory Acts: Law, exploitation, and class struggle

Daniel McLoughlin and Talina Hürzeler

INTRODUCTION

Gary Young notes that there are two different types of writing on law that one finds in Marx's work: 'abstract, programmatic statements about the place and function of law in social structure' and 'accounts of a few relatively specific bourgeois legal institutions and laws'.[1] Young goes on to write that Marxist theories of law have tended to focus on the first of these, while the latter are '[r]arely studied'.[2] In this chapter, we provide something of a remedy to this tendency by examining Marx's account of the English Factory Acts, which is one of his most important analyses of specific bourgeois laws.

Over three decades in the middle of the nineteenth century, the British Parliament passed a series of laws limiting the length of the working day across various industries. In chapter ten of the first volume of *Capital*, Marx provides a detailed account of the politics surrounding these laws, in what Alan Hunt rightly describes as a 'classic study of the interrelation and interaction of class forces'.[3] While Marx never articulated a theory of the 'place and function of law' in *Capital*, his analysis of the Factory Acts is informed by a sophisticated account of the relationship between law, politics, and the capitalist mode of production. In this chapter, we suggest that Marx's analysis undermines the liberal belief in the autonomy of the juridical order, and, more importantly, the economistic and voluntarist theories of law that have tended to dominate the Marxist tradition.[4] Marx shows that the Factory Acts were neither simply a reflection of an 'economic base' nor an instrument in the hands of the bourgeoisie. Instead, legislation limiting the working day was the product of a political struggle that occurred on a social and economic terrain shaped by the capitalist mode of production.

Marx's analysis of the Factory Acts in *Capital* also suggests that law can play an important role in the struggle against capitalism. Indeed, in instructions that Marx wrote for delegates to the 1866 Geneva Congress of the International Workingmen's Association, he states that the legal regulation of the working day is the 'preliminary condition' for the emancipation of the working class, 'without which all further attempts at improvement and emancipation

---

[1]   Gary Young, 'Marx on Bourgeois Law' (1979) 2 *Research in Law and Sociology* 133, 133.

[2]   Young, 'Marx on Bourgeois Law', 133.

[3]   Alan Hunt, 'Law, State and Class Struggle' (1976) 20 *Marxism Today* 178, 186. Marx's analysis of the Factory Acts in *Capital* is similar, in style and methodology, to some of his earlier close studies of class struggle. See e.g., Karl Marx, 'The Class Struggles in France: 1848 to 1850' [1850] and 'The Eighteenth Brumaire of Louis Napoleon' [1852] in Karl Marx, *Political Writings*, vol 2: *Surveys from Exile* (David Fernbach ed, Verso 2010) 35 and 143.

[4]   These have often been read out of what Young calls Marx's 'abstract' and 'programmatic' statements about law.

must prove abortive'.[5] Yet Marx is also well known for his often strident criticisms of law. We explain the seeming contradiction between these two positions in the final section of the chapter. We argue that both Marx's critique of bourgeois legality and his endorsement of the Factory Acts are underpinned by an analysis of the role that different kinds of law play in the context of class struggle.

THE ENGLISH FACTORY ACTS AND THE STRUGGLE FOR THE 'NORMAL WORKING DAY'

In *Capital*, Marx traces the legislative history that helped to establish a 'normal working day' in English 'modern industry' from 1833 to 1864. In 1833 Parliament imposed the first effective limitations on working hours in factories: it forbade the employment of children under nine; the law limited the work of children between nine and 13 to eight hours a day; and those between 13 and 18 to 12 hours a day. However, no limits were placed on the freedom of capital to exploit the labour of adults.[6] In 1844 a further Factory Act was adopted, placing women over the age of 18 under protection by limiting their employment to 12 hours per day and forbidding night work. In practice, the working day for adult males was subject to the same limitations because factory work depended on the simultaneous labour of women and children. However, the manufacturers 'did not allow this "progress" without a compensating "retrogression"',[7] and during the period of 1844–47 the minimum age for exploitable children was reduced from nine to eight.

In June 1847 a third Factory Act was adopted that limited the working day to ten hours. While manufacturers resisted this law by a range of legal and political means, it nonetheless came into force on 1 May 1848. Manufacturers then challenged the validity of the Act by questioning whether it strictly prohibited the use of the relay system, a management technique that shifted workers around different factories to make it more difficult for inspectors to keep track of their hours. In 1850 the Court of Exchequer, whose principal function was to 'protect, enforce and administer the collection of public revenues',[8] upheld the manufacturer's challenge, finding that the Act contained 'certain words that rendered it meaningless'.[9] Yet this legal victory generated serious problems for the capitalist class as workers, who felt that they had been cheated, began to threaten strikes. In response, an additional Factory Act was passed that brought the working day to ten and a half hours and put an end to the relay system by specifying that meals should be held at the same time for all workers.[10] However, the Act contained a loophole allowing manufacturers to continue their exploitation of children; this was closed by a further act in 1853 forbidding 'employment of children before and in the evening after

---

[5]   Karl Marx, 'Instructions for Delegates to the Geneva Congress' [1866] in Karl Marx, *Political Writings, vol 3: The First International and After* (David Fernbach ed, Verso 2010) 85, 87.

[6]   Between 1802 and 1833 Parliament passed five labour laws. However, these were a 'dead letter', as no funds were allocated for their enforcement. Karl Marx, *Capital: A Critique of Political Economy*, vol 1 (first published 1867, Ben Fowkes tr, Penguin 1990) 390.

[7]   Marx, *Capital*, vol 1, 395.

[8]   Bradley Selway, 'Of Kings and Officers—The Judicial Development of Public Law' (2005) 33 *Federal Law Review* 187.

[9]   Marx, *Capital*, vol 1, 404.

[10]   Marx, *Capital*, vol 1, 405.

young persons and women'.[11] Over the next ten years, a series of acts extended the regulation of the working day to sectors of industry that had been exempt from the 1850 Act, including dye-works and bleach-works, baking, and the manufacture of earthenware and lace.[12]

The legislative history of the Factory Acts can only be adequately understood in the context of the development of the capitalist mode of production, which created the social, economic, and political conditions to which the legal regulation of the working day responded. Marx's analysis of the working day follows upon three chapters on the problem of surplus value. To make a profit, the capitalist needs to 'produce a commodity greater in value than the sum of the values of the commodities used to produce it, namely the means of production and the labour-power he purchased with his good money in the open market'.[13] The value of labour-power is determined, as with all other commodities, by the amount of socially necessary labour-time required to produce it. This is the total value of the 'bundle of commodities' (food, rest, housing, reproduction, entertainment, etc.) that the worker needs to replenish themselves so that they can turn up to work again the next day. But while the worker may need the monetary equivalent of six hours of labour to survive, this does not prevent the capitalist, who has purchased their labour-power for the working day, from asking them to work additional hours. These hours are what Marx calls surplus labour-time, and this creates surplus value, which is realised by the capitalist as profit. Labour-power is thus a unique commodity that has the capacity to produce more value than it costs to purchase.[14]

Marx's analysis of surplus value shows that within the capitalist mode of production, the material interests of the proletariat and bourgeoisie are fundamentally opposed: the labourer has an interest in working only those hours necessary to reproduce their labour-power; the capitalist, on the other hand, has an interest in extending the working day to extract greater profits. Moreover, capitalists need to extract ever greater levels of surplus value because the viability of their business depends on it being the most competitive and profitable in the marketplace.[15] Capital thus acts like a 'vampire'[16] that lives by sucking labour from workers without any concern for their physical or moral well-being.[17] The decisive question, given this conflict of interests between wage-labourer and employer, is: what actually determines the length of the working day? Marx's response to this question is one of his most memorable, and pithiest, statements on law: 'between equal rights, force decides'.[18] The two parties to the wage contract have equal rights under the law: the capitalist has the right to use labour-power in the way that they see fit; and the worker has a right to preserve their labour-power to sell it again in the future. What ultimately determines the length of the working day is thus not the appeal to legal rights, but rather a 'struggle between collective capital, i.e., the class of capitalists, and collective labour, i.e., the working-class'.[19]

---

[11]   Marx, *Capital*, vol 1, 408.

[12]   Marx, *Capital*, vol 1, 409–11.

[13]   Marx, *Capital*, vol 1, 293.

[14]   Marx, *Capital*, vol 1, 136.

[15]   For Marx's claim that the unrelenting drive to extract ever greater levels of surplus labour is unique to the capitalist mode of production, see 'The Voracious Appetite for Surplus Labour' in Marx, *Capital*, vol 1, 344–53.

[16]   Marx, *Capital*, vol 1, 342.

[17]   Marx, *Capital*, vol 1, 341.

[18]   Marx, *Capital*, vol 1, 344.

[19]   Marx, *Capital*, vol 1, 344.

Bob Jessop writes that, as Marx describes it in *Capital*, the capitalist mode of production is characterised by 'tendencies and counter-tendencies which together constitute its "laws of motion"'.[20] However, as Jessop also points out, the way that these tendencies play out in practice depends upon the interaction among them, and the specific conditions in which they are realised.[21] Marx's analysis of the struggle over the working day is a perfect illustration of this theoretical point. The analysis of surplus value shows that the capitalist organisation of production generates a tendency to extend the working day as much as possible. However, the way that this plays out in practice depends upon the struggle between the bourgeoisie and the working class. The actual length of the working day under capitalism is therefore dependent not only upon the laws of motion that are immanent to this mode of production, but also upon the amount of force that each of the contending classes is able to bring to bear in the course of that struggle.

The development of the capitalist mode of production not only generates class conflict; it also influences the balance of forces between classes as the struggle between them unfolds. Immediately prior to his discussion of the attempt to place legal limits on the working day, Marx analyses the history of labour laws from the fourteenth to seventeenth centuries that extended the length of the working day. Capital was in its 'embryonic state' during this period, which meant that it could not 'yet use the sheer force of economic relations to secure its right to absorb a sufficient quantity of surplus labour', and so it needed to be 'aided by the power of the state'.[22] However, even when backed by the state, the power of capital to extend the working day in this period was limited. As late as 1770, the anonymous author of *An Essay on Trade and Commerce* argued that the ideal workhouse would work people for 12 hours a day. Yet this 'House of Terror' proved to be positively mild when compared to the factory system of the early nineteenth century.[23]

The legal limitation of the working day only became a political demand in the early nineteenth century because the development of capitalism had strengthened the capacity of the bourgeoisie to exploit the working class. The most immediate cause of the extension of the working day in this period was the way that large-scale industry transformed the labour process. Until this time, craft workers played a central role in the manufacturing process. Their skills gave them some control over their work, and meant they could not easily be replaced at the whim of their employer. However, the development of technology allowed capitalists to replace craft labour with the power of machines, and, as a result, the individual worker became a replaceable cog in a system of production planned and organised by the capitalist. This radically undermined the power of the working class, which was 'stunned ... by the noise and turmoil' of the 'new system of production', and was only capable of offering resistance once it had 'recovered its senses'.[24] The Industrial Revolution thus led to 'an avalanche of violent and unmeasured encroachments' through which 'every boundary set by morality and nature, age and sex, day and night was broken down' by capital.[25]

---

[20]   Bob Jessop, 'Regulation Theories in Retrospect and Prospect' (1990) 19 *Economy and Society* 153, 163.

[21]   Jessop, 'Regulation Theories'; Bob Jessop, *The Capitalist State: Marxist Theories and Methods* (New York University Press 1982).

[22]   Marx, *Capital*, vol 1, 382.

[23]   Marx, *Capital*, vol 1, 387–89.

[24]   Marx, *Capital*, vol 1, 390.

[25]   Marx, *Capital*, vol 1, 390.

However, technological transformation was only able to rewrite the relations between labour and capital because of social conditions in which the 'free worker' was obliged, as Marx points out, 'to sell the whole of his active life, his very capacity for work, for the price of the necessaries of life, his birth-right for a mess of pottage'.[26] This is a reference to the process of primitive accumulation, which created the prerequisites for capitalist production, namely, 'considerable masses of capital and labour-power in the hands of commodity producers'.[27] The 'tender annals of political economy'[28] explain the emergence of these conditions through a moral fable in which wealth is accumulated through diligence and frugality, while poverty is a result of laziness and 'riotous living'.[29] In *Capital*, by contrast, Marx turns to the historical record to show that both the proletariat and industrial capital were the result of a process of expropriation that is 'written in the annals of mankind in letters of blood and fire'.[30]

Marx argues that the genesis of the industrial capitalist is to be found in the violence of colonialism and slavery: 'the treasures captured outside Europe by undisguised looting, enslavement and murder, flowed back to the mother-country and were turned into capital there'.[31] However, capital is 'not a thing, but a social relation', which means that the riches stolen from the colonies could only function as capital if they could be used to extract surplus value.[32] Industrial capitalism thus required not only vast quantities of capital, but a huge army of wage-labourers. Marx traces the origins of this workforce to the last third of the fifteenth century, when feudal lords began to enclose common land, and to clear the peasantry from the newly privatised estates, so that they could pursue profits in the wool trade through large-scale agriculture.[33] This theft of the commons, and the corresponding depopulation of the country-side, continued for centuries, and was accompanied by considerable state violence, including the use of the British Army to clear the Scottish Highlands in the early nineteenth century,[34] and the passage, in the sixteenth and seventeenth centuries, of a series of laws prescribing brutal punishments for begging and vagabondage.[35] The proletarian class was thus a product of 'the expropriation of the agricultural producer, the peasant, from the soil',[36] which separated workers from 'the ownership of the conditions for the realisation of their own labour'.[37]

The Industrial Revolution, taking place in the context of the centuries-long process of prim-itive accumulation, put the labouring class in a position of extreme weakness with respect to

---

[26]   Marx, *Capital*, vol 1, 382.

[27]   Marx, *Capital*, vol 1, 873.

[28]   Marx, *Capital*, vol 1, 874.

[29]   Marx, *Capital*, vol 1, 873.

[30]   Marx, *Capital*, vol 1, 875.

[31]   Marx, *Capital*, vol 1, 918. The origins of the industrial capitalist are different from the capitalist farmer, who gradually emerged through the transformation of labour relations in the countryside along-side the process of the enclosure of the commons. See *Capital*, vol 1, 905–7.

[32]   Marx devotes the very last chapter of the first volume of *Capital* to a discussion of EG Wakefield's analysis of the colonies. Wakefield argued that it was difficult for capitalist production to take hold in the colonies because the availability of land meant that the working class did not have to rely upon wage labour to survive. He proposed a policy of 'systematic colonisation' that would ensure a supply of wage labour by placing an artificial price on land. See Marx, *Capital*, vol 1, 931–40.

[33]   Marx, *Capital*, vol 1, 511.

[34]   Marx, *Capital*, vol 1, 889–93.

[35]   Marx, *Capital*, vol 1, 896–99.

[36]   Marx, *Capital*, vol 1, 876.

[37]   Marx, *Capital*, vol 1, 874.

their employers. The development of heavy industry put the control of production in the hands of the capitalist, and meant that manufacturing was no longer dependent upon craft workers who were noted for their 'habits of indiscipline'.[38] Meanwhile, a now landless peasantry provided a vast pool of cheap labour that was compelled, by both economic circumstances and punitive legislation, to accept waged exploitation on the factory floor.[39] However, Marx argues that the development of capitalism also created the material conditions through which this way of organising production might be overcome.[40] Under feudalism, workers had enjoyed private ownership of some of the means of production. This created a barrier to their ability to act together as a class, as peasants were separated from one another by working different plots of land, and craft workers laboured in small-scale workshops organised by guilds. However, the development of capitalism generated ever greater concentrations of capital, and, along with it, an increasingly large-scale and socialised labour process in which the instruments of labour could only be used in common.[41] This meant that, at the same time capitalism immiserated the working class, it made it easier for workers to organise collectively by ensuring that they were 'disciplined, united, organised by the very mechanism of the process of production itself'.[42] The socialisation of labour thus created the potential for a new political subject to emerge and assert its power: as Marx and Engels put it in *The Communist Manifesto*, 'with the development of industry the proletariat not only increases in number; it becomes concentrated in greater masses, its strength grows, and it feels that strength more'.[43]

Nonetheless, the organisation of production under capitalism gave the bourgeoisie the upper hand in their struggle with the nascent proletariat. In the first place, the bourgeoisie had control over the labour process, which gave it the power to circumvent laws even when they were in full force. While the most important of the managerial tactics adopted by capitalists was the relay system, Marx discusses a range of other techniques used to circumvent the Factory Acts, including setting clocks to the wrong time, forcing workers to take mealtimes outside the working day, replacing workers who were protected to some degree by law (such as women and children) with men who were not, and changing the definition of 'child' to include younger workers. The power that capitalists had over the factory also gave them the opportunity to use the wage relation to try and control the political activity of the working class. For example, manufacturers exploited the fact that workers were recovering from the 1846–47 economic crisis by cutting wages as much as 25 per cent, in an attempt to get workers to agitate against the restriction of hours under the 1848 Act.[44]

The growing economic power of the bourgeoisie also gave it substantial influence over the state. As Douglas Booth writes, by the 1830s 'the power of the old landed aristocracy over the

---

[38]   Henry Heller, 'Marx's *Capital* as History' (2014) 4 *International Critical Thought* 38, 46.

[39]   Marx, *Capital*, vol 1, 896–99.

[40]   Marx, *Capital*, vol 1, 541–42.

[41]   Marx, *Capital*, vol 1, 542. See also the analysis of co-operation in ch 13 of Marx, *Capital*, vol 1, 439–54.

[42]   Marx, *Capital*, vol 1, 542.

[43]   Karl Marx and Friedrich Engels, *The Communist Manifesto* (first published 1848, Gareth Stedman Jones ed, Penguin 2002) 229.

[44]   This strategy was, however, of little effect. Despite such efforts, which were accompanied by frenzied media propaganda, 70 per cent of workers declared that they remained in favour of the ten-hour working day. See Marx, *Capital*, vol 1, 397.

political apparatus had begun to weaken'.[45] The electoral changes that resulted from the Great Reform Act of 1832 had undermined the parliamentary power of the aristocracy and increased that of the bourgeoisie, while the working class remained excluded from the franchise. The political dominance of the industrial bourgeoisie at the time was reflected in the shift towards free trade policy in 1846–47, including, most importantly, the repeal of the Corn Laws that had regulated the grain trade. These changes undermined the economic base of the aristocracy by decreasing profits derived from agriculture, while at the same time increasing those from manufacture.[46] The industrial bourgeoisie had substantial influence over not only Parliament but also the judiciary: Marx points out that the magistrates in the county courts, which heard cases under the 1844 Factory Act, were often manufacturers themselves, who tended to find their commercial brethren not guilty.[47]

Given the political influence of the bourgeoisie, it is unsurprising that the creation and application of labour law should be heavily shaped by their economic interests. However, Marx also shows, at a number of important points in his narrative, that countervailing social and political forces placed important limits on the ability of the capitalist class to pursue these interests through the state. For example, capitalists waged a campaign against the 1833 Factory Act both within and outside Parliament, and this was so successful that, by 1835, the Whig government proposed lowering the age of childhood from 13 to 12.[48] However, Marx writes that the government 'lost its nerve' once the '"pressure from without" became more threatening'.[49] While Marx does not specify what form the pressure took, this suggests that some combination of class forces was sufficiently strong to prevent the state from acting in the immediate economic interests of industrial capital.

Marx provides a more comprehensive account of the class politics that surrounded the 1844 Factory Act. The Chartist movement emerged as a major political force in the late 1830s and early 1840s, demanding the franchise for workers, and making the Ten Hours Bill its 'economic … election cry'.[50] While the passage of the 1844 Act was opposed by most capitalist manufacturers, the Whig government backed these reforms to gain the support of the now politically organised working class, which it needed in its own conflict with the Tories over the repeal of the Corn Laws.[51] The 1844 Act was also supported by some industrialists, who, having complied with previous laws, complained that competitors who ignored it had received an unfair advantage.[52]

However, there was soon a dramatic reversal in the balance of class forces, as the state repressed the Chartist Party by imprisoning its leaders and dismembering its organisation,

---

[45]   Douglas E Booth, 'Karl Marx on State Regulation of the Labor Process: The English Factory Acts' (1978) 36 *Review of Social Economy* 137, 151.

[46]   Marx, *Capital*, vol 1, 393.

[47]   Marx, *Capital*, vol 1, 401–2.

[48]   Marx, *Capital*, vol 1, 392.

[49]   Marx, *Capital*, vol 1, 392.

[50]   Marx, *Capital*, vol 1, 393.

[51]   Marx, *Capital*, vol 1, 393. In their discussion of the ten hours agitation in *The Communist Manifesto*, Marx and Engels state that the bourgeoisie 'supplies the proletariat with its own elements of political and general education' by enlisting it in its struggle against the aristocracy. Marx and Engels, *Communist Manifesto*, 230.

[52]   Marx, *Capital*, vol 1, 393.

a move that 'shattered the self-confidence of the English working class'.[53] Subsequent insur-
rections on the continent, in June 1848, then united 'all fractions of the ruling class' against
the working class, which was everywhere 'outlawed, anathematized, placed under the "*loi des
suspects*"'.[54] This allowed manufacturers to mobilise around what Marx calls a 'pro-slavery
rebellion in miniature'.[55] On this occasion, capital's insurrection was pursued not through
parliamentary means but direct control over the labour process, with manufacturers exploiting loopholes that allowed them to fulfil the letter of the law while violating its spirit. The
courts also played a crucial role in the campaign against the working class. It is in the context
of his discussion of this capitalist revolt that Marx discusses the bias of the county courts.
And as noted earlier, it was in response to a case brought by manufacturers that the Court
of Exchequer rendered the 1848 Act null and void. Yet as was also noted, what seemed like
a thorough victory for the bourgeoisie produced another rapid reversal as the working class
shifted from depression in the wake of the 'fiasco of the Chartist party' to outraged militancy.
Factory inspectors began to warn that class antagonism had 'reached an unheard of degree
of tension',[56] and, faced with the threat of major industrial and political unrest, the British
government finally adopted an act that met the demands of the working class, doing away with
the relay system by imposing consistent mealtimes and a fixed working day of ten and a half
hours.

THE FACTORY ACTS AND THE POLITICS OF LAW

What does Marx's history of the Factory Acts teach us about law—and, more specifically,
about Marx's own approach to the law? To begin with, his analysis undermines the belief in
the autonomy of law and the state that characterises liberal jurisprudence and pluralist political
theory. The Factory Acts emerged from a political struggle shaped by class antagonism and
economic power, rather than a rational bureaucratic and parliamentary process that reflected
the greatest good for the greatest number. The application of the laws limiting the working day
was also irremediably influenced by class politics, with the judiciary displaying a substantial
bias in favour of the bourgeoisie. Yet these are rather generic insights that characterise all
Marxist theories of law; what is more important about Marx's account of the legal limitation
of the working day is that it also undermines some of the more simplistic theories of law that
have emerged from the Marxist tradition.

Perhaps the central problem in Marxist analyses of law is the relationship between the
juridical order and the mode of production. There are a range of different approaches to this
issue in the work of Marx and Engels, and those that have followed in their wake. Nonetheless,
analysis of law within the Marxist tradition has tended to be dogged by two forms of reductionism: economism and voluntarism.[57] Economistic theories of law generally argue that the

---

[53]   Marx, *Capital*, vol 1, 397.
[54]   Marx, *Capital*, vol 1, 397. For Marx's work on the 1848 revolutions and their aftermath see Karl
Marx, *Political Writings*, vol 1: *The Revolutions of 1848* (David Fernbach ed, Verso 2010); Marx, 'Class
Struggles in France'; Marx, 'Eighteenth Brumaire'.
[55]   Marx, *Capital*, vol 1, 398.
[56]   Marx, *Capital*, vol 1, 397.
[57]   For analyses of the role that these two forms of reductionism have played in Marxist legal theory,
see Richard Kinsey, 'Marxism and the Law: Preliminary Analyses' (1978) 5 *British Journal of Law and*

juridical 'superstructure' reflects the economic 'base', and that the driving force of legal change is the development of productive forces.[58] Yet this analysis tends to assume that the form and substance of law can simply be extrapolated from the system of production; what is rarely clear is the causal mechanism through which the economic base has this effect on the juridical superstructure.[59]

The voluntarist theory of law, on the other hand, tends to accompany the instrumental theory of the state that has been read out of Marx and Engels' claim that the 'executive of the modern state is nothing more than the executive committee for managing the common affairs of the whole bourgeoisie'.[60] On this account, the organisation of production divides society between a working class and those who exploit it; the potential for conflict between these two classes then creates the need for a state that can pacify society; and this state is used by the economically dominant class to pursue its interests and oppress the working class.[61] The voluntarist theory of law thus compensates for the limitations of economism by presenting politics as the means by which the mode of production influences the law; what tends to remain unclear in such analyses, however, is exactly how the bourgeoisie controls the state and its laws, particularly given that political and economic power are separated within the capitalist mode of production.[62]

Both of these accounts of law contain important insights, inasmuch as they contest the idea that law and state are autonomous with respect to productive relations and class forces. Yet they do not provide an especially detailed analysis of the relationship between economic structures and the legal system. As a result, they can be used to provide support for the common claim that Marxist thought is reductionist and deterministic. Economism suffers from these problems insofar as it does not afford law and politics any independence with respect to the economic base, the development of which is thought to be determined by economic 'laws' that are immanent to the system of productive relations. Meanwhile, voluntarist theories of law and state do not acknowledge that they can function as anything other than instruments of bourgeois oppression.

Society 202, 203–7; Hugh Collins, *Marxism and Law* (OUP 1982) 22, 22–34; Andrew Vincent, 'Marx and Law' (1993) 20 *Journal of Law and Society* 371, 379–87. On the dominance of the instrumental theory of law for much of the twentieth century, see Maureen Cain and Alan Hunt, *Marx and Engels on Law* (Academic Press 1979) x–xi. These approaches to law and state have by now been thoroughly contested within the Marxist tradition. In the anglophone world, this occurred in the flowering of debates in Marxist jurisprudence during the 1970s and early 1980s, particularly in the wake of Althusser's structuralist Marxism.

[58] While the metaphor of base and superstructure became central to the way that the relationship between law and production has been understood within the Marxist tradition, it only appears a few times in Marx's work. The most important is in the preface to 'A Contribution to the Critique of Political Economy' [1859] in Karl Marx, *Later Political Writings* (Terrell Carver ed, CUP 1996) 159–60.

[59] Steven Spitzer, 'Marxist Perspectives in the Sociology of Law' (1983) 9 *Annual Review of Sociology* 103, 104–5.

[60] Marx and Engels, *Communist Manifesto*, 221.

[61] For the canonical account of the state in these terms see VI Lenin, 'The State and Revolution' [1917] in VI Lenin, *Essential Works of Lenin: 'What is to be Done?' and Other Writings* (Henry M Christman ed, Dover 1966) 271.

[62] For a critique of the instrumental conception of the state on the basis of the specificities of the capitalist state, and in particular the separation of the political and the economic under capitalism, see Nicos Poulantzas, *State, Power, Socialism* (first published 1978, Patrick Camiller tr, Verso 2000) 12–13, 18–19.

How does Marx's analysis of the Factory Acts stand with respect to these two interpretations of his thinking on law? Marx displays a certain measure of economism when he states
that the substantive content of the Acts—detailed specifications with respect to stop times,
meal breaks, and which categories of workers can be employed at which times and for which
purposes—was not a 'fantasy of a Member of Parliament', but emerged as a kind of 'natural
law' from the 'modern mode of production'.[63] Yet the story that he tells in chapter ten is not
one in which law is simply a passive reflection of changes in the base of productive relations.
While the Acts regulated the organisation of the factory system, their existence and enforcement were the contingent result of political struggles in which unexpected events and shifting
class alliances played a major role. But while the development of the capitalist mode of production did not lead to the Factory Acts as a matter of necessity, it did have a profound impact
upon the course of the class struggle from which they emerged. As we have seen, by the early
nineteenth century, the development of capitalism had radically transformed the balance of
forces between the working class and the capitalist class by driving the peasantry off their land,
replacing craft work with machinery and proletarian labour, and giving the bourgeoisie control
over production, as well as a profound influence over the state. Yet industrial capitalism had
also expanded the ranks of the proletariat, whose immiseration bolstered their interest in the
struggle against the bourgeoisie, while the socialisation of labour placed the working class in
an unprecedented position to develop a unified political organisation. Meanwhile, competition
between capitalists, and differences in the economic interests of different fractions of capital
(in particular between agricultural capital and the newly ascendant industrialists), created
opportunities for the working class to 'compel legislative recognition of the particular interests
of workers, by taking advantage of the divisions within the bourgeoisie itself'.[64]

The voluntarist theory of law is thus correct to emphasise that politics plays a crucial role
in mediating between the organisation of production and the content of at least some kinds of
law. However, Marx's detailed account of the class politics that surrounded the Factory Acts
does not demonstrate that law or the state are simply instruments in the hands of capitalist
class. Indeed, if law were simply a tool for oppressing the working class, one would expect
the alliance between the Whigs and industrial capital to have led to the curtailment of legal
restrictions on the working day after the 1832 Reform Act. While the manufacturers were
certainly able to slow the passage of factory legislation, to shape its content, and to radically
undermine its application, effective limitations on the working day were eventually adopted by
Parliament and enforced by the British state. On Marx's account, this only came about because
the parliamentary representatives of the bourgeoisie acted against the wishes of industrial
capitalists when the exigencies of the political situation called for it. This occurred, as we have
noted, when the Whig government needed the political support of the working class for their
'free trade' reforms, and it happened again in 1848 to head off industrial and political unrest.

Marx's analysis of the Factory Acts is underpinned by a sophisticated account of the relationship between law and class antagonism, in which the law is neither just a reflection of the
economic base nor simply an instrument in the hands of capitalists who control the state. Marx
shows that the legal regulation of the working day was the contingent result of class struggles
that unfolded on a social and political terrain contoured by the economic development of capitalism, which determined the class composition of British society, defined the material inter-

---

[63]   Marx, *Capital*, vol 1, 394–95.
[64]   Marx and Engels, *Communist Manifesto*, 230.

ests of the contending classes, and shaped the political possibilities available to them in the conjunctures in question. The history of this struggle shows that the economically dominant class wields a decisive political influence over the capitalist state which, for the most part, acts in their immediate economic interests. However, the fact that political and economic power are to some degree distinct under capitalism means that the proletariat may be able to compel the adoption of laws that promote their own ends, depending in part upon their own level of political organisation and the divisions within the bourgeoisie.

Marx endorsed the legal limitation of the working day in his own political activism around the time he was completing the first volume of *Capital*, describing it as the 'preliminary condition' for any further emancipation of the working class.[65] This might seem surprising in light of the well-known criticisms of law that can be found throughout his work. Perhaps the most famous of these appears in his 1843 essay 'On the Jewish Question', where he argues that the supposedly universal rights of 'equality, liberty, security, property' in the 1789 Declaration of the Rights of Man and Citizen are nothing but 'the rights of the member of civil society, i.e. of egoistic man, of man separated from other men in the community'.[66] One also finds a critique of bourgeois rights in *Capital*, with Marx writing that the realm of exchange is the 'very Eden of the innate rights of man. There alone rule Freedom, Equality, Property and Bentham.'[67] For bourgeois thought, worker and capitalist meet each other in the sphere of exchange as equal legal subjects, each freely choosing to pursue their interests and dispose of their property (capitalist on the one hand, worker on the other) through the wage contract. Yet Marx argues that when we turn our attention to the 'hidden abode of production',[68] we quickly see that the relationship between worker and capitalist is one of exploitation and domination:

> he who was previously the money-owner, now strides out in front as a capitalist; the possessor of labour-power follows as his labourer. The one smirks self-importantly and is intent on business; the other is timid and holds back, like one who has brought his own hide to market and has nothing to expect but—a tanning.[69]

Towards the end of his analysis of the Factory Acts, however, Marx distinguishes between the 'pompous catalogue of the "inalienable rights of Man"' and the 'modest Magna Carta of the legally limited working day'.[70] Marx views the bourgeois rights associated with contract law as an essential component of capitalist exploitation, as they make wage dependence legally

---

[65] See Marx, 'Instructions for Delegates to the Geneva Congress', 78–80. This resolution was adopted by the Geneva Congress of the IWA. Marx and Engels are also very positive about the struggle to limit the working day by the British working class in *The Communist Manifesto*, which informs their comments on the growing strength of the working class. They do not, however, explicitly endorse the limitation of the working day as a political tactic in this work. Marx and Engels, *Communist Manifesto*, 230.

[66] Karl Marx, 'On the Jewish Question' [1843] in Karl Marx, *Early Writings* (Rodney Livingstone and Gregor Benton tr, Penguin 1975) 211, 229. Another famous example is found in his 1875 'Critique of the Gotha Programme', which criticises the bourgeois conception of equal rights for applying the same standard to different individuals, and argues that this idea must be overcome in the transition to communism: see 'A Contribution to the Critique of Political Economy' [1859] in Karl Marx, *Later Political Writings* (Terrell Carver ed, CUP 1996) 208, 213–15.

[67] Marx, *Capital*, vol 1, 280.

[68] Marx, *Capital*, vol 1, 280.

[69] Marx, *Capital*, vol 1, 280.

[70] Marx, *Capital*, vol 1, 416.

enforceable while presenting it as an expression of freedom and equality. By contrast, the laws limiting the working day emerged directly from the historical experience of exploitation, which taught workers that they had to 'put their heads together and, as a class, compel the passing of a law, an all-powerful social barrier by which they can be prevented from selling themselves and their families into slavery and death by voluntary contract with capital'.[71] Marx's critique of the rights of man and his endorsement of the legal limitation of the working day are thus grounded in an analysis of the role that each form of law plays within the political economy of capitalism. Where bourgeois rights present an illusory account of the exploitative social relations they help to maintain, the Factory Acts intervene in the sphere of production to limit the tendency to increase the working day.

However, Marx's endorsement of the legal limitation of the working day does not provide theoretical or political grounds for fetishising law reform as an antidote to the ills generated by the capitalist mode of production. While Marx's analysis of the Factory Acts shows that law may be useful in the political struggle against capitalism, it also shows that the most effective counter to exploitation is an organised and militant proletariat. Legal regulation may check some of capitalism's destructive tendencies if it is supported by a social and political force antagonistic to capitalism, or at least to specific capitalist interests. However, Marx's analysis also shows that capitalism generates incentives for the bourgeoisie to circumvent legal regulations, which means that the workers' movement must be eternally vigilant if it is to protect its living and working conditions (which is why Rosa Luxemburg described the work of trade unions under capitalism as the 'Labour of Sisyphus').[72] Further, Marx's critique of political economy shows that the capitalist organisation of production limits the capacity of legal reform to improve the lot of the proletariat, regardless of the strength of the labour movement. So long as the bourgeoisie controls the means of production, it wields substantial power over the working class, which remains exploited for the sake of surplus value production.

Marx once wrote that 'to be radical means to grasp things by the root'.[73] His political response to the exploitation of the working class was not, then, to make capitalism more humane by legally limiting exploitation. Instead, he sought to address the root of this problem by socialising production and abolishing exploitative labour as such. On Marx's account, this could only be achieved through a class struggle that led to the conquest of state power and the dictatorship of the proletariat. However, he believed that the struggle for the legal regulation of the working day made a vital contribution to this revolutionary political and economic project.

Marx notes that while manufacturers fought the Factory Acts tooth and nail, these laws generated a boom for those sectors of industry that were effectively regulated.[74] While the extension of the working day was in the immediate economic interests of individual capitalists, it gradually sapped the health of the workforce and the profitability of the capitalist system as a whole. The legal limitation of the working day thus led to the 'physical and moral regeneration of the factory workers', and, along with it, the 'wonderful development' of industry.[75]

---

[71]   Marx, *Capital*, vol 1, 416.
[72]   Rosa Luxemburg, 'Reform or Revolution' [1900] in Helen Scott (ed), *The Essential Rosa Luxemburg: Reform or Revolution & The Mass Strike* (Haymarket 2008) 83.
[73]   Karl Marx, 'A Contribution to the Critique of Hegel's Philosophy of Right. Introduction' [1844] in Karl Marx, *Early Writings* (Rodney Livingstone and Gregor Benton tr, Penguin 1975) 243, 251.
[74]   Marx, *Capital*, vol 1, 408–9.
[75]   Marx, *Capital*, vol 1, 408.

While saving capitalism from its own crisis tendencies could be regarded as self-defeating for the workers' movement, Marx saw it as a political victory for the working class because, as he states in his Inaugural Address to the IWA in 1864, 'it was the first time in broad daylight that the political economy of the middle class succumbed to that of the working class'.[76] Booth glosses this point nicely, suggesting that for Marx the economic boom that followed from the regulation of the working day provided 'historical proof of the superiority of social regulation and control over the blind functioning of *laissez faire* capitalism'.[77]

Nonetheless, a victory for socialism on the level of ideas would be meaningless without forms of organisation that could supplant the political economy of the middle class. In his 1864 address, Marx states that the co-operative movement had shown that it was possible for large-scale production to be carried out without masters.[78] However, he also argues that these experiments in workers' control over production could not challenge the power of industrial capital by themselves. To do this Marx believed that it was necessary for the proletariat to conquer political power and use it to foster co-operative production. On this front, he believed that the struggle for the legal limitation of the working day was a success because it mobilised the working class, provided it with experience in political organising, and brought it a significant political victory. The process of fighting for law reform had therefore transformed the balance of class forces between the capitalist class and the proletariat:

> after the factory magnates had resigned themselves and submitted to the inevitable, capital's power of resistance gradually weakened, while at the same time the working classes power of attack grew with the number of its allies in those social layers not directly interested in the question.[79]

CONCLUSION

The history of English factory legislation in the middle of the nineteenth century reveals much about the spirit of capital and, at the same time, about the 'spirit of the laws'. Marx's account of the Factory Acts renders liberal ideas of legal equality and state neutrality highly questionable by showing the power that law and the state give to the bourgeoisie in a capitalist society. Marx's analysis is also underpinned by an account of the relation between the capitalist mode of production, class struggle, and legal order which undermines many of the reductionist interpretations of his work that have dominated Marxist thought. The laws regulating the working day were not simply mechanical reflections of economic forces. Nor were they simple instruments of bourgeois oppression. Instead, they were products of a class struggle in which the balance of forces was heavily conditioned by the development of capitalism, but whose result was a contingent outcome of political events.

Although Marx's analysis of the Factory Acts clearly demonstrates that the capitalist legal and political system favours the bourgeoisie, it also suggests that law can make an important

---

[76]   Marx, 'Instructions for Delegates to the Geneva Congress', 79.

[77]   Booth, 'Karl Marx on State Regulation of the Labor Process', 155. Marx makes a similar point in *Capital*, where he states that the 'principle' of the fixed working day had triumphed, as evidenced by the fact that industrialists now trumpeted its virtues, and that the 'Pharisees of political economy' claimed the idea as a new discovery of their so-called science. See Marx, *Capital*, vol 1, 409.

[78]   Marx, 'Instructions for Delegates to the Geneva Congress', 79.

[79]   Marx, *Capital*, vol 1, 409.

contribution in the struggle against capitalism. However, it also shows that the political possibilities that law generates for the workers' movement, and indeed social movements more broadly, are dependent upon the kind of law that they seek to mobilise, and the particular politico-economic circumstances in which they do so. Marx's own analysis of the development of capitalism and the course of the class struggle led him to maintain a long-standing hostility towards the 'rights of man' because of the ideological and institutional role they play in maintaining the wage relation. At the same time, he supported the struggle for the legal limitation of the working day because it helped to undermine bourgeois ideology, politically mobilised the proletariat, and transformed the balance of class forces. For Marx, what was important about the legal regulation of the working day was not simply that it improved the living conditions of the proletariat, but that, in so doing, it strengthened their hand in the struggle for communism.

4. 'Putting weapons into the hands of the proletariat': Marx on the contradiction between capitalism and liberal democracy

August H Nimtz

INTRODUCTION

Forced to withdraw from the battlefield of the 1848–49 European Spring, Karl Marx and Frederick Engels were obligated as communists to draw a balance sheet on what had transpired in those momentous revolutionary events—in order to prepare for an expected revival. Marx's 'The Class Struggles in France, 1848 to 1850' was the most famous first fruit of their new literary task. About a third of the way into the text, he opined on the constitution that issued from the revolution:

> The fundamental contradiction of this constitution ... consists in the following: The classes whose social slavery the constitution is to perpetuate, proletariat, peasantry, petty bourgeoisie, it puts in possession of political power through universal suffrage. And from the class whose old social power it sanctions, the bourgeoisie, it withdraws the political guarantees of this power. It forces the political rule of the bourgeoisie into democratic conditions, which at every moment help the hostile classes to victory and jeopardise the very foundations of bourgeois society. From the first group it demands that they should not go forward from political to social emancipation; from the others that they should not go back from social to political restoration.[1]

This chapter argues that this was Marx's first explicit recognition of the 'fundamental contradiction' between capitalism and liberal democracy as universal suffrage, and that this is what the French experience of the European Spring taught him. Implicit in Marx's comment, I also argue, was his recognition that this contradiction could not endure indefinitely—that something had to give.

Marx's pregnant comment motivated an influential research agenda in the field of comparative politics. Political scientist Adam Przeworski revealed in a retrospective on his career that a major component of it was intended to refute Marx's point. As he explained, 'there is a passage by Marx wrote [sic] from 1850 in *Class Struggles in France* that says that the combination of private property and universal suffrage is impossible ... This phrase, which Marx repeats in other works, was my target'.[2] His own political agenda, he said, was to vindicate twentieth-century social democracy, and the reformist rather than revolutionary choices it

---

[1]   Karl Marx, 'The Class Struggles in France, 1848 to 1850' [1850] in Karl Marx and Frederick Engels, *Collected Works*, vol 10 (International Publishers 1975) 45, 79.
[2]   Adam Przeworski, 'Capitalism, Democracy, and Science' in Gerardo L Munck and Richard Snyder (eds), *Passion, Craft, and Method in Comparative Politics* (The Johns Hopkins University Press 2007) 456, 464. My 'Marx and Engels's Electoral Strategy: The Alleged and the Real' (2010) 32 *New Political Science* 367, disputes Przeworski's distorted reading of them.

made. Twenty-first century social democracy has experienced an unexpected revival—and by no means only in the United States, owing to the Bernie Sanders phenomenon. If it owes its success even marginally to a Przeworskian reading—or misreading—of Marx's point, then this exposition, what Marx really meant, has more significance than just interesting intellectual history. The political economy of late capitalism, I argue, reveals that Marx's claim, Przeworski's challenge notwithstanding, has more currency than ever.

I begin by distilling Marx's earlier views on constitutions and political democracy in order to determine if prior thinking in any way informed his point. Did he begin, in other words, with prior assumptions? Most importantly, to what extent did subsequent events in that historical moment bear out Marx's claim? How prescient was Marx? What actually happened in France? I then address contemporaneous and later comments that both he and Engels made on constitutions, universal suffrage, and the electoral process. How much did Marx's observation inform those comments? And how accurate did he prove to be?[3] Lastly, I attempt to make a case for the validity of Marx's insight by considering two prominent issues in capitalism's recent history.

Regarding this chapter in Marx's life, a new biographer claims that it was characterised by his 'hostility towards the modern representative state[,] ... with consequent belittlement of the significance of manhood suffrage and the democratic republic [and] ... disregard of political and legal forms'.[4] At the end of this chapter, the reader will be able to determine if this is true or simply a reiteration of an oft-repeated tale from the Marx-bashing enterprise.[5]

THE 'SOLVED *RIDDLE* OF ALL CONSTITUTIONS': EARLY MARX

Commenting on his university education two decades earlier, Marx noted in 1859 that though he had 'studied jurisprudence, I pursued it as a subject subordinated to philosophy and history'.[6] The privileging of the latter two subjects exposed him to the best that Western thought had to offer on the subject: he stood on the shoulders of Hegel, who had brilliantly digested and commented on the jurisprudence literature—'its most consistent, richest and final formulation', as Marx put it in the 'Introduction' to his *Contribution to the Critique of Hegel's Philosophy of Law* in 1843.[7] Marx's incomplete manuscript, for which the 'Introduction' was intended, is replete with his earliest ideas about constitutions, private property, elections, and democracy (as well as other topics such as bureaucracy). What follows can only be a distillation.

---

[3]   I include Engels in the discussion. He and Marx constituted a political partnership and there is nothing to suggest they were not on the same political page, particularly for the matters addressed here.

[4]   Gareth Stedman Jones, *Karl Marx: Greatness and Illusion* (Harvard University Press 2016) 307. For a recent and convincing refutation of such claims see Igor Shoikhedbrod, *Revisiting Marx's Critique of Liberalism: Rethinking Justice, Legality and Rights* (Palgrave Macmillan 2019).

[5]   About this enterprise, see Hal Draper's still insightful foreword to *Karl Marx's Theory of Revolution*, vol 1 (Monthly Review Press 1977).

[6]   Karl Marx, 'Preface' in Karl Marx, *A Contribution to the Critique of Political Economy* (International Publishers 1989) 19.

[7]   Karl Marx, 'Contribution to the Critique of Hegel's Philosophy of Law. Introduction' [1844] in Karl Marx and Frederick Engels, *Collected Works*, vol 3 (International Publishers 1975) 175, 181. On the significance of Hegel's book, see Shlomo Avineri, *Karl Marx: Philosophy and Revolution* (Yale University Press 2019) ch 2.

The practical experience of the newly minted PhD is crucial to understanding Marx's interrogation of Hegel's *Philosophy of Law*. His 11-month stint as a cub reporter and editor for the liberal *Rheinische Zeitung* in Cologne until March 1843 taught him what no doctoral philosophy education could. 'I first found myself', he later admitted, 'in the embarrassing position of having to discuss what is known as material interests'.[8] He got the job owing in part to a remarkable letter of recommendation from Moses Hess, six years Marx's senior and author, at that point, of two books on philosophy.

> Be prepared to meet the greatest, perhaps the only real philosopher living now ... Dr. Marx ... is still a young man, barely 24 years old, but he will give the final blow to all medieval religion and politics; he combines the deepest philosophical seriousness with a cunning wit. Can you imagine Rousseau, Voltaire, Holbach, Lessing, Heine, and Hegel combined—not thrown together—in one person? If you can—you have Dr. Marx.[9]

Hess' letter reveals what the young Marx brought to his interrogation of Hegel.

Along with the problem of press censorship, Marx reported on the plight of landless peasants and impoverished grape growers at the mercy of the wealthy, issues that required him to address the legal and thus political framework within which these developments unfolded. This, in turn, obligated him to take on Hegel's defence of constitutional monarchy, which Marx opposed, and therefore also Hegel's theory of constitutions.[10] Hegel's basic problem, Marx argued, is that he began with 'the idea' of the state and its constitution. 'If Hegel had set out from real subjects as the bases of the state he would not have found it necessary to transform the state in a mystical fashion into a subject.'[11] Marx therefore dismissed as a 'trivial truth' Hegel's point that a constitution could be out of sync with the 'customs and consciousness of any given people' at any determinant moment, 'a heavy fetter on an advanced consciousness'.[12] The solution, he replied, 'would be simply the demand for a constitution which contains within itself the designation and the principle to advance along with consciousness, to advance as actual men advance, this is only possible when "man" has become the principle of the constitution'.[13] Therein lay the premise of Marx's alternative theory.

The 'man' Marx had in mind was the 'sovereignty of the people', 'the democracy' in the parlance at that time. 'Democracy', he argued, 'is the solved *riddle* of all constitutions'.[14] If understood that way, he continued, 'the constitution is constantly brought back to its actual basis, the *actual human being,* the *actual people,* and established as the people's *own* work'.[15] To get the attention of the audience of his time—and maybe even today for those who treat constitutional instruments like the US Constitution as if they were religious texts—Marx asserted: 'Just as it is not religion which creates man but man who creates religion, so it is not

---

[8]   Marx, 'Preface', 19.

[9]   Avineri, *Karl Marx*, 56.

[10] Avineri, *Karl Marx*, ch 2, is a useful introduction to Marx's critique. Draper, *Karl Marx's Theory of Revolution*, vol 1, ch 3, is still the best summary.

[11] Karl Marx, 'Contribution to the Critique of Hegel's Philosophy of Law' [1843] in Karl Marx and Frederick Engels, *Collected Works*, vol 3 (International Publishers 1975) 3, 23.

[12] Marx, 'Contribution to the Critique of Hegel's Philosophy of Law', 19.

[13] Marx, 'Contribution to the Critique of Hegel's Philosophy of Law', 19.

[14] Marx, 'Contribution to the Critique of Hegel's Philosophy of Law', 29 (original emphasis).

[15] Marx, 'Contribution to the Critique of Hegel's Philosophy of Law', 29 (original emphases).

the constitution which creates the people but the people which creates the constitution'.[16] The basis of all constitutions, in other words, were 'the people', either their consent for democratic ones, in both 'content and form', or their passive compliance with constitutional monarchies or even tyrannies.[17]

As for constitutional change, Marx rejected Hegel's category of:

> *gradual* transition … [I]t explains nothing … Posed correctly, the question is simply this: Has the people the right to give itself a new constitution? The answer must be an unqualified 'Yes', because once it has ceased to be an actual expression of the will of the people the constitution has become a practical illusion.[18]

But 'for a *new* constitution', as France 1789 taught, 'a real revolution has always been required'.[19] Given the world in which he lived and his experience as a cub reporter, Marx had no illusions about 'the people' vis-à-vis the constitution. 'The political constitution at its highest point is therefore the *constitution of private property*', especially '*landed property*'. No friend of private property given its '*barbarism … against family life*', Marx thought more consequential 'the power of *abstract private property* over the *political state*'.[20] The oppression of landless peasants and small grape growers in the Rhineland no doubt informed Marx's harsh judgment.

It was in the legislative arena that the 'power of *abstract private property*' was conspicuously on display.[21] That had a lot to do with the electoral laws. For that reason, 'the question here is not whether civil society [*bürgerliche Gesellschaft* in the original, literally bourgeois society] shall exercise the legislative power through representatives or by all individually; the question is rather one of the *extension* and greatest possible *generalisation* of *election* both of the right to vote and the right to be *elected*'.[22] In anticipation of the European Spring, 'this is the real point of dispute concerning political reform, in France as in England'.[23] In a series of subsequent articles titled 'On the Jewish Question', Marx revealed that he had been reading extensively about the reality of liberal democracy on the other side of the Atlantic, the best extant example. The United States, including its electoral system, taught the young Marx that something more fundamental was needed to bring about 'human emancipation' if this were the best that liberal democracy had to offer.[24] This was of crucial importance for the communist conclusions he would soon begin to draw explicitly.[25]

At the heart of Marx's critique of Hegel was the philosopher's claim that he had found the solution to the problem of the particularism and 'egoism' of civil society—a society that prioritised individual and private rights, especially the private ownership of property, and which

---

[16]   Marx, 'Contribution to the Critique of Hegel's Philosophy of Law', 29.

[17]   Marx, 'Contribution to the Critique of Hegel's Philosophy of Law', 29.

[18]   Marx, 'Contribution to the Critique of Hegel's Philosophy of Law', 57 (original emphasis).

[19]   Marx, 'Contribution to the Critique of Hegel's Philosophy of Law', 56 (original emphasis).

[20]   Marx, 'Contribution to the Critique of Hegel's Philosophy of Law', 98–99 (original emphases).

[21]   Marx, 'Contribution to the Critique of Hegel's Philosophy of Law', 99 (original emphasis).

[22]   Marx, 'Contribution to the Critique of Hegel's Philosophy of Law', 120 (original emphases).

[23]   Marx, 'Contribution to the Critique of Hegel's Philosophy of Law', 120.

[24]   Karl Marx, 'On the Jewish Question' [1843] in Karl Marx and Frederick Engels, *Collected Works*, vol 3 (International Publishers 1975) 146.

[25]   See August H Nimtz, *Marx, Tocqueville, and Race in America: The 'Absolute Democracy' or 'Defiled Republic'* (Lexington 2003) ch 1.

had been lauded by liberal philosophers like Thomas Hobbes, John Locke, and Adam Smith. While Hegel correctly diagnosed the problem—'his major contribution to modern political philosophy' in Avineri's opinion[26]—his solution to 'individualism', Marx argued, was bogus. The bureaucracy, according to Hegel, was 'the universal class', supposedly representing the interests of society as a whole. Marx's dissection of it, long before that of Max Weber, suggested otherwise. Clearly his reporter/editor experience was informative. If not the bureaucracy, then which class? Certainly not the bourgeoisie—'universal egoism' par excellence. Once Marx moved to Paris and completed his critique of Hegel, he discovered the 'universal class'. His advice for Germany was direct: only that social stratum 'which cannot emancipate itself without emancipating itself from all other spheres of society and thereby emancipating all other spheres of society' could claim a universal status, and this was 'the proletariat'.[27] Only the proletariat had a class interest in '*general human* emancipation'.[28] This discovery was the *sine qua non* for all of Marx's subsequent analyses *and* actions.[29]

LESSONS OF THE EUROPEAN SPRING: FIRST EDITION

Universal male suffrage—seen as universal suffrage or its advent—only became a constitutional right in 1793 during the French Revolution.[30] But it was never realised. Napoleon's overthrow of the First Republic took the issue off the table until the plebeian masses in Paris took to the streets in February 1848, the commencement of the Second Republic. In the lead-up to the February Revolution, liberals vacillated on electoral reform. This included Alexis de Tocqueville, the famous author of *Democracy in America*.[31] The right to vote had always been a class issue, as debates during the English Civil War in the seventeenth century had made clear. The most radical voice in those debates, Gerard Winstanley, a Digger or True Leveller, argued that universal suffrage, were it ever granted, could not guarantee democracy as long as inequalities in wealth persisted.[32] The incompatibility between social inequality and political democracy would mark the course of the European Spring, not only in France but elsewhere—and it has done so ever since. But Winstanley's prescient insight could only be verified if universal suffrage became a reality.

With France's last monarch, Louis-Philippe, unceremoniously sent packing, a provisional government composed of various political tendencies, including socialists, took the reins on

[26] Avineri, *Karl Marx*, 31.
[27] Marx, 'Contribution to the Critique of Hegel's Philosophy of Law. Introduction', 186.
[28] Marx, 'Contribution to the Critique of Hegel's Philosophy of Law. Introduction', 184 (original emphasis).
[29] Spurred no doubt by his critique of Hegel, Marx planned to write, according to a 'Draft Plan', a 'Work on the Modern State' that included many of the topics in the critique, as well as others such as 'judicial power and law', 'nationality and the people', and 'political parties'. Karl Marx, 'Draft Plan for a Work on the Modern State' [1844–47] in Karl Marx and Frederick Engels, *Collected Works*, vol 4 (International Publishers 1975) 666.
[30] Greece, for a brief period in the first half of the nineteenth century, was the exception. See Daniele Caramani, *Elections in Western Europe Since 1815* (Macmillan 2000) 47–54.
[31] On Tocqueville's reluctance to support universal suffrage see August H Nimtz, *Marxism versus Liberalism: Comparative Real-Time Political Analysis* (Palgrave Macmillan 2019) ch 2.
[32] For an informative account of the English Civil War, with specific reference to the question of suffrage, see Paul Foot, *The Vote: How It Was Won and How It Was Undermined* (Viking 2005).

24 February. The latter's presence registered the all-important fact that in addition to political rights Paris' proletariat sought social rights. Key to spurring the overturn was the economic crisis the country and much of western Europe was facing—the first transnational capitalist depression. The immediate issue facing unemployed Parisian workers was the need for a job, so that they and their families might eat. Most, no doubt, saw the right to vote as a means toward that end. The elections at the end of April 1848 for a constituent assembly allowed many of them to do so for the first time. This marked the realisation of the constitutional right of universal male suffrage promised in 1793. Until then only roughly 240 000 men out of a population of 36 million could vote.

While the Parisian proletariat was striving to put its stamp on the February Revolution, Marx and Engels were knee-deep in the German edition of the European Spring. They too fought for a working-class perspective, as outlined in the just published *Communist Manifesto*.[33] In addition to actions on the streets and barricades, their efforts involved detailed attention to constitution-writing, suffrage, and electoral politics. Only when it was clear 14 months later that the German Revolution had stalled did they retreat from the battlefield. On the way to exile in London, they stopped in Paris to assess developments there. Marx, who arrived in June, wrote to his partner, still in Germany, that 'never has a colossal eruption of the revolutionary volcano been more imminent than in Paris today'.[34] If the French struggle was still alive, there was hope for Germany. Thus the commencement of their balance sheets on the French Revolution.

Engels arrived in Paris after Marx and family left for London in August 1849. He filed his first report on 20 December 1849. A month later in another article for the Chartist monthly, *The Democratic Review*, he pointed to a local election in which 'the great majority' of the vote went 'for a thoroughly Red candidate' in what had been historically a reactionary stronghold.[35] For Engels, this was evidence that the revolution was indeed alive. Elections on 10 March gave him further cause for optimism despite the fact that in Paris 'some sixty thousand working men have been, under a variety of pretexts, struck off the voting register'.[36] Only in hindsight would Engels and Marx see the purge as the beginning of the end of the world's first experiment in universal suffrage. Engels reported that owing to expected gains of 'the Social-Democratic party' in the elections, the:

> government ... prepared a measure for doing away with what is now openly called the conspiracy of 'Universal Suffrage'. They intend to make the suffrage indirect; the voters to elect a limited number of electors, who again name the representative. In this the government are sure of the support of the majority.[37]

---

[33]   See August H Nimtz, *Marx and Engels: Their Contribution to the Democratic Breakthrough* (State University of New York Press 2000) chs 3–4, for details about their participation in the German theatre.

[34]   Karl Marx, 'Karl Marx to Frederick Engels, in Kaiserslautern, 7 June 1849' in Karl Marx and Frederick Engels, *Collected Works*, vol 38 (International Publishers 1975) 198, 199.

[35]   Frederick Engels, 'Striking Proofs of the Glorious Progress of Red Republicanism!' [1850] in Karl Marx and Frederick Engels, *Collected Works*, vol 10 (International Publishers 1978) 21, 22.

[36]   Frederick Engels, 'Signs of the Times.—The Anticipated Revolution' [1850] in Karl Marx and Frederick Engels, *Collected Works*, vol 10 (International Publishers 1978) 24, 26.

[37]   Engels, 'Signs of the Times', 26.

But thinking that the revolution was still alive, Engels mistakenly assumed that the regime would not be able to get away with this sleight of hand.

'*Victory!* Victory!' Engels happily reported in his article on 22 March 1850. Three 'representatives of the people for Paris', one of whom was 'an openly pronounced communist of long standing', were elected on 10 March to the National Assembly, 'from 127,000 to 132,000 votes'.[38] Further, the 'elections in the departments … have been very favourable to the Red party. They having carried two-thirds, the [Party of Order] one-third of their candidates'.[39] But Engels, a month later, was sober about the victory. For a run-off election in Paris, '*from twenty to thirty thousand working men struck off* under various pretexts' the voting lists. And neither was there a revolutionary leadership in place for 'the Paris movement'. Yet the moment could be saved. 'The fact remains that with universal suffrage, they [the Party of Order] can no longer govern France … And the government, forced to attack universal suffrage, will thereby give the people an occasion for a combat, in which there is for the proletarians the certainty of victory.'[40] The 'ordermongers', as Marx called them (or the Party of Order, as they would come to be known), were composed of the 'two great royalist factions', the most conservative bourgeois forces in opposition to the revolutionary proletariat.[41] Though never an official member, Tocqueville was effectively one of their enablers.[42] Like his partner, Engels too held there to be an incompatibility between liberal democracy-cum-universal suffrage and the interests of capital represented by the Party of Order. Again, something had to give. When the government did resolve the problem on 31 May 1850, Engels, contrary to what he expected, was at pains to explain 'the indifference displayed by the people, at the destruction of Universal Suffrage'.[43] Time now to bring Marx into the conversation.

Now settled in London, Marx began writing in January 1850 the articles for what became 'The Class Struggles in France, 1848 to 1850'.[44] Their purpose, Marx explained, was to 'prove' how the defeat effectively put the proletarian revolution on France's political agenda for the first time. The first article sought to explain the reason for the February Revolution, which initiated the European Spring, and its contours in class terms with particular focus on the proletariat, its strengths and limitations. The proletariat and not the bourgeoisie, he argued, demanded that the February uprising result in 'the proclamation of the republic on the basis of universal suffrage'.[45]

> By dictating the republic to the Provisional Government, and through the Provisional Government to the whole of France, the proletariat immediately stepped into the foreground as an independent party, but at the same time challenged the whole of bourgeois France to enter the lists against it. What it won

---

[38] Frederick Engels, 'The Elections.—Glorious Victory of the Reds.—Proletarian Ascendancy.—Dismay of the Ordermongers.—New Schemes of Repression and Provocations to Revolution' [1850] in Karl Marx and Frederick Engels, *Collected Works*, vol 10 (International Publishers 1978) 27, 27 (original emphasis).
[39] Engels, 'The Elections', 28.
[40] Engels, 'The Elections', 30–32 (original emphasis).
[41] Marx, 'The Class Struggles in France, 1848 to 1850', 101.
[42] Nimtz, *Marxism versus Liberalism*, ch 2.
[43] Engels, 'The Elections', 35.
[44] Originally written for Marx and Engels' short-lived journal the *Neue Rheinische Zeitung*, the articles were republished in 1895 with an introduction by Engels under the present title.
[45] Marx, 'Class Struggles in France, 1848 to 1850', 54.

was the *terrain* for the fight for its revolutionary emancipation, but by no means this emancipation itself.[46]

Four decades later, in 1892, when an opponent accused Marx and Engels of having ignored forms of democratic governance, Engels responded as follows: 'Marx and I, for forty years, repeated *ad nauseam* that for us the democratic republic is the only political form in which the struggle between the working class and the capitalist class can first be universalised and then culminate in the decisive victory of the proletariat.'[47] He could have rightly pointed to Marx's argument about the democratic 'terrain' the proletariat needed for its liberation as evidence for his claim.

Marx then addressed the significance of the '*direct general elections*' to the Constituent Assembly that convened on 4 May 1848—the first anywhere in Europe.[48]

> But if universal suffrage was not the miracle-working magic wand the republican worthies had taken it for, it possessed the incomparable higher merit of unchaining the class struggle, of letting the various middle strata of bourgeois society rapidly get over their illusions and disappointments, of tossing all the sections of the exploiting class at one throw to the apex of the state, and thus tearing from them their deceptive mask, whereas the monarchy with its property qualifications had let only certain factions of the bourgeoisie compromise themselves, allowing the others to lie hidden behind the scenes and surrounding them with the halo of a common opposition.[49]

Unlike the 'republican worthies', Marx the communist viewed universal suffrage not as an end but as a means, in this case to politically educate the proletariat and learn who its true allies were.

The life-and-death lessons of the Constituent Assembly elections for the Parisian proletariat arrived with a vengeance on 22 June. When the Provisional Government reneged on its promise to provide jobs for the unemployed, they took to the streets again. 'The workers', Marx wrote, 'were left no choice; they had to starve or let fly. They answered on June 22 with the tremendous insurrection in which the first great battle was fought between the two classes that split modern society. It was a fight for the preservation or annihilation of the *bourgeois* order. The veil that shrouded the republic was torn asunder.'[50] The uprising was brutally suppressed, 'the bourgeoisie ... massacring over 3,000 prisoners', compelled to do so because the alternative, Marx continued, meant 'the bold slogan of revolutionary struggle: *Overthrow of the bourgeoisie! Dictatorship of the working class!*'—his first usage of the term.[51] The terrain on which the proletariat was defeated was 'the birthplace of the *bourgeois republic*', which required in 'its pure form' a 'state whose admitted object it is to perpetuate the rule of

---

[46]   Marx, 'Class Struggles in France, 1848 to 1850', 54 (emphasis added).

[47]   Frederick Engels, 'Reply to the Honourable Giovanni Bovio, 16 February 1892' in Karl Marx and Frederick Engels, *Collected Works*, vol 27 (International Publishers 1990) 270, 271.

[48]   Marx, 'Class Struggles in France, 1848 to 1850', 65 (original emphasis).

[49]   Marx, 'Class Struggles in France, 1848 to 1850', 65.

[50]   Marx, 'Class Struggles in France, 1848 to 1850', 67 (original emphasis).

[51]   Marx, 'Class Struggles in France, 1848 to 1850', 68–69 (original emphasis). For the most exhaustive treatment of how Marx and Engels employed the 'dictatorship of the proletariat', see Hal Draper, *Karl Marx's Theory of Revolution*, vol 3 (Monthly Review Press 1986), and in this first instance at 175–81. The only qualification I would add to Draper's otherwise erudite exposition is that rather than just the rule of majority, as Draper argues, 'force' and 'despotic means' were essential to their usage of 'dictatorship', as seen in their *Communist Manifesto*.

capital, the slavery of labor'—a 'bourgeois dictatorship'.[52] The defeat had clarified, in other words, not only what was now at stake in France but in all of Europe—either the rule of the working class or the rule of capital.

Once the Parisian proletariat had been slain, imprisoned, and exiled, the Constituent Assembly could get back to writing the kind of constitution for the kind of state it wanted—to represent not 'the people' but only a portion of them, the propertied. This is a central theme in Marx's second article in 'Class Struggles', where his weighty point about the 'fundamental contradiction of this constitution' appears. He completed the article about 4 March 1850, a fact that is of significance because the actual abolition of universal suffrage took place two months later on 31 May.[53] This means that Marx could not have made his prescient point with the advantage of hindsight.

Marx noted that before the June slaughter the architects of the constitution considered incorporating into it a 'right to work' provision, 'the first clumsy formula wherein the revolutionary demands of the proletariat are summarised'.[54] Specifically, the relevant text stated that 'the right of labour is the right of every member of society to live by labour. Therefore it is the duty of society to supply with work all able-bodied persons who cannot otherwise obtain it'.[55] But such a provision, he argued, was incompatible with capitalist relations of production. Tocqueville, a key architect of the constitution, later admitted that only because of 'fear of outside events and the excitement of the moment[,] … this pressure of revolutionary ideas', was the provision entertained.[56] The first time the bourgeoisie ever considered enshrining 'the right to work' in one of its constitutions was therefore when the plebeian masses took to the streets. Their brutal repression, which Tocqueville had a hand in, meant that such a concession was no longer necessary.[57]

Nevertheless, the document still displayed contradictions between the interests of the bourgeoisie and those of workers. The most important was the subject of Marx's key point. Again:

> [t]he fundamental contradiction of this constitution, however, consists in the following: The classes whose social slavery the constitution is to perpetuate—proletariat, peasantry, petty bourgeoisie—it puts in possession of political power through universal suffrage. And from the class whose old social power it sanctions, the bourgeoisie, it withdraws the political guarantees of this power. It forces the political rule of the bourgeoisie into democratic conditions, which at every moment help the hostile classes to victory and jeopardise the very foundations of bourgeois society. From the first group it demands that they should not go forward from political to social emancipation; from the others that they should not go back from social to political restoration.[58]

---

[52] Marx, 'Class Struggles in France, 1848 to 1850', 69 (original emphasis).

[53] Hal Draper, *The Marx-Engels Chronicle: A Day-by-Day Chronology of Marx and Engels' Life and Activity* (Schocken 1985) 48, n 10.

[54] Marx, 'Class Struggles in France, 1848 to 1850', 77–78.

[55] Karl Marx, 'The Constitution of the French Republic Adopted November 4, 1848' [1851] in Karl Marx and Frederick Engels, *Collected Works*, vol 10 (International Publishers 1978) 567, 567.

[56] Nimtz, *Marxism versus Liberalism*, 50–51.

[57] On Tocqueville's role in the repression, see Nimtz, *Marxism versus Liberalism*, 48. Tocqueville's admission is indispensable, I argue, for understanding the modern politics of the social safety net—granted under 'pressure' or the threat thereof. Social benefits are not the default position of the capitalist mode of production.

[58] Marx, 'Class Struggles in France, 1848 to 1850', 79.

Private property, whose protection the constitution guaranteed, ensured that the proletariat, peasantry, and petit bourgeoisie were bounded through the wage-relation (and debt) to the bourgeoisie, and therefore unable to realise 'social emancipation'. On the other hand, these three classes now had the right to vote, putting the political power of the bourgeoisie, a monopoly it enjoyed before February 1848, in jeopardy.

The rest of the article is mainly about the growing contest between Louis Bonaparte, elected president on 10 December 1848, a product of the constitution, and the National Assembly, newly elected on 14 May 1849, in which the Party of Order became the leading faction. The struggle registered, owing to universal suffrage, the emergence of two:

> quite different periods in the life process of the republic; the one, the small republican faction of the bourgeoisie that alone could proclaim the republic, wrest it from the revolutionary proletariat by street fighting and a reign of terror [over the June insurgency in Paris], and draft its ideal basic features in the constitution; and the other, the whole royalist mass of the bourgeoisie that alone could rule in this constituted bourgeois republic, strip the constitution of its ideological trimmings, and realise by its legislation and administration the indispensable conditions for the subjugation of the proletariat.[59]

Tocqueville, a key architect of the final document, took the lead in stripping 'the constitution of its ideological trimmings' especially the 'right to work' provision.[60]

The elections to the National Assembly in May 1849 resulted in the '*social-democratic party*, that is, the *Red* Party', as Marx put it, taking second place behind the Party of Order with a third of the vote.[61] Its leader, Alphonse Ledru-Rollin, organised a mass protest on 13 June, against Bonaparte's government for its counter-revolutionary role in Rome's edition of the European Spring—in violation of the constitution. Poorly organised, however, Ledru-Rollin and company were routed and forced to flee. Although the Parisian proletariat abstained from the protest—payback for Ledru-Rollin's Montagnard party not coming to its defence a year earlier—the spectre of another June 1848 uprising steeled the Party of Order and the Bonaparte government to have the National Assembly enact measures to severely limit democratic space guaranteed by the constitution. Tocqueville, the foreign minister in Bonaparte's government, enthusiastically supported the measures. It was a needed 'parliamentary dictatorship', as he called it.[62] For Marx, 'the 13th of June ... makes the *legislative dictatorship* of the [Party of Order] a *fait accompli*'.[63]

But the 'fundamental contradiction' was still in place. Marx's third article in 'Class Struggles', completed about the end of March, accurately anticipated how the contradiction would be resolved.[64] Despite the Party of Order's victory over Ledru-Rollin's faction, universal suffrage, increasingly threatened and degraded, as Engels had noted in his 20 December 1849 article, was still in place. And as executive and legislative policies increasingly alienated the lower classes, especially the peasantry, 'the votes that the peasant casts into the ballot box' could be determinant and radicalising.[65] Crucial here was the 'peasants' actual experience of

---

[59]   Marx, 'Class Struggles in France, 1848 to 1850', 85–86.
[60]   See Nimtz, *Marxism versus Liberalism*, 49–50.
[61]   Marx, 'Class Struggles in France, 1848 to 1850', 97 (original emphases).
[62]   Tocqueville, *Recollections*, 220.
[63]   Marx, 'Class Struggles in France, 1848 to 1850', 107 (original emphasis).
[64]   Draper, *The Marx-Engels Chronicle*, 48, n10.
[65]   Marx, 'Class Struggles in France, 1848 to 1850', 122.

using the vote, and the successive disappointments it rained down blow by blow with revolutionary speed upon them. *Revolutions are the locomotives of history.*'[66]

Among the various tendencies that called themselves 'socialist' was one in which 'the *proletariat* increasingly organises itself around *revolutionary Socialism*, around *Communism* … This Socialism is the *declaration of the permanence of the revolution*, the *class dictatorship* of the proletariat as the necessary transit point to the *abolition of class distinctions generally*'—that is, to a communist society.[67] For Marx, needless to say, that was the real socialist party. When elections were scheduled for 10 March 1850 to replace Ledru-Rollin and the other Montagnard deputies who were expelled due to the 13 June demonstration, that tendency put forward three candidates to represent the Parisian proletariat. The results were what moved Engels to declare '*Victory!* Victory!' in his aforementioned 24 April article. Not only did the three revolutionary socialist-endorsed candidates win their races, but beyond Paris the Montagnards made major gains.

The victories left the bourgeoisie fuming. Marx and also Engels concluded that the gains for the 'party of anarchy', as the Party of Order called the socialists, were intolerable not only for the bourgeoisie but also for Bonaparte. Only one outcome was possible.

> The foundation of the constitution … is *universal suffrage. Annihilation of universal suffrage*—such is the last word of the party of Order, of the bourgeois dictatorship … By repudiating universal suffrage, with which it hitherto draped itself and from which it sucked its omnipotence, the bourgeoisie openly confesses, '*Our dictatorship has hitherto existed by the will of the people; it must now be consolidated against the will of the people.*'[68]

The solution to the 'fundamental contradiction' was now in sight.

Marx's forecast was prescient. On 31 May 1850, the National Assembly, under the leadership of the Party of Order, effectively ended after two years not only France's but the world's first experiment with universal suffrage.[69] It took him seven months to get back into print to report and assess what had happened.

A digression is needed here. As Marx was making his comments on universal suffrage and liberal democracy, and the 10 March special elections were being arranged, he and Engels were just issuing their first statement on how the revolutionary proletariat should conduct itself in the electoral process. Their March 1850 'Address of the Central Authority to the League' was a balance sheet—and self-criticism—for the German theatre of the European Spring. Marx, who had leadership responsibilities for Germany's first communist party, apparently dissolved the organisation into the broader democratic movement sometime during the 13-month convulsions. That decision, the document admits, had been a mistake. In (unfulfilled) anticipation of a new upsurge, it sketched out a course of independent working class political action. Along with urging alternative governing institutions and popular militias in the next upheavals, Marx and Engels prescribed that the workers' party run its own candidates

---

[66] Marx, 'Class Struggles in France, 1848 to 1850', 122 (original emphasis).

[67] Marx, 'Class Struggles in France, 1848 to 1850', 127 (original emphases).

[68] Marx, 'Class Struggles in France, 1848 to 1850', 130–31 (original emphases).

[69] Though Tocqueville was not present when the vote was taken, owing to illness, a later comment suggests he was not opposed to the decision. Alexis de Tocqueville, *Selected Letters on Politics and Society* ed. Roger Boesche (University of California Press 1985) 268. By July 1850, he was having second thoughts on the need to maintain the constitution (see 249).

in future elections regardless of their chances for winning. Doing so would give the party an opportunity 'to count their forces and to lay before the public their revolutionary attitude and party standpoint'.[70] Participation in elections was obligatory for communists but only if done independently—a word that appears on every page of the 11-page document—of the bourgeoisie and petit bourgeoisie.[71] They could have pointed to the candidacy of François Raspail in the presidential elections in France on 10 December 1848, as an example—'the first act', Marx noted in his 'Class Struggles', 'by which the proletariat, as an independent party, declared its separation from the democratic party', whose candidate was Alexandre Ledru-Rollin.[72] At the same moment, therefore, that the first opportunity for the European proletariat to participate in elections was under threat, Marx and Engels insisted that they continue to do so when possible. Any anarchist/ultra-leftist or liberal claim that they belittled working-class involvement in the electoral process flies in the face of the evidence from the very beginning.[73]

Marx's last article in 'Class Struggles', completed sometime in October 1850, offered an explanation why, contrary to Engels' expectation, no mass rebellion took place to oppose the 31 May law abolishing universal suffrage. The government's decision to put 'an army of 150,000 men in Paris' in position, along with 'the long deferment of the decision, the appeasing attitude of the press, the pusillanimity of the [Montagnards] and of the newly elected representatives, the majestic calm of the petty bourgeoisie', were all determinant.[74] But 'above all, the commercial and industrial prosperity, prevented any attempt at revolution on the part of the proletariat'—something Marx had learned during the course of the research he had been conducting since his arrival in London.[75] If it took a capitalist crisis, a deep recession, to push the working class into the streets of Paris in February 1848, such conditions no longer existed two years later. Nevertheless, there was a lesson worth noting here. 'Universal suffrage had fulfilled its mission. The majority of the people had passed through the school of development, which is all that universal suffrage can serve for in a revolutionary period. It had to be set aside by a revolution or by the reaction.'[76] For Marx and Engels, again, the electoral process was not an end in itself but a means to an end, namely proletarian emancipation. And only the class struggle, their frame of analysis, would determine if a revolutionary period had exhausted itself.

Marx ended the article by analysing the growing conflict between Bonaparte and the Party of Order. 'The party of Order regarded the [31 May] election law … as a victory over Bonaparte', who owed his presidency to universal suffrage; 'Bonaparte, on his part, treated the election law as a concession to the [Party of Order-led National] Assembly, with which he claimed to

---

[70]   Karl Marx and Frederick Engels, 'Address of the Central Authority to the League, March 1850' in Karl Marx and Frederick Engels, *Collected Works*, vol 10 (International Publishers 1978) 277, 284.

[71]   I argue that the document became Lenin's playbook for the drama of 1917 in Russia; August H Nimtz, '"The Bolsheviks Come to Power": A New Interpretation' (2017) 81 *Science & Society* 478.

[72]   Marx, 'Class Struggles in France, 1848 to 1850', 81.

[73]   For a summary of their views, see August H Nimtz, *The Ballots, the Streets—or Both? From Marx and Engels to Lenin and the October Revolution* (Haymarket 2019) ch 1. Stedman Jones' claim that they belittled 'the significance of manhood suffrage' is due, therefore, not to ignorance but rather dishonesty, since he pretends to have read the March 1850 address. Stedman Jones, *Karl Marx*, 299–300, 307.

[74]   Marx, 'Class Struggles in France, 1848 to 1850', 137.

[75]   Marx, 'Class Struggles in France, 1848 to 1850', 137.

[76]   Marx, 'Class Struggles in France, 1848 to 1850', 137.

have purchased harmony between the legislative and executive powers'.[77] But the bourgeoisie, represented by the Party of Order, was limited in its ability to wage a successful fight against Bonaparte precisely because it was a minority class in society, ever fearful of the plebeian masses. 'In its struggle', Marx perceptively saw, 'the party of Order is compelled constantly to increase the power of the executive. Every increase of the executive's power increases the power of its bearer, Bonaparte. In the same measure, therefore, as the party of Order strengthens its joint [dynastic] might, it strengthens the fighting resources of Bonaparte's dynastic pretensions, it strengthens his chance of frustrating a constitutional solution by force on the day of the decision.'[78] And hanging over the whole problem like the sword of Damocles was the 'first Sunday in May 1852', Bonaparte's constitutionally designated expiration date.[79]

Although Marx mistakenly thought both protagonists would figure out a way to postpone a solution, until a new economic crisis would fuel a working-class solution, his point about the Party of Order enabling Bonaparte was prescient. Tocqueville, one of those enablers, later admitted that the efforts of him and his Party of Order allies to humour Bonaparte only whetted the appetite of what Marx termed 'the vulgar adventurer'.[80] On 2 December 1851, Bonaparte carried out a *coup d'état*, overthrowing the National Assembly and constitutional government. A year later, he made his 'dynastic pretensions' official; he declared himself Emperor of France, in the footsteps of his more worthy uncle. It obligated Marx to write one of his most famous works to explain the entire drama that began on 22 February 1848.

LESSONS OF THE EUROPEAN SPRING: SECOND EDITION

A year after the effective abolition of universal suffrage in France, Marx dissected the constitution that was still in force. Written for the vanguard of the English proletariat, the Chartists, who were fighting for a democratic 'charter' for their country, Marx was consciously pedagogical.[81] His detailed analysis gives lie to the time-worn fable that he dismissed constitutional matters, including civil liberties such as freedom of the press and association. The article is too rich to be digested fully here. One point, though, is worth noting—his reaction to the provision in the document that 'the division of powers is the primary condition of a free government'. 'Here', Marx retorts, 'we have the old constitutional folly. The condition of a "free government" is not the division, but the unity of power. The machinery of government cannot be too simple. It is always the craft of knaves to make it complicated and mysterious'—an insight as current as when originally written.[82] Not for naught did Marx criticise the liberal professoriat in Frankfurt who were writing 1848–49 Germany's edition of the French Constitution and their seduction by 'the Montesquieu-[Jean Louis] Delolme worm-eaten theory of division of powers'.[83] To advocate, as they did, for the separation of powers between the Prussian 'Crown' and the 'Assembly' after the 18 March Revolution in Berlin, was to stifle the revolution, to

---

[77]   Marx, 'Class Struggles in France, 1848 to 1850', 139.
[78]   Marx, 'Class Struggles in France, 1848 to 1850', 142.
[79]   Marx, 'Class Struggles in France, 1848 to 1850', 142.
[80]   For details see Nimtz, *Marxism versus Liberalism*, 57.
[81]   The venue was the Chartist organ, *Notes to the People*.
[82]   Marx, 'The Constitution of the French Republic', 570.
[83]   Karl Marx, 'The Crisis and the Counter-Revolution' [1848] in Karl Marx and Frederick Engels, *Collected Works*, vol 7 (International Publishers 1977) 427, 430.

place obstacles in the way of extending democracy. 'Democracy is the solved *riddle* of all constitutions'; Marx's 1843 *Critique of Hegel's Philosophy of Law*, still informed him.

More pertinent for present purposes is Marx's commentary on the electoral law provisions in the constitution, which he reproduced in full:

> The above articles are conceived in exactly the same spirit, as all the rest of the constitution. 'All Frenchmen are electors, who enjoy their political rights' — but 'the electoral law' is to decide what Frenchmen shall *not* enjoy their political rights! The electoral law of March 15, 1849, reckoned under this category all criminals, but not political offenders. The electoral law of May 31, 1850, added not only the political offenders, all those who had been convicted of 'offending against old-established opinions', and against the laws regulating the press, but it actually established domiciliary restrictions, by which two-thirds of the French people are incapable of voting! That is what 'the electoral franchise, direct and universal', means in France.[84]

Ever careful about the wording of the laws to illustrate the duplicity of the bourgeoisie, Marx emphasised that the 31 May electoral law did not explicitly abolish universal suffrage. Rather, the subtraction of two-thirds of the population from the electorate for insufficient resident requirements, a less obvious solution, effectively did the job. The electoral law revisions, he concluded, instantiated the reality of a bourgeois constitution.

> The eternal contradictions of this Constitution of Humbug, show plainly enough, that the middle-class can be democratic in *words*, but will not be so in deeds—they will recognise the truth of a principle, but never carry it into practice—and the real 'Constitution' of France is to be found, not in the Charter we have recorded, but in the *organic laws* enacted on its basis, an outline of which we have given to the reader. The *principles* were there—the *details* were left to the future, and in those details a shameless tyranny was re-enacted![85]

One of those 'eternal contradictions' was 'the fundamental contradiction' that this article highlights. Marx thought it important to educate the most politically conscious of the English proletariat, the Chartists, about the implications of that contradiction, one of the key lessons of the European Spring.[86]

Speculation on the 'shameless re-enactment of a tyranny' is the last subject in Marx's article:

> The only alternative for Bonaparte is, therefore, to defy the constitution, take up arms, and fight it out, or a legitimate surrender of his functions at the time prescribed ['the second Sunday in May 1852']... The game of Napoleon, therefore, now is, to work on the discontent of the people. The middle-class are the enemies of Napoleon,—the people know it, and there is one bond of sympathy between them. He, however, shares the odium of oppression jointly with the middle-class; if he can cast it off his shoulders entirely on theirs, one great obstacle will have been removed.[87]

---

[84]   Marx, 'The Constitution of the French Republic', 571 (original emphasis).

[85]   Marx, 'The Constitution of the French Republic', 578 (original emphases).

[86]   Marx followed European Spring constitutional developments elsewhere, specifically Denmark. See his informed remarks about counter-revolutionary developments there, especially the eroding of the liberal electoral laws by various restrictions on who could vote. Karl Marx, '[Arrest of Delescluze.—Denmark.—Austria.—The Times on the Prospects of War Against Russia]' [1853] in Karl Marx and Frederick Engels, *Collected Works*, vol 12 (International Publishers 1979) 421.

[87]   Marx, 'The Constitution of the French Republic', 579.

At the end, Marx offered, with remarkable prescience, a concise first definition of what came to be called 'Bonapartism': 'The game of Napoleon, is, first to play off the People against the middle-class. Then to play off the middle-class against the people and to use the army against them both.'[88] Marx finished the article on 8 June. Seven months later Bonaparte played the army option card.

'FIRST TRAGEDY, SECOND FARCE'—'THE EIGHTEENTH BRUMAIRE'

As soon as Louis Bonaparte staged his *coup d'état* on 2 December 1851, Marx began to draw up a balance sheet—an elementary communist task to prepare the proletariat for the next round in the class struggle. Basically, he sought to put the entire drama, in a more distilled way than the 'Class Struggles' articles, in deep historical context, in the spirit of *The Communist Manifesto* written four years earlier.

If Marx thought that liberal-democratic conditions, especially universal suffrage, jeopardised the social power of the bourgeoisie, their property—'the fundamental contradiction of this constitution'—then his claim ought to have figured significantly, if not centrally, in his 'Eighteenth Brumaire of Louis Bonaparte'. The main research question of Marx's approximately 100-page pamphlet, after all, was why France's Second Republic so easily succumbed to a 'swindler', and later a 'grotesque mediocrity'. Despite its famous introductory sentence about 'world history' appearing 'the first time as tragedy, the second as farce'—an aphorism he employed in his 1843 critique of Hegel—Marx's claim was indeed on centre stage in the text. A telling signal for what was to come, he pointed out mid-way into the narrative, was when the Party of Order's parliamentary deputies in fall 1849 became fixated on 'socialism', lambasting even the mildest of liberal measures.

> [B]y … stigmatising as 'socialistic' what it had previously extolled as 'liberal', the bourgeoisie confesses that its own interests dictate that it should be delivered from the danger of its own rule; that to restore tranquillity in the country its bourgeois parliament must, first of all, be laid to rest; that to preserve its social power intact its political power must be broken; that the individual bourgeois can continue to exploit the other classes and to enjoy undisturbed property, family, religion, and order only on condition that their class be condemned along with the other classes to like political nullity; that in order to save its purse it must forfeit the crown, and the sword that is to safeguard it must at the same time be hung over its own head as a sword of Damocles.[89]

Fearful of another June uprising, the bourgeoisie began to rethink the new political space that came with the February Revolution. The proletariat, too, could make use of it. The need to sacrifice parliamentary democracy, the ideal political form for bourgeois rule, became an increasingly attractive option. If the alternatives were either the maintenance of the National

---

[88]   Marx, 'The Constitution of the French Republic', 580. Draper, *Karl Marx's Theory of Revolution*, vol 1, chs 15–18, remains the most thorough exposition of the topic.

[89]   Karl Marx, 'The Eighteenth Brumaire of Louis Bonaparte' [1852] in Karl Marx and Frederick Engels, *Collected Works*, vol 11 (International Publishers 1979) 99, 142–43. Draper argues that 'here', a preceding related point, 'Marx is making his first detailed analysis of the basic incompatibility of capitalism with democracy'. *Karl Marx's Theory of Revolution*, vol 1, 398. My claim is that his pregnant insight in 'Class Struggles', the focus of this article, anticipated the point.

Assembly or the security of the bourgeoisie's private property, then the answer—the way to resolve 'the fundamental contradiction of this constitution'—was clear. Bonaparte increasingly recognised that the bourgeoisie had no great love for liberal democracy. One of the 'confessors' was Tocqueville. His *Souvenirs*, published long after his death in 1859, revealed how, as a fellow-traveller of the Party of Order in the National Assembly, his fear of 'socialism' and the plebeian masses enabled Bonaparte's *coup d'état*.[90]

The spectre of 'socialism' became real once again with 'an unexpected event ... the *by-elections on March 10, 1850*', not only for the bourgeoisie but also for Bonaparte himself.[91] 'Paris elected only Social-Democratic candidates. It even concentrated most of the votes on an insurgent of June 1848'.[92] This frightened the bourgeoisie with what could be another June. To head off that possibility, the Party of Order initiated on 8 May what would become law on 31 May.

> The law of May 31, 1850, was the *coup d'état* of the bourgeoisie. All its conquests over the revolution hitherto had only a provisional character ... They depended on the hazards of a new general election, and the history of elections since 1848 irrefutably proved that the bourgeoisie's moral sway over the mass of the people was lost in the same measure as its actual domination developed. On March 10 universal suffrage declared itself directly against the domination of the bourgeoisie; the bourgeoisie answered by outlawing universal suffrage. The law of May 31 was therefore one of the necessities of the class struggle ... [I]t did everything to smuggle the election of the President out of the hands of the people and into the hands of the National Assembly.[93]

That legerdemain undermined whatever remaining legitimacy the National Assembly had in the eyes 'of the people', about which Bonaparte was all too aware. 'The electoral law was followed by a new press law, by which the revolutionary newspapers were entirely suppressed.'[94] With the enactment of the 31 May electoral law, the die had been cast.

The next chapter in the narrative summarised the renewed 'struggle between the National Assembly and Bonaparte'.[95] The former thought it could deal successfully with the latter by confining the fight to the parliamentary arena, dealing with narrow matters rather than the need to limit executive power and thereby making 'the cause of the National Assembly' the 'cause of the nation'.[96] The Party of Order that led the National Assembly refused to do so because it would have required giving 'the nation its marching orders, and it fears nothing more than that the nation should move'.[97] Tocqueville, in a private communication, admitted as much, observing that Bonaparte's *coup d'état* 'is inevitable, unless resisted by an appeal to revolutionary passions, which I do not wish to rouse in the nation'.[98] It is as if Marx had read Tocqueville's letter. Tocqueville and colleagues were afflicted with, in Marx's words, 'a peculiar malady which since 1848 has raged all over the Continent, *parliamentary cretinism*', the

---

[90]   Nimtz, *Marxism versus Liberalism*, ch 2, 46, 49.
[91]   Marx, 'Eighteenth Brumaire', 143 (original emphasis).
[92]   Marx, 'Eighteenth Brumaire', 143–44.
[93]   Marx, 'Eighteenth Brumaire', 146–47.
[94]   Marx, 'Eighteenth Brumaire', 145.
[95]   Marx, 'Eighteenth Brumaire', 147.
[96]   Marx, 'Eighteenth Brumaire', 155.
[97]   Marx, 'Eighteenth Brumaire', 155.
[98]   Quoted in Nimtz, *Marxism versus Liberalism*, 59.

mistaken belief that what took place inside the legislative arena was the beginning and end of politics, ignoring, to their peril, 'the rude external world'.[99]

By enacting the 31 May electoral law, the National Assembly had 'subordinated the Constitution to the parliamentary majority', rather than to a supermajority as stipulated in the constitution itself. It gave license to Bonaparte to do the same with his *coup d'état*. Specifically, the supermajority rejected the Party of Order's bill—the only time Marx mentioned 'their reporter Tocqueville'—to revise the constitution to allow Bonaparte to serve for a second term. 'He therefore acted in the sense of parliament when he tore up the Constitution, and he acted in the sense of the Constitution when he dispersed parliament.'[100]

Tellingly, Tocqueville was the architect of the constitution's provision for an elected president, inspired no doubt by the US example but more advanced due to its provision of direct election. An elected president would be, in Tocqueville's calculus, a check on the National Assembly, and also elected by universal suffrage.[101] Earlier in the narrative, Marx addressed the pitfalls of France's new presidential system. The 'Constitution here abrogates itself once more by having the President elected by all Frenchmen through direct suffrage'. Sarcastically, Marx wrote that '*he* is the elect of the nation and the act of his election is the trump that the sovereign people plays once every four years … As against the Assembly, he possesses a sort of divine right; he is President by the grace of the people'.[102] Europe's first experiment with an elected president taught the ever-vigilant Marx that the apparent 'sovereignty of the people' could be deceiving.

Marx returned to 'the fundamental contradiction' in his penultimate chapter. He reminded the reader about his insight, and then strengthened his claim by looking at the 'Party of Order *outside* parliament'.[103]

> While the *parliamentary Party of Order*, by its clamour for tranquillity, as I have shown, committed itself to quiescence, while it declared the political rule of the bourgeoisie to be incompatible with the safety and existence of the bourgeoisie[,] … the *extraparliamentary mass of the bourgeoisie*, on the other hand, by its servility towards the President, by its vilification of parliament, by its brutal maltreatment of its own press, invited Bonaparte to suppress and annihilate its speaking and writing section, its politicians and its *literati*, its platform and its press, in order that it might then be able to pursue its private affairs with full confidence in the protection of a strong and unrestricted government. It declared unequivocally that it longed to get rid of its own political rule in order to get rid of the troubles and dangers of ruling.[104]

In other words, actually existing capitalism, as it might be called today, was unequivocal in its willingness to sacrifice the niceties of bourgeois democracy at the altar of profit-making.

One last scene in the drama is worth recounting. 'On the very first day of its re-opening [4 November 1851], the National Assembly received the message from Bonaparte in which he demanded the restoration of universal suffrage and the abolition of the law of May 31,

---

99 Marx, 'Eighteenth Brumaire', 161 (original emphasis).
100 Marx, 'Eighteenth Brumaire', 168–69. Tocqueville later admitted, in hindsight, that the proposal only whetted Bonaparte's appetite for wanting to stay in office. See Nimtz, *Marxism versus Liberalism*, 57–58.
101 Nimtz, *Marxism versus Liberalism*, 51.
102 Marx, 'Eighteenth Brumaire', 116–17 (original emphasis).
103 Marx, 'Eighteenth Brumaire', 169–70 (original emphasis).
104 Marx, 'Eighteenth Brumaire', 172–73 (original emphases).

1850.'[105] The National Assembly rejected the demand, leaving it bereft of moral authority with the masses. This is why Bonaparte was then able to pretend that his coup was done in the interest 'of the people'. It is also why he was able to stage, with his troops still in place, a successful yes-or-no referendum three weeks later to approve his coup. The final chapter of the narrative speculated on the course of Bonaparte's rule and the prospects of the proletariat taking centre stage once again and staying there for the first time.

Marx did not pretend to be more prescient than anyone else about the *dénouement* of the drama. 'If ever an event has, well in advance of its coming, cast its shadow before it', he wrote, 'it was Bonaparte's *coup d'état*[,] ... a necessary, inevitable result of antecedent developments.'[106] What he uniquely did was to demonstrate why the outcome was inevitable. In the game Bonaparte was playing, Marx predicted seven months earlier that if the National Assembly—that is, the parliamentary bourgeoisie—thought 'the people were about to conquer, [they would] prefer the lesser of two evils. They would prefer an Empire or a Dictatorship of Napoleon, to a Democratic and Social Republic, and would, therefore, come to terms with the President'.[107] Marx was mistaken about parliamentary representatives of the bourgeoisie like Tocqueville; they never did. But the bourgeoisie '*outside* parliament' was a different story; they applauded Bonaparte's coup. While parliamentary democracy and civil liberties served their collective interests, the laboratory of the class struggle taught that the bourgeoisie was not wedded ineluctably to them. If necessary, they were willing to subordinate—indeed, sacrifice—them to their private interests, to protect their property from 'the people'; a lesson as current, I argue, as when Marx discovered it. Stedman Jones' recent reading of the 'Eighteenth Brumaire' asserts that Marx's 'refusal to think of universal suffrage as anything other than a pathological symptom imposed serious limitations upon his understanding of the sequence of events. It led him to underestimate the ways in which the suffrage issue pushed the revolution in directions different from anything encountered in 1789 or 1830'.[108] A claim so breathtakingly dishonest can only assume its readers have not and will never read what Marx actually wrote.

SOME ADDENDA TO A PRESCIENT INSIGHT

Marx's characterisation of Bonaparte's coup, 'when he tore up the Constitution', anticipated similar wording he would employ a decade later. The setting now was the US Civil War, which, in Marx's opinion, was on the centre stage of world politics. He dropped everything, including the writing of *Capital*, to campaign against bourgeois opinion in England that apologised for the slavocracy, and also to mobilise working-class opinion there and elsewhere to side with the Union and Abraham Lincoln against the 'slave power'. For Marx and many other Union partisans, the war was an echo of the hopes of the European Spring. Arguably the same may be said for Lincoln himself, as he spoke during his famed Gettysburg Address about 'whether ... any nation so conceived [dedicated to the proposition that all men are created equal] can

---

[105]   Marx, 'Eighteenth Brumaire', 177–78.
[106]   Marx, 'Eighteenth Brumaire', 176–77.
[107]   Marx, 'The Constitution of the French Republic', 580.
[108]   Stedman Jones, *Karl Marx*, 342.

long endure'. Lincoln scholars agree that the failed republican revolutions in Europe were very much on his mind in this passage.[109]

Less than a year earlier, on 22 September 1862, Lincoln issued an executive order, *The Emancipation Proclamation*. It declared that if the rebel Confederate states did not end their secessionist movement by 1 January 1863, their slaves would then be free. Its issuance was the key moment in the war because it proclaimed that the Union cause was no longer about putting an end to secession but rather about the abolition of slavery as such. Marx was elated—'the most important document in American history since the establishment of the Union, tanta-mount to the tearing up of the old American Constitution ... Lincoln's place in the history of the United States and of mankind will ... be next to that of Washington!'[110] 'Wars of this kind', he advised a couple of months earlier, 'ought to be conducted along revolutionary lines, and the Yankees have so far been trying to conduct it along constitutional ones'.[111]

If Marx was critical of Bonaparte for 'tearing up' the constitution, he applauded Lincoln for doing the same. Among other things, this meant that he did not fetishise constitutional texts; the social context was all-important. His critique of Hegel two decades earlier had made that clear. Elsewhere in his critique of Hegel, he wrote that 'the constitution which was the product of a bygone consciousness can become a heavy fetter on an advanced consciousness ... What would really follow would be simply the demand for a constitution which contains within itself the designation and the principle to advance along with consciousness, to advance as actual men advance'.[112] In 'Class Struggles', in the article in which 'the fundamental contradiction' appears, Marx noted that the US republic represented a more conservative version of republi-can governance, unlike what had just appeared in France. It is unclear whether he had in mind the outcome of the 1787 Philadelphia Convention as an example of a 'bygone consciousness' when applauding Lincoln for 'tearing up' the 'Old American Constitution'.[113] But in substance that is what the Civil War represented and promoted: an 'advance' in 'consciousness'. Thus the need to 'tear up' the old document and replace it with one that represented an 'advance as actual men advance'.

Marx also recognised that constitutions are not set in stone. On the topic of how con-stitutions change, he wrote that 'for a *new* constitution a real revolution has always been required'.[114] This is exactly what the defeat of the 'slave power' registered, a second American revolution.[115] Marx was more positive about the 1776 Declaration of Independence, represent-ative of a more 'advanced consciousness'. Two years later, in 1864, when he congratulated Lincoln on his reelection on behalf of the International Working Men's Association, he called the document 'the first Declaration of the Rights of Man[,] ... the first impulse given to the

---

[109] See e.g., Don Doyle, *The Cause of All Nations: An International History of the American Civil War* (Basic Books 2015) 281–84.

[110] Karl Marx, 'Comments on the North American Events' [1862] in Karl Marx and Frederick Engels, *Collected Works*, vol 19 (International Publishers 1984) 248, 250.

[111] Karl Marx, 'Marx to Engels, in Manchester, 7 August 1862' in Karl Marx and Frederick Engels, *Collected Works*, vol 41 (International Publishers 1985) 399, 400.

[112] Marx, 'Contribution to the Critique of Hegel's Philosophy of Law', 19.

[113] For the argument that the Philadelphia meeting was effectively a counter-revolution, see Michael J Klarman, *The Framer's Coup: The Making of the United States Constitution* (OUP 2016).

[114] Marx, 'Contribution to the Critique of Hegel's Philosophy of Law', 56 (original emphasis).

[115] Marx, 'Contribution to the Critique of Hegel's Philosophy of Law', 56.

European revolution of the eighteenth century'.[116] The Civil War amendments to the US Constitution, made possible by the revolution Lincoln led, constituted a radical rewriting of the original document—what Marx would have expected.

Not unlike the drama of the European Spring, this second American Revolution was followed by counter-revolution. The 'fundamental contradiction' goes a long way in explaining why. The armed overthrow of the slavocracy by small white farmers and former slaves paved the way for universal male suffrage for the first time in the United States. Even white males at the bottom of the social ladder in a number of slave-holding states could not vote—an important fact that convinced the young Marx to consider the communist road to 'human emancipation'.[117] Former slaves took advantage of the new political space and began exercising democratic rights even before the ratification in 1870 of the Fifteenth Amendment to the Constitution, which granted them the right to vote. Although no longer chattel slaves, they increasingly became slaves of debt and wages, as tenant farmers and workers for their former masters. Such was Marx's 'social slavery'. Democratic rights like civil liberties and the right to vote were a threat to the new masters of their sweat and toil. Something had to give—forward or backward. There is credible evidence that what galvanised the post-Civil War elite to begin the process of dismantling Radical Reconstruction was, ironically, another proletarian revolution in France—the Paris Commune of 1871.[118] Though a quarter of a century late, Marx and Engels had argued that the defeat of 1848 had set the stage for such a development. The northern liberal bourgeois feared that something similar could happen in the United States, involving free labour in white skin and, most ominously, in alliance with those in black skin. This was a scenario too scary to be permitted. Even more ironic, the individual who led the charge to defang Radical Reconstruction, Liberal Republican Carl Schurz, had bitterly opposed Marx and Engels two decades earlier for wanting to keep the 'revolution in permanence' in Europe.[119] He probably knew his old nemeses were actively hoping for the same in the new American theatre.[120] In 1896 the US Supreme Court gave its imprimatur to what was by then the system of Jim Crow racial segregation—in order to assure such a white-black alliance could never materialise. As in the lead-up to the 31 May 1850 electoral law, the denial of the right to vote for former slaves came in piecemeal—law by law, murder by murder—until by the beginning of the twentieth century only a tiny minority of former slaves and their descendants were entitled to vote. It would take the Second Reconstruction, a half century away, to overcome that historic defeat.

Marx, like Lincoln, did not live to see the bloody end of Radical Reconstruction—a process which, unlike what happened to the Second Republic, took almost two decades to be completed. In 1877, six years before his death, he and his partner welcomed the news of the first

---

[116] Karl Marx, 'Marx to Abraham Lincoln, President of the United States of America, 22–29 November 1864' in Karl Marx and Frederick Engels, *Collected Works*, vol 20 (International Publishers 1985) 19, 19.

[117] Alexander Keysaar, *The Right to Vote: The Contested History of Democracy in the United States* (Basic Books 2000) ch 3.

[118] Heather Cox Richardson, *The Death of Reconstruction: Race, Labor, and Politics in the Post-Civil War North, 1865–1901* (Harvard University Press 2001).

[119] I spent an afternoon in 2011 skimming Schurz's papers at the US Library of Congress but could not find a smoking gun to make connections. Many of his papers, unfortunately, were lost to a fire.

[120] For their activities see August H Nimtz, *Marx, Tocqueville, and Race in America: The 'Absolute Democracy' or 'Defiled Republic'* (Lexington 2003) ch 4, 164–68.

general strike in the United States. Marx optimistically speculated that the 'policy of the new President [Hayes to end Radical Reconstruction] will turn the negroes ... into militant allies of the workers'.[121] Engels, too, was 'delighted' by the strike: 'Only twelve years since slavery was abolished and already the movement has got to such a pitch.'[122] That kind of alliance was indispensable for preventing a counter-revolution. Note how, as in the 1848 French Revolution, Marx and Engels were optimistic about the American version of the European Spring. In hindsight, they were mistaken. Real-time politics, their starting-point, taught that only the class struggle would settle the question whether the revolution would advance.

For the American scene, no issue was as challenging in forging multi-racial proletarian unity than that of race. Marx's congratulatory letter to Lincoln in 1864 was insightful on the point.

> While the working men, the true political powers of the North, allowed slavery to defile their own republic, while before the Negro, mastered and sold without his concurrence, they boasted it the highest prerogative [read privilege] of the white-skinned labourer to sell himself and choose his own master, they were unable to attain the true freedom of labour, or to support their European brethren in their struggle for emancipation.[123]

Note how Marx, like Lincoln, connected the republican struggle on both sides of the Atlantic. Three years later he refined the comment in *Capital*: 'In the United States of America, every independent movement of the workers was paralysed so long as slavery disfigured a part of the Republic.' In the next sentence, he shifted to his present, 1867: 'Labour cannot emancipate itself in the white skin where in the black it is branded.'[124] It would take a second Reconstruction before the most conscious of the proletariat in all skin colours understood the significance of Marx's point. His advice is as current now as when he first uttered it. Think: when Black lives matter, all lives matter!

Universal male suffrage did not become a reality in any other major European country until Prussian Prime Minister Otto Bismarck, representative of the feudal-bureaucratic elite, declared that this was so in 1866. His was a demagogic move not unlike the manoeuvres of Louis Bonaparte in respect of universal suffrage, designed to frighten the bourgeoisie. A year before Bismarck's decree, Engels had warned German workers as much in his pamphlet, *The Prussian Military Question and the German Workers' Party*: '[O]ne has only to go to France to realise what tame elections [universal direct suffrage] can give rise to, if one has only a large and ignorant rural population, a well-organised bureaucracy, a well-regimented press, associations sufficiently kept down by the police and no political meetings at all.'[125] Such was the reality of universal suffrage under Bonaparte's dictatorship. Yet, Engels argued, there were invaluable lessons from France for the German proletariat—lessons that had to do with 'the fundamental contradiction'. Pedagogically, with Marx's input, he explained that '[t]he bourgeoisie cannot win political power for itself nor give this political power constitutional

---

[121] Karl Marx, 'Marx to Engels, in Ramsgate, 25 July 1877' in Karl Marx and Frederick Engels, *Collected Works*, vol 45 (International Publishers 1985) 250, 251.

[122] Frederick Engels, 'Engels to Marx, in London, 31 July 1877' in Karl Marx and Frederick Engels, *Collected Works*, vol 45 (International Publishers 1985) 254, 255.

[123] Marx, 'Marx to Abraham Lincoln', 20.

[124] Karl Marx, *Capital: A Critique of Political Economy*, vol 1 (first published 1867, International Publishers 1972) 301.

[125] Quoted in Frederick Engels, 'On the Dissolution of the Lassallean Workers' Association' [1868] in Karl Marx and Frederick Engels, *Collected Works*, vol 21 (International Publishers 1985) 20, 21.

and legal forms without at the same time putting weapons into the hands of the proletariat'.[126] This was exactly Marx's point. Engels continued as follows:

> To be consistent, it must therefore demand universal, direct suffrage, freedom of the press, associ- ation and assembly and the suspension of all special laws directed against individual classes of the population ... But the proletariat will thereby also acquire all the weapons it needs for its ultimate victory. With freedom of the press and the right of assembly and association it will win universal suffrage, and with universal, direct suffrage, in conjunction with the above tools of agitation, it will win everything else.[127]

Workers, therefore, were obligated 'to support the bourgeoisie in its struggle against all reac- tionary elements, *as long as it remains true to itself.* Every gain which the bourgeoisie extracts from reaction, eventually benefits the working class, if that condition is fulfilled'.[128]

Encapsulated here was the very core of Marx and Engels' perspective on the relationship between the fight for liberal democracy and proletarian revolution. Because of what occurred in France, bourgeois fear of democratic 'weapons into the hands of the proletariat', German workers should, Marx argued, be under no illusion that their bourgeoisie would have more spine than their French cohorts. Have not, Marx cautioned, one iota of trust in the German bourgeoisie; this was exactly why the working class should be organised independent of the bourgeoisie, as the March 1850 address advised. But neither, he suggested, should German workers be seduced by Bismarck. Only as long as the Junkers' representative thought he could use the workers' movement against the bourgeoisie, in good Bonapartist fashion, would it be tolerated: 'From the moment that this movement turns the workers into an independent force, and thereby becomes a danger to the government, there will be an abrupt end to it all.'[129] A year later Bismarck decreed universal male suffrage. Germany's first working-class party was formed in 1869, becoming the largest such party in the world. In 1878, as Engels had predicted, it was outlawed. Not without reason did Engels end his pamphlet with a line from an ancient German epic: 'With the spear one should accept gifts, point against point.'[130]

Despite Bismarck's Bonapartist agenda in decreeing universal male suffrage, Marx and Engels enthusiastically encouraged the German proletariat to take advantage of the opportunity—but, again, only if done on the basis of independent working-class political action.[131] They encouraged fledgling parties elsewhere to emulate the German party. The all-important qualification of independence, however, came under pressure as the German party won seats in the Reichstag. The gains were seductive, seen increasingly as ends in them- selves rather than as means toward the end of 'win[ning] everything else', that is, proletarian revolution. The two founders of modern communism wrote a sharp rebuke of that course of action in a memorandum meant only for the eyes of the party's leadership, 'The Circular Letter of 1879'. It emphasised two interrelated points: the continuing currency of proletarian revo- lution, and the need to subordinate the party's parliamentary representatives to its rank and

[126]   Frederick Engels, 'The Prussian Military Question and the German Workers' Party' [1865] in Karl Marx and Frederick Engels, *Collected Works*, vol 20 (International Publishers 1985) 37, 77.
[127]   Engels, 'The Prussian Military Question', 77.
[128]   Engels, 'The Prussian Military Question', 77 (original emphasis).
[129]   Engels, 'On the Dissolution of the Lassallean Workers' Association', 20.
[130]   Engels, 'The Prussian Military Question', 79.
[131]   Nimtz, *The Ballot, the Streets*, ch 1 provides the details upon which the following is based.

file. Marx and Engels thought their rebuke had reined in the German party's leadership—an assumption that proved erroneous in hindsight.[132]

Marx died in 1883 and it fell to Engels to advise the increasing number of European workers' parties how to comport themselves in the electoral or parliamentary arena. No comment captures his opinion better than a congratulatory reply to Paul Lafargue, one of the leaders of the French Workers Party, about its gains in a recent election in 1892:

> Do you realise now what a splendid weapon you in France have had in your hands for forty years in universal suffrage; if only people knew how to use it! It's slower and more boring than the call to revolution, but it's ten times more sure, and what is even better, it indicates with the most perfect accuracy the day when a call to armed revolution has to be made; it's even ten to one that universal suffrage, intelligently used by the workers, will drive the rulers to overthrow legality, that is, to put us in the most favourable position to make the revolution.[133]

Arguably Engels' most pithy comment on universal suffrage in his final years (he died in 1895), this passage distils the essence of his and Marx's views on the topic, as captured in the 'March 1850 Address' and *The Prussian Military Question*. Rather than an end in themselves, elections, as they put it in 1850, were a means to an end for the workers' party, 'to count their forces and to lay before the public their revolutionary attitude and party standpoint'—in other words, to determine when best to utilise armed struggle to take state power. Only with state power could the proletariat, the true 'universal class', begin the process of dismantling class society, the necessary condition for '*general human* emancipation'. Lenin, I claim, understood that perspective better than any of Marx and Engels' students.[134]

LESSONS FROM THE TWENTIETH AND TWENTY-FIRST CENTURIES: A FEW CONCLUDING THOUGHTS

If it is true that there is a 'fundamental contradiction' between capitalism and liberal democracy, why have they apparently co-existed since at least the First World War, when universal suffrage became for the first time an international norm if not a reality? This is the puzzle that informed Przeworski's research and political agenda.[135] Further, are there other potential lessons from the European Spring for current political reality? Although what follows cannot deal with these questions exhaustively, I can suggest two prominent issues. Both prioritise the US reality, where the contradiction between liberal democracy and capitalism has global import more than ever.

The most consequential institution in any advanced capitalist country today is arguably its central bank, an institution which is tellingly, and purposely, sealed off from the electorate (twice removed in the case of the European Central Bank). The US example, the prototype

---

[132] Karl Marx and Frederick Engels, 'Circular Letter to August Bebel, Wilhelm Liebknecht, Wilhelm Bracke and Others' [1879] in Karl Marx and Frederick Engels, *Collected Works*, vol 24 (International Publishers 1989) 253.
[133] Frederick Engels, 'Engels to Paul Lafargue at Le Perreux, 12 November 1892' in Karl Marx and Frederick Engels, *Collected Works*, vol 50 (International Publishers 2004) 29.
[134] See, again, Nimtz, '"The Bolsheviks Take Power": A New Interpretation'.
[135] Adam Przeworski and Michael Wallerstein, 'The Structure of Class Conflict in Democratic Capitalist Societies' (1982) 76 *American Political Science Review* 215.

for the twentieth century, is instructive. Founded in 1913, in response to a banking panic, the Federal Reserve Bank was constituted to ensure significant independence from the two elected branches of government, Congress and the Presidency—though its power derives from the backing of the 'full faith and credit' of the US government. Appointment by the White House of its board members was designed to minimise the impact of presidential elections on its decisions—the only way that Wall Street gave its approval to the project. Making it difficult, if not impossible, for the proletariat to vote on key decisions that affected their livelihood was the US bourgeoisie's early twentieth-century solution to 'the fundamental contradiction'.

Similar arrangements, such as the 1887 Interstate Commerce Commission and the 1914 Federal Trade Commission, were designed to minimise the impact of working-class voters on major economic policies. In the name of 'clean and efficient government' and 'taking politics out of governance', council-manager forms of government increasingly came into place at the local level, comprising an unelected executive. The rationale was often that 'big city' political machines, frequently associated with minority working-class voting blocs, needed to be eliminated or at least controlled. The class biases of the middle-class reformers were less transparent than the business of party politics that they sought to cleanse.[136]

Another phenomenon regarding local governments has reared its ugly head in late capitalism, putting them in receivership when they cannot pay their bills. Effectively, their elected officials no longer make vital decisions. Unelected boards under the authority of state governments become the real decision-makers, with numerous serious consequences such as the lead-poisoning tragedy in Flint, Michigan. New York City was governed by such a board in the mid-1970s owing to the capitalist crisis of the period. Covid-19 is generating another financial crisis and threatening a similar arrangement. But it is a phenomenon not just at the state level. James Copland's just published *The Unelected: How an Unelected Elite is Governing America* provides rich details about what he calls 'the regulatory state'. Evidence for his thesis is this sobering fact: 'Among the estimated 300,000 federal crimes on the books, 98 percent were never voted on by Congress.'[137] Copland, a conservative, convincingly documents how unelected boards and other mechanisms at all levels of governance have been able to avoid democratic accountability.

The last time the world and the United States faced a deep economic depression, like the one presently unfolding, was, of course, the Great Depression. And the only time a US president raised the spectre of suspending the Constitution was in the early years of the crisis as a way to solve it. In his inaugural address in March 1933, newly elected Franklin Delano Roosevelt, did just that. 'It is to be hoped', he said, 'that the normal balance of executive and legislative authority may be wholly adequate to meet the unprecedented task before us.' But in case the legislative branch did not measure up, he continued, 'I shall ask the Congress for the one remaining instrument to meet the crisis—broad Executive power to wage a war against the emergency, as great as the power that would be given to me if we were in fact invaded by a foreign foe.'[138] Not even the Civil War, the gravest crisis in the country's history, caused

---

[136] Ira Katznelson's *City Trenches: Urban Politics And The Patterning Of Class In The United States* (Pantheon 1981) is instructive.

[137] James Copland, *The Unelected: How an Unelected Elite is Governing America* (Encounter 2020) 7.

[138] 'First Inaugural Address of Franklin D. Roosevelt' [4 March 1933], https://avalon.law.yale.edu/20th_century/froos1.asp accessed 7 April 2021.

Lincoln to entertain such a proposal. It would be naïve to think that another Great Depression would not move another president to make a similar proposal, and with the approval of the US capitalist class.

The Federal Reserve may be formally independent of the electorate, but it is certainly not indifferent to it. Exigencies like wars and economic crises, particularly the latter, obligate it to make decisions that often make its 'independence police', like the editorial page of *The Wall Street Journal*, cringe. That has certainly been true since the 2007–08 recession. To maintain economic activity the Federal Reserve has engaged in policies that encourage 'moral hazards' like keeping alive 'zombie' companies that ordinarily would have been allowed to die as part of capitalism's 'creative destruction'. But the political costs that would come with the unemployment consequences are too high. The ideals of the market, the drive for efficiency at any human and social cost, are incompatible with liberal democracy, which includes the right of working people to vote—as long as they can exercise those rights. 'Kicking the can down the road' rather than resolving the dilemma is the new normal—only delaying the day of reckoning.

The European Central Bank purports to play a similar role for the capitalist classes of Europe (and beyond). Unable to persuade Europe's working class masses to vote to lower their own standard of living (the austerity drive) and thereby resolve the Great Recession crisis, the European Union's leadership sought to impose its decisions on them by fiat. But that came with a political price—the 'Brexit' and 'populist' reactions. And the promotion of such policies by social-democratic governments has provided an opening to more right-wing parties. The irony is that it was the first iteration of such governments, the Provisional Government in France, which instituted modernity's first social safety net, a jobs program for the unemployed. But as Marx pointed out then, the 'right to work' is incompatible with the capitalist mode of production. Twenty-first century social democracy has proven to be no more willing to be an existential threat to capital than its nineteenth-century forebears.

Lastly, there is the election of Donald Trump in 2016, a product of the Great Recession—the American version of Europe's Brexit/populist reaction. The lead-up to his victory was most instructive. In remarkable Tocqueville-like fashion, a wing of US rulers decided that they would rather take a risk with a 'grotesque mediocrity'—Marx's priceless characterisation of Louis Bonaparte—than with the 'socialist' Bernie Sanders. The 'anyone but Sanders' camp was not as candid—at least publicly—as was Tocqueville. Even if it meant the end of the Second Republic, Tocqueville thought a Bonaparte regime was preferable to 'the mob', the 'Party of Anarchy'. In choosing Joe Biden as its candidate in 2020, the anti-Sanders Democratic Party establishment continued to engage in risky behaviour. Doing so threatened the alienation of the party's most ardent activists, the pro-Sanders youth, and thus the possibility of a second Trump presidency—someone whose Bonapartist tendencies were no longer in doubt. Whatever the outcome of the election (three weeks from when this is being written), the crisis of late capitalism guarantees that not only will 'bourgeois socialism' à la Bernie Sanders, as Marx and Engels in *The Communist Manifesto* would have defined his politics, continue to get a hearing, but that the real deal, the 'communist' alternative, will do so as well.

Alexander Keysaar concludes his magisterial and still authoritative 2000 survey, *The Right to Vote: The Contested History of Democracy in the United States,* with this point: 'The history of the right to vote is a record of the slow and fitful progress of the [democratic] project, progress that was hard won and often subject to reverses.'[139] The reason for the combination of setbacks and gains is due, I argue, to 'the fundamental contradiction'; capitalism and liberal democracy co-exist in constant tension, an 'eternal contradiction', as Marx once put it—as in plate tectonics. This tension, in other words, can be—and nearly always is—in place long before it erupts and achieves its social and historical resolution. Przeworski's positivist reading of Marx's prescient comment is therefore blind to the subtlety of Marx's realist dialectics.

That the word 'democracy' has never found its way into the US Constitution—even after the Civil War—is no accident. The world's first experience with universal suffrage teaches that the bourgeoisie will seek to undermine or overthrow democracy whenever it feels its class interests are threatened. Whether that happens, and whether the bourgeoisie can get away with it, depends in the final analysis on 'the people'. This, again, is 'the solved *riddle* of all constitutions'.

---

[139] Keysaar, *The Right to Vote*, 324.

5.   Marx's concept of dictatorship

Cosmin Sebastian Cercel

INTRODUCTION

In his famous misquotation of Hegel,[1] Marx wrote that 'all facts and personages of great importance in world history occur … twice … the first time as tragedy, the second as farce'.[2] The rise of authoritarianism today, and the politico-juridical disarray with which it is associated, invites a host of historical comparisons. It is a stark reminder for those in the global North that history has a movement of its own. It is also a reminder that the Great Depression and the rise of right-wing authoritarianism are not simply matters of historiographical concern, but that they are subject to repetition, often farcically.[3]

It is high time that we return to Marx in order to reflect upon his understanding of dictatorship. This choice of focus seems obvious at this moment. Not only are we facing a constant presence of exceptional and extraordinary measures augmenting the state's traditional repressive mechanisms, but state repression has begun to dispense with legal forms and regulations altogether. The current surge of authoritarianism, which many have hastened to analyse on the basis of the vague and uncertain concept of 'populism',[4] adds considerable urgency to the question. Under the strain of contemporary developments, we need to assess both the nature and the form of current threats to nominally liberal states. Mainstream approaches to law and politics are not able to account for the historical significance of these developments, tending to misunderstand the current crisis as either a new example of 'constitutions under stress'[5] or a new form of 'populist constitutionalism'.[6] While relying on a selective reading of history, and offering different explanations of liberal democracy, these accounts agree on a central point: liberal legality as such is innocent. In the words of Gábor Halmai, 'liberalism is … a constitutive precondition for democracy, which provides for the rule of law, checks and balances, and guaranteed fundamental rights'.[7] As such, it is not responsible for having produced the conditions that generated the contemporary rise of authoritarianism.

---

[1]   Bruce Mazlich, 'The Tragic Farce of Marx, Hegel and Engels: A Note' (1972) 11 *History and Theory* 335.

[2]   Karl Marx, 'The Eighteenth Brumaire of Louis Bonaparte' [1852] in Karl Marx and Frederick Engels, *Collected Works*, vol 11 (Lawrence & Wishart 1979) 99, 103.

[3]   Enzo Traverso, *The New Faces of Fascism: Populism and the Far Right* (first published 2017, David Broder tr, Verso 2019) 5.

[4]   Jan-Werner Müller, *What is Populism?* (University of Pennsylvania Press 2016).

[5]   András Sajó and Renáta Uitz, *The Constitution of Freedom: An Introduction to Legal Constitutionalism* (OUP 2017) 419–44.

[6]   Paul Blokker, 'Varieties of Populist Constitutionalism: The Transnational Dimension' (2019) 20 *German Law Journal* 332.

[7]   Gábor Halmai, 'Populism, Authoritarianism and Constitutionalism' (2019) 20 *German Law Journal* 296, 311.

As against this mainstream view, this chapter argues that a more refined reading of law, politics, and history is required to understand the limits of liberal legality. I claim that Marx is a helpful resource for understanding the present, not only as a social theorist and economist but also as a keen observer of history and law, if not as a 'legal scholar' per se. Specifically, I recuperate Marx's unorthodox understanding of law, history, and politics by focusing upon the concept of dictatorship. The main sources on which I draw are the political writings from 1848 to 1871, particularly 'The Class Struggles in France',[8] 'The Eighteenth Brumaire of Louis Bonaparte',[9] and 'The Civil War in France'.[10] This chapter is thus mainly a work of reconstruction. It aims to capture the structure and meaning of dictatorship, and also to render it serviceable for a jurisprudential understanding of law and politics in our time. Consequently, it seeks to clarify and reinterpret Marx's understanding of dictatorship with a view to problematising the status of law in disruptive moments such as the present one. My aim is to capture Marx's historical encounter with dictatorship and dictatorial practices. His discussion of the dictatorship of the proletariat during a 'period of ... revolutionary transformation' is beyond the scope of this investigation.[11]

This chapter is both a disciplinary inquiry and a response to a specific intellectual context in which Marxism has returned after a long period of neglect and effacement. I first respond to a number of jurisprudential and general philosophical questions that have either sidelined or obfuscated the relevance of Marx's work. By addressing these questions within the context of the ongoing crises of capitalism and liberalism,[12] the chapter argues that revisiting Marx's concept of dictatorship is necessary as a response to the constitutional theories that continue to dominate contemporary discourse and that often seek to explain the so-called 'populist turn'. I then argue that a move away from the Schmittian paradigm,[13] which was embraced by critical legal scholars,[14] is also necessary to understand the current conjuncture. Moreover, I argue that Marx's call for a historical-materialist understanding of dictatorship is crucial for breaking with the Agambenian paradigm of the state of exception,[15] sometimes used for the purpose of analysing neoliberal legality.[16] After addressing this theoretical and jurisprudential context, I shall analyse, by means of a close reading, Marx's uses of the concept of dictatorship

[8]   Karl Marx, 'The Class Struggles in France, 1848 to 1850' [1850] in Karl Marx and Frederick Engels, *Collected Works*, vol 10 (Lawrence & Wishart 1978) 45.
[9]   Marx, 'Eighteenth Brumaire'.
[10]   Karl Marx, 'The Civil War in France' [1871] in Karl Marx and Frederick Engels, *Collected Works*, vol 22 (Lawrence & Wishart 1986) 307.
[11]   Karl Marx, 'Critique of the Gotha Programme' [1875] in Karl Marx and Frederick Engels, *Collected Works*, vol 24 (Lawrence & Wishart 1989) 75, 95.
[12]   István Mészáros, *The Structural Crisis of Capital* (Monthly Review Press 2009) 33.
[13]   Carl Schmitt, *Dictatorship* (first published 1921, Michael Hoelzl and Graham Ward tr, Polity Press 2014); Carl Schmitt, *Political Theology* (first published 1922, George Schwab tr, MIT Press 1985); Carl Schmitt, *The Concept of the Political* (first published 1929, George Schwab tr, University of Chicago Press 1996).
[14]   Matilda Arvidsson, Leila Brännström, and Panu Minkkinen (eds), *The Contemporary Relevance of Carl Schmitt: Law, Politics, Theology* (Routledge 2016).
[15]   Giorgio Agamben, *Homo Sacer: Sovereign Power and Bare Life* (first published 1995, Daniel Heller-Roazen tr, Stanford University Press 1998); Giorgio Agamben, *State of Exception* (first published 2003, Kevin Attell tr, University of Chicago Press 2005).
[16]   Daniel McLoughlin, 'Giorgio Agamben on Security, Government and the Crisis of Law' (2012) 21 *Griffith Law Review* 680.

in three distinct historical and constitutional moments that marked French history during the nineteenth century: the repression of the proletarian uprising of June 1848, the rise to power of Louis Bonaparte in 1852, and the Paris Commune of 1871. In doing so, I also aim to connect Marx's analysis with the historical and legal developments of his time.

THE FADING MEANING OF DICTATORSHIP

In the opening lines of the 'Eighteenth Brumaire of Louis Bonaparte', Marx notes—in what would become an oft-quoted paragraph—that 'the tradition of all the dead generations weighs like a nightmare on the brain of the living'.[17] It is indeed the nightmarish weight of history that separates us from Marx's own writings which has obscured the core meaning of dictatorship in his work as well as the actual political practice of dictatorship. To put it simply, after the experiences of the past century, dictatorship has seemingly vanished as an explanatory model for the exercise of power, and even more so as a description of a specific configuration of juridico-political power. However, the demise of 'state communism' and of the authoritarian regimes of the past century does not imply a disappearance of either political or legal practices related to dictatorial powers. It simply attests to the continual degradation of their use and meaning.[18]

After a career in public law and political theory,[19] the concept of dictatorship is now generally relegated to a merely derogatory use.[20] This has been the case since the first decade after the Second World War, when its use was reserved almost exclusively for socialist states and often in conjunction with the concept of totalitarianism, with which it came to be associated closely.[21] Dictatorship was stripped of much of its explanatory force through fusion with totalitarianism,[22] and both concepts came to be used as rather blunt weapons in a Cold War war of ideas, with significant implications for the humanities and social sciences.[23] The fall of the Berlin Wall did very little to alter the situation, as both concepts continued to be distorted. The concept of dictatorship was reserved for 'rogue' regimes falling outside—or afoul of—a then triumphant liberal order.[24] Moreover, it lost within this process any technical legal meaning, let alone a jurisprudential one.

It is thus not surprising that when cracks started to show in the 'global constitutional order', and serious threats emerged to constitutional institutions and distributions celebrated by the

---

[17] Marx, 'Eighteenth Brumaire', 103.

[18] Alain Badiou, *D'un désastre obscur: sur la fin de la vérité d'État* (Editions de l'Aube 1998) 24; Cosmin Cercel, *Towards a Jurisprudence of State Communism: Law and the Failure of Revolution* (Routledge 2018) 99–105.

[19] Théodore Reinach, *L'Etat de siège: étude historique et juridique* (Librairie Cotillon 1885); Schmitt, *Dictatorship*; Clinton L Rossiter, *Constitutional Dictatorship: Crisis Government in the Modern Democracies* (Princeton University Press 1948).

[20] There are also notable exceptions; see e.g., Jack M Balkin and Sanford Levinson, 'Constitutional Dictatorship: Its Dangers and Its Design' (2010) 94 *Minnesota Law Review* 1789.

[21] Carl J Friedrich and Zbigniew Brzezinski, *Totalitarian Dictatorship and Autocracy* (Praeger 1966).

[22] John Armstrong, 'Conclusion' (1967) 26 *Slavic Review* 27.

[23] Domenico Losurdo, *War and Revolution: Rethinking the Twentieth Century* (first published 1996, G Elliott tr, Verso 2015) 26.

[24] Traverso, *New Faces of Fascism*, 150–58.

ideology of the rule of law, constitutional and legal theorists were in want of an adequate name for the phenomena they were facing. 'Dictatorship' was a term whose value had fallen significantly during the preceding half century, and it was essentially of no more than antiquarian interest to many. Referring to 'stealth authoritarianism',[25] 'autocratic legalism',[26] or 'populist constitutionalism'[27] was not only more fashionable, but enabled one to avoid glaring historical parallels with moments of turmoil in the not-so-distant past. The slow erasure of the concept of dictatorship was also useful for avoiding thorny questions about the historical continuities of dictatorial projects at the core of many liberal democracies.[28]

These were precisely some of the questions that a specific strand of critical legal scholarship was also reluctant to ask. Multifaceted, transnational, and interdisciplinary, this body of legal critique rediscovered the works of the interwar Carl Schmitt shortly after 1991, mainly as a critique of the then triumphant liberalism.[29] The concept of dictatorship now piqued the interest of many in the critical legal movement, as a kind of dark supplement lurking beneath reflections on the force of law and the poetry of undecidability.[30] It gathered significant interest among these scholars during the *fin de siècle* years,[31] and reached its peak with the US-led 'war on terror'.[32] The late translation into English of much of Schmitt's work did not prevent his reflections on dictatorship from being circulated, often in a style and vocabulary marked by his political-theological ruminations. The core of the concept—safeguarding the legal order with little or no effective legal constraints—was largely kept alive. However, direct engagement with the social and historical contexts of actual dictatorships was generally eschewed in favour of a focus on its performative functions or an attempt to reconstruct related jurisprudential debates.[33] What was generally left outside the scope of this discussion was the historical trajectory of dictatorship and its continuity within the legal mechanisms of the liberal state. More importantly, the coupling of dictatorship and the economy was absent from these analyses, a testament perhaps to Schmitt's avowed 'anti-economism'.[34]

More directly, Giorgio Agamben's analysis of the limits of law—an analysis conducted in part on the basis of Schmitt and by way of the concept of the state of exception—has revived interest in dictatorship. Yet his account of the concepts of the exception, *nomos basileus*,[35]

---

[25]   Ozan O Varol, 'Stealth Authoritarianism' (2015) 100 *Iowa Law Review* 1673.

[26]   Kim Lane Scheppele, 'Autocratic Legalism' (2018) 85 *University of Chicago Law Review* 545.

[27]   David Landau, 'Populist Constitutionalism' (2018) 85 *University of Chicago Law Review* 521.

[28]   For a line of analysis documenting this continuity, see Christian Joerges and Navraj Singh Ghaleigh (eds), *Darker Legacies of Law in Europe: The Shadow of National Socialism and Fascism Over Europe and Its Legal Traditions* (Hart 2003); Stephen Skinner (ed), *Fascism and Criminal Law: History, Theory, Continuity* (Hart 2015).

[29]   Chantal Mouffe, 'Penser la démocratie moderne avec, et contre, Carl Schmitt' (1992) 42 *Revue française de science politique* 83.

[30]   Jacques Derrida, *Force de loi* (Galilée 1994).

[31]   John P McCormick, *Carl Schmitt's Critique of Liberalism* (CUP 1997) 121–48; William E Scheuerman, *Carl Schmitt: The End of Law* (Rowman & Littlefield 1999) 28–34.

[32]   Gopal Balakrishnan, *The Enemy: An Intellectual Portrait of Carl Schmitt* (Verso 2000); Sylvie Delacroix, 'Schmitt's Critique of Kelsenian Normativism' (2005) 18 *Ratio Juris* 1.

[33]   Lars Vinx, *The Guardian of the Constitution: Hans Kelsen and Carl Schmitt on the Limits of Constitutional Law* (CUP 2015).

[34]   Carl Schmitt, *Roman Catholicism and Political Form* (first published 1923, Gary L Ulmen tr, Grenwood Press 1996) 14.

[35]   Agamben, *Homo Sacer*, 30–38.

and *homo sacer*,[36] as embodiments of the structural imbalance between legal normativity and political power, misses a key point, namely the modern significance of this suspension of the law.[37] Agamben's genealogical account of the exception and his re-reading of Aristotle's relationship between life and politics both elide the specifically modern features of dictatorship, obfuscating their legal significance in the name of broader philosophical reflections on law's relation to life.[38] It is against this background that the importance of Marx's reading of dictatorship today reveals itself most clearly.

The concept of dictatorship has two meanings in Marx's writings, both of which were articulated in much of the legal and political thought with which he engaged. First, dictatorship has had an important place in the history of European legal systems since the Roman Republic. Its technical legal meaning can be summed up as a temporary suspension of law and the corresponding delegation of unlimited powers to a specific body or person in order to preserve the existing system of legality. In this sense, dictatorship is both inside and outside the law, an operation which Agamben, following Schmitt, has astutely observed: '[s]ince "there is no rule that is applicable to chaos", chaos must first be included in the juridical order through the creation of a zone of indistinction between outside and inside, chaos and the normal situation—the state of exception'.[39] Historical examples of this meaning abound, from the time of Sulla to the fall of the Roman Empire and from the Thirty Years' War to the French Revolution.[40] Dictatorship was used and theorised with a view to protecting the existing legal order, often through acts unjustifiable on the basis of existing legal rules. In this sense, dictatorship is a response to an 'extraordinary' situation that takes the form of internal strife or external military threat. It is explicitly connected to martial law and other legal mechanisms such as the state of siege, the state of emergency, and the state of exception.

A second meaning of dictatorship captures the excess of power related to the use of such extraordinary powers. While closely related to the first and explicitly legal meaning, this meaning builds on the supplementary authority vested in the body or person exercising dictatorial power. In this sense, it fixes the boundary between what is already inscribed in the legal order and the a-legal, if not illegal, 'excess' this body or person is bound to exercise. Hal Draper suggested that these two meanings do not originally seem to be accompanied by any clear ideological baggage, but instead simply describe different constitutional realities and political situations.[41] Indeed, both dictatorship and its dictatorial supplement have been used for a variety of projects throughout the nineteenth and twentieth centuries.

[36]   Agamben, *Homo Sacer*, 71–74.
[37]   Cosmin Cercel, 'Law's Disappearance: The State of Exception and The Destruction of Experience' in Simone Glanert and Fabien Girard (eds), *Law's Hermeneutics: Other Investigations* (Routledge 2016) 186.
[38]   Agamben, *Homo Sacer*, 13–14.
[39]   Agamben, *Homo Sacer*, 19.
[40]   Reinach, *L'Etat de siège*, 11–87; Schmitt, *Dictatorship*, 34–64.
[41]   Hall Draper, *Karl Marx's Theory of Revolution*, vol 3 (Monthly Review Press 1986) 28–32.

RULE BY SWORD: REVOLUTION, DICTATORSHIP, AND THE LAW

In order to appreciate Marx's understanding of dictatorship and this concept's usefulness for contemporary analysis, we need to situate Marx's work in its material and intellectual context. It is not coincidental that Marx's body of work on the topic of dictatorship concerns France, examining the outcome of the 1848 Revolution, the emergence of the Second Empire, and the Paris Commune. Many of Marx's writings attempt to theorise revolutionary practices in light of the failures of proletarian uprisings and movements in nineteenth-century France. Given Marx's commitment to the view that history is the history of class struggle, what we are faced with is an analysis of the position in which the French proletariat found itself in the wake of the bourgeois revolution of February 1848. It is worth recalling that by the time he wrote these historico-sociological studies of France, Marx had already arrived at the view that the proletariat is capitalism's most promising and significant agent of social and historical progress, both in his 'Critique of Hegel's Philosophy of Right'[42] and within the framework of *The Communist Manifesto*. Given the overtly strategic and tactical features of his writings, we are a step away from the philosophical insights in his critique of Hegel, and also a step away from his early theorisation of historical materialism in the 'Preface to a Contribution to the Critique of Political Economy'.[43]

Marx seeks here to draw political lessons from the limits and failures of the French proletariat's participation in the revolution. In France the 1848 Revolution had two distinct moments—the February Revolution, which abolished the July Monarchy of Louis Phillipe of Orléans, and the June Days Uprising, which opposed the Paris proletariat to the bourgeois provisional government. On a larger historical scale, the 1848 Revolution followed the two monarchical regimes of restoration after Napoleon's rule. From 1814 onwards France was ruled twice in accordance with a charter that was revised in 1830 and that sought to reconcile constitutional monarchy with the fundamental rights enshrined in the various instruments concluded following the 1789 revolution.[44] Within the domain of dictatorial powers, detailed legislation regulating the state of siege was in place. Its own history is indicative for extending the scope of application of siege measures to civilian contexts. In essence, this legislation granted military authorities judicial and police powers otherwise within the remit of civilian authorities. In its initial form, the practical application of the state of siege was limited to fortifications and fortified cities in territories bordering enemy countries.[45] It evolved to a point of general application, within any territory under actual military threat. Even under the more relaxed conditions made possible by an 1811 decree, the state of siege was limited by a tellingly vague declaration that the state was confronted with a real and serious military or insur-

---

[42]   Karl Marx, *Critique of Hegel's 'Philosophy of Right'* (first published 1927, Annette Jolin and Joseph O'Malley tr, CUP 1977).

[43]   Karl Marx, 'A Contribution to the Critique of Political Economy' [1859] in Karl Marx and Frederick Engels, *Collected Works*, vol 29 (Lawrence & Wishart 1987) 257.

[44]   Alain Laquièze, *Les origines du régime parlementaire en France, 1814–1848* (Presses Universitaires de France 2002) 77–80.

[45]   Art 10, Loi du 10 juillet 1791 sur la conservation et le classement des places de guerre et postes militaires, reproduced in *Bulletin des lois depuis le mois du juin 1789 jusqu'au mois d'août 1830*, vol 2 (Paul Dupont 1834) 235.

rectional threat.[46] In this respect, the measures taken under the state of siege were considered to be outside the purview of the governing French Constitution.[47]

Not long before the period Marx analysed, a state of siege had been declared under the Charter of 1830 regime in response to several riots that had commenced in 1832 (and to which Marx alludes).[48] On this occasion, one Geoffroy, a participant in the riots, was brought before a war council and judged according to the rules of martial law. Facing a death sentence, he filed for constitutional review before the civil Court of Cassation, which held the greatest authority over such matters. On this occasion, the court made two important points which illustrate vividly the status of dictatorial powers prior to 1848. On the one hand, the court refused to examine the legality or constitutionality of the king's declaration of a state of siege. On the other hand, it found that the war council had no jurisdiction over Geoffroy insofar as he was not a member of the military.[49] This judgment shows the internal antinomy of a nascent liberal legality. Such a regime is split between the sovereign exercise of the declaration of siege—an act of sovereign power that is placed beyond judicial scrutiny—and the residual constitutional protection offered by the available body of law.

The antinomies of liberal legality formed the substance of Marx's 'Critique of Hegel's Philosophy of Right'. They also occupied an important place in his early and pivotal writings on the statute relating to the theft of wood.[50] In the case of the latter, Marx described legality's debasement by private groups and their affirmation in law. Whether in the form of the private warden of forests, as in the case of the law on the theft of wood, or in the form of the state as such, the affirmation of the bourgeoisie's class interests was, he argued, necessarily connected to a demotion of the legal system officially authorised to uphold the public interest.

It is worth noting that Marx had been involved in legal analysis since his early writings, and indeed had studied the law formally. Likewise, it should be borne in mind that he was also subject to the power of the law in the context of the 1848 Revolution, the charge in question being incitement to revolt in connection with the Committee of Rhenish Democrats' position on the refusal to pay taxes.[51] Acquitted, as no legally valid ground for an indictment could be found, Marx offered important insights during the trial's proceedings into the structure and operation of the law. He wrote sharply: 'society is not founded upon the law; that is a legal fiction. On the contrary, the law must be founded upon society'.[52] His position later evolved past this refusal of legal determinism and the longstanding belief that law regulated society by virtue of its normative power.[53] As an accused, subject to Prussian law, and also as a revolu-

---

[46]   Arts 53, 101, Décret du 24 décembre 1811 relatif à l'organisation et au service des états-majors des places, reproduced in *Bulletin des lois*, 511.

[47]   Michel Teyssier-Desfarges, 'De l'état de siège' (1848) 5 *Revue de droit français et étranger* 498, 500.

[48]   Marx, 'Class Struggles in France', 48.

[49]   Teyssier-Desfarges, 'De l'état de siège', 507–8.

[50]   Karl Marx, 'Proceedings of the Sixth Rhine Province Assembly: Third Article—Debates on the Law on Thefts of Wood' [1842] in Karl Marx and Frederick Engels, *Collected Works*, vol 1 (Lawrence & Wishart 1975) 224.

[51]   Karl Marx, 'The Trial of the Rhenish District Committee of Democrats' [1849] in Karl Marx and Frederick Engels, *Collected Works*, vol 8 (Lawrence & Wishart 1977) 323.

[52]   Marx, 'Trial of the Rhenish District Committee of Democrats', 327.

[53]   Hans Kelsen, *Introduction to the Problems of Legal Theory* (first published 1934, Bonnie Litchewski Paulson and Stanley Paulson tr, OUP 1992) 60.

tionary, Marx described the law as a machinery serving the interests of the landed propertied classes.[54]

In the context of the Prussian Revolution, the law that was arguably applicable to Marx's situation was even worse, a remnant of the estate society specific to the feudal mode of production. Consequently, Marx observed, '[t]he maintenance of the legal basis is therefore in constant conflict with the existing needs, it hampers commerce and industry, it prepares the way for *social crises*, which erupt in *political revolutions*'.[55] In a revolutionary situation, the very meaning of legality may be at stake, becoming a point of wide-ranging contestation: 'The struggle between two political powers lies neither within the sphere of civil law, nor within the sphere of criminal law.'[56] From this perspective, the question of legality is both superfluous and misleading. At the end of the struggle, the consequence is an assertion of power on which the law shall be constructed. As Marx would still recall in the pages of *Capital*, '[b]etween equal rights, force decides'.[57]

At the core of the 1848 revolutionary situation within the German states, Marx found two opposing classes caught in a struggle that was yet to find its resolution, namely the landed aristocracy and the industrial bourgeoisie. Despite his acquittal on the grounds of non-retroactivity and lack of legal basis, that is through the operation of the law caught between the opposing sides of class struggle, Marx's position within this context is revelatory for problematising the explicit relationship between law, revolution, class struggle, and unmediated force.

The situation in France, as reflected in 'Class Struggles', was quite different. In that work, Marx seemed to suggest that among the opposing factions in any given configuration of social power, the proletariat may constitute a distinct and specific force, even if one involved in a failed revolution. In February 1848, with the support of the proletariat, a heterogeneous alliance of bourgeois parties was able to topple the financial aristocracy that supported Louis Philippe's July Monarchy.[58] Indeed, Marx goes to great lengths to uncover the heterogeneity of the new regime emerging from the barricades. His account paints a vivid picture of the various factions of the new regime: royalists (legitimists and Orléanists) forming the Party of Order, bourgeois of either Jacobin or moderate convictions, and socialists forming the Party of Anarchy. The provisional government brought about this regime change was a reflection of the tensions traversing its structures; 'it could not', Marx wrote, 'be anything but a *compromise between the different classes*'.[59] This motley crew draped in the gowns of Order and legal legitimacy was able to sideline and alienate the proletariat, limiting its representation and silencing its demands.[60]

There were two key reforms that directly engaged the proletariat and that were accommodated by the bourgeoisie, albeit reluctantly: the institution of universal male suffrage, and the guarantee of the right to work.[61] The institution of the *ateliers nationaux*, people's workshops maintained by the state through nationally levied taxes in support of the proletariat's right to

---

[54]   Marx, 'Trial of the Rhenish District Committee of Democrats', 327.

[55]   Marx, 'Trial of the Rhenish District Committee of Democrats', 328 (original emphases).

[56]   Marx, 'Trial of the Rhenish District Committee of Democrats', 325.

[57]   Karl Marx, *Capital: A Critique of Political Economy*, vol 1 (first published 1867, Ben Fowkes tr, Penguin 1976) 344.

[58]   Marx, 'Class Struggles in France', 53.

[59]   Marx, 'Class Struggles in France', 53 (original emphasis).

[60]   Marx, 'Class Struggles in France', 55–56.

[61]   Marx, 'Class Struggles in France', 57–60.

work present in Paris and its urban agglomerations, is illustrative here.[62] The *ateliers* antagonised the rural provinces and the newly created National Assembly refused to support the project, as well as the Commission of Luxembourg's related proposals for the reorganisation of labour relations.[63] The opposition of the peasantry and the petty bourgeoisie to the *ateliers* testified to their reactionary positions, as well as to the division of class interests within the proletariat generally. More broadly, it bore witness to the suspicion the new regime had for the very form of the social demands, particularly in regard to workers' rights, insofar as they were able to upset existing relations of production. As Marx observes, '[t]he emancipation of the workers—even as a *phrase*—became an unbearable danger to the new republic, for it was a standing protest against the restoration of credit, which rests on undisturbed and untroubled recognition of the existing economic class relations'.[64]

The government's reaction, which hastened to rescind funding for and ultimately decided to close down the *ateliers* (i.e., to engage in a direct attack on the already limited rights granted to workers), was a matter of historical necessity inscribed in the class struggle. Accordingly, 'it was necessary *to have done with the workers*'.[65] Through these actions, taken by the provisional government with the assent of the National Assembly, the newly created republic revealed itself to be a 'bourgeois republic', not a means of furthering the revolutionary goals of the proletariat but 'a *republic with social institutions*' that are 'the political reconsolidation of bourgeois society'.[66] Faced with this dire reality, no longer veiled under the guise of post-revolutionary transitional reforms, the French proletariat was forced into an open conflict.

In the wake of the *ateliers*' closure,[67] workers opposed the government in an uprising. The reaction was swift and merciless: dictatorial powers were entrusted to General Louis Eugène Cavaignac, who built his career in the colonial wars in Algeria.[68] Paris was placed under a state of siege,[69] while a newly formed 'Mobile Guard', comprised largely of workers and supplementing the police and armed forces, took control of the streets of Paris. Through this intervention, '[t]he veil that shrouded the republic was torn asunder',[70] and the republic came out 'in its pure form as the state whose admitted object it is to perpetuate the rule of capital, the slavery of labour'.[71] The proletarian uprising of June 1848, an act into which it was forced by the very logic of class antagonism, was able to unveil the enmity between the two camps.[72] Consequently, the government abolished the last institutional limits in the face of this threat. By the very act of dispensing with such legality, 'bourgeois rule, freed from all

[62] Marx, 'Class Struggles in France', 63.
[63] Marx, 'Class Struggles in France', 61.
[64] Marx, 'Class Struggles in France', 62 (original emphasis).
[65] Marx, 'Class Struggles in France', 62 (original emphasis).
[66] Marx, 'Class Struggles in France', 66 (original emphasis).
[67] Marx, 'Class Struggles in France', 67.
[68] Jennifer Session, 'Colonizing Revolutionary Politics: Algeria and the French Revolution of 1848' (2015) 33 *French Politics, Culture & Society* 75, 78–83.
[69] Décret par lequel l'Assemblée nationale se maintient en permanence, met Paris en état de siège, et délègue les pouvoirs exécutifs au général Cavaignac, 24 juin 1848, reproduced in Jean-Baptiste Duvergier (ed), *Collection complète des lois, décrets, ordonnances, réglements, et avis du Conseil d'Etat*, vol 48 (Charles Noblet 1848) 354.
[70] Marx, 'Class Struggles in France', 67.
[71] Marx, 'Class Struggles in France', 69.
[72] Marx, 'Class Struggles in France', 68.

fetters, was bound to turn immediately into *bourgeois terrorism*'.[73] The terror raised by the Second Republic under the form of the 'rule by sword' is not an exceptional moment in a new order supporting bourgeois rule and its legality.[74] Cavaignac's defence of dictatorial powers before the National Assembly—an act intended to underline the limited and therefore purely commissarial and temporary nature of this rule—does not signify its end. Once the uprising was quelled, with the rioters shot on the spot, sent to the colonies, or delivered to the discretion of military courts, the National Assembly took on its work as a constituent assembly. It began to engage in a purge of its socialist-leaning members by investigating the June Days Uprising, and also wrote a constitution under the state of siege, which followed it closely.[75] As such:

> [t]he Constituent Assembly resembled the Chilean official who wanted to regulate property relations in land more firmly by a cadastral survey just at the moment when subterranean rumblings announced the volcanic eruption that was to hurl away the land from under his very feet. While in theory it accurately marked off the forms in which the rule of the bourgeoisie found republican expression, in reality it held its own only by the abolition of all formulas, by force *sans phrase* [without any exceptions], by the *state of siege*.[76]

In sum, Marx's account of the events of June 1848 offers a study of the political significations of the juridico-political dictatorship. The dictatorial powers entrusted to General Cavaignac under the supervision of the National Assembly, as well as the various measures that complemented it—the declaration of a state of siege, expedited trials, and deportation of insurgents, among others—were at the core of the new regime of legality created by the February Revolution. Such legal practices revealed the republic's dependence upon the bourgeoisie's class power, as well as tensions between the formal character of constitutional law and its material foundations, themselves little more than military force.

THE PATH TO BONAPARTISM: CONSTITUTION AND DICTATORSHIP

Dictatorship reveals the social forces on which juridico-political order rests. Understood in the light of class struggle, dictatorship unveils the objective historical meaning of the law. In the context of the 1848 events, it undermined public law's pretence of neutrality and illuminated the reactionary nature of the new regime. As Marx notes, '[t]his constitution … did not sanction any social revolution; it sanctioned the momentary victory of the old society over the revolution'.[77] It should therefore come as no surprise that the new constitution was effectively mirrored in new laws concerning the press and the state of siege, with the latter stretching the conditions for the declaration of a siege even further by eliminating the material and political requirements necessary for its formal institution.[78] As a result, the National Assembly—or, in

---

[73]   Marx, 'Class Struggles in France', 69 (original emphasis).
[74]   Marx, 'Class Struggles in France', 107.
[75]   Marx, 'Class Struggles in France', 77.
[76]   Marx, 'Class Struggles in France', 77 (original emphasis).
[77]   Marx, 'Class Struggles in France', 77.
[78]   Loi du 9 août 1849 sur l'état de siège, reproduced in *Bulletin des lois*, 146.

the event of its prorogation, the President of the Republic—was able to declare the state of siege without any factual requirement for its justification.[79]

Although Marx does not explain the full effects of these developments, which had important and far-reaching constitutional consequences, he does explore their political significance when analysing the rise to power of Napoleon III, the 'nephew' who emerged on the stage of history in a farcical re-enactment of his illustrious ancestor. While 'Class Struggles' offers a cartography of the legal institution of dictatorship, 'Eighteenth Brumaire' illustrates the excesses it made possible and its importance for sustaining France's bourgeois legal order. This dictatorial regime emerged as an uneasy compromise between a terrified bourgeoisie and the smallholding peasantry, aided by the sword of the lumpenproletariat. An exercise in the political anatomy of Caesarism, 'Eighteenth Brumaire' is often read retrospectively as a disclaimer about the limits of revolutionary struggle, as well as a text that anticipates twentieth-century models of right-wing dictatorships.[80] Such readings are valuable, but they obscure Napoleon III's dictatorial regime's legal underpinnings, as well as the constitutional drama that brought him to power. Napoleon emerges from the pages of 'Eighteenth Brumaire' as a figure of particular moral depravity and political ruthlessness. Yet what is often elided is the fact that his rule affected—and was made possible by—the juridico-political structure of the state, whose power was certainly 'not suspended in mid air'.[81] Napoleon represented the class of smallholding peasants, and his rule was also a response on the part of the bourgeoisie to the constitutional problems of the Second Republic. In this sense, there is a clear line of continuity between the proletariat's repression in June 1848 and the military takeover on 2 December 1852, both in Marx's own discussion and in the historical course of the political events.[82] The continuity is that between the legal institution of dictatorship and the dictatorial regime that it conveys. For its part, such a dictatorial regime is not the legal exercise of dictatorial powers, but their thwarting and inscription within the regular functioning of the constitutional order. If Napoleon III is a proto-authoritarian leader, as Marx's analysis suggests, it is crucial to grasp the relation that Marx posits between the existing legal-dictatorial framework and the emergence of the dictatorial regime. Marx's insight is unambiguous on this point: it is the very possibility of dictatorial powers inscribed in the constitution that acted as a precondition for their transformation into a 'norm'. This is an insight that many contemporary commentators on authoritarian (or so-called 'populist') regimes seem to elide, and that has significant implications for law's participation in the creation of dictatorial regimes.

Elected president by way of direct vote and with an overwhelming majority, Bonaparte—a military figure boasting at least two failed coup attempts in the preceding decade—soon started upending existing constitutional arrangements. This was achieved by quelling the revolutionary insurrection in Rome,[83] a clear violation of Articles 5 and 54 of the French Constitution of 1848, which were designed to prevent wars of aggression and vested war powers in the

---

[79] Louis-Joseph Gabriel de Chénier, *De l'État de siège, de son utilité et de ses effets* (Librairie Militaire de J Dumaine 1849) 27–31.

[80] Martin Kitchen, *Fascism* (Macmillan 1976) 71–82.

[81] Marx, 'Eighteenth Brumaire', 186.

[82] Marx, 'Eighteenth Brumaire', 182–84.

[83] Following the 1848 Revolution, Pope Pius IX was expelled from Rome and a constitutional assembly proclaimed the republic in February 1849. The Pope pleaded for support from Catholic powers, and the republic sent in an expeditionary force. Karl Marx described the proclamation of the republic in Rome as 'the beginning of the revolutionary drama of 1849': Karl Marx, 'Proclamation of a Republic in

National Assembly rather than the president.[84] Yet this violation of the constitution should not be overstated as a foundational event. As Marx observes, the constitution was marred by contradictions arising from subsequent laws and practices, but these antinomies were already inherent in republican legal arrangements: 'each paragraph of the Constitution contains its own antithesis, its own Upper and Lower House, namely, freedom in the general phrase, abrogation of freedom in the marginal note'.[85] These antinomies reflected the internecine tension between the various factions of the bourgeoisie. They also revealed a deeper systemic imbalance within the structure of bourgeois legality: 'so long as the *name* of freedom was respected and only its actual realisation prevented, of course in a legal way, the constitutional existence of liberty remained intact, inviolate, however mortal the blows dealt to its existence *in actual life*'.[86] Put differently, as a matter of constitutional normative reality freedom was protected, while as a matter of objective legal and sociological fact it was limited, thwarted, or effectively disregarded. What is important to note here is that this peculiar functioning of the law is not a mere distinction between the norm and its application, but part of a constitutional structure that supports the belief in bourgeois promises. As Marx observed in the 'Critique of Hegel's Philosophy of Right', this procedure, which is specific to bourgeois constitutional thought and practice, 'is not a question of developing the determinate idea of the political constitution, but of giving the political constitution a relation to the abstract Idea, of classifying it as a member of its (the Idea's) life history'.[87] It is thus by way of this operation that an objectionable reality is elevated furtively to the level of an 'abstract Idea'. The fundamental limit of the bourgeois state is further explored by Marx in 'On the Jewish Question', where he examines the survival of status society within the framework of the modern state as a necessary precondition for its existence. As he writes:

> [t]he state abolishes ... the distinctions established by *birth, social rank, education, occupation* ... But the state, none the less, allows private property, education, occupation, to *act* ... as private property, education, occupation, and to manifest their *particular* nature. Far from abolishing these *effective* differences, it only exists so far as they are presupposed; it is conscious of being a *political state* and it manifests its *universality* only in opposition to these elements.[88]

These internal tensions were furthered by the arrangement of powers which sought to offer the National Assembly the upper hand in counterbalancing presidential powers. As such, while the assembly could remove the president constitutionally, the president could remove the assembly only unconstitutionally, 'by setting aside the Constitution itself'.[89] This is precisely what Bonaparte ended up doing by coup in December 1851. Even more strikingly, the blind spot of the republican order was the constitution's structural reliance on dictatorial powers: '[t]he state of siege of Paris was the midwife of the Constituent Assembly in its travail of republican

---

Rome' [1849] in Karl Marx and Frederick Engels, *Collected Works*, vol 8 (Lawrence & Wishart 1977) 414, 414.

[84]   Marx, 'Eighteenth Brumaire', 131.
[85]   Marx, 'Eighteenth Brumaire', 115.
[86]   Marx, 'Eighteenth Brumaire', 115 (original emphases).
[87]   Marx, *Critique of Hegel's 'Philosophy of Right'*, 14.
[88]   Karl Marx, 'On the Jewish Question' [1843] in Robert C Tucker (ed), *The Marx-Engels Reader* (2nd edn, WW Norton & Co 1978) 26, 32 (original emphases).
[89]   Marx, 'Eighteenth Brumaire', 115.

creation'.[90] The constitutionalism of the republic was thus, in essence and as a matter of legal practice, connected to military power. When Bonaparte, securing the support of parts of the military—and especially factions of the colonial army in Algiers—arrested the members of the National Assembly and declared himself a 'prince-president', he was acting in accord with the logic already on display in the constitution: 'If the Constitution is subsequently put out of existence by bayonets, it must not be forgotten that it was likewise by bayonets, and these turned against the people, that it had to be protected in its mother's womb, and by bayonets that it had to be brought into existence.'[91]

The establishment of the Second Empire under Napoleon III followed the suppression of the June Days Uprising, against the background of growing militarisation and repressive force. Bonaparte's rise revealed what the constitution kept secret. The coup would replace the republican slogan of '*Liberté, Égalité, Fraternité*' by the unambiguous words: 'Infantry, Cavalry, Artillery!'[92] Such a shift was rightly described as a farce, as a long literary tradition defined the features of this genre by an excess in representation of the characters' traits. Just as in classic farces, where one witnesses the soldier, merchant, or king,[93] the Second Empire embodied the rule of the bourgeoisie in its alliance with the peasantry that was not yet caught within capitalist relations of production.[94] The dictatorship thus exposes the difference between the social power exercised by the bourgeoisie and its politico-legal status. On the one hand, the social dominance of the bourgeoisie was limited to urban areas where capitalist relations of production had taken root. On the other hand, its politico-legal power was already challenged by the proletariat. Accordingly, the dictatorship operated as a means of defending the social power of the bourgeoisie at the expense of politico-legal power. Therefore, 'in order to preserve its social power intact, its political power must be broken; … in order to save its purse, it must forfeit the crown, and the sword that is to safeguard it must at the same time be hung over its own head as a sword of Damocles'.[95]

The constitutional embodiment of this political stand took the form of a significant growth in executive power. The state of siege, as the nexus between the law, the state, and the military, is also the most extreme form of the return of the unlimited sovereign power of absolutism operating under 'liberal' conditions. As Marx observes, the 1848 Revolution transformed 'the motley pattern of conflicting medieval plenary powers into the regulated plan of a state authority whose work is divided and centralised as in a factory'.[96] This move was closely related to dictatorship's role as the legal basis for state repression. By directing its power against the rising and increasingly self-conscious proletariat, the bourgeoisie 'found itself compelled to strengthen, along with the repressive measures, the resources and centralisation of governmental power'.[97] This reliance upon force culminated in the creation of the Second Empire, with its jingoistic attitude and unfettered repression of political opponents.

---

[90]   Marx, 'Eighteenth Brumaire', 118.

[91]   Marx, 'Eighteenth Brumaire', 118.

[92]   Marx, 'Eighteenth Brumaire', 137 (original emphases).

[93]   Robert S Stephenson, 'Farce as Method' (1960) 5 *The Tulane Drama Review* 85.

[94]   Terrell Carver, 'Marx's Eighteenth Brumaire of Louis Bonaparte: Democracy, Dictatorship, and the Politics of Class Struggle' in Peter Baehr and Melvin Richter (eds), *Dictatorship in History and Theory* (CUP 2004) 103, 115.

[95]   Marx, 'Eighteenth Brumaire', 143.

[96]   Marx, 'Eighteenth Brumaire', 185.

[97]   Marx, 'Eighteenth Brumaire', 186.

20 years later, when Marx was reflecting on the experience of another failed revolution, that of the Paris Commune, this trend was even clearer.[98] In its attempt to quell the rising proletariat, the bourgeoisie increased the powers of the executive, while disarming the National Assembly of legal means to restrict the scope of dictatorial power. The Second Empire was born from the support of the Party of Order, the bourgeois republic's reliance on repression and dictatorial power.[99] However, it is not only the bourgeoisie who brought about the new regime. As already mentioned, the smallholding peasants were at the core of the popular support behind Napoleon III.[100] Yet the proletariat, in disarray after the June events, was also partly caught under the spell of the new regime, first by falling prey to the national path underway since the 1848 Revolution, second through its support of the breakdown of parliamentarism. By obfuscating class contradictions under 'the chimera of national glory',[101] the empire reconstructed France, entrenching the bourgeoisie's social power.[102] Liberated from its political duties and constitutional shackles, the bourgeoisie was able to build and develop the material basis of the new regime by supporting exploitation internally and imperialism externally.[103]

However, when faced with the rise of German imperialism, the Second Empire fell after a short and extremely bloody war against Prussia and its allies. The Third Republic, acting through the provisional governments of the national bourgeoisie, hastened to seek an armistice with the enemy and tried to impose its rule on a divided France, torn by war. It was under these conditions that the Paris Commune, the 'positive form' of the 'social republic' heralded by the 1848 Revolution, first began to emerge. For Marx the Commune was nothing short of the antithesis of the Second Empire, involving universal suffrage, internationalism, opposition to nationalistic jingoism, and even socialism. As such, it reversed the repressive apparatus and put under political scrutiny both the police and the judiciary. Yet given the prevailing balance of forces, and partly on account of the disorganisation in its own ranks, the Commune came under attack by the bourgeois government in Versailles. In the last chapter of Marx's account of this process, in which repression unfettered by law was once again exacted on the proletariat, Marx attempts to trace the origins of this practice:

> To find a parallel for the conduct of Thiers and his bloodhounds we must go back to the times of Sulla and the two Triumvirates of Rome … There is but this difference, that the Romans had no mitrailleuses for the despatch, in the lump, of the proscribed, and that they had not 'the law in their hands,' nor on their lips the cry of 'civilization.'[104]

CONCLUSION

Marx's understanding of dictatorship is neither purely political nor strictly jurisprudential. Rather, it nests itself at the intersection between politics, law, and history. Such an intellectual device appears at first glance at best perplexing, if not utterly unrefined. It does not offer an

---

[98]   Marx, 'Civil War in France', 329–30.
[99]   Marx, 'Civil War in France', 329.
[100] Marx, 'Civil War in France', 329.
[101] Marx, 'Civil War in France', 330.
[102] Marx, 'Civil War in France', 330.
[103] Marx, 'Civil War in France', 330.
[104] Marx, 'Civil War in France', 348–49.

explicit definition of dictatorial powers, nor does it tackle frontally law's structural limits in grasping historical turns. It is thus not a reflection on the conundrum between the validity of the law and its efficacy, although it implicitly invites one. However, such an intellectual apparatus is still able to relate the sphere of law to the unfolding of a historical trajectory. It thus situates legality in a broader framework that takes into account not only ostensible aspects of class antagonism, but the moments of minute construction of a regime of legality within the history of class struggle. Dictatorship emerges as a legal apparatus that suspends the norms—the liberal pledges of public interest and reason—and exposes the naked material power on which these pledges are built. At the same time, it reveals the tensions traversing the ruling classes and the differences within their interests, while being a reminder that disruptions in constitutional arrangements are a signifier of deeper economic and political divisions.[105]

If the current structural crisis is read with a limited focus on the otherwise obscure figures of the countless authoritarians emerging seemingly out of nowhere on the surface of constitutional arrangements, what Marx's reading of dictatorship can offer us is the lacking context. The emphasis on the material conditions that have produced such figures and have brought them to the helms of our polities, is able to act as a sobering reminder that the very legality we still blissfully support is at least a part of the ideological superstructure of this reality. With specific reference to the case of France, as Alain Badiou rightly noted in an otherwise unpopular intervention, there is a need to return to the classical Marxist categories, be it only for gaining a level of orientation.[106] The rise of the far right, the overt presence of symbols of national sovereignty, and the confused popular contestation of a government described as Caesarist,[107] all emerge on the background of a declared state of emergency that has lasted for two years and which was again contemplated as a possibility in the wake of the *gilets jaunes* protests, and finally declared in response to the Covid-19 pandemic.[108] In order to understand the meaning of state violence and the roots of the ideological confusion still dominating French politics, one has to trace the history of class relations within this country and ask a series of difficult questions about class interest, the status of the nation-state within contemporary capitalism, and the repressed history of collaboration and colonialism. Ultimately, one would need to engage in an archaeology of dictatorship and dictatorial powers. In light of recent constitutional developments generated by the pandemic, such an exercise would certainly be beneficial also beyond the French context. Not only have constitutional protections concerning the exercise of fundamental rights been suspended, as emergency legislative mechanisms have been put in place, but executives in and beyond Europe have secured sweeping powers through various legal devices, ranging from exceptional regulations to blank cheques for executive power in ensuring public health and safety.

What Marx is able to offer for an understanding of our constitutional present is thus an impetus to move away from models of political takeover in which a malevolent figure or faction skilfully exploits 'gaps' in legality. Rather, he enables us to reflect on the flaws within

---

[105] Franz Neumann, 'Economics and Politics in Twentieth Century' [1951] in Franz Neumann, *The Democratic and the Authoritarian State: Essays in Political and Legal Theory* (Herbert Marcuse ed, Free Press 1957) 257.

[106] Alain Badiou, *Méfiez-vous des blancs, habitants du rivage* (Fayard 2019) 53.

[107] Alain Badiou, *Eloge de la politique* (Flammarion 2017) 123.

[108] See e.g., the French statute of emergency concerning the Covid-19 epidemic of 23 March 2020: JORF, No. 0072 du 23 March 2020.

the very normative structure that is supposed to guarantee freedom and equality. Moreover, as a matter of historical inquiry, his reading is able to document the nexus between nascent liberal constitutionalism and legality and the remnants of the unbound exercise of power which has survived within the texture of modern legality. While such a reading does indeed expose a structural fault line within the rule of law, it is also the expression of a historical trajectory, and not of an ahistorical limit of Western legality bestowed from immemorial times on our polities. Entangled in the history of class struggle, the rule by sword captures that side of the law which has remained 'the prerogative of kings or nobles',[109] even under conditions of liberal legality.

---

[109] Walter Benjamin, 'Critique of Violence' [1921] in Marcus Bullock and Michael W Jennings (eds), *Walter Benjamin: Selected Writings*, vol 1 (Harvard University Press 1996) 236, 249.

6.   Revolution, Lenin, and law
Michael Head

INTRODUCTION

Any appraisal of the Marxist approach to law must be placed in the context of the 1917 Russian Revolution. In relation to political and legal theory and practice, the revolution launched the boldest and most far-reaching experiment of the twentieth century. The Soviet government headed by Lenin, the chairman of the Council of People's Commissars, took steps without precedent. It dispensed with the previous courts, legal system, and legal profession, and sought to fashion a radically new approach to the state, law, and legal theory, with some striking results in many fields, including criminal and family law. Moreover, it attempted to create the conditions for the fading away (or 'withering away') of law and the state.

Despite the oft-repeated claim that Marx and Engels failed to elaborate a full theory of law and the state, and therefore provided no blueprint for a victorious working-class socialist revolution, the Bolshevik Party, led by Lenin, was grounded in the key programmatic concepts fashioned by Marx and Engels. In fact, during the final tumultuous months leading up to the October Revolution, Lenin was preoccupied with reinforcing these concepts in his pamphlet, *The State and Revolution*, drawing directly from their writings, in order to prepare the party for the seizure of power, the complete abolition of the old tsarist-capitalist state, and the establishment of a totally new kind of state.

Lenin's focus on this issue, even as he was in hiding from the police of the unelected provisional government formed after the February Revolution, also exemplified his role in constantly seeking to clarify the immense political issues and tasks confronting the Bolshevik Party and the working class. Knowing that the question of actually overthrowing the provisional government and leading the seizure of power by the soviets, or workers' councils, would produce pressure in his own party to pull back and compromise with supposedly democratic elements within the provisional capitalist government, Lenin was acutely concerned with the need to 're-establish' the principles elaborated by Marx and Engels.[1]

Directly answering opportunist social-democratic revisions of the writings of Marx and Engels, especially by Karl Kautsky,[2] Lenin quoted extensively from their original writings. For example, he re-emphasised the need for a genuine mass revolution to entirely overthrow the bourgeois state: 'According to Marx, the state is an organ of class *rule*, an organ for the *oppression* of one class by another; it is the creation of this "order", which legalises and perpetuates this oppression by moderating the conflict between the classes'.[3] Against reformist conceptions, Lenin also reiterated that when Engels foreshadowed the 'withering away' of the state he was speaking about the workers' state established by a socialist revolution, not the

---

[1]   VI Lenin, *The State and Revolution: The Marxist Theory of the State and the Tasks of the Proletariat in the Revolution* (first published 1917, Progress Publishers 1970) 12.

[2]   Lenin, *State and Revolution*, 8–9.

[3]   Lenin, *State and Revolution*, 14 (original emphases).

capitalist state: 'According to Engels, the bourgeois state does not "wither away", but is abolished by the proletariat in the course of the revolution. What withers away after this revolution is the proletarian state or semi-state.'[4]

Never before had a mass revolution, involving millions of people, placed in power an administration whose avowed intent was to dissolve itself into a classless, stateless society. One chronicler of the Russian Revolution, Isaac Deutscher, noted that in October 1917 Lenin's Bolsheviks spoke of a 'great vision':

> Theirs was to be a state without a standing army, without police, without bureaucracy. For the first time in history, the business of government was to cease to be the professional secret and privilege of small groups of people, elevated above society. It was to become the daily concern of the ordinary citizen ... To be sure, this was the ideal state of the future, not the Russian state of 1917. But the Soviet republic, as it emerged from the revolution, was to be directly related to the ideal.[5]

This program of state disappearance was enshrined as a constitutional principle. In the words of Article 9 of the first constitution of the Russian Socialist Federal Soviet Republic (RSFSR), adopted in 1918:

> [t]he principal aim of the constitution of the RSFSR, which is designed for the present transition period, consists in the establishment of the dictatorship of the urban and rural proletariat and the poorest peasantry in the form of a strong all-Russian Soviet power for the purpose of complete crushing of the bourgeois, the destruction of the exploitation of man by man, and the establishment of socialism, under which there will be neither division into classes nor state power.[6]

Conscious of the international character of the political perspective animating Lenin and other Soviet leaders, another historian of the Bolshevik Revolution, EH Carr, argued that '[s]ince, however, "the establishment of socialism" could be conceived only as an international event, the Russian federation was merely the first unit of an eventual world federation of socialist republics. In this sense, too, it marked a "transitional period"'.[7] Although not a Marxist, Carr was a knowledgeable and meticulous scholar, familiar with the historically derived concepts and terminology adopted by Marx, Engels, and Lenin. Carr noted that:

> [t]he emotional overtones of the word 'dictatorship' as associated with the rule of the few or of one man were absent from the minds of the Marxists who used the phrase. On the contrary, the dictatorship of the proletariat was the rule of the vast majority, it would require, once the bourgeoisie was struck down, less compulsion to maintain it than any previous order of society. Far from being a rule of violence, it would pave the way for the disappearance of the use of violence as a social sanction, i.e., for the dying away of the state.[8]

Such an heroic vision—the elimination of exploitation and the creation of a stateless society— should not be lightly dismissed as utopian, despite the subsequent betrayal of the revolution by the nationalist bureaucracy that emerged under Stalin after the revolution failed to spread beyond the borders of the first isolated workers' state. In many ways, the Marxist vision built

---

[4]   Lenin, *State and Revolution*, 28.
[5]   Isaac Deutscher, *The Prophet Armed, Trotsky: 1879–1921* (OUP 1954) 318.
[6]   Cited in EH Carr, *A History of Soviet Russia*, vol 1 (Macmillan 1950) 129.
[7]   Carr, *History of Soviet Russia*, vol 1, 129–30.
[8]   Carr, *A History of Soviet Russia*, vol 1, 151.

upon—and also advanced further—the epic aims of the great democratic revolutions of the seventeenth and eighteenth centuries in England, America, and France.[9]

Moreover, as Trotsky argued, this perspective was based upon the development of humanity's productive capacities, on a global scale, to such a level that scarcity was eliminated for all practical purposes, permitting a voluntary, egalitarian, democratic, and collaborative approach to production and distribution:

> The material premise of communism should be so high a development of the economic powers of man that productive labor, having ceased to be a burden, will not require any goad, and the distribution of life's goods, existing in continual abundance, will not demand—as it does not now in any well-off family or 'decent' boardinghouse—any control except that of education, habit and social opinion.[10]

Trotsky documented how the nationalist, autarchic, and repressive program of the Stalinist bureaucracy prevented the material and political conditions for this vision to be realised.[11] Nevertheless, the early, pre-Stalinist record of Soviet Russia provides insight into the emancipatory potential of a future socialist society.[12]

TUMULTUOUS EVENTS

In examining early Bolshevik legal policy, one factor must not be overlooked, flowing from the mass character of the October Revolution. Well before the Soviet government was formed, and decreed the abolition of the tsarist courts, in key areas the working people themselves had already swept aside the authority of the old police agencies and courts. For example, immediately after the February Revolution, in Kronstadt and the Vyborg side of Petrograd, the workers had ignored the tsarist courts and begun to set up their own revolutionary courts.[13] Trotsky recorded that on 1 March 1917 the Provisional Government had issued an order for the arrest of all police officers, but the gesture was 'purely platonic in character, for the police were already being arrested and the jails were their only refuge from massacre'.[14] By April Trotsky reported that, under the pressure of the masses, 'the soviets were becoming organs of administration', interfering in all aspects of government, 'even in the courts of justice'. In Tiflis (Tbilisi), for example, the local soviet 'confiscated a private printing establishment for its own uses, made arrests, took charge of investigations and trials for political offences, established a bread ration, and fixed the prices of food and the necessaries of life'.[15]

After seizing power in October, the Bolsheviks initially lagged with respect to the courts. Judges continued to act in the name of the overthrown Provisional Government. Writing in *Pravda* in November 1917, Pyotr Stuchka, the first Soviet Commissar of Justice, stated: 'We

---

[9]   Michael Head, *Evgeny Pashukanis: A Critical Reappraisal* (Routledge-Cavendish 2008) 3–4.

[10]   Leon Trotsky, *The Revolution Betrayed: What is the Soviet Union and Where is it Going?* (first published 1936, Pathfinder 1972) 45–46. See also Lenin, *State and Revolution*, 117–43, on the economic basis of the withering away of the state.

[11]   Trotsky, *Revolution Betrayed*, 45–64.

[12]   Head, *Pashukanis*, 1–15.

[13]   PI Stuchka, *Selected Writings on Soviet Law and Marxism* (Robert Sharlet, Peter B Maggs, and Piers Beirne ed and tr, ME Sharpe 1988) 3.

[14]   Leon Trotsky, *The History of the Russian Revolution* (first published 1930, Pluto Press 1977) 200.

[15]   Trotsky, *History*, 371–72.

must concede that the Russian Revolution acts very slowly with respect to the old apparatus of power; except for the commanding heights, all the old apparatus is intact.' Under the headline 'A Class Court or a Democratic Court?', he complained that judges were continuing to preside over cases, even though they were not yet subjected to democratic election and recall.[16]

As an interim measure, Stuchka proposed transferring the following cases from the courts: agrarian cases (to land committees), apartment disputes (to apartment house mediation committees), and all other civil cases (to special workers' institutions). He observed that the overall volume of cases would also diminish significantly with the removal of such obsolete institutions as tribal property and predetermined inheritance, the abolition of political and religious crimes, and the simplification of the penal system.

Stuchka proposed the election of all judges, the equalisation of all judicial salaries, and the earliest possible replacement of the old legal institutions with revolutionary courts. But there were heated discussions among the Bolsheviks about how to proceed. One faction urged the retention of the pre-revolutionary courts during the period of socialist transition. Another faction insisted that all existing legal institutions and law should be abolished because they were incompatible with socialism.[17]

Lenin effected a compromise with the enactment of Decree No. 1 on the courts on 24 November 1917. First, this decree abolished most of the old legal system, including the district courts, military and naval courts, commercial courts, court chambers, the departments of the Ruling Senate, the Procuracy, and justices of the peace. Second, it declared that all laws were invalid if they contradicted the decrees of the Central Executive Committee or the minimum programs of the two parties in the ruling coalition—the Russian Social Democrats (Bolsheviks) and the Left Social Revolutionaries. Third, it instituted a system of local (later people's) courts and revolutionary tribunals. The former were to hear civil cases and minor criminal trials; the latter were to consider offences of a counter-revolutionary character. Both were to be democratically elected, and their members were to be guided by revolutionary consciousness.[18]

According to Stuchka, Lenin supported Stuchka's first draft of the decree and worked on it personally, adding a note to Article 5. The original draft stated as follows: 'Local workers and peasants revolutionary courts are approved, guided in their decisions and sentences not by the written laws of the overthrown governments, but by the decrees of the Council of People's Commissars, revolutionary conscience and revolutionary legal consciousness.'[19]

Concerned that insufficient decrees existed and that the terms 'revolutionary conscience' and 'revolutionary legal consciousness' were too abstract and vague, and facing opposition from the Social Revolutionaries and among the Bolsheviks to the sweeping nature of the proposal, Lenin added a note specifying that all laws would be regarded as repealed that contradicted the Soviet government's decrees or the minimum programs of the ruling coalition partners (the Bolsheviks and Left Social Revolutionaries). Lenin also delayed the measure by two days and asked Anatoly Lunacharsky to write an article in *Pravda*, the Bolshevik Party's

---

[16] Stuchka, *Selected Writings*, 7.
[17] Stuchka, *Selected Writings*, 4.
[18] Stuchka, *Selected Writings*, 4.
[19] Stuchka, *Selected Writings*, 90.

newspaper, in support of the decree.[20] Thus, from the first days of the revolution, lively and considered debates erupted over legal policy.

LENIN'S ROLE

As even these early legal experiences illustrate, Lenin was undoubtedly the most important figure in the October Revolution. Arguably, Trotsky had a more profound impact by elaborating the international paradigm—the theory of permanent revolution—that clarified the necessity for a socialist revolution in Russia as part of a worldwide overthrow of capitalism. But Lenin provided the pivotal theoretical, political, and practical leadership in the establishment and administration of the Soviet government. This was not simply a product of his formal position as chairman of the Council of People's Commissars. His record since the 1890s, his leadership in forging the Bolshevik tendency from 1903, combined with his exacting attention to the strategic experiences of the international working-class movement, gave him enormous political authority within the ruling party. While he strenuously opposed all forms of formal glorification and personal deference, he exercised critical intellectual authority, backed by widespread popular support.[21]

Lenin's pre-eminent role continued until his first stroke in May 1922, and resumed before his second stroke of December that year. That is not to say that Lenin's views prevailed automatically. They were invariably the topic of considerable discussion and subject to variations in implementation. The Bolshevik Party was far from the monolithic apparatus that it later became under Stalin, and Lenin often had to overcome deep differences and sharp resistance within the government. But time and again, he would write an article, deliver a speech, or give a lecture that would lead to specific policy shifts. On occasions, he would write or amend decrees or other declarations himself.

More fundamentally, Lenin's capacity to direct the trajectory of Soviet Russia was deeply limited by the underlying and often dire circumstances of the Russian Revolution, rooted in the economic backwardness and isolation of the first socialist-inspired state. These problems dominated the last part of his active political life, from January to March 1923, when he suffered a third stroke that effectively incapacitated him until he died in January 1924. During that period, in alliance with Trotsky, he fought to combat the Russian nationalism and bureaucratism that he thought to be imperilling the entire revolution under the pressure of foreign capitalist powers.[22]

LENIN'S ANALYSIS OF THE STATE AND LAW

Because of his pivotal role, a brief review of Lenin's positions on the state and law is essential to understanding the debates over early Soviet law, as well as the subsequent degeneration

---

[20]   Stuchka, *Selected Writings*, 220.
[21]   Trotsky, *History*, 343–44; Trotsky, *Lenin* (Blue Ribbon Books 1925); Head, *Pashukanis*, 43–44.
[22]   See generally Moshe Lewin, *Lenin's Last Struggle* (Faber & Faber 1969); EH Carr, *History of Soviet Russia*, vol 4 (Macmillan 1954).

under Stalin.[23] Between 1917 and 1923, Lenin intervened continuously on issues large and small that impinged on legal policy and administration, often cutting across the niceties of theoretical discourse. More generally, his views shaped the overall theoretical and practical terrain within which debates unfolded.

In general, Lenin regarded law as a residual, essentially bourgeois, instrument that a socialist state was obliged to use as long as it remained incapable of achieving the conditions for genuine communism. Second, Lenin emphasised in *The State and Revolution* that the old capitalist state, with its apparatus of police, spies, military forces, courts, and prisons, could not be reformed or adapted to socialist purposes. It had to be abolished completely. Third, the new state formed after a socialist revolution must begin to wither away immediately. To the extent that a coercive and distributive state apparatus continued to exist, it remained a 'bourgeois' state. Fourth, Lenin arrived at that position during the course of 1917, following the February Revolution and his April Theses, where he revised his strategic conception of the Russian Revolution. Until then, he conceived of the Russian Revolution as a radical bourgeois-democratic revolution led by the working class, not as a socialist revolution.[24]

The single most consistent theme running through Lenin's relevant writings is that law and the state machinery are not neutral and necessary instruments of social regulation but historical products of class society. They are essentially mechanisms whereby the most powerful social class enforces its economic and political rule. When the working classes and other oppressed masses seize power through revolutionary means, leading to the eventual creation of a classless society, the need for law and an enforcing state apparatus begin to fade away.

These views saturate *The State and Revolution*, written during the months following the February 1917 revolution. Lenin insisted that a socialist revolution could not adapt the old state machinery of capitalist society to its needs, but would instead need to abolish the existing legal and bureaucratic apparatus and create a unique new system. This regime would be required to overcome the resistance of the old ruling class, but it would be democratic for the majority of the population and it would be transitional, leading to the emergence of a classless society. Lenin emphasised that even under the temporary dictatorship of the proletariat, the state would begin to die away, and would ultimately 'wither away' altogether when communism was really achieved—when, that is, the productive forces of humans had developed and been rationally planned to such a degree that scarcity and inequality were for all practical purposes eliminated. 'According to Marx', wrote Lenin, 'what the proletariat needs is only a state in process of withering away, i.e., so constituted that it will at once begin to wither away and cannot help wither away'. He added: 'The proletarian state will begin to wither away immediately after its victory, since in a society without class contradictions, the state is unnecessary and impossible.'[25]

Lenin did not expect an isolated revolution in underdeveloped Russia, followed by a prolonged capitalist encirclement. He insisted that a revolution in Russia could only succeed if it were the opening shot of a Europe-wide and ultimately worldwide socialist revolution. Nevertheless, even in the most favourable circumstances, he did not expect the process of withering away to be automatic. Drawing from Marx's writings on the Paris Commune, he advocated the introduction of definite protections against the misuse of official power: polit-

---

[23]   For the debates and subsequent degeneration see Head, *Pashukanis*, chs 1, 6–8.
[24]   Head, *Pashukanis*, ch 3.
[25]   Lenin, *State and Revolution*, 37, 43.

ical representatives would be paid no more than the average worker's wage; they would be subject to instant recall by their electors; and representatives would be obliged to participate in administrative work.[26]

Only with the advent of true communism would the root causes of social antagonisms— private and conflicting ownership of the productive forces, the division of the globe into nation-states, and the social inequality produced by the capitalist market—be overcome. By then the great majority of working people would be accustomed to administering their own affairs and those of society as a whole without the need for legal and physical coercion. This would eventually dispense with the need for a state—that is, a separate body of politicians, bureaucrats, judges, and armed personnel—'the special bodies of armed men having prisons, etc. at their command'.[27]

Lenin drew a further remarkable conclusion from Marx's analysis—that not only law but the workers' state itself would be 'bourgeois' during the transition to communism:

> As regards the distribution of products of consumption, bourgeois law, of course, inevitably presup-poses the *bourgeois* state as well, because law is nothing without a mechanism capable of *compelling* the observance of legal norms. It follows that under communism not only does bourgeois law remain for a certain time but so does the bourgeois state, without the bourgeoisie![28]

BOLSHEVIK LAW: THE RECORD

In its initial phases, the Russian Revolution bore witness to far-reaching efforts to end the old legal order based on private property, de-legalise all aspects of family and social life, and pave the way for a self-governing society without a separate legal apparatus of lawyers, judges, police, and prisons. These were unprecedented endeavours at the time, and remain unparal-leled to this day, in the sense that their full liberating sweep has not been matched anywhere in the world. This chapter can only examine three areas in which there were notable implications that remain relevant in the twenty-first century.[29]

Family Law

One of the most revealing and emblematic areas of Bolshevik legal theory and practice was family law. In general, the Bolsheviks sought to free women from domestic drudgery. They gave women equal political and legal rights with men, liberalised divorce rules, and legalised abortion. More fundamentally, they sought to transform the material conditions of family life. They set about providing universal social care and accommodation: maternity houses, nursery schools, kindergartens, schools, social dining rooms, social laundries, first-aid stations, and hospitals.[30]

---

[26] Lenin, *State and Revolution*, 62–65.
[27] Lenin, *State and Revolution*, 17.
[28] Lenin, *State and Revolution*, 138 (original emphasis).
[29] See further Head, *Pashukanis*, ch 5.
[30] Trotsky, *Revolution Betrayed*, 144–46; Head, *Pashukanis*, 5–6; John Quigley, *Soviet Legal Innovation and the Law of the Western World* (CUP 2007) 17–26.

In this sphere, as in others, the Bolsheviks were guided by the critique and analysis conducted by the Marxist movement. Most notable in this field was Engels' *The Origin of the Family, Private Property and the State*. Drawing upon the research of Lewis Morgan, Engels traced the origins of patriarchal society and its associated conception of the family as a monogamous economic unit to the emergence of surplus value, private property, and the state. To summarise his conclusions somewhat simplistically, Engels argued that the accumulation of private property gave rise to the need for a father to pass his estate onto his children.

More fundamentally, on the basis of a certain historical level of development of productive capacity, society became divided into classes. Through the different phases of class society— slavery, feudalism, and capitalism—the family evolved in line with the requirements of production and the interests of the ruling strata. In the classless society of the future, the economic basis and dictates of the nuclear family would fade away and with it the supremacy of men and the legal enforcement of marriage, together with the consequent problems of infidelity, prostitution, and the degradation of divorce and custody battles. Bound only by love, affection, and mutual respect, personal relations, including monogamous partnerships, would be truly free and enjoyable.

Engels poured scorn on the notion that by beginning to provide formal legal equality to women, Western capitalist governments were 'removing all cause for complaint on the part of the woman'. He pointed out that the legislative reforms, insofar as they modified marriages into voluntary agreements with equal rights and obligations on both sides, brought family law in line with the transformation of commercial law from status, under feudalism, to contract.[31] Marriage arrangements remained tied up with private property rights:

> As far as marriage is concerned, even the most progressive law is fully satisfied as soon as the parties formally register their voluntary desire to get married. What happens behind the legal curtains, where real life is enacted, how this voluntary agreement is arrived at—is no concern of the law and the jurist. And yet the simplest comparison of laws should serve to show the jurist what this voluntary agreement really amounts to. In countries where the children are legally assured of an obligatory share of their parents' property and thus cannot be disinherited—in Germany, in the countries under French law, etc.—the children must obtain their parents' consent in the question of marriage. In countries under English law, where parental consent to marriage is not legally requisite, the parents have full testatory freedom over their property and can, if they so desire, cut their children off with a shilling.[32]

Whether or not formal property and inheritance rights were still enforced, Engels insisted, the formally equal and free appearance of marriage would remain a charade as long as personal relations were dominated by economic considerations. Although he was writing of the conditions of the late nineteenth century, his observations were certainly applicable to early twentieth-century Russia and remain substantially valid.

> Today, in the great majority of cases, the man has to be the earner, the breadwinner of the family, at least among the propertied classes, and this gives him a dominant position which requires no special legal privileges. In the family, he is the bourgeoisie; the wife represents the proletariat.[33]

---

[31] Frederick Engels, *The Origin of the Family, Private Property and the State* (first published 1884, Progress Publishers 1948) 72, 79–82.

[32] Engels, *Origin*, 73.

[33] Engels, *Origin*, 74.

Only under a socialist society would the underlying source of oppression of both women and men be removed:

> With the passage of the means of production into common property, the individual family ceases to be the economic unit of society. Private housekeeping is transformed into a social industry. The care and education of the children becomes a public matter. Society takes care of all children equally, irrespective of whether they are born in wedlock or not. Thus, the anxiety about the 'consequences', which is today the most important social factor—both moral and economic—that hinders a girl from giving herself freely to the man she loves, disappears.[34]

Engels emphasised that these processes did not dictate the end of monogamous partnerships. Instead, they would create the conditions for genuine, loving relationships for the first time in human history. Marriages would be freed from the hypocrisy of 'extra-marital affairs' and the recourse by men to the services of prostitutes. Partnerships would be amicably entered into and would last as long as the love which sustained the marriage continued: 'A definite cessation of affection, or its displacement by a new passionate love, makes separation a blessing for both parties as well as for society. People will only be spared the experience of wading through the useless mire of divorce proceedings.'[35] At the same time, Engels refused to attempt to predict or prescribe the future evolution of human and sexual relations under socialism:

> That will be settled after a new generation has grown up: a generation of men who never in all their lives have had occasion to purchase a woman's surrender either with money or with any other means of social power, and of women who have never been obliged to surrender to any man out of consideration other than that of real love, or to refrain from giving themselves to their beloved for fear of the economic consequences. Once such people appear, they will not care a rap about what we today think they should do. They will establish their own practice and their own public opinion, conformable therewith, on the practice of each individual—and that's the end of it.[36]

In tsarist Russia, the law conceived the family in religious or sacramental terms. A religious marriage ceremony was required. Marriage between members of the Eastern Orthodox or Roman Catholic churches and non-Christians was prohibited, as was marriage between Protestants and pagans. The prevailing doctrine, as stated at a synod of 1744, was that 'marriage is established by God for the increase of the human race'. Women, therefore, were under a duty to bear children. Grounds for divorce varied according to religious faiths and suits for divorce were heard only in ecclesiastical courts.[37]

Among their first initiatives, the Bolsheviks secularised marriage, liberalised divorce, and permitted abortions, as initial steps toward liberating women and children (and men) from the confines of semi-feudal and capitalist family relations. For the first time in Russian history, the Family Code introduced in 1918 recognised civil (non-religious) marriages, granted the absolute right of divorce, and abolished illegitimacy as a legal category.[38]

---

[34]   Engels, *Origin*, 76.
[35]   Engels, *Origin*, 82.
[36]   Engels, *Origin*, 82–83.
[37]   Harold Berman, *Justice in the USSR: An Interpretation of Soviet Law* (Harvard University Press 1963) 331–32.
[38]   On this debate generally see Lewis Siegelbaum, *Soviet State and Society Between Revolutions, 1918–1929* (CUP 1992) 149–56.

Some historians have acknowledged the progressive character of the 1918 Family Code, and attributed its enlightened content to the Marxist tradition of the party. Both Quigley and Goldman describe it as an intensely revolutionary document that reflected the 'socialist-libertarian heritage of the Bolsheviks'.[39] Others have judged it to be 'no more than modern and Western', rather than 'socialist'.[40] But there is no doubt that the Bolsheviks themselves saw the emancipation of women, the equality of the sexes, freedom of human and sexual relations, and the removal, so far as it was possible, of economic pressures from family and social life, as integral aspects of creating the conditions for a genuinely socialist society. In Trotsky's view:

> [t]he October revolution honestly fulfilled its obligation in relation to woman. The young government not only gave her all political and legal rights in equality with man, but, what is more important, did all that it could, and in any case incomparably more than any other government ever did, actually to secure her access to all forms of economic and cultural work ... The revolution made a heroic effort to destroy the so-called 'family hearth'—that archaic, stuffy and stagnant institution in which the woman of the toiling masses performs galley labour from childhood to death. The place of the family as a shut-in petty enterprise was to be occupied, according to the plans, by a finished system of social care and accommodation: maternity houses, crèches, kindergartens, schools, social dining rooms, social laundries, first-aid stations, hospitals, sanatoria, athletic organisations, moving-picture theatres, etc. The complete absorption of the housekeeping functions of the family by institutions of the socialist society, uniting all generations in solidarity and mutual aid, was to bring to woman, and thereby to the loving couple, a real liberation from the thousand-year-old fetters.[41]

Liberating human relations from the economic burdens, as well as legal restrictions, associated with capitalist private property was essential to the socialist project, Trotsky insisted, writing that socialism, 'if it is worthy of the name, means human relations without greed, friendship without envy and intrigue, love without base calculation', and that the 'genuinely socialist family, from which society will remove the daily vexation of unbearable and humiliating cares, will have no need of any regimentation'.[42]

As materialists, the Bolsheviks recognised that the nuclear family and its exploitative character were rooted in deep economic and social pressures produced by money and class relations. Marriage vows and family ties could not be simply abolished. Rather, the Family Code sought to end the church's control over marriage and end the legal and social bondage of women. Alexander Goikhbarg, responsible for the committee that drafted the code, summarised this position starkly, stating that Soviet state institutions of guardianship 'must show parents that social care of children gives far better results than the private, individual, inexpert and irrational care by individual parents who are "loving", but in the matter of bringing up children, ignorant'.[43]

---

[39]   John Quigley, 'The 1926 Soviet Family Code: Retreat from Free Love' (1979) 6 *Soviet Union* 166, 174; Wendy Goldman, 'Freedom and its Consequences: The Debate on the Soviet Family Code of 1926' (1984) 11 *Russian History* 364.

[40]   Beatrice Farnsworth, 'Bolshevik Alternatives and the Soviet Family: The 1926 Marriage Law Debate' in Dorothy Atkinson, Alexander Dallin, and Gail Warshofsky Lapidus (eds), *Women in Russia* (Harvester Press 1978) 139, 140–41.

[41]   Trotsky, *Revolution Betrayed*, 144–45.

[42]   Trotsky, *Revolution Betrayed*, 155–57.

[43]   Zigurds Zile, *Ideas and Forces in Soviet Legal Theory: Statutes, Decisions and Other Materials on the Development and Processes of Soviet Law* (College Printing & Publishing 1970) 36.

Given the extraordinary financial, economic, and cultural difficulties confronting the new order, the Code did not attempt to provide for public maintenance of children—parents remained responsible for the upbringing of children, with the assistance of state facilities.[44] In 1920, a further step was taken to free women (and men) from economic and social pressure—abortion was legalised for the first time. Trotsky insisted that under conditions of poverty and family distress, abortion was one of women's 'most important civil, political and cultural rights'.[45]

According to the available evidence, these unprecedented reforms began to have a significant impact on social and family life. They contributed to a rise in registered marriages, a decline in church weddings in urban areas, higher ages of marriage, smaller families, and rising divorce rates.[46] However, the privations and shortages of the civil war, followed by drastic cuts in childcare and other social services under the New Economic Policy (NEP), generated increased pressures on working class women and children. War, unemployment, and food and housing shortages added to family breakups and a growth in the number of orphaned children.

Two diverging responses emerged. Some party leaders, such as Nikolai Bukharin, blamed lax sexual morals and excessive consumption of alcohol, an early warning of a tendency to turn back to family authority as a means of social control. At a Komsomol congress in 1922, Bukharin attacked 'anarchy in the realm of conduct'.[47] By contrast, Trotsky stressed the need for expanding and improving the stock of housing, public dining facilities, organised leisure activities, and other services to alleviate the burdens of working class and peasant women, together with higher levels of literacy, education, and cultural development.

In 1923 Trotsky sought to address anxieties about the disintegration of traditional family authority. 'There is no denying', he wrote, 'that family relations, those of the proletarian class included, are shattered', and gave examples of many 'domestic tragedies'. He argued that this crisis was symptomatic of the death of the old family and the birth pangs of the new, while urging party members to work for 'the development of the individual[,] ... raising the standard of his requirements and inner discipline'.[48]

Against this background, the RSFSR Commissariat of Justice prepared a draft of a new family code, which became the subject of wide and democratic discussion, notwithstanding the intense factional war that had been waged by Stalin, Grigory Zinoviev, and Lev Kamenev against Trotsky since late 1923. The draft was canvassed in the media and debated in regional and district executive committees before it was submitted to the RSFSR Central Executive Committee in October 1925.

---

[44]   For an English translation of the 1918 Code and parts one and two of the 1926 Code, see Rudolf Schlesinger (ed), *Changing Attitudes in Soviet Russia: The Family in the USSR—Documents and Readings* (Routledge & Kegan Paul 1949) 33–40, 154–68.

[45]   Trotsky, *Revolution Betrayed*, 149.

[46]   Barbara Clements, 'The Effects of the Civil War on Women and Family Relations' in Diane P Koenker, William G Rosenberg, and Ronald Grigor Suny (eds), *Party, State and Society in the Russian Civil War: Explorations in Social History* (Indiana University Press 1989) 105, 107–9.

[47]   Siegelbaum, *Soviet State and Society*, 151.

[48]   Leon Trotsky, *Problems of Everyday Life* (first published 1923, Pathfinder 1973) 36–47. See also Leon Trotsky, 'Address to the Third All-Union Conference on Protection of Mothers and Children' [1925] in Leon Trotsky, *Women and the Family* (Pathfinder 1970) 34–36.

This draft went significantly beyond the 1918 Family Code in several respects. It recognised de facto marriage as legally equivalent to registered marriage, extending property and alimony rights to de facto wives, making the Soviet Union the first country to do so. Second, it established joint ownership of property acquired during marriage and its equal division in case of divorce. Third, it simplified divorce proceedings, entrusting them to the civil registry offices (ZAGS) instead of the courts and also allowing for notification of divorce via mail.

An extensive debate ensued in the 434-member Central Executive Committee, ranging over a broad range of issues, including the legal criteria for marriage, childrearing, and the role of law in the transition to a socialist society. It cut across factional lines, with Left Oppositionists and supporters of the party majority among the proponents and critics of the draft. Rather than imposing a position, the Central Executive Committee postponed a decision until after local soviets had considered the draft. More than 6000 village meetings were held.[49] Peasant representatives and working class women expressed considerable opposition to the liberalisation of divorce and recognition of de facto marriages, reflecting concerns about the insecurity of their economic circumstances.[50]

Before the Central Executive Committee resumed its consideration of the draft in November 1926, Aleksandra Kollontai, a leading Bolshevik who briefly returned from her diplomatic post in Norway, argued that it was demeaning to women and a negation of socialist principles to oblige them to plead before the courts for support from their former husbands. She also pointed to the plight of women who had borne children outside any form of marriage, who were not covered by the 1918 code. Kollontai proposed a General Insurance Fund, based on contributions from the working population.[51] This proposal ignited a lively debate in the press, winning support from young activists and several leading figures, Trotsky among them, but encountered strong criticism, including from female factory workers, for fostering irresponsibility among men. The draft was adopted with only minor revisions in November 1926 and went into effect in January 1927.

The RSFSR was the only Soviet republic to fully recognise de facto marriages, suggesting both a sensitivity to peasant sentiment and a tendency to compromise with traditional elites in the less economically developed republics. However, from 1926 to 1929, an official campaign was waged in the Central Asian republics against the veiling of women, which included legal and administrative measures to break the resistance of mullahs and village and clan elders.[52]

Significantly, the open and lively discussion on the 1926 Code on Marriage, Family, and Guardianship was one of the last to occur before the 1927–28 repression of the Left Opposition. Within a decade the egalitarian and liberating features of the 1926 code were among the first social gains reversed by Stalin's regime. Given the continuing relative backwardness of Soviet society, the gains for peasant and working women and their families had been limited in any case. As Trotsky noted, by 1935 there were only 1 181 000 children in kindergarten, a 'drop in

---

[49]   Schlesinger, *Changing Attitudes in Soviet Russia*, 107–20.

[50]   Wendy Goldman, 'Working-Class Women and the "Withering Away" of the Family: Popular Responses to Family Policy' in Sheila Fitzpatrick, Alexander Rabinowitch, and Richard Stites (eds), *Russia in the Era of NEP: Explorations in Soviet Society and Culture* (Indiana University Press 1991) 125, 138–39.

[51]   Farnsworth, 'Bolshevik Alternatives', 149–52.

[52]   Siegelbaum, *Soviet State and Society*, 155–56.

the ocean' of more than 40 million Soviet families, especially given that the lion's share would undoubtedly go to the families of party and administrative bureaucrats.[53]

But the Stalinists systematically demolished the gains of Bolshevik family law, re-criminalising non-therapeutic abortions in 1936, followed by new laws, adapted from the capitalist West, to restrict divorce and reinforce the sanctity of marriage.[54] Berman suggests that these reversals were intended to lift the birth rate and halt the disintegration of the family, which was 'endangering the stability of Soviet social relations'.[55] He points to 'alarming' rates of juvenile delinquency, soaring abortion rates, and an 'extraordinarily high' number of registered and de facto divorces. By comparison, Trotsky argued that the changes not only expressed the material interests of the new privileged caste, which revived nepotism and other family favouritism, but also the political calculations of the ruling stratum: 'The most compelling motive of the present cult of the family is undoubtedly the need of the bureaucracy for a stable hierarchy of relations, and for the disciplining of youth by means of 40,000,000 points of support for authority and power.'[56]

Indeed, the Stalinist doctrine of the 'sacredness' of the Soviet family contained definite echoes of the tsarist sacramental conception of marriage. 'Soviet marriage reveals the spiritual side of marriage, its moral beauty, inaccessible to capitalist society', the official newspaper *Pravda* declared in 1936, during the debates on the law restricting abortion. Another official commentary insisted that '[a]ssertions that socialism brings the withering away of the family are profoundly erroneous and harmful … The family under socialism does not wither away, but is strengthened. Comrade Stalin, the Party, and the government are giving much attention to questions of strengthening the Soviet family.'[57] Again in 1944, welcoming the restoration of judicial control over divorce, *Pravda* emphasised the 'spiritual side' of family law, stating that '[a] mother who has not yet known the joy of motherhood has not yet realised all the greatness of her calling'.[58] The 1944 decree subjected divorce to rigorous judicial procedure and high fees. De facto marriages ceased to be recognised as legal. The right of illegitimate children to inheritance from their father was ended.[59]

These shifts matched a new stress on personal ownership of one's home, of one's savings, and government bonds. Greater freedom of inheritance was introduced in 1945, permitting Soviet citizens to not only become wealthy but to pass their wealth on to their heirs with a maximum inheritance tax of 10 per cent.[60] Stalin's denunciation of 'equality-mongering' and exultation of personal rewards sanctified the abandonment of any goal of social equality and the emergence of a new privileged caste, whose interests were anchored in both testation and marriage arrangements.

By 1934 Stalin had repudiated Marxist egalitarianism, declaring 'equality in the sphere of requirements and individual life' to be 'a piece of reactionary petty-bourgeois absurdity worthy of a primitive sect of ascetics, but not of a socialist society organized on Marxian

[53] Trotsky, *Revolution Betrayed*, 147.
[54] Trotsky, *Revolution Betrayed*, 151–53.
[55] Berman, *Justice in the USSR*, 49.
[56] Berman, *Justice in the USSR*, 153.
[57] Robert V Daniels, *Trotsky, Stalin, and Socialism* (Westview 1991) 154.
[58] Berman, *Justice in the USSR*, 332–33.
[59] Daniels, *Trotsky, Stalin, and Socialism*, 155.
[60] Berman, *Justice in the USSR*, 51; Daniels, *Trotsky, Stalin, and Socialism*, 155.

lines'.[61] While these transformations were carried out in the name of Marxism-Leninism, they were an ironic, negative, confirmation of Engels' analysis of the relationship between private property and the nuclear family.

'Crime' and 'Punishment'

On crime and punishment too, Marx and Engels had sketched, at least in outline form, a communist approach. In essence, they drew out that so-called criminal conduct was the product of several factors. In part, it expressed an elemental protest by the poor and working people at the rampant inequality and oppression of capitalist society. Insofar as it consisted of anti-social behaviour, its roots substantially lay also in social conditions. At the same time, 'crime' was socially and legally defined by the ruling class of any society in order to protect its propertied interests. In addition, different punishments were meted out to the rich and poor. For all these reasons, Marx and Engels vehemently opposed the 'purely *police* character'[62] of the harsh and revengeful response, particularly reliance upon the death penalty.

Drawing on the English crime statistics of his day, Engels noted the rapid growth of crime under capitalism ('the British nation has become the most criminal in the world') and the extraordinarily high proportions of prisoners who had poor education levels, an indication of poverty, while only 0.22 per cent had enjoyed a higher education.[63] While stressing that impoverishment and want drove some ordinary people to theft, Engels noted that crime also contained an element of social protest. In tracing the emerging revolt of the British working class, which later took the form of industrial strikes and the Chartist movement for voting rights, Engels wrote as follows:

> The earliest, crudest, and least fruitful form of this rebellion was that of crime. The working-man lived in poverty and want, and saw that others were better off than he. It was not clear to his mind why he, who did more for society than the rich idler, should be the one to suffer under these conditions. Want conquered his inherited respect for the sacredness of property, and he stole. We have seen how crime increased with the extension of manufacture; how the yearly number of arrests bore a constant relation to the number of bales of cotton annually consumed.[64]

Elsewhere, Engels observed that criminality was also rooted in capitalism's transformation of human relations into cash relations. Paraphrasing Thomas Carlyle, he noted that cash payment became more and more 'the sole nexus between man and man', with cut-throat competition, cheating, corruption, and adulterous marriages of commercial convenience—most of which practices were not, of course, classified as crimes—prevailing.[65]

Engels observed that when it came to conviction, sentencing, and imprisonment, the poor in England invariably fared worse than the rich, despite the pretence of formal legal equality. In

---

61   Daniels, *Trotsky, Stalin, and Socialism*, 158.
62   Karl Marx, 'The Bourgeoisie and the Counter-Revolution' [1848] in Karl Marx and Frederick Engels, *Collected Works*, vol 8 (Lawrence & Wishart 1977) 154, 172 (original emphasis).
63   Frederick Engels, 'The Condition of the Working-Class in England' [1845] in Karl Marx and Frederick Engels, *Collected Works*, vol 4 (Lawrence & Wishart 1975) 295, 424–27.
64   Engels, 'The Condition of the Working-Class', 502–4.
65   Frederick Engels, 'Socialism: Utopian and Scientific' [1880] in Karl Marx and Frederick Engels, *Collected Works*, vol 24 (Lawrence & Wishart 1989) 281, 288.

a passage that—with allowances for wit and popularity of style—is indicative of his underlying analysis of law, as well as his observations of its application, he wrote:

> Laws are only necessary because there are persons in existence who own nothing; and although this is directly expressed in but few laws, as, for instance, those against vagabonds and tramps, in which the proletariat as such is outlawed, yet enmity to the proletariat is so emphatically the basis of the law that the judges, and especially the Justices of the Peace, who are bourgeois themselves, and with whom the proletariat comes most in contact, fund this meaning in the laws without further consideration. If a rich man is brought up, or rather summoned, to appear before the court, the judge regrets that he is obliged to impose so much trouble, treats the matter as favourably as possible, and, if he is forced to condemn the accused, does so with extreme regret, etc., etc., and the end of it all is a miserable fine, which the bourgeois throws upon the table with contempt and then departs. But if a poor devil gets into such a position as involves appearing before the Justice of the Peace—he has almost always spent the night in the station-house with a crowd of his peers—he is regarded from the beginning as guilty; his defence is set aside with a contemptuous 'Oh! We know the excuse', and a fine imposed which he cannot pay and must work out with several months on the treadmill.[66]

From their earliest writings, Marx and Engels denounced the punitive outlook of the prevailing regimes as cruel, vindictive, and counter-productive. In *The Holy Family*, they related the official attitude to the theology of the Church, with its insistence on purging humanity's 'original sin'. They wrote that 'vengeance on the criminal' was linked with 'penance and consciousness of sin in the criminal, corporal punishment with spiritual punishment, sensuous torture with the non-sensuous torture of remorse'.[67] Marx declared that history and statistics had proven that punishment neither deterred crime nor ameliorated its social causes, strongly condemning capital punishment. He asked rhetorically, 'is there not a necessity for deeply reflecting upon an alteration of the system that breeds these crimes, instead of glorifying the hangman who executes a lot of criminals to make room only for the supply of new ones?'[68]

Marx and Engels predicted that communist society would mean an immense reduction, if not eventual elimination, of crime and, along with it, the need for a vast police and an elaborate judicial and penal system. In one speech, Engels outlined their argument as follows:

> Present-day society, which breeds hostility between the individual man and everyone else, thus produces a social war of all against all which inevitably in individual cases, notably among uneducated people, assumes a brutal, barbarously violent form—that of crime… In communist society … we eliminate the contradiction between the individual man and all others, we counterpose social peace to social war, we put the axe to the *root* of crime—and thereby render the greatest, by far the greatest, part of the present activity of the administrative and judicial bodies superfluous. Even now, crimes of passion are becoming fewer and fewer in comparison with calculated crimes, crimes of interest— crimes against *persons* are declining, crimes against *property* are on the increase. Advancing civilization moderates violent outbreaks of passion even in our present-day society, which is on a war footing; how much more will this be the case in communist, peaceful society! Crimes against property cease of their own accord where everyone receives what he needs to satisfy his natural and spiritual urges, where social gradations and distinctions cease to exist. Justice concerned with criminal cases ceases of itself, that dealing with civil cases, which are almost all rooted in the property relations or

---

66   Engels, 'The Condition of the Working-Class', 567–68.
67   Karl Marx and Frederick Engels, 'The Holy Family, or Critique of Critical Criticism Against Bruno Bauer and Company' [1845] in Karl Marx and Frederick Engels, *Collected Works*, vol 4 (Lawrence & Wishart 1975) 5, 178–79.
68   Karl Marx, 'Capital Punishment' [1853] in Karl Marx and Frederick Engels, *Collected Works*, vol 11 (Lawrence & Wishart 1979) 495, 497–98.

at least in such relations as arise from the situation of social war, likewise disappears; conflicts can then be only rare exceptions, whereas they are now the natural result of general hostility, and will be easily settled by arbitrators.[69]

As far as possible, the Bolsheviks sought to implement this approach. One of the earliest legal debates concerned the pace at which the new government could abolish criminal punishment, under extraordinarily difficult conditions. Given the deprivations faced by millions of people after years of war, the levels of robbery and murder rose sharply both before and after the October Revolution. By 1918 the levels in Moscow were said to be ten to 15 times the pre-war levels.[70] Despite this social strife, the first Criminal Code made criminal law hinge on 'social danger' and 'measures of social defence', rejecting the notions of 'crime' and 'punishment'.[71] Soviet leaders drew the conclusion that these terms, together with 'guilt', functioned to obscure the social causes of crime.[72]

Drafted by Stuchka, the 'Guiding Principle of Criminal Law of the RSFSR' of 1919 defined criminal law as 'made up of rules of law and other legal measures by which the system of social relations of a particular "class society" is protected against infringement (crime) through the application of repressive measures (punishment)'.[73] Notably, the terms 'crime' and 'punishment' were placed in parantheses. These traditional notions were rejected for socialist society. As Stuchka also explained, this flowed from the view that the state's role was social protection, not the assignment of individual guilt and retribution.

The 'Guiding Principle' described penalties as compulsory measures by which the government protects a certain order of social relations against future infringements by the offender or by others. In a class-divided society, crime originated from the social structure, not individual 'guilt'. Therefore, penalties ought not to 'redeem the guilt' but be restricted to the demands of expediency, without inflicting injurious and needless sufferings. Penalties ought to re-educate, not just deter. The range of penalties included compulsory attendance at evening classes. In sentencing, courts should consider the class position and personality of the offender, as well as the degree of danger to society. The criminal law's operation was regarded as *transitional*.[74] Thus, the criminal law's acknowledged purpose was to help attain definite economic and social purposes, rather than to punish individuals. The Communist Party program of the same year looked ahead to when 'the entire working population will participate in administering justice and punishment will be replaced once and for all by educational measures'.[75]

These efforts were, however, cut short by the Civil War, in which the policy of Red Terror was advanced to counter the sabotage, summary executions, and reprisals by the White Army and their allies. One of the worst examples of the White Terror was the British

---

[69]   Frederick Engels, 'Speeches in Elberfeld' [1845] in Karl Marx and Frederick Engels, *Collected Works*, vol 4 (Progress Publishers 1975) 243, 248–49 (original emphasis).

[70]   Peter Juviler, *Revolutionary Law and Order: Politics and Social Change in the USSR* (Simon & Schuster 1976) 18–19.

[71]   Berman, *Justice in the USSR*, 35.

[72]   Raymond Bauer, *The New Man in Soviet Psychology* (Harvard University Press 1959) 38.

[73]   Bauer, *New Man*, 50.

[74]   'Soviet criminal law has the task of protecting the system of social relations which correspond to the interests of the working masses who are being organised into the ruling class under the dictatorship of the proletariat during the period of transition from capitalism to communism.' Rudolf Schlesinger, *Soviet Legal Theory: Its Social Background and Development* (OUP 1945) 74–75.

[75]   Juviler, *Revolutionary Law and Order*, 25.

military-organised execution of 26 Bolsheviks in Baku.[76] These conditions led to a wider adjustment of the early emphasis on avoiding criminal punishments. When an official in the Revolutionary Tribunal system argued that 'the Socialist criminal code must not know punishment as a means of influence on the criminal', representatives of the Commissariat of Justice rebuked him. Kozlovsky derided 'sentimental notions of re-education', saying that during the time it would take to create socialism, and until 'remnants of the past, crime and the need for punishments disappear', the government would need decisive measures of terror and isolation. Savrasov, head of the Commissariat's Penal Department, agreed that the Bolsheviks could not 'soften' the regimen in places of confinement. Lenin also declared that to curb:

> increases in crime, hooliganism, bribery, speculation, outrages of all kinds ... we need time and *we need an iron hand...* We would be laughable utopians if we imagined that such a task can be accomplished the day after the fall of the bourgeois regime, that is, in the first stage of the transition from capitalism to socialism, or that it can be accomplished without repression.[77]

These statements, however, need to be placed in the context of the Civil War, in which revolutionary tribunals were established to deal with serious counter-revolutionary activities. Even so, their jurisdiction was strictly confined to counter-revolution, pogroms, corruption, forgery, and espionage. No tribunal judgment could be carried out before the defendant or any other interested citizen could appeal to a special Court of Cassation.[78]

During the early revolutionary period, the debates over criminal law occurred at several levels. For example, from 1917 to 1927 a number of disputes arose over the right of necessary defence (usually referred to as self-defence in Western jurisprudence). The primary issue was the extension of the right to the defence of collective and societal, rather than individual, interests. Article 19 of the 1922 RSFSR Criminal Code permitted defence against infringements of both the person and the rights of the defender or of other persons. AA Piontkovsky, a legal theorist, criticised it for following 'bourgeois law, bourgeois codes', whose provisions were 'usually intended merely to protect individual interests'. As he observed, the code was silent 'about protecting the interests of the collective'.[79] Later, in 1926–27, a 'lively' debate occurred before the words 'revolutionary legal order' were deleted from the necessary defence clauses of the Soviet codes because they were excessively broad and vague as criteria for justifying defensive conduct.[80]

These initial efforts to develop an enlightened criminal law were repudiated under Stalin. His 1936 Constitution restored the words 'crime' and 'punishment'. The 'formal-juridical' element was emphasised as having equal importance to the 'material' element of social danger and social defence.[81] While Berman suggests that this reversal, like that in family law, was in response to a social crisis, including high crime rates,[82] Huskey argues that the restoration of

[76] Leon Trotsky, *Social Democracy and the Wars of Intervention in Russia 1918–1921* (New Park 1975) 31–32.
[77] This and preceding quotations in Juviler, *Revolutionary Law and Order*, 19.
[78] Schlesinger, *Soviet Legal Theory*, 77.
[79] Quoted in William Butler, 'Necessary Defense, Judge-Made Law, and Soviet Man' in William E Butler, Peter B Maggs, and John B Quigley Jr (eds), *Law After Revolution: Essays on Socialist Law in Honor of Harold J Berman* (Oceana 1988) 99, 103.
[80] Butler, 'Necessary Defense', 104–5.
[81] Berman, *Justice in the USSR*, 56.
[82] Berman, *Justice in the USSR*, 49.

'bourgeois' conceptions of punishment by Andrey Vyshinsky was related to the consolidation of political and social power in the hands of the nascent Stalinist bureaucracy.[83] For his part, Trotsky drew attention to the mounting inequality and social antagonisms that produced discontent and police repression.[84]

Mental Illness

There was a similar trajectory on questions of mental illness. The early Soviet approach to criminal law extended to the removal of questions of mental health from courts altogether. Article 14 of the 'Leading Principles of Criminal Law' of 1919 stated: 'A person shall not be subject to trial and to punishment for a deed which was committed in a condition of mental illness ... To such persons shall be applied only medical measures and measures of precaution.' In effect, all accused who pleaded mental illness were immediately under the jurisdiction of the medical administration.[85] This was in line with the view that the roots of anti-social behaviour lay primarily in the socio-economic conditions of society, and, in some instances, the complex interaction of these conditions with mental illnesses.[86] Again, the emphasis was not 'individual' culpability and punishment but treatment—and, where necessary, confinement to address the underlying mental problem and protect society.

The First All-Union Conference on Psychiatry and Neurology in 1925 adopted a resolution 'On Legislation and the Criminal Question' that opposed the notion of 'imputability'—that is, mental capacity to incur criminal guilt—and advocated its replacement by the ideas of 'social dangerousness and socially dangerous conditions' and attention to the 'neuropsychiatric deprivations of the criminal'.[87] The concept of legal insanity was reintroduced in the criminal codes of 1923 and 1926, but until the mid-1930s the question of criminal insanity was still determined by a psychiatric expert. Article 10 of the 1926 Criminal Code provided that 'measures of social defence of a judicial-correctional character' may be applied to persons who have committed 'socially dangerous acts' only where they acted intentionally (they foresaw the socially dangerous nature of their acts) or acted negligently (they should have foreseen the socially dangerous consequences of their acts). Article 11 stated that judicial and correctional measures may not be applied to persons who act while in a condition of chronic mental illness or temporary derangement, if they could not realise the nature of their acts or control them. Article 11 also applied to persons who, although they acted in a condition of mental balance, had become mentally ill at the time of sentencing. 'To such persons', it stated, 'may be applied only measures of social defence of a medical character'.[88]

Until the mid-1930s, as provided by the Code of Criminal Procedure, a psychiatric expert was summoned whenever the issue of mental health was raised, whether at a pre-trial hearing or during the trial itself. Courts rarely rejected the psychiatrist's conclusions. Thus, although the Criminal Code provided for tests of mental health in terms of will and intellect, the tests

---

[83]   Eugene Huskey, 'Vyshinsky, Krylenko, and Soviet Penal Politics in the 1930s' in Piers Beirne (ed), *Revolution in Law: Contributions to the Development of Soviet Legal Theory* (Routledge 1990) 173.

[84]   Trotsky, *Revolution Betrayed*, 115–70.

[85]   Trotsky, *Revolution Betrayed*, 315.

[86]   See generally Bauer, *New Man*.

[87]   Berman, *Justice in the USSR*, 315.

[88]   This provision did not apply to persons who were intoxicated. Berman, *Justice in the USSR*, 315–16.

that were actually applied were psychiatric tests for mental illness. But from 1935, there was a sharp shift, corresponding to the overall shift to 'stability of laws' demanded by Stalin. Soviet psychiatrists, like jurists and members of every other intellectual discipline, became victims of Stalin's purges to the extent that they clung to any residue of a genuinely Marxist approach. They were denounced as 'wreckers', clumped together with 'Trotskyites' and the disgraced former Justice Commissar Nikolai Krylenko.

In 1938, the Director of the Serbskii Institute of Forensic Psychiatry, the leading agency involved in the psychiatric examination of accused persons, was denounced for 'failing to draw any conclusions for himself from the break in the legal front of wrecking'. According to the authorities, '[t]he treatment of the problems of imputability and non-imputability by the Institute of Forensic Psychiatry coincided in fact with the wrecking tendencies of Krylenko'.[89] This turn corresponded to the reversal of Soviet criminology, attributing 'crime' to evil persons and substantially denying the impact of both social conditions and mental impairment. Taking a quote from Engels on 'free will' entirely out of context, the official 1948 textbook on criminal law declared that Marxism placed 'freedom of the human will' at 'the basis of criminal responsibility'.[90] The practical effects of this reversal were felt starkly. In 1922 46.5 per cent of all psychopaths examined by the Serbskii Institute were declared non-imputable, and 29.3 per cent 'partly imputable'. By 1945 only 12 per cent were judged non-imputable, and the 'partly imputable' category had long been abolished.[91]

STALINISM AND 'SOCIALIST LEGALITY'

With Lenin largely incapacitated by illness, however, from the time of his first stroke in 1923, the 'NEPmen' and bureaucrats who had prospered under the partial restoration of market relations, introduced to try to cope with the ravages of the Western-sponsored 1918–21 Civil War, found a champion in Stalin. By autumn 1924, less than a year after the defeat of the October 1923 German Revolution and eight months after Lenin's death, Stalin had unveiled the new doctrine of 'socialism in one country'.[92] This new nationalist program appealed to a mood of exhaustion in the country, abandoning the struggle for international socialism and instead concentrating on constructing a strong national state. It became the ideological and material underpinning of the bureaucrats who assumed the role of presiding over terrible scarcity and inequality, all the while declaring these social conditions to be necessary for the forging of socialism.[93]

According to Carr, the consolidation of a corresponding legal regime was a sign of the emergence of the elite layer and its nationalist doctrine, 'one of the most striking symptoms of the change in the climate of opinion which paved the way for the doctrine of socialism in one country'.[94] This change is key for analysing the early Soviet debates about law. The reversal of earlier aspirations of a transition to a classless, stateless society led to the consolidation of

---

[89]   Berman, *Justice in the USSR*, 317–18.
[90]   Berman, *Justice in the USSR*, 317–18.
[91]   Berman, *Justice in the USSR*, 318–19.
[92]   Trotsky, *Revolution Betrayed*, 291–301.
[93]   Trotsky, *Revolution Betrayed*, 88–94.
[94]   Carr, *History of Soviet Russia*, vol 5, 88.

state authority, which, in turn, was bound up with the emergence of a nationalist outlook. After 1924, from enlightened legislation and vibrant legal debates, the climate shifted dramatically to repressive laws and mindless diatribes.[95] One of the central features of that reversal was the adoption of what the regime called 'socialist legality'. Ironically, as the regime became increasingly lawless in practice—seen, for example, in the show trials of 1934–37—it proclaimed the construction of a new permanent legal system, overturning the previous emphasis on moving toward the disappearance of the state and law.

By 1936 the Stalinist regime had not only trampled but formally repudiated the basic Marxist conception of the withering away of the state. While claiming to have created socialism and dissolved antagonistic social classes, the regime denied that the legal institutions and state apparatus would disappear, even in the final stage of communism. This abandonment of Marxist precepts flowed organically from the doctrine of 'socialism in one country' adopted by Stalin in 1924. The formal reason given for the new policy of 'socialist legality' was the existence of socialism in one country, encircled by capitalist powers, making it essential to strengthen the state power.

In the midst of the Great Purges of 1936–37, directed against all socialist opposition, Stalin emphasised the need for stability, orthodoxy, and legality for consolidating power. 'We need stability of laws now more than ever', he said in his Report on the Draft Constitution in 1936.[96] Over the following two years, every surviving feature of Bolshevik jurisprudence was overturned. 'Crime' and 'punishment' were restored, as were 'judicial authority', the sanctity of marriage and contracts, and individual fault as chief criterion of personal injury liability.[97]

Correspondingly, Soviet legal theory became reduced to self-serving and platitudinous gibberish. In a series of articles and a book on Soviet public law published in 1938, Procurator-General Andrey Vyshinsky denounced Stuchka and Evgeny Pashukanis, a prominent early Soviet jurist, and their insistence that genuine socialism would mean the end of law. 'History demonstrates that under socialism, on the contrary, law is raised to the highest level of development', he stated, claiming further that '[o]ur laws are the expression of the will of our people as it directs and creates history under the leadership of the working class. The will of the people with us is fused with the will of the whole people'.[98]

As Western legal observers have noted, these banalities cannot compare to the theoretical work of Pashukanis,[99] let alone provide a coherent conception of law. Berman, like many other scholars and commentators, has pointed to the relationship between the lawless despotism of the Stalinist regime, its annihilation of the Bolshevik Party, and its increasing need for the political prop of 'socialist legality'.[100] Indeed, as Trotsky observed in *The Revolution Betrayed,* the evolution of the Soviet state into an ever more totalitarian regime under Stalin could not be reconciled with the classical Marxist conception of the withering away of the state. Referring to the 1918 program adopted by the Bolshevik Party, he wrote that:

> [t]he state as a bureaucratic apparatus begins to die away the first day of the proletarian dictatorship. Such is the voice of the party program—not voided to this day. Strange: it sounds like a spectral voice

---

[95]   Head, *Pashukanis*, chs 6, 7.
[96]   Berman, *Justice in the USSR*, 53.
[97]   Berman, *Justice in the USSR*, 57.
[98]   Quoted in Berman, *Justice in the USSR*, 55.
[99]   See generally Head, *Pashukanis*.
[100]   Berman, *Justice in the USSR*, 64.

from the mausoleum. However you may interpret the nature of the present Soviet state, one thing is indubitable: at the end of its second decade of existence, it has not only not died away, but not begun to 'wither away'. Worse than that, it has grown into a hitherto unheard of apparatus of compulsion … While continuing to publish the works of Lenin (to be sure, with excerpts and distortions by the censor), the present leaders of the Soviet Union and their ideological representatives do not even raise the question of the causes of such a crying divergence between program and reality.[101]

Stalin's nationalist doctrine of building socialism in just one country became intertwined with the development of a totalitarian order and the reversal of the early legal initiatives. It reversed the Marxist conception that the transition to communism required overcoming scarcity, instead holding out the prospect of gradually building socialism, even on an impoverished basis. 'Stalinist legality' was a terrible demonstration of the truth of the Marxist analysis of law as a defender and facilitator of privilege, inequality, and private property interests.

---

[101] Trotsky, *Revolution Betrayed*, 51–52.

7. Marx, Engels, Lenin, and the right of peoples to self-determination in international law

Bill Bowring

INTRODUCTION

The right of peoples to self-determination is a continuing scandal at the heart of post-Second World War international law. Prior to the Second World War, collective self-determination was a revolutionary principle deployed by Marx, Engels, and Lenin, and was enshrined as such in the first constitutions of Soviet Russia and the Soviet Union.[1] With the establishment of the United Nations in 1945, self-determination found expression in that organisation's founding constitutional instrument, the UN Charter, including among its four 'purposes' a provision that spoke of the need '[t]o develop friendly relations among nations based on respect for the principle of equal rights and self-determination of peoples, and to take other appropriate measures to strengthen universal peace'.[2] In 1945 self-determination was therefore a 'principle', but not a 'right' under international law. Nevertheless, as a result of the hard-fought 'battle for international law' in the context of decolonisation,[3] the legal right of peoples to self-determination was enshrined in the two 1966 human rights covenants, both of which are legally binding multilateral treaties ratified by most of the 193 current members of the United Nations.[4] As a result, self-determination was controversially confirmed as a human right, at the foundations of both civil and political rights, going back to the 1789 Déclaration des droits de l'homme et du citoyen, and to social, economic, and cultural rights, first grudgingly conceded by Western capitalist states in 1919 with the creation of the International Labour Organisation in response to the Russian Revolution.[5] Indeed, the right to self-determination is not simply enshrined in binding treaty law; it enjoys an even higher status, being understood by most international lawyers as a norm of customary international law, binding on all states. It is also understood as an *erga omnes* obligation—an obligation owed by states to the international community as a whole, intended to protect and promote the basic values and common interests of all.

---

[1] Bill Bowring, 'The First Soviet Constitutions, Self-Determination and the Rights to Secession' (2019) *SCRSS Digest*, 8–10, http://www.scrss.org.uk/Documents/SCRSSDigest_Autumn2019 _Supplement.pdf accessed 7 April 2021.

[2] Art 1(2), Charter of the United Nations, 1 UNTS xvi.

[3] Bill Bowring 'The Soviets and the Right to Self-Determination of the Colonized: Contradictions of Soviet Diplomacy and Foreign Policy in the Era of Decolonization' in Jochen von Bernstorff and Philipp Dann (eds), *The Battle for International Law: South-North Perspectives on the Decolonization Era* (OUP 2019) 404.

[4] International Covenant on Economic, Social and Cultural Rights [ICESCR], 993 UNTS 3, https:// www.ohchr.org/en/professionalinterest/pages/cescr.aspx accessed 7 April 2021; International Covenant on Civil and Political Rights [ICCPR], 999 UNTS 171, https://www.ohchr.org/EN/ProfessionalInterest/ Pages/CCPR.aspx accessed 7 April 2021.

[5] The ILO's structure is tripartite, involving states, employers, and trade unions.

In my 2008 book, *The Degradation of the International Legal Order?*,[6] I wrote that:

> [t]he Bolshevik and then Soviet doctrine of the right of nations to self-determination had its origin in the uncompromising pre-World War I struggle between Lenin, Stalin and Trotsky (and orthodox Marxists with Karl Kautsky at their head) on the one side, and the Austro-Marxist theorists such as Karl Renner and Otto Bauer on the other.[7]

The 'right of nations to self-determination' was a key element of Lenin's policy from 1914 onwards. In fact, the right of 'nations' (a term that is now often replaced by 'peoples') to self-determination has a long history, and was an important matter of principle for Marx and Engels.

This chapter proceeds in three parts. First, I begin by considering recent orthodox accounts of self-determination in international law, which generally seek to downplay the importance and content of the right of peoples to self-determination. I pay particularly close attention to the role of Marx and Lenin—and also, paradoxically, the Soviet Union—in propagating the concept of self-determination and related political programmes. I also pay close attention to the success of the Soviet Union and other 'socialist' states in making self-determination a core element of international law after the Second World War. Second, I turn to the mid-life conversion of Marx and Engels to support national self-determination in the cases of Poland and Ireland, and the vexed question of whether this simply amounted to a rehearsal of the Hegelian (and Eurocentric) theory of historical and non-historical nations. Engels inherited the concept of non-historical peoples from Hegel, who had identified nationhood with a tradition of statehood.[8] Third, I examine Lenin's principled support of the right of nations to self-determination, his return to Marx's position, and his decisive role in placing the right at the centre of early Soviet policy and constitutionalism. Finally, I trace the role of the Soviet Union in helping to bring about a revolution in international law, and at the same time securing its own downfall.[9]

SELF-DETERMINATION AND INTERNATIONAL STRUGGLE, 2004 AND 2019

The right to collective self-determination was recently—and clearly—reaffirmed by the International Court of Justice (ICJ) in two advisory opinions, dealing with two exemplary instances of the anti-imperialist struggle, itself an aspect of the class struggle. These two opinions were delivered in 2004 (on the question of Israel's construction of its West Bank wall,

---

[6]   Bill Bowring, *The Degradation of the International Legal Order? The Rehabilitation of Law and the Possibility of Politics* (Routledge-Cavendish 2008).

[7]   Bowring, *Degradation*, 13.

[8]   'A nation with no state formation has, strictly speaking, no history—like the nations which existed before the rise of states and others with still exist in a condition of savagery'. GWF Hegel, *Hegel's Philosophy of Mind: Part Three of the Encyclopaedia of the Philosophical Sciences* (first published 1817, William Wallace and AV Miller tr, Clarendon Press 1971) para 549.

[9]   For Putin's denunciation of Lenin's policy, and his blaming Lenin for the destruction of the Russian Empire and the collapse of the Soviet Union, see Bowring 'First Soviet Constitutions'.

which runs through occupied Palestinian territories)[10] and in 2019 (on the United Kingdom's violation of the Chagos Islanders' right to self-determination).[11]

In its 2004 advisory opinion on the West Bank wall, the ICJ recalled[12] that common article 1 of the ICESCR and ICCPR 'reaffirms the right of all peoples to self-determination', and lays upon all states parties to these instruments the obligation to promote the realisation of that right and to respect it, in conformity with the UN Charter. The ICJ held that Israel had violated the right to self-determination of the Palestinian people by constructing a wall, which it termed a 'separation barrier', through occupied Palestinian territories.

In its more recent advisory opinion on 'the legal consequences of the separation of the Chagos Archipelago from Mauritius by the United Kingdom in 1965', the ICJ held that '[t]he nature and scope of the right to self-determination of peoples, including respect for "the national unity and territorial integrity of a State or country", were reiterated in the 1970 Declaration on Principles of International Law concerning Friendly Relations and Co-operation among States in accordance with the Charter of the United Nations', which 'confirmed its normative character under customary international law'.[13] Further, the ICJ stated that '[s]ince respect for the right to self-determination is an obligation *erga omnes*, all States have a legal interest in protecting that right'.[14] The ICJ held that the United Kingdom violated this right when it separated the Chagos Islands from Mauritius prior to the latter's independence in March 1968. On 8 November 1965, the islands were formally established as part of an overseas territory of the United Kingdom—that is, a new British colony—to be known as the 'British Indian Ocean Territory'. In 1971 the United Kingdom and the United States concluded a treaty to lease the island of Diego Garcia, the largest of the Chagos Islands, to the United States, so that the latter might build an air and naval base on the island. The inhabitants of the Chagos Islands were subsequently exiled in secret to Mauritius, where they became chronically impoverished.[15] The ICJ concluded that 'the United Kingdom has an obligation to bring to an end its administration of the Chagos Archipelago as rapidly as possible, and that all Member States must co-operate with the United Nations to complete the decolonization of Mauritius'.[16]

On 22 May 2019 the UN General Assembly adopted a resolution welcoming the ICJ's advisory opinion on the legal consequences of the Chagos Archipelago's separation from Mauritius, and also demanding that the United Kingdom unconditionally withdraw its colonial administration from the area within six months.[17] The vote was 116 in favour of the resolution to six against, with 56 abstentions.[18] The right of peoples to self-determination continues, it

[10]   Legal Consequences of the Construction of a Wall in the Occupied Palestinian Territory, Advisory Opinion [2004] ICJ Reports 136, https://www.icj-cij.org/en/case/131/advisory-opinions accessed 7 April 2021.
[11]   Legal Consequences of the Separation of the Chagos Archipelago from Mauritius in 1965, Advisory Opinion [2019] ICJ Reports 95, https://www.icj-cij.org/en/case/169/advisory-opinions accessed 7 April 2021.
[12]   ICJ, Wall Advisory Opinion, para 88.
[13]   ICJ, Chagos Advisory Opinion, para 155.
[14]   ICJ, Chagos Advisory Opinion, para 180.
[15]   Stephen Allen, *The Chagos Islanders and International Law* (Hart 2014).
[16]   ICJ, Chagos Advisory Opinion, para 182.
[17]   UNGA Resolution 73/295 (22 May 2019). For a summary of statements see https://www.un.org/press/en/2019/ga12146.doc.htm accessed 7 April 2021.
[18]   Samuel Osborne, 'Chagos Islands: UN Officially Demands Britain and US Withdraw From Indian Ocean Archipelago' *The Independent* (22 May 2019), https://www.independent.co.uk/news/

would seem, to retain its importance—indeed, its revolutionary anti-colonial power—today. It is unlikely that the United Kingdom will acquiesce in the General Assembly's demand, or that the United States will be made to leave Diego Garcia. It is now known that the island has played a central role in the United States' policies of torture and rendition to Guantánamo Bay,[19] in which the United Kingdom has colluded.[20]

Umut Özsu contends that the development of international human rights law since 1945 should not be explained either as 'an incremental unfolding of some inexorable logic' or as a hierarchy of norms, but rather as 'an outgrowth of a series of wide-ranging but systemically constrained struggles over which social claims and relations were to receive legal sanction'.[21] I argue more concretely that the right of peoples to self-determination is a hotly contested irruption of politics into law, with its roots in the nineteenth century—and that while it is uncontestably a legal right in international law, both as enshrined in treaties and as customary international law, it is by no means accepted as such. Self-determination struggles continue to rage throughout the world, for example in the ongoing cases of the Basque, Irish, Kurdish, and Palestinian peoples.[22] I contend that the claim to a right of peoples to self-determination had its origins entirely outside any discussion of international law. Marx, Engels, and Lenin had no interest whatsoever in international law, and what was for a long period a political slogan or demand only acquired legal status in the context of struggles for decolonisation and the break-up of colonial empires. And in the context of the United Nations.

DOWNGRADING SELF-DETERMINATION?

Although the Soviet Union, paradoxically and hypocritically, was instrumental in transforming the principle of self-determination into a legal right, a central norm of international law, most orthodox texts on international law portray the Soviet approach to the right to self-determination as merely hypocritical and contradictory.

---

world/americas/chagos-islands-uk-un-resolution-general-assembly-vote-indian-ocean-a8924656.html accessed 7 April 2021.

[19]   Cori Crider, '7 Things You Should Know About Diego Garcia and Renditions' *The Guardian* (11 July 2014), https://www.theguardian.com/commentisfree/2014/jul/11/7-things-diego-garcia-rendition-flights-documentaton-water-damage accessed 7 April 2021. Crider heads the abuses-in-counterterrorism team at Reprieve, where she serves as Guantánamo attorney, legal director, and strategic director.

[20]   James Hanning, 'British Government Suppressing Key Documents on Allegations of UK Collusion in Torture and Rendition: Files Reveal Tony Blair and Jack Straw Discussed Treatment of British Detainees in Guantanamo with US Officials' *The Independent* (5 March 2016), https://www.independent.co.uk/news/uk/politics/british-government-suppressing-key-documents-on-allegations-of-uk-collusion-in-torture-and-rendition-a6914666.html accessed 7 April 2021.

[21]   Umut Özsu, 'The Necessity of Contingency: Method and Marxism in International Law' in Ingo Venzke and Kevin Jon Heller (eds) *Contingency in International Law: On the Possibility of Different Legal Histories* (OUP 2021) 60, 75.

[22]   See 'The Right to Self-Determination' (2009) 53 *Socialist Lawyer* 18–29, https://www.haldane.org/s/SocialistLawyer53.pdf accessed 7 April 2021. The symposium contains Bill Bowring 'Self-Determination', 18–20; Tim Potter, 'Basques: Battle for Identity Endures Struggle', 20–22; Sean Oliver, 'Irish: "United Ireland" is Back on the Agenda', 22–23; Alex Fitch, 'Kurds: A Marginalised and Criminalised People', 24–25; Annie Rosa Beasant, 'Palestinians: Resisting Israel's Illegal Occupation', 26–28.

The entry for 'self-determination' in the *Max Planck Encyclopedia of International Law*, for example, maintains that, according to Soviet doctrine, self-determination existed 'only for cases where it served the cause of class struggle and so-called socialist justice; it was only a tactical means to serve the aims of world communism and not an end in itself'.[23] Stefan Oeter passes a similar judgment in a well-known commentary on the UN Charter, characterising Lenin's insistence on the right of 'nations' to self-determination as nothing more than a 'political weapon', whereas Woodrow Wilson, with his 'Fourteen Points' on the reorganisation of Europe after the First World War, is presented as the political actor who enabled self-determination to make its way from politics to international law.[24] In a similar vein, Lauri Mälksoo, an Estonian scholar of international law, has suggested that it is 'misleading to pick and choose certain pro self-determination moves by the Bolsheviks in 1917 and 1920, and then conclude that the Soviets advanced this right in international law'.[25]

In order to get a broader sense of the role of socialist states in shaping the international law of self-determination, it is useful to consider two recent books that engage closely with self-determination: Jörg Fisch's *The Right of Self-Determination of Peoples: The Domestication of an Illusion*,[26] and Fernando Tesón's edited volume, *The Theory of Self-Determination*.[27] Both books recognise the significance of the contradictory role played by the Soviet Union in decolonisation.

Fisch's book starts by recognising Lenin's contribution: 'Lenin's position on the right to self-determination was already clear in 1914, while Wilson probably did not even know of the expression "right of self-determination of peoples" in 1914', Fisch suggests controversially, adding that because the Second World War was a 'traditional power struggle' the right to self-determination might have disappeared 'definitively'.[28] However, the victorious powers were unable to keep their colonies in check, and in the summer of 1945, when the Soviet Union introduced the 'principle of self-determination' into the UN Charter,[29] '[t]his secured the Soviet Union the approval of the colonial regions'.[30] Fisch adds that '[t]he Soviet bloc and the Third World took over the substance of the concept that had been created in the Americas between 1776 and 1865, but had not yet been designated as self-determination'.[31] According to Fisch, the Third World, supported by the Soviet Union and its allies, succeeded after 1945 in 'monopolising the discourse of self-determination and the right to self-determination for

---

[23]   Daniel Thürer and Thomas Burri, 'Self-Determination' in Rüdiger Wolfrum (ed), *Max Planck Encyclopedia of Public International Law* (online edn), MN 3, https://opil.ouplaw.com/view/10.1093/law:epil/9780199231690/law-9780199231690-e873 accessed 7 April 2021.

[24]   Stefan Oeter, 'Self-Determination', in Bruno Simma et al (eds), *The Charter of the United Nations: A Commentary*, vol 1 (3rd edn, OUP 2012), MN 5. On Wilson see e.g., Michla Pomerance, 'The United States and Self-determination: Perspectives on the Wilsonian Concept' (1976) 70 *American Journal of International Law* 1, 16–20; Anthony Whelan, 'Wilsonian Self-determination and Versailles Settlement' (1994) 43 *International and Comparative Law Quarterly* 99.

[25]   Lauri Mälksoo, 'The Soviet Approach to the Right of Peoples to Self-determination: Russia's Farewell to *jus publicum europaeum*' (2017) 19 *Journal of the History of International Law* 200, 214.

[26]   Jörg Fisch, *The Right of Self-Determination of Peoples: The Domestication of an Illusion* (Anita Mage tr, CUP 2015).

[27]   Fernando R Tesón (ed), *The Theory of Self-Determination* (CUP 2016).

[28]   Fisch, *Right of Self-Determination of Peoples*, 121, 190.

[29]   UN Charter, arts 1, 55.

[30]   Fisch, *Right of Self-Determination of Peoples*, 191.

[31]   Fisch, *Right of Self-Determination of Peoples*, 191.

itself'.[32] He concludes that 'Lenin's venture in 1917–1918 was a resounding success', and that 'Wilson became a prophet of the right of self-determination, but not of his own concept of it, but rather Lenin's'.[33]

Tesón's collection, by contrast, has very little to say about the decolonisation period, save only for a chapter authored by Patrick Macklem.[34] Unlike Fisch, Macklem seems determined to ensure that the Soviet Union should disappear from the history of common article 1 of the two 1966 human rights covenants. Thus, he begins by informing his reader that it was Arab, Asian, and Latin American delegations that began to press for recognition of a legal right to self-determination during the 1950s, much to the alarm of 'European officials', who saw this as a pretext for attacks on colonial powers.[35] Lenin and the Soviet Union make no appearance in Macklem's account of the emergence of the concept, as a discourse justifying the liberation of eastern European peoples.[36] He asserts that '[a]fter a decade of efforts by the African, Arab, Asian, and Latin American delegations to attempt to persuade numerous UN bodies to recognize self-determination as a human right', the General Assembly adopted Resolution 1514 (XV).[37] And he further adds that '[t]he elevation of self-determination to the status of a human right was a spectacular political achievement by the Arab, Asian, and Latin American delegations' at the United Nations.[38]

It is worth comparing these recent additions to the literature on decolonisation with Antonio Cassese's magisterial 1995 book on the topic, *Self-Determination of Peoples: A Legal Reappraisal*.[39] Cassese was clear that 'Lenin was the first to insist, to the international community, that the right of self-determination be established as a general criterion for the liberation of peoples'.[40] He engages in detail with the positions of Lenin and Wilson, Lenin's call for the immediate liberation of those living under colonial rule, and Wilson's championing of 'orderly liberal reformism'.[41] Cassese's claim that it was the Soviet Union that insisted on the proclamation of the right to self-determination in the text of the UN Charter is supported by several sources and discussed in detail.[42] Cassese gives the 1955 Bandung Conference its proper place as an important contributor to a legal right to self-determination. But he maintains that the socialist countries were the most active advocates of anti-colonial self-determination, and 'adopted and developed Lenin's thesis that self-determination should first and foremost be a postulate of anti-colonialism'.[43] Further, it was the Soviet Union, he argues, that 'strongly advocated the need for both Covenants formally to enshrine the right of peoples to self-determination, which, in the Soviet view, was a precondition for the respect

---

[32]   Fisch, *Right of Self-Determination of Peoples*, 218.
[33]   Fisch, *Right of Self-Determination of Peoples*, 240.
[34]   Patrick Macklem, 'Self-Determination in Three Movements' in Fernando R Tesón (ed), *The Theory of Self-Determination* (CUP 2016) 94.
[35]   Macklem, 'Self-Determination', 94.
[36]   Macklem, 'Self-Determination', 97.
[37]   Macklem, 'Self-Determination', 99.
[38]   Macklem, 'Self-Determination', 100.
[39]   Antonio Cassese, *Self-Determination of Peoples: A Legal Reappraisal* (2nd edn, CUP 1995).
[40]   Cassese, *Self-Determination of Peoples*, 14.
[41]   Cassese, *Self-Determination of Peoples*, 14–23, with Wilson quoted at 21, n 30.
[42]   Cassese, *Self-Determination of Peoples*, 38.
[43]   Cassese, *Self-Determination of Peoples*, 44.

of individual rights'.[44] Self-determination, for Cassese, is an 'international political postulate' with a revolutionary content.[45]

MARX ON SELF-DETERMINATION

Marx himself used the phrase 'self-determination', of peoples or nations, on at least three occasions. First, in his 1843 'Contribution to the Critique of Hegel's Philosophy of Right', Marx wrote that '[i]n democracy the constitution, the law, the state itself, insofar as it is a political constitution, is only the self-determination of the people, and a particular content of the people'.[46] Marx's phrase 'self-determination of the people', in the context of democratic struggles, is significant in relation to positions he would adopt later in life. It was shortly before this passage that Marx added his famous statement about democracy:

> Democracy is the solved *riddle* of all constitutions.[47] Here, not merely *implicitly* and in essence but *existing* in reality, the constitution is constantly brought back to its actual basis, the *actual human being*, the *actual people*, and established as the people's *own* work. The constitution appears as what it is, a free product of man.[48]

Marx's use of 'self-determination of nations' in a more directly political, and less theoretical, sense may be seen at least as early as 1865. In his letter of 20 November 1865, Marx referred, under the heading 'International Politics', to '[t]he need to eliminate Muscovite influence in Europe by applying the right of self-determination of nations, and the re-establishment of Poland upon a democratic and social basis'.[49] Additionally, on 22 February 1866, the Belgian newspaper *L'Echo de Verviers* published a letter Marx had helped to write, containing the following language: 'The Central Council ... has founded three newspapers in Switzerland[,] ... one in Britain, *The Workman's Advocate*, the only English newspaper which, proceeding from the right of the peoples to self-determination, recognises that the Irish have the right to throw off the English yoke'.[50]

The cause of Poland, subject to three partitions by Russia, Austria, and Prussia during the course of the eighteenth century (in 1772, 1793, and 1795 respectively), and complete elimination in the final partition, engaged Marx's particular enthusiasm. Marx was a passionate enemy of the Russian Empire, the 'gendarme of Europe', as the following passage from 1856–57 shows: 'It is in the terrible and abject school of Mongolian slavery that Muscovy was nursed and grew up. It gathered strength only by becoming a *virtuoso* in the craft of serfdom.

---

[44]   Cassese, *Self-Determination of Peoples,* 47.
[45]   This is the title of ch 2 of Cassese, *Self-Determination of Peoples.*
[46]   Karl Marx, 'Contribution to the Critique of Hegel's Philosophy of Law' [1843] in Karl Marx and Frederick Engels, *Collected Works*, vol 3 (Lawrence & Wishart 1975) 3, 31.
[47]   Susan Marks drew upon this passage for the title of her *The Riddle of All Constitutions: International Law, Democracy, and the Critique of Ideology* (CUP 2000).
[48]   Marx, 'Contribution', 29 (original emphases).
[49]   Karl Marx, 'Marx to Hermann Jung, in London, 20 November 1865' in Karl Marx and Frederick Engels, *Collected Works*, vol 42 (Lawrence & Wishart 1987) 200.
[50]   H Jung, 'To the Editor of *L'Echo de Verviers*' [1866] in Karl Marx and Frederick Engels, *Collected Works*, vol 20 (Lawrence & Wishart 1985) 392, 399.

Even when emancipated, Muscovy continued to perform its traditional part of the slave as master.'[51]

Furthermore, in a speech on Poland delivered on 22 January 1863, Marx once again referred to self-determination in strong terms:

> What are the reasons for this special interest of the Working Men's Party in the fate of Poland? Firstly, of course, sympathy for a subjugated people, which by continuous heroic struggle against its oppressors has proved its historic right to national independence and self-determination. It is by no means a contradiction that the *international* Working Men's Party should strive for the restoration of the Polish nation.[52]

Needless to say, Poland was not the only nation for the liberation of which Marx became a strong advocate. Ireland was another.

Marx underwent a dramatic change of mind (not the only occasion on which he did so) concerning Ireland, in 1867. As Lenin made a point of noting, prior to the 1860s Marx thought that Ireland 'would not be liberated by the national movement of the oppressed nation, but by the working-class movement of the oppressor nation'. 'However', he noted, 'it so happened that the English working class fell under the influence of the liberals for a fairly long time, became an appendage to the liberals, and by adopting a liberal-labour policy left itself leaderless. The bourgeois liberation movement in Ireland grew stronger and assumed revolutionary forms. Marx reconsidered his view and corrected it.'[53] Lenin cited a letter from Marx to Engels of 2 November 1867,[54] in which Marx wrote as follows:

> The Fenian trial in Manchester was exactly as was to be expected. You will have seen what a scandal 'our people' have caused in the Reform League. I sought by every means at my disposal to incite the English workers to demonstrate in favour of Fenianism ... I once believed the separation of Ireland from England to be impossible. I now regard it as inevitable, although Federation may follow upon separation.[55]

The trial in question was that of the 'Manchester martyrs': William Philip Allen, Michael Larkin, and Michael O'Brien, all members of the Irish Republican Brotherhood. These three were executed after having been found guilty of the murder of a police officer during an escape from prison that took place close to Manchester's city centre in 1867.[56] For his principled position on the matter, Marx would now be prosecuted for 'glorifying terrorism'.[57]

---

[51]   Karl Marx, 'Revelations of the Diplomatic History of the 18th Century' [1856] in Karl Marx and Frederick Engels, *Collected Works*, vol 15 (Lawrence & Wishart 1986) 25, 87 (original emphasis).

[52]   Karl Marx and Frederick Engels, 'For Poland' [1875] in Karl Marx and Frederick Engels, *Collected Works*, vol 24 (Lawrence & Wishart 1989) 55, 57 (original emphasis).

[53]   VI Lenin, 'The Right of Nations to Self-Determination' [1914] in VI Lenin, *Collected Works*, vol 20 (3rd edn, Progress Publishers 1977) 393, 440.

[54]   Lenin, 'Right of Nations to Self-Determination', 440.

[55]   Karl Marx, 'Marx to Engels, in Manchester, 2 November 1867' in Karl Marx and Frederick Engels, *Collected Works*, vol 42 (Lawrence & Wishart 1987) 458, 460.

[56]   Owen McGee, *The IRB: The Irish Republican Brotherhood from the Land League to Sinn Féin* (Four Courts Press 2005) 36.

[57]   Eric Barendt, 'Incitement to, and Glorification of, Terrorism' in Ivan Hare and James Weinstein (eds), *Extreme Speech and Democracy* (OUP 2009) 445, 445:

Jeremy Smith, writing on the 'national question',[58] notes that in 1848 Marx blamed the Irish for the chauvinism of British workers, viewing the English Chartist movement as the only force capable of liberating the Irish people. But the rise of the Fenian movement in the 1860s forced Marx to urge the English workers to support them, and to recognise that revolution in Ireland might even precede and encourage revolution in England. Marx and Engels' new position was that all national liberation movements were by nature revolutionary and should therefore in every case be supported by communists. Nigel Harris also contends that the views of Marx and Engels changed 'quite radically'. On his account, '[i]n 1848 Engels was completely insensitive to the complicated class issues of the Austrian Empire, subordinating all to the fate of Magyars, Poles, and Italians, and the need to stop Russia'; all other nations were 'reduced to the non-historical, the rubbish of ages', with '[a]ll Slavs except the Poles bec[oming] "Panslavists"'. However,'for Marx and Engels the discovery of Ireland changed the motivation, not simply the strategic balance'.[59]

As to Marx's radical change of position, Michael Heinrich has rightly argued that rather than a single, consistent oeuvre, or (as for Althusser) a simple break between a younger, more philosophical Marx and a later, properly scientific one focused on political economy, 'we find in Marx a whole series of attempts, discontinuations, shifts, new concepts and new beginnings'.[60] Indeed, 'there are no texts to be found that show directly or indirectly that he wanted to build any kind of -ism'.[61]

THE DEBATE CONCERNING MARX AND THE 'NATIONAL QUESTION'

At this point I have referred to the positions of Marx and Engels with respect to the right to self-determination of Ireland and Poland. In his 1991 *Marxism and Nationalism*,[62] Ephraim Nimni, the leading scholar of the Austro-Marxists Otto Bauer and Karl Renner and their approach to the question of non-territorial cultural autonomy, accuses Marx and Engels of 'superficial discussions, apparent conceptual gaps and great differences of interpretation from one historical context to another'.[63] This he ascribes to their adherence to Hegel's theory, referred to above, of 'historical versus non-historical nations'.[64] He attributes their support for Polish and Irish self-determination and their strong opposition to any such right for the

---

The Terrorism Act 2006 introduced into UK law a new offence of encouragement of terrorism. Statements which are likely to be understood as a direct or indirect encouragement or other inducement to the commission of terrorist acts may be caught by the offence. One clause in the Act was particularly controversial: it provides that among the statements likely to be understood as indirectly encouraging an act of terrorism are those glorifying such acts, at least where members of the public would reasonably infer that they should emulate them.

[58]   Jeremy Smith, *The Bolsheviks and the National Question 1917–1923* (Macmillan 1999) 9.
[59]   Nigel Harris, *National Liberation* (Penguin 1990) 47.
[60]   Michael Heinrich, 'A Short History of Marx's Economic Critique' in Sara R Farris (ed), *Returns of Marxism: Marxist Theory in a Time of Crisis* (Haymarket 2016) 63, 72.
[61]   Heinrich, 'A Short History', 66.
[62]   Ephraim Nimni, *Marxism and Nationalism: Theoretical Origins of a Political Crisis* (Pluto Press 1994).
[63]   Nimni, *Marxism and Nationalism*, 17.
[64]   Nimni, *Marxism and Nationalism*, 17.

Slavic peoples of the Balkans to their 'rigid evolutionary model, epiphenomenal economism, and the Eurocentric approach which permeated their interpretations of the processes of social change'.[65]

Nimni accuses Marx and Engels of adhering to Hegel's position in his *Philosophy of History*—a position according to which, as Nimni himself puts it, 'peoples ("Völker") who had been proven incapable of building a state will never be able to do so and are damned culturally to vanish in the stream of history'.[66] He cites the scathing remarks of Marx and Engels, often in their pre-1860s journalism, about Mexicans,[67] Scandinavians,[68] the Chinese (their 'hereditary stupidity'),[69] and North African Bedouins[70] as only a few samples, arguing that 'Marx and Engels were, to put it mildly, impatient with and intolerant of ethnic minorities'.[71]

Kevin Anderson notes Nimni's use of the phrase 'hereditary stupidity' as an example of Marx's 'abusive language' and 'intense hostility' to many non-Western 'national communities', but insists that Marx's real target in this newspaper article about China was British imperialism and what he saw as its unconscionable opium trade.[72] He cites the editor of Marx's journalism, James Ledbetter, to the effect that with the possible exception of human slavery, 'no topic raised Marx's ire as profoundly as the opium trade with China'.[73] He acknowledges the troubling nature of Marx's language about 'hereditary stupidity', but argues that Marx's focus was 'not Chinese backwardness, but a Chinese national awakening'.[74]

The African-American Marxist scholar August Nimtz has also addressed what he calls the 'myth' of Marx's Eurocentrism.[75] Nimtz explains how, from 1870 onwards, Marx and Engels ceased to expect the rebirth of a revolutionary movement in England, following the demise of the Chartists. Instead, they turned to Russia as the revolutionary vanguard, despite the fact that Russia was an overwhelmingly peasant country that had only one foot in Europe, and not the Europe that the Eurocentric charge refers to, that is, western Europe with its developed capitalist industry and world-wide colonies.[76] He recalls that in 1849 Marx and Engels insisted that only a world war could provide the Chartists with the opportunity for a successful upris-

---

[65] Nimni, *Marxism and Nationalism*, 25.

[66] Nimni, *Marxism and Nationalism*, 28. Nimni does not give a reference to Hegel for this passage.

[67] Nimni, *Marxism and Nationalism*, 29.

[68] Nimni, *Marxism and Nationalism*, 29–30.

[69] Nimni, *Marxism and Nationalism*, 30. Marx's remark concerning the Chinese appeared in a newspaper article published in 1853: Karl Marx, 'Revolution in China and in Europe' [1853] in Karl Marx and Frederick Engels, *Collected Works*, vol 12 (Lawrence & Wishart 1979) 93, 94.

[70] Nimni, *Marxism and Nationalism*, 30.

[71] Nimni, *Marxism and Nationalism*, 30.

[72] Kevin Anderson, *Marx at the Margins: On Nationalism, Ethnicity and Non-Western Societies* (University of Chicago Press 2016). Anderson 'upholds a view of Marx as a multilinear, non-determinist thinker who over time became increasingly sensitive to the need for a variety of pathways of development and toward revolution for societies outside Western Europe and North America' (xii). As to Marx's condemnation of Sir John Bowring, the erstwhile radical and literary executor of Jeremy Bentham, and his role in perpetrating the Opium Wars, see Bill Bowring, 'Did the States Which Founded the UN Have Liberal or Illiberal Governments?' (2016) 15 *Baltic Yearbook of International Law* 31.

[73] James Ledbetter (ed), *Dispatches for the New York Tribune: Selected Journalism of Karl Marx* (Penguin 2007) 1.

[74] Anderson, *Marx at the Margins*, 31.

[75] August Nimtz, 'The Eurocentric Marx and Engels and Other Related Myths' in Crystal Bartolovich and Neil Lazarus (eds), *Marxism, Modernity and Postcolonial Studies* (CUP 2002) 65.

[76] Nimtz, 'The Eurocentric Marx and Engels', 66.

ing, and that any European war in which England was involved would be a world war, since world-wide colonies would be involved.[77]

Nimtz shows how Marx and Engels reversed their earlier position and gave support to religious-led Arab resistance to French imperialism in Algeria in 1857; expressed strong sympathy for the Sepoy Mutiny (uprising) against Britain in India in 1857–59; and by 1861 wrote, as the US Civil War loomed, that US expansion into Texas and what is now Arizona and New Mexico brought with it slavery and the rule of the slaveholders.[78] At the same time, they were quite clear that the 'booty of British imperialism' had begun to corrupt and compromise the English proletariat.[79]

For his part, Pranav Jani focuses on Marx's response to the 1857 revolt in British India, the so-called 'Indian Mutiny'.[80] Jani maintains that 'under the impact of the Revolt, Marx's articles increasingly turned from an exclusive focus on the British bourgeoisie to theorize the self-activity and struggle of colonized Indians'.[81] He demonstrates that Marx's historical-materialist methodology allowed him to move beyond his prejudices and weak formulations and develop a more complex understanding of the relation between coloniser and colonised, in much the same way that the Paris Commune forced him to reassess his theory of the state.[82] For Jani, Marx was thereby transformed from a 'mere observer' of the anti-colonial struggle into an active participant in the ideological struggle over the meaning of the revolt. This also enabled him to refute racist representations of Indian violence in the British press, 'by drawing a sharp division between the violence of the oppressed and that of the oppressor, and dialectically linking the two'.[83] Jani concludes that if Eurocentrism makes western Europe the centre of the globe, then the Marx he presents is not Eurocentric.

LENIN AND SELF-DETERMINATION

I return to the context in which Lenin engaged in his polemic against Rosa Luxemburg, and, as I noted above, explained the radical change in Marx's position. It was in December 1913 that Lenin began to write on the question of the 'right of nations to self-determination'. In a short polemic on the question of independence for Ukraine, he insisted on '*freedom* to secede, for the *right* to secede', while conceding that '[t]he *right* to self-determination is one thing, of course, and the *expediency* of self-determination, the secession of a given nation under given circumstances, is another'.[84] Later that month he again declared that '[a] democrat could not remain a democrat (let alone a proletarian democrat) without systematically advocating, precisely among the Great-Russian masses and in the Russian language, the "self-determination"

---

[77]   Nimtz, 'The Eurocentric Marx and Engels', 71.
[78]   Nimtz, 'The Eurocentric Marx and Engels', 68–69.
[79]   Nimtz, 'The Eurocentric Marx and Engels', 71.
[80]   Pranav Jani, 'Karl Marx, Eurocentrism, and the 1857 Revolt in British India' in Crystal Bartolovich and Neil Lazarus (eds), *Marxism, Modernity and Postcolonial Studies* (CUP 2002) 81.
[81]   Jani, 'Karl Marx', 82.
[82]   Jani, 'Karl Marx', 83.
[83]   Jani, 'Karl Marx', 90–91.
[84]   VI Lenin, 'The Cadets and "The Right of Nations to Self-Determination"' [1913] in VI Lenin, *Collected Works*, vol 19 (4th edn, Progress Publishers 1977) 525, 525–26 (original emphases).

of nations in the political and not in the "cultural" sense'.[85] The latter, he said, meant only freedom of languages.

In mid-1914 Lenin published 'The Right of Nations to Self-Determination', a substantial work on the question and a polemic against Luxemburg, who opposed the breakup of the tsarist empire and instead urged the creation of autonomies within the existing empires. In his first chapter, Lenin insisted that 'it would be wrong to interpret the right to self-determination as meaning anything but the right to existence as a separate state'.[86] He further argued that 'the national state is the rule and the "norm" of capitalism; the multi-national state represents backwardness, or is an exception. From the standpoint of national relations, the best conditions for the development of capitalism are undoubtedly provided by the national state'.[87] Lenin's understanding of the historical significance of the demand is highly significant, and merits substantial citation here:

> The epoch of bourgeois-democratic revolutions in Western, continental Europe embraces a fairly definite period, approximately between 1789 and 1871. This was precisely the period of national movements and the creation of national states. When this period drew to a close, Western Europe had been transformed into a settled system of bourgeois states, which, as a general rule, were nationally uniform states. Therefore, to seek the right to self-determination in the programmes of West-European socialists at this time of day is to betray one's ignorance of the ABC of Marxism.
>
> In Eastern Europe and Asia the period of bourgeois-democratic revolutions did not begin until 1905. The revolutions in Russia, Persia, Turkey and China, the Balkan wars—such is the chain of world events of *our* period in our 'Orient'. And only a blind man could fail to see in this chain of events the awakening of a *whole series* of bourgeois-democratic national movements which strive to create nationally independent and nationally uniform states. It is precisely and solely because Russia and the neighbouring countries are passing through this period that we must have a clause in our programme on the right of nations to self-determination.[88]

Thus, Lenin's conception of self-determination in 1914 was intended to apply not only to the Russian Empire, or the Austro-Hungarian Empire, but also to the colonial empires of European states. This was one of the key differences between him and Wilson, who contemplated self-determination mainly for the new central and eastern European states emerging from the ruins of those two empires, as well as the Ottoman Empire. Otto Bauer, Karl Renner, and the Jewish Bund all proposed forms of autonomy within the existing states.[89]

Lenin returned to this question in 1916, in the midst of the First World War and before the October Revolution, and summed up his thoughts on the question of self-determination, writing that autonomy might enable a nation, until then forcibly retained within an existing state such as Russia, to 'crystallise into a nation' entitled to self-determination and independence as a sovereign state.[90] He had in mind Norway's declaration of independence from

---

[85]   VI Lenin, 'National-Liberalism and the Right of Nations to Self-Determination' [1913] in VI Lenin, *Collected Works*, vol 20 (3rd edn, Progress Publishers 1977) 56, 57.

[86]   Lenin, 'Right of Nations to Self-Determination', 397.

[87]   Lenin, 'Right of Nations to Self-Determination', 400.

[88]   Lenin, 'Right of Nations to Self-Determination', 405–6 (original emphases).

[89]   See e.g., Roni Gechtman, 'A "Museum of Bad Taste"?: The Jewish Labour Bund and the Bolshevik Position regarding the National Question, 1903–14' (2008) 43 *Canadian Journal of History* 31.

[90]   VI Lenin, 'The Discussion on Self-Determination Summed Up' [1916] in VI Lenin, *Collected Works*, vol 22 (4th edn, Progress Publishers 1977) 320.

Denmark in 1814, and envisaged a declaration by a multi-ethnic Poland that it would no longer be ruled by the Russian tsar.

In May 1917 the issue of independence for Poland and Finland was again at the forefront of European political and diplomatic attention in a hotly contested debate within the Bolshevik Party. Lenin drafted a resolution on the 'national question'.[91] His starting-point was clear: recognition of the right of all nations forming part of Russia freely to secede and form independent states. To deny them such a right, or to fail as a Russian government to take the necessary measures to guarantee the realisation of the right to secede in practice, would in effect be to support a policy of forcible seizure or annexation. For Lenin, opposed by a number of leading Bolsheviks including Nikolai Bukharin and Georgy Pyatakov, the right to self-determination was not a mere slogan but a policy to be put into practice with immediate effect within the former Russian Empire after the Bolshevik Revolution.

Igor Blishchenko, in his time one of the most authoritative Soviet scholars of international law,[92] wrote, in a text ironically published in 1968, the year the Soviet Union crushed the 'Czech Spring', that it was the 'Decree on Peace' of 26 October 1917, drafted by Lenin,[93] which for the first time explicitly extended the principle of the right to self-determination to all nations, thereby discarding the imperialist distinction between 'civilised' and 'uncivilised' nations.[94] In response to Western scholars who claimed that this decree was hypocritical, having no application to peoples within the Soviet Union and applicable only to Finland in the former tsarist empire, Blishchenko pointed to the 1924 Soviet constitution (which remained in force until Stalin's 1936 constitution). Article 4 of that constitution enshrined the right of the Soviet Union's constituent republics freely to leave the union, this being a point on which Lenin had insisted.[95] More importantly, Blishchenko underlined the degree to which the principle was indeed put into practice by Lenin during the early years of the Soviet Union. Poland, Finland, and the three Baltic countries, until then part of the Russian Empire, became independent sovereign states. Writing 30 years later in a collection published by the Russian human rights non-governmental organisation Memorial, after the Soviet Union collapse in 1991, Blishchenko argued that the early Soviet government was remarkably consistent in implementing self-determination.[96]

---

[91]   VI Lenin, 'Resolution on the National Question' [1917] in VI Lenin, *Collected Works*, vol 24 (4th edn, Progress Publishers 1977) 302.

[92]   Blishchenko's best-known work, translated into English, is *International Humanitarian Law* (Progress Publishers 1987). I worked with Blishchenko for a number of years, in particular on the draft of the Rome Statute of the International Criminal Court. For a touching obituary by the International Committee of the Red Cross, see Jose Doria, Aslan Khuseinovich Abashidze, and Vassily Fyodorovich Poriouvaev, 'Igor Pavlovich Blishchenko, 1930–2000' (2001) 83 *International Review of the Red Cross* 885.

[93]   VI Lenin, 'Report on Peace, October 26 (November 8)' [1917] in VI Lenin, *Collected Works*, vol 26 (Progress Publishers 1964) 249.

[94]   IP Blishchenko, *Antisovetizm i mezhdunarodnoe pravo* [*Antisovietism and International Law*] (Mezhdunarodnye otnosheniia 1968) 69.

[95]   The Russian-language text of the constitution is available at http://constitution.garant.ru/history/ussr-rsfsr/1924/ accessed 7 April 2021. An abridged English-language translation is available at http://pwerth.faculty.unlv.edu/Const-USSR-1924(abridge).pdf accessed 7 April 2021.

[96]   IP Blishchenko, 'Soderzhaniye prava narodov na samoopredeleniye' [The Content of the Right of Peoples to Self-determination] in AG Osipov (ed), *Pravo narodov na samoopredeleniye: ideya i voploshcheniye* [*Right of Peoples to Self-Determination: Idea and Realisation*] (Memorial 1997) 71. On national

According to Blishchenko, it was clear even before the October Revolution that Lenin and the Bolsheviks favoured not only a right of secession from Russia by the 'captive nations' but also a right to territorial autonomy for minorities that did not enjoy the status of nationhood. In 'The Tasks of the Revolution', published in October 1917, Lenin declared that a democratic peace would be impossible without explicit renunciation of annexation and seizure. He emphasised that every nation without exception, whether in Europe or in the colonial world, should have the right to decide for itself whether it should form a separate state.[97] This right was enshrined in the 1918 constitution of the Russian Soviet Federated Socialist Republic (RSFSR), which stated that every nation was entitled to decide whether it wished to participate in the RSFSR and on which basis.[98] This was the only basis for creating a 'free and voluntary state' as proclaimed in the 1918 constitution.

What Blishchenko failed to point out in 1968, writing in the Soviet Union, where Lenin had been in effect deified, with Stalin as his true disciple, was the fact that one of Lenin's most bitter struggles with Stalin concerned the question of independence for Georgia. As Moshe Lewin described in detail, Lenin was strongly in favour of Georgia's right to independence— just as he had been for Finland, the Baltic states, and Poland.[99] Stalin, of Georgian origin, was opposed. As Lewin points out, Lenin's criticism of Stalin's national policy and of his treatment of the Georgians explains how he changed his mind about Stalin, and urged that Stalin should be deprived of his post.[100] On 31 December 1922, shortly before his death, in 'The Question of Nationalities or "Autonomisation"', Lenin warned against Stalin:

> It is quite natural that in such circumstances the 'freedom to secede from the union' by which we justify ourselves will be a mere scrap of paper, unable to defend the non-Russians from the onslaught of that really Russian man, the Great-Russian chauvinist, in substance a rascal and a tyrant, such as the typical Russian bureaucrat is.[101]

Lenin regarded Stalin as just such a 'Great-Russian chauvinist'. Stalin was utterly opposed to self-determination for Georgia. Lenin supported Georgia's secession, even if it were under Menshevik rule.[102]

---

liberation movements see also DI Baratashvili, 'Natsionalno-osvoboditel'noye dvizheniye i razvitiye mezhdunarodnogo prava' [The National Liberation Movement and the Development of International Law] (1967) *Sovyetskoye gosudarstvo i pravo* 69.

[97]   VI Lenin, 'The Tasks of the Revolution' [1917] VI Lenin, *Collected Works,* vol 26 (Progress Publishers 1964) 59, 62.

[98]   The Russian-language text of the constitution is available at http://constitution.garant.ru/science -work/modern/3988990/ accessed 7 April 2021. An English translation is available at https://www .marxists.org/history/ussr/government/constitution/1918/ accessed 7 April 2021.

[99]   Moshe Lewin, *Lenin's Last Struggle* (University of Michigan Press 2005).

[100]   Lewin, *Lenin's Last Struggle,* 89.

[101]   VI Lenin, 'The Question of Nationalities or "Autonomisation"' [1922] in VI Lenin, *Collected Works,* vol 36 (4th edn, Progress Publishers 1977) 605, 606.

[102]   Lewin, *Lenin's Last Struggle,* 61. More recently, Nikolay Svanidze has argued that Lenin and Stalin had very different positions on the nationalities question, and that Lenin's views on the rights of nations were irreproachable. See Paul Goble, 'Putin's Criticism of Lenin on Nationality Issues about More than Federalism, Svanidze Says', *Window on Eurasia* (5 February 2020), https://windowoneurasia2 .blogspot.com/2020/02/putins-criticism-of-lenin-on.html accessed 7 April 2021.

SELF-DETERMINATION, INTERNATIONAL LAW, AND THE SOVIET UNION

The right of peoples to self-determination is the 'revolutionary kernel' of post-Second World War international law, and is both reflected in and energised by the struggles of national liberation movements for independence from colonial empires.[103] The Soviet Union played a leading role in bringing about this development, in the teeth of fierce resistance from colonial powers. It is particularly noteworthy that the Soviet Union gave significant support to national liberation movements and the newly independent states, engaging in a sustained diplomatic effort to secure legal recognition for an international right of collective self-determination. At the same time, Soviet tanks appeared in 1956 and 1968, in Budapest and Prague, in order to extinguish any signs of self-determination in Hungary or Czechoslovakia. The Crimean Tatars, who suffered genocide at the hands of Stalin in 1944 and were deported en masse to central Asia, only won the right to return to their homeland in the late 1980s, and since the annexation of Crimea by Russia in 2014 are once again finding themselves persecuted.[104]

The role of the Soviet Union could, of course, be dismissed as blatant hypocrisy, given that it, together with the territories it occupied as a result of the Yalta and Potsdam agreements, constituted the greatest territorial expanse of any Russian-dominated polity. There was at the very least a stark contradiction between Soviet theory and practice with respect to self-determination.[105] Writing in 1976, Boris Meissner emphasised that the opposition of non-Russian ethnic groups in the Soviet Union to Brezhnev's policies of centralisation and Russification grew significantly after 1968.[106] Soviet dissidents like Andrei Sakharov often took up the injustice suffered by the Crimean Tatars, deported from their homeland to central Asia in 1944, and the Meskhetians, who had been similarly expelled from Georgia. On 19 March 1970, two years after first mentioning the Crimean Tatars in writing, Sakharov sent a letter to the Soviet leadership demanding full restoration of all rights—including rights of national autonomy and the right to return to ancestral homelands—for those nations that had been forcibly resettled under Stalin. These demands were reiterated in a further memorandum from Sakharov to Brezhnev of 5 March 1971.[107]

Then, in his book published in English in October 1975, entitled *My Country and the World*,[108] Sakharov again expressed his opposition to the oppression of the non-Russian nationalities. He drew attention to the fact that many political prisoners were so-called 'nationalists' from Ukraine, the Baltic republics, and Armenia. These individuals had originally been

---

[103]   Bowring, *Degradation,* ch 1; Harris, *National Liberation.*

[104]   Bill Bowring, 'Who Are the "Crimean People" or "People of Crimea"? The Fate of the Crimean Tatars, Russia's Legal Justification for Annexation, and Pandora's Box' in Sergey Sayapin and Evhen Tsybulenko (eds), *The Use of Force Against Ukraine and International Law: Jus Ad Bellum, Jus In Bello, Jus Post Bellum* (TMC Asser/Springer 2018) 21.

[105]   Bill Bowring, 'Positivism versus Self-Determination: The Contradictions of Soviet International Law' in Susan Marks (ed), *International Law on the Left: Re-examining Marxist Legacies* (CUP 2008) 133.

[106]   Boris Meissner, 'The Soviet Concept of Nation and the Right of National Self-Determination' (1976–77) 32 *International Journal* 56.

[107]   Meissner, 'The Soviet Concept', 76. See also FJM Feldbrugge, *Samizdat and Political Dissent in the Soviet Union* (Brill 1975) 219.

[108]   Andrei Sakharov, *My Country and the World* (Guy V Daniels tr, Harvill Press 1975).

brought to trial principally because of their concern for the preservation of their national culture in the face of Russification, and had been given particularly heavy sentences. In addition to the Crimean Tatars, the fate of the Volga Germans and the Jews were the subject of Sakharov's attention.[109] Thus the seeds were sown for the 'parade of sovereignties' that followed the collapse of the Soviet Union in 1991,[110] a development that threatened the continuing existence of the Russian Federation itself and the continuing relevance of self-determination to Russia's actions in Crimea, eastern Ukraine, Abkhazia, Transnistria, South Ossetia, and elsewhere.[111]

It is clear to Russia's present rulers that Lenin's wholehearted advocacy and implementation of the right to collective self-determination played a crucial role in the destruction of the Russian Empire and in the collapse of the Soviet Union, and continues to pose an existential threat to contemporary Russia. On 25 January 2016 Putin accused Lenin of placing an 'atomic bomb' under Russia.[112] In Putin's opinion Lenin was responsible for destroying, with German support for his move from Switzerland to Russia in 1917, the great Russian Empire. He was also responsible for preparing the destruction of the great Soviet Union. Putin was particularly critical of Lenin's concept of a federal state whose constituent entities enjoyed the right to secede, stating that this had heavily contributed to the breakup of the Soviet Union in 1991. He added that Lenin was wrong in his dispute with Stalin, who, in Putin's words, advocated a unitary state model. For Putin Stalin was in the line of great tsars, from Ivan IV to Peter I to Catherine II. Putin also claimed that Lenin's government had whimsically drawn borders between different parts of the Soviet Union, placing the Donbass under Ukrainian jurisdiction to increase the percentage of the proletariat, in a move that Putin called 'delirious'.[113]

These statements were made not long after Russia argued that Crimea's secession from Ukraine and its accession to the Russian Federation in March 2014 were the result of the 'people of Crimea' exercising their right to self-determination. This position was legally incorrect,[114] and has opened something of a Pandora's box, since there are many peoples in Russia, not least 5.5 million Tatars, with strong and long-standing claims to self-determination—claims of the kind that Lenin recognised and supported.[115]

---

[109]   Meissner, 'Soviet Concept', 76–77.

[110]   For a detailed account see Bill Bowring, 'The Russian Constitutional System: Complexity and Asymmetry' in Marc Weller and Katherine Nobbs (eds), *Asymmetric Autonomy and the Settlement of Ethnic Conflicts* (University of Pennsylvania Press 2010) 48.

[111]   Bill Bowring, 'International Law and Non-Recognized Entities: Towards a Frozen Future?' in Benedikt Harzl and Roman Petrov (eds), *Non-Recognised Entities in International and EU Law* (Brill Nijhoff, forthcoming). For news and commentary on the future of Russian federalism, see also the website 'After Empire: Regionalism and Federalism in Russia', http://afterempire.info/2016/11/02/why-after-emp/ accessed 7 April 2021.

[112]   See the transcript of a meeting of the President's Council on Science and Education, held on 21 January 2016, http://kremlin.ru/events/councils/by-council/6/51190 accessed 7 April 2021.

[113]   See 'Vladimir Putin Accuses Lenin of Placing a "Time Bomb" Under Russia' *The Guardian* (25 January 2016), https://www.theguardian.com/world/2016/jan/25/vladimir-putin-accuses-lenin-of-placing-a-time-bomb-under-russia accessed 7 April 2021.

[114]   See e.g., Khazar Shirmammadov, 'How Does the International Community Reconcile the Principles of Territorial Integrity and Self-Determination? The Case of Crimea' (2016) 4 *Russian Law Journal* 61.

[115]   Bowring, 'Who Are the "Crimean People" or "People of Crimea"?'

CONCLUSION

In this chapter I have paid particular attention to the surprisingly Marxist content of a corner-stone of post-Second World War international law. In doing so, I have grappled with the vexed question for Marxism of the 'national question', and also with claims that Marx and Engels were Eurocentric and subscribed, at least tacitly, to Hegel's discredited theory of 'historical' and 'non-historical' nations.

Lenin's life and legacy have become increasingly controversial, not least as new evidence has emerged of the slaughter that followed the 1920 to 1921 Tambov (or Antonov) peasant uprising against the Bolsheviks, suppressed by the Red Army using chemical weapons, with 100 000 arrested and 15 000 killed.[116] This was in addition to the well-known suppression of the 1921 Kronstadt uprising. Official Soviet figures claimed that approximately 1000 rebels were killed, 2000 wounded, and between 2300 and 6528 captured, with 6000 to 8000 defecting to Finland, while the Red Army had 527 killed and 3285 wounded.[117] Lenin then turned to the partial restoration of capitalism in Russia, the New Economic Policy from 1921 to 1928.[118] However, one of Lenin's lasting legacies pertained to his implementation of his controversial policy of the 'right of nations to self-determination', and his insistence on a federal structure for the new Soviet Union. His mummified remains are still resting in his mausoleum in Red Square, but he is anathematised by the Putin regime for precisely these policies.

This chapter has shown that although Soviet diplomacy, based as it firmly was on the principles propounded by Marx and Lenin, was key to the recognition of the right to self-determination as a specifically legal right under international law. It has also shown that the Soviet Union made enormous contributions to the process of decolonisation, both materially and diplomatically, and that it did so notwithstanding significant contradictions in its positions with respect to self-determination, contradictions which ultimately helped to bring about the collapse of the Soviet Union itself.

---

[116]   Eric C Landis *Bandits and Partisans: The Antonov Movement in the Russian Civil War* (University of Pittsburgh Press 2018).

[117]   Paul Avrich, *Kronstadt 1921* (Princeton University Press 2006).

[118]   Alan M Ball, *Russia's Last Capitalists: The Nepmen, 1921–1929* (University of California Press 1990); Sheila Fitzpatrick, Alexander Rabinowitch, and Richard Stites (eds), *Russia in the Era of NEP: Explorations in Soviet Society and Culture* (Indiana University Press 1991).

8. Pashukanis' commodity-form theory of law

Matthew Dimick

INTRODUCTION

Evgeny Bronislavovich Pashukanis has been called the 'only more or less original thinker of Soviet jurisprudence'[1] and his critique of jurisprudential thought, *The General Theory of Law and Marxism*, has been described as 'groundbreaking'[2] and 'the most significant Marxist work on the subject'.[3] Writing during the era of the Soviet Union's New Economic Policy, between the Russian Civil War and the rise of Stalin's bureaucratic collectivism, Pashukanis developed what has come to be known as the 'commodity-form theory of law'.[4] Pashukanis was a victim of Stalin's purges in the late 1930s, but his theory survived the attempt to bury it, along with its author.[5] The commodity-form theory draws recurring attention, and interest in it has followed the trend of Marxist scholarship more generally, which experienced a resurgence in the late 1960s through to the early 1980s, and again today.

Two features define Pashukanis' theory of law. First, Pashukanis directs his analysis to the law's form, not just its content as a collection of legal rules. Pashukanis never precisely defines the legal form, but he generally describes it as an historically specific form for the regulation of social relations. As such, the legal form is a specific form of practice, in the Marxist sense,[6] one characterised by the identification and deployment of rights, duties, and claims that individu-

---

[1] Stephen J Powell, 'The Legal Nihilism of Pashukanis' (1967) 20 *University of Florida Law Review* 18, 19.

[2] China Miéville, 'The Commodity-Form Theory of International Law' (2004) 17 *Leiden Journal of International Law* 271, 276.

[3] Chris Arthur, 'Editor's Introduction' in Evgeny B Pashukanis, *Law and Marxism: A General Theory* (Chris Arthur ed, Barbara Einhorn tr, Pluto 1983) 9.

[4] Pashukanis never referred to his theory as the 'commodity-form theory of law'. One wonders whether a better description would be the 'value-form theory of law', particularly in light of recent scholarship on the 'value-form' approach to Marx's theory of value. (I refer to 'value-form theory' ecumenically, including members of the 'New Marx Reading', such as Hans-Georg Backhaus, 'On the Dialectics of the Value-Form' (1980) 1 *Thesis Eleven* 99, as well as those associated with the 'New Dialectic', such as Christopher J Arthur, *The New Dialectic and Marx's* Capital (Brill 2004).) The value-form approach owes much of its perspective to Pashukanis' contemporary, Isaac I Rubin, and his classic *Essays on Marx's Theory of Value* (first published 1924, Black Rose Books 1973) 11. As Arthur notes, Rubin's ideas have 'interesting points of contract' with Pashukanis' work. Arthur, 'Editor's Introduction', 9. In this chapter, I will refer to the 'commodity-form theory of law', because a change would require substantiating a claim that would take us beyond the scope of this chapter.

[5] For an intellectual biography of Pashukanis see Michael Head, *Evgeny Pashukanis: A Critical Reappraisal* (Routledge 2008).

[6] The starting-point for Marx's theory of practice is his *Economic and Philosophical Manuscripts of 1844* as well as his *Theses on Feuerbach*. See Karl Marx, *Early Writings* (Rodney Livingstone and Gregory Benton tr, Penguin 1974). This concept of practice is further developed in Georg Lukács, *History and Class Consciousness: Studies in Marxist Dialectics* (first published 1923, Rodney Livingstone tr, MIT Press 1972).

als, as abstract 'legal subjects', have against other legal subjects within some larger political community, however defined.

Second, Pashukanis insists on going beyond the functional relationship between law and capitalism; he also wants to understand the forms of consciousness associated with law and the legal form, above all the categories created and used by jurists and legal philosophers. Although scholars often refer to Pashukanis' theory of the legal form as a 'homology' of the commodity form, the relationship is both more and less than that.[7] It is more in the sense that there is an *internal* relation between commodity form and legal form. It is also less in the sense that there is nevertheless a non-identity between the legal form and the commodity form that derives from the legal form's *abstract* character. In that one-sidedness lies the difference that accounts for the ideological character of the legal form.[8]

This chapter will aim to explicate these two features of Pashukanis' commodity-form theory of law. The first section states the basic theory, showing how Pashukanis' theory builds on Marx's theory of the commodity to explain the legal form, the existence of formal-legal equality, and the basic categories of private and public law under capitalism. Next, the chapter will explore some of the various criticisms and debates that this theory has stimulated. Pashukanis has been criticised both for being idealist as well as for being crudely materialist. He has also been criticised for a key implication of his theory: that the law would 'wither away' with the abolition of capitalism. To show my cards at the outset, this presentation will be mainly sympathetic to Pashukanis' project. However, I do not wish to imply that his theory of law is finished, complete, or flawless. There remains much work to be done in Marxist legal theory. I hope at the very least to convince the reader that any such future project should seriously consider the foundation laid by Pashukanis.

THE COMMODITY-FORM THEORY OF LAW

What makes Pashukanis' theory of law so innovative is that he is not concerned solely with demonstrating that the content of the law—specific legal doctrines, standards, or rules—serves the interests of this or that social group or class. Rather, he goes beyond the content of the law to interrogate the form in which the rules are applied and have validity. The inspiration for this approach, as Pashukanis himself makes clear, is none other than Marx's *Capital*.[9] It is Marx's key contention in that work that capitalism, as a mode of production, is an historically specific social form of production. Similarly, Pashukanis' central argument is that the legal form is also an historically specific form for the regulation of social relations. This is not to deny that

---

[7]   See e.g., Colin Sumner, 'Pashukanis and the "Jurisprudence of Terror"' (1981) 11 *Insurgent Sociologist* 99, 99.

[8]   Pashukanis, *Law and Marxism*, 70:
       The legal relation is, to use Marx's expression, an abstract, one-sided relation, which is one-sided not as a result of the intellectual labour of a reflective subject, but as the product of social development. … What Marx says here about economic categories is directly applicable to juridical categories as well. In their apparent universality, they in fact express a particular aspect of a specific historical subject, bourgeois commodity-producing society.

[9]   Pashukanis' fidelity to Marx's method is most clearly laid out in the 'Introduction' and the chapter, 'Methods of Constructing the Concrete in the Abstract Sciences', in the *General Theory*. See Pashukanis, *Law and Marxism*, 47–64, 65–72.

law, like commodity exchange or even specific forms of capital (e.g., merchants' or usurers' capital), precedes capitalism, both historically and conceptually. But it is to claim that the legal form—again, like capital itself—does become both dominant and especially sophisticated under capitalism. The attention to the legal form is also not to denigrate the analysis of law's content, the particular legal rules themselves. Rather, Pashukanis did not preoccupy himself with the law's content both because he thought that previous scholars had already covered this ground and because he believed this mode of analysis by itself dissolved jurisprudence into sociology or psychology.[10] He wanted to push a Marxist argument further, to show that Marx's analysis of capitalism could account not just for the class character of legal rules but also for the predominant form of regulation under capitalist social relations.

Before proceeding, I signal two notes of caution. First, the following exposition is inevitably interpretative. As Pashukanis himself acknowledged, *The General Theory* was a work-in-progress.[11] Clear, definitive statements are rare, and claims are more often made in the course of critiquing some other theory rather than in their own positive exposition. I will endeavour to note where I make claims that go beyond Pashukanis' own. Second, one has to accept a considerable degree of abstraction in Pashukanis' argument. Pashukanis' analysis is not only explanatory, it is also an immanent critique. He also wants to explain hermeneutically the legal categories and forms of consciousness, the *Verstehen*, that participants in legal relations hold—judicial actors and legal theorists above all. In the following description, therefore, one must resist the urge to *peremptorily* 'get behind' the appearance of the commodity form, for it is precisely on this level that the legal form works, both as a real regulator of capitalist relations of production—which *are* exchange relations—and as a source of legal and liberal ideology.[12]

This approach finds its roots in Marx's own method. Famously, Marx's *Capital* begins with a discussion not of capital but of the commodity—the form that wealth takes under capitalism. There are several reasons Marx starts his analysis of capitalism in this way, the most important being that it is part of his dialectical method of presentation.[13] However, another reason is as part of a critique of ideology under capitalism. As Patrick Murray explains, 'because commodity circulation is an easily recognizable and understandable moment of the circulation of capital where liberty, equality, property and Bentham appear to reign, it is easily mistaken

---

[10] Consider e.g., Pashukanis, *Law and Marxism*, 53–57 (discussing various 'sociological and psychological theories of law', which are characteristically preoccupied with the law's content: 'Yet legal regulation itself has still not been analysed as a form, despite the wealth of historical content with which we imbue it' (at 55)).

[11] Pashukanis, *Law and Marxism*, 36, 37.

[12] For Hegel, as for Marx, the appearance-essence distinction is not some claim about the essence being real and the appearance being somehow 'unreal' or pure illusion. Rather, essence exists concretely only in and through its appearances. Hegel says that the 'essence must *appear* [*erscheinen*]', and explains that '[t]he essence is thus not *behind* or *beyond* the appearance; instead, by virtue of the fact that it is the essence that exists concretely, concrete existence is appearance'. Georg Wilhelm Friedrich Hegel, *Encyclopedia of the Philosophical Sciences in Basic Outline. Part I: Science of Logic* (first published 1817, Klaus Brinkman and Daniel O Dahlstrom tr and ed, CUP 2010) 174, 197 (original emphases). Similarly, one can say that '[a]ppearance is always also an appearance of essence and not mere illusion. Its changes are not indifferent to essence'. Theodor W Adorno, 'Sociology and Empirical Research' in *The Positivist Dispute in German Sociology* (Glyn Adey and David Frisby tr, Heinemann 1976) 68, 84.

[13] Michael Heinrich, *An Introduction to the Three Volumes of Karl Marx's* Capital (first published 2004, Alexander Locascio tr, Monthly Review 2012) 36–38.

for an independent sphere and even for the full reality of capitalist society'.[14] Quite similar concerns motivate Pashukanis' commodity-form theory of law. The commodity form, the exchange relation under capitalism, can explain the legal form as a social practice and the forms of legal thought, the latter of which, given their abstract nature, obscure the 'full reality' of social relations under capitalism.

According to Marx, a commodity is a unity of use-value, its qualitatively distinct utility or usefulness, and value, the product of 'homogeneous' labour, labour in the abstract.[15] A commodity's use-value is derived from the concrete, particular qualities that make it an object of utility, whether that use is in satisfying hunger (e.g., a hamburger), thirst (e.g., Coca-Cola), mobility (e.g., an automobile), vanity (e.g., a haircut), or in the production of some other use-value (e.g., an automobile-assembling robot). However, says Marx, if 'we disregard the use-values of commodities, only one property remains, that of being products of labour'.[16] In other words, if one abstracts from the use-value characteristic of commodities, one also abstracts 'from the material constituents and forms' that make them use-values, including the distinct forms of labour required to produce them. In that case, commodities 'can no longer be distinguished, but are all together reduced to the same kind of labour, human labour in the abstract'.[17]

Marx famously asserts that what makes commodities *values* is the property of being products of abstract labour. The quantity of abstract labour-time socially—not individually—necessary to produce the commodity, measured in units of time, constitutes the magnitude of value. It is extraordinarily important to emphasise this social dimension of abstract labour. As Michael Heinrich puts it, '[a]bstract labour is a *relation of social validation (Geltungsverhältnis)* that is constituted in exchange'.[18] Abstract labour is not just labour-time expended in production because this magnitude only becomes meaningful—that is, socially validated—when brought into relation with other commodities in exchange. Thus, the magnitude of value is an important part of commodities' exchange-value, the ratio at which one commodity exchanges for another. Finally, Marx calls money the 'universal measure of value'.[19] Even in the analysis of the commodity, Marx already hints at how 'objectified' value serves as the basis for the liberal, bourgeois ideal of legal equality. As Marx writes, '[e]quality in the full sense between different kinds of labour can be arrived at only if one abstracts from their real inequality, if one reduces them to the characteristic they have in common, that of being the expenditure

---

[14]   Patrick Murray, *The Mismeasure of Wealth: Essays on Marx and Social Form* (Brill 2016) 59.
[15]   Karl Marx, *Capital: A Critique of Political Economy*, vol 1 (first published 1867, Ben Fowkes tr, Penguin 1976) 126–28.
[16]   Marx, *Capital*, vol 1, 128.
[17]   Marx, *Capital*, vol 1, 128.
[18]   Heinrich, *Introduction,* 50 (original emphasis). It is worth quoting the passage in full:
    Accordingly, it is exchange, that consummates the abstraction that underlies abstract labour (independent of whether the people engaged in exchange are aware of this abstraction). But then *abstract* labour cannot be measured in terms of hours of labour: every hour of labour measured by a clock is an hour of a particular *concrete* act of labour, expended by a particular individual, regardless of whether the product is exchanged. Abstract labour, on the other hand, cannot be 'expended' at all. Abstract labour is a *relation of social validation (Geltungsverhältnis)* that is constituted in exchange.
    For a similar distinction, using 'abstract labour' for labour-time and 'practically abstract labour' for abstract labour that is socially validated in exchange, see Murray, *Mismeasure*, 124–29, 158–60.
[19]   Marx, *Capital*, vol 1, 188.

of human labour-power, of human labour in the abstract'.[20] Despite the radically unequal, concrete characteristics of commodities' use-values, they are equalised as abstract labour in exchange.

Pashukanis' central argument is simply that the legal subject and the legal form are also results of the abstraction of social relations that emerge in and through the exchange of commodities. Just as exchange is constitutive of the abstractness of value, so it is also constitutive of the legal subject, a 'free and equal', abstract subject with the capacity to possess rights. As exchange and the division of labour expand, value 'acquires objective economic significance'.[21] As it asserts its objectivity, value becomes the predominant basis for mediating between commodity exchangers. '[S]ocial life disintegrates', says Pashukanis, leaving the kind of social relation where people are 'defined only by contrast with an object, that is, as a subject'.[22] 'At this point', Pashukanis says, 'the capacity to be a legal subject is definitely separated from the living concrete personality' and the 'capacity to act is itself abstracted from the capacity to possess rights'.[23] The liberal ideals of freedom and equality—where every person owns themselves, and, by extension, the products of their labour, and is free to act as long as they respect the freedom of others—is, according to Pashukanis, 'nothing but the idealised market, transported to the nebulous heights of philosophical abstraction'.[24]

To help clarify the idea of the legal subject, Pashukanis contrasts it with the existence of 'privileges' or 'prerogatives' in the medieval period. In this period, Pashukanis suggests, the 'abstract concept of the legal subject' did not exist. Instead, the 'objective norm' existed as part of the 'establishment of concrete privileges and freedoms'.[25] Grants of such privileges were more akin to conveyances of land to specific individuals—say, to Godfried and his heirs—than to the establishment of general norms.[26] Even under today's supposedly more substantive legal rules, for example, legislation intended to protect employees (e.g., minimum wage legislation)—where 'employee' would seem to be a more concrete designation than the abstract legal subject—is still more general than these medieval conveyances because they refer to no particular employees. After all, today's employee is tomorrow's capitalist.[27] It is

---

[20]   Marx, *Capital*, vol 1, 166.

[21]   Pashukanis, *Law and Marxism*, 115.

[22]   Pashukanis, *Law and Marxism*, 113. Marx agrees, writing that in a fully developed system of exchange, the 'money relation', relations of personal dependence, and distinctions of 'blood, education, etc.', are 'exploded, ripped up'. Individuals are then independent, 'free to collide with one another and to engage in exchange within this freedom'. However, this is only a 'seeming', illusory independence, and only appears as such for someone who 'abstracts' from these individuals' *'conditions of existence'*, conditions which likewise appear as *'natural conditions*, not controllable by individuals'. In fact, these 'external relations' between abstracted individuals 'are very far from being an abolition of "relations of dependence"', and are really a generalisation of relations of dependence, 'a general form' of dependence. These *'objective* dependency relations' are the 'antithesis of those of *personal* dependence ... in such a way that individuals are now ruled by *abstractions*, whereas earlier they depended on one another'. Karl Marx, *Grundrisse: Foundations of the Critique of Political Economy* (first published 1939, Martin Nicolaus tr, Penguin 1973) 163–65 (original emphases).

[23]   Pashukanis, *Law and Marxism*, 115.

[24]   Pashukanis, *Law and Marxism*, 114.

[25]   Pashukanis, *Law and Marxism*, 120.

[26]   Nigel Simmonds, 'Pashukanis and Liberal Jurisprudence' (1985) 12 *Journal of Law and Society* 142.

[27]   Of course, it is generally not acknowledged that this option to become a capitalist is not available to all workers simultaneously. Marx, *Grundrisse,* 285–86. For an interesting interpretation of this

only with the generalisation of commodity production that 'every subject becomes an abstract legal subject' and law takes on its 'perfected' form as 'abstract universal law'.[28]

The relation between commodity exchange and the legal subject (and, by extension, the legal form) is more than just an homology, as sometimes claimed. Pashukanis in fact argues that they are 'extremely closely linked'. The social relations of generalised commodity production present themselves 'simultaneously in two absurd forms': the value of commodities, on the one hand, and the capacity to be a bearer of rights, on the other.[29] Value, as abstract labour, and the legal subject are better conceived, not as an homology, but as an internal relation. Social relations of exchange presuppose a certain form of regulation, a certain legal structure if that phrase can be used without already supposing too much. On this point, Pashukanis relies on Marx,[30] who points out that for commodities to be exchanged, their 'guardians' must bring them to market, recognising each other as owners of private property, and alienate them without appropriating the property of the other, except through an act of consent.[31] Because the commodity is a 'born leveller and cynic', the regulation of exchange relations also presupposes a necessary amount of abstraction, disregarding individuals' personal status, whims, or preferences, as well as the characteristics that mark their commodities as use-values.[32] Commodity exchange is general, and requires a suitably abstract form of regulation appropriate to that generality.

It is possible to see the legal subject as a more refined product of what Pashukanis calls the legal form. By 'legal form' Pashukanis means an historically specific form for the regulation of social relations, one characterised by claims one person can make against another, however concretely or abstractly this takes place across history. Pashukanis constantly says that 'the juridical factor' in the regulation of social relations, as a distinct kind of social regulation, arises when 'the differentiation and opposition of interests begin'.[33] Although Pashukanis does not explicitly state it, one gets the sense that the differentiation and opposition of interests to which he refers exists not only under capitalism, but in any type of class society in which forms of private property, and hence private interests, obtain.[34] For this reason, the 'juridical factor' in social life appears wherever private exchange or private property exist, in however rudimentary a form. Nevertheless, given conditions for the emergence of the legal subject, Pashukanis also claims that exchange relations under capitalism sharpen and purify this differentiation and

---

passage, see James Furner, *Marx on Capitalism: The Interaction-Recognition-Antinomy Thesis* (Brill 2018) 260–64. See also GA Cohen, 'The Structure of Proletarian Unfreedom' (1983) 12 *Philosophy & Public Affairs* 3.

[28]   Pashukanis, *Law and Marxism*, 120–21.
[29]   Pashukanis, *Law and Marxism*, 113.
[30]   Pashukanis, *Law and Marxism*, 112.
[31]   Marx, *Capital*, vol 1, 178.
[32]   Marx, *Capital*, vol 1, 179.
[33]   Pashukanis, *Law and Marxism*, 81, also 93, 104, n 32. See also Arthur, 'Editor's Introduction', 13.
[34]   See e.g., Pashukanis, *Law and Marxism*, 44–45, 58. For example, Pashukanis says that a 'basic prerequisite for legal regulation' is not commodity exchange, but the 'conflict of private interests'. Because 'conflict of private interests' is a broader category than commodity exchange—which would certainly still imply the conflict of private interests, but in a more specific, socially situated sense—the legal form, or the 'juridical factor', applies in social formations other than capitalism. Pashukanis, *Law and Marxism*, 81. Alan Norrie also recognises this point. Alan Norrie, 'Pashukanis and the "Commodity Form Theory": A Reply to Warrington' (1982) 10 *International Journal of the Sociology of Law* 419, 430–31.

opposition of interests to an unprecedented degree. Commodity exchange is therefore a crucial condition for a more sophisticated development of the legal form because it brings individuals' distinct interests into sharp relief. Within commodity exchange, 'the general interest', Marx remarks, is nothing more than the 'generality of self-seeking interests', a mutual recognition of instrumental rationality where parties to transactions recognise themselves as ends only by treating themselves and others as means to those ends.[35] Hence, the legal form under capitalism takes shape in the form of rights and duties between 'autonomous', abstract legal subjects, who require only the capacity to possess these rights and duties.[36]

Because the legal form under capitalism corresponds to a society of autonomous legal subjects, law is linked with a certain kind of individualism. As Pashukanis explains, '[c]ommodity exchange presupposes an atomised economy. ... The legal relation between subjects is simply the reverse side of the relation between products of labour which have become commodities.'[37] For Pashukanis, the legal relation therefore has the same individual-level locus as the exchange relation. That is, an exchange economy implies a form of regulation in which individuals make claims against one another as 'atomised' legal personalities. One should not be misled that 'atomised' here refers to 'individuals' in the biological sense, such that the legal recognition of collective or corporate actors would create a problem for the theory.[38] Indeed, as Pashukanis himself remarks, it is constitutive of the legal subject that it exists in abstraction from 'a zoological individual'.[39] Thus, that a corporation acquires legal personality is not a refutation of Pashukanis' theory but, in fact, is a striking confirmation of it.[40] Despite

---

[35] Marx, *Grundrisse*, 241–43. Elsewhere in the *Grundrisse*, Marx says that the:
economists express this as follows: Each pursues his private interest and only his private interest; and thereby serves the private interests of all, the general interest, without willing or knowing it. The real point is not that each individual's pursuit of his private interest promotes the totality of private interests, the general interest. One could just as well deduce from this abstract phrase that each individual reciprocally blocks the assertion of the others' interests, so that, instead of a general affirmation, this war of all against all produces a general negation. The point is rather that private interest is itself already a socially determined interest, which can be achieved only within the conditions laid down by society and with the means provided by society.
Marx, *Grundrisse*, 156.
[36] 'The subject as representative and addressee of every possible claim, the succession of subjects linked together by claims on each other, is the fundamental legal fabric which corresponds to the economic fabric, that is, to the production relations of a society based on division of labour and exchange.' Pashukanis, *Law and Marxism*, 99.
[37] Pashukanis, *Law and Marxism*, 85.
[38] Hunt writes that 'it is simply wrong to contend that the legal form restricts recognition to atomised economic agents' in contrast to corporations, trade unions, voluntary associations, charities, and other 'collective' actors. Alan Hunt, 'A Socialist Interest in Law' (1992) 192 *New Left Review* 105, 116. Hunt's implicit assumption is that there is a well-defined distinction between 'atomised' and 'collective' agents. There is, however, no such distinction, as even in liberal political and legal theory what constitutes the individual is contested terrain. Consider, for example, the status of the moral individual in liberal theory: does it include a person's 'natural' endowment of talents and intelligence, as it does for Robert Nozick, or does it not, as is John Rawls' position? See Simmonds, 'Pashukanis', 146–48. And just as there are competing ideas of the individual in *bourgeois* moral and legal theory, so too is there an idea of communist individualism. See Marx, *Capital*, vol 1, 739.
[39] Pashukanis, *Law and Marxism*, 115.
[40] Norrie puts it this way:
Hence, the question whether the state recognises the juridical subject as a concrete legal subject in one guise (the human subject) or another (the corporate entity) does not affect the basic validity

the enormous, concrete differences between the corporation and other legal subjects, those differences are abstracted away, and each legal subject is treated as equal before the law, endowed with the capacity to sue, to be sued, to acquire and alienate property, to possess rights and duties, and so on. Furthermore, the acquisition of legal subjectivity by a corporation is precisely the legal construction of 'atomisation' at work, in the following sense: by becoming a legal subject, the corporation can act in an 'autonomous' way with respect to and in the same way as other legal subjects.

To highlight the legal form is necessarily to draw a contrast with its content—though it is not to dismiss that content, as '[t]he form is of no value if it is not the form of the content'.[41] The distinction is both crucial for Pashukanis' argument and is the clearest reason why his theory of law is not a reductionism, as often claimed.[42] It is as the legal form that law becomes autonomous.[43] While the legal form is an essential precondition for exchange, the law's content refers to specific legal rules and their function in, for example, regulating exchange. However, although there is a necessary, internal relation between the legal form and exchange, this is not true of law's content or function. Thus, commodity exchange is only one area of legal regula-tion, although certainly an important one.[44] Pashukanis remarks that the capacity to engage in exchange transactions 'is only one of various concrete manifestations of the general capacity to act and of legal capacity'.[45] Just as the value form itself 'assumes ... derived ... forms of expression' (such as land, which is not a product of labour), so too 'the universality of the legal form' does not imply that inquiry into those relations—that is, exchange relations—on which the legal form is actually based should be limited.[46] To put this another way, in its nature the legal form expresses the commodity form. However, in its function, as regulation, the legal form moves well beyond the level of commodity exchange *stricto sensu*.[47] One example, about which Pashukanis is emphatic, is public law: in this case, 'this basis', the commodity form, 'is *not* synonymous with those relations known as public-law relations'.[48] To be sure, this strong form-content distinction poses a challenge for Pashukanis. What warrant does he have saying the legal form derives from commodity exchange when it is applied to content that is not commodity exchange in nature? Pashukanis never quite gives a fully satisfactory answer to this question, but I will consider some possibilities when discussing public law and public

---

of the 'commodity exchange theory' for the theory already presupposes the constitution of the juridical subject by the state in one way or another.
Norrie, 'Pashukanis', 424.
[41] Karl Marx, 'Proceedings of the Sixth Rhine Province Assembly: Third Article—Debates on the Law on Thefts of Wood' [1842] in Karl Marx and Frederick Engels, *Collected Works*, vol 1 (International Publishers 1975) 224, 261.
[42] Paul Hirst, *On Law and Ideology* (Macmillan 1979) 110.
[43] 'It is dispute, conflict of interest, which creates the legal form, the legal superstructure. In the lawsuit, in court proceedings, the economically active subjects first appear in their capacity as parties, that is, as participants in the legal superstructure. Even in its most primitive form, the court is legal super-structure par excellence. The legal differentiates itself from the economic and appears as an autonomous element through legal proceedings.'
Pashukanis, *Law and Marxism*, 93.
[44] Norrie, 'Pashukanis', 426.
[45] Pashukanis, *Law and Marxism*, 118.
[46] Pashukanis, *Law and Marxism*, 60.
[47] Norrie, 'Pashukanis', 427.
[48] Pashukanis, *Law and Marxism*, 60–61 (original emphasis).

administrative law below. Nevertheless, given the form-content distinction, it is a misreading of Pashukanis to claim that he 'reduces all legal phenomena to the domain of private law'.[49]

Viewing the legal form through an institutional lens can also give the reader a clearer angle on it. Although it would be wrong to reduce the legal form to any particular institutional manifestation, Pashukanis claims that it is within the judicial process and the law court that its 'consummate' expression is found.[50] Pashukanis explains this as follows: 'It is dispute, conflict of interest, which creates the legal form … In the lawsuit, in court proceedings, the economically active subjects first appear in their capacity as parties, that is, as participants in the legal superstructure.'[51] It is important to keep this institutional perspective in mind because it helps to ground the more general category of the legal form. Indeed, by doing so, it deflects the criticism that Pashukanis' theory of legal form, and particularly of the abstract legal subject, is a theory of law as legal formalism. That would be a drawback for Pashukanis, of course, insofar as legal formalism was an adequate description of law perhaps only during the nineteenth-century period of so-called *laissez-faire* capitalism. However, although he does not focus on legal content for the reasons already given, it is clear that Pashukanis believes that the legal form can be filled with any content whatsoever.[52] Using contract law as an example, Pashukanis writes that the '[p]olitical power can, with the aid of laws, regulate, alter, condition and concretise the form and content of this legal transaction in the most diverse manner. The law can determine in great detail what may be bought and sold, how, under what conditions, and by whom'.[53] Thus, for example, the fact that regulation of the employment contract gives explicit recognition to the 'employer' and 'employee' does not defeat the theory of the legal form insofar as it still presupposes that form, namely the existence of rights, duties, claims, and a forum in which to make them.

The diverse applications of the legal form raise a question about the inclusiveness of the legal subject in capitalist history. De jure legal exclusion is said to pose a problem for Pashukanis' theory insofar as American plantation slavery, South African *apartheid*, Nazi race laws, or colonial preference for white settler minorities, for example, co-existed with widespread commodity exchange.[54] Pashukanis never addressed this objection, so it is impossible to say how he would answer it. However, Pashukanis' theory is not necessarily incompatible with various forms of race domination. Charles Post, for instance, pointing to the research of Barbara J Fields, Edmund Morgan, and Theodore Allen, argues that race ideology, which reifies race as an immutable characteristic of an individual, 'only emerges as a way of classifying humanity when legal-juridical equality becomes the *norm* and only distinctive groups (African slaves, Irish tenant-peasants) are *unfree'*.[55] The idea is that law requires special justification for de jure exclusions once the legal form and legal subjectivity become dominant. This is unlike

---

[49]   Igor Shoikhedbrod, *Revisiting Marx's Critique of Liberalism: Rethinking Justice, Legality, and Rights* (Palgrave Macmillan 2019) 97.

[50]   Pashukanis, *Law and Marxism*, 43.

[51]   Pashukanis, *Law and Marxism*, 93.

[52]   On this point see also Norrie, 'Pashukanis', 428–29.

[53]   Pashukanis, *Law and Marxism*, 93.

[54]   Nancy E Anderson and David F Greenberg, 'From Substance to Form: The Legal Theories of Pashukanis and Edelman' (1983) 1 *Social Text* 73.

[55]   George Souvlis and Charlie Post, 'Class, Race, and Capital-centric Marxism: An Interview with Charlie Post' *Salvage* (19 January 2018) (original emphasis), https://salvage.zone/online-exclusive/class-race-and-capital-centric-marxism-an-interview-with-charlie-post/ accessed 7 April 2021.

medieval society, where relations of domination are simply assumed as the natural state of affairs. In that sense, exceptions to being a legal subject presuppose the widespread, baseline existence of the abstract legal subject.

Although Pashukanis' attention is directed to the legal form, thinking about the law's content helps illuminate the reach, and limits, of his argument. As for private law, the relevance of his commodity theory of law is immediately apparent.[56] Given the centrality of exchange for Pashukanis, property and contract law are the pre-eminent examples. Although specific types of contracts are extensively regulated by the state in our contemporary time, legal formalism still exerts itself in at least two ways. First, contract law applies to any exchange of promises and, second, it either disregards the adequacy of consideration (common law) or dispenses with the requirement of consideration altogether (civil law). In other words, contract law makes no judgment about the substantive fairness or justice of contracts. Tort law (or delict) is likewise essential for the functioning of commodity exchange even though it involves civil wrongs such as nuisance or negligence, not 'economic' activity as such. Along with criminal law, tort law can be understood as the regulation of involuntary transactions, as it has by generations of legal thinkers, from Aristotle[57] to Posner.[58] Because consent is the principal criterion of freedom in liberal-legal thought, the law cannot countenance involuntary transfers or destructions of wealth; the protection of private property remains the bedrock of a system of commodity exchange between free and equal legal subjects.

Remember that for Pashukanis exchange relations are emphatically not the content of public law relations. Nevertheless, generalised commodity production, and the formal kind of freedom and equality it produces, have inevitable consequences for state-society relations. Pashukanis' discussion of constitutional law and public law is rather limited. However, his most important remarks are directed toward the fascinating point that legal theorists have a particularly tough time grappling with public law. The division itself between public law and private law makes it difficult to articulate an overarching principle that can ground both. A legal theory cannot equate the rights of the 'legislator' with the rights of the 'creditor' because this 'would imply substituting isolated private interest for the dominance of the universal, impersonal interest of state assumed by bourgeois ideology'.[59] Pashukanis arguably remains relevant for understanding why administrative law faces continuing crises of legitimacy in a society founded on generalised commodity production.[60]

---

[56]   Powell, 'Legal Nihilism', 20.

[57]   Pashukanis, *Law and Marxism*, 169.

[58]   Richard A Posner, 'The Concept of Corrective Justice in Recent Theories of Tort Law' (1981) 10 *Journal of Legal Studies* 187.

[59]   Pashukanis, *Law and Marxism*, 103. For some contemporary reflections on this point, see Simmonds, 'Pashukanis', 144–46. Whether Pashukanis' theory can itself account for the dichotomy between public and private law is another matter. Pashukanis appears to regard 'authoritarian regulation' and an 'external norm-setting authority', such as the 'military unit set out in formation' or a 'Jesuit order', as a completely distinct form of social regulation, one that 'has nothing whatever to do with the legal form'. If that is the case, the public-private law contradiction then resides solely with universalistic theories of law, whose attempts to subsume authoritarian regulation under the legal form are inevitably incompatible. Pashukanis, *Law and Marxism*, 101.

[60]   For an overview of current literature on administrative law's legitimacy crisis in the United States, see K Sabeel Rahman, 'Reconstructing the Administrative State in an Era of Economic and Democratic Crisis' (2018) 131 *Harvard Law Review* 1671.

In order to understand the relevance of Pashukanis' theory for public law, some extrapolation is required. He never denies that some form of enforcement is required for the functioning of commodity exchange, and therefore that a division between private actors and an 'impersonal apparatus of public power' is necessary for capitalism.[61] At the very least, then, the theory is consistent with the idea that a commodity-producing society will necessarily generate a separation between private and public law, between civil society and the state.[62] Therefore, under capitalism the relationship between the ruling class and the state assumes an entirely new form. In terms of function, the capitalist ruling class requires a 'restrained state', a state that will simultaneously deploy its violence to enforce contracts and protect property rights vis-à-vis other legal subjects, but also limit the state from deploying that violence to interfere with these property rights on behalf of some collective or sovereign interest. In terms of law's own self-presentation, the legal form presents these constitutional restraints as general limitations on the state's authority to interfere with or deprive legal subjects of their universal rights to 'life, liberty, and property'. Understood in these terms, Pashukanis does have some warrant for regarding the legal form as intrinsically related to commodity exchange, even when the content is not. One might say that private-public opposition of interests have a second-order nature: the conflict between public and private interests that constitutional law regulates (1) derives from the separation of the state and civil society peculiar to capitalism and generalised commodity production, and (2) is only intelligible in a system of generalised commodity production that makes production for the sake of profit a way of life.[63]

In terms of the law's content, criminal law is routinely posed as the commodity-form theory's biggest challenge.[64] Yet, as I have shown, the legal form can be applied to an indeterminate range of content. And insofar as criminal law protects persons and property from involuntary transfer or destruction, its connection to exchange is hardly remote. Pashukanis also admits that criminal law is a manifestation of law in its most unmediated, class-based expression: '[c]riminal justice in the bourgeois state is organised class terror'.[65] Yet what is perhaps most puzzling about the criminal law is not its content, which overlaps to a considerable extent with tort law, but its distinctive remedies (which may result in the deprivation of liberty[66]) and its

---

[61]   Pashukanis, *Law and Marxism*, 134–36, 139.

[62]   Under capitalism, the domination of capitalists over workers is mediated by the value form and the capitalists' ownership of the means of production. This is unlike slavery and serfdom, where domination rests on immediate, direct, 'political' coercion. Pashukanis explicitly posed the question of the 'separation' of the economic from the political in capitalist society, a question which has fuelled much discussion in subsequent scholarship. Pashukanis, *Law and Marxism*, 139. See e.g., John Holloway and Sol Picciotto (eds), *State and Capital: A Marxist Debate* (Edward Arnold 1978).

[63]   Pashukanis also remarks: 'But the very thing which characterises bourgeois society is that universal interests are disengaged from, and set in opposition to, private interests. In this antithesis, they themselves involuntarily assume the form of private interests, that is, legal form. As could be expected, the juridical factors in state organisation are primarily those which can be adapted to the framework of conflicting isolated private interests.'
Pashukanis, *Law and Marxism*, 104.

[64]   Warrington states that the application of the commodity-form theory to criminal law has only 'a spurious theoretical consistency', 'clearly has no place' in the larger theory, and is 'faintly comic'. Ronnie Warrington, 'Pashukanis and the Commodity Form Theory' (1981) 9 *International Journal of the Sociology of Law* 1, 19.

[65]   Pashukanis, *Law and Marxism*, 173.

[66]   Jeffrey Reiman, 'The Marxian Critique of Criminal Justice' (1987) 6 *Criminal Justice Ethics* 30, 42.

mode of enforcement (namely, prosecution through state authorities representing the community rather than by individual, civil plaintiffs). Pashukanis addresses these issues in at least two ways.[67] First, and most forcefully, he emphasises the 'equivalence' between the punishment levied and the criminal act, which he interprets as isomorphic to the act of exchange.[68] Second, Pashukanis highlights the formal separation between the prosecutor, as representative of 'the people', and the judge, as the impersonal power of the state.[69] Whether Pashukanis is successful in these arguments, I leave it for others to assess.[70]

The 'Withering Away' Thesis

One more implication of Pashukanis' theory is worth considering. Pashukanis is also well-known for extending Engels' remarks about the 'withering away' of the state to the law.[71] If law is the dominant form of regulating social relations under capitalism, then it follows that a socialist or communist society would be one in which the law will 'wither away'. At first, the idea that there could be a 'proletarian' or socialist law sounds 'revolutionary par excellence', Pashukanis notes.[72] In fact, he continues, 'this tendency proclaims the immortality of the legal form', the mistaken assumption of bourgeois thought that the legal form is an 'eternal' form for the regulation of social relations.[73] For Pashukanis, '[t]he withering away of the categories of bourgeois law will, under these conditions, mean the withering away of law altogether, that is to say the disappearance of the juridical factor from social relations'.[74] A post-capitalist society may well have law, but this implies a form of regulation inherited from the immediate bourgeois past, a form that the new society must strive to overcome rather than one to which it must remain subservient.

But would a society without law even be possible? Society needs rules and governance, does it not? Remember that for Pashukanis, law is only one, historically specific form for the regulation of social relations. He writes that it is only 'under certain conditions [that] the *regulation* of social relations assumes a *legal character*'.[75] He points out that in many pre-capitalist societies social relationships are regulated in a meaningfully non-legal, or at least pre-legal, way.[76] He describes 'authoritarian regulation', as found in the military or a 'Jesuit order', to

---

[67]   Pashukanis also contends that unlike pre-capitalist criminal liability, the requirement of criminal intent is unique to an age of free will and legal subjectivity. Pashukanis, *Law and Marxism*, 178.

[68]   Pashukanis, *Law and Marxism*, 168–70.

[69]   Pashukanis, *Law and Marxism*, 177. Pashukanis also attempts to draw a line between the regulation of criminality in capitalist and post-capitalist societies, not all that successfully in my view.

[70]   For a defence see Norrie, 'Pashukanis', 431–34. For an elaboration see Reiman, 'Marxian Critique', 39–45.

[71]   Frederick Engels, 'Anti-Dühring: Herr Eugen Dühring's Revolution in Science' [1877–78] in Karl Marx and Frederick Engels, *Collected Works*, vol 25 (International Publishers 1987) 1, 268.

[72]   Pashukanis, *Law and Marxism*, 61.

[73]   Pashukanis, *Law and Marxism*, 61.

[74]   Pashukanis, *Law and Marxism*, 61. Pashukanis also grounds this discussion in 'Critique of the Gotha Programme', where Marx remarks that a society in the 'first phase' of communism would be constrained by the 'narrow horizon of bourgeois right'. Karl Marx, 'Critique of the Gotha Programme' [1875] in Karl Marx and Frederick Engels, *Collected Works*, vol 24 (International Publishers) 75, 87.

[75]   Pashukanis, *Law and Marxism*, 79 (original emphases).

[76]   Pashukanis, *Law and Marxism*, 58, 79.

be yet another kind of social regulation.[77] Even in bourgeois society, law is not the exclusive form of regulation. In an oft-discussed passage, Pashukanis states that '[t]rain timetables regulate rail traffic in quite a different sense than, let us say, the law concerning the liability of the railways regulates its relations with consigners of freight. The first type of regulation is predominantly technical, the second primarily legal.'[78] Returning to his assertion that the 'prerequisite for legal regulation' is the 'conflict of private interests', he says that this 'is both the logical premise of the legal form and the actual origin of the development of the legal superstructure'.[79] By contrast, the prerequisite for 'technical regulation' is 'unity of purpose'. 'For this reason', continues Pashukanis, 'the legal norms governing the railways' liability are predicated on private claims, private, differentiated interests, while the technical norms of rail traffic presuppose the common aim of, say, maximum efficiency of the enterprise'.[80]

Pashukanis' point, then, is not that socialist or communist society is a society without rules, but that the form of social regulation will be fundamentally different than law. Rather than organising social life around the conflict of private interests, with social reproduction a seemingly incidental outcome of such conflict, socialist or communist society will instead be co-ordinated in accordance with those considerations of collective outcomes consciously in mind from the beginning.

CRITICISMS OF THE COMMODITY-FORM THEORY OF LAW

This section addresses some of the criticisms that Pashukanis' theory has encountered. Four main criticisms are addressed: (1) the commodity-form theory of law prioritises exchange over production in a way that is inconsistent with Marx's basic theory of capitalism; (2) because law is a bourgeois institution, Pashukanis' legal theory is too idealist, presenting law as nothing more than an ideological fetish; (3) the commodity-form theory of law depends too much on its relationship with the economic activity of exchange, and is therefore reductionist and crudely materialist; (4) Pashukanis' prediction that law will 'wither away' in communist society downplays politics to a dangerous degree, so much so that he was in part responsible for Stalin's 'jurisprudence of terror'.

Prioritising Exchange over Production?

One common objection to Pashukanis' theory of law is that, as a *commodity*-form theory of law, it is inherently limited in its explanatory scope. As summarised by Alan Hunt, 'the standard Marxist criticism of Pashukanis is that he reverses Marx's priority of production relations over commodity relations'.[81] Hunt suggests that this error results from a 'simplistic reading of Marx'.[82] However, it is arguably Hunt that is guilty of a 'simplistic reading' of Marx. The

---

[77]   Pashukanis, *Law and Marxism*, 101.
[78]   Pashukanis, *Law and Marxism*, 79.
[79]   Pashukanis, *Law and Marxism*, 81.
[80]   Pashukanis, *Law and Marxism*, 81.
[81]   Alan Hunt, 'Marxist Theory of Law' in Dennis Patterson (ed), *A Companion to Philosophy of Law and Legal Theory* (Blackwell 1996) 355, 360.
[82]   Hunt, 'Marxist Theory', 360.

problem is in hypostatising production as somehow 'separate' from distribution or exchange. This is an error for which Marx attacked bourgeois political economy with effective incisiveness.[83] There is certainly a sense in which production has a sort of ontological primacy over exchange in Marx's analysis. But as the best readings of Marx make clear, the production of value under capitalism can only be co-constituted in and through exchange.[84] As shown earlier, the amount of labour-time necessary for the production of a commodity, the magnitude of value, is a social category, fully and finally determined only when commodities are put into relation with one another in exchange.

It is common to question Pashukanis' Marxist *bona fides* in this inversion-of-exchange-over-production critique.[85] Yet Pashukanis is merely elaborating a point made by Marx in the *Grundrisse*. I provide the quote in full, both because it is characteristically insightful for Marx and because it establishes a crucial link between Marx's and Pashukanis' thinking. Marx writes as follows:

> Therefore, when the economic form, exchange, posits the all-sided equality of its subjects, then the content, the individual as well as the objective material which drives towards the exchange, is *freedom*. Equality and freedom are thus not only respected in exchange based on exchange values but, also, the exchange of exchange values is the productive, real basis of all *equality* and *freedom*. As pure ideas they are merely the idealized expressions of this basis; as developed in juridical, political, social relations, they are merely this basis to a higher power.[86]

Marx continues, conjecturing about the historical development of the legal form in exactly the same way that Pashukanis does:

> In Roman law, the *servus* is therefore correctly defined as one who may not enter into exchange for the purpose of acquiring anything for himself (see the *Institutes*). It is, consequently, equally clear that although this legal system corresponds to a social state in which exchange was by no means developed, nevertheless, in so far as it was developed in a limited sphere, it was able to develop the *attributes of the juridical person, precisely of the individual engaged in exchange*, and thus anticipate (in its basic aspects) the legal relations of industrial society, and in particular the right which rising bourgeois society had necessarily to assert against medieval society.[87]

For Pashukanis it is not the commodity-theory of law but law itself that prioritises exchange over production. The law is able to achieve this because under capitalism labour-power *is* a commodity, exchanged on the market. Unlike societies based on either slave or serf labour, it is an endlessly 'interesting'[88] fact of capitalist domination over the worker that it has 'no kind

---

[83]   For example, in the introduction of the *Grundrisse*, Marx analyses consumption, distribution, and exchange as different moments within the totality of production, in distinction to the bourgeois political economists, who analyse each as a self-sufficient, eternal category. Marx, *Grundrisse*, 83–100.

[84]   Marx, *Capital*, vol 1, 166: 'The substance of value … is not inherent to individual commodities, but is bestowed *mutually* in the act of exchange.' Heinrich, *Introduction*, 53 (original emphasis), also 48–52.

[85]   Steve Redhead, 'The Discrete Charm of Bourgeois Law: A Note on Pashukanis' (1978) 7 *Critique* 113.

[86]   Marx, *Grundrisse*, 245 (original emphases).

[87]   Marx, *Grundrisse*, 245–46 (original emphasis).

[88]   Arthur, 'Editor's Introduction', 30.

of official legal expression at all'.[89] Whereas the slave or the serf has a distinct legal status, the wage-labourer is not legally compelled to work for any particular capitalist. Rather, the formal legal relationship between capitalist and labourer is one of free and equal owners (of means of production and labour-power, respectively) engaged in commodity exchange, the 'very Eden of the innate rights of man', as Marx says in *Capital*. Under capitalism, the capitalist's domination over the worker (and the state, Pashukanis adds) is secured through the extra-legal monopolisation of the means of production by the capitalist class.[90] But unlike pre-capitalist forms of exploitation, these relations are mediated through the anonymous institutions of the law and the market (in, for example, the form of the contract), in which real relations of exploitation are elided with abstract relations between employer and employee, buyer and seller of labour-power.[91] All of this raises the 'fundamental question', says Pashukanis: why does class rule under capitalism remain factual? Why 'does the machinery of state coercion not come into being as the private machinery of the ruling class; why does it detach itself from the ruling class and take on the form of an impersonal apparatus of public power separate from society?'[92] It is unclear to me how a theory that wants to 'prioritise' production can answer this question. On the other hand, these facts of capitalism are perfectly consistent with Pashukanis' commodity-form theory of law.

Legal Fetishism

Another criticism of Pashukanis is that his theory of law is fundamentally idealist. For Pashukanis, the criticism goes, the social being of law emerges from forms of consciousness, rather than the other way around, as a good materialist analysis should demonstrate. For example, Steve Redhead complains that Pashukanis' 'work produced a conception of law as a mystification of social relations which simply requires a process of "uncovering" for the real content to be revealed. The *reality* of appearances is thus not sufficiently theorised in' Pashukanis' work.[93] Giorgio Del Vecchio describes 'the commodity exchange theory as evincive of the principle that law to Pashukanis is nothing more than a "bourgeois fetish"'.[94]

One can respond to these criticisms of Pashukanis in several ways. In point of fact, Pashukanis specifically denies that 'the categories of law have absolutely no significance other than an ideological one'.[95] Pashukanis also insists that a Marxist analysis of law cannot be 'used *only* to expose the bourgeois ideology of freedom and equality'.[96] Moreover, the criticism of idealism is surprising in light of the fact that Pashukanis is at pains at various points to emphasise the 'material' or 'real' fundamentals of the legal relations he describes. For

---

[89] Pashukanis, *Law and Marxism*, 138.

[90] Arthur, 'Editor's Introduction', 30. There is nothing in the law that guarantees that the means of production would be entirely owned by a single class or other social group within society. In fact, in capitalism's fantasy everyone owns a share of the means of production, whether that is, variously with different stages of capitalism, the yeoman farmer, the skilled artisan, the independent professional, or the household that simultaneously supplies labour and owns shares in firms.

[91] Pashukanis, *Law and Marxism*, 110, 140–41.

[92] Pashukanis, *Law and Marxism*, 139.

[93] Redhead, 'Discreet Charm', 118 (original emphasis).

[94] Powell, 'Legal Nihilism', 31. This is Powell's paraphrase of Del Vecchio's argument.

[95] Pashukanis, *Law and Marxism*, 73.

[96] Pashukanis, *Law and Marxism*, 40 (original emphasis).

example, most of the third chapter of Pashukanis' *General Theory* is devoted to his objections against bourgeois legal theories that seek to derive basic legal categories from the commands of the sovereign, the 'pure sphere of the normative', or 'the "pure" category of the *Ought*'.[97] Pashukanis' approach is the opposite of this: 'If we wish to expose the roots of some particular ideology, we must search out the material relations which it expresses.'[98]

Pashukanis' actual analysis of the relationship between law, ideology, and social reality is also a good deal subtler than the law-as-fetishism criticisms suggest. For an interesting example of this, Pashukanis contrasts the nature of the ideology that undergirds law and the state in medieval European societies with the reigning ideology of modern capitalist societies. He claims that in 'the former interpretation [of medieval society] we are dealing with fetishism of the first order; consequently we shall not succeed in discovering anything at all in the corresponding ideas and concepts other than an ideological reproduction of reality, in other words the same factual relations of dominance and subservience'.[99] Medieval serfs were legally unfree, and their domination and exploitation was apparent and conspicuous.[100] Medieval political ideology resorts to metaphysically invariant claims for these explicit differences in status and social relations, referring to the divine right of kings, patriarchal conceptions of the monarch as father-king, and the naturalised station of the aristocracy. Under capitalism, on the other hand, wage earners are formally and legally free, and the commodity form obscures the time workers spend between producing value for themselves and surplus value for the capitalist. This marks an important difference to the nature of legal ideology under capitalism: 'In contrast to [the medieval] conception, the legal view is one-dimensional; its abstractions are the expression of only one of the facets of the subject as it actually exists, that is, of commodity-producing society.'[101]

This is the real thrust of the ideological dimension of Pashukanis' theory of the legal form. On this account, the law is contradictory, presenting a view of social relations that is simultaneously true and false. As Pashukanis insists, law only exists in concrete social relations and practices. The specific rights that legal subjects enjoy with respect to one another are certainly real; violating them can have severe and material consequences. They are, in that sense, adequate to the social functions they serve.[102] At the same time, these legal relations are abstract, and therefore present only a partial representation of social reality. Thus, despite vast social differences, and however the law regulates the terms of trade, roughly the same basic rules of contract formation that govern exchange relations among capitalists also govern relations between capitalists and workers. More generally, everyone stands in a free and equal relationship to anyone else simply by virtue of being a legal subject, to which general laws apply and specify various rights and duties. In that sense, the law distorts reality, mystifying relations of domination. Pashukanis writes that the law treats heterogeneous and particular commodity

---

[97]   Pashukanis, *Law and Marxism*, 52 (original emphasis).

[98]   Pashukanis, *Law and Marxism*, 139.

[99]   Pashukanis, *Law and Marxism*, 139.

[100]   As Marx says '[t]he *corvée* can be measured by time just as well as labour which produces commodities, but every serf knows that what he expends in the service of his lord is a specific quantity of his own personal labour-power.' Marx, *Capital*, vol 1, 170.

[101]   Pashukanis, *Law and Marxism*, 139.

[102]   Cf Jacques Bidet, *Exploring Marx's* Capital: *Philosophical, Economic, and Political Dimensions* (David Fernbach tr, Brill 2006) 200–1.

exchangers as free and equal 'only in the abstract relation of appropriation and alienation'.[103] In reality these individuals are subject to varying relations of domination, subordination, and dependence. Pashukanis gives as examples the retailer and the wholesaler, the peasant and the landowner, the debtor and the creditor, and the worker and the capitalist. Yet, despite all these 'innumerable relationships of actual dependence', 'for the juridical theory of the state it is as if they did not exist'. They are 'incomprehensible'.[104]

In this light, it falls short of the mark to take Pashukanis to task for allegedly not theorising 'the reality of appearances'. If he had done only that, he would not have given us a complete account of the law. Instead, he would not have got beyond an analysis of the political economy of commercial exchange, the anthropology of debt, or the sociology of class struggle. These are crucial parts of the analysis, to be sure, but that analysis must also seek to interrogate the categories of bourgeois jurisprudence and 'lay bare the historically limited nature of the legal form'. The analysis of law must be an immanent critique. This means that a Marxist theory of law must necessarily 'venture into enemy territory'.[105]

Finally, it is this aspect of Pashukanis' thought—an explanation of law that includes not just its functional content but also its internal structure—that accounts for its 'bourgeois' appeal. Pashukanis is sometimes reproached for finding more appreciation from liberal legal philosophers than from Marxists. For example, Steve Redhead writes that 'Pashukanis ... has received acclaim from bourgeois jurisprudence ... and that at least might make readers of *The General Theory of Law and Marxism* suspicious'.[106] But why has Pashukanis had such a strong 'bourgeois' appeal? One possibility is its formal character, of a piece with bourgeois legal philosophy. But this again is to mistake Pashukanis' historical and materialist method with the object of critique itself: the law. A better answer to the question of Pashukanis' bourgeois appeal is that by placing the legal form at the centre of his analysis, Pashukanis is able to say something about the nature and identity of law itself. And this matters because only by understanding law's nature can one expose its reified character. This realisation, in turn, has all sorts of practical consequences—from avoiding liberal legalistic fallacies to escaping traps like 'proletarian law', and from grasping law's historical nature to understanding the limitations of law in constructing a communist society. Arthur hits this squarely on the head: 'If law is not explored in terms of its internal structure, then its peculiar character will be dissolved away into some vaguer notion of social control. This is all most Marxists provide.'[107] Thus, most Marxists approach the law in purely functional terms: the law is important only insofar as it replicates or reproduces other forms of domination. Such Marxists believe, as Leslie Green and Thomas Adams observe, 'that the specific nature of law casts little light on their primary concerns'.[108] Green and Adams' reply, in which they specifically exempt Pashukanis, is devastating: 'But one can hardly know that in advance; it depends on what the nature of law actually

---

[103] Pashukanis, *Law and Marxism*, 147.

[104] Pashukanis, *Law and Marxism*, 147.

[105] Pashukanis, *Law and Marxism*, 64.

[106] Redhead, 'Discreet Charm', 113. For two examples of 'bourgeois' scholars with deep appreciation for Pashukanis, see Lon L Fuller, 'Pashukanis and Vyshinsky: A Study in the Development of Marxian Legal Theory' (1949) 47 *Michigan Law Review* 1157; Simmonds, 'Pashukanis'.

[107] Arthur, 'Editor's Introduction', 12.

[108] Leslie Green and Thomas Adams, 'Legal Positivism' (Winter 2019) *Stanford Encyclopedia of Philosophy*, https://plato.stanford.edu/archives/win2019/entries/legal-positivism/ accessed 7 April 2021.

is.'[109] Green and Adams are saying that Pashukanis is the only Marxist legal theorist to give an answer to the question: what is the nature of law? In light of the other extraordinary insights provided by a multitude of Marxist legal thinkers, that assertion may sound presumptuous. But it need not: for some Marxists, questions about the nature of law are essentialist and therefore not even worth asking.[110] But if the implications are as important as Pashukanis suggests, the question of law's nature remains a compelling one.

Crude Materialism

At the other end of the idealist-materialist spectrum, Hugh Collins writes that Pashukanis' 'analysis is limited to a crude materialist explanation of the content of law'.[111] Collins says his analysis 'lacks an account of the mechanisms by which social practices determine conscious action, and is thus fatally flawed'.[112] Furthermore, 'consequent upon his crude materialism, Pashukanis indulged in all the vices of reductionism, that is, he purported to explain all legal rules as reflections of commodity exchange'.[113] The charge of economism, and especially reductionism, has likewise been a point of critique from the Althusserians. Paul Hirst writes that '[p]ossessive right, the essence of the legal form, is a derivative of commodity relations between economic subjects. One reductionism, of law to class oppression, is rejected in the interests of another, of legal form to commodity form.'[114]

The answer to the charge of vulgar materialism is to recognise it as implicitly informed by a positivist and narrowly causal problematic. For Collins the problem is the lack of a 'mechanism', one that causally explains conscious action in terms of economic practice. For Hirst the problem is more directly one of reductionism, in which legal relationships are merely 'derivative' of economic relationships.

Both of these objections misinterpret Pashukanis' approach. As I have demonstrated, the distinction between legal form and legal content is extraordinarily important for Pashukanis—in that distinction lies law's autonomy. As form, the law detaches itself from the 'base', so to speak, and becomes part of the legal 'superstructure'.[115] There is an internal relation between the commodity form and the legal form: the legal form is the necessary form that the regulation of commodity exchange takes. However, the relation between legal form and its content is contingent. For that reason, one cannot simply 'reduce' the law to its base, nor explain its content as a mechanical cause of the economy. At the same time, there is still a relation—an ontological imbrication—between law and economy, one that avoids a sociological structural-functionalism giving rise to a vaguely causal notion of 'relative autonomy'.

These objections also ignore the earlier chapters (especially chapters two and three) of *The General Theory*, where Pashukanis critiques different schools of bourgeois legal thought for denying 'the relation between subjects', actively engaged in various social practices, and

---

[109]   Green and Adams, 'Legal Positivism'.
[110]   Hirst, *On Law and Ideology*, 111–12.
[111]   Hugh Collins, *Marxism and Law* (OUP 1982) 108.
[112]   Collins, *Marxism and Law*, 109.
[113]   Collins, *Marxism and Law*, 109.
[114]   Hirst, *On Law and Ideology*, 110. See also Nicos Poulantzas, 'Marxist Examination of the Contemporary State and Law and the Question of the "Alternative" [1964] in James Martin (ed), *The Poulantzas Reader: Marxism, Law, and the State* (Verso 2008) 25, 28.
[115]   Pashukanis, *Law and Marxism*, 93.

'preferring to concentrate their undivided attention on the formal relevance of the norms'.[116] By contrast, Pashukanis says, '[i]n material reality, the relation has primacy over the norm. If no debtor repaid his debts, the relevant regulation would have to be considered as non-existent in real terms'.[117] Here social relations are primary, but in an ontological rather than a causal or deterministic sense. Pashukanis continues, '[l]aw as an objective social phenomenon cannot be *exhaustively* defined by the norm or regulation—whether it be written or unwritten'.[118] I emphasise this passage to indicate that Pashukanis believes that the norm (whether legal or customary) is a constitutive feature of the legal relation. This is underscored when Pashukanis writes that 'to assert the objective existence of law, it is *not enough* to know its normative content, rather one must know too whether this normative content materialises in life, that is in social relations'.[119]

My interpretation of these passages is as follows: the legal (or at the very least, the normative) is constitutive of social practices because social action is incomprehensible without purposes and expectations—that is, forms of consciousness. At the same time, if these norms are not observed in practice, they cannot be said to exist. Norms and social practices are therefore mutually constitutive; or, as Alan Norrie writes of Pashukanis, '[b]oth logically, and historically, the relationship between law and exchange is one of mutual entailment'.[120] 'Mutual entailment' is itself support for the claim that the relation between norm and social practice should not be thought of in limited causal terms, as if one mechanistically determined the other. Simmonds sums up the response to the crude-materialism charge:

> It is perfectly true that Pashukanis had no account of how 'social practices determine conscious action', but this is because he did not imagine that the relationship between social practice and conscious action could be a causal one. Social practices *consist of* conscious actions and are structured by purposes and expectations.[121]

All of these passages demonstrate that Pashukanis has a far more sophisticated sense of social practice, the relationship between materiality and consciousness, than the charge of crude materialism gives him credit for.

The 'Withering Away' Thesis Revisited

Pashukanis' thesis that the law will 'wither away' in a communist society has been subjected to fierce criticism. For many critics, the thesis is wrong simply because of the way that Pashukanis defines the law. If the law is simply what is generally called the regulation of social relations under capitalism, then, simply by definitional fiat, law will cease to exist when capitalism ceases to exist.[122] This goes along with scepticism about the meaningfulness of the distinction that Pashukanis drew between legal rules, on the one hand, and technical regulations, on the other. Collins, for instance, finds this distinction 'extremely vague', writing that

---

[116] Pashukanis, *Law and Marxism*, 85.
[117] Pashukanis, *Law and Marxism*, 87.
[118] Pashukanis, *Law and Marxism*, 87 (emphasis added).
[119] Pashukanis, *Law and Marxism*, 87 (emphasis added).
[120] Norrie, 'Pashukanis', 424.
[121] Simmonds, 'Pashukanis', 136 (original emphasis).
[122] Collins, *Marxism and Law*, 110.

it can hardly 'provide the analytic basis for a definition of law'.[123] Are tax laws, for example, technical regulations intended to serve a single purpose in financing the government, or are they legal rules governing the claims between government and citizen?

An even more trenchant criticism concerns the alleged political implications of the withering away thesis. This is the idea that by impugning the law as something inherently capitalist and by counterposing law with 'technical' regulation, Pashukanis at a minimum dangerously denigrated the role of politics in a post-capitalist society and, at worst, paved the way for the rise of the monstrous totalitarianism of Stalin and the Soviet state. Peter Binns links the two ends of this claim, arguing that stressing the 'technical as opposed to political nature of decisions under socialism ... could not but help Stalin'.[124] More acidly, Dean Roscoe Pound commented that 'if there had been law instead of only administrative orders, it might have been possible for [Pashukanis] to lose his job without losing his life'.[125]

Starting with the second argument, one has to remember that Pashukanis was 'liquidated' precisely because his withering away thesis was incompatible with Stalin's bureaucratic-collectivist objectives. Pashukanis was opposed to the idea of 'proletarian law', but proletarian law is exactly what Stalin needed to justify the massive deployment of coercion in his bureaucratic state-building project.[126] The argument that Pashukanis' rejection of proletarian law paved the way to Stalin's 'jurisprudence of terror'[127] is therefore not entirely persuasive.[128]

The other claim—that Pashukanis' withering away thesis offered a vision of socialist regulation only weakly distinguishable from bourgeois law, while also dangerously ignoring politics—has more force. Pashukanis too hastily saw purposive, technical regulation—as opposed to the purposeless private law—as marking a post-capitalist form of regulation.[129] Ironically, he places too much weight on the rules' function, rather than their form, in making this distinction. Unsurprisingly, the distinction fails to carry weight, especially in light of our contemporary experience with the administrative state and the demise of legal formalism.

In response to these criticisms, it is necessary to reconstruct Pashukanis' idea of socialist or communist regulation. The way to do this, I suggest, is to focus on the basic component of what he calls regulation, which is 'unity of purpose'. Unity of purpose is hardly compatible with, for example, Pound's description of technical regulation as an 'administrative order'. An

---

[123]   Collins, *Marxism and Law*, 110.

[124]   Peter Binns, 'Law and Marxism' (1980) 4 *Capital & Class* 100, 100.

[125]   Quoted in Powell, 'Legal Nihilism', 30.

[126]   Joseph Stalin, 'Report to the XVIII Party Congress' [1939] in John Hazard (ed), *Soviet Legal Philosophy* (Hugh W Babb tr, Harvard University Press 1951) 343.

[127]   Sumner, 'Pashukanis', 103.

[128]   John Hazard, one of Pashukanis' 'bourgeois' admirers, remarked on the reasons for Pashukanis' arrest: 'He was criticized primarily for having preached a philosophy of law which, had it been followed to its conclusions, would have undermined the foundations of the Soviet state, and it was hinted that his theory had been developed for the purpose of bringing about the end of the Soviet system of government.' John N Hazard, 'Pashukanis Is No Traitor' (1957) 51 *American Journal of International Law* 385, 385–86.

[129]   Karl Korsch's assessment was similar, accusing Pashukanis of putting the cart before the horse and interpreting the Soviet Union's efforts at socialist construction (which relied heavily on the market-oriented New Economy Policy) idealistically, 'in light of the subjectively posed goal', rather than materialistically, in terms of their 'concrete nature', thereby hinting at their role in market regulation and hence their legal 'form-ness'. Karl Korsch, 'Appendix: An Assessment by Karl Korsch' [1930] in Pashukanis, *Law and Marxism*, 193.

order, administrative or otherwise, immediately implies some sort of duty; to speak of a duty, in turn, is only valid where there is the potential for the opposition of interests, not their unity. To return to Pashukanis' example, timetables for railways are completely devoid of any sense of right or obligation. In this respect, a closer analogy to post-legal regulation might be, not a 'technical regulation', but a 'co-ordinating convention'. Another present-day example of a co-ordinating convention would be rules specifying which side of the road to drive on. Such rules are in a certain sense self-enforcing because no distributive consequences flow from them. Thus, it is in everyone's interest to follow the 'rules of the road', simply so that they can co-ordinate their behaviour, and the choice of which side to drive on is in a strong sense arbitrary. Because of their lack of distributive consequences, such conventions often arise spontaneously, without the need for authoritative declaration and enforcement—the state.[130] However, under capitalism, such co-ordinating conventions are rare, and certainly not typical, because in an accumulation-oriented, commodity-producing society where everyone is market dependent, most rules have distributive consequences and therefore generate opposition of interests.

To explore this idea in more detail, consider the fate of tort law (or delict) in a society where production is primarily oriented towards satisfying basic needs, rather than towards profit, and the means of production are under common ownership. Along with Marx and Engels after the Paris Commune, I assume that common ownership does not mean state ownership,[131] and that, along with the socialists and communists of the German Revolution of 1918–19, there exists a robust system of workers' councils that regulates independently of the state.[132] As in Marx's 'first phase of communist society', the worker 'receives a certificate *from society* [not from a firm or an enterprise] that he has furnished such-and-such an amount of labour … and with this certificate, he draws from the social stock of means of consumption as much as the same amount of labour cost'.[133] Already, the implication of Marx's argument is that tort law would not make much sense in this kind of society, because even '[b]efore' the means of consumption are 'divided among the individuals', 'funds for those unable to work' are deducted from the total social product.[134] Under this sort of plan, injured workers are compensated by 'society' for their injuries; there would be no rationale for a lawsuit to compensate for medical costs or lost wages, nor would the injured worker be compelled to work when injured to satisfy their needs. Tort law would also lack a rationale because the enterprises where workers work and are injured are publicly owned (and worker-managed): seeking compensation from their 'employer' would be seeking compensation, retrospectively, from society itself—but society's members have already, prospectively, chosen to compensate for workers' injuries.[135] With respect to the law of torts, in a socialised economy, neither worker nor enterprise is an

---

[130] 'Such conventions' does not *necessarily* include the rules of the road, which often are regulated by traffic rules.

[131] Karl Marx and Frederick Engels, 'Manifesto of the Communist Party' [1848] in Karl Marx and Frederick Engels, *Collected Works*, vol 6 (International Publishers 1976) 477.

[132] Nicholas Vrousalis, 'Council Democracy and the Socialisation Dilemma' in James Muldoon (ed), *Council Democracy: Towards a Democratic Socialist Politics* (Routledge 2018) 89.

[133] Karl Marx, 'Critique of the Gotha Programme' [1875] in Karl Marx and Frederick Engels, *Collected Works*, vol 24 (International Publishers 1989) 75, 86 (emphasis added).

[134] Marx, 'Critique of the Gotha Programme', 85.

[135] This thought experiment would be worth further exploration. Should the enterprise pay 'punitive' damages for encouraging particularly dangerous working conditions? Would such conditions be chosen

independent, private, or autonomous legal subject. Rather, the injured worker's means of life are met by society itself.[136]

The critique applies not just to private law, but to public law as well. Consider, for example, workplace safety standards.[137] Under capitalism, the regulation of occupational health and safety necessarily takes the form of state-imposed, regulatory duties on private producers, backed by coercive sanctions. This form of regulation is inevitable where the law of value's own coercive objectivity compels capitalists to reduce costs and externalise workplace hazards onto workers. Asking capitalists to self-regulate would result in a severe under-provision of workplace safety and a substantial increase in industrial accidents, compared to current levels (which themselves are probably still unacceptable). But self-regulation is not such an impossibility where the means of production are socially owned and the law of value does not dominate. Because their labour is compensated by society, workers in self-managed firms will not be compelled to sacrifice their physical well-being in order to remain competitive. Safety standards will be self-enforcing because workers will have no profit motive to evade them; likewise, coercive duties will be inapposite because the only duty owed would be to workers themselves, who already have a primary interest in workplace safety. If there is a problem, there may be an over-provision of workplace safety, but this problem pales in comparison to the lack of safety under capitalism. More importantly, it is not a problem the law is well equipped to address.[138]

Other examples could be multiplied, as assuredly as could counter-examples. What about traffic rules? What about acts of irrational and indiscriminate violence, however much communism reduces property crime? But the demonstration of the continuing, interstitial need for law is misplaced, and misconstrues both Pashukanis and Engels. The point is that generalised commodity production generates a set of oppositional interests that are pervasive, necessitating the widespread use of law as the dominant mode of social regulation. Likewise, the transformation to a socially owned economy freed from market imperatives will have an

---

and would punitive damages make sense if a representative workers' council—at the firm level, sector level, or both—was empowered and responsible for choosing the pace and nature of work?

[136] Another private law example would be contract law. Worker-managed firms may indeed make agreements to provide inputs to other firms or retailers, but disputes over, say, failures of substantial performance (which under capitalism reduce to disputes about lost profits among 'private, isolated' economic producers) would be as meaningless as the '"undiminished" Lassallean "proceeds of labour"'. Marx, 'Critique of the Gotha Programme', 84. Instead, if such a dispute arose, the same council of workers planning production in the relevant industries would decide the best course of action that would save on social resources. Workers at the different worker-managed firms would have an incentive to comply with these decisions because their consequences would not individually affect one's material well-being: having supplied one's labour, one is compensated by 'society' rather than by the firm where one works. That one's firm loses or gains is irrelevant because what will increase each worker's labour certificate is the decision that saves society economic resources.

[137] Shoikhedbrod claims that Pashukanis' theory 'cannot make independent theoretical sense of public law', using 'workplace safety standards' as an example of public law. Shoikhedbrod, *Revisiting Marx's Critique of Liberalism*, 104–5.

[138] The over-provision of workplace safety arises because it is not obvious that workers' interest in safety will align with society's interest in efficient production. But unless one wants a repressive society which, Stakhanov-like, enforces duties upon workers to achieve a certain level of output, law will not be the solution to this problem. Rather, it will require the elaboration of standards by both workers and consumers, and 'soft' competitive constraints on enterprises rather than workers.

equally profound effect on the regulation of social relations.[139] Engels' remark that victims would be able to appeal to arbitrators[140] is not an evasive attempt, like Pashukanis' idea of technical regulation, to draw a dubious distinction between law and arbitration.[141] Rather, the claim is that resort to conflict resolution would be rare, and therefore appropriately handled by arbitrators, because the propensity for conflict would lessen in a society where needs are no longer systematically shunted. Legal regulation will become the exception rather than norm.

Likewise, the other side of Engels' 'withering away' of the state is precisely the admission that communism would not and could not *abolish* the law—that is, make the law simply disappear as with the stroke of a pen. There is a larger point to Engels' claim, which is that the rights and duties associated with the legal form can only be made real with the use of violence, and the use of violence makes the law a repugnant, debasing form of social regulation. Reverent intonations to rule of law's transhistorical significance obscure its premise: the existence of an organisation wielding violence and therefore in need of restraint. Legitimate violence is still violence.[142] By all means, state violence should be restrained by the rule of law. But the more fundamental aim is to build a society without violence.

There will, of course, be 'politics' in communist society because the social objectives will have to be decided upon in advance. This will involve highly charged decisions about how much to produce and its impact on the environment, how much (potential labour) time to devote to consumption rather than leisure, and how much labour to invest in cost-saving technology versus how much to allocate to present consumption. There will even be contested choices, especially in Marx's 'first phase of communist society', about how much labour-time should be devoted to the production of commodified versus de-commodified use-values. But the point is that the form of these disputes will not take the form of law. In fact, they will be more transparently political than in present-day, capitalist society.[143] If there is an institutional analogy, regulation will take the form of the assembly rather than the court.

CONCLUSION

Perhaps the most important insight gained from Pashukanis' *General Theory* is that the legal form marks an historically specific form for the regulation of social relations, one that achieves predominance in society with the rise of capitalism, the universalisation of exchange relations, and abstract legal subjectivity. Emphasising the law's form-ness foregrounds its historicity

---

[139] Pashukanis writes that the 'real prerequisite for such an abolition of the legal form and of legal ideology is . . . a society in which the contradiction between individual and social interests has been broken down'. Pashukanis, *Law and Marxism*, 103–4.

[140] Frederick Engels, 'Speeches in Elberfeld, February 8, 1845' in Karl Marx and Frederick Engels, *Collected Works*, vol 4 (International Publishers 1975) 243, 248.

[141] This is how Shoikhedbrod construes Engels' comment. Shoikhedbrod, *Revisiting Marx's Critique of Liberalism*, 122.

[142] Theodor W Adorno, *Negative Dialectics* (first published 1966, EB Ashton tr, Continuum 1973) 309.

[143] 'One side of the "bifurcation of the political" [the differentiation of the economic and the political under capitalism] is a depoliticisation of the inherently political class relations of the economy. The other is a "political" realm impoverished by the exclusion of inherently political matters.' Tony Smith, *Beyond Liberal Egalitarianism: Marx and Normative Social Theory in the Twenty-First Century* (Brill 2017) 190.

and provides the basis for its autonomy as a social practice distinct from, say, production or aesthetics.

Pashukanis did not live to further develop his theory and, given the Soviet political climate, was essentially forced to withdraw some of his stronger claims. This has left the commodity-form theory in an open, unfinished state. Pashukanis' remarks about constitutional law and public law are tantalising, but incomplete. Whether the legal form or commodity relations can account for the criminal law and administrative law are highly contested questions. Pashukanis' emphasis on exchange relations can be questioned, but several currents in the revival of Marxist thought, from the New Marx Reading to the New Dialectic, suggest, along with Lukács, that 'there is no solution that could not be found in the solution to the riddle of commodity-*structure*'.[144] It is up to future scholars to revisit those open questions and see what fresh insights can be drawn from this line of thinking.

---

[144] Lukács, *History and Class Consciousness*, 83 (original emphasis).

9. Thinking in a Gramscian way: Reflections on Gramsci and law

Pablo Ciocchini and Stéfanie Khoury

INTRODUCTION

This chapter examines the political thought of Italian Marxist Antonio Gramsci as it relates to socio-legal analyses of law, particularly courts in capitalist societies. Law has the ability to 'mystify social life'[1] and reify social relations. It is a complex phenomenon that takes on diverse forms and meanings depending on circumstances. A Marxist analysis of law is one that is historically situated, that factors in the specific material conditions of the period in question, and that has the ultimate objective of achieving or contributing to real social change. In this respect, Gramsci's thought informs our consideration of law by way of his call for transformative politics.

In this chapter, we consider the law in two respects. First, we examine law as legislation, i.e., state-sanctioned rules, which is how Gramsci generally understands law. Second, we examine law as the outcome of judicial decisions. Even in civil law countries, where precedents are not strictly binding, judges' interpretations of the written law can and do shape their implementation, as well as the way in which it is understood by different people. We argue that the process (or struggle) undertaken to pass legislation or attain a judicial outcome is particularly significant, because that process represents a condensation of forces from above and below. It is in that dynamic of struggle that the potential for social change emerges.

A Gramscian approach inspires us to take up 'a point of view that is "critical", which for the purpose of scientific research is the only fertile one'.[2] This is an approach that is not blindly optimistic, but nor does it fall into a pessimism that might paralyse collective action. Instead, it seeks to exploit the internal contradictions of a system that is otherwise inherently oppressive in order to advance the emancipation of subaltern social groups.[3] Gramsci remains relevant

---

[1] Steven Spitzer, 'Marxist Perspectives in the Sociology of Law' (1983) 9 *Annual Review of Sociology* 103, 114.

[2] Antonio Gramsci, *Selections from the Prison Notebooks of Antonio Gramsci* (Quintin Hoare and Geoffrey N Smith eds and tr, International Publishers 1971) 344.

[3] 'Subaltern' is a term coined by Gramsci to refer to politically and socially marginalised groups in society; see Leandro Galastri, 'Social Classes and Subaltern Groups: Theoretical Distinction and Political Application' (2018) 42 *Capital & Class*, 1, 43–62. Guido Liguori argues that Gramsci used the concept in three different ways. Firstly, he used it to refer to sections of the population that are politically marginalised. Secondly, he applied the term 'subaltern class' to the industrial proletariat that reached the level of political organisation required to challenge the hegemony of the dominant class. And lastly, he used it in a pejorative sense in reference to the cultural limitations of individual subjects (e.g., in a personal communication with his spouse). See Guido Liguori, 'Conceptions of Subalternity in Gramsci' in Mark McNally (eds), *Antonio Gramsci: Critical Explorations in Contemporary Political Thought* (Palgrave Macmillan 2015) 118. The concept is particularly useful for recognising the different degrees of subalternity, from the complete disaggregation to the achievement of political unification

today because his concepts can help to illuminate strategies of subversion, ones that work inside and outside the law and courts. In the spirit of Stuart Hall, we can '"think" our problems in a Gramscian way',[4] since, as he suggests, Gramsci 'gives us, not the tools with which to solve the puzzle, but the means with which to ask the right kinds of questions'.[5]

This chapter begins by briefly introducing Gramsci, focusing in particular on two major events in his life that are significant interpretative keys to his writings: his devoted militancy in the Italian Communist Party (Partito Comunista Italiano, or PCI) and the decade he spent in prison under the Italian fascist regime.[6] This is followed by an outline of a selection of Gramsci's major concepts and ideas. These include 'hegemony',[7] 'organic intellectual', 'integral state', 'civil society', 'moral and intellectual leadership', 'historical bloc', 'praxis', 'passive revolution', 'war of position', and 'war of manoeuvre'. Each of these concepts, as we shall see, is significant for socio-legal analyses of the state, law, and social order. While there is no dearth of literature on Gramsci, less scholarship is available for 'thinking' in a Gramscian mode about law and in socio-legal studies.[8] We seek to contribute to the process of filling this gap by reflecting on two issues: first, the role of law (understood as both legislation and judicial rulings) in maintaining hegemony; second, the extent that legal battles can be effective tactics in the larger project of challenging the hegemony of the dominant class.

---

as a social class; see Galastri, 'Social Classes', 45. Furthermore, together with hegemony, subalternity underscores the cultural and ideological aspect of political domination, and also of possible challenges to that domination. It is important to differentiate this use of the concept of subaltern from the way a sector of academia has applied the concept, with an overemphasis on the cultural dimension to the detriment of the economic one. This interpretation reduces subaltern to a mere reference to any oppressed group in society; see Liguori, 'Conceptions of Subalternity'.

4   Stuart Hall, *The Hard Road to Renewal: Thatcherism and the Crisis of the Left* (Verso 1988) 161.

5   Hall, *The Hard Road to Renewal*, 162.

6   For a comprehensive biography, see Alastair Davidson, *Antonio Gramsci: Towards an Intellectual Biography* (Brill 2016). For a political biography, see e.g., Walter L Adamson, *Hegemony and Revolution: A Study of Antonio Gramsci's Political and Cultural Theory* (University of California Press 1980).

7   Gramsci acknowledged that 'hegemony' was Lenin's term and was used by Marxists before him, remarking that 'I have referred elsewhere to the philosophical importance of the concept and the fact of hegemony, for which Ilich [Lenin] is responsible' (Gramsci, *Selections from the Prison Notebooks*, 381). However, Gramsci gave 'hegemony' an original meaning and application in his writing; see Perry Anderson, *The Antinomies of Antonio Gramsci* (Verso 2017).

8   For notable exceptions, see e.g., Stuart Hall et al, *Policing the Crisis: Mugging, the State, and Law and Order* (Macmillian Press 1978); David Litowitz, 'Gramsci, Hegemony and the Law' (2000) 2 *Brigham Young University Law Review* 1, 515–51; Duncan Kennedy, 'Antonio Gramsci and the Legal System' (1982) 6 *ALSA Forum* 1, 32–37; Boaventura de Sousa Santos, 'Popular Justice, Dual Power and Socialist Strategy' in Bob Fine et al (eds), *Capitalism and the Rule of Law: From Deviancy Theory to Marxism* (Hutchison & Co 1979) 151–63; Alan Hunt, *Explorations in Law and Society: Towards a Constitutive Theory of Law* (Routledge 1993); Boaventura de Sousa Santos, *Toward a New Legal Common Sense: Law, Globalization and Emancipation* (2nd edn, Butterworths/LexisNexis 2002); Boaventura de Sousa Santos and César A Rodríguez-Garavito (eds), *Law and Globalization From Below: Towards a Cosmopolitan Legality* (CUP 2005); Claire Cutler, 'Gramsci, Law, and the Culture of Global Capitalism' (2005) 8 *Critical Review of International Social and Political Philosophy* 4. Nicos Poulantzas is also worth considering here; for a discussion see Bob Jessop, *The Capitalist State: Marxist Theories and Methods* (Martin Robertson 1982).

GRAMSCI'S MILITANCY AND PRISON YEARS

Antonio Gramsci was a Sardinian-born Marxist whose most lasting influence can be found in his political philosophy. Gramsci's political awakening was rooted in his analysis of the divide in Italy, between the northern bourgeoisie and the southern peasantry. This is what he called the 'Southern Question'. In 1915 Gramsci became an active member of the Italian Socialist Party (Partito Socialista Italiano, or PSI), and began a career in journalism writing for the socialist newspapers *Grido del Popolo* and *Avanti!*. During his early career as a journalist, Gramsci lived among the working class in Turin and became increasingly engaged in working-class activities and life.[9] His journalistic writing was informed by the 'Southern Question', and it continued to illuminate his political thought throughout his life. According to Gramsci, the structural composition of capitalist society, such as it was in the Italian industrial North, subjugated the Italian South and retained it in an agrarian, pre-capitalist state. Through his study of the 'Southern Question', Gramsci identified the existence not only of class-based oppression but also of inter- and intra-class struggles, a theme that endured in his political writings.

Gramsci's militancy and his proximity to the communist minority of the PSI led him to side with the communists during the party's political split in 1921. He later assumed the role of the PCI's general secretary. The 1917 Revolution was a key moment for Gramsci, one in which his political thought began taking form. In 1919, together with four close friends, he founded *L'Ordine Nuovo: Rassegna Settimanale di Cultura Socialista* (The New Order: A Weekly Review of Socialist Culture), an influential revolutionary periodical. The early 1920s were a key time in the shaping of Gramsci's political outlook in which he was committed to the development of the factory council movement and militant journalism. In 1922, Gramsci travelled to Russia as a representative of the newly founded PCI. The year coincided with Mussolini's rise to power in Italy. Two years later, Gramsci became leader of the PCI, launching a political attack on fascism and calling for a left united front to return democracy to Italy. Upon his return from Russia, and despite the immunity afforded to him as a parliamentary deputy, he was arrested on 8 November 1926. The prosecutor at his trial famously (and disturbingly) remarked 'We must prevent this brain from functioning.'[10] He was sentenced to solitary confinement and died in 1937. He spent the last decade of his life in prison, although this did not stunt his intellectual prowess. It was during his prison years that Gramsci laid out a sophisticated, if fragmentary and dispersed, political philosophy in what became known as his *Prison Notebooks*; these texts only became available after the Second World War, first in Italian and translated into English in the late 1950s.

Gramsci's prison years were his most intellectually fruitful. Working from memory and under bitter censorship, he developed the ideas that continue to inspire academics and activists. His analysis of revolution led him to consider alternative strategies to achieving socialism in industrially advanced countries, and he developed a political strategy to achieve social transformation. His emphasis on the political and ideological dimensions of class struggle broke with the 'economism' associated with many of his Marxist contemporaries. The foundation of his theory of Marxist politics lies in his insight that a socialist revolution could not occur in

---

[9]   Alistair Davidson, *Antonio Gramsci: The Man, His Ideas* (Australian Left Review 1968).
[10]   Adamson, *Hegemony and Revolution*, 101.

Europe's capitalist states in the same way as it had in tsarist Russia, partly because of the existence of a stronger 'civil society' in the former. Gramsci's analysis led him to the conclusion that the industrialised powers of western Europe would not cede to a seizure of the state but would require the elaboration of and struggle for a new ideology or 'common sense'. Strong ideological leadership within civil society, reinforced by the legitimate threat of force by the state, created what Gramsci defined as 'hegemony', arguably his most significant contribution to modern political thought. Hegemony, as one historian has observed, is the 'unifying thread of Gramsci's prison notes'.[11] Although Gramsci did not examine the connection between law and hegemony at length, a specifically Gramscian approach to law can help us understand not only how power and domination are expressed but also how they may be countered and subverted. It is to a discussion of a selection of Gramsci's central concepts that we now turn.

GRAMSCI'S POLITICAL THOUGHT

Shortly before his death, Marxist historian Eric Hobsbawm praised Gramsci as 'the most original thinker produced in the West since 1917'.[12] Several decades earlier, while commenting on Gramsci's concept of 'hegemony', he had observed that the concept permeates Marxist and non-Marxist politics.[13] Indeed, 'hegemony' has been a key point of reference in cultural studies, postcolonial studies, and Subaltern Studies, as well as in disciplines such as sociology, anthropology, criminology, political science, and international relations.[14] While the concept of hegemony has been examined to some degree from the perspective of legal, particularly socio-legal, studies, we agree with Litowitz's suggestion that hegemony 'deserves broader consideration from the legal academy because it is a critical tool that generates profound insights about the law's ability to induce submission to a dominant worldview'.[15]

Gramsci defined hegemony as, firstly, '[t]he "spontaneous" consent given by the great masses of the population'; and, secondly '[t]he apparatus of state coercive power which "legally" enforces discipline on those groups who do not "consent" either actively or passively'.[16] The means of achieving consent, he argued, is (physical) 'domination' and (moral) 'intellectual leadership'.

---

[11]   Thomas R Bates, 'Gramsci and the Theory of Hegemony' (1975) 36 *Journal of the History of Ideas* 351, 351.

[12]   Eric Hobsbawm, *How to Change the World: Tales of Marx and Marxism* (Abacus 2011) 316.

[13]   Eric Hobsbawm, 'Gramsci and Political Theory' (July 1977) *Marxism Today* 205.

[14]   See e.g., Lee Artz and Bren Ortega Murphy, *Cultural Hegemony in the United States* (SAGE 2000); Christine Buci-Glucksmann, *Gramsci and the State* (Lawrence & Wishart 1980); Noam Chomsky, *Hegemony or Survival: America's Quest for Global Dominance* (Henry Holt 2003); Kate Crehan, *Gramsci, Culture and Anthropology* (Pluto Press 1988); Robert Cox, 'Gramsci, Hegemony and International Relations: An Essay in Method' in Steven Gill (ed), *Gramsci, Historical Materialism and International Relations* (CUP 1993) 49; Cutler, 'Gramsci'; Stuart Hall, 'Gramsci's Relevance for the Study of Race and Ethnicity' (1986) 10 *Journal of Communication Inquiry* 2; James Lull, *Media, Communication, Culture: A Global Approach* (Polity Press 1995); Anne Showstack Sassoon, *Gramsci's Politics* (2nd edn, University of Minnesota Press 1987).

[15]   Litowitz, 'Gramsci', 516.

[16]   Gramsci, *Selections from the Prison Notebooks*, 12.

A social group dominates antagonistic groups, which it tends to 'liquidate', or to subjugate perhaps even by armed force; it leads kindred and allied groups. A social group can, and indeed must, already exercise 'leadership' before winning governmental power (this indeed is one of the principal conditions for the winning of such power); it subsequently becomes dominant when it exercises power, but even if it holds it firmly in its grasp, it must continue to 'lead' as well.[17]

In other words, hegemony consists, first, of the ability of a dominant group to impose its leadership upon other groups and to inculcate the latter with particular values and beliefs, even (or especially) when those values and beliefs work against them. For Gramsci, this was 'spontaneous consent' achieved through 'leadership'. Second, hegemony involves the coercive or repressive power of the state.[18] In his own words, Gramsci tells us that 'State = political society + civil society, in other words hegemony protected by the armour of coercion'.[19] As such, consent through hegemony (civil society) and coercion through force (the state) exist in a dialectical relationship, and together they represent the integral state.

The concept of the integral state was taken up decades later by other scholars, such as Foucault, who emphasised the importance of non-state institutions for governance.[20] The same formulation was later critiqued for de-emphasising the state.[21] Indeed, the idea that the state is undergoing 'retreat' is touted by liberals who suggest that the market is independent of the state, rather than acknowledging that the market exists *by and through* the state.[22] David Whyte argues that states are juxtaposed with markets in zero-sum terms: the power of the state diminishes as the power of the market rises, and vice versa.[23] This argument draws attention to a key, but often overlooked, point about the limitations of the view that Gramsci referred to as the 'State as policeman'. Whyte usefully points out that Gramsci did not view the function of the state one-dimensionally, or as 'limited to the safeguarding of public order and of respect for the laws',[24] since it obscures 'the important interconnections between the policing/social control/criminal justice functions of the state and the broader social ordering functions of the state'.[25] The point Gramsci was making was that no line can be drawn between the state

---

[17]   Gramsci, *Selections from the Prison Notebooks*, 57–58.

[18]   Herman and Chomsky analyse the way in which the supposedly 'spontaneous' consent of the masses is 'manufactured' by the mass media, composed of 'effective and powerful ideological institutions that carry out a system-supportive propaganda function by reliance on market forces, internalized assumptions, and self-censorship, and without significant overt coercion'. Edward S Herman and Noam Chomsky, *Manufacturing Consent: The Political Economy of Mass Media* (Pantheon 1988) 306.

[19]   Gramsci, *Selections from the Prison Notebooks*, 263.

[20]   See e.g., Michel Foucault, *Discipline and Punish: The Birth of the Prison* (first published 1975, Alan Sheridan tr, Random House 1995).

[21]   See e.g., Bob Jessop, 'Bringing the State Back In (Yet Again): Reviews, Revisions, Rejections, and Redirections' (2001) 11 *International Review of Sociology* 2.

[22]   For more on this see e.g., Frank Pearce and Steve Tombs, *Toxic Capitalism: Corporate Crimes and the Chemical Industry* (Ashgate 1998); Steve Tombs and David Whyte, 'Capital Fights Back: From Cullen to Crime in the Offshore Oil Industry' (1998) 57 *Studies in Political Economy* 73.

[23]   David Whyte, 'The Paradox of Regulation: The Politics of Regulating Global Markets' in Simon Mackenzie and Penny Green (eds), *Criminology and Archaeology: Studies in Looted Antiquities* (Hart 2009) 127.

[24]   Gramsci, *Selections from the Prison Notebooks*, 261.

[25]   Whyte, 'Paradox of Regulation', 128; Whyte points out that Poulantzas also noted the danger of an understanding of state activity based upon 'repression-ideology', in that it diminishes the economic role of the state. See also Steve Tombs, 'State-Corporate Symbiosis in the Production of Crime and Harm' (2012) 1 *State Crime Journal* 170.

(repressive force) and civil society (ideology), because the historical development of the state depends upon civil society (or private force).

This point is illustrated in Gramsci's discussion of legislators. Legislators play an important role as intellectuals because they generate consensus for laws that are touted as 'equal' and 'fair', thus contributing to social cohesion through a particular ideology or hegemony. Gramsci notes that 'every man, in as much as he is active ... tends to establish "norms", rules of living and of behaviour'.[26] The greatest legislative power, he notes, belongs to state legislators, those with direct access to the state's coercive powers, though he acknowledges that 'private' organisations also have such powers at their disposal. And in this brief discussion of legislators, Gramsci makes a key point about consent, consensus, and coercion. He suggests that we are all legislators, even when we accept directives from others. Indeed, as legislators, we all contribute to building a social consensus: we conform to, and ensure that others abide by, norms, including those produced by private organisations, and laws, enacted by state institutions. This contributes to the production of 'spontaneous consent' and can also be conceptualised as what Gramsci refers to as a 'war of position' since social struggles waged by subaltern groups and fought out in legal arenas may contest consensus. Ultimately, these struggles demonstrate lack of consent.

The scholarship on hegemony has generally focused upon leadership emanating from civil society. Civil society, Gramsci notes, includes such institutions as the Church, trade unions, schools, and the media. Analysis of civil society institutions therefore lies at the root of any analysis of how to attain and consolidate hegemony. According to Gramsci, a social revolution materialised in Russia because the void created by the disintegration of the tsarist state was filled by communist revolutionaries. However, in the West, when the state faltered, civil society stepped in to reinforce capitalist society, defusing or absorbing revolutionary demands. Of course, every theory of the state is situated within a specific historical period, and within specific material conditions that reflect specific configurations of social power.[27] In considering his own historical moment, Gramsci sought to demystify the liberal capitalist state and the ideological separation between the state and civil society, as well as the emphasis upon equality and neutrality in the liberal legal system. That the relation between the state and civil society is far tighter than traditionally described is illustrated by the legal profession: oftentimes, as part of the same career path, lawyers move between state (e.g., law commissions, civil service, judiciaries) and civil, or 'private', society (e.g., law firms, autonomous legal bodies such as law societies, arbitrators).[28]

The analysis of the separation between the state and civil society was later taken up by Poulantzas, who sought to move past the instrumentalism of orthodox Marxist accounts of the state by developing a theory of 'relative autonomy'. Poulantzas argued that the state is not a tool of the dominant class. Rather, the 'relative autonomy' of the state 'regulates the variations of intervention and non-intervention of the political in the economic, and of the economic

---

[26]   Gramsci, *Selections from the Prison Notebooks*, 265.
[27]   Susanne Soederberg, *Corporate Power and Ownership in Contemporary Capitalism: The Politics of Resistance and Domination* (Routledge 2010) 51.
[28]   We are grateful to David Whyte for offering this example of lawyers. The example serves as a useful illustration of the false separation between public and private in the liberal capitalist state.

in the political'.[29] The state, in Poulantzas' theory, acts to 'legitimize and reproduce the conditions and relations of domination and exploitation by which the ruling class is constituted'.[30] The law is not a direct instrument of the dominant class but is related to economic conditions through values upheld by the dominant class and eventually shared by the masses—what Gramsci referred to as 'common sense'.[31] Gramsci explained 'the juridical problem' as:

> the problem of assimilating the entire grouping to its most advanced fraction; it is a problem of education of the masses, of their 'adaptation' in accordance with the requirements of the goal to be achieved. This is precisely the function of law in the State in society; through 'law' the State renders the ruling group 'homogeneous', and tends to create a social conformism which is useful to the ruling group's line of development.[32]

The law—by which we mean law-making processes, the legal profession, law enforcement, prisons and other punitive institutions—contributes to the development of 'common sense' by helping to generate and sustain a shared worldview that responds to the needs of capitalist social reproduction.[33] Like Gramsci, Poulantzas argued that '[a] theory of the capitalist State must be able to elucidate the metamorphoses of its object'.[34] The implication is that a Marxist approach to law must be able to identify the complex ways in which it mutates under the contradictions of the system exposed in the different balance of forces, to the point of offering a certain autonomy from the economic forces in a given situation, while maintaining a tendency to support the dominant class hegemony.

Gramsci's state theory is informed by his concept of the 'historical bloc'[35]—a strategy for hegemony—as a base for building a strategy for revolutionary *praxis*. He describes 'praxis' as 'the concept of the unity of theory and practice'.[36] At the heart of any revolutionary social transformation is a participatory democracy with a new historical bloc—a dialectical relationship that Gramsci identifies as material forces (content) and ideology (form).[37] The historical bloc is 'exactly the concept that enables us to think the unity and interrelation between eco-

---

[29]   Nicos Poulantzas, *Political Power and Social Classes* (first published 1968, Timothy O'Hagan ed and tr, Verso 1978) 143.

[30]   Robert P Resch, *Althusser and the Renewal of Marxist Social Theory* (University of California Press 1992) 329–30.

[31]   James Martin, 'Introduction' in James Martin (ed), *The Poulantzas Reader: Marxism, Law and the State* (Verso 2008) 4.

[32]   Gramsci, *Selections from the Prison Notebooks*, 195.

[33]   Bob Jessop, *State Theory: Putting Capitalist States in Their Place* (Polity Press 1990) 51. See also Pablo Ciocchini and Stéfanie Khoury, 'A Gramscian Approach to Studying the Judicial Decision-Making Process' (2017) 26 *Critical Criminology* 75.

[34]   Nicos Poulantzas, *State, Power, Socialism* (first published 1978, Patrick Camiller tr, Verso 2000) 123.

[35]   In the words of Panagiotis Sotiris,
> [t]he historical bloc is a strategic, not a descriptive or an analytical, concept. It does not define a social alliance, but a social and political condition, namely the condition when hegemony has been achieved. The concept of the historical bloc refers to a strategy for hegemony. The struggle for hegemony means a struggle for the formation of a new historical bloc.

Panagiotis Sotiris, 'Gramsci and the Challenges for the Left: The Historical Bloc as a Strategic Concept' (2018) 82 *Science & Society* 94, 95.

[36]   Gramsci, *Selections from the Prison Notebooks*, 334.

[37]   Gramsci, *Selections from the Prison Notebooks*, 377.

nomics, politics and ideology, within Gramsci's theory of hegemony and the integral State'.[38] This unity is echoed in Karl Polanyi's idea of 'embeddedness', a condition in which economic relations are immersed in and constrained by non-economic institutions.[39] Gramsci's idea of the 'historical bloc' thus incorporates the recognition that hegemony does not imply homogeneity, and that intra-class struggles always occur alongside inter-class struggles.

In developing this theory, Gramsci identified two modes or phases of class struggle that he called the 'war of manoeuvre' (consisting of direct conflict or revolution) and the 'war of position' (a discrete conflict in which a class attempts to acquire hegemonic power). A war of position led by dominated classes consists of struggles that contest the hegemonic ideology. Gramsci believed that a war of position was key to a successful revolution, and that it generally needed to occur in advance of direct conflict. And although the war of position involves a struggle without direct conflict, this does not imply that Gramsci believed in reform rather than revolution. Indeed, he denounced reformism, which he referred to as a 'passive revolution',[40] and which he distinguished analytically from the process of revolution led by the dominated classes. According to Gramsci, passive revolutions are social processes in which the dominant classes, or in some cases the state itself, lead a series of molecular changes that result in a significant modification of the pre-existing configuration of forces but that restore dominant social relations while diffusing dominated pressures.[41] That said, Gramsci's rejection of reformist processes cannot be equated with a rejection of specific struggles by the dominated—a war of position. The fundamental difference is the leading role of those classes. In other words, a war of position is part of a larger strategy of producing revolution and transforming the social order. By contrast, passive revolutions are processes led by the dominant classes to adapt the social order to changing material conditions while maintaining their own hegemony.

Both statutes and case law contribute to the production and reproduction of hegemony. Both contribute to producing consent among the dominated, including competing factions of the dominant class, and they establish the coercive apparatuses of the state to protect dominant social arrangements when sufficient consent is not present. What concerns us here is whether legal struggles are strategically worthwhile when engaging in a war of position. All Marxists agree that systemic change will not happen through the courts alone. But legal struggles may nurture resistance or at the very least draw attention to gross injustices. The impact of certain landmark cases, such as the US Supreme Court's 1954 decision in *Brown v Board of Education of Topeka*, simply cannot be denied.[42] Some legal challenges have resulted in profound implications for civil rights and continue to influence social movements, for example, in the strug-

[38]   Sotiris, 'Gramsci', 102.
[39]   Karl Polanyi, *The Great Transformation: The Political and Economic Origins of Our Times* (Beacon Press 1944).
[40]   Gramsci, *Selections from the Prison Notebooks*, 106–14.
[41]   See Alex Callinicos, 'The Limits of Passive Revolution' (2010) 34 *Capital & Class* 3; Chris Hesketh, 'From Passive Revolution to Silent Revolution: Class Forces and the Production of State, Space and Scale in Modern Mexico' (2010) 34 *Capital & Class* 3. Although not necessarily referring to Gramsci, or to passive revolution, criminologists in particular have examined how this strategy plays out in capitalist states through *re-regulation* for the purpose of protecting capitalism from itself. See e.g., Frank Pearce, *Crimes of the Powerful: Marxism, Crime, and Deviance* (Pluto Press 1976).
[42]   *Brown v Board of Education of Topeka* [1954] 347 US 483. This is the landmark ruling that dismantled systematic segregation in schools.

gle for same-sex marriage.[43] Although systemic racism, homophobia, and inequality continue, these cases have at the very least provided a platform for struggle, a space for contestation and debate. A counter-argument is that these are examples of civil society 'stepping in' to reinforce capitalist domination. However, there are also examples of revolutionary movements using courts subversively, such as the Black Panthers (a legal strategy seen through partly by Angela Davis) or Euskadi Ta Askatasuna in the Basque Country (especially during Franco's dictatorship and the Burgos trials). Furthermore, sex workers have used courts in several jurisdictions to decriminalise their activities and demand fairer and safer working conditions. More recently, we can point to a number of cases from the #MeToo movement that question the violence of patriarchal understanding of sexual relationships while challenging specific laws, the legal system, and arguably also, at least to some degree, the legal form itself.[44] Thus, in addition to potentially creating a 'safe space' for survivors to come forward about sexual assault, #MeToo also highlights the inadequacies and contradictions of the law, a development which, in turn, may encourage more general suspicions about law's claim to justice and neutrality. In the United Kingdom, for instance, the number of complaints of sexual assault have increased, which is perhaps an indication that a 'safe space' has indeed been fostered, but there has also been a surge in defamation cases, which is perhaps not surprising given the tension between #MeToo and many defamation laws.[45] Rather than demonstrating that all are equal before the law, as the bourgeoisie claims the legal system does, these cases illustrate the fallacy of liberal notions of equality before the law. While we do not claim that such legal battles will of themselves suffice to produce systemic change, we submit that such legal battles can help to destabilise the status quo, therefore creating political conditions favourable to those challenging the dominant social order.

The challenge to the dominant social order requires leadership. The emergence of subaltern leadership in a war of position requires 'organic intellectuals'—social agents speaking for the interests of a specific class (dominant or dominated)—to play a crucial role in developing a unifying ideology. Gramsci believed that '[a]ll men [sic] are intellectuals' but noted that not everyone has the function of 'intellectual' in society.[46] He determined that there were both 'traditional' and 'organic' intellectuals who play different roles in class struggle. The former think of themselves as autonomous from any class-specific struggle; Gramsci rejected this independence, suggesting instead that traditional intellectuals serve the dominant class. He argued that the ideological assimilation of the traditional intellectual is key to the consolidation of hegemony, although it is most successful when the class vying for hegemony elaborates its own organic intellectuals.[47] Thus, organic intellectuals have structural ties to a particular

---

[43] See e.g., *Goodridge v Department of Public Health* [2003] 798 NE 2d 941 (Mass). For a discussion of the implications of *Brown* on social movements and litigation strategies, see David S Meyer and Steven A Boutcher, 'Signals and Spillover: *Brown v. Board of Education* and Other Social Movements' (2007) 5 *Perspectives on Politics* 81.

[44] See Catherine A MacKinnon, '#MeToo Has Done What the Law Could Not' *New York Times* (4 February 2018), https://www.nytimes.com/2018/02/04/opinion/metoo-law-legal-system.html accessed 7 April 2021.

[45] See Owen Bowcott, '#MeToo and the Justice System: Complaints Up, But Convictions Down' *The Guardian* (15 October 2019), https://www.theguardian.com/world/2019/oct/15/metoo-justice -system-complaints-up-convictions-down accessed 7 April 2021.

[46] Gramsci, *Selections from the Prison Notebooks*, 9.

[47] Gramsci, *Selections from the Prison Notebooks*, 10.

class and create legitimacy for that class. In the case of the subaltern, their organic intellectuals have an important role in developing strategies for revolution.

The strategic importance of the war of position makes it vital to identify and understand the mechanisms, institutions, and organisations that contribute to that struggle. This is so since, as Hall pointed out, '[t]he question of hegemony is always the question of a new cultural order'.[48] That said, law and legal actors have largely been overlooked as exclusively belonging to the realm of the 'state'. In his important and controversial critique of Gramsci, Perry Anderson has suggested that this might be due to disregard of the state apparatus' cultural influence:

> [It is] impossible to partition the ideological functions of bourgeois class power between civil society and the state, in the way that [Gramsci] initially sought to do. The fundamental form of the Western parliamentary state—the juridical sum of its citizenry—is itself the hub of the ideological apparatuses of capitalism.[49]

While Anderson recognises the importance of cultural control within civil society, he also recognises that we cannot underestimate the 'cultural-ideological role of the state itself'.[50] The cultural role of the judiciary, which has been on the rise in many spheres since the 1990s, is evidence for Anderson's observation. Elsewhere we have considered hegemony beyond 'private' organisations, examining the moral and intellectual leadership of the judiciary, which, over the past 30 years, has acquired significant cultural influence, not least in the realm of human rights.[51]

The analytical importance of focusing on the judicial elite stems from the fact that judicial decisions often enjoy a significant measure of social influence, including influence over the development of social and legal norms. While judges do not formally 'make' law—an authority reserved to legislators in the liberal tradition—the role of judges in law-making, including 'judicial activism', has been widely studied.[52] The role of law and legal actors in shaping ideology and contributing to common sense should neither be ignored nor underestimated, since judges can be considered moral and intellectual leaders—actors who produce and legitimate the values of the dominant social order.[53] Judges are thus at once 'traditional intellectuals' who self-identify as 'autonomous and independent of the dominant social group',[54] and also 'organic intellectuals'. We have argued elsewhere that '[t]his dual functionality means that judges can serve a particularly important role in the hegemonic project because the illusion of the neutrality of the traditional intellectual allows judges to carry out an ideological project within civil society (as opposed to political society), despite their work remaining highly political'.[55] A Gramscian approach is useful to examine the system-preserving and system-reproducing capacities of laws and courts, because it takes seriously the possibility that

---

[48]   Hall, *The Hard Road to Renewal*, 170.

[49]   Anderson, *Antinomies of Antonio Gramsci*, 66.

[50]   Anderson, *Antinomies of Antonio Gramsci*, 66.

[51]   Ciocchini and Khoury, 'A Gramscian Approach'.

[52]   For a valuable discussion of the concept of 'judicial activism', see Keenan D Kmiec, 'The Origin and Current Meanings of Judicial Activism' (2004) 92 *California Law Review* 5.

[53]   Ciocchini and Khoury, 'A Gramscian Approach'.

[54]   Gramsci, *Selections from the Prison Notebooks*, 7.

[55]   Ciocchini and Khoury, 'A Gramscian Approach'.

hegemony may change hands rather than focusing solely on the question of how to oppose the existing hegemony. In this sense, it may be characterised as an optimistic approach.

A GRAMSCIAN APPROACH TO LAW: OPTIMISM OF THE INTELLECT[56]

Marxist theory has always struggled with questions of law. As Cain and Hunt note, this is in part because 'no theory of law as such is constructed by Marx and Engels'.[57] Considerations of law are fundamental to Marxism, not least since the 'wage contract', key to Marx's analysis of capitalism, is itself a *legal* construct.[58] Many Marxist theories of law focus on the legal form, and much recent work is on questions of international law and their relation to questions of global political economy.[59] As Paul O'Connell notes, Marxist analyses of law have typically sought to expose the fraudulence of the liberal insistence of 'law as natural, neutral and conducive to equality and freedom'. Indeed, 'a central task of Marxist analyses of law, state and rights is to highlight the role they play in structuring and legitimating societies riven with class inequalities and contradictions'.[60]

Gramsci adds significantly to this task, despite the brevity and often obscurity of his remarks on law (there are two pages fully devoted to law and a few scattered references throughout his *Notebooks*). He refers to:

[t]he general activity of law (which is wider than purely State and governmental activity and also includes the activity involved in directing civil society, in these zones which the technicians of law call legally neutral—i.e. in morality and in custom generally) serves to understand the ethical problem better, in a concrete sense.[61]

And rather than focusing on the question of whether law will 'wither away' with the advent of an entirely new, anti-capitalist society,[62] he offers a broader, more capacious 'conception of the Law', an 'essentially innovatory one [that] is not to be found, integrally, in any pre-existing doctrine'.[63] Consequently, although he does not discuss law extensively, it is clear that Gramsci

---

[56]   Gramsci attributed the statement 'pessimism of the intellect, optimism of the will', with which he would come to be associated, to Romain Rolland and referred to it in a letter to his brother on 19 December 1929. Gramsci, *Selections from the Prison Notebooks*, 173–75.

[57]   Maureen Cain and Alan Hunt, *Marx and Engels on Law* (Academic Press 1979) xiii.

[58]   Spitzer, 'Marxist Perspectives'.

[59]   For examples of legal form analysis see e.g., Evgeny Pashukanis, *Law and Marxism: A General Theory* (Chris Arthur ed, Barbara Einhorn, tr, Pluto Press 1978); China Miéville, *Between Equal Rights: A Marxist Theory of International Law* (Brill 2005). For examples of recent work on international law, see e.g., Cutler, 'Gramsci'; Stephen Gill, *Power and Resistance in the New World Order* (2nd edn, Palgrave Macmillan 2008); Robert Knox, 'Marxist Theories of International Law' in Anne Orford and Florian Hoffmann, *The Oxford Handbook of the Theory of International Law* (OUP 2016) 306; Umut Özsu, 'Grabbing Land Legally—A Marxist Analysis' (2019) 32 *Leiden Journal of International Law* 215.

[60]   Paul O'Connell, 'Law, Marxism and Method' (2018) 16 *tripleC* 647, 653.

[61]   Gramsci, *Selections from the Prison Notebooks*, 195.

[62]   On the 'withering away' of law, together with the state, after a communist revolution, see Christine Sypnowich, 'The "Withering" Away of Law' (1987) 33 *Studies in Soviet Thought* 4.

[63]   Gramsci, *Selections from the Prison Notebooks*, 246.

retains for law a critical role in capitalist society. Some of his most pertinent observations in the *Notebooks* are worth reproducing at length here:

> If every State tends to create and maintain a certain type of civilisation and of citizen (and hence of collective life and of individual relations), and to eliminate certain customs and attitudes and to disseminate others, then the Law will be its instrument for this purpose (together with the school system, and other institutions and activities). It must be developed so that it is suitable for such a purpose—so that it is maximally effective and productive of positive results. The conception of law will have to be freed from every residue of transcendentalism and from every absolute ... In reality, the State must be conceived of as an 'educator', in as much as it tends precisely to create a new type or level of civilisation ... [The State] operates according to a plan, urges, incites, solicits, and 'punishes'; for once the conditions are created in which a certain way of life is 'possible', then 'criminal action or omission' must have a punitive sanction, with moral implications, and not merely be judged generically as 'dangerous'. The Law is the repressive and negative aspect of the entire positive, civilising activity undertaken by the State. The 'prize-giving' activities of individuals and groups, etc., must also be incorporated in the conception of the Law; praiseworthy and meritorious activity is rewarded, just as criminal actions are punished (and punished in original ways, bringing in 'public opinion' as a form of sanction).[64]

In the several paragraphs that surround this passage, Gramsci sketches a new 'conception of law', focusing upon the manifold ways in which law, rooted in state and civil society alike, provides the repressive and regulatory mechanisms of control and ideological rationalisation necessary to capitalism. Thus, he highlights the relevance of the role of law in shaping 'customs, ways of thinking and acting, morality',[65] and, by doing so, consolidating the hegemonic project by the application of 'pressure on individuals so as to turn necessity and correction in apparent freedom'.[66]

A Gramscian approach is one that is not entirely pessimistic about law. Gramsci understood the law as a space to 'struggle for the creation of new customs',[67] and indeed the consequences of legal disputes spread over broader social life.[68] This is to some degree what Maureen Cain had in mind when observing that Gramsci's 'question is "what can law do for us"—a positive and open approach' that seeks to elaborate an effective strategy to dismantle capitalism.[69] This, however, does not imply that a Gramscian approach is reformist. Rather, Gramsci was interested in a political strategy that would successfully bring about revolutionary social transformation. For that reason, we disagree with Litowitz's critique that 'Gramsci's work provides important insights for understanding how the law sustains unequal power relations, but it offers scant direction for reforming the law'.[70] As a revolutionary, Gramsci sought to locate

---

64   Gramsci, *Selections from the Prison Notebooks*, 246–47.

65   Gramsci, *Selections from the Prison Notebooks*, 242.

66   Barbara Emadi-Coffin, *Rethinking International Organisation: Deregulation and Global Governance* (Routledge 2002) 55.

67   Antonio Gramsci, *Prison Notebooks*, vol 3 (Joseph Buttigieg ed and tr, Columbia University Press 2005) 83.

68   Sonja Buckel and Andreas Fischer-Lescano, 'Gramsci Reconsidered: Hegemony in Global Law' (2009) 22 *Leiden Journal of International Law* 437.

69   Maureen Cain, 'Gramsci, the State and the Place of Law' in David Sugarman (ed), *Legality, Ideology and the State* (Academic Press 1983) 95, 101.

70   Litowitz, 'Gramsci', 518.

and devise tools of systemic social transformation, not piecemeal reform.[71] Hall cogently high-lights the significance of Gramsci's approach to ideology, writing that this is an approach that:

> replaces the notion of fixed ideological meanings and class-ascribed ideologies with the concepts of ideological terrains of struggle and the task of ideological transformation. It is the general movement in this direction, away from an abstract general theory of ideology, and towards the more concrete analysis of how, in particular historical situations, ideas 'organize human masses, and create the terrain on which men move, acquire consciousness of their position, struggle, etc.'[72]

As Hall notes elsewhere, Gramsci invites us to think about 'how different forces come together, conjuncturally, to create the new terrain on which a different politics must form up'.[73] It is possible to extend this insight to law. Although law is typically understood first and foremost as state-sanctioned law, it is much broader and comprises forms of social power, including pre-capitalist forms of law, customary and Indigenous legal traditions, and legal norms generated by and circulating outside formal state institutions. There may be common elements to all legal orders, but some aspects of law produced 'privately' or beyond formal state channels may be useful for challenging key elements of the legally encased capitalist system. A notable example is the *Pachamama*, the 'Mother Earth' goddess of the Indigenous peoples of the Andes, and the rights of nature invoked by other Indigenous peoples of South America. In Bolivia and Ecuador, *Pachamama* was integrated into state law and given constitutional rights during the 2000s.[74] While the economies of both countries remain heavily dependent upon the extractive industry, the constitutional entrenchment of the *Pachamama* has arguably helped to alter 'common sense' views about an economic model based on unbridled consumption and the extraction of natural resources. Specifically, the constitutional recognition of *Pachamama* has served as a springboard for understanding links between different forms of oppression: the systematic violation of nature is linked to the inequalities and injustices of racism, patriarchy, and capitalism.[75] The importance of analysing the role of law in social struggles through a Gramscian lens, attending to wars of position as well as manoeuvre, is that Gramsci provides us with resources to eschew defeatism and lay the groundwork for breaking away from capitalism to a freer and fairer society.

In an essay in the *Socialist Register* Leo Panitch argues convincingly that we need optimism that is 'intellectually tempered by a sober recognition of the great barriers to positive transformative change, to make whatever positive contribution we can to overcoming those

---

[71]   Gramsci's categorisation as a 'revolutionary' has been debated. Gramsci was misappropriated by the proponents of Eurocommunism in the mid-1970s to justify their parliamentarian adventurism. Like Anderson's *Antinomies of Antonio Gramsci*, Peter Thomas argues that this was an intentional misinter-pretation that exploited the lack of direct reference to revolution in Gramsci's writings, which he did in order to avoid censorship during his prison years. Peter Thomas, *The Gramscian Moment: Philosophy, Hegemony and Marxism* (Brill 2009) 63–67.

[72]   Stuart Hall, 'The Problem of Ideology: Marxism Without Guarantees' (1986) 10 *Journal of Communication Inquiry* 28, 40 (quoting Gramsci, *Selections from the Prison Notebooks*, 377).

[73]   Hall, *The Hard Road to Renewal*, 163.

[74]   Daniel Bonilla-Maldonado, 'Environmental Radical Constitutionalism and Cultural Diversity in Latin America: The Rights of Nature and Buen Vivir in Ecuador and Bolivia' (2019) 42 *Revista Derecho del Estado* 3.

[75]   Eduardo Gudynas, 'Buen Vivir: Today's Tomorrow' (2011) 54 *Development* 441.

barriers, including in ourselves and our institutions'.[76] He goes on to appeal to faith in 'the capacities of collective human agency as especially crucial variable factors in developing transformative institutional forms'.[77] This is not reformism but an important reminder that we need to be creative and especially optimistic to achieve real social transformation.

A Gramscian approach to law is one that is realistic—that is, it is fully conscious of the repressive nature of law in a capitalist society—but also optimistic—aware that struggles in and around law have in some cases resulted in real change (e.g., struggles for civil, LGBTQ+, and women's rights). Of course, these are far from complete social transformations. But they have had an important effect upon those affected. That said, perhaps the most important revelation of these legal 'victories' is that compartmentalising struggles has in general limited challenges to oppressive systems, further underscoring the need for an intersectional approach in the battle for social transformation.[78] Hall summarises the position well when he argues that 'the civil rights and freedoms which make our society what it is are rights which were defined and won in struggle against the dominant interests in society, not bestowed on society by theory'.[79] In other words, although those transformations unfold within the parameters of a specific set of capitalist social relations, the optimism that a Gramscian perspective brings to these struggles is that each might serve to bring us closer to creating the conditions necessary for a revolutionary transformation of capitalist social relations in their entirety. If domination is based on a combination of consent and coercion, a legal strategy that manages to exploit the internal contradictions of the legal system (and it will be successful only if it also exploits the intra-class contradictions that feed such legal contradictions) may successfully turn law's power against the ruling class itself. Such strategies are not solely based on strategic litigation but might use litigation to legitimise other political strategies while delegitimising the ruling class' reaction to them. This is in fact the strategy used by numerous social movements in the global South, especially Indigenous communities facing the exploitation of their lands by large corporations.[80]

Gramsci recognised that 'material forces would be inconceivable historically without form'.[81] Neither the state nor the law, and their specific social forms, should be conceived as mere reflections of 'deeper' economic structures. Rather, they need to be understood as inseparable from the material forces they help to constitute, organise, and manifest. No struggle in or around the law by the subaltern classes is ever undertaken strictly within a legal arena. Whenever these struggles engage with the law, they simultaneously confront the 'political'

---

[76]   Leo Panitch, 'On Revolutionary Optimism of the Intellect' (2017) 53 *Socialist Register* 356, 357.
[77]   Panitch, 'On Revolutionary Optimism', 360.
[78]   For a discussion see Sharon Smith, 'A Marxist Case for Intersectionality' *SocialistWorker.Org* (1 August 2017), https://socialistworker.org/2017/08/01/a-marxist-case-for-intersectionality accessed 7 April 2021. The concept of intersectionality was proposed by African-American legal scholar Kimberlé Crenshaw in her groundbreaking essay, 'Demarginalizing the Intersection of Race and Sex: A Black Feminist Critique of Antidiscrimination Doctrine, Feminist Theory and Antiracist Politics' (1989) 1 *University of Chicago Legal Forum* 139.
[79]   Spitzer, 'Marxist Perspectives', 112 (quoting Stuart Hall).
[80]   For an insightful analysis of the strategic use of law by the Indigenous peoples of Ecuador against a large-scale open-pit copper mining project, see Esben Leifsen, Luis Sánchez-Vázquez, and Maleny Gabriela Reyes, 'Claiming Prior Consultation, Monitoring Environmental Impact: Counterwork by the Use of Formal Instruments of Participatory Governance in Ecuador's Emerging Mining Sector' (2017) 38 *Third World Quarterly* 1092.
[81]   Gramsci, *Selections from the Prison Notebooks*, 377.

and 'economic', as these are necessarily interconnected. As such, legal struggles may to a certain extent create opportunities to contest hegemonic structures expressed in and through law, contributing to a war of position. This suggests that under favourable conditions, given a favourable balance of forces, legal struggles may prove tactically useful as part of a larger political strategy to contest hegemonic 'common sense' and raise the subaltern classes' consciousness of the ideological character of the dominant ideas protected by the legal system. As EP Thompson suggested, in certain conditions, law can be 'a genuine forum within which certain kinds of class conflict [can be] fought out'.[82] Those legal struggles can help to galvanise support among the dominated, based on the recognition that any improvement of their position can only be achieved through collective organisation and sustained legal and political confrontation. This point is made convincingly by Honor Brabazon, who suggests that:

> rather than using legal channels in order to legitimise and institutionalise counter-neoliberal goals, there is potential for law to be used in a manner that additionally exploits the ubiquity of the logic of the legal form, incorporating a critique of law into attempts to use legal channels subversively to debate and challenge neoliberalism.[83]

In contrast with this position, Marxist social and legal theorist Isaac Balbus believed that '[t]he homology between the legal form and the commodity form guarantees both that the legal form, like the commodity form, functions and develops autonomously from the preferences of social actors *and* that it does *not* function and develop autonomously from the system in which these social actors participate'.[84] As such, he argued that 'those who would simultaneously uphold this [legal] form and condemn the capitalist mode of production which "perverts" it simply fail to grasp that part they uphold is inextricably tied to the very system they condemn'.[85] For Balbus, the legal form cannot be part of a genuine socialist society, because individuals in a 'truly socialist society … are bound by neither interest nor obligation [law] but rather by the *concrete universal* of *social need*'.[86] However invaluable, Balbus' position may be reconciled with a Gramscian perspective. First, Balbus' criticisms are directed toward the idea that legal recognition of the subaltern's social needs may ensure their satisfaction. Second, Balbus believes that the gap or contradiction between the law 'on the books' and the law 'in practice' does not delegitimise the dominant legal and political system.[87] While we agree with both such claims, we argue, following Gramsci, that legal struggles may be useful tactically as part of a larger political strategy even if they are not necessarily themselves goals. This is compatible with Balbus' claim that it is possible to 'decode' the commodity form of law in order to reunite the abstract and the concrete, and consequently to restore the hidden meaning of the social relation concealed by the legal form.[88] Balbus argues that the process of decodification will empower individuals and enable the delegitimation of both the legal form and the capitalist

[82]   EP Thompson, *Whigs and Hunters: The Origin of the Black Act* (Allen Lane 1975) 265.
[83]   Honor Brabazon, 'Dissent in a Juridified Political Sphere' in Honor Brabazon (ed), *Neoliberal Legality: Understanding the Role of Law in the Neoliberal Project* (Routledge 2017) 167, 184.
[84]   Isaac D Balbus, 'Commodity Form and Legal Form: An Essay on the "Relative Autonomy" of the Law' (1977) 11 *Law & Society Review* 571, 585 (original emphases).
[85]   Balbus, 'Commodity Form and Legal Form', 580.
[86]   Balbus, 'Commodity Form and Legal Form', 580 (original emphases).
[87]   Balbus, 'Commodity Form and Legal Form', 581.
[88]   Balbus, 'Commodity Form and Legal Form', 585.

mode of production.[89] Although he never clarifies what concrete form this decodification might take, we suggest it can take place by tactically using legal struggles in a larger political strategy under the right correlation of forces. Thus, as long as legal struggles are part of the process and not the goal, they can help unveil the asymmetrical social relationships hidden by the legal form, and by doing so enable a political challenge to them.

Of course, to recognise that some bourgeois tenets and commitments are questioned does not necessarily mean that the bourgeoisie's class leadership is at risk. This is partly because the consent required for effective control does not require active consensus from the subaltern. As Gramsci points out, the subaltern has:

> for reasons of submission and intellectual subordination, adopted a conception which is not its own but is borrowed from another group; and it affirms this conception verbally and believes itself to be following it, because this is the conception which it follows in 'normal times'—that is when its conduct is not independent and autonomous, but submissive and subordinate.[90]

Robert Cox, a neo-Marxist influenced by Gramsci, has written extensively on the question of popular legitimacy in the political order. It is this question of legitimacy—that is, understanding how a mixture of coercive practices and popular consent produces the conditions for dominant groups to rule—which is prominent in Gramsci, who points to conflict rather than convergence between (and within) social classes as a key mechanism for shaping the political order. Although focused above all upon the international order, Cox makes an interesting point that is equally relevant in the national context: he argues that consensus often occurs at a level removed from the public sphere, suggesting that it is frequently an intra- rather than inter-class consensus.[91] While this provides a basis for hegemonic cohesion at the ideological level, bids for hegemony appear to be constrained by ideas and practices developed by elites.[92] Legal struggles may become part of a larger strategy in challenging capitalist bids for hegemony, despite the conservatism of law and courts within capitalist states. That is not to say that those legal struggles will of their own accord lead to the achievement of transformative social change. But it does mean that the subaltern may operate politically within the contradictions of the capitalist state.

---

[89]   Balbus, 'Commodity Form and Legal Form', 580.

[90]   Gramsci, *Selections from the Prison Notebooks*, 327.

[91]   Cox argues that in the corporatist form of polity that reigned for much of the twentieth century, consensus was achieved behind closed doors, between authorised unions and large businesses. These meetings excluded large numbers of workers who were not represented by those highly bureaucratised unions. But with increased internationalisation of production from the 1970s onwards, those same unions lost their place, and consensus is instead now achieved among central agencies of advanced capitalist states (e.g., presidential office, central bank, etc.), largely in interactions that are channeled through international institutions such as the IMF or the World Bank. In none of these political models is consensus with subaltern groups actually sought; see Robert Cox, *Production, Power and World Order: Social Forces in the Making of History* (Columbia University Press 1987) 186–18, 259–61.

[92]   For a discussion see Stéfanie Khoury and David Whyte, 'The Rarefied Politics of Global Legal Struggles' in Willem de Lint, Marinella Marmo, and Nerida Chazal (eds), *Criminal Justice in International Society* (Routledge 2014) 227.

CONCLUSION

This chapter has sought to contribute to Marxist analyses of law by reflecting upon the relevance of Gramsci's political strategy to legal struggles today, and by arguing that Gramsci's work can inform critical analyses of the role of law and contribute to the development of a transformative politics. Cain rightly points out that Gramsci 'emphasized the importance of law, but it did not occupy a specific place in his political strategy, or a significant place in his theory'.[93] Yet it is still possible to draw upon Gramsci to think differently about political and legal strategies, especially because, as Joseph Buttigieg has put it, his work is an invitation 'to become involved in an active—one could even say participatory—encounter with ideas and lines of thinking which, in the case of the *Prison Notebooks*, remain always in a fluid process of elaboration, reformulation, revision, amplification, etc'.[94]

The continued relevance of Gramsci for law and socio-legal studies is twofold. First, by making clear the interdependence between civil society and the state (that is, the integral state), it helps us to appreciate the significance that strategic litigation can have in particular political circumstances. If the subaltern are able to organise themselves in support of a significant cause, legal struggles can become useful tactics in a larger strategy of a war of position to dispute the moral and intellectual leadership of the dominant class. Even if such contestation does not encompass all structures of oppression, it can help to weaken consent among the subaltern for dominant ideas, and by extension for the latter's hegemony. Second, because Gramsci's strategy is premised upon hope for social change, it distances us from defeatist approaches. The final objective is always social change and the overcoming of capitalism. In the words of Tony Benn, 'social change ha[s] two prerequisites: the burning flame of anger at injustice, and the burning flame of hope at a better world'.[95] Thinking in a Gramscian way fuels both of these flames.

---

[93]   Cain, 'Gramsci', 101.

[94]   Joseph A Buttigieg, 'Foreword: Antonio Santucci and Antonio Gramsci: An Open Dialogue' in Antonio A Santucci (ed), *Antonio Gramsci* (first published 2005, Graziella Di Mauro and Salvatore Engel-Di Mauro tr, Monthly Review Press 2010) 9, 11.

[95]   Quoted in Owen Jones, 'Tony Benn: Defiant Until the End' *The Guardian* (5 October 2014), https://www.theguardian.com/politics/shortcuts/2014/oct/05/tony-benn-defiant-until-the-end accessed 7 April 2021.

10. Poulantzas' changing views on law and the state

Bob Jessop

INTRODUCTION

Nicos Aristides Poulantzas was a Greek Marxist whose influential intellectual and political career was spent in Paris. His father was a practising lawyer, and Poulantzas qualified to practise law in Greece but chose an academic career. His legal background was central to his subsequent critique of political economy and the state, and played a key role in his analyses of the rule of law, liberal democracy, exceptional regimes, and the rise of authoritarian statism. This chapter plots continuities and discontinuities in his account of law and the state. It addresses three phases in his work: (1) an early existentialist-Marxist phase; (2) the discovery of Antonio Gramsci and Althusserian structuralism; and (3) the relational turn. It also relates these shifts to the intellectual climate and political conjuncture in Europe.[1]

THE EXISTENTIALIST-MARXIST PHASE

Poulantzas' early work on law is little known today.[2] This may be related to the fact that he disavowed his doctoral dissertation and refused to allow its republication as interest grew in his studies of the state. His early work was written at a time of growing rapprochement between existentialism and 'Western Marxism'. These two currents shared similar views on the human subject as author of social relations, and they both rejected the dehumanising mechanical materialism of orthodox Marxism.[3] Two texts that significantly shaped Poulantzas' work on law were Jean-Paul Sartre's *The Problem of Method* (1957) and *Critique of Dialectical*

---

[1]   This contribution draws on, but also updates, my previous analysis of Poulantzas' work, notably by showing continuities across different stages in his critique of law and the state; see Bob Jessop, *Nicos Poulantzas: Marxist Theory and Political Strategy* (Macmillan 1985).

[2]   For some recent translations into English, see James Martin (ed), *The Poulantzas Reader: Marxism, Law, and the State* (Verso 2008). This includes English translations of some key early texts: 'L'examen marxiste de l'État et du droit actuels et la question de l'alternative' (1964) 219–20 *Les Temps Modernes* 274; '*La critique de la raison dialectique* de J-P Sartre et le droit' (1965) 10 *Archives de philosophie du droit* 83; 'Préliminaires à l'étude de l'hégémonie dans l'État' (1965) 234 *Les Temps Modernes* 862 and (1965) 235 *Les Temps Modernes* 1048 (in two parts); 'À propos de la théorie marxiste du droit' (1967) 12 *Archives de philosophie du droit* 145. These articles are at Martin (ed), *The Poulantzas Reader*, 25, 47, 74, and 139, respectively.

[3]   Cf Jean-Paul Sartre, *Being and Nothingness: A Phenomenological Essay on Ontology* (first published 1943, Hazel E Barnes tr, Methuen 1963) and Perry Anderson, *Considerations on Western Marxism* (New Left Books 1976).

Reason (1960).[4] The first emphasised the need to overcome a generic economic determinism, displaying concern for the distinctive logic of specific fields within the social whole and how the relations among these fields are mediated through individual projects. This required a 'progressive-regressive' method that moves in a spiral fashion to establish the relation between the objective and subjective, capitalism and workers' experiences. Sartre's *Critique* focused on the Marxist pole of this rapprochement, calling for a shift from concern with static totalities to the exploration of totalisation and arguing that only dialectical reason can comprehend this process. Moreover, since Sartre believed that a disinterested observer employing analytical reasoning could never produce value-free knowledge, he also believed that observers should explore totalisation from within history by engaging with totalising projects.

Poulantzas' earliest analysis of law was contained in his initial proposal for his doctorate. This text, which was published in 1962, was entitled 'The Rebirth of Natural Law in Germany After the Second World War'. Poulantzas argued that this rebirth reflected a rejection of the extreme positivism of Nazi law. In exploring this topic, Poulantzas aimed to synthesise existentialism and Marxism, overcome the dualism between fact and value, and establish an axiological basis for political practice based on the promotion of human freedom. This required the replacement of German with French existentialism. While the former regarded all social relations as inauthentic, the latter offered a sociological account of authenticity.[5] These arguments informed Poulantzas' doctoral dissertation.

'THE NATURE OF THINGS'

In his dissertation, Poulantzas developed an existentialist-Marxist approach to law inspired by Sartre. This project rested on three premises: first, existentialism supplies an ontology of human action that implies the unity of fact and value; second, a critical reinterpretation of base-superstructure relations may help to locate law in the social totality; and third, these elements can be synthesised using Sartre's method of dialectical reason. This analysis rejected the neo-Kantian antinomy of fact and value. Instead, Poulantzas wanted to establish the dialectical unity of fact and value immanent both in individual action and collective praxis. He relied here on the concept, then current in German and French legal theory, of the *Natur der Sache* or *nature des choses*, but gave it a strong Marxist inflection. Specifically, he argued the factual and ideal are *naturally* linked in human action, and that this is grounded materially in the dialectic of labour and needs, with labour being primary.[6]

Poulantzas developed this argument in two ways. First, he used the concept of *la nature des choses* to capture the social character of 'the activity of man-in-association-with-others'. Human beings can only exist and act by virtue of values embodied in projects. For in order to exist, they must look towards an as yet unrealised but valued future. Because humans are ontologically free, liberty is the only authentic expression of their nature. Moreover, because

---

[4]   Jean-Paul Sartre, *The Problem of Method* (first published 1957, Hazel E Barnes tr, Vintage 1963); Jean-Paul Sartre, *The Critique of Dialectical Reason*, 2 vols (first published 1960 and 1968, Alan Sheridan-Smith and Quintin Hoare tr, New Left Books, 1976 and 1991).

[5]   Nicos Poulantzas, *La renaissance du droit naturel en Allemagne après la seconde guerre mondiale* (np [mémoire polycopié] 1962) 7–10, 148–49.

[6]   Poulantzas, 'L'examen marxiste de l'État'; Poulantzas, 'La critique de la raison dialectique'.

they are always already social, this liberty must take account of others' liberty. This excludes on axiological grounds the typical bourgeois concern with individual liberties and the legal necessity of private property.[7]

Second, Poulantzas emphasised that society is a structural totality based on the unity of internally stratified infra- and super-structures, each of which has its own particular properties and reciprocal influence in that totality. Nonetheless, the overall structure of society is determined in the last instance by the economic level, because it is only there that the primary needs of humans can be satisfied.[8] It is in this context that he considered the historically specific features of the modern juridical system. These comprised abstraction, generality, formalism, and *réglementation* (i.e., a codified system of rules that provides for the legitimate transformation of the law and that also prohibits illegitimate change). These properties are both internal attributes of modern law and an externally determined effect of the economic base.

Thus, Poulantzas rejected both a purely internalist *Normlogik* à la Hans Kelsen and a simplistic economic reductionism. Even limit-case examples of a clear fit between a given legal rule or juridical principle and an immediate infrastructural need must still be integrated into the legal system as a whole and made to conform to the specific formal characteristics of the modern legal system, namely, calculation, anticipation, and stability.[9] Furthermore, the relation between base and juridico-political superstructure is mediated through the worldview of the dominant economic class. This finds its particular juridical expression in general legal principles and the priority given to the juridical concept of public order, which underpins the unity of juridical structures and accords them substantive ideological content.[10] These principles, and the meaning of public order, nonetheless change as capitalism evolves. An example is the shift from the 'night-watchman' constitutional state of nineteenth-century France to contemporary *étatisme*, which subordinates individual liberties to the dictates of economic planning and state intervention.[11]

Pursuing the axiological implications of this existentialist-Marxist approach to the unity of fact and value in the legal realm, Poulantzas argued that legal institutions and norms are not equally valuable. On the contrary, a juridico-political order is valuable 'only to the extent that it reflects directly and immediately the historically given possibilities (at a given moment and in regard to the future of man) of abolishing a universe of alienation and reification'.[12]

OTHER EARLY PHILOSOPHICAL AND LEGAL STUDIES

Besides articles that anticipated, reprised, or revised arguments from his dissertation, Poulantzas explored methodological problems in Marxist juridico-political theory. He did this in several different ways. First, he criticised phenomenological analyses for failing to explain

---

[7]   Nicos Poulantzas, *Nature des choses et droit: Essai sur la dialectique du fait et de la valeur* (R Pichon et R Durand-Avzias 1965) 105–52.

[8]   Poulantzas, *Nature des choses et droit*, 167–85, 212–38.

[9]   Poulantzas, *Nature des choses et droit*, 251–79.

[10]   Poulantzas, *Nature des choses et droit*, 289–94.

[11]   Poulantzas, *Nature des choses et droit*, 295–342.

[12]   Poulantzas, *Nature des choses et droit*, 348 (translation mine).

the place of law in the social totality.[13] Second, he criticised Sartrean existentialism for its *sur-ontologisme*—its overly ontological treatment of the generic 'species-being' of man as the sole basis of legal norms.[14] Instead, he saw social intercourse as a general substratum of legal norms and practices that acquired definite form and content only in specific social and historical conditions. Only Marxism could explain these conditions and their implications for law and the state.[15]

Third, without citing specific texts,[16] Poulantzas condemned other Marxist approaches to law for economism (e.g., Piotr Stuchka and Evgeny Pashukanis) or voluntarism.[17] Against these competing approaches, Poulantzas proposed the study of the articulation of the material base and its axiological-normative superstructure. This approach would explore both the internal structuration of each level and their reciprocal influence within the dialectical totality formed by a human community.[18] Capitalist commodity production and exchange, for example, shape modern property and contract law. This, for Poulantzas, is mediated by the fundamental reality and value (*realité-valeur*) of the individualistic voluntarism generated by the bourgeois legal order, and the more general reification of bourgeois social relations.

Fourth, in turn, law has a reciprocal role in structuring capitalist society because it provides the framework of calculability and forecasting (*prévision*) necessary to monopoly capitalism.[19] To explain this adequately requires an 'internal-external' dialectical method. Internally, the juridical system reveals a specific axiomatisation, hierarchisation of powers, and logical coherence, such that superior norms validate inferior norms.[20] Externally, this system rests on the exploitation of oppressed classes backed by the state's repressive power. In summary, this implies a need to show how each juridical norm engendered by economic imperatives gains its distinctive place in the legal universe and is overdetermined by the overall legal order.[21]

---

[13]   Nicos Poulantzas, 'Notes sur la phénoménologie et l'existentialisme juridiques' (1963) 8 *Archives de philosophie du droit* 213.

[14]   Marx employs the term 'species-being' (*Gattungswesen*) in several early writings. See e.g., Karl Marx, 'Economic and Philosophic Manuscripts of 1844' [1844] in Karl Marx and Frederick Engels, *Collected Works*, vol 3 (Lawrence & Wishart 1975) 229, 275–77, 333.

[15]   Poulantzas, 'La phénoménologie et l'existentialisme juridiques', 213–35.

[16]   Representative texts include Piers Beirne, *Revolution in Law: Contributions to the Development of Soviet Legal Theory, 1917–1938* (ME Sharpe 1990); John N Hazard (ed), *Soviet Legal Philosophy* (Harvard University Press 1951); Mikhail A Reisner, 'Right, Our Right, Someone Else's Right, Common Law' [1925] in John N Hazard (ed), *Soviet Legal Philosophy* (Harvard University Press 1951) 83; Piotr I Stuchka, *Selected Writings on Soviet Law and Marxism* (Robert Sharlet, Peter B Maggs, and Piers Beirne tr, ME Sharpe 1988); Andrey Y Vyshinksy, *The Law of the Soviet State* (first published 1938, Hugh W Babb tr, Macmillan 1948).

[17]   Voluntarism sees law as the product of the will of a rational sovereign legal subject. See Reisner, 'Right, Our Right'; Vyshinksy, *Law of the Soviet State*, 275–78.

[18]   Poulantzas, 'L'examen marxiste de l'État', 278–82.

[19]   Poulantzas, 'L'examen marxiste de l'État', 283–90.

[20]   Frederick Engels, 'Engels to Conrad Schmidt, in Berlin, 27 October 1890' in Karl Marx and Frederick Engels, *Collected Works*, vol 49 (Lawrence & Wishart 2001) 57. See also Hans Kelsen, *General Theory of Law and the State* (Anders Wedberg tr, Harvard University Press 1945); Hans Kelsen, *Introduction to the Problems of Legal Theory* (first published 1934, Bonnie Litschewski Paulson and Stanley L Paulson tr, Clarendon 1992).

[21]   Poulantzas, 'L'examen marxiste de l'État', 290–94.

Fifth, Poulantzas applied this internal-external dialectic to the state in its public law aspect—that is, as a juridical order with its own hierarchy of institutions and practices regulated according to their respective competences and the separation of powers:

> From the internal viewpoint, the state presents itself as the axiological-normative order of rules and juridical institutions taken as a whole (state-organization); from the external viewpoint, the state presents itself as the repressive force that, through its rules and juridical institutions, aims at class exploitation (state-organization as instrument).[22]

This approach has clear and important implications for political strategy. To break out of its subaltern status and conquer power, the working class must transform the state internally into a democratic power that integrates the people. It must also establish a dictatorship over the bourgeoisie, using it as an external power to break bourgeois domination.[23]

OBSERVATIONS ON THE EARLY WORK

Poulantzas made important, if today largely unrecognised, contributions to legal philosophy during his existentialist-Marxist phase. His interests in the rebirth of natural law theory in Germany stimulated his search for axiological bases to distinguish good from bad law. He employed the phenomenological concept of the 'nature of things' to address this problem. A further influence was the rapprochement in France between existentialism and Western Marxism. This mattered for three reasons. First, it informed Poulantzas' novel approach to the unity of fact and value, its relevance to the field of law, and its role in an axiology of law. Notably, Poulantzas started not from the isolated individual responding to individual scarcity, but from situated existential action, through which humans make themselves, in terms of socialised labour and socialised needs. Second, he historicised the nature of things, relating it to changing divisions of labour and material interests. And third, he reinterpreted Sartre's internal-external dialectic to produce useful results in analysing the modern state and modern law in ways more complex and sophisticated than envisaged by Sartre himself.

In another respect, German legal theory pervades all of Poulantzas' work. As a neo-Kantian positivist, Kelsen argued that an effective legal order must be hierarchically unified under a fundamental legal norm (*Grundnorm*) backed by effective coercive sanctions. He declared that the state and law are identical, and insisted that there can only be one sovereign, compulsory legal order in any given society. For the state to be able to appear to act *as if* it were a unified national sovereign, its power must be backed by a valid and effective legal order, materially personified in a unified bureaucracy. Kelsen further argued that the division between public and private law is ideological and simply serves to dissimulate private law as located beyond politics.[24]

---

[22]   Poulantzas, 'L'examen marxiste de l'État', 297 (translation mine).
[23]   Poulantzas, 'L'examen marxiste de l'État', 299.
[24]   Kelsen, *General Theory*, 18–22, 45, 110–35, 181–87, 194, 202–5, 255 ff; see also Kelsen, *Introduction*.

While Poulantzas denied that Kelsen's formal, logical account of law holds for all legal systems, he declared its validity for the *modern* legal system.[25] The latter corresponds historically to key features of the capitalist mode of production. Poulantzas thereby resolved the key problem with Kelsen's pure theory of law, namely, the source of the *Grundnorm* from which all other legal principles can be derived. He could then use Kelsen's work to explain how the juridical logic of the modern legal system shapes the operation of law, economy, and civil society. This critical recontextualisation of Kelsen's pure theory of law was elaborated, albeit in other ways, in all of Poulantzas' subsequent work on law and the state.

Sartre's analysis of the state likewise anticipated some key themes that Poulantzas would later elaborate in his own fashion. Specifically, Sartre (1) identified the state's role in transcending the internal divisions within the dominant classes; (2) emphasised the links between its sovereign authority and institutional unity; (3) noted how the latter depends on the seriality (isolation and mutual separation) of the dominated and dominant classes alike; (4) referred to the heterogeneity (institutional separation) and autonomy of the state in pursuing the national interest; and (5) observed that the state's maintenance of the established order also serves the interest of the dominant classes.[26] Obvious parallels in Poulantzas' work are the state's role in organising the dominant classes, the *normlogisch* foundations of sovereign authority, the 'isolation effect' in the economic sphere and civil society, the relative autonomy of the state as a condition of exercising power in the name of a national-popular interest, and the manner in which the state's role as a factor of social cohesion also serves to reproduce capitalism.

After Poulantzas turned to structuralism, these parallels or continuities became less evident. Earlier arguments were developed without retaining what, as his own harshest critic, he now rejected as their humanist and historicist underpinnings. He could now exploit the *normlogisch* approach (and legal theory more generally) and integrate it with his Marxist sociology of law and the state. This was enabled by his engagement with two further key influences: Antonio Gramsci's philosophy of praxis and Louis Althusser's structuralist reading of Marx. Gramsci provided the substantive theoretical concepts for locating Poulantzas' emerging ideas about law and the state in the context of capitalist societies. Althusser, in turn, provided the philosophical means to break with the *sur-ontologisme* of Sartrean existentialism and its humanist and historicist assumptions and connotations. Marx remained decisive in Poulantzas' critique of political economy, of course, mediated by Althusser's reading of *Capital* and later his own re-reading of Marx and later work on imperialism.[27]

APPROPRIATING GRAMSCI AND ALTHUSSER

Commenting on the mid-1960s, Mark Poster once remarked that 'just when existential Marxism emerged, there was an abrupt shift in the French intellectual mood towards struc-

---

[25]   Nicos Poulantzas, 'La dialectique hégélienne-marxiste et la logique juridique moderne' (1966) 11 *Archives de philosophie du droit* 149, 154–57.

[26]   Sartre, *Critique of Dialectical Reason*, 635–42; cf Poulantzas, '*La critique de la raison dialectique de J-P Sartre*', 100–1.

[27]   Cf Bob Jessop, 'Poulantzas über den Imperialismus' in Tobias Boos, Hanna Lichtenberger, and Armin Puller (eds), *Mit Poulantzas Arbeiten um aktuelle Macht- und Herrschaftsverhältnisse zu verstehen* (VSA 2018) 77.

turalism'.[28] Poulantzas participated in this and was influenced, but not fully converted, by the Althusserian school. For Poulantzas, this shift began shortly before his dissertation was published in 1965.

A key transitional text was 'Preliminaries to the Study of Hegemony in the State'. This article rejected the orthodox Marxist view of the state as an instrument of repression controlled by the economically dominant class.[29] In response, Poulantzas made two points. First, the state is a specific structural ensemble with its own effects on the reproduction of a society divided into classes. Second, classes do not have a pre-given, unifying consciousness, but are constituted as political forces through the state itself.[30] Reflecting his existentialist-Marxist approach to legal analysis, Poulantzas employed the 'external-internal' method to analyse state power. Whereas the dominant mode of production is externally determinant, the institutional structure of the state is internally determinant. For example, the capitalist mode of production rests on the individual 'freedom' of producers, so that economic exploitation is based on exchange relations rather than extra-economic coercion to control what happens in the labour process. This also permits the autonomisation of politics from economics. Thus, as formally free and equal individuals, the 'people' participate in politics as *citizens*, through universal suffrage, rather than as *producers*. Accordingly, the 'hegemonic' bourgeois state must appear to mediate the competing 'private' interests of its citizens and counterpose them to their general, 'public' interest. In short, politics is constituted as the field of struggles over hegemony. To be able to impose short-term economic sacrifices on a dominant fraction or class and thereby secure its long-term political power, the state must have a definite institutional unity and a certain measure of autonomy. Intellectuals and ideological class struggle are crucial here because, following Gramsci, Poulantzas argued that the modern state must be analysed as a contradictory unity of direction-domination,[31] organisation-coercion, in all areas of social relations.[32]

Poulantzas extended the notion of hegemony (*direzione*, leadership) from the political relation between dominant and dominated classes to that between different fractions of capital and other dominant classes. These forces cannot be unified through mechanical compromise or temporary tactical alliances. Instead, a specific fraction must advance the interests of all or most fractions, not by imposing its narrow economic-corporate interests but by exercising hegemony within a power bloc (*bloc au pouvoir*). This is facilitated by its hold over key positions inside the state apparatus, which enables it to exploit the state's apparatus unity and sovereign authority.[33] Here Poulantzas' analysis clearly puts Kelsen in dialogue with Gramsci.

This article also affirmed that Althusser's structural Marxism offered a sound alternative to both Hegelian essentialism (with each part an expression of the same essence) and crude 'base-superstructure' analyses. In contrast, for Althusser, a social totality has different levels, each with its own relative autonomy and reciprocal effects on others. Its unity is secured by the dominance of one level (not necessarily the economic), as determined in the last instance

---

[28]   Mark Poster, *Existential Marxism in Postwar France: From Sartre to Althusser* (Princeton University Press 1975) 306.

[29]   Poulantzas, 'Préliminaires à l'étude de l'hégémonie'.

[30]   Poulantzas, 'Préliminaires à l'étude de l'hégémonie', 866–69.

[31]   The French term, *direction*, clearly refers to Gramsci's notion of *direzione*, or leadership, just as *domination* corresponds to the Italian *dominio*.

[32]   Sartre, *Critique of Dialectical Reason*.

[33]   Poulantzas, 'Préliminaires à l'étude de l'hégémonie', 1048–66.

by the relations of production.[34] Poulantzas' approach could provide a more adequate Marxist interpretation of law, politics, and ideology. Yet he also criticised Althusser for failing to explain how the economic region could be determinant in the last instance of other social relations.[35] Thus, while he retained Althusser's overall conceptual vocabulary for the moment, Poulantzas looked elsewhere for the concepts needed to develop the hitherto underdeveloped field of Marxist state theory. His legal training proved useful here as he re-read the Marxist classics on this topic.

TOWARDS A REGIONAL THEORY OF THE POLITICAL

Poulantzas presented his first monograph on the state and state power, *Political Power and Social Classes* (*PPSC*), as an attempt to develop a scientific theory of the state and state power in capitalist social formations.[36] This required a complex work of theoretical elaboration that was attentive to the precise location and function of various concepts within the structural Marxist framework.[37] In this context, he suggested that an 'autonomous science of politics' should move from more abstract-simple concepts to more complex-concrete ones. This process would be presented in three main steps: (1) the general theory of modes of production, class-divided societies, states, and politics; (2) the particular theory of the capitalist mode of production, which determines the exact place and function of the state and politics in its overall structural—or regional—matrix; and (3) a specific theory of the capitalist state and politics as a distinct region with its own logic that is different, and potentially dissociated, from the economic and ideological regions.[38] Steps one and two were based on Althusserian structuralism, which claimed that Marx's *Capital* presents both the particular theory of the capitalist mode of production and an account of the autonomous logic of the economic region. Specifically, it argued that the economic region was uniquely self-governing because economic exploitation and capital accumulation were based on market relations rather than extra-economic coercion.[39] Poulantzas concluded that the autonomy of the economic region in the capitalist mode of production enabled the political region to be self-governing too. This justified his effort to develop a regional theory of the capitalist type of state and its exercise of state power.

The first step in this ambitious analysis was the general theory of politics, classes, and state power. As Poulantzas had not yet introduced concepts relating to particular modes of production and their corresponding forms of state, this general theory focused on the fundamental class character and functions of the state and politics. At this stage all that could be said was

---

[34]   Poulantzas, 'Préliminaires à l'étude de l'hégémonie', 200–17.

[35]   Poulantzas, 'À propos de la théorie marxiste du droit', 145–62, 145–49, 159–60; Nicos Poulantzas, *Political Power and Social Classes* (first published 1968, Timothy O'Hagan tr and ed, New Left Books 1973) 256–57 [*PPSC*].

[36]   Poulantzas, *PPSC*.

[37]   See Louis Althusser, *For Marx* (first published 1965, Ben Brewster tr, New Left Books 1969). See also Louis Althusser et al, *Lire le Capital* (Maspero 1965), translated as Louis Althusser et al, *Reading Capital: The Complete Edition* (first published 1965, Ben Brewster and David Fernback trs, Verso 2015).

[38]   Poulantzas, *PPSC*, 12, 16–18, 142.

[39]   Althusser, *For Marx*, 1965; Poulantzas, *PPSC*, 16, 20–21, 25–33; cf Nicos Poulantzas, 'Brèves remarques sur l'objet du *Capital*' in Vincent Fay (ed), *En partant du Capital* (Anthropos 1968) 235, 243–47.

that the state's global (in this context, general or overall) function is to serve as the factor of social cohesion in class-divided societies. Otherwise Poulantzas simply advanced three propositions: (1) the state reflects and condenses all the contradictions in a class-divided society, thereby constituting the terrain for the most comprehensive political struggles; (2) political practices are always class practices; and (3) state power is always the power of a definite class to whose interests the state corresponds. These propositions exclude a role for the state as a mere tool of the dominant class. Instead, the state must try to manage the equilibrium of compromise among classes in struggle on the political field.[40]

In step three, following Althusser's (mis)interpretation of Marx,[41] Poulantzas argued that the self-valorisation of capital, secured through the dull compulsion of market forces, enabled the state to monopolise and constitutionalise extra-economic coercion and focus on its overall political task to maintain social cohesion in bourgeois society. This, in turn, implies that the political region can be treated as a distinct scientific object to be analysed using distinctive political concepts.[42] The rest of *PPSC* develops these concepts based on Poulantzas' reading of Marx, Engels, Lenin, and Gramsci. He shows how, facilitated by its internal organisational principles, the state shapes the balance of class forces in the interests of capital.[43]

THE 'ISOLATION EFFECT', CLASS RELATIONS, AND THE STATE

The juridico-political region of the capitalist mode of production constitutes economic agents as individual juridical subjects rather than as members of antagonistic classes.[44] This disorganises economic classes and promotes economic competition within their ranks. Something similar occurs in the political region. Law and juridico-political ideology duplicate the 'fracturing' of the 'private' sphere by constituting the public sphere, too, as a field of relations among mutually isolated, individual 'citizens' and political categories. In the political sphere, however, this is coupled with what we might term the 'unifying effect' of the capitalist state. The capitalist state presents itself as the strictly political (that is, non-economic) public unity of the people-nation, considered as the abstract sum of formally free and equal legal subjects. In turn, a formally sovereign state is the 'classless' embodiment of the unity of the people-nation.[45] This promotes social cohesion, and thereby provides a stable social framework for capitalist reproduction.

---

[40]   Poulantzas, *PPSC*, 37–119.

[41]   Poulantzas later abandoned his assumption that the economic region was self-reproducing and always dominant (as opposed to determinant in the last instance); he then explored the state's changing roles in reproducing the economic region, notably in different periods of imperialism and crisis conjunctures (see *Fascism and Dictatorship: The Third International and the Problem of Fascism* (first published 1970, Judith White tr, New Left Books 1974) [*FD*]; *Classes in Contemporary Capitalism* (first published 1974, David Fernbach tr, New Left Books 1975) [*CCC*]; *The Crisis of the Dictatorships* (first published 1975, David Fernbach tr, New Left Books 1976) [*CD*]; and *State, Power, Socialism* (first published 1978, Patrick Camiller tr, New Left Books 1978) [*SPS*]).

[42]   Poulantzas, *PPSC*, 17, 21, 29–32, 46, 50–51, 129–31, 143n, 190, 226–27, 282.

[43]   Poulantzas, *PPSC*, 75–77, 135–37, 143, 148–51, 187–88, 309.

[44]   Poulantzas, *PPSC*, 130–31, 213–14, 275–76, 310; cf Evgeny B Pashukanis, *Law and Marxism: A General Theory* (first published 1924, Barbara Einhorn tr, InkLinks 1978).

[45]   Poulantzas, *PPSC*, 125, 133–34, 188–89, 213–16, 223–24, 276–79, 288, 291, 310, 348–50.

This global political function can only be performed when the state can (1) disorganise the dominated classes, reinforcing their economic isolation and political fragmentation, and (2) organise the dominant class fractions or classes in order to secure the unity of the power bloc and its hegemony over the popular masses.[46] This involves the continual negotiation of interests in an 'unstable equilibrium of compromise' and requires real (albeit limited) material concessions to the 'economic-corporate' interests of subordinate classes.[47] This is hard to achieve. Indeed, explicitly echoing Pashukanis, Poulantzas suggests that the capitalist type of state is characterised by a fundamental contradiction. It must function as a class state while also being formally democratic.[48]

FUNDAMENTAL CHARACTERISTICS OF THE CAPITALIST TYPE OF STATE

PPSC focused on the administrative and representational features of what Poulantzas called the theoretically 'typical' capitalist state. These include: (1) the centralisation of political power implied in state sovereignty; (2) a legitimate monopoly on force, which displaces open class struggle into trade-unionist, electoral, and other forms of organisation, against which open violence is less effective; (3) commitment to the rule of law, which, as the 'code of organized public violence',[49] serves, among other things, to sanction capitalist relations of production and exploitation through their juridical representation as rights attached to private property, organises the sphere of circulation through contract and commercial law, and regulates the state's economic interventions;[50] (4) bourgeois adherence to democratic institutions based on 'parliamentary representation, political liberties, universal suffrage, popular sovereignty, etc.', which underpin and build on the 'isolation effect' and provide the conditions for struggles to define the national-popular interest;[51] and (5) the role of juridico-political ideology (at least in liberal capitalism, with its appeal to legality and rule of law) in contributing to the 'isolation effect', legitimating state power, and framing the struggle for hegemony.[52] All these features involve legal aspects of the state, reaffirming the role of juridico-political concepts in Poulantzas' analysis. Together they help to organise the power bloc under the hegemony of one class fraction, disorganise subordinate classes, and organise bourgeois hegemony vis-à-vis the popular masses. The reasons for this had already been set out in Gramscian terms in Poulantzas' 1965 article on hegemony, and earlier still in his comments on Kelsen and Sartre. Nevertheless, bourgeois hegemony is not guaranteed—and political crises are always possible.[53]

---

[46] Poulantzas, *PPSC*, 136–37, 140–41, 188–89, 284–85, 287–89.
[47] Poulantzas, *PPSC*, 137, 190–91.
[48] Poulantzas, *PPSC*, 189.
[49] Poulantzas, *SPS*, 77.
[50] Poulantzas, *PPSC*, 53, 163, 214, 228; Poulantzas, *FD*, 320, 324.
[51] Poulantzas, *PPSC*, 113, 157–58, 160–61, 166–67, 183.
[52] Conversely, crises can lead to a resort to open violence, surveillance, the withering of law, the redeployment of the judicial and police apparatuses, etc., to provide a new form of legitimation (*FD*, 316–28; *SPS*, 236–37). On hegemony see further *PPSC*, 195, 211–16, 221–27, 310–12, 356–57; FD, 76–78, 143–47, 151, 240–43, 302, 306–9, 320–30; *SPS*, 82.
[53] Poulantzas, *PPSC*, 191–93.

Poulantzas suggested that the two kinds of hegemony *tend* to be exercised by the same class or fraction. In developing this argument, Poulantzas introduced more concrete and complex concepts, drawn from the Marxist classics, to analyse the 'political scene', that is, the struggle between social forces organised as parties. These include blocs of parties, party ententes, and electoral alliances; the ruling class, whose political party (or parties) dominate the 'political scene'; and the class in charge of the state, 'from which the political, bureaucratic, military, etc., personnel is recruited and which occupies the "heights" of the state'.[54] He noted that the ruling class or class in charge need not be hegemonic, and indeed that it may not even participate in the power bloc or be allied with it. This is particularly clear for the petty bourgeoisie. At best, it can be an ally of the power bloc, and, more typically, it serves only as a *supporting class*—as may peasants and the *Lumpenproletariat*. Their support for the power bloc does not require real political sacrifice by the power bloc and its allies, but is often based on 'ideological illusions'. In addition, such support may be motivated by fear of the working class and is typically expressed in support for the current form of state as their protector against that class.[55]

STATE UNITY AND RELATIVE AUTONOMY

The characteristic unity and relative autonomy of the capitalist state is based, as noted above, on the 'specific coherence of an autonomised juridico-political superstructure'.[56] It is reinforced, in democratic regimes, by the sovereignty of the people-nation. These features allow the state to present itself as defending the general interest against all particular interests, even overruling the dominant classes and fractions when necessary to secure social cohesion.[57] This requires a dominant branch, apparatus, or power centre within the overall state apparatus that can control what other branches or apparatuses do. This role is typically associated with the branch, apparatus, or power centre that crystallises both the political unity of the power bloc and its hegemony over the people-nation and that seeks to organise the unstable equilibrium of compromise to this end. Other branches merely act as supports,[58] or resistances to the dominant centre of power.[59] The state's operational autonomy is further enhanced by the institutional separation of economic and political class struggles, the political manoeuvrability involved in democratic structures, and the ideological opportunities for the state to present itself as the political representative of the dominated classes.[60]

JURIDICO-POLITICAL INSTITUTIONS AND CLASS PRACTICES

As already mentioned, Poulantzas identified the political region in terms of the juridico-political instance of the state, and even noted, echoing Kelsen, Gramsci, and Althusser, that it was hard to distinguish the legal order and the state. He identified different forms of the 'normal' state

---

[54]   Poulantzas, *PPSC*, 245–49.
[55]   Poulantzas, *PPSC*, 243–44.
[56]   Poulantzas, *PPSC*, 256.
[57]   Poulantzas, *PPSC*, 255–57, 275–79, 282–85, 287–89.
[58]   Poulantzas, *PPSC*, 42n.
[59]   Poulantzas, *PPSC*, 303–6, 310–17.
[60]   Poulantzas, *PPSC*, 258–62, 279–87, 302.

in terms of the relative weight of the legislative and executive branches, and distinguished political regimes by reference to their respective systems of party representation.[61] In this context, he discussed how the institutions of representative democracy affect political class relations. Although social antagonisms are grounded in class relations, the latter are affected by institutions. Institutions influence the forms in which class antagonisms manifest, as well as the capacities of different classes to pursue their interests. Thus, although institutions do not, strictly speaking, have any power, they do constitute centres for the exercise of class power.[62] In other words, institutions are a crucial mediating link between the abstract structure of the capitalist mode of production and the concrete field of class struggle. So important did Poulantzas consider juridico-political ideology in capitalist societies that he described it as the dominant 'region' in the dominant ideology.[63]

BUREAUCRACY AND BUREAUCRATISM

PPSC ends abruptly, with some brief remarks on these two topics. Poulantzas regarded the bureaucracy (including bureaucrats, judges, police, and other functionaries) as a particular social category rather than as a class, class fraction, or social stratum. Its capacity to act as a unified force depends on shared commitments to the dominant juridico-political ideology, which justifies its activities with a discourse of public service, general interest, and the maintenance of national unity and social order.[64] State personnel need not share a common class affiliation by virtue of shared social origins. As long as they follow the commands of the dominant branch, apparatus, or power centre, they also serve the interests of the hegemonic power bloc, if any. Indeed, the state bureaucracy 'accurately reflects the political power of the dominant classes and represents their interests in the particular economic, political, and ideological conditions of the class struggle'.[65] That said, Poulantzas concedes that an overblown administration may transform the classes that supply the lower echelons of the bureaucracy into significant sources of support for the state and the power bloc.[66] Conversely, where state personnel do play a limited independent political role, this stems from their institutional position and correlative powers of resistance. In turn, bureaucratism is a specifically political deformation in the capitalist type of state, and is rooted in its formal, hierarchical, and rational-legal administration as well as its claim to represent the people-nation.

THE RELATIONAL TURN AND FOUCAULT

The collapse of dictatorships in southern Europe in 1975 (in Greece, Portugal, and Spain, to be exact) reinforced Poulantzas' emerging view, rooted above all in Marx and Gramsci, that the state is best considered a social relation. In each case, the collapse was due to growing conflicts

---

[61]   Poulantzas, *PPSC,* 308–21, 318–19.
[62]   Poulantzas, *PPSC*, 115–16, 315–16; Poulantzas, *CD*, 25–26; Poulantzas, *SPS,* 39, 41, 45.
[63]   Poulantzas, *PPSC*, 195, 211–15, 221–23, 310–12, 356–57. See also *FD*, 76–78, 143–47, 151, 240–43, 302, 306–9; *CCC*, 286–89.
[64]   Poulantzas, *PPSC*, 348, 353–54; Poulantzas, *FD*, 317, 327.
[65]   Poulantzas, *PPSC*, 354.
[66]   Poulantzas, *PPSC*, 332–40, 344–46, 352–79.

within a power bloc in crisis, internal contradictions within the state, and mobilisation of the popular masses at a distance from the state. This led Poulantzas to a more precise formulation of his relational approach. Specifically, in *State, Power, Socialism* (*SPS*), he proposed that, 'like "capital"', the state is '*a relationship of forces, or more precisely the material condensation of such a relationship among classes and class fractions, such as this is expressed within the State in a necessarily specific form*'.[67] In other words, for Poulantzas, state power (not the state apparatus) is a form-determined condensation of the changing balance of forces in political and politically relevant struggle. This underpins his bold claim to have finally completed Marx's theory of the state.[68]

A further theoretical influence in developing this approach was Foucault's work on power as a social relation, the dialectic of power and resistance, and the coupling of power and knowledge.[69] Poulantzas acknowledged this influence and freely admitted to employing Foucault's language and ideas (just as, one might note, Marx coquetted with Hegelian language in *Capital*). But he stressed that his inspiration came from Foucault as an analyst of power, not as an epistemologist or methodologist. Foucault's reflections reinforced Poulantzas' developing insights that the state's structural powers and capacities cannot be understood by focusing on the state alone—even assuming one could define its institutional boundaries precisely. For the exercise of state power depends on material and symbolic inputs (including knowledge production) produced beyond as well as within the state apparatus. Moreover, although the ensemble of state apparatuses has distinctive powers and resources, it also has distinctive weaknesses and always encounters resistance within and beyond its boundaries. State powers are therefore always conditional and relational.

That said, Poulantzas criticised Foucault for overemphasising the role of disciplines and normalisation, and also for neglecting the importance of law and coercion in the capitalist state, which Poulantzas regarded as crucial for the effective functioning of disciplinary normalisation and governmentality.[70] Moreover, he noted, law is not purely negative; it also has positive roles and features. It provides the dominated classes with real rights and liberties through which to pursue their economic and other interests. In this way, it helps to organise consent. But, Poulantzas added, the capitalist state is not a pure *Rechtsstaat*. For it also performs actions which are not subject to legal sanctions. It can change the law subject to limits set by class struggle, and it often infringes its own legality.[71]

---

[67]   Poulantzas, *SPS*, 128–29 (original emphasis).

[68]   Nicos Poulantzas, 'Les théoriciens doivent retourner sur terre' (26 June 1978) *Les nouvelles littéraires*. Rafael Khachaturian's chapter in this volume provides an elegant analysis of Poulantzas' relational approach to the state and should be read in conjunction with the present chapter.

[69]   Michel Foucault, *Surveiller et punir: Naissance de la prison* (Gallimard 1975); Michel Foucault, *Histoire de la sexualité,* vol 1: *La volonté de savoir* (Gallimard 1976); Michel Foucault, *Power/ Knowledge: Selected Interviews and Other Writings. 1972–1977* (Colin Gordon ed, Harvester Wheatsheaf 1980).

[70]   Poulantzas, *SPS*, 81.

[71]   Poulantzas, *SPS*, 82–84.

Table 10.1 Normal states and exceptional regimes

Normal States	Exceptional Regimes
Liberal democracy with universal suffrage and formally free elections	Suspend elections (except for top-down plebiscites, referenda)
Power is transferred between parties and/or governments in a stable way in line with rule of law	There is no legal regulation of power transfer ('might is right', state of exception, state of siege)
Pluralistic series of ideological apparatuses that mostly operate relatively independently of the core 'repressive' state apparatus	Ideological apparatuses are integrated into (or newly created by) the official state to legitimate its enhanced societal power
Separation of powers	Concentration of powers
Power circulates organically, thereby enabling its flexible reorganisation	These regimes freeze the extant balance when exceptional regimes are introduced

EXCEPTIONAL REGIMES AND AUTHORITARIAN STATISM

PPSC assumed that the capitalist type of state would generally function smoothly as a political apparatus, and that bourgeois hegemony would generally be secured. Poulantzas would modify this position in later work by exploring the economic functions of the state, the dynamics and effects of political and ideological crises, and the importance of exceptional political regimes. This is seen in his next three monographs: *Fascism and Dictatorship* (*FD*), *Classes in Contemporary Capitalism* (*CCC*), and *The Crisis of the Dictatorships* (*CD*).[72] These three books examine the emergence of exceptional regimes (regimes that suspended democratic rule, whether fascist, military, or Bonapartist), the changing forms of economic intervention in the normal state, and the paradox that exceptional regimes appear stronger, but are actually more fragile, than democratic regimes.

FD, the first of these three books, presented a detailed account of successive phases of fascism as a social movement and political regime and how these corresponded to offensive and defensive steps in the class struggle. It also emphasised the historical specificity of fascist regimes as weak links in the imperialist chain during the transition to the dominance of monopoly capitalism and its associated interventionist state. Fascism emerged because normal (democratic) means for the circulation of hegemony were blocked by complex political and ideological crises and because the prevailing balance of forces excluded resort to military dictatorship or Bonapartist bureaucratic despotism. German and Italian fascist regimes aimed not only to shift the domestic balance of forces in favour of monopoly capital, but also to advance their interests in the inter-imperialist struggle for domination. Poulantzas' analysis highlighted the complexity of the multiple crises that affected these weak links, and their (in)ability to resolve these crises through the normal play of class forces in democratic regimes. Poulantzas classified exceptional regimes in terms of the dominant branch of the state: the political police in fascism, the military in military dictatorships,[73] and the bureaucrats in Bonapartism. These ideas were further developed in his comments on the crisis of dictatorships in southern Europe. He drew some general conclusions about the contrast between exceptional regimes and normal states (see Table 10.1).

Poulantzas' book on fascism argued that the dominance of the political police modifies the juridical system and the role of the judiciary. Law no longer regulates the relations among

---

[72] Poulantzas, *FD*; Poulantzas, *CCC*; Poulantzas, *CD*.
[73] Poulantzas, *FD*, 323–24.

different parts of the state system or sets limits to the state's interventions in the wider society. Instead, the rule of law in civil and constitutional matters is displaced by the cult of *Il Duce* or the *Führerprinzip* (leadership principle). An orderly bureaucratic hierarchy and distinct spheres of competence are displaced by the arbitrary, ad hoc control of the political police. Likewise, the administration of law emphasises ideological soundness rather than objective guilt.[74] That said, the political police have limited influence in economic management. This is controlled closely by the fascist party leadership and subject to the influence of corporatist organisations dominated by monopoly capital.[75] This protected status is also reflected in the field of business law, which retains its formal, rational-legal qualities.

Exceptional regimes develop in response to political and ideological crises that cannot be resolved through the normal, democratic play of class forces. Democratic institutions must be suspended or eliminated in such cases and the crises resolved through an open 'war of manoeuvre' that ignores constitutional niceties. But the very act of abolishing democratic institutions tends to congeal the balance of forces prevailing when the exceptional state is stabilised. In turn, this makes it harder to react to fresh crises and contradictions through routine and gradual policy adjustments that could establish a new equilibrium of compromise. Thus, Poulantzas concluded that the professed strength of the exceptional state is superficial. For it actually disguises brittle qualities. These make the exceptional state vulnerable to a sudden collapse in the face of growing contradictions and pressures. Accordingly, just as the movement from a normal to an exceptional state involves political crises and ruptures, so the transition from an exceptional to a normal form also involves a series of breaks and crises rather than a simple process of self-transformation. In contrast, the apparently weak democratic state bends under the strain. It therefore proves more flexible in organising political class domination.[76] This said, exceptional regimes vary in their capacity to deal with crises. Whereas fascism illustrates the most flexible type of exceptional regime, the least flexible type is illustrated by military dictatorship.[77]

SPS built on these analyses and other work to propose that a new 'normal' type of capitalist state was emerging to replace the interventionist state characteristic of monopoly capitalism. This is authoritarian statism. This is now 'permanently and structurally characterised by a peculiar sharpening of the generic elements of political crisis and state crisis' rather than showing intermittent signs of short-term, conjunctural crisis. In brief, authoritarian statism involves 'intensified state control over every sphere of socio-economic life combined with radical decline of the institutions of political democracy and with draconian and multiform curtailment of so-called "formal" liberties'.[78] Specifically, Poulantzas argued that its principal elements and its implications for representative democracy comprise: first, a transfer of power from the legislature to the executive and the concentration of power within the latter; second, an accelerated fusion between the three branches of the state—legislature, executive, and judiciary; third, a decline in the rule of law and in judicial punishment of well-defined offences in favour of surveillance and pre-emptive policing of the potentially disloyal and deviant;

---

74   Poulantzas, *FD*, 320–23, 343–44, 353–54.
75   Poulantzas, *FD*, 112–13, 134, 194–95, 221–22, 344.
76   Poulantzas, *CD*, 30, 38, 48–50, 90–93, 106, 124.
77   Poulantzas, *PPSC*, 79, 107–8, 180, 243–44, 258–61, 282–83, 302, 320, 357–59; Poulantzas, *FD*, 87, 113.
78   Poulantzas, *SPS*, 203–4.

fourth, the functional decline of political parties as the major forces in organising hegemony and the main channel for the masses to engage in political dialogue with the administration; and finally, the growth of parallel power networks cross-cutting the formal organisation of the state and holding a decisive share in its various activities and linking the state to capitalist interests.[79] Authoritarian statism could take different forms: more neoliberal in France, for example, more authoritarian in Germany.[80]

CONCLUSION

There are major areas of continuity across the three main phases in Poulantzas' work on law and the state (existentialist-Marxist, a structuralist moment influenced by legal theory and Gramsci, and the relational turn). Especially relevant to the aims of this volume are the influence of juridico-political theory and analysis on Poulantzas' work, and his abiding interest in the historical specificity of bourgeois legal and political forms. The latter include, but are not exhausted by, the following: (1) the distinction between private and public law; (2) the institutionalised separation of the economic and political spheres; (3) the absence of a formal monopoly of class power in a representative constitutional state, creating the necessity of struggles for hegemony within the power bloc and over the people-nation; (4) the juridico-political architecture of the capitalist type of state, based upon hierarchically organised powers and competences subordinate to a single sovereign authority; and (5) the content and impact of juridico-political ideology on the forms and stakes of economic, political, and ideological class struggles. This influence persisted as Poulantzas shifted politically from a humanist-existentialist position to a Gramscian inflection of Marxism-Leninism which called for working-class hegemony led by a vanguard party, and finally to a left Eurocommunist position committed to cross-class alliances, co-operation among left parties, and close articulation of direct and representative democracy. The influence of legal theory is evident in all three stages, and Gramscian concepts and arguments help to organise Poulantzas' analysis in the second and third stages. This suggests that structural Marxism is not as decisive in Poulantzas' theory of law, the state, and state power as many have claimed. Although it led to misleading arguments about the self-organising logic of capital accumulation in the economic region,[81] structural Marxism merely provided an intellectually fashionable framework within which to present his autonomous science of politics.

The major innovations in stage three are: (1) the distinction between normal states and exceptional regimes, and the associated concept of authoritarian statism as the 'new normal' with a mix of normal and exceptional elements; (2) recognition that law has a politically useful as well as a repressive role in bourgeois societies, and that states can and do infringe their own legality; (3) analyses of the state's role in constituting the 'nation' and its 'national territory' as an organising matrix of class power and capitalist competition; (4) an account of state forms

---

[79]   Poulantzas, *CCC*, 55–57; *SPS*, 217–31.
[80]   Cf Nicos Poulantzas, 'Interview with Nicos Poulantzas' (July 1979) *Marxism Today* 194, 199.
[81]   It also led to a tortured discussion organised around a reified distinction between class structures and class practices in each region of the capitalist mode of production. This was fully resolved in the relational approach developed in *SPS*.

and intervention in different stages of capitalism and locations within the imperialist chain; and (5) a nuanced account of the specificity of political crises.[82]

Finally, following the collapse of the Soviet Union and his publicly voiced concerns about the 'boat people' fleeing the Pol Pot regime in Cambodia, Poulantzas no longer dismissed the distinction between the public and private as an ideological illusion but affirmed the value of so-called 'formal liberties'. Given the crisis of Fordism (including peripheral Fordism in southern Europe), Poulantzas paid increased attention to new social movements, the crisis in the traditional party form, and the need to form *pluri-partiste* (multi-party) and *pluri-classiste* (cross-class) alliances that could integrate new social movements. This would be the basis for developing a democratic socialism that would combine direct and representative democracy in ways that ensured continuing popular pressure on the sovereign state.

---

[82] Nicos Poulantzas, 'The Political Crisis and the Crisis of the State' [1976] in James Martin (ed), *The Poulantzas Reader: Marxism, Law, and the State* (Verso 2008) 294.

11. The state as social relation: Poulantzas on materiality and political strategy

Rafael Khachaturian

INTRODUCTION

Nicos Poulantzas' work remains, 40 years after his untimely death, one of the most innovative contributions to Marxist political sociology and political theory. In what is still the only English-language biography of Poulantzas, Bob Jessop called him 'the single most important and influential Marxist theorist of the state and politics in the postwar period'.[1] More recently, Poulantzas has influenced discussions of 'authoritarian neoliberalism',[2] political ecology,[3] and the surveillance state.[4] Translations of secondary literature, from German[5] and French,[6] have steadily increased his profile in the English-speaking world and cultivated an international dialogue on his contemporary relevance.

Poulantzas' theoretical interventions came at a particularly fertile time for Marxist debates about the capitalist state. These debates spanned the 1970s and were responses to the political reverberations of 1968, the internal reckoning of Western communist parties on the legacies of Stalinism, and the dual crises of accumulation and legitimation in advanced capitalist states.[7] However, Poulantzas' analysis stands out because of his distinctive class theoretical approach, which rejected attempts to treat the state as either an object or a subject. Instead, Poulantzas advanced a conception of the capitalist state as a constellation of social forces and powers, to which the class struggle was immanent. He thus challenged both Leninist 'revolutionary' and social-democratic 'reformist' orthodoxy about the capitalist state, all with the purpose of theorising the ruptural strategies involved in the political and social transition from capitalism to socialism.

In this chapter, I discuss Poulantzas' work through this lens of the materiality of the capitalist state. I examine how Poulantzas situated his intervention in relation to existing treatments of the state as either an instrument/object or a subject; the impact of this framework on the law and juridical personhood; and the relevance of this account for political strategy, in particular

---

[1] Bob Jessop, *Nicos Poulantzas: Marxist Theory and Political Strategy* (St Martin's Press 1985) 5.

[2] Ian Bruff, 'The Rise of Authoritarian Neoliberalism' (2014) 26 *Rethinking Marxism* 113.

[3] Bob Jessop, 'Nicos Poulantzas on Political Economy, Political Ecology, and Democratic Socialism' (2017) 24 *Journal of Political Ecology* 186.

[4] Christos Boukalas, 'No Exceptions: Authoritarian Statism: Agamben, Poulantzas, and Homeland Security' (2014) 7 *Critical Studies on Terrorism* 112.

[5] Alexander Gallas, Lars Bretthauer, John Kannankulam, and Ingo Stützle (eds), *Reading Poulantzas* (Merlin Press 2011).

[6] Jean-Numa Ducange and Razmig Keucheyan (eds), *The End of the Democratic State: Nicos Poulantzas, a Marxism for the 21st Century* (Palgrave Macmillan 2019).

[7] Martin Carnoy, *The State and Political Theory* (Princeton University Press 1984); Clyde W Barrow, *Critical Theories of the State: Marxist, Neomarxist, Postmarxist* (University of Wisconsin Press 1993); Raju Das, 'State Theories: A Critical Analysis' (1996) 60 *Science & Society* 27.

the transitions to liberal democracy in southern Europe and the opportunities for a transition to democratic socialism in the European and North American capitalist core. I argue that by theorising the state as a social relation—more specifically, as a material condensation of a relationship of forces between classes and class fractions—Poulantzas was able to sidestep the theoretical dilemmas that confounded prior Marxist thinking about the state. Furthermore, Poulantzas' account of political strategy follows from his treatment of the state as a material condensation of social forces. In particular, his conception of the state as a contradictory and uneven terrain that is potentially open to the intervention of the 'popular classes' into a given conjuncture continues to provide a foundation for a distinctly Marxist theory of politics.

BEYOND STATE-AS-THING AND STATE-AS-SUBJECT

Apart from his first book *Nature des choses et droit*,[8] Poulantzas developed his arguments over the course of five major books and a substantial number of essays. While they share an overarching concern with the theorisation of the capitalist state, the scope and focus of Poulantzas' arguments varies across these works. *Fascism and Dictatorship* and *The Crisis of the Dictatorships* (*CD*) are studies of distinct exceptional forms taken by the capitalist state.[9] Poulantzas characterised the remaining three books as approaching the same problem—the peculiar structures of the capitalist state—through distinct vantage points.[10] Thus, the main focus of *Political Power and Social Classes* (*PPSC*) was a general theory of the capitalist state based on the separation of the economic and the political levels that was peculiar to the capitalist mode of production.[11] In *Classes in Contemporary Capitalism* (*CCC*),[12] Poulantzas addressed how the division of labour influenced the constitution of social classes. In his final work, *State, Power, Socialism* (*SPS*), the same lens of the division of labour was then applied to the institutional materiality of the capitalist state itself.

The relationship between Poulantzas' earlier and later writings has been a matter of some debate. Poulantzas' reputation as a structuralist Marxist was based on a (largely one-sided) reading of *PPSC*, published soon after the events of May 1968. There, he began from the distinct requirements of the capitalist mode of production and the role of the political level within a social formation, eventually proceeding to an account of the state as the 'factor of cohesion between the levels of a social formation' and the 'structure in which the contradictions of the various levels of a formation are condensed'.[13] Due to this influence of Althusserian termi-

---

[8]   Nicos Poulantzas, *Nature des choses et droit: essai sur la dialectique du fait et de la valeur* (Librairie générale de droit et de jurisprudence 1965). See also James Martin, 'Ontology and Law in the Early Poulantzas' (2009) 35 *History of European Ideas* 465.

[9]   Nicos Poulantzas, *Fascism and Dictatorship: The Third International and the Problem of Fascism* (first published 1970, Judith White tr, New Left Books 1974) [*FD*]; Nicos Poulantzas, *The Crisis of the Dictatorships* (first published 1975, David Fernbach tr, New Left Books 1976) [*CD*]. On Poulantzas' earlier writing and his theory of the fascist type of state, see Bob Jessop's chapter in this volume.

[10]   Nicos Poulantzas, *State, Power, Socialism* (first published 1978, Patrick Camiller tr, Verso 1980) 53 [*SPS*].

[11]   Nicos Poulantzas, *Political Power and Social Classes* (first published 1968, Timothy O'Hagan tr and ed, New Left Books 1973) [*PPSC*].

[12]   Nicos Poulantzas, *Classes in Contemporary Capitalism* (first published 1974, David Fernbach tr, New Left Books 1974) [*CCC*].

[13]   Poulantzas, *PPSC*, 44–45.

nology, Poulantzas' contemporaries, especially in the English-speaking world, saw him as exemplary of structural Marxist approaches to the state—a reputation that he retains today.[14]

However, Poulantzas' indebtedness to Althusser has often been overstated, partly as a result of his famous debate with Ralph Miliband in the early 1970s, which helped popularise the schematic distinction between instrumentalist and structuralist approaches to the state.[15] Jessop argues that Poulantzas shed much of the Althusserian conceptual framework after *PPSC*, as he moved toward a relational account of the state.[16] In addition, Barrow points out that even in his most structuralist phase Poulantzas had already registered his differences with the positions taken by Althusser and Balibar in *Reading Capital*.[17] These differences became more pronounced in his later writings, as Poulantzas criticised their reduction of the state to the function of repression and ideology, as well as their treatment of the political and economic levels in the capitalist mode of production as self-generating and independently functioning instances that were then mechanically 'combined' with each other.[18]

What is truly distinctive about Poulantzas' contribution is not the 'structuralism' of his account of the capitalist state, but rather the innovative way he framed the relationship between social forces and political structures. Despite the changing nuances in his thought between *PPSC* and the appearance of *SPS* ten years later, Poulantzas consistently rejected the 'false dilemma' between the state understood as a thing/instrument and as a subject.[19] His conception of the relative autonomy of the state, for which he is best known, must be seen in light of his critique of these two dominant approaches to the state within Marxist thought, corresponding to its Leninist and social-democratic variants.

First, Poulantzas rejected a tendency that saw the state as a thing, instrument, machine, or tool. This view, which he associated with both the legacy of economism and voluntarism in Marxist thought, saw the state as a 'mere tool of domination, manipulable at will' by the dominant class.[20] The unity of the state was derived from the assumed unified will of the dominant class, thereby reducing the state to an instrument of organised coercion wielded for the purpose of class rule. Understood in this way, the state had no autonomy, since it was merely the superstructural expression of class interests originating from the base of the combined forces and relations of production.[21] Poulantzas attributed this 'instrumentalist' conception

---

[14]   Amy Beth Bridges, 'Nicos Poulantzas and the Marxist Theory of the State' (1974) 4 *Politics & Society* 161; David A Gold, Clarence YH Lo, and Erik Olin Wright, 'Recent Developments in Marxist Theories of the Capitalist State' (1975) 27 *Monthly Review* 29.

[15]   See Nicos Poulantzas, 'The Problem of the Capitalist State' [1969] in James Martin (ed), *The Poulantzas Reader: Marxism, Law and the State* (Verso 2008) 172. See also Clyde W Barrow, *Toward a Critical Theory of States: The Poulantzas-Miliband Debate After Globalization* (State University of New York Press 2016) ch 2.

[16]   Jessop, *Nicos Poulantzas*, 81–82.

[17]   Barrow, *Toward a Critical Theory of States,* ch 2; Louis Althusser et al, *Reading Capital: The Complete Edition* (first published 1965, Ben Brewster and David Fernbach trs, Verso 2015).

[18]   Nicos Poulantzas, 'The Capitalist State: A Reply to Miliband and Laclau' [1976] in James Martin (ed), *The Poulantzas Reader: Marxism, Law and the State* (Verso 2008) 270, 286–93; Nicos Poulantzas, 'The State, Social Movements, Party: Interview with Nicos Poulantzas' *Viewpoint* (18 December 2017), https://www.viewpointmag.com/2017/12/18/state-social-movements-party-interview-nicos-poulantzas-1979/ accessed 7 April 2021.

[19]   Poulantzas, 'The Capitalist State: A Reply to Miliband and Laclau', 283.

[20]   Poulantzas, *PPSC*, 256.

[21]   Poulantzas, 'The Capitalist State: A Reply to Miliband and Laclau', 283.

of the state alternately to Lenin, the Third International, and contemporary analyses of 'state monopoly capitalism'.

By contrast, the social-democratic tradition tended to see the state as a subject. This conception, said to originate with Hegel, later re-emerged in the Second International and interwar German social democracy, as well as in the thought of Max Weber and the 'institutionalist-functionalist' political sociology of the 1960s and 1970s.[22] Here the unity of the state was not premised on a direct expression of a specific class, but on corporatist institutional arrangements that allowed it to balance and harmonise competing societal interests.[23] The state, imbued with metaphysical principles of a 'personality' and 'will', was seen as the 'rationalising instance of civil society' and as 'incarnated in the power of the group that concretely represents this rationality/power (bureaucracy, elites)'.[24] The state-as-subject had absolute autonomy, acting as the neutral arbitrator between contending classes, and thus could incorporate working class interests into a pluralistic consensus.

Poulantzas rejected both the premise that the state derived its unity from a presupposed dominant class will, and that it possessed a unity insofar as it was an integral subject 'animated' by a professional bureaucratic cadre. This left open the matter of explaining *how* and *why* it was still possible to discuss 'the capitalist state' as a coherent and unified entity. What criteria enabled us to speak of the unity of the state and its capitalist character, such that it was neither reducible to direct control by a single class nor reified into a transhistorical or metaphysical entity?

Poulantzas' innovation in the face of this dilemma was to advance a conception of the capitalist type of state as a material condensation of social/class forces—one that acted as the privileged terrain for the formation and consolidation of capitalist class hegemony. Initially, Poulantzas expressed this view via his theory of the relative autonomy of the state, as found in *PPSC*. In this framework, the state's relative autonomy from the dominant classes and fractions was a structural feature stemming from the distinctive separation taken by the political and the economic levels in the capitalist mode of production. As the instance tasked with maintaining the cohesion of the different levels of the capitalist mode of production, the capitalist state had a structural unity that allowed it a degree of independence from the immediate interests of any particular class or faction. More concretely, the capitalist state was the nexus on which the competing interests of different fractions of the bourgeoisie could be organised, mediated, and reconciled under the hegemony of a dominant power bloc (including through political parties). Just as it consolidated the political power of the dominant classes, the state also disorganised the working classes, through mechanisms both ideological (e.g., educational institutions, the legal system) and repressive (e.g., the army, the police, prisons, and other carceral institutions).

Following *PPSC*, as his arguments became less marked by structuralist terminology, Poulantzas placed greater emphasis on the capitalist state understood as a material, social relation that was affected by class struggles. Jessop suggests that Poulantzas' previous reliance on the notion of relative autonomy would later present a theoretical problem, as it was difficult to reconcile with the contingency implied by the class struggle approach.[25] From this

---

[22]   Poulantzas, 'The Capitalist State: A Reply to Miliband and Laclau', 281.
[23]   Poulantzas, *PPSC*, 270.
[24]   Poulantzas, 'The Capitalist State: A Reply to Miliband and Laclau', 283.
[25]   Jessop, *Nicos Poulantzas*, 98–102.

he concludes that the residue of the relative autonomy argument undercut the real insight of Poulantzas' subsequent, relational approach to the state. Conversely, Barrow has argued for greater continuity in Poulantzas' thought, pointing to the role he assigned to class practices even in his more overtly 'structuralist' phase and his differences with Althusser and Balibar.[26] While it is true that relative autonomy is less emphasised in *SPS*, this can partly be explained by changing social and political contexts. After 1968 the effectiveness of the capitalist state in the reproduction of hegemony came into question. This new reality required an explanation not only of the state's role in creating political stability and social reproduction, but also how its failure to do so under certain conditions gave rise to political crises.

Despite this change of emphasis from a regional account of the state to the state understood as a relational, strategic field, what remained consistent in Poulantzas was a rejection of earlier Marxist problematics. He consistently adhered to a view of the capitalist state whose task was the organisation (and disorganisation) of social classes, and whose unity was the product of an ongoing interaction between structures and practices.[27] If, in its attempt to fill the textual lacunae in Marx's writings on the state, the Marxist tradition had come to alternate between treating the state as either a superstructural derivative of ruling class interests or as a neutral institutional apparatus, then Poulantzas' theoretical intervention can be seen as a materialist dialectical *inversion* or *displacement* of this dichotomy.

THE MATERIALITY OF THE STATE

Despite their differences, the Leninist and social-democratic views both tended to see the state in a relation of externality to the class struggle, in which 'either the dominant classes submit the state (thing) to itself by a game of "influences" and "pressure groups" or the state (subject) submits the dominant class to itself'.[28] Instead, Poulantzas suggested that the capitalist state was always already at work in forging and reproducing class power, because state institutions were the crucial sites where hegemony was constructed and consolidated. Classes did not first constitute themselves 'outside' the state (e.g., in the workplace, civil society, or the domestic sphere), and only subsequently 'encounter' the state. Rather, the capitalist state was itself the fusion of social/class forces, both acting upon and being affected by them. It was not merely that class contradictions and struggles traversed the previously-constituted terrain of the state, but that 'class contradictions are the very stuff of the State: they are present in its material framework and pattern its organisation; while the State's policy is the result of their functioning within the State'.[29]

Poulantzas thus sought to develop a conception of the *interiority* and *immanence* of power relations between class and state. As he wrote:

the political field of the State (as well as the sphere of ideology) has always, in different forms, been present in the constitution and reproduction of the relations of production ... The position of the State

---

[26]   Barrow, *Toward a Critical Theory of States*, ch 2.

[27]   For a self-clarification of Poulantzas' occasionally abstruse discussion of structures and practices, see Poulantzas, 'The Capitalist State: A Reply to Miliband and Laclau', 292.

[28]   Nicos Poulantzas, 'The Political Crisis and the Crisis of the State' [1976] in James Martin (ed), *The Poulantzas Reader: Marxism, Law and the State* (Verso 2008) 294, 308.

[29]   Poulantzas, *SPS*, 132.

vis-à-vis the economy is never anything but the modality of the State's presence in the constitution and reproduction of the relations of production.[30]

The implication of this argument was monumental: the traditional Marxist problematic of base and superstructure, with all of the theoretical dilemmas it raised, needed to be put to rest, in favour of a model in which the economic, political, and ideological levels were fused into a unity.[31]

How are class forces present in this material framework of the state? The state is fundamentally a relation, like capital. More specifically, it is a 'material condensation (apparatus) of a relation of force between classes and fractions of classes as they are expressed in a specific manner (the relative separation of the state and the economy giving way to the very institutions of the capitalist state) at the very heart of the state'.[32] In *SPS* Poulantzas identified four key aspects of the state's institutional materiality: the division between manual and intellectual labour; the individualisation and regimentation of the social body; law and state-sanctioned violence; and the ideology of the nation, with its particular temporality and spatiality. These are material practices, stemming from the relations of production and the social division of labour, through which the capitalist state perpetuates itself. Together, they contribute to the capitalist state being a:

> specialized and centralized apparatus of a peculiarly political nature, comprising an assemblage of impersonal, anonymous functions whose form is distinct from that of economic power; their ordering rests on the axiomatic force of laws-rules distributing the spheres of activity or competence, and on a legitimacy derived from the people-nation.[33]

Poulantzas' stress on the interiority of the state and class distinguishes his account from neo-Weberian institutionalist frameworks that sought to identify the scope of state autonomy from society, largely by investigating its bureaucratic capacity and ability to resist capture by any particular class.[34] These accounts have tended to define the state not as a relation but as a set of concrete institutions, thereby returning to a conception of class-state (or society-state) exteriority.[35] While state apparatuses are indeed 'material condensations of relations', they are material only insofar as they are crystallised expressions of the dynamics of class struggles.[36] As Demirović puts it, 'the state is a space determined by the class struggle, in which the power relations among the classes materialize and become sedimented, thus also determining the class struggles of the future'.[37]

---

[30] Poulantzas, *SPS*, 17.

[31] Albert Bergesen, 'The Rise of Semiotic Marxism' (1993) 36 *Sociological Perspectives* 1.

[32] Poulantzas, 'The Political Crisis and the Crisis of the State', 307–8.

[33] Poulantzas, *SPS*, 54.

[34] Theda Skocpol, *States and Social Revolutions: A Comparative Analysis of France, Russia and China* (CUP 1979); Theda Skocpol, 'Political Response to Capitalist Crisis: Neo-Marxist Theories of the State and the Case of the New Deal' (1980) 10 *Politics & Society* 155.

[35] Rafael Khachaturian, 'Bringing What State Back In? Neo-Marxism and the Origin of the Committee on States and Social Structures' (2019) 72 *Political Research Quarterly* 714.

[36] Nicos Poulantzas, 'Interview with Nicos Poulantzas' [1979] in James Martin (ed), *The Poulantzas Reader: Marxism, Law and the State* (Verso 2008) 387, 397.

[37] Alex Demirović, 'The Capitalist State, Hegemony, and the Democratic Transformation Toward Socialism', in Jean-Numa Ducange and Razmig Keucheyan (eds), *The End of the Democratic State: Nicos Poulantzas, a Marxism for the 21st Century* (Palgrave Macmillan 2019) 43, 56.

Here we can note a main point of contention in Poulantzas' debate with Miliband about the distinction between state power and state apparatuses. Miliband had famously argued that Poulantzas' 'structural superdeterminism' reduced the state to class power, thereby undercutting the very concept of state autonomy that Poulantzas had tried to establish in *PPSC*.[38] Yet Miliband's criticism was largely misguided, for while the state was the locus of class practices, its makeup eluded any direct determination by a particular class or fraction. As Poulantzas later clarified, 'state apparatuses do not possess a "power" of their own, but materialise and concentrate class relations ... The state is not an "entity" with an intrinsic instrumental essence, but it is itself a relation, more precisely a condensation of a class relation'.[39] Later, he suggested that the state exhibits a 'peculiar material framework' where the phenomenon of state power could not be reduced to the state apparatus; rather, 'political domination is itself inscribed in the institutional materiality of the State'.[40]

Class struggles thus adapted themselves to 'the materiality of the various state apparatuses, only becoming crystallised in the State in a refracted form that varies according to the apparatus'.[41] The administration of the capitalist state is organised at 'nodes and focuses of real power located at strategic points of the various state branches and apparatuses', including the executive, the parliament, army, judiciary, ministries, regional and municipal administrations, and the ideological institutions.[42] Together, they act as multiple points from which the various fractions of the dominant classes organised their interests into a hegemonic power bloc. Since it is a tenuous unity of contradictory processes, the capitalist state's various apparatuses are constantly engaged in a process of 'structural selectivity', making decisions and non-decisions, determining their own priorities, and processing and interpreting the information gathered by the other apparatuses.[43]

These functions also require the existence of state personnel (politicians, bureaucrats, judges, military and police personnel, etc.), individuals who are members of a specific social category, the state bureaucracy, that links them across their class positions. By virtue of the organisational framework of the capitalist state, these state apparatuses have a relative autonomy from the economically dominant classes. At the same time, their personnel may be divided both 'vertically' (as upper and lower echelon civil servants), and 'horizontally' (through rivalries between the different organisations and apparatuses making up the state). The capitalist state's various organs and branches (ministries and government offices, executive and parliament, central administration and local and regional authorities, army, judiciary, etc.) thus reveal 'major contradictions among themselves, each of them frequently constituting the seat and the representative—in short, the crystallization—of this or that fraction of the

---

[38]   Ralph Miliband, 'The Capitalist State: Reply to Nicos Poulantzas' (1970) 59 *New Left Review* 63.

[39]   Poulantzas, *CCC*, 26.

[40]   Poulantzas, *SPS*, 14.

[41]   Poulantzas, *SPS*, 131.

[42]   Poulantzas, *SPS*, 139.

[43]   Poulantzas, 'The Political Crisis and the Crisis of the State', 309. Poulantzas borrowed the concept of 'structural selectivity' from Claus Offe, 'Structural Problems of the Capitalist State: Class Rule and the Political System. On the Selectiveness of Political Institutions' in Klaus von Beyme (ed), *German Political Studies*, vol 1 (SAGE 1974) 31. However, as Jessop suggests, his own approach to the term is better understood as strategic selectivity; see Bob Jessop, 'The Strategic Selectivity of the State: Reflections on a Theme of Poulantzas' (1999) 25 *Journal of the Hellenic Diaspora* 1.

power bloc, this or that specific and competing interest'.[44] Put differently, state institutions take on a materiality as they mediate and channel the dynamics of the class struggle, from the micro-processes of subject-formation all the way to the macro-processes of national economic management and engagement with other states in the transnational sphere.

Developing this account of the materiality of the state allowed Poulantzas to avoid the dichotomy of treating the capitalist state as either a monolithic bloc in the hands of monopoly capital, or a neutral apparatus that pursues policies of functional integration which reproduce capitalist class rule. It is important to note the element of contingency in Poulantzas' framework, for he understood class conflict as a material but decisively non-teleological dynamic. Readings of Poulantzas as a functionalist have suggested that the relative autonomy of the capitalist state consistently enables it to effectively co-ordinate the long-term hegemony of the power bloc.[45] However, the fact that its materiality is derived from a relation of class forces makes any such 'state project' uneven and uncertain, although its strategic selectivity still favours the capitalist class. Poulantzas does not simply derive the operations of the state from what is predetermined as necessary for the reproduction of the capitalist mode of production.[46] Instead, he focuses on the materiality of capitalist states in their concrete, historical form, which are not fixed in advance but depend on social struggles. In his words, 'the relation of the masses to power and the State—in what is termed among other things a *consensus*—*always possesses a material substratum* ... the State acts within an unstable equilibrium of compromises between the dominant classes and the dominated'.[47] Correspondingly, the notion of hegemonic crisis plays a more pronounced role in his later writings.[48] Both the constitutive makeup of the state and the policies that it produces are susceptible to shifts, interventions, and transformations, albeit their specific nature will vary depending on the conjuncture.

Here we return to the question of the state's unity and capitalist character. If Poulantzas' earlier works were criticised for their 'structural superdeterminism' and 'structural abstractionism',[49] a directly opposite criticism was made of the 'class struggle' approach found in *CCC* and *SPS*. This line of criticism asked whether, by making room for class struggle, Poulantzas had not undermined his own claims about the necessarily capitalist character of the state.[50] However, as Demirović observes, while the state does express a relationship of forces, it is not merely 'the momentary result of the conflict between various groups' different interests'.[51] This neo-pluralist approach misses important elements of the state's institutional permanence, including the persistence of its apparatuses and their role in organising and disorganising particular class fractions. This role of disorganisation, which remained consistent across

    44   Poulantzas, 'The Capitalist State: A Reply to Miliband and Laclau', 284.
    45   Simon Clarke, 'Marxism, Sociology, and Poulantzas' Theory of the State' (1977) 1 *Capital & Class* 1; Skocpol, 'Political Response to Capitalist Crisis'.
    46   Lars Bretthauer, 'Materiality and Condensation in the Work of Nicos Poulantzas' in Alexander Gallas et al (eds), *Reading Poulantzas* (Merlin Press 2011) 72, 74.
    47   Poulantzas, *SPS*, 30–31 (original emphasis).
    48   Jessop, *Nicos Poulantzas*, 84.
    49   Miliband, 'The Capitalist State: Reply to Nicos Poulantzas'; Ralph Miliband, 'Poulantzas and the Capitalist State' (1973) 1 *New Left Review* 83.
    50   Axel van den Berg, *The Immanent Utopia: From Marxism on the State to the State of Marxism* (Princeton University Press 1988); Kenneth Finegold and Theda Skocpol, *State and Party in America's New Deal* (University of Wisconsin Press 1995).
    51   Demirović, 'The Capitalist State', 56.

Poulantzas' writings, was accomplished not only through the state's material apparatuses but also through the social relations articulated in its juridical structures, to which I now turn.

LAW AND THE CAPITALIST STATE

Poulantzas understood law (the state's juridico-political structures) as a central element in the organisation of hegemony and as a technique for the creation of cohesion and consensus, both within the power bloc and between the power bloc and the dominated classes.[52] This argument was already being developed in his earliest work but acquired a more elaborate, and persuasive, form in *PPSC*.[53] The dual function of the capitalist state in relation to class struggles was 'to disorganize the dominated classes politically, and at the same time to organize the dominant classes politically'. By virtue of its juridical and ideological structures, the capitalist state concealed from its subjects their socio-economic relations as agents participating in a socialised form of production. Through this 'effect of isolation', individuals experienced these relations as a 'specific fragmentation and atomization'.[54]

This atomisation is not merely an ideological mystification at the individual level. It is perpetuated through concrete state institutions and mass material practices of a political and juridical nature, including parliamentary representation and universal suffrage. Through these practices, as well as pronouncements of popular sovereignty and the collective will, the state-nation came to represent a collective unity. The state's political legitimation through popular sovereignty created a collective subject—the people—as an 'empirical, abstract mass of individuals-citizens whose mode of participation in a national political community as expressed by the state is manifest in universal suffrage'.[55] To subjects constituted in this manner, the capitalist state then appears as a political unity representing the general interest, complete with the universal values of formal abstract liberty and equality, as the 'incarnation of the popular will of the people/nation'.[56] These universals are codified in a juridical system of state apparatuses, whose objective function is to preserve and maintain the fragmentation of civil society, and to organise its operation within the exchange-based capitalist mode of production.[57]

However, by *SPS*, Poulantzas' treatment of the juridico-political level as one of working-class atomisation and disorganisation gave way to a qualified support for elements of the modern *Rechtsstaat*. On the one hand, the repressive and productive capacities of the law were now seen as a 'constitutive element of the politico-social field'.[58] In the capitalist mode of production, law replaces religion as the dominant discourse for the reproduction of ideology. In the context of the capitalist state, 'abstract, formal, universal law is the truth of

---

[52] Sonja Buckel, 'The Juridical Condensation of Relations of Force: Nicos Poulantzas on Law' in Alexander Gallas et al (eds), *Reading Poulantzas* (Merlin Press 2011) 154.

[53] Poulantzas, *PPSC*, 189. See further Bob Jessop's chapter in this volume.

[54] Poulantzas, *PPSC*, 189.

[55] Nicos Poulantzas, 'Preliminaries to the Study of Hegemony in the State' [1965] in James Martin (ed), *The Poulantzas Reader: Marxism, Law and the State* (Verso 2008) 74, 85.

[56] Poulantzas, *PPSC*, 133.

[57] Poulantzas, 'Preliminaries to the Study of Hegemony in the State', 83–85. See also Bob Jessop's chapter in this volume on the echoes of this juridical theory of the state in Hans Kelsen.

[58] Poulantzas, *SPS*, 83.

subjects: it is knowledge (in the service of capital) which constitutes juridical-political subjects and which establishes the difference between private and public'.[59] The productive processes of capitalism in its monopoly phase, and the corresponding social division of labour, require the law to individualise agents, once again constituting them as juridico-political subjects and re-aggregating them within the fictitious unity of the people-nation-state.

However, Poulantzas also modified this account of atomisation by noting that in certain cases the abstract and general norms of the law allowed it to act as a mechanism through which the exercise of state power could be regulated, if highly imperfectly. Since the capitalist state was the condensation of social forces and articulated the form taken by class struggles, the 'material concessions imposed on the dominant classes by popular struggle' also became inscribed within the juridical domain.[60] The 'formal' and 'abstract' liberties of the *Rechtsstaat* were also historical victories of the popular masses. Treating the institutions of representative democracy and civil rights as the historic gains of the oppressed classes, Poulantzas argued that these concessions were the means by which popular struggles and resistances were inscribed into the materiality of the capitalist state. While he acknowledged that there remained a constant gap between their codification and their application in practice, he nevertheless insisted that the rights of the dominated classes were real, insofar as they were embedded as practices within the material structures of the state itself.

Because of these gains, Poulantzas suggested that modern law could 'set the limits of the exercise of power and of intervention by the state apparatuses'.[61] Rather than seeking to politicise all existing social relations as a mode of revolutionary strategy, Poulantzas came to speak of the limits to the 'politics of politicization', in part because such politicisation was likely to take the form of the modern state's impingement on the sphere of individuality.[62] As evidenced by his discussion of 'authoritarian statism' as the new tendency of the capitalist state, Poulantzas' views about the political and strategic importance of juridical personhood, including civil freedoms and political rights, and as a space to be defended from state encroachment, eventually came to play a larger role in his thought.

IMPLICATIONS FOR POLITICAL STRATEGY

Poulantzas' theoretical shift in conceptualising the state not as a thing or subject but as a relation had strategic implications. If the 'normal' (non-exceptional) capitalist state was not an instrument in the hands of any specific fraction of the bourgeoisie, but was nevertheless structured in such a way as to give them an institutional advantage, what opportunities for intervention would the popular classes have? In *PPSC* the atomising effects of the capitalist state and its relative autonomy were largely seen as excluding the possibility of a struggle on the terrain of the state. That conception of the state as an institutionally fragmented but func-

[59]   Poulantzas, *SPS*, 89.
[60]   Poulantzas, *SPS*, 84.
[61]   Poulantzas, *SPS*, 92.
[62]   Nicos Poulantzas, 'The Loss of Nicos Poulantzas: The Elusive Answer' *Legal Form* (7 December 2017), https://legalform.blog/2017/12/07/the-loss-of-nicos-poulantzas-the-elusive-answer-a-translation-by-rafael-khachaturian/ accessed 7 April 2021.

tionally unified entity implied that only an intervention by a revolutionary party could act as a counterweight to the state's advantages in the organisation of hegemony.

However, as suggested by Poulantzas' changing account of juridical subjectification and ideology, the importance of the state's materiality as an absorber of popular struggles became strategically more pronounced in *CD* and *SPS*. Although Poulantzas initially began to think of the state as a condensation or relation of forces in *CCC,* a major impetus for the shift in his thinking on the strategic view of the state can be attributed both to the crisis of the Leninist party model and the transitions from military dictatorship to constitutional democracy in Portugal, Spain, and Greece.[63] Rather than being internally coherent entities positioned 'above' civil society, these regimes were riven by social contradictions. The enlistment of the popular classes and the petty bourgeoisie into the lower ranks of the military created internal contradictions at the core of the state apparatus between the lower/intermediate and top ranks of the military.[64] Lacking mass parties that could link the competing fractions of the bourgeoisie into a common hegemonic project (as was the case with fascism), and having to rely directly on the military cadres and loyal bureaucrats to implement state policies, these regimes' state apparatuses were toppled by an alliance of the popular classes and the national bourgeoisie. While popular struggles were not the direct or principal factors in the overthrow of the southern European dictatorships, they were the determining ones.[65] Such popular interventions, therefore, could have second-order effects on the state apparatuses and on the balance of power within them.

The balance of class forces that constituted the state were not expressed directly in the state, but at a certain distance, mediated and channelled by its many institutions. Nevertheless, because the state was both constituted and divided by class contradictions, it could never be 'a monolithic bloc without cracks, whose policy is established, as it were, in spite of its own contradictions'.[66] State institutions are not static nuclei of coercive and ideological power, upon which externally formed and reproduced classes then act. Precisely because the state is a condensation of the balance of forces, it reproduces within itself these class contradictions and social struggles, which permeate and run through the state apparatuses as fissures within the power bloc. Inscribed in the state in this manner, contending social forces and interests could create cleavages and contradictions within state institutions leading to political crises. As Poulantzas noted, 'the shift in the relationship of forces within the State touches its apparatuses and mechanisms as a whole … Any struggle at a distance always has effects within the State: it is always there, even if only in a refracted manner and through intermediaries'.[67]

The southern European transitions illustrated Poulantzas' argument that pitting social classes against the state in a relationship of externality led to seeing the state either as a subject or a thing, either the 'embodiment of the general will in the face of atomized individuals', or a machine 'that can be manipulated at will by the dominant classes, and whose relationship of representation with their class interests is supposedly due to their "grip" on this inert instrument'.[68] Maintaining that the capitalist state was a condensation of class struggles, in contrast

---

[63]   Poulantzas, 'Interview with Nicos Poulantzas', 394.
[64]   Poulantzas, *CD*, 85.
[65]   Poulantzas, *CD*, 78.
[66]   Poulantzas, *SPS*, 132.
[67]   Poulantzas, *SPS*, 259.
[68]   Poulantzas, *CD*, 81.

to Hans Kelsen's formal-juridical account of the state's uniformity, Poulantzas argued that we should 'discard once and for all the view of the State as a completely united mechanism, founded on a homogeneous and hierarchical distribution of the centres of power moving from top to bottom of a uniform ladder or pyramid'.[69] The latter was a strategic oversight that foreclosed the ability to read the state's internal contradictions, and specifically the class contradictions that cut through the state, which are 'expressed, in a specific way, as internal contradictions within the state, which never is and can never be a monolithic bloc devoid of fissures'.[70]

Rejecting the Leninist view of the state as a repressive monolith also meant rejecting its corresponding political strategy: the concentration of a parallel, dual power in the soviets in preparation for a 'frontal' assault on the capitalist state. As a member of the KKE Interior (the breakaway, Eurocommunist part of the Communist Party of Greece) and a supporter of the 'Common Programme' between the French Communist Party and the Socialist Party during the late 1970s, Poulantzas sided with the PCF's decision to formally abandon the notion of the dictatorship of the proletariat. He saw the latter as an impediment to the process of making successful alliances across various classes and class fractions at the base of the party. While the 'social democratisation' of labour parties in Western capitalist democracies turned them into custodians of the state, the Leninist call for soviet democracy, absent the existence and balance of representative democratic institutions, would soon consolidate into a 'dictatorship of the party' and a conflation of party and state rather than any genuine dictatorship of the proletariat.

With regard to the popular classes, the view of the state as a social relation required a strategy where the purpose was 'to modify the balance of power [*le rapport de force*] within the state, and furthermore, radically modify the materiality of the state'.[71] In very general terms, this required a tactical combination of organised, electoral participation by a unified left on the terrain of the state, and—equally importantly—popular struggles outside the state apparatuses via new structures of direct democracy at the base exerting continuous pressure on existing state institutions.[72] Such an approach could make possible a novel articulation of representative democracy on the level of the state with direct democratic struggle originating outside the state. Struggles that by all accounts appeared 'external' to the state could actually reverberate within it by exacerbating its existing internal contradictions—not only through class-based appeals, but also through the development of hegemonic projects relying on invocations of democracy and 'the people'. Here too we can note the shift in the conception of popular sovereignty, from that of atomised juridical subjects aggregated and represented by the legal institutions of the state, to the prominent role played by the 'popular classes' and cross-class alliances in the undercutting of the authoritarian state. The materiality of the capitalist state enabled the advancement of collective rights claims not only by the working classes, but also by the post-1968 'new social movements' advocating such previously 'secondary' concerns as feminism and environmentalism. Together, these popular alliances, which linked the working classes to the growing strata of white collar workers and the downwardly mobile fractions of

---

[69]   Poulantzas, *SPS*, 133.

[70]   Poulantzas, *CD*, 82.

[71]   Poulantzas, 'The Loss of Nicos Poulantzas: The Elusive Answer'.

[72]   Nicos Poulantzas, 'The State and the Transition to Socialism' [1977] in James Martin (ed), *The Poulantzas Reader: Marxism, Law and the State* (Verso 2008) 334, 338.

the petty bourgeoisie, would displace the traditional understandings of the proletariat and the party form as the privileged subjects of the struggle.

Because of this position, Poulantzas has often been associated with left Eurocommunism. *SPS* was praised by one author at the time as perhaps the most theoretically sophisticated document of Eurocommunist political strategy.[73] However, for critics such as Ellen Meiksins Wood, Poulantzas was the bridge between the Marxist tradition of class analysis and the identity-based new social movements that had begun to emerge in the 1970s.[74] Similarly, in his dialogue with Poulantzas, Henri Weber had suggested that by having rejected Lenin's theory of the state as a repressive apparatus, he had arrived at electoral reformism.[75]

Indeed, during this period, Poulantzas suggested that representative democratic institutions, 'formal' rights and liberties, and a plurality of political parties would remain key elements of a successful transition to socialism. However, he differed from other Eurocommunist theoreticians such as Santiago Carrillo and Pietro Ingrao on the question of the seizure of state power. Identifying fissures within the state did not mean that the popular classes could seize the state in a piecemeal manner as part of an extended transition to socialism. The capitalist state was a strategic terrain on which social relations could be modified. But it nevertheless remained a relation of material forces premised on the social division of labour, the concentration of repressive power, and juridical subject-formation. All of this skewed the state's terrain in favour of the dominant class. The presence of a plurality of parties inherently swung the balance of power in favour of the status quo and risked the stagnation of the movement into parliamentary reformism unless it was buttressed by institutions of self-management and rank-and-file democracy at the base. Even more dangerously, since power was distributed through numerous nodes across the different state apparatuses, a left government gaining control of some parts of the state apparatus also enabled other apparatuses to become privileged sites of resistance by the power bloc.[76] As the Chilean example tragically illustrated, the repressive apparatuses often remained the privileged site of the state's relative autonomy, staying mostly insulated and resistant to popular pressures.[77] Poulantzas had also diagnosed a new set of tendencies emerging in the period of capitalist crisis during the 1970s. This new modality of the capitalist state, which he called authoritarian statism, featured 'intensified state control over every sphere of socio-economic life combined with radical decline of the institutions of political democracy and with draconian and multiform curtailment of so-called "formal" liberties'.[78] Authoritarian statism was characterised by the establishing of new power techniques, practices, and channels to create 'a new materiality of the social body upon which power is exercised'.[79] Among these were the shift of power from parties and the parliament to the executive and administration; the emergence of parallel administrative, coercive, and surveillance networks not susceptible to legislative oversight; the decline of the rule of law and curtailment of civil and political liberties; and the insulation of the state apparatuses from

---

[73]   George Ross, 'Nicos Poulantzas, Eurocommunism, and the Debate on the Theory of the Capitalist State' (1979) 9 *Socialist Review* 143.

[74]   Ellen Meiksins Wood, *The Retreat from Class: A New 'True' Socialism* (first published 1986, Verso 1998).

[75]   Poulantzas, 'The State and the Transition to Socialism'.

[76]   Poulantzas, *SPS*, 138–39.

[77]   See Poulantzas, *CD*, 156–57.

[78]   Poulantzas, *SPS*, 203–4.

[79]   Poulantzas, *SPS*, 238.

political interventions by the popular masses. Yet this was also the form of state on whose terrain the struggle for democratic socialism would have to occur. Contradictions between fractions of the bourgeoisie could reverberate within the authoritarian state, politicising layers of the middle and lower ranks of the administration, and leading to a legitimation crisis on which broader interventions by the popular classes could occur.

Equally rejecting social-democratic reformism, dual power, and the piecemeal 'occupation' of state institutions, Poulantzas stressed that a transition to democratic socialism would be brought about by a '*stage of real breaks*, the climax of which—and there has to be one—is reached when the relationship of forces on the strategic terrain of the State swings over to the side of the popular masses'.[80] Culminating in this ruptural transition characterised by a crisis of the capitalist state, the balance of forces would ostensibly give way to a new form of political organisation, based on the already existing mechanisms of direct workers' democracy. Critics of Poulantzas as a Eurocommunist reformist have thus ignored his insistence that the democratic transition to socialism still required a 'moment of rupture ... a profound crisis of the state, with a shift in the balance of forces inside the state itself'.[81]

There were clear risks involved in this strategy of strategic escalation, in expanding and deepening the insufficient formal-representative democracy found in capitalist states. However, Poulantzas maintained that a more militant strategy would doom a movement to failure, for no capitalist state, not even one undergoing a crisis such as Portugal in 1974, would allow the establishment of a true dual power situation without resorting to an armed intervention. Prematurely rushing into such a ruptural break, including by dismantling the state's economic apparatus at the first opportunity, would only paralyse the state and mobilise the bourgeoisie in opposition.[82] The best chance for success remained in a left parliamentary coalition, such as the *Programme commun* of French socialists and communists in the early 1970s, supplemented by widespread social mobilisation and popular democratic initiatives, which would act as an extra-parliamentary catalyst to prevent social-democratic stagnation.[83]

TOWARD A DEMOCRATIC STATE?

I have argued that Poulantzas' approach to the capitalist state as a material condensation of social forces was a key intervention within Marxist discussions of the state, with important theoretical and practical consequences. I wish to conclude by suggesting that Poulantzas' insights about the materiality of the state allow us to pose a speculative and open-ended question—one concerning the controversial notion of the withering away of the state, but also extending beyond it to the issue of democracy as a political form.

Interspersed in Poulantzas' writings are references to a number of different state forms, corresponding to distinct phases of capitalism. Thus, alongside authoritarian statism, there are accounts of absolutist, liberal, monopoly capitalist, fascist, Bonapartist, and totalitarian states, among others. However, there is no discussion of the democratic state, such as that may emerge during or after the transition to democratic socialism. Here the notion of a democratic

---

[80]   Poulantzas, *SPS*, 258–59 (original emphasis).
[81]   Poulantzas, 'Interview with Nicos Poulantzas', 391.
[82]   Poulantzas, *SPS*, 198.
[83]   Poulantzas, 'The State and the Transition to Socialism', 359.

socialist state is conspicuously absent, being at most a latent theoretical and historical *possibility* rather than a necessity or guarantee.

What institutional forms could we expect social relations under a democratic state to take? Here neither the examples of the Paris Commune nor the Soviet Union clearly suffice. Even Gramsci, the intellectual inspiration of Eurocommunism, was said by Poulantzas to lack 'a positive theory of the exercise of power, of the institutions of representative democracy in the transition to democratic socialism', in part because of his disinterest in the plurality of parties and the *Rechtsstaat*.[84] We have seen that by the end of his life, Poulantzas came to suggest that a successful transition to democratic socialism could only entail a combination of parliamentary-representative and direct democratic institutions, along with a plurality of parties and autonomous social movements and forms of contestation that extended beyond the traditional concerns of the organised labour movement. Alongside these conditions, we could expect a democratic state to retain a constitution combining socialist, republican, and liberal elements (as did the new Portuguese constitution adopted in 1976), and also to oversee the radical democratisation and transformation of the previous state's repressive and ideological apparatuses.

Yet the notion of the democratic state is not exhausted by these cursory institutional elements. Approaching the state as a material condensation of social forces means that any post-transitional democratic state would exist as a concrete and specific articulation of social and political struggles. It would be a political formation within which a variety of contestatory social movements could seek to challenge and modify existing social structures and the balance of social forces as expressed through state institutions, particularly if advanced in the name of greater universality and inclusion. In different ways, theorists like Étienne Balibar and Chantal Mouffe have built on Poulantzas' contributions to present accounts of democracy as an ongoing project. For Balibar, who eventually came to adopt Poulantzas' view of the state, these struggles would be expressions of a popular demand for the democratisation of democracy—a dynamic between constituent and constituted power animated by what he terms 'equaliberty'.[85] In turn, Mouffe has recently suggested that the state is a 'crystallization of the relations of forces and a terrain of struggle', upon which discourses of liberty and equality are articulated in different ways.[86]

Crucial to both cases is an expanded field of struggles that traverse state institutions, and in which the language of citizenship and the paradoxes of inclusion and exclusion from the *demos* are among the principal ways in which the state's materiality is organised. Viewed through this lens, the democratic state would not be an alienated, parasitic body superimposed upon civil society, but a material constitution immanent to the balance of forces and popular struggles within a social formation.[87] We may thus suggest that a consequence of Poulantzas'

---

[84] Poulantzas, 'The Loss of Nicos Poulantzas'.

[85] Étienne Balibar, 'Communism and Citizenship: On Nicos Poulantzas' in Étienne Balibar, *Equaliberty* (first published 2010, James Ingram tr, Duke University Press 2014) 145; Étienne Balibar, *Citizenship* (Polity Press 2015).

[86] Chantal Mouffe, *For a Left Populism* (Verso 2018) 46. For a critical discussion, see Rafael Khachaturian, review of *For a Left Populism* (2021) 1 *Philosophy and Global Affairs* 168.

[87] See Rob Hunter, 'Constitutionalism: Appearance, Form, and Content' *Legal Form* (3 December 2017), https://legalform.blog/2017/12/03/constitutionalism-appearance-form-and-content-rob-hunter/ accessed 7 April 2021; Rob Hunter, 'Elaborating the Material Constitution: A Response to Marco Goldoni' *Legal Form* (30 June 2018), https://legalform.blog/2018/06/30/elabourating-the-material

intervention is the displacement of the traditional Marxist problematic of the abolition or transcendence of the state with a different problematic: that of the state's ongoing and perpetual democratisation.[88]

While a unified Marxist theory of the state is likely impossible, largely because of the internal diversity of Marxist approaches, Poulantzas' contribution to a rethinking of the Marxist tradition in the postwar period is significant.[89] It is ironic that his theoretical breakthrough came on the threshold of the irreversible decline of communist regimes. Nevertheless, his work opened a path toward a rethinking of the state, law, and politics. Writing from the vantage point of the 1970s, Poulantzas was preoccupied with the transformation of the capitalist state during that decade's accumulation and legitimation crises, and the political possibilities that these opened. His conception of the state as a social relation was an innovation that identified the dilemmas reached by then-existing approaches, and provided the lasting elements of a research agenda for studying the nature and functions of the capitalist state and its relationship to social struggles. Today, Poulantzas' insights remain crucial from the perspective of political strategy and democratic agency, capturing how an abstract—yet nevertheless material—entity like the state can be engaged, challenged, and potentially transformed.

-constitution-a-response-to-marco-goldoni-rob-hunter/ accessed 7 April 2021; Marco Goldoni, 'Introduction to the Material Constitution: Traditions and Constitutive Elements' *Legal Form* (9 February 2018), https://legalform.blog/2018/02/09/introduction-to-the-material-constitution-traditions -and-constitutive-elements-marco-goldoni/ accessed 7 April 2021.

[88]   In at least one place Poulantzas (*SPS*, 262) suggests that the articulation of struggles to transform the state with struggles for direct democracy opens up a 'global perspective of the withering away of the State'. Yet he does not elaborate on this idea, in part because his theory rests on a rather different problematic concerning the state's emergence, function, and transformation.

[89]   Clyde W Barrow, 'The Marx Problem in Marxian State Theory' (2000) 64 *Science & Society* 87.

PART II

CONTEMPORARY MARXIST ANALYSIS OF LAW, RIGHTS, AND THE STATE

12. Marx's critique and the constitution of the capitalist state

Rob Hunter

INTRODUCTION

Constitutionalism is a globally distributed practice of depoliticisation that appears as the regulation of governance and the structuration of formal political and legal institutions. Constitutional law institutionalises the depoliticisation of the capitalist state, typically by restricting the legislative pursuit of legal or institutional change.[1] It thereby secures the conditions for capital accumulation against the politicisation of capitalism's inverted and antagonistic social relations. The constitutional state is both conditioned by, and a form of, class struggle and social antagonism.[2] It is bound up with the reproduction of 'the notional separation of political and economic power'[3] (or the 'bifurcation of the political'[4]), in which social relations of production and exchange are depoliticised[5]—while, simultaneously, a set of formal institutions and practices centred on the state are regarded as comprising the full scope

---

[1] Constitutionalism erects and patrols the 'boundaries of "politics" and the law'. Simon Clarke, 'The State Debate' in Simon Clarke (ed), *The State Debate* (Macmillan 1991) 1, 33. Often, the most consequential kind of constitutional constraint is that of constitutional courts exercising powers to review the constitutionality of legislation. On constitutional review see Michel Troper, 'The Logic of Justification of Judicial Review' (2003) 1 *International Journal of Constitutional Law* 99; Víctor Ferreres Comella, 'The Rise of Specialized Constitutional Courts' in Tom Ginsburg and Rosalind Dixon (eds), *Comparative Constitutional Law* (Edward Elgar 2011) 265; Tom Ginsburg and Mila Versteeg, 'Why Do Countries Adopt Constitutional Review?' (2014) 30 *The Journal of Law, Economics, & Organization* 587; Conrado Hübner Mendes, *Constitutional Courts and Deliberative Democracy* (OUP 2014).

[2] On the capitalist state as the political form of capitalist social relations, see Simon Clarke, 'State, Class Struggle, and the Reproduction of Capital' in Simon Clarke (ed), *The State Debate* (Macmillan 1991) 183. For additional perspectives, see Werner Bonefeld, 'Social Constitution and the Form of the Capitalist State' in Werner Bonefeld, Richard Gunn, and Kosmas Psychopedis (eds), *Open Marxism 1: Dialectics and History* (Pluto Press 1992) 93; Soichiro Sumida, 'Die Zusammenfassung der bürgerlichen Gesellschaft in der Staatsform' (2018) 2017 *Marx-Engels Jahrbuch* 41; Alex Demirović, 'The Capitalist State, Hegemony, and the Democratic Transformation Toward Socialism' in Jean-Numa Ducange and Razmig Keucheyan (eds), *The End of the Democratic State: Nicos Poulantzas, a Marxism for the 21st Century* (Palgrave Macmillan 2019) 43, 56 ff.

[3] Marco Goldoni and Michael A Wilkinson, 'The Material Constitution' (2018) 81 *Modern Law Review* 567, 583.

[4] Justin Rosenberg, *The Empire of Civil Society: A Critique of the Realist Theory of International Relations* (Verso 1994).

[5] The reproduction of the separation of formal politics from the (inherently political) domination inherent in relations of production and exchange is immanent to the concept of the capitalist state. Tony Smith, *Beyond Liberal Egalitarianism: Marx and Normative Social Theory in the Twenty-First Century* (Brill 2017) 187–89. See also Ellen Meiksins Wood, *Democracy Against Capitalism: Renewing Historical Materialism* (CUP 1995) 10–12, 19–48.

of politics—an 'institutionalised illusion'[6] that defines the capitalist state form[7] and is characteristic of liberal constitutional polities. Constitutionalism is best understood as a specific form of struggle over the reproduction of capitalist social relations, not simply as an apparent 'legal technology for structuring state power'.[8] The critique of the constitution of the capitalist state form consists in the study of legal and political institutions' formation through the dynamics of antagonistic social relations—not the study of the putative power of constitutions to constrain social antagonism.

Within the constrained analytic framework of liberal constitutional theory, however, constitutionalism consists in systems, practices, and imaginaries[9] through which public power and political authority are both constituted and limited; or it consists in formal texts, social contracts, or collective decisions that delimit power through the specification of legitimate authority. In the former case, constitutions are held to subsist in logics and rationalities of symbols, meanings, and the representation or objectification of reality; in the latter, constitutions are abstracted from the social relations in which they are embedded and with which they are mutually constitutive. In either case, liberal constitutional theory has a pronounced 'normativist'[10] bent. It is preoccupied with the reconciliation of the contrary poles of 'democratic constitutionalism': the affirmation of both individual rights and majoritarian legitimation of public power.[11] As such, it evinces an enduring preoccupation with the project of justification, not critique.

This chapter rejects such conceptions of constitutionalism and traces the outline of a critique of constitutionalism and of liberal constitutional theory. Constitutionalism must be investigated as part of the broader project of interpreting, elaborating, and critically engaging with Marx's critique of capitalist society. Constitutionalism is a form of struggle, not a formal puzzle. Liberal constitutional theory's inability to forgo an 'obscurantist celebration of the "paradoxes" of constitutionalism'[12] can be overcome only by apprehending constitutionalism as a form of social antagonism.

Constitutional texts prescribe institutional boundaries and describe legal frameworks[13] in order to mediate the exercise of formal political power, but constitutions—in the senses of

---

[6] Patrick Murray, *Marx's Theory of Scientific Knowledge* (Humanities Press 1988) 32.

[7] Clarke, 'State Debate', 9–10.

[8] Aslı Bâli and Aziz Rana, 'Constitutionalism and the American Imperial Imagination' (2018) 85 *University of Chicago Law Review* 257.

[9] On images, symbols, and the representation of social reality in constitutional theory, see Charles Taylor, *Modern Social Imaginaries* (Duke University Press 2004); Zoran Oklopcic, *Beyond the People: Social Imaginary and Constituent Imagination* (OUP 2018); Jiří Přibáň, 'Constitutional Imaginaries and Legitimation: On *Potentia, Potestas*, and *Auctoritas* in Societal Constitutionalism' (2018) 45 *Journal of Law and Society* S30.

[10] Martin Loughlin, 'The Concept of Constituent Power' (2014) 13 *European Journal of Political Theory* 218.

[11] Nimer Sultany, 'The State of Progressive Constitutional Theory: The Paradox of Constitutional Democracy and the Project of Political Justification' (2012) 47 *Harvard Civil Rights–Civil Liberties Law Review* 371.

[12] Oklopcic, *Beyond the People*, 350.

[13] The prototypical case is the empowerment of a constitutional court to conduct constitutional review. This model necessarily privileges the drafting, interpretation, and elaboration of legal texts. The contrast with the Westminster model—legislative sovereignty and the persistence of an 'unwritten constitution'—has been blurred by the adoption of bills of rights and moves toward constitutional review in Commonwealth countries. Mark Tushnet, 'The Rise of Weak-Form Judicial Review' in Tom Ginsburg

political communities or legal orders—are themselves constituted only through struggle and antagonism. Texts like constitutional provisions, statutes, and doctrines figure prominently in constitutional theory, but they do not exhaust its scope. Adequately apprehending constitutionalism is possible only by situating constitutional law in its historical specificity, and by illuminating the ways in which law and the state are reproduced as specific moments in the totality of capitalist social relations. Some of the roots of such a critique are already present in constitutional theory. The study of constitutionalism has often been characterised by a contradictory duality between formality and materiality[14]—not just between constitutional text and constitutional form, but also between the fragmentation of constitutional law among and within national and international jurisdictions, on the one hand, and the global scope of constitutionality concomitant with the reach of the world market and the global expansion and intensification of capital accumulation, on the other. The territorial fragmentation of nation-states is the political expression of the global unity of value relations.[15] The constitution of this form of social relations must be subject to further critique—critique that is articulated with Marx's critique of political economy.[16]

In this chapter I present the outline of such a critique as a contribution to the sustained critique of constitutionalism conjoined with the Marxian critique of political economy. I adumbrate the theoretical traditions and debates that I consider to be the most important for the critique of the capitalist state in its appearance as a constitutional state. I then explore the reproduction of constitutionalism as a practice of depoliticisation, with a focus on the constitution of political and legal relations (including the constitution of juridical relations and subjects), and the link between constitutionalism and the reproduction of the capital relation. Inquiry into these processes and relations is necessary for a critical understanding of constitutionalism. I also argue that crises are constitutive of and central to constitutionalism, rather than inimical to it. I conclude by briefly considering the broader implications of the critique of constitutionalism.

BACKGROUND THEORETICAL CONSIDERATIONS

My approach in this chapter is informed by the contributions to critical state theory found in the perspective of Open Marxism[17] as well as by proponents of form-analytic approaches to

---

and Rosalind Dixon (eds), *Comparative Constitutional Law* (Edward Elgar 2011) 5; Stephen Gardbaum, *The New Commonwealth Model of Constitutionalism: Theory and Practice* (CUP 2013).

[14]   Goldoni and Wilkinson, 'Material Constitution'.

[15]   Simon Clarke, 'Class Struggle and the Global Overaccumulation of Capital' in Robert Albritton and others (eds), *Phases of Capitalist Development: Booms, Crises and Globalizations* (Palgrave Macmillan 2001) 76; Rodrigo Pascual and Luciana Ghiotto, 'The State and Global Capital: Revisiting the Debate' in Ana Cecilia Dinerstein et al (eds), *Open Marxism 4: Against a Closing World* (Pluto Press 2020) 109.

[16]   For a broad, introductory overview of this articulation, see Emilios Christodoulidis and Marco Goldoni, 'Marxism and the Political Economy of Law' in Emilios Christodoulidis, Ruth Dukes, and Marco Goldoni (eds), *Research Handbook on Critical Legal Theory* (Edward Elgar 2019) 95.

[17]   See e.g., Bonefeld, 'Social Constitution'; Simon Clarke, 'The Global Accumulation of Capital and the Periodisation of the Capitalist State Form' in Werner Bonefeld, Richard Gunn, and Kosmas Psychopedis (eds), *Open Marxism 1: Dialectics and History* (Pluto Press 1992) 133. For a contemporary perspective, see Chris O'Kane, 'Capital, the State, and Economic Policy: Bringing Open Marxist

the critique of capitalism.[18] According to the former, the state is the political form of capitalist society. Capitalist social relations appear as a fragmented and contradictory unity in which social individuals experience impersonal domination through the mediation of abstract social forms—a theme that I elaborate by drawing upon form-analytic theories that stress that capitalist society is constituted by 'historically specific social forms'.[19] My aim is not to gloss Marx's scattered remarks on constitutionality and democratic institutions, but rather to explore the ways in which a critical analysis of constitutionalism can draw upon—and inform and extend in turn—the critique of capitalist social relations.

The critique of capital requires the critical apprehension of the dominating forms assumed by capitalism's constituent social relations in their contradictory and conflict-laden reproduction. Within the critique of capital, both capitalists and workers are regarded as personifications of historically specific social categories.[20] Their relations with one another are mediated by value,[21] the production of which is socially validated through money-mediated exchange.[22] The relations of the production and realisation of value are global in scope, and are extended and consolidated by state violence.[23] Under capitalism, social production is undertaken, not in order to fulfil human needs, but on an antagonistic basis among capitals that are structurally compelled to compete with one another. The imperative to valorise capital[24] compels capitalists to purchase labour-power as cheaply as possible (and to pursue commodity production on a private basis—that is, without regard to the risk of crises). Most individuals are separated from the means of production; their access to any portion of the total social product—which 'presents itself as an "immense accumulation of commodities"'[25]—is mediated by money. They can reproduce themselves only by obtaining money, by selling labour-power to those who own the means of production. And yet both capitalist and worker contribute to the reproduction of the capital relation and capitalism's constituent social forms—the essential determinations of capitalism that mediate social individuals' activity (and dominate them). These include commodities, money, and capital—but also law and the state as well.[26]

Within capitalist society, the political is fragmented, such that relations of production and exchange are commonly represented as merely economic and outside the realm of politics—the latter being reduced to a depoliticised state form that is abstracted from the social relations

Critical Political Economy Back into Contemporary Heterodox Economics' (2020) 54 *Review of Radical Political Economics* 684.

[18] See esp. Murray, *Marx's Theory*, 31–33, 35–39; Werner Bonefeld, *Critical Theory and the Critique of Political Economy: On Subversion and Negative Reason* (Bloomsbury 2014) 165–92; Smith, *Beyond Liberal Egalitarianism*, 183–91; Paul Mattick, *Theory as Critique: Essays on* Capital (Brill 2018) 72–122.

[19] Use of the term 'form' in this context does not connote a featureless universality; rather, it is an acknowledgement that all social relations assume 'historically specific social forms'. Patrick Murray, *The Mismeasure of Wealth: Essays on Marx and Social Form* (Brill 2016) xi.

[20] Karl Marx, *Capital: A Critique of Political Economy*, vol 1 [1867] in Karl Marx and Frederick Engels, *Collected Works*, vol 35 (Lawrence & Wishart 1996) 10; Mattick, *Theory as Critique*, 106.

[21] Smith, *Beyond Liberal Egalitarianism*, 83–4.

[22] Michael Heinrich, *An Introduction to the Three Volumes of Karl Marx's* Capital (first published 2004, Alexander Locascio tr, Monthly Review Press 2012) 48–70; Mattick, *Theory as Critique*, 102–22.

[23] Bonefeld, *Critical Theory*, 79–95, 165–85.

[24] Smith, *Beyond Liberal Egalitarianism*, 106–8 ff.

[25] Marx, *Capital*, 45.

[26] Smith, *Beyond Liberal Egalitarianism*, 183–92.

with which it is mutually constitutive. The capitalist state is in no way a mere agent of a unified ruling class. Nevertheless, the capitalist state is immanent to value relations, such that state actors must seek to maintain the conditions for capital accumulation.[27] As such, the capitalist state is directly implicated in the reproduction of the separation of producers from the means of production;[28] in the struggles that attend the reproduction of the capital relation;[29] and in the maintenance of the depoliticising separation of the political and the economic (the 'bifurcation of the political').[30] Through its maintenance of the bifurcation of the political, the capitalist state is crucial to the reproduction of capital as a social relation. It 'insulates'[31] capitalist production and exchange relations from political contestation—indeed, it cannot do otherwise and remain a capitalist state.[32]

Law and the state are moments in the contradictory totality of capitalist social relations.[33] A 'moment' in this sense is not a temporal unit. It is 'an element considered in itself that can be conceptually isolated and analysed as such but that can have no isolated existence' in actual social life outside of a broader totality.[34] But law and the state are not only moments in the contradictory totality of capitalist social relations; they are also, themselves, sites of the constitution of social relations (including those of production and exchange). Relations of production and exchange are mutually constitutive with legal and political relations. They are neither natural nor trans-historically valid.[35] The critique of capitalist society is incomplete without critical inquiry into the legal constitution of juridical subjects, relations of property and contract, and the legal articulation of production and exchange relations. Since they number among capitalism's essential social forms; the analysis and critique of law and the state are neither secondary to, nor separable from, the analysis and critique of capital.

Some Marxists have recommended viewing law and the state as 'relatively autonomous'[36] from other social relations[37]—meaning that the content of political relations at the level of

---

27   Heinrich, *Introduction*, 203–13.

28   Bonefeld, *Critical Theory*, 79–100.

29   Clarke, 'State, Class Struggle'.

30   Smith, *Beyond Liberal Egalitarianism*, 187–91.

31   Werner Bonefeld, 'European Integration: The Market, the Political and Class' (2002) 26 *Capital & Class* 117, 118.

32   Smith, *Beyond Liberal Egalitarianism*, 190.

33   '[T]he capitalist mode of production can only be grasped as a complex totality. However, this is not the complexity of relations of structural interdependence, it is the complexity of an historical process, a process of class struggle which develops on the basis of contradictory historical foundations'. Clarke, 'Global Accumulation of Capital', 149.

34   Geert Reuten, 'The Difficult Labor of a Social Theory of Value' in Fred Moseley (ed), *Marx's Method in Capital: A Reexamination* (Humanities Press 1993) 89, 92. See also Geert Reuten, 'An Outline of the Systematic-Dialectical Method: Scientific and Political Significance' in Fred Moseley and Tony Smith (eds), *Marx's* Capital *and Hegel's* Logic*: A Reexamination* (Brill 2014) 241, 249 (noting that, although moments must be presented sequentially, when it comes to apprehending totalities 'we always have the simultaneity of all moments').

35   'The capitalist state is neither independent from the economy nor does it derive from it, nor does the economy comprise a structured system of independent economic laws'. Bonefeld, *Critical Theory*, 182.

36   Christopher Tomlins, 'How Autonomous Is Law?' (2007) 3 *Annual Review of Law and Social Science* 45.

37   Nicos Poulantzas, *State, Power, Socialism* (Patrick Camiller tr, New Left Books 1978); Bob Jessop, *State Theory: Putting the Capitalist State in Its Place* (Polity Press 1990) 24–47; Sonja Buckel,

the state is neither fully separate from, nor fully determined by, relations of production and exchange. But the endeavour to specify the limits of the state's autonomy is fraught. There is always the danger of reproducing liberalism's fetishistic conception of the state as an institution standing apart from value relations.[38] This risk can be avoided by viewing the state as the political form of capitalist social relations, as one moment in a contradictory social totality. The capitalist state is not anterior to capitalist production; it is mutually constitutive with exchange relations, the world market, and the global expansion of capital accumulation.[39] It is necessary to resist the temptation to accept liberal thought's naturalisation of its own categories. We must not accept the separation of state and civil society as a brute fact. It is constituted by and valid for (and only for) capitalist social relations.[40] It is important to attend to the specificity of the political and the legal within the totality of capitalist social relations. The constitutional state is not a distinct level of society, but neither is it smoothly continuous with other social relations. State and law are forms of struggle and domination in their own right, ones through which the depoliticisation of society obtains, and the conditions for the reproduction of capital accumulation are secured.

THE PRACTICE OF CONSTITUTIONALISM

Constitutionalism warrants sustained critical inquiry in conjunction with the critique of political economy. A number of contradictions in liberal social thought converge within the scope of constitutional theory. It is formal and prescriptive, but it is also focused on the material contours of the social constitution of the state. Critical constitutional theory's task is to apprehend the relationship between the formal and the material constitution in the context of the critique of political economy. It must illuminate the ways in which constitutionalism is implicated in attempts to constrain or delimit struggles over the reproduction of capitalist social relations. Normativist theories of constitutionalism tend to become ensnared by 'constitutional fetishism'[41]—the tendency for constitutional theorists to abstract constitutional provisions and

'The Juridical Condensation of the Relations of Forces: Nicos Poulantzas and Law' in Alexander Gallas et al (eds), *Reading Poulantzas* (Merlin Press 2011) 154.

[38] Simon Clarke, 'Marxism, Sociology, and Poulantzas's Theory of the State' in Simon Clarke (ed), *The State Debate* (Macmillan 1991) 70 (arguing that Poulantzas' approach tends to reproduce the categories of bourgeois social thought rather than produce immanent critiques of them); Bob Jessop, 'Globalization and the National State' in Stanley Aronowitz and Peter Bratsis (eds), *Paradigm Lost: State Theory Reconsidered* (2002) 185, 198–200. See also EP Thompson, *The Poverty of Theory, or, An Orrery of Errors* (first published 1978, Merlin Press 1995) 130–32.

[39] Cf Clarke, 'State, Class Struggle'; 'Global Accumulation of Capital'; and 'Class Struggle'; Bonefeld, *Critical Theory*, 79–95, 147–85.

[40] John Holloway and Sol Picciotto, 'Introduction: Towards a Materialist Theory of the State' in John Holloway and Sol Picciotto (eds), *State and Capital: A Marxist Debate* (Edward Arnold 1978) 1, 3–10. Cf Bonefeld, *Critical Theory*; Smith, *Beyond Liberal Egalitarianism*.

[41] Franz L Neumann, *The Democratic and the Authoritarian State: Essays in Political and Legal Theory* (Herbert Marcuse ed, Free Press, 1957) 199. WEB Du Bois first explored the fetishism of 'constitutional metaphysics' in 1935 in his magisterial *Black Reconstruction*. WEB Du Bois, *Black Reconstruction in America* (first published 1935, Free Press 1998) 366 and passim; see also Allison Powers, 'Tragedy Made Flesh: Constitutional Lawlessness in Du Bois's Black Reconstruction' (2014) 34 *Comparative Studies of South Asia, Africa and the Middle East* 106.

structures from the social relations which alone provide them with meaning. Constitutional fetishism is closely related to the conceit that formal and normative constitutional systems are self-reproducing and self-referential,[42] rather than manifested in, and reproduced through, contradictory and conflictual social relations. A consequence of constitutional fetishism is the belief in, or the desire for, the routinisation of the political through constitutional order and thoughtful institutional design. Rather than prescribe constitutional measures to contain conflict, the critique of constitutional theory must apprehend the constitutive role of struggle in the constitutional state.

Happily, such a critique can draw—selectively—upon more recent and innovative trends in comparative constitutional scholarship, which balance attention to constitutions as formal-juristic constructs with attention to questions of political economy, social movements, and the study of culture.[43] These trends are welcome correctives to the formalist and normative-justificatory impulses that, historically, have dominated constitutional theory. Importantly, contemporary scholars of comparative constitutionalism refuse to be limited by territorial and jurisdictional boundaries and include international institutions and networks of capital, firms, and organisations within their ambit of study.[44] Such attentiveness to the inadequacy of textually- and territorially-bound analysis is salutary. Additionally, much of this scholarship stresses constitutionalism's insulation of markets from mechanisms of democratic decision-making, accomplishing the extension of state capacities through the elevation of market discipline as a political rationality or embedding states in transnational frameworks;[45] or it stresses that constitutionalism is not merely political but social—such that rules and norms can never be adequately apprehended in abstraction from their social context.[46] Finally, some contributions to this scholarship acknowledge constitutions as 'conscious projects to insulate the economy and private power from any potential for democratisation of control and, if necessary, to do so with punitive disciplinary measures'.[47] These 'conscious projects' are accomplished through various means, such as the elaboration of regimes of property relations, the judicialisation of policy, or the insulation of accumulation regimes from democratic oversight through the transference of regulatory competencies from national parliaments to

---

[42]   See e.g., Gunther Teubner, *Law as an Autopoietic System* (Blackwell 1993).

[43]   Ran Hirschl, 'The Realist Turn in Comparative Constitutional Politics' (2009) 62 *Political Research Quarterly* 825; Tom Ginsburg and Rosalind Dixon (eds), *Comparative Constitutional Law* (Edward Elgar 2011); Roger Masterman and Robert Schütze (eds), *The Cambridge Companion to Comparative Constitutional Law* (CUP 2019).

[44]   See e.g., Petra Dobner and Martin Loughlin (eds), *The Twilight of Constitutionalism?* (OUP 2010); Christine EJ Schwöbel, 'Situating the Debate on Global Constitutionalism' (2010) 8 *International Journal of Constitutional Law* 611; Gunther Teubner, *Constitutional Fragments: Societal Constitutionalism and Globalization* (OUP 2012); Stephen Gill and A Claire Cutler (eds), *New Constitutionalism and World Order* (CUP 2014); Turkuler Isiksel, *Europe's Functional Constitution: A Theory of Constitutionalism Beyond the State* (OUP 2016); Marco Goldoni, 'Introduction to the Material Study of Global Constitutional Law' (2019) 8 *Global Constitutionalism* 71.

[45]   See e.g., Jessop, 'Globalization and the National State', 207 ff; Gill and Cutler (eds), *New Constitutionalism*.

[46]   Chris Thornhill, *A Sociology of Constitutions: Constitutions and State Legitimacy in Historical-Sociological Perspective* (CUP 2011); Paul Blokker and Chris Thornhill (eds), *Sociological Constitutionalism* (CUP 2017).

[47]   Stephen Gill and A Claire Cutler, 'New Constitutionalism and World Order: General Introduction' in Stephen Gill and A Claire Cutler (eds), *New Constitutionalism and World Order* (CUP 2014) 1, 11.

supranational institutions. Nevertheless, such contributions do not conduce to a critique of constitutionalism articulated with the critique (rather than the application) of political economy.[48] The task remains to apprehend and elucidate the systematic character of constitutionalism as a form of continuing struggles over the reproduction of capitalist social relations; in other words, the task is to engage in the critique of constitutionalism with reference to, and for the sake of, the critique of political economy and the emancipatory abolition of capitalist social relations.

Constitutional theory—in any register, whether justificatory or critical—requires an appreciation of tensions and oppositions. It 'deals with the structure of relationships *within* the state … [as well as] the relationship *between* the state and the other organizations and associations in society'.[49] The term 'constitutional' may be applied to a form of government, but also to a particular and historically specific pattern of social relations. That is, constitutionalism, like the state, cannot be posited *a priori*.[50] This remains a challenge for liberal constitutional theory, which is an intensely normative and prescriptive affair. It focuses on questions of institutional design, prescriptions for drafting and interpreting texts, and prescribing specific practices and norms. It places special emphasis on the normative justification of constitutional constraints on public power for the sake of securing the endurance of formal democratic politics. Liberal constitutional theory is vexed by the contradiction between the containment of politics by law and the breaching of legal boundaries by politics.[51]

Even so, constitutions persistently wobble between the political and the legal.[52] They define institutional boundaries and the rights and duties of subjects; they are treated (or are intended by their drafters to be treated) as wellsprings of legal validity and legitimate authority; and they place obstacles in front of the legislative pursuit of legal change. There is a ceaseless tension between the material constitution (a matrix of social relations in which the formal constitution is embedded and through which the constitutional norms, meanings, and institutions are

---

[48] Many such contributions are premised on the claim that the extension of the world market and the expanding scope of capital accumulation (and the legal insulation of both) are recent phenomena. Werner Bonefeld, 'Social Constitution and the Spectre of Globalization' in Andreas Bieler and others (eds), *Global Restructuring, State, Capital and Labour: Contesting Neo-Gramscian Perspectives* (Springer 2006) 45. However, 'capital's process of internationalisation is inherent to capitalism and not a novelty'. Pascual and Ghiotto, 'The State and Global Capital', 117. As Marx emphasised, '[t]he tendency to create the world market is inherent directly in the concept of capital itself'. Karl Marx, 'Economic Manuscripts of 1857–58' in Karl Marx and Frederick Engels, *Collected Works*, vol 28 (Lawrence & Wishart 1986) 335.

[49] John Dearlove, 'Bringing the Constitution Back in: Political Science and the State' (1989) 37 *Political Studies* 521, 533 (original emphasis).

[50] 'Constitutions do not form but rather follow from social situations'. David T ButleRitchie, 'Organic Constitutionalism: Rousseau, Hegel and the Constitution of Society' (2005) 6 *Journal of Law and Society* 36.

[51] Some liberals insist on the primacy of ultimate normative principles in order to reject a dualism between law and politics. See e.g., David Dyzenhaus, 'The Politics of the Question of Constituent Power' in Martin Loughlin and Neil Walker (eds), *The Paradox of Constitutionalism: Constituent Power and Constitutional Form* (OUP 2007) 129.

[52] Goldoni, 'Introduction', 80.

manifested)[53] and the formal constitution (of juridical rationality and discursive resources).[54] The formal constitution is definitional, but it is definitional for the sake of material ends. The material constitution is constituted through social relations; but it can also be, in its own way, as resistant to change as the formal constitution, and it contributes to the demarcation of the boundaries of social validity.[55]

A considerable degree of policy variation is possible within constitutional boundaries (institutional as well as jurisdictional). This variability illustrates the duality of constitutions, the contradictory character of which appears in liberal constitutional theory as a paradox. Constitutions are at once rigid and plastic—rigid because they are expressed and socially recognised as formal containers for permissible political activity, and plastic insofar as regimes and orders must constantly be reproduced through struggle and political antagonism. Such a contradiction between the formal and the material is perpetually obscured by the analytic frame of liberal constitutional theory, which tends to privilege the former.

The scope of constitutional theory is not exhausted by jurisprudence and institutional design. In neither their legal nor their political valences can constitutions be reduced to basic laws. Nor are constitutional orders blunt instrumentalities of elite rule. As such, critical inquiry into constitutionalism must also attend to questions of the production of subjectivity, the specification of the content of the state and legal forms, and the trajectory of class struggle. Examining these processes illuminates constitutions' mediation between politics and law within the context of unfolding struggles over the reproduction of capitalist social relations. Constitutions' formal characters do not exhaust their materiality.

On the liberal account, constitutions ground the legal and constrain the political. They discipline the exercise of public power, establish the parameters of legal validity, and legitimate governance. The mechanisms for accomplishing these tasks include the specification of institutional boundaries, powers, and competencies through inscriptive formalisation (such as the separation of powers, schedules of rights and privileges, and amendment procedures); constitutional review of legislation for constitutional validity; and discourses and rationalities of constitutional identity, values, or patriotism. This account may be given additional texture by apprehending constitutionalism as a complex of institutions and practices—as a field within which regimes pursue legitimation, and in which subjects are encouraged to identify with (or are disassociated from) the social order.[56] Indeed, it has been suggested that constitutions may be seen as vehicles of hegemonisation—that is, that they are the juridico-political

---

[53]   As an example, the materiality of the constitution may be understood with reference to the contested political membership of wage-labourers in industrialising societies—as when EP Thompson referred to the unemployed who resorted to Luddism against liberalised labour relations as having been 'thrust beyond the pale of the constitution'. EP Thompson, *The Making of The English Working Class* (Victor Gollancz 1963) 546. On '[t]he admission of the working class to the constitution' see Simon Clarke, *Keynesianism, Monetarism and the Crisis of the State* (Edward Elgar 1988) 19 ff.

[54]   Goldoni and Wilkinson, 'Material Constitution', 569. '[T]he material constitution is not the opposite nor the hidden engine of the formal constitution. ... [T]he relation ... is one of integration, not of stark opposition'. Goldoni, 'Introduction', 85.

[55]   On social validity and its boundaries, see Bonefeld, *Critical Theory*, 25.

[56]   On law's role in constituting subjects and integrating them into capitalist social relations, see Robert Knox, 'Law, Neoliberalism and the Constitution of Political Subjectivity: The Case of Organised Labour' in Honor Brabazon (ed), *Neoliberal Legality: Understanding the Role of Law in the Neoliberal Project* (Routledge 2017) 92.

entrenchment of settlements of social conflict.[57] In this sense, constitutions could be clues to the dynamics of past and continuing political conflicts.

Settlement is a mirage, however. Constitutionalism is contestation.[58] Constitutional texts bear the marks of histories of antagonism and contestation, but they also fulfil specific roles in the antagonism that is constitutive of capitalist social relations. This is not to reduce them to merely technical instruments—far from it. Constitutionalism is a practice of depoliticisation, in which capital accumulation is secured and relations of production and exchange are fetishised. The illumination that is cast by a strategic conception of constitutions as fields or terrains does not extend to the full scope of constitutionalism. Constitutionalism is not just a field for struggle; it is, itself, struggle. Consider three examples:

First, constitutions are, quite simply, relations of struggle over the constitution, disposition, and reproduction of the capital relation. It is true that constitutions are often understood as defining state capacities—for example, through the separation of powers (explicitly demarcating institutional competencies and boundaries); the identification of juridical subjects (citizens, aliens, the marginalised and the excluded); and the specification of procedures whereby constitutional provisions may themselves be altered. But these are not mere limits on state capacities. Constitutional restrictions on state power may (or, in the event, may not) restrain domination by particular fractions; but they refine and reproduce capital's social domination of individuals. The separation of powers can serve to conceal—rather than eliminate—the production and operation of power in capitalist society.[59] More fundamentally, however, the formal separation of powers should not be considered a fiction; it is a constitutive determination of bourgeois society. The demarcation of institutional boundaries—which must be understood as an ongoing and contested process rather than an event—is a regularly celebrated achievement of political liberalism. Separated powers do not map neatly onto discernibly distinct power blocs. Rather, their creation and contested reproduction are gambits in the contest over whether and how capitalist society shall be reproduced. In that contest, dispersing formally specified administrative or bureaucratic capacities, or entrenching particular institutional boundaries, can be of decisive importance. The activity of placing formal barriers in front of legal change through parliamentary politics is always a potent tool in the struggle over the continuity and content of the capital relation.

The production of subjectivity is another example. The marks of juridical subjectivity are typically foregrounded in constitutional texts. In fact, constitutional law does not simply address subjects; it purports to name them into being. In truth, however, constitutions are made through social activity.[60] Constitutional texts and international treaties may describe juridical

---

[57] 'Every political-constitutional doctrine (or ideology) has an enemy or, more precisely, a threat that it seeks to avert'. Pasquale Pasquino, 'One and Three: Separation of Powers and the Independence of the Judiciary in the Italian Constitution' in John Ferejohn, Jack N Rakove, and Jonathan Riley (eds), *Constitutional Culture and Democratic Rule* (CUP 2001) 205, 214.

[58] 'The fact that constitutions serve a contradictory role—simultaneously limiting and empowering—opens spaces for political contestation'. Nimer Sultany, 'Arab Constitutionalism and the Formalism of Authoritarian Constitutionalism' in Helena Alviar García and Günter Frankenberg (eds), *Authoritarian Constitutionalism: Comparative Analysis and Critique* (Edward Elgar 2019) 292, 293.

[59] Cf Jules Lobel, 'The Political Tilt of Separation of Powers' in David Kairys (ed), *The Politics of Law: A Progressive Critique* (3rd edn, Basic Books 1998).

[60] James Tully, *Strange Multiplicity: Constitutionalism in an Age of Diversity* (CUP 1995) 30 ff. Constituent power is, in other words, constantly exercised by a variety of actors in many dif-

subjects, but the reproduction of capitalist social relations is what actually produces them (and it is produced by them in turn).[61] It would be better to say that constitutional law consists, in part, in patterns of subjectivation that yield juridical persons who may or may not be citizens, and who become bearers of the social categories constitutive of capitalism.[62] Constitutions, as relations of struggle, encompass citizens and the excluded alike.

As a third example, consider constitutional amendment. The specification of amendment procedures is crucial to any attempt at constitutional formalisation.[63] Such procedures are both an acknowledgement of the inevitability of legal change and an attempt to control (or at least regularise) it. They are technical expedients for marginal changes to constitutional provisions or structures—but at the same time, they are also obdurate barriers to the extension or intensification of political antagonism. The bare existence of amendment procedures can be made to serve as a legitimation discourse in its own right. Amendment procedures are also implicit acknowledgements of the awkward contradiction produced by the merger of constitutional law and political liberalism through which 'peoples' allegedly authorise their self-rule.[64] At the conceptual level, amendment is closely related to constitutional fetishism—the notion that constitutions are self-reproducing rather than socially determined, informing the conceit that they are persistently stable during periods between drafting and amendment. But constitutions are not final events—although they are often construed as such by their authors and interpreters, through reliance on performances of finality and fixity in inscriptive spectacles of drafting and ratification. Instead, constitutions are social relations, reproduced through social activity. The articulation of liberalism with formal democracy that is characteristic of many (though not all) periods in the historical trajectories of capitalist polities is managed through constitutionalism.

Constitutions are both declarations and effacements of class struggle. Constitutionalism naturalises and obscures social domination and state violence—through appeals to the fictive unity of popular sovereignty[65] or popular constituent authority; through the invocation of trans-historical principles of rights and justice; or through the construction of ideological objects such as the general interest. Constitutionalism depoliticises politics. It channels social conflict into technical questions. It anticipates and constrains democratic and emancipatory contestation from below.[66] It also furnishes alternative narratives about the origins, purposes,

---

ferent ways. See e.g., Martin Loughlin and Neil Walker (eds), *The Paradox of Constitutionalism: Constituent Power and Constitutional Form* (OUP 2007); Richard Albert and Joel I Colón-Ríos (eds), *Quasi-Constitutionality and Constitutional Statutes: Forms, Functions, Applications* (Routledge 2019).

[61] Cf Chris Thornhill, 'Contemporary Constitutionalism and the Dialectic of Constituent Power' (2012) 1 *Global Constitutionalism* 369, 374 and passim (arguing that constituent power is 'juridified' and not anterior to law).

[62] Goldoni and Wilkinson, 'Material Constitution', 587; on capitalism's social categories, see Mattick, *Theory as Critique*, 102–22.

[63] Yaniv Roznai, *Unconstitutional Constitutional Amendments: The Limits of Amendment Powers* (OUP 2017); Richard Albert, *Constitutional Amendments: Making, Breaking, and Changing Constitutions* (OUP 2019).

[64] Benedict Anderson, *Imagined Communities: Reflections on the Origin and Spread of Nationalism* (Verso 1983); Oklopcic, *Beyond the People*.

[65] On the historical development of 'popular sovereignty' (rather than democracy) see Daniel Lee, *Popular Sovereignty in Early Modern Constitutional Thought* (OUP 2016).

[66] The Indian experience presents a particularly vivid example; see Sandipto Dasgupta, 'India's Constitution and the Missing Revolution' in Alf Gunvald Nilsen, Kenneth Bo Nielson, and Anand Vaidya (eds), *Indian Democracy: Origins, Trajectories, Contestations* (Pluto Press 2019) 13.

and justifications of state power. Constitutionalism's partisans present it as a self-evidently good thing, as the necessary form of the institutionalisation of a well-ordered democratic polity (rather than an historically specific form of struggle). However, far from simply being obdurate and rigid bulwarks, constitutions are potent and generative in their capacity to produce power relations, subjectivities, and the porous border between the political and the legal. Their reproduction is susceptible to contestation and transformation.

THE REPRODUCTION OF CONSTITUTIONALISM

The totality of capitalist social relations is not a harmonious whole. Its constituent moments and relations are reproduced through contingent and contradictory historical processes: the formal constitution of politics (including the production of constitutional subjectivity) as well as the reproduction of the capital relation itself. In this section I explore the conjoined reproduction of the constitutional state and capitalist social relations more generally.

Constitutional texts present themselves as sources of—or guides to—legal validity and political authority. But the specification of formal power is closely bound up with the production and reproduction of juridico-political relations. This is true not simply for constitutional jurisprudence, but for the social relations that are intended to be governed by—and are purportedly logically subsequent to—constitutional provisions. The practice of constitutionalism is crucial to the reproduction of the 'radical separation of the state from civil society'.[67] This occurs not only at the national but at the international level. Political institutions and communities are indeed constituted through public law, but this is not, as liberal theory imagines, because constitutional law is the product of exercises of constituent power, affirmed by popular sovereigns. Rather, the constitutional state—an historically specific instantiation of the political form of capitalist society[68]—is constituted through (and constitutive of) social relations.

Formality must be distinguished from writtenness. The production and mediation of legal relations through textuality—through practices of meaning-making, and through inscription and interpretation—are always social acts and hence subject to contestation and transformation. Constitutional texts are not self-enacting or self-enabling. A text is no sure guide to the structure of a polity.[69] Nevertheless, textuality remains central to contemporary constitutional practice and the production of constitutional forms within and across state boundaries. Within the liberal constitutional imagination, obvious departures from what is commanded or required by comparatively unambiguous texts are often treated as aberrant pathologies. Constitutional texts are potent resources in the symbolic economy of politics. Stories about constitution-drafting are crucial episodes in state and regime legitimation narratives. In many polities, appeals to constitutional patriotism or constitutional morality are crucial to the pro-

---

[67] Clarke, 'Global Accumulation of Capital', 140.

[68] '[C]apitalist society is fundamentally a world-market society and the national state is the political form of this society'. Bonefeld, *Critical Theory*, 197–98.

[69] '[N]o constitutional document long remains coextensive with the constitutional order'. Walter F Murphy, *Constitutional Democracy: Creating and Maintaining a Just Political Order* (Johns Hopkins University Press 2007) 14.

duction of constructs such as the 'national interest'. To understand this phenomenon more fully, however, it must be considered in conjunction with the production of subjectivity.

The production and reproduction of juridico-political relations is not an achievement of institutional design or constitution-drafting. It is a process that is bound up with the reproduction of social relations in their historical specificity. The constitutional orders of liberal states produce individuated legal subjects, and they articulate contradictory unities among those subjects, in forms such as peoples and nation-states. Such unities are riddled with contradictions—and the statist rhetoric of political unity privileges social cohesion over the satisfaction of particular collective claims on or against the polity as a whole. What's more, the construction of constitutional law can be as much the product of mass activity as it is the product of elite draftspersonship[70]—such that it is also possible to speak of subjects producing constitutions. That is, constitutional subjects also make constitutions, but this does not occur through idealised moments of unmediated constitutional creation through constituent assemblies. Rather, it is immanent to the practice of constitutionalism. For example, the peculiar character of US constitutionalism—a 'covenantal' cultural project, complete with saints and hagiographies[71]—cannot be explained without reference to the subjectivities it shapes and the subject experiences that sustain that project.[72] The study of constitutions as forms of social relations includes the investigation of constitutional subjectivation: 'the formation of collective political actors and their contribution to constitutional change'.[73] Constitutional orders, basic laws, and the arrangement and competencies of institutions are often claimed to be the products of the expression of popular sovereignty—but historical examples of such exercises of constituent power can be hard to find.[74] The constitutional state persists through mutual constitution with juridical subjects. This, in turn, may only be understood by attending to the contested and contradictory reproduction of capitalist social relations.

In their capacity as legal constructs, constitutional forms provide the appearance of mass consent to capitalist social relations within a given polity.[75] Moreover, constitutional law, particularly in countries with courts exercising constitutional review, tends to acquire its own justificatory logic over and against formally democratic institutions. However, constitutionalism's historical emergence as a political ideal and a social fact is inseparable from the conflicts constituting political liberalism and bourgeois society.[76] Constitutional law, in other words, is not self-grounding. Constitutional states are not exogenous or anterior to social relations. They

---

[70]   See e.g., Rohit De, *A People's Constitution: The Everyday Life of Law in the Indian Republic* (Princeton University Press 2018).
[71]   Roxanne Dunbar-Ortiz, *An Indigenous Peoples' History of the United States* (Beacon Press 2014) 47.
[72]   Michael Kammen, *A Machine That Would Go of Itself: The Constitution in American Culture* (Alfred A Knopf 1986); Sanford Levinson, *Constitutional Faith* (Princeton University Press 1988).
[73]   Goldoni and Wilkinson, 'Material Constitution', 587.
[74]   András Sajó, 'Constitution without the Constitutional Moment: A View from the New Member States' (2005) 3 *International Journal of Constitutional Law* 243.
[75]   'The constitutional state (*Rechtsstaat*) is a mirage, but one which suits the bourgeoisie very well, for it replaces withered religious ideology and conceals the fact of the bourgeoisie's hegemony from the eyes of the masses'. Evgeny B Pashukanis, *Law and Marxism: A General Theory* (Pluto Press 1989) 146. Compare with Niklas Luhmann, *Law as a Social System* (first published 1993, Klaus A Ziegert tr, Fatima Kastner et al ed, OUP 2004) 381.
[76]   See e.g., RC van Caenegem, *An Historical Introduction to Western Constitutional Law* (CUP 1995) 194–247; Thornhill, *Sociology of Constitutions*, 77–251.

can neither ignore, nor disarticulate themselves from, capitalist social relations of production. The capitalist 'state form restricts the (nonetheless indeterminate) range of state policies in the following sense: *the capitalist state cannot introduce reforms that overcome the bifurcation of the political without dismantling itself*'.[77] Put differently, the capitalist state 'is the political form of capitalist society'.[78] It is inextricable from the capitalist mode of production. It engages in primitive accumulation; it (re)produces (and coercively regulates) the working class and guarantees the formal equality of capital and wage labour.[79] Constitutional states and capitalist production are co-constitutive.

Investigation of this relationship hinges, of course, on questions of historical specificity. To say that state and capital are co-constitutive is not to suggest that their reproduction is an orderly process that is free of contradiction. The capitalist state does not simply serve a putative 'general interest' of capital or capitalists—something which may be illustrated by attending to the constitution of class through struggle.[80] No unambiguous 'general interest' of all capitalists obtains within capitalism; there are only the particular and contingent interests of various fractions, whose interests must be constituted and moulded through conflict.[81] All the same, the fact that capitalist states do not simply busy themselves with carrying out the edicts of the ruling class[82] does not mean that such states lack a class character. Contestation over policy and conflict within the state do not indicate the absence of a constitutive relationship between the state form and other social relations. This could only be the case if there were an objectively discernible class interest shared by all possessors of capital, frustrated by the state's apparent failure to manifest it.

The apparent disjuncture between state action and class interests is a manifestation of the contradictions attending capitalist social relations' constitutive antagonisms. Interests must always be articulated; they are not discovered or revealed. Identities, solidarities, and alliances are not ready-made; they are produced through the contingency and conflict of politics. The constitutional state is as much the stage for such contestation and antagonism as is any other moment in the totality of capitalist social relations. The continuous reproduction of direct producers' separation from the means of production,[83] the expansion of the world market, and the global scope of value relations all entail the continued relevance of 'the state form of the class struggle'[84] even if it assumes distinctive or novel appearances. Social antagonism is instead cabined and transformed, through the mediation of social relations such as juridico-political boundaries and structures—much like the continued reproduction of the capital relation is accomplished through the dull compulsion of the market (including competition among wage-labourers) rather than direct coercion on the part of the controllers of the means of production. Constitutionalism disciplines and curtails political conflict, securing the

---

[77] Smith, *Beyond Liberal Egalitarianism*, 190 (original emphasis).

[78] Bonefeld, *Critical Theory*, 166.

[79] Bonefeld, *Critical Theory*, 165–192. For another perspective on primitive accumulation, see William Clare Roberts, 'What Was Primitive Accumulation? Reconstructing the Origin of a Critical Concept' (2020) 19 *European Journal of Political Theory* 532.

[80] Richard Gunn, 'Notes on "Class"' (1987) 2 *Common Sense* 15; Salar Mohandesi, 'Class Consciousness or Class Composition?' (2013) 77 *Science & Society* 72.

[81] Heinrich, *Introduction*, 208–9.

[82] Pashukanis, *Law and Marxism*, 139.

[83] Bonefeld, *Critical Theory*, 79–100.

[84] Clarke, 'State, Class Struggle', 194. Cf Clarke, 'Global Accumulation of Capital'.

order in which it is possible for state activities such as bureaucratic administration, dispute adjudication, and the deployment of repressive violence to maintain the necessary conditions for continued accumulation.

However, it is not sufficient to merely posit the state as the administrator of social reproduction.[85] This would seem to entail that the state is logically anterior to its own constitution through historically specific processes. It is indisputable that bourgeois states are implicated in the reproduction of capitalist society. But arguments that are expressed logically rather than with reference to historical experience risk becoming 'schematic' or otherwise susceptible to 'politicism'.[86] Charting the specification of the roles of constitutional states in the reproduction of capitalist sociality remains a major task for critical inquiry into law and state. It is indeed the case that '[t]he state cannot stand above value relations, for the simple reason that the state is inserted in such relations as one moment of the class struggle over the reproduction of capitalist relations of production'.[87] But such a proposition can only serve as the beginning and not the end of an attempt to trace the specificity of constitutionalism.

There is another sense in which the logical must not be allowed to crowd out the historical: constitutional states frequently fail to produce political order or constrain contestation. Here it must be remembered that the possibility of crisis is always present in the reproduction of the capital relation. 'The reproduction of capitalist social relations of production is only achieved through a class struggle in which their reproduction is always in doubt'.[88] Constitutional law is an example of such uncertain struggle. No critique of the place of constitutional states in the reproduction of capital as a totality of social relations is adequate without an account of constitutional crises.

CRISIS

Conflict and antagonism are constitutive of the practice of constitutionalism. Constitutional codification and amendment are both responses to, and manifestations of, conflict.[89] In other words, crisis is immanent to the concept of constitutionalism. Marx's own critique highlights the socially constitutive character of conflict and contradiction.[90] Capitalist production's contradiction-driven tendency toward crises—episodes 'when value considerations block the production and use of use values'[91]—'is a necessary form of capitalist social reproduc-

---

[85]   Cf Joachim Hirsch, 'The State Apparatus and Social Reproduction: Elements of a Theory of the Bourgeois State' in John Holloway and Sol Picciotto (eds), *State and Capital: A Marxist Debate* (Edward Arnold 1978) 57.

[86]   Clarke, 'State Debate', 13–16.

[87]   Clarke, 'State Debate', 51.

[88]   Clarke, 'State Debate', 63. Compare with Alexander Gallas, 'Reading "Capital" with Poulantzas: "Form" and "Struggle" in the Critique of Political Economy' in Alexander Gallas et al (eds), *Reading Poulantzas* (Merlin Press 2011) 89, 96.

[89]   Cf Bob Jessop, *The State: Past, Present, Future* (Polity Press 2016) 56; Demirović, 'Capitalist State', 56.

[90]   'For Marx, crises were not the ultimate truth of capitalism... Crises were the superficial and transient expression of the most fundamental contradiction of the capitalist mode of production. But at the same time, the tendency to crisis is inherent in every aspect of the everyday reality of capitalist social existence...' Simon Clarke, *Marx's Theory of Crisis* (Palgrave Macmillan 1993) 280.

[91]   Mattick, *Theory as Critique*, 57.

tion'.[92] Similarly, the perpetuation of the constitutional form of appearance of the capitalist state is in no way immune from crisis tendencies. Elaborating the ways in which crisis is internal to the constitutional dynamics of the capitalist state is a major task for the critique of constitutionalism.

In liberal constitutional theory, crises are often viewed as pathologies to be anticipated, managed, or thwarted. Indeed, liberal social theory tends to pathologise conflict, at least when it breaches certain parameters. And yet constitutional design is rarely equal to constitutional ambition; one study indicates that the average lifespan of a national constitution is only 19 years.[93] Constitutional codification and entrenchment are pursued in the context of specific conflicts and disputes. Moreover, the invocation of the notion of crisis is often merely a gambit in the cut-and-thrust of parliamentary politics, not an expression of dismay at constitutional infidelity. Indeed, constitutional crises must also be distinguished from constitutional violations. The latter occur frequently, both in the polity at large and within the formal boundaries of the state. In neither case are such violations necessarily harbingers of crisis. The internal logic of constitutionalism itself presupposes the regularity of conflict across institutional boundaries. Far from being accidental to the reproduction of constitutionality, constitutional violations are integral to it. And so are constitutional crises themselves. Nevertheless, many liberal constitutional theorists often insist on demarcating mere constitutional conflicts from constitutional crises, denying any smooth continuity between conflict and crisis; they 'reserve the term for a more special class of situations'.[94]

Constitutional crises might be thought of either as occurring either (i) *within* or (ii) *over* the reproduction of constitutionalism. That is, (i) struggle and contestation may intensify within the parameters of established constitutional forms, such that the reproduction of con- stitutionality is possible only through its (perhaps profound and destructive) reorganisation; or (ii) struggle and contestation may disrupt the continuity of the reproduction of a particular constitution. In both cases political struggle breaches constitutionalism's boundaries of depo- liticisation—be it (i) political struggles within and about constitutions or (ii) political struggle over and against the reproduction of capitalist social relations. It should be remembered, however, that such politicisation does not automatically conduce to struggle over capitalism's social form. Indeed, it is more often likely to conduce to struggles to refashion capitalist social relations rather than to overcome them.

In no instance is crisis mere illegality. Nor is constitutionality simply legality; it is not unmade by coercion or violence—not least because coercion and violence are constitutive of legal orders.[95] The constitutional state 'makes order by means of the force of law-making violence'.[96] Laws are routinely broken and yet the reproduction of social relations endures. Antagonism is constitutive rather than corrosive of the social. Constitutional crises are periods in which constitutions, as relations of struggle, are contested from within and without. As such,

---

[92] Bonefeld, *Critical Theory*, 155.
[93] Zachary Elkins, Tom Ginsburg, and James Melton, *The Endurance of National Constitutions* (CUP 2009) 129.
[94] Sanford Levinson and Jack M Balkin, 'Constitutional Crises' (2009) 157 *University of Pennsylvania Law Review* 707, 712.
[95] '[S]tate illegality is always inscribed in the legality which it institutes ... The activity of the State always overflows the banks of law...'. Poulantzas, *State, Power, Socialism*, 84–85.
[96] Bonefeld, *Critical Theory*, 184.

it is not necessarily a straightforward exercise to ascertain whether or not a crisis is a catastrophe or a strategic opportunity.

Constitutional crises are continuous with constitutional conflict, not sharply demarcated from it. Constitutions sometimes fail to delimit the scope of political conflict. As forms of depoliticisation they are susceptible to the politicisation of social antagonism. But the possibility of that happening is immanent to the practice of constitutionalism, not a threat to it. Recently bruited concerns[97] about the stability or longevity of constitutionalism notwithstanding, crises and extra-legality are central to the endurance of constitutionalism. In the present moment, it is not constitutionalism itself that is at risk, but rather particular constitutional orders, regimes, norms, and practices. Indeed, constitutionalisation is likely to be central to projects to further delimit and constrain the already truncated space of politics in capitalist society. It is possible that democratic institutions will be etiolated to the point that a 'minimalist' conception of democracy[98] seems hopelessly maximalist. If this comes to be, it will be accomplished in part through the strengthening, not the erosion, of constitutional constraints on democratic politics. The eclipse of constitutional democracy does not betoken the abandonment of constitutionalism. It betokens the strengthening of constitutional constraints (both formal and material) on politics—at the expense of democracy within social relations writ large.[99] A crisis in the institutions of parliamentary democracy need not be a crisis of constitutionalism.

Ultimately, constitutional crises disclose the contradictory character of constitutionalism: it is made and re-made through social relations, interests, and experiences—and consequently reproduced through antagonism and conflict, not stasis.[100] Constitutionalism consists simultaneously in the social objectivity of particular relations and in subjective experience.[101] As such, the possibility of crisis is always present in the practice of constitutionalism. Crises are possible both within constitutionalism and in the reproduction of constitutionalism. The full strategic and normative implications of this claim cannot be explored fully here, but it is important to note that it clearly forbids the critical constitutional theorist from treating crises as pathologies or defects, either in a given constitution or in constitutionalism *per se*. Crisis is an essential property of both constitutionalism (as the mediating form between political and legal relations) and of the material constitution (as the conjunction of state- and legal-form with subjectivity). Abstract analysis of the stakes of crises in general have some role to play, but they have important limitations: whether a given crisis represents a strategic opportunity, a moment of confusion, or a threat—and for whom—cannot be known outside of historical experience. In turn, that experience must itself be interpreted and theorised.

---

[97]   Tom Ginsburg and Aziz Z Huq, *How to Save a Constitutional Democracy* (University of Chicago Press 2018); Mark A Graber, Sanford Levinson, and Mark Tushnet (eds), *Constitutional Democracy in Crisis?* (OUP 2018); Kim Lane Scheppele, 'The Opportunism of Populists and the Defense of Constitutional Liberalism' (2019) 20 *German Law Journal* 314.

[98]   Adam Przeworski, 'The Minimalist Conception of Democracy: A Defense' in Ian Shapiro and Casiano Hacker-Cordón (eds), *Democracy's Value* (CUP 1999) 23.

[99]   'The great danger for the democratic state is the democratization of society'. Bonefeld, *Critical Theory*, 180.

[100]   Dysfunctional, contested, or failing constitutional orders are all possibilities in 'the general condition of constitutions'. Sultany, 'Arab Constitutionalism', 295.

[101]   The concept of crisis links social form and subjective experience. Brian Milstein, 'Thinking Politically about Crisis: A Pragmatist Perspective' (2015) 14 *European Journal of Political Theory* 141.

Recognising that crisis is constitutive of constitutionalism entails acknowledgment that crises are neither aberrant nor unusual. They are not even infrequent. They express the contradictions of constitutionalism—which both presupposes and suppresses conflict—and are, in a sense, banal. Recent constitutional changes, conflicts, and struggles in India,[102] Turkey,[103] the European Union[104] (including the departure of the United Kingdom,[105] as well as the consolidation of authoritarian regimes in Hungary[106] and Poland[107]), and elsewhere have attracted considerable attention in contemporary constitutional scholarship, much of which emphasises that constitutions are not exclusive to liberal polities, and that liberalism and authoritarianism are by no means necessarily in opposition.[108] But the conflicts attending the crisis-prone reproduction of the US constitution ought to attract attention as well—in spite of the self-congratulatory register adopted by most US constitutional theorists.[109] The US constitution was created and has been reproduced through struggles to preserve specific social relations, including settler colonialism, chattel slavery, and domination through ascription to hierarchies of race.[110] Its reproduction is attended by crisis tendencies, and it is presently articulated with the coercive reproduction of global capital accumulation through state violence.[111] Such articulation also suggests that the concept of constitutional crisis cannot be neatly mapped onto territorial or jurisdictional frameworks. Nor are they independent or separate from crises attending the reproduction of capitalist social relations more generally. Within capitalism, constitutional crises are always global. As of this writing, interlaced and contagious crises of production, debt, and novel pathogens are demonstrating the planetary scope of the subordination of the social good to the valorisation of capital and are exposing the contradictions that inhere in constitutionalism's depoliticisation of society. And yet this is just one thread out of many in the tapestry of catastrophe.

---

[102] Alf Gunvald Nilsen, Kenneth Bo Nielson, and Anand Vaidya (eds), *Indian Democracy: Origins, Trajectories, Contestations* (Pluto Press 2019).

[103] Pınar Bedirhanoğlu, Çağlar Dölek, Funda Hülagü, and Özlem Kaygusuz (eds), *Turkey's New State in the Making: Transformations in Legality, Economy and Coercion* (Zed Books 2020).

[104] Michael A Wilkinson, 'Authoritarian Liberalism in Europe: A Common Critique of Neoliberalism and Ordoliberalism' (2019) 45 *Critical Sociology* 1023; Werner Bonefeld, 'European Economic Constitution and the Transformation of Democracy: On Class and the State of Law' (2015) 21 *European Journal of International Relations* 867. See also Eva Nanopoulos' contribution to the present volume.

[105] Tawihda Ahmed and Elaine Fahey (eds), *On Brexit* (Edward Elgar 2019).

[106] Adam Fabry, *The Political Economy of Hungary: From State Capitalism to Authoritarian Neoliberalism* (Palgrave Macmillan 2019).

[107] Wojciech Sadurski, *Poland's Constitutional Breakdown* (OUP 2019).

[108] Alviar García and Frankenberg, *Authoritarian Constitutionalism.*

[109] In a classic statement, Karl Llewellyn noted that a wide (and hence crisis-prone) fissure between grand constitutional narratives and the realities of constitutional functioning has been a persistent feature of the US as a polity. Karl N Llewellyn, 'The Constitution as an Institution' (1934) 34 *Columbia Law Review* 1.

[110] Beard's 'economic interpretation' is woefully inadequate precisely because of its inattention to these essential elements of US constitutionalism. Charles A Beard, *An Economic Interpretation of the Constitution of the United States* (Free Press 1913). Du Bois provided posterity with the closest thing to a definitive critique of US constitutional culture in his *Black Reconstruction.* For background see Robert L Tsai, *America's Forgotten Constitutions* (Harvard University Press 2014); Michael J Klarman, *The Framers' Coup: The Making of the United States Constitution* (OUP 2016); Adam Dahl, *Empire of the People: Settler Colonialism and the Foundations of Modern Democratic Thought* (University Press of Kansas 2018).

[111] Bâli and Rana, 'Constitutionalism'.

CONCLUSION

Contemporary constitutionalism is riven with contradictions. Anti-democratic projects of depoliticisation are pursued through the constitutionalisation of policy, such as judicial supremacy,[112] 'juristocracy',[113] or the legal insulation of particular relations of production and exchange in supra- or transnational institutions or international legal frameworks.[114] Liberal constitutional frameworks are currently in free fall in numerous polities, both established and relatively new. Often, many of those who criticise liberal constitutionalism from the left find themselves defending constitutional law—despite its manifest flaws and contradictions—against a global tide of reaction.

At one point Marx did, of course, identify democracy as the solution to the '*riddle* of all constitutions'.[115] As always, it must be remembered that the democratisation of social relations (which must not be confused with parliamentary democracy) is inseparable from the struggle to transform capitalist social relations. Defences of liberal constitutionalism against reaction—whether they are strategic or sincere, principled or instrumental—are not themselves adequate tactics of emancipatory contestation. Constitutions are relations of struggle and made through struggle. The barriers they erect in the place of the democratisation of social relations can themselves only be unmade through struggle.

Constitutional law is a rich area for further analysis and inquiry by students of Marx's critique. But, as ever, it remains the point to change the world and not only to interpret it—necessary though the latter may be to the former. All too often, constitutional theorists go no further than the contemplation of the puzzles and riddles posed by the practice and theory of constitutionalism. Leaning back in contented repose does not become those who inquire into the law for the purposes of emancipatory social transformation. The critique of constitutionalism is not simply an exercise in debunking. It should be undertaken with the transformation of social relations and emancipatory struggle in mind.

---

[112] Gordon Silverstein, *Law's Allure: How Law Shapes, Constrains, Saves, and Kills Politics* (CUP 2009).

[113] Ran Hirschl, *Towards Juristocracy: The Origins and Consequences of the New Constitutionalism* (HUP 2004).

[114] For a recent example see Tom Chodor, 'The Rise and Fall and Rise of the Trans-Pacific Partnership: 21st Century Trade Politics through a New Constitutionalist Lens' (2019) 26 *Review of International Political Economy* 232.

[115] Karl Marx, 'Contribution to the Critique of Hegel's Philosophy of Law' [1843] in Karl Marx and Frederick Engels, *Collected Works*, vol 3 (Lawrence & Wishart 1975) 3, 29 (original emphasis). Cf Igor Shoikhedbrod, *Revisiting Marx's Critique of Liberalism: Rethinking Justice, Legality and Rights* (Palgrave Macmillan 2019) 191–205.

13. Marx and critical constitutional theory
Nimer Sultany

INTRODUCTION

The poverty of contemporary liberal constitutional theory is evident. It misdescribes political reality because it deploys anachronistic principles like the 'separation of powers'.[1] It also proffers a limited range of institutional templates that are titled towards domesticating popular mobilisation and containing 'the transformative uses of governmental power'.[2] This limited ambition for reform and fear of democracy are also evident in the 'single-minded focus' on developing theories and arguments addressing higher judges and supreme courts.[3] They are also palpable in the absence of a macro-level analysis of the role of concentrated wealth in politics, the class-based and unequal allocation of power and privilege, and the disempowerment of the poor.[4] Consequently, liberal constitutional theory does not adequately address the 'social question'.[5] Nineteenth-century reformers and revolutionaries expressed their dissatisfaction with the status quo, partly through the 'social question', and highlighted the discrepancy between 'ruling ideas' and the reality of poverty, inequality, and injustice that pervaded the conditions of the working classes since the advent of wage labour.[6] Contemporary constitutional debates reduce the 'social question' to the desirability of judicially enforced 'social rights' in a counter-majoritarian constitution. In other words, the attempt to improve the conditions of the working class is not accompanied with a democratisation of political structures in order to ensure the effective attainment of these rights.[7] Progressive constitu-

---

[1] Daryl J Levinson and Richard H Pildes, 'Separation of Parties, Not Powers' (2006) 119 *Harvard Law Review* 2311; Daryl J Levinson, 'Foreword: Looking for Power in Public Law' (2016) 130 *Harvard Law Review* 33; Mogens Herman Hansen, 'The Mixed Constitution versus the Separation of Powers: Monarchical and Aristocratic Aspects of Modern Democracy' (2010) 31 *History of Political Thought* 509; Kate Andrias, 'Separations of Wealth: Inequality and the Erosion of Checks and Balances' (2015) 18 *University of Pennsylvania Journal of Constitutional Law* 419.

[2] Roberto Mangabeira Unger, *What Should Legal Analysis Become?* (Verso 1996) 16; Roberto Mangabeira Unger, *The Critical Legal Studies Movement* (Harvard University Press 1983) 28–29.

[3] Unger, *What Should Legal Analysis Become?*, 73, 112.

[4] Ganesh Sitaraman, 'The Puzzling Absence of Economic Power in Constitutional Theory' (2016) 101 *Cornell Law Review* 1445; Stephen Loffredo, 'Poverty, Inequality, and Class in the Structural Constitutional Law Course' (2007) 34 *Fordham Urban Law Journal* 1239; William E Forbath, 'Caste, Class and Equal Citizenship' (1999) 98 *Michigan Law Review* 1.

[5] Marx prefers 'the existing class struggle' to 'the social question'. Karl Marx, 'Critique of the Gotha Program' [1875] in Robert C Tucker (ed), *The Marx-Engels Reader* (2nd edn, WW Norton & Co 1978) 525, 536.

[6] See e.g., Holly Case, 'The "Social Question," 1820–1920' (2016) 13 *Modern Intellectual History* 747; Jan Breman et al (eds), *The Social Question in the Twenty-First Century: A Global View* (University of California Press 2019).

[7] Roberto Gargarella, *Latin American Constitutionalism, 1810–2010: The Engine Room of the Constitution* (OUP 2013) 130–31, 138, 137, 142–43; Roberto Gargarella, *The Legal Foundations of Inequality: Constitutionalism in The Americas, 1776–1860* (CUP 2014) 246. For a discussion of the

tionalists often reduce constitutional theory to constitutional interpretation to the detriment of examining persistent and inhospitable structures.[8] They offer progressive interpretations of constitutions without much attention to the 'institutional prerequisites of social democracy'.[9] Similarly, while progressive liberals like John Rawls recognise that welfare state capitalism is unjust, they continue to defend constitutional arrangements that enable the injustices they decry.[10] The critique of these arrangements is even more urgent today in light of the emergence of transnational regulations (the 'new constitutionalism' or 'supra-constitutionalism') that entrench capitalist economic structures, constrain democratic politics, and shape domestic constitutions.[11]

This impoverished state of constitutional theory requires critical scholars to bring Marx to constitutional theory. Surprisingly, Marx is rarely discussed in connection with questions of constitutional law and theory. Nevertheless, throughout his life, Marx examined the subject of the constitution, both theoretically and historically. On the basis of these interventions, this chapter argues that Marx proffers important resources to develop a critical constitutional theory that questions the fetishism and mystifications of modern constitutionalism and whose goal is to deepen democracy. In particular, it argues that Marx's critical theory of constitutional law is political, social, socialist, and anti-systemic.

Marx's theory of constitutional law is political in three ways. First, it analyses constitutional puzzles as socio-political rather than as mere theoretical puzzles, because the latter mystify reality. Second, it is anti-foundationalist in the sense of discarding the constitution's 'sacred origins', 'singular foundings', and venerated 'founding fathers', who are supposed to impose moral or structural limits on future generations. Instead of elevating the constitution above the people, Marx insists on openness and experimentation. Third, it rejects normative reductionism (the view that the constitution constitutes a 'higher' law or a 'normative contract' that binds ordinary politics) and conceives the constitution as embedded in a web of social relations and as an outcome of class struggle.

Marx's theory is social because it subjects abstractions to critical scrutiny and insists on concrete analyses as the basis for theoretical elaboration.[12] In particular, Marx argues 'that

---

difficulties facing rights-based attempts to tackle economic inequality within liberal constitutionalism see: Rosalind Dixon and Julie Suk, 'Liberal Constitutionalism and Economic Inequality' (2018) 85 *University of Chicago Law Review* 369.

[8]   Mark A Graber, 'Social Democracy and Constitutional Theory: An Institutional Perspective' (2001) 69 *Fordham Law Review* 1969, 1975, 1977–78.

[9]   Graber, 'Social Democracy', 1977.

[10]   Nimer Sultany, 'What Good is Abstraction? From Liberal Legitimacy to Social Justice' (2019) 67 *Buffalo Law Review* 823; Tony Smith, *Beyond Liberal Egalitarianism: Marx and Normative Social Theory in the Twenty-First Century* (Brill 2017).

[11]   David Schneiderman, 'Investment Rules and the New Constitutionalism' (2000) 25 *Law & Social Inquiry* 757; Danny Nicol, *The Constitutional Protection of Capitalism* (Hart 2010); Christine Schwöbel-Patel, 'The Political Economy of Global Constitutionalism' in Anthony F Lang Jr and Antje Wiener (eds), *Handbook on Global Constitutionalism* (Edward Elgar 2017) 407.

[12]   Following Hegelian dialectics, one may distinguish between 'abstraction' and 'critical abstraction' (or dialectical abstraction). The former (which is characteristic of one-sided 'understanding') is a flight from reality. Empiricist and positivist critics of abstraction err in reducing reality to appearances and 'common sense'. On the other hand, dialectical abstraction (which is characteristic of 'reason') 'is the reduction of the diverse forms and relations of reality to the actual process in which they are constituted' and to their essence. Herbert Marcuse, *Reason and Revolution: Hegel and the Rise of Social Theory* (first published 1941, Routledge 1955) 44–47, 156–58. Marx distinguishes between abstractions that mystify

the activities and agencies of the state are human activities', and that they are 'nothing but the modes of existence and operation of the social qualities of men'.[13] In order to avoid mystification, one needs to start from 'real subjects as the bases of the state'.[14] In the context of constitutional law and politics, Marx questions invocations of the 'people' and its 'constituent power' by analysing social locations, competing interests, and power struggles. Of particular relevance here is the relation between Marx and the tradition of political and legal republicanism that grounds political legitimacy in popular sovereignty and encourages political participation by public-spirited citizens who pursue the common good. Marx is often accused of being committed to two contradictory propositions, neither of which is accurate: either he is accused of having neglected the impact of the republican tradition by emphasising possessive individualism,[15] or his thought is reduced to a republican critique of liberal constitutional orders.[16] Yet while Marx draws upon republican discourse and participated in its debates and struggles, he recognises and highlights its limitations in order to develop a socialist critique of republicanism.[17]

Republicans and liberals routinely argue about institutional arrangements within the constitutional democratic state and the meaning of democracy and constitutionalism (e.g., reform of the House of Lords in the United Kingdom and the Senate in the United States; the counter-majoritarian difficulty; political versus legal constitutionalism).[18] These debates, however, have been 'wholly inattentive to the realities of elite economic domination in politics'.[19] Both defenders and critics of judicial empowerment overlook 'the overwhelming influence of unequal wealth' on the political system in capitalist societies.[20] Marx, in contrast, goes beyond these debates' limited framework by examining the ideologies that they embody, the frameworks they justify or obscure, and the political economies they enable. Bringing Marx to constitutional theory is even more crucial today because 'liberal constitutional theorists have largely abandoned the poor',[21] and because liberal republicans—whose institutional prescriptions are hardly distinguishable from those of most other liberals—have deradicalised

---

and those that represent real knowledge. For discussion see Étienne Balibar, *The Philosophy of Marx* (first published 1994, Gregory Elliot and Chris Turner tr, Verso 2007) 36.

[13]   Karl Marx, *Critique of Hegel's Philosophy of Right* (first written 1844, Joseph O'Malley ed, Annette Jolin and Joseph O'Malley tr, CUP 1970) 22.

[14]   Marx, *Critique of Hegel's Philosophy of Right*, 23, 24. See also Thesis VIII in Karl Marx, 'Theses on Feuerbach' [1888] in Robert C Tucker (ed), *The Marx-Engels Reader* (2nd edn, WW Norton & Co 1978) 143, 145 ('Social life is essentially *practical*. All mysteries which mislead theory into mysticism find their rational solution in human practice and in the comprehension of this practice.' (original emphasis)).

[15]   JGA Pocock, 'Authority and Property: The Question of Liberal Origins' in Barbara Malament (ed), *After the Reformation: Essays in Honor of JH Hexter* (University of Pennsylvania Press 1980) 338, 350.

[16]   Recent scholarship that seeks to frame Marx within the republican tradition highlights that Marx's is an 'alternative republicanism' or 'radical republicanism'. See William Clare Roberts, *Marx's Inferno: The Political Theory of Capital* (Princeton University Press 2018) 8; Michael J Thompson, 'The Radical Republican Structure of Marx's Critique of Capitalist Society' (2019) 47 *Critique* 391.

[17]   Jeffrey Isaac, 'The Lion's Skin of Politics: Marx on Republicanism' (1990) 22 *Polity* 461.

[18]   For a criticism of the US constitution see Sanford Levinson, *Our Undemocratic Constitution: Where the Constitution Goes Wrong (And How We the People Can Correct It)* (OUP 2008).

[19]   Sitaraman, 'Puzzling Absence', 1477, 1488.

[20]   Loffredo, 'Poverty, Inequality, and Class', 1250.

[21]   Loffredo, 'Poverty, Inequality, and Class', 1243.

republicanism.[22] Indeed, the absence of adequate attention to class may be explained, in part, by the 'republican revival' that privileged an ideological analysis over an economic analysis of constitutional thought and history.[23]

As this chapter shows, Marx's overall critique diverges from liberal and republican criticisms of the extant political order. Marx is a democrat who criticises both authoritarian centralism (of the Jacobins, Louis Bonaparte, Simón Bolívar, and others) and judicial empowerment. Yet he does not presuppose a Weberian state that is separate from society,[24] or a Hegelian state whose universality transcends social conflict in 'civil society' (the sphere of economic relations). His critique is not merely concerned with the separation of powers within the state or with inclusion (i.e., struggle over access to the state). Rather, it is concerned with extending democracy to the economic and not only the political sphere.[25] It thus seeks both social control of the state and 'free and associated labour' in order to overcome 'alienation'.[26] Democracy thus becomes synonymous with socialism, and Marx's critique is driven by the necessity and possibility of establishing an alternative to capitalism.[27]

Consequently, a project of critical constitutional theory is not merely one of internal critique of constitutionalism, but one that seeks to overcome its limitations in a 'political constitution'. Marx expresses this approach when he states, 'We, gentlemen, are not constitutionalists, but we take up the standpoint of the gentlemen who are accusing us in order to beat them on their own ground with their own weapons. Hence we appeal to constitutional usage'.[28] Accordingly, Marx's theory is anti-systemic because it foregrounds persistent alienation under capitalism in the face of invocations of constitutional legitimacy or the common good. Rather than searching for a stable form of constitutional legitimacy, this critical constitutional theory seeks to overcome alienation.[29] Thus, Marx puts forward a radical critique of existing arrangements that goes further than liberal and republican criticisms of extant constitutional arrangements within the capitalist mode of production.[30]

This chapter is organised as follows. The first section highlights Marx's attention to the antinomy of constitutionalism in his engagement with Hegel's theory of the state. In the

---

[22]   See e.g., Philip Pettit, *On the People's Terms: A Republican Theory and Model of Democracy* (CUP 2013); Cass R Sunstein, 'Beyond the Republican Revival' (1988) 97 *Yale Law Journal* 1539. But see Bruno Leipold, Karma Nabulsi, and Stuart White (eds), *Radical Republicanism: Recovering the Tradition's Popular Heritage* (OUP 2020).

[23]   Sitaraman, 'Puzzling Absence', 1492–93.

[24]   Bob Jessop, *The State: Past, Present, Future* (Polity Press 2010).

[25]   Terry Eagleton, *Why Marx Was Right* (Yale University Press 2011) 201.

[26]   Marx, 'Critique of the Gotha Program', 537; Karl Marx, 'The Civil War in France' [1871] in Robert C Tucker (ed), *The Marx-Engels Reader* (2nd edn, WW Norton & Co 1978) 618, 635–36; Karl Marx, 'Contribution to the Critique of Hegel's *Philosophy of Right*: Introduction' [1844] in Robert C Tucker (ed), *The Marx-Engels Reader* (2nd edn, WW Norton & Co 1978) 53, 54; Karl Marx, *Capital: A Critique of Political Economy*, vol 1 (first published 1867, Ben Fowkes tr, Penguin 1976) 173.

[27]   Ellen Meiksins Wood, *Democracy Against Capitalism: Renewing Historical Materialism* (Verso 1995).

[28]   Karl Marx, 'The First Trial of the *Neue Rheinische Zeitung*, Speech by Karl Marx' [1849] in Karl Marx and Frederick Engels, *Collected Works*, vol 8 (Lawrence & Wishart 2010) 304, 307.

[29]   Marx, 'Contribution', 54.

[30]   For the argument that Marx condemns capitalist exploitation as 'unjust' despite his aversion to moralistic discourse, see Norman Geras, 'The Controversy About Marx and Justice' (1985) 150 *New Left Review* 47; Norman Geras, 'Bringing Marx to Justice: An Addendum and Rejoinder' (1992) 195 *New Left Review* 37.

course of this engagement, Marx contrasts the political constitution (both monarchical and republican) with 'democracy' in order to foreground the constitution's limitations and point the way toward the resolution of the paradox by centring the people's constituent power and subjecting the constitution to popular will at all times. The second section examines alienation and the abstraction of popular sovereignty under a political constitution that emanates from the separation of state and 'civil society'. The third section argues that the limitations and mystifications of 'the paradox of constitutionalism' are rooted in the political (or partial) revolution that generates the constitution. Instead of a class-neutral constituent power leading a political revolution, Marx envisions a social revolution in which the proletariat is the constituent power. In order to illustrate the false promises of political revolutions, the fourth and fifth sections focus on the failings of constituent assemblies. These constitution-making assemblies do not live up to the ideal of constituent power, either because their politics is non-revolutionary or because the pre-revolutionary constitutional order imposes constraints on their work to prevent revolutionary rupture. The sixth section highlights Marx's analysis of the incoherence and contradictions of the political revolution's constitution. The fact that the constitution is ultimately based on *modus vivendi* because it accommodates competing interests and embodies a class compromise generates this incoherence. The seventh section returns to the paradox of constitutionalism in order to highlight Marx's conclusion, following his analysis of bourgeois revolutionary constitutions, that the fundamental contradiction consists in the blockage of social emancipation, and that the constitutional incoherence and instability are better understood as emanating from the unresolved paradox of constitutionalism. In order to overcome the paradox of constitutionalism, one needs to move beyond liberalism; and in order to overcome the fundamental contradiction, one needs to move beyond capitalism. The eighth (and penultimate) section explores elements of an alternative radical constitutionalism that Marx identifies in the experience of the Paris Commune in order to chart a path beyond the alternatives of despotism and class rule. The conclusion reflects on Marx's continued relevance.

THE ANTINOMY OF CONSTITUTIONALISM

Long-running debates in constitutional law and legal theory identify and then purport to resolve a 'paradox of constitutionalism' arising from efforts to reconcile the people's unlimited power to establish their mode of government with its subjection to the constitution it has created.[31] In these debates, the distinction between constituent power and constituted power responds to the question of the legitimacy of the constitutional order (who authorises the constitution?) by grounding it in an originary power and separating it from the question of legality once constitutional legitimacy is established.[32]

The paradox of constitutionalism is central to Marx's early engagement with Hegel's theory of the state.[33] Hegel's dialectical theory is highly critical of the resignation to facts and

---

[31] Martin Loughlin and Neil Walker (eds), *The Paradox of Constitutionalism: Constituent Power and Constitutional Form* (OUP 2007).

[32] EJ Sieyès, 'What is the Third Estate?' [1789] in EJ Sieyès, *Political Writings: Including the Debate Between Sieyès and Tom Paine in 1791* (Michael Sonenscher ed, Hackett 2003) 136; Hannah Arendt, *On Revolution* (first published 1963, Penguin 1990) 162–63.

[33] Marx, *Critique of Hegel's Philosophy of Right*.

customs, and the reification of the world through 'common sense' and traditional logic.[34] It is not content with surface appearances but highlights the gap between existence and essence, reality and potentiality.[35] Hegel rejects the two dominant methods of German constitutional law, the normative-idealist and the positivist-empiricist.[36] The first of these two approaches is content with the 'ought', pronouncing principles. The latter, for its part, is concerned with the 'is', describing the status quo. Hegel is further credited with shifting political philosophy's focus from legitimacy to historicity and change, and away from single and legendary founders or legislatures who legitimate the polity.[37]

Yet, Marx finds Hegel's attempt to resolve the paradox wanting. In Hegel's formulation, the paradox relates to the role and status of the legislature, whose power lies both outside and inside the constitution. On the one hand, legislative power is the 'power to determine and establish the universal',[38] and is thus the 'power of the constitution' (which is understood as the universal determination of rational will).[39] On the other hand, the legislature presupposes the constitution and is a constitutional power, as one of the branches of the state within the separation of powers.[40] It is the whole, but it is part of the whole (or the 'organic unity' of the state).[41] Historically, legislatures presuppose constitutions they did not themselves make. Yet the constitution, Marx says, is 'certainly not self-generating'.[42] Thus, there must be a lawmaker that precedes the constitution and stipulates legislative powers: 'A legislature must exist or have existed before and outside of the constitution. There must exist a legislature outside of the actual, empirical, established legislature'.[43]

Hegel's resolution of this antinomy, the 'opposition between constitution and legislature', simply restates the question, Marx argues.[44] Formally, according to Hegel, the legislature cannot alter the constitution. But 'materially', it effectively and indirectly amends it through legislative clarification and application of constitutional norms. Thus, there is a contradiction between constitutional form and 'constitutional effect', or between the 'is' and the 'ought' (the empirical reality and the normative ideal of legislative power).[45]

In light of this gap between the constitution's form and its actuality, it is difficult to explain constitutional change. Marx objects to the view of 'gradual' constitutional change. According to Hegel, the organic constitution 'advances and matures' through legislative work, without a need to make this change formally explicit. Yet, for Marx, 'the category of gradual transition is, first of all, historically false; and secondly, it explains nothing'.[46] It explains nothing because it does not explain the legislature's ability to do informally what it is not supposed to

---

[34]   Marcuse, *Reason and Revolution*, 16–20, 112–13.

[35]   Marcuse, *Reason and Revolution*, 44–47.

[36]   Shlomo Avineri, *Hegel's Theory of the Modern State* (CUP 1972) 39.

[37]   See e.g., Avineri, *Hegel's Theory*, x.

[38]   GWF Hegel, *Elements of the Philosophy of Right* (first published 1820, Allen W Wood ed, HB Nisbet tr, CUP 1991) 308.

[39]   Marx, *Critique of Hegel's Philosophy of Right*, 55.

[40]   Hegel, *Elements of the Philosophy of Right*, 336; Marx, *Critique of Hegel's Philosophy of Right*, 55.

[41]   Hegel, *Elements of the Philosophy of Right*, 339.

[42]   Marx, *Critique of Hegel's Philosophy of Right*, 55.

[43]   Marx, *Critique of Hegel's Philosophy of Right*, 55.

[44]   Marx, *Critique of Hegel's Philosophy of Right*, 56.

[45]   Marx, *Critique of Hegel's Philosophy of Right*, 56.

[46]   Marx, *Critique of Hegel's Philosophy of Right*, 57.

do formally, and because resultant constitutional change is unconscious. The formal and actual constitution will correspond only when it is understood that the people are the 'real corner stone of the constitution', and that constitutional change is a product of conscious democratic will. With the achievement of such correspondence, 'progress' (i.e., 'the movement of the constitution') will become 'itself ... the constitution'.[47] In other words, the constitution should always be subject to the people's power to establish it and change it.[48]

Conscious change invites the role of the legislature as a constitution-maker. The gradual transition thesis is historically false because Marx is alive to the necessity of revolutionary ruptures in the presumed linearity of historical time. This position differs from Hegel's attempt to 'legitimize the revolutionizing of reality, while discounting the revolution itself',[49] or his preference for 'revolutions from above'.[50] While 'entire state constitutions' have been modified when new conditions arise, Marx argues, a 'new constitution' has historically required a 'real revolution'.[51] The French Revolution illustrates this point because the legislature 'produced' the revolution and rejected the 'antiquated constitution'.[52] It also illustrates the difference between the legislature, which represented popular will, and executive power, which represented particular interests and 'produced the small, retrograde revolutions'.[53]

In light of this, the opposition between the legislature and the constitution is in fact an internal paradox to the very idea of the constitution (revolutionary or antiquated, actual or formal, universal or particular, changing or fixed, democratic or non-democratic):

> Posed correctly, the question is simply this: Does a people have the right to give itself a new constitution? The answer must be an unqualified yes, because the constitution becomes a practical illusion the moment it ceases to be a true expression of the people's will. The collision between the constitution and the legislature is nothing more than a conflict of the constitution with itself, a contradiction in the concept of the constitution. The constitution is nothing more than an accommodation between the political and non-political state [i.e., civil society]; hence it is necessarily in itself a treaty between essentially heterogeneous powers. Here, then, it is impossible for the law to declare that one of these powers [namely, the legislature], which is part of the constitution, is to have the right to modify the constitution, which is the whole. In so far as we speak of the constitution as a particular thing, however, it must be considered a part of the whole. ... The resolution of this conflict has been attempted by differentiating between *assemblée constituante* and *assemblée constituée*.[54]

Republicans' answer to the dilemma at the basis of Hegel's paradox of the legislature is to split the power of the legislature into a constituent assembly (the power to establish the constitution) and a legislative assembly (a constitutional power within the established constitution). For republicans, constituent power to establish the mode of government belongs to the people.[55] Yet the distinction between constituent power and constituted power (between

[47] Marx, *Critique of Hegel's Philosophy of Right*, 57.
[48] Stathis Kouvelakis, *Philosophy and Revolution: From Kant to Marx* (GM Goshgarian tr, Verso 2003) 298.
[49] Jürgen Habermas, *Theory and Practice* (first published 1963, John Viertel tr, Beacon Press 1974) 131.
[50] Kouvelakis, *Philosophy and Revolution*, 296.
[51] Marx, *Critique of Hegel's Philosophy of Right*, 57.
[52] Marx, *Critique of Hegel's Philosophy of Right*, 57–58.
[53] Marx, *Critique of Hegel's Philosophy of Right*, 58.
[54] Marx, *Critique of Hegel's Philosophy of Right*, 58.
[55] Sieyès, 'What is the Third Estate?', 136.

making the constitution and being constrained by it, between the revolutionary power of the people to reconstitute their polity and the forms of government they create) does not resolve the mystery. As the following sections illustrate, the paradox of constitutionalism is an antinomy because it fails to illuminate the historical realities of social and political conflicts. It idealises constituent power by abstracting it from class conflict, and by portraying it as an unlimited creative power, notwithstanding limitations of constituent assemblies during revolutionary processes. Despite these limitations, constituent power is conceived as a one-time event that imposes—by laying down the constitution—a 'pre-commitment' or a 'dead hand' of the past generations that limits the openness of the social and constitutional order to conscious transformation. Theoretical attempts to resolve the paradox through a reconciliation that leads to a universally accepted or normatively acceptable constitution mystify these realities. This is so given the debates' limitation to a 'political constitutional' paradigm in which the people's constituent power is class-neutral, popular sovereignty is abstract, and the political is separated from the economic.[56]

ALIENATION AND THE ABSTRACTIONS OF POPULAR SOVEREIGNTY

One of the primary abstractions that grounds and legitimates the 'political constitution' is 'popular sovereignty'. Marx shares with the republican tradition the rejection of monarchical sovereignty and the endorsement of popular sovereignty, but he parts with republicanism by refusing to fetishise either the people or sovereignty. Marx's criticism of the monarchical constitution is analogous to his criticism of the republican constitution; one abstraction simply replaces another. Modern republicanism criticises the first abstraction, monarchy, but not the second, the people. In fact, 'the struggle between monarchy and the republic' is limited, because it is 'still a struggle within the abstract form of the state'.[57] Both cases evidence a state formalism in which the state's form is separated from its materiality, and the state's content (namely, the rules of property and contract that govern relations within civil society) is external to the constitution (because they are isolated from state intervention).[58] A 'democratic' state is different from all other forms of state. In non-democractic forms, 'the state, the law, the constitution is dominant without really governing, that is, materially permeating the content of the remaining non-political spheres'.[59]

In contrast to Hegel's conception of sovereignty as embodied in the monarch who represents the unity of the state, Marx argues that sovereignty belongs to the people because the 'state is an abstraction; the people alone is the concrete'.[60] Monarchical sovereignty and popular sovereignty are 'two completely opposed concepts of sovereignty'.[61] While Marx considers monarchical sovereignty a 'fiction' or 'illusion', he recognises that it is an 'existing

---

[56]   For a critical discussion of the debates on the paradox of constitutionalism see Nimer Sultany, *Law and Revolution: Legitimacy and Constitutionalism After the Arab Spring* (OUP 2017) ch 10.

[57]   Marx, *Critique of Hegel's Philosophy of Right*, 31.

[58]   Marx, *Critique of Hegel's Philosophy of Right*, 31.

[59]   Marx, *Critique of Hegel's Philosophy of Right*, 31.

[60]   Marx, *Critique of Hegel's Philosophy of Right*, 28.

[61]   Marx, *Critique of Hegel's Philosophy of Right*, 29.

fiction'—in other words, a fiction that has socio-political consequences.[62] In particular, this fiction disempowers the people. The state is mystified, the constitution becomes mysterious, and sovereignty turns monarchical, but only if one abstracts these concepts from their bases in historical reality and concrete human activity. Instead of analysing them as the 'free product of men', they are conceived as products of abstract universal rationality. Instead of representing the 'whole', they present the 'part' as if it were the 'whole':

> In monarchy the whole, the people, is subsumed under one of its modes of existence, the political constitution; in democracy the constitution itself appears only as one determination, and indeed as the self-determination of the people. In monarchy we have the people of the constitution, in democracy the constitution of the people. Democracy is the resolved mystery of all constitutions. ... The constitution appears as what it is, the free product of men. ... [H]ere the constitution is in general only one moment of the people's existence, that is to say the political constitution does not form the state for itself.[63]

The 'mystery of all constitutions' is resolved by 'democracy'. This is because the monarchy denies the people their right and power to determine their constitution—that is, to organise their polity. Thus, the constitution constitutes the people ('the people of the constitution'). In democracy, however, the people determine the constitution and it belongs to them ('the constitution of the people'). Moreover, the monarchical constitution is 'political', and as such is a partial representation of reality. Indeed, the people is the 'whole' (the social totality), and under a democratic rule the political constitution (i.e., the organisation of the state) is only one part of this social totality. The constitution becomes reified under a monarchy because the part (the monarch) seeks 'to determine the character of the whole'.[64] Democracy 'is the generic constitution' and the monarchical constitution is a perversion of this constitution. The democratic constitution is the only one that gives an account of the social totality and resolves the contradiction of monarchy (a rule without *demos*; a misplaced sovereignty; a constitution unfreely determined).[65] Under popular sovereignty, there is a unity of ruler and ruled in the sense that the people author the constitution under which they live. Under monarchical sovereignty, however, the monarch usurps sovereignty from the people and they are ruled by an alien constitution.[66]

Democracy resolves the paradox of constitutionalism because it 'redefines politics in terms of constitutive power' or 'permanent revolution'.[67] In other words, it maintains the people's constituent power (revolution is a process rather than an event) and the constitution is always subject to the people's revolutionary power to change it. Other political forms, however, elevate the constitution above the people as a fetter on their power. Thus, the constitution is fetishised when it is thought to have powers it does not possess:

> Just as it is not religion that creates man but man who creates religion, so it is not the constitution that creates the people but the people which creates the constitution. ... Man does not exist because

---

[62]   Marx, *Critique of Hegel's Philosophy of Right*, 28–29.
[63]   Marx, *Critique of Hegel's Philosophy of Right*, 29–30.
[64]   Marx, *Critique of Hegel's Philosophy of Right*, 29.
[65]   Marx, *Critique of Hegel's Philosophy of Right*, 29.
[66]   Marx, *Critique of Hegel's Philosophy of Right*, 28.
[67]   Kouvelakis, *Philosophy and Revolution*, 297.

of the law but rather the law exists for the good of man. Democracy is *human existence*, while in the other political forms man has only *legal* existence. That is the fundamental difference of democracy.[68]

Under democracy a 'socialised' person exists.[69] In other constitutional orders (e.g., liberal and republican), there is only the abstract legal person. The socialised person represents the full range of human existence, whereas the legal person represents only a formal part of this existence. Marx's position on the bifurcation of human consciousness and political organisation, which generates alienation, differs from Hegel's position.

At the centre of Hegel's theory of freedom, and his criticism of the French Revolution's inability to achieve this freedom,[70] is an account of alienation that offers an alternative to conceptions of sociological legitimacy,[71] and that Marx takes up and develops. For Hegel, alienation of this kind arises when public institutions and practices no longer command citizens' allegiance. Citizens come to be alienated because they are unable to identify with the norms these public institutions and practices embody.[72] In other words, there is a mismatch between the constitution and its social and political basis. The constitution, the political organisation of social life, is experienced as something foreign and as a fetter on free human development. Accordingly, Hegel rejects the superficial Enlightenment view of rational engineering of society, in which a model constitution is designed and then imposed externally.[73]

For Marx, humans alienate their powers to the state, and thus the political constitution is the sphere of alienation.[74] They attribute to (or project onto) the political sphere and to their citizen status what they lack in real life: equality, fraternity, and community. Thus, the political constitution plays in the political sphere an analogous role to religion's role in civil society—a role that involves self-estrangement and projecting upon an external entity the powers that we actually possess. In civil society, the sphere of the war of all against all, humans are separated from themselves: they lose their communal being, reduce themselves into means, and treat others as means for their material pursuits.[75] Instead of freeing humans from religion, the political constitution grants freedom of religion. Instead of freeing them from egoism, it grants them freedom of business. And instead of freeing them from property, it grants them freedom of property.[76] The liberal state presents itself as universal and sovereign. However, all these premises are false: this universality is unreal; the public is separated from the private, and the human leads a double life, as a citizen and private individual. And this sovereignty is imaginary, since political freedom is separated from the reality of economic dependence and exploitation, and thus citizens are not equal partners in popular sovereignty.[77]

---

[68]   Marx, *Critique of Hegel's Philosophy of Right*, 30 (original emphases).
[69]   Marx, *Critique of Hegel's Philosophy of Right*, 30.
[70]   Joachim Ritter, *Hegel and the French Revolution: Essays on The Philosophy of Right* (first published 1957, Richard Dien Winfield tr, MIT Press 1984).
[71]   Charles Taylor, *Hegel and Modern Society* (CUP 1979) 122–24.
[72]   Taylor, *Hegel and Modern Society*, 88–89; Hegel, *Elements of the Philosophy of Right*, 311–13.
[73]   Hegel, *Elements of the Philosophy of Right*, 311–13; Taylor, *Hegel and Modern Society*, 120.
[74]   Marx, *Critique of Hegel's Philosophy of Right*, 31.
[75]   Karl Marx, 'On the Jewish Question' [1844] in Robert C Tucker (ed), *The Marx-Engels Reader* (2nd edn, WW Norton & Co 1978) 26, 34.
[76]   Marx, 'Jewish Question', 45.
[77]   Marx, 'Jewish Question', 33–34. On alienation of labour see Karl Marx, 'Economic and Philosophic Manuscripts of 1844' in Robert C Tucker (ed), *The Marx-Engels Reader* (2nd edn, WW Norton & Co 1978) 66, 74–77.

The reason for the difference between democracy and other forms of political organisation is that democracy alone challenges the separation between political and civil society, between the 'political' and 'private' human. Hegel recognises the separation between citizen and private person, following the necessary separation between state and church.[78] Nevertheless, for Hegel, this separation of state and civil society is not to be transcended. Classes are part of the division of labour within the social totality, and as such are not to be overcome.[79] Importantly, there is no account of the working class in Hegel's account of social classes.[80]

For Marx, in contrast, democratising the constitution would require not only returning it to its creators (the *demos*) and extending self-government,[81] but also resocialising members of the community by recognising that they are embedded in social structures and that their abstract legal status conceals class inequality, so that they can 'reclaim in their daily lives the powers that the state had appropriated from them'.[82] The negation of 'political alienation, unlike that [of] religious alienation, requires a real revolution—a collective act whereby the citizens repossess the social power externalized in state institutions'.[83] In democracy the formal status attends to the material conditions. In contrast, other ('political') regimes institutionalise a gap between formal status and material conditions.[84] The abstraction of the state, Marx argues, is a modern evolution. Only in the modern state is there an abstract opposition between material and political life, and thus the 'political state' appears 'as the form of the material state'.[85]

There are two main difficulties with the separation between political and civil society, as presented in Hegel's exposition.[86] The first is that Hegel assumes this separation and then essentialises it in thought. While this separation certainly exists, it is not an eternal and historically universal necessity. Rather, it emerged as part of the historical development of modern states and capitalist societies. A theoretical exposition should not transform the historically contingent into the essential and necessary expression of universal rationality. Second, despite taking this separation for granted, Hegel presents the state as a unity. He does this although it is merely a part of this dualism. Thus, he ends up reproducing the same dualism in the sphere of the state by including elements of civil society ('the Estates') in the sphere of legislative and parliamentary activity. In the course of theoretical exposition, the initially presupposed dichotomy collapses. Rather than resolving the dualism between civil and political society, it is merely reintroduced. In democracy, this dualism needs to be dialectically sublated.

The experience of the French Revolution illustrates these criticisms. Both Hegel and Marx argue that the French Revolution's liberal abstractions are inimical to the creation of a community.[87] They also criticise the Jacobins for their authoritarian centralism and for the state's invasion of civil society. For Hegel, the centralisation of all aspects of social life and the sti-

[78] Avineri, *Hegel's Theory*, 32.
[79] Avineri, *Hegel's Theory*, 104.
[80] Avineri, *Hegel's Theory*, 108–9.
[81] Marx, *Critique of Hegel's Philosophy of Right*, 32 ('Monarchy is the fullest expression of this estrangement. The republic is the negation of this estrangement within its own sphere').
[82] Eagleton, *Why Marx Was Right*, 202.
[83] Robert C Tucker, 'Introduction' in Robert C Tucker (ed), *The Marx-Engels Reader* (2nd edn, WW Norton & Co 1978) xix, xxiv.
[84] Marx, *Critique of Hegel's Philosophy of Right*, 30.
[85] Marx, *Critique of Hegel's Philosophy of Right*, 32.
[86] Marx, *Critique of Hegel's Philosophy of Right*, 72–74.
[87] Kouvelakis, *Philosophy and Revolution*, 29–33; Marx, 'Jewish Question'.

fling of voluntary associations exhibit the continuity between the republic and the monarchy.[88] The Reign of Terror embodies a one-sided negative freedom ('freedom of the void'), in which all particular differences are obliterated in the pursuit of abstract universality: 'This is why the people, during the French Revolution, destroyed once more the institutions they had themselves created, because all institutions are incompatible with the abstract self-consciousness of equality'.[89]

For Marx, the Jacobin terror is a misguided 'attempt to realize a political order still lacking its socio-economic preconditions'.[90] The Jacobins' efforts to forcibly 'overcome the antagonism between state and civil society' are 'one-sided' endeavours to impose universality, as opposed to a dialectical resolution of the conflict 'by the recognition of the universality of the individual'.[91] Instead of merely negating civil society, what is needed is a dialectical incorporation and transcendence of its achievements.[92]

BETWEEN POLITICAL CONSTITUTION AND SOCIAL REVOLUTION

In light of this separation between the political constitution and the socio-economic reality, the main mystifying abstractions in constitutional debates are the 'people' and its 'constituent power'. Early republican theorists presented a 'class-specific', as opposed to class-neutral, understanding of the people.[93] By contrast, modern republican constitutions 'invariably treat the people as a homogenous unit: the people are a unitary and socio-economically anonymous collection of individual citizens, formally equal under the law'.[94] More generally, it is rare for contemporary constitutions or constitutional courts' jurisprudence to recognise the existence of social classes.[95] This lack of attention to class (in anti-discrimination law, for instance) overlooks the ways in which the class structure gets reproduced and social apartheid persists (such as through private education). It thus 'deflects attention from the institutional structure of society to which our interests, ideals, and group identities remain fastened'.[96]

Against this modern trend, Marx highlights that in a bourgeois revolution the republican bourgeoisie exercises constituent power and establishes a constitution that embodies the achievements—and limitations—of this revolution. The invocation of an imaginary, class-neutral 'people' founders on the reality of '*real* people [,]... that is, representatives of

---

[88]   GWF Hegel, 'The German Constitution' [1802] in GWF Hegel, *Political Writings* (Lawrence Dickey and HB Nisbet ed, CUP 1999) 6, 22–25, 89; Avineri, *Hegel's Theory*, 48–49.

[89]   Hegel, *Elements of the Philosophy of Right*, 38–39; Taylor, *Hegel and Modern Society*, 115–16.

[90]   Shlomo Avineri, *The Social and Political Thought of Karl Marx* (CUP 1968) 188.

[91]   Avineri, *Karl Marx*, 189.

[92]   Avineri, *Karl Marx*, 190–91.

[93]   John P McCormick, 'People and Elites in Republican Constitutions, Traditional and Modern' in Martin Loughlin and Neil Walker (eds), *The Paradox of Constitutionalism: Constituent Power and Constitutional Form* (CUP 2007) 107.

[94]   McCormick, 'People and Elites in Republican Constitutions', 107.

[95]   Günter Frankenberg, *Comparative Constitutional Studies: Between Magic and Deceit* (Edward Elgar 2018) 246–47; Unger, *What Should Legal Analysis Become?*, 83–104; Mario L Barnes and Erwin Chemerinsky, 'The Disparate Treatment of Race and Class in Constitutional Jurisprudence' (2009) 72 *Law and Contemporary Problems* 109.

[96]   Unger, *What Should Legal Analysis Become?*, 95.

the different classes into which it falls'.[97] Universal suffrage and direct elections bring forward this reality and undermine the '*cult of the people*', in French republicanism for instance, which posits 'at least in the majority of Frenchmen, *citoyens* with the same interests, the same understanding, etc.'[98]

The paradox of constitutionalism is unresolvable because constituent power is conceived within a 'partial, *merely* political revolution which leaves the pillars of the building standing'. In a political revolution, 'a *section of civil society* emancipates itself and attains universal domination; a determinate class undertakes, from its *particular situation*, a general emancipation of society'.[99] However, the claims of one class to represent the general interests of the people in a political revolution generate an unresolved tension between the particularity of the liberating class and the universality of its claims. The only way for this tension to be resolved is for the dehumanised proletariat to lead the revolution towards emancipation and a '*total redemption of humanity*':

> A class must be formed which has *radical* chains, a class in civil society which is not a class of civil society, a class which is the dissolution of all classes, a sphere of society which has a universal character because its sufferings are universal, and which does not claim a *particular redress* because the wrong which is done to it is not a *particular wrong* but *wrong in general*. ... This dissolution of society, as a particular class, is the proletariat.[100]

The proletariat 'is the right name, discovered at last (and substituted for "Third Estate", "people", "*sans-culotterie*", etc.), for the antagonism immanent in modern society'.[101]

Marx does not draw a rigid distinction between political and social revolution. Instead, he conceives each as part of a process that requires going beyond political emancipation toward human emancipation:

> Every revolution dissolves the *old society* and to that extent it is *social*. Every revolution overthrows the *old power* and to that extent it is *political*... Revolution in general—the *overthrow* of the existing power and *dissolution* of the old relationships—is a *political act*. But *socialism* cannot be realised without *revolution*. It needs this *political* act insofar as it needs *destruction* and *dissolution*. But where its organising activity begins, where its *proper object*, its *soul*, comes to the fore—there socialism throws off the *political* cloak.[102]

This 'political cloak' is inclusive of liberal and republican political constitutions. In fact, despite the emancipatory potential of these abstractions, they too have negative consequences. For Marx, republicanism is an ideology whose 'notions of citizenship and community are constitutive of reality at the same time that they misdescribe it'.[103] By emphasising formal citizenship, '[i]t functions as an ideological legitimation of the *bellum omnes contra omnes*

---

[97]   Marx, 'The Class Struggles in France, 1848 to 1850' [1850] in Karl Marx and Frederick Engels, *Collected Works*, vol 10 (Lawrence & Wishart 2010) 45, 65 (original emphasis).

[98]   Marx, 'Class Struggles in France', 65 (original emphasis).

[99]   Marx, 'Contribution', 62 (original emphases).

[100]   Marx, 'Contribution', 64 (original emphases).

[101]   Kouvelakis, *Philosophy and Revolution*, 236.

[102]   Karl Marx, 'Critical Marginal Notes on the Article "The King of Prussia and Social Reform"' [1844] in Robert C Tucker (ed), *The Marx-Engels Reader* (2nd edn, WW Norton & Co 1978) 126, 132 (original emphases).

[103]   Isaac, 'Lion's Skin', 475.

which constitutes civil society, compensating for the practical debasement of ordinary life by elevating the alienated man to the status of species-being'.[104]

Accordingly, the call to overthrow this cloak is an invitation to go beyond the struggle over access to the state toward transforming the state and its relation to society. The following section shows that constituent assemblies in political revolutions often fail to produce the required social change and democratisation.

CONSTITUENT ASSEMBLIES DURING A POLITICAL REVOLUTION

Marx agrees with republicans that 'sovereign dictatorship' is necessary during a revolution.[105] In a moment of founding, popular sovereignty cannot be limited by pre-existing procedures and principles.[106] Power struggles between opposing parties cannot be regulated, let alone resolved, through existing institutions and principles. Marx's commentary on the 1848 revolutionary process in Germany sets out this view, but it also highlights his scepticism about constituent power in concrete historical contexts, given the performance of actual constituent assemblies that fail to attain the ideal of constituent power. In contrast to this ideal, which presumes unlimited power to reconstitute the polity and enact the new constitution, constituent assemblies do not act in a vacuum and do not create the constitution *ex nihilo*.[107]

The Frankfurt Assembly is a case in point. As the assembly attempted to purify the army of officers who were not sympathetic to the revolution, the cabinet—backed up by Frederick William IV—refused to pass these measures and consequently resigned. The constitutional crisis thus involved a struggle between the king and his executive power on the one hand and the elected assembly on the other. For Marx, this struggle presents a stark choice between 'recognition of popular sovereignty' and 'sham constitutionalism', between democratic freedom and military dictatorship. In particular, Marx argues that the monarch does not have the right to dissolve the Frankfurt Assembly on the basis of the pre-existing constitutional order. This is because the assembly as a revolutionary constituent power is tasked with writing the constitution. In other words, pre-existing constituted bodies cannot limit its power. It is akin to a sovereign dictator reconstituting the polity:

> [I]t has been convened not on the basis of a Constitution, but on that of a *revolution*. It received its mandate by no means from the Crown or from the Ministers answerable to the Crown, but from those who elected it and from the Assembly itself. The Assembly was sovereign as the legitimate expression of the revolution. ... A sovereign assembly ... cannot be dissolved by anybody, and cannot be given orders by anybody.[108]

---

[104]   Isaac, 'Lion's Skin', 476.

[105]   Cf Andrew Arato, 'The Link Between Revolution and Sovereign Dictatorship: Reflections on the Russian Constituent Assembly' (2017) 24 *Constellations* 493.

[106]   Sieyès, 'What is the Third Estate?', 139.

[107]   Cf Claude Klein and András Sajó, 'Constitution-Making: Process and Substance' in Michel Rosenfeld and András Sajó (eds), *The Oxford Handbook of Comparative Constitutional Law* (OUP 2012) 419, 421.

[108]   Marx, 'The Crisis and the Counter-Revolution' [1848] in Karl Marx and Frederick Engels, *Collected Works*, vol 7 (Lawrence & Wishart 2010) 427, 428–29 (original emphasis).

In light of this position, Marx mocks the invocation of 'constitutional principles'. The cabinet and the monarchists argued that the assembly violated the principle of separation of powers, usurping the executive branch's powers. But these arguments conflate the constituent assembly (during a revolution) with a legislative assembly (under an established constitution). They thereby ignore the fact that the revolution is a process rather than an event, and that the new constitutional order is yet to emerge. As such, the revolution is still underway and requires reconstitution of the polity rather than reliance upon the very constitutional order whose bankruptcy the revolution foregrounds and whose substance it seeks to change.[109]

The 'constitutional fantasies' that Marx criticises are prevalent during 'ordinary' times. Even under such conditions, these principles are myths that conceal the actual operation of the state. Consider, for instance, liberal constitutionalists' admission that the 'rule of law' is 'merely a slogan', and 'mere rhetoric', and that the ideal of 'government of laws and not of men' is 'an impossibility'.[110] In capitalist states, neoliberal austerity undermines minimal promises of the rule of law (such as in criminal procedure),[111] and wealth inequality leads to unequal application of the law and the privileging of the affluent (such as the financial sector).[112] Consider further that the principle of separation of powers is 'outdated' and 'must be scrapped' because it is not consistent with constitutional democratic practice and does not accurately reflect political reality.[113] Indeed, Madisonian political theory is 'clearly anachronistic' with respect to its 'vision of legislative-executive separation of powers'.[114] Thus, 'constitutional law and theory have been looking for power in the wrong places',[115] because 'the distribution of power at the structural level seldom bears any systematic relation to the distribution of power at the level of interests'.[116] Thus, 'the problem of concentrated wealth and its organization to achieve political ends' is the primary reason for the failure of effective 'checks and balances', rather than partisanship.[117] Maintaining this constitutional fiction is even less justifiable under revolutionary conditions, when the reconstitution of the polity requires redistribution of power.[118] In fact, such assertions of constitutional continuity often seek to delimit the potentialities of revolutionary change.

Marx defends constituent power against constitutional arguments that seek to constrain it, but he is cognisant of the fact that the 1848 Constituent Assembly failed to assert itself as a constituent power with sufficient force. It was, he suggests, a 'parody' of constituent

---

[109] Marx, 'Crisis and the Counter-Revolution', 430–31. Marx makes a similar point elsewhere arguing that the struggle between the Assembly and the monarch is not a constitutional power struggle between two branches or authorities (executive versus legislature). Rather, in the absence of a constitution, the Assembly is a sovereign and unlimited power tasked to establish the constitutional order. Marx, 'The Trial of the Rhenish District Committee of Democrats' [1849] in Karl Marx and Frederick Engels, *Collected Works*, vol 8 (Lawrence & Wishart 2010) 323.

[110] Martin Loughlin, *Foundations of Public Law* (OUP 2010) 312–13.

[111] The Secret Barrister, *Stories of the Law and How It's Broken* (Pan Macmillan 2018).

[112] Joseph E Stiglitz, *The Price of Inequality: How Today's Divided Society Endangers Our Future* (WW Norton & Co 2012) 496–541.

[113] Hansen, 'Mixed Constitution', 516.

[114] Levinson and Pildes, 'Separation of Parties, Not Powers', 2313.

[115] Levinson, 'Foreword', 38.

[116] Levinson, 'Foreword', 40.

[117] Andrias, 'Separations of Wealth', 421.

[118] See e.g., Sultany, *Law and Revolution* (on the struggle over 'judicial independence' and 'rule of law' in the Arab Spring).

power.[119] This lack of constituent action emboldens counter-revolutionary forces. Marx also criticises the lack of early action by the GL Camphausen government (March–June 1848) to destroy the remnants of old institutions.[120] Marx reminds his reader that pre-revolutionary governments did not shy away from invoking public interest—through appeals to 'public safety'—against democratic forces. The government could have done the same in 1848 against the revolution's enemies. Yet the cabinet refrained from following this course of action during a revolutionary process.[121] Indeed, the resurgence of the reactionary forces turned out to be only a matter of time. By April 1849, the revolution was defeated and monarchical regimes were restored in Germany and elsewhere in Europe.

This weakness in the performance of constituent assemblies invites the question of the limits to their mandate. By November 1848 Marx was thoroughly disillusioned with the Frankfurt Assembly. In particular, it decided to rebuke the Berlin Assembly by rejecting its determination that the refusal to pay taxes was a method of lawful resistance to the king. Such a decision was a betrayal of the German people and an endorsement of the very monarchical regime against which they had revolted. Marx declared that the representatives ought to be put on trial, and also called upon them to resign.[122] For Marx, who defends the masses' right to pressure constituent assemblies by attending their deliberations,[123] the people maintain their right to step forward if a constituent assembly violates the terms of its mandate, namely by establishing a new constitution that befits the new social order that the revolution brought forward: 'If the Assembly does not act in accordance with the mandate it has received, then this mandate lapses. The people then takes stage itself and acts on its own'.[124]

LEGAL CONTINUITY AND THE COUNTER-REVOLUTION

The fact that constituent assemblies may fail to establish new orders under revolutionary conditions invites questions about the legal and institutional continuities that impede their action. On the one hand, it is sobering as it enables a realistic assessment of the work needed for the revolutionary change to materialise. On the other hand, the imposition of legal continuity is objectionable (because it relies on a fiction and seeks to abort revolutionary change) and thus should be rejected.

In his speech during the 'Tax-Refusal Trial', Marx discussed the legal ramifications of the power struggle between the crown and the Constituent Assembly, the question of legal continuity, and the relation between taxes and constitutionalism. His prosecution related to the public 'appeal' he had published in the *Neue Rheinische Zeitung* on 18 November 1848,

---

[119]   Marx, 'Crisis', 432.

[120]   Marx, 'Crisis', 431. Similarly, he criticises the Frankfurt Assembly for its failure to promptly and clearly endorse the principle of popular sovereignty as the basis for the new constitutional order and to act against reactionary counter-revolutionary forces. Karl Marx and Frederick Engels, 'The Assembly at Frankfurt' [1848] in Karl Marx and Frederick Engels, *Collected Works*, vol 7 (Lawrence & Wishart 2010) 16.

[121]   Marx, 'Crisis', 431.

[122]   Marx, 'Assembly'.

[123]   Karl Marx, 'Freedom of Debate in Berlin' [1848] in Karl Marx and Frederick Engels, *Collected Works*, vol 7 (Lawrence & Wishart 2010) 436.

[124]   Marx, 'Trial', 339.

on behalf of the 'Rhenish District Committee of Democrats'.[125] This appeal had invoked the Prussian National Assembly's resolution and urged 'all democratic associations in the Rhine province' to refuse to pay taxes and to resist 'their forcible collection ... everywhere and in every way'.[126]

The prosecution relied on two organic laws enacted in April 1848, following the 1848 March Revolution. Marx disputed the validity of these organic laws on two grounds. First, even if one assumes *arguendo* that the organic laws were procedurally valid, they were suspended by the fact of the counter-revolution (the overthrow of the constitutional order that the March Revolution brought into place). More importantly, they were null and void because they had been enacted by unauthorised bodies that did not possess sovereign power, and were in fact overthrown by the revolution. The attempt to 'preserve a semblance of legal continuity' despite this rupture was absurd, Marx argued.[127]

The monarchy had effectively suspended the legal order by its counter-revolutionary act. As a result, Marx stated, 'it cannot appeal to the laws it has itself so scandalously annulled'.[128] The organic laws were not mere ordinary laws, and by violating them the monarchy had invalidated the constitutional order they embodied. This included the fact that the electoral and parliamentary system, which the organic laws prescribed, was not respected. The monarchy had introduced an upper chamber in the legislative branch based on property qualifications. Marx's argument was that although these legal instruments could still be formally valid (since they were not annulled), they were effectively or substantively invalid (since they lacked factual power and social efficacy during a societal upheaval or revolutionary turmoil). The government could not pick and choose among legal provisions, treating some as valid while ignoring and violating others.

If a revolutionary change occurred, then the monarchy was better off invoking 'necessity' (violating 'legal formula to save the country').[129] Instead, the monarchy chose the opposite route of assuming the 'pretense of legality': rather than executing its opponents, the regime chose to prosecute them; rather than considering them political enemies, it sought to criminalise them.[130] According to Marx, the regime could not prosecute him because he was its political enemy and his call for resistance (his refusal to pay taxes) was part of the struggle between the monarchy and the Constituent Assembly. In such a struggle, 'only power can decide between two powers'.[131] Marx sided with the National Assembly because it represented the people.

Marx's second argument was that the laws in question were *formally* invalid. Institutionally, the Universal Provincial Diet was not an authoritative legislative organ because it represented the old social order (namely, the landed gentry and feudal lords) which the March 1848 Revolution had overthrown along with the absolute monarchy.[132] Substantively, this obsolete state organ represented anachronistic interests. Maintaining legal continuity in this context meant preserving the interests of the old social order in the face of the emerging social order

---

[125] Karl Marx, 'Appeal' [1848] in Karl Marx and Frederick Engels, *Collected Works*, vol 8 (Lawrence & Wishart 2010) 41.

[126] Marx, 'Appeal', 41.

[127] Marx, 'Trial', 326.

[128] Marx, 'Trial', 324.

[129] Marx, 'Trial', 324.

[130] Marx, 'Trial', 324.

[131] Marx, 'Trial', 325.

[132] Marx, 'Trial', 326–27.

(given industrialisation and the rise of the bourgeoisie). This did not make sense for Marx, who thought that law should maintain its relation to social needs and interests.[133] Otherwise, priorities were flipped and law was fetishised:

> Society is not founded upon the law; this is a legal fiction. On the contrary, the law must be founded upon society, it must express the common interests and needs of society—as distinct from the caprice of individuals—which arise from the material mode of production prevailing at the given time.[134]

The maintenance of legal continuity, then, meant that the law advanced minority over majority interests, despite changing social bases, and that there was a disconnect between law and 'the conditions of life'.[135] The law became unfit for purpose and could hamper social and economic developments, leading to crisis. This is why the March 1848 Revolution sought to reconstitute the polity, establishing a new constitution befitting the new order.[136] The April 1848 organic laws sought to undermine the revolution and shackle the Constituent Assembly, which was tasked with establishing a new constitution for the new polity.

For Marx, legal continuity could not be maintained because the struggle was not a conflict within the same society or the same framework of principles.[137] Rather, it was a conflict between two opposing visions of social order, competing interests, and contradictory principles:

> What took place was not a political conflict between two parties within the framework of *one* society, but a *conflict between two societies*, a social conflict, which assumed a political form; *it was the struggle of the old feudal bureaucratic society with modern bourgeois society*, a struggle between the society of *free competition* and the *society of guild system*, between the society of landownership and the industrial society, between a religious society and a scientific society.[138]

This also showed that the National Assembly's conciliatory efforts to resolve the conflict amicably were misguided, since there could be no reconciliation in the context of such conflict with the monarchy. The assembly thereby underestimated the lurking danger of the monarchical counter-revolution, which was a 'constantly recurrent condition … after every revolution'.[139] 'Hence no peace is possible between these two societies. Their material interests and needs bring them into mortal combat. One side must win, the other must lose. That is the only reconciliation possible between them.'[140]

Indeed, the 1848 Revolution did not produce the kind of rupture necessary to ensure success, and different forms of institutional continuity undermined it. On February 1849 Marx would reflect as follows:

---

[133]   For Marx, the duty to bridge the gap between law and social needs is not merely the task of the constituent assembly, but also an interpretive duty on those who apply the law like the jury. Marx, 'First Trial', 304.

[134]   Marx, 'Trial', 327.

[135]   Marx, 'Trial', 328.

[136]   Marx, 'Trial', 328.

[137]   Thus, there can be no Dworkinian continuity based on a background shared scheme of abstract principles. Sultany, *Law and Revolution*, ch 5.

[138]   Marx, 'Trial', 335 (original emphases).

[139]   Marx, 'Trial', 336.

[140]   Marx, 'Trial', 336.

What caused the defeat of the *March revolution*? It reformed only the highest political summit, it left all the groundwork of this summit intact—the old bureaucracy, the old army, the old boards of prosecuting magistrates, the old judiciary which had been created, had developed and grown grey in the service of absolutism.[141]

Herein lies the limitation of the political revolution and the political constitution it engenders: it underestimates the magnitude of social struggle by wrongly assuming a shared abstract framework that ignores the conflicting material interests at stake, and it further limits its aspirations for reform, thus failing to achieve genuine rupture from the old regime.

THE POLITICAL CONSTITUTION IN CONTEXT

The limitations of the political constitution require further elaboration. Constitutional scholars often approach the constitution as a higher law or normative contract. Yet constitutional experiences are varied and not reducible to this approach.[142] Moreover, the ability of the abstract normative constitution to legitimate the juridico-political order, by subjugating it to a higher law of lawmaking, is questionable even within the frameworks of liberal thought.[143] The line between normativity and *modus vivendi* is often overstated, because abstract rights require social and political struggles to be actualised.[144] Constitutions are based on a *modus vivendi* because they are an outcome of class struggle rather than a binding normative agreement against the backdrop of a 'social contract' between the capitalist class and the working class.[145]

For Marx, the constitution embodies a compromise.[146] This is not simply a matter of political compromise, in the sense of bringing a variety of different groups together for constitution-making purposes.[147] Instead, it is first and foremost a class compromise.[148] Thus, Marx's answer to the question 'what is a constitution' is that the constitution is a class-based compromise. This is reflected in his brief commentary on the uncodified British constitu-

---

[141] Marx, 'First Trial', 316–17 (original emphasis).

[142] Jorge González-Jácome, 'From Abusive Constitutionalism to a Multilayered Understanding of Constitutionalism: Lessons from Latin America' (2017) 15 *International Journal of Constitutional Law* 447; Günter Frankenberg, 'Comparing Constitutions: Ideas, Ideals, and Ideology—Toward a Layered Narrative' (2006) 4 *International Journal of Constitutional Law* 439.

[143] Frank I Michelman, 'Human Rights and the Limits of Constitutional Theory' (2000) 13 *Ratio Juris* 63; Frank Michelman, 'Is the Constitution a Contract for Legitimacy?' (2003) 8 *Review of Constitutional Studies* 101; Louis Michael Seidman, *On Constitutional Disobedience* (OUP 2013).

[144] See e.g., Marx's discussion of the class struggle over the regulation of the working day, describing resistance, setbacks, and legal loopholes: Marx, *Capital*, 382, 390, 394–95, 404–5, 408–9. See also Sultany, *Law and Revolution*, ch 2.

[145] See e.g., Richard Miller, 'Rawls and Marxism' (1974) 3 *Philosophy & Public Affairs* 167, 170; Louis Michael Seidman, *Our Unsettled Constitution: A New Defense of Constitutionalism and Judicial Review* (Yale University Press 2001).

[146] Marx, *Critique of Hegel's Philosophy of Right*, 58 ('is nothing more than an accommodation between the political and non-political state; hence it is necessarily in itself a treaty between essentially heterogeneous powers').

[147] Carl Schmitt, *Constitutional Theory* (first published 1928, Jeffrey Seitzer ed and tr, Duke University Press 2008) 82–88, 112–24.

[148] See discussion in Ernst-Wolfgang Böckenförde, 'The Historical Evolution and Changes in the Meaning of the Constitution' in Ernst-Wolfgang Böckenförde, *Constitutional and Political Theory: Selected Writings* (Mirjam Künkler and Tine Stein eds, OUP 2017) 152, 162–65.

tion.[149] For Marx, the 'essential features' of this constitution are not merely formal or textual.[150] In particular, he maintains that what distinguishes this constitution from others are not those rules that regulate political representation and the exercise of executive power. Rather, the British constitution is a historic compromise ('antiquated and obsolete') between the bourgeoisie and the landed aristocracy that was subsequently modified in accordance with changes in social relations to accommodate rising social powers, such as the financial aristocracy after the Glorious Revolution of 1688.[151]

In light of the fact that constitutions are based on a *modus vivendi* within a class-based social order, it is unsurprising that they generate contradictions and incoherence, or that they over-promise and under-deliver. Marx's analysis of the French Constitution of 1848 reveals that such compromise is unstable and generates an incoherent constitutional order whose practice falls short of its proclaimed ideals, as evident in the disenfranchisement of the poor. The constitutional order thus seeks to stabilise itself through reliance on violence (such as through the deployment of emergency powers), constitutional entrenchment, and irremovability of judges.

To begin with, Marx takes note of the gap between constitutional texts and practices, the failure to deliver on the promises of formal rights of equality, and the existence of ambiguities and contradictions in constitutional orders. Although the 1848 French Constitution was a republican instrument, the legal order to which it gave expression limited universal suffrage through excluding criminals and stipulating a residency requirement that disenfranchised a large number of people.[152] The revolution created a new constitution, but this constitution fell short of establishing a new polity. Constitutional discontinuity co-existed with continuity in state administration because the 'old organisation of the administration', such as the judiciary and the military, remained unreformed.[153] The constitution declared the rights of the citizen 'absolute', but the 'equal rights of others' and considerations of 'public safety' limited these rights, or they awaited further elaboration in legislation that effectively undermined them.[154] Constitutional practice was discriminatory: the organic laws privileged the bourgeoisie because their exercise of rights was not limited by the rights of other classes, and the 'public safety' proviso effectively meant 'bourgeois safety'.[155]

For Marx, these conditions show that the constitution is not simply a document, but also the web of laws that purport to implement it but may in fact undermine the rights and freedoms it ostensibly protects:

> [T]he real 'Constitution' of France is to be found, not in the Charter we have recorded, but in the organic laws enacted on its basis … The *principles* were there—the *details* were left to the future, and in those details a shameless tyranny was re-enacted![156]

---

[149]   Marx, 'The British Constitution' [1855] in Karl Marx, *Surveys from Exile* (Verso 2010) 281.

[150]   Marx, 'British Constitution'.

[151]   Marx, 'British Constitution'.

[152]   Karl Marx, 'The Eighteenth Brumaire of Louis Bonaparte' [1852] in Karl Marx and Frederick Engels, *Collected Works*, vol 11 (Lawrence & Wishart 1979) 109, 114.

[153]   Marx, 'Eighteenth Brumaire', 114

[154]   Marx, 'Eighteenth Brumaire', 114–15.

[155]   Marx, 'Eighteenth Brumaire', 115.

[156]   Karl Marx, 'The Constitution of the French Republic Adopted November 4, 1848' in Karl Marx and Frederick Engels, *Collected Works*, vol 10 (Lawrence & Wishart 2010) 567, 578 (original emphases).

As a result, it is not sufficient to agree on abstract principles, and it is necessary to be aware of the institutional organisation of the constitutional order: 'People! Make up your minds as to *details*, as well as to principles, before you come to power'.[157] Agreement on an abstract constitution may be meaningless.[158]

The 1848 French Constitution was a site for conflicting demands and aspirations. It was utilised by different parties to achieve different ends. This was not because of abuse or violations of the constitution, but because the constitution itself contained contradictory provisions: 'For each paragraph of the Constitution contains its antithesis, its own Upper and Lower House'.[159] Indeed, 'from beginning to end it is a mass of fine words, hiding a most treacherous design. From its very wording, it is rendered *impossible* to violate it, for every one of its provisions contains its own antithesis—utterly nullifies itself'.[160]

One of the principal conflicts Marx identifies is between different branches of government. Despite a well-crafted constitutional text, it was 'like Achilles, vulnerable in one point, not in the heel, but in the head, or rather the two heads'.[161] Marx describes the deadlock to which the constitutional separation of powers led, discussing tensions between the presidential and parliamentary, executive and legislative, branches. The constitution 'not only sanctifies the division of powers', he writes, but also 'widens it into an intolerable contradiction'.[162] It grants the president 'actual power', and the legislature (the National Assembly) a 'moral power'. According to Marx, there are two primary problems with this arrangement. First, 'it is impossible to create a moral power by paragraphs of law'.[163] Second, by providing for direct election of the president, the constitution-maker (the constituent assembly) opened the door for undermining the constitutional order. This is because the president was the only constitutional power representing the unity of the people, whereas the divided legislative assembly represented a variety of competing interests. The assembly represented the nation in a 'metaphysical sense', but the president directly and 'personally' represented the nation.[164] This constitutional arrangement granted the president the upper hand in the battle against the assembly, and thus facilitated the overthrow of the constitution itself. A major reason for the inability to resolve the political conflict constitutionally was the difficulty in amending the constitution.

Marx critiques the constitutional entrenchment effort as a failed attempt to stabilise the political order. The ruling majority expected to lose power and wanted to immunise its achievements from the vagaries of electoral politics. It thus 'sought to cheat destiny by a catch in the Constitution'.[165] It placed a high threshold for constitutional amendment, making the constitution virtually unamendable.[166] This was one of the few constitutional provisions that Marx thought open to violation because it was not contradictory.[167] Yet the virtual impossibility of constitutional amendment prevented the possibility of changing the constitutional order

---

[157]   Marx, 'Constitution of the French Republic', 578 (original emphases).
[158]   See e.g., Michelman, 'Human Rights and the Limits of Constitutional Theory'.
[159]   Marx, 'Eighteenth Brumaire', 115.
[160]   Marx, 'Constitution of the French Republic', 577 (original emphasis).
[161]   Marx, 'Eighteenth Brumaire', 115.
[162]   Marx, 'Eighteenth Brumaire', 115–16.
[163]   Marx, 'Eighteenth Brumaire', 116.
[164]   Marx, 'Eighteenth Brumaire', 117.
[165]   Marx, 'Eighteenth Brumaire', 117.
[166]   Art §111, as quoted in Marx, 'Constitution of the French Republic', 577.
[167]   Marx, 'Constitution of the French Republic', 578.

without overthrowing the constitution. Indeed, these attempts to fix the constitutional order did not survive the political turmoil. The constitution lasted until 2 December 1851, when Louis Bonaparte staged a *coup d'état* after refusing to leave office at the end of his constitutionally prescribed (non-renewable) term.[168] The constitution, then, is not above politics, and it cannot be a guarantee against it.[169]

Marx also points out the role of violence in stabilising the constitutional order. The constitution-making process co-existed with the declaration of the 'state of siege' in Paris. A state of siege empowers the military and its tribunals to suspend constitutional guarantees during an emergency period, thereby often allowing them to violate citizens' rights. For Marx, this is another demonstration of the fact that general proclamations in legal texts can be, and often are, superseded in practice. The role of violence suggests two further insights.

First, the constitution of the parliamentary republic was neither an exclusive outcome of the democratic exercise of free will, nor a product of a rational exercise of the human faculties. Rather, it was written during social unrest and supported by force and violence.[170] The 'state of siege of Paris was the midwife of the Constituent Assembly in its travail of republican creation'.[171] Bayonets protected the establishment of the constitution, and bayonets overthrew it.[172] Indeed, during the constitution-making process, the government ruthlessly crushed the working class' June 1848 insurrection.[173] However, this deployment of violence, far from stabilising the political order, actually destabilises it. The state of siege was normalised because it was 'periodically employed in every ensuing crisis in the course of the French Revolution'.[174] The risks of deployment by competing factions in the service of their own interests is that it may pave the way for the military itself to capture power by using the device of the state of siege.[175]

Second, Marx takes up the question of prolonging the state of siege as preceding and accompanying constitution-making in order to distinguish between revolutionary and counter-revolutionary constitutions. Revolutionary constitutions sanction a social revolution once social relations stabilise and a compromise among different factions of the ruling classes is concluded to the exclusion of the masses. The counter-revolutionary constitution, however, affirms the 'momentary victory of the old society over the revolution'.[176] Marx finds evidence for the counter-revolutionary orientation of the Constituent Assembly in the removal of

[168] Eugénie Mérieau, 'French Authoritarian Constitutionalism and Its Legacy' in Helena Alviar García and Günter Frankenberg (eds), *Authoritarian Constitutionalism: Comparative Analysis and Critique* (Edward Elgar 2019) 185, 196.

[169] See also Seidman, *Our Unsettled Constitution*, 7, 21–22.

[170] Marx, 'Eighteenth Brumaire', 118. See also Marx, 'Freedom of Debate in Berlin', 436–38. For additional examples for this proposition see Jon Elster, 'Constitution-Making and Violence' (2012) 4 *Journal of Legal Analysis* 7; and Gregory Ablavsky, 'The Savage Constitution' (2014) 63 *Duke Law Journal* 999.

[171] Marx, 'Eighteenth Brumaire', 118.

[172] Marx, 'Eighteenth Brumaire', 118.

[173] Marx, 'Eighteenth Brumaire', 109–11.

[174] Marx, 'Eighteenth Brumaire', 118. For an analysis of the contemporary normalisation of emergency powers, see Günter Frankenberg, *Political Technology and the Erosion of the Rule of Law: Normalizing the State of Exception* (Edward Elgar 2014).

[175] Marx, 'Eighteenth Brumaire', 118.

[176] Marx, 'Class Struggles in France', 77.

the right to work and progressive taxation,[177] as well as the right to education and the right of orphans to state support, which appeared in an earlier draft that predated the June 1848 insurrection.[178]

A final stabilising device, and another manifestation of the counter-revolutionary character of the constitution, is juristocracy—the rule of judges. Its objective is to immunise the old order from democratic elements by empowering the judiciary and isolating it from political influence:

> While the tricolor constitution … was unable to win the attachment of any new social element to the new form of government, it hastened, on the other hand, to restore its traditional inviolability to a body that constituted the most hard-bitten and fanatical defender of the old state. It raised the *irremovability of judges*, which had been questioned by the Provisional Government, to an organic law. The *one* king whom it had removed rose again, by the score, in these irremovable inquisitors of legality.[179]

Absent broad social support for the new constitutional order, the irremovability of judges—who are closely associated with the pre-existing regime and notions of law and order—becomes a primary stabilising mechanism. While the constitution grants universal suffrage, it excludes various classes, including the proletariat and peasantry, from the political process. It prevents these classes from gaining significant electoral and parliamentary power, or using such power to radically change the constitutional order or replace the professional class tasked with applying and interpreting the constitution. Such an anti-majoritarian juristocracy, which limits the efficacy of electoral and participatory politics, continues to be a major feature of modern constitutional orders.[180]

FROM CONCEPTUAL PARADOXES TO MATERIAL CONFLICTS

These criticisms of disenfranchisement, constitutional entrenchment, judicial empowerment, and the role of violence may be familiar to those who object to anti-democratic measures and counter-majoritarian structures in liberal and republican constitutional orders. Marx, however, goes beyond the criticisms of counter-majoritarianism and authoritarian centralism. Unlike other commentators at the time, Marx is not content with analysing the power struggle between two branches of government—the legislative/sovereign assembly (National Assembly) and the executive (president)—over the final decision-making authority.[181] This is not, Marx argues, the constitution's 'fundamental contradiction'. He warns against conflating 'language of the struggle on the platform' with 'its real content'.[182] As in the case of the German Revolution,

---

[177]   Marx, 'Class Struggles in France', 78.

[178]   Marx, 'Constitution of the French Republic', 567.

[179]   Marx, 'Class Struggles in France', 78–79 (original emphases).

[180]   Ran Hirschl, *Towards Juristocracy: The Origins and Consequences of the New Constitutionalism* (Harvard University Press 2007); JAG Griffith, *Politics of the Judiciary* (5th edn, Harper Collins 1997); Nimer Sultany, 'The State of Progressive Constitutional Theory: The Paradox of Constitutional Democracy and the Project of Political Justification' (2012) 47 *Harvard Civil Rights—Civil Liberties Law Review* 371.

[181]   Marx, 'Class Struggles in France', 79, 85.

[182]   Marx, 'Class Struggles in France', 85.

framing the revolutionary situation in constitutional terms is a misconception and amounts to an abdication of constituent power. Properly understood, the constitutional conflict is actually a conflict between two societies (and different interests) rather than within one society. Thus, and in contrast to liberal constitutional theory,[183] there is no harmonious unfolding of the relation between constituent power and constituted power. Instead, they may well be—and often are—in direct conflict. This is an historical conflict, and not merely a conceptual or logical puzzle. Accordingly, it is embodied in real conflict between different social forces that capture different state institutions and have competing visions of the social and constitutional order.

Marx argues that the fundamental contradiction is embodied in the separation between social and political emancipation. On the one hand, the French Constitution entrenches the class-based social order (under which workers are dependent on capital and forced into exploitative wage labour); on the other hand, it extends the right to vote to all citizens. It grants political emancipation but forestalls social emancipation:

> The fundamental contradiction of this constitution, however, consists in the following: The classes whose social slavery the constitution is to perpetuate, proletariat, peasantry, petty bourgeoisie, it puts in possession of political power through universal suffrage. And from the class whose old social power it sanctions, the bourgeoisie, it withdraws the political guarantees of this power. It forces the political rule of the bourgeoisie into democratic conditions, which at every moment help the hostile classes to victory and jeopardise the very foundations of bourgeois society. From the ones it demands that they should not go forward from political to social emancipation; from the others that they should not go back from social to political restoration.[184]

The contradiction thus is the one between capitalism and liberal democracy.[185] Capitalism increases the separation between class power and state power, i.e., economic structures of exploitation are divorced from direct political coercion.[186] In contrast to feudalism, the centralisation of the state dispossesses 'the appropriating class of direct political powers ... leaving them with private exploitative powers purified of public, social functions'.[187] This is not merely a question of separating the economic and political as much as redrawing the boundaries of the political.[188]

The very constitution that establishes an electoral democracy inhibits the ability of the masses' political power to fundamentally change the social order (because it protects property rights and erects counter-majoritarian structures). Despite the achievements of the political revolution (democratising the constitutional order), it is an incomplete revolution that seeks to block further democratisation. It attempts to deprive the proletariat, peasantry, and petty bourgeoisie of the power to transform their society by democratising the economy. Put differently, the masses are denied their constituent power to expand the political and deepen democracy because the constitution entrenches the socio-political order and blocks a further revolution.

---

[183] See e.g., Hans Lindahl, 'Constituent Power and Reflexive Identity: Towards an Ontology of Collective Selfhood' in Martin Loughlin and Neil Walker (eds), *The Paradox of Constitutionalism: Constituent Power and Constitutional Form* (OUP 2008) 9, 11.

[184] Marx, 'Class Struggles in France', 79.

[185] See August H Nimtz's chapter in this volume.

[186] Wood, *Democracy Against Capitalism*, 33–34.

[187] Wood, *Democracy Against Capitalism*, 39.

[188] Wood, *Democracy Against Capitalism*, 44.

Marx adds that the nature of the constitutional contradiction between executive and legislative powers is better understood as originating in the unresolved paradox of constitutionalism—the struggle between constituent and constituted power in a revolutionary situation. On the one hand, the establishment of the constitution displaces the constituent assembly: 'The first day of the realisation of the constitution was the last day of the rule of the Constituent Assembly'.[189] On the other hand, the creator refuses to leave the political scene; constituent power seeks to remain active after the constitution of the new form of government:

> from the hour when the National Assembly had installed Bonaparte ... France stepped out of the period of republican constitution into the period of the constituted republic. And what place was there for a Constituent Assembly in a constituted republic? After the earth had been created, there was nothing else for its creator to do but flee to heaven. The Constituent Assembly was determined not to follow his example; the National Assembly was the last asylum of the party of the bourgeois republicans.[190]

The reason for this is that the constitutional and legal guarantees installed by the drafters of the constitution failed to achieve the intended consequences. Despite setting a high threshold of number of votes (two million) for presidential candidates, Louis Bonaparte swept the vote and therefore nullified the need to resort to a choice of president by the Constituent Assembly itself.[191] The drafters had an imaginary people in mind, but what the electoral process reflected was the 'real people' in their divisions, their perceived or even misconceived interests.[192] For a variety of reasons, different classes of the people imagined Bonaparte to represent their interests.[193]

The constituted power sought to wrest the polity away from the hands of constituent power. The latter, for its part, wanted to prevent the degeneration of its constitutional designs to trajectories it did not anticipate or welcome:

> Louis Bonaparte as against the Constituent National Assembly—that was not one unilateral constitutional power as against another; that was not the executive power as against the legislative. That was the constituted bourgeois republic itself as against the intrigues and ideological demands of the revolutionary faction of the bourgeoisie that had founded it and was now amazed to find that its constituted republic looked like a restored monarchy, and now desired forcibly to prolong the constituent period with its conditions, its illusions, its language, and its personages and to prevent the mature bourgeois republic from emerging in its complete and peculiar form ... Thus on January 29 [1849], it was not the President and the National Assembly of the *same* republic that were face to face; it was the national assembly of the republic that was coming into being and the President of the republic that had come into being, two powers that embodied quite different periods in the life process of the republic.[194]

Thus, this case is inconsistent with the general argument that constituent power finds its termination in the establishment of the constitution (and thus the paradox of constitutionalism

---

[189] Marx, 'Class Struggles in France', 80.
[190] Marx, 'Class Struggles in France', 83–84.
[191] Marx, 'Class Struggles in France', 79.
[192] Marx, 'Class Struggles in France', 65.
[193] Marx, 'Class Struggles in France', 80.
[194] Marx, 'Class Struggles in France', 85 (original emphasis).

Table 13.1   *Constituent power and constituted power*

	Constituent Power	Constituted Power
Stage of Development	Becoming	Being
Social Force	Republican bourgeoisie	Royalist bourgeoisie
Institutional Site	National Assembly	President
Nature of Power	Legitimacy (authorial powers/ authoritative source)	Legality (power to rule)
Type of Constitution	Ideal constitution	Non-ideological (actual) constitution

is resolved).[195] It is also inconsistent with the idea that constituent power (embodied in a popularly elected constituent assembly) brings forward a higher form of representation than in electoral politics because it overcomes the divisibility of the nation into competing interests.[196] In lieu of these mystifications of political conflict, Marx outlines the differences in a way that lends itself to visualisation (see Table 13.1).[197]

The 'overthrow of the parliamentary republic' by Bonaparte meant executive usurpation of the 'general will'.[198] While the 'general will' may be criticised as a universalisation of the ruling classes' interests, the republic can no longer be said to be self-governing after the coup.

> In parliament the nation made its general will the law, that is, it made the law of the ruling class its general will. Before the executive power it renounces all will of its own and submits to the superior command of an alien will, to authority. The executive power, in contrast to the legislative power, expresses the heteronomy of a nation, in contrast to its autonomy. France, therefore, seems to have escaped the despotism of a class only to fall back beneath the despotism of an individual, and, what is more, beneath the authority of an individual without authority.[199]

Bonaparte finalised the process of state centralisation that the 1789 French Revolution inaugurated. Under his rule, the state machinery—the bureaucracy—increasingly separated itself from civil society.[200] The fact that the French masses who initially propelled Bonaparte to power, consisting primarily of smallholding peasants, failed to articulate a coherent interest and represent themselves facilitated such domination of society by the state.[201] The bourgeoisie could not blame the 'stupidity of the masses' for Bonaparte's ascendancy because they were complicit in it: their policies of punishing the peasantry through violent repression and the imposition of the states of siege undermined revolutionary forces within the peasantry and strengthened traditional and 'imperial sentiments'.[202]

The critique of the concentration of power in the hands of the executive is a recurrent theme in Marx. For instance, Marx attacks (1858) the Latin American leader Simón Bolívar as

---

[195]   For examples of this argument, see Arendt, *On Revolution*; Ulrich K Preuss, 'Constitutional Powermaking for the New Polity: Some Deliberations on the Relations Between Constituent Power and the Constitution' in Michel Rosenfeld (ed), *Constitutionalism, Identity, Difference, and Legitimacy: Theoretical Perspectives* (Duke University Press 1994) 143.

[196]   Sultany, *Law and Revolution*, 292–93.

[197]   Marx, 'Class Struggles in France', 85–86.

[198]   Marx, 'Eighteenth Brumaire', 184.

[199]   Marx, 'Eighteenth Brumaire', 184–85.

[200]   Marx, 'Eighteenth Brumaire', 185–86.

[201]   Marx, 'Eighteenth Brumaire', 187–88.

[202]   Marx, 'Eighteenth Brumaire', 188–89.

a Bonapartist dictator who concentrated power in the executive branch.[203] However, the Paris Commune provides Marx with an opportunity to illustrate the contours of the democratic constitution beyond the bad alternatives of authoritarian centralism ('despotism of an individual') and impersonal class rule ('despotism of a class'). This constitutional experiment charts the path towards solving the 'fundamental contradiction' by expanding the political and deepening democracy. It also solves the paradox of constitutionalism because there is no mystery in the constitution (it is no longer a sphere of alienation) because it is subjected to the constituent power of the working class. For Marx, in order to overcome the paradox of constitutionalism, one needs to move beyond liberalism; and in order to overcome the fundamental contradiction, one needs to move beyond capitalism.

MARX AND THE PARIS COMMUNE 1870–71: ELEMENTS OF THE RADICAL CONSTITUTION

The radicalism of the Commune's short-lived constitutional experiment bears a family resemblance to radical experiments in the Americas during the eighteenth and nineteenth centuries. Radicals and republicans in the Americas espoused participatory, inclusive, majoritarian decision-making (as opposed to elitist and exclusionary decision-making).[204] They distrusted the representative system and pursued a closer relationship between people and representatives (short mandates; annual elections; mandatory rotations; written instructions to representatives; large representative bodies; and unicameral rather than bicameral legislatures).[205] They rejected the concentration of powers in the hands of the few, reserved the right of the people to abolish government, preferred a weak executive, and called for decentralisation.[206] Their understanding of a strict separation of powers, as opposed to a mixed arrangement of 'checks and balances', implied an exogenous popular restriction rather than judicial review or other counter-majoritarian measures.[207]

Theirs was a substantive, not procedural, majoritarianism.[208] It was concerned with the necessary preconditions for the emergence of the general will and establishment of democracy. These included not only universal suffrage (right to vote) and social welfare (rights to guarantee people's subsistence) but also an objection to wage labour and large-scale manufacture as well as a demand for far-reaching redistribution of land to tackle economic inequality (by redistributing land to those who worked on it, taxing non-resident landowners, and imposing limits on land ownership).[209] They highlighted the influence of different economic models on

---

[203] Hal Draper, 'Karl Marx and Simón Bolívar: A Note on Authoritarian Leadership in a National-Liberation Movement' (1968) 7 *New Politics* 64.

[204] Gargarella's survey of 'American constitutionalism' includes 'the constitutional developments that took place in the United States [1776–1801] and in nine Latin American countries, namely, Argentina, Bolivia, Colombia, Chile, Ecuador, Mexico, Peru, Uruguay, and Venezuela [1810–1860]'. Gargarella, *Legal Foundations of Inequality*, 2.

[205] Gargarella, *Legal Foundations of Inequality*, 23–30, 45–49.

[206] Gargarella, *Legal Foundations of Inequality*, 48.

[207] Gargarella, *Legal Foundations of Inequality*, 58.

[208] Gargarella, *Legal Foundations of Inequality*, 45.

[209] Gargarella, *Legal Foundations of Inequality*, 78–82.

citizens' moral character (consumption; agrarian versus commercial). They thus employed the discourse of vice and virtue, and sought a moral regeneration of society.[210]

While Marx shares (and even inspires) some of these positions,[211] republicanism, populism, majoritarianism, and radicalism are occasionally used interchangeably in discussing these constitutional experiments and scholarly approaches.[212] The Paris Commune echoes some of the above mentioned constitutional proposals but it is clearly distinct from most approaches to republicanism in its social content. While the communitarian strand in republican conceptions may also be related to Hegel's view of the state as an ethical community, this ethical discourse can be employed as a republican defence of counter-majoritarian judicial power.[213] Rousseau's distrust of the representative system and his distinction between 'general will' and 'will of all' can also be deployed to justify judicial power as a vindication of past abstract commitments that limit the politics of the day.[214] In addition to these anti-majoritarian constitutional arrangements, republicanism underestimates the persistence of social and political conflict because it presumes 'the existence of shared values and the possibility of a common good', and thus envisages the emergence of 'a social consensus' through rational 'deliberation by individuals ... who are capable of abstracting from their private experiences'.[215] Finally, the concern with economic conditions cannot be reduced to a juridical question of social and economic rights in a generally liberal or conservative constitution. This not only leads to inconsistency, inefficacy, and deradicalisation of social demands,[216] but also leaves unanswered the economic structures that render these rights ineffective and unrealisable.[217] Thus, it is crucial to ground the different proposals for constitutional change in a comprehensive view of the socio-political order, and the role of the constitution in it, that seeks to radically transform it.

There are several key socialist and democratic elements that Marx extrapolates from the Commune's experiment. First, Marx is clear that the Communal Constitution foregrounds social control over the state:

> The unity of the nation was not to be broken, but, on the contrary, to be organised by the Communal Constitution and to become a reality by the destruction of the State power which claimed to be the

---

[210]   Gargarella, *Legal Foundations of Inequality*, 33–38.

[211]   Such as the critique of wage labour: Marx, 'Critique of the Gotha Program'.

[212]   Gargarella writes as follows: 'Radical or majoritarian or populist constitutions may be characterized by their political majoritarianism and their normally implicit defense of moral populism. They try to strengthen the authority of the people'. Gargarella, *Legal Foundations of Inequality*, 3. This lumping together is justified under the rubric of 'ideal types' of radicalism, conservatism, and liberalism. Gargarella, *Legal Foundations of Inequality*, 4.

[213]   Frank Michelman, 'Law's Republic' (1988) 97 *Yale Law Journal* 1493. See also Sultany, 'Progressive Constitutional Theory', 394–99.

[214]   Bruce A Ackerman, 'The Storrs Lectures: Discovering the Constitution' (1984) 93 *Yale Law Journal* 1013. See also Sultany, 'Progressive Constitutional Theory', 399–402.

[215]   Derrick Bell and Preeta Bansal, 'The Republican Revival and Racial Politics' (1988) 97 *Yale Law Journal* 1609, 1610.

[216]   Gargarella, *Latin American Constitutionalism*, 137, 142–43; Gargarella, *Legal Foundations of Inequality*, 246.

[217]   Paul O'Connell, 'The Death of Socio-Economic Rights' (2011) 74 *Modern Law Review* 532; Paul O'Connell, 'On Reconciling Irreconcilables: Neo-liberal Globalisation and Human Rights' (2007) 7 *Human Rights Law Review* 483.

embodiment of that unity independent of, and superior to, the nation itself, from which it was but a parasitic excrescence.[218]

In other words, Marx calls for 'popular control from below'.[219] This includes not only the election of all public servants but also community control of the police: instead of an agent of the government, the police turn into a 'responsible and at all times revocable agent of the Commune'.[220]

Second, the fiction of judicial independence impedes social control and democratisation of the state. Thus, judges should be elected in order to be politically accountable:

> The judicial functionaries were to be divested of that sham independence which had but served to mask their abject subserviency to all succeeding governments to which, in turn, they had taken, and broken, the oaths of allegiance. Like the rest of public servants, magistrates and judges were to be elective, responsible, and revocable.[221]

Third, there are limits to the emancipatory potential of universal suffrage, including because of careerism and corruption in politics.[222] Thus, there is a need for a closer relationship between the people and their representatives: 'each delegate to be at any time revocable [i.e., subject to recall] and bound by the *mandat impératif* (formal instructions) of his constituents'.[223] The required form of representation is egalitarian and rejects attempts 'to supersede universal suffrage by hierarchical investiture'.[224]

Fourth, this egalitarian governance is clear in Marx's call for decentralisation. It should be clear, however, that what he means is not a federalism of state units. The concern is not merely with centralisation and the existence of an over-powerful executive (that would be a question of internal organisation of the state or of separation of powers) but in the negation of alienation by bringing state structures under social control:

> [T]his new Commune, which breaks the modern State power, has been mistaken for a reproduction of the medieval Communes, which first preceded, and afterwards became a substratum of, that very State power. The Communal Constitution has been mistaken for an attempt to break up into a federation of small States, as dreamt of by Montesquieu and the Girondins, that unity of great nations which... has now become a power coefficient of social production. The antagonism of the Commune against the State power has been mistaken for an exaggerated form of the ancient struggle against over-centralisation.[225]

---

[218] Marx, 'Civil War in France', 633. See also Marx, 'Critique of the Gotha Program', 537.

[219] Hal Draper, 'Marx on Democratic Forms of Government' (1974) 11 *Socialist Register* 101, 111, 122.

[220] Marx, 'Civil War in France', 632. For contemporary calls to defund and disband the police in the United States, see Alex S Vitale, *The End of Policing* (Verso 2018); Anthony O'Rourke, Rick Su, and Guyora Binder, 'Disbanding Police Agencies' (2021) 121 *Columbia Law Review* 1327.

[221] Marx, 'Civil War in France', 632.

[222] Marx, 'Civil War in France', 628.

[223] Marx, 'Civil War in France', 633.

[224] Marx, 'Civil War in France', 633.

[225] Marx, 'Civil War in France', 633–34.

Fifth, what is distinctive about the constitution is the emancipation of labour, which Marx calls a 'thoroughly expansive political form' as opposed to other 'repressive' forms of government.[226] This democratic form is a working class rule:

> Its true secret was this. It was essentially a working-class government, the produce of the struggle of the producing against the appropriating class, the political form at last discovered under which to work out the economic emancipation of labour. Except on this last condition, the Communal Constitution would have been an impossibility and a delusion. The political rule of the producer cannot coexist with the perpetuation of social slavery. The Commune was therefore to serve as a lever for uprooting the economical foundations upon which rests the existence of classes, and therefore of class-rule. With labour emancipated, every man becomes a working man, and productive labour ceases to be a class attribute.[227]

The nature of this emancipation lies in the transformation from 'private property' to 'free and associated labour':

> the Commune intended to abolish that class-property which makes the labour of the many the wealth of the few. It aimed at the expropriation of the expropriators. It wanted to make individual property a truth by transforming the means of production, land and capital, now chiefly the means of enslaving and exploiting labour, into mere instruments of free and associated labour.[228]

Finally, and in contrast to the settled legitimacy of revolutionary constitutions in liberal and republican thought, which presuppose a singular act of founding and a sacred origin,[229] and seek to settle political conflict by theoretical constructs and meta-rules that subordinate politics,[230] Marx emphasises that there are no ready-made utopias. Instead, there is only continuous struggle and openness to self-questioning, improvement, and experimentation:

> The working class did not expect miracles from the Commune. They have no ready-made utopias to introduce *par décret du people*. They know that in order to work out their own emancipation, and along with it that higher form to which present society is irresistibly tending by its own economical agencies, they will have to pass through long struggles, through a series of historic processes, transforming circumstances and men.[231]

Similarly, in 'The Eighteenth Brumaire', Marx writes that unlike the 'short-lived' bourgeois revolutions of the eighteenth century:

> proletarian revolutions, like those of the nineteenth century, criticise themselves constantly, interrupt themselves continually in their own course, come back to the apparently accomplished in order to begin it afresh, deride with unmerciful thoroughness the inadequacies, weaknesses and paltriness of their first attempts ... until a situation has been created which makes all turning back impossible, and the conditions themselves cry out: Hic Rhodus, hic salta![232]

---

[226]   Marx, 'Civil War in France', 634.
[227]   Marx, 'Civil War in France', 634–35.
[228]   Marx, 'Civil War in France', 635.
[229]   Angelica Maria Bernal, *Beyond Origins: Rethinking Founding in a Time of Constitutional Democracy* (OUP 2017).
[230]   Seidman, *Our Unsettled Constitution*, 21–22.
[231]   Marx, 'Civil War in France', 635–36.
[232]   Marx, 'Eighteenth Brumaire', 106–7.

The historical struggle thus continues in order to create the conditions that facilitate the emergence of the new society that would enable human flourishing, without exploitation or alienation, here and now.

CONCLUSION

Legal and political developments since Marx's death both vindicate his insights and show the importance of bringing those insights into constitutionalism. Recent research illustrates Marx's continued relevance as it showcases the general historical tendency of capitalist societies to increase inequality in wealth and income.[233] It thus shows a persistent failure of capitalist constitutional democracies to address the question of poverty and inequality. Although the lines between the political and economic, public and private, have been redrawn in order to justify state intervention in the economy, these achievements were momentary. Political and economic developments in the last few decades have rolled back many of the welfare state's achievements, and welfare state capitalism increasingly looks like a short-lived experiment.[234]

In legal theory, private law—the traditional sphere of 'freedom and equality'—was transformed through its 'socialisation' (the sociological criticism of the formalism of classical legal thought to justify social law, such as labour law) and its subsequent 'politicisation' (the legal realist criticism of *laissez-faire* capitalism and of the public/private distinction).[235] For instance, legal realists point out that coercion is ubiquitous under capitalism both in the public sphere and the private sphere, and the seemingly free contract to sell labour-power conceals the coercion of property.[236] Indeed, the legal protection of private property is a form of delegation of sovereignty to private owners of the means of production.[237] This legal protection has constrained redistributive policies in capitalist societies like the United States, which have 'featured a continuing struggle between majority will and property rights'.[238] Despite this politicisation of private law, attempts to reconstruct the distinction between the public/private and political/economic persist. This persistence merely undermines the coherence of the distinction and underscores the futility of reconstruction.[239]

Crucially, these developments in legal theory after Marx led to the 'constitutionalisation' of private law, and thus empowered the judiciary to police the public/private distinction, thereby inviting the spectre of juristocracy.[240] They thus increased the importance of constitutional

---

[233] Thomas Piketty, *Capital in the Twenty-First Century* (first published 2013, Arthur Goldhammer tr, Harvard University Press 2014).

[234] See David Harvey, *A Brief History of Neoliberalism* (OUP 2005).

[235] Gonçalo de Almeida Ribeiro, *The Decline of Private Law: A Philosophical History of Liberal Legalism* (Hart 2019).

[236] Robert Hale, 'Coercion and Distribution in a Supposedly Non-Coercive State' (1923) 38 *Political Science Quarterly* 470.

[237] Morris R Cohen, 'Property and Sovereignty' in Morris R Cohen, *Law and the Social Order: Essays in Legal Philosophy* (Harcourt, Brace 1933) 41.

[238] Michael J Klarman, 'The Degradation of American Democracy—and the Court' (2020) 134 *Harvard Law Review* 1, 135.

[239] Duncan Kennedy, 'The Stages of the Decline of the Public/Private Distinction' (1982) 130 *University of Pennsylvania Law Review* 1394.

[240] Mattias Kumm, 'Who's Afraid of the Total Constitution? Constitutional Rights as Principles and the Constitutionalization of Private Law' (2006) 7 *German Law Journal* 341.

debates because the argument turned 'from substance to procedure—from the content of the law to the authority to make laws'.[241] These debates over the paradox of constitutionalism have failed hitherto to produce a conclusive answer to the question of political justification. The crisis of private law becomes the crisis of public law, and the question of legitimacy of the constitutional order remains unresolved.[242] The ideological nature of contemporary debates over the paradox, which pit majoritarian democrats against constitutionalists, is evident in their limited and narrow scope, as well as in the attempt to wish away contradictions and quiet anxieties about the incoherence of the constitutional order.[243] Yet the legitimacy question is disquieting precisely because of the coercive power of the law and repressive function of the capitalist state, which through policing, surveillance, and incarceration subdues 'collective forms of opposition to corporate power' and controls 'discarded workers and marginalized populations'.[244]

It is against this backdrop that Marx offers important contributions to critical constitutional analysis. Such analysis is crucial because it exposes the poverty of liberal constitutional theory. Liberal scholarship presents constitutionalism as a departure from the excesses of right-wing conservatives and left radicals alike. It positions itself as a theory and practice that possesses the best of both worlds, or at least as a kind of optimal centre.[245] This idealised portrait merely cements the 'dictatorship of no alternatives', preventing the kind of radical change that alone may transform social reality.[246] It papers over the incoherence and contradictory character of liberal constitutionalism itself.[247] If anything, the experience of the past decades shows that the view of the liberal constitution as non-ideological and stable is no longer, if it ever was, tenable.[248] Even prior to the appearance of Donald Trump and far-right populism, scholars in the United States had noted that their own liberal 'triumphalism' is misplaced in light of the structural deficiencies of the liberal order,[249] and that the distinction between liberal democracy and dictatorship 'is greatly overstated'.[250] At root, then, liberal theory is yet to respond convincingly to Marx's challenge.

One of the weaknesses of liberal claims is exhibited in the unreflective mantra that the far right and far left coincide, in their basic concerns and strategies.[251] Yet it cannot be seriously argued that because Marx and Edmund Burke are both critics of the abstraction of rights that they aspire to the same social and political order, or that their claims are equally objec-

---

[241]   Ribeiro, *Decline of Private Law*, 11.

[242]   Sultany, 'Progressive Constitutional Theory', 455; Ribeiro, *Decline of Private Law*, 12.

[243]   Sultany, 'Progressive Constitutional Theory', 455.

[244]   Harvey, *Brief History*, 77.

[245]   See e.g., Gargarella, *Legal Foundations of Inequality*. For a classical statement of this position see Arthur Schlesinger Jr, *The Vital Center: The Politics of Freedom* (first published 1949, Transaction 1997) (defending 'the free society' against the 'totalitarian temptation' of progressives and conservatives).

[246]   Roberto Mangabeira Unger, *The Left Alternative* (Verso 2005).

[247]   Mark Tushnet, 'Truth, Justice, and the American Way: An Interpretation of Public Law Scholarship in the Seventies' (1979) 57 *Texas Law Review* 1307.

[248]   Sultany, 'What Good is Abstraction?'; Klarman, 'Degradation of American Democracy'.

[249]   Bruce Ackerman, *The Decline and Fall of the American Republic* (Harvard University Press 2010).

[250]   Sanford V Levinson and Jack M Balkin, 'Constitutional Dictatorship: Its Dangers and Its Design' (2010) 94 *Minnesota Law Review* 1789, 1790.

[251]   For a classical statement, see Schlesinger, *The Vital Center*, 278–79 (arguing that the opposition between left and right is not linear but circular).

tionable.[252] Burke and most other conservatives are fundamentally anti-egalitarian, seeking to preserve inherited social privileges and exclusionary political orders. Marx, on the other hand, is a radical democrat who attacks elite privilege and defends the rights of the poor, the excluded, and the dispossessed.[253] The value of his critique of constitutional law and theory is to chart a path towards a more democratic and egalitarian organisation of political power and social order than is possible under the abstractions and ideological illusions of liberalism and republicanism alike.

---

[252] Edmund Burke, *Reflections on the Revolution in France* (first published 1790, LG Mitchell ed, OUP 1993).

[253] Karl Marx, 'Proceedings of the Sixth Rhine Province Assembly: Third Article—Debates on the Law on Thefts of Wood' [1842] in Karl Marx and Frederick Engels, *Collected Works*, vol 1 (Lawrence & Wishart 2010) 224.

14. The reproduction of moral economies in capitalism: Reading Thompson structurally

Nate Holdren

INTRODUCTION

The Marxist historian and polemicist EP Thompson is often remembered today for having offered an analysis of what he termed the 'moral economy' in a series of writings from 1963 to 1971.[1] For Thompson, a moral economy was a food market in which each commodity is bought and sold at a 'fair price' instead of a 'free price' determined purely by the market. In this way, the 'moral economy' subordinates profit-making to the need to avoid hunger and ultimately starvation. Thompson offered his analysis of the 'moral economy' in the context of a broader examination of popular riots in eighteenth-century England. He referred to these riots as a 'pattern of social protest'[2] consisting of specific 'forms of [collective] action' which 'depended upon a particular set of social relations'.[3] 'Moral economy' was his term for that 'particular set of social relations', and in his view it offered ordinary people ideological resources for transgressing prevailing social norms and engaging in acts of collective resistance. For Thompson, a 'moral economy' existed, and it facilitated collective action, when it was generally believed that food prices should be regulated to ensure subsistence, when legal authorities were widely believed to enforce this norm, and when certain food vendors violated the expectations the norm generated by pricing bread and other food too high. Under these conditions, the popular classes could step in to punish vendors for departing from general norms relating to bread-pricing, thus enforcing the 'moral economy' as the background normative condition for food markets.

While Thompson's investigation was time- and place-specific, he regarded the eighteenth-century riots—and their analysis—as being of broad significance. In this chapter, I reformulate and examine Thompson's account of moral economies, and the various struggles he explained with that concept. The goal of the chapter is to explain the analytical potential of Thompson's investigations and to extend the usefulness of 'moral economy' as a concept for Marxist analysis of law and society. I argue that moral economies recur in capitalist societies, meaning that areas of economic life in capitalist society are often subject in part to norms beyond narrowly economic imperatives. I also argue that moral economies are generally

---

[1]   This work has generated a voluminous body of scholarship. The best review of that scholarship remains Thompson's own from two decades later; see EP Thompson, 'The Moral Economy Reviewed' in EP Thompson, *Customs in Common: Studies in Traditional Popular Culture* (Merlin Press 1991) 259. For reviews of subsequent developments, see Elizabeth Harrison, '"People Are Willing to Fight to the End": Romanticising the "Moral" in Moral Economies of Irrigation' (2020) 40 *Critique of Anthropology* 194. For recent reappraisal see 'The Moral Economy' (symposium) (2020) 11 *Humanity*.

[2]   EP Thompson, 'The Moral Economy of the English Crowd in the Eighteenth Century' in EP Thompson, *Customs in Common: Studies in Traditional Popular Culture* (Merlin Press 1991) 185, 247.

[3]   Thompson, 'The Moral Economy of the English Crowd', 249.

opposed by capitalists and therefore tend to be merely temporary in duration. As a result, conflicts in which people draw on the normative structures of a given 'moral economy' for collective action—I use the term 'moral economy struggles' for these forms of collective action—also recur in capitalist society. Understanding the recurrence of 'moral economy struggles' requires examination of both continuities and changes in the institutionalisation of capitalist social relations, above all in the form of law. The account of social unrest provided here calls attention to problems that repeatedly confront law, as well as the role of law in actively producing both social order and social unrest. In particular, I argue that Marxists should not view 'moral economy struggles' overly optimistically, as they tend not to generate new political possibilities.

This chapter begins with what might be called 'Thompsonology', explaining what Thompson thought and what his writing suggested. It then transitions to develop a Thompsonian theory of capitalism.[4] First, I summarise Thompson's original argument. Second, I draw out some of the implications of this argument, arguing that the eighteenth-century English moral economy Thompson examined can be fruitfully understood as an example of what the Marxist sociologist Göran Therborn terms an 'ideological apparatus'.[5] I emphasise that moral economies are partly composed of legal institutions and forms of legal consciousness. I also discuss how moral economies can, under specific circumstances, generate social conflicts such as the riots that Thompson analysed, conflicts that concern official legal actors greatly. Third, I consider moral economies more generally, as a distinct kind of phenomenon in capitalist societies. Fourth, I discuss the basic social relations that define capitalism and changes across time and place in the institutions that express capitalism's fundamental conditions. That discussion provides an account of capitalist development that I use to show that moral economies emerge with some regularity in the history of capitalism. These recurrent developments are due in part to law's role in promoting the reproduction of capitalist social relations, even when that reproduction takes conflict-laden forms. Fifth, I briefly apply this analysis to events in Madison, Wisconsin in 2011, as an example of the light these concepts can shed, before discussing why Marxists should see moral economy struggles as politically limited, in keeping with Gramsci's recommendation that we opt for pessimism of the intellect. Moral economy struggles are an important recurring pattern in the history of capitalist society, but they tend not to generate significant anti-capitalist political victories.

THOMPSON'S ACCOUNT OF THE MORAL ECONOMY IN EIGHTEENTH-CENTURY ENGLAND

The English Moral Economy

Thompson drew on the concept of moral economy in his magisterial *The Making of the English Working Class*, first published in 1963, and also in 'The Peculiarities of the English', pub-

---

[4]   To be clear, I regard Thompson as a Marxist, unlike Gaspar Tamás' thoroughly unjustified claim that he 'believed' that he was a Marxist without actually being one. GM Tamás, 'Telling the Truth About Class' in Leo Panitch and Sam Gindin (eds), *Socialist Register 2006: Telling the Truth* (Merlin Press 2005) 228, 228–29.

[5]   Göran Therborn, *The Ideology of Power and the Power of Ideology* (Verso 1980) 85–86.

lished in 1965.[6] He fully developed the concept in a long essay published in 1971, entitled 'The Moral Economy of the English Crowd in the Eighteenth Century'.[7] In this essay, Thompson argued that other scholars too often understood bread riots in eighteenth-century England through a kind of caloric deprivation theory of collective action: when hungry enough, people will riot for food. For example, Thompson quotes the historians TS Ashton and J Sykes, referring to food riots as an 'instinctive reaction' to the brute fact of hunger.[8] Thompson rejected this view, arguing that it was false and pernicious insofar as it reduced people to ambulatory stomachs and ignored their minds. This view stood as an example of what Thompson called in *The Making of the English Working Class* 'the enormous condescension of posterity'.[9] Furthermore, he argued, those who held this reductionist view were too taken by the ideology of classical political economy. Thompson saw the scholars he criticised as having a mistaken and economistic picture of society, 'a picture which is itself a product of a political economy which diminished human reciprocities to the wages-nexus'.[10]

What in fact explained bread riots, Thompson argued, was not hunger but rather outrage. Bread rioters were people enraged by what they understood as an injustice. Riots did not arise from stomachs, but from hearts and minds. Understanding bread riots thus required analysing why people were outraged, and how they authorised themselves to take action as a result of that outrage. Thompson argued that what made hunger an outrage for the bread rioters he examined was that their hunger resulted specifically from the makers and sellers of bread raising bread prices. To render people hungry in pursuit of profit was unacceptable to many people in eighteenth-century England, because there was a set of norms in place regarding practices of making and selling food, norms holding that practices of exchange should be reined in when the subsistence of ordinary people was at stake. Bread sellers could profit so long as it was not at the expense of hunger for ordinary people. When makers and sellers of food increased prices enough to generate hunger, they violated those norms, creating a sense of outrage that sometimes generated riots.

Rioters opposed the introduction of a new norm of price-setting, one indifferent to the old norm of preserving people's access to food. According to this new putative norm, bread buyers could eat, but not necessarily at the expense of profits for bread sellers. Rioters and the sellers they rioted against were thus embroiled in a dispute over whether access to bread should be determined entirely according to depoliticised ideas like market price, or whether prices should instead be regulated in accordance with considerations of public right and social justice. Rioters saw the new practices of bread-pricing, and the hunger that resulted from it,

---

[6]   EP Thompson, *The Making of the English Working Class* (Penguin 1968); EP Thompson, 'The Peculiarities of the English' (1965) 2 *Socialist Register* 311.

[7]   EP Thompson, 'The Moral Economy of the English Crowd'.

[8]   Quoted in Thompson, 'The Moral Economy of the English Crowd', 186.

[9]   Thompson, *The Making of the English Working Class*, 12.

[10]   Thompson, 'The Moral Economy of the English Crowd', 258. While the 1971 essay focused on other academics, it is worth noting that this essay strongly echoed Thompson's criticisms of what he saw as distortions in Marxism introduced by Stalin and Stalinist political culture. EP Thompson, 'Socialist Humanism' in Cal Winslow (ed), *E.P. Thompson and the Making of the New Left* (Monthly Review Press 2014) 49. In addition, his use of the concept of moral economy in 'The Peculiarities of the English' was dedicated to contributing to debates within the emerging New Left about how to understand the present and the contemporary practice of revolutionary politics. Thompson seems to have understood his moral economy analysis as having political significance beyond a narrow academic debate. Thompson's anti-economistic Marxism is part of why he remains a relevant author in the present.

as an injustice. That sense of injustice, in turn, served as one of the 'legitimating notion[s]' of 'the common people' who took part in food riots.[11]

As already noted, Thompson used the term 'moral economy' to refer to the particular kind of food markets that were successfully held to standards of 'fair price', so as to allow poor people to subsist. He also used the term to refer to a normative market that existed as a kind of picture in the social imagination of working people. In practice, food-selling was generally conducted in ways that fostered ordinary people's subsistence. Thompson argued at length in 'The Moral Economy of the English Crowd' that this form of subsistence-permitting food-selling was widely approved—viewed as how society ought to be—according to a widespread social consensus in eighteenth-century England. When there were departures from actual practices of subsistence-permitting food sales, crowds acted prescriptively, taking collective action to enforce the moral economy, thereby seeking to make social relations return to conforming with the normative market that existed in their social imagination.

Thompson's primary interest was in understanding collective action, particularly working-class agency. It is important to note, however, that he explained that collective action by recourse to pre-existing social conditions. That is, on Thompson's account, there was a kind of social structure that served as the precondition for working-class agency. This is in keeping with Marx's famous statement: while people make history, 'they do not make it under self-selected circumstances, but under circumstances existing already, given and transmitted from the past'.[12] Thompson made a similar point when he suggested that moral economy struggles 'depended upon a particular set of social relations'. Law played an important role in this 'set of social relations'.

Law in/as Thompson's Moral Economy

Law was a central component of Thompson's understanding of the moral economy. The moral economy was in part a consensus shared by ordinary people and legal authorities that market practices should be regulated in accordance with extra-market norms, including notions of distributive justice. Legal authorities helped to legitimate and spread—that is, to enrol people within—the norms of the moral economy. Furthermore, legal vocabularies and concepts formed part of how ordinary people expressed their understanding of that consensus.

Thompson cited formal legal texts that codified the norms of the moral economy and he referred repeatedly to legal and state personnel as taking action to maintain bread-pricing, including state inquiries to investigate whether bread-sellers were pricing as they should and prosecuting people who violated the moral economy's rules.[13] In some instances, crowds 'attempted to enlist' local state authorities such as magistrates and constables into their efforts to impose price reductions on sellers who were pricing foodstuffs too highly, and sometimes succeeded in this enlisting.[14] Thompson also cited popular actions that used legal terms and

---

[11]   Thompson, 'The Moral Economy of the English Crowd'; Thompson, 'The Moral Economy Reviewed'.

[12]   Karl Marx, *The Eighteenth Brumaire of Louis Bonaparte* (first published 1852, International Publishers 1963) 15.

[13]   Thompson, 'The Moral Economy of the English Crowd', 193–94, 222. On state action see 192, 197, 200.

[14]   Thompson, 'The Moral Economy of the English Crowd', 229–30.

concepts to express their outrage. For instance, they sometimes accused bread sellers of 'unlawfull Dealing' and warned them to lower prices accordingly.[15] Thompson also cited numerous calls for legal personnel to step in against bread-sellers, with crowds enforcing the law when legal personnel would not do so.[16] Often 'the crowd claimed that since the authorities refused to enforce "the laws" they must enforce them for themselves'.[17] That they understood bread prices to be not only too high but illegally high was often a 'legitimizing notion' people used to authorise themselves to act collectively in ways that transgressed the norm for public behaviour, including seizing or destroying goods and threatening bread sellers.[18]

Moral economy struggles violated legal standards of behaviour, which is part of why they were often called riots. The response of state personnel to those behavioural violations varied considerably—sometimes standing aside and permitting the rioters to act, sometimes directly opposing the rioters. Thompson argued that later legal authorities in England began to take a more consistently repressive response to popular disturbances, in part out of fear of the French Revolution. This repressive response helped reduce the numbers and efficacy of these riots, without eliminating them altogether.[19] For Thompson this change signalled the opening of a new period, a change in the specifics of the set of social relations in the background that explained the collective action he examined.

I refer to these points in Thompson's discussion in part to underline the fact that, on his account, law is a constitutive element of the moral economy. That is to say, the moral economy, as a social phenomenon, is already in part a legal one, and Thompson's is in part a legal analysis. Legal authorities often enforced the norms of the moral economy upon the bread sellers, and to an important degree they had to do so, compelled by institutional arrangements and the popular consensus to which they too belonged. As Thompson wrote, legal authorities were often 'prisoners of the people', who had little choice other than to enforce the moral economy's norms.[20] This point helps to distinguish the claim that law is socially constitutive from claims about law's autonomy from society. Some legal scholars have overestimated law's independence from society.[21] A moral economy analysis of law suggests that, to allude to Marx's phrase, law constitutes the social, but not in circumstances of law's own choosing: path dependencies limit the law's malleability and the room for manoeuvre available to those who draw upon it.[22]

---

[15]   Thompson, 'The Moral Economy of the English Crowd', 214.
[16]   Thompson, 'The Moral Economy of the English Crowd', 196, 198, 216.
[17]   Thompson, 'The Moral Economy of the English Crowd', 227.
[18]   Thompson, 'The Moral Economy of the English Crowd', 188.
[19]   Thompson, 'The Moral Economy of the English Crowd', 249–50.
[20]   Thompson, 'The Moral Economy of the English Crowd', 189.
[21]   See Christopher Tomlins, 'What is Left of the Law and Society Paradigm After Critique? Revisiting Gordon's "Critical Legal Histories"' (2012) 37 *Law & Social Inquiry* 155. Tomlins criticises Robert Gordon's 'Critical Legal History' specifically, and critical legal studies more generally, for overstating the indeterminacy of law, which is for my purposes here a synonym for legal autonomy. For another such overestimation, see Mark Tushnet, 'Marxism as Metaphor' (1983) 68 *Cornell Law Review* 282; Mark Tushnet, 'Is There a Marxist Theory of Law?' in J Ronald Pennock and John W Chapman (eds), *Marxism: Nomos XXVI* (New York University Press 1983) 171. For a critique of Tushnet see Nate Holdren and Eric Tucker, 'Marxist Theories of Law Past and Present: A Meditation Occasioned by the 25th Anniversary of *Law, Labor, and Ideology*' (2000) 45 *Law & Social Inquiry* 1142.
[22]   This is not to deny that law has some autonomy from the economy or from the capitalist class. Rather, the point is to emphasise the limits to law's autonomy. Law is a moment within the totality of

The moral economy was a legally formalised institutional arrangement that acted on people of all class positions and acted back upon the law as well. As suggested by the title of Thompson's essay, his real object of analysis was collective action, which the concept of moral economy was intended to explain. He studied what he called the 'moral economy of the crowd' in order to understand the crowd as a form of collective action.[23] Implied in his analysis, however, was a moral economy of the action of legal authorities as well. Indeed, the changing effects of the moral economy on legal authorities and on popular mobilisations shaped one another over time.

Phases of Moral Economies

Thompson argued that the moral economy's grip on English legal authorities gradually eroded over the course of the eighteenth century. As a consequence, these authorities tended to do less to enforce standards of fair pricing. As that happened, the mobilisations of the crowd stepped into the space left by reduced enforcement, with two effects. First, moral economy struggles shored up, temporarily and partially, the moral economy's hold on legal authorities. Second, they created an independent enforcement mechanism for the moral economy's norms.

It is analytically helpful to consider an abstract schema of the sequence of events that give rise to a moral economy struggle. This schema describes in the broadest strokes the patterns Thompson found in his fine-grained examinations of actual moral economy struggles, while removing all situational particularity. Doing so can help delineate more clearly what constitutes, so to speak, moral economy-ness. In all the moral economy struggles Thompson described, for a time a moral economy existed and was relatively stable, with legal authorities and informal social pressures compelling conformity to the moral economy's norms. Periodically, that moral economy faced violations from some capitalists, who generally were successfully disciplined back into following the norms of the moral economy. Eventually, violations increased, sometimes in a collective and co-ordinated fashion and sometimes with an effort to justify those violations ideologically through pamphlets and speeches. Alongside and perhaps as partial cause of increasing violations, legal enforcement became less frequent and effective over time. At that point, moral economy struggles became more frequent as ordinary people sought to defend the moral economy.[24]

This schema divides into two basic stages or periods—a period of relative stability and legitimacy of the moral economy, and a period during which the moral economy is unstable

---

capitalist social relations and has some autonomy within that totality but not autonomy from that totality. That is to say, in capitalism law is constrained to foster the reproduction of capitalist social relations, but there are a range of possibilities for exactly how law serves that reproduction. Indeed, as Isaac Balbus and Nicos Poulantzas have argued, law's ability to serve the reproduction of capitalist social relations requires this kind of relative autonomy. Isaac Balbus, 'Commodity Form and Legal Form: An Essay on the "Relative Autonomy" of the Law' (1977) 11 *Law & Society Review* 571; Nicos Poulantzas, *State, Power, Socialism* (first published 1978, Patrick Camiller tr, Verso 2014) 127–29. See also Tony Smith, *Beyond Liberal Egalitarianism: Marx and Normative Social Theory in the Twenty-First Century* (Brill 2017) 183–85, 190–92 (arguing for some autonomy of law and the state—Smith's own term is 'indeterminacy'—but stressing that this autonomy is limited by the totality of capitalist social relations).

[23]   Thompson, 'The Moral Economy of the English Crowd', 185–258.

[24]   I treat moral economies as singular here for analytical purposes. I will note that it is entirely possible that multiple moral economies could exist or even overlap with one another in a given time and place.

and embattled. Moral economy struggles in the first period help to preserve its stability and legitimacy. In effect, they prevent or delay the outbreak of the second kind of period. During that second period, capitalists are afforded the opportunity not only to profit individually by violating the moral economy's norms, but to push those norms aside in their entirety. That is, capitalists are sometimes capable of creating a new 'set of social relations', like the institutional order in which the authoritative norm is bread priced for greater profit.[25] In eighteenth-century England, moral economy struggles belonging to the second period involved attempts to restore the previous condition of the moral economy's stability and legitimacy, thereby preventing the emergence of a new institutional order.

The Moral Economy was Not Pre-capitalist: An Aside on Agrarian Capitalism

The purpose of this chapter is to argue that the concept of the moral economy is helpful for thinking about patterns and modalities of class struggle in capitalist society, in contexts well beyond eighteenth-century England. As such, I must address directly a possible misreading of Thompson's own account. Thompson's analysis of class struggles in eighteenth-century England involves close examination of a society that was already subject to capitalism, and thereby displaying dependency on the market and the drive to produce and accumulate surplus value. The people whose outrage and collective resistance Thompson examines lived in a specifically agrarian rather than industrial capitalism. This is certainly an important distinction, but it is a distinction between varieties of capitalism, not one between a capitalist society on the one hand and a pre- or non-capitalist society on the other.

Ellen Meiksins Wood places the emergence of English agrarian capitalism in the sixteenth century. She refers to the eighteenth century, the era Thompson examined in his 1971 essay on the moral economy, as 'the golden age of agrarian capitalism' in England.[26] Moral economy struggles in this 'golden age' were not a holdover from the pre-capitalist period, but rather of a piece with the capitalist character of that era's social relations. As noted above, Thompson discussed ways that English legal authorities tended to intervene to regulate markets in food in order to preserve subsistence. This regulatory action, like all active state regulatory intervention into the economy, is not anti- or non-capitalist but rather constitutive of a particular kind of capitalism. What moral economy struggles in late eighteenth-century England contested was not the rise of capitalism as such, but rather the rise of a specific institutional regime of capitalism, one that knew few regulations and was oriented more or less entirely to market demands.

In this section I have described Thompson's account of one particular moral economy, the one in eighteenth-century England, in a way that has highlighted both the explicit and implicit elements of his understanding of moral economy. My goal has been to describe the concept in a way that enhances its applicability to other contexts while emphasising that my own formulation of the concept is broadly in keeping with Thompson's own understanding of the concept. Moral economy struggles are always part of the self-preservation of a specific institutional order. That self-preservation takes the form of appearance of social unrest. Still,

---

[25]   My reading of Thompson here is influenced by Nancy Fraser and Rahel Jaeggi, *Capitalism: A Conversation in Critical Theory* (Polity Press 2018). Thompson can be read as anticipating some of their points.

[26]   Ellen Meiksins Wood, 'The Agrarian Origins of Capitalism' (1998) 50 *Monthly Review* 14.

in important respects, moral economy struggles are not forces of disorder so much as they are forces of order. They have typically constituted a kind of self-deputised police action from below, aimed at keeping an existing institutional regime in place.

INSTITUTIONALISED FORMS OF CLASS DOMINATION: THE STRUCTURAL REPRODUCTION OF MORAL ECONOMIES

In this section I move from Thompson's examination of a particular moral economy to presenting in greater detail my schematisation of the concept of the moral economy as a recurring phenomenon in capitalist societies. I examine this more general account of moral economies and moral economy struggles, and explain why they are both integral to the social ontology of actually existing capitalism.[27] More specifically, I argue that moral economies tend to be structurally reproduced over the life of capitalist societies.

Two Kinds of Structure: Systemic Continuities and Institutional Variations

All capitalist societies share certain basic characteristics, one especially key trait being dependence upon the market for access to subsistence. Among other things, market dependence is a condition in which a significant quantity of the goods and services people need to live are unavailable except through sale and purchase. Under these conditions, market participation—and by extension the possession of money—is socially compulsory. The working class and the capitalist class are both dependent on the market, as is the state to an important degree, and therefore exposed to competitive pressures to maximise profits and accumulate capital.[28]

At any given moment, any capitalist society has in place institutions through which capitalist social relations are produced and reproduced. As political scientist and historian Ira Katznelson has put it, while 'capitalism is structured everywhere in coherent ways, it is also structured in particular manners' that vary by time and place.[29] That variation is somewhat (but only somewhat) open-ended. Capitalism's fundamental characteristics and tendencies constrain the range of institutional variations that are possible in capitalist societies: the fundamental traits of capitalist societies create a set of issues, so to speak, that all capitalist societies need to deal with. Institutions combine into ensembles or regimes that are time- and place-specific ways to deal with those issues. Above all, regimes of institutions serve, in the

---

[27]   On Marxism and capitalism's social ontology see Tony Smith, *Beyond Liberal Egalitarianism*, 52–61, 110–12, 129–32.

[28]   This paragraph is drawn from the work of Wood, who argues that markets must be understood 'as not only a simple mechanism of exchange or distribution but as the principal determinant and regulator of social reproduction', and that '[t]his unique system of market-dependence entails some very distinctive "laws of motion," specific systemic requirements and compulsions shared by no other mode of production'. Wood, 'Agrarian Origins', 16. See further Ellen Meiksins Wood, 'From Opportunity to Imperative: The History of the Market' (1994) 46 *Monthly Review* 14, 25. For a recent reformulation of Wood's position, and also that of Robert Brenner, see John Clegg, 'A Theory of Capitalist Slavery' (2020) 33 *Journal of Historical Sociology* 74.

[29]   Ira Katznelson, 'Working-Class Formation: Constructing Cases and Comparisons' in Ira Katznelson and Aristide Zolberg (eds), *Working-Class Formation: Nineteenth-Century Patterns in Western Europe and the United States* (Princeton University Press 1986) 3, 15.

words of economist David Kotz, to 'stabilize class conflict and channel it in directions that are not unduly disruptive'.[30] Marxist sociologist and theorist Simon Clarke has argued convincingly that we should understand these regimes as 'institutional forms of class domination'.[31]

By identifying various differences between regimes of institutionalised class domination, scholars have been able to create time- and place-specific accounts of different forms of capitalist society, and to identify and track changes over time. Scholars have discussed 'war capitalism', 'merchant capitalism', 'monopoly capitalism', 'state-managed capitalism', and 'neoliberalism', among many others.[32] The history of changes in capitalism's institutional regimes following from crises and class struggles strongly suggests that one of capitalism's fundamental characteristics is that institutional regimes in any capitalist society are temporary, because all forms of capitalism eventually wear out their current institutions and create new ones. The wearing out of institutions occurs in part through class struggle: the institutionalised forms of class domination in place in any given capitalist society are objects of class struggle, shaped by class struggle, and important determinants of the time- and place-specific forms that class struggle takes. Absent a workers' revolution, any given form of capitalism will eventually break down and be replaced with another form of capitalism, though when and how this will happen, and which new kind of capitalism will emerge, are mostly under-determined.

The concept of moral economy is useful in connection with the analysis of regimes of institutionalised class domination. We can identify greater and lesser degrees of subordinating individual capitalists to norms other than those associated with the drive to accumulate and reinvest capital. For example, in most states today, child labour laws regulate the age at which people may enter labour markets, and basic labour and employment law prohibits discrimination on the part of employers when making decisions about whose labour-power they will purchase, on the basis of race, gender, ability, religion, and other grounds. Laws that regulate wage rates and work hours are also exceedingly common.

Differences in the degree to which individual capitalists are constrained and find their authority curtailed, and differences in the manner of producing those constraints, are part of what distinguish different regimes of institutionalised class domination. The kinds of regulation that produce different degrees of constraints on individual capitalists should be considered a matter of allocating directive authority.[33] It is tempting to treat a society that allocates greater authority to individual capitalists as 'more capitalist' than one that allocates less authority to

---

[30]   David M Kotz, 'Interpreting the Social Structure of Accumulation Theory' in David M Kotz, Terrence McDonough, and Michael Reich (eds), *Social Structures of Accumulation: The Political Economy of Growth and Crisis* (CUP 1994) 55.

[31]   Simon Clarke, 'Overaccumulation, Class Struggle and the Regulation Approach' (1998) 12 *Capital & Class* 59, 84.

[32]   Nancy Fraser and Rahel Jaeggi examine different kinds of capitalism, such as merchant capitalism, state-managed capitalism, and neoliberal capitalism. *Capitalism: A Conversation in Critical Theory*, 64–65. See also Sven Beckert's account of what he calls 'war capitalism' in *Empire of Cotton: A Global History* (Knopf 2014). The Social Structures of Accumulation School is particularly useful for analysing changing institutional structures in capitalist society. See David M Kotz, Terrence McDonough, and Michael Reich (eds), *Social Structures of Accumulation: The Political Economy of Growth and Crisis* (CUP 1994); Terrence McDonough, Michael Reich, and David M Kotz (eds), *Contemporary Capitalism and its Crises: Social Structure of Accumulation Theory for the 21st Century* (CUP 2010). In this chapter I use the term 'regime' for the sake of consistency and concision.

[33]   Christopher Tomlins, 'Subordination, Authority, Law: Subjects in Labor History' (1995) 47 *International Labor and Working-Class History* 56.

individual capitalists, particularly when these limits on capitalists' authority have resulted from struggles between workers and capitalists. But it is a mistake to treat the degree of capitalist authority as an indicator of a 'more' or 'less' capitalist society. A society with child labour laws and minimum wage legislation is not for that reason 'less capitalist'. As Marx's analysis of the English Factory Acts indicates, new forms of limitations on capitalists may well foster new forms of capitalist production, which ultimately benefit the capitalist class and further the reproduction of capitalist social relations.[34] Rather than these kinds of regulation indicating that a given society is less capitalist, they should be understood as producing co-ordination among the capitalist class, and so as a kind of class formation or class consciousness that disciplines individual capitalists to act in line with the interests of the capitalist class or capitalist society as a whole, with those interests in large part produced through law.[35]

The moral economy, then, should be understood as an institution that limits the authority of capitalists over some aspects of social life. But that limitation should be treated as a variation on capitalist social relations, rather than as an alternative to capitalism. What is specific to the moral economy is not that capitalists are subject to discipline, but that this discipline is suffused with a particular kind of normativity and public legitimacy, a normativity and legitimacy upon which working people can sometimes draw for popular mobilisations.

Ideological Apparatus and Tactical Reversal

Moral economy struggles break out in the face of challenges to an existing regime of institutionalised class domination, and they are especially frequent during periods when one regime is breaking down and another is emerging. That said, moral economy struggles do not break out under all regimes or in response to all challenges to them, since not all regimes include moral economies. Identifying when a moral economy has coalesced is a task for careful empirical inquiry. Generally speaking, moral economies can be understood as ideological institutions, and the norms of the moral economy should be understood as an ideology.[36]

In the words of Althusser, ideology imposes 'self-evident facts as self-evident facts (without in the least seeming to, since they are "self evident") which we cannot *not* recognize and before which we have the inevitable and eminently natural reaction of exclaiming (aloud or in

---

[34]   Marx's treatment of the origins of the English Factory Acts provides a good example. See chapters ten through fifteen of Marx's *Capital*, especially the tenth and fifteenth chapters. Karl Marx, *Capital: A Critique of Political Economy*, vol 1 (first published 1867, Ben Fowkes tr, Penguin 1976) 340–642. See also Nate Holdren, *Injury Impoverished: Workplace Accidents, Capitalism, and Law in The Progressive Era* (CUP 2020), for an analysis of US workers' compensation laws conducted in a similar spirit.

[35]   Göran Therborn has argued that interests must be understood not as given but historically and socially constituted, so that it is a mistake to appeal to structural positions like class as generating interests in any meaningful sense. Therborn, *The Ideology of Power and the Power of Ideology*, 4–5, 10.

[36]   Althusser used the term 'ideological state apparatus', often shortened to 'ISA', including churches, families, unions, 'press, radio and television', and 'literature, the arts, sports, etc' in his general definition. Louis Althusser, *On the Reproduction of Capitalism: Ideology and Ideological State Apparatuses* (first published 1995, GM Goshgarian tr, Verso 2014) 243. Therborn has criticised the concept of the ISA on the grounds that it is overly broad, arguing that Althusser himself abandoned it, at least in his private correspondence. Therborn himself prefers 'ideological apparatus', which he defines as 'settings of clustered discourse and related non-discursive practices, and settings or sites of ideological conflict'. Therborn, *The Ideology of Power and the Power of Ideology*, 85–86.

"the silence of consciousness"): "That's obvious! That's right! That's true!"'.[37] Ideology facilitates the creation of a kind of implicit 'of course' or taken-for-grantedness. Thompson's work on moral economies demonstrates that it was self-evident for many, obviously good and right, that bread should be priced in accordance with human need, with profit partially subordinated to that need. The moral economy resulted not simply from this being self-evident, but from the process whereby that fact came to be regarded as self-evident. One of the roles that the moral economy played, then, as an ideological institution, was to promote social order.

Ideological institutions foster, in Althusser's words, the 'reproduction of [the working class'] submission to the rules of the established order'.[38] The moral economy reproduced this submission, promoting social stability, until such time as capitalists mounted widespread attacks on the moral economy. The moral economy struggles that broke out were not causes of disorder, but attempts at restoring an order unsettled by capitalist-initiated disruptions of the prevailing regime of class domination. When moral economy struggles break out, they in effect are instances of people taking an existing ideology and turning it into a source for engaging in collective action. That collective action is in one sense a social disruption but in another important sense this action is order-conserving, aimed at preserving an existing but embattled institutional order. Moral economy struggles, then, are local and tactical reversals of ideology.[39]

In the words of legal scholar Robert Knox, 'one of law's key roles is to integrate the working class into capitalism'.[40] The specific features of this legal integration, Knox explains, change over time, but what does not change is the presence of processes that press the working class to remain 'within the coordinates of capitalist social relations'.[41] When moral economy struggles break out, people draw on the legally underwritten norms of the moral economy in order to give themselves permission to violate other legal rules regarding acceptable behaviour. That is, people in moral economy struggles draw on some elements of a mode of legality in order to authorise themselves to violate some laws regarding behaviour: they protest vociferously, perhaps harming some individual people or damaging some property. At the same time, moral economy struggles do not tend to signal a general crisis of legal authority or a threat to the capitalist social order which law helps to constitute and uphold. This is a difficult claim to

---

[37]   Althusser, *On the Reproduction of Capitalism*, 189. Thompson would likely have not accepted my use of Althusser, having written a book-length polemical response to Althusser. See EP Thompson, *The Poverty of Theory and Other Essays* (Merlin Press 1978). I agree with Thompson's criticisms of Althusser's actual politics. See also the theoretical and political criticisms of Althusser in Jacques Rancière, *Althusser's Lesson* (first published 1974, Emiliano Battista tr, Bloomsbury 2011) and Jacques Rancière, 'On the Theory of Ideology: Althusser's Politics' in Terry Eagleton (ed), *Ideology* (Routledge 2014) 141.

[38]   Althusser, *On the Reproduction of Capitalism*, 51.

[39]   I take the term 'tactical reversal' from the first volume of Michel Foucault's *History of Sexuality*, but my use of the term does not presume any Foucaultian theoretical perspective, nor any criticism of Foucault. Michel Foucault, *The History of Sexuality: Volume I: An Introduction* (first published 1976, Robert Hurley tr, Vintage 1990) 157.

[40]   Knox develops this analysis as part of a discussion of law and trade unions in the twentieth-century United Kingdom, but his points apply to the eighteenth-century English moral economy as well. See Robert Knox, 'Law, Neoliberalism and the Constitution of Political Subjectivity: The Case of Organised Labour' in Honor Brabazon (ed), *Neoliberal Legality: Understanding the Role of Law in the Neoliberal Project* (Routledge 2017) 92, 95.

[41]   Knox, 'Law, Neoliberalism and the Constitution of Political Subjectivity', 95.

substantiate with evidence, given that the claim asserts an absence. Yet moral economy struggles tend to end in a resumption of the order prior to that conflict. Indeed, the heart of a moral economy conflict is precisely the demand for the return to a prior normal.[42] The historical pattern seems that at most these struggles can prevent the emergence of specific kinds of institutional regimes or encourage the emergence of different regimes, as state personnel respond to moral economy struggles with efforts to either repress or placate people.

Not all ideology is tactically reversible in the way that moral economy struggles tend to be. As Therborn has written, class domination may be ideologically secured through a variety of means: the installing of fear of the potential consequences of contesting domination, a sense that domination is natural, or a more general sense of resignation, among many others.[43] These ways of securing class domination ideologically are not tactically reversible, because fear, resignation, and the naturalisation of domination do not permit claims-making or offer the dominated resources to draw upon for collective mobilisation. Other ways of securing class domination ideologically are, however, subject to tactical reversals on occasion. Sometimes, though, social practices are ideologically coded as good and right, presenting domination as relatively acceptable and generating a sense of being heard or adequately represented. These ideologies are subject to tactical reversals, because they appeal to notions of consent and the acceptability of the social order. These appeals allow people to make claims and offer resources with which to mobilise. These reversal-prone forms of ideology are key parts of moral economies.

Moral economies include a specific kind of ideology, as indicated in the term 'moral' itself. At root, moral economies present capitalist markets as good, right, and fair, as long as market practices ensure that most people continue to enjoy a certain standard of living. Thompson depicted collective action by people who were angry that market practices and previous standards of living had begun to come apart, as bread-sellers began to set prices in ways that placed food out of reach for many people, producing widespread hunger. Under those conditions, a moral economy might seem subversive, even revolutionary. Prior to such departures, however, when market practices and standards of living generally aligned, as Thompson suggested they did in eighteenth-century England, the ideology of the moral economy was not at all subversive. Under those conditions, the moral economy depicted the economy as moral and unobjectionable, thus promoting working-class obedience and minimising working-class challenges to the existing institutional order. Another way to think about this is to ask who is disciplined, and in which ways, by the moral economy, understood as an ideological institution.

Generally speaking, we should expect moral economy struggles to break out when we find four factors present: first, forms of regulation that limit the authority of powerful market actors; second, an ideology that treats the economy that results from those limits as morally good, right, just, and so on; third, challenges by some capitalists or state personnel to those forms of regulation; and fourth, no other enforcement of the limits upon those powerful market actors. When all four of these conditions obtain, actions of the powerful come to be understood as outrageously immoral by a great many, and what I have called a moral economy struggle—collective action to enforce the embattled limitations—may ensue. The first two of those factors, moral economies, recur in capitalist society with some regularity, but their

[42] Thompson, 'The Moral Economy Reviewed'; Harrison, "'People Are Willing to Fight to the End'".
[43] Therborn, *The Ideology of Power and the Power of Ideology*, 99.

reproduction is not necessarily guaranteed.[44] Such reproduction results, among other things, from ideas and practices in the legal profession and within the state bureaucracy, the processes of electoral politics, and the politico-economic orientation of existing social protests and movements. I am sceptical that the presence of moral economies can be theoretically predicted with any degree of certainty; investigating their presence or absence is the work of empirical and historical investigation. Still, the concept deserves a greater place in Marxist social and socio-legal theory.

Moral economies are artefacts of a particular kind of regime of institutionalised class domination. They mitigate the power of market actors and introduce priorities beyond those of short-term transactions, in effect demoting individual capitalists and reducing their ability to make decisions about how to act within market transactions. A regime that limits the individual authority of some capitalists is not 'less capitalist' than a regime that allows capitalists greater authority. Different regimes of institutionalised class domination organise capitalist social relations differently. It is certainly the case that some may be preferable to others, but it is a mistake to treat one regime as 'less capitalist' than another. The institutional regimes in which we find moral economies act ideologically, encouraging people to see the regulated market that results from limits on capitalists' authority as moral in character, as good, right, just, and so on. When moral economies exist, if capitalists or state personnel seek to depart from or revise the regime of institutionalised class domination, the ideological picture of the regulated market as moral becomes a liability for those actors. That ideological picture helps people authorise themselves to engage in collective action to defend the existing, if embattled, regime of class domination.

TYPES OF SOCIAL CONFLICT AND THE LIMITS OF MORAL ECONOMY STRUGGLES

Moral economies and moral economy struggles have serious limitations from a Marxist perspective. While moral economy struggles might well involve the breaking of specific rules, they are not themselves threats to the rule of law or the capitalist social order. Moral economy struggles are important examples of working-class resistance endemic to capitalism's unfolding, but that resistance is often merely friction. That a tank may spin its treads and rattle a little

---

[44]   My argument that moral economies tend to recur is similar to what Karl Polanyi called 'a counter-movement' seeking to check the expansion of market relations. Karl Polanyi, *The Great Transformation: The Political and Economic Origins of Our Time* (first published 1944, Beacon 2001) 136. Nancy Fraser and Rahel Jaeggi articulate a partly Polanyian account of what they call 'boundary struggles'. Fraser and Jaeggi, *Capitalism: A Conversation in Critical Theory*, 54. For an important critique of Fraser's work, emphasising problems arising from her proximity to Habermas, see Chris O'Kane, 'Critical Theory and the Critique of Capitalism: An Immanent Critique of Nancy Fraser's "Systematic" "Crisis-Critique" of Capitalism as an "Institutionalized Social Order"' (2021) 85 *Science & Society* 207. What I have called 'moral economy struggles' could also be called 'boundary struggles' or 'Polanyian popular struggles'. However, my argument differs from those of Polanyi, Fraser, and Jaeggi. For one thing, 'moral economy struggle' is a narrower term, referring specifically to collective action by workers. For another, I do not (and Thompson did not) counterpose 'market' and 'society' in the way that Polanyi did. The people about whom Thompson wrote were already market-dependent and therefore operated in a (capitalist) market society already. Moral economy struggles are conflicts over the details of institutional regimes, which makes them conflicts over which types of market society will prevail.

as it advances over mud, rocks, and the dead is not evidence that the tank is meaningfully vulnerable to those obstacles. To put it another way, long-term social orders can accommodate short-term and local disorders. Moral economy struggles are local and short-term instances of apparent disorder that are at a systemic level not disorder at all, but rather recurring and orderly occurrences. This is in part because moral economy struggles tend to be confined to specific kinds of conflict, due to their reliance upon order-conserving moral economies. I explore these claims in this section, including a brief analysis of events in Madison, Wisconsin in 2011. These events were an important example of moral economy struggles, and they help to illustrate the limits of such struggles.

Modes of Social Conflict

It is possible to sort social conflict in capitalist society into three general types. I call these 'tactical conflicts', 'institutional framework conflicts', and 'social form conflicts'.[45] A tactical conflict is small, in scale but also in demand (e.g., seeking to make immediate social superiors use their discretion in one way rather than another). This kind of activity is about navigating rather than challenging the social-structural positions to which people are consigned. It is about coping with, rather than overcoming or restructuring, existing social arrangements. For their part, institutional framework conflicts raise issues over the distribution of power and what rules should or should not be in place in a given workplace, industry, or area. These kinds of conflicts may involve aggressive lobbying and protests demanding that the law change or not change, unionisation drives, demands during contract negotiations for or against changes in specific language in a collective bargaining agreement, or demands that a company change some set of policies. Finally, social form conflicts relate to how capitalist society might ultimately be abolished. These are exceedingly rare, and the results of both theory and practice regarding social form struggles are distressingly inconclusive.[46] But the difference between changing a law and changing the mode of production is a crucially important one for Marxists of nearly all stripes. It may be one of the few genuinely defining traits of what it is to be a Marxist, as it is hard to imagine the point of any Marxism that abandoned the sense that a non-capitalist society is possible and ultimately necessary.

Analysis of moral economies and moral economy struggles directs our attention to a kind of instability inherent in capitalist society. This instability is a kind of friction built into the process of institutional reorganisation, and is itself constrained. Moral economy struggles involve fighting for elements of a given institutional structure, but not necessarily a struggle on the level of social form. This means that moral economy analysis helps us to understand conflict over the institutional specifics of a regime of class domination and conflict during times when one regime is being taken apart and another is being constructed. This analysis does not

---

[45]   These categories are inspired by Erik Olin Wright's discussion of three visions of the sociology of class. See Erik Olin Wright, *Understanding Class* (Verso 2015) x–xi, 118–25.

[46]   On these questions I have benefited from the communisation current in Marxist theory, of which the journal *Endnotes* has been a particularly visible English-language exponent. The core of this vision of social transformation is that, like the state, dependence on the market does not 'wither away'. An anti-capitalist social transformation only materialises when market-dependency is brought to an end definitively. See Mac Intosh, 'Communization Theory and the Abolition of the Value-Form' (2012) 57 *Internationalist Perspective* 11. See also 'Communisation and Value Form Theory' (2) *Endnotes*, https://endnotes.org.uk/issues/2/en/endnotes-communisation-and-value-form-theory accessed 7 April 2021.

identify—and the presence of moral economy struggles does not indicate—instability within the fundamental social relations that define capitalist societies. Moral economy struggles can be quite intense, even bloody, and have tremendous consequences. They include conflicts over who will occupy positions of state and class power, and which forms of capitalism will predominate. That said, these struggles are ultimately conflicts between two or more different kinds of capitalism, not conflicts relating to the abolition of capitalism as such. At most, moral economy struggles offer raw materials in support of social form struggles.

Social Form Struggles and the Limits of Law

A social form struggle is one that has some real chance of actually contributing to abolishing capitalist social relations. Law will not contribute to the outbreak of social form struggles. At most, legal institutions, legal ideology, and legal professionals can help carry out tactics of defence and survival, as occur during moral economy struggles, prior to the outbreak of a social form struggle. Preventing major social ruptures is a key project of law. Law faces the task of channelling struggles in specific directions, maintaining social control, and preventing social form conflicts from emerging. One of the roles of law in preserving social order is to encourage social conflict to express itself within the contours of existing moral economies and to not go beyond those contours.[47]

A social form struggle will not arise based on moral economies and moral economy struggles. Moral economy struggles are limited by their legally constituted starting-point: law constructs moral economy struggles as wrong-footed from the outset, directing them to preserve an existing social settlement. Moral economy struggles are also limited by the limits that law imposes on which kinds of collective actions are and are not permissible. Were a social form conflict to arise, it would likely involve illegal activities, such as the unlawful expropriation of private property. It might be possible in very specific contexts to legalise that expropriation. Certainly such efforts would face important counter-efforts designed to keep expropriation illegal. The history of capitalist counter-offensives against working-class movements is replete with an instructively long list of arsons, shootings, and bombings, some of which have been illegal and some of which have been carried out in and through the law. Were a specific social form conflict to begin to emerge, law's response would likely be swift and brutal, and also authorised and rhetorically sanitised by legal speech.

Moral Economy Conflicts in Madison, Wisconsin

In early 2011, Wisconsin's state legislature, controlled by the US Republican Party, launched an attack on public-sector unionism in the state, notably through a budget bill proposed by the state's governor, Scott Walker, that sought to effectively end public-sector unionism except among emergency personnel.[48] The bill included a cap on public employees' ability to negotiate pay rises, placed pensions and job conditions outside the purview of collective bargaining, made collection of public-sector union dues more difficult, and required annual recertification

---

47   For an analysis supporting this point see Knox, 'Law, Neoliberalism and the Constitution of Political Subjectivity'.

48   Jason Stein and Patrick Marley, *More Than They Bargained For: Scott Walker, Unions, and the Fight for Wisconsin* (University of Wisconsin Press 2013) 49.

of public-sector unions.[49] The bill included provisions that would allow the state to fire any public employees who struck or otherwise disrupted government operations, including by unexcused absence.[50] The budget bill was part of a long-term process of undeclared yet ferocious class war in the United States. Walker praised President Ronald Reagan's 1981 attack on the federal air traffic controllers union and expressed a desire to emulate Reagan.[51] Yet the bill still came as a surprise to many people in the state, including some Republicans in the Wisconsin state legislature itself, because it had been prepared quickly and in relative secrecy.[52]

Equally surprising was the resistance that the labour movement, and working-class people more generally, were able to muster in response. Ground zero for this resistance was Wisconsin's capitol city, Madison. The protests in Madison numbered 100 000 people on multiple occasions. This was in a city of under 300 000, and a state of under six million. Furthermore, they lasted for months, and were attended by a large number of people outside the activist left. Workers engaged in sick-outs. Protesters occupied the state capitol building for three weeks.[53] Labour union officials began to speak openly of a general strike, something unheard of in the United States for many decades. And activists made the same call in larger numbers via protest chants, posters, and pamphlets.

Numerous commentators, many of them life-long radicals, spoke about the unexpected size and duration of what some would later call the 'Wisconsin Uprising'.[54] These events were especially heady because they broke out early in the process that would soon come to be called the 'Arab Spring', and as those events were receiving increasing attention in the United States news media. That concurrence gave the impression that a global wave of popular unrest was brewing. Many people expressed hope at the time that the Wisconsin events might renew the US labour movement.[55] In conversations I had at the time with fellow radicals and activists, many people expressed even larger hopes. Perhaps neoliberal austerity might be beaten back

---

[49] Alexis N Walker, *Divided Unions: The Wagner Act, Federalism, and Organized Labor* (University of Pennsylvania Press 2020) 3.

[50] Stein and Marley, *More than They Bargained For*, 69.

[51] Walker, *Divided Unions*, 1. For a history of the air traffic controllers' strike see Joseph A McCartin, *Collision Course: Ronald Reagan, the Air Traffic Controllers, and the Strike that Changed America* (OUP 2011).

[52] Stein and Marley, *More than They Bargained For*, 49–50.

[53] Walker, *Divided Unions*, 1.

[54] Michael D Yates (ed), *Wisconsin Uprising: Labor Fights Back* (Monthly Review Press 2011). I happened to be in Madison doing archival research the week the 'uprising' commenced, and I remained loosely involved afterwards through a network of activists across the US Midwest supporting those events within our limited abilities. I have attended many picket lines as well as large demonstrations and protests, including the protests against the IMF and World Bank in Washington, DC in 2000, estimated at 15 000 attendees, and the Chicago demonstration against the Iraq War on the international day of protest in February 2003, estimated at 6000 attendees. (See, respectively, Socialism Today, 'A16, Washington DC', http://socialismtoday.org/archive/47/a16.html accessed 7 April 2021; Antiwar.com, 'February 2003 Antiwar Demonstrations', https://www.antiwar.com/feb03demos.html accessed 7 April 2021.) The Wisconsin events were like nothing I had ever seen, and I have never seen anything like them since. I still get goosebumps when I recall the marching band of the firefighters' union circling the crowded and cheering square, then marching, while playing, straight into the capitol building. To be clear, while I have some basis for comparison in finding the Madison events exceptional, I did not personally play any important role in these events.

[55] Yates, *Wisconsin Uprising*.

entirely. Perhaps a reenergised socialist movement, or even a revolutionary situation might break out.

The Madison protests failed, heartbreakingly. The Wisconsin legislature passed their anti-union legislation, fostering a rapid drop in unionisation in Wisconsin. Wisconsin's public-sector union density had been at approximately 50 per cent in early 2011, significantly higher than the national average of 34 per cent. By 2017, the state's public-sector union density had fallen to just under 19 per cent.[56]

The Madison events can be understood as expressing and drawing on a moral economy of public-sector unionism. Public-sector employees believed that they had a deal, concretised in their collective bargaining agreements, and that they had held up their end of the agreement. This was a sensibility along the lines of 'we worked hard and were told we would get pensions and insurance; we did our part of that bargain and now the government is backing out!'

I spoke to many unemployed people and private-sector workers who rallied in Madison. They tended to see public-sector workers as 'ordinary' people. They did so because, like public-sector employees themselves, they saw the legislative attack on public-sector workers as fundamentally unjust. They also saw these attacks as part of a class war waged by the state and corporations against ordinary people. In this latter view, people expressed a second moral economy, one of public services and citizenship. This was a sensibility along the lines of 'we were told that the American Dream meant we would have better lives as Americans, but austerity has denied us those lives'. The distinction between these two moral economies should not be exaggerated. The essential point is that many private-sector employees saw the Wisconsin budget bill as an unjust attack on a group to which they did not belong—public-sector employees—and an injustice worth rallying around, while also seeing the budget bill as an attack on themselves as citizens who made use of public services. There were thus a number of reasons behind the mass mobilisation in Wisconsin. The latter sensibility, the moral economy of public services and citizenship, seems to have persisted long after the Madison events died down, helping to animate Occupy Wall Street.[57]

The Madison protests had a chance to stop Walker's budget bill and thus to slow or even put an end to austerity politics in the state.[58] That said, many radicals were given to overestimating the political potential in Wisconsin, perhaps understandably given how heady these events were. The Madison events were a moral economy struggle to defend the specific rights to public-sector unionism and public services within a regime of institutionalised class domination. This moral economy struggle was directed against the Walker government's attempt to reorganise the regime of institutionalised class domination with a view to introducing a new and more coercive regime of class domination, an attempt that ultimately proved successful. But it was not itself a social form struggle. The human stakes of moral economy struggles are significant. They are grounded in a commitment to defend rights and access to goods and

---

[56]   Jill Manzo et al, *The State of the Unions 2018: A Profile of Unionization in Wisconsin and in the United States* (Midwest Economic Policy Institute 2018).

[57]   This is my impression as a participant-observer. I do not mean to be reductive or to simplify the complexity of Occupy so much as to explain that this sensibility seems to have been one factor in Occupy's development.

[58]   For an important contribution to understanding how austerity politics has often been specifically legal politics, see Robert Knox, 'Against Law-Sterity' (2018) 6 *Salvage*, https://salvage.zone/in-print/against-law-sterity/.

services, the loss of which is a major harm and injustice. That said, moral economy struggles do not eliminate class domination as such.

CONCLUSION

The perspective I have elaborated in this chapter matters in part because it helps us identify processes and practices that are part of people's relationship to law in capitalist society. It also matters because moral economy conflicts may be significant conflicts, always a matter of interest to law and thus to analysts of law. In certain respects, moral economy struggles are in part within and in part against the law, and vice versa: law is in part within and in part against moral economy struggles. Understanding this dialectic of conflict and consensus matters for analysts of law. This matters especially for Marxists, as it helps to illuminate ongoing class conflicts within capitalism, and their possibilities and limits.

This perspective also helps to make clear that in specific contexts the working class appears as an interest group jockeying for position within capitalism, a view akin to pluralism within industrial relations.[59] That condition, in which the working class appears as a system-immanent interest group, occurs in conditions historically produced by the development of capitalism over time. Other contexts might be produced, wherein the working class could become not a class with interests within a social system, but a class opposed to the social existence of class. Part of the force of the concept of moral economy as reformulated here is to underscore that moral economy struggles are not struggles against class—that is to say, not social form conflicts—and do not give rise to those struggles of their own unfolding. The point of doing so is to call our attention to the need to attend to the project of giving rise to social form conflicts.[60]

This chapter's formulation of moral economy can help us think in a way that bridges structure and agency, helping us to see the potential for agency that exists in capitalism's social structure, to see that kind of agency as itself structurally produced and structurally limited. That kind of agency can only become radical if dramatically expanded and repurposed to be turned against capitalist social structure. This perspective helps us to think both conjuncturally and structurally.[61] Conjuncturally, this concept of moral economy may help us see the type of situation we are in, and help make clear some of the basics of that situation in a way that informs further thought and action. Structurally, this concept can help explain the systemic recurrence of specific kinds of conjuncture, and why these conjunctures generally tend to play out in certain ways, and will continue to do so unless the pattern can be broken by conscious and radical class struggle.

---

[59] On industrial pluralism see Christopher Tomlins, *The State and the Unions: Labor Relations, Law, and the Organized Labor Movement in America, 1880–1960* (CUP 1985).

[60] Throughout this chapter I have connected Marxist analysis as an intellectual project with socialist practice as a political project. Part of the force of my argument is that socialists ought to continue to consider questions about what we mean by social revolution, and political questions about how such a revolution might occur. These questions cannot be left to any spontaneous or automatic process, as if moral economy struggles will give rise to social form conflicts simply of their own accord.

[61] I owe this formulation to Umut Özsu; see Umut Özsu, 'The Necessity of Contingency: Method and Marxism in International Law' in Ingo Venzke and Kevin Jon Heller (eds), *Contingency in International Law: On the Possibility of Different Legal Histories* (OUP 2021) 60.

As I write, it seems as if attacks on working class standards of living will continue to be the order of the day. Some of the time these attacks will elicit moral economy struggles in response, wherein working class people perceive themselves as having been loyal subjects of a prior order which has suddenly been revised unilaterally in a way that produces outrage. Some of that outrage will eventuate into struggle. Unfortunately, these struggles will likely take the form of tactical conflicts and occasionally institutional conflicts. Of course, Marxists hope for working class people to succeed in their struggles, but until a successful social form struggle, all class struggles end in a kind of defeat.

It is likely that for the foreseeable future the best we can realistically hope for are rule changes, but we need to remain aware that this is the case and to hold out hope for more fundamental social change. For such change to take place, the working class will need to disentangle itself from moral economies and from laws. At the least, the working class will need to find ways to supplement moral economies by developing new, future-centred norms and self-authorisation for struggles, in order to fight for more than just holding onto prior deals, and, hopefully, coming to struggle for the end of the capitalist social form altogether.

When moral economy struggles succeed, they are likely to produce, among other things, a legitimation of the social order they defended, rather than a challenge to that order. When moral economy struggles fail, on the other hand, those failures are likely to have other ideological effects, namely the production of fear or resignation, which serve the current institutional regimes of class domination and make it easier for other, even worse regimes to be introduced in the future. As such, Marxists should hope, and in their limited capacities act to help, moral economy struggles to succeed, without having illusions as to what that success will produce.

All of this said, some of the values and practices that are sometimes found within or produced by people in moral economy struggles—such as internationalism, solidarity, opposition to oppression—are, in Simon Clarke's words, 'the expression of human needs and aspirations, which alone point the way forward to socialism'.[62] Moral economy struggles sometimes allow people a small glimpse of social practices animated by those values and can deepen the felt importance of those values for some people. That matters a great deal, but it is only through organised and deliberate efforts to wrest control of society from the imperatives of capital and install those other values in society's operating principles—that is, through social form struggles—that a truly better society can be made. Moral economies at best underline the importance of social form struggles, but they do not have internal tendencies to generate such struggles.

---

[62]   Clarke, 'Overaccumulation, Class Struggle and the Regulation Approach', 89.

15. Law and the state in Frankfurt School critical theory
Chris O'Kane

INTRODUCTION

Originally the retrospective designation of a number of thinkers associated with the Institut für Sozialforschung (Institute for Social Research) during the 1930s and 1940s, Frankfurt School critical theory is now an interdisciplinary theoretical and methodological orientation that has been developed by scholars in virtually every academic discipline. From the so-called 'first generation' of critical theorists, through the 'second', 'third', and now the 'fourth', Frankfurt School critical theory has been broadly defined as consisting of the analysis of society from an emancipatory perspective.[1]

Yet the array of secondary literature that treats critical theory in this manner tends also to treat the development of Frankfurt School critical theory as the refinement of social analysis and emancipatory perspectives by the leading thinkers of each 'generation'.[2] Adorno and Horkheimer are said to have abandoned Marx for a critique of instrumental reason and total administration that led the first generation to a social-theoretical and emancipatory 'cul de sac'.[3] Jürgen Habermas' theory of communicative action identified an emancipatory type of reason distinct from instrumental reason, introducing social complexity and a normative theory of democratic emancipation, and leading the second generation's resuscitation of critical theory.[4] Axel Honneth's theory of recognition has deepened Habermas' social theory and his conception of emancipation.[5] As a consequence, the predominant approach to critical

---

[1] Nancy Fraser and Rahel Jaeggi, *Capitalism: A Conversation in Critical Theory* (Polity Press 2018).

[2] Although I have been unable to ascertain who coined the term 'generations', or who began to interpret the development of Frankfurt School critical theory in this progressive manner, the convention had been established by the time David Held's influential *Introduction to Critical Theory: Horkheimer to Habermas* (Polity Press 1980) and Ralf Wiggershaus' *The Frankfurt School: Its History, Theories, and Political Significance* (first published 1986, Michael Robertson tr, MIT Press 1994) were published.

[3] This interpretation of the development of Adorno and Horkheimer's work was popularised by what is still to this day the most influential account of the development of Frankfurt School critical theory in the anglophone world: Martin Jay, *The Dialectical Imagination: A History of the Frankfurt School and the Institute of Social Research, 1923–1950* (University of California Press 1973). It is echoed in influential works by other notable critical theory scholars, such as Richard Wolin, 'Critical Theory and the Dialectic of Rationalism' (1987) 23 *New German Critique* 23. Recent work, notably Howard Prosser, *Dialectic of Enlightenment in the Anglosphere* (Springer 2020), draws on these sources to continue to advance this interpretation. The term 'cul de sac' is used in Martin Jay, *Marxism and Totality: The Adventures of a Concept from Lukács to Habermas* (University of California Press 1984) 256.

[4] As demonstrated by Prosser, *Dialectic of Enlightenment*, this interpretation was popularised in the late 1970s and early 1980s.

[5] Exemplary of this approach are Joel Anderson's account of the development of the Frankfurt School in 'The "Third Generation" of the Frankfurt School' (2000) 22 *Intellectual History Newsletter*,

theory today is the one developed by Habermas and refined by Honneth and their friendly interlocutors (such as Nancy Fraser) and the critical theory of the 'first generation' is generally assessed from this perspective.

The anglophone secondary literature on critical theory, the state, and law exemplifies this approach to Frankfurt School critical theory. Habermasian critical theory is often treated as synonymous with Frankfurt School critical theory as a whole, especially with respect to questions of the state and law. Not only is Habermas' work treated as epitomising the 'second generation' of critical theory, but if 'first generation' critical legal or state theory receives any mention at all, it is typically associated with the work of Otto Kirchheimer, Franz Neumann, and Friedrich Pollock, which is treated as a footnote to Habermasian theory. In leading works on Marxist state and legal theory, Kirchheimer, Neumann, and Pollock's theories are either relegated to conjunctural debates about the relation between capitalism and fascism,[6] or else passed over in favour of a concerted focus on the early Habermas[7] or the early Habermas and Claus Offe's neo-Marxist state theory.[8] The secondary literature on the Frankfurt School's engagement with questions of law focuses on Kirchheimer and Neumann's writings, which are generally treated as having been superseded by the legal theory of the late Habermas and his followers.[9] Inasmuch as the state theory of the 'first generation' is examined in this secondary literature on the Frankfurt School, the focus is generally on Pollock's theory of state capitalism, which is held to have underpinned the development of Adorno and Horkheimer's social theory.[10]

In contrast to these hegemonic interpretations, the heterodox Marxist approach to critical theory (represented in Best, Bonefeld, and O'Kane)[11] argues that Adorno and Horkheimer did not abandon Marx for a one-dimensional theory of instrumental reason. Instead, they sought to develop an heterodox and critical interpretation of Marx that differed from classical Marxism and explained the failures of the German and Russian revolutions, the rise of fascism, and the persistence of capitalism.[12] This heterodox Marxist approach has also identified what I have

---

https://www.phil.uu.nl/~joel/research/publications/3rdGeneration.htm accessed 7 April 2021. See also the analysis of Honneth's thought in Joel Anderson, 'Situating Axel Honneth in the Frankfurt School Tradition' in Danielle Petherbridge (ed), *Axel Honneth: Critical Essays, With a Reply by Axel Honneth* (Brill 2011) 31.

[6]   Bob Jessop, 'The State' in Ben Fine and Alfredo Saad-Filho (eds), *The Elgar Companion to Marxist Economics* (Edward Elgar 2012) 333.

[7]   See Clyde W Barrow, *Critical Theories of the State: Marxist, Neo-Marxist, Post-Marxist* (University of Wisconsin Press 1993).

[8]   See e.g., Jessop, 'The State'; Barrow, *Critical Theories of the State*.

[9]   See esp. William E Scheuerman, *Between the Norm and the Exception: The Frankfurt School and the Rule of Law* (MIT Press 1994); William E Scheuerman, 'Critical Theory and the Law' in Peter E Gordon, Espen Hammer, and Axel Honneth (eds), *The Routledge Companion to the Frankfurt School* (Routledge 2018) 486.

[10]   Tobias ten Brink, 'Economic Analysis in Critical Theory: The Impact of Friedrich Pollock's State Capitalism Concept' (2015) 22 *Constellations* 333; Manfred Gangl, 'The Controversy over Friedrich Pollock's State Capitalism' (2016) 29 *History of the Human Sciences* 23.

[11]   Beverley Best, Werner Bonefeld, and Chris O'Kane (eds), *The SAGE Handbook of Frankfurt School Critical Theory* (SAGE 2018).

[12]   Beverley Best, Werner Bonefeld, and Chris O'Kane, 'Introduction' in Best, Bonefeld, and O'Kane, *The SAGE Handbook*, 1. On the relationship between Adorno's interpretation of Marx and his critical theory see Christian Lotz, *The Capitalist Schema: Time, Money, and the Culture of Abstraction* (Lexington 2014); Werner Bonefeld, 'Negative Dialectics and the Critique of Economic Objectivity'

termed a 'subterranean' line of critical theory, neglected in the relevant secondary literature, that developed Adorno and Horkheimer's critique of traditional theory and their interpretation of the critique of political economy as a critical theory of society outside and against Habermasian critical theory and traditional Marxism.[13]

This chapter further develops this heterodox Marxist interpretation of Frankfurt School critical theory by aiming to establish the heterodox Marxist critique of the state and law as a Frankfurt School critical theory approach to the state and law that also amounts to a distinct contemporary Marxist analysis of the state and law. In order to do so, the chapter reconstructs the heterodox Marxist approach of Adorno and Horkheimer's critical theories of the state and law, and argues that thinkers associated with Open Marxism develop this approach.[14] The chapter also distinguishes this heterodox Marxist critique of the state and law from classical Marxism, traditional Marxism,[15] and Habermasian critical theory.

The chapter's first part focuses on Horkheimer and Adorno's heterodox Marxist conceptions of the state and law in the context of their critiques of traditional theory and capitalist society. Horkheimer and Adorno hold that traditional theory involves viewing the state and law as neutral instruments that may be wielded irrationally, leading to social disorder, or rationally, leading to the progressive attainment of social harmony. By contrast, their own critical theory conceives the state and law as inherent in the reproduction of the negative totality of capitalist

---

(2016) 29 *History of the Human Sciences* 60; Chris O'Kane, 'Introduction to "Theodor W. Adorno on Marx and the Basic Concepts of Sociological Theory. From a Seminar Transcript in the Summer Semester of 1962"' (2018) 26 *Historical Materialism* 154; Charles Prusik, *Adorno and Neoliberalism: The Critique of Exchange Society* (Bloomsbury 2020). Due to the focus of the chapter, I refrain from discussing *Dialectic of Enlightenment*, which has little concentrated theoretical discussion of the state and law. I focus instead on passages that substantiate Horkheimer and Adorno's heterodox Marxist critical theory of the state and law. However, it should be noted that, in contrast to this dominant interpretation, *Dialectic of Enlightenment* should not be read as representing Adorno and Horkheimer's substitution of the critique of instrumental reason for the critique of political economy, but as an attempt to deepen the critique of political economy against classical Marxism into an heterodox Marxist critical theory of society, a project that was further developed in Adorno's later work. See Marcel Stoetzler, 'Dialectic of Enlightenment: Philosophical Fragments' in Best, Bonefeld, and O'Kane, *The SAGE Handbook,* 142; Massimiliano Tomba, 'Adorno's Account of the Anthropological Crisis and the New Type of Human' in Jernej Habjan and Jessica Whyte (eds), *Misreadings of Marx in Continental Philosophy* (Palgrave 2014) 34; Robert Zwarg, 'Half a Heart and Double Zeal: Critical Theory's Afterlife in the United States' (2017) 132 *New German Critique* 225.

[13]   Chris O'Kane, 'On the Development of the Critique of Political Economy as a Critical Social Theory of Economic Objectivity' (2018) 26 *Historical Materialism* 175. See also Riccardo Bellofiore and Tommaso Redolfi Riva, 'The *Neue Marx Lektüre*: Putting the Critique of Political Economy Back into the Critique of Society' (2015) 189 *Radical Philosophy* 24.

[14]   'Open Marxism' refers to a critical approach to Marx and Marxism that developed out of the Conference of Socialist Economists. I discuss the development of Open Marxism and its critical interpretation of Marx in more detail in the third section. See also Christos Memos, 'Open Marxism and Critical Theory: Negative Critique and Class as a Critical Concept' in Best, Bonefeld, and O'Kane, *The SAGE Handbook,* 1314, for an overview of Open Marxism as a critical theory.

[15]   I use 'classical Marxism' in reference to social-democratic and revolutionary interpretations of Marx from the Second and Third Internationals by figures such as Karl Kautsky, VI Lenin, and Leon Trotsky. By 'traditional Marxism' I refer to recent interpretations of Marx and Marxism that follow these interpretations.

society.[16] As I demonstrate, such a distinction is spelled out, *contra* traditional theory, in Horkheimer and then Adorno's critique of German idealism, social democracy, and classical Marxism, as well as their critiques of Soviet state socialism and Keynesian state capitalism.

The second part of the chapter turns to Habermas, Honneth, and Fraser's critical theories, paying particular attention to their views on law and the state. I argue that Habermasian critical theory rests on certain assumptions about progressive historical development, as well as the view that the state and law are best understood as neutral instruments. Habermasian critical theory contends that the state has become socially 'decoupled' from the democratic 'lifeworld', leading to laws that codify social disorder. However, it also argues that contemporary society is marked by emancipatory intersubjective norms of reason that could and should facilitate the rule of democratic reason via the state and law. I show how this approach to critical theory is developed in Habermas' theory of legitimation crisis and communicative action, Honneth's theory of recognition and freedom, and Fraser's crisis-critique of capitalism and expanded idea of socialism.

The third part turns to the subterranean strand of Open Marxist critical theory, examining the work of Johannes Agnoli, Simon Clarke, and Werner Bonefeld. I establish these thinkers' continuity with Horkheimer and Adorno by providing an overview of their distinctions between traditional and critical theory, as well as their criticisms of traditional Marxism and Habermasian critical theory. I also discuss how this subterranean line of Marxist critical theory developed a critique of the capitalist state and of law, a critique in which the capitalist state form and the state's law-making and -enforcing capacities are integral to the contradictory, antagonistic, and crisis-ridden reproduction of capitalist society. I do so by focusing on Agnoli's critique of the constitutional state and his notions of 'statification' and 'involution', Clarke's critical account of the role that monetary, economic, and social policies play in the dynamic of accumulation and reproduction, and Bonefeld's critique of the state as the political form of capitalist social relations and the moralising function of law-making violence.

The fourth part draws together the preceding account of Adorno and Horkheimer, Habermasian critical theory, and Open Marxism's conceptions of the state and law. It does so in order to contribute further to the heterodox Marxist perspective on Frankfurt School critical theory that contrasts with the predominant literature on the Frankfurt School and Marxism. I initially provide an account of the development of the Frankfurt School critical theory of the state and law, from an heterodox Marxist critical theory perspective. I then critically distinguish the heterodox Marxist critique of the state and law from Habermasian and traditional Marxist theories of the state and law. I thereby establish the former as both a specific approach to Frankfurt School critical theory and a contemporary Marxist analysis of the state and law.

---

[16]   In what follows, 'negative totality' and 'negative universality' are used to convey the double-faceted character of heterodox Marxist critical theory's engagement with German idealism and classical Marxism and their critiques of capitalist society. As I show below, according to critical theory, German idealism and classical Marxism had philosophical histories of the progressive development of social totality that would culminate in freedom when subject (humanity) and object (the social spheres of modern society) were reconciled. Heterodox Marxist critical theory developed a regressive philosophy of history in which subject and object were reconciled in unfreedom. Hence, according to heterodox Marxist critical theory, historical development, totality, and universality are 'negative' rather than 'positive'.

HORKHEIMER AND ADORNO'S CRITICAL THEORY

Horkheimer

As its title clearly suggests, Max Horkheimer's 1937 essay 'Traditional and Critical Theory' laid out the fundamental distinction between traditional and critical theory.[17] In this essay, Horkheimer argued that traditional theories of the capitalist state and society, including law, proceeded from a standpoint within capitalist society itself, employing rational and scientific thought as a normative and diagnostic tool to identify and promote the progressive elements of such a society while minimising or even eliminating its abuses. By advocating measures to ensure that rational thought formed the basis of capitalist society's basic norms and institutions, traditional theory intended to dispel social disorder, realise social harmony, and contribute to the further realisation of social progress. The aim of the critical theory of society, on the other hand, was 'not simply to eliminate one or other abuse' within capitalist society, since it understood 'such abuses as necessarily connected with the way in which the social structure is organized'.[18] In contrast to traditional theory, the critical theory of society, as Horkheimer understood it, drew on a critical interpretation of Marx's critique of political economy to examine the misery and domination intrinsic to the organisation of capitalist society from the perspective of its emancipatory transformation.

Horkheimer's writings on political economy, the state, and law took up this distinction. Horkheimer argued that German idealism and classical Marxism were all forms of traditional theory. Each was committed to philosophical histories of progressive development that would supposedly culminate in the achievement of social harmony through the embodiment of reason in the state and its laws. Such a traditional approach stood in marked contrast to Horkheimer's own interpretation of Marx and his critical theory of society. For while in 'the Idealist dialectic ... *[t]he identity of the ideal and the real is considered the presupposition and the goal of history*', for the 'materialist dialectic ... [t]he identity of the ideal and reality is universal exploitation'. Consequently, 'Marxist science constitutes the critique of bourgeois economy and not the expounding of a socialist one; Marx left that task to Bebel'.[19]

According to Horkheimer, classical Marxism was premised on an interpretation of progressive historical development. According to this interpretation, history was driven by contradictions between forces and relations of production, but these contradictions would ultimately be overcome when a worker state was established and acquired control and direction of production. This would unleash the productive forces. By contrast, Horkheimer argued that following an initial period of progressive development, capitalism had 'hind[ered] further development and driv[en] humanity into a new barbarism'.[20] Moreover, in distinction to classical Marxism's understanding of socialism as involving the proletarian state's control of economic processes, 'the critical theory of society ... has for its object men as producers of their own historical way

---

[17]   Max Horkheimer, 'Traditional and Critical Theory' [1937] in Max Horkheimer, *Critical Theory: Selected Essays* (Matthew J O'Connell et al tr, Continuum 2002) 188. John Abromeit's *Max Horkheimer and the Foundations of the Frankfurt School* (CUP 2011) provides the best account of Horkheimer's critical theory.

[18]   Horkheimer, 'Traditional and Critical Theory', 206–7.

[19]   Max Horkheimer, 'The Authoritarian State' (1975) 15 *Telos* 3, 13 (original emphasis).

[20]   Horkheimer, 'Traditional and Critical Theory', 227.

of life in its totality'.[21] Consequently, he argued that '[e]conomism, to which the critical theory is often reduced, does not consist in giving too much importance to the economy, but in giving it too narrow a scope'.[22] Instead, following Marx, critical theory 'held on to the realization that the free development of individuals depends on the rational constitution of society. In radically analyzing present social conditions it became a critique of the economy'.[23]

In opposition to classical Marxist theories of the base and superstructure, Horkheimer argued that the reified social spheres of the economy, state, and household mutually mediated each other in the process of capital accumulation and reproduction.[24] Yet Horkheimer's conception of reified totality also stood in contrast to Lukács' account, which fused Hegelian and classical Marxist assumptions and held that the progressive development of history would culminate in the proletariat's seizure of the reified totality it had created.[25] *Contra* Lukács, Horkheimer thought that the reified totality of capitalist society was constituted by humanity's capitalist metabolic interaction with nature, and perpetuated by the internal relationship between the economy, the state, and the household. In contrast to Hegel's understanding of totality, which focused on the development of the interrelated spheres of the state, civil society, and the family as (subjective-objective) expressions of the realisation of freedom, and also Lukács' belief that the proletariat—as the subject/object of history—would actualise freedom by seizing the totality, Horkheimer conceived of capitalist society as a negative totality. Accordingly, for Horkheimer, the subjective-objective development of the interrelated spheres of capitalist society express and reproduce unfreedom in a regressive historical trajectory. As Horkheimer put it, the critical theory of society thus expounds a 'single existential judgement' by understanding present conditions as a 'new barbarism' that is unfolded from the concept of simple exchange, itself arising from the 'enormous extension of human control over nature'.[26]

Horkheimer's distinction between these 'traditional' and 'critical-theoretical' approaches to the state and law were further demonstrated in his critique of state capitalism. Traditional theory—in the guise of social democracy and classical Marxism—saw the emergence of 'Keynesian' state policies in Western democracies and socialism in the Soviet Union as signs of progress. Yet Horkheimer argued that these policies had led to the perpetuation of capitalist society in the form of state capitalism. What Horkheimer termed the 'integral state's' administration of the economy had created a 'prestablished harmony' integrating the different classes and spheres of capitalist society. Rather than freedom, this stage of history typified unfreedom. For in contrast to social democracy or classical Marxism, from the perspective of critical theory, '[t]he takeover of what belongs to the individual into the state's keeping, the spread of industry, even in the widespread satisfaction of the masses are tacts whose historical significance is determined only by the nature of the totality to which they belong'.[27] Consequently, no matter the extent of nationalised industries, state planning, redistributive policies, electoral reforms, or party rule, 'the change to a new state of society ... contains more than elements

---

[21]   Horkheimer, 'Traditional and Critical Theory', 244.
[22]   Horkheimer, 'Traditional and Critical Theory', 249.
[23]   Horkheimer, 'Traditional and Critical Theory', 246.
[24]   See Chris O'Kane, 'Reification and the Critical Theory of Contemporary Society' (2021, forthcoming) 8 *Critical Historical Studies*.
[25]   See O'Kane, 'Reification'.
[26]   Horkheimer, 'Traditional and Critical Theory', 227.
[27]   Max Horkheimer, 'Postscript' [1937] in Max Horkheimer, *Critical Theory: Selected Essays* (Matthew J O'Connell et al tr, Continuum 2002) 244, 248–49.

from political economy or jurisprudence' and 'does not depend simply on ... a change in certain property relations or on increased productivity in new forms of social collaboration'. Rather, '[i]t depends just as much on the nature and development of the society in which all these particular developments are taking place. The issue, then, is the real nature of the new relations of production'.[28] From this it follows, in further contrast to classical Marxism, that the 'dependence of politics on the economy is' the 'object [of critical theory] not its program'.[29]

Hence, in contrast to the traditional theories of German idealism and classical Marxism, emancipation is not achieved through the state rule of capitalist totality on a democratic or socialist basis, but the abolition of this totality. Rather than a constitution or bureaucracies ruling the economy in the interests of the people or the workers, for Horkheimer, a free society would have no state, no constitution, and no bureaucracy. It would consist of workers' councils, and decisions would be made on the basis of 'free agreement'.[30] As against traditional theory, '[s]uch an outcome is not a further acceleration of progress, but a qualitative leap out of the dimension of progress'.[31]

Adorno

Adorno's late work in the 1960s developed these aspects of critical theory. For Adorno, the 'golden years' of capitalism did not mark the further realisation of progress, but regression and the persistent domination of outer and inner nature through the reproduction of capitalist society. Classical Marxism notwithstanding, the development of the productive forces had not led to the development of class consciousness and the revolutionary overthrow of capitalism. Nor did Keynesianism result in working-class gains. Instead, it led to the integration of class consciousness and the proletariat's increased dependence on capitalism. Moreover, unlike what Kant had suggested, the faculties of human reason possessed by autonomous individuals were not increasingly expressed in the rational state and laws of an enlightened society. Finally, departing from Hegel, Adorno held that the particular spheres of modern society were not moments of a totality that expressed itself in the state's universal legislative acts progressively realising freedom. Rather, reason and law were supraindividual forms of negative universality that dominated particularity and expressed unfreedom. No matter which class or type of reason ruled the state and legislate laws, even according to 'its very form, before class-content and class-justice', the state and its law 'expresses domination'. This is because 'the system of self-produced concepts, which slides a full-fledged jurisprudence over the life-process of society, decides in advance, by means of the subsumption of everything individual under the category, in favor of the social order which the classificatory system is formed in the image of'; law (and, by extension, the state) is the 'Ur-phenomenon of irrational rationality'.[32] In combination with 'exchange', whose properties they mirrored, 'law' and identity thinking were moments of a negative totality that was created and reproduced through

---

28   Horkheimer, 'Postscript', 249–50.
29   Horkheimer, 'Postscript', 251.
30   See Felix Baum, 'The Frankfurt School and Council Communism' in Best, Bonefeld, and O'Kane, *The SAGE Handbook*, 1160, for a more in-depth discussion of the relationship between the Frankfurt School and council communism.
31   Horkheimer, 'The Authoritarian State', 12.
32   Theodor W Adorno, *Negative Dialectics* (first published 1966, 2001 trans by Dennis Redmond, available at http://libcom.org/library/negative-dialectics-theodor-adorno).

the unconscious collective activities of individuals in class society, realising unfreedom in a regressive historical trajectory of permanent catastrophe.

Such a theoretical perspective was reflected in Adorno's critique of contemporary capitalist and 'socialist' societies. In 'Late Capitalism or Industrial Society?', mirroring Horkheimer's critique of Keynesianism, Adorno argued that the state contributed to reproducing 'late' capitalist society through Keynesian fiscal and monetary policies that had counteracted capitalism's crisis tendencies and raised standards of living. However, this had not led to the progressive realisation of freedom. Late capitalism had not overcome social domination, class antagonism, or misery, all of which continued to persist. Rather, Keynesianism had led to total integration and to the subsumption of the state, household, and subjectivity to the reproduction of capital by virtue of the internal relation between these spheres. In late capitalism, '[m]aterial production, distribution, consumption are administered in common. Their borders, which once separated from inside the total process of externally separated spheres, and thereby respected that which was qualitatively different, are melting away. Everything is one.'[33] The 'totality of the process of mediation, in truth', was thus 'that of the exchange-principle',[34] which 'confronts' everyone as a 'doom' cultivating thinking identical to the exchange principle, crippling autonomy, and rendering individuals reliant on their own unfreedom.[35]

Adorno also claimed that '[i]n the Soviet Union something similar is at work, despite the removal of the market economy'. Under the 'dictatorial administration' of the party, the unfettering of forces of production had renewed the relations of production under different conditions, hindering 'fully-realized freedom'. Hence 'an unmistakable convergence' had occurred between the United States and the Soviet Union, for '[u]nder both systems, the capitalist concept of socially essential work is reduced to a satanic parody' wherein the state and laws administer the development of the productive forces to perpetuate class antagonism and unfreedom rather than realise freedom.[36] Hence, building on Horkheimer, Adorno argued that the 'harmony' of late capitalist society and Soviet socialism was one of negative totality. Emancipation thus consisted in the abolition of such a totality and the creation of a non-dominative relationship between inner and outer nature and the realisation of the realm of freedom.

In sum, Horkheimer and Adorno's critical theory does not seek to use a normative conception of the historical development of reason to advocate social harmony under capitalism. In opposition to classical Marxism, Horkheimer and Adorno's critical theory does not conceive history in terms of the progressive development of the forces of production, nor of the distinction between capitalism and socialism amounting to which class rules the economy and the state. According to Adorno and Horkheimer, these theories are traditional theories. In contrast, critical theory is 'concerned with society as a whole',[37] or with demonstrating how the organisation of capitalist society is realised in the semi-autonomous spheres of capitalist society, which compels individual action within these spheres, restricting human freedom and driving

---

[33]   Theodor W Adorno, 'Late Capitalism or Industrial Society? Opening Address to the 16th German Sociological Congress' (first published 1968, 2001 trans by Dennis Redmond, available at https://www.marxists.org/reference/archive/adorno/1968/late-capitalism.htm).

[34]   Adorno, 'Late Capitalism'.

[35]   Adorno, 'Late Capitalism'.

[36]   Adorno, 'Late Capitalism'.

[37]   Adorno, 'Postscript', 249.

humanity as a whole into crises and catastrophes. The state and law are not neutral instruments that can either lead to social disorder if wielded irrationally or remedy these conditions if wielded rationally. Rather, the state and law are inherent in the negative totality of capitalist society, and both must be abolished to realise freedom.

HABERMASIAN CRITICAL THEORY

Habermas

Habermas endeavoured to provide the normative standpoint, sociological complexity, and democratic theory he claimed were lacking in both classical Marxism and Adorno and Horkheimer's critical theory.[38] This led Habermas to develop an approach to critical theory distinct from Adorno and Horkheimer, an approach which has been developed further by Honneth, Fraser, and others. In his early work, Habermas developed a social-theoretical framework that he held supplemented Marx, Adorno, and Horkheimer. Habermas contended that essential components of modern society which he argued Marx had neglected—the state, law, and democratic reason—were essential to understanding capitalism and emancipation.[39] In these works—particularly *Legitimation Crisis* and 'Towards a Reconstruction of Historical Materialism',[40] Habermas adapted Marxist categories to elaborate a normative democratic theory of progressive social evolution.[41] Habermas' theory held that components of society he characterised as part of the 'system' (e.g., money, the state, and technology) had developed out of step with the 'lifeworld', leading to periodic crises that threatened social integration. In advanced capitalist societies, economic crises had been forestalled through state management of the economy, leading to 'rationality', 'legitimation', and 'motivation' crises tendencies. Such problems could and should be resolved by anchoring the disembedded 'system' in the practical moral consciousness of communicative action, and by overseeing institutional

---

[38] For overviews of the development of Habermas' critical theory that stress these underlying commitments, see Christoph Henning, 'Jürgen Habermas: Against Obstacles to Public Debates' in Best, Bonefeld, and O'Kane, *The SAGE Handbook*, 402; Matthew G Specter, *Habermas: An Intellectual Biography* (CUP 2010).

[39] Consider William Scheuerman's illuminating comment: 'As Habermas noted with evident frustration in a 1963 essay, Marx "went beyond Hegel to discredit so enduringly for Marxism both the idea of legality itself and the intention of Natural Law as such that ever since the link between Natural Law and revolution has been dissolved". Accordingly, the young Habermas tried to correct for this analytic rupture within Marxism by highlighting the rule of law's implicit normative and political potential. By showing how it could be reconceived as a politically progressive *social* rule of law, Habermas hoped to overcome the unfortunate delineation of legality (and its origins in modern natural law) from radical politics. An updated version of the rule of law, in short, was indispensable to radical reform.'
Scheuerman, 'Critical Theory and the Law', 492 (original emphasis, citations omitted).

[40] Jürgen Habermas, *Legitimation Crisis* (first published 1973, Thomas McCarthy tr, MIT Press 1975); Jürgen Habermas, 'Towards a Reconstruction of Historical Materialism' (1975) 2 *Theory and Society* 287.

[41] Helmut Reichelt, 'Jürgen Habermas' Reconstruction of Historical Materialism' in Werner Bonefeld and Kosmas Psychopedis (eds), *The Politics of Change: Globalization, Ideology and Critique* (Palgrave 2000) 105, for a critical account of Habermas' interpretation of Marx. Reichelt's article also demonstrates the continuity between the traditional theoretical elements of Habermas' early and late theory, upon which this section draws.

regulation through the state and law. The state and law thus played a key role in Habermas' early critical theory. On the one hand, the crises tendencies of advanced capitalism ultimately consisted in the unmooring of the state from the 'lifeworld'. On the other hand, the normative role of the state and law pointed to how the state and law should be grounded in substantive democracy premised on communicative reason.

Habermas' later work made the underlying differences between Habermas' earlier approach to critical theory, Marx, Adorno, and Horkheimer more explicit. *The Theory of Communicative Action* marked his formal break from reconstructing historical materialism, jettisoning his interpretation of Marxist categories in favour of a normative democratic theory of socio-logical complexity explicitly premised on addressing what Habermas perceived as Adorno and Horkhiemer's normatively deficient social theory. Like his earlier work, the distinction between 'system' and 'lifeworld', and a philosophical history of the evolution of modern society, lies at the heart of Habermas' later work. However, in this later work, Habermas' 'system' now consisted of the structurally differentiated institutions of market and state, which he now explicitly held to be necessary elements of contemporary societies. The 'lifeworld' was now the realm of intersubjective communicative reason shorn of any vestige of class antagonism. Such a theory was said to provide an understanding of society as one of 'complex differentiation' rather than 'one-dimensionality'.[42]

Habermas' understanding of the state and law was the fulcrum on which this normative social theory turned. What Habermas termed 'social pathologies' referred to conditions in which the state becomes 'unmoored' from the public sphere, and rules on the basis of 'power' pure and simple. This leads to the adoption of laws that allow the 'system', in particular the state and the economy, to transcend their normative boundaries, in which market and state activity are appropriate, 'colonising the lifeworld'. As a result, communicative reason is trammelled, undermining political will-formation and democratic practice. Such laws—and, by extension, the political regimes that adopt them—are fundamentally illegitimate. Indeed, Habermas argues that juridico-political orders are legitimate only so long as they adhere to their basic normative commitments, ideally by way of a constitution that enshrines legal norms and establishes state institutions as a kind of 'transmission belt' between the 'system' and the 'lifeworld'. This, in turn, will ensure that the state and its laws are not engulfed by money and power and may act as democratic 'steering mechanisms', restricting money and power to their prescribed spheres and enabling them to fulfil their normative functions on the basis of communicative democracy. Hence the emancipatory and normative role the state and law play in Habermas' democratic critical theory.

Honneth

Honneth has deepened Habermas' normative social theory, replacing his neo-Kantian focus on reason and discourse with a neo-Hegelian understanding of recognition and freedom.[43] Yet, following the later Habermas, Honneth treats the social spheres of capitalist society as

---

    [42] Jürgen Habermas, *The Theory of Communicative Action*, 2 vols (first published 1981, Thomas McCarthy tr, Beacon 1985).

    [43] For critical overviews of Honneth's critical theory, see Anita Chari, *A Political Economy of the Senses: Neoliberalism, Reification, Critique* (Columbia University Press 2015); Michael J Thompson, 'Axel Honneth and Critical Theory' in Best, Bonefeld, and O'Kane, *The SAGE Handbook*, 564.

necessary components of *any* complex modern society. Moreover, Honneth's conception of recognition is grounded in Habermas' conception of evolutionary historical development and functional differentiation.

Like Habermas, Honneth does not argue for the abolition of capitalist society.[44] Instead, mirroring Habermas, he argues that the miseries of modern life stem from disequilibria within and between the spheres of modern society—disequilibria that arise when the types of systemic rationality appropriate to specific spheres are disembedded from the normative structures that should anchor them. Further, although Honneth argues that norms in each of these spheres are essential to remedying social disorder, the state and law play a superordinate role in his theory. This is because, like Habermas, Honneth views the state as a neutral institution and law as a neutral means of co-ordination, demarcation, and norm-realisation. 'Social pathologies' thus arise when systemic activities become decoupled from norms in their respective spheres. 'Misdevelopments' stem from the state failing to play its own normative role, namely aligning laws with norms and containing them within their respective spheres. This leads to boundary transgressions and laws that codify misrecognition. According to Honneth's progressive philosophy of history, these types of misrecognition have been—and will continue to be—overcome when the state plays its proper role: codifying norms of recognition demanded by social movements in laws. In a socialist society, the state would ultimately serve as a 'co-ordinating mechanism' or 'steering authority', establishing norms of recognition conceived by the political will within the political sphere and between the spheres of the market and family through the freedom-realising capacities of law.

Fraser

Fraser has been an interlocutor of both Habermas and Honneth, pointing to gaps in their theories.[45] Her early work argued incisively against Habermas' indifference toward the private sphere and gender in his account of the public sphere.[46] Her work in the early 2000s further argued that Honneth's theory of recognition does not account for the important and ultimately complementary idea of redistribution.[47] Over the past decade Fraser has worked on a crisis critique of capitalism that attempts to incorporate these interests with Habermas' early work, her traditional interpretation of Marx, and a variety of traditional forms of Marxist scholarship into an 'expanded' theory of capitalism as an 'institutionalized social order'.[48]

---

[44] The following discussion draws upon Axel Honneth, *Freedom's Right: The Social Foundations of Democratic Life* (first published 2011, Joseph Ganahl tr, Columbia University Press 2014) and Axel Honneth, *The Idea of Socialism: Toward a Renewal* (first published 2015, Joseph Ganahl tr, Polity Press 2017).

[45] Despite Fraser's debates with leading figures in the second and third generations, and a formidable body of work, the only overview of Fraser's critical theory is Claudia Leeb, 'Radical Political or Neo-Liberal Imaginary? Nancy Fraser Revisited' in Best, Bonefeld, and O'Kane, *The SAGE Handbook*, 550.

[46] Nancy Fraser, 'What's Critical About Critical Theory? The Case of Habermas and Gender' (1985) 35 *New German Critique* 97; Nancy Fraser, 'Rethinking the Public Sphere: A Contribution to Actually Existing Democracy' (1990) 25/26 *Social Text* 56.

[47] Nancy Fraser and Axel Honneth, *Redistribution or Recognition? A Political-Philosophical Exchange* (Joel Golb, James Ingram, and Christiane Wilke tr, Verso 2003).

[48] Fraser has developed this theory across a number of publications. For the most developed account of this theory, see Fraser and Jaeggi, *Capitalism: A Conversation in Critical Theory*. For an immanent cri-

However, despite her incisive criticisms of Habermas and Honneth, Fraser's work has adhered to the Habermasian paradigm. Like Habermas and Honneth, Fraser conceives of misrecognition, maldistribution, and crises as 'social pathologies' that arise from the lack of proper democratic state co-ordination. This is exemplified by her critique of capitalism, according to which the unmooring of the market and state enforcement of neoliberal policies have led to widespread and significant institutional disorder. Her solution follows Habermas and Honneth in conceiving the state and law as neutral instruments that can and should represent and codify the social-democratic political consensus, which in turn represents the basic normative structure of capitalist society. Fraser's early criticisms of Habermas adapted his ideas. During the early 2000s, in her debates with Honneth, Fraser argued that the establishment of 'participatory parity', which would enable all citizens to participate in the democratic process, would assure that policies of redistribution and recognition would be enacted into law, achieving justice. In the expanded conception of socialism developed in her recent work, mirroring Honneth, Fraser has also argued that capitalism and its crisis tendencies can be overcome by the state mooring the market, protecting the boundaries between the market, state, and household, and enacting laws that realise the norms inherent in each of these spheres.

Habermasian critical theory thus departs from Adorno and Horkheimer's critical theory. Following Habermas, such an approach to critical theory attempts to overcome Adorno and Horkheimer's supposedly one-dimensional and non-normative social theory by developing a complex normative democratic theory premised on the state and law within the context of modern society's progressive development. Mirroring, and drawing upon, the traditional theories of German idealism and classical Marxism, the state is posited as the neutral instrument that can and should resolve 'social pathologies' created by the disembedding of the 'system' from the 'lifeworld'. It should do so by expressing the types of reason that are active but not yet fully realised in modern society. This, in turn, will be achieved through the neutral medium of law, which will sanctify and protect fundamental norms, leading to the realisation of a free, just, and democratic society. Habermas' neo-Kantian critical theory reflects such a paradigm in his early work on the theory of legitimation crises and in his later development of the theory of communicative action. Honneth's neo-Hegelian reconstruction of the historical realisation of freedom draws on and deepens the Habermasian paradigm, as does Fraser's view of justice, her conception of capitalism as an institutionalised social order, and her expanded vision of socialism.

OPEN MARXIST CRITICAL THEORY

The term 'Open Marxism' was first used by Johannes Agnoli to distinguish his critical approach to Marx from Ernest Mandel's traditional Marxism.[49] A number of key participants in the Conference of Socialist Economists (CSE)—notably Sol Picciotto, John Holloway, and Simon Clarke—later developed an interpretation of Marx with parallels to Agnoli's critical

---

tique of Fraser's theory see Chris O'Kane, 'Critical Theory and the Critique of Capitalism: An Immanent Critique of Nancy Fraser's "Systematic" "Crisis-Critique" of Capitalism as an "Institutionalized Social Order"' (2021) 85 *Science & Society* 207.

[49]   See Memos, 'Open Marxism'.

theory. Starting in the journal *Common Sense*, and then proceeding in a number of edited collections, Open Marxism brought together and drew on the work of these and other figures.

While Open Marxism has received ample attention in secondary literature on Marxism,[50] it is generally not discussed in the dominant anglophone literature on the history of critical theory. Following and building on the work of Bonefeld, Best, and Memos, this section shows that Open Marxism is a subterranean strand of critical theory that has developed Horkheimer and Adorno's heterodox Marxist critique of the state and law, in opposition to traditional Marxism and Habermasian theory. I unpack these aspects of Open Marxism's heterodox Marxist theory by focusing on Agnoli's critique of the constitutional state and his concepts of 'involution' and 'statification'. I also examine Clarke's critical account of the forms of the state, law, and policy in perpetuating the crisis-ridden dynamic of accumulation and reproduction, as well as Bonefeld's conception of the state as the political form of capitalist social relations.

Agnoli

Agnoli developed his 'destructive' critique of the state in opposition to traditional Marxism and Habermas. As against these interpretations of historical development, Agnoli argued that history was not a process of evolution, but was instead a process of what he termed 'involution'. The emancipatory promise of feudalism's demise was eclipsed by the development of capitalist societies and states. This led to the 'liberation of production, but not … to the emancipation of individuals', and had significant implications for the 'form in which socio-economic structures of domination were translated into politics, that is, the form of the state'.[51] For Agnoli social misery is not characterised by a process of decoupling, with the neutral subsystems of the economy and the state colonising the 'lifeworld' due to a lack of democratic co-ordination. Nor is progress characterised by the concessions granted by the capitalist state as a result of class struggle or the spread of democracy and the enshrinement of rights in the laws of a democratic state. Rather, the separation of the economy from the state means that the democratic capitalist state works in tandem with the capitalist economy, as a peacemaker that pacifies the workers' movement and the women's movement by absorbing and neutralising them. Mirroring Adorno and Horkheimer, 'involution' refers to the regressive march of history, as characterised by the expansion and consolidation of capitalist social relations.

In further contrast to Habermas, Agnoli does not criticise contemporary society or its institutions on the basis of some set of pre-existing and unrealised norms. Rather, mirroring Adorno, he stresses that norms specific to different spheres of capitalist society are indeed capitalist norms, and argues that giving expression to these norms in the form of law, 'democratic' or otherwise, simply reproduces capitalism. This is because 'capitalist producing and bourgeois constituted society, needs a political form … It needs … a form that is the master of

---

[50]   See e.g., John M Roberts, 'From Reflection to Refraction: Opening Up Open Marxism' (2002) 26 *Capital & Class* 87; Andreas Bieler and Adam David Morton, 'Globalisation, the State and Class Struggle: A "Critical Economy" Engagement with Open Marxism' (2003) 5 *British Journal of Politics and International Relations* 467; Frederick Harry Pitts, *Critiquing Capitalism Today: New Ways to Read Marx* (Palgrave Macmillan 2018).

[51]   Johannes Agnoli, 'Emancipation: Paths and Goals' in Werner Bonefeld and Sergio Tischler (eds), *What Is To Be Done? Leninism, Anti-Leninist Marxism and the Question of Revolution Today* (Routledge 2018) 187, 187.

the law, a master who possesses authority, offices and institutions for the implementation and imposition of law'.[52] This political form is the capitalist state.

It follows from Agnoli's interpretation of the capitalist state and capitalist law that a democratic constitution 'guarantees the predominance of the capitalist mode of production and, at the same time, satisfies the demand for mass political participation by the population', establishing the 'framework' for a 'peaceful order' that 'guarantees' and 'safeguards' the 'organization of social reproduction'.[53] This occurs on the basis of norms of liberty and freedom that preserve private property and class antagonism, while transforming emancipatory struggles into political contests between juridically equal citizens, principally over the persons who will be authorised to represent them and their interests.

In further opposition to traditional Marxism and Habermasian critical theory, this means that mass political participation neutralises emancipatory social movements: class struggle is transformed into representative democratic contests; the 'progressive' laws that states adopt absorb social movements. This process, which Agnoli terms 'statification', is presupposed by the separation of the economic and political, and also codified in the constitution, which guarantees that 'all opportunities, beyond the democratic virtue of "voting", of active meddling in politics are excluded from the "liberal democratic" principles of government'.[54] Consequently, class antagonism and anti-capitalist politics are displaced and depoliticised in the political sphere, in which different parties compete for the votes of citizens whom they ostensibly represent. The policies these parties support are already limited by the constitution. But Agnoli also argues that even the most 'progressive' reformist movements are neutralised by the state: the citizenry's active participation is replaced by an electoral platform extolled by a single representative; concrete policies are transformed 'into bureaucratic apparatuses of integration'.[55] As a consequence, '[e]ach parliamentary reform that is realized within states ... serves not to expand the possibility for the masses to take part in decision-making processes, but rather to contain that possibility by intensifying parliament's function of domination'.[56] Agnoli's conclusion is clear: 'Even where there exists a political articulation of a free public sphere, it cannot use parliament as a tool to implement itself practically.'[57]

In sum, as with traditional Marxism, and Habermas and his followers, Agnoli conceives the state as separate from the economy. Yet, unlike Habermas and his followers, this demarcation is the basis for critiquing how the realisation of the norms of liberty, equality, and democracy in the form of the capitalist state and law perpetuate and reproduce capitalist social relations. Hence, in contrast to the neutral-instrumentalist view of the state:

> [s]tate institutions do not allow themselves to be used in any manner whatsoever, for their logic is not their own, but is determined by the reality whose functioning they serve. State institutions are not

---

[52]   Johannes Agnoli, 'The Market, the State and the End of History' in Werner, Bonefeld and Kosmas Psychopedis (eds), *The Politics of Change: Globalization, Ideology and Critique* (Palgrave 2000) 196, 199.

[53]   Agnoli, 'Market', 200–2.

[54]   Agnoli, 'Market', 201.

[55]   Johannes Agnoli, 'Theses on the Transformation of Democracy and on the Extra-Parliamentary Opposition' (2014) *Viewpoint*, https://www.viewpointmag.com/2014/10/12/theses-on-the-transformation-of-democracy-and-on-the-extra-parliamentary-opposition/ accessed 7 April 2021.

[56]   Agnoli, 'Theses'.

[57]   Agnoli, 'Theses'.

there to realize either freedom or human rights, not to mention social emancipation; rather they have solely the responsibility of organizing and securing the social reproduction of a capitalist society.[58]

As a consequence, the '*multitudo*, then, loses out to the authority of the state' while political power amounts to different strategies for managing the state and the economy.[59] For Agnoli '[t]he true characterization of "liberal democracy" is thus *constitutional oligarchy*'.[60] This is why '"liberal democracy" and the capitalist form of social reproduction do quite well together'.[61]

Clarke

Mirroring Agnoli, Horkheimer, and Adorno, Marxist sociologist Simon Clarke offers a critique of both 'traditional' and 'constructive' theories of society. In *Marx, Marginalism and Modern Sociology*, an overlooked masterpiece of Marxist critical theory, Clarke differentiates Marx's critique of political economy from classical political economy and traditional interpretations of Marx as a classical political economist.[62] Clarke also demonstrates convincingly that the post-Parsonian sociology of Habermas, and by extension of Honneth and Fraser, is grounded in a number of unsubstantiated dualisms—between, in particular, 'system' and 'lifeworld', and 'instrumental' and 'communicative' rationality—which stem from the marginalist tradition. According to Clarke, traditional Marxism and Habermas' critical theory are thus premised on traditional social theories that naturalise the institutions of capitalist society, failing to grasp its constitution and antagonistic, crisis-ridden reproduction. In other work, such as *Keynesianism, Monetarism and the Crisis of the State*, and his contributions to *The State Debate*, Clarke made a similar argument in regard to a number of other contemporary traditional interpretations of Marx and Marxist theories of the state.[63] As he noted, in further contrast to traditional Marxism and Habermasian critical theory, '[t]he theoretical conclusion of the CSE contribution was that we have to look behind the institutional separation of economics, law and politics to see money, law and the state as complementary economic, legal and political forms of the power of capital'.[64] The 'underlying unity of these differentiated, and complementary, forms of capitalist power was explained by Marx's theory of value, the three aspects being united in capitalist property, money representing the most abstract form of capital, whose power is institutionalised in the law and enforced by the state'.[65]

Clarke's critical theory of the capitalist state and law proceeds from this specific understanding of Marx's theory of value, which is distinct from traditional Marxism. In Clarke's view, Marx's critique was grounded in capitalism's historically specific social form of class antagonism. This antagonistic social form constitutes capitalist society in its totality, including

---

[58] Agnoli, 'Emancipation', 190–91.

[59] Agnoli, 'Market', 201.

[60] Agnoli, 'Market', 201 (original emphasis).

[61] Agnoli, 'Market', 200.

[62] Simon Clarke, *Marx, Marginalism and Modern Sociology: From Adam Smith to Max Weber* (2nd edn, Macmillan 1991).

[63] See Simon Clarke, *Keynesianism, Monetarism and the Crisis of the State* (Edward Elgar 1988); Simon Clarke, 'Introduction' in Simon Clarke (ed), *The State Debate* (Macmillan 1991) 1.

[64] Clarke, *Keynesianism*, 15.

[65] Clarke, *Keynesianism*, 15.

the supraindividual forms of money, the law, and the world market. These forms of negative universality mediate—and are mediated by—the acts of individual workers, capitalists, and states, and are realised in the antagonistic, contradictory, and crisis-ridden process of capital accumulation and social reproduction.

This crisis-prone process is 'imposed on individual capitals by the pressure of competition, [and] is the tendency for capital to develop the productive forces without limit'.[66] This leads individual capitalists to seek out 'new markets by commercial expansion and by displacing backward forms of production, and to reduce costs by lengthening the working day, forcing down wages, intensifying labour and, above all, by transforming methods of production'.[67] For Clarke this crisis-ridden dynamic likewise underlies the tendency for 'capital, from its earliest stages, to develop the world market and to generalise capitalist social relations of production on a global scale'.[68] Clarke further argues that 'the tendency to develop the productive forces without regard to the limit of the market also underlies the tendency to the global overaccumulation and uneven development of capital, as the development of social production confronts the limits of its capitalist form as production for profit'.[69] Crucially, in Clarke's interpretation, this propensity to overaccumulation 'appears in its most dramatic form' in the eruption of a 'generalised crisis of overproduction', but it is also 'the everyday reality of accumulation, as the pressure of competition leads to an intensification of class struggle, the devaluation of backward capitals, the destruction of productive capacity and the displacement of labour'.[70]

For Clarke this contradictory dynamic is mediated by the form of the state.[71] And since the state is fundamentally mediated by this dynamic, it is also unable to resolve its contradictions. Rather, it is intrinsic to this contradictory, antagonistic, and crisis-prone social process. Like Agnoli, Clarke understands '[t]he class character of the state' not in a traditional Marxist manner, but on the basis of the formal 'separation of the state from civil society, and the corresponding subordination of state and civil society to the rule of money and the law'.[72] Crucially, the state:

> secures the general interest of capital in the first instance not by overriding the rule of the market, but by enforcing the rule of money and the law, which are the alienated forms through which the rule of the market is imposed not only on the working class, but also on all particular capitals.[73]

Thus, contra traditional Marxism, '[t]he class character of the state does not lie in its expressing the interests of capitalists, but in the duality of money and the state as the complementary forms of existence of capital-in-general'.[74]

---

[66]   Simon Clarke, 'The Global Accumulation of Capital and the Periodisation of the State Form' in Werner Bonefeld, Richard Gunn, and Kosmas Pyschopedis (eds), *Open Marxism 1: Dialectics and History* (Pluto Press 1992) 133, 135.

[67]   Clarke, 'Global Accumulation', 135.

[68]   Clarke, 'Global Accumulation', 135.

[69]   Clarke, 'Global Accumulation', 135.

[70]   Clarke, 'Global Accumulation', 135.

[71]   Clarke, 'Global Accumulation', 135.

[72]   Simon Clarke, 'Class Struggle and the Global Overaccumulation of Capital' in Robert Albritton, Makoto Itoh, Richard Westra, and Alan Zuege (eds), *Phases of Capitalist Development: Booms, Crises and Globalizations* (Palgrave 2001) 76, 79.

[73]   Clarke, *Keynesianism*, 124.

[74]   Clarke, *Keynesianism*, 125.

Consequently, the liberal form of the state secures the mutual subordination of civil society and the state to the anonymous rule of money and the law. For Clarke the 'independence' of the judiciary and the central bank is the most adequate institutional form of the alienated power of money and the law. These institutions do not simply express 'the complementarity of civil society and the state'; they also 'provid[e] the constitutional guarantee of the integrity of its form'.[75] The 'formal and abstract character of the law' is then 'the complement of the abstract form of property as money', and the institutions of the state act to guarantee the persistence of these forms and with it the persistence of capitalist society.[76] However, these forms inhere in capitalism's crisis-ridden process of reproduction on the world market. They express contradictory and antagonistic class relations, which the state attempts to defuse and control through a number of institutional and political means, which themselves are contradictory and antagonistic. This is because '[t]he national form of the state requires it to express, politically and ideologically, the national interest, against all particular interests', so that '[t]he reproduction of the state correspondingly requires it to resolve this contradiction'.[77] The state must not only act as capital in general against the demands of particular capitals, but must also strive to overcome the crisis-laden process of accumulation by managing class antagonism.

Such a 'contradiction appears to the state in the form of the social and political aspirations of the working class, to which it has to respond within the limits of its form, confining the working class within the form of the wage and the constitutional form of the state'.[78] The state responds by providing concessions, such as constitutional rights, social programs, trade unions, and bargaining rights and powers, in the name of an illusory common interest that depoliticises class struggle and undermines autonomy. Yet this does not resolve the struggle or the contradictions. Instead, these programs increase the pressure on the state to secure the sustained accumulation of domestic productive capital in the context of a further contradiction, this one 'between the national form of the state and the global character of capital accumulation'.[79]

In sum, the contradictory social form of capitalism consists in the reified social spheres of the economy and state, and the reified social forms of money, property, and law which express and are expressed in the class-antagonistic, crisis-prone process of capital accumulation. The state and law thus act in the general interest of capital, utilising policies to attempt to counteract crises and depoliticise class struggle. Yet since the state form and its institutional capacities are developed by this very dynamic, the state cannot overcome or even effectively counteract it. Only the emancipatory abolition of the capitalist social form, including the state, can overcome contradiction, class struggle, and recurrent crisis.

Bonefeld

Bonefeld's work builds on Agnoli and Clarke's critique of the state and law, developing this subterranean heterodox Marxist critical theory even further while also criticising the further

---

[75] Clarke, *Keynesianism*, 127.
[76] Clarke, *Keynesianism*, 127.
[77] Clarke, *Keynesianism*, 18.
[78] Clarke, *Keynesianism*, 18–19.
[79] Clarke, *Keynesianism*, 19.

development of traditional Marxist state theory.[80] In his earlier work, Bonefeld translated Agnoli, edited the Open Marxist collections, and developed a critique of the state that criticised some of the premises of normative political theory and traditional Marxist state theory.[81] In his recent work, notably *Critical Theory and the Critique of Political Economy*, Bonefeld has more forthrightly aligned this critique of the state with Adorno and Horkheimer's critical theory, developing a critical theory of economic objectivity.

Such a critical theory is premised on conceiving capitalist society as a historically specific negative totality of separated unity created by primitive accumulation. In Bonefeld's account, the separation of workers from the means of production and the accumulation of surplus value and private property by capitalists is mirrored in the constitution of capitalist society's separate but structurally related spheres. Yet traditional economic and political theory, and by extension traditional Marxism and Habermasian critical theory, offers only constructive criticisms within the parameters of these distinct spheres, drawing on their specific norms and laws to develop progressive ideas and policies. Bonefeld's critical theory, by contrast, conceives the reproduction of capitalist society as the reproduction of these separations. This leads him to distinguish classical political economy and traditional Marxist theories of the state from an heterodox Marxist critical theory of the state which understands the form of the state and its law as integral to the process of reproducing capitalism's logic of separation.

Following Agnoli and Clarke, Bonefeld views the state, not as an institution that is 'accountable to capital', but 'the political form of the capitalist social relations'.[82] As the political form of capital, the 'cohesion, organization, integration and reproduction' of the capitalist economy 'are matters of state'.[83] Here Bonefeld succinctly formulates the ends of such a political practice: 'Crudely put, the purpose of capital is to accumulate extracted surplus value, and the state is the political form of that purpose'.[84] He also provides an account of how this purpose is achieved by state policies enacted for the purpose of furthering accumulation. The state, he argues, 'facilitates the order of economic freedom ... by means of the force of law-making violence'; sustains capitalist relations of production and exchange by depoliticising 'socio-economic relations'; guarantees 'contractual relations of social interaction'; seeks further development of the system of free labour through 'cheapness of provision'; and extends these relations by securing 'free and equal market relations'.[85]

In yet another departure from Habermasian theory, and continuity with Adorno and Horkheimer, Bonefeld argues that the strong (neo)liberal state functions as a 'market facilitating state' not because it is decoupled from morality, but because it does so through moralising law. In Bonefeld's view, such a technique consists in the moralising social policy of 'vital politics' (*Vitalpolitik*) as a 'market facilitating, enabling and embedding policy, which, in the face of the destructive sociological and moral effects of the free economy, has to be pursued

---

[80]   See O'Kane, 'On the Development of the Critique of Political Economy'.

[81]   See e.g., Werner Bonefeld, 'Reformulation of State Theory' (1987) 33 *Capital & Class* 96; Werner Bonefeld, 'The Capitalist State: Illusion and Critique' in Werner Bonefeld (ed), *Revolutionary Writing: Common Sense Essays in Post-Political Politics* (Autonomedia 2003) 201.

[82]   Werner Bonefeld, *Critical Theory and the Critique of Political Economy: On Subversion and Negative Reason* (Bloomsbury 2014) 160.

[83]   Bonefeld, *Critical Theory*, 182.

[84]   Bonefeld, *Critical Theory*, 168.

[85]   Bonefeld, *Critical Theory*, 183–85.

relentlessly to sustain and maintain the free economy'.[86] Vital politics act as a 'market police' by using the instrument of depoliticising social policy in order to eliminate 'the proletariat by means of a "market-conforming" social policy,' which facilitates 'freedom and responsibility' in a way that transforms 'recalcitrant workers into willing entrepreneurs of their own labour power'.[87] In other words, the norms of freedom and responsibility are capitalist norms: the 'social element of the market economy … connects market freedom with individual responsibility, sets out to reconcile workers with the law of private property, promotes enterprise, and delivers society from proletarianised social structures'.[88] The 'strong state' thus utilises the form-determined capacities of 'law-making violence' in an instrumental manner, in order to organise, integrate, sustain, and extend the social relation at the heart of the peculiar dynamic of valorisation for the purpose of accumulating surplus value. In so doing it perpetuates the separated unity of the negative totality of capitalist society.

Taken as a whole, in contrast to traditional Marxism and Habermasian critical theory, Open Marxism does not conceive of history as the progressive development of the productive forces or as a process of complex differentiation leading to the formation of a functionally differentiated contemporary society characterised by competing types of social co-ordination. Nor does Open Marxism view the economy and state as neutral instruments inherent in all societies, characterised by class rule or 'decoupling', miscoordination, and misrule. Finally, Open Marxism does not criticise specific laws and rulers with a view to determining which laws should be promulgated by which rulers to spur some form of progressive realisation of freedom. Instead, following Horkheimer's notion of traditional theory, Open Marxism designates these Habermasian and traditional Marxist approaches as what Agnoli terms 'constructive critique', which 'constantly makes positive proposals and seeks to improve and consolidate existing conditions'. Open Marxism, in contrast, follows Horkheimer's notion of critical theory, engaging in 'destructive critique', which aims to 'demolish[] existing conditions'.[89] Open Marxism also develops Adorno and Horkheimer's critique of the state and law as inherent in the organisation and reproduction of capitalist society. Open Marxism critiques the form of the state as integral to the historically specific social form of capitalism, and law (exemplified by constitutions, social and fiscal policy) as the means whereby the state contributes to the reproduction of antagonistic, contradictory, and crisis-ridden capitalist society. Consequently, the state and law are a part of capitalist society and must be abolished, so that freedom and human flourishing may be realised.

THE DISTINCT APPROACH OF THE HETERODOX MARXIST CRITICAL THEORY OF THE STATE AND LAW

I now cash out the distinctions I have made between classical Marxist, traditional Marxist, heterodox Marxist, and Habermasian approaches to the state and law. I do so by considering

---

[86] Werner Bonefeld, *The Strong State and the Free Economy* (Rowman & Littlefield 2017) 7.
[87] Werner Bonefeld, 'Freedom and the Strong State: On German Ordoliberalism' (2012) 17 *New Political Economy* 633, 635, 644.
[88] Bonefeld, 'Freedom', 646–47. See also Bonefeld, *Strong State*.
[89] Johannes Agnoli, 'Destruction as the Determination of the Scholar in Miserable Times' (1992) 12 *Common Sense* 43, 50.

their ramifications for understanding the development of Frankfurt School critical theory, the Frankfurt School critical theory approach to the state and law, and contemporary Marxist analyses of the state and law. I first provide an heterodox Marxist account of the development of the Frankfurt School critical theory of the state and law, going against the grain of dominant accounts in the secondary literature. I then distinguish the heterodox Marxist conception of critical theory from traditional Marxism and Habermasian critical theory. I do so by focusing on their different conceptions of the state, law, society, and emancipation in order to establish the former as a distinct approach to Frankfurt School critical theory and contemporary Marxist analysis of the state and law.

As I have shown, Horkheimer and Adorno opposed critical theory to traditional theory. Traditional theory understood the state and law as neutral instruments that could be wielded in an irrational matter, but also could—and should—be wielded at the behest of the progressive historical development of reason to realise social harmony. Horkheimer and Adorno's theory critiqued the state and law as inherent in the reproduction of the negative totality of capitalist society. They likewise criticised classical Marxism and German idealism as emblematic of traditional theory, and the Soviet Union and Keynesianism as emblematic of negative totality.

In distinction to Adorno and Horkheimer, the critical theories of Habermas, Honneth, and Fraser draw on traditional Marxism, social democracy, and German idealism, understanding modern society to have been created through a process of progressive historical development. Habermasian critical theory holds that the institutions within such a society are fundamentally neutral. What it terms 'social pathologies' are 'misdevelopments' that have arisen during the course of this historical process, as a result of which the state has become 'disembedded' from its rational basis. These pathologies have been—and should and will continue to be—remedied by anchoring the state in the inherent intersubjective rationality of modern society and transforming law into a conduit for such rationality. This will lead to social harmony and enhanced freedom.

By contrast, Open Marxist critical theory develops the approach of Adorno and Horkheimer. Open Marxism's critique of traditional Marxism and of Habermasian critical theory continues Adorno and Horkheimer's critique of traditional theory. Open Marxism's critique of the state and law also develops Horkheimer and Adorno's critical theory of the negative totality of capitalist society. As Agnoli, Clarke, and Bonefeld argue, the form of the state and law (exemplified by constitutions and economic and social policies) are intrinsic to the crisis-racked process of capitalist accumulation and reproduction. Moreover, since the norms of capitalist society are just that, capitalist norms, norms of equality and democracy upheld by the state and enshrined in its laws are not only inhibited by the irrational rule of the state and law, but ultimately express capitalist rationality. The progressive policies of traditional theory reproduce social domination, crises, and misery while depoliticising class struggle. Hence, rather than history being marked by the progressive realisation of democratic freedom, it is marked by the crisis-ridden involution of capitalist society.

In contrast to dominant accounts of the development of Frankfurt School critical theory, and its account of the state and law, as consisting in the evolutionary development of social analysis from an emancipatory perspective, there is a fundamental discontinuity between Adorno and Horkheimer's critique of the state and law and Habermas' normatively oriented critical theory of the state and law in complex society. At the same time, there is continuity between Adorno and Horkheimer's critical theory and Open Marxism's critique of the state and law in the negative totality of capitalist society. Building on the heterodox Marxist approach to

Frankfurt School critical theory, the Open Marxist critique of the state and law should then be seen as a 'subterranean strand' of Frankfurt School critical theory that develops Adorno and Horkheimer's analysis of the state and law.

Moreover, rather than conceiving the Frankfurt School critical theory of the state and law as leading to Habermas' normative theories of law, democracy, and the state, the heterodox Marxist critique of the state and law and Habermas' normative democratic theory should be seen as fundamentally distinct modes of critical theory. By virtue of its critique of traditional Marxism and its distinct understanding of the state, law, capitalist society, and human emancipation, the heterodox Marxist critical theory of the state and law should be seen as a distinct approach to contemporary Marxist analysis. As I have shown, traditional Marxism conceives crises and domination as the capitalist rule of the state and economy, and emancipation as the proletarian rule of the state and economy. Habermasian critical theory provides normative theories of crises and domination as 'social pathologies' generated by the unmooring and irrational rule of the state and law from the perspective of emancipatory democratic rule. Both traditional Marxism and Habermasian theory see these types of state rule as the culmination of progressive historical development. In contrast to these traditional theories, heterodox Marxist critical theory provides a destructive critique of capitalist society, one which critiques the state and law as inherent in the reproduction of the negative totality of capitalist society. In further distinction to these traditional theories, heterodox Marxist critical theory analyses the persistence of such a totality as that of crisis-ridden 'statification' and permanent catastrophe from the perspective of its emancipatory abolition. Habermasian critical theory and heterodox Marxist critical theory are thus distinct approaches to Frankfurt School critical theory. Moreover, by virtue of its differences with classical and traditional Marxism, the heterodox Marxist approach to critical theory amounts to a unique contemporary approach to the Marxist analysis of the state and law.

CONCLUSION

As Nancy Fraser indicates, Frankfurt School critical theory is broadly defined as an interdisciplinary analysis of society from an emancipatory perspective. The development of Frankfurt School critical theory is generally portrayed as the evolutionary development of this emancipatory analysis. While Adorno and Horkheimer are held to have abandoned Marx for a one-dimensional social theory of instrumental reason that lacked a normative theory of emancipation, Habermas and the leading figures of successive generations that build on his work are said to have provided a more complex account of social analysis and a normative democratic theory of emancipation.

Moreover, the Frankfurt School critical theory of the state and law is also generally associated with the work of Habermas and those who draw on and develop Habermas' work. The legal theory and state theory of the first generation is tied to Neumann, Kirchheimer, and Pollock, and it is either treated as addressing particular historical issues, such as the rise of fascism, or as a precursor that pales in comparison to Habermasian state and legal theory. Yet as I have demonstrated, these approaches neglect Adorno and Horkheimer's heterodox Marxist critique of the state and law and the development of such a critique by the subterranean strand of Open Marxist critical theory.

This chapter has sought to establish this heterodox Marxist lineage. In so doing, it has not only sought to undermine the hegemonic understanding of the Frankfurt School approach to these topics as synonymous with Habermas and Habermasian theory. It has also elaborated an approach to critical theory that is distinct from classical and traditional Marxism and Habermasian theory. In disentangling this heterodox Marxist critical theory of the state and law from Habermasian theory, classical Marxism, and traditional Marxism, the chapter has thus identified and exposited a distinct contemporary Marxist approach to the critique of the state and law that contributes to the secondary literature on critical theory. It is my hope that disentangling the development of these traditions, and identifying this distinct approach to contemporary Marxist theories of the state and law, will contribute to greater reliance upon the heterodox Marxist aspect of Frankfurt School critical theory in Marxist studies of the state and law.

16. Feminist materialism and the laws of social reproduction

Miriam Bak McKenna

INTRODUCTION

In early 2017 a short cartoon drawn by a French computer scientist went viral. 'The Mental Load' and its depiction of the unequal burden of domestic labour performed by women struck a chord with many, who no doubt discerned similar patterns in their own homes.[1] The limits of liberal feminism's clarion call to equality, based on access to the labour market, have been clear for decades, highlighted by successive waves of feminist scholars, but sometimes it takes a cartoon to crystallise latent frustrations into public debate. The asymmetries of unpaid care and domestic work, now widely debated in the context of the Covid-19 pandemic, have been well documented in recent years.[2] A 2018 report by the International Labour Organisation (ILO) stated that 16.4 billion hours are spent each day in unpaid care work, amounting to roughly 2 billion people working eight hours per day for no pay.[3] Unsurprisingly, women share the bulk of this burden, performing on average 76.2 per cent of total hours of unpaid care work.[4] This imbalance is not, however, confined to the home. Capitalism's dependence upon unwaged, under-waged, and reproductive labour extends to labour relations fed by global patterns of exploitation, from slavery to migrant labour.

None of this is news to Marxist feminists, who have spent the better part of the last century highlighting the hierarchies and divisions engendered by a system that depends upon the devaluation of human activity and the exploitation of labour. Decades of interventions, ranging from radical proposals like the 'Wages for Housework' campaign in the 1970s to attempts to disrupt gendered narratives that present women's care work as a given, have sought to address the constitutive function of social reproduction for capital accumulation.[5]

---

[1]   Emma, 'The Gender Wars of Household Chores: A Feminist Comic' *The Guardian* (26 May 2017), https://www.theguardian.com/world/2017/may/26/gender-wars-household-chores-comic accessed 7 April 2021.

[2]   UN Secretary-General António Guterres recently noted that 'COVID-19 could reverse the limited progress that has been made on gender equality and women's rights.' António Guterres, 'Put Women and Girls at the Centre of Efforts to Recover From COVID-19' (9 April 2020), https://www.un.org/en/un-coronavirus-communications-team/put-women-and-girls-centre-efforts-recover-covid-19 accessed 7 April 2021.

[3]   ILO, Care Work and Care Jobs For the Future of Decent Work (2018), https://www.ilo.org/asia/media-centre/news/WCMS_633284/lang--en/index.htm accessed 7 April 2021.

[4]   Patricia Espinoza Revollo, 'Time to Care: Unpaid and Underpaid Care Work and the Global Inequality Crisis—Methodology Note' (Oxfam 2020), https://dx.doi.org/10.21201/2020.5419 accessed 7 April 2021.

[5]   On the Wages for Housework campaign, see especially Silvia Federici, *Wages Against Housework* (Power of Women Collective and Falling Wall Press 1975); Mariarosa Dalla Costa and Selma James, *The Power of Women and the Subversion of the Community* (Falling Wall Press 1972); Silvia Federici,

While some countries have made improvements in their recognition of care work, progress has been slow and now seems to be stalling. Moreover, against the backdrop of neoliberalism, the reduction of state investment in social services and welfare programs, and the deregulation of labour markets, the amount of domestic work performed by women, both paid and unpaid, has actually begun to increase.[6] The result, as Prabha Kotiswaran explains, is an eroded and unjust infrastructure of social reproduction in which women are increasingly expected to shoulder the dual pressures of performing paid work for transnational markets and the mounting burdens placed upon them with regard to unwaged labour.[7] In this context, the flow of global labour and the increasing use of female migrant workers, particularly for domestic work and childcare, highlights one of the normative gaps in the contemporary feminist movement: when women undertake paid employment, they often enter into an exploitative relationship with other women (and men) with less social power, whose labour, bodies, and time provide the means for access to better conditions within the labour market.[8]

Against this background, integrating social reproduction theory (SRT) into feminist jurisprudence is useful for analysing the legal and political complexity of the global labour market, the social relations which sustain it and which often lie beyond the point of production, and how these systems of exploitation unfold at the intersections of gender, class, race, and nationality.[9] This chapter explores gendered materialisms in law in order to gain a clearer understanding of how legal norms and mechanisms operate as instruments of domination and accumulation, as well as the limits of dominant models of liberal feminism as means of securing women's empowerment.

'Putting Feminism Back on Its Feet' [1984] in Silvia Federici, *Revolution at Point Zero: Housework, Reproduction, and Feminist Struggle* (PM Press 2012) 54.

[6]   Nicole Busby, 'Unpaid Care, Paid Work and Austerity: A Research Note' (2014) 4 *Feminists@ law*, https://journals.kent.ac.uk/index.php/feministsatlaw/article/view/100/259 accessed 7 April 2021. This has been especially true in countries subjected to structural adjustment programs, which have been compelled to reduce public spending for health care, education, infrastructure, and basic necessities.

[7]   Prabha Kotiswaran, 'The Laws of Social Reproduction: A Lesson in Appropriation' (2013) 64 *Northern Ireland Legal Quarterly* 317.

[8]   See Barbara Ehrenreich and Arlie Russell Hochschild, *Global Woman: Nannies, Maids, and Sex Workers in the New Economy* (Henry Holt 2002).

[9]   SRT has been the subject of substantial popular and academic interest in recent years. See Werner Bonefeld, 'Global Capital, National State, and the International' (2008) 36 *Critique* 63; Johanna Brenner, *Women and the Politics of Class* (Monthly Review Press 2000); Tithi Bhattacharya (ed), *Social Reproduction Theory: Remapping Class, Recentering Oppression* (Pluto Press 2017); Kirstin Munro, 'Unwaged Work and the Production of Sustainability in Eco-Conscious Households' (2018) 50 *Review of Radical Political Economics* 675; Kirstin Munro, '"Social Reproduction Theory," Social Reproduction, and Household Production' (2019) 83 *Science & Society* 451; Miriam Bak McKenna, 'Blood, Breastmilk, and Dirt: Silvia Federici and Feminist Materialism in International Law', *Legal Form* (12, 15 July 2018), https://legalform.blog/2018/07/12/blood-breastmilk-and-dirt-silvia-federici -and-feminist-materialism-in-international-law-part-one-miriam-bak-mckenna/ and https://legalform .blog/2018/07/15/blood-breastmilk-and-dirt-silvia-federici-and-feminist-materialism-in-international -law-part-two-miriam-bak-mckenna/ accessed 7 April 2021.

SOCIAL REPRODUCTION: A MARXIST FEMINIST METHODOLOGY

At its core, SRT proposes a broad approach to analysing the capitalist system, one that includes all forms of labour involved in the regeneration of the worker and of society as a whole, stressing that the 'production of goods and services and the production of life are part of one integrated process'.[10] Many advocates of SRT therefore claim that it moves beyond traditional Marxist approaches to the reproduction of labour-power, according to which the worker's 'maintenance' arguably requires no more than 'a certain quantity of the means of subsistence',[11] to include a wide range of emotional, generational, and everyday labour activities, performed both inside and outside the home. As Johanna Brenner and Barbara Laslett explain, this includes:

> the activities and attitudes, behaviors and emotions, and responsibilities and relationships directly involved in maintaining life on a daily basis and intergenerationally. It involves various kinds of socially necessary work—mental, physical, and emotional—aimed at providing the historically and socially, as well as biologically, defined means for maintaining and reproducing populations. Among other things, social reproduction includes how food, clothing, and shelter are made available for immediate consumption, how the maintenance and socialization of children is accomplished, how care of the elderly and infirm is provided, and how sexuality is socially constructed.[12]

Many traditional Marxist approaches tend to categorise labour of this kind as productive of use-value but not necessarily of exchange-value, assuming that it takes place outside the direct relationship between capital and wage-labourer. For social reproduction theorists, however, these processes are not secondary to but inherent in the very core of commodity production.[13] Most social reproduction theories concern most or all of the following: (1) the biological reproduction of human beings; (2) unpaid work in the home, such as cooking and cleaning; (3) social provisioning and care work (for children, the elderly, and disabled persons, for instance, as well as voluntary work to meet the needs of the community); (4) sexual, emotional, and affective relations (to maintain families and intimate ties).[14] SRT arose in response to a widely shared conviction that an explanation of capitalism which does not include these processes— processes relating to reproductive labour that falls outside the conventional relationship between capitalist and wage-labourer—fails to account fully for the multiple spaces in which capitalist exploitation materialises.

Driven by a frustration with traditional Marxist conceptions of women and gender in capitalist society, social reproduction theorists sought to bring to light not only the multiple

---

[10]   Meg Luxton, 'Feminist Political Economy in Canada and the Politics of Social Reproduction' in Kate Bezanson and Meg Luxton (eds), *Social Reproduction: Feminist Political Economy Challenges Neo-Liberalism* (McGill-Queen's University Press 2006) 11, 36.

[11]   Karl Marx, *Capital: A Critique of Political Economy*, vol 1 (first published 1867, Ben Fowkes tr, Penguin 1990) 274. See also Louis Althusser, *On the Reproduction of Capitalism: Ideology and Ideological State Apparatuses* (first published 1995, GM Goshgarian tr, Verso 2014).

[12]   Johanna Brenner and Barbara Laslett, 'Gender, Social Reproduction, and Women's Self-Organization: Considering the US Welfare State' (1991) 5 *Gender & Society* 311, 314.

[13]   Federici, *Wages Against Housework*.

[14]   Isabella Bakker and Stephen Gill (eds), *Power, Production and Social Reproduction: Human In/security in the Global Political Economy* (Palgrave Macmillan 2003) 32.

sources of women's oppression but also the critical function played by women's work at home in chains of production and accumulation. In their view, such labour—which is largely invisible in most economic analyses—is central not only to capitalist commodity production but also women's oppression under capitalism.[15] Alongside the development of SRT, which rose to prominence in the late 1960s and 1970s,[16] the concept of patriarchy—that is, the 'manifestation and institutionalisation of male dominance over women and children in the family and the extension of male dominance over women in society in general'[17]—was also gaining influence as a means of understanding and addressing asymmetries in gender relations. Both radical feminists and socialist feminists proposed that patriarchy's relationship to capitalism was a defining aspect of women's oppression; however, they differed as to how they defined and understood this relationship. Some social reproduction theorists proposed a 'dual-system theory', in which capitalism and patriarchy are distinct systems that were fused together in the pre-industrial era to create the system of exploitation (along class, gender, and other lines) we see today.[18] Others developed a 'single-system theory', in which capitalism and patriarchy 'are not autonomous, nor even interconnected systems, but the same system'.[19]

Since the 1960s Marxist-feminist scholars and movements such as Wages for Housework, Lotta Femminista and Rivolta Femminile in Italy, Midnight Notes in the United States, and the Power of Women Collective in the United Kingdom, have continued debates about the relations between patriarchy, capitalism, and social reproduction.[20] Their contributions and insights have led to a new understanding of the history of capitalist development and the class struggles with which it is punctuated. This new understanding encompasses issues of primitive accumulation, imperialist aggression, and ecological degradation,[21] and it examines how economic and social conditions shape women's oppression through the overlapping dimensions of imperialism, race, gender, class, and nationality.

---

[15]   Zillah R Eisenstein (ed), *Capitalist Patriarchy and the Case for Socialist Feminism* (Monthly Review Press 1979) 25.

[16]   The publication of Margaret Benston's seminal article 'The Political Economy of Women's Liberation' marked a key moment; see Margaret Benston, 'The Political Economy of Women's Liberation' (1969) 21 *Monthly Review* 13.

[17]   Gerda Lerner, *The Creation of Patriarchy* (OUP 1986) 239.

[18]   See e.g., Heidi Hartmann, 'The Unhappy Marriage of Marxism and Feminism: Towards a More Progressive Union' in Lydia Sargent (ed), *Women and Revolution: A Discussion of the Unhappy Marriage of Marxism and Feminism* (South End Press 1981) 1; Sylvia Walby, *Gender Segregation at Work* (Open University Press 1988).

[19]   Pat Armstrong and Hugh Armstrong, 'Class is a Feminist Issue' in Althea Prince and Susan Silva-Wayne (eds), *Feminisms and Womanisms: A Women's Studies Reader* (Women's Press 2004) 317, 317. See also Lise Vogel, *Marxism and the Oppression of Women: Toward a Unitary Theory* (first published 1983, Brill 2013); Iris Marion Young, 'Beyond the Unhappy Marriage: A Critique of Dual Systems Theory' in Lydia Sargent (ed), *Women and Revolution: A Discussion of the Unhappy Marriage of Marxism and Feminism* (South End Press 1981) 43.

[20]   The literature includes Veronica Beechey, *Unequal Work* (Verso 1987); Dorothy E Smith, 'Feminist Reflections on Political Economy' (1989) 30 *Studies in Political Economy* 37; Brenner, *Women and the Politics of Class*; Antonella Picchio, *Social Reproduction: The Political Economy of the Labor Market* (CUP 1992).

[21]   See e.g., Maria Mies, *Patriarchy and Accumulation on a World Scale* (Zed Books 1986); Ariel Salleh, *Ecofeminism as Politics* (Zed Books 1997); Silvia Federici, *Caliban and the Witch: Women, the Body, and Primitive Accumulation* (Autonomedia 2004).

SOCIAL REPRODUCTION THEORY: A BRIEF OVERVIEW

While SRT is multifaceted, it is possible to sketch its basic parameters and explain the kinds of questions it seeks to answer, particularly in light of concerns raised in the current politico-economic conjuncture.

The Relationship between Reproductive and Productive Labour

SRT posits that a central yet overlooked aspect of the capitalist system is the production and reproduction of labour outside formal sites of capitalist production. Under capitalism, this is a process that is generative of commodity value and indeed of society as a whole. As Lise Vogel explains, '[r]eproduction of labour-power is a condition of production, for it *re*posits or *re*places the labour-power necessary for production'.[22] In doing so, SRT reveals not only that paid and unpaid labour are part of the same socio-economic process, but that both spheres are governed by the same logic of exploitation and surplus value extraction.[23] Capitalism's dependence upon the constant reproduction of labour-power is both driven and tempered by workers' needs for wages, as well as for social conditions that will enable them to satisfy their basic subsistence needs. Capitalism thus subordinates the satisfaction of human needs to the imperative of surplus value production and capital accumulation.

One of the ways in which such subordination is achieved is the 'value transfer' secured through the use of devalued and large invisible labour, primarily in the home. Early social reproduction theorists therefore focused their analysis on the home and on the family unit, particularly women's biological capacity for human reproduction, as vital to maintaining capitalist society generally.[24] Crucially, as with formal labour relations, capitalism creates the conditions for exploiting (and regulating) such care and reproductive work. This is achieved primarily through its undervaluation and naturalisation as non-work—through, for example, narratives that stress women's natural predisposition to care work or their biological destiny as mothers, as well as strict distinctions between the factory (understood as the principal sphere of production) and the household (understood as the principal sphere of reproduction) as a means of supporting gendered divisions of labour.[25] Given the biological aspects of pregnancy, childbirth, and care, the wedge that was driven between the workplace and the home during the Industrial Revolution, the rise of the atomised household, and the loss of collective solutions for the provision of care meant that women were increasingly confined to providing unpaid care within the home.[26] This sexual division of labour—structural and ideological—has continued to define women and men in their respective hierarchical roles, within and outside

---

[22]   Vogel, *Marxism and the Oppression of Women,* 144 (original emphases).

[23]   Susan Ferguson, 'Social Reproduction: What's the Big Idea?' Pluto Press, https://www.plutobooks .com/blog/social-reproduction-theory-ferguson/ accessed 7 April 2021.

[24]   Lindsey German, *Sex, Class and Socialism* (Bookmarks 1989) 40. See also Tony Cliff, *Class Struggle and Women's Liberation* (Bookmarks 1984); Sheila McGregor, 'Marxism and Women's Oppression Today' (2013) 138 *International Socialism* 95; Judith Orr, *Marxism and Women's Liberation* (Bookmarks 2015).

[25]   Nicole Cox and Silvia Federici, *Counterplanning from the Kitchen: Wages for Housework, A Perspective on Capital and the Left* (Falling Wall Press 1975) 4.

[26]   According to Chris Harman: '[i]n the mid 19th century, the reproduction of the labour force was only possible if the average working class wife had eight or ten pregnancies (in London nearly 60 percent

the home. In particular, women's reproductive capacity continues to limit their social and economic opportunities, excluding them from production and public life and providing a steady stream of free labour. 'Capital', as Silvia Federici writes, 'has made and makes money out of our cooking, smiling, fucking'.[27]

While the household is vital for social reproduction and the replenishment of labour-power, childcare, health care, education, prisons, and aged care facilities are also crucial to these processes. Immigrant and coerced labour also provide a continual source of unwaged and undervalued labour. On the one hand, capital is largely indifferent in regard to the sources of the labour it exploits. However, as Susan Ferguson explains:

> the *fact* of capital's need does explain why a highly effective institution—the privatised household—is trumpeted and reinforced (through sexist legislation, educational systems, social-welfare practices, for example), and thereby entrenched in capitalist societies (as much as it was inherited from pre-capitalist societies and reshaped through time).[28]

Capitalism may not have created the family unit, but its structural dependence on the unwaged labour of women, and the interdependence of household and workplace, ensures that the family, as a form of socio-economic organisation, remains both central and beneficial to capital accumulation.

Unitary Materialist Theory

By adopting a broad approach to labour and value production, and situating these processes at the intersection of the market, state, and household, SRT underscores the socially situated character of labour. It also provides a framework for explaining the relationship between labour exploitation and the (racial, gendered, sexualised, etc) social relations that make such exploitation possible. As Tithi Bhattacharya explains, 'SRT treats questions of oppression (gender, race, sexuality) in distinctly nonfunctionalist ways precisely because oppression is theorized as structurally relational to, and hence shaped by, capitalist production rather than on the margins of analysis or as add-ons to a deeper and more vital economic process.'[29] Not every form of oppression pervading contemporary capitalist societies originated with capitalism, but focusing on the relation between oppression and exploitation helps us to address the question of how the logic of capital accumulation is itself reproduced through the social relations it sustains.[30]

---

of infants died by the age of five in 1850) and so spent virtually all her life after marriage either pregnant or nursing young children.'

Chris Harman, 'Women's Liberation and Revolutionary Socialism' (1984) 23 *International Socialism* 3, 9. See also Johanna Brenner and Maria Ramas, 'Rethinking Women's Oppression' (1984) 144 *New Left Review* 33.

[27]   Federici, *Wages Against Housework*, 5.

[28]   Susan Ferguson, 'Intersectionality and Social-Reproduction Feminisms: Toward an Integrative Ontology' (2016) 24 *Historical Materialism* 38, 50 (original emphasis).

[29]   Tithi Bhattacharya, 'Mapping Social Reproduction Theory' Verso (15 February 2018), https://www.versobooks.com/blogs/3555-mapping-social-reproduction-theory accessed 7 April 2021.

[30]   See Meg Luxton, 'Feminist Political Economy in Canada and the Politics of Social Reproduction' in Kate Bezanson and Meg Luxton (eds), *Social Reproduction: Feminist Political Economy Challenges*

A key aspect of this explanation relates to capitalism's production of a particular type of worker as part of its regulation of social reproduction generally.[31] What is produced and reproduced is not simply labour-power but the subjectivity of workers themselves.[32] This is a process that cannot be explained solely by reference to biological or physiological factors.[33] The traditional division of labour between genders, and the way in which women have been socialised to perform care work, is emblematic of this process. As Federici writes, housework has not simply 'been imposed on women', but 'has been transformed into a natural attribute of our female physique and personality, an internal need, an aspiration, supposedly coming from the depth of our female character'.[34] In other words, in conceiving housework and care work not as productive of value, but as a matter of biological destiny or simply as a labour of love, women come to be understood as unskilled 'non-workers'. Even when entering the paid workforce, women are on average paid less than men, while still generally being expected to undertake the bulk of labour within the home. At the level of the state, the drive to control women's lives and confine them to the home has been supported through legal and social policies on marriage and the family, as well as prohibitions against abortion.[35] These dynamics also extend to the way that workers are valued according to race and class.[36] Discourses and practices surrounding race, borders, immigration, and social inclusion and exclusion are shaped to help legitimise and systematise this inequality (with, for instance, the categories of 'temporary worker' and 'illegal immigrant'), which has important and wide-ranging implications for access to health care, education, and other social services, and basic rights and freedoms.[37] As Ferguson explains:

> the socio-geographic location of bodies—and the labour involved in socially reproducing those bodies—matters: ostensibly similar and equal bodies *become* different, and differently valued, bodies within capitalist societies. Existing discourses and practices of racialisation and racism are reshaped to help justify and systematise this inequality, just as new such discourses and practices are invented.[38]

Neo-Liberalism (McGill-Queen's University Press 2006) 36–37. See also Maria Mies, Patriarchy and Accumulation on a World *Scale: Women in the International Division of Labour* (Zed Books 1986).

[31]   Antonio Gramsci, *Selections from the Prison Notebooks* (Geoffrey N Smith and Quintin Hoare tr, International Publishers 1971) 352.

[32]   Ben Fine and Alfredo Saad-Filho, *Marx's 'Capital'* (6th edn, Pluto Press 2017) 60.

[33]   Ferguson, 'Intersectionality and Social-Reproduction Feminisms'.

[34]   Federici, *Wages Against Housework*, 2.

[35]   See e.g., Antonella Picchio, *Social Reproduction: The Political Economy of the Labour Market* (CUP 1992).

[36]   Zillah R Eisenstein, 'Some Notes on the Relations of Capitalist Patriarchy' in Zillah R Eisenstein (ed), *Capitalist Patriarchy and the Case for Socialist Feminism* (Monthly Review Press 1979) 362. See also Robert Miles, *Racism* (Routledge 1989) 70.

[37]   Ferguson, 'Intersectionality and Social-Reproduction Feminisms', 52. See also Susan Ferguson, 'Canadian Contributions to Social Reproduction Feminism: Race and Embodied Labor' (2008) 15 *Race, Gender & Class* 42; Susan Ferguson and David McNally, 'Capital, Labour-Power, and Gender Relations: Introduction to the *Historical Materialism* Edition of *Marxism and the Oppression of Women*' in Lise Vogel, *Marxism and the Oppression of Women: Toward a Unitary Theory* (first published 1983, Brill 2013) xvii.

[38]   Ferguson, 'Intersectionality and Social-Reproduction Feminisms', 53 (original emphasis).

New Sites of Struggle

SRT focuses on the dialectical relationship between different forms of oppression and the socio-economic system that creates the material conditions for such oppression. It also expands sites of anti-capitalist resistance. According to SRT, confronting capitalism in isolation will not eliminate the oppression of women and other vulnerable groups.[39] Zillah Eisenstein, for example, argues that the struggle against gendered divisions of labour, and for the redistribution of care work, poses a threat to patriarchy as well as capitalism.[40] The control that women retain over their lives and bodies (via control over their sexual and physical health, choice of partner and living conditions, etc) may become a dynamic force for change as they struggle against the demands placed upon them in 'production, reproduction and consumption'.[41] In Nancy Hartsock's formulation, 'the power of feminism grows out of contact with everyday life'.[42] Organising around issues that affect women's daily lives would, Eisenstein argues, provide a more unified and coherent political strategy for the women's movement. Resisting capital's attempts to regulate the private sphere, and in particular women's bodies through the fight for abortion, sexuality, and reproductive health, are important sites of resistance.[43] Moreover, the importance of integrating a class analysis into any discussion of women's oppression, along with other intersecting forms of oppression, is also crucial when pursuing reforms to ensure the buck is not simply passed on to other subordinated groups. Failure to understand SRT when pursuing reforms will simply provide women with a bigger share of the cake while 'creat[ing] gradations among the underprivileged'.[44]

THE LAWS OF SOCIAL REPRODUCTION IN THE NEOLIBERAL ERA

SRT's approach to capitalism and the social dynamics of the economy, together with belief in relational, overlapping forms of oppression, promotes critical insights into the law and the way in which discourses and techniques of power intertwine in the legal field, at the domestic and also the international level. This approach integrates gendered relations, practices, and

---

[39]   As Juliet Mitchell has written: 'the overthrow of the capitalist economy and the political challenge that effects this do not in themselves mean a transformation of patriarchal ideology'. The way to address the subordination of women, she argues, is to analyse the condition of women in four spheres: production, reproduction, sex, and the socialisation of children. Women's liberation may be achieved only through the transformation of all four structures; reforms in one sphere alone would otherwise be offset by changes in another. Juliette Mitchell, *The Longest Revolution: Essays on Feminism, Literature and Psychoanalysis* (first published 1966, Virago 1984) 29.

[40]   Zillah Eisenstein, 'Constructing a Theory of Capitalist Patriarchy and Socialist Feminism' (1999) 25 *Critical Sociology* 211.

[41]   Eisenstein, 'Constructing', 206–7.

[42]   Nancy Hartsock, 'Feminist Theory and the Development of Revolutionary Strategy' (unpublished paper, 1975) 19.

[43]   Ferguson, 'Intersectionality and Social-Reproduction Feminisms', 50.

[44]   Sheila Rowbotham, *Woman's Consciousness, Man's World* (first published 1973, Verso 2015) 123. Cf Nancy Fraser, 'Social Justice in the Age of Identity Politics: Redistribution, Recognition, and Participation' in Nancy Fraser and Axel Honneth, *Redistribution or Recognition? A Political-Philosophical Exchange* (Joel Golb, James Ingram, and Christiane Wilke tr, Verso 2003) 7.

structures into Marxist analysis, but does not reduce all relations, practices, and structures to capitalism pure and simple. Nor does it depict the social order as a single, monolithic entity. Rather, SRT understands capitalism as a complex and multifaceted system of domination and exploitation, in which patriarchy, racism, imperialism, and other forms of oppression are fundamental constitutive elements.

Law and Social Reproduction

Law's role in the regulation and devaluation of social reproduction has been highlighted by a small yet influential group of feminist legal scholars.[45] Underlining the numerous deficiencies of liberal-feminist approaches to women's empowerment, they have offered a number of critical reflections on the structural impediments to women's empowerment which are contained within current legal discourse. This includes consideration of the way in which law (particularly tax, family, employment, and social welfare law) reinforces the gendered division of labour and women's categorisation as 'secondary' workers, 'naturally' suited to care work, thus enabling the appropriation of women's labour.[46] These scholars have also explored the way that legal protections of the institutions of marriage and the family reinforce social reproduction processes.[47]

Marxist-feminist critiques of law emerged simultaneously with the broader feminist movement of the 1960s, which was largely centred on securing women's access to waged labour as a means of ensuring their equality and independence. For liberal-feminist lawyers, this movement involved removing what they understood as the key impediments to women's immersion in the labour force, namely discriminatory laws and policies.[48] By the 1960s, the model of the 'single breadwinner', centred around providing high wages and secure employment to men (a system supported by tax, labour, family, and social welfare law), was beginning to stall. Women were beginning to enter the paid workforce in greater numbers. By the 1970s women made up nearly half of the workforce in the United States,[49] yet their responsibilities within the

---

[45]   See e.g., Joanne Conaghan, 'Introduction' (2007) 58 *Northern Ireland Legal Quarterly* 245; Shirin M Rai, Catherine Hoskyns, and Dania Thomas, 'Depletion: The Costs of Unpaid Domestic Work', *E-International Relations*, https://www.e-ir.info/2012/03/19/depletion-the-costs-of-unpaid-domestic -work/ accessed 7 April 2021; Simone Wong, 'Would You "Care" to Share Your Home?' (2007) 58 *Northern Ireland Legal Quarterly* 268; Joanne Conaghan and Emily Grabham, 'Sexuality and the Citizen Carer' (2007) 58 *Northern Ireland Legal Quarterly* 325; Hila Shamir, 'Between Home and Work: Assessing the Distributive Effects of Employment Law in Markets of Care' (2009) 30 *Berkeley Journal of Employment and Labor Law* 404; Miriam Bak McKenna, 'Queering the Crisis of Care: The Role of Families in the Legal Recognition of Reproductive Labour' *Women, Gender & Research* (forthcoming).

[46]   Jill Steans and Daniela Tepe-Belfrage, 'The New Materialism: Re-Claiming a Debate from a Feminist Perspective' (2016) 40 *Capital & Class* 324.

[47]   See esp. Kerry Quinn, 'Mommy Dearest: The Focus on the Family in Legal Feminism' (2002) 37 *Harvard Civil Rights Civil Liberties Law Review* 447; Anne Barlow, 'Configuration(s) of Unpaid Caregiving within Current Legal Discourse In and Around the Family' (2007) 58 *Northern Ireland Legal Quarterly* 251.

[48]   Johanna Brenner argues that despite the opening of 'higher-paid occupations' to women, 'male dominance continues, because feminism has been signally unable to win significant changes in the organization of social reproduction. Caregiving remains the privatized responsibility of family/households'. Brenner, *Women and the Politics of Class*, 308.

[49]   Theodore Caplow et al, *Recent Social Trends in the United States, 1960–1990* (McGill-Queen's University Press 1991) 123.

home remained largely unchanged. This 'second shift' of labour, Marxist feminists assumed, would prove a unifying force for the women's movement to push for social and economic reform, exposing cracks in the reigning ideologies of patriarchy and capitalism.[50] However, this assumption greatly underestimated capital's capacity to disarticulate the composition of the workforce while reproducing the sexual division of labour. The shortage of unpaid labour not only resulted in an increase in the number of hours women worked, but paved the way for the commodification of social reproduction outside the home, exposing vulnerable workers, particularly non-white and immigrant workers, to even further exploitation.[51] Indeed, since the 1980s, economic restructuring and neoliberal policies designed to promote flexible employment have led to a deterioration in employment standards, dropping unionisation rates, declining real wages, the spread of precarious work, and the fragmentation of the workforce through deindustralisation and globalisation.[52] Against this background, a high degree of reproductive work has been removed from the home and reorganised on a market basis through the expansion of the service industry, now one of the dominant forms of paid employment. This is often the least secure and lowest paid of all such industries, and one in which women predominate.[53]

Law's contradictory role in this context was highlighted by Eisenstein in *The Radical Future of Liberal Feminism*.[54] Given its central role in organising and regulating gender relations, law, Eisenstein argued, was capable of restructuring existing divisions of reproductive labour. The US Supreme Court's 1973 ruling in *Frontiero v Richardson*, which repudiated the 'separate spheres' approach that confined women to the role of unpaid caregiver, offers one example of how law could prove useful in this regard.[55] However, the liberal and individualist underpinnings of law, and its commitment to the separation of the public and private spheres, would, Eisenstein argued, largely subordinate wider class struggles to considerations of individual gain.[56] Indeed, the emphasis on legal norms for women's employment based upon formal equality quickly proved insufficient for tackling the broader structural barriers of the market, the family, and the wider community. As Julie Suk explains, '[t]he law of sex equality struck at the outdated and deteriorating infrastructure of social reproduction by disapproving of gender stereotypes based on traditional roles in the family, but it did not mandate the creation of an alternative infrastructure'.[57] While the legalisation of abortion, the provision of reliable and effective mechanisms for reproductive control, and the liberalisation of divorce laws were all major victories, providing women with greater control over their reproductive choices, formal legal equality did not address the gendered division of labour. Even the fight to demand publicly supported daycare, so that women could more easily gain employment

---

[50]   Zillah R Eisenstein, *The Radical Future of Liberal Feminism* (Longman 1981) 220–28.

[51]   Kim Moody, *On New Terrain: How Capital is Reshaping the Battleground of Class War* (Haymarket 2017) 20.

[52]   Judy Fudge, 'The New Workplace: Surveying the Landscape' (2009) 33 *Manitoba Law Journal* 131.

[53]   Judy Fudge and Rosemary Owens (eds), *Precarious Work, Women, and the New Economy: The Challenge to Legal Norms* (Hart 2006).

[54]   Eisenstein, *Radical Future of Liberal Feminism*.

[55]   *Frontiero v Richardson* 411 US 677 (1973).

[56]   Eisenstein, *Radical Future of Liberal Feminism*, 223, 228.

[57]   Julie Suk, 'Gender Equality as Social Reproduction Infrastructure' LPE Blog (20 June 2018), https://lpeblog.org/2018/06/20/gender-equality-as-social-reproduction-infrastructure/ accessed 7 April 2021.

outside the home, did not always attend to the underlying dynamics of undervalued labour, simply shifting these problematic dynamics into new domains and onto other classes of women. As Martha Gimenez notes, 'the "liberation" of professional and career women and the ability of vast numbers of working women to work is predicated on the labor of other women, a large proportion of which are immigrant and non-white women'.[58]

Furthermore, equality laws are ill-equipped to prevent the move towards different—and inferior—employment conditions for women. Industries dominated by women quickly became associated with lower pay, weaker benefits, and more precarious employment conditions, particularly as they tend to mirror traditional forms of social reproductive work like teaching, nursing, and related health and service occupations. Women were also far more likely to work in non-unionised jobs in the service sector on a part-time or temporary basis.[59] The gender wage gap continues to present a major hurdle to the economic equality of women today. While the gap has narrowed from 40 to around 22 per cent in the past four decades, the rate of narrowing has slowed considerably since the 1980s.[60] This broader pattern of discrimination, particularly evident in rates of sexual and workplace harassment and in relation to women's maternity and caring commitments, reveals the continuing interconnectedness of patriarchy and capitalism.

Various attempts have been made to counter these trends by means of substantive and transformative equality, especially employment laws to combat indirect or adverse-effects discrimination in the 1980s and 1990s. However, Marxist-feminist critiques of law have underlined the limitations of this approach, particularly as such legal protections are centred around waged employment and are thus unable to address inequalities that arise outside formal employment relationships. Moreover, as research into 'family-friendly' policies has revealed, the allocation of labour in proportion to the unpaid work of women has not in fact changed significantly, with legal responses tending to entrench rather than redress such gender differences. In their study of European laws on work and family obligations, for example, León and Millns demonstrate that the legal framework of maternity rights is much stronger than its parental rights counterpart.[61] This, in turn, helps to enshrine in domestic law a gendered conceptualisation of childcare, in which greater legal and financial protection is conferred upon working mothers, giving fathers little incentive to become more involved in childrearing. Similarly, Hila Shamir points to the impact of accommodations for working families provided by employment law, which were meant to recognise care responsibilities but may in fact often

---

[58]   Martha E Gimenez, 'The Dialectics of Waged and Unwaged Work: Waged Work, Domestic Labor and Household Survival in the United States' in Jane L Collins and Martha Gimenez (eds), *Work Without Wages: Domestic Labor and Self-Employment within Capitalism* (State University of New York Press 1990) 25, 42.

[59]   Judy Fudge, 'From Segregation to Privatization: Equality, Law and Women Public Servants, 1908–2000' in Brenda Cossman and Judy Fudge (eds), *Privatization, Law and the Challenge to Feminism* (University of Toronto Press 2002) 86.

[60]   Heidi Hartman, Stephen Rose, and Vicky Lovell, 'How Much Progress in Closing the Long-Term Earnings Gap?' in Francine D Blau, Mary C Brinton, and David B Grusky (eds), *The Declining Significance of Gender?* (Russell Sage Foundation 2006) 125, 126; Francine D Blau and Lawrence M Kahn, 'The Gender Pay Gap: Going, Going … But Not Gone' in Francine D Blau, Mary C Brinton, and David B Grusky (eds), *The Declining Significance of Gender?* (Russell Sage Foundation 2006) 37, 41.

[61]   Margarita León and Susan Millns, 'Parental, Maternity and Paternity Leave: European Legal Constructions of Unpaid Care Giving' (2007) 58 *Northern Ireland Legal Quarterly* 343.

consolidate and entrench class and gender disparities.[62] Even when women are compensated for their reproductive labour through childcare and household subsidies, this has little effect on the achievement of gender equality in the workplace, resulting in a 'motherhood gap'.[63] Socially and culturally within the workplace, women are still largely viewed as primary carers for children, and their responsibility for childcare is typically seen as an individual choice. From her study of the generous support provided to women in France and Sweden, Nancy Dowd concludes that '[w]omen [are still] paid less, on the whole, than men, are concentrated in a small number of occupations, and are at the bottom of the occupational and managerial hierarchies'.[64] In jurisdictions where pregnancy accommodation is unpaid, brief, or only attracts minimal levels of welfare benefits (such as those for work-incapacitated persons), mothers are pushed out of the labour market and become reliant upon others for their economic survival. The low level of legally guaranteed parental benefit, in a market in which women generally earn less than their male partners, also means that for economic reasons a supposedly gender-neutral policy of parental leave ensures that the burden falls upon women.[65]

These policies maintain a gendered division between the compliant worker and the marginalised caregiver. However, as an analysis of the dynamics of social reproduction suggests, the prevailing undervaluation of reproductive labour is also maintained across other legal regimes, including property, tax, welfare, and inheritance law, as well as laws and regulations relating to social security provision. For example, in their study of the judicial discourse surrounding marital disputes, some scholars reveal how 'indirect', care-based contributions to homemaking are unlikely to translate into legal property and financial rights. This is seen most clearly and prominently in divorce proceedings, where the wage-earning spouse generally retains the majority benefit of their waged labour.[66] Such analysis also highlights the hierarchy of relationships emerging from legal constructions of unpaid caregiving, with heterosexual patriarchal relationships being privileged above all others, and questions the moral implications of a distributive regime which allocates rewards on the basis of conformity with traditional gender roles. This analysis reveals the broader legal framework that entrenches the division of labour in the home, assumes women's caregiving as a given, and ensures its undervaluation in both status and compensation.

---

[62]   Shamir, 'Between Home and Work'.

[63]   Claire Cain Miller, 'The 10-Year Baby Window That Is the Key to the Women's Pay Gap' *New York Times* (9 April 2018), https://www.nytimes.com/2018/04/09/upshot/the-10-year-baby-window-that-is-the-key-to-the-womens-pay-gap.html accessed 7 April 2021.

[64]   Nancy E Dowd, 'Envisioning Work and Family: A Critical Perspective on International Models' (1989) 26 *Harvard Journal on Legislation* 311, 336.

[65]   Linda Dickens, 'Re-Regulation for Gender Equality: From Either or to Both' (2006) 37 *Industrial Relations Journal* 306.

[66]   Allen M Parkman, 'Bargaining Over Housework: The Frustrating Situation of Secondary Wage Earners' (2004) 63 *American Journal of Economics and Sociology* 765 (arguing that it is too easy for men to leave marriage without compensating women adequately); Katharine Silbaugh, 'Turning Labor into Love: Housework and the Law' (1996) 91 *Northwestern University Law Review* 1 (arguing that because women's household labour is not valued as real work, women are undercompensated at the time of divorce).

The Commodification of Social Reproduction on the Global Legal Plane

SRT also reveals that capitalism's structural dependence on unwaged and reproductive labour is reflected at the level of international law, as facilitated by states, international organisations, and international legal regimes. Considering the gendered and racialised dynamics of globalisation, for example, it is possible to examine the way that the devaluation of women's labour has been facilitated by international institutions, notably the World Bank and International Monetary Fund, through development initiatives like micro-finance and poverty-reduction strategies that reject non-market-oriented economic activities.[67] Similar insights can be gained by analysing international legal norms and mechanisms in contemporary regimes of trade, property, human rights, and immigration law, which perpetuate or facilitate patterns of domination and accumulation. These dynamics are ultimately rooted in law's power to constitute, sustain, and reproduce capitalist social relations. The transformations of the labour market during the neoliberal era, which have been fuelled by the drive to harness and exploit labour in its unpaid and low-paid dimensions, are important here.[68]

Migration has proven to be one of the biggest generators of cheap labour, spurred by economic inequalities between high- and low-income countries, as well as vulnerabilities linked to the legacies of colonialism, economic imperialism, and international economic restructuring.[69] The response by Western states in particular has typically taken the form of new, and largely repressive, immigration laws designed to control this increased flow between borders. As David McNally argues, this ensures migrants from the global South enter countries 'frightened, oppressed, vulnerable', ready to accept low-wage, insecure jobs.[70] Domestic legal regimes in other areas, such as employment, family, and welfare law, do not afford immigrants the same legal and social protections as citizens, which helps to ensure that their secondary status benefits the market. Capitalism, Federici argues, depends not only on unwaged housework but on a global strategy of underdevelopment in the global South.[71]

Federici cites increased dependence upon migrant labour in affluent countries as evidence of this 'new international division of labour', which furthers the expropriation of the wealth of the formerly colonial world.[72] As she explains, 'through emigration, third world women directly contribute to the accumulation of wealth in the "advanced" capitalist countries, not

---

[67]   Among the reforms prescribed by this approach are land privatisation (the abolition of communal land tenure), trade liberalisation, the downsizing of the public sector, and the defunding of public services. Silvia Federici, 'Reproduction and Feminist Struggle in the New International Division of Labor' [1999] in Silvia Federici, *Revolution at Point Zero: Housework, Reproduction, and Feminist Struggle* (PM Press 2012) 65.

[68]   Ferguson and McNally argue that the neoliberal era has been marked by the 'globalization of primitive accumulation'. Susan Ferguson and David McNally, 'Precarious Migrants: Gender, Race and the Social Reproduction of a Global Working Class' in Leo Panitch and Greg Albo (eds), *Socialist Register 2015: Transforming Classes* (Merlin Press 2015) 1, 9.

[69]   Judy Fudge, 'Global Care Chains: Transnational Migrant Care Workers' (2012) 28 *International Journal of Comparative Labour Law & Industrial Relations* 63; Judy Fudge, 'Gender, Equality and Capabilities' in Tonia Novitz and David Mangan (eds), *The Role of Labour Standards in Sustainable Development: From Theory to Sustainable Pratice?* (OUP 2011) 41.

[70]   David McNally, *Another World is Possible: Globalization and Anti-Capitalism* (Arbeiter Ring 2006) 190.

[71]   Federici, 'Reproduction and Feminist Struggle'.

[72]   Federici, 'Reproduction and Feminist Struggle'.

only as producers of goods but also as (re)producers of workers, for the factories, the hospitals, agriculture and commerce'.[73] In the commodification of care in particular, the loss of some women's reproductive labour in the home has been offset by poor women, illustrating what Hester Eisenstein has called the 'dangerous liaison' between second wave feminism and global capitalism, which consists of the fetishism of waged labour on the one hand and the marketisation and attenuation of care provision on the other.[74] As Rosemary Hennessy notes, 'the emergence of feminism and the category of the "independent woman" in the west is related to colonial expansion and the re-construction of an "other" woman "elsewhere"'.[75] Women's transnational migration creates a global 'care chain', especially for care of children and the elderly, with significant social and economic effects in migrants' home countries. Much of this work often takes place informally, and is therefore not protected by labour law, exposing workers to increased risks of exploitation. Given that many women are motivated to work abroad in order to provide for their families, earning perhaps more than they would at home but far below the median income in the countries in which they are employed, the result is an exploitative relationship which has disastrous consequences for health and social care provision in developing countries.[76] It also entrenches the division of labour alongside hierarchies of class, race, and gender, weakening the struggle against the division of labour in the family and stalling the achievement of gender equality in developing countries.[77]

Other forms of social reproductive labour are also increasingly commodified in the global market and tied to flows of female migrant labour. Law's undervaluation of women's reproductive labour within the home also extends to market-based reproductive labour, such as surrogacy and sex work.[78] When combined with persistent social stigma, criminalisation, and lack of labour and other legal protections, workers in these industries are made vulnerable to still further exploitation. Racialisation (particularly in the form of immigration rules) only adds to this precarity and potential for abuse.[79] As Katie Cruz explores in her examination of migrant sex workers' socially reproductive paid and unpaid labour, immigration law sets 'limits on a migrant worker's ability to commodify her labour power', while also threatening arrest, detention, and removal, and severely restricting access to public funds.[80]

---

[73]   Silvia Federici, 'Reproduction and Feminist Struggle in the New International Division of Labor' in Mariarosa Dalla Costa and Giovanna F Dalla Costa (eds), *Women, Development and Labor of Reproduction: Struggles and Movements* (Africa World Press 1999) 47, 57. See also Hannah Lewis et al, 'Hyper-Precarious Lives: Migrants, Work and Forced Labour in the Global North' (2014) 39 *Progress in Human Geography* 580.

[74]   Hester Eisenstein, 'A Dangerous Liaison? Feminism and Corporate Globalization' (2005) 69 *Science & Society* 487.

[75]   Rosemary Hennessy, 'Materialist Feminism and Foucault: The Politics of Appropriation' (1990) 3 *Rethinking Marxism* 251, 261.

[76]   David E Staples, *No Place Like Home: Organizing Home-based Labor in the Era of Structural Adjustment* (Routledge 2006) 1.

[77]   Ann Stewart, 'Who Do We Care About? Reflections on Gender Justice in a Global Market' (2007) 58 *Northern Ireland Legal Quarterly* 359.

[78]   See Kotiswaran, 'The Laws of Social Reproduction'.

[79]   Judy Fudge, 'Precarious Migrant Status and Precarious Employment: The Paradox of International Rights for Migrant Workers' (2013) 34 *Comparative Labor Law & Policy Journal* 95, 99; Katie Cruz, 'Unmanageable Work, (Un)liveable Lives: The UK Sex Industry, Labour Rights and the Welfare State' (2013) 22 *Social & Legal Studies* 465.

[80]   Katie Cruz, 'Beyond Liberalism: Marxist Feminism, Migrant Sex Work, and Labour Unfreedom' (2018) 26 *Feminist Legal Studies* 65, 80.

NEW SPHERES OF ENCLOSURE

Over the past several decades, a new trend has also become relevant to law's relationship to social reproduction. This trend is characterised by the sudden interest shown by international organisations in the inequalities of unpaid care and domestic work, and a new political rhetoric that frames women's unpaid work as a barrier to their 'economic empowerment' and their further integration into the paid labour force. The United Nations, European Union, Organisation for Economic Co-operation and Development, and other international organisations discuss the 'unused potential' of social reproduction in their social and development policies, within the broader discourse about enhancing productivity and competitiveness.[81] This development is understandably greeted with considerable scepticism by women's rights activists, who fear it simply replicates the liberal-feminist approach to employment-centred liberation popularised in the 1970s. Like the failure of liberal legal approaches to rectify the structural inequalities of reproductive labour, these market-based approaches, rooted in increased participation of women in the labour market, fail to address the wider social framework underpinning processes of social reproduction. This, in turn, leads to further gender-wage disparities and exploitative working conditions for women, particularly in the informal sector. For instance, the integration of unpaid care and housework into the UN Sustainable Development Goals (SDGs) is framed predominantly as a means of integrating women into the paid global workforce. Target 5.4 of the SDGs stresses the need to '[r]ecognize and value unpaid care and domestic work through the provision of public services, infrastructure and social protection policies and the promotion of shared responsibility within the household and the family as nationally appropriate'.[82]

However, as Colleen O'Manique and Pieter Fourie argue, the SDGs largely ignore the 'material and ideological spaces where the demands of socially necessary labour, much of it unwaged, have intensified over the past four decades of neoliberalism'.[83] This is true not only of continued disparities of unpaid care in the home, which have intensified under austerity, but also in relation to the growing global care chain, and the exploitation of migrant women in low or unpaid precarious jobs in the care sector to mitigate the crisis of social reproduction in the global North.[84] The failure to address the structural and ideological dynamics of social reproduction is particularly visible in the contradictory role played by the private sector and multinational corporations in the SDGs, which tend to brush over their role in the amplification of inequality, environmental destruction, and gender injustice. The tendency to depict social reproduction as a barrier to productivity also reinforces the idea that social reproductive work has no independent value or worth. Alongside the emphasis on the 'unused economic

---

[81]   See e.g., European Union, *Report on Equality between Women and Men 2015* (2016), https://op.europa.eu/en/publication-detail/-/publication/2ca44101-173b-11e6-ba9a-01aa75ed71a1 accessed 7 April 2021; Gaëlle Ferrant, Luca Maria Pesando, and Keiko Nowacka, *Unpaid Care Work: The Missing Link in the Analysis of Gender Gaps in Labour Outcomes* (OECD Policy Brief 2014), https://www.oecd.org/dev/development-gender/Unpaid_care_work.pdf accessed 7 April 2021.

[82]   UN Sustainable Development Goals, 'Transforming Our World: The 2030 Agenda for Sustainable Development', UNGA Resolution 70/1 (25 September 2015).

[83]   Colleen O'Manique and Pieter Fourie, 'Affirming Our World: Gender Justice, Social Reproduction, and the Sustainable Development Goals' (2016) 59 *Development* 121, 122.

[84]   Friederike Beier, 'Marxist Perspectives on the Global Enclosures of Social Reproduction' (2018) 16 *tripleC* 546, 555.

potential' of unpaid care work, this approach simply leads to further expropriation of women's labour, with women expected to enter the paid labour market on the basis of their so-called 'economic empowerment', while the failure to address the broader social implications of social reproduction helps to maintain the status quo.[85]

CONCLUSION

As this brief overview has revealed, attending to the dynamics of social reproduction in legal analysis generates numerous insights into the ways legal norms and frameworks regulate and facilitate the exploitation of women's (and other vulnerable groups') unpaid work. In particular, SRT recovers the messy relations between state, market, and household, and the complicated lived reality of human beings who find themselves located within multiple rubrics of class, race, gender, and nationality.

This is particularly significant for understanding the persistent limitations of the liberal-feminist approach to gendered power relations. Considered from a legal standpoint, the focus on waged employment as a goal may have provided some women with a basis for material equality. But the focus on individual choice has come at the price of understanding broader structures of exploitation. Broader structural problems, particularly the persistence of gendered divisions of labour in the home and capitalism's systemic dependence on unpaid labour, ensure that the happy marriage of patriarchy and capitalism remains relatively undisturbed. As long as legal norms and mechanisms maintain the undervaluation of social reproductive labour, capital will continue to find new ways to exploit it by way of law, ensuring that women, particularly those from the global South, are subject to extreme social and economic vulnerability. Given new processes of accumulation, there is an even greater need to integrate struggles over social reproduction into legal-theoretical accounts of capital, particularly in order to foster new sites of co-operation against the logic of capital. Moving forward, a feminist materialism attuned to social reproduction also raises important questions about strategies for countering these relations of exploitation, particularly within the framework of law. As the pitfalls of liberal feminism have shown, an approach that foregrounds redistribution alone, without attending to the underlying normative frameworks that maintain the devaluation of unwaged labour, will simply shift the problem to another group of workers. SRT forces us to re-evaluate the human costs of capitalism and pose the question of how a new paradigm could better meet the needs of all people.

---

[85]   Beier, 'Marxist Perspectives', 547.

17. Marxism, labour and employment law, and the limits of legal reform in class society

Ahmed White

INTRODUCTION

It is well known that neither Marx nor Engels nor any other classical exponent of what we know today as 'Marxism' developed a comprehensive theory of law. Not until the 1920s and 1930s, through figures like Karl Renner, Evgeny Pashukanis, and Franz Neumann, did Marxists really begin to give the topic of law sustained attention.[1] Even today this project of divulging Marxism's considerable contributions to the understanding of law remains, as the various chapters in this handbook reveal, both important and incomplete.

Explorations of the connection between law and Marxism have been especially weak in regard to the relation between law and the labour process. At various times, Marx and Engels confronted this issue. But their work on the topic was sporadic. Over the years, many Marxists have participated in debates about law and the workplace, but without ever developing a broad theory or explanation of law and labour.[2] Nevertheless, as is often the case with Marxism, what commentary there is on this topic provides the basis for a useful inquiry into the origins and functions of law in this realm, one that in turn reveals much about the place of law itself in a class society.

It must be said that to broach this subject is to acknowledge inherent—and very Marxist—uncertainties about what constitutes the law, and also which laws are relevant to this discussion. In this regard, one may recall, for instance, the introduction to the *Grundrisse*, where Marx at once comprehends the law and ideology of property in a textured way, and yet also sees in them the juridical foundations of capitalism and wage labour.[3] One may also recall his earlier judgments about the labour-regulating functions of laws that punished the theft of wood—and, for that matter, controlled hunting, fishing, and other modes of subsistence.[4] And

---

[1] Hugh Collins, *Marxism and Law* (Clarendon 1982); Andrew Vincent, 'Marx and Law' (1993) 20 *Journal of Law and Society* 371.

[2] See e.g., Alexis Cukier, 'Exploitation, marxisme et droit du travail' *Contretemps: Revue de critique communiste* (13 October 2016), http://www.contretemps.eu/exploitation-marxisme-droit-travail/ accessed 7 April 2021. The relative underdevelopment of work on this topic might be contrasted with the more thoroughly explored, and somewhat related, issue of Marxism and welfarism. See e.g., Victor George, *Major Thinkers in Welfare: Contemporary Issues in Historical Perspective* (Policy Press 2009) 201–32.

[3] Karl Marx, *Grundrisse: Foundations of the Critique of Political Economy* (first published 1939, Martin Nicolaus tr, Penguin 1993) 85–111.

[4] Karl Marx, 'Proceedings of the Sixth Rhine Province Assembly. Third Article—Debates on the Law on Thefts of Wood' in Karl Marx and Frederick Engels, *Collected Works*, vol 1 (Lawrence & Wishart 1975) 224.

then, too, there is *The Origin of the Family, Private Property, and the State*, where Engels identifies the juridical foundations of class society partly with the law of the family.[5]

It is with precisely this sense of the law's contingent meaning and its complex functions that later Marxists have demonstrated how even areas of law that might seem quite distant from the front lines of economic production, like modern criminal law, are often quite impossible to understand except as means of regulating labour.[6] All of this lends great support to the more fundamental point, which is central to this chapter, that while the meaning of the term 'law' is necessarily contingent, it is quite certain that the law's nature can only be grasped by examining its relationship to social structure and class conflict.

Focusing on the core of the subject, which consists of those statutes, court rulings, and decrees that are generally known today as labour and employment law, this chapter presents a critical review of the history of labour and employment law and its functions in capitalist society. It reveals how laws like these, which have long been propagated by both liberals and leftist reformers, have been widely affirmed by international law and adopted by states around the world. It recognises how this proliferation of legal 'protections', which must be seen against the backdrop of an overall improvement in the conditions of labour in society, appears not only to most liberals but also to some leftists in two ways—first, as proof of a state-mediated settlement or compromise between labour and capital regarding the terms and conditions of capitalist exploitation; second, as confirmation that this kind of reform is an effective and essential forum for advancing workers' interests.[7]

However, as this chapter also makes clear, it would be wrong to overestimate what workers have won through these legal reforms, to exaggerate the role of the law in achieving these gains, or to ignore what the law is really bound to accomplish on this front. Not only is this body of law embedded in a larger legal system that has done nothing to abolish class conflict and exploitation, but these laws themselves, and the reformist protections they ratify, are also captive to a logic that limits the reach of legal reform in class society. Labour and employment law remains, no less than wage labour itself, circumscribed by the dictates of capitalism. It is, to put it simply, capitalist law, with all that this implies about what it is destined to mean and how it is destined to function.

---

[5]   Friedrich Engels, *The Origin of the Family, Private Property, and the State* (first published 1884, Penguin 2010).

[6]   Georg Rusche and Otto Kirchheimer, *Punishment and Social Structure* (first published 1939, Transaction 2003). See also Francis Snyder and Douglas Hay (eds), *Labour, Law, and Crime: An Historical Perspective* (Tavistock 1987); Douglas Hay et al (ed), *Albion's Fatal Tree: Crime and Society in Eighteenth-Century England* (Pantheon 1975).

[7]   With respect to the United States, see e.g., Alan Matusow, *The Unraveling of America: A History of Liberalism in the 1960s* (Harper & Row 1986). As Nelson Lichtenstein notes, the notion of such a settlement emerged in the United States as article of faith among liberals, who later made charges that employers and the state had breached this accord a centrepiece of their call for better support for workers. Nelson Lichtenstein, *State of the Union: A Century of American Labor* (Princeton University Press 2002) 98–99. Outside the United States, this concept of settlement on the labour front is typically folded into discourses on the rise (and decline) of social democracy, 'embedded liberalism', and 'social partnership'. See e.g., Lowell Turner, *Fighting for Partnership: Labour and Politics in United Germany* (Cornell University Press 1998); Stefan Berger and Hugh Compston (eds), *Policy Concertation and Social Partnership in Western Europe: Lessons for the 21st Century* (Berghahn 2002); Hugh Compston and Justin Greenwood (eds), *Social Partnership in the European Union* (Palgrave 2001).

This reading of labour and employment law rests on a view of law and its position in class society that emerges from important texts like Marx's 'On the Jewish Question', his 'Contribution to the Critique of Political Economy', and Engels' *Family, Private Property, and the State*. It aligns with the insights that inhere in Marx's more specific engagements with questions of labour and law. And in the fashion of Marxism's most potent critiques, it is also founded on a broad understanding of the ways that law and labour have evolved together through history.

LAW, CLASS, AND THE EMERGENCE OF FREE LABOUR

It is obvious that some manifestations of what could be called labour and employment law are as old as civilisation. The laws of ancient Mesopotamia regulated wages, and to some degree hours of work; Jewish law broadly legislated in the interests of poor workers; and Roman law established a diversity of technical rules governing labour contracts.[8] But although it sometimes benefited workers, the law in ancient (and, later, pre-industrial) societies was also a means of effectuating class rule and supporting the dominant means of exploitation. So it was that the same laws which protected workers also legislated their status as slaves, serfs, and other types of bondmen—and, in so doing, affirmed their general social subordination.[9]

This contradictory feature of these older iterations of labour and employment law is not an artefact of these archaic times. As a review of the history of law in this realm makes clear, the whole project of legal reform of the workplace has always been marked not only by the persistence of laws of property and contract that provide a robust juridical foundation for class rule, but also by the equally important fact that even its reformist guise, labour and employment law itself, has always been reconciled to the dictates of class society.

So it is that even with the emergence of capitalism and the emergence of what Marx called 'formally free labour' that the regulation of labour remained immersed in a dialectic that merged the protective with the authoritarian, the compensatory with the exploitative, and the truly free with the unfree, in line with the needs of capitalist social order.[10] This is evident, for instance, in the complicated and decidedly unfree array of work qualifications, ethnic or clan limitations, and price and quality controls of the sort imposed by the English guild and indenture systems, the labour corporation system on the European continent, the *taille* and *corvée* systems that European states extended to their colonies, or the *Jātis* of India, for instance.[11] These systems were also rooted in legal traditions that protected workers in various ways. But

---

[8]   For a useful sketch of the early development of employment and labour law see Matthew W Finkin, 'Labour Law, Introduction' in *International Encyclopedia of Comparative Law*, vol 15 (Mohr, Siebeck 2014) 3.

[9]   See e.g., Edward B Rugemer, *Slave Law and the Politics of Resistance in the Early Atlantic World* (Harvard University Press 2018); Thomas D Morris, *Southern Slavery and the Law* (University of North Carolina Press 1996).

[10]   Karl Marx, *Capital: A Critique of Political Economy*, vol 1 (first published 1867, Penguin 1992) 928.

[11]   On the global prevalence of guilds and their kin, see Jan Lucassen, Tine De Moor, and Jan Luiten van Zanden, 'The Return of the Guilds: Towards a Global History of the Guilds in Pre-Industrial Times' (2008) 53 *International Review of Social History* 5. With respect to the United States, see e.g., Alan Matusow, *The Unraveling of America: A History of Liberalism in the 1960s* (Harper & Row 1986).

as Marx rather dolefully chronicled in *Capital* (and as many historians have since confirmed), the law in these areas imposed on the freedoms of wage labour in a great number of even more coercive ways, at various times limiting wages, mandating work, punishing vagrancy and vagabondage, and criminalising 'combinations of workers'.[12]

An even more salient example of this dialectic is the doctrine of 'master and servant'. Developed in England in the sixteenth century and expanded by both common law and statute, the doctrine had come by the nineteenth century to prevail not only throughout its former colonies but also in many civil law jurisdictions, as it emerged as the prominent legal framework for the regulation of wage labour. The doctrine obligated masters to ensure the welfare of their servants, even to protect them from physical attack.[13] But this hardly eliminated that regime's oppressive and exploitative features, any more than the obligation of masters to support their chattel slaves negated that institution's crudely exploitative and dehumanising features. Its ostensible service to free labour notwithstanding, the doctrine recognised masters' very definite prerogative to 'correct' workers, one that was backed by the legal authorisation to whip, incarcerate, and fine workers, as well as force them to work.[14]

So pronounced were the law's oppressive functions that the struggle to expand labour's freedom took shape, inevitably, as a legal project. This perspective was central not only to classical liberalism, with its consummate tendency to fetishise rights, but also to the utopian pseudo-socialism of Henri de Saint-Simon and his followers. Marx himself saw in the rise of 'free labour', as a juridical category, a step toward the emancipation of the worker. But for him, of course, this move was destined to remain as incomplete as capitalism's overall contributions to human freedom.

Evident in Marx's rejoinder to Bruno Bauer in 'On the Jewish Question', where he at once celebrates and condemns the implications of bourgeois emancipation, this perspective is also reflected in the first preface to volume one of *Capital*. There, in the course of explaining the historical significance of the reformist English Factory Acts, Marx speaks of the clearing of 'all the legally removable obstacles to the development of the working class', which included the US War of Independence and US Civil War, as central to the development of capitalism, and as events whose brutality or inhumanity would reflect nothing so much as 'the degree of development of the working class itself'.[15]

When the Industrial Revolution brought about the maturation of capitalism and the rise of what Marx often called 'modern industry', the generalisation of wage labour, and the restructuring of social relations around the conflict between the proletariat and bourgeoisie, it

---

[12]   Marx, *Capital*, vol 1, 896–904. See e.g., AL Beier and Paul Ocobock (eds), *Cast Out: Vagrancy and Homelessness in Global and Historical Perspective* (Ohio State University Press 2014); Patricia Fumerton, *Unsettled: The Culture of Mobility and the Working Poor in Early Modern England* (University of Chicago Press 2006); Judith M Bennett, 'Compulsory Service in Late Medieval England' (2010) 209 *Past & Present* 7.

[13]   On the nature and extent of this mutual obligation, see e.g., William Blackstone, *Blackstone's Commentaries* (William Young Birch and Abraham Small 1803) bk 1, ch 14, 428–29; Francis Raleigh Batt, *The Law of Master and Servant* (Pitman 1967) 288.

[14]   On this doctrine see e.g., Douglas Hay and Paul Craven (eds), *Masters, Servants, and Magistrates in Britain and the Empire, 1562–1955* (University of North Carolina Press 2004); Philip Selznick, *Law, Society, and Industrial Justice* (Russell Sage Foundation 1969) 122–37; Robert J Steinfeld, *The Invention of Free Labour: The Employment Relation in English and American Law and Culture, 1350–1870* (University of North Carolina Press 2002).

[15]   Marx, *Capital*, vol 1, 92.

also reformed the legal landscape. As not only Marx but Locke, Rousseau, Montesquieu, and Weber all understood, the triumph of capitalism was accompanied by a fundamental change in jurisprudence and juridical thought. 'Rule of law' norms, which had initially emerged as effective ways of undermining the authority of the old aristocratic and mercantilist order, were refashioned into the legal foundations of bourgeois rule.[16]

Premised on a reification of law as the true sovereign, and on various assumptions about the legitimacy of bourgeois conceptions of property, the state, and personhood, the 'rule of law' was operationalised in separation-of-powers doctrines, the idea that law is universal and non-retroactive, and the concept of formal equality under the law. It was also grounded in notions of individual rights and in the veneration of semi-democratic and constitutional (or quasi-constitutional) administration. In the context of labour and employment law, these norms gave credence to the idea—aligned closely with the interests of bourgeois employers— that labour's emancipation consisted above all of labour's freedom from regulation, at least beyond that agreed by contract.

Just as the 'rule of law' had to be created—often in the guise of its 'discovery'—the concept of free labour also had to be 'invented', as an alternative to the entrenchment in legal doctrine of the idea that labour was unfree.[17] Not by coincidence, this project was most fully realised in the United States, where, in Marx's words, bourgeois society had, unfettered by a feudal past and unreconciled to slavery, 'developed to hitherto unheard-of dimensions'.[18] And not by coincidence, either, it was in the United States that the concept of free labour was most fully institutionalised in the doctrine of 'employment-at-will'.

Devised in the late nineteenth century, employment-at-will affirmed the right of both worker and employer, absent contractual terms to the contrary, to terminate the employment relationship at will. It also implied a prerogative to insist upon the modification of terms of employment, at any time and for any reason. The doctrine's main propagandist was an American lawyer named Horace Wood, who in his 1877 treatise *Master and Servant* cited a handful of cases to present this new formulation as consistent with the doctrine of master and servant.[19] Wood's reconceptualisation of this relationship was not so much an endorsement of liberty as a powerful confirmation of capitalist employers' prerogative, backed by their economic power, to use threats of harsh discipline, onerous workplace rules, and job loss to control the industrial workplace.[20] So it was that this reform, too, even more so than older notions of master and servant, endorsed workers' bondage by making it an implication of their freedom.

The doctrine of employment-at-will in its strictest sense was always a uniquely American rule and the principle underlying it was less relevant in civil law jurisdictions, which were, of their nature, more disposed to the idea that law intruded into the employment relationships. But the basic idea that an employer could generally terminate a contract with a worker without

---

[16]   For a critical review of this thesis see e.g., Franz L Neumann, 'The Change in the Function of Law in Modern Society' [1937] in Herbert Marcuse (ed), *The Democratic and the Authoritarian State: Essays in Political and Legal Theory* (Free Press 1957) 22.

[17]   Steinfeld, *The Invention of Free Labour*.

[18]   Marx, *Grundrisse*, 884.

[19]   HG Wood, *A Treatise on the Law of Master and Servant* (John D Parsons Jr 1877) 272–73.

[20]   Jay Feinman, 'The Development of the Employment at Will Rule' (1976) 20 *American Journal of Legal History* 118.

incurring any particular liability, and that this confirmed the freedom of both, quickly became dominant, even in civil law countries.[21]

As Marx fully recognised, the appeal to formal equality and the fiction of free contract as a means of justifying wage labour, an institution built on coercion and inequality, was essential to the juridical legitimacy of industrial capitalism and therefore universal in substance if not form or degree. It was with a clear sense of this nexus of legal freedom and economic exploitation that Marx, in *The German Ideology*, pronounced the essence of free labour as the freedom to serve as one's own enslaver—an insight that aligns with Pashukanis' famous judgment that the general structure of bourgeois law, including its system of rights and its pretence of formal equality, represents a formalisation of the social relations of capitalist society.[22] And it is consistent with recent work that documents the central role that legally sanctioned coercion played in labour markets well into the industrial age.[23]

FREE LABOUR AND THE LIMITS OF LEGAL REFORM IN CAPITALIST SOCIETY

As the development of capitalism reformed the law of the workplace around the prerequisites of wage labour, it also transformed the worker organisations around which modern labour law would evolve. From the mid-1800s onwards, when labour organisations began to emerge in their modern form as ways of contesting the terms of capitalist exploitation, they took shape as more or less free associations of free labourers, shorn of the complicated and rigid strictures of the guilds and the 'labour corporations'—and often suspicious of the law and circumspect about the wisdom of advancing their members' interest through the law.[24]

The ability of workers to join these unions would seem to have been an inarguable and legally enforceable implication of free labour, not to mention the 'rule of law' and the broader, ideological pretentions of bourgeois liberalism. And in fact, by the late nineteenth century, union membership was legally tolerated in most industrial societies—a development which, as Marx noted when he described how England's repeal of the anti-union Combination Acts in 1824 occurred 'in the face of the threatening attitude of the proletariat'.[25] But if the threats posed by worker agitation encouraged reform, they also ensured that the emerging tolerance of organised labour would unfold haltingly and incompletely, and would be marked by important exceptions that anticipated the very contingent support for labour rights among employers and their allies in liberal society today.

---

[21]   Bruno Veneziana, 'Formation, Modification and Termination of Employment Contracts' in *International Encyclopedia of Comparative Law*, vol 15 (Mohr, Siebeck 2014) ch 4, 3–6.

[22]   Karl Marx and Friedrich Engels, *The German Ideology* (first published 1932, Clemens Dutt, W Lough, and CP Magill tr, Prometheus 1998) 220–21; Evgeny Pashukanis, *Law and Marxism: A General Theory* (first published 1929, Ink Links 1978).

[23]   Marc Steinberg, *England's Great Transformation: Law, Labor, and the Industrial Revolution* (University of Chicago Press 2016).

[24]   To be sure, this often occurred despite the struggles of many workers, particularly skilled workers who cherished their traditional control of work and who clung to the old structures that had once benefited them. Nevertheless, as capitalism steadily undermined the relevance of such workers, the trend in this direction proved largely inexorable.

[25]   Marx, *Capital*, vol 1, 903.

Indeed, it became typical for notions of liberty in the broad sense, like the concept of free labour, to be construed as a mandate against labour rights. For instance, with the Decree of 14 June 1791—*la loi Le Chapelier*, as it was commonly known—the revolutionary regime in France simultaneously outlawed labour 'corporations' and repealed the right of association, which were deemed contrary to revolutionary values. Enacted alongside *la loi d'Allarde*, which consecrated the freedom of commerce and trade, this law would stand until 1864. In the United States unions inhabited a 'legal twilight zone' from the late nineteenth century into the twentieth century. A variety of doctrines, including conspiracy and laws banning combinations, allowed the criminal and civil prosecution of even the most conventional trade unions, often on the similar ground that unionists were threats to the liberty of others.[26] Marrying concerns about liberty with concerns about state security, as well as the claim that workers needed to be protected from their fellow workers' destructive ideals, many American jurisdictions in the late nineteenth and early twentieth centuries essentially outlawed radical unions by enacting and enforcing laws relating to 'criminal syndicalism' and other forms of sedition. Likewise, the 1878 German Anti-Socialist Law broadly repressed unions, until its expiration in 1890. In other cases, an even cruder approach prevailed. Imperial Russia made little pretence about liberty when it deemed unions of just about all kinds unlawful until the 1905 Revolution and declared them only semi-lawful thereafter.[27]

Just as important as these impositions on the 'right of association' were restrictions on the right to strike. Representing a somewhat different way that free labour could be a self-negating limit on labour rights, this concept was fashioned to deny prisoners, agricultural workers, sailors, and workers under contract or in debt the right to quit work, let alone engage in strike action. Free labour was realised, in part, by what it was not. In a similar way, labour laws were reconciled with capitalist rule through the legal validation of employers' prerogative to treat strike action as an act of permanent resignation, and also through their ability to secure labour contracts that barred striking and even outlawed union membership itself.[28] These too were presented as consistent with the implications of free labour.

While the notion that strikes were criminal conspiracies or illegal combinations (popular in both England and the United States for a time) did not survive the maturation of capitalism, it gave way to the view—entirely consistent with emerging notions of free labour—that even lawful strike action could be criminalised because of how, when, or where strikes occurred. In particular, strikes could be prohibited if they impinged on market freedoms, coerced a 'neutral' or 'secondary' employer to win greater leverage, constituted a prohibited restraint of trade, impeded the delivery of 'essential' goods or services, or otherwise prevented people from running their businesses or going to work. With similar justification, they could also be prohibited because they were conducted in a criminal or excessively disorderly fashion.

This new framework for regulating strikes in 'reasonable' ways had important and lasting political implications. For it presented employers' opposition to labour rights as an exercise

---

[26] Christopher L Tomlins, *The State and the Unions: Labor Relations, the Law, and the Organized Labor Movement in America, 1880–1960* (CUP 1985) 33.

[27] See e.g., Robert Justin Goldstein, *Political Repression in 19th Century Europe* (Barnes & Noble 1983); Robert Justin Goldstein, 'Labour History Symposium: Political Repression of the American Labour Movement During its Formative Years—A Comparative Perspective' (2010) 51 *Labour History* 271.

[28] See e.g., Chad Pearson, *Reform or Repression: Organizing America's Anti-Union Movement* (University of Pennsylvania Press 2015).

that at once honoured the principle of free labour and protected public safety and the common good. Although this artifice might not withstand critical reflection on how capitalism and the legal system actually work, it was buttressed by bourgeois devotion to the 'rule of law'. For in the scheme of things, it was always workers who were obliged to challenge the status quo and nearly always they who initiated labour conflict in the first place, creating disorder, disturbing the flow of commerce, and threatening the sovereignty of the law itself. It was also workers—particularly dissatisfied and militant workers—who could then be blamed and have their rights curtailed.

If strikes could be declared illegal, so could workers' transgressions be used to justify violent repression, both extra-legal and state-sponsored. When justification seemed necessary, it was largely by appeals to the 'rule of law' and the idea of protecting free labour from transgression that labour conflict in the age of industrial capitalism descended into a condition of sustained and open warfare, with tragic results. In this regard, it is revealing that in the United States, where the politics of free labour flourished and where employers prevailed against a post-Civil War struggle by workers, the toll of injured and dead in labour disputes reached extraordinary levels—exceeded in the industrial world only by imperial Russia. Between 1870 and 1940 it is likely that around 2000 people were killed in these struggles, alongside countless others who were assaulted, arrested, and imprisoned.[29]

Of course, workers also faced other injuries at the hands of industrial capitalism. By reducing the economic value of workers to their ability to sell their capacity to work, industrial capitalism absolved employers of any obligations to support the workers they employed, and positioned capitalists and workers as implacable adversaries in a contest that the latter were destined to lose, at least short of revolution. For workers the results were poverty, inequality, and alienation in the context of extraordinary increases in social wealth, as well as exposure to a host of other perils and burdens. These, in turn, became focal points for further agitation, and ultimately legislation.

One area where this was certainly true was with respect to workplace injuries and deaths. This was the major theme of Engels' *The Condition of the Working Class in England*, whose grim statistics about worker mortality provided him and Marx with an empirical foundation for their critiques of capitalism. And as industrial capitalism consolidated itself, so did these dire consequences proliferate. In the United States, around the turn of the last century, one worker

---

[29]   Goldstein, 'Labour History Symposium'; Daniel R Brower, 'Labor Violence in Russia in the Late Nineteenth Century' (1982) 41 *Slavic Review* 417; Paul F Lipold, '"Striking Deaths" at Their Roots: Assaying the Social Determinants of Extreme Labor–Management Violence in US Labor History—1877–1947' (2014) 38 *Social Science History* 541. To be sure, the violent repression of unions tended to be less common in other parts of the industrialising world, including much of northern Europe. But Spain and Hungary, for instance, were also the scene of considerable repression. Repression was also far from uncommon in countries like France, Italy, and Austria. To a degree that defies measurement, it was also commonplace throughout much of the colonial world and the periphery of the industrialising global North, where, amid the persistence of the *corvée* system, the convict labour system, peonage, and statutory labour, the pretence of free labour arrived much later than the mandates to fully exploit the resources at hand. See e.g., Pia Maria Jolliffee, *Prisons and Forced Labour in Japan: The Colonization of Hokkaido, 1881–1894* (Routledge 2019) 159–172; AT Nzula, II Potekhin, and AZ Zusmanovich, *Forced Labour in Colonial Africa* (Zed Press 1979); Christian G De Vito and Alex Lichtenstein, 'Writing a Global History of Convict Labour' (2013) 58 *International Review of Social History* 285; Stephen J Rockel, 'New Labor History in Sub-Saharan Africa: Colonial Enslavement and Forced Labor' (2014) 86 *International Labor and Working Class History* 159.

in 50 was killed or disabled for a month or more because of an accident on the job.[30] Workers were left to suffer these fates in the name of freedom as employers indulged an indifference to them that was confirmed in common law countries with doctrines like assumption of risk, contributory negligence, and the so-called 'fellow-servant' rule, as it was elsewhere by statute or by the simple lack of any legal recourse for workers.[31]

In a similar way, the new social order also exposed workers to unemployment, which industrial capitalism, with its unrelenting cycles of expansion and contraction, its constant introduction of labour-replacing machinery, and its mandate that human needs yield to the needs of capital and the dictates of accumulation, transformed from a relatively uncommon product of social catastrophe, disaster, or local misfortune into a recurrent and perfectly normal fact of life. In this Marx saw not only capitalism's capricious indifference to the human needs of working people but a structural reality that benefited capitalists by setting before them a 'reserve army of labour', whose existence has always made effective worker protests and bargaining that much more difficult.[32]

Another prominent legacy of industrial capitalism was a world of work riven by inequality based on race, gender, and ethnicity. And here, too, the contradictory logic of free labour held sway. Although typically enforced as much by custom as by law, workplace inequality of these kinds proliferated in the late nineteenth and early twentieth centuries, spurred on by the manifold ways that capitalism accelerated the movement of people all over the globe, drawing millions into a system that generated deep inequalities and resentments while inviting workers (sometimes propelled by employers) to see themselves as each other's competitive rivals. This trend reached its apotheosis in the US South and in the industrialising parts of the colonial world, like South Africa, where it evolved into a more or less comprehensive and legally sanctioned system of racial apartheid.[33]

In this last respect, workplace inequality took its place alongside new management practices and strategies that displaced older, reciprocal structures bound up with custom and supplanted workers' own control over production. To this end, employers repudiated or undermined union representation and hired armies of foremen and managers, who were charged with enforcing comprehensive workplace standards and rules that the employers themselves had devised.[34] In many ways a reflection of how fully industrial capitalism endowed employers with the power

---

[30] John Fabian Witt, *The Accidental Republic: Crippled Workingmen, Destitute Widows, and the Remaking of American Law* (Harvard University Press 2006) 2. On the prevalence of workplace perils in this period see also Jamie L Bronstein, *Caught in the Machinery: Workplace Accidents and Injured Workers in Nineteenth-Century Britain* (Stanford University Press 2008).

[31] See e.g., Michael Ashley Stein, 'Victorian Tort Liability for Workplace Injuries' (2008) 2008 *University of Illinois Law Review* 933; Finkin, 'Labour Law', 14.

[32] Frederick Engels, *The Condition of the Working Class in England in 1844* (first published 1845, Florence Kelley Wischnewetzky tr, Swan Sonnenschein & Co 1892) 84–85, 90.

[33] See e.g., Oliver Cox, *Caste, Class and Race* (Monthly Review Press 1948); Harold Wolpe, *Race, Class and the Apartheid State* (James Currey 1988); Frederick Johnstone, *Class, Race and Gold* (Routledge & Kegan Paul 1976). For a recent argument that race and racism are embedded in the logic of capital see David Roediger, *Class, Race and Marxism* (Verso 2017).

[34] Among the important works in this extensive area of research are Richard Edwards, *Contested Terrain: The Transformation of the Workplace in the Twentieth Century* (Basic Books 1980); Dan Clawson, *Bureaucracy and the Labor Process* (Monthly Review Press 1980); David Montgomery, *Workers' Control in America: Studies in the History of Work, Technology and Labor Struggles* (CUP 1979); Harry Braverman, *Labor and Monopoly Capital: The Degradation of Work in the Twentieth*

to legislate their own private law in the workplace—a practice entirely consistent with the logic of free labour, and one that informed apt depictions of industrial work as 'wage slavery' or a 'new feudalism'—this approach likewise served to accommodate new forms of production and the intensified exploitation of labour.

To the extent that unions survived in this period as authentic champions of their members' interests, they were at once bound to oppose these conditions and constrained by the same underlying realities of capitalist rule from achieving a great deal in this direction. Their members being mindful of this dilemma, more than a few such organisations emerged with revolutionary purpose. Such was the case with the Industrial Workers of the World, or, in its early years, the French Confédération générale du travail. Indeed, as in revolutionary Russia, where a massive strike wave preceded the 1917 Revolution, or in Mexico, where the Casa del Obrero Mundial supported revolution in that country, unions sometimes did play a direct role in challenging capitalist rule.

Such radicalism would prove largely fleeting, though—a fact evidenced, for instance, in the Casa del Obrero Mundial's counter-revolutionary turn. Factionalism and opportunism were common factors. But so was the simple fact that unionists who embraced revolution faced repression in its most acute, often life-destroying forms. Another, more ironic reason is that the threat of revolution, which radical unionists stoked, gave impetus to an important current of bourgeois reformism according to which capitalists acceded to the legitimacy of unions willing to repudiate radicalism and find some accommodation with the prevailing economic order. Many unions did just that.

These contradictory tendencies were evident to Marx and Engels, who were famously equivocal about unions. At times, especially in their youth, they viewed these organisations as important to the class struggle. A young Engels, for instance, famously described unions as a 'military school of the workers'.[35] But Marx and Engels became more sceptical about unions, wary of their penchant for compromise and convinced that they were unequal to the task of leading any revolution.[36] As Marx put it in 1865, the problem with unions, even when they had not been corrupted, was that they 'fail generally from limiting themselves to a guerrilla war against the effects of the existing system, instead of simultaneously trying to change it, instead of using their organised forces as a lever for the final emancipation of the working class, that is to say, the ultimate abolition of the wages system'.[37]

This circumspect view of unions, which situated these organisations, like the law, amid the constraints of more powerful social forces, was shared by other revolutionary Marxists, including, for instance, Lenin and Luxemburg. And it remains a dominant perspective among many Marxists, not least because the course of events has confirmed it.[38] By the late nineteenth century the great majority of unions had committed themselves to reformism, even if many

---

Century (Monthly Review Press 1975); David Nelson, *Managers and Workers: Origins of the New Factory System in the United States* (University of Wisconsin Press 1975).

[35]   Engels, *The Condition of the Working Class*, 224.

[36]   Kenneth Lapides (ed), *Marx and Engels on the Trade Unions* (Praeger 1987).

[37]   Karl Marx, 'Wages, Price and Profit' [1865] in Karl Marx and Frederick Engels, *Collected Works*, vol 20 (Lawrence & Wishart) 101, 149.

[38]   See e.g., Richard Hyman, *Marxism and the Sociology of Trade Unionism* (Pluto Press 1971); Perry Anderson, 'The Limits and Possibilities of Trade Union Action' in Robin Blackburn and Alexander Cockburn (eds), *The Incompatibles: Trade Union Militancy and the Consensus* (Penguin 1967) 263; Rosa Luxemburg, *The Mass Strike: The Political Party and the Trade Unions* (first published 1906,

continued for a time to profess their ultimate commitment to revolution, and even if reform was the foundation, in practice, of reaction. In so doing, they reconciled themselves to changes in capitalism that had further reshaped the legal system to the same counter-revolutionary ends.

LEGAL REFORMS, FREE LABOUR, AND THE CONTRADICTIONS OF MODERN LABOUR AND EMPLOYMENT LAW

As it consolidated its reign, the newly ascendant bourgeoisie altered the *laissez-faire* liberalism that had so well served its own revolution into a program suited to the more active management of capitalist society. In so doing, this class and its champions in government and the intelligentsia embraced the power and legitimacy of the state as a means of better sustaining the preconditions of capital accumulation, even if this implied a good measure of compromise and reform, and especially if the costs could be placed on the working class. And they also modified the 'rule of law', such that its libertarian and anti-statist mandates, like the idea of formal equality, which had served so well the bourgeoisie's struggle against the old aristocratic order, would now better endorse the state's intervention into economic matters. In the course of this transformation, many capitalists came to appreciate not only the legitimacy of unions that were willing to acquiesce to capitalist rule, but also the value of adopting legal reforms about the workplace, including both measures to lessen repression and explicitly remedial legislation that more or less directly redressed some of capitalism's glaring injustices.[39]

Although one early expression of this was the near-simultaneous adoption of the English Factory Acts and repeal of that country's Combination Laws, the move towards reform did not gain great momentum until after Marx's death. But in the late nineteenth century it surged forward, unfolding under the larger banners of 'progressivism', 'liberalism', 'social democracy', or even 'socialism'. By the early twentieth century, legal reform of labour and employment conditions was central to a broader platform of bourgeois reformism that emerged as the leading mode of governance in capitalist societies, rivalled only for a time by fascism, and utterly dominant today.[40]

Labour Law

To a great extent, the success of reforms on this front must be understood as a victory for workers, the culmination of a sustained and wide-ranging surge in labour organising and social protest that extended across the industrial world from the first years of the twentieth century to the Second World War. But reform in this area also represented for capitalists

Harper & Row 1971). On the continuing debate of this topic see John McIlroy, 'Marxism and the Trade Unions: The Bureaucracy versus the Rank and File Debate Revisited' (2014) 42 *Critique* 497.

[39] See Gabriel Kolko, *The Triumph of Conservatism: A Reinterpretation of American History, 1990–1916* (Free Press 1963); James Kloppenberg, *Uncertain Victory: Social Democracy and Progressivism in European and American Thought, 1870–1920* (OUP 1988); Pearson, *Reform or Repression*; Sheldon Stormquist, *Re-Inventing 'The People': The Progressive Movement, the Class Problem, and the Origins of Modern Liberalism* (University of Illinois Press 2006).

[40] It was from this fact that many communists' otherwise dubious dismissal of reform liberalism as 'social fascism' drew, for a time, an element of truth.

a way to forestall the threat of radicalism apparent in this 'Great Upsurge'. And it clearly represented a means, too, of rationalising the workings of the profit system, including the aim—prominently intellectualised as Keynesian economics—to better manage capitalism's crisis tendencies through government-sponsored efforts to sustain demand. These efforts were made in the context of the rapid increases in productivity and capital accumulation which defined capitalist production through much of the twentieth century.[41]

Moreover, these later reforms, like their predecessors, continued to subordinate labour rights to the essential needs of capital. So it is that limits on the right to strike have extended into the present day. Even in countries whose labour laws are relatively generous to workers, it is quite common for government workers or other ostensibly 'essential' employees to be denied the right to strike or required to serve notice or undergo mediation before striking. And it is not uncommon for these workers to be subjected to criminal prosecution if they defy these strictures. Indeed, all relevant jurisdictions broadly limit the right to strike, and do so with respect to all workers. Labour laws worldwide prohibit strikes that occur while collective bargaining agreements are pending, that are conceived as 'sympathy' strikes or otherwise undertaken in a way that implicates 'neutral' employers, or that impinge on national interests. Every jurisdiction also permits a considerable degree of police intervention in strikes, as well as criminal and sometimes civil prosecution of strikers or unions themselves for violence or other disruptive behaviour on picket lines. In line with the persistence of employers' free labour prerogatives, and the conceit of protecting workers' freedom not to strike, the right to strike also entails some range of authority for employers to discharge unruly strikers as well as those who participate in illegal strikes.[42]

In fact, in continued deference to either the letter or spirit of employment-at-will, quite a few jurisdictions broadly recognise the right of employers to constructively discharge strikers even without any particular cause. In some cases, this prerogative is limited to the use of temporary replacements who must make way for the strikers when the strike ends. In other jurisdictions—notably, the United States—employers may hire permanent replacement workers, effectively making job loss an immediate risk of going out on strike. Of course, no jurisdiction that broadly recognises the right to strike simply precludes employers from hiring replacement workers. Doing so would essentially guarantee the success of most every strike, and also violate the basic prerogatives of capital and the conception of free labour that is essential to its juridical legitimacy. Instead, those that prohibit the use of replacement workers, whether temporary or permanent, typically impose significant limits on when workers can strike, often by subjecting labour disputes to the jurisdiction of more elaborate administrative or judicial proceedings that closely involve the state in arbitrating the merits of the underlying

---

[41]   On the role of labour militancy in the development of labour law, see e.g., Michael Goldfield, 'Worker Insurgency, Radical Organization, and New Deal Labor Legislation' (1989) 83 *American Political Science Review* 1257; Michael Goldfield and Cody Melcher, 'The Myth of Section 7(a): Worker Militancy, Progressive Labor Legislation, and the Coal Miners' (2019) 16 *Labor: Studies in Working-Class History* 49; George Feldman, 'Unions, Solidarity, and Class: The Limits of Liberal Labor Law' (1994) 15 *Berkeley Journal of Employment and Labor Law* 187.

[42]   See e.g., Bernard Gernigon, Alberto Odero, and Horacio Guido, *ILO Principles Concerning the Right to Strike* (International Labour Office 1998); Ruth Beth-Israel, 'Strike, Lockouts and Other Kinds of Hostile Actions' in *International Encyclopedia of Comparative Law*, vol 15 (Mohr, Siebeck 2014) ch 15, 9–13, 15–16, 18–21, 34–37.

conflict and resolving competing claims within a framework that presupposes capitalist rule.[43] The state thereby protects workers and employers alike from the implications of free labour, preserving the functionality of the market by subjecting all parties to explicitly authoritarian control.

These different approaches to the right to strike reflect a broader distinction that emerged in the mid-twentieth century between systems of labour law whose strongly interventionist tendencies lend them a corporatist character and those at the opposite extreme, which render the state a more distant referee of labour disputes. This difference in approach extends beyond the handling of strikes to include whether the state takes an active role in the collective bargaining process and the enforcement of any contracts that the parties might enter. Some jurisdictions leave these matters to be decided by the relative economic power of the parties while others reserve to the state the authority to intervene. But despite a rough correlation between a country's commitment to labour corporatism and overall union membership, the logic of this approach is also compromise. It seems clear that neither approach accords workers any decisive advantage over their capitalist employers in the struggle to define the terms of exploitation.

The result is a system of labour rights which, despite ubiquitous rhetoric about the 'co-operation' or 'partnership' that the law supposedly ensures, affirms the fundamentally subordinate position of workers. And still, worldwide, employers' support for this system remains quite contingent. In the face of escalating opposition to unions, shaped around changes in political economy, union membership and collective bargaining have declined dramatically since the 1970s. It is telling that in the United States and France, where many of the freedoms thought essential to capitalism were forged, membership has reached negligible levels.[44]

Employment Law

Although these developments in labour law reflected early notions of free labour, they were also premised juridically on a partial repudiation of the doctrine of employment-at-will. This change in the degree of deference to employment-at-will was in turn reflected in an expansion of employment law, which is to say a broad constellation of 'protective' legislation and legal rules oriented around individual employee rights or imposed outside the parameters of collective bargaining.

---

[43]   See e.g., Kenneth G Dau-Schmidt, 'Labor Law and Industrial Peace: A Comparative Analysis of the United States, the United Kingdom, Germany, and Japan under the Bargaining Model' (2000) 8 *Tulane Journal of International and Comparative Law* 117.

[44]   International Labour Organisation, *Presentation of the Committee on Freedom of Association: Annual Report for the Period 2018* (2019); Organisation for Economic Co-operation and Development, 'Collective Bargaining Coverage', https://stats.oecd.org/Index.aspx?DataSetCode=CBC accessed 7 April 2021; International Labour Organisation, *Issue Brief No.1, Trends in Collective Bargaining Coverage: Stability, Erosion or Decline?* (2017). On the role of escalating opposition to unions in causing their decline in the United States, see Michael Goldfield, *The Decline of Organized Labor in the United States* (University of Chicago Press 1987). For an alternative view focusing on economic developments, compare e.g., Henry Farber and Bruce Western, 'Accounting for the Decline of Unions in the Private Sector, 1973–1998' (2001) 22 *Journal of Labor Research* 459. For a review of this issue in the European context see Bernhard Ebbinghaus and Jelle Visser, 'When Institutions Matter: Union Growth and Decline in Western Europe, 1950–1995' (1999) 15 *European Sociological Review* 135.

Among the earliest of these laws were those concerning excessive hours of work. The English Statute of Artificers of 1562, for instance, limited hours of work. But like many early enactments on this front, that statute had a narrow jurisdiction. Broader legislation would not come until later, in the nineteenth century, and particularly in Australia and New Zealand, where more or less comprehensive minimum wage laws were enacted in the 1890s. England followed with a similar regime in 1909, and so did France, adopting in 1919 a law decreeing an eight-hour working day. Revolutionary Mexico went even further, legislating both a living wage and an eight-hour day in its 1917 constitution.[45]

Not until 1938 did the United States effectively legislate on this front, with Congress enacting the Fair Labor Standards Act. The statute combined regulations of wages and hours, but its approach to the latter was relatively weak, as it did not set upper limits on hours of work. Instead, in a compromise with capital that also accommodated the practical interests of reformist labour organisations that wished to preserve an option to bargain over such matters, the statute addressed the problem of overwork by mandating overtime compensation.[46]

The Fair Labor Standards Act was one of many statutes that advanced the agenda of the International Labour Organisation (ILO). Established in 1919 at the Versailles Peace Conference and under the umbrella of the League of Nations, and now the United Nations, the ILO has been, from its inception, a tireless proponent of bourgeois reformism in this realm.[47] Indeed, the organisation was established around an endorsement of a 'living wage', which it affirmed by its Minimum Wage-Fixing Machinery Convention Number 26 of 1928. Having already endorsed a similar position on hours of work in its Conventions Number 1 and 30, the ILO adopted in 1936 Convention Number 47, the Forty-Hour Week Convention, which 'declares its approval of ... the principle of a forty-hour week applied in such a manner that the standard of living is not reduced in consequence'.

Since its inception, the ILO has adopted nearly 400 conventions, recommendations, and protocols on labour and employment. These are not directly enforceable against employers, however. Instead, the ILO relies on a 'principle-agent' relationship to enforce its standards, a scheme by which the organisation's 185 member countries are obliged to report on their efforts to enforce ILO standards and the ILO is authorised to investigate complaints about their violation. The organisation has no authority over private employers, and cannot impose any sanctions on countries either, even if they or their employers violate these standards. Its power, such as it is, resides mainly in the force of negative publicity.

By the end of the twentieth century, the vast majority of countries had adopted statutes regulating both hours and wages, with the most notable exceptions being those that relied on labour unions to maintain labour standards in these realms. Today about 75 per cent of countries limit weekly hours of work for workers employed outside the home, usually by statutes restricting 'normal' weekly employment at any one employer (and sometimes overall weekly

---

[45]   Finkin, 'Labour Law', 10–14.

[46]   Fair Labor Standards Act, Public Law 75–718, ch 676, 52 *US Statutes at Large* 1060 (25 June 1938).

[47]   On the history of the ILO and the evolution of its social vision, see e.g., Guy Standing, 'The ILO: An Agency for Globalization?' (2008) 39 *Development and Change* 355. On its reconciliation with capitalist precepts see Joshua Taversima Yange, Dokun Oyeshola, and Ayodeji Anthony Aduloju, 'The Politics of Workers Rights Protection: International Labour Organisation and Promotion of Labour Rights in Manufacturing Industry in Nigeria' (2016) 44 *Critique* 267.

employment) to some particular number of hours—usually between 40 and 49.[48] A majority of countries have also adopted legislation establishing a minimum wage, at least for some workers.[49]

Reforms on this front have been more the product of worker agitation and calculated attempts by capitalists and their allies to forestall revolutionary uprisings, rationalise labour markets, and sustain their legitimacy than they have been the result of ILO agitation or other exogenous expressions of bourgeois concern for workers. They also reflect the interests of capital in another, very direct way: by ensuring the efficiency, and even survival, of the people on whom capital relies for labour-power. Indeed, a similar point can be made about the practical function of child labour laws, which also, with the backing of the ILO, flourished in this period, and which not only advanced the interests of children but facilitated their better training for future employment. As Marx observed in volume one of *Capital*, '[t]he maintenance and reproduction of the working class remains a necessary condition for the reproduction of capital'. And while some of this might be left to the workers' 'drives for self-preservation', this approach to the problem would only go so far.[50]

Indeed, what Marx called the 'reproduction of the working class' is essential to the reformist logic of modern labour and employment law—and not just in regard to workers' need for rest, sustenance, shelter, and the like, or even education at a young age, but also in the most basic sense of human reproduction, which emerged at an early stage as an area of both agitation and accommodation. Industrial capitalism, at its most anarchical and rapacious, had proved relatively incompatible with the efficient employment of women. Among the reasons for this was that pregnancy, child-rearing, and care for male workers conflicted with the commodification of women's working time, especially as industrial capitalism reordered work around rigid schedules. These conflicts unfolded in a context in which motherhood and domestic work remained socially necessary labour, which it fell to women to perform.[51]

The English Factory Acts, which reduced the maximum working time of women and children, represented a compromise on this issue, albeit one that conceded much to a sexual division of labour under capitalism. Amid continued growth in the demand for labour-power and the progressive evisceration of extended family structures and customary privileges in the workplace, reconciling the burdens of maternity with the mandates of production remained important. The result was a long struggle for further reforms, spearheaded by women themselves, which developed in earnest during the late nineteenth century. As reflected in the ILO's early and consistent support for its initiatives, this broad agenda was largely endorsed by bourgeois reformers by the 1920s. But this did not mean that capitalists simply acceded to this program, least of all when it imposed on them direct costs that they, as individuals or entities, would just as soon let someone else bear. Nevertheless, by the end of the last century, an overwhelming majority of states had adopted laws requiring pregnancy or maternity (and

---

[48]   ILO, *ILO Working Conditions Laws Report, 2012* (2013) 6–19.
[49]   ILO, *ILO Working Conditions Laws Report, 2012*, 52–63. For a review of recent activism on this front see Deborah M Figart, *Living Wage Movements: Global Perspectives* (Routledge 2004).
[50]   Marx, *Capital,* vol 1, 718.
[51]   Among many informative discussions of this topic see e.g., Johanna Brenner, *Women and the Politics of Class* (Monthly Review Press 2000); Robert Albritton and Dennis Badeen, 'Political Economy and Childcare: A Levels-of-Analysis Approach' (2017) 29 *Rethinking Marxism* 384; Lindsey German, 'Marxism, Class and Women's Oppression' (2008) 6 *Critical and Radical Social Work* 141; Margaret Benston, 'The Political Economy of Women's Liberation' (1969) 21 *Monthly Review* 13.

sometimes paternity) leave, usually with some measure of continued compensation, just as they adopted child labour laws paired with compulsory, usually state-subsidised education systems.[52]

These developments demonstrate clearly that the reformist impulses underlying labour and employment law remain captive to the mandates of capitalism, even when they yield tangible improvements for workers. On the one hand, reforms have proven to be of immeasurable value in protecting childhood from the most destructive effects of wage labour and abetting the liberation of women from what Lenin famously characterised as domestic slavery.[53] On the other hand, these same reforms made it possible for women to occupy the ranks of wage labour, and to be exploited in that capacity, that much more effectively.

The incorporation of women, especially married women, into the capitalist labour market subjected many more women to the same inexorable exploitation that men experienced. But it also eroded the cultural and political foundations of the 'family wage', leaving capitalists free to pay all workers less without compromising the ability of the working class to reproduce itself.[54] Yet, despite this, as bourgeois reformers with the ILO readily acknowledge, the conditions of women workers remain worse than those of men, and not only because of wage discrimination between men and women in similar jobs but also because of the continued exclusion of women from the more lucrative jobs that remain relatively scarce in capitalist society.[55]

The effort to redress racial, ethnic, and gender inequality in the workplace unfolded even later—and to different, though similarly contradictory, ends. Although the roots of reform in this field can be traced back to the political revolutions of the eighteenth and nineteenth centuries, including the US Civil War, a more immediate impetus can be found in the proliferation of human rights concepts in the wake of the Second World War. Especially important in this regard was the ILO and its Convention on Discrimination in Respect of Employment and Occupation Number 111, which the ILO adopted in 1958.[56]

It was in this period that national legislation also began to proliferate, with the United States leading the way (outside the Soviet bloc) by enacting a spate of 'fair employment' statutes that sought to uproot inequitable workplace practices. Driven partly by a desire to parry criticisms about the treatment of women and racial minorities in the United States by Soviet diplomats and representatives of national liberation movements, these laws were promoted domestically by shifting coalitions of liberal and left-wing unions, civil rights organisations, and liberal reformers.[57] They began to come into their own in the early 1960s, when the US Congress

[52]   ILO, *ILO Working Conditions Laws Report, 2012*, 33–41; ILO, *ILO World Social Protection Report, 2017–2019* (2017) 28–43. For revealing examples from an extensive literature that documents the complicated politics behind the adoption of these laws, see Natalie M Fousekis, *Demanding Child Care: Women's Activism and the Politics of Welfare, 1940–1971* (University of Illinois Press 2011); Rob Clark, 'Child Labor in the World Polity: Decline and Persistence, 1980–2000' (2011) 89 *Social Forces* 1033.
[53]   VI Lenin, 'Capitalism and Female Labour' in VI Lenin, *Collected Works*, vol 36 (first published 1913, Progress Publishers 1971) 230.
[54]   Brenner, *Women and the Politics of Class*, 11–58.
[55]   See e.g., ILO, *Women at Work: Trends, 2016* (2016).
[56]   Roger Blanpain, 'Equality of Treatment in Employment' in *International Encyclopedia of Comparative Law*, vol 15 (Mohr, Siebeck 2014) ch 10, 3–6.
[57]   See e.g., Mary L Dudziak, 'Desegregation as a Cold War Imperative' (1988) 41 *Stanford Law Review* 61; Meredith L Roman, *Opposing Jim Crow: African Americans and the Soviet Indictment of U.S. Racism, 1928–1937* (University of Nebraska Press 2012).

enacted the Equal Pay Act of 1963, followed by the more effective Civil Rights Act of 1964, Title VII of which directly concerned employment discrimination.[58]

Over the next 50 years, most countries followed the United States in enacting their own laws to address problems of workplace inequality. Like US laws, such legislation initially focused on race, sex, religion, and national origin, before expanding also to include disability, age, gender and sexual orientation, and political opinion. These systems vary widely in how they have proposed to remedy inequality, some by means of civil penalties and others with 'affirmative action' schemes. They also differ in their administrative structures, with some embracing private litigation against individual employers and others putting the state in the position of prosecuting violations. Running through most every country's approach to these issues, though, is the practice, pioneered in America and endorsed by the ILO, of conceptualising inequality above all as *discrimination*.[59]

This emphasis on discrimination has proved both uniquely problematic and uniquely revealing of the limits of reform within the framework of capitalism and wage labour. Because institutional employers proliferate, decision-making is complicated, and actors often effectively conceal or do not even comprehend their own biases, courts and legislatures have been able to preserve the functionality of laws premised on discrimination only by conjuring a dizzying array of doctrines that establish what it means to discriminate in the first place.[60] Precisely because these efforts to operationalise discrimination have not been—and could never have been—fully successful, this area of law remains mired in unrelenting complaints about over-inclusiveness, as exemplified by strident charges that it has placed excessive burdens on business or caused 'reverse discrimination'. This is true even as other critics argue with good reason that the law in this area has not gone far enough to address problems of workplace inequality.[61]

At the same time, the conceptual difficulties inherent in rooting out discrimination have shaped employment inequality as a problem that consists less of structural issues like the accumulated effects of racial or sexual divisions of labour, the scarcity of decent employment, or the long-standing efforts of capitalists to divide the working class, than of issues involving racism, sexism, and other deviations from what is presumed to be the legitimate way that the capitalist labour market should function.[62] In modern workplaces, it is typical for workers to be each other's managers and supervisors, who are likely in any case to have conflicts among themselves. In this context, developing the law around the concept of discrimination has the further effect of presenting the problem of workplace inequality as a set of dysfunctions among

---

[58]   Blanpain, 'Equality of Treatment in Employment', 3–10; Equal Pay Act, Public Law 88–3877, *US Statutes at Large* 56 (10 June 1963); Civil Rights Act, Public Law 88–352, 78 *US Statutes at Large* 241 (2 July 1964).

[59]   Evelyn Ellis and Philippa Watson, *EU Anti-Discrimination Law* (OUP 2012); Blanpain, 'Equality of Treatment in Employment'.

[60]   Ellis and Watson, *EU-Anti-Discrimination Law*, 143–69; Blanpain, 'Equality of Treatment in Employment', 11–21, 52–54.

[61]   On the resulting controversies, see Robert K Fullinwider, *The Reverse Discrimination Controversy: A Moral and Legal Analysis* (Rowman & Littlefield 1980).

[62]   Among critiques of this kind, see e.g., Ellen Berrey, 'Breaking Glass Ceilings, Ignoring Dirty Floors: The Culture and Class Bias of Diversity Management' (2014) 58 *American Behavioral Scientist* 347. See also Judith Stein, *Running Steel, Running America: Race, Economic Policy, and the Decline of Liberalism* (University of North Carolina Press 1998).

workers that employers may address by reframing their appetite to control and exploit workers in the language of civil rights, 'inclusion', and 'diversity'.[63] From a critical perspective, this entire system looms as dysfunctional, if not fraudulent. But then is there any other way to legislate workplace fairness or equality within the context of an economic order that is inherently unfair, exploitative, and ultimately little more than an engine of inequality?

A similar judgment may be made about attempts to redress related problems of unemployment and retirement with government-sponsored benefits. First instituted locally in Belgium and Switzerland in the 1890s, these systems also proliferated throughout much of Europe in the early twentieth century, before eventually being adopted in the United States through the 1935 Social Security Act. They have since spread over much of the world. However, unlike legal accommodations for pregnancy and maternity, for instance, regulation in these areas has remained limited in scope. Today only about half of the world's states provide some measure of legal protection against unemployment at the national level. Among these countries, insurance programs represent the dominant approach, alongside severance and mandatory employment schemes and savings plans, often backed by government-sponsored pension programs.[64]

That support for the unemployed and the aged is so limited no doubt reflects the fact that such benefits are costly and yet neither central to the reproduction of the working class nor an area of sustained working-class agitation. Unemployed workers, like those who are retired, are of no direct value to capitalists. And while they have at times posed enough of a threat of disorder to warrant some accommodation, they have never been as well-organised—and therefore as threatening—as unions.[65]

Regulation in this context is particularly vulnerable to a dynamic that generally discourages the provision of benefits to poor and working people. From the outset, policies that aid workers and other marginalised persons have operated on the principle of distinguishing 'sturdy beggars' from the 'undeserving'. They have thereby maintained, as Jeremy Bentham—a man whose own intellectual life was an evolving testament to the contradictions of capitalism and free labour—put it, the 'lesser eligibility' of drawing benefits compared to unsupported labour market participation. From the vantage point of capitalists, this is often best served by providing workers with the most limited of benefits, if any at all.

When benefits are extended for unemployment or retirement, they are often secured through insurance schemes. This reflects a different way that class interests prevail, notwithstanding the modest benefits of reform and the rhetoric of social settlement. Insofar as labour is the source of all value, every benefit that workers receive is ultimately paid by the working class itself. But how this happens varies; and with insurance systems, the costs are borne directly by the workers themselves.

No less problematic have been legal reforms that address workplace injuries and deaths. By the middle decades of the twentieth century, laws that mandated inspection of risks and compensation for workplace injuries and deaths, and that operationalised the principle that

---

[63]   Ahmed A White, 'My Coworker, My Enemy: Solidarity, Workplace Control, and the Class Politics of Title VII' (2015) 63 *Buffalo Law Review* 1061. See also Vicki Schultz, 'The Sanitized Workplace' (2003) 112 *Yale Law Journal* 2061.

[64]   ILO, *ILO World Social Protection Report, 2017–2019*, 44–99.

[65]   On the role of threats of social disorder in the rise of welfare policies, see e.g., Frances Fox Piven and Richard A Cloward, *Poor People's Movements: Why They Succeed, How They Fail* (Vintage 1978); Ian Levitt, *Poverty and Welfare in Scotland 1890–1948* (Edinburgh University Press 1988).

employers had some duty to protect their workers from such risks, were embraced by all industrialised countries.[66]

Importantly, at the centre of these schemes was a move to socialise, rationalise, and to some degree limit the costs that injuries and illnesses imposed on employers.[67] Despite the prevalence of workers' compensation, as well as vast improvements in science, engineering, and medicine, between two and three million people die each year from occupational accidents and diseases.

Nearly 300 million in total incur serious non-fatal injuries at work.[68] It is probably true that these numbers would be much higher in the absence of all regulations. Still, it is hard not to understand these tolls as further proof of how unfree labour is destined to remain when legal reforms yield to the mandates of capital accumulation, and when the 'freedom' authorised by free labour consists above all in the freedom to submit to a system premised on alienation and exploitation.

CONCLUSION

In one of the many richly ironic passages that can be found in the first volume of *Capital*, Marx observes that the capitalist 'profits not only by what he receives from the worker, but also by what he gives him'.[69] Marx's main concern in saying this was to underscore the contradictions inherent in wage labour, and the way the dependencies it created ultimately inured to the benefit of the capitalists. But these words have a transcendent relevance for understanding the essential nature of labour and employment law in capitalist society.

What employers have given in the name of reform and the freedom of labour remains just that—a set of concessions that may benefit workers, but never to the point of stifling the process of capital accumulation, and which serve a vision of freedom that is itself captive to the logic of capitalist social order.

It may be foolish to discount the value of legal reforms. But it seems even more foolish to mistake them as means of genuine change. In this light, it seems essential to recognise that if this chapter's review of labour and employment law is a lesson in the limits of legal reform in this realm, it is also a reminder of the true prerequisites of real change. And in this regard, nothing is so apt in closing this chapter as Lenin's admonition to the comrades, in *The State and Revolution*, to remember that 'bourgeois states are exceedingly variegated, but their

---

[66] Charles H Verrill, Lindley Daniel Clark, and Royal Meeker, *Workmen's Compensation Laws of the United States and Foreign Countries* (GPO 1914); ILO, *Factory Inspection: Historical Development and Present Organization in Certain Countries* (Kundig 1923); Waclaw Szubert, 'Safety and Health at Work' in *International Encyclopedia of Comparative Law*, vol 15 (Mohr, Siebeck 2014) ch 7, 4–6; Guy Perrin, 'Occupational Risks and Social Security' in *International Encyclopedia of Comparative Law*, vol 15 (Mohr, Siebeck 2014) ch 8; John G Fleming, 'Tort Liability for Workplace Injury' in *International Encyclopedia of Comparative Law*, vol 15 (Mohr, Siebeck 2014) ch 9.

[67] For a critical review of the history of these schemes, see Grant Duncan, 'Workers' Compensation and the Governance of Pain' (2003) 32 *Economy and Society* 449, 450–54.

[68] ILO, 'Safety and Health at Work', https://www.ilo.org/global/topics/safety-and-health-at-work/lang--en/index.htm accessed 7 April 2021; ILO, *ILO Report for World Day for Safety and Health at Work* (2007). On improvements in developed countries, see Ussif Al-Amin, 'An International Analysis of Workplace Injuries' (2004) 127 *Monthly Labor Review* 41.

[69] Marx, *Capital*, vol 1, 718.

essence is the same: in one way or another, all of these states are in the last analysis inevitably a dictatorship of the bourgeoisie'.[70]

---

[70]   VI Lenin, *State and Revolution* (first published 1917, International Publishers 2011) 31.

18. Karl Marx, Douglass North, and postcolonial states: The relation between law and development

BS Chimni

INTRODUCTION

The relation between law and development has been examined by a great many social, political, and economic theorists, from Adam Smith through Karl Marx to Max Weber and ultimately more recent scholars such as Douglass North. This chapter offers a *preliminary* appreciation and critique from a Marxist perspective of Douglass North's views on the relation between law and legal institutions and development in postcolonial states. There are at least four reasons that compel engagement with North's work. First, his views on the significance of law and legal institutions for development 'permeate institutional economics and economic history' and have become part of the common sense of contemporary governance.[1] Second, he has 'had an important policy influence over the World Bank and other major institutions involved in economic development'.[2] While the policies and approaches of the World Bank have undergone change, the core insight that effective laws and legal institutions, or more broadly the prevalence of 'rule of law', are crucial to the development process remains.[3] Third, North has drawn from Marxism to focus in his work on 'institutions, property rights, the state, and ideology'.[4] However, importantly, he has also departed from Marxism by jettisoning much that is significant to its understanding of the role of law and legal institutions in the development process. These include Marxism's central insights on the nature of capitalism, the significance of the social category 'class', and the internal relationship between capitalism and imperialism. Fourth, North's work helps to shed light on the unfortunate neglect by left parties

---

[1] Geoffrey M Hodgson, 'Introduction to the Douglass C. North Memorial Issue' (2017) 13 *Journal of Institutional Economics* 1, 2. Alvaro Santos has written that: '[t]he idea that the legal system is crucial for economic growth now forms part of the conventional wisdom in development theory. This idea's most common expression is the "rule of law" (ROL): a legal order consisting of predictable, enforceable and efficient rules required for a market economy to flourish.'
   Alvaro Santos, 'The World Bank's Uses of the "Rule of Law" Promise in Economic Development' in David Trubek and Alvaro Santos (eds), *The New Law and Economic Development: A Critical Appraisal* (CUP 2006) 253, 253. North's views have been developed further by others; see e.g., Daron Acemoglu and James A Robinson, *Why Nations Fail: The Origins of Power, Prosperity and Poverty* (Profile Books 2012).
[2] Hodgson, 'Introduction', 2.
[3] For changing World Bank approaches to the relationship between 'law' and 'development', see Shalini Randeria and Lys Kulamadayil, 'Promise and Pitfalls of Polytheism: A Critique of The World Development Report 2017' (2020) 12 *Revue internationale de politique de développement*, https://journals.openedition.org/poldev/3227 accessed 7 April 2021; Santos, 'The World Bank's Use of the "Rule of Law" Promise'.
[4] Douglass C North, *Structure and Change in Economic History* (WW Norton & Co 1981) 61.

and movements, especially in many postcolonial nations, of the important role of law and legal institutions in resisting and reforming the capitalist dispensation. For all these reasons it is worth making a critical assessment of his work.[5]

The chapter proceeds as follows. First, I touch on North's contention that effective institutions matter in promoting economic growth. More specifically, I note North's argument that the presence of a legal system that effectively enforces contractual and property rights, reducing transaction and production costs, are crucial to the development prospects of postcolonial nations. I contend that while North's views on the role of law and legal institutions are important, he does not fully appreciate the nature and working of capitalism. Above all, he does not consider the impact of imperialism, eliminating an important basis of analysis of the role of laws and legal institutions in postcolonial states. North also works with a narrow concept of development and a formalist definition of the state that do not take seriously class, gender, and other divides in capitalist societies, thereby neglecting the distributive outcomes resulting from the functioning of laws and legal institutions in postcolonial states. Second, I argue that it would nevertheless be a mistake to dismiss North's stress on the role of law and legal institutions in the development process. I offer in this context some reflections on Marx and Engels' views on the relative autonomy of law and legal institutions in a capitalist system. I conclude that parties and movements of the left must take law and legal institutions seriously as these can have a significant impact on the development prospects of postcolonial states, explaining why they have emerged as a key site of struggle. Third, and finally, I argue that this view is strengthened by the vision of development which accompanies the peoples' democratic revolutions (PDRs), the programmatic goal of many left movements in postcolonial nations, such as the Communist Party of India (Marxist).[6] I argue that North unfortunately equates

---

[5]   For a general assessment of different law-and-development approaches to nations of the global South, albeit from a non-Marxist perspective, see generally Bui Ngoc Son, 'Law and Development Theory: A Dialogical Engagement' (2019) 51 *George Washington International Law Review* 65; Yong-Shik Lee, 'General Theory of Law and Development' (2017) 50 *Cornell International Law Journal* 415.

[6]   The meaning of 'people's democratic revolution' is spelled out in the Party Programme of Communist Party of India (Marxist), Part VI of which is titled 'People's Democracy and Its Programme' and states that the Party: 'places before the people as the immediate objective, the establishment of people's democracy based on the coalition of all genuine anti-feudal, anti-monopoly and anti-imperialist forces led by the working class on the basis of a firm worker-peasant alliance. This demands first and foremost the replacement of the present bourgeois landlord State by a State of people's democracy. This alone can complete the unfinished democratic task of the Indian revolution and pave the way for putting the country on the road to socialism.'

The text of the programme is available at https://cpim.org/party-programme accessed 7 April 2021. Prabhat Patnaik provides a useful commentary: 'The people's democratic revolution is a rich and complex concept. Since it entails a carrying forward of the democratic revolution i.e., completion by the proletariat of the task that the bourgeoisie historically had undertaken, its objective is to remove the fetters upon the most through-going bourgeois development; *it creates therefore the conditions for the most vigorous and the most broad-based capitalist development.* At the same time, since it is the proletariat that leads the people's democratic revolution, it is not content only to create conditions for the most through-going capitalist development, and then sit back and watch capitalism unfold in its full vigor; rather, it unleashes a historical process where the people's democratic revolution leads on to the socialist revolution. Once the proletariat has acquired a "subject" role, it does not withdraw from that role; rather it uses that role to ensure that the people's democratic revolution leads on to the socialist revolution over a more or less protracted period of time.'

development with capital accumulation and economic growth; his focus is on increased productivity, technological progress, and economic 'performance'. On the other hand, left visions of development in postcolonial states tend to subscribe to some variant of Amartya Sen's idea of 'development as freedom'.[7] The latter models of development foreground the need to enhance individual capabilities through an affirmation of civil and political rights on the one hand and social, cultural, and economic rights on the other.[8] It is also pointed out that Marx did not reject but merely exposed the limits of bourgeois rights, these being dispensable only in a communist society.

A CRITIQUE OF NORTH'S THESIS

A central question that sociologist Max Weber addressed in his work on legal institutions is their nature and relationship to development in Western societies. As law-and-development scholar David Trubek has observed, Weber believed that 'European law was more "rational" than the legal systems of other civilizations, that is, it was more highly differentiated (or autonomous), consciously constructed, general, and universal'.[9] It was his view that other civilisations 'failed to develop the religious ideas, political structures, and economic interests which facilitated the growth of rational law in Europe'.[10] Like Weber, North believed that Western societies had grasped the significance of institutions, including legal institutions, to the growth process. North defined 'institutions' as consisting of both formal and informal constraints: 'Institutions are the *humanly devised constraints* that structure political, economic and social interaction. They consist of both *informal constraints* (sanctions, taboos, customs, traditions, and codes of conduct), and *formal rules* (constitutions, laws, property rights).'[11] In his view, institutions are important because they 'enable ordered thought, expectation, and action by

---

Prabhat Patnaik, 'The CPI (M) and the Building of Capitalism' International Development Economics Associates blog (30 January 2008), available at http://www.networkideas.org/news-analysis/2008/01/the-cpim-and-the-building-of-capitalism/ accessed 7 April 2021 (original emphasis). For a classic study see Francis J Kase, *People's Democracy: A Contribution to the Study of the Communist Theory of State and Revolution* (Leyden 1968).

[7] Amartya Sen, *Development as Freedom* (OUP 1999).

[8] To be sure, there are areas of divergence arising from Sen's attempt to combine the insights of both Smith and Marx. What he also does not do is to indicate how the goal of 'development as freedom' is to be realised in a capitalist society that is constrained by imperialism. Prabhat Patnaik, 'Amartya Sen and the Theory of Public Action' (1998) 33 *Economic & Political Weekly* 2855; BS Chimni, 'The Sen Conception of Development and Contemporary International Law: Some Parallels' (2008) 1 *Law and Development Review* 2.

[9] David M Trubek, 'Max Weber on Law and the Rise of Capitalism' (1972) 1972 *Wisconsin Law Review* 720, 724.

[10] Trubek, 'Max Weber', 724.

[11] Douglass C North, 'Institutions' (1991) 5 *Journal of Economic Perspective* 97, 97 (emphases added). Elsewhere he has also written as follows: 'Institutions are the rules of the game in society or, more formally, are the humanly devised constraints that shape human interaction. In consequence they structure incentives in human exchange, whether political, social, or economic. ... Conceptually, what must be clearly differentiated are the rules from the players. The purpose of the rules is to define the way the game is played. But the objective of the team within that set of rules is to win the game. ... Modeling the strategies and the skills of the team as it develops is a separate process from modeling the creation, evolution, and consequences of the rules.'

imposing form and consistency on human activities'.[12] They can thereby play a crucial role in reducing transaction and production costs:

> Together with the standard constraints of economics they [i.e., institutions] define the choice set and therefore determine transaction and production costs and hence the profitability and feasibility of engaging in economic activity. They evolve incrementally, connecting the past with the present and the future; history in consequence is largely a story of institutional evolution in which the historical performance of economies can only be understood as a part of a sequential story.[13]

In sum, by enforcing contract and property rights, both tangible and intangible, the legal system promotes economic growth, facilitating the smooth flow of goods, services, investment, and finance within and across borders. The role of the state in creating and sustaining effective institutions is crucial. But the state, for new institutional economists like North, is a neutral actor which stands above social divides.[14] In other words, North emphasised that economic growth was facilitated by a robust legal system and a neutral state enforcing contractual and property rights.[15] It is evident that North's claims essentially concern the conditions for the operation of an efficient market economy. Indeed, new institutional economists have defined the market:

> as a set of social institutions in which a large number of commodity exchanges of a specific type regularly take place, and to some extent are facilitated, and structured by these institutions. Exchange ... involves contractual agreement and the exchange of property rights, and the market consists in part of mechanisms to structure, organize, and legitimate these activities. Markets, in short, are organized and institutionalized exchange.[16]

But it is recognised that for effective enforcement of contractual and property rights, a number of other legal initiatives may have to be taken, including but not limited to 'a corporate law regime that facilitates the capital investment function; a bankruptcy regime that induces the exit of inefficient firms and rapid redeployment of their assets to higher valued uses; and

---

Douglass C North, *Institutions, Institutional Change and Economic Performance* (CUP 1990) 3–5. There is, however, no consensus on the meaning and scope of application of the term 'institution'. Hodgson defines 'institutions' as 'systems of established and prevalent social rules that structure social interactions. Language, money, law, systems of weights and measures, table manners, and firms (and other organizations) are thus all institutions'. An institution is also 'a special type of social structure that involves potentially codifiable and (evidently or immanently) normative rules of interpretation and behavior'. Geoffrey M Hodgson, 'What are Institutions?' (2006) 40 *Journal of Economic Issues* 1, 2, 4.

[12]   Hodgson, 'What are Institutions?', 2.

[13]   North, 'Institutions', 97. See also Acemoglu and Robinson, *Why Nations Fail*, 73–75.

[14]   Sean P Stacy, 'Government vs. Private Ownership—A Fresh Look at the Merits of Bank Privatization in Developing Economies' (2012) 12 *UC Davis Business Law Journal* 243, 245.

[15]   Elsewhere, North has written that: 'well-specified and enforced property rights, a necessary condition for economic growth, are only secure when political and civil rights are secure; otherwise arbitrary confiscation is always a threat. Also credible commitment—an essential condition for the creation of capital markets—is not possible without an effective legal system, one that will impartially and systematically enforce agreements across time and space.'

Douglass C North, 'The Paradox of the West' in RW Davis (ed), *The Origins of Modern Freedom in the West* (Stanford University Press 1995) 7, 7–8.

[16]   Geoffrey M Hodgson, *Economics and Institutions: A Manifesto for a Modern Institutional Economics* (Polity Press 1988) 174.

a non-punitive, non-distortionary tax regime'.[17] It is in the matrix of this neo-institutionalist thinking that the World Bank attempted to identify key indicators of successful markets by way of its 'Ease of Doing Business' index.[18] North's view of the positive relationship between effective legal institutions and socio-economic development also explains why the World Bank has spent billions of dollars on exporting its law-and-development project to postcolonial nations. The World Bank, however, focuses on a range of issues, including 'enhancing legal education; implementing judicial reform; constitution or code drafting; transplanting laws and institutions; law enforcement training; combating corruption; educating lay people about the law; providing access to the law for the poor; and supplying material assistance for legal institution building (including basics like office supplies, computers, and legal materials)'.[19] The underlying vision of its law-and-development program is currently promulgated through, among other things, its 'Global Forum on Law, Justice and Development'.[20] This forum has fostered knowledge initiatives in the area of law, justice, and development, such as an annual 'Law, Justice, and Development Week' and the publication of the *World Bank Legal Review*.

Before turning to the critique of North, two additional points are in order. First, North admits that a simple change in formal legal rules may not suffice to facilitate the lowering of transaction or production costs. Informal rules or societal culture are just as important, sometimes even more so. In this view societies that are underdeveloped embody belief systems that 'fail to confront and solve new problems of societal complexity'.[21] As a result, 'efforts to reform simply by establishing or changing formal (legal) rules have been … unsuccessful'.[22] For North, 'culture defines the way individuals process and utilize information and hence may affect the way informal constraints get specified'.[23] Societal culture can therefore either undermine or reinforce formal rules. In the case of India, for instance, the oppressive caste system which seeks to confine Dalits, lowest in the caste hierarchy, to particular professions distorts the operations of legal institutions. The concept of culture is inclusive of 'legal culture', which can 'include underlying values or principles of a legal system, as well as traditions, shared

---

[17] Kevin E Davis and Michael J Trebilcock, 'Legal Reforms and Development' (2001) 22 *Third World Quarterly* 21, 23.

[18] World Bank, *Doing Business 2020: Comparing Business Regulation in 190 Economies* (2020), http://documents.worldbank.org/curated/en/688761571934946384/pdf/Doing-Business-2020 -Comparing-Business-Regulation-in-190-Economies.pdf accessed 7 April 2021. This report states that '[r]esearch demonstrates a causal relationship between economic freedom and gross domestic product (GDP) growth, where freedom regarding wages and prices, property rights, and licensing requirements leads to economic development' (2).

[19] Brian Z Tamanaha, 'The Primacy of Society and the Failures of Law and Development' (2001) 44 *Cornell International Law Journal* 209, 217.

[20] See the website of the World Bank's Global Forum on Law, Justice and Development, http:// globalforumljd.com/new/ accessed 7 April 2021. The preamble of its charter states that 'strong legal and judicial institutions are an important cornerstone of sustainable economic and social development'. World Bank, Global Forum on Law, Justice and Development—Charter of the GFLJD (2014) 2, http:// globalforumljd.com/new/sites/default/files/documents/aboutUs/gfljd-charter.pdf accessed 7 April 2021.

[21] Douglass C North, 'Economic Performance Through Time' (1994) 84 *American Economic Review* 359, 364.

[22] Hodgson, 'Introduction', 7.

[23] North, *Institutions, Institutional Change and Economic Performance*, 42.

beliefs, common ways of thinking, constellations of interests or patterns of allegiances of lawyers, lawmakers, and citizens'.[24]

Second, North understands organisations to be a special kind of institution.[25] According to Geoffrey Hodgson, another prominent institutional economist, North recognised that 'it is possible for organizations to be treated as actors in some circumstances *and* generally to be regarded as institutions'.[26] North described organisations as follows:

> Organizations are the players: groups of individuals bound by a common purpose to achieve objectives. They include political bodies (political parties, the senate, a city council, a regulatory agency); economic bodies (firms, trade unions, family farms, cooperatives); social bodies (churches, clubs, athletic associations); and educational bodies (schools, colleges, vocational training centers).[27]

On the international plane, examples of such organisations can be said to include the United Nations, the International Monetary Fund, the World Bank, and the World Trade Organisation.

To sum up, North's aim in emphasising the role of institutions in the development process is not to replace market or neoclassical economics with new institutional economics but simply to offer 'a modification of neoclassical theory'.[28] He only wishes to point to mainstream neoclassical economic theory's failure to appreciate the historical significance of institutions in the development process. More specifically, he argues that such theory is based on 'two erroneous assumptions: (i) that institutions do not matter and (ii) that time does not matter'.[29] In turning to the role of institutions and history North borrows from historical materialism. But he invokes Marx's insights highly selectively, entirely ignoring his incisive critique of capitalism.[30] North thereby neglects the fact that the shape and content of institutions reflect

---

[24]   Roger Cotterrell, 'Comparative Law and Legal Culture' in Mathias Reimann and Reinhard Zimmermann (eds), *The Oxford Handbook of Comparative Law* (2nd edn, OUP 2019) 710, 711.

[25]   'Starting with a definition of institutions as socially embedded systems of rules, it is evident that organizations are a special kind of institution, with additional features. Organizations are special institutions that involve (a) criteria to establish their boundaries and to distinguish their members from nonmembers, (b) principles of sovereignty concerning who is in charge, and (c) chains of command delineating responsibilities within the organization.'
Hodgson, 'What are Institutions?', 8.

[26]   Hodgson, 'What are Institutions?', 10 (original emphasis).

[27]   Douglass C North, 'The New Institutional Economics and Development', 6, http://www2.econ .iastate.edu/tesfatsi/NewInstE.North.pdf accessed 7 April 2021.

[28]   North, 'Economic Performance Through Time', 359. As Milonakis and Fine observe, 'even when he [North] departs from the neoclassical framework through the introduction of institutions and ideology, he does so in a complementary way, to make up for some deficiency in this underlying framework'. Dimitris Milonakis and Ben Fine, 'Douglass North's Remaking of Economic History: A Critical Appraisal' (2007) 39 *Review of Radical Political Economics* 27, 32.

[29]   North, 'Economic Performance', 359.

[30]   According to North, '[t]he Marxian framework is the most powerful of the existing statements of secular change precisely because it includes all of the elements left out of the neoclassical framework: institutions, property rights, the state, and ideology'. North, *Structure and Change in Economic History*, 61. North says of his college experience at the University of California at Berkeley: 'While I was there my life was completely changed by my becoming a Marxist'. He continues: 'Marxism was attractive because it appeared to provide answers to the pressing questions of the time, including the Great Depression that we were in—answers missing from the pre-Keynesian economics that I was taught in 1939–1940'. See 'Douglas C. North' in Roger W Spencer and David A Macpherson (eds), *Lives of the Laureates: Twenty-Three Nobel Economists* (MIT Press 2014) 161, 162. North has also observed that

the distribution of economic and political power in society, both domestic and international. Recognising this problem, even the World Bank has attempted to factor 'power' into its analyses. For instance, the World Bank's 2017 *World Development Report* (WDR17), devoted to the general theme of 'governance and the law', attempts, among other things, to take into account power asymmetries between hegemonic and subaltern social and political forces, both at the national and the international levels. The aim is to meet the objection of critics that earlier the World Bank was narrowly focused on the instrumental dimensions of the rule and role of law.[31] However, the report falls short because it does not address the question as 'to what extent power asymmetries themselves are created by law'.[32] Furthermore, insofar as the World Bank is concerned, since it emphasises economic growth to a greater degree than socially inclusive development, it is unable in practice to take the theme of law and power seriously.[33] Unsurprisingly, WDR17 advances the same prescriptions as it always has:

---

he 'drifted into being a Marxist. Not a Communist, a Marxist. That's a big difference.' North continues: 'I read lots of Marx. That was a big influence on my life, and it still is. I'm not a Marxist any more, but still, he had an enormous impact. Anyway, I went through school and thus became a leader in left-wing activities. Then, World War II came along.' Karen Ilse Horn, 'Douglas C. North' in Karen Ilse Horn, *Roads to Wisdom, Conversations with Ten Nobel Laureates in Economics* (Elgar 2009) 153, 160. But as has been pointed out: 'the major differences which divide North's framework from even the most liberal version of historical materialism can be reduced to their differing choice as to what constitutes the most appropriate basic unit of analysis: The instinct of Marxists is to reach for the group as a place to begin one's analysis, even though not all continue to insist that the most appropriate basic unit of analysis must always be class ... North's neoclassical instincts, by contrast, prompt him to reach for the individual as the appropriate unit of analysis.'

Jon D Wisman, John Willoughby, and Larry Sawers, 'The Search for Grand Theory in Economic History: North's Challenge to Marx' (1988) 55 *Social Research* 747, 751.

[31]   It is 'an attempt to please a variety of constituencies with divergent expectations'. Randeria and Kulamadayil, 'Promise and Pitfalls', para 16. They summarise the discussion of the theme 'law and development' in earlier *World Development Reports* as follows: 'WDR17 is not the first Report to consider the link between law and development. If WDR02 highlighted the importance of the judicial system as an institution necessary for the building of markets, WDR04 and WDR06 underlined the significance of judicial institutions in the delivery of basic services and in securing fair process. And WDR11 alerted us to the weakness or failure of legal institutions being a cause of violence and insecurity. What is distinctive of WDR17 is that it places the role of law at the centre of its thinking on equity, in terms of wealth and power.'

Randeria and Kulamadayil, 'Promise and Pitfalls', para 2.

[32]   Randeria and Kulamadayil, 'Promise and Pitfalls', para 19.

[33]   Elaborating the role of legal institutions, the 2017 *World Development Report* emphasises the significance of both 'rule of law' and the 'role of law': 'Ultimately, the *rule of law*—the impersonal and systematic application of known rules to government actors and citizens alike—is needed for a country to realize its full social and economic potential'. World Bank, *World Development Report 2017: Governance and the Law*, 14 (original emphasis), https://www.worldbank.org/en/publication/wdr2017 accessed 7 April 2021. It continues as follows: 'The WDR 2017 proposes three simple principles to guide those thinking about reform. First, it is important to think not only about what form institutions should have, but also about the *functions* that institutions must perform—that is, think not only about the form of institutions but also about their functions. Second, it is important to think that, although capacity building matters, how to use capacity and where to invest in capacity depend on the relative bargaining powers of actors—that is, think not only about capacity building but also about *power asymmetries*. Third, it is important to think that in order to achieve the rule of law, countries must first strengthen the different roles of law to enhance contestability, change incentives, and reshape preferences—that is, think not only about the rule of law but also about the *role of law*.'

World Development Report 2017, 29 (original emphases).

'A credible commitment to pro-growth policies and property rights is … essential to ensure macroeconomic stability and enable growth'.[34] The critique of North therefore also applies to the current World Bank view on the relationship between law and development.

CAPITALISM AND LEGAL INSTITUTIONS

Nearly all states today are capitalist, of one or another variety.[35] An important shortcoming in North's work is that he relies upon a partial understanding of the capitalist mode of production. He understands capitalism as production for the market by predominantly private enterprises, and the role of legal institutions to be the creation of the appropriate conditions for the efficient functioning of a system premised upon capital accumulation through protecting contractual and property rights.[36] In contrast to this is the explanation of 'capitalism' offered by Marx, which captures its principal feature: '[t]he capitalist mode of production … rests on the fact that the material conditions of production are in the hands of non-workers in the form of property in capital and land, while the masses are only owners of the personal condition of production, of labour power'.[37] Using this understanding, two points need to be made about North's view of the role of law and legal institutions under capitalism. First, while North emphasises the importance of protecting contract rights, he does not appreciate the fact that contracts—and the body of law that sanctifies and enforces them—assumes significance under capitalism from the fact that labour-power is transformed into a commodity which is exchanged on the market.[38] As Soviet legal theorist Evgeny Pashukanis pointed out in his work *The General Theory of Law and Marxism*,[39] it is on account of the fact that under capitalism labour-power is bought and sold on the market that contracts enjoy the status of 'one of the central concepts of law'.[40] The contract between the worker and the capitalist is not just another kind of contract. It represents the legal foundation of capitalism, producing and legitimising in the final analysis

---

[34]   *World Development Report* 2017, 5.

[35]   This understanding is an extension at the global level of Marx's view that '[i]n all forms of society there is one specific kind of production which predominates over the rest, whose relations thus assign rank and influence to the others. It is a general illumination which bathes all the other colours and modifies their particularity.' Karl Marx, *Grundrisse: Foundations of the Critique of Political Economy* (first published 1939, Martin Nicolaus tr, Penguin 1993) 106–7.

[36]   North works with a definition of capitalism advanced by Milton Friedman in his well-known book *Capitalism and Freedom*, namely the 'organization of the bulk of economic activity through private enterprise operating in a free market'. Milton Friedman, *Capitalism and Freedom* (University of Chicago Press 1962) 4.

[37]   Karl Marx, 'Critique of the Gotha Programme' [1875] in Karl Marx and Frederick Engels, *Selected Works*, vol 2 (Foreign Languages Publishing House 1951) 13, 23.

[38]   'Marx viewed the buying and selling of labor power as fundamentally different from the exchange of other goods. The reason is that the former establishes the buyer's right to control human activity within the workplace. And the deal which workers and capitalists strike in the labor market is dependent upon their relative class power. Thus for Marx, beneath the surface reality of markets lies the more causally important social relations of production. It is for this reason that he viewed capitalism as characterized by a distinct class relation rather than a distinct set of property rights.'
Wisman, Willoughby, and Sawers, 'Grand Theory', 767.

[39]   Evgeny Pashukanis, 'General Theory of Law and Marxism' [1924] in Piers Beirne and Robert Sharlet (eds), *Pashukanis: Selected Writings on Marxism and Law* (Academic Press 1980) 37.

[40]   Pashukanis, 'General Theory', 82.

the generation of surplus value, the basis of capital accumulation. In the words of Marx, 'the consumption of labor-power is at one and the same time the production of commodities and of surplus-value'.[41] Similarly, according to political economist Maurice Dobb, what makes labour-power 'unique' among commodities is 'its capacity for yielding a surplus value when put to use'.[42] In other words, the centrality of the contract under capitalism is to be traced to the fact that it is the fundamental basis for generating surplus value, which is then safeguarded by the effective enforcement of property rights.[43] Therefore, any serious proposal to renegotiate distributive outcomes is regarded—certainly by capitalists but also, due to ideological inculcation, by many workers and peasant groups—as threats to the legal institutions requisite for the development process. As a result, trade unions and collective bargaining mechanisms are also often regarded as obstacles in the way of socio-economic development, particularly where the capitalist class has thrown its weight, as it does, behind flexible labour regimes. In short, Marx's account of capitalism explains why North assigns a critical and constitutive role to law and legal institutions in capitalist societies. Capitalist relations of production cannot be sustained without effective contract and property laws in place. If Marx's account is fundamentally correct, and it is, then the left needs to engage in a sustained way with law and legal institutions in order to reconfigure them to the extent possible to the advantage of the labouring classes.

Second, North neglects the internal and historical relationship between capitalism and imperialism. He therefore largely ignores the role of international law and organisations in sustaining the exploitative relations between advanced capitalist states and postcolonial nations. The reality is that contemporary international law and organisations have considerably reduced the policy space available to postcolonial nations, preventing the adoption of legal measures that promote development.[44] Even if it is accepted that North integrates questions of 'interstate conflict fully into his model',[45] what he does not adequately explain is the historical domination and exploitation of some nations by others.[46] This 'omission' is crucial, since imperialism has been the defining feature of international relations since the sixteenth century.[47] In other words, the causes of underdevelopment of postcolonial states are not entirely internal; they are also external, and international law and international organisations have over the centuries

[41]   Karl Marx, *Capital: A Critique of Political Economy*, vol 1 (first published 1867, Samuel Moore and Edward Aveling tr, Progress Publishers 1977) 172.

[42]   Maurice Dobb, 'Introduction' in Karl Marx, *A Contribution to the Critique of Political Economy* (first published 1859, Maurice Dobb ed, SW Ryazanskaya tr, Lawrence & Wishart 1971) 5, 15.

[43]   Of course, there are innumerable kinds of contracts that are entered into in any modern society. Not all contracts are associated with the generation of surplus value. What is being discussed is the principal role of contracts in a capitalist society.

[44]   BS Chimni, 'International Institutions Today: An Imperial State in the Making' (2004) 15 *European Journal of International Law* 1.

[45]   Wisman, Willoughby, and Sawers, 'Grand Theory', 761. Insofar as classical Marxism is concerned, it is Luxemburg who should be credited with having theorised the internal relationship between capitalism and imperialism most thoroughly, though the relevant writings of Lenin, Hilferding, and others should not be forgotten.

[46]   Acemoglu and Robinson concede that 'the profitability of European colonial empires was often built on the destruction of independent polities and indigenous economies around the world'. *Why Nations Fail*, 271. The case of India is discussed at 272. What they do not do is to recognise the phenomenon of imperialism or neocolonialism today.

[47]   Antony Anghie, *Imperialism, Sovereignty, and the Making of International Law* (CUP 2005).

played a critical role in sustaining and legitimising imperialism.[48] So much so that the current phase of international law, and the history of its organisations, could even be dubbed 'legal imperialism'. Yet as law-and-development scholar Chantal Thomas has noted, in North's work, '[i]nternational law and policy tends to be treated as exogenous to analysis, with doctrinal or empirical assessment following from exogenously given rules and institutions'.[49] In general, North is reminiscent of John Rawls, who discusses the virtues of Western liberal democracies without so much as mentioning imperialism in his theory of justice.[50] As political theorist Seyla Benhabib has observed in response, in Rawls' account:

> the plunder of Africa by all western societies is not mentioned even once; the global character of the African slave trade and its contribution to the accumulation of capitalist wealth in the United States and the Caribbean basin are barely recalled; the colonization of the Americas disappears from view; and it is as if the British never dominated India and exploited its riches.[51]

MARX ON LAW AND LEGAL INSTITUTIONS

In contrast to North, who underlines the constitutive role of legal institutions under capitalism, movements of the left in postcolonial states have not paid adequate attention to how such institutions help to entrench capitalist relations of production. A sustained engagement with legal institutions is also necessary because, as Banerjee and Duflo observe, 'details matter. Institutions are no exception. To understand the effect of institutions on the lives of the poor, what is needed is a shift in perspective from INSTITUTIONS in capital letters to institutions in lower case—the "view from below"'.[52] But the fact that Marx famously appeared to confine the role of legal institutions to the 'superstructure' has led the left to disregard its importance, at both the macro and the micro levels, for bringing about social change. Therefore, for any attempt to identify the tasks before the left, a few observations are in order to demonstrate that Marx did in fact understand the complex role of law and legal institutions in bourgeois societies.

If Marx contended that relations of production precede legal relations, it is only in a purely (and unhelpfully) conceptual sense. In concrete reality, the two are joined at the hip, and emerge in parallel. As the historian EP Thompson put it, '[p]roductive relations themselves are, in part, only meaningful in terms of their definitions at law'.[53] That is to say, law consolidates and reinforces relations of production in great part by validating and formalising

---

[48]   For a sketch of this history see BS Chimni, *International Law and World Order: A Critique of Contemporary Approaches* (2nd edn, CUP 2017) 477–99.

[49]   Chantal Thomas, 'Law and Neoclassical Economic Development in Theory and Practice: Toward an Institutionalist Critique of Institutionalism' (2011) 96 *Cornell Law Review* 967, 1023.

[50]   John Rawls, *A Theory of Justice* (Harvard University Press 1971); John Rawls, *The Law of Peoples* (Harvard University Press 2001).

[51]   Seyla Benhabib, *The Rights of Others: Aliens, Residents, and Citizens* (CUP 2004) 99–100. In addition to these two points, it should also be noted that North works with a growth-centric conception of development that does not take into account the importance of (and intersections between) class, gender, and race.

[52]   Abhijit V Banerjee and Esther Duflo, *Poor Economics: Rethinking Poverty and the Ways of Ending It* (Random House 2013) 357–58.

[53]   EP Thompson, *Whigs and Hunters: The Origin of the Black Act* (Pantheon 1975) 267.

specific sets of property claims. This objective was historically achieved through the use of pre-existing or already available legal concepts and categories. As capitalism emerged and developed in northern and western Europe, rules and principles from Roman law, among other sources, were used to protect property entitlements. This was most certainly the case in countries like France and the Netherlands. In *The German Ideology*, Marx and Engels write that:

> [a]s soon as industry and trade developed private property further, first in Italy and later in other countries, the highly developed Roman civil law was immediately adopted ... and raised to authority. When later the bourgeoisie had acquired so much power that the princes took up its interests in order to overthrow the feudal nobility by means of the bourgeoisie, there began in all countries—in France in the sixteenth century—the real development of law, which in all countries except England proceeded on the basis of the Roman Codex. In England, too, Roman legal principles had to be introduced to further the development of civil law (especially in the case of movable property).[54]

In the *Grundrisse*, Marx adds that Roman law 'anticipate[d] (in its basic aspects) the legal relations of industrial society'.[55] In fact, Marx was intrigued by the fact that a capitalist society could use legal concepts and categories first developed in earlier modes of production, but he postponed the matter for reflection in his promised volume on the state. Later, the important Austro-Marxist Karl Renner developed this insight further, arguing that socialism did not call for a dramatic modification of the categories of bourgeois law in his well-known *The Institutions of Private Law and Their Social Functions*. Renner's thesis in this regard is '*that fundamental changes in society are possible without accompanying alterations of the legal system*'.[56] Indeed, he goes so far as to describe some forms of law as 'empty frame[s]', with the norms composing the institution of property itself apparently being 'neutral like an algebraic formula'.[57] Tracing the history of the legal institution of private property from simple commodity production to fully fledged capitalist production and exchange, Renner attempts to show that although the social functions performed by property have undergone transformation, there has been no corresponding change in legal norms. He goes on to argue, more controversially, that the construction of a socialist society is capable of being worked out from within the law. '[N]early all the legal norms which would be applicable in a socialist commonwealth, are already now in existence', Renner writes, adding 'though their functions have not been fully developed'.[58] Renner believed that law and the legal institutions of capitalist society could play an effective role in its transformation to a socialist society. A combination of reformist and revolutionary methods, including the growing powers of the state and its interventions, could make a peaceful transition to 'socialism' possible, a process that did not always and necessarily rule out 'defensive violence'.[59]

---

[54] Karl Marx and Frederick Engels, 'The German Ideology' [1846] in Karl Marx and Frederick Engels, *Selected Works*, vol 1 (Progress Publishers 1973) 16, 78.

[55] Marx, *Grundrisse*, 246.

[56] Karl Renner, *The Institutions of Private Law and Their Social Functions* (first published 1929, O Kahn-Freund ed, Agnes Schwarzschild tr, Routledge & Kegan Paul 1976) 252 (original emphasis).

[57] Renner, *Institutions*, 112, 225. 'Empty frame' is Kahn-Freund's summary description of Renner's position.

[58] Renner, *Institutions*, 83.

[59] Tom Bottomore, 'Introduction' in Tom Bottomore and Patrick Goode (eds), *Austro-Marxism* (Clarendon Press 1978) 1, 40 ff.

In affirming the relative autonomy of law and legal institutions in bourgeois societies, Marx and Engels made a number of observations. In particular, Marx and Engels noted the dialectical relation between the categories 'economic structure' and the different elements of the 'superstructure'; underscored that a legal system has its own internal logic and dynamics, which cannot be disregarded opportunistically; suggested that the legal profession, the judiciary, and 'legal culture' have an important role to play in the shaping of the law and legal institutions; and argued that capitalist law can be reformed, in however limited a manner, to benefit the working classes.[60] Lenin, for his part, also underlined the need for revolutionary parties to work in parliamentary institutions, and also in other legal bodies. In *The State and Revolution*, Lenin writes that 'in the first phase of Communist society (usually called Socialism) "bourgeois right" is *not* abolished in its entirety, but only in part'.[61] Indeed, he goes on to observe that 'not only bourgeois right, but even the bourgeois state for a certain time remains under Communism, without the bourgeoisie!'[62] He also acknowledges the educational value of legislated rights, as can be seen from the spate of legislations, proclamations, decrees, and other legal instruments after the October Revolution.[63] After introducing the New Economic Policy in 1921 as a temporary retreat from the nascent Soviet Union's socialist policies with respect to nationalisation of all means of production, Lenin notes that there was the need to 'work out a *new* civil law, a new attitude to "private" contracts, etc'.[64] He also recognises the need to educate courts on the state of the revolution during the period of state capitalism.[65] Like Marx, after all, Lenin had been trained as a lawyer and was never dismissive of the role of law and legal institutions, neither in capitalist nor in revolutionary societies.

Finally, it is worth noting that in order to promote rapid development, China reconstructed its legal institutions in the aftermath of the Cultural Revolution of the 1960s and 1970s.[66] A large number of legal reforms have been undertaken since 1978, when Deng Xiaoping established himself as China's paramount political leader. Many changes have been introduced in the Chinese legal system since then, especially in regard to the protection of private property. Importantly, many of these reforms are reflected in the 1982 Chinese Constitution, which has been amended five times since first entering into force (in 1988, 1993, 1999, 2004,

[60]   Chimni, *International Law and World Order*, 449–61.
[61]   VI Lenin, 'The State and Revolution' [1917] in VI Lenin, *Selected Works*, vol 2 (Foreign Languages Publishing House 1947) 141, 205 (original emphasis).
[62]   Lenin, 'The State and Revolution', 208.
[63]   See generally John Quigley, *Soviet Legal Innovation and the Law of the Western World* (CUP 2007).
[64]   VI Lenin, 'On the Tasks of the People's Commissariat for Justice under the New Economic Policy' [1922] in VI Lenin, *Collected Works*, vol 36 (Progress Publishers 1966) 560, 562 (original emphasis).
[65]   While Lenin correctly assessed that it was important to use legal forums for exposing bourgeois regimes, he did not, given the historical situation of the times, fully appreciate the importance of legal institutions in limiting the powers of the Soviet state for the production of democratic socialism. This subsequently had important consequences as the Soviet state conflated the idea of rule of law with the rule of the party.
[66]   Liu Dongjin, 'China's Economic Legal System in Changing Times' in David K Linnan (ed), *Legitimacy, Legal Development and Change: Law and Modernization Reconsidered* (Ashgate 2011) 123; Perry Keller (ed) *Law and the Market Economy in China* (Ashgate 2011); Perry Keller (ed), *Obligations and Property Rights in China* (Ashgate 2011); Perry Keller (ed), *The Citizen and the Chinese State* (Ashgate 2011).

and 2018 respectively).[67] They are also reflected in the Chinese Property Rights Law of 2007.[68] Numerous judicial institutions have been created anew during this period.[69] The efforts that Chinese authorities have taken to protect property and contractual rights does not necessarily validate the law-and-development model that North espoused.[70] The experience can well demonstrate the Renner thesis that bourgeois legal categories and institutions can be used in a non-capitalist society with transformed social relations. That China cannot be described as a socialist society, what with its denial of civil and political rights to Chinese citizens, is another matter. But there is no denying the importance of an effective legal system.

It is against the backdrop of these views and practices that underscore the relative autonomy of law and legal institutions that the tasks of the left in postcolonial states need to be identified. It is also useful to keep in mind that such an exercise is supported by the reality that in recent years legal institutions have become key sites of social struggle in many postcolonial states.[71] Summarily stated, the tasks of the left include taking law-making seriously to bring benefits to poor and marginalised groups, ensuring that employment contracts do not result in the full subordination of the working class to capital, unpacking and reconfiguring property rights in favour of the weak and for the promotion of the common good (e.g., through remunicipalising services that are being privatised), safeguarding both civil and political rights and social, economic, and cultural rights contained in domestic law and international conventions, retrieving policy space from international law and institutions so that an independent path of development can be pursued, and critically reviewing the state of legal education and legal scholarship. There is no excuse for not paying enough attention to legal battles in the postcolonial world, as the concept of development the left supports in the context of PDRs focus on the realisation of bourgeois rights. Towards that end, struggles around laws and legal institutions assume a certain salience. A few words may therefore be said on the vision of development that is most often embraced by the left.

---

[67] An English translation of the Constitution of the People's Republic of China is available at http://english.www.gov.cn/archive/lawsregulations/201911/20/content_WS5ed8856ec6d0b3f0e9499913.html accessed 7 April 2021.

[68] An unofficial English translation of the act, which was revised in 2015, is available at http://www.lehmanlaw.com/fileadmin/lehmanlaw_com/laws___regulations/Propoerty_Rights_Law_of_the_PRC__LLX__03162007.pdf accessed 7 April 2021. For a summary, see Laney Zhang, 'Chinese Law on Private Ownership of Real Property' (2015), available at https://blogs.loc.gov/law/2015/03/chinese-law-on-private-ownership-of-real-property/ accessed 7 April 2021.

[69] See generally Randall Peerenboom, 'Social Foundations of China's Living Constitution' in Tom Ginsburg (ed), *Comparative Constitutional Design* (CUP 2012) 138.

[70] For a variety of hypotheses see Gregory M Stein, *Modern Chinese Real Estate Law: Property Development in an Evolving Legal System* (Ashgate 2012) ch 12.

[71] Thus, for instance, in a recent essay social scientist Nandini Sundar has written that in India: '[t]he struggle today is as much a struggle between laws, as people seek to defend rights enshrined in earlier laws against new legislation that seeks to diminish these as privileges or deny them altogether, or make fresh laws to reflect the democratic aspirations of a postcolonial age. In other words, "legal mobilization" is an important part of social mobilization in a way it has rarely been before.'

Nandini Sundar, 'The Rule of Law and the Rule of Property: Law-Struggles and the Neo-Liberal State in India' in Akhil Gupta and K Sivaramakrishnan (eds), *The State in India after Liberalization: Interdisciplinary Perspectives* (Routledge 2012) 175, 176–77.

THE CONCEPT OF 'DEVELOPMENT AS FREEDOM'

It is commonplace to state that the concept of development is an essentially contested concept. A wide range of different meanings may be attributed to the concept of development, including but not limited to development as growth, development as basic needs, and 'development as freedom'. Famously, the last of these, 'development as freedom', was first articulated and advanced by Amartya Sen. It radically departs from approaches to development that identify this concept with the growth of gross national product, some form of technological progress, or simply mass-scale industrialisation.[72] Instead, development is viewed 'as a process of expanding the real freedoms that people enjoy', mainly to offer an inclusive and humanistic approach.[73] Sen himself defines freedom as 'the "capabilities" of persons to lead the kind of lives they value—and have reason to value'.[74] To this end, a rights-based system, protecting both negative and positive liberties, needs to be established.[75] As Thomas has observed, in Sen's view:

> economic growth was *internally dependent* on the protection of human rights…Whereas the neoclassical vision of good governance focused on the enforcement of property rights and the stability of private commercial law, the vision informed by Sen's theory of capabilities focused on respect for human rights.[76]

By contrast, North:

> flatly dismisses the notion that the introduction of a bill of rights or the universal franchise in a developing country would improve the chances of development. In this he is not restating the undisputed platitude that the enactment of legal rules is insufficient to bring about social and economic change. Instead, his statement suggests that he categorically dismisses even the possibility of a legal mechanism as important as the bill of rights having an impact on the process of political and economic development.[77]

From a left perspective, a critical question that arises is whether the understanding of 'development as freedom' or rights-based development is an ideal that Marxists can subscribe to. More narrowly still, we might simply ask: 'can a Marxist believe in human rights?'[78]

Notwithstanding Marx's incisive critique of rights and legalism, this question must be answered in the affirmative. It is certainly true that in the essay 'On the Jewish Question' Marx argues that rights, particularly civil and political rights, are based 'on the separation of man from man', and that the 'practical application of man's right to liberty is man's right to *private property*'.[79] In the final analysis, the realisation of most rights in capitalist societies is

---

[72]   Sen, *Development as Freedom*, 3.
[73]   Sen, *Development as Freedom*, 3.
[74]   Sen, *Development as Freedom*, 18.
[75]   Sen, *Development as Freedom*, 212.
[76]   Thomas, 'Law and Neoclassical', 988 (emphasis added).
[77]   Julio Faundez, 'Douglass North's Theory of Institutions: Lessons for Law and Development' (2016) 8 *Hague Journal on the Rule of Law* 373, 408.
[78]   Steven Lukes, 'Can a Marxist Believe in Human Rights?' (1981) 4 *Praxis International* 334.
[79]   Karl Marx, 'On the Jewish Question' [1843] in Karl Marx and Frederick Engels, *Collected Works*, vol 3 (International Publishers 1975) 146, 162–63 (original emphasis).

constrained by the right of each individual to enjoy their property and to dispose of it at their own discretion, 'without regard to other men, independently of society'.[80] As Marx observes:

> [n]one of the so-called rights of man, therefore, go beyond egoistic man, beyond man as a member of civil society, that is, an individual withdrawn into himself, into the confines of his private interests and private caprice, and separated from the community. In the rights of man, he is far from being conceived as a species-being; on the contrary, species-life itself, society, appears as a framework external to the individuals, as a restriction of their original independence. The sole bond holding them together is natural necessity, need and private interest, the preservation of their property and their egoistic selves.[81]

Later, in the 'Critique of the Gotha Programme', Marx claims that '[r]ight can never be higher than the economic structure of society and its cultural development conditioned thereby'.[82] While these and other passages seem to suggest that Marx was dismissive of rights (and that Engels followed him in this regard), this is in reality very far from being the case. While it is not possible to canvass the entirety of Marx's writings on the subject of rights here,[83] it should be noted that Marx stressed the importance of free speech and a free press on several occasions, and he understood these freedoms to be worth defending as part of class struggles in a capitalist state.[84] He also went to great lengths to describe in detail the struggle of the British working class to achieve the ten-hour working day, demonstrating the importance he attached to the rights that workers were able to secure for improved working conditions. In other words, Marx 'supported the pursuit of legal reforms in the nature of rights victories', even as he was 'always cognizant that these were limited, and potentially limiting, victories'.[85] The pursuit of rights-based development in postcolonial nations is particularly salient because of the programmatic goal of PDRs. It is no accident that Prabhat Patnaik, the Indian Marxist political economist, has been vocal in his support for the project of rights-based development.[86] It is also useful to recall that since the days of Marx, the theory and practice of human rights has greatly expanded. To be sure, a growing literature continues to point to the limitations and even the many dark sides of human rights law. These include the displacement of the discourse of justice by that of human rights and legitimisation of armed interventions by imperialist states in post-colonial nations.[87] But it is vital not to be dismissive of the progressive role of human rights. What is called for is their decolonisation and reimagination with a clearer focus in practice on the rights of subaltern classes.[88] But even as presently framed and implemented, human rights law help safeguard the rights of the working and marginalised classes through

---

[80]   Marx, 'On the Jewish Question', 163.

[81]   Marx, 'On the Jewish Question', 164.

[82]   Marx, 'Critique of the Gotha Programme', 23.

[83]   I have attempted to do so elsewhere; see Chimni, *International Law and World Order*, 534–43.

[84]   Chimni, *International Law and World Order*, 534–43.

[85]   Amy Bartholomew, 'Should a Marxist Believe in Marx on Rights?' (1990) 26 *Socialist Register* 244, 253.

[86]   Prabhat Patnaik, 'A Left Approach to Development' (2010) 45 *Economic & Political Weekly* 33.

[87]   Samuel Moyn, *Not Enough: Human Rights in an Unequal World* (Harvard University Press 2018); David Kennedy, 'The International Human Rights Movement: Part of the Problem?' (2002) 15 *Harvard Human Rights Journal* 101.

[88]   José-Manuel Barreto, *Human Rights from a Third World Perspective: Critique, History and International Law* (Cambridge Scholars Publishing 2013); Susan Marks, *A False Tree of Liberty: Human Rights in Radical Thought* (OUP 2019) 18; Boaventura de Sousa Santos, 'Human Rights as an

identifying relevant norms and providing forums at the national, regional, and international levels for canvassing their enforcement. What is more, as scholars like Allen Buchanan, Christine Sypnowich, and Rodney Peffer have shown, a certain social space needs to be created for rights to resolve certain conflicts even in socialist societies.[89] Buchanan in particular has demonstrated convincingly that rights are also necessary under socialism. Among other things, rights under socialism would continue to prove useful, in this case as a set of legal and political constraints: on democratic procedures (e.g., for the purpose of protecting the rights of minorities) or to guarantee equal access to and participation in such procedures; on paternalistic limitations imposed by the state on personal freedoms, or attempts to use state power to dictate what may or must be done to maximise welfare or other public or social goods; on the use of coercion in the provision of public goods; and on the extent and limits of sacrifices for future generations.[90] On the other hand, many 'actually existing socialist' states subscribed to the view that individual rights-based claims against the state constituted threats to the very project and process of socialism. It is the practice of these societies which gave credence to the erroneous view that Marx was opposed to rights, human and otherwise.

CONCLUSION

This chapter has argued that North made out a persuasive case that institutions matter in the development process. But in primarily focusing on the effective enforcement of contractual and property rights, he overlooked the nature of capitalism and the role of imperialism in hampering development prospects in postcolonial states. On the other hand, the left in postcolonial nations has often failed to take seriously the role of laws and legal institutions in both the struggle for resisting the policies of ruling classes and in bringing a modicum of welfare to marginalised and oppressed groups. In this regard, the observations of Marx, Engels, and Lenin underscoring the relevance of legal institutions and legal struggles deserve to be revisited. Such an exercise is important not only because they stressed the relative autonomy of the legal sphere, but also because legal institutions are increasingly becoming sites of key struggles. Furthermore, the left in postcolonial nations relies on the vocabulary of human rights to advance the cause of the PDRs. Given the fact that bourgeois rights and accompanying institutions may need to be preserved even after the socialist revolution, we urgently need to develop a Marxist theory of law and legal institutions for our times.

Emancipatory Script? Cultural and Political Conditions', in Boaventura de Sousa Santos (ed), *Another Knowledge is Possible: Beyond Northern Epistemologies* (Verso 2007) 3.

[89]   See Allen E Buchanan, *Marx and Justice: The Radical Critique of Liberalism* (Rowman & Littlefield 1982) 163; Christine Sypnowich, *The Concept of Socialist Law* (OUP 1990) ch 5; RG Peffer, *Marxism, Morality, and Social Justice* (Princeton University Press 1990) 325.

[90]   Buchanan, *Marx and Justice*, 165.

19. Transcending disciplinary fetishisms: Marxism, neocolonialism, and international law

Radha D'Souza

INTRODUCTION

The relations between international law, international institutions, and Third World states[1] that came to be established after the end of the two world wars are the structural pillars of neocolonialism. For Kwame Nkrumah, who coined the term, '[t]he essence of neo-colonialism is that the State which is subject to it is, in theory, independent and has all the outward trappings of international sovereignty. In reality its economic system and thus its political policy is directed from outside'.[2] Neocolonialism is a mode of governance that Nkrumah called 'Invisible Government'. 'This Invisible Government', he wrote, 'is a relatively new institution', one that 'appear[s] outwardly to be a normal part of the conventional government'.[3]

How does this 'invisible government' operate? How is an independent state 'directed' from the outside? Who directs it, and how do they do so? Why do legally independent sovereign states allow themselves to be directed from the 'outside' in an interstate international legal and institutional order which, unlike European imperial arrangements of the past, expressly affirms the sovereign equality of all states? What makes some states 'directors' and others 'directed', in a global order nominally founded on the equality of states? Above all, what makes this government 'invisible', and in what sense exactly? In attempting to answer such questions from a Marxist perspective, we are immediately confronted with a host of daunting theoretical and methodological challenges. Whose Marxism? Which kind of Marxism? Marxism to what end?

The historical trajectory of Marxist theory and praxis means that it is no longer possible to speak of Marxism as a unified theoretical approach. After the end of the Second World War, Marxism trifurcated and developed distinct trajectories of theories and practices. The

---

[1] Since the end of the Cold War, the term 'Third World', which refers to formerly colonised nations that won independence after the conclusion of the Second World War, has largely given way to the more popular 'global South' as a non-geographical descriptor in the 'West and the Rest' framing of international order. I continue to use the term 'Third World' for two reasons. First, the Soviet Union's implosion has not erased structural relations between advanced capitalist states (the 'First World'), Russia and other formerly socialist states (the 'Second World'), and formerly colonised nations that have secured statehood (the 'Third World'). Second, the term 'global South' renders invisible the histories of the anti-imperialist struggles that continued after the end of the Second World War. Those histories and struggles remain important and continue to inform international law, international politics, and international political economy, all of which are relevant to this chapter.

[2] Kwame Nkrumah, *Neo-colonialism: The Last Stage of Imperialism* (first published 1965, Heinemann 1968) ix.

[3] Nkrumah, *Neo-colonialism*, 240. Nkrumah was quoting here from David Wise and Thomas B Ross, *The Invisible Government* (Random House 1964) 4.

success of the Bolshevik Revolution meant that Marxists had to attend to rebuilding the state and economy destroyed by the First World War. Marxist legal thinkers endeavoured to adapt Marxist theory to experiments with socialist construction. The victory of the Allies over fascism in the capitalist West strengthened the social-democratic strand in political practices and 'Western' (or 'Critical') Marxism in theory.[4] Social democracy informed different typologies of social welfare states and models of capitalism. The genesis of social democracy as a strand in Marxism was already present in the Second International, which was wound up in 1916 largely because of differences within Marxism about nationalism and colonialism.[5] Western/Critical Marxism developed against the backdrop of what Philip McMichael calls the 'development project', 'an internationally orchestrated program of *national* economic growth, with foreign financial, technological and military assistance under conditions of the Cold War'.[6] This 'development project' is the lynchpin of the international political economy which the Third World understands as 'neocolonialism'.[7]

Finally, the success of the Chinese Revolution produced what has often been called 'Third World Marxism'; its unambiguous anti-imperialist thrust, and its reliance on peasant struggles as a revolutionary social force for change, resonated powerfully across Asia, Africa, and Latin America, bolstering the decisions and operations of many liberation movements.[8] Third World Marxism was at best ambivalent about law and legal relations, and this ambivalence was broadly shared wherever its influence came to be felt.[9] Marxism's trifurcation after the Second World War—into Soviet-bloc Marxism, Western Marxism, and Third World Marxism, respectively—has profoundly influenced the way in which scholars understand and speak about Marxism, as well as the multiple meanings its categories and methods have come to acquire, especially within and in relation to the Third World. Finding a common conceptual vocabulary and understanding of history between the three strands is fraught with difficulties.

As if to compound these problems, the boundaries between Marxist and non-Marxist critiques of capitalism were themselves blurred with the emergence of postmodernism in the West, along with its Third World variant, postcolonial theory. Referring to Fredric Jameson's essays on postmodernism, Marxist historian and social theorist Arif Dirlik writes about the blurring of 'the distinction between a Marxist discourse on postmodernism and an appropriation of Marxism into the discourse of postmodernity'.[10] A similar confounding of boundaries between Marxism and postmodernism occurred in their application to the Third World, in the form of postcolonial theories and other Marxist-inflected or influenced theories.[11] The end of

---

    [4]   Perry Anderson, *Considerations on Western Marxism* (New Left Books 1976).
    [5]   VI Lenin, 'Imperialism and the Split in Socialism' [1916] in VI Lenin, *Collected Works*, vol 23 (Progress Publishers 1967) 105.
    [6]   Philip McMichael, *Development and Social Change: A Global Perspective* (Pine Forge Press 2008) 21 (emphasis added).
    [7]   I use the terms 'development' and 'development project' in the sense developed by McMichael, *Development and Social Change*.
    [8]   Arif Dirlik, 'Mao Zedong Thought and the Third World/Global South' (2013) 16 *Interventions: International Journal of Postcolonial Studies* 233.
    [9]   Carlos Wing-Hung Lo, 'Socialist Legal Theory in Deng Xiaoping's China' (1997) 11 *Columbia Journal of Asian Law* 469; Suzanne Ogden, 'Sovereignty and International Law: The Perspective of the People's Republic of China' (1974) 7 *NYU Journal of International Law and Politics* 1.
    [10]   Arif Dirlik, *The Postcolonial Aura: Third World Criticism in the Age of Global Capitalism* (first published 1998, Routledge 2018) 1.
    [11]   Dirlik, *Postcolonial Aura*, ch 3.

the Cold War saw the emergence of writings by a small group of international law scholars who claimed to be Marxists.[12] However, boundary questions about what is and is not Marxism have left us with more debates and less clarity about Nkrumah's 'invisible government'. 'What's Left?', asks Barbara Stark, in an extended review of Susan Marks' *International Law on the Left*, punning on the title of the edited collection.[13] Seeking to understand relations between neocolonialism, international law, and Third World statehood in the maze that is the contemporary Marxist theoretical landscape could well be akin to the proverbial fool rushing in where scholarly Marxists fear to tread.

This chapter examines the effect of the trifurcation, arguing that the left has succumbed to a number of important disciplinary fetishisms as a result. These fetishisms have prevented an explanatory critique of the place of law in neocolonialism from Marxist perspectives. The first such fetishism is none other than 'legal fetishism', which arises when social relations of production, circulation, exchange, and consumption—in short, capitalist social relations—are left out of consideration in legal analysis. Legal fetishism deflects attention from capitalism, transforming law into an object of independent inquiry and impeding appreciation of the fact that legal relations are one among a variety of different social relations under capitalism. The second fetishism relates to the mischaracterisation of the state, in particular its role as an institutional actor in capitalism and imperialism, and, related to this, the failure to differentiate between the (neo)colonial states of the periphery and the capitalist/imperialist states of the core.[14] This mischaracterisation produces what I call 'state fetishism'. State fetishism is implicit in Nkrumah's 'invisible government'. The third and final fetishism, which I call 'market fetishism', relates to a way of engaging with political economy while ignoring the legal and institutional preconditions of political and economic relations. Market fetishism arises when the veil over institutional actors is not lifted to reveal the real people behind the institutional façade.[15]

Together these three disciplinary fetishisms render invisible 'national oppression', a central theme in Third World Marxism.[16] National oppression is oppression of nations as nations, irreducible to class, race, or other social categories. By way of analogy, if the oppression of labour by capital is the axis of capitalist social relations, the oppression of a large number of nations by a small group of powerful nations is the axis of imperialist and neocolonial social relations. One of Marx's principal commitments is to lift the veil over manifest phenomena, revealing the conflictual social relations that underpin the capitalist social order. Likewise,

---

[12]   See e.g., BS Chimni, *International Law and World Order: A Critique of Contemporary Approaches* (SAGE 1993); China Miéville, *Between Equal Rights: A Marxist Theory of International Law* (Haymarket 2006); Susan Marks (ed), *International Law on the Left: Re-examining Marxist Legacies* (CUP 2008).

[13]   Barbara Stark, 'What's Left? A Review of *International Law on the Left*' (2010) 42 *George Washington International Law Review* 191.

[14]   Radha D'Souza, 'Imperial Agendas, Global Solidarities, and Third World Socio-Legal Studies: Methodological Reflections' (2012) 49 *Osgoode Hall Law Journal* 6.

[15]   A fourth type of fetishism, 'technology fetishism', applies to neocolonial relations, involving the notion that social problems generated by capitalism are capable of being addressed by 'technology fixes' or through scientific and mathematical reasoning. Due to space constraints, I do not discuss this fourth fetishism in this chapter.

[16]   For an extended discussion of imperialism and the national oppression see Radha D'Souza, 'Imperialism and Self-Determination: Revisiting the Nexus in Lenin' (2013) 48 *Economic & Political Weekly* 60.

Marxists who are committed to putting imperialism and neocolonialism to an end must lift the veil over manifest phenomena and reveal the conflictual social relations that underpin the imperialist international order. Disciplinary fetishism acts as the veil that conceals the conflicts that underpin social relations of capitalism generally and post-1945 imperialism and neocolonialism specifically. Disciplinary knowledge is incompatible with Marxist epistemology.

MARXISM AND DISCIPLINARY FETISHISM

In his account of the history of the social sciences, published in 1987, philosopher of science Peter Manicas argues that disciplinary divisions in the social sciences, at least as we know them today, came into existence only at the turn of the twentieth century, taking shape largely during its first 30 years. Since that time, Manicas maintains, disciplinary formations have remained essentially stable.[17] Notwithstanding the emergence of a variety of new sub-fields and intra-disciplinary orientations since 1987, the architectures of most disciplines have remained remarkably unchanged over time. Modern universities, founded on modern disciplines and each in possession of distinct theories, methods, and vocabularies, mirror the widespread social, political, economic, and cultural transformations that accompanied the emergence of transnational monopoly finance capitalism in the early twentieth century.[18] Disciplinary fetishism fragments reality into distinct social segments.

Elsewhere I have argued that disciplines mirror divisions of labour in capitalist societies.[19] As philosopher of science Steve Fuller argues, disciplines operate on the understanding that different aspects of reality require different procedures of inquiry and different conceptual resources.[20] Knowledge of reality produced within fragmented disciplines becomes an object of contemplation, and is disengaged from social practices. In contrast, Marx and the Marxist tradition focus on social relations—economic and political, legal and institutional, scientific and technological, cultural and ideological relations, under capitalism and imperialism.

---

[17]   Peter Manicas, *A History and Philosophy of the Social Sciences* (Basil Blackwell 1987).

[18]   Lenin's views on imperialism and the sense in which it is an 'epoch' are addressed in the last section of this chapter. Lenin argued that capitalism began to undergo profound transformations at the turn of the twentieth century. From being national, competitive, and industrial, capitalism became transnational, monopolistic, and dominated by finance capital. Lenin called this new stage of capitalism 'the epoch of capitalist imperialism'. VI Lenin, 'Imperialism, the Highest Stage of Capitalism' [1917] in VI Lenin, *Selected Works,* vol 1 (Progress Publishers 1970) 643, 747–50. Indeed, throughout the text, he uses the term 'epoch' and views (finance capitalism-led) monopolies and colonialism as comprising economic, political, legal, diplomatic, class, and cultural relations that are different from those associated with previous stages of capitalism. National oppression, new forms of colonialism, and the imperialist aspect of capitalism become dominant social relations during the 'epoch of capitalist imperialism'. Throughout this chapter, I use Lenin's expression 'epoch of capitalist imperialism' interchangeably with the expression 'transnational monopoly finance capitalism'. For an extended discussion of Lenin's analysis of imperialism and transnational monopoly finance capitalism, see Radha D'Souza, *What's Wrong With Rights? Social Movements, Law and Liberal Imaginations* (Pluto Press 2018). For an extended discussion of the centrality of national oppression in the imperialist stage of capitalism, see D'Souza, 'Imperialism and Self-Determination'.

[19]   D'Souza, *What's Wrong With Rights?*, ch 3.

[20]   Steve Fuller, 'Disciplinary Boundaries: A Critical Synthesis' (1985) 3 *4S Review* 2.

What does it mean to be a Marxist? Marx himself writes that it is not enough for critique to reverse a given argument. In a simple inversion of this kind, critique remains on the same level as the argument it critiques. Put differently, it is not enough for critique to remain on the level of an argument abstracted from social reality. Instead, critique must be oriented toward the explanation and transformation of that social reality.

> The weapon of criticism cannot, of course, replace criticism of the weapon, material force must be overthrown by material force; *but theory also becomes a material force as soon as it has gripped the masses*. Theory is capable of gripping the masses as soon as it *demonstrates ad hominem*, and it demonstrates ad hominem as soon as it becomes radical. *To be radical is to grasp the root of the matter*. But, for man, the root is man himself.[21]

Grasping the 'root of the matter' requires interrogating the whys and wherefores of social phenomena—not by reference to another person's argument, but rather by reference to the lived experiences of the masses of working people who produce and reproduce the conditions necessary for human existence. Marxism is about nothing if not about (capitalist and imperialist) social relations. In the 'epoch of capitalist imperialism', people's lives become enmeshed in a complex web of international, interstate, and nation-class contradictions. How does Nkrumah's 'invisible government' work? What are the social relations under transnational monopoly finance capitalism that produce and reproduce neocolonial relations? Marxist scholars must explain—not only to other scholars but to people more generally—how national oppression occurs, its modus operandi, and the effects it has on their lives.

The *Oxford English Dictionary* defines 'fetish' as a 'thing to which more respect or attention is given than is normal or sensible'.[22] In his trilogy on the conceptual history of the fetish, intellectual historian William Pietz traces its origins to the coast of West Africa during the colonial encounters of the sixteenth and seventeenth centuries, its permeation into Enlightenment thinking in the eighteenth and nineteenth centuries, and its percolation into different disciplines in the twentieth century.[23] According to Pietz, Enlightenment thinkers were intrigued by the problem of 'how *any* personal or social value could be attributed to material objects whose only "natural" values were instrumental and commercial'.[24] Marx brought the 'fetish home' from the colonies, as it were, by using the concept to explain commodity production under conditions of European capitalism. Capitalism transformed the commodity, an object of instrumental and commercial value, into a fetish.

For Marx, 'commodity fetishism' reduces the complex web of social relations necessary for commodity production under capitalism to exchange relations pure and simple. In a similar vein, the three interrelated forms of disciplinary fetishism stem from the reduction of a complex web of social relations necessary for transnational monopoly finance capitalism to

---

[21]   Karl Marx, 'Contribution to the Critique of Hegel's Philosophy of Law. Introduction' [1844] in Karl Marx and Frederick Engels, *Collected Works*, vol 3 (Lawrence & Wishart 1975) 175, 182 (emphases added).

[22]   *Oxford English Dictionary*, 'Fetish' in A Cowie (ed), *Oxford Advanced Learner's Dictionary of Current English* (OUP 1989) 449.

[23]   William Pietz, 'The Problem of the Fetish, I' (1985) 9 *RES: Anthropology and Aesthetics* 5; William Pietz, 'The Problem of the Fetish, II' (1987) 13 *RES: Anthropology and Aesthetics* 23; William Pietz, 'The Problem of the Fetish, IIIa: Bosman's Guinea and the Enlightenment Theory of Fetishism' (1988) 16 *RES: Anthropology and Aesthetics* 105.

[24]   'The Problem of the Fetish, II', 45 (original emphasis).

a single aspect of it, which is objectified as such in different disciplines. In addition, knowledge itself becomes a commodity and scholars the wage-labourers who are alienated from the products of their labour,[25] with little or no control over who uses their knowledge and for what purposes disciplinary knowledge becomes a fetish.[26]

LEGAL FETISHISM

The expansion of capitalism beyond the limits of laws and institutions of established states and empires necessitated the development of new legal and institutional forms for transnational capitalism to operate on a global plane. By the turn of the twentieth century, 'the undifferentiated state of international law, as it was then', in the words of Irwin Abrams,[27] began to emerge from the shadows of law, philosophy, and the social sciences. In Europe the 1870–71 Franco-Prussian War, the Paris Commune uprising that followed in 1871, and the attendant expansion of capitalism meant that tensions between market-building and peace-building shaped international law's doctrinal and institutional developments.[28] In the United States, with its numerous revolving doors between business, state bureaucracy, the defence establishment, academia, and the legal profession, tensions between business and national interests were less fraught. For example, the genesis of the American Society of International Law (ASIL) established in 1906 lies in the US foreign policy establishment's need to 'foster … the study of international law and promote the establishment of international relations on the basis of law and justice'.[29] From its inception the ASIL has promoted academic scholarship on international law, publishing the widely read *American Journal of International Law*. At the same time, it provides a platform for businesspersons, state bureaucrats, legal practitioners, the defence establishment, and academics to congregate and debate US interests, greasing the revolving doors through which people and ideas circulate. Many of the ASIL's office holders, beginning with Robert Lansing, one of its founders, have gone on to become significant state officials and diplomats.[30] If critique of international law is to demonstrate '*ad hominem*' the role it has played—and that it continues to play—in colonialism and imperialism, light must be shed on the nexus between legal discourse and the people and institutions who animate the law. Instead, Marxist international law scholars most often work to defend the discipline.

---

[25]   See e.g., Bronwyn Davies and Peter Bansel, 'Governmentality and Academic Work: Shaping the Hearts and Minds of Academic Workers' (2010) 26 *JCT: Journal of Curriculum Theorizing* 5; Emilo Luque, 'Whose Knowledge (Economy)?' (2001) 15 *Social Epistemology* 187; Mark Olssen and Michael A Peters, 'Neoliberalism, Higher Education and the Knowledge Economy: From the Free Market to Knowledge Capitalism' (2005) 20 *Journal of Education Policy* 313; Peter Scott, 'Prospects for Knowledge Work: Critical Engagement or Expert Conscription?' (2004) 53 *New Formations* 28.

[26]   For a discussion on the appropriation of knowledge produced by scientists in the academy after the Second World War, see Gary Werskey, 'The Marxist Critique of Capitalist Science: A History in Three Movements?' (2007) 16 *Science as Culture* 397.

[27]   Irwin Abrams, 'The Emergence of the International Law Societies' (1957) 19 *Review of Politics* 374.

[28]   Abrams, 'The Emergence'. See also Martti Koskenniemi, *The Gentle Civilizer of Nations: The Rise and Fall of International Law 1870–1960* (CUP 2001).

[29]   American Society of International Law, 'History of the Organization of the American Society of International Law' (1907) 1 *American Society of International Law Proceedings* 23, 28.

[30]   American Society of International Law, 'History of the Organization'.

China Miéville declares that his book, *Between Equal Rights: A Marxist Theory of International Law*, 'is resolutely on international law itself'.[31] Although he acknowledges that wider discussions within Marxism on social forms and value forms are important, he makes it clear that the legal form is the focus of his study. Having carved out the disciplinary domain of international law as the site for his engagement with Marxism, the legal form becomes his object. After a vigorous theoretical defence of Pashukanis' theory of the legal form,[32] Miéville's arguments proceed at a high level of abstraction. For example, Miéville argues that the universalisation of commodity exchange leads to 'abstraction of the state' as a 'third force' to 'stabilise relations', and states become subjects of international law.[33] What kind of relations? Exchange relations? Production relations? Inter-state relations? How do they play out in the 'invisible government'? Miéville writes that '[m]odern capitalism is an imperialist system, and a juridical one',[34] in which the 'fundamental subjects of international law are the sovereign states, which face each other as property owners' having ownership over their own territory.[35] How did Britain, a small island state with limited territorial 'property', become a global empire, whereas India, a vast subcontinent, become a colony? How did states, particularly colonial states, acquire subjectivity after the Second World War, and why? Why is the juridical form so central to post-war capitalism? And how does the form facilitate unequal relations between imperial and neocolonial states? The narrow focus on legal forms takes Miéville to a level of abstraction that makes it difficult to lift the veil on manifest phenomena and reveal the conflictual imperial-neocolonial relations that have underpinned capitalism since the end of the Second World War.[36] Miéville takes attention away from the role of international law in the social relations of imperialism and neocolonialism, and focuses instead on the theoretical positions of other scholars. Pashukanis, by contrast, cautioned Marxists to keep their understanding of legal forms close to their historical substance.[37]

BS Chimni, another leading Marxist scholar of international law, devotes significant attention to Myres McDougal's contributions to international law.[38] But he does not explain fully the role that McDougal and his New Haven School of International Law, with its 'policy-oriented' approach to jurisprudence, played in augmenting the legal aspects of the American empire. McDougal developed his theories as an administrator of the US lend-lease programs at a critical moment in the Second World War, and as general counsel for the US State Department's Office of Foreign Relief and Rehabilitation Operations. A contextual analysis of McDougal's theories could help to shine light, *ad hominem*, on the role of international

---

[31]   Miéville, *Between Equal Rights*, 4.
[32]   Miéville, *Between Equal Rights,* ch 3.
[33]   Miéville, *Between Equal Rights*, 139.
[34]   Miéville, *Between Equal Rights*, 290.
[35]   Miéville, *Between Equal Rights*, 291–92.
[36]   For an extended discussion of the role of international law in transnational monopoly finance capitalism after the Second World War, see D'Souza, *What's Wrong With Rights?*
[37]   Evgeny B Pashukanis, *Law and Marxism: A General Theory* (first published 1929, Barbara Einhorn tr, Pluto Press 1989) ch 1.
[38]   BS Chimni, *International Law and World Order: A Critique of Contemporary Approaches* (2nd edn, CUP 2017) ch 3.

law and the significance of his theories for the consolidation of the US empire after the Second World War.[39]

Robert Knox quotes from Marx to argue that legal relations comprise only one kind of the many social relations in each historical stage of capitalism, that they need to be considered in their entirety, and that their roots lie 'in the material conditions of life'.[40] At the same time, Knox claims that '[t]he writings of Marx and Engels have almost no *systematic* engagement with legal questions, instead making only scattered and fragmentary references', a shortcoming in Knox's view.[41] Knox also quotes extensively from Lenin on imperialism and international organisations like the League of Nations. He bemoans the fact that Lenin does not provide 'any deeper materialist theory *of* international law'.[42] Having paid his tributes to Marx, Engels, and Lenin by restating key propositions of Marxism about legal relations being one of many social relations of capitalism, Knox is disappointed that they did not write about international law as such, as an independent object of analysis.

Susan Marks notes that Marxism, rather paradoxically, witnessed a revival after the dissolution of the Soviet bloc. This development 'liberated' Marxism from old dogmas and orthodoxies, opening up the possibility of rediscovering the relevance of Marxism in new ways, in international law and other disciplines.[43] Marks' earlier monograph, *The Riddle of All Constitutions*, aimed 'to reawaken a sense of the progressive possibilities which the[se] two concepts—democracy and ideology—*could help to open up within international law*'.[44] Marks defends international law as an object of inquiry in its own right.

Although he writes from a non-Marxist Third World perspective, Antony Anghie's approach is also popular among many Marxist scholars of law, particularly international law.[45] For Anghie the imperialism of international law is reducible to cultural difference. Indeed, Anghie puts race at the centre of his theory of imperialism and largely removes capitalist political economy and the histories of national oppression, long understood by most Marxists as the drivers of imperialism and indeed racism. The primacy of racial and cultural difference in Anghie's account of the history of international law, the amount of work it is made to do in his explanation of inequality between peoples and states, leaves us with moralistic solutions and voluntarist calls for solidarity.

It is possible to expand on the disciplinary orientations and loyalties of Marxist international law scholars. What is 'radical' about 'radical international law', asks Bill Bowring, replying that:

> [m]y own answer to the question is that almost all 'critical' or 'radical' approaches to international law are firmly located in the academy, or the 'discipline', or the 'field' as it is often called. These

---

[39]   Andrew R Willard, 'Myres Smith McDougal: A Life of and About Human Dignity' (1999) 108 *Yale Law Journal* 927.

[40]   Robert Knox, 'Marxist Theories of International Law' in Anne Orford and Florian Hoffmann (eds), *The Oxford Handbook of the Theory of International Law* (OUP 2016) 306, 307.

[41]   Knox, 'Marxist Theories of International Law', 306 (original emphasis).

[42]   Knox, 'Marxist Theories', 315 (original emphasis).

[43]   Susan Marks, 'Introduction' in Susan Marks (ed), *International Law on the Left: Re-Examining Marxist Legacies* (CUP 2008) 1, 16.

[44]   Susan Marks, *The Riddle of All Constitutions: International Law, Democracy, and the Critique of Ideology* (OUP 2003) 7 (emphasis added).

[45]   Antony Anghie, *Imperialism, Sovereignty and the Making of International Law* (CUP 2005).

approaches are often marked by the eclecticism and the closely related pragmatism which traditionally emanate from the United States, just as British mainstream thinking is often termed 'empiricism'.[46]

Even within the narrowly disciplinary debates of Western academia, Marxist international law scholars generally accept the division of law into public and private, choosing for the most part to focus on questions of public international law. The multifaceted relationship between public and private international law, so central to the history of Third World state-formation and neocolonial governance, is missing from most such scholarship. Equally, barring exceptions, a systematic critique of international economic law in the context of transnational monopoly finance capitalism escapes Marxist international law scholarship.[47]

Marxists have tended on the whole to ignore important developments even within the disciplinary domain of international law. For example, there is very little engagement by Western Marxist scholars with the work of Soviet Marxist international law scholarship after the Second World War. In the first edition of his book *International Law and World Order*, published in 1993, BS Chimni engages with the work of GI Tunkin, a Soviet international law scholar.[48] It is through Tunkin that Chimni makes the argument that international law is 'bourgeois democratic' in character. In the reworked 2017 edition of his book, Chimni dismisses Tunkin in a footnote, on the grounds that his writings are 'less theoretical exercises and more attempts at justifying Soviet foreign policy in the vocabulary of international law'.[49] How is Tunkin different from McDougal, who also defended US foreign policy? The real question is whether Soviet international law contributed to the consolidation of neocolonialism.

Bill Bowring is among the few who consider the influence of Soviet legal practices on the right to self-determination, and the way those practices helped to shape the international legal order.[50] However, Bowring does not consider the ramifications of the restoration of capitalism in the Soviet Union for the Third World, or the rise of what Chinese Marxists characterised as 'Soviet social imperialism'—that is, socialism in words, capitalism in deeds. Consequently, Soviet practice appears contradictory to Bowring, espousing legal positivism in theory and democratic freedoms for the Third World in practice. What this position obfuscates is the consequences for neocolonialism of 'Soviet social imperialism', the international legal order, and a Cold War that was in actuality anything but cold in two-thirds of the world. Not surprisingly, Nkrumah's 'invisible government' remains 'invisible'.

China's move away from the Soviet model to socialism with 'Chinese characteristics' had a profound influence on imperialism and neocolonialism in the Third World. Deng's reforms

---

[46] Bill Bowring, 'What Is Radical in "Radical International Law"?' (2011) 22 *Finnish Yearbook of International Law* 3, 3.

[47] For instance, Chimni writes on international trade and economic law; see e.g., BS Chimni, 'The World Trade Organization, Democracy and Development: A View from the South' (2006) 40 *Journal of World Trade* 5; BS Chimni, 'WTO and Environment: Legitimisation of Unilateral Trade Sanctions' (2002) 37 *Economic & Political Weekly* 133. In *International Law and World Order,* he characterises the world economy as 'neocolonial' and international law as 'bourgeois democratic' between 1945 and 1985, after which he characterises the global economy as a form of '[g]lobal imperialism' and international law as '[g]lobal international law' (477–99).

[48] Chimni, *International Law and World Order*, 242–70.

[49] Chimni, *International Law and World Order*, 462 n.

[50] Bill Bowring, 'Positivism Versus Self-Determination: The Contradictions of Soviet International Law' in Susan Marks (ed), *International Law on the Left: Re-examining Marxist Legacies* (CUP 2008) 133.

entailed widespread legal transformations that included a radically different approach to international law, taking it away from the 'legal nihilism' of the Mao era to the 'rule of law with Chinese characteristics' approach that came to characterise the Deng era.[51] The implications of the transformations in China for the international legal order and for neocolonialism specifically remain to be studied by Marxist international law scholars.

The most significant omission here is the absence of engagement with the transformations in the institution of statehood engineered by expanding international legal relations since the League of Nations era.[52] Given that the state is a basic building-block of international law, and that statehood has been normalised and universalised by the United Nations, this absence leaves a gaping hole at the heart of Marxist international legal studies. Indeed, Marxist international legal scholarship has to date left analysis of statehood largely to the social sciences.

STATE FETISHISM

Anthony Carty makes an important point about statehood in the context of modern Europe. Referring to nineteenth-century European jurists who considered the existence of states to be a fact, he writes that:

> [s]tates ... do not have their statehood conceded to them by a higher authority. ... The great nineteenth-century jurists insisted there could be no legally rational justification for the configuration of States. This is the profound meaning of the concept of the State as a fact.[53]

In the case of Third World states, the 'factual existence' of statehood was historically an outcome of inter-imperialist rivalry.[54] It continues to be contingent on recognition, in particular by the 'big five' veto-bearing powers on the UN Security Council, qualifying the rights of nations and peoples to self-determination. After 75 years and countless UN General Assembly resolutions on Israeli occupation, Palestine is not yet a fully fledged state under international law. 'Regime change', crucial to the establishment and dissolution of colonial states and administrations in the past,[55] continues in new forms within the present international legal order. For example, regime change was the rationale for the invasion of Iraq. In the Third World, statehood continues to be vulnerable to imperialist intervention and therefore unstable.

State fetishism arises when a Third World state is considered to be an 'actually existing entity' dehors its history. Incorporating different historical and sociological understandings of states in theories of capitalism and imperialism complicates disciplinary approaches to

---

[51]   Lo, 'Socialist Legal Theory'; Ogden, 'Sovereignty and International Law'.

[52]   See Radha D'Souza, 'International Law and Development: From Company Raj to Network Governance via Indirect Rule' in Samuel Adelman and Abdul Paliwala (eds), *Limits of Law and Development: Neoliberalism, Governance and Social Justice* (Routledge 2020) 167.

[53]   Anthony Carty, *The Decay of International Law: A Reappraisal of the Limits of Legal Imagination in International Affairs* (2nd edn, Manchester University Press 2019) 1.

[54]   For an account of South Asian state formations see Radha D'Souza, 'Wars Beyond the Armed Forces: Colonialism and Militarisation of Ethno-National Conflicts in Contemporary South Asia' in Jude Lal Fernando (ed), *Resistance to Empire and Militarization: Reclaiming the Sacred* (Equinox 2020) 25.

[55]   Charles Arnold-Baker, 'Resident, Residency' in Charles Arnold-Baker, *The Companion to British History* (2nd edn, Routledge 2001); Michael Grow, *U.S. Presidents and Latin American Interventions: Pursuing Regime Change in the Cold War* (University Press of Kansas 2008).

statehood. If we instead take capitalism and imperialism as the two formative historical and sociological mechanisms that structure modern states, it is possible to distinguish between two broad typologies of state.[56] The first type of state was established during the course of the internal transformation of European societies from feudalism to capitalism. In contrast, the second type of state was established through rivalries between empires and their colonial allies; external relations between European powers were the critical formative factors that forced internal changes within colonial societies. The colonial state is not identical to the capitalist state, except in the purely juridical sense of being an institutional form.[57] When histories of state formations are hollowed out of the concept of statehood, the state form is privileged over the historical and class content of states. Privileging state form over inter-state and intra-state relations obfuscates neocolonial relations of domination and subordination.

What stands between the colonialisms of the eighteenth and nineteenth centuries and the neocolonialism of the epoch of transnational monopoly finance capitalism is the colonial state's transformation into the neocolonial state, retaining or even reinforcing the power of imperial states to subjugate Third World states. Third World leaders clearly recognised the transformations. Barely had the ink on the treaties establishing the Bretton Woods and United Nations organisations dried than Raúl Prebisch introduced dependency theory into discussions of the UN's Economic Commission for Latin America.[58] Indonesia's Sukarno opened the 1955 Bandung Conference with a warning:

> We are often told 'Colonialism is dead.' Let us not be deceived or even soothed by that. I say to you, colonialism is not yet dead. … I beg of you, do not think of colonialism only in the classic form which we of Indonesia, and our brothers in different parts of Asia and Africa, knew. Colonialism has also its modern dress, in the form of economic control, intellectual control, actual physical control by a small but alien community within a nation. It is a skilful and determined enemy, and it appears in many guises. It does not give up its loot easily. Wherever, whenever and however it appears, colonialism is an evil thing, and one which must be eradicated from the earth.[59]

Critical accounts that present imperialism as involving the oppression of nations and peoples lost their ground in much of academia with the rise of postmodernism and postcolonialism in the 1980s. Elsewhere I have argued that national liberation struggles were composed of alliances between multiple social forces oppressed by imperialism.[60] Dismantling the class alliances forged during the course of national liberation struggles was precisely the goal of the United States and other imperialist powers.

---

[56] Radha D'Souza, 'Imperialism and Self-Determination', 60.

[57] For an extended argument see Radha D'Souza, 'Imperial Agendas, Global Solidarities'. For an analysis of India as a specific case, see Radha D'Souza, 'The "Third World" and Socio-Legal Studies: Neo-Liberalism and Lessons From India's Legal Innovations' (2005) 14 *Social & Legal Studies* 487.

[58] HW Arndt, *Economic Development: The History of an Idea* (first published 1978, University of Chicago Press 1987) 120–22. These ideas would go on to dominate discussions in the context of the UN Conference on Trade and Development in the 1960s and would eventually lay the groundwork for much of the New International Economic Order project of the 1970s.

[59] Achmed Sukarno, 'Speech at the Opening of the Bandung Conference, 18 April 1955' in Indonesian Ministry of Foreign Affairs, *Africa-Asia Speaks from Bandung* (Government of Indonesia 1955) 19.

[60] D'Souza, 'Imperial Agendas'; and also D'Souza. *What's Wrong With Rights?*

The dismantling of such class alliances in order to roll back the gains of the national liberation struggles was realised through a combination of political, economic, legal, and ideological
interventions. On the political front, regime changes were achieved through *coup d'états* and
political assassinations. Sukarno was murdered, we now know by the CIA and with the support
of the British government, along with over one million other Indonesians.[61] After several
targeted assassination attempts, Nkrumah was overthrown by a CIA-supported coup in 1966.[62]
Around the world, Third World government after Third World government was overthrown
or subverted behind the façade of the Cold War.[63] In each case, 'regime change' was at issue,
and internal class forces acted in concert with imperial states and organisations—Suharto in
Indonesia, Kotoka and Afrifa in Ghana, among many others. These 'regime changes' rolled
back any aspirations of freedom that Third World peoples may have harboured. On the economic front, the World Bank and IMF stepped in to design the political economy of Third
World states with the aid of the allies of imperial powers who were installed after the regime
changes.[64] Multilateral and bilateral aid with conditions attached was provided by the United
States and other imperial powers.[65] These economic interventions made Third World states
vulnerable to economic domination by transnational corporations and global investors. On
the legal front, the World Bank and IMF developed the legal and institutional structures that
facilitated the operation of transnational corporations and other foreign investors. While some
organs of the United Nations, notably the Commission on Human Rights, continued to reaffirm the rights of nations to self-determination in international law, the Economic and Social
Council, an important organ of the organisation, continued to adopt the agendas of the World
Bank and IMF in their development programs for the Third World.[66] On the ideological front,
'democratic development' became an important rhetorical device for rationalising the economic and political interventions. Development, as McMichael explains, was understood as
'an internationally orchestrated program of *national* economic growth, with foreign financial,
technological, and military assistance under the conditions of the Cold War'.[67] Democracy
meant the freedom of corporations and foreign investors to exploit nature and people around
the world.[68]

The rise of postmodernism in the First World and postcolonialism in the Third World gave
voice to the new class alliances within and between First World and Third World states.[69] The
growing academic popularity of postmodernism and postcolonialism mirrored the reconstitution of Third World states through the expansion of transnational monopoly finance capitalism. 'A striking feature of the debate between modernism and postmodernism', wrote Jan

---

[61]   For a graphic portrayal of the events see John Pilger, *The New Rulers of the World* (2001), documentary film available at http://johnpilger.com/videos/the-new-rulers-of-the-world accessed 7 April
2021.

[62]   Boni Yao Gebe, 'Ghana's Foreign Policy at Independence and Implications for the 1966 Coup
d'État' (2008) 2 *Journal of Pan African Studies* 160.

[63]   William Blum, *Killing Hope: U.S. Military and CIA Interventions Since World War II* (Zed Books
2003).

[64]   Pilger, *The New Rulers of the World*.

[65]   See 'The Reality of Aid Network', https://realityofaid.org/ accessed 7 April 2021.

[66]   D'Souza, *What's Wrong With Rights?*, chs 6, 7.

[67]   McMichael, *Development and Social Change*, 21 (original emphasis).

[68]   D'Souza, *What's Wrong With Rights?*, ch 4.

[69]   Dirlik, *Postcolonial Aura*; cf Vivek Chibber, *Postcolonial Theory and the Specter of Capital*
(Verso 2013).

Nederveen Pieterse in 1990, 'is that it is being conducted with the backs turned to the Third World'.[70] Deliberately misreading Ella Shohat's question, '[w]hen exactly … does the "post-colonial" begin?', Dirlik responds by stating that it began 'when Third World intellectuals have arrived in First World academe'.[71] The need to find answers for the paradoxical nature of independence—highlighted by Third World leaders like Sukarno, Nkrumah, and many others—is thereby overshadowed by Third World scholars' need to gain recognition within Euro-American academia.[72] Applauding the rise of Subaltern Studies, arguably the most influential school within postcolonial theory, Ronald Inden writes that 'Indians are, for perhaps the first time since colonization, showing sustained signs of reappropriating the capacity to represent themselves'.[73] Vivek Chibber adds wryly, 'better late than never'.[74] If regime changes in the Third World invite attention to classic Marxist questions about the class character of new neocolonial states, the rise of postcolonial studies invites attention to the articulation of those class interests in the international domain, including within the world of academia.

Dirlik identifies three epistemological premises of postcolonial critique. The first is the 'affirmation of "difference"' in which 'linguistic encounters become[] a metaphor for all encounters … including the encounters of political economy', so that the 'metaphorization of social encounters' produces 'a conviction that literary works suffice as evidence for what goes on in the world'.[75] Historical thinking is transformed with the postcolonial emphasis on 'narrativization and representation'.[76] The second is the idea that meanings are negotiated by speakers as equals in such linguistic encounters. The third is the emphasis on 'porosity of boundaries', 'border crossings', 'hybridity', and 'in-betweenness'.[77] With these epistemological tools, postcolonial critique repudiates all 'foundational historical writing',[78] 'Orientalism' as well as its 'Other', namely Third World nationalism. It also repudiates 'master narratives' about modes and relations of production. It is no longer possible to say anything definitive about the positionality of the Third World state within the international imperial economy, or about the historical trajectory that 'othered' it. So pervasive have these modes of thinking become that in 2003, when the United States openly engineered regime change in Iraq, the erasure of 'foundational historical writing' meant that even some Marxists were alarmed by what they saw as the rise of the American Empire,[79] an empire that had by then been in existence for at least 53 years. Few recognised that regime change, far from being something that emerged in 2003, was as old as colonialism itself. Postcolonial studies evacuated the Third World state of its historical, geopolitical, and economic substance.

Postcolonial theorists have consistently targeted Marxist analyses of the Third World state, typified by Nkrumah's *Neo-colonialism* and Walter Rodney's *How Europe Underdeveloped*

---

[70] Jan Nederveen Pieterse, *Empire and Emancipation: Power and Liberation on a World Scale* (Pluto Press 1990) 51.

[71] Dirlik, *Postcolonial Aura*, 52.

[72] Dirlik, *Postcolonial Aura*, ch 3.

[73] Ronald Inden, 'Orientalist Constructions of South Asia' (1986) 20 *Modern Asian Studies* 401, 445.

[74] Chibber, *Postcolonial Theory*, 8 n.

[75] Dirlik, *Postcolonial Aura*, 5.

[76] Dirlik, *Postcolonial Aura*, 5.

[77] Dirlik, *Postcolonial Aura*, 6.

[78] Dirlik, *Postcolonial Aura*, 56.

[79] See e.g., Michael Hardt and Antonio Negri, *Empire* (Harvard University Press 2000).

Africa.[80] These intellectual developments reflected a resurgence of liberation struggles in many parts of the Third World, including Cambodia, Colombia, India, Indonesia, Nepal, Peru, Philippines, Vietnam, and elsewhere. With nation and nationalism under attack, the state became the universalising demon of modernity, one devoid of class content. Third World Marxist concepts like 'comprador bourgeoisie' disappeared from the vocabularies of many Marxists. The concepts of class and class struggle were widely dismissed as 'essentialist', and often replaced with the concept of 'the subaltern', with the concept of the mode of production itself rejected as a 'totalising idea'. Similarly, questions of production, consumption, and distribution were frequently ignored, and the very idea of a Third World state that is structured by colonialism, past and present, became difficult to articulate. We were thereby left with a way of speaking about the state as a kind of personified being—a hypostatised entity that 'acts' and 'behaves' in different, sometimes terrible ways. The state form of Marxist and non-Marxist social science dovetails the concept of state as juridical entity formalised in the international legal order. How do these abstract concepts 'do' the things they do and 'behave' in the way they do? We are left without conceptual tools to connect the dots between the international political economy, international law, and international institutions, as well as the Third World state that sits at the intersection of the three.

MARKET FETISHISM

In this section, I turn the spotlight on disciplinary fetishism in political economy, the foundation on which neocolonialism stands. According to Karl Polanyi, capitalist societies are 'market societies', and 'market econom[ies] can only function in market societies'; that is, 'market economies' entail the 'running of society as an adjunct to the market'.[81] 'The' market, Alan Aldridge argues, 'has become one of the key concepts through which Western societies understand themselves', adding that discourses about markets are entangled in an 'intricate bundle of description, analysis and prescription', implicitly or explicitly carrying 'visions of the good society' and serving as ideological devices that mystify the inequalities of capitalism.[82] When Adam Smith wrote about the 'invisible hand of the market' in *The Wealth of Nations* in 1776, he was referring to thousands of everyday transactions between buyers and sellers in the marketplace, who 'truck, barter and exchange one thing for another'.[83] These everyday transactions were *sui generis*, Smith argued, and market transactions were self-regulating mechanisms for setting commodity prices. Marx stripped the mystique off the 'invisible hand' as a regulator of commodity prices, revealing the real social relations that were concealed by the façade of 'the' market. Marx argued that behind the veneer of self-regulating markets, understood as price-setting mechanisms by classical political economists like Smith, David Ricardo, and others, were real social relations involving real producers and appropriators of

---

[80]   Walter Rodney, *How Europe Underdeveloped Africa* (first published 1972, rev edn, Howard University Press 1981). For South Asia see Hamza Alavi, 'India and the Colonial Mode of Production' (1975) 10 *Economic & Political Weekly* 1235.

[81]   Karl Polanyi, *The Great Transformation: The Political and Economic Origins of Our Time* (first published 1944, Beacon Press 1957) 60.

[82]   Alan Aldridge, *The Market* (Polity Press 2005) 2, 6.

[83]   Adam Smith, *The Wealth of Nations, Books I-III* (first published 1776, Penguin 1982) 91.

surplus value: workers and capitalists. Marx explained the relations between wages, prices, and profits. Furthermore, he worked out how social relations between labour and capital transformed European societies from a feudal social order based on land relations to a capitalist order based on commodity exchange relations.

For Marx, legal and institutional changes were instrumental in the shift from feudal to capitalist society. Marx never misses the 'who' and 'how' questions when analysing the 'what', 'where', and 'when' of capitalist social developments. As a result, law is ever-present in Marx's analysis of capitalist social relations, but without becoming an independent object of inquiry as such. Polanyi's *The Great Transformation* tracks the legal and institutional changes that accompany the displacement of the peasantry in England and the establishment of labour markets, a necessary condition of the development of capitalist social relations.[84] By the turn of the twentieth century, the expansion of national, competitive industrial capitalism led to its qualitative transformation. The new form of capitalism that emerged as a result of this process had the effect of transnationalising many previously national markets. Oligarchies and monopolies displaced thousands of small firms. New forms of property, particularly in the form of financial instruments, were created through legal changes. Insurance products were perhaps amongst the first financial products to be traded as virtual property in the early twentieth century.[85] Classical political economy, with its focus on labour, capital, and production, had by this time already given way to neoclassical political economy, in which price, utility, and exchange relations were the chief concerns.[86] Neoclassical economics' mathematical methods, statistical modes of reasoning, *ceteris paribus* derivations, and imagined states of 'market equilibrium' endowed 'the' market with a mystical, transcendental status, one very different from Smith's 'invisible hand'. The mysticism concealed the new actors behind a new type of expanded market façade that operated across national boundaries.

How did Marxists address the new type of capitalism that emerged in the early twentieth century? The work of Paul Baran, John Bellamy Foster, Paul Sweezy, Harry Magdoff, and others associated with the *Monthly Review* school of neo-Marxism arguably goes furthest in analysing this new type of capitalism.[87] Although the works of Baran, Sweezy, and others pursue the 'when', 'where', and 'what' of transnational monopoly finance capital, they do not address how relations between the economic and the political are established and reproduced through law, legal relations, and legal institutions. Marxist political economy becomes an object of inquiry at the intersection of wider disciplinary fields like economics, political science, sociology, and history. Omitting law from our understanding of the new type of capitalism in the twentieth century has important political consequences, not the least of which is that it conceals imperialist and neocolonial relations. Law, legal relations, and legal

---

[84]   Polanyi, *Great Transformation*, esp ch 7.

[85]   Richard V Ericson, Aaron Doyle, and Dean Barry, *Insurance as Governance* (University of Toronto Press 2003); Robin Pearson, 'Towards an Historical Model of Services Innovation: The Case of the Insurance Industry, 1700–1914' (1997) 50 *Economic History Review* 235.

[86]   David Dequech, 'Neoclassical, Mainstream, Orthodox, and Heterodox Economics' (2007) 30 *Journal of Post Keynesian Economics* 279.

[87]   Paul Baran, *The Political Economy of Growth* (Monthly Review Press 1967); Paul A Baran and Paul M Sweezy, *Monopoly Capital: An Essay on the American Economic and Social Order* (first published 1966, Monthly Review Press 1996); John Bellamy Foster, *The Theory of Monopoly Capitalism: An Elaboration of Marxian Political Economy* (first published 1986, Monthly Review Press 2014); Harry Magdoff, *Imperialism Without Colonies* (Monthly Review Press 2003).

institutions are especially important in the transnational monopoly finance stage of capitalism, because classical colonialism is further legalised and institutionalised under neocolonialism. These transformations were the basis of the 'new world order' established after the Second World War.[88] The 'relations of production' about which Marx and Marxists write are established by law. Law creates institutions, constitutes legal subjects, and establishes relations between those subjects. Leaving out legal and institutional relations obfuscates the actors in transnational monopoly finance capitalism. This results in a kind of 'market fetishism', in which markets are personified as hypostatised entities that 'act' and 'behave' like human beings, developing wills of their own and acquiring mystical qualities. Marx's call for a form of critique that is *ad hominem* becomes an incantation, a form of obeisance to Marx.

In contrast, neoliberals and others on the political right have devoted attention to laws and institutions. For instance, the Mont Pèlerin Society, established in 1947, was a particularly influential forum for discussion and political strategising on the transatlantic political right. The society focused on establishing new legal regimes and actors. Among its aims were (i) a 'redefinition of the functions of the state so as to distinguish more clearly between the totalitarian and the liberal order'; (ii) '[m]ethods of reestablishing the rule of law and of assuring its development'; (iii) 'establishing minimum standards' for 'the functioning of the market'; and (iv) the creation of 'an international order conducive to … the establishment of harmonious international economic relations'.[89] Similarly, the 'law and economics' movement emerged as a new disciplinary field during the latter half of the twentieth century.[90] It has focused on ironing out legal questions arising from transnational monopoly finance capitalism, questions involving the expansion of the legal personality of corporations, democratisation of the rights of incorporation, popularisation of new management systems, and creation of new financial products (new types of property), financial regulation, and rules about competition.[91] Established to study and describe 'a suitable legal and institutional framework of an effective competitive system', the 'Chicago School' of law and economics has played an especially important role in developing legal frameworks for post-war capitalism.[92] Friedrich Hayek, who played a leading role in developing a new liberalism for conditions of transnational monopoly finance capitalism, gave law a central place and reformulated classical liberal legal principles.[93] He was one of the founders and leading members of the Mont Pèlerin Society,

---

[88]   See D'Souza, *What's Wrong With Rights?*

[89]   Dieter Plehwe, 'Introduction' in Philip Mirowski and Dieter Plehwe (eds), *The Road from Mont Pèlerin: The Making of the Neoliberal Thought Collective* (Harvard University Press 2009) 1, 25.

[90]   Rob van Horn and Philip Mirowski, 'The Rise of the Chicago School of Economics and the Birth of Neoliberalism' in Philip Mirowski and Dieter Plehwe (eds), *The Road from Mont Pèlerin: The Making of the Neoliberal Thought Collective* (Harvard University Press 2009) 139.

[91]   On the development of legal personality of corporations see Sanford A Schane, 'The Corporation Is a Person: The Language of a Legal Fiction' (1987) 61 *Tulane Law Review* 563.

[92]   See Rob van Horn, 'Reinventing Monopoly and the Role of Corporations: The Roots of Chicago Law and Economics' in Philip Mirowski and Dieter Plehwe (eds), *The Road from Mont Pèlerin: The Making of the Neoliberal Thought Collective* (Harvard University Press 2009) 204, 205. See also Alain Marciano and Giovanni B Ramello (eds), 'Law and Economics: The Legacy of Guido Calabresi' (symposium) (2014) 77 *Law and Contemporary Problems*. For later developments see David Singh Grewal and Jedediah Purdy (eds), 'Law and Neoliberalism' (symposium) (2014) 77 *Law and Contemporary Problems*.

[93]   See FA Hayek, *Law, Legislation and Liberty: A New Statement of the Liberal Principles of Justice and Political Economy* (3rd edn, Routledge 1998).

as well as of the 'Chicago School'.[94] In the political sphere, neoliberalism surfaced in full force during the 1980s, with the Reagan and Thatcher administrations. By then the political economy of transnational monopoly finance capitalism, and its legal and institutional preconditions, were firmly in place and had essentially become a *fait accompli*. As Pashukanis had noted generations earlier, new social relations precede their formalisation in law.[95]

Left scholarship devotes considerable space to demonstrating the connections between 'politics' and 'economics'.[96] Conundrums about how the two might be (re)connected arise because many in the post-war era, including some Marxists, tended to juxtapose markets and states, as directly antithetical social artefacts.[97] Legal liberalism is premised upon the dualism of markets and states, and has helped to reproduce that dualism in social theory. Uncritically accepting the division between private and public law as two separate legal spaces, each with its own independent social sphere, leads Marxists into endless debates about how to connect 'politics' and 'economics', theoretically and methodologically. 'The' market is fetishised as a result, and new actors and agents who 'truck, barter and exchange'—monopolistic corporations, financial oligarchies, states, and a civil society largely organised as legal entities (NGOs, charities, trusts)—thereby become opaque. In the transnational monopoly capitalism stage, the creation of new, non-human 'persons' as rights-bearing legal subjects, with independent legal personalities and the legal capacity to enter into contract, transforms both the character of 'market actors' and 'the marketplace' in which they operate.[98]

Markets and states are partly legal artefacts, both being complexes of laws. Both establish the social conditions necessary for capitalism to function. Transnational monopoly finance capitalism eroded the market-state dualism of nineteenth-century capitalism, in which markets were founded on private law, in particular contract law, and states on public law, especially constitutional law. Transnational monopoly finance capitalism has blurred the boundaries between public and private law,[99] even as corporatism, welfarism, and fascism further integrated states, economies, and civil societies on the ground.[100] Equally, the new capitalism blurred the national/international divide by furthering the reduction of statehood to formal legal criteria (formalised in the 1933 Montevideo Convention on the Rights and Duties of States) and reorganising the international legal order around the United Nations.[101]

Polanyi opens *The Great Transformation* with the following statement:

---

[94] Horn, 'Reinventing Monopoly'.

[95] Pashukanis, *Law and Marxism*.

[96] See e.g., David Harvey, *The New Imperialism* (OUP 2003); Ellen Meiksins Wood, *Democracy Against Capitalism: Renewing Historical Materialism* (CUP 1995).

[97] See e.g., Susan Strange, *States and Markets* (2nd edn, Continuum 1994).

[98] See D'Souza, *What's Wrong With Rights?*

[99] For debates and discussions on the public/private divide, see the articles in (1982) 130 *University of Pennsylvania Law Review*. See also Dawn Oliver, *Common Values and the Public-Private Divide* (Butterworths 1999); Michael Taggart, 'The Nature and Functions of the State' in Peter Cane and Mark Tushnet (ed), *The Oxford Handbook of Legal Studies* (OUP 2003) 101; Margaret Thornton (ed), *Public and Private: Feminist Legal Debates* (OUP 1995).

[100] See Daniel Chirot, 'The Corporatist Model and Socialism' (1980) 9 *Theory and Society* 363; James Q Whitman, 'Of Corporatism, Fascism, and the First New Deal' (1991) 39 *American Journal of Comparative Law* 747.

[101] D'Souza, 'Imperialism and Self-Determination'.

Nineteenth-century civilization has collapsed. ... Nineteenth-century civilization rested on four institutions. The first was the balance-of-power system which for a century prevented the occurrence of
any long and devastating war between the Great Powers. The second was the international gold standard which symbolized a unique organization of world economy. The third was the self-regulating
market which produced an unheard-of material welfare. The fourth was the liberal state. Classified
in one way, two of these institutions were economic, two political. Classified in another way, two of
them were national, two international. Between them they determined the characteristic outlines of
the history of our civilization.[102]

All four of these collapsed institutions were rebuilt on new foundations after the two world
wars. This rebuilding process established new institutions, brought forth new actors, and built
new relations between them. As with the earlier transformations from feudalism to capitalism
and from mercantile capitalism to industrial capitalism, law was once again the mechanism
that established these institutions and created new actors and legal subjectivities. Unlike in
earlier stages of capitalism, though, the legal and institutional transformations of the twentieth
century were from the very outset transnational in scope. The balance-of-power system of the
'great powers' of the nineteenth century—mainly involving Britain, France, Austria, Prussia,
and Russia—was replaced by the UN Security Council, where the veto-bearing powers were
the United States, Britain, France, the Soviet Union (now Russia), and finally China, which
was allowed to take its seat at the Security Council after the rapprochement between the United
States and China.[103] All five of these new 'great powers' were victors in the world wars. The
veto power at the centre of the international legal order, with its roots in the post-Napoleonic
War settlement between the European 'great powers',[104] continues the old balance-of-power
system under the new conditions of post-Second World War capitalism. Under post-war capitalism, the US dollar replaced the British-dominated gold standard. The US dollar continues
to set many of the conditions for engaging in 'truck, barter and exchange' for peoples around
the world. The dollar is managed internationally with the assistance of the IMF—a legal
artefact fabricated by the Allies during and after the Second World War to control the international monetary system. As a legal entity it must operate in accordance with its Articles of
Agreement, which set the terms under which the organisation was established and pursuant to
which it operates. The IMF's 'stabilisation loans' take the form of legal contracts with Third
World states, whereby the latter undertake specific contractual obligations and agree to certain
penalties in the event of default. In addition, these contractual obligations require Third World
states to adopt laws conducive to the operation of transnational corporations and the dominance of 'governance by contracts' in the economic sphere.[105]

During the late twentieth century, the 'self-regulating markets' of classical political
economy mythology were belied at every turn by the outright price-fixing of monopolies and
oligarchies operating transnationally.[106] Legal relations were central to enabling such monop-

---

[102] Polanyi, *Great Transformation*, 3.

[103] Evelyn Goh, *Constructing the U.S. Rapprochement with China, 1961–1974: From 'Red Menace'
to 'Tacit Ally'* (CUP 2005).

[104] Gerry Simpson, *Great Powers and Outlaw States: Unequal Sovereigns in the International Legal
Order* (CUP 2004).

[105] D'Souza, *What's Wrong With Rights?* See also A Claire Clutter and Thomas Dietz (eds), *The
Politics of Private Transnational Governance by Contract* (Routledge 2017).

[106] Baran, *Political Economy of Growth*; Baran and Sweezy, *Monopoly Capital*.

olistic practices, with 'anti-trust' legislation providing much of the façade.[107] Some scholars have argued that this period witnessed the onset of 'warfare states'.[108] The international legal order privileges warfare states, enabling them to organise and discipline other states through treaties and other instruments on a range of issues, including but not limited to disarmament, military aid, lease of territories for military bases, and nuclear non-proliferation. Unlike earlier stages of capitalism, transnational monopoly finance capitalism is characterised by the fact that all four institutions are international in scope, and also that all four are institutionalised. Each of these transformations has been facilitated by mechanisms of law and through significant changes in legal systems. These legal relations form the preconditions necessary for capitalism to operate in systemic ways across the globe. Equally, these legal relations are not an 'autonomous sphere' that exists outside relations of production, consumption, and exchange. Market fetishism obfuscates the real actors in the (ongoing) epoch of imperialism in ways that subvert the development of an agenda for revolutionary political change. Marxist debates on whether or not law is an epiphenomenon, whether it is base or superstructure, miss the real issues relevant for any anti-imperialist political mobilisation to occur. Consequently, neocolonialism becomes invisible, a liturgical reference to statistics operationalised by mysteries of 'the market'. It is necessary to lift the veil over this statistical façade, which clouds the critique of political economy, and examine the ways in which transnational monopoly finance capitalism operates in the real world.

MARXISM, NEOCOLONIALISM, AND INTERNATIONAL LAW

How, then, are we to understand Marxism, international law, and neocolonialism? I wish to return to basics by drawing attention to insights from Lenin that are relevant for this chapter. Lenin's views on imperialism are often read narrowly by relying on one pamphlet, *Imperialism, the Highest Stage of Capitalism*.[109] The weight placed on this single text does disservice to Lenin's analysis of imperialism, reducing it to a discussion of either inter-imperialist war or imperialist political economy. Lenin understood imperialism to be an extended period of time, and called it 'the epoch of capitalist imperialism'.[110] 'We cannot say how long this epoch will last', Lenin is reported to have said.[111] Lenin did not write as a scholar. His analysis is scattered in different pamphlets, speeches, and interventions in political debates. While Lenin changed his mind on a large number of issues over time, often as part of a direct tactical response to shifting circumstances, there is a high degree of coherence in his basic analysis of relations

---

[107] Robert Bork, 'Vertical Integration and the Sherman Act: The Legal History of an Economic Misconception' (1954) 22 *University of Chicago Law Review* 157.
[108] David Edgerton, *Warfare State: Britain, 1920–1970* (CUP 2005); Brian Waddell, 'Limiting National Interventionism in the United States: The Warfare-Welfare State as Restrictive Governance Paradigm' (2001) 25 *Capital & Class* 109.
[109] Lenin, 'Imperialism'.
[110] Lenin, 'Imperialism', 734.
[111] VI Lenin, 'Lecture on "The Proletariat and the War", October 1(14), 1914, Newspaper Report' in VI Lenin, *Collected Works*, vol 36 (first published 1914, Progress Publishers 1971) 297, 299.

between law and the state under conditions of transnational monopoly finance capitalism.[112] 'Imperialism', Lenin wrote, 'is oppression of nations on a *new* historical basis'.[113]

Writing about the Monroe Doctrine, first articulated in 1823 but revived during Woodrow Wilson's presidency, Lenin argued that it merely formalised an existing system of protectorates.[114] Lenin opposed the Wilsonian idea of self-determination as a legal right of nations, a view supported by many Marxists at the time including Rosa Luxemburg.[115] Lenin argued that the meaning of self-determination could not be deduced 'by juggling with legal definitions, or "inventing" abstract definitions', but only by 'examining the historical and economic conditions of the national movements',[116] organised through the expansion of capitalism, that called forth the 'nation-state' as a universal political form. Real self-determination was about the ability to exist as an independent state, free of 'alien national bodies'.[117] The formal equality promised by the right to self-determination did not guarantee real equality. For Lenin, the unequal development of capitalism meant that older capitalist states, with 'long-established constitutional regime[s]',[118] were able to mobilise a range of military, diplomatic, economic, and ideological resources to dominate newer, more fragile states. During the epoch of imperialism, advanced capitalist states had become 'rentier' or 'usurer' states, and '[t]he world has become divided into a handful of usurer states on the one side, and a vast majority of debtor states on the other'.[119] Thus, while the historical expansion of capitalism universalised the nation-state form, it also called forth asymmetrical relations between 'usurer states' and 'debtor states'. Lenin discussed different ways in which some states might be subordinated to stronger ones, including by way of colonies, semi-colonies, settler colonies, protectorates, and various combinations of these and other legal forms.[120] Referring to Portugal, which had effectively become something of a British protectorate, Lenin writes as follows:

> Relations of this kind have always existed between big and little states. But during the period of capitalist imperialism *they become a general system*, they form part of the process of 'dividing the world,' they *become a link in the chain of operations of world finance capital.*[121]

How have developments since the First World War transformed relations between powerful and less powerful states into what Lenin here calls 'a general system', one in which national

---

[112]   For an expanded discussion see D'Souza, 'Imperialism and Self-Determination'.

[113]   VI Lenin, 'Notebooks on Imperialism' [1915–16] in VI Lenin, *Collected Works*, vol 39 (Progress Publishers 1974) 27, 736 (original emphasis).

[114]   Lenin, 'Notebooks on Imperialism', esp 752.

[115]   VI Lenin, 'Second Congress of the Communist International, July 19–August 7, 1920' in VI Lenin, *Selected Works*, vol 3 (Progress Publishers 1971) 389, 395–96. See also The Communist International, *Second Congress of the Communist International: Proceedings of Petrograd Session of July 17th and Moscow Sessions of July 19th—August 7th, 1920* (Publishing Office of the Communist International 1921) 128.

[116]   VI Lenin, 'The Right of Nations to Self-Determination' [1914] in VI Lenin, *Selected Works*, vol 1 (Progress Publishers 1970) 564, 565.

[117]   Lenin, 'The Right of Nations to Self-Determination', 565. For a critique of the Treaty of Versailles, and the roles of John Maynard Keynes and Woodrow Wilson in the post-First World War settlement, see 'Speech at the Second Congress of the Communist International', 392–33, 395–97.

[118]   Lenin, 'Right of Nations to Self-Determination', 568.

[119]   Lenin, 'Imperialism', 718.

[120]   Lenin, 'Imperialism', 702 ff.

[121]   Lenin, 'Imperialism', 707 (emphases added).

oppression is a feature of the divisions fostered by finance capital? Marxism's fragmentation has deflected attention from this central question. Instead, ambivalence towards international law and international organisations has mystified their role in imperialist and neocolonialist relations. If Marxists are to return to the question more than a century after Lenin, a new research agenda is needed that confronts developments since the First World War, highlighting international law's role in the 'oppression of nations on a *new* historical basis'.

How does international law establish the 'oppression of nations on a *new* historical basis'? Pursuant to the Monroe Doctrine, the United States claimed sole hegemony over the Americas, discouraging European powers from contesting its political and economic control of the Western hemisphere. By 1933 the doctrine had come to be integrated into international law in the view of many.[122] To some degree, it even helped to lay the foundations for the 1933 Montevideo Convention,[123] which offered a formal definition of statehood and furthered the universalisation of the juridical state form beyond the Americas. The formal equality of states by no means ended US domination in Latin America.[124] If anything, notions of sovereign equality facilitated the expansion of US domination internationally.

If we are to pick up the threads where Lenin left off, the central question of Marxism's relation to international law and questions of neocolonialism is clear: how do states become 'link[s] in the chain of operations of world finance capital'? How does transnational monopoly finance capitalism assign a place to each state in the link? What role does the class composition of each state have in the place that states occupy in the imperial chain? What types of conflicts, contradictions, and forms of collaboration ensue between states as a consequence of their different positions in the imperial chain? Above all, at least for present purposes, how does international law establish states, how does it link them together in an imperialist chain, and how does it keep these chains from breaking up? Satisfactory answers to these questions require a comprehensive research agenda for understanding relations of imperialism and neo-colonialism generally and the role of international law in these relations specifically.

CONCLUSION

A new research agenda for Marxism, law, and neocolonialism, of the kind outlined above, holds out the possibility of a new radicalism. It enables Marxists to assert that if 'the roots of man is man himself', then legal persons are not real 'men'. It enables Marxists to put people and their struggles at the centre of the critique of capitalist society, and also articulate a critique of imperialism transcending academic disciplines. When all is said and done, though, whether Marxists can—and will—return to a radical critique of international law and neocolonialism will depend on the course of anti-imperialist struggles in the 'new colonies', where the struggle against imperialism is a daily struggle for survival of millions of working people.

---

[122] See Philip C Jessup, 'The Generalization of the Monroe Doctrine' (1935) 29 *American Journal of International Law* 105; Juan Pablo Scarfi, 'In the Name of the Americas: The Pan-American Redefinition of the Monroe Doctrine and the Emerging Language of American International Law in the Western Hemisphere, 1898–1933' (2016) 40 *Diplomatic History* 189.

[123] James J Lenoir, 'The Monroe Doctrine and International Law: 1933–1941' (1942) 4 *Journal of Politics* 47.

[124] Lenoir, 'Monroe Doctrine and International Law'.

20. Taking political economy seriously: *Grundriss* for a Marxist analysis of international law

Rémi Bachand

INTRODUCTION

Over the last few decades, critical international lawyers have invested significant energy attempting to unveil how international law has historically contributed to reproducing and consolidating the social structures of capitalism and imperialism.[1] Insightful work has been produced showing how human rights,[2] the right to democracy,[3] global governance (and the international organisations that promote it),[4] and the so-called 'responsibility to protect'[5] do not enjoy the kind of emancipatory power that mainstream international lawyers generally accord them. This development is clearly to be welcomed, since it undermines the idyllic liberal view that international law is a peaceful force for the emancipation of subaltern classes and peoples.

Surprisingly, critical scholars of international law have generally failed to engage with questions of political economy.[6] Still more remarkable is the fact that this is also the case

---

[1]   To take only some of the most famous examples, see Antony Anghie, *Imperialism, Sovereignty and the Making of International Law* (CUP 2005); Martti Koskenniemi, *The Gentle Civilizer of Nations: The Rise and Fall of International Law 1870–1960* (CUP 2001); Sundhya Pahuja, *Decolonising International Law: Development, Economic Growth, and the Politics of Universality* (CUP 2011); James Thuo Gathii, *War, Commerce, and International Law* (OUP 2010).

[2]   Amy Bartholomew, 'Empire's Law and the Contradictory Politics of Human Rights' in Amy Bartholomew (ed), *Empire's Law: The American Imperial Project and the 'War to Remake the World'* (Pluto Press; Between the Lines 2006) 161; Makau Mutua, *Human Rights Standards: Hegemony, Law, and Politics* (State University of New York Press 2016); Costas Douzinas, *Human Rights and Empire: The Political Philosophy of Cosmopolitanism* (Routledge-Cavendish 2007); Radha D'Souza, *What's Wrong with Rights? Social Movements, Law and Liberal Imaginations* (Pluto Press 2018); David Kennedy, 'The International Human Rights Movement: Part of the Problem?' (2002) 15 *Harvard Human Rights Journal* 125; David Kennedy, 'The International Human Rights Regime: Still Part of the Problem?' in Robert Dickinson et al (eds), *Examining Critical Perspectives on Human Rights* (CUP 2012) 19; José-Manuel Barreto (ed), *Human Rights from a Third World Perspective: Critique, History and International Law* (Cambridge Scholars Publishing 2012); Upendra Baxi, *The Future of Human Rights* (OUP 2006).

[3]   Susan Marks, *The Riddle of All Constitutions: International Law, Democracy, and the Critique of Ideology* (OUP 2000); Susan Marks, 'What Has Become of the Emerging Right to Democratic Governance?' (2011) 22 *European Journal of International Law* 507.

[4]   Antony Anghie, 'Civilization and Commerce: The Concept of Governance in Historical Perspective' (2000) 45 *Villanova Law Review* 911; James Thuo Gathii, 'Neoliberalism, Colonialism and International Governance: Decentering the International Law of Governmental Legitimacy' (2000) 98 *Michigan Law Review* 1996.

[5]   Anne Orford, *International Authority and the Responsibility to Protect* (CUP 2011).

[6]   Exceptions include Anthony Carty, 'Marxism and International Law: Perspectives for the American (Twenty-First) Century' (2004) 17 *Leiden Journal of International Law* 247; Mark Neocleous,

for many scholars of international law who are inspired by Marxism. More often than not, when critical scholars engage with political economy, they subscribe to an understanding of the field that is surprisingly wide and abstract. They are, for instance, sometimes satisfied with the simple statement that political economy is the study of how wealth is created and distributed.[7] On this definition, demonstrating that international law plays a role in producing and distributing wealth is enough to claim that one is providing a politico-economic analysis (or even a critique of political economy). Moreover, when critical international legal scholars actually do relate international law directly to questions of political economy, they tend to assume that capitalism is always and necessarily in need of the same types of institutions for its reproduction[8]—or, at best, they use a very broad periodisation in an effort to demonstrate how international law has been important for the successful operation of capitalism in its different stages.[9] It is also common to start from a rather broad description of capitalism,[10] and then to claim that international law is useful for protecting and promoting some of its essential institutions,[11] such as private property or free mobility of capital,[12] or the interests of the capitalist class.[13] Hence, such approaches tend oftentimes not to be based upon a real interdisciplinary method grounded in direct engagement with political economy as a distinct discipline that can shed light on the formation and operation of law.[14]

Yet, for any Marxist, understanding why international law's institutions are used one way or another requires a deeper and more accurate understanding of how the global economy works in a specific context. It requires an understanding not only of how the dominant mode of production works in general, but also of its specificities and complexities in the particular era

---

'International Law as Primitive Accumulation; Or, the Secret of Systematic Colonization' (2012) 23 *European Journal of International Law* 941; Orford, *International Authority*; Martti Koskenniemi, 'It's Not the Cases, It's the System' (2017) 18 *Journal of World Investment and Trade* 343; Umut Özsu, 'Grabbing Land Legally—A Marxist Analysis' (2019) 32 *Leiden Journal of International Law* 215; Ntina Tzouvala, *Capitalism as Civilization: A History of International Law* (CUP 2020).

[7]   For a particularly well-known example, see David Kennedy, *A World of Struggle: How Power, Law, and Expertise Shape Global Political Economy* (Princeton University Press 2016).

[8]   See e.g., Tzouvala, *Capitalism as Civilization*, though it should also be noted that Tzouvala offers an historical analysis that distinguishes between different periods in the history of international law.

[9]   BS Chimni, *International Law and World Order: A Critique of Contemporary Approaches* (2nd edn, CUP 2017).

[10]   BS Chimni, 'Capitalism, Imperialism, and International Law in the Twenty-First Century Symposium' (2012) 14 *Oregon Review of International Law* 17.

[11]   BS Chimni, 'Third World Approaches to International Law: A Manifesto' in Antony Anghie et al (eds), *The Third World and International Order: Law, Politics, and Globalization* (Martinus Nijhoff 2003) 47, 52–58.

[12]   BS Chimni, 'An Outline of a Marxist Course on Public International Law' (2004) 17 *Leiden Journal of International Law* 1, esp 10.

[13]   BS Chimni, 'International Institutions Today: An Imperial Global State in the Making' (2004) 15 *European Journal of International Law* 1. Chimni is one of the few international legal scholars who identifies as a Marxist and who has attempted to examine the link between capitalism (from a politico-economic standpoint) and international law. The point I make here is that more work is required to expand our understanding of how capitalism works, how it changes over time, and how international law is involved in its reproduction and transformation.

[14]   John Haskell and Akbar Rasulov, 'International Law and the Turn to Political Economy' (2018) 31 *Leiden Journal of International Law* 243.

under scrutiny.[15] The analysis of capitalism as a mode of production must also offer an analysis of its historical and geographic variations.

This chapter's chief objective is to propose a research agenda whose goal would be to examine how the economic particularities of each historical period influence international law, and how the latter affects the global economy differently depending upon the period in question. In other words, the chapter takes a closer look at the co-constitution of international law and international economy. This research agenda would operate at a lower level of abstraction than what has generally been the case in recent critical international legal scholarship. The chapter is divided into two parts. I first discuss some Marxist and neo-Marxist theoretical frameworks of political economy that might be useful for such a research agenda. I then discuss how some of their relevant portions might be integrated into a framework for analysing international law.

MARXIST POLITICAL ECONOMY: SOME USEFUL CONTRIBUTIONS

In this part, I begin by exploring the neo-Gramscians. I then explore two trends in what is sometimes called 'radical political economics'[16]—the École de la régulation (ÉR) and the Social Structure of Accumulation Theory (SSAT), which share a number of similarities despite slightly different conceptual frameworks. I conclude this section by considering scholars who emphasise variations in the rate of profit when analysing the economic history of the past 70 years.

Neo-Gramscian Critics of Global Political Economy

To some degree, this first approach is best understood as a broad introduction to the ones that follow, rather than a distinct theoretical framework of political economy per se. Indeed, the neo-Gramscian school, developed by the late Robert Cox and some of his York University colleagues in the 1980s, was originally a theory of international relations (IR), having as its initial objective the criticism of realist and neo-realist theories of IR.[17] Since then, it has been

---

[15]   See also Akbar Rasulov, 'CLS and Marxism: A History of an Affair' (2014) 5 *Transnational Legal Theory* 622, 639 (stating that 'to understand how the economic base really works, one needs to study the way in which the particular underlying regime of property and contract are configured').

[16]   Marlene Kim, 'What Is Radical Political Economics?' (2018) 50 *Review of Radical Political Economics* 576.

[17]   Robert W Cox, 'Social Forces, States and World Orders: Beyond International Relations Theory' (1981) 10 *Millennium* 126.

widely used by academics working in fields such as sociology of international relations,[18] political economy,[19] and also international law.[20]

Using the work of the Italian philosopher and activist Antonio Gramsci, the neo-Gramscians theorise the role of hegemony in the reproduction and stabilisation of a social order that conforms in the main to the fundamental interests of its dominant class. This concept of hegemony, they argue, is especially useful for understanding the role of international organisations (and, by extension, international law) in international relations.[21]

First, for Cox, hegemony:

> means dominance of a particular kind where the dominant state creates an order based ideologically on a broad measure of consent, functioning according to general principles that in fact ensure the

[18]   Ted Hopf, 'Common-Sense Constructivism and Hegemony in World Politics' (2013) 67 *International Organization* 317; William I Robinson, 'Gramsci and Globalisation: From Nation-State to Transnational Hegemony' (2005) 8 *Critical Review of International Social and Political Philosophy* 559; William I Robinson, 'The Transnational State and the BRICS: A Global Capitalism Perspective' (2015) 36 *Third World Quarterly* 1; William I Robinson, 'Global Capitalism Theory and the Emergence of Transnational Elites' (2012) 38 *Critical Sociology* 349; William I Robinson and Jerry Harris, 'Towards a Global Ruling Class? Globalization and the Transnational Capitalist Class' (2000) 64 *Science & Society* 11; Leslie Sklair, *The Transnational Capitalist Class* (Blackwell 2001); Leslie Sklair and Peter T Robbins, 'Global Capitalism and Major Corporations from the Third World' (2002) 23 *Third World Quarterly* 81; Upendra D Acharya, 'Globalization and Hegemony Shift: Are States Merely Agents of Corporate Capitalism?' (2013) 36 *Boston College International and Comparative Law Review* 937; Mark Rupert, 'Reading Gramsci in an Era of Globalising Capitalism' (2005) 8 *Critical Review of International Social and Political Philosophy* 483; Andreas Bieler and Adam David Morton, 'The Gordian Knot of Agency—Structure in International Relations: A Neo-Gramscian Perspective' (2001) 7 *European Journal of International Relations* 5; Kees van der Pijl, 'Gramsci and Left Managerialism' (2005) 8 *Critical Review of International Social and Political Philosophy* 499; Steen Fryba Christensen and Xing Li (eds), *Emerging Powers, Emerging Markets, Emerging Societies: Global Responses* (Palgrave Macmillan 2016); Joe Wills, 'The World Turned Upside Down? Neo-Liberalism, Socioeconomic Rights, and Hegemony' (2014) 27 *Leiden Journal of International Law* 11.
[19]   Adam David Morton, 'Social Forces in the Struggle over Hegemony: Neo-Gramscian Perspectives in International Political Economy' (2003) 15 *Rethinking Marxism* 153; Stephen R Gill and David Law, 'Global Hegemony and the Structural Power of Capital' (1989) 33 *International Studies Quarterly* 475; Andreas Bieler and Adam David Morton, 'Globalisation, the State and Class Struggle: A "Critical Economy" Engagement with Open Marxism' (2003) 5 *British Journal of Politics and International Relations* 467.
[20]   Sonja Buckel and Andreas Fischer-Lescano, 'Gramsci Reconsidered: Hegemony in Global Law' (2009) 22 *Leiden Journal of International Law* 437; James D Fry, 'Legitimacy Push: Towards a Gramscian Approach to International Law' (2008) 13 *UCLA Journal of International Law and Foreign Affairs* 307; A Claire Cutler, 'Artifice, Ideology and Paradox: The Public/Private Distinction in International Law' (1997) 4 *Review of International Political Economy* 261; A Claire Cutler, 'Gramsci, Law, and the Culture of Global Capitalism' (2005) 8 *Critical Review of International Social and Political Philosophy* 527; A Claire Cutler, 'Global Capitalism and Liberal Myths: Dispute Settlement in Private International Trade Relations' (1995) 24 *Millennium* 377; Rémi Bachand, 'Le droit international et l'idéologie droits-de-l'hommiste au fondement de l'hégémonie occidentale' (2014) 2014 *Revue québécoise de droit international* 69.
[21]   Robert W Cox, 'Gramsci, Hegemony and International Relations: An Essay in Method' (1983) 12 *Millennium* 162, 162.

continuing supremacy of the leading state or states and leading social classes but at the same time offer some measure or prospect of satisfaction to the less powerful.[22]

The effect of hegemony is consequently to ensure domination, the 'continuing supremacy' of a specific actor over the rest of society. At first glance, in the international context, this actor could be a dominant state. Nevertheless, coming from a Marxist background and being critical of the state-civil society separation assumed by mainstream theories of IR,[23] Cox relies upon Gramsci's concept of the 'historic bloc',[24] reminding us that state and civil society form a single and 'solid structure' and cannot easily be distinguished from each other.[25] Consequently, hegemony is not the supremacy of a state, but of a dominant social class that succeeds in expanding its internal hegemony on a global scale. To be more accurate, '[h]egemony at the international level … is an order within a world economy with a dominant mode of production which penetrates into all countries and links into other subordinate modes of production'.[26] Hegemony, then, is the result of a social class exporting a mode of production (favourable to its own interests) to the entire world, thereby succeeding in convincing other actors that it is also beneficial for them. For Cox, one cannot understand international relations without first understanding political economy, and how social relations are organised in the dominant states of the era under scrutiny.

Cox then examines the role of international organisations in the construction and reproduction of hegemony, stating that 'international organisation functions as the process through which the institutions of hegemony and its ideology are developed'.[27] More precisely, international organisations play various roles to facilitate the reproduction of hegemony: '(1) they embody the rules which facilitate the expansion of hegemonic world orders; … (3) they ideologically legitimate the norms of the world order; (4) they co-opt the elites from peripheral countries and (5) they absorb counter-hegemonic ideas'.[28] Stephen Gill adds another dimension that could easily be added to this list. Writing about the 'new constitutionalism', understood as the 'political-judicial counterpart' of a certain 'discourse of political economy' (and specifically 'disciplinary neoliberalism'),[29] Gill underlines the different mechanisms used to create 'a new constitutional framework to separate economic institutions … from political influence of elected politicians and more generally the wider public, and so "depoliticize" the question of money',[30] as well as many other social, economic, and political problems. In other words, international organisations create a 'common sense',[31] one that excludes some

[22]   Robert W Cox, *Production, Power, and World Order: Social Forces in the Making of History* (Columbia University Press 1987) 7.

[23]   Cox, 'Social Forces, States and World Orders', 127.

[24]   Antonio Gramsci, *Cahiers de prison: Cahiers 6, 7, 8 et 9* (Monique Aymard and Paolo Fulchignoni tr, Gallimard 1983) 186, 362.

[25]   Cox, 'Gramsci, Hegemony and International Relations', 167.

[26]   Cox, 'Gramsci, Hegemony and International Relations', 171.

[27]   Cox, 'Gramsci, Hegemony and International Relations', 172.

[28]   Cox, 'Gramsci, Hegemony and International Relations', 172.

[29]   Stephen Gill, 'Constitutionalizing Inequality and the Clash of Globalizations' (2002) 4 *International Studies Review* 47, 47.

[30]   Gill, 'Constitutionalizing Inequality', 49.

[31]   Stephen Gill and A Claire Cutler (eds), *New Constitutionalism and World Order* (CUP 2015).

questions from the universe of possibilities, from what can be democratically put in place or even imagined by citizens.[32]

Even without being a political economy theoretical framework per se, the neo-Gramscian school is useful because it stresses the importance of the link between legal institutions and concrete politico-economic structures. It shows how much a dominant state's economic structures and ruling classes have the capacity to influence the international economic order, as well as the international law that formalises and organises it. It highlights that international law facilitates the globalisation by capitalist classes in dominant states of economic structures that are responsible for their hegemonic power at home. This framework also offers an understanding of the 'rise and fall' of some institutions: when they are not able to reproduce the interests of the hegemonic class, they may face contestation, and their very existence may become endangered.[33]

As already noted, hegemony for Cox involves the entry of a dominant mode of production into other countries or societies. In other words, it concerns its worldwide expansion. Cox explains the concept of 'mode of production' in *Production, Power, and World Order*, where he writes as follows: 'Production of physical goods plus the production of historical structures together constitute the material reproduction of society. It would seem that Marx meant something like this when he wrote about the mode of production.'[34]

Earlier in this book, Cox lists some characteristics that distinguish the specific ways that physical goods are produced—the 'kinds of things [that] are produced and [the way] they are produced', 'the complementarity of roles required in most production', and 'the distribution of the rewards of production'.[35] According to Cox, hegemony is the expansion of a specific form of organisation of production, of a distinctive form of *social relations of production*. Thus, if hegemony depends, as Cox believes it does, upon international organisations for its reproduction and social and spatial expansion, this also means that the latter are linked directly to the way the hegemonic country organises its production. Yet the neo-Gramscians, Cox in particular, do not offer details about what precisely must be analysed to understand Cox's understanding of modes of production. Consequently, a turn to political economy is necessary to have a clear view of the link between the organisation of production on the one hand and international law and organisations on the other. In order to complement neo-Gramscian analysis, the next section will explore two additional theories: the ÉR and the SSAT. Their theoretical similarities are close and important enough to allow for comparative analysis.[36]

---

32   See also Cutler, 'Artifice, Ideology and Paradox'.
33   Christensen and Li, *Emerging Powers*.
34   Cox, *Production, Power, and World Order*, 396.
35   Cox, *Production, Power, and World Order*, 11–12.
36   Allan Coblan, 'La Régulation et l'école radicale américaine' in Robert Boyer and Yves Saillard (eds), *Théorie de la régulation: l'état des savoirs* (2nd edn, La Découverte 2002); David M Kotz, 'A Comparative Analysis of the Theory of Regulation and the Social Structure of Accumulation Theory' (1990) 54 *Science & Society* 5; Terrence McDonough, Michael Reich, and David M Kotz, 'Introduction: Social Structure of Accumulation Theory for the 21st Century' in Terrence McDonough, Michael Reich, and David M Kotz (eds), *Contemporary Capitalism and Its Crises: Social Structure of Accumulation Theory for the 21st Century* (CUP 2010) 1, 4–8.

The École de la Régulation and the SSAT

The ÉR and SSAT developed in parallel on both sides of the Atlantic during the second half of the 1970s. Facing the end of the *Trente glorieuses*, they both tried to understand the crisis that was emerging at that time from a theoretical standpoint that was critical of mainstream economics. More precisely, and quoting David Kotz, one of the principal participants in the debate:

> The [ÉR] and the SSAT seek to explain long-run patterns of capital accumulation by analyzing the relation between the capital accumulation process and a set of social institutions which affect that process. The central idea is that crucial features of the trajectory of the capital accumulation process, over a long time period, are the product of the supporting role played by a set of social institutions.[37]

For international lawyers, the relevance of this is immediately evident, since it points towards a research agenda whose main questions are: How does international law contribute to capital accumulation during different periods? What is the influence of capital accumulation on the development of international law?

The basic *problématique* and theoretical orientation of ÉR emerged in the doctoral dissertation of Michel Aglietta, defended in 1974 and published in 1976.[38] Theorising the contradictions at the basis of capitalism's crises, Aglietta starts his work with the following hypothesis:

> [C]apitalism is a force for change that does not have a principle of regulation by itself. This principle lies in the coherence of social mediations that direct the accumulation of capital in the sense of progress. ... Consequently, the dysfunction of the growth should be sought in the distortions between changes provoked by capitalism and the incapacity of existing institutions to deal with them within the framework of established macroeconomic regulation.[39]

Aglietta's research agenda then focuses on the different forms taken by the capitalist mode of production, how each succeeded for a while, before entering into crisis just to be replaced by another form of capitalism. At the core of the analysis lies the fact that different institutions operate as mediators to help reproduce the specific form of capital accumulation.

Two important concepts are at the centre of this agenda. The first is 'accumulation regime', which refers to a pattern of regularities that ensures the relatively stable and coherent accumulation of capital.[40] Aglietta argues that the concept is useful for understanding how capitalism works, and how capital accumulation is organised in a particular period of time and in a specific area. For ÉR economists, understanding a regime of accumulation requires analysis of its specific social patterns. Five such patterns are generally identified. First, the organisation of production, more specifically the relation between labour and capital. Second, the 'temporal horizon for the valorization of capital', that is, the extent of time that the owners of a production unit (and in particular the shareholders) are willing to wait before their investments generate profits. Notably, this characteristic will play an important role on management principles.

---

[37]   Kotz, 'A Comparative Analysis', 7.
[38]   Michel Aglietta, *Régulation et crises du capitalisme* (first published 1976, 2nd edn, Jacob 1997).
[39]   Aglietta, *Régulation*, 437–38. This and the following translations are mine.
[40]   Aglietta uses the term 'growth regime' where his followers talk about 'accumulation regime'. I prefer the latter since the ultimate *raison d'être* of capitalism is the capital accumulation, even if growth is an important element for the achievement of this purpose.

Third, the way that wealth is distributed between classes. Fourth, a particular composition of socio-economic demand that determines the path and development of production. Fifth, the specific way in which capitalist and non-capitalist social dynamics interact.[41]

An accumulation regime is supported and legitimised by a 'mode of regulation'. This is the second important concept of Aglietta's agenda. A 'mode of regulation' includes a 'set of individual and collective procedures and behaviours' whose functions are to (1) 'reproduce the fundamental social relations of the mode of production through the conjunction of historically determined institutional forms'; (2) 'to sustain and "pilot" the present accumulation regime'; (3) and 'to ensure the dynamic compatibility of an array of decentralized decisions without requiring the internalization, by the economic actors, of whole system-adjustment principles'.[42] These 'individual and collective procedures and behaviours', also called 'institutional forms', include a monetary regime, a wage form, forms of competition, international insertion modalities (i.e., the rules that regulate relations between the state and the rest of the world with regard to trade in goods, services, finance, investment, and so on), and a state form.[43] These 'institutional forms' are important. When they no longer work, when they fail to mediate between contradictory forces inherent in an accumulation regime, the latter faces a crisis that can ultimately lead to its replacement by an entirely different regime, or even the collapse of the mode of production itself.[44]

The ÉR, then, offers a two-step analysis which can be summarised as follows: (1) study how capital accumulation works in a particular economic formation (that is, how surplus value is extracted and how profits are reaped); (2) study how this process is regulated (that is, how it is legitimised and how its inherent problems and contradictions are managed and postponed). Even if its adherents often insist that the institutional forms constituting the mode of regulation are not all legal forms, this agenda is useful for this chapter. Indeed, it is an invitation to compare and link the evolution of legal institutions with the historically and geographically located organisations of the capitalist mode of production, specifically their modes of regulation.

However, this conceptual apparatus comes with certain difficulties. One of these difficulties is that if we take the definitions offered of 'accumulation regime' and of 'mode of regulation', it is not always self-evident that each of the elements the authors use to exemplify them (the particular way to divide value between classes, the specific organisation of social demand, the monetary regime, and so on) fits in the category (of the 'accumulation regime' or 'mode of regulation') they have put them in. For example, it is not obvious that the organisation of the relation between labour and capital, which is placed in the 'accumulation regime' category, is not an important agent of regulation, especially since one can argue that it is the product of some 'individual and collective procedures and behaviours' (i.e., the definition of the 'mode of regulation') and that it can help to legitimise capital accumulation. The bottom line here is that we may be better off avoiding overly strict reliance upon this school's conceptual apparatus; we may instead want to adapt it loosely.

[41]   Robert Boyer, *La théorie de la régulation: une analyse critique* (La Découverte 1986) 46.
[42]   Boyer, *La théorie de la régulation*, 54.
[43]   Robert Boyer, *Économie politique des capitalismes: théorie de la régulation et des crises* (La Découverte 2015) 40–52.
[44]   Boyer, *Économie politique des capitalismes*, 82.

The SSAT, for its part, offers a simpler and more workable conceptual framework, and one with significant explanatory power in its own right. First, its objective is to 'explain both the long periods of more rapid expansion and the long periods of stagnation or contraction'.[45] Drawing from Marxist and Keynesian theories, it argues that capitalism is 'an inherently conflictual system', but that:

> these inherent problems can be attenuated through the construction of sets of institutions that mitigate and channel class conflict and stabilize capitalists' long-run expectations. Institutions in this sense are conceived of broadly and can be economic, political, ideological, or cultural in character. ... [These institutions] are mutually compatible and generally supportive of each other as well as supportive of the accumulation process.[46]

Thus, the SSAT uses the 'social structure of accumulation' concept to examine this 'coherent institutional structure ... [that is] cent[red] around promoting profit-making and a stable capital accumulation process'.[47] In a sense, this bears similarities to the Gramscian concept of 'historic bloc'; since the SSA is a historically situated configuration of institutions, its main feature is to stabilise social conflicts and to solve the problems caused by the contradictions inherent in capitalism.[48]

Somewhat similar to the ÉR, the SSAT distinguishes between two kinds of 'processes'. To quote David Gordon, Richard Edwards, and Michael Reich, authors of a book that quickly became an early reference of SSAT literature, '[t]he inner boundary of the social structure of accumulation, then, divides the capital accumulation process itself (the profit-making activities of individual capitalists) from the institutional (social, political, legal, cultural and market) context within which it occurs'.[49] Thus, the SSAT encourages analysts to put economic activities directly related to capital accumulation to one side and the institutional phenomena that legitimise such accumulation to another. Now, what are the institutions that should be considered in such research? Gordon, Edwards, and Reich continue as follows:

> In the other direction we specify the outer boundary so that the social structure of accumulation is not simply shorthand for 'the rest of society.' We do not deny that *any* aspect or relationship in society potentially and perhaps actually impinges to *some* degree upon the accumulation process; nonetheless, it is not unreasonable to distinguish between those institutions that directly and demonstrably condition capital accumulation and those that touch it only tangentially. Thus, for example, the financial system bears a direct relation whereas the character of sports activity does not.[50]

David Kotz, Terrence McDonough, and Michael Reich give another idea of the content of these institutions:

---

[45]   McDonough, Reich, and Kotz, 'Introduction', 1.

[46]   McDonough, Reich, and Kotz, 'Introduction', 2.

[47]   David M Kotz, *The Rise and Fall of Neoliberal Capitalism* (Harvard University Press 2017) 3.

[48]   David M Kotz, 'Interpreting the Social Structure of Accumulation Theory' in David M Kotz, Terrence McDonough, and Michael Reich (eds), *Social Structures of Accumulation: The Political Economy of Growth and Crisis* (CUP 1994) 50, 55.

[49]   David M Gordon, Richard Edwards, and Michael Reich, *Segmented Work, Divided Workers: The Historical Transformation of Labor in the United States* (CUP 1982) 25.

[50]   Gordon, Edwards, and Reich, *Segmented Work, Divided Workers*, 25 (original emphases).

The institutions comprising a SSA include both domestic and international arrangements. The domestic institutions may include the state of labor-management relations; the organization of the work process; the character of industrial organization; the role of money and banking and their relation to industry; the role of the state in the economy; the line-up of political parties; the state of race and gender relations; and the character of the dominant culture and ideology. The international institutions may concern the trade, investment, monetary-financial, and political environments.[51]

For example, in his later analysis of the institutions that characterised neoliberalism, Kotz insists on four in particular: '1) the global economy; 2) the role of government in the economy; 3) the capital-labor relation; and 4) the corporate sector'.[52]

As under ÉR models, once a SSA is in place, accumulation, according to the SSAT, is secured. Nevertheless, after some time, profit-making and accumulation slow down due to a variety of factors, such as an intensification of class struggles, the rise of competition for access to resources, and the saturation of available markets. This decline in the rate of profit and accumulation brings the SSA through a period of crisis, and leads to a new struggle between classes and social forces, which eventually leads to a new SSA.[53] The study of this pendulum between 'long swings' of growth and capital accumulation on the one hand and crisis and recession on the other is the focus of the SSAT's work.

Given that they share the same *problématique* and a very similar way of analysing it (despite differences in conceptual framework), it is probably unsurprising that the SSAT and the ÉR suffer from the same shortcomings for a project like mine. For example, both theories focus on the national sphere, leaving the international sphere mostly undertheorised.[54] Additionally, neither of them really addresses the role of the dominant state and its hegemonic social classes in the evolution of capital accumulation at the international level. Another criticism that can be made of both schools is that they postulate that a SSA (or regime of accumulation) may only change following a crisis. Yet it is hard to see why such a change could not happen in another situation, for example in a context where a crisis *is expected* to happen, or because of the arrival of some new competitors.

In conclusion, both the ÉR and the SSAT offer the advantage of focusing on the crucially important topic of capital accumulation. Both recognise that this process works differently depending upon the period and place in question, and accept the idea that capital accumulation needs some institutions to be secured. Their pairing with neo-Gramscians allows us to emphasise the role of international law and institutions in the expansion and promotion of the regime of accumulation (a concept similar to the 'mode of production' in Cox's analysis) of the hegemonic state of a given epoch. Considered from this perspective, both invite international lawyers to examine the processes whereby international law contributes to the promotion and expansion of capital accumulation.

---

[51] David M Kotz, Terrence McDonough, and Michael Reich, 'Introduction' in David M Kotz, Terrence McDonough, and Michael Reich (eds), *Social Structures of Accumulation: The Political Economy of Growth and Crisis* (CUP 1994) 1, 1.

[52] Kotz, *The Rise and Fall of Neoliberal Capitalism*, 12.

[53] McDonough, Reich, and Kotz, 'Introduction', 3.

[54] *Contra* Emlyn Nardone and Terrence McDonough, 'Global Neoliberalism and the Possibility of Transnational State Structures' in Terrence McDonough, Michael Reich, and David M Kotz (eds), *Contemporary Capitalism and its Crises: Social Structure of Accumulation Theory for the 21st Century* (CUP 2010) 168.

Now, it bears reminding that the expansion of a specific regime of accumulation is not important *in abstracto*. It is important, and crucially so, because it promotes the interests (e.g., the accumulation of capital) of the hegemonic social class of the dominant state or states. Capital accumulation is premised upon the production and exploitative appropriation of surplus value, and international law plays an important role in facilitating it. As a result, international law and international organisations need to be analysed with a view to illuminating the history of the rate of profit of capitalists in dominant states. Some of the scholars whose work will be addressed in the following subsection focus specifically on this aspect.

Theorising the Rate of Profit, Overproduction, and Over-Accumulation

The framework put in place by the ÉR and the SSAT is complemented by work in political economy focusing on the rate of profit, a phenomenon related to the overproduction and over-accumulation of capital. This body of literature is rooted in the third volume of *Capital*, where Marx explains that since profit is derived from the exploitation of labour, the historical trend of the rise of constant capital[55] (the proportion of capital devoted to the cost of purchasing raw and ancillary materials, as well as purchasing and maintaining equipment and other work implements) in relation to variable capital (the proportion of capital devoted to wages for purchasing human labour-power) generates a tendency of the rate of profit to fall.[56] In other words, 'it has been shown to be a law of the capitalist mode of production that its development does in fact involve a relative decline in the relation of variable capital to constant, and hence also to the total capital set in motion',[57] the consequence of this law being that the 'gradual growth in the constant capital, in relation to the variable, must necessarily result in a *gradual fall in the general rate of profit*, given that the rate of surplus-value, or the level of exploitation of labour by capital, remains the same'.[58]

For Marx the tendency for the rate of profit to fall is a basic law of capitalism, and it has a number of important consequences. First, the growing quantity of constant capital 'enables more raw and ancillary materials to be transformed into products',[59] increasing labour productivity. This rise in productivity, in turn, creates the conditions for a rise in surplus value, profit, and total capital. Once again, in Marx's words:

> the same development in the social productivity of labour is expressed, with the advance of the capitalist mode of production, on the one hand in a progressive tendency for the rate of profit to fall and on the other in a constant growth in the absolute mass of the surplus-value or profit appropriated; so that, by and large, the relative decline in the variable capital and profit goes together with an absolute increase in both. This two-fold effect, as explained, can be expressed only in a *growth in the total capital that takes place more rapidly than the fall in the rate of profit.*[60]

---

[55]   Karl Marx, *Capital: A Critique of Political Economy*, vol 3 (first published 1894, David Fernbach tr, Penguin 1981) 318.

[56]   Marx, *Capital*, vol 3, ch 13.

[57]   Marx, *Capital*, vol 3, 318.

[58]   Marx, *Capital*, vol 3, 318 (original emphasis).

[59]   Marx, *Capital*, vol 3, 318.

[60]   Marx, *Capital*, vol 3, 329–30 (emphasis added).

This growth of the total amount of capital creates what Marx calls overproduction, or the over-accumulation of capital, a situation in which 'no further additional capital could be employed for the purpose of capitalist production'.[61] Under these conditions, a growing part of capital 'would lie completely or partially idle (since it would first have to expel the capital already functioning from its position, to be valorized at all), while the other portion would be valorized at a lower rate of profit, owing to the pressure of the unoccupied or semi-occupied capital'.[62] This creates considerable pressure on capitalists and exacerbates competition between them (which degenerates into a 'struggle of enemy brothers'[63]), the consequence of which is that they have less opportunity to invest capital and also to sell commodities.[64]

The tendency of the rate of profit to fall, and the overproduction and over-accumulation with which it is associated, has been at the centre of a large and important body of literature in recent years. While some scholars have adhered closely to Marx's original theoretical exposition,[65] many have distanced themselves from it, adopting an empirical methodology to demonstrate the historical existence of a tendency for the rate of profit to fall.[66]

In an article published a few years ago, I also moved in this direction, linking the development of international law to the evolution of the rate of profit in capitalist states since 1945, with an emphasis on the United States as the period's dominant power.[67] I divided the post-1945 period into four sub-periods: 1945–71 (the *Trente glorieuses*, when rates of profit were very high in advanced capitalist countries); 1971–82 (the years of recession and stagflation in the advanced capitalist economies); 1982–97 (a period full of optimism in the United States, notwithstanding economic ups and downs in other advanced capitalist countries); and 1997 to the present (a period marked by the proliferation of economic crises, structural uncer-

---

[61] Marx, *Capital*, vol 3, 360.

[62] Marx, *Capital*, vol 3, 360.

[63] Marx, *Capital*, vol 3, 362.

[64] Marx, *Capital*, vol 3, 364 ('Overproduction of capital never means anything other than over-production of means of production—means of labour and means of subsistence—that can function as capital, i.e. can be applied to exploiting labour at a given level of exploitation.')

[65] Michael Roberts, *The Long Depression: Marxism and the Global Crisis of Capitalism* (Haymarket 2016).

[66] Erdogan Bakir, 'Capital Accumulation, Profitability, and Crisis: Neoliberalism in the United States' (2015) 47 *Review of Radical Political Economics* 389; Erdogan Bakir and Al Campbell, 'Is Over-Investment the Cause of the Post-2007 U.S. Economic Crisis?' (2015) 47 *Review of Radical Political Economics* 550; Karl Beitel, 'The Rate of Profit and the Problem of Stagnant Investment: A Structural Analysis of Barriers to Accumulation and the Spectre of Protracted Crisis' (2009) 17 *Historical Materialism* 66; Gérard Duménil and Dominique Lévy, *The Crisis of Neoliberalism* (Harvard University Press 2011); John Bellamy Foster and Fred Magdoff, *The Great Financial Crisis: Causes and Consequences* (Monthly Review Press 2009); Vladimiro Giacché, 'Marx, the Falling Rate of Profit, Financialization, and the Current Crisis' (2011) 40 *International Journal of Political Economy* 18; David McNally, *Global Slump: The Economics and Politics of Crisis and Resistance* (PM Press 2011); David M Kotz, 'The Current Economic Crisis in the United States: A Crisis of Over-Investment' (2013) 45 *Review of Radical Political Economics* 284; Robert Brenner, 'What Is Good for Goldman Sachs Is Good for America: The Origins of the Present Crisis', UCLA Center for Social Theory and Comparative History (2009), https://escholarship.org/uc/item/0sg0782h accessed 7 April 2021; Robert Brenner, *The Boom and the Bubble: The US in the World Economy* (Verso 2003); Robert Brenner, *The Economics of Global Turbulence: The Advanced Capitalist Economies from Long Boom to Long Downturn, 1945–2005* (Verso 2006); David Harvey, *The New Imperialism* (OUP 2005).

[67] Rémi Bachand, 'Suraccumulation du capital, surproduction, impérialisme et droit international' (2015) 28 *Revue québécoise de droit international* 1.

tainties, and the 'emergence' of various BRIC-style 'rising powers'). A central aspect of my theoretical framework was what Marx called the 'counteracting factors' to the fall of the rate of profit.[68] For Marx, these factors have the function of 'checking and cancelling the effect of the general law and giving it simply the character of a tendency'.[69] The thesis of my article was that these counteracting factors are still relevant for analysing the development of international law and international relations, in the sense that capitalist states continue to look for tools and strategies to put them to work when the rate of profit falls.

The different theoretical frameworks canvassed earlier in this chapter illustrate that overemphasising the rate of profit may be misleading, since it may set aside some elements that are also relevant to the political economy of international law, such as the specific way the dominant economy is organised, or even the competition between competing and largely different regimes of accumulation. Consideration of these other contributions encourages us to add additional factors to our analysis. This is precisely what the next section will try to achieve.

GRUNDRISS FOR A MARXIST POLITICAL ECONOMY ANALYSIS OF INTERNATIONAL LAW

The approaches and contributions discussed thus far point towards a common methodology for understanding the political economy of international law. Concretely, this political economy literature helps to explain how the accumulation of capital works in specific contexts, and how such accumulation is related to the development of international legal rules and institutions. In return, these aspects can benefit from international law to reproduce or transform themselves. Nevertheless, one of my conclusions was that since the ÉR and the SSAT concentrated their efforts on national economies, some of the factors on which they focus are not as relevant to an analysis of international law as one would hope. I also concluded that analyses focusing essentially on the rate of profit, over-accumulation, and overproduction put aside important factors (such as the organisation of production in a specific era and particular region) that need to be included to achieve our goal. It is consequently impossible to rely solely on existing frameworks to understand the historical development of international law from the perspective of Marxist and neo-Marxist political economy. As a result, in this section, I provide a brief list (incomplete and preliminary due to limited space) of economic factors integral to a 'regime of accumulation',[70] which Marxists should keep in mind when analysing the evolution of rules and practices of international law. I rely here on the neo-Gramscian thesis that the primary function of international institutions is to expand, reproduce, and protect the 'regime of accumulation' of dominant states. For each of the listed factors, I provide examples to show how

---

[68]   Marx, *Capital*, vol 3, ch 10. For Marx the most general such tendencies are as follows: (1) the rise in the intensity of exploitation of labour; (2) the reduction of wages; (3) the cheapening of elements of constant capital (raw material, energy sources, and so on); (4) the growth of the industrial army of labour; (5) foreign trade; and (6) an increase of capital stock (e.g., financialisation).

[69]   Marx, *Capital*, vol 3, 339.

[70]   Without denying my important intellectual debt to the ÉR, it is to be noted that my use of the concept of 'regime of accumulation' is slightly different from theirs. In this section, I will move closer to the approach taken by Gordon, Edwards, and Reich and associate that concept with the economic phenomena associated with the capital accumulation process, distinct from the institutional forms that legitimate and contribute to the reproduction of it.

they have influenced international law (or how they could theoretically do so), how international law can play a role similar to that of the 'mode of regulation' for them, and what kind of questions should be the starting-point of reflection on these factors.

The Rate of Profit

From the outset, the generation of profit and accumulation of capital remain the most important factors in a 'regime of accumulation'. As such, it is useful to ask, as Aglietta once did, 'what is the required rate of return?'[71]—or, put differently, how can one know that a particular rate of profit is satisfactory for a given set of capitalists? To answer this question, it is also useful to consider another element of the ÉR 'regime of accumulation' theory—the 'temporal horizon for the valorization of capital', this being determined by the way in which corporations are structured and managed. In other words, even if the definition of what is a sufficient rate of profit is determined mainly by the objective necessity of accumulation under capitalism, it is also in part a social construction linked to the organisation of corporations specific to a particular period.[72] For instance, in regard to neoliberalism, Aglietta writes that:

> there was ... a dramatic change in the ownership structure of corporations, that has shifted business strategy from 'insider productivity-sharing' to shareholder value-optimizing'. The norm of profitability has changed altogether. Market-value accounting has replaced reproduction-cost accounting as the yardstick of corporate performance. ... Combined with the long ascending wave in the stock market, the imperative of shareholder value gave rise to a much higher required rate of return than in the heyday of post-war growth.[73]

This transformation in governance structures had an important effect on how businesses are managed on a day-to-day basis, with related political and economic effects on the global plane. Indeed, since CEO performance is no longer evaluated on the basis of the long-term health of the enterprise but rather on quarterly financial results, significant pressure is applied on CEOs to maximise short-term profits even if the actions taken to achieve these results can have pernicious effects on its long-term success, or are ethically dubious.

In any case, a rate of return that a given set of capitalists deem unsatisfactory puts great stress on the capitalist class, as well as on states. I have already noted that many scholars have sought to explain the neoliberal reforms of the past half century as an attempt to counteract the fall in the rate of profit that commenced in many advanced capitalist countries in the late 1960s. Interestingly, international law is crucial for some of these scholars, notably because some international institutions (such as the International Monetary Fund) have promoted the privatisation of public-held assets in developing countries since the 1980s. Such privatisation offers new investment possibilities with the potential for significant profit. Elsewhere I have attempted to explain the effects of the rate of profit on the behaviour of states, as well as the configuration and use of international economic organisations.[74] During a period in which the

---

[71]   Michel Aglietta, 'Into a New Growth Regime' (2008) 54 *New Left Review* 61, 69.
[72]   On this topic see also Duménil and Lévy, *Crisis of Neoliberalism*; Lorraine Talbot, 'Why Shareholders Shouldn't Vote: A Marxist-Progressive Critique of Shareholder Empowerment' (2013) 76 *Modern Law Review* 791.
[73]   Aglietta, 'New Growth Regime', 69.
[74]   Bachand, 'Suraccumulation du capital'.

rate of profit is thought satisfactory, the capitalist class tends to collaborate especially closely with each other, the result being an inclination for more liberal policies and the creation of organisations for their realisation. Conversely, during periods in which the rate of profit falls, such collaboration may not necessarily be as close, competition and protectionism tending to be the norm.

That said, the Marxist theory of the falling rate of profit raises some important questions for international lawyers. Does its rise and fall have a real effect on the behaviour of states? Does it have a real effect on the configuration of international rules and institutions? Beyond economic institutions, does it have an impact, for instance, on the development of legal rules that may be used to justify military interventions?

The Competition Form

For the ÉR, an important topic is the competition form, in which rivalries between independent producers in a given market are mediated and structured.[75] For ÉR scholars, this concept is key to understanding processes of price formation.[76] Nevertheless, one can use the concept in a broader sense to explain relations between different centres of accumulation in the global economy.

At a very high level of abstraction, the arrival of new foreign competitors means the contestation of control over existing markets, and the challenge by new capital of existing investment opportunities. This means that previously dominant capitalists will have to reaffirm their comparative advantages by cutting the prices of the commodities they sell, offering goods and services of better quality, and so on. It also means that they will have to find new ways to invest their capital, potentially in places where the rate of return is significantly lower than before. Finally, increased competition will potentially lead to over-accumulation (some capital not being able to find satisfying places to invest) and overproduction (capitalists being unable to use their production capacities optimally), which will affect the rate of profit even further. Thus, the state of rivalry in the global economy exerts a significant effect on the rate of profit of capitalists all around the world, and it constitutes a factor which should be central to any theoretical framework explaining the political economy of international law.

Historically, we can illustrate this link between the competition form and the evolution of international legal practices and institutions by comparing two periods since the Second World War: the 1970s and the current era. First, a common interpretation of the crisis of the 1970s is that the fall in the rate of profit of US enterprises was provoked by the arrival of new Japanese and European competitors benefiting from the sustained growth of their economies after the 1950s. This downturn had significant effects on international law. Above all, it forced the US government to sacrifice the Bretton Woods monetary system between 1971 and 1973, then to adopt some protectionist measures that influenced the results of the Tokyo Round of the General Agreement on Tariffs and Trade, and finally to turn towards a neoliberal program that was ultimately adopted and imposed all across the world by international financial institutions.[77]

---

[75]   Robert Boyer and Yves Saillard, 'Un précis de la régulation' in Robert Boyer and Yves Saillard (eds), *Théorie de la régulation: l'état des savoirs* (2nd edn, La Découverte 2002) 62.
[76]   Boyer, *Économie politique des capitalismes*, 26.
[77]   Brenner, *The Boom and the Bubble*, 16 ff.

Second, an important characteristic of the current period is the transformation of the competition form, specifically with the rise of the so-called 'emerging economies', China being the most important among them.[78] This event is incontestably at the heart of the crisis experienced by the World Trade Organisation (WTO) at the moment of writing.[79] It also seems to be crucial to the conclusion and negotiation of regional and bilateral (rather than multilateral) free trade agreements, every country trying to position itself in relation to its competitors, so as to guarantee its capitalists better market access than their rivals.

This topic also raises a number of important questions: What are the relations between dominant economic states and their challengers? Do the former exercise real hegemonic power (in the Gramscian sense)? Do the challengers contest the world order currently in place?[80] What are the effects of the arrival of new challengers on the capacity to find investment opportunities? To sell a larger or smaller proportion of production capacities? In other words, on the state of over-accumulation and overproduction? And, subsequently and more importantly, how does international law contribute to the resolution (or exacerbation) of these problems?

The Role of the State in the Capital Accumulation Process

The mode of state involvement in the process of capital accumulation is another pivotal factor, both for the ÉR[81] and the SSAT.[82] Both schools put the state at the core of their analysis of how contradictions of capitalism are resolved. Hence, when comparing Fordism with neoliberalism as regimes of accumulation, one finds that both emphasise how the redefinition of the mandate of the state significantly and structurally impacted almost every aspect of economic relations in the relevant states.

Perhaps the most important of these aspects is that the way the state intervenes in the economy will have a predominant effect on the values accompanying the production and redistribution of wealth in society. For one thing, in a context where state involvement is minimal, market forces will be predominant in the economic decision-making process and it is highly probable that the only considered value will be the search for profits. Now, it is possible for the state to interfere with that logic thanks to regulation, for instance in matters of environmental, consumer, or labour protection. This involvement can also include the protection of national capitalists against foreign competition. Finally, a direct involvement via public-private partnership, parastatal enterprises, or direct participation in private corporations can help to promote other values, such as regional development for example. Of course, every option will

---

[78]   Giovanni Arrighi, *Adam Smith à Pékin: les promesses de la voie chinoise* (Nicolas Vieillescazes tr, M Milo 2009); Bachand, 'Suraccumulation du capital', 28–34.

[79]   Tetyana Payosova, Gary Clyde Hufbauer, and Jeffrey J Schott, 'The Dispute Settlement Crisis in the World Trade Organization: Causes and Cures', Peterson Institute for International Economics Policy Brief (March 2018), https://www.piie.com/publications/policy-briefs/dispute-settlement-crisis-world -trade-organization-causes-and-cures accessed 7 April 2021; Rémi Bachand, 'What's Behind the WTO Crisis? A Marxist Analysis' (2020) 31 *European Journal of International Law* 857.

[80]   Kristen Hopewell, *Breaking the WTO: How Emerging Powers Disrupted the Neoliberal Project* (Stanford University Press 2016).

[81]   Boyer, *Économie politique des capitalismes*, 34–39; Alessandra Devulsky da Silva Tisescu, 'Aglietta e a Teoria da Regulação: Direito e Capitalismo' (PhD dissertation, Universidade de São Paulo 2014), https://www.teses.usp.br/teses/disponiveis/2/2133/tde-13022015-135600/publico/INTEGRAL _ALESSANDRA_D_DA_SILVA_TISESCU.pdf accessed 7 April 2021.

[82]   Kotz, *The Rise and Fall of Neoliberal Capitalism*, 14–26.

have an impact on who will benefit from production and the final result will inevitably be the consequence of a political struggle, if not a class struggle.

The absence of a state at the global level has some methodological implications. It is crucial to understand the role of the state in the dominant economy because it is a core aspect of the regime of accumulation that its dominant social classes try to extend around the world. A relatively shared conception between dominant and concurrent economies will probably render this topic insignificant. That being said, major differences in this conception can have a huge impact. Besides, an important aspect of the neoliberal program of the Washington Consensus revolved precisely around the withdrawal of the state from the economy.[83] In other words, the depoliticisation of economies signified the expansion of an important aspect of the new mode of accumulation adopted by the United States, the United Kingdom, and others. This was in the interest of their capitalist classes, because it facilitated the penetration of new markets for their goods, services, and investments. More recently, it can be argued that a crucial aspect of the conflict between the United States and China actually concerns the place of the state in the latter's economy,[84] especially with the apparent success it has had in regard to development and its potential to become a model for other countries.

In summary, questions related to this topic should include: What is the involvement of the state in the economy in dominant capitalist states? What about their main competitors? Which social classes are the main beneficiaries of such models? Are alternative conceptions widely or only slightly different? Are they considered to be efficient? Do they constitute a real alternative to the hegemonic model? What is their potential to influence other countries in adopting the same model? Are international organisations biased in regard to different models? Do they promote some at the expense of others? Is competition between different models an important factor in international relations, and by extension international law?

Organisation of Production

Another aspect concerns the way that production is organised, or, more specifically, the dominant schemes that define the links between economic units. This aspect raises questions such as: What is the level of competition between these economic actors (in that sense, it is directly related to the competition form)? How is the relation between each step of the production of a particular product organised? Is production concentrated in a single or a small number of economic units, or is its final production fragmented between a large variety of independent producers? Is production essentially organised on a national, regional, or international scale? What are the effects of each model on the capital-labour relation? Is fragmented and decentralised production exacerbating competition between workers from different countries, consequently negatively affecting their balance of power against capital?

---

[83]   John Williamson, 'A Short History of the Washington Consensus' (2009) 15 *Law and Business Review of the Americas* 7; Quinn Slobodian, *Globalists: The End of Empire and the Birth of Neoliberalism* (Harvard University Press 2018).

[84]   Barry Naughton, *The Chinese Economy: Adaptation and Growth* (2nd edn, MIT Press 2018); Mark Wu, 'The China, Inc. Challenge to Global Trade Governance' (2016) 57 *Harvard International Law Journal* 261; Li-Wen Lin, 'A Network Anatomy of Chinese State-Owned Enterprises' (2017) 16 *World Trade Review* 583.

The relation between international law and these aspects can be extremely close. For instance, a meaningful characteristic of the global economy at the end of the 1990s was the importance of mergers and acquisitions. This had a major impact on Third World countries and it was greatly facilitated by the multiplication of bilateral investment treaties.[85] On the other hand, production has increasingly been organised around 'global value chains' since the 1980s, despite WTO rules that are not, in the opinion of some experts,[86] well adapted for that reality. What conclusions can be drawn from that apparent incoherence between legal framework and production organisation? What can be said of the multiplication of regional free-trade agreements with regards to this issue? What should be the political position of labor movements concerning this topic? What is at stake for Third World countries?[87]

CONCLUSION

Because of limitations of space, the list proposed in this chapter is not exhaustive and some other important questions should be added concerning topics such as what the ÉR calls the 'monetary regime', the form taken by the capital-labour relation, or the ecological limits that constitute important constraints on the accumulation of capital. This list's exhaustiveness is likely not important here if it serves as a strong argument for the relevance of a detailed study of the different forms historically taken by capitalism to reproduce itself.

Such an analysis is important for at least two reasons. The first reason is that, for a Marxist, 'neither legal relations nor political forms could be comprehended whether by themselves or on the basis of a so-called general development of the human mind, but that on the contrary they originate in the material conditions of life', that is, in the mode of production.[88] Even if this statement is regularly used in general explanations of the legal form in capitalist societies, it can also be extremely useful to interpret legal variations in the light of cyclical transformations of how production evolves, and of how capital accumulation is organised. This appears to be particularly true at the international level. The first goal is then descriptive and helps the legal scholar to undertake a 'concrete analysis of the concrete situation' when analysing international law and institutions.

The second reason—untouched in this chapter—is political and related to the political positions, strategies, and tactics that should be adopted by labour and anti-imperialist movements concerning international law. Let us take only one example: for at least a decade and a half, left-wing and far-left-wing activists have largely been opposed to free trade agreements. This position has been justified through a concrete analysis of the concrete situation at a particular moment, roughly the end of the 1990s. We currently face a situation in which free trade institutions like the WTO are under fire, notably in the United States, from right-wing populism

---

[85]   UNCTAD (ed), *Cross-Border Mergers and Acquisitions and Development* (United Nations 2000).

[86]   David A Gantz, *Liberalizing International Trade after Doha: Multilateral, Plurilateral, Regional, and Unilateral Initiatives* (CUP 2013).

[87]   Victor Ramiro Fernández, 'Global Value Chains in Global Political Networks: Tool for Development or Neoliberal Device?' (2015) 47 *Review of Radical Political Economics* 209; Erik van der Marel, 'Positioning on the Global Value Chain Map: Where Do You Want to Be?' (2015) 49 *Journal of World Trade* 915.

[88]   Karl Marx, 'A Contribution to the Critique of Political Economy' [1859] in Karl Marx and Frederick Engels, *Collected Works*, vol 29 (Lawrence & Wishart 1987) 257, 262.

and a variety of other forces. The revelation of this surprising 'new ally' may be an opportunity to take a step back and undertake a new concrete analysis of the actual situation and see if the latter is still the same as it was 20 years ago. This reflection could be led by various questions, the first and most important being: has globalisation not sufficiently transformed regimes of accumulation to reshape the objective interests of the working classes towards the international trade regime? Would the working classes really benefit from a return to a protectionist organisation of global economy? To an economic world order in which the hegemonic power can decide at any moment and with impunity to prevent imports from sensitive sectors, notwithstanding effects on employment? Should we militate for new forms of agreements? With social and environmental provisions? Should we advocate new forms of international trade? For a trade that is organised on a local scale? How can we strategically link radical and anti-capitalist economic objectives with analyses of and strategies with regard to international trade law? Answers to these crucial questions start from a detailed and serious understanding of how capitalism works, not only in general but also within the specific period concerned.

21. From class-based project to imperial formation: European Union law and the reconstruction of Europe

Eva Nanopoulos

INTRODUCTION

According to the political economist Magnus Ryner, the 'merging of Marxism and European integration has been a case of mutual neglect'.[1] In particular, he notes, there was until recently a 'striking lack of interest by Marxists to develop a rigorous analysis of the *specificity* of the European Union'.[2] Within legal studies, neglect is somewhat of an understatement.[3] The European Union (EU) and European Union law (EU law) continue to be viewed primarily through a liberal lens. European integration is typically presented as a peace project that brought the continent's long history of violence to an end—a peace that the EU is now seeking to export through the promotion of the core values that have shaped its evolution, including democracy, human rights, and the rule of law.[4] Law is regarded as having played a crucial role in these processes. Internally, this is reflected in the concept of 'integration through law', which posits that the law is not only an object but also an agent of integration.[5] In the sphere of external relations, it finds expression in models of the EU as a normative power,[6] which exports and diffuses liberal norms and values.

This chapter does not purport to provide a fully fledged Marxist theory of EU law. Rather, it is a first attempt to read legal developments in the EU and think about the role of law in the European project with reference to existing Marxist analyses of European integration. Although the legal dimension of the project has received scant attention, some Marxists have drawn upon regulation theories to link different modes of EU regulation to different 'socioeconomic epochs (phases) of transnational capitalism'.[7] Ryner and Cafruny, for example, identify three main epochs of European integration: the Fordist period of the 1960s and early 1970s,

---

[1] Magnus Ryner, 'European "Integration"' in Matt Vidal, Tony Smith, Tomás Rotta, and Paul Prew (eds), *The Oxford Handbook of Karl Marx* (OUP 2019) 519, 519.

[2] Ryner, 'European "Integration"', 520 (emphasis added).

[3] For some exceptions see e.g., Gustav Peebles, '"A Very Eden of the Innate Rights of Man"? A Marxist Look at the European Union Treaties and Case Law' (1997) 22 *Law & Social Inquiry* 581.

[4] See in particular arts 3 and 21 of the Consolidated Version of the Treaty on European Union [2008] OJ C115/13 [TEU].

[5] See e.g., Daniel Augenstein (eds), *'Integration through Law' Revisited: The Making of the European Polity* (Ashgate 2012); Mauro Cappelletti, Monica Seccombe, and Joseph Weiler (eds), *Integration Through Law: Europe and the American Federal Experience*, vol 1 (De Gruyter 1985).

[6] Ian Manner, 'Normative Power Europe: A Contradiction in Terms?' (2002) 40 *Journal of Common Market Studies* 235.

[7] Magnus Ryner and Alan Cafruny, *The European Union and Global Capitalism: Origins, Development, Crisis* (Palgrave 2017) 31; H Buch-Hansen and A Wigger, 'Revisiting 50 Years of

the ascendency of neoliberalism in the 1980s, and the consolidation of neoliberalism following the 'eurozone crisis' or 'eurocrisis'.[8] To each phase there corresponds a particular form of regulation—from the permissibility of national regulatory autonomy during Fordism to tighter and disciplinary legal constraints under neoliberalism, and to authoritarian and coercive forms of rule in the present.

The historical overview offered in this chapter builds on this periodisation, but also refines, nuances, and extends it. Section one shows the intimate links between the original project of European integration, EU law, and the reproduction of capitalist social relations. Section two examines how, even during the Fordist period, the class dimensions of EU law and the increased transnationalisation of capitalist relations had important consequences for domestic legal systems, imposing important formal limitations on national regulatory autonomy. Section three revisits the transition to neoliberalism, showing how legal developments in the 1970s sowed the seeds for its consolidation in the 1980s. Section four places the neoliberal 'turn' of the organisation in the context of a deeper transformation of the EU's 'constitution', designed to secure the general conditions of coercion and consent necessary for the reproduction of the neoliberal order. Section five considers the 'external' dimensions of integration and how the growing hegemony of finance capital began to produce a distinct form of European imperialism. Sections six and seven, finally, turn to the eurocrisis and its aftermath, with a focus on the role of law in the emergence of authoritarian neoliberalism and the constraints it places on attempts to reverse the status quo.

Before I move on to the analysis, however, I wish to make four clarifications. First, although a historical periodisation frames the discussion offered in this chapter, the analysis should not be taken to support a linear, stageist, or teleological reading of European integration. Legal developments certainly highlight important continuities between different phases of integration, which the chapter attributes to the long-term structural connection between EU integration, EU law, and the evolution of capitalism on the European continent. However, a legal history of the EU also brings to the fore the ambivalent and multifaced character of EU law and hence the multiple contradictions that underpin the European project. Some commentators have mapped Marxist debates about the EU onto classic distinctions between 'supranationalists' and 'intergovernmentalists'.[9] Yet, this analogy is somewhat misguided. If anything, the strength of a class analysis of the EU and EU law is precisely that it transcends these dichotomies and allows for the many paradoxes, dysfunctionalities, and contingencies

---

Market-Making: The Neoliberal Transformation of European Competition Policy' (2010) 17 *Review of International Political Economy* 20.

[8]   Ryner and Cafruny, *The European Union and Global Capitalism,* ch 2. Their co-authored book only briefly addresses this third phase, but Ryner analyses it in greater depth in subsequent work. See e.g., Magnus Ryner, 'The Authoritarian Neoliberalism of the EU: Legal Form and International Politico-Economic Sources' in Eva Nanopoulos and Fotis Vergis (eds), *The Crisis Behind the Eurocrisis: The Eurocrisis as a Multidimensional Systemic Crisis of the EU* (CUP 2019) 89.

[9]   Anton Jäger, 'Visions of Europeanism in the Mandel-Poulantzas Debate, 1967–1979', https://www.academia.edu/30258064/Visions_of_Europeanism_in_the_Mandel-Poulantzas_Debate_1967-1979 accessed 7 April 2021.

that define the EU to be adequately theorised.[10] And this is also why, I argue, it offers a more convincing explanation of integration than traditional theories[11] or neoclassical economics.[12]

Second, the chapter's focus on these structural connections and contradictions across different phases of European capitalism is not intended to downplay the role of agency and class antagonism in the development of the EU and EU law. Neo-Gramscian approaches to integration have done much to advance our understanding of the social forces that have shaped the contemporary form of the EU. Chief among these was the European Round Table of Industrialists (ERI).[13] A forum of Europe's largest business leaders created in 1983, the ERI helped to co-ordinate the interests of big industrial and financial capital and played a key role in the neoliberal re-orientation of the EU.[14]

Third, by mapping legal developments onto different phases of capitalist development, this chapter does not suggest adherence to the 'base-superstructure' motif—the idea that the capitalist mode of production is distinguished above all by an economic foundation (or 'base') to which legal and political arrangements ('the superstructure') merely correspond. If anything, the evolution of the EU demonstrates that the two are indissociable elements of a complex and mutually constitutive totality.

Fourth and finally, I should note that the title of the chapter is not intended to suggest that we reject the imperial dimensions of the original common market. On the contrary, Marxist theories of imperialism provide important analytical tools for theorising both the inception and evolution of European integration. Rather, the title's reference to the development of the EU from a 'class-based project' to an 'imperial formation' aims to highlight the dialectic between the internal and external dimensions of the European project and the ways in which the internal consolidation of European capitalism affects the EU's relations with the outside world.

PEACE PROJECT AS CLASS PROJECT

As in many other areas to which Marxist analytical tools have been applied, there is no single Marxist theory of European integration. Instead, a variety of approaches have been developed to unearth the class dimensions of what is today the EU. However, contrary to idealist framings of the EU as a peace project, Marxists have all shared a commitment to placing integration in its specific historical context,[15] beginning with the socio-economic and geopolitical factors that led to the conclusion of the Treaty Establishing the European Coal and Steel Community

---

[10] See e.g., Alex Callinicos, 'Brexit and the Imperial Constitution of Europe' in Eva Nanopoulos and Fotis Vergis (eds), *The Crisis Behind the Eurocrisis: The Eurocrisis as a Multidimensional Systemic Crisis of the EU* (CUP 2019) 419.

[11] Ryner and Cafruny, *European Union and Global Capitalism*.

[12] Guglielmo Carchedi, *For Another Europe: A Class Analysis of European Economic Integration* (Verso 2001).

[13] See e.g., Bastiaan van Apeldoorn, *Transnational Capitalism and the Struggle over European Integration* (Routledge 2002).

[14] This was also due to changes in the balance of forces within the ERI characterised by the growing dominance of a global neoliberal fraction over a European protectionist fraction. See Bastiaan van Apeldoorn, 'Transnational Class Agency and European Governance: The Case of the European Round Table of Industrialists' (2000) 5 *New Political Economy* 157.

[15] See e.g., Charalampos Kouroundis, 'The Roots of the European Crisis: A Historical Perspective' in Eva Nanopoulos and Fotis Vergis (eds), *The Crisis Behind the Eurocrisis: The Eurocrisis as*

(ECSC Treaty) in 1951 and the Treaty Establishing the European Economic Community (EEC Treaty) in 1957, the two founding treaties of the modern EU (also known as the 'original EU Treaties'). The first instrument aimed to integrate the coal and steel industries of the six founding members—Germany, France, Italy, and the so-called 'Benelux' countries. The second laid the foundations for the creation of a customs union and a common market in goods, labour, services, and capital. Key to the conclusion of these treaties, for Marxist scholars, was the economic imperative of restoring competitiveness and the need to tackle growing unemployment, inflation, social discontent, and working-class radicalism. Also crucial was the geopolitical support of the United States. Rivalries between Washington and European capitals notwithstanding, the United States saw European integration as part of a broader set of international institutional innovations designed to counter Soviet expansionism, contain the communist threat, and further the worldwide dominance of a Western-led capitalism under US leadership.

These factors all shaped the form and content of the original EU Treaties. Chris Harman may have stepped too far in the direction of economic determinism by concluding that these treaties amounted merely to a 'business arrangement, an agreement between different capitalist ruling classes, relating to the way in which they organise their markets'.[16] The project of integration was, after all, embraced by socialists, social democrats, liberals, and conservatives alike, even if they did so for different reasons. Still, there was no popular input in the drafting or conclusion of these instruments; the 'Founding Fathers', as they have come to be known, were notoriously averse to the masses.[17] And as Bernard Moss recounts, the EEC was 'supported not only by exporters looking for outlets, but by the entire capitalist class, financiers, merchants, employers, large and small, because it was the optimal regime for the exploitation of labor free from state interference'.[18]

In regard to their content, the pooling of coal and steel, two key sectors for states' military capabilities, was designed to tame the long-standing and destructive antagonism between France and Germany. The idea that free trade would reduce conflict, both within the state and on the plane of international relations, boasted a long-standing pedigree in liberal political theory, stretching back to the sixteenth century.[19] To keep the ECSC from becoming a 'gigantic European cartel for coal and steel producers', however, the United States pressed for the inclusion of strict rules on antitrust.[20] The common market, on the other hand, began to create the legal preconditions for enhancing the mobility and competitiveness of European capitals. The 'four freedoms' enabled the factors of production—goods, services, labour, and capital—to move freely across national borders. The rules on competition prohibited conduct which may distort competition and hinder trade. Guardianship over this construct was transferred to

a Multidimensional Systemic Crisis of the EU (CUP 2019) 51; Alex Callinicos, *Imperialism and Global Political Economy* (Polity Press 2009) 169–78.

[16]   Chris Harman, 'The Common Market' (1971) 49 *International Socialism* 6, https://www.marxists .org/archive/harman/1971/xx/eec-index.html accessed 7 April 2021.

[17]   Turkuler Isiksel, *Europe's Functional Constitution* (OUP 2016) 11.

[18]   Bernard H Moss, 'Introduction: The EU as a Neo-liberal Construction' in Bernard H Moss (ed), *Monetary Union in Crisis: The European Union as a Neo-liberal Construction* (Palgrave 2005) 1, 9.

[19]   See e.g., Debra P Steger, *Peace Through Trade: Building the World* (Cameron May 2004); Alexis Dalem, 'Guerre et économie: le libéralisme et la pacification par le marché' (2003) 9 *Raisons politiques* 49.

[20]   Buch-Hansen and Wigger, 'Revisiting 50 Years of Market-Making', 28.

a set of supranational institutions over which democratic forces would have limited control, insulating 'the "free market" from working class aspirations'.[21]

Ideologically, this legal 'superstructure' took at least some inspiration from ordoliberal,[22] if not neoliberal, thinking—which several of the early negotiators of the EU Treaties espoused. Contrary to classic *laissez-faire* liberalism, ordoliberals do not conceive the market as a spontaneous order. Rather, the institutional preconditions of competition need to be created through the establishment of an 'economic constitution'.[23] In the case of the common market, this was to be guaranteed by a supranational structure, which would legally anchor markets and protect them from political and social struggles at both the national and international levels.

To be sure, rooted as they are in broader Marxist debates about the nature of class, the capitalist state, and the imperial state system, disagreements over the structural causes and dynamics of European integration are by no means trivial. An early example is the debate between Ernest Mandel and Nicos Poulantzas.[24] In line with classic theories of imperialism, Mandel saw the process of economic integration as a product of three factors: (a) the development of the productive forces on the European continent, which had largely 'outgrown the framework of the national state';[25] (b) the growing concentration and interpenetration of capital on an international scale; (c) and increased competition between American and European capitals. For Poulantzas, by contrast, classic theories of imperialism based on inter-imperialist rivalries and core-periphery relations could not explain the post-Second World War conjuncture. In his view, we had now reached a new phase of imperialism characterised by the dominance of monopoly capital over competitive (national) capitalisms and a growing subordination of the European imperial metropolis to US imperialism. Far from creating class-driven geopolitical rivalries, this led to the emergence of a new class, the 'interior bourgeoisie', which was structurally dependent upon and increasingly integrated with American capital.[26]

As the Mandel-Poulantzas debate illustrates, moreover, such theoretical differences can have significant implications for our understanding of EU law. For Mandel, the legal and political superstructure would adapt gradually to 'changed property relationships, i.e. the appearance of a type of capitalist property having outgrown the limits of the old national state on the European continent',[27] opening the prospect for a pan-European state designed to secure the interests of a unified European capital. For Poulantzas, this analysis was based on an erroneous view of the state as an instrument of the ruling classes. While he agreed that European integration would lead the state to assume increased 'responsibility for the inter-

---

[21]   Werner Bonefeld, 'European Integration: The Market, the Political and Class' (2002) 26 *Capital & Class* 117, 118.

[22]   Bonefeld, 'European Integration', 118.

[23]   On which see e.g., Wolf Sauter, 'The Economic Constitution of the European Union' (1998) 4 *Columbia Journal of European Law* 27.

[24]   On which see Ryner, 'European "Integration"'; Jäger, 'Visions of Europeanism'; Tristan Auvray and Cédric Durand, 'A European Capitalism? Revisiting the Mandel–Poulantzas Debate' in Jean-Numa Ducange and Razmig Keucheyan (eds), *The End of the Democratic State: Nicos Poulantzas, a Marxism for the 21st Century* (Palgrave 2019) 145.

[25]   Ernest Mandel, 'International Capitalism and "Supra-Nationality"' (1967) 4 *Socialist Register* 27, 27. See also Ernest Mandel, *Europe Versus America? Contradictions of Imperialism* (Merlin Press 1968).

[26]   Nicos Poulantzas, 'Internationalisation of Capitalist Relations and the Nation-State' (1974) 3 *Economy and Society* 145.

[27]   Mandel, 'International Capitalism', 35.

nationalisation of public functions with respect to capital',[28] he argued that this new phase of imperialism would reshape, rather than supersede, its internal structures. This conclusion resonates with ordoliberal thinking, in which supranationalisation was not designed to weaken the nation state as much as to consolidate its ability to constitute and reproduce capitalist social relations.[29] Nonetheless, Marxist approaches to integration all serve to highlight that Europe's peace project was fundamentally a class project and that EU law was from the outset tied inextricably to the reproduction of capitalist social relations.

SUPRANATIONALISM AND THE TRANSNATIONALISATION OF EUROPEAN CAPITAL

The implications of the connections between EU law and European capitalism, particularly for domestic political and legal structures, became evident shortly after the adoption of the EEC Treaty. Although it was concluded as a classic international law treaty, a number of key decisions of the European Court of Justice in the 1960s radically altered the constitutive features of European Community law. The doctrine of EU law's direct effect enabled individuals to enforce their economic rights directly before national courts.[30] The doctrine of EU law's supremacy ensured that these rights took precedence over conflicting national laws, including those of a constitutional nature.[31] These doctrinal developments were linked directly to the building of the common market. Any other arrangement, the Court explained, would call into question the legal basis of the European Community itself.[32]

Pashukanis' commodity-form theory of law offers valuable insights into the connections between the class dimensions of EU law and its transformation into a 'new legal order',[33] which now claimed autonomy from both national and international law. Pashukanis sought to demonstrate the specificity of the legal form, which he linked to the commodity form. Pursuant to his theory, the legal form is homologous to commodity exchange, which requires commodity owners to meet in the market as abstract and formally equal legal subjects.[34] He also transposed this logic to the international sphere, where, he argued, '[s]overeign states co-exist and are counterposed to one another in exactly the same way as are individual property owners with equal rights'.[35] The supranational form of the EU could be seen as an intermediate form between the domestic and the international legal form. On one level, the specific features of EU law could be conceived as a further stage in the development of the international legal form (EU law is, after all, a subset of international law). That stage would be characterised by the recognition of individuals, alongside states, as subjects of international law. And, following Mandel, it would express the increased interpenetration of capital across national borders. On

---

28   Poulantzas, 'Internationalisation', 173.
29   Alan S Milward, *The European Rescue of the Nation-State* (Routledge 1992).
30   Case 26/62 *Van Gend en Loos v Nederlandse Administratie der Belastingen* [1963] ECR 1.
31   Case 6/64 *Costa v ENEL* [1964] ECR 1207 [*Costa v ENEL*].
32   *Costa v ENEL.*
33   *Costa v ENEL.*
34   Evgeny Pashukanis, 'General Theory of Law and Marxism' [1924] in Piers Beirne and Robert Sharlet (eds), *Pashukanis: Selected Writings on Marxism and Law* (Academic Press 1980) 37.
35   Evgeny Pashukanis, 'International Law' [1925–26] in Piers Beirne and Robert Sharlet (eds), *Pashukanis: Selected Writings on Marxism and Law* (Academic Press 1980) 168, 176.

another level, EU law could be seen as a further stage in the development of the domestic legal form. The more capitalist social relations are reorganised across national borders, the more national laws are drawn into an embryonic post-national (European) law shaping—without necessarily superseding—domestic legal systems in line with Poulantzas' predictions. Either way, in both cases, supranationalism can be seen as the specific legal expression of the increased transnationalisation of capitalist social relations on the European continent.

With time this 'constitutionalisation' of the treaties itself contributed considerably to the project of market building, and therefore the reconfiguration of capitalist social relations both within and across national borders. The treaties set up a number of enforcement mechanisms. The European Commission, in particular, was endowed with considerable powers to police the conditions for competition, combining investigative, judicial, and enforcement functions, even if, in the early days, the need to enhance the EU's competitiveness meant that it was relatively permissive towards state intervention and capital concentration. Yet there were—and remain—considerable normative and practical limitations to what 'public' enforcement through ad hoc infringement proceedings are capable of achieving. By empowering private parties to challenge national regulations that impede their economic freedom, the European Court of Justice thus created a new and powerful mechanism for ensuring compliance with market rules, transforming transnational economic operators into an 'army of vigilant police'.[36]

In the early days, the class content of EU law was perhaps less visible. The concept of the common market was sufficiently ambiguous to ensure consensus and supranational institutions retained a relatively low profile. However, if, as Nicol points out, the 'Treaty left unresolved the balance between market forces and state intervention that would be permissible in the new EEC',[37] there were early signs that the market would prevail—or at least that the state's ability to legislate unconstrained by market imperatives would be severely curtailed. The European Court of Justice's 1964 *Costa v ENEL* decision is a case in point. The judgment is primarily remembered for having established the principle of supremacy. But *Costa v ENEL* also involved one of the most radical renationalisation programs of the post-Second World War era. The program granted a single state-owned company, ENEL, exclusive rights over the production and distribution of electricity and was introduced by the Italian Christian Democratic Party in exchange for the support of the Socialist Party. Costa's challenge was ultimately unsuccessful, perhaps unsurprisingly so given the charged political context and the need for the Court to establish its authority. Yet the Court's reasoning alleviated Costa's lawyer's fear that the plan would 'undermine Italy's free market economy' and 'pave the way to the implementation of the doctrines of Marx, Engels, and Lenin'.[38] The Court certainly appeared to embrace a relatively narrow view of the common market, defined by the aim of unifying national markets and removing discriminatory barriers to trade. At the same time, neither did it rule that the public provision of electricity fell outside the scope of the rules on freedom of establishment or competition. This forewarned what would soon become all too apparent—that no national regulation or practice would be immune to the rules of the internal market, save for limited exceptions. This tendency was even more pronounced in the field of

[36] Stephen Weatherhill, *The Internal Market as a Legal Concept* (OUP 2017) 65.
[37] Danny Nicol, *The Constitutional Protection of Capitalism* (Hart 2010) 86.
[38] Quoted in Amedeo Arena, 'How European Law Became Supreme: The Making of *Costa v. ENEL*', Jean Monnet Working Paper No 5/2018, 13, https://jeanmonnetprogram.org/wp-content/uploads/JMWP-05-Amedeo-Arena.pdf accessed 7 April 2021.

382 Research handbook on law and Marxism

competition, where the Court held as early as 1966 that it was sufficient for an agreement to be 'capable of constituting a threat, either direct or indirect, actual or potential, to freedom of trade between member states in a manner which might harm the attainment of the objectives of a single market between States', for it to be caught by the rules prohibiting anti-competitive behaviour.[39]

THE ROAD TO NEOLIBERALISM: JUDICIALISATION AND LIBERALISATION

The conditions warranting a more interventionist approach to market building would soon materialise. By the 1970s capitalism was again in crisis and the conditions that enabled the early phase of integration began to crumble. The Fordist model of mass production and consumption was characterised by high levels of growth, wages, and employment. This enabled a compromise between capital and labour, expressed in the consolidation of the welfare state. With the collapse of the Bretton Woods monetary system in 1971, the oil crisis of 1973–74, and the global recession that followed, these trends were effectively reversed, setting the stage for the transition to a finance-led neoliberal regime of accumulation as a way to restore conditions of profitability.[40]

Legally this transitory phase was characterised and indeed enabled by two interconnected trends, which transformed both the locus of EU law-making and the content of EU law. On the one hand, power shifted decisively toward the two institutions that were most remote from domestic and transnational class conflicts, the supranational and unaccountable European Court of Justice and the European Commission. Throughout the 1960s and 1970s, national governments sitting in the Council were paralysed by continuing antagonisms between powerful states and growing social unrest in a number of member states. Under those conditions, the two institutions took it upon themselves to push forward the completion of the common market. Partly as a result, on the other hand, market building shifted from a project of so-called 'positive' integration, involving the adoption of common standards at the European level, to a project of 'negative' integration based on the dismantling of barriers to trade.

These changes had significant implications and ushered in a more fundamental transformation of the state. In its 1974 *Dassonville* decision, the Court took a very broad view of barriers to trade which were said to include 'all trading rules enacted by Member States which are capable of hindering, directly or indirectly, actually or potentially, intra-Community trade'.[41] This shifted the focus from the form of the measure to its effects on the internal market,[42] opening up to scrutiny any form of public or social regulation. In *Cassis de Dijon*, decided five years later,[43] the Court further drew a presumption that products which had been lawfully

---

[39]   Joined Cases 56 and 58/64 *Consten and Grundig v Commission* [1966] ECR 299, cited in Weatherhill, *The Internal Market*, 58.

[40]   On neoliberalism as a class project see, among others, Gérard Duménil and Dominique Lévy, *The Crisis of Neoliberalism* (Harvard University Press 2011); David Harvey, *A Brief History of Neoliberalism* (OUP 2007).

[41]   Case 8/74 *Procureur du Roi v Benoît and Gustave Dassonville* [1974] ECR 837, para 5.

[42]   Weatherhill, *Internal Market*, 52.

[43]   Case 120/78 *Rewe-Zentral AG v Bundesmonopolverwaltung für Branntwein* ('*Cassis de Dijon*') [1979] ECR 649.

marketed in one of the member states should enjoy unimpeded access to the market of other states. Obstructive national laws and practices could be maintained if they were justified by a 'mandatory requirement'. But this became subject to a strict proportionality test and the reversed burden of proof essentially transferred the power to determine the legality of national regulation to the Court of Justice. As Nicol points out, this was not ideologically neutral. Instead, it created a hierarchy of values, typical of neoliberal policy, under which the free market would prevail over other public considerations.[44] These cases also made clear—if it was not clear already—that economic freedoms were not merely rights to equal treatment with domestic goods or operators, but rather 'free-standing substantive rights'.[45] Their content and scope would be determined by EU bodies, and they would override national laws and regulations that interfere with the market, even if these were not discriminatory.

In parallel with these developments, a far more aggressive campaign against cartels, state aid, and anti-competitive behaviour by the Court-backed European Commission also had important consequences for the form, content, and reach of EU competition law.[46] The latter gradually grew into a European-wide regime that superseded national policies and embraced a far more pervasive logic of economic efficiency that targeted not only private activity but also public regulations.[47] Together internal market law and competition law effectively acted as 'can openers', cracking the public sector open to marketisation.[48]

The deepening of the state's configuration along market lines was not always smooth and generated its own set of contradictions and counter-movements. Coupled with the doctrines of direct effect and supremacy, pursuant to which rights under EU law can be enforced directly by domestic courts regardless of countervailing domestic law, the Court's pro-market interpretation prompted increased levels of litigation against a wide range of national laws. Famously, the Court felt compelled to lay down some limits to the reach of the market, after a series of controversial cases that challenged non-discriminatory 'selling arrangements' such as Sunday trading rules.[49] A degree of European regulation of labour relations, mostly in the form of individual workers' rights, also followed the dismantling of collective rights and social regulation at the domestic level. Challenges by domestic courts to the overreach of EU law, finally, led the Court in the early 1970s to recognise that fundamental human rights formed an integral part of the European Community legal order.

Yet none of these developments challenged the expansion and deepening of the market. The internal market case law would continue to further greater liberalisation, and litigation would remain instrumental for the dismantling of regulations inhospitable to market forces. 'Social Europe', meanwhile, could hardly be disaggregated from concerns about integrating the working classes more firmly into transnational capitalist relations. EU labour law was not the product of social struggles from below, nor did it aim to protect workers or enhance the power of labour vis-à-vis capital. Instead, it was a largely top-down enterprise meant to incentivise

---

[44]   Nicol, *Constitutional Protection of Capitalism*, 97.
[45]   Agustín José Menendez, 'A European Union Founded on Capital? The Fundamental Norms Organising Public Power in the European Union' in Céline Jouin (ed), *La constitution matérielle de l'Europe* (Pedone 2019) 147.
[46]   Buch-Hansen and Wigger, 'Revisiting 50 Years of Market-Making'.
[47]   Menendez, 'A European Union'.
[48]   The expression was used by Commissioner Karel van Miert; see Nicol, *Constitutional Protection of Capitalism*, 107.
[49]   Case C-267/91 *Keck and Mithouard* [1993] ECR I-6097.

the movement of labour—which had remained rather limited—and facilitate its incorporation into an increasingly flexible labour market,[50] designed to support the mobility of capital and boost competitiveness. Not all states agreed with the Thatcherite line that this process had necessarily to involve mass deregulation and strict limitations on collective bargaining. Yet, as Bob Hepple notes, these differences were not 'in the direction of change—reducing real costs of labour and enhancing employers' ability to respond effectively to new markets and processes—but in the methods necessary to achieve it'.[51] The market's structural primacy would become even clearer in the Court of Justice's case law, where the rights to collective bargaining and industrial action were explicitly subordinated to the economic freedoms,[52] emptying them of much of their content and social purpose.[53] Similarly, the gradual 'constitutionalisation' of EU Treaties, which entrenched liberal values as founding principles of the EU Constitution, supported the expansion of market principles. The connection between the development of human rights and the construction of the common market was already clear in the early case law. Were breaches of fundamental rights to be judged in light of national constitutional law instead of Community law, the Court explained, 'the substantive unity and efficacy of Community law' would be damaged and the 'unity of the Common Market' destroyed.[54] More generally, the EU's commitment to principles of liberal constitutionalism would over time fulfil an important ideological function, concealing the class nature of the project, and in the face of mounting criticism about its democratic deficit, providing it with much-needed legitimacy and stability.

THE CONSTITUTIONALISATION OF NEOLIBERALISM

By the mid-1980s, neoliberalism became politically entrenched in most politico-economically 'core' European countries and explicitly inscribed into the constitutional DNA of the European project.[55] At Maastricht, the liberalisation of capital movements[56] was complemented with the introduction of the Economic and Monetary Union (EMU), finally paving the way for a single currency after protracted negotiations throughout the late 1960s and 1970s, a constitutional commitment to 'the principle of an open market economy and free competition',[57] and the establishment of an autonomous and unaccountable European Central Bank (ECB) responsible for maintaining price stability.

---

50   Gareth Dale and Nadine El-Enany, 'The Limits of Social Europe: EU Law and the Ordoliberal Agenda' (2013) 14 *German Law Journal* 613.
51   Bob Hepple, 'The Crisis in EEC Labour Law' (1987) 16 *Industrial Law Journal* 77, 82.
52   See Case C-438/05 *International Transport Workers' Federation v Viking* [2007] ECR I-10779; Case C-341/05 *Laval v Svenska Byggnadsarbetare* [2007] ECR I-11767.
53   Among the many discussions of the cases see Maria Tzanakopoulou, *Reclaiming Constitutionalism: Democracy, Power and the State* (Hart 2018) 74–78.
54   Case 44/79 *Liselotte Hauer v Land Rheinland-Pfalz* [1979] ECR 3727, para 14.
55   See e.g., Nicol, *Constitutional Protection of Capitalism*, ch 3.
56   Council Directive 88/361/EEC for the Implementation of Article 67 of the Treaty [1988] OJ L178/5.
57   Consolidated Version of the Treaty on the Functioning of the European Union [2008] OJ C 115/49, art 119 [TFEU].

Several political and socio-economic factors explain Maastricht's constitutional embrace of neoliberal ideas, including the influence of the ERI and the 'U-turn' of François Mitterrand's government in France, which abandoned even its moderate nationalisation plans. But the constitutionalisation of neoliberalism cannot be divorced from the class character of EU law. Far from ensuring prosperity and greater competitiveness for the mutual benefit of all eurozone members, the EMU reflected and facilitated the entrenchment of the core-periphery dynamic that had begun to shape European enlargement. Although the rules of the EMU formally applied to all states equally, by fixing exchange rates and preventing devaluation, Maastricht institutionalised the interests of the dominant factions of European capital as against the less developed economies of the newly acceding states. The arrangement also deepened the structural imbalance between labour and capital. Particularly for countries of the periphery, maintaining competitiveness under a single currency required greater extraction of surplus value at the point of production, putting increased pressure on wages. Guglielmo Carchedi summarised the class content of the EMU, and hence of EU law, well: 'The economic significance of the EMU and of the Euro for labour cannot but be negative. The more the EU countries are tied to Germany (i.e. to the project of Europe's advanced capital under the leadership of the German one), the greater the expropriation of value from labour.'[58] Ideologically, moreover, this constitutional construct made monetarism appear as the product of a technical economic policy imposed by a 'distant bureaucracy',[59] rather than a strategy designed to weaken organised labour. Finally, the single currency aimed to make the eurobloc more competitive with—and independent from—US capital, even though, as Carchedi predicted, absent a strong political and military power, the euro is yet to pose a serious challenge to US dominance.

The widespread embrace of neoliberal policies also required a more significant overhaul of the EU's Constitution. Subjection to market rules was secured by what neo-Gramscian scholar Stephen Gill has termed the 'new constitutionalism', namely the 'construction of legal or constitutional devices to remove or insulate substantially the new economic institutions from popular scrutiny or democratic accountability'.[60] This was achieved by various means. One was the unaccountability of the ECB and the limited powers of the European Parliament. Another was the establishment of a tight system of rules on public debt and budget deficits.[61] Also crucial was the prohibition of the ECB to act as a lending institution, which made member states dependent on markets for their financing.[62] As a result, while states remained formally responsible for economic policy, their power was heavily policed and normalised by a combination of institutional, legal, and market mechanisms designed to overcome domestic pressures.

Other constitutional changes were designed to ensure the legitimacy of, and support for, the neoliberal construct. One example is the introduction of EU citizenship. If it found root in the ordoliberal and neoliberal distrust for the masses, the 'new constitutionalism' also reflected the EU's deeper political malaise. This was already apparent in the Danish rejection of the

---

[58]   Carchedi, *For Another Europe*, 140.
[59]   Carchedi, *For Another Europe*, 143.
[60]   Stephen Gill, 'The Emerging World Order and European Change: The Political Economy of European Union' (1992) 28 *Socialist Register* 157, 165. See also Stephen Gill, 'European Governance and New Constitutionalism: Economic and Monetary Union and Alternatives to Disciplinary Neoliberalism in Europe' (1998) 3 *New Political Economy* 5.
[61]   TFEU, art 126.
[62]   TFEU, arts 123, 125.

Maastricht Treaty, and it was confirmed by the resistance to the austerity measures member states sought to impose after the world recession of the early 1990s in order to abide by the Maastricht convergence criteria.[63] At Maastricht, EU citizenship came to supplement early efforts to build a common sense of identity, history, and belonging and produce an 'ideology of Europeanism' capable of yielding popular support for the European endeavour.[64]

However, EU citizenship would struggle to become for the EU what national citizenship was for the capitalist state. As the notion of 'market citizenship' illustrates, EU citizenship remained closely tied to market participation.[65] Even to the present date, social entitlements such as welfare benefits depend on the fulfilment of conditions chiefly defined by the pursuit of economic activity.[66] EU citizenship thus primarily protects wealthy, mobile agents of production rather than precarious or vulnerable labour. More generally, other entitlements that attach to European legal subjecthood are subordinate to the status of the EU citizen as *homo economicus*: fundamental rights are triggered only in cases falling within the scope of EU law (i.e., in situations of cross-border economic activity), and do not automatically prevail over economic freedoms. As such, EU citizens are primarily seen as personifications of a commodity, whether 'the commodity labor power or the commodity money',[67] not as political agents or human beings.

This framework differs considerably from the context in which Marx engaged with law and rights.[68] First, notwithstanding Marx's critique of political emancipation, which fell short, in his view, of real human (social) emancipation, Marx still viewed the granting of equal citizenship rights as a great achievement.[69] The same conclusion could not automatically apply to EU citizenship. Rights of political participation are limited and other entitlements do not apply equally to all citizens. Second, one of the reasons why, for Marx, citizenship rights did not guarantee human emancipation (and why Marx was so critical of the rights of man, such as the right to property and security) is that they were subordinate to—and indeed a means of conserving—the rights of 'egoistic man',[70] that is, the rights of individuals as bourgeois individuals pursuing their own interests. In the EU, this subordination runs even deeper. The citizen is not simply the 'servant of egoistic man';[71] to the extent that citizenship rights include rights that are key to the pursuit of cross-border economic activity, such as the right to residence and movement, the EU citizen *is* Marx's egoistic man.

The entrenchment of neoliberalism, finally, also prompted the constitutionalisation of an embryonic European repressive apparatus designed to secure the stability of the neoliberal

[63]   Christakis Georgiou, 'The Euro Crisis and the Future of European Integration' (2010) 128 *International Socialism* 81, https://isj.org.uk/the-euro-crisis-and-the-future-of-european-integration/ accessed 7 April 2021.

[64]   Céline Cantat, 'Narratives and Counter-Narratives of Europe: Constructing and Contesting Europeanity' (2015) 3 *Cahiers: Mémoire et Politique* 5.

[65]   Niamh N Shuibhne, 'The Resilience of EU Market Citizenship' (2010) 47 *Common Market Law Review* 1597.

[66]   Charlotte O'Brien, 'I Trade, Therefore I Am: Legal Personhood in the European Union' (2013) 50 *Common Market Law Review* 1643.

[67]   Peebles, 'A Marxist Look', 590.

[68]   Karl Marx, 'On the Jewish Question' [1844] in Karl Marx, *Early Writings* (Rodney Livingstone and Gregor Benton tr, Penguin 1990) 211.

[69]   Marx, 'On the Jewish Question', 221.

[70]   Marx, 'On the Jewish Question', 230.

[71]   Marx, 'On the Jewish Question', 231.

order as a whole. Mark Neocleous explains the problem of the modern police as a consequence of the structural separation between the economic and political spheres under capitalism. As serfdom 'was simultaneously a form of economic exploitation and politico-legal coercion',[72] feudalism was characterised by the 'unity of economic and political domination'.[73] The separation between the two spheres under capitalism raised the question of how to preserve a peaceful order, particularly under conditions of increased social instability. This is by and large when modern notions of the police entered the scene. Similarly, as the movement towards market building and expansion deepened, the difficulties arising from the separation between the European economic order and the political sphere became more apparent. Despite being closely intertwined with Westphalian ideas of sovereignty, the disjuncture between the economic base of society and its political apparatus, much of which continued to be organised domestically, eventually became untenable, requiring new forms of policing that transcended state boundaries.

Maastricht took a more decisive step in that direction, constitutionalising a set of more informal forms of co-operation that had begun in the early 1970s in the fields of criminal law, civil law, and asylum and immigration on the one hand and foreign and security policy on the other—two of the so-called 'pillars' of the EU that stood alongside the central pillar of integration, now renamed the 'European Community'. Over the course of the EU's subsequent development, these two policy fields evolved at very different paces and followed different trajectories. The former was fully integrated into the supranational economic pillar. By contrast, under the 2009 Treaty of Lisbon, the 'Common Foreign and Security Policy' (CFSP) continues to be subject to special rules and procedures. The provisions on the CFSP are located in a different treaty, namely the TEU, rather than the TFEU. And their content differs from the arrangements traditionally associated with the supranational governance characterising the core economic pillar, such as qualified majority voting, judicial review, or directly effective regulations and directives.

These differences in institutional forms and legal tools can be explained by the different socio-economic contents of each pillar. Internally, the completion of the internal market and the creation of monetary union required rapid and expansive integration in matters traditionally belonging to the realm of criminal justice.[74] Several factors also prompted greater co-ordination in matters of foreign policy and security. The constitutionalisation of a neoliberal model of accumulation supported by a single market and currency promoted capital investment beyond the European borderland. Geopolitical developments, such as the war in Kosovo, also forced major European powers to set aside some of their differences and commit to greater integration. However, other factors militated against the development of an independent European 'police power', a power to secure the interests of European capital abroad. One such factor is the continued existence of competing national imperialisms with long historical roots and interests in specific regions. France, for example, continues to have a strong

---

[72] Mark Neocleous, *The Fabrication of Social Order: A Critical Theory of Police Power* (Pluto Press 2000) 1.

[73] Neocleous, *Fabrication of Social Order*, 1.

[74] On relations between the internal market and EU criminal law, see e.g., Massimo Fichera, 'Sketches of a Theory of Europe as an Area of Freedom, Security and Justice' in Maria Fletcher, Ester Herlin-Karnell, and Claudio Matera (eds), *The European Union as an Area of Freedom, Security and Justice* (Routledge 2017) 34.

military presence in its old colonial territories, as captured by the term 'Françafrique'. Another is the leading role of the United States in policing the global capitalist order. These factors are particularly prevalent in matters of defence, in relation to which the treaties clarify that the EU's defence policy 'shall not prejudice the specific character of the security and defence policy of certain Member States' and 'shall respect the obligations of certain Member States … under the North Atlantic Treaty'.[75] The differences between the CFSP and other EU policies, however, are gradually fading and there are increased calls for a greater juridification of foreign and security policy.[76] As we will see, this coincides with a changing and increasingly unstable geopolitical environment, illustrating how extra-economic 'external' factors can have important and sometimes unpredictable effects on the evolution of the EU.

CLASS PROJECT AS IMPERIAL PROJECT

Nonetheless, the creation of the CFSP still expressed the gradual emergence of a distinct, if imperfect, European imperialism, one that intertwines with national imperialisms but called forth novel institutions at the EU level to secure and further the interests of European capitalism as a whole. In BS Chimni's materialist theory of international law, neoliberalism's consolidation corresponds to the rise of 'imperial' international law, a 'global state formation' or 'nascent global state' that realises the 'interests of transnational capital and powerful states in the international system to the disadvantage of third world states and peoples'.[77] International institutions play a central role in that constellation, not only as 'institutions of continuing informal imperialism' but as active agents in the process of state reconfiguration.[78]

The EU can certainly be understood as an element of this embryonic structure. European integration transformed European (and non-European) states, facilitating their integration into a global network of capitalist production. Yet states retain an important role in the contemporary imperial system.[79] And as Carchedi reminds us, the EU is anything but identical to international organisations like the International Monetary Fund and World Bank, which 'act as the agents of capital in the centre' but do not pursue 'their own imperial policies'.[80] Indeed, the EU both mediates 'contradictory national interests' and pursues a 'relatively independent formulation of common interests by EU institutions'.[81]

These insights allow for a reconstruction of the imperial dimensions of European integration and the different forms European imperialism has taken over time. From its inception, the

---

[75]   TEU, art 42.

[76]   See e.g., Annegret Bendiek, 'A Paradigm Shift in the EU's Common Foreign and Security Policy: From Transformation to Resilience' (2017) Stiftung Wissenschaft und Politik Research Paper, https://www.swp-berlin.org/fileadmin/contents/products/research_papers/2017RP11_bdk.pdf accessed 7 April 2021.

[77]   BS Chimni, 'International Institutions Today: An Imperial Global State in the Making', (2004) 15 *European Journal of International Law* 1, 1–2 (de-emphasised from original).

[78]   James Tully, 'On Law, Democracy and Imperialism', Twenty-First Annual Public Lecture Centre for Law and Society University of Edinburgh (10–11 March 2005) 18.

[79]   See e.g., Alex Callinicos, *Imperialism and Global Political Economy*; Ellen Meiksins Wood, *The Empire of Capital* (Verso 2003).

[80]   Bruno Carchedi and Guglielmo Carchedi, 'Contradictions of European Integration' (1999) 67 *Capital & Class* 119, 122.

[81]   Carchedi and Carchedi, 'Contradictions', 122.

European Community was never a purely European endeavour. Through special arrangements with 'associate states', which were granted preferential access to the European market, the original EEC Treaty incorporated the colonies of France, Belgium, and the Netherlands into the newly created economic area. Access to Africa's natural resources was essential to the project of rebuilding Europe into a geopolitical and geoeconomic 'power bloc', whilst European integration helped to stabilise the African colonial system.[82] After decolonisation, 'Eurafrica' took on a different legal form.[83] The integration of African markets was furthered by a series of treaties, commencing with the 1963 Treaty of Yaoundé. Far from marking the end of empire, these instruments formalised a new set of neocolonial arrangements, premised on the political independence of African countries but rooted in old patterns of exploitation and economic dependency.[84] Throughout the Fordist period, African countries acted as key market outlets for the European imperial core, providing Europe with raw materials and primary commodities and generally experiencing little large-scale industrialisation.[85]

With the completion of the internal market, the interpenetration of European capital accelerated, the power of finance capital grew, and European capital became increasingly internationalised. Nowhere is this clearer than in the Treaty of Lisbon, which granted the EU exclusive competence over foreign direct investment.[86] As part of that process, the EU began to develop its own 'territorial logic',[87] linked partly to the interests of the hegemonic faction of European capital, namely finance capital, and partly to other capitalist interests, notably military-industrial capital.[88] Legally this process took various forms across time and space, from formal accession through association agreements to traditional international treaties (e.g., the Cotonou Agreement with the African, Caribbean, and Pacific Group of States) and other forms of semi-institutionalised co-operation (e.g., the European Neighbourhood Policy). These arrangements differ considerably, including in the economic relations they help to foster. But to a greater or lesser extent, they have all been shaped by a core-periphery dynamic that tends to subordinate the needs of EU 'partners' to those of European capital.[89] And in all cases, the law has played a crucial role in enabling and consolidating economic expansion.

'Classic' Marxist theories of imperialism of the early twentieth century had already highlighted that the shift from the export of commodities—which characterised early forms of capitalist expansion through trade and the extraction of raw materials and which required

---

[82]   Peo Hansen and Stefan Jonsson, 'European Integration as a Colonial Project' in Olivia U Rutazibwa and Robbie Shilliam (eds), *Routledge Handbook of Postcolonial Politics* (Routledge 2018) 32.

[83]   Quinn Slobodian, *Globalists: The End of Empire and the Birth of Neoliberalism* (Harvard University Press 2018) 183. See more generally Peo Hansen and Stefan Jonsson, *Eurafrica: The Untold History of European Integration and Colonialism* (Hart 2014) 40.

[84]   Slobodian, *Globalists*, 216.

[85]   Giuliano Garavini, 'The Colonies Strike Back: The Impact of the Third World on Western Europe, 1968–1975' (2007) 16 *Contemporary European History* 299, 301. See also Ryner and Cafruny, *European Union and Global Capitalism*, ch 8, esp 195–200.

[86]   Auvray and Durand, 'European Capitalism'.

[87]   On the development of the EU into a new form of empire see in particular Jan Zielonka, *Europe as Empire: The Nature of the Enlarged European Union* (OUP 2006).

[88]   Iraklis Oikonomou, 'A Historical Materialist Approach to CSDP' in Xymena Kurowska and Fabian Breuer (eds), *Explaining the EU's Common Security and Defence Policy* (Palgrave 2012) 162.

[89]   Raffaella A Del Sarto, 'Normative Empire Europe: The European Union, Its Borderlands, and the "Arab Spring"' (2016) 54 *Journal of Common Market Studies* 1.

control over foreign territories—to the export of capital would necessitate the 'export [of] *capitalism* (as a form of social organisation)'.[90] In this instance, this was achieved by various forms of conditionality—from integration of the community *acquis* through structural adjustment-style reforms to the promotion of 'good governance'—which opened up markets in relevant states and created the internal conditions for finance-led accumulation. Accession, for instance, was preceded by a 'transition period of institutional restructuring towards market capitalism', including through the institutionalisation of 'market freedoms and ownership rights'.[91] Ideologically, moreover, this was justified by a liberal discourse that resembled the old standard of civilisation, which was always closely intertwined with the expansion of the capitalist mode of production.[92]

AUTHORITARIAN CONSTITUTIONALISM: THE EUROCRISIS AND THE RADICALISATION OF NEOLIBERALISM

More than any other crisis of capitalism, the 2007–08 financial crash brought into the open the many contradictions at the heart of European integration. Given the EU's entanglement in 'global networks of capitalist production and finance', the crisis spread to European markets quickly, culminating in the eurocrisis, the sovereign debt crisis of the EU periphery. The specific form the crisis of global capital took on the European continent reflected the imbalances and uneven development that had come to define the eurozone.[93] Spatially, the bloc was divided between Germany and other capital-exporting countries that maintained surpluses by lending money to the periphery to buy their exports and capital-importing countries that ran deficit accounts and depended upon debt-driven growth.

The EU's interpretation of and response to the crisis were both shaped by neoliberal ideology. According to the EU establishment, the eurocrisis was not intrinsic to global capitalism or the contradictions of the EMU, but the product of reckless borrowing and 'overspending by irresponsible governments'.[94] Partly as a result, the response was not based on any form of collective responsibility or social solidarity, through, say, the mutualisation of debt. Instead, the burden was borne by the European periphery. These 'recalcitrant' states had to be disciplined and restructured, resulting once again in labour paying the price for the crisis of capital. Echoing old colonial tropes, the acronyms PIGS—Portugal, Ireland, Greece, and Spain—or PIIGS—which adds Italy to the list—provided the medium through which core-periphery relations of exploitation were refashioned as a moralised distinction between virtuous and vicious states and austerity was justified.

---

[90]   Robert Knox, 'A Critical Examination of the Concept of Imperialism in Marxist and Third World Approaches to International Law' (PhD dissertation, London School of Economics and Political Science 2014) 43.

[91]   Angela Wigger, 'The External Dimension of EU Competition Policy: Exporting Europe's Core Business?' in Jan Orbie (ed), *Europe's Global Role: External Policies of the European Union* (Routledge 2008) 181, 186.

[92]   See e.g., Gerrit W Gong, *The Standard of 'Civilization' in International Society* (OUP 1984).

[93]   Bastiaan van Apeldoorn, 'The Transnational Political Economy of European Integration: The Future Socio-Economic Governance in the Enlarged Union' in Richard Stubbs and Geoffrey RD Underhill (eds), *Political Economy and the Changing Global Order* (3rd edn, OUP 2005) 306, 308.

[94]   Dale and El-Enany, 'Limits of Social Europe', 627.

Legally, the response to the eurocrisis followed various stages. The immediate response took the form of emergency measures enacted mostly outside the EU legal framework. In order to restore market confidence, the countries of the periphery—or, in reality, the French and German banks which held their debt—were bailed out and subject to the shock therapy first applied by the International Monetary Fund across the global South, through a mixture of EU law and international law instruments.[95] Recourse to these 'abnormal' measures was not accidental. They allowed limitations to the powers of the ECB to be circumvented. They also helped to shift the blame for the debt crisis, and the humanitarian crises that followed the dismantling of social protection, onto the relevant states. According to the EU institutions, given that these measures were not based on the EU Treaties, the EU's 'social constitution' did not apply and securing compliance with human rights was the sole responsibility of national authorities. That they had limited leeway to do so, given the detailed and prescriptive nature of the memoranda of understanding, did not appear to create a paradox, for those states had 'voluntarily' asked for financial assistance, agreed to the terms of the bailouts, and supposedly retained a level of discretion in their implementation.[96]

In a second stage, this legal paradigm was normalised and expanded. The legality of the 'abnormal' measures was upheld by EU courts,[97] the EU Treaties were amended,[98] and some of these instruments were brought within the scope of EU law. However, the loaning facility, now renamed the European Stability Mechanism, continued to rest on an international agreement, an enduring sign of the extraordinary character of the EU's response. In parallel, the EU establishment seized upon the emergency narrative to push through a more fundamental change in the regulation of the eurozone. The 'new economic governance'—a series of measures amending the Stability and Growth Pact—tightened fiscal discipline, enhanced the supervisory powers of the European Commission over state budgets, and strengthened monitoring procedures by introducing monetary fines. Again, some of these measures, such as the Fiscal Compact, were concluded outside the EU legal framework, while those formally adopted as EU laws—the so-called 'Six-Pack' and 'Two-Pack'—lacked a clear basis in the EU Treaties. For example, the EU has no express competence in the budgetary field and the introduction of reverse majority voting[99]—pursuant to which fines are deemed to be approved unless a qualified majority of states in the Council reject them—appears to go against the

---

[95] Claire Kilpatrick, 'Abnormal Sources and Institutional Actions in the EU Sovereign Debt Crisis—ECB Crisis Management and the Sovereign Debt Loans' in Marise Cremona and Claire Kilpatrick (eds), *EU Legal Acts: Challenges and Transformations* (OUP 2018) 69.

[96] Claire Kilpatrick, 'Are the Bailouts Immune to EU Social Challenge Because They Are Not EU Law?' (2010) 10 *European Constitutional Law Review* 393, 394–96.

[97] Case C-370/12 *Thomas Pringle v Government of Ireland* ECLI:EU:C:2012:756; Case C-62/14 *Peter Gauweiler and Others v Deutscher Bundestag* ECLI:EU:C:2015:400.

[98] A paragraph was added to Art 136 of the TFEU, which reads: 'The member states whose currency is the euro may establish a stability mechanism to be activated if indispensable to safeguard the stability of the euro area as a whole. The granting of any required financial assistance under the mechanism will be made subject to strict conditionality.'
See Decision of the European Council Amending Article 136 of the Treaty on the Functioning of the European Union With Regard To a Stability Mechanism For Member States Whose Currency is the Euro [2011] OJ 91/1.

[99] Pursuant to art 3 of Regulation 1174/2011, 'decisions shall be deemed adopted by the Council unless it decides, by qualified majority, to reject the recommendation within 10 days of its adoption by the Commission'. See Regulation 1174/2011 (EU) of the European Parliament and of the Council on

Treaty requirement that they be approved by qualified majority in the Council.[100] The result is a further shift in power from the intergovernmental Council to the supranational Commission.

To the extent that they deepened the subjection of the state (and politics) to the demands of the market by undemocratic means, these developments could be read as continuations of 'disciplinary neoliberalism' and 'new constitutionalism'. Yet a closer look at the form and content of post-crisis EU law also makes it clear that they set in motion a deeper qualitative change. Numerous legal scholars have characterised the management of the eurocrisis as a form of emergency law or authoritarian rule.[101] Equally clear from such analyses is that these modes of regulation did not only involve a temporary circumvention of the EU Treaties (whether through the conclusion of international agreements or the adoption of EU legislation stretching the formal boundaries of legality) but also a more fundamental 'constitutional mutation'.[102] From a formal perspective, the executive branch, particularly its financial arm, was reinforced and democratic processes were sidelined at both domestic and European levels.[103] From a substantive perspective, the de facto constitutionalisation of austerity and dismantling of social rights at the national level[104] deepened the structural asymmetries at the heart of the European construct: that between core and periphery on the one hand and that between labour and capital on the other.

Lukas Oberndorfer drew on Poulantzas' theory of authoritarian statism to explain these changes and their interconnection.[105] In his view, these developments are best understood as a shift from 'new constitutionalism' to 'authoritarian constitutionalism',[106] which forms part of a new stage in the development of neoliberalism in Europe, from disciplinary neoliberalism to authoritarian competitive statism. The neoliberal turn of the EU had already required a sidelining of substantive democracy via the mechanisms and institutions of 'new constitu-

---

Enforcement Measures to Correct Excessive Macroeconomic Imbalances in the Euro Area [2011] OJ L306/8.

[100]   Rainer Palmstorfer, 'The Reverse Majority Voting under the "Six Pack": A Bad Turn for the Union?' (2014) 20 *European Law Journal* 186.

[101]   See e.g., Cristian Kreuder-Sonnen, 'Beyond Integration Theory: The (Anti-)Constitutional Dimension of European Crisis Governance' (2016) 54 *Journal of Common Market Studies* 1350, 1354–55.

[102]   Robert Pye, 'The EU and the Absence of Fundamental Rights in the Eurozone: A Critical Perspective' (2017) 24 *European Journal of International Relations* 567.

[103]   See e.g., Christian Joerges and Maria Weimer, 'A Crisis of Executive Managerialism in the EU: No Alternative?' in Gráinne de Búrca, Claire Kilpatrick, and Joanne Scott (eds), *Critical Legal Perspectives on Global Governance: Liber Amicorum David M Trubek* (Hart 2015) 295.

[104]   See e.g., Floris de Witte, 'EU Law, Politics, and the Social Question' (2013) 14 *German Law Journal* 581.

[105]   See Nicos Poulantzas, *State, Power, Socialism* (first published 1978, Patrick Camiller tr, Verso 2014) 203–16. Others, too, adapted Poulantzas' theory to the European context. See e.g., Etienne Schneider and Sune Sandbeck, 'Monetary Integration in the Eurozone and the Rise of Transnational Authoritarian Statism' (2019) 23 *Competition & Change* 138.

[106]   Lukas Oberndorfer, 'From New Constitutionalism to Authoritarian Constitutionalism: New Economic Governance and the State of European Democracy' in Johannes Jäger and Elisabeth Springler (eds), *Asymmetric Crisis in Europe and Possible Futures: Critical Political Economy and Post-Keynesian Perspectives* (Routledge 2016) 184. See also Michael Wilkinson, 'Authoritarian Liberalism in the European Constitutional Imagination: Second Time as Farce?' (2015) 21 *European Law Journal* 313; Ian Bruff, 'The Rise of Authoritarian Neoliberalism' (2014) 26 *Rethinking Marxism* 113.

tionalism'. The deepening of the neoliberal agenda now necessitated a more radical incursion into the 'procedures of formal democracy and the rule of law'.[107] The reason, according to Oberndorfer, was increased resistance to the neoliberal project and the EU's deeper political crisis:

> While up until the European crisis of hegemony, national compromise balances were circumvented and challenged by the shifting of policy fields into European law, *now even the power relations condensed in the European legal form are becoming too tight for the radicalization of the neoliberal project.*[108]

Other Marxists also drew the connections between the economic and political dimensions of the eurocrisis, linking them to conditions that are intrinsic to European capitalism. Razmig Keucheyan and Cédric Durand, for example, developed the notion of 'bureaucratic Caesarism'—a coercive, undemocratic form of dictatorial power which Gramsci associated with crises of hegemony and which is exercised in this instance by an impersonal, bureaucratic institution rather than a charismatic individual—to capture the authoritarian form that the crisis of capital took in the European context.[109]

However, Oberndorfer's analysis helpfully highlights both the legal dimensions *of* the European crisis and the crucial role that law has played *in* producing and legitimising it. It also makes clear that these developments are far from temporary. Contrary to the narrative put forward by EU institutions, the radicalisation of the neoliberal project was not necessitated by the eurocrisis. Rather, as Oberndorfer reminds us, it is intrinsic to the class character of the EU, its internal contradictions, and the pressures produced by its integration in the competitive world market. As such, if authoritarian constitutionalism was precipitated by the eurocrisis and the decline of the neoliberal consensus, it is also on course to becoming the new form of European (neoliberal) governance.[110]

FUTURE TRAJECTORY?

In the last few years, Europe's new existential crisis has deepened. The 'morbid symptoms' are visible at both national and European levels. At the national level, it has facilitated the rise and appeal of far-right parties and racist ideologies. At the European level, the authoritarian character of the EU has been arguably normalised and expanded. The two, moreover, feed one another. Commentators often remark that the eurocrisis helped fuel nationalistic sentiments and practices. But there are also signs that EU law is now developing to accommodate and legitimise these trends. As Charlotte O'Brien brilliantly documents, the European Court of

---

[107] Oberndorfer, 'From New Constitutionalism', 202.
[108] Oberndorfer, 'From New Constitutionalism', 202 (emphases added).
[109] Razmig Keucheyan and Cédric Dunand, 'Bureaucratic Caesarism' (2015) 23 *Historical Materialism* 23.
[110] Lukas Oberndorfer, 'Crisis of Hegemony in Europe—Heading Towards Authoritarian Competitive Statism?' (2015) Nicos Poulantzas Institute, https://poulantzas.gr/wp-content/uploads/2015/04/Oberndorfer-Crisis-of-Hegemony-in-Europe-Heading-Towards-Authoritarian-Competitive-Statism.pdf accessed 7 April 2021.

Justice has offered decreasing levels of resistance to various forms of discrimination based on nationality in domestic welfare policies and laws, particularly as regards precarious labour.[111]

Again, from a Marxist perspective, this would be another illustration of Europe's deepening crisis of hegemony. Contrary to conceptualisations of the EU as a cosmopolitan post-national experiment,[112] securing the consent of the popular masses has always involved a dangerous process of exclusionary identity-building: historically, the emergence of 'Fortress Europe' and the securitisation of migration from outside the EU was closely linked to the creation of EU citizenship and the completion of the internal market.[113] As the EU's legitimacy weakens, playing the 'subaltern off against each other as competitive "people-nations"' is emerging as a new way of minimising popular resistance.[114] The language of 'PIGS' (i.e., Portugal, Italy, Greece, and Spain), and the attendant narrative that the ordinary European taxpayer had to bear the cost of the crisis, thereby pitching (mostly German) workers against (Greek) workers, were striking examples of this phenomenon.

However, the overall future trajectory of the EU project remains uncertain. Constitutional developments at the European level lend little support to Mandel's belief in the inevitability of full supranationalisation. Legal integration has certainly advanced, including in the aftermath of the eurocrisis. One example is the creation of the Banking and Financial Union. Yet legal integration has never entailed the full absorption of national legal systems into EU law. And the EU's constitutional architecture is characterised by increased flexibility and differentiation—an idea captured by expressions like 'variable geometry' and 'multi-speed Europe'[115]—between different policy areas or member states. Perhaps the most dramatic expression was the introduction of a withdrawal clause in 2009 and the United Kingdom's decision to leave the EU, which shattered the EU's constitutional commitment to an 'ever closer Union'.

At first sight, Poulantzas' view that integration involves a transformation, rather than a displacement, of the nation-state, appears to capture the complex relation between national and European legal structures.[116] The same is true of his prognosis that the internationalisation of capital would produce increasing levels of uneven development. At least part of the 'variable geometry' characterising the European legal construct reflects the deepening of cleavages between core and periphery. At the same time, the Poulantzasian approach may not capture the full range of contradictions that beset the European project and that are likely to shape its future development, particularly, as predicted by 'classic' Marxist theories of imperialism, the continuing relevance of national antagonisms and geopolitical rivalries, among the member states and between the EU and other states in the global imperialist chain.

Poulantzas' understanding of the 'interior' European bourgeoisie produced by US hegemony suggested that European capital would develop a uniform set of interests. That this process

---

[111] Charlotte O'Brien, 'Civis Capitalist Sum: Class as the New Guiding Principle of EU Free Movement Rights' (2016) 53 *Common Market Law Review* 937.

[112] See e.g., Joseph HH Weiler and Marlene Wind (eds), *European Constitutionalism Beyond the State* (CUP 2003).

[113] See Jef Huysmans, 'The European Union and the Securitisation of Migration' (2000) 38 *Journal of Common Market Studies* 751.

[114] Oberndorfer, 'Crisis of Hegemony'.

[115] Eric Maurice, 'Macron Revives Multi-Speed Europe Idea', *EUObserver* (30 August 2017), https://euobserver.com/institutional/138832 accessed 7 April 2021.

[116] See Christopher J Bickerton, *From Nation States to Member States* (OUP 2012).

of class formation would face obstacles was already apparent in the early days of integration. One need only recall Charles de Gaulle's veto of the United Kingdom's two applications for membership of the EU in the 1960s. But it is equally visible today. Many of the EU's constitutional arrangements, such as the 'opt-outs' and exemptions negotiated by several member states, can be explained by concerns about accommodating national differences and disagreements over the EU's future trajectory.

Similarly, whilst the United States undoubtedly exerted decisive influence over the creation of the EU, it is not clear that this remains true today. There certainly is evidence that the amalgamation of US and European capital—and hence the latter's dependency on US capital—has continued to deepen.[117] Yet European imperialist powers in recent years have also sought greater strategic autonomy. The latest version of the EU's Security Strategy is replete with references to the EU's role in protecting 'our citizens', 'our principles', and 'our values'.[118] This discourse, moreover, has been accompanied by increased EU interventionism and militarisation. These developments can be linked to the consolidation and internationalisation of European capital. But they have also been driven by the changing and increasingly unstable geopolitical context. This includes the migration crisis, generalised insecurity in Europe's wider periphery, the geopolitical rivalry with Russia over the question of Ukraine and control of Russian oil and gas resources, and disagreements with the United States over Iran. The latter, in particular, has re-opened calls for a strengthening of the euro as a counterweight to US geo-economic power.[119] These changes to the socio-economic and political content of the EU's constitutional structures should be cause for concern. The common market may have helped to mediate capitalism's competitive and expansionist tendencies without recourse to military force. But as 'their Europe', to borrow from Harman, consolidates, classic Marxist theories of imperialism suggest that we should be wary of the idealist correlation between economic integration and international peace.[120]

All this raises the question of whether such trends can be reversed. Many on the left hold onto the possibility that the European project might eventually be democratised and socialised. This position, which is carried forward at the European level by groups such as the 'Democracy in Europe Movement 2025' (or 'DiEM25'), gained importance in the context of Britain's decision to leave the EU, where broad alliances were formed around the strategy of 'remain and reform'. However, the brief historical overview and analysis of EU law I have provided in this chapter raises serious doubts about the prospects of radical change in the nature of the EU and hence also the viability of strategies to reform it.

Constitutional developments do not support the view that the neoliberal and increasingly authoritarian character of the EU involves a radical break with the original European project. Maastricht may have sealed the neoliberal character of the organisation. But it built on long-term developments that are inseparable from the class nature of the European project and its position in global networks of production and exchange. To the extent that calls for

---

[117] Auvray and Durand, 'European Capitalism'.

[118] European Union, 'Shared Vision, Common Action: A Stronger Europe—A Global Strategy for the European Union's Foreign and Security Policy' (June 2016), https://eeas.europa.eu/archives/docs/top_stories/pdf/eugs_review_web.pdf accessed 7 April 2021.

[119] Caroline de Gruyter, 'The Omnipotent Dollar: US Sanctions and the Euro Problem' European Council on Foreign Relations (22 May 2018), https://ecfr.eu/article/commentary_the_omnipotent_dollar_us_sanctions_and_the_euro_problem/ accessed 7 April 2021.

[120] Harman, 'The Common Market'.

reform assume that the EU was hijacked by neoliberal forces, they neglect the historical and structural connections between the development of the EU and the reproduction of capitalist social relations on the European continent and beyond.

More importantly, the specific characteristics and historical development of EU law suggest that it imposes serious, and perhaps unique, procedural and substantive limitations to projects that radically challenge the EU's structural subordination of labour to capital. Notwithstanding their differences, both Mandel and Poulantzas stressed 'the difficulties that internationalization poses for revolutionary strategies'.[121] In particular, both pointed to the state's endurance as the primary site of class struggle, and the limitations faced by the pursuit of revolutionary strategies at the European level. In line with his supranationalisation thesis, Mandel recognised that there would come a point at which it was no longer 'objectively possible' for socialists to work for the 'overthrow of capitalism within the boundaries of their "own" country'.[122] Where the interpenetration of capital and the supranationalisation of power would give rise to a unified transnational capitalist class, he explained, 'the whole struggle for socialism will have to be lifted to the new international dimension'. However, uneven socio-economic development, as well as significant differences in internal conditions, meant that he did not believe such a transformation of the European space to be imminent. Nor did he think that, when the time came, the cross-border co-ordination of working-class struggles would be easy.[123] Similarly, Poulantzas wrote that 'in the current phase of internationalisation, the rupture of the imperialist chain in one of its link becomes terribly difficult'.[124] Again, this was due not simply to dependence on US capital, but also to the fact that 'the national form [still] prevails' in the essentially international character of the class struggle, despite increased international solidarity between workers.[125] This remains largely true today.

Mandel and Poulantzas both placed the difficulties involved in the co-ordination of the class struggle at the European level in the context of their theories of the state and the internationalization of capital. Building on their work, Durand and Keucheyan helpfully linked their persistence—which, in their view, also explains the absence of a European state—to the specific characteristic of the contemporary EU.[126] As they explain, the EU 'is not a sufficiently open political space to be able to allow different social forces to enter into conflict and establish compromises, as historically the modern nation-state has done.' The 'hegemony of transnational and financial capital at the EU level' and the 'cumulative process of exclusion of labour', in their view, prevent 'the institutional crystallization of conflicting European class relations and the substantiation of democratic processes at this level'.[127] These processes are not the product of the law alone. Other modes of soft or disciplinary governance, and a 'European elite' composed of domestic actors and the European bureaucracy, contribute to the entrenchment of a status quo that consolidates capital's hegemony and deflates popular revolt. Yet the structural biases encoded in the EU's constitutional structures play a key role in the dynamics Durand and Keucheyan describe.

---

[121] Auvray and Durand, 'European Capitalism', 149.
[122] Mandel, 'International Capitalism', 38 (de-emphasised from original).
[123] Mandel, 'International Capitalism', 39.
[124] Poulantzas, 'Internationalisation', 177.
[125] Poulantzas, 'Internationalisation', 171.
[126] Cédric Durand and Razmig Keucheyan, 'Financial Hegemony and the Unachieved European State' (2015) 19 *Competition & Change* 129, 130.
[127] Durand and Keucheyan, 'Financial Hegemony', 130.

On the one hand, EU law creates and organises the conditions for the reproduction of capital's hegemony. In the absence of a genuine set of social policies and labour laws at the European level, EU law rights and the supranational legal form mainly serve to advance the interests of capital and deepen its structural primacy over labour. On the other hand, EU law plays a key role in thwarting the formation of a collective political subject that could act as an agent of systemic change at the European level.[128] As Tzanakopoulou observes, for all the EU's rhetorical commitment to democracy, the absence of a European *demos* does not reflect 'national heterogeneity' but is instead the direct result of 'material practices that have divested European people of the power to identify with one another'.[129] If anything, the prospect of creating a European space for political contestation and social struggle continues to diminish as EU law evolves towards an increasingly 'elitist model of free movement' and EU citizenship.[130]

We might also add, to complement Durand and Keucheyan's analysis, that EU law also simultaneously impoverishes democracy at the national level and contributes to shrinking the space for the pursuit of socialist projects. There are many stories to tell, and lessons to be learned, from the experience of the left-wing SYRIZA government from 2015 to 2019 in Greece. One is a story of how an anti-austerity agenda was defeated by the EU's constitutional radicalisation of neoliberalism. Another, however, is a story of how left politics, if not democracy more generally, was set aside as a viable project, squeezed in a false choice between the European 'cosmopolitan' ideal and the nationalist, isolationist dystopia.

The issue, then, is not, or not only, that the EU Treaties are difficult to amend,[131] precluding a more fundamental overhaul of the organisation. If only because of state consent, that is the case for *all* international law. Nor is the issue that progressive social movements can have no influence at all in the passing of EU legislation. Popular resistance to the so-called Bolkestein Directive, which aimed to fully liberalise the movement of services, including public services, led to some tempering of the principle that states could not impose their national regulations on service providers located in a different member state.[132] Again, this relative 'openness' is not unique to EU law: even at the international level, Marxists have recognised the possibility of tactical resistance to and uses of law to advance the interests of the subaltern classes.[133] The issue, rather, is that EU law actively produces and sustains the hegemony of the main factions of European capital through mechanisms that continuously weaken the power of labour and impoverish the public sphere at both the European and national levels.

Commentators on the left routinely characterise the contemporary EU as the actualisation of Hayek's vision of the inter-state federation.[134] This diagnosis would only tend to confirm

---

[128]   Tzanakopoulou, *Reclaiming Constitutionalism*, 95.

[129]   Tzanakopoulou, *Reclaiming Constitutionalism*, 95.

[130]   O'Brien, 'Civis Capitalist Sum', 937.

[131]   See Danny Nicol, 'Is Another Europe Possible?' UK Constitutional Law Association blog (29 February 2016), https://ukconstitutionallaw.org/2016/02/29/danny-nicol-is-another-europe-possible/ accessed 7 April 2021.

[132]   Although it should be said that this already followed from the Court's judgment in *Cassis de Dijon*.

[133]   Robert Knox, 'Marxism, International Law, and Political Strategy' (2009) 22 *Leiden Journal of International Law* 413.

[134]   See Wolfgang Streeck, *Buying Time: The Delayed Crisis of Democratic Capitalism* (2nd edn, Patrick Camiller and David Fernbach trs, Verso 2017). For Hayek's vision on interstate federations see FA Hayek, *Individualism and Economic Order* (Routledge & Kegan Paul 1952).

the difficulties involved in reversing the dynamics described in this section, as well as the role of law and institutions in their reproduction. At least part of Hayek's support for the federal model was rooted in his belief that it was the best means of containing threats to the market. On the one hand, the federal supranational element would guard the economy against redistributive policies, cementing the structural primacy of capital over labour. On the other hand, the retention of the nation-state as a constituent element of the federation would prevent the emergence of transnational forms of solidarity.[135]

CONCLUSION

This chapter could only offer a brief snapshot of the historical interconnections between EU law and the reproduction of capitalist social relations, and the specific ways in which EU law played a role in the reconstitution of European capitalism after the Second World War. Marxist analyses of EU law have much to contribute to our understanding of European integration, especially its historical development and its juridico-political specificity. But more importantly, they also assist in the process of articulating strategies and visions of European and international solidarity that could truly transform Europe from an imperialist project to a genuinely peace-oriented project.

---

[135] Bojan Bugaric, 'Europe Against the Left? On Legal Limits to Progressive Politics' (2013) LSE 'Europe in Question' Discussion Paper Series, Paper No 61, http://eprints.lse.ac.uk/53186/1/LEQSPaper61.pdf accessed 7 April 2021.

PART III

FUTURE ORIENTATIONS OF
MARXIST LEGAL ANALYSIS

22. From free time to idle time: Time, work-discipline, and the gig economy

Rebecca Schein

INTRODUCTION

In his classic 1967 essay, 'Time, Work-Discipline, and Industrial Capitalism', EP Thompson identifies changes in the experience of time as a key feature of the transition to industrial capitalism in England. 'Those who are employed', he writes, 'experience a distinction between their employer's time and their "own" time'.[1] With the rising importance of 'free labour' in the organisation of different kinds of work in the eighteenth and nineteenth centuries, Thompson argues that the distinction of 'ownership'—whose time is it?—displaced task-oriented, nature-driven modes of organising and experiencing time, in which daily or seasonal tasks seemed to 'disclose themselves, by the logic of need, before the crofter's eyes'.[2] Proletarianisation, in other words, entailed a transition in people's consciousness of time, which became an abstract, divisible currency: time 'is not passed, but spent'.[3]

For Thompson the transformation of working class people's internalised experience of time was a manifestation of the 'new human nature' required and created by a 'severe restructuring of working habits' in the transition to industrial capitalism—a human nature upon which the new incentives and disciplines of the age could 'bite effectively'.[4] Soon enough, the new temporal regime of industrial capitalism came to be experienced simply as Time—natural, objective, and immutable—just as the 'new human nature' came to be understood simply as Human Nature writ large. From today's vantage point—a moment in which the disciplines of precarious employment, 'gig-work', and other types of non-standard employment increasingly shape work culture and class expectations for both workers and capitalists—Thompson's analysis invites us to consider the role of time in the expansion and entrenchment of neoliberal work arrangements. In other words, if the transition to industrial capitalism established and naturalised a new temporal regime, reshaping workers' relationship to time, to what extent has the proliferation and normalisation of precarious and 'non-standard' employment in the neoliberal era entailed a parallel temporal transformation?

The transition Thompson describes hinges on the inauguration of bourgeois time, which posits a sharp distinction between 'work time' and 'free time', distinguished by who has the right to allocate and control workers' capacity to labour.[5] This distinction, of course, is itself a mystification foundational to capitalism: the allocation of workers' time into 'work time'

---

[1]   EP Thompson, 'Time, Work-Discipline, and Industrial Capitalism' (1967) 38 *Past & Present* 56, 61.

[2]   Thompson, 'Time', 59.

[3]   Thompson, 'Time', 61.

[4]   Thompson, 'Time', 57.

[5]   I prefer this distinction to the more conventional divide between 'work time' and 'leisure time', as it more accurately encompasses the range of activities that workers must allocate to the time they have

and 'free time' belies the total annexation of workers' time by their reliance on wages, which compels them both to relinquish hours of their day to the boss' control and to squeeze into the time that remains the satisfaction of all their human needs—whether for sleep, sustenance, or society.[6] Bourgeois time—regimented, abstract, fungible—undergirds one of Marx's most consequential observations about the terrain of class confrontation, namely, that the fulcrum of antagonism between workers and capitalists takes place at the production site, in the form of both organised battles over the length and intensity of the official working day and individualised, micro-level skirmishes over the allocation of minutes formally constituting that work day.[7] As Marx famously observes in the first volume of *Capital,* the length of the working day is 'not a constant'.[8] Although it is constrained by both 'natural' and 'moral' considerations regarding individuals' capacities to work and their need to replenish themselves, these limits are 'very elastic in nature, and allow a tremendous amount of latitude'.[9] Without legal constraint, Marx notes, the 'werewolf-like hunger' of capital for surplus labour drives the extension of the working day in nineteenth-century industry towards the 'slow sacrifice of humanity'—whether the stunted development of 'untaught children', or the 'bodily suffering and early death' of working people generally.[10] Working-class resistance, political agitation, and moral outrage over this sacrifice, particularly regarding the effects of unfettered industry on child workers, led in Marx's time to a succession of Factory Acts, which regulated everything from the start and end of the working day for men, women, and children of specified ages, to the provision of meal breaks, to the use of a 'public clock' such as 'a nearby railway clock' to set factory work hours.[11] Conversely, each effort to regulate and restrict working hours generated its own response by capital—extending working hours for men when women's and children's hours were legally restricted, reducing wages in order to pressure workers into accepting longer workdays, shortening or eliminating meal breaks, and generally exploiting every legal loophole in order to bring the working day as close to its natural limit as factory inspectors and workers' resistance would allow, all while working to repeal the Factory Acts outright and limit their enforceability in the interim.[12] In short, the history of struggle over the length of the working day is the story of how the ascendence of bourgeois time not only signalled the effective transformation of peasants and artisans into workers, but also established a new terrain of class antagonism, as both workers and capitalists recognised their stake in maximising the time under their legal and de facto control.

In a context in which cutting-edge legal battles are as likely to relate to the regulation of Uber drivers as they are to work schedules in auto plants, how similar are contemporary experiences

---

outside the paid workday, including both the time and the unpaid labour they must expend to reproduce themselves daily and generationally.

6   Karl Marx, *Capital: A Critique of Political Economy*, vol 1 (first published 1867, Ben Fowkes tr, Penguin 1992) 341.

7   See e.g., Stephen Ackroyd and Paul Thompson's discussion of 'workplace misbehaviour' and various forms of workplace resistance in 'Unruly Subjects: Misbehaviour in the Workplace' in Stephen Edgell, Heidi Gottfried, and Edward Granter (eds), *The SAGE Handbook of the Sociology of Work and Employment* (SAGE 2016) 185.

8   Marx, *Capital*, vol 1, 341.
9   Marx, *Capital*, vol 1, 341.
10   Marx, *Capital*, vol 1, 353–54, 356.
11   Marx, *Capital*, vol 1, 394.
12   Marx, *Capital*, vol 1, 396, 398–99.

of class struggle over the ownership of time? Today's 'non-standard employment' encompasses a wide array of working arrangements, most of which presuppose an almost infinite availability of work, absent a contractual promise of actual work—whether temporary agency employment, serial or overlapping short-term contracts, 'zero-hour', on-call, or 'umbrella' contracts, or what the International Labour Organisation calls 'disguised employment relationships' and 'dependent self-employment', especially characteristic of work in the gig (or 'sharing') economy and in multi-level marketing schemes.[13] How do such arrangements—and the disciplines and incentives they produce—modify the experiential distinction between 'worker-owned' and 'boss-owned' time that was so crucial to the legal and political battles of the past? What can we learn both about the tactical manoeuvres available to workers and capitalists in today's environment and about the mechanisms by which neoliberal working arrangements are naturalised and internalised (or denaturalised and contested)?

Tracing the emergence and naturalisation of a new temporal regime represents, on one level, an instructive way to characterise an age, whether the emerging dominance of the wage relation with the rise of industrial capitalism or the growing significance of the 'precariat' in the neoliberal era. Thus, we might usefully be able to describe a transition from 'artisanal time' to 'bourgeois time', or from 'industrial time' to 'neoliberal time', as a way to deepen our understanding of the relationship between a mode of production and the norms, expectations, alliances, and antagonisms they generate. The reordering of time that attends the restructuring of work regimes represents, in other words, a powerful way to understand the intimate mechanisms of hegemony, the displacement of one common-sense regime by another, as a new economic order embeds itself in workers' consciousness and transforms their relationship to something as elemental as the passing minutes and hours of their lives. On a deeper level, this transformation of time consciousness is uniquely significant in the context of a capitalist order—whether industrial or neoliberal—in which time is the stolen substance that constitutes capitalist exploitation. For Marx time is both mystified and tangible: its standardised, abstract measurement provides the basis for the fiction of a 'fair wage'—a day's pay for a day's labour—and yet time also functions as the experiential locus of class conflict, as both workers and capitalists understand that 'moments are the elements of profit', and that each has an interest in owning those minutes.[14] Time consciousness, in other words, is a corollary of class consciousness, though both are subject to misapprehension and mystification.

What, then, can an analysis of time in the era of gig-work teach us about class consciousness, mystification, and common sense under current conditions of production? How have the most recent iterations of 'just-in-time labour' transformed workers' experience of the distinction between time contracted to an employer and time that is still, perhaps regrettably, theirs to spend? This chapter examines some of the ways in which one of the signature innovations of neoliberal employment relations treats the question of time. Like Marx and Thompson, I am interested in the transformation and normalisation of the temporal regime governing workers' lives. Unlike Thompson, however, who wrote centuries after the transition he describes, my analysis is very much *in medias res,* examining novel and contingent work arrangements that are still defined in opposition to the 'standard employment relationships' which continue to dominate our regulatory regimes and class imaginaries, despite their steady decline since

---

[13]   Valerio De Stefano, 'Non-Standard Work and Limits on Freedom of Association: A Human Rights-Based Approach' (2017) 46 *Industrial Law Journal* 185, 188.

[14]   Marx, *Capital*, vol 1, 352.

the economic transitions of the 1970s and early 1980s.[15] By proposing a kind of Thompson redux, identifying in today's work world an emergent temporal regime, I do not mean to suggest a direct parallel between the intensification of capitalist dynamics in the neoliberal era and the dramatic social ruptures associated with proletarianisation in the transition to capitalism. Indeed, let me stipulate that many of the signature features of working life under neoliberalism—day-to-day uncertainty, irregular hours, limited or non-existent benefits, lack of union representation, limited capacity to refuse work, and a disproportionate allocation of risk from the capitalist class to workers—have been the norm for many categories of workers throughout the history of capitalism.[16] Furthermore, notwithstanding the novelty of technologically enabled gig-work like Uber and TaskRabbit, trends toward low-paid service-sector jobs and increased casualisation have been underway for decades in the global North, attendant with deindustrialisation and the rise of financial capitalism. The 'norm' of long-term employment associated with the post-war boom looks increasingly like a blip in the longer history of capitalism, in which work has more closely resembled the fragmented, episodic, and atomised character of today's gig-work than the conditions of a unionised auto plant of the 1960s. Yet an examination of contemporary gig-work is still instructive: fewer workers now expect their working lives to be dominated by stable, long-term employment with a single employer in a single industry, including those whose education, whiteness, or other social capital might have bolstered their employment expectations in the past. The technological novelty of today's platform-enabled gig-work, as well as our increased reliance on various tech platforms as consumers, have perhaps contributed to a heightened sense that micro-managed, heavily surveilled, highly individualised precarious employment represents the present and future of work, posing both tactical and strategic challenges for building and sustaining working-class power after decades of defeat and retrenchment. Under these conditions, workers' experience of time may still represent a key to understanding both the mystification and revelation of class antagonism, with implications for understanding—and perhaps transforming—the balance of class power.

'YOUR DAY BELONGS TO YOU!': RE-MYSTIFYING THE WAGE RELATION

In their landmark study of the history of American labour organising, *Our Own Time*, David Roediger and Philip Foner describe the clock tower erected in 1828 by Pawtucket mill workers—with US$500 they raised among themselves—in order that 'the clock [would] no longer be figured to suit the owner'.[17] Along similar lines, EP Thompson recounts how English factory owners banned the use of pocket watches among their workers and ordered 'that no person ... doth reckon by any other clock, bell, watch or dyall but the Monitor's', which would

---

[15]   Katherine VW Stone, 'The Decline in the Standard Contract of Employment in the United States: A Socio-Regulatory Perspective' in Katherine VW Stone and Harry Arthurs (eds), *Rethinking Workplace Regulation: Beyond the Standard Contract of Employment* (Russell Sage 2013) 58.

[16]   For a discussion of the limited scope of standard employment norms even in the 'Golden Age of Capitalism', see Ursula Huws, 'Logged Labour: A New Paradigm of Work Organisation?' (2016) 10 *Work Organisation, Labour & Globalisation* 7.

[17]   David R Roediger and Philip S Foner, *Our Own Time: A History of American Labor and the Working Day* (Greenwood Press 1989) 20.

never 'be altered but by the clock-keeper'.[18] Concern about who controls the clock—and hence the time that is the basic currency underwriting the wage contract—runs through the history of labour struggles, as workers fought against 'factory time' and for 'solar time', disputed the boss' calculation of when the sun could be said to be risen (when the sun touched the church spire, or when it lit the factory floor?), and challenged the artificial extension of the winter workday by the use of artificial light.[19]

The history of time-theft by capital—and of workers' efforts to counter it through appeals to objective, mutually transparent time-keeping—offers a clear illustration of the antagonistic relationship underlying the wage contract. For Marx, of course, bourgeois theft of workers' time is built into the wage relation in the form of uncompensated surplus labour-time, even without the brazen dishonesty of manipulating clocks to lengthen the workday. The notion of theft here is characteristically double-edged, on the one hand signalling actual violations of legal contracts governing the quantity of workers' time duly purchased by their employers, and on the other hand the legally sanctioned exploitation hidden in the way '[s]urplus labour and necessary labour are mingled together', while only the latter is represented in workers' wages.[20] Time is at the centre of Marx's famous observation that class struggle presents itself as 'an antinomy, of right against right, both equally bearing the seal of the law of exchange', as both buyers and sellers of labour-power lay legitimate claim to their rightful property.[21] From this observation flows Marx's attitude towards both the necessity and the inadequacy of legal battles for the limited, regulated workday: 'For "protection" against the serpent of their agonies, the workers [must] … as a class, compel the passing of a law, an all-powerful social barrier by which they can be prevented from selling themselves and their families into slavery and death'.[22] At the same time, Marx sardonically characterises this struggle for the legally limited work-day as a 'modest Magna Carta', which necessarily displaces apparently more ambitious declarations of the 'inalienable rights of man'.[23] Representing a rather pallid vision of freedom, such a law would nonetheless 'at last make[] clear "when the time which the worker sells is ended, and when his own begins"'.[24]

Both overt and hidden, legal and extra-legal, battles over the length of the working day have always been significant as a marker of workers' and capitalists' contrary interests. At its most basic, the wage contract is a negotiation over time—who owns it, for how long, and with what kind and amount of compensation. Through its apparent similarity with other market transactions between formally equal buyers and sellers, the wage relation mystifies the special feature of the commodity at stake: the value-producing labour-power of the worker. But the negotiation of wage contracts also foregrounds and personifies an adversarial, power-inflected confrontation between workers and capitalists. In this negotiation, time represents an objective, measurable, and divisible substance, the allocation of which is irrevocable; time cannot be given or taken back. And as Roediger and Foner argue, this feature of time has made

---

[18]   Thompson, 'Time', 82.
[19]   Roediger and Foner, *Our Own Time*, 20.
[20]   Marx, *Capital*, vol 1, 346.
[21]   Marx, *Capital*, vol 1, 344.
[22]   Marx, *Capital*, vol 1, 416.
[23]   Marx, *Capital*, vol 1, 416.
[24]   Marx, *Capital*, vol 1, 416.

struggles over its regulation a critical dimension of labour struggles, elemental to what might appear more explicitly to be struggles over wage rates, benefits, and working conditions.

Among the many mystifications associated with the so-called 'sharing economy' is its ostensible subversion of the wage relation and the contradictory interests it contains. It has been widely noted that Uber, the US$70 billion ride-sharing company operating in more than 700 cities worldwide, prefers to describe itself as 'a technology company' rather than a mere transportation service.[25] Uber provides a software platform that enables its users to connect to each other—easily, efficiently, and relatively safely; horizontal connectivity is the service the company provides, not rides, the argument goes.[26] Both riders and drivers are 'Uber customers' insofar as they are users of the app, which generates a commission for the company with each transaction it facilitates between purchaser and provider. Uber's role is not that of an employer, whose bottom-line interests necessarily run counter to those of its workers/drivers, but that of a technoservice provider, benefitting alongside the 'independent contractors' who use its platform to connect with other users willing to pay for their time, skills, and the use of their vehicle.

Multiple lawsuits have focused on Uber's refusal to apply for taxi licenses or to accept designation as either an employer or a transportation company[27]—a refusal central to what Calo and Rosenblat describe as a strategy of 'regulatory arbitrage' characteristic of the so-called 'sharing economy'.[28] This is a business model organised around 'reproducing existing services without the same societal restrictions' that constrain their competitors, whether labour regulations or industry standards.[29] Uber's desire to avoid the costs and risks associated with employer status is perhaps unremarkable. Indeed, the company's effort to evade the obligations associated with maintaining a regular workforce—whether workers' compensation, sick pay, minimum-wage and overtime pay, or covering drivers' insurance, vehicle maintenance, and fuel expenses—represents the culmination of a strategy of casualisation that firms have been pursuing since the steady profits of the post-war period began to waver and fall in the late 1960s.[30] What has emerged to new prominence in the age of Uber,

---

[25]   See e.g., Joel Rosenblatt, 'Uber's Future May Depend On Convincing the World Drivers Aren't Part of its "Core Business"' *Time* (12 September 2019), https://time.com/5675637/uber-business-future/ accessed 7 April 2021; Enrique Dans, 'There Are Tech Companies and Then There Are Uber-Tech Companies …' *Forbes* (12 April 2019), https://www.forbes.com/sites/enriquedans/2019/04/12/there-are -tech-companies-and-then-there-are-uber-tech-companies/?sh=2db1179d4be6.

[26]   Ryan Calo and Alex Rosenblat, 'The Taking Economy: Uber, Information, and Power' (2017) 117 *Columbia Law Review* 1623, 1646.

[27]   In 2017, for instance, the European Court of Justice rejected Uber's self-designation as a digital technology company, holding that the firm must be understood and regulated as a transportation service. See *Asociación Profesional Elite Taxi v Uber Systems Spain, SL*, European Court of Justice (Grand Chamber), Case C-434/15 (20 December 2017), https://eur-lex.europa.eu/legal-content/EN/TXT/?uri= CELEX%3A62015CJ0434 accessed 7 April 2021. More recently, the Supreme Court of Canada held that Uber's arbitration agreements with drivers were unconscionable and therefore legally invalid. See *Uber Technologies Inc v Heller*, 2020 Supreme Court of Canada 16 (26 June 2020), https://decisions.scc-csc .ca/scc-csc/scc-csc/en/item/18406/index.do accessed 7 April 2021.

[28]   Calo and Rosenblat, 'The Taking Economy', 1645.

[29]   Calo and Rosenblat, 'The Taking Economy', 1627.

[30]   Louis Hyman, *Temp: How American Work, American Business, and the American Dream Became Temporary* (Viking 2018), which examines the emergence of both the management consulting giant McKinsey and the temping agency Manpower in the late 1960s, observing their dual role in a corporate strategy to erode the norms of full-time employment established in the postwar period.

however, is the centrality of the 'disguised employment relationship' to the broad strategy of normalising and legitimising capital's long-term push for workforce casualisation.[31] Uber's repudiation of the employer-employee relationship has been a key feature both of its legal and marketing strategies and of its app design, which is the principal way it interacts with its drivers. Uber has thus gone further than previous efforts by firms simply to 'downsize' or 'streamline' permanent workforces by proportionally increasing their reliance on temporary, part-time, sub-contracted, and deskilled workers. Not content with the wholesale replacement of permanent workers with flexible, just-in-time labour, Uber has demonstrated a commitment to mystifying its relationship with those very workers, disavowing the existence of the employment relationship itself and of any contradiction between the company's interests and those of its workers/'users'.

'Your day belongs to you', reads the banner text addressing prospective drivers on Uber's homepage. Like other crowdwork platforms, Uber's pitch to the public hinges on its promise of paid work without the constraints of traditional employment. As Arun Sundararajan notes in *The Sharing Economy: The End of Employment and the Rise of Crowd-Based Capitalism*, proponents of gig-work tend to emphasise the provision of horizontal networks in place of hierarchical employment relationships, scaling up and commercialising 'peer-to-peer' transactions that would otherwise take place only within the relatively limited circuits and transactional norms of people's 'real-life' social networks.[32] Gig-work platforms not only promise opportunities for individuals to leverage 'idle assets'—an unused vehicle, an empty passenger seat, an apartment unoccupied for the weekend, or an as-yet-unremunerated skill-set—but also to do so under conditions of maximum flexibility and autonomy. Work as much or as little as you like; choose your own hours; customise your schedule according to your family obligations, other work commitments, or simply your whims and preferences. Underlying these promises of autonomy is the intimation that Uber claims no interest in controlling when and how often individual drivers choose to log on to the app and accept rides. Treating its drivers as independent entrepreneurs who use Uber's app as part of their business, Uber disavows the existence of any relationship of negotiated trade-offs between the company and the people who deliver services through its platform. Such negotiated trade-offs, of course, are intrinsic to the employment contract, in which each party recognises that they have a compelling incentive to enter an agreement—whether to earn a wage or to direct another's labour-power—and also that such an agreement will necessarily represent a compromise between fundamentally conflicting interests. In denying an employment relationship, Uber denies this fundamental conflict between the company and its workers.

But to what extent are drivers' interests aligned with those of the company? And absent an acknowledged employment contract, how are any conflicting interests negotiated? As Calo and Rosenblat note, Uber has been a pioneer in the use of both technological and psychological tactics to direct drivers' choices about when and how much to drive.[33] A one-off calculation of the relationship between Uber's interests and those of any individual driver is,

---

[31]   For a discussion of 'disguised employment relations', see International Labour Organisation, 'Disguised Employment/Dependent Self-Employment', https://www.ilo.org/global/topics/non-standard -employment/WCMS_534833/lang--en/index.htm accessed 7 April 2021.

[32]   Arun Sundararajan, *The Sharing Economy: The End of Employment and the Rise of Crowd-Based Capitalism* (MIT Press 2016).

[33]   Calo and Rosenblat, 'The Taking Economy', 1630.

of course, highly misleading. While it is true that Uber earns money when the driver does, Uber's service model relies on fast pick-up times, which means more idling drivers. Drivers' uncompensated time waiting for a ride is essential to Uber's capacity to meet riders' expectations for quick response times. In order to maintain riders' loyalty, Uber needs drivers to be available even when and where ride frequency—and thus drivers' earnings—are likely to be low. Uber invests heavily in data analysis in order to understand and optimise, with local and temporal specificity, the relationship between price, rider demand, and driver supply.[34] In fact, continuous experimentation and data analysis is central to Uber's business model, as it regularly modifies its app and varies its policies and incentives across the municipalities where it operates, constantly refining its understanding of both drivers' and riders' behaviour. As the *New York Times* reported in 2017, this experimentation often involves the use of 'video game techniques, graphics and non-cash rewards of little value that can prod drivers into working longer and harder—and sometimes at hours and locations that are less lucrative for them'.[35]

Uber's in-app income-targeting features are a good example of a situation in which the company uses psychological tools to encourage drivers to work against their own interests. Through in-app pop-ups reminding users that they are, say, US$30 from meeting their daily average or exceeding their highest daily intake, Uber encourages drivers to stay on the road for a few more fares, even when demand might be low. Working to such targets might feel like driver-led decision-making and goal-setting about when and how much to work, but its function is to encourage drivers to accept more unpaid time idling, reducing their hourly intake while they wait for a few more fares to meet a daily target. Like all other service industry firms, Uber has had to find a way to keep its doors open for business even at times of the day when business is slow, or risk losing a loyal consumer base. But where a traditionally structured service business—a coffee shop or 'bricks-and-mortar' retail store, for example—must continue to pay staff to accept customers even during slow periods, Uber has offloaded the daily costs of intermittent 'overstaffing' onto its just-in-time workforce, idling in their cars while they wait for the next fare, even though their own best strategy for maximising their average income rate would be to work exclusively at busy hours.

Not all of the incentives embedded in the Uber app are carrots—whether encouragement to set and meet daily income targets, pop-up notices flagging the start of rush-hour or the release of crowds from a stadium at the end of a game, or messages discouraging users from logging off and 'leaving money on the table' in the form of queued ride requests or anticipated surges in demand (and price). Uber closely monitors both ride-cancellation rates and ride-acceptance rates of drivers in each city where it operates, punishing drivers who fall outside its targets— whether by automatically logging them out of the app, effectively pausing their earning capacity, or by 'deactivating' (firing) them as drivers.[36] 'I cannot refuse a job without the fear of deactivation, even for 10 minutes', a 39-year-old European gig-worker for an unnamed company, complains. 'If I don't accept the job three times, the [platform] deactivates me for

---

[34]   Calo and Rosenblat, 'The Taking Economy', 1651.

[35]   Noam Schreiber, 'How Uber Uses Psychological Tricks to Push Its Drivers' Buttons' *New York Times* (2 April 2017), https://www.nytimes.com/interactive/2017/04/02/technology/uber-drivers-psychological-tricks.html accessed 7 April 2021.

[36]   Uber, 'Uber Community Guidelines', https://www.uber.com/legal/community-guidelines/us-en/ accessed 7 April 2021.

10 minutes. If you are consistent … they will deactivate you permanently.'[37] Uber drivers have complained both that the speed and obligatory character of the 'automatic queuing feature' means that accepting subsequent rides is physically easier than turning down a fare or logging out, making it difficult to avoid rejecting or cancelling rides when they do in fact want to stop work, or even pause for a break.[38] Drivers also are given no information about the upcoming fares in their queue, requiring them to make blind decisions about accepting a ride that may be minimally lucrative, or which may take them far from home or from high-demand areas with little opportunity to earn money on the return trip. In a 2017 report on Uber's efforts to 'gamify' worker incentives, sometimes to their own detriment, the *New York Times* observed that such manipulation often takes place 'without the whiff of coercion'.[39] An Uber spokesperson notes that the company finds ways to 'show drivers areas of high demand or incentivise them to drive more', but emphasises that 'any driver can stop work literally at the tap of a button—the decision whether or not to drive is 100 percent theirs'.[40]

Drivers may well respond to the push and pull of Uber's tactics—whether in-app prompts to set and meet daily earnings goals, or the automatic queuing feature called 'forward dispatch', which prompts riders to accept upcoming fares before their current ride is complete—but they are not unconscious of the costs that come with their compliance with these incentives.[41] Not only do drivers admit to finding it difficult to ignore the automatic queuing prompt, even when they need to stop to find a restroom or when they have driven longer than they intended, but they also know that the advertised flexibility of gig-work is limited by the daily and weekly ebb and flow of earning opportunities. A respondent in a European study of gig-workers notes that when the platform 'claims like you can start anytime, finish anytime—yes, you can start the app any time and finish the app, close the app at any time but it doesn't mean you are going to make any money … So if you are a driver, a real driver, and you want to make money, you have to work on the busiest hour'.[42] Another observes:

> Once I work, I don't really stop. That's because I'm working at the peak times … and yeah, I mean, there's been some times, like, for example, when I used to work the lunch time shift, that was really slow … but the weekend evening shifts, so yeah, you have no control.[43]

Between gamified incentives to continue to drive through slow periods and tangible pressure to capitalise on periods of peak demand, the constraints on drivers' real experience of choice, autonomy, and flexibility are quickly felt. What is ostensibly hidden is the role of an employer—a boss—who is entitled to direct workers' energies for a negotiated period of time. Instead, workers feel themselves to be responding directly to the market itself, unmediated by a capitalist interlocutor whose interests stand in opposition to their own. As

---

[37]   Ursula Huws, Neil H Spencer, Dag S Syrdal, and Kaire Holts, *Work in the European Gig Economy: Research Results from the UK, Sweden, Germany, Austria, The Netherlands, Switzerland and Italy* (FEPS/UNI Europa/University of Hertfordshire 2017) 39, https://uhra.herts.ac.uk/bitstream/handle/2299/19922/Huws_U._Spencer_N.H._Syrdal_D.S._Holt_K._2017_.pdf?sequence=2 accessed 7 April 2021.
[38]   Schreiber, 'Psychological Tricks'.
[39]   Schreiber, 'Psychological Tricks'.
[40]   Schreiber, 'Psychological Tricks'.
[41]   Schreiber, 'Psychological Tricks'.
[42]   Huws et al, *Work in the European Gig Economy*, 41.
[43]   Huws et al, *Work in the European Gig Economy*, 47.

single-operator 'entrepreneurs', Uber drivers ostensibly stand alone amidst the ebb and flow of consumer demand, negotiating not with an employer through a contract, but between their own subsistence needs and the opportunities afforded by un-personified market forces. This is a powerful form of mystification: rather than the employer qua capitalist appearing simply as a commodity-purchaser like any other—the mystification embedded in the wage relation—the employer seems to disappear altogether. Thus Uber's disavowal of the wage relation not only frees the company from the legal and regulatory obligations of employment, but, on a broader scale, also helps to render natural, immutable, and incontestable the de-personified market forces that are in fact a set of historically specific class relations. How, then, do drivers experience this mystification of their relationship with the company and its influence on the allocation of the hours and minutes of their days?

THE TEMPORAL REGIME OF GIG-WORK

It is in his discussion of the working day that class struggle makes its first appearance in the first volume of *Capital*. Marx's explanation of the nature and appearance of class struggle hinges on what David Harvey calls his 'deep theorization of the nature of time and tempo-rality under capitalism'.[44] In the form of 'the working day', time appears at once as a natural phenomenon, directly experienced by the senses and constrained by the immutable rhythms of sun, earth, and human physiology, and as a thoroughly social phenomenon, shaped by and subject to moral judgment, political power, and physical force.[45] The essential mystification of capitalist accumulation hinges on the fact that 'the working day' is both limited and elas-tic.[46] The 'day's wage' straddles a fixed, objective reality—the 24-hour period during which workers must replenish themselves for another day's labour—and the immensely variable norms and expectations regarding the nature and extent of that replenishment, which, Marx argues, depend on the balance of class power and the 'level of civilization' of a given society.[47] These determine, for instance, whether the daily replenishment of the workers includes 'time in which to satisfy [their] intellectual and social requirements', not to mention the vast range within which workers' physical needs for rest and sustenance are said to be met.[48] '[T]he peculiar nature of the commodity sold', Marx writes, 'implies a limit to its consumption by the purchaser'.[49] The sellers of labour-power must attempt to preserve their capacity to sell their commodity again in the future, and thus must confront and resist the buyers' compulsion to 'extract the maximum possible benefit from the use-value of' the commodity they have purchased, by maximising the length and intensity of 'a day's work'.[50]

These countervailing compulsions on the part of workers and capitalists are exposed both in overt contract negotiations and in daily efforts to enforce (or violate) the contract to the advan-tage of one party or the other. In other words, both legal and extra-legal strategies and tactics

[44] David Harvey, *A Companion to Marx's* Capital, vol 1 (Verso 2010) 135.
[45] Marx, *Capital*, vol 1, 341.
[46] Marx, *Capital*, vol 1, 341.
[47] Marx, *Capital*, vol 1, 275.
[48] Marx, *Capital*, vol 1, 341.
[49] Marx, *Capital*, vol 1, 344.
[50] Marx, *Capital*, vol 1, 342.

are always a part of class struggle on the battlegrounds of day-to-day workplace tussles and in formal and implicit contract negotiations, as well as in legislative and regulatory wrangling. But how do these compulsions appear when the capitalist appears to have 'exited the stage'— to borrow Marx's dramaturgical metaphor—leaving the worker as the apparent master of the entirety of their own time? How does class consciousness emerge, and in what form, absent the structures signalling a continuously negotiated settlement between adversaries? In the 'frictionless economy' touted by boosters of technology-enabled gig-work, where do workers still experience the friction that stems from incompatible claims on the finite, unrecoverable hours and minutes of their days?[51] Gig-work seems to hide from workers the capitalist parties to the employment contract, encouraging workers to view themselves as independent entrepreneurs responding directly to market demand, rather than negotiating with an employer over compensation for their labour-time: in this way, the daily structure of workers' 'free' time in the gig-economy may be experientially different from that of workers governed by standard employment contracts, in which their time is divided into larger and more regular parcels of 'working time' and 'free time'. Nonetheless, in gig-work as in all forms of wage labour, time represents a site of friction and conflict, at once objective, immutable, and accessible to the senses and subject to manipulation, subterfuge, and the exercise of power. The next three sections explore three experiential dimensions of time within a gig-work regime: the first explores worker/company conflicts over objective, measurable 'clock time'; the second examines the transformation of 'free time' into uncompensated 'idle time'; the third looks at the subdivision of the traditional 'day's work' into a series of micro-contracts governing disparate hours and minutes, with new demands on workers for contract-negotiation, contract-enforcement, and risk-management.

Clock Time

As in the industrial era described by Thompson, the literal regulation of the clock is one of the places in which Uber drivers encounter themselves in conflict with the company—a conflict that feels to drivers like a gratuitous exercise of company power, and which reveals Uber's obligatory interests as a capitalist employer, despite its disavowal of the role. Like the nineteenth-century factory owners who declared sole authority over the factory clock, banned pocket watches among workers, and manipulated 'factory time' to shorten meal breaks and extend working hours, Uber's power over workers is expressed in part through its control over time-keeping.

Time-keeping disputes between Uber and its drivers take place most visibly in relation to Uber's cancellation fee policy, which is intended to compensate drivers who are dispatched to a pick-up location only to find that their passengers have failed to show up as expected. No-show passengers are charged a cancellation fee through their online Uber account, and drivers receive a flat fee for each cancellation, provided they wait for five minutes at the pick-up location before leaving to accept another fare. Online forums of Uber drivers include recurrent reports of the company withholding cancellation fee payments, as well as widespread frustration when drivers' own time-keeping differs from the in-app clock that the company uses to determine whether the driver has waited the requisite five minutes in the pick-up

---

51   Sarah Kessler, *Gigged: The End of the Job and the Future of Work* (St. Martin's Press 2018) 228.

location.[52] When drivers have contacted the company to inquire about missing cancellation fee payments, they have been told by company representatives that the app indicated that they had not waited the full five minutes required to earn a cancellation fee, despite drivers reporting that by their own time-keeping, they had waited six or seven minutes. Drivers who requested Uber's time stamps were told that the company was 'unable to provide screenshots of our software', and that the cancellation fees were automatically dispensed or withheld according to the system's internal clock.[53] One driver Calo and Rosenblat spoke with reported that an Uber rep informed him that he had only waited '4 minutes and 59 seconds', and thus was not entitled to a cancellation fee.[54]

Like the Pawtucket mill workers who erected their own town clock—dubbed the 'ten-hour clock' and later the 'nine-hour clock' and the 'liberty bell'—to counter the distortions of 'factory time', Uber drivers in this situation have no authorised access to the company's time-keeping: Uber's software, like the factory-owner's clock, functions as an inscrutable, inaccessible authority governing drivers' compensation.[55] (It is also worth keeping in mind that the cost of unpaid cancellation fees is not only the US$5 or $10 flat fee drivers are promised, but also the additional minutes they might wait to ensure that they satisfy the company clock, as well as the general costs of uncompensated driving time en route to and from no-show locations.) Drivers who dispute the company's time-keeping accuracy are confronted—via ostensibly powerless service reps—with the objective, impersonal authority of Uber's software. But unlike the mill workers, whose experience of stolen time was collective, simultaneous, and geographically fixed, Uber workers have no obvious technological analogue to the shared public clock with which their nineteenth-century counterparts disputed the authority of factory time. Instead, they confront Uber as individual users whose experiences of stolen time are neither physically proximate nor temporally synchronised to the similar experiences of other drivers. Consequently, the drivers interviewed by Calo and Rosenblat could only appeal feebly to their own private time-keeping devices against the power of the company clock.

Clock time disagreements encapsulate the contradictory character of time as the fulcrum of class antagonism within the wage relation. On the one hand, negotiations about clock time—and, especially, manipulations of clock time—are starkly revealing, exposing what Carole Pateman and others regard as a 'relation of command and obedience' that is the essential precondition for the exploitation embedded in the employment relationship.[56] Although Marxist analyses of the wage relationship have tended to focus more on exploitation than domination, an unmistakeable feature of the wage contract is the submission of the worker's will, energy, and capacity to the wishes of the capitalist—for a specified, limited period of time. At one level, time-theft can be read merely as a corollary of wage-theft, which we take to be reason enough to inspire workers' righteous outrage. But perhaps more profoundly, time-theft represents an encroachment on workers' freedom, an exercise of domination that is quickly, deeply, and intuitively identified and resented. Where the exploitation of surplus value extraction remains behind the curtain of the 'fair wage', the employer's attempt to control workers' will

---

[52] Calo and Rosenblat, 'The Taking Economy', 1666–67.
[53] Calo and Rosenblat, 'The Taking Economy', 1666.
[54] Calo and Rosenblat, 'The Taking Economy', 1666.
[55] Roediger and Foner, *Our Own Time*, 20.
[56] Kathi Weeks, *The Problem with Work: Feminism, Marxism, Antiwork Politics, and Postwork Imaginaries* (Duke University Press 2011) 21.

beyond the limited temporal terms of the contract exposes an unmistakably antagonistic political relationship, in which workers' freedom is at stake.

Thus, clock disputes push the capitalist from the shadows back onto the stage, scripting the wage contract as a drama of domination, submission, and resistance. At the same time, however, by holding out the possibility of objectivity and transparency, the clock functions as an alibi for the wage contract's essential premise of fairness and equality and the mystification of both domination and exploitation. Uber workers resent the inaccessibility of Uber's time-keeping and wish for more transparent, independently verifiable and arbitrable systems for record keeping and dispute settlement. But the clock itself—like the mill workers' liberty bell—seems like it *could* be a tool for ensuring precisely this kind of fairness, if only it were more objective, more visible, more mutually controlled. In this way, the clock by turns reveals and obscures what is at stake in the promise of a 'day's wage'.

Idle Time

Disputes about the in-app clock perhaps represent the most obvious analogue between old-fashioned forms of industrial time-theft and the restructuring of time by platform-mediated gig-work. Such disputes quite obviously re-centre Uber the employer as the antagonist, wielding power over them via the implacable, depersonalised authority of the app's invisible time-keeper. The signature temporal feature of gig-work, however, is not this old-fashioned form of clock-mediated time-theft, but the restructuring of unpaid time from 'non-work time'/'leisure time' to idle or on-call time. Across all kinds of platforms and services— driving, cleaning, deliveries, data entry, small home repairs, flat-pack furniture assembly, and even more specialised gigs including editing, software development, and graphic design— gig-workers describe the rising importance of time that is unpaid yet unfree. One data-entry worker for Amazon's 'Mechanical Turk' platform has described her efforts to win as many of her preferred gigs as possible: doing so involved programming a script that would cause her computer to alert her the second a new job matching her criteria is posted to the site.[57] This gig-worker 'didn't feel like she could leave her apartment, or even her computer, lest she miss out on an opportunity to work on good tasks', often choosing to sleep next to her computer rather than lose an opportunity to work.[58] A driver describes how he and the drivers he knows spend 70 or 80 hours a week in their cars, sleeping and eating in their vehicles in order to avoid missing a fare.[59] Another gig-worker speaks longingly of the rare opportunities afforded by a 'long job'.[60]

> Obviously, I would be very happy if I could have a long job every day. For example, if I could have an eight-hour job every day that will be perfect, because then I will have no problems. ... I would start work, I would finish and I could have even a private life during the week, but that doesn't often happen. I will tell you, based on this week I had. I was almost not booked at all. I only had—I was only booked for one job on Friday and then today I was booked for two jobs, and two of them are big

---

[57]   Kessler, *Gigged*, 73.
[58]   Kessler, *Gigged*, 74.
[59]   Huws et al, *Work in the European Gig Economy*, 46.
[60]   Huws et al, *Work in the European Gig Economy*, 47.

jobs on Monday and Tuesday. ... and I don't know what is going to happen on Wednesday/Thursday. I am still waiting.[61]

One worker puts it bluntly: 'Well I don't think I'm as happy as I used to be, because I have no free time. Anytime I am free, I actually have to work for [name of platform].'[62] Hardly the vaunted freedom to 'own their day', the flexibility of platform-based gig-work means rather an endless workday and workweek that is remunerated only intermittently. Gig-workers speak longingly of the regular eight-hour day, both for the relative security and predictability it would afford and because it, ironically, represents the possibility of freedom from work.

Like time-theft, of course, just-in-time labour is not a new phenomenon, nor is it limited to technology-enabled gig-work. Long before and alongside the existence of 'platform capitalism', day-labourers have assembled near garden centres, farm stands, and hardware stores to win a day's work as farm-hands, landscapers, or construction workers.[63] Freelance workers in a variety of fields—including relatively highly-paid, high-status, and technical areas—have competed for short-term contracts, bearing the costs and time-effects both of continuously pursuing and securing work and of idle time between gigs.

Struggles to mitigate the vicissitudes of just-in-time work represent a dimension of labour history less often remembered, though perhaps equally important as struggles for the legally limited working day. In their account of the 1934 longshoreman strikes up and down the west coast of the United States, Stan Weir describes the significance of workers' demand for control over the allocation of what was essentially just-in-time piecework.[64] Like today's manual day-labourers, unorganised dockworkers acquired work only through an employer-controlled 'shape-up', congregating daily at the shipyards and hoping to be among those assigned to unload whatever ships were in harbour that day.[65] Not only did this system ensure that workers felt pressure to compete with each other when work was scarce and to curry individual favour with the boss, but it also meant hours of idle time assembling on the docks with no promise of daily work. Further, workers had limited capacity to refuse dangerous work, or to demand additional hands to reduce the risks of a particularly awkward or heavy job. The just-in-time system for assigning work on the docks was thus foundational to the balance of power between capital and workers and became a central focus for dockworkers' organising demands.

The imposition of the worker-controlled 'low-man-out system' was among the most significant victories of the 1934 dockworker strikes.[66] In lieu of the daily shape-up, in which the employer chose which men would work that day, the low-man-out system imposed a system of worker-regulated turn-taking: those who had worked most recently were bumped to the bottom of the list, guaranteeing a more even distribution of work and eliminating the power to punish or reward individuals by assigning or withholding assignments.[67] When workers 'gained control over the hiring process by creating hiring halls with [their own] elected dispatchers', they not only freed themselves from a daily situation of 'humiliating subordination' to their employer, but they also transformed the temporal structure of their working

---

[61] Huws et al, *Work in the European Gig Economy*, 47.
[62] Huws et al, *Work in the European Gig Economy*, 47.
[63] Hyman, *Temp*.
[64] Stan Weir, *Singlejack Solidarity* (George Lipsitz ed, University of Minnesota Press 2004).
[65] Weir, *Singlejack Solidarity*, 351.
[66] Weir, *Singlejack Solidarity*, 352.
[67] Weir, *Singlejack Solidarity*, 352.

lives.[68] As Weir argues, the low-man-out system heralded a new social warrant that enabled longshoremen to become 'different kinds of people'.[69] Turn-taking wrested a degree of predictability from an unpredictable industry, freeing workers from fruitlessly assembling on the docks when they knew their name was still low on the priority list for a day's work. Idle time was transformed into free time, or what their union counterparts in limited-hours movements regularly demanded as time to labour, time to rest, and time for 'what we will'.[70] Weir credits the low-man-out system for the flourishing of a vibrant working-class culture in coastal cities affected by dockworker militancy.[71] As he puts it, a 'proliferation of small magazines, theater groups, camera clubs, dance troupes, and musical ensembles threw forth egalitarian opinions and ideas that permeated commercial culture and high art as well as vernacular expressions for decades to follow'.[72]

If the low-man-out system illustrated the emergence of new norms and expectations for work and leisure time in the mid-twentieth century, we can identify its inverse in the current expansion and normalisation of highly atomised, competitive forms of just-in-time labour through technology-enabled gig-work. Like their unorganised counterparts on the docks, gig-workers' time is divided not between work time and free time, but between remunerated work time and uncompensated idle time, during which they are not effectively free to do 'what they will'. But where dockworkers' idle time was temporally and spatially bound in the communal space of the docks, gig-workers spend their idle time alone in their cars or by their computers, regularly confronting neither a personified employer nor a fellow worker. Although the employer-controlled shape-up fostered competition and resentment among unorganised dockworkers, their idle time was nonetheless spent in congregation, just as their work was necessarily carried out co-operatively. The replacement of the daily shape-up with the low-man-out system was no doubt facilitated by the collective character of both work and idle time, as workers confronted—daily and collectively—capital's effective control over their time, whether they were working or not. Wresting control over idle time from the company thus represented an obvious sphere in which to contest the boss' power. Today's gig-workers have no trouble recognising the financial, physical, and psychological costs of idle time—perhaps spent literally idling in their cars—but their experience of idle time, like their experience of time-theft, is a solitary one.

Micro-contracts

Among the many terms used to describe the restructuring of work by platforms like Uber, Handy, or the Mechanical Turk—'gig-work', 'the sharing economy', 'platform capitalism', 'crowd-work', 'micropreneurship', and so on—the most descriptively accurate term, 'micro-contracting', is relatively absent from the popular lexicon. Recent lawsuits against Uber and other gig-work platforms have focused on the classificatory distinction between a regular employment relationship and the attenuated mutual obligations associated with independent contractor status, irrespective of the length of gig-work contracts. Amidst the disputes

---

[68]   Weir, *Singlejack Solidarity*, 352.
[69]   Weir, *Singlejack Solidarity*, 352.
[70]   Weeks, *Problem with Work*, 162.
[71]   Weir, *Singlejack Solidarity*, 353.
[72]   Weir, *Singlejack Solidarity*, 353.

about the misclassification of gig-workers, much of the focus has been on the way contractor status allows companies to circumvent minimum wage laws and other worker protections that are required in standard employment relationships. Somewhat lost in these disputes are the particular ways in which the extremely short length of gig-work contracts sharpen even further the asymmetries of power, information, and risk between gig-workers and the companies they contract with, as well as the experiential dimension of the way micro-contracts restructure time for gig-workers.

As Ursula Huws and co-authors note in their 2017 study of European gig-workers, '[a] major cause of frustration was the frequency with which changes were made to the online procedures as well as to payment and reward systems'.[73] One driver estimated that the platform he relied on for gig-work had changed its terms of service 50 to 70 times in the period since he began driving for them: 'Every single month, almost every single week they change something new, they bring something new for the drivers.'[74] Uber drivers complain about the 'dizzying' frequency with which they encounter changes in the app, as fare rates fluctuate, new fare-structures are piloted, and new 'features' are added that transform the driver or rider experience.[75] As Calo and Rosenblat observe, Uber's business model involves complex transactions, time- and location-specific agreements, and constant experimentation to enable the company to learn from the data generated by rider and driver behaviours.[76] 'Drivers', they write, 'must perennially agree to new terms of service in order to log in to work—akin to signing a new employee manual every few days'.[77] Commission structures, fare rates, and the assorted incentive schemes that Uber continuously pilots change regularly, and drivers may find it impossible to avoid blindly accepting terms and conditions as a routine part of logging into the app. This constant churn of micro-contracts means that drivers' disputes with the company almost always involve after-the-fact disagreements about whether specific terms and conditions have been satisfied, rather than meaningful up-front negotiations about contract terms. 'The way the platform works is changing from update to update', one gig-worker complains. 'So sometimes after one month with the next update they change something and the way you can get the work is changing ... But it's like I feel like nothing I say or do has any impact on the company which I rely on ... I have nothing to say about the rules of the platform and my impact is zero.'[78]

As is the case with disputes over cancellation fees, drivers regularly find themselves in conflict with Uber over whether they have satisfied the company's requirements. A good example of one such micro-contract is the 'hourly-rate option', which ostensibly guarantees select drivers a predetermined hourly take, provided they meet key criteria set by the app. From Uber's perspective, guaranteed hourly rates are a tool to incentivise drivers to be on-call during specified hours and in particular locations, which might not otherwise be sufficiently covered. For drivers, the hourly-rate option means the possibility of mitigating—for an hour or two—the income fluctuations that are among the defining characteristics of gig-work. Drivers are promised the hourly guarantee provided they accept 90 per cent of ride requests;

73 Huws et al, *Work in the European Gig Economy*, 42.
74 Huws et al, *Work in the European Gig Economy*, 42.
75 Calo and Rosenblat, 'The Taking Economy', 1630.
76 Calo and Rosenblat, 'The Taking Economy', 1661.
77 Calo and Rosenblat, 'The Taking Economy', 1661.
78 Huws et al, *Work in the European Gig Economy*, 42.

complete a minimum of two rides per hour; remain logged-in to the app during a specified priority time frame; operate within a specified priority location; and maintain high average customer ratings. But drivers complain that they are at times unable to meet the criteria due to the functioning of the app itself, which may flash ride requests so quickly across their screens that they cannot accept them in time to maintain their acceptance rate, or which logs them out automatically and jeopardises their capacity to satisfy the company's terms.[79] Or as in the case with disputed cancellation fees, drivers report accepting 100 per cent of rides during the specified period, only to find that the company has denied them the guaranteed hourly wage.

The hourly-rate guarantee, like Uber's cancellation fee policy, regularly puts drivers in conflict with the company over its automated record-keeping, but it also highlights the complexity of the time scales drivers are juggling as they carry out their work with Uber. Drivers are effectively entering agreements with Uber when they log in to the app, when they accept an individual ride, and when they opt-in to an offer for the hourly-rate guarantee. The vaunted autonomy of driving for Uber amounts to making contract decisions multiple times a day, often with very limited information and few or onerous mechanisms of accountability and transparency when it comes to record-keeping and contract enforcement. Drivers are acutely aware of both the impersonal, episodic nature of their relationship to the company, and the mismatch between their fleeting micro-contracts with the company and the risks they assume through the car leases, insurance plans, cell phone contracts, and mobile data plans that make Uber driving possible. One worker describes her feeling that gig-work platforms can 'flick a kill switch and take your job away', noting that 'there's no face-to-face relationship, no face-to-face contact ... not the kind of normal social etiquette that goes along with taking someone's income away'.[80] Drivers fear deactivation, which they often perceive to be arbitrary and difficult to challenge.

These fears are especially acute when drivers have made financial commitments—sometimes mediated through Uber itself—that are measured in months and years, not minutes. As Kessler has argued, Uber encourages current drivers to sign up other drivers, offering them a small commission when their recruits complete a minimum number of rides on the app.[81] Of course, such recruitments rely heavily on new drivers' earnings expectations, which are not only unpredictable but are affected by both rider demand and driver supply. Especially in its early days, Uber 'pitched aggressively', promising new drivers that they would be able to earn as much as US$6000 a month, and even offering access to sub-prime car loans that could be paid back through Uber earnings.[82] While partisans of the 'sharing economy' have often depicted gig-work as leveraging idle assets that workers were already paying for as consumers, not entrepreneurs—an already insured family car, for instance, or an existing mobile data plan—Uber anticipated that new drivers would take on entrepreneurial risks for the opportunity to drive for the company. While more than half of Uber drivers use the platform to supplement income from other full-time or part-time jobs, or from other gig-work platforms (including other ride-sharing platforms), almost 20 per cent of American Uber drivers report

---

[79]   Calo and Rosenblat, 'The Taking Economy', 1664.
[80]   Huws et al, *Work in the European Gig Economy*, 42.
[81]   Kessler, *Gigged*, 68.
[82]   Kessler, *Gigged*, 16.

spending more than 35 hours a week driving for the company.[83] For such drivers especially, the long-term burdens of consumer contracts—now transformed into business expenses—stand in sharp contrast to fleeting and inscrutable commitments Uber is willing to entertain with its drivers, sometimes with devastating financial consequences. One gig-worker for an unnamed driving service in the United Kingdom describes the situation of a fellow driver, who was enticed into a car lease by the promise of rideshare earnings:

> So, he bought that car … then suddenly they deactivate him. They deactivate him without giving him any warning, any grievance procedure, anything. When he woke up and he looked at his app and the app was saying, oh you're not allowed to activate. So, every single day when I go to bed, I pray, I pray to my god, like probably tomorrow is the customers going to complain.[84]

TIME AND GRIEVANCE

In *The Problem with Work*, Kathi Weeks makes the case for an 'anti-work politics' as the terrain of class struggle in the contemporary economy. In contrast to the 'labourist ethic' of the Marxist tradition—a tradition that associates labour with human creativity, dignity, and sociality, calling for labour's liberation from alienation and exploitation—Weeks' analysis focuses on the political promise of liberating life from its encroachment by work. '[F]ocusing on work', she writes, 'is one politically promising way of approaching class—because it is so expansive, because it is such a significant part of everyday life, because it is something we do rather than a category to which we are assigned'.[85] Across a range of incomes, industries, and professional identities, Weeks notes, the increasing dominance of work in people's lives represents a potential site of common grievance—and thus a potential site for common demands, analysis, and subject-formation. My focus on the restructuring of time within contemporary work regimes is driven by a similar set of concerns and intuitions regarding both the experience of class grievance and the internalisation of new expectations, incentives, and forms of work-discipline.

The impact of gig-work on workers' experience of time represents a particularly profound and insidious manifestation of the dominance of life by work that Weeks shorthands as the 'work society'.[86] But perhaps more deeply, the encroachments, transformations, and outright theft of time experienced by gig-workers manifest both the mystification of class domination and its revelation. It is no surprise that gig-economy boosters present the fleeting bonds of serial micro-contracts as the essence of autonomy and freedom—'freedom from the tyranny of the punch clock, the autocratic boss, the finite wages and limited opportunities of the 9-to-5 job'.[87] Few who rely on income from gig-work would fail to recognise the narrow kind of 'freedom' promised by Uber's slogan, 'no shifts, no boss, no limits'. And yet the discourse and practice of making choices, weighing costs, assessing risks, and allocating resources is very powerful, particularly when the employer seems to have left the scene of the action, leaving

---

[83]   Jonathan V Hall and Alan B Krueger, 'An Analysis of the Labor Market for Uber's Driver-Partners in the United States' (2018) 71 *ILR Review* 705.

[84]   Huws et al, *Work in the European Gig Economy*, 43.

[85]   Weeks, *Problem with Work*, 20.

[86]   Weeks, *Problem with Work*, 8.

[87]   Kessler, *Gigged*, 11.

workers ostensibly responding directly, as autonomous agents, to de-personified market forces. In this context, the transformations of time experienced by gig-workers offer a window into the naturalisation of a precarious, relentless work regime that arguably extends far beyond technologically enabled gig-work.

The emergence of the distinction between work time and free time examined by Thompson was a consequential feature of proletarianisation not only because it reorganised daily temporal rhythms in enduring ways, but also because it reoriented prevailing conceptions and experiences of freedom and domination. The time that workers owned for themselves became a measure of freedom, the portion of their days during which they were the subjects of their own will, rather than that of the employer. The drive to reduce working hours represented, perhaps, a still limited conception of freedom, given the continued necessity of subjection to capital's demands as the condition for subsistence. Nonetheless, the experience of and demand for 'time to do what we will', founded on a conception of ownership of one's own time, became a powerful force for recognising shared class grievances and advancing reforms oriented by a conception of countervailing class interests.

With the erosion of the work-time/free-time distinction—both for the large range of contract workers whose time is now divided between work time and idle time, and, arguably, for the many waged and salaried workers whose availability to employers has been increased dramatically by new communications technologies and related workplace norms—the sharp distinction between freedom and subjection (even of this limited kind) has also been attenuated. Workers have long been encouraged to perceive their employers' interests and desires as coterminous with their own, significantly through the cultivation of professional identities, acculturation to workplace norms, and the internalisation of financial and interpersonal incentives.[88] The emergent temporal regime I have been describing represents a different strategy for scrambling the distinction between the interests of capital and the will of workers. As I have argued, when 'free time' is replaced with 'idle time', and the 'day's wage' is replaced by a succession of fleeting, kaleidoscopically changing micro-contracts, the discipline of the boss seems to be replaced by a direct encounter with the discipline of the market itself. The work-time/free-time dichotomy described by Thompson inaugurated both the mystifications associated with the wage relation and the structure of a shared experience of class grievance, with attendant demands and acts of individualised and collective resistance. By the same token, the temporal regime emblematised by the 'sharing economy' has not only shifted the way in which class antagonism is disappeared from view, but also the way workers frame their resentments, frustrations, and desires for alternatives to the status quo. In both cases, workers' time represents the material substance through which these resentments, frustrations, and desires are felt. We could say that workers' grievances, and their dreams for alternatives, take place *in time*—time stolen and transformed, time which is never fully theirs, time which is divided and subdivided without reference either to immutable, natural daily rhythms, basic

---

[88]   See e.g., Arlie Hochschild's important work on the emotional labour of flight attendants and others in the service industry: *The Managed Heart: Commercialization of Human Feeling* (University of California Press 1983). Among her key insights is that it is easier for such workers to cultivate in themselves the feelings that the job requires than to resist the requirement or attempt to display feelings inauthentically. Aligning their own feelings with those demanded of them comes at less cost to themselves than the effort of faking it.

human needs, or the temporal structure of the consumer contracts, family obligations, and interpersonal commitments that govern their subsistence lives.

The story that Thompson tells about time and work-discipline is double-edged. On the one hand, it is a story of an emergent hegemony, an expression of the naturalisation of capitalist social relations, to the point where even freedom is largely imagined within the constraints of the new regime—as simply more 'worker-owned time', a shifting ratio of autonomy to subjection. On the other hand, as I have argued, the sharp distinction between 'our time' and 'their time' also sharpened the distinction between 'our interests' and 'their interests', dramatising the relationship of class conflict embedded in the wage contract. This dual character remains true of the emergent temporal regime emblematic of today's precarious work, in the 'sharing economy' and beyond. Time, I have argued, is an irreducible medium for experiencing class grievance, whether as nineteenth-century mill workers locked in factories for 16-hour days, or as Uber drivers idling in vehicles for 20 hours. But where the temporal grievances of traditional workplaces were likely to be witnessed and experienced collectively, today's precarious workers are far more likely to be atomised, isolated from each other, apparently confronting an algorithm rather than an employer. Even as gig-workers and other members of the precariat may identify stolen and transformed time as a visceral way in which their lives are twisted and diminished by the status quo, there are few obvious contemporary analogues to the liberty bell or the low-man-out system. Indeed, one of the effects of the 'disguised employment' structures Uber epitomises is that workers are encouraged to recognise conflict not with their employer, but rather with competing 'contractors'; to focus their resentment not on the impersonal algorithm on their mobile interface, but on the taxes they must manage and pay as 'independent contractors', or on the lucky workers who still enjoy predictable working hours, regular wages, and standard employment protections.

How, then, to collectivise the temporal experiences of the precarious workforce? What would transform these individualised experiences of theft, vulnerability, and domination into a shared sense of class grievance, which might make possible shared analysis, action, and demands? Kathi Weeks' analysis of the 'work society' suggests two key ways to pursue answers to this question: first, she turns to basic income as a demand that could loosen the grip of work over time, arguing for the utility of the demand not only once achieved, but also as a way of articulating grievances and desires against a deeply naturalised, internalised status quo. Second, by approaching class through her extremely capacious concept of the 'work society'—which signifies not only the obligatory character of waged work for most people, but also its centrality to liberal ideals of citizenship, morality, and social responsibility— Weeks goes some way towards decentring the production site as the sphere where '[c]lass identities and relations are made and remade'.[89] These insights are clearly connected: the demand for basic income is not directed at employers, nor is it limited to a single industry or category of workers; hence agitating for a basic income, articulating the grievances it might mitigate, and imagining its reverberating effects are activities not limited to workplace confrontations, but potentially taking place in the other shared spaces where class identities and relations are made.

The temporal shifts I have described among gig-workers clearly reverberate to sites beyond the production sphere, compressing and distorting the time spent 'not at work', whether caring

---

[89]   Weeks, *Problem with Work*, 9.

for family or other community members, commuting, performing the 'work of consumption', or participating in civic life. Rather than searching for direct analogues to the liberty bell and the low-man-out system suitable to the gig-economy, perhaps the task is to identify a set of policy demands that similarly decentre employment relations as the site not only of class confrontation but of basic social provision. Efforts to conceptualise unionism beyond the workplace— bus riders' unions, for example, or student or neighbourhood assemblies—represent one step in this direction, as do some recent attempts by traditional unions to focus on the defence and advancement of public services as a core piece of their mandate.[90] Experiments in freelancers' unions, interns' unions, and gig-workers' unions, while still oriented around employment relations, necessarily locate specific grievances against individual employers within the broader frame of workforce casualisation, within and across industries.[91] But these efforts still confront a crucial set of challenges: where and how do workers congregate, commiserate, and recognise their own grievances as part of a larger pattern of class antagonism? The hypothesis of this chapter is that workers' temporal experiences are key to asking and answering this question.

---

[90]   I am thinking here particularly of Canadian public sector unions' interest in demands that clearly extend beyond their direct membership: public pension expansion, say, or the extension of Canada Post's mandate to include basic banking services that would reach communities underserved by conventional banks or vulnerable to the predatory practices of pay-day lenders and other commercial financial services.

[91]   Some relatively modest policy proposals that might function across employers and industries to offer more protection for precarious workers include 'portable benefits', stricter classification requirements, and improved resources for arbitrating and enforcing existing labour protections.

23. Greening anti-imperialism and the national question

Max Ajl

The Green New Deal (GND) burst into popular consciousness in autumn 2018, when Representative Alexandria Ocasio-Cortez (working with Senator Edward Markey) submitted a non-binding draft resolution under that name to the US Congress.[1] The document emerged from debates about 'jobs-for-all' programs, intended to guarantee a decent job to any resident of the United States who wanted one. More broadly, the proposal was part of a process of transforming rising economic and social discontent into policy. The 'green' aspect of such programs had long been present in efforts to bring together the labour movement—concerned with jobs, often in industry—and the environmental movement—concerned with protecting the natural world, with little attention to social issues. One of the most prominent of these efforts was the 'Apollo Alliance', which began in 2003 as an attempt to bring together labour unions like the United Auto Workers, United Steelworkers, and International Union of Machinists and Aerospace Workers, and big green foundation-funded pro-capitalist environmental organisations like the Sierra Club, Greenpeace, and the Natural Resources Defence Council. It called for an 'Apollo Project' to rejuvenate the US economy through a ten-year, $300 billion initiative to transition to clean energy.

The push to 'do something' about the climate crisis received additional support from the 2018 Intergovernmental Panel on Climate Change (IPCC) report, which for the first time used language departing from the placid bureaucratese of previous syntheses. That document argued for 'rapid and far-reaching transitions in energy, land, urban and infrastructure (including transport and buildings), and industrial systems', noting that 'systems transitions are unprecedented in terms of scale, but not necessarily in terms of speed, and imply deep emissions reductions in all sectors'. It added that 'there is no documented historic precedent for their scale'.[2] With the addition of this potent institutional-intellectual fertiliser, thinking about transformative ecological politics bloomed across the imperialist core, well beyond the isolated cloisters of environmental activism and climate science. The clarion call to remake society attracted attention to environmental concerns—and to eco-socialism—on an unprecedented scale. In its wake, a huge raft of documents with barely a whisper of egalitarian pretensions have emerged from the vanguard of the capitalist class, which is currently using a variety of institutions, from the World Economic Forum to the Climate Finance Leadership Initiative, to manage the great transition.

---

[1]   Alexandria Ocasio-Cortez, 'H.Res.109–116th Congress (2019–2020): Recognizing the Duty of the Federal Government to Create a Green New Deal' (12 February 2019), https://www.congress.gov/bill/116th-congress/house-resolution/109/text accessed 7 April 2021.

[2]   Intergovernmental Panel on Climate Change, 'Global Warming of 1.5 °C' (2018), https://www.ipcc.ch/sr15/chapter/spm/ accessed 7 April 2021.

The increasingly wide-ranging debate over humans' relationship with their natural environment is a debate about 'managing the future'.[3] The outlines of that future are yet to be drawn, but this does not mean that the world lacks for blueprints. Current intellectual and political struggles over those schemes sweep across the social and ideological landscape, from rival visions of the GND through 'Half-Earth' eidolons which aim to turn half the Earth into a biodiversity reserve based on the false idea that humans need to be walled off from nature, to The Red Nation's 'Red Deal', an ambitious proposal from a communist Indigenous group in the present-day United States that aims to decolonise those lands, introduce eco-socialism, and abolish the police and military. Other plans exist, too, from the world's poorest and richest alike. The debate ranges across a spectrum of possibilities for the future of redistribution, internationalism, racist and nationalist chauvinism, and, of course, capitalism itself. Many far-right proposals imagine an entirely greened capitalism, with the current ruling classes continuing to dominate advanced capitalist states, many of them settler states, and climate change moderated enough to stave off unmanageable waves of climate refugees. The material for these partial curatives is to be secured through environmental imperialism—taking resources from, and dumping waste in, the global South. There are also proposals for the replacement of current energy sources with renewables in the global North (alongside increased energy use in the global South)—the standard left-liberal response, roughly what Ocasio-Cortez represents. A third kind of position argues for lower energy use through the retrofitting of energy infrastructures in core capitalist countries, substantial domestic redistribution to recover 1950s-era levels of (in)equality, and an ambiguous call for grants to help Southern countries transition. This is the green social-democratic, or 'being nice to the South', solution.[4] A fourth type of approach, this one revolutionary, suggests considerably lower energy use in the core alongside de-commodified social infrastructure, guaranteed social well-being, and massive technology grants to the Third World. This is a form of what has come to be called 'degrowth eco-communism', or simply 'eco-communism'. As we shall see, it intertwines with renewed defence of sovereignty, leaning on Indigenous and agro-ecological land management, demilitarisation, and decolonisation.

This chapter surveys the debate. In particular, it highlights the social content and context of the far-right and left-liberal GND, or great transition, programs.[5] It extracts some themes that touch upon questions of nationalism, internationalism, (settler) colonialism, land, and reparations. It also offers some ideas from an anti-systemic perspective on these issues, which, though often sidelined, are fundamental to a just global transition.

LEFT-LIBERAL GREEN NEW DEALS

The GND and *the* GND, of Markey/Ocasio-Cortez fame, are frequently conflated, with one becoming a reference point for the other. The Markey/Ocasio-Cortez GND crystallised many emergent contradictions of left-liberal thought, the current historical moment, and the

---

[3]   Philip McMichael, 'Commentary: Food Regime for Thought' (2016) 43 *Journal of Peasant Studies* 648, 660.

[4]   Robert Pollin, 'De-Growth vs a Green New Deal' (2018) 112 *New Left Review* 5.

[5]   I draw here on small portions of chapters one and three, and all of chapter seven, of Max Ajl, *A People's Green New Deal* (Pluto Press 2021).

management of the ecological crisis. The text of this draft non-binding resolution must be examined, as must the way it illustrates certain key aspects of the broader debate. In this latter sense, it serves as a shorthand for a mixture of domestic redistribution and environmental protection through cessation of polluting activities, the cleaning up of existing pollution, and, more generally, the transition away from CO_2 production in the core. Yet the actual scope of distribution and the international dimensions of this change have generally gone unmentioned or under-analysed.

As it happens, the idea of a GND is not new. One of the earliest references to it came from the pen of Thomas Friedman, the imperialist core's in-house deadpan comic relief. That GND was meant to be 'geostrategic, geoeconomic, capitalistic and patriotic', because 'living, working, designing, manufacturing and projecting America in a green way can be the basis of a new unifying political movement for the 21st century'.[6] Such a scheme was GND as indus-trial renaissance, shoring up weak points in the edifice of US power. It was a 'trade'-centred proposal for *imperium*, creating more jobs in the United States in order to generate significant reinvestment in domestic capitalist enterprises, as a way of preparing for the looming climate crisis. Kindred proposals came from more populist perspectives, proposing that green and trade union movements join forces for a kind of renewables moonshot.[7] A later GND, calling for immediate emissions reductions, food sovereignty, and eventually even eco-socialism, emerged from the US Green Party, although without much popular resonance (or, indeed, audibility).[8]

Ocasio-Cortez's GND emerged in a starkly different political environment. First, after the 2008 financial crisis and the subsequent Occupy Wall Street protests, capitalism was ideolog-ically concussed as a system of rule. Marxism gained popularity as a way of understanding and acting in the world. In this new environment, brimming with openness to redistributive politics, political avatars of nebulous socialisms, nearly all strictly anti-communist, have arisen across the North Atlantic, from the SYRIZA movement to Podemos and Jeremy Corbyn to Bernie Sanders. The ruling classes have shattered and evaporated such challengers one after another, forcing them into compromise, co-optation, or irrelevance.

Against this background, Ocasio-Cortez joined Markey to introduce a non-binding resolu-tion calling for a GND. With massive marketing, fluency in social media, and the backing of the US 'Justice Dems' (an effort, closely linked to the Sanders candidacy, to put progressive candidates in office), Ocasio-Cortez introduced the GND, a compact crystallisation of emer-gent trends in social-democratic and left-liberal politics in the United States. This resolution emerged from earlier ideas about a 'jobs-for-all' program, a sweeping populist remedy for an underpaid and underemployed middle class and working class. The Markey/Ocasio-Cortez document referred, first, to 'wage stagnation, deindustrialization, and antilabor policies', as well as the need to limit the rise in global temperatures to no more than 1.5° C above pre-industrialised levels.[9] Second, the document called for a 'new national, social, industrial,

---

[6]   Thomas L Friedman, 'The Power of Green' *New York Times* (15 April 2007), https://www.nytimes.com/2007/04/15/opinion/15iht-web-0415edgreen-full.5291830.html accessed 7 April 2021.

[7]   Apollo Alliance, 'The New Apollo Program: Clean Energy, Good Jobs' (2008), https://community-wealth.org/content/new-apollo-program-clean-energy-good-jobs accessed 7 April 2021.

[8]   Green Party of the United States, 'The Green New Deal', https://gpus.org/organizing-tools/the-green-new-deal/ accessed 7 April 2021.

[9]   For this and all other references to the document in this and the following paragraph, see Ocasio-Cortez, 'H.Res.109–116th Congress (2019–2020)'.

and economic mobilization', along the lines of the original, anti-communist New Deal, with sweeping notions of a new corporatist social pact. Third, it was clearly non-socialist, and did not diagnose capitalism as the source of social ills or the sower of social antagonism. Instead, it suggested 'transparent and inclusive consultation … and partnership with … businesses', as well as the allocation of 'adequate capital … [to] businesses working on the Green New Deal mobilization', coupled with a murky call for public 'appropriate ownership stakes and returns on investment' in such capital grants. Fourth, it gestured toward 'consultation, collaboration, and partnership with frontline and vulnerable communities'. But each of those last three nouns are amorphous. Everyone is vulnerable. All people are members of communities. And 'frontline' is an index of spatial or geographical risk. While these words give off a warm aura of concern, they are denuded of class content. Fifth, it noted the 'historic oppression' of the poor and of low-income workers. But it sought to address that oppression while keeping the fundamental property structures of the country intact. What was remarkable, then, is how much has been made of what little was actually explicitly offered in Ocasio-Cortez's GND—and, further, how little attention has been paid to what the resolution actually states. Capital grants to businesses constitute an existing policy of US capitalism. To 'green' it is simply to 'green' capitalism.

The question of US interaction with the periphery, or internally colonised nations, entered the Markey/Ocasio-Cortez GND on two fronts. First, supporting the industrial green renaissance interpretation, the resolution called for '[p]romoting the international exchange of technology, expertise, products, funding, and services, with the aim of making the United States the international leader on climate action'. This anticipated likely future manoeuvering on the national and international stage: a new 'space race'-type competition for leadership and monopoly control over the technology for a green transition. The second and more surprising aspect of the GND was its stated commitment to 'protecting and enforcing the sovereignty and land rights of indigenous peoples', a truly capacious demand which in theory—given the scope of those land rights and depending on who is interpreting them, and keeping in mind the history of disregarded treaties between Indigenous peoples and the US government—pointed towards revolutionary horizons.

ELITE TRANSITIONS ON THE RIGHT

Meanwhile, from the right, there emerged a different set of proposals, mostly consonant with the Markey/Ocasio-Cortez GND but far more brazen, for managing the great transition. Authors of these proposals ranged from Breakthrough (National Centre for Climate Restoration), based in Melbourne, to the Energy Transitions Commission (ETC), an international think tank. Such proposals shared several traits: partnerships between corporations and the state, and also between corporations and communities, an embrace of the national security sector and national security discourse, commitment to technological salvation, the opening of new frontiers of land-based accumulation in the global South, and the further hollowing out of Third World sovereignty. Many converged on what the economist Daniela Gabor calls the 'Wall Street Consensus'—reorganising 'development interventions around selling development finance to the market', 'escorting' capital into bonds, and remaking Third World states by demanding that their treasuries and national budgets bear the burden of risks.[10]

Such reports generally set the stage for their analysis and recommendations by invoking concern about climate change, often in apocalyptic or eco-nationalist terms. Consider a few examples. A recent Brookings Institution report discussed rising 'droughts, fire', and natural disasters, plagues that translated into 'risks to economies and livelihoods'. Furthermore, the '*current growth path*' generated significant pressures on water, land, and biodiversity, causing 'accelerated loss of natural capital'.[11] Words like 'economies' and 'livelihoods', 'community' and 'frontline', are in many ways optical illusions. They suggest great concern for human needs, particularly food, shelter, and a decent life. However, none of these words implies a particular pattern of power. 'Class, not as an institutional context variable, but as a relational concept, is absent from the discourse of livelihoods', for example, as the sociologist Bridget O'Laughlin argues.[12] Those using such concepts frequently do not wish to question the existing maldistribution of wealth. Or consider the example of Breakthrough, which, in a May 2019 report titled *Existential Climate-Related Security Risk: A Scenario Approach*, gave expression to the views of David Spratt, the institute's research director, and Ian Dunlop, a former international oil, coal, and gas industry executive (and the current chief executive of the Australian Institute of Company Directors).[13] The foreword, written by Admiral Chris Barrie, demanded 'strong, determined leadership in government, in business and in our communities' to combat the cataclysm of climate change.[14] The report warned of 'existential risk', and urged that steps be taken to avoid it. How? Under a scenario better than the current trajectory, with emissions peaking at 2030 and declining 80 per cent by 2050, '[d]eadly heat conditions persist for more than 100 days per year in West Africa, tropical South America, the Middle East and South-East Asia, contributing to more than a billion people being displaced from the tropical zone'.[15] Water availability decreases in the dry tropics and subtropics, parching two billion. Agriculture becomes 'nonviable in the dry subtropics'.[16] As watersheds and the temperature bands within which humans have flourished for millennia shift northward, all societies built on essentially stable climactic foundations are shaken and perhaps collapse.

Such national security bureaucrats and intellectuals know that climactic shifts threaten to change the planet's environment enough to evaporate the gossamer flows and political scaffoldings of global capitalism. They have written, thought, and planned accordingly. These reports were not the work of earnest do-gooders, but the written calculations of steel-souled

---

[10] Daniela Gabor, 'The Wall Street Consensus', 1, https://osf.io/preprints/socarxiv/wab8m/ accessed 7 April 2021.

[11] Amar Bhattacharya et al, 'Aligning G20 Infrastructure Investment with Climate Goals & the 2030 Agenda', *Foundations 20 Platform: A Report to the G20* (Brookings Institution & Global Development Policy Center 2019) 3 (emphasis added).

[12] Bridget O'Laughlin, 'Book Reviews' (2004) 35 *Development and Change* 385, 387.

[13] David Spratt and Ian Dunlop, 'Existential Climate-Related Security Risk: A Scenario Approach' Breakthrough (National Centre for Climate Restoration) (2019), https://apo.org.au/node/239741 accessed 7 April 2021. See also David Spratt and Ian Dunlop, 'What Lies Beneath: The Understatement of Existential Climate Risk' Breakthrough (National Centre for Climate Restoration) (2018), https://climateextremes.org.au/wp-content/uploads/2018/08/What-Lies-Beneath-V3-LR-Blank5b15d.pdfaccessed 7 April 2021.

[14] Spratt and Dunlop, 'Existential Climate-Related Security Risk', 3.

[15] Spratt and Dunlop, 'Existential Climate-Related Security Risk', 8.

[16] Spratt and Dunlop, 'Existential Climate-Related Security Risk', 8.

strategists shocked at the sluggishness with which the greater part of ruling classes and governments are acting. To head off the massive human migrations such a scenario would entail, the Breakthrough report called for 'a zero-emissions industrial system [to] set in train the restoration of a safe climate'.[17]

On the accumulation side of the ledger, the Climate Finance Leadership Initiative (CFLI) laid out the economic and environmental aspects of the ruling class agenda.[18] The CFLI was an initiative of United Nations Secretary-General António Guterres. Guterres asked Michael R Bloomberg, billionaire former mayor of New York City and UN Special Envoy for Climate Action, to chart the path toward a wide mobilisation of private finance to respond to the crisis. Executives of seven key institutions—Allianz Global Investors, AXA, Enel, Goldman Sachs, HSBC, Japan's Government Pension Investment Fund (GPIF), and the Macquarie Group—joined Bloomberg in this effort.

The CFLI clarified that it is the state's job to guarantee 'revenue security': the constant flow of value. To do so, 'development finance institutions' will open 'new markets' by encouraging a suitable investment climate. Socio-politically as well as ecologically, the global South and global North are different. In the latter, various political structures ensure that wind and solar installation costs are now below the cost of new investments in hydrocarbon-based energy and fuel. There are also mechanisms that secure prices and ensure payment for energy, stabilising flows of revenue. But in the 'emerging markets' of the South:

> DFIs can leverage private investment through risk-sharing tools, such as guarantees and political risk insurance, and their ability to source and coordinate catalytic finance from donors and third parties .... Policy stability is also critical. Reversals or renegotiations of PPAs, tax incentives, or other agreements—particularly in the early stages of market development—can have a long-lasting negative impact on future investor interest.[19]

The anodyne term 'political risk insurance' means that presiding governments in sovereign states must effectively guarantee that future governments—more 'populist', nationalist, or sovereignist, perhaps—will not move to renegotiate electricity rates. States would become liable for redistributive action in international tribunals, placing them under the jurisdiction of courts in which corporations can sue states for reducing or eliminating their profits. Green financing mechanisms rest, then, on the capitalist enclosure and evaporation by the North of the sovereignty of the South, subordinating the latter once again by colonisation through financial chicanery. These great transitions aim to eliminate sovereignty, making the battlefield of sovereignty—the national question, or the set of political issues dealing with self-determination domestically and internationally—a critical one for anti-systemic ecological movements. The gains of decolonisation, including putting an end to colonial famine and de-development, are at risk.[20]

17   Spratt and Dunlop, 'Existential Climate-Related Security Risk', 10.
18   Climate Finance Leadership Initiative, 'Financing the Low-Carbon Future: A Private-Sector View on Mobilizing Climate Finance' (2019), https://assets.bbhub.io/company/sites/55/2019/09/Financing-the-Low-Carbon-Future_CFLI-Summary-Booklet_September-2019.pdf accessed 7 April 2021.
19   Climate Finance Leadership Initiative, 'Financing the Low-Carbon Future', 14.
20   I discuss these at greater length in Max Ajl, 'The Arab Nation, the Chinese Model, and Theories of Self-Reliant Development' in İlker Cörüt and Joost Jongerden (eds), *Beyond Nationalism and the Nation-State: Radical Approaches to Nation* (Routledge 2021) ch 7 (and sources cited therein).

When it comes to land, proposals of this kind envisage the forests and grasslands of the periphery for use primarily outside the needs of the people who inhabit them. Some imagine biodiversity corrals, relying on the idea of separating humanity from 'wild nature', a hallucination of colonial-capitalist ideologues for aeons.[21] These views, which extend to the self-described left, elide the fact that the history of humanity is the history of managed landscapes, and that humans are indeed some of the very best managers and guardians of biodiversity.[22] These individuals, especially but not only those on the capitalist right, have called for fantastical afforestation, plopping trees where they have never been, or reforestation, based on reductionist ecology, or reducing complex questions about the ecological effects of tree planting to the simple benefit of CO_2 sequestration. They are based on fantasies about lost sylvan Arcadias which justified one after another colonial incursion.[23] Never mind that closed-canopy forests are probably a myth in their supposed heartland of western Europe, that 'the natural vegetation' in central and western Europe and the western United States 'is a mosaic of grasslands, scrub, trees and groves',[24] and, furthermore, that willy-nilly tree planting can be environmentally disastrous.[25]

When land is not to be allotted for deadened deciduous or coniferous plantations, it will be for biofuels, a 'clean' energy source. Of course, all such reports, the ETC's included, gesture at how biofuels can compete with food, and also address issues of carbon drawdown and biodiversity. Such homages to the warnings in the IPCC report are mandatory and customary caveats—forcefields of deniability around any capitalist discussion of biofuels. But the ETC program pointedly states that '[s]ustainable biofuels or synthetic fuels will need to scale up from today's trivial levels to play a major role in aviation and perhaps shipping', less hesitant than the full-throttle embrace that is inevitable if these programs are implemented.[26] Accordingly, the ETC national manifesto for the Australian leap to sustainability states that '[f]ull decarbonisation for industries such as steel, cement and chemicals require the use of electrification, hydrogen, bioenergy and carbon capture and storage (CCS)'.[27]

[21] Dina Gilio-Whitaker, *As Long as Grass Grows: The Indigenous Fight for Environmental Justice from Colonization to Standing Rock* (Beacon Press 2019); Carolyn Merchant, *The Death of Nature: Women, Ecology, and the Scientific Revolution* (HarperCollins 1990).

[22] Troy Vettese, 'To Freeze the Thames' (2018) 111 *New Left Review* 63; William M Denevan, *Cultivated Landscapes of Native Amazonia and the Andes* (OUP 2001); William M Denevan, 'The Pristine Myth: The Landscape of the Americas in 1492' (1992) 82 *Annals of the Association of American Geographers* 369.

[23] Diana K Davis, *Resurrecting the Granary of Rome: Environmental History and French Colonial Expansion in North Africa* (Ohio University Press 2007).

[24] William J Bond, *Open Ecosystems: Ecology and Evolution beyond the Forest Edge* (OUP 2019); Franciscus WM Vera, *Grazing Ecology and Forest History* (CABI 2000) 379.

[25] Fred Pearce, 'In Israel, Questions Are Raised About a Forest That Rises from the Desert', Yale Environment 360 (30 September 2019), https://e360.yale.edu/features/in-israel-questions-are-raised-about-a-forest-that-rises-from-the-desert accessed 7 April 2021; Oswald Schmitz, 'How "Natural Geoengineering" Can Help Slow Global Warming', Yale Environment 360 (25 January 2016), https://e360.yale.edu/features/how_natural_geo-engineering_can_help_slow_global_warming accessed 7 April 2021.

[26] Energy Transitions Commission, 'Making Mission Possible: Delivering a Net-Zero Economy' (2020) 42, https://www.energy-transitions.org/publications/making-mission-possible/#download-form accessed 7 April 2021.

[27] Energy Transitions Commission, 'Program Overview' (2020) 7, https://www.energy-transitions.org/wp-content/uploads/2020/08/Australian-Industry-ETI-Program-Overview-July-2020.pdf accessed 7 April 2021.

Similarly, the EU's energy transitions plan moots massively increasing the biofuel mix in hard-to-decarbonise sectors like maritime and airborne transport.[28] But using land for growing biofuels and planting trees for the express purpose of pulling in CO_2 from the atmosphere means that such land will not be used for crops. Even under the most optimistic scenarios, shifting all of the world's hydrocarbon use to biofuels would cut savagely into agricultural production and water use. For India, where farmland for food has been dragooned into use for tropical export crops while peasants starve, the ETC identified biomass as a possible power source for Indian metallurgy.[29] Furthermore, the slippage is not hypothetical. One quarter of EU-funded bio-based industry projects are based on agricultural biomass, while a large portion of the money from EU projects goes to agriculture-based biomass initiatives. Just 10 per cent of coordinators associated with biomass-based industries have anticipated positive results from biodiversity, and just a hair more than a quarter anticipate more sustainable management of planetary natural resource.[30]

Clearly, the land question remains central to any great transition: as a frontier for accumulation, as a realm for possible use-values for capitalism (or whatever system replaces it), and as a source for securing social needs like food, shelter, and heating, the primary elements of a people's ecological civilisation in the periphery. In that sense, the agrarian question of land, like the agrarian question of nation, also remains central to any possible GND.

THE NATIONAL QUESTION

The agrarian question of nation refers to the political parameters within which peoples can resolve their own internal social, ecological, and gender contradictions. It is a subset of the broader national question, the set of political problems concerning oppressed nationalities within nations, colonialism, self-determination, and national liberation. The 'question' surfaced throughout the history of the socialist movement. In particular, it arose as the Third International, led by Lenin, was trying to achieve a principled policy towards colonised and dependent nations. In this context, the national question was a way of understanding the political topography of imperialism. One central 'national question' emerges out of the 'distinction between the oppressed, dependent and subject nations and the oppressing, exploiting and sovereign nations', the latter of which carry out the 'colonial and financial enslavement of the vast majority of the world's population'.[31] That is, the national question was articulated alongside the class struggle and the pursuit of popular emancipation. Today the national question takes

---

[28]   European Commission, 'Powering a Climate-Neutral Economy: An EU Strategy for Energy System Integration' (2020), https://eur-lex.europa.eu/legal-content/EN/ALL/?uri=COM:2020:299:FIN accessed 7 April 2021.

[29]   Energy Transitions Commission, 'Towards a Low-Carbon Steel Sector: Overview of the Changing Market, Technology, and Policy Context for Indian Steel' (2019), https://www.energy-transitions.org/publications/towards-a-low-carbon-steel-sector/ accessed 7 April 2021.

[30]   Corporate Europe Observatory, 'Research and Destroy: The Factories of the Industrial Bioeconomy Threaten the Climate and Biodiversity' (2020), https://corporateeurope.org/sites/default/files/2020-05/BBI-report-final_0.pdf accessed 7 April 2021.

[31]   VI Lenin, 'Preliminary Draft Theses on the National and the Colonial Questions for the Second Congress of the Communist International' [1920] in VI Lenin, *Collected Works*, vol 31 (Progress Publishers 1965) 144, 145.

a variety of forms, including the ongoing struggles for decolonisation and self-determination, in the sense of achieving de jure political and economic sovereignty, in settler colonies like Israel and the United States.[32] Struggles to end the transfer of value from South to North are also part of the national question, and they are the phenomenon that constituted the essence of the relation between oppressing and oppressed nations that Lenin identified.[33] For those reasons, the national question arises in South and North alike. It is not surprising, then, that it should also be the foundation of a people's GND. This might seem an odd foundation-stone for a people's agenda in a settler-colonial empire like the United States, which runs roughshod over the sovereignty of other states. But that is precisely the point. Other peoples' national questions, especially those of Indigenous peoples, must form the basis of a people's GND within the territory of the United States and in other settler colonies, since building ecological societies requires popular control by the most excluded over their national productive resources.

It can be all too easy to sidestep or suppress the national question, in favour of a sort of easy ecologism, or a compression or reduction of fundamentally political questions to environmental management. To that end, one response has been to argue that reducing the rate at which the imperial core spills out CO_2 and other environmental toxins into the world is internationalist by definition, and that we had therefore better focus on that mission. Many then suggest that degrowth in the wealthier world, which would reduce its material impact on the remainder of the planet, is the most effective internationalism, leaving greater space for others to live.[34] But there is a thin line between modesty and myopia, an inwards-looking ostrich syndrome, in a country marked by imperial modes of living.[35] Such a move may reduce political choices and demands about paths forward to simply retooling the machinery of growth. Such an internationalism can inadvertently silence demands for climate reparations. A similar but more Eurocentric arrogance claims that an ecological politics for 'the working class' means a politics for the Northern industrial and service sectors (cotton farmers in India, pomegranate farmers in Iran, phosphate miners in Tunisia, and many others do not on this view figure as 'working class'). This approach deliberately disdains any transformative aspirations as it effectively erases ecological debt, offering another version of green pseudo-social democracy in its praise for the Markey/Ocasio-Cortez GND.[36] A third approach looks to supply chain

---

[32]   Sam Moyo, Praveen Jha, and Paris Yeros, 'The Classical Agrarian Question: Myth, Reality and Relevance Today' (2013) 2 *Agrarian South: Journal of Political Economy* 93; Amílcar Cabral, *Unity and Struggle: Speeches and Writings of Amilcar Cabral* (Monthly Review Press 1979).

[33]   Enrique Dussel, *Hacia un Marx desconocido: un comentario de los manuscritos del 61–63* (Siglo XXI 1988) 312–61.

[34]   It is striking that one of the serious interventions on this front, Corinna Dengler and Lisa Marie Seebacher, 'What About the Global South? Towards a Feminist Decolonial Degrowth Approach' (2019) 157 *Ecological Economics* 246, is silent on climate and ecological debt, barely mentions the word 'imperialism', and states that '[c]olonialism and Northern expansionary politics set the basis for today's hierarchically structured global system, in which territorial imperialism has largely been replaced with policies of economic re-structuring under the guise of "sustainable development"' (249). This is not a reality-based account of United States/European Union foreign policy.

[35]   Ulrich Brand and Markus Wissen, 'Crisis and Continuity of Capitalist Society-Nature Relationships: The Imperial Mode of Living and the Limits to Environmental Governance' (2013) 20 *Review of International Political Economy* 687.

[36]   Matt T Huber, 'Ecological Politics for the Working Class' (2019) 3 *Catalyst: A Journal of Theory and Strategy*, https://catalyst-journal.com/vol3/no1/ecological-politics-for-the-working-class accessed 7 April 2021.

justice and cross-national worker solidarity for just transitions 'from below' as the basis for developmental convergence and unity-in-difference, while equally eliding entirely the historic language of climate debt, and transmogrifying the national question into aesthetic gestures about imperialism and colonialism.[37] And a fourth and final approach, coming from institutions like the UN Conference on Trade and Development,[38] entertains 'foist[ing] Northern ideas and ideological framings of green transitions centred on techno-optimist imaginings about renewable energy futures onto the South' that are 'unsuited to the realities of the global South'.[39]

While supporters of degrowth are most sympathetic toward, if not outright supportive of, the payment of climate debt, and while they are the most open to Third World Marxism, other internationalisms sidestep serious engagement with the past, present, and future of an hierarchical international system organised around nation-states. These other internationalisms deny that polarisation is inherent in the capitalist world-system, green or otherwise. And they reject the national question as necessary for organising thinking about autonomous forms of resistance towards emancipatory horizons. Discussions about GNDs in the United States are never—and can never simply be—about the United States alone, because US capitalism is not and never has been just about the United States itself. US wealth is built on a continental process of primitive accumulation of land and continuous wars that transmute lost lives into the stock market valuations of US corporations.[40] Its circuits of accumulation cut across borders and crosshatch the world. Its long tradition of burning cheap petroleum and coal to build up an immense and convenient infrastructure has come at the cost of denying other countries the capacity to choose the same resource-use path. That history of large-scale burning of resources cascades into developmental disarray and de-development even now, from millennial cyclones in Mozambique to deluges in Bangladesh and the looming submersion of the Seychelles. Future decisions about how much lithium to use, whether to pay or not pay climate debt, and how much energy to allot to each inhabitant of this territory inevitably reverberate globally.

THE NATIONAL QUESTION: THEORY

In an imperialist world, environmental politics have a specifically national aspect. Because imperialism, the transfer of value from South to North and the uneven development accompanying it, continued long after the end of the major wave of formal decolonisation, the national question is not a historical curio, antiquated and anachronistic.

---

[37]   Transnational Institute, 'Just Transition: How Environmental Justice Organisations and Trade Unions Are Coming Together for Social and Environmental Transformation' (2020), https://www.tni.org/files/publication-downloads/web_justtransition.pdf accessed 7 April 2021.

[38]   UNCTAD, 'Financing a Global Green New Deal' (2019), https://unctad.org/system/files/official-document/tdr2019ch3_en.pdf accessed 7 April 2021.

[39]   Keston K Perry, 'Financing a Global Green New Deal: Greening Capitalism or Taming Financialization for a New "Civilizing" Multilateralism?' (2021) 52 *Development and Change* 1022, 1031.

[40]   Glen Sean Coulthard, *Red Skin, White Masks: Rejecting the Colonial Politics of Recognition* (University of Minnesota Press 2014); Ali Kadri, *Imperialism with Reference to Syria* (Springer 2019).

First, colonialism itself is not over. It endures de jure in a plethora of settler states, and its afterlives haunt the periphery.[41] As formal and legal decolonisation gave way to neocolonialism, nations lost control over their economic sovereignty, the pot of gold they had hoped to find at the end of national liberation. Nation-states, the political containers through which accumulation on a world scale and uneven development endure, persevere, and deepen, structure uneven access to the fruits of world production. Countries like the Democratic Republic of the Congo, Iraq, Venezuela, and Yemen face national losses in their productive forces, not to mention sanctions and the threat or actuality of war. The national question endures for these reasons too. The nation is one of the political and social units within which people organise to resist oppression. A large number of the most dynamic struggles from the 1980s to the present, from Venezuela to Bolivia, have used a national-popular idiom to articulate their politics and place domestic wealth at the service of the peasantry and working and marginalised classes.[42] It is perhaps underappreciated that the most cherished struggle for liberation and justice in the world today, that of the Palestinians, is that of a subjugated *nation* fighting for land, liberation, and return. And there is no hope that Palestinians—or Yemenis—will receive and control climate debt reparations unless they have de facto and de jure national sovereignty, the political shells within which thinking about the future can occur.

It is in and through the national political sphere that decisions about rates of investment and disbursement of social goods must be made, alliances built, and internationalisms constructed. It matters, for instance, who is at the helm of the Bolivian state. It was Bolivia, a sovereign and national-popular Indigenous-led state, that was the sanctuary for the Cochabamba documents, which emerged from meetings in late April 2010 and demanded wide-ranging payments from North to South alongside a radical climate agenda to meet the needs of Mother Earth and poor humanity alike.[43] And it is through the state system that ecological debts are calculated and demands for debt repayments are made in world-political fora. Focusing on the national question underscores the right to regain control of a people's historical process, for people to decide how and with whom they want to live. This includes Indigenous peoples, who cannot be reduced to any kind of beneficiary of a restored prelapsarian ecology, but who are, as Indigenous scholars Andrew Curley and Majerle Lister write, emphatically 'modern peoples whose greatest threats are political marginalization at the hands of continued colonial processes'.[44]

---

[41]   Samir Amin, *Accumulation on a World Scale: A Critique of the Theory of Underdevelopment* (Monthly Review Press 1974).

[42]   Chris Gilbert, 'To Recover Strategic Thought and Political Practice' *Monthly Review Online* (29 September 2015), https://mronline.org/2015/09/29/gilbert290915-html/ accessed 7 April 2021; Sam Moyo and Paris Yeros, 'The Fall and Rise of the National Question' in Sam Moyo and Paris Yeros (eds), *Reclaiming the Nation: The Return of the National Question in Africa, Asia and Latin America* (Pluto Press 2011) 1; Álvaro García Linera, 'El evismo: lo nacional-popular en acción' (2006) 7 *OSAL— Observatorio Social de América Latina* 25.

[43]   World People's Conference on Climate Change and the Rights of Mother Earth, 'People's Agreement of Cochabamba' (24 April 2010), https://pwccc.wordpress.com/2010/04/24/peoples -agreement/ accessed 7 April 2021; World People's Conference on Climate Change and the Rights of Mother Earth, 'Rights of Mother Earth' (4 January 2010), https://pwccc.wordpress.com/programa/ accessed 7 April 2021.

[44]   Andrew Curley and Majerle Lister, 'Already Existing Dystopias: Tribal Sovereignty, Extraction, and Decolonizing the Anthropocene' in Sami Moisio, Natalie Koch, Andrew EG Jonas, Christopher

Insisting on the importance of the national question does not require denial of social or democratic questions: who gets what within nations, who decides who gets what within nations, and who gets to shape the ecological architecture of production and distribution within and across nations. It affirms that the world-system is hierarchically structured. The United States' exercise of extra-territorial violence and value drain has created a significant 'sovereignty deficit' in many other states, limiting their power and authority. This is a continuous feature of settler colonialism, pacted decolonisation—or decolonisation which occurred only through extensive dialogue with the colonial force and led to significant surrenders of national sovereignty—and neocolonialism, which has reduced the physical resources available for poor people to build up their own lives.[45] Indeed, even during the brilliant noon of decolonisation from 1947 to 1980, farmlands, forests, banks, currencies, factories, salt and iron mines, quarries, and oil seams remained in the hands of the colonisers. Almost never was decolonisation so successful as to allow peoples to fully determine their own histories, even within the nation-state. All peoples have the right, morally and legally, to determine their own histories in the face of imperialism. Such a right, however, requires struggle. The national question is a coin with two faces, imposing distinct political and social burdens of transformation, planning, and struggle in the North and the South, including the 'Fourth World' of Indigenous peoples.[46] That is because rights are neither possessions nor abstractions. Rights are relationships. Any right of the Third or Fourth World implies First World respect for that right, including the political struggle to secure such respect. That is, rights imply responsibilities—Sioux rights at Standing Rock meant people of all kinds had to go and stand with the Sioux, Lakota, and other Indigenous peoples to fight for those rights. If one believes that Palestinians have a right to national liberation and self-determination against imperialism and colonialism, there is an implied obligation for everyone, from their own specific locations, to assist that struggle, including identifying the manacles forged by core nations that enchain the Palestinians. Whether GNDs take the form of local planning or a new global architecture for just transition, all parties must shoulder the burden of that transformation, which involves assessing how much the First World as it currently exists—its skyscrapers, mass transit systems, beautifully wired metropolises of marble and granite, and a countryside increasingly sanitised of ecologically ruinous industrial production—has been based on a relationship which denies many rights to Indigenous peoples and peoples on the periphery of the world economic order, and trying to make amends for those denials.

At least three elements of the national question are central to just transition. First, the push to have the concepts of climate and ecological debt taken seriously and acted upon. Second, movements in favour of demilitarisation and the construction of a peacetime economy in the metropolitan core. Third, struggles against settler colonialism, which are connected to attempts to reinvigorate sovereignty and safeguard our common home: the world and the global environment. These three elements overlap in their promise of an entirely different world. Demilitarisation redirects social spending away from destructive and towards productive (and even creative) endeavours, liquidating the material foundations for the core's denial

---

Lizotte, and Juho Luukkonen (eds), *Handbook on the Changing Geographies of the State: New Spaces of Geopolitics* (Edward Elgar 2020) 251, 251.

[45]   Sit Tsui et al, 'The Development Trap of Financial Capitalism: China's Peasant Path Compared' (2013) 2 *Agrarian South: Journal of Political Economy* 247.

[46]   George Manuel and Michael Posluns, *The Fourth World: An Indian Reality* (Free Press 1974).

of peripheral sovereignty and popular development. 'Land back' projects do so too, since land is the principal physical basis for decolonisation. By definition, reinvigorated sovereignty for Indigenous peoples means 'land back'. Ecological debt is the means whereby sovereign and appropriate industrialisation, and increasingly humane and popular development itself, becomes possible for peripheral countries looted through generations of colonial and neocolonial drain. It is the organic fertiliser which allows economic sovereignty to finally bloom.

CLIMATE AND ECOLOGICAL DEBT

The concept of ecological debt is based on the diagnosis that capitalist accumulation, production, and consumption has vastly overrun the world's space for waste, including the atmospheric space for that all-important by-product of fossil capitalism, carbon dioxide. The concept of climate debt concerns the appropriation, or enclosure, of the world's capacity to absorb greenhouse gases, with staggering implications for the development prospects and pathways of the world's poor. Some also refer to what is often termed 'adaptation debt', the resources needed for poor countries to control or otherwise respond to rising sea levels, increased typhoons, and other outgrowths of environmentally destructive capitalism.[47]

Settling climate debt is a material implementation of the international legal principle of 'common but differentiated responsibilities', which stipulates that all states are responsible for addressing the destruction of the global environment but in different ways and to different degrees, depending partly on their history and level of industrialisation. Economic and other disparities between countries must be considered when designing legal obligations or responsibilities appropriate to their economic resources and institutional capabilities. The frequent erasure or muffling of calls for climate debt in much Northern climate discourse is inseparable from the contemporary rise of social democracy, with avatars like Jean-Luc Mélenchon, Jeremy Corbyn, and Bernie Sanders. Policy intellectuals accompanying these developments have put forward a climate discourse which is largely silent on climate debt. And if social democracy in its classic form has been a prophylactic against revolution, it makes sense that climate debt, a Third World working-class demand par excellence, has been largely absent from most GND manifestoes. While genuflections to internationalism abound, and proposed programs refer frequently to settler colonialism, global racism, and apartheid, beneath them lies denial of responsibility for colonialism, neocolonialism, and imperialism.

These new positions are in stark contrast to previous left climate politics. Over a decade ago, the Cochabamba people's process took place. When socialist states like Bolivia, Cuba, and Venezuela resisted the 2009 Copenhagen Accord, Evo Morales, Bolivia's president, called for a 'World People's Conference on Climate Change and the Rights of Mother Earth', which was held in April 2010 in the Bolivian city of Cochabamba. In contrast to the top-down and comfortable-with-capitalism Copenhagen summit, this counter-summit intended, among other things, '[t]o work on the organization of the World People's Referendum on Climate Change',

---

[47]   Matthew Stilwell, *Climate Debt–A Primer* (Third World Network 2009); Republic of Bolivia, 'Commitments for Annex I Parties under Paragraph 1(b)(i) of the Bali Action Plan: Evaluating Developed Countries' Historical Climate Debt to Developing Countries—Submission by the Republic of Bolivia to the AWG-LCA', https://unfccc.int/files/kyoto_protocol/application/pdf/bolivia250409.pdf accessed 7 April 2021.

to 'analyze and develop an action plan to advance the establishment of a Climate Justice Tribunal', and to 'define strategies for action and mobilization to defend life from Climate Change and to defend the Rights of Mother Earth'.[48]

That meeting devoted a working group to tackling the issue of climate debt, building upon two of the core principles of the United Nations Framework Convention on Climate Change: the principle of common but differentiated responsibilities, and the principle of equity. The UN Framework Convention, a multilateral treaty which had been opened for signature in June 1992, reflected state-of-the-art political and scientific understandings of a remarkable array of different topics: climate change; uneven incorporation into the capitalist world-system; the complex and multiple legacies of colonialism; the state-based organisation of global politics; the sovereign rights of states to develop their resources; and these states' obligations to ensure that such rights were not exercised in such a way as to harm their neighbours 'beyond the limits of national jurisdiction'.[49] The 1992 Framework Convention declared that the climate must be safeguarded:

> [f]or the benefit of present and future generations of humankind, on the basis of equity and in accordance with their common but differentiated responsibilities and respective capabilities. Accordingly, the developed country Parties should take the lead in combating climate change and the adverse effects thereof.[50]

Countries listed in Annex I of the Framework Convention were industrialised members of the Organisation for Economic Co-operation and Development (OECD) or 'economies in transition' (i.e., undergoing transition from state socialism). These countries were categorised as having historic responsibility for emissions and were required to commit to specific emissions reduction targets. Bolivia and other so-called 'petrostates' committed to 'extractivist' industries and seeking to lift millions of people out of poverty were not categorised as Annex I countries. Nor was China.[51]

Building upon the treaty, the Cochabamba working group laid out a five-point program based on honouring climate debts—not merely finance, but on 'restorative justice', or:

> a means by which all peoples—particularly those who are mainly responsible for causing climate change and with the capacity to correct it—can honour their historical and current responsibilities, as part of a common effort to address a common cause. Ultimately, the compensation of climate debt is about keeping all of us safe.[52]

This is an internationalist and eco-socialist updating of 'from each according to their ability, to each according to their needs', and a material and working-class demand: what do oppressed people want and need more than to be safe, at home and in life generally? The five key

---

[48]   World People's Conference on Climate Change and the Rights of Mother Earth, 'Call' (15 January 2010), https://pwccc.wordpress.com/2010/01/15/call/ accessed 7 April 2021.

[49]   United Nations Framework Convention on Climate Change, entered into force 21 March 1994, 1771 UNTS 107, 166 ('UNFCC').

[50]   UNFCC, 169.

[51]   UNFCC, 189.

[52]   World People's Conference on Climate Change and the Rights of Mother Earth, 'Final Conclusions Working Group 8: Climate Debt' (30 April 2010), https://pwccc.wordpress.com/2010/04/30/final-conclusions-working-group-n°-8-climate-debt/ accessed 7 April 2021.

demands were, first, the Olympian task of returning 'occupied' atmospheric space—that is, to 'decolonise' the atmosphere by reducing and removing emissions, to allot atmospheric space fairly, and to account for dual and potentially duelling needs for 'development space and equilibrium with Mother Earth'. The second demand was to honour debts that reflect lost development opportunities, since the cheap development paths blazed by the wealthy countries to build up their infrastructures cannot be walked again by poor countries. The third was to honour debts related to the destruction caused by climate change, including lifting migration restrictions. The fourth was to honour 'adaptation debts', the costs of providing people with the resources to stay at home and have decent lives within their own countries. The fifth and final demand was to repudiate all efforts to segregate the climate crisis from the broader ecological crisis, and to honour adaptation and climate debts as a promissory note on the 'broader ecological debt to Mother Earth'.[53]

The history of battles over debt at climate change-related conferences is the history of battles over the poor's right to the future. In Bolivia, the radical leadership of Evo Morales and Álvaro García Linera was deposed by a US-backed coup. (Their party has since returned to power in a brilliant display of popular organisation.) That coup was preceded and made possible by a discourse of their ecological mismanagement, a mixture of outright falsehoods and quarter truths about the burning Amazon. Indeed, on a world scale, Bolivia's environmental programs are not damaging but dazzling. Part of Bolivia's contributions to the fight for humanity's future was a call for significantly larger transfers of technology and financial resources than have traditionally been considered. Their proposals were designed to curb emissions in developing countries while realising their right to development.[54]

A Swedish social scientist, Rikard Warlenius, has taken the Cochabamba positions as the basis for quantifying the climate debt. He argues that if space in the atmosphere had been calculated fairly, on the basis of how much CO_2 could have been safely emitted and absorbed by sinks, 'the North' (or Annex I countries) would only have emitted 15 per cent of what it actually has emitted. 'The South', by contrast, could have emitted more carbon dioxide than they have so far emitted, but not a lot: only about 4.4 per cent more in total. In numerical terms, as of 2008, the North had over-emitted 746.5 $GtCO_2$ (gigatons of carbon dioxide).[55] As of 2008, at a carbon price of $50 per ton of CO_2 the value of the historical carbon debt would have been around $37.325 trillion. The Intergovernmental Panel on Climate Change estimates that a carbon price of between $150 and $600 is required to keep global warming below 1.5°. Those numbers would increase the size of the debt owed to the South enormously—to $111.975 trillion, at the low end, or to $447.9 trillion, at the high end.[56] More concretely, Bolivia has demanded '[p]rovision of financial resources by developed countries to developing countries amounting to at least 6% of the value of GNP of developed countries, for adaptation, technology transfer, capacity building and mitigation'.[57] The GNP of the United

[53]   'Final Conclusions Working Group 8'.

[54]   Republic of Bolivia, 'Commitments for Annex I Parties under Paragraph 1(b)(i) of the Bali Action Plan'.

[55]   Rikard Warlenius, 'Decolonizing the Atmosphere: The Climate Justice Movement on Climate Debt' (2018) 27 *Journal of Environment & Development* 131.

[56]   IPCC, 'Global Warming of 1.5 °C', 80–81.

[57]   Republic of Bolivia, 'Submission by the Plurinational State of Bolivia to the Ad-Hoc Working Group on Long-Term Coooperative Action', 8, https://unfccc.int/files/meetings/ad_hoc_working _groups/lca/application/pdf/bolivia_awglca10.pdf accessed 7 April 2021.

States in 2019 was $21.584 trillion, 6 per cent of which is $1.29 trillion. In that same year, the GNP of the entire OECD, comprising the bulk of Annex 1 countries, was about $54 trillion, 6 per cent of which is $3.24 trillion per year.

Two facets of those bogglingly huge numbers are especially important. First, they indicate that as of 2008, the former Third World taken as a collective, including the mammoth China, had clean hands when it came to the climate crisis (although China's continued emissions since then slightly change the picture). It had not emitted CO_2 beyond its fair share of the environment's absorption capacity. Hence, the climate crisis until that point was the child of Northern imperialism, pure and simple. Second, 6 per cent of GNP per year far exceeds annual 'growth' in the industrialised world. Although numerical indicators of growth are messy and map untidily over increases in the amount of physical material usage per unit of GNP, it is clear that considerable quantities of assets, technology, and rights (to timber, water, farmland, wheat, pomegranates, shawls, and transistors, the things for which GNP stands) would pass from North to South under such an arrangement.

The numbers in the Bolivian proposal are staggering—and probably deliberately so. They are compatible neither with capitalism nor with a polarised and highly unequal world-system. They are arithmetic proof of the need for worldwide ecological and socialist revolution, including in North-South relations. For that reason, climate debt has been described as a 'bomb'.[58] The violence of the metaphor is appropriate because it is very hard to imagine a world-system based on polarisation between the South and the North enduring amidst massive debt payments going from North to South.

And because these numbers cannot be argued with or dismissed, the North has generally ignored them, or tried to muffle and stifle them through the most effective way possible, a *coup d'état*. If the South has no strong and sovereign states, but merely neo-colonies, climate debt loses some of its most powerful champions and social agents.

DEMILITARISATION AND A PEACETIME ECONOMY

For any serious response to the climate crisis, a key arena of structural transformation in the North is the removal of the US military from its role as a global police force and the United States' concomitant conversion into a peacetime economy. That shift must be part and parcel of the augmentation of Southern sovereignty, the furtherance of decolonisation, and widespread acceptance of the need to take climate debt seriously. Such struggles are interwoven, composing the social and political fabric of profoundly systemic changes.

Aside from the fact that the US military is a means of constraining the sovereign power of Southern states, it is a tremendous fountain of CO_2 pollution. If the US military were an independent state, it would be the 47th largest polluter in the world, slotted between Peru and Portugal. It produces uncounted quantities of waste the world over: heavy metals and pollution in waterways and grasslands. Jet fuel contaminates drinking water. Military bases are frequently Superfund sites—locations polluted so thoroughly that they require a long-term process of cleaning up hazardous materials. White phosphorus and depleted uranium are left behind by US weaponry in Fallujah, Raqqa, and the Gaza Strip, with a dark bloom of birth

---

58   Warlenius, 'Decolonizing the Atmosphere', 151.

defects. The Grants Mineral Belt in New Mexico remains one of the best endowed uranium deposits anywhere, providing the raw material for the world-killing weapons. The mining takes place close to homes and communities of the Diné people, and those who have laboured in the industry include Diné, Acoma, Laguna, Zuni, and Hispanic peoples, forcing upon them the social and ecological costs of US colonial-capitalist domination.[59]

It is urgent that the US military be eliminated as a major producer of waste, and it is crucial to retool the labour it employs and the industrial plants it keeps occupied into socially useful goods, like solar panels and wind turbines and high-speed trains. This demand connects to the time scale of change. We ought to oppose technocratic or 'pragmatic' time scales, since they tend to rest on economistic habits of thought and political practice. If far too much CO_2 has already been spilled into the atmosphere—and there has been, needless to say, far too much death at the hands of imperialism and capitalism—then the Pentagon system of global security must be eliminated immediately. The Pentagon produces not merely physical waste, but the waste of destroyed human lives. This churn of waste is the flipside of accumulation on a world scale. Furthermore, much of US industrial capacity should be devoted to producing clean technology for global systems change. As a fundamental demand of the climate justice movement, the Pentagon system and its sprawling manufacturing nodes ought to be converted to clean-tech plants.

In this context, it is worth recalling the appeals to security in Markey/Ocasio-Cortez's 'eco-socialist' GND. Indeed, that GND was virtually silent on the question of the national security state. Similarly, but also dissimilarly, consider Bernie Sanders, who recommended '[s]caling back military spending on maintaining global oil dependence'.[60] In fact, Sanders called more broadly for redirecting the $1.5 trillion in annual global military spending towards a clean fossil fuel infrastructure, but that number was not the basis for policy.[61] Meanwhile, the current Biden administration wallows in national-security appeals: 'regional instability … could make areas more vulnerable to terrorist activities', it warns. The response? 'Invest in the climate resilience of our military bases', which will be needed in case there is a need for 'military response'.[62] The US Green Party's GND has been clearer and firmer, advocating that the Pentagon budget be halved from its current titanic one trillion to a paltry $500 billion.[63] The Indigenous group The Red Nation has been bolder still, declaring that 'capitalism-colonialism on a global level' must be brought to an end, and that this includes 'divestment away from police, prisons, military, and fossil fuels'.[64] These differences matter. They have to do with whether the GND will be a vehicle for green social democracy in the United States, alongside

---

[59] Curley and Lister, 'Already Existing Dystopias', 256.

[60] Cited in Michael Barnard, 'Bernie Sanders' Climate Plan: Excellent On Electrification, But Concerningly Authoritarian & Populist—#Election2020' *CleanTechnica* (28 September 2019), https://cleantechnica.com/2019/09/28/bernie-sanders-climate-plan-excellent-on-electrification-but -concerningly-authoritarian-populist-election2020/ accessed 7 April 2021.

[61] Max Ajl, 'Report Card on Bernie Sanders' Green New Deal' *Uneven Earth* (27 August 2019), http://unevenearth.org/2019/08/report-card-on-bernie-sanders-green-new-deal/ accessed 7 April 2021.

[62] 'The Biden Plan for a Clean Energy Revolution and Environmental Justice', https://joebiden.com/ climate-plan/ accessed 7 April 2021.

[63] US Green Party, 'The Green New Deal'.

[64] The Red Nation, 'The Red Deal: Indigenous Action to Save Our Earth—Part One' (2020) 8, 11 (de-emphasised from original), http://therednation.org/wp-content/uploads/2020/04/Red-Deal_Part -I_End-The-Occupation-1.pdf accessed 7 April 2021.

superficial and largely tokenistic forms of anti-racism and 'decolonisation', or whether it will instead belong to a broader anti-imperialist program, involving the decolonisation of settler states in the Western hemisphere and elsewhere, alongside opposition to imperialism and the Pentagon system.

SOVEREIGNTY

Under colonialism peoples were denied their right to history—their right to control their history and social and economic life, including what to do with the land and its resources.[65] Oftentimes the consequence of this denial of history included 'late Victorian holocausts' and massive wealth drain and colonial famine.[66] People were super-exploited: they were paid wages below those needed for their day-to-day survival and well-being.[67] The anti-colonial struggle, in the words of the outstanding anti-colonial theorist and leader Amílcar Cabral, was the 'national liberation of a people', the 'regaining of the historical personality of that people, it is their return to history through the destruction of the imperialist domination to which they were subjected'.[68] And it did not end with the extirpation of formal colonial rule.

Even in the eyes of those who had led the most brilliant struggles for national liberation, formal decolonisation was only an initial step. Throwing off the shackles of direct colonialism shifted the political apparatus, but it often left the economic apparatus under the control of the 'former' colonial power.[69] Across the South, many understood that independent development—*al-tanmiya al-mustaqila*, as it was known in the Arab region—was the logical continuation of breaking the colonial apparatus.[70] Struggles over the contours and shape of development stepped into the space previously occupied by calls for liberation.[71]

The world counter-revolution soon unfurled from the imperial core to the Third World and the heartlands of actually existing communism. It dispelled dreams of development, most of which imagined, as had Bandung-style projects, a non-aligned third way for the Third World, one involving national capitalist development within, against, and beyond the

---

[65]   Cabral, *Unity and Struggle*.

[66]   Utsa Patnaik, 'Revisiting the "Drain", or Transfers from India to Britain in the Context of Global Diffusion of Capitalism' in Shubhra Chakrabarti and Utsa Patnaik (eds), *Agrarian and Other Histories: Essays for Binay Bhushan Chaudhuri* (Tulika Books 2017) 277; Utsa Patnaik, 'Profit Inflation, Keynes and the Holocaust in Bengal, 1943–44' (2018) 53 *Economic & Political Weekly* 33; Alec Gordon, 'A Last Word: Amendments and Corrections to Indonesia's Colonial Surplus 1880–1939' (2018) 48 *Journal of Contemporary Asia* 508; Mike Davis, *Late Victorian Holocausts: El Niño Famines and the Making of the Third World* (Verso 2002).

[67]   Ruy Mauro Marini, *Subdesarrollo y Revolución* (Siglo Veintiuno Editores 1969).

[68]   Cabral, *Unity and Struggle*, 130.

[69]   Max Ajl, 'Farmers, Fellaga, and Frenchmen' (PhD dissertation, Cornell University 2019); Sam Moyo, *The Land Question in Zimbabwe* (Sapes Books 1995); Sam Moyo, 'Three Decades of Agrarian Reform in Zimbabwe' (2011) 38 *Journal of Peasant Studies* 493.

[70]   Ajl, 'The Arab Nation'; Ismail-Sabri Abdallah, 'Al-tanmīyya al-mustaqila: muḥāwala litaḥdīd mafhūm mujahal' [Independent Development: An Attempt to Define an Unknown Concept] in Nader Fergany (ed), *Al-tanmīyya al-mustaqila fi al-waṭan al-ʿarabī* [*Independent Development in the Arab Nation*] (Center for Arab Unity Studies 1987) 25.

[71]   Frantz Fanon, *The Wretched of the Earth* (first published 1963, Richard Philcox tr, Grove Press 2004).

world-system.[72] As it happened, wars, invasions, hot capital flows, financialisation, and coups burnt such hopes to ash. The heat of US global counter-insurgency warped even the steeliest nationalist-communist projects, setting some on the way to 'market reform' and 'market socialism', inciting full-bore Thermidor in others.[73] These national liberation struggles and non-aligned socialists were, for the most part, far too radical for the imperialists and not radical enough to ride out the imperialist storm (the lodestar of Cuba, the most ecologically advanced state on the planet, has been exceptional in its resilience).[74]

Slowly, imperialists undid these governments, through the financial hook of neoliberal reforms and structural adjustment or the violent crook of war, coup, siege, or sanctions.[75] They rejected their right to set their political and economic paths, to choose their alliances and friends, to weigh in on colonialism elsewhere on the globe, to carry out redistributive reforms, and to recover the land that had been seized by settlers. As the 1990s dawned, rights to protect and intervene, responsibilities to protect, and the rest of the cant of imperialism had become the dominant chatter of a new 'civilising mission'.[76] In the dawn and dusk of the 2010s, ecological mismanagement and accusations of extractivism soften up Western public opinion for the twenty-first century's gunboat diplomacy and *coup d'états*.[77] By the dawning of the third decade of the third millennium, there is very little substantive concern for the right to self-determination or sovereignty in large swathes of Western public opinion. Of course, few say as much openly. Such rights are formally accepted. But the notion that the United States and European Union must be prevented from violating those rights is scarcely present in Western political life.

A major element of this new imperialist consensus is the political organisation of extraction from nature: green accumulation, environmental service commodification, monocrop tree plantations, and biofuels.[78] This occurs by gutting states and reconfiguring their internal structures in order to turn them into conveyor belts for Northern capitalist interests, narrowing 'the scope for a green developmental state that could design a just transition to low-carbon

---

[72]   Max Ajl, 'The Hidden Legacy of Samir Amin: Delinking's Ecological Foundation' (2021) 48 *Review of African Political Economy* 82; Samir Amin, *Delinking: Towards a Polycentric World* (Zed Books 1990).

[73]   Max Ajl, 'The Political Economy of Thermidor in Syria: National and International Dimensions' in Linda Matar and Ali Kadri (eds), *Syria: From National Independence to Proxy War* (Springer 2019) 209; Linda Matar, *The Political Economy of Investment in Syria* (Palgrave Macmillan 2016); Matteo Capasso, 'The War and the Economy: The Gradual Destruction of Libya' (2020) 47 *Review of African Political Economy* 545.

[74]   Helen Yaffe, *We Are Cuba!: How a Revolutionary People Have Survived in a Post-Soviet World* (Yale University Press 2020).

[75]   Peter Gowan, *The Global Gamble: Washington's Faustian Bid for World Dominance* (Verso 1999).

[76]   Diana Johnstone, *Fools' Crusade: Yugoslavia, Nato, and Western Delusions* (Monthly Review Press 2002); Edward S Herman, David Peterson, and Noam Chomsky, *The Politics of Genocide* (Monthly Review Press 2010).

[77]   Federico Fuentes, 'Bolivia: NGOs Wrong on Morales and Amazon' *Green Left* (24 September 2011), https://www.greenleft.org.au/content/bolivia-ngos-wrong-morales-and-amazon accessed 7 April 2021.

[78]   Archana Prasad, 'Ecological Crisis, Global Capital and the Reinvention of Nature' in Praveen Jha, Paris Yeros, and Walter Chambati (eds), *Rethinking the Social Sciences with Sam Moyo* (Tulika Books 2020).

economies'.[79] When Southern states need to compensate foreign investors when they exercise their sovereignty through acts of nationalisation or heavy taxation, their sovereignty is to an important degree diminished. It is turned into faded words on tattered paper, as its substance returns to the monopolies and the Northern states with which they are intertwined.

The struggle against such institutions requires overlapping and complementary South-North struggles to open political space for—and prevent reprisals against—Southern states which institute humane wages, nationalise production processes, widen the scope of national control over productive forces, and ensure that popular classes are able to exercise such control through increased social power. Sovereignty must be strengthened because states are necessary vehicles for popular interests in our current historical moment. This is especially the case when it comes to the climate, not least because legal treaties and other instruments take the state to be central. States cannot demand, let alone receive, climate reparations unless they act collectively on the world stage. From the perspective of the South, this means national-popular environmentalism of the poor and eco-socialism. From that of the North, it means acknowledging that this must be the case, and struggling against violations of sovereignty and self-determination in the South. It is not meaningful to discuss debt payments without respecting the sovereignty of the states to which those debts are owed.[80]

SETTLER COLONIALISM

Sovereignty connects to a different national question: settler colonisation and decolonisation within the First World, and the breaking of the social order in the settler colonies of the Third World. Such demands concern first and foremost land and the environment, the two very tightly bound, since land alienation through settler colonialism has had direct and profound environmental effects. As a political process, Kyle Powys Whyte argues, '[s]ettler colonialism can be interpreted as a form of *environmental injustice* that wrongfully interferes with and erases the socioecological contexts required for indigenous populations to experience the world as a place infused with responsibilities to humans, nonhumans and ecosystems'.[81] Anti-colonial struggle for control of the land is, then, a pathway to world-wide environmental restoration.

And in other settler states or politically decolonised settler states, national demands concern land first of all. In Zimbabwe, for instance, there unfolded the most radical post-Cold War agrarian reforms, eliciting a 'cold' campaign of demonisation, isolation, and arguably rollback.[82] In South Africa, agrarian reform is on the table, and is a vibrant political demand

---

[79]   Gabor, 'The Wall Street Consensus', 1.

[80]   Batul Suleiman, 'al-wahidat al-sha'biyya «al-muslaha»... waraqa al-yasar «alrabiha» fi amrika al-latiniyya' *Al-Akhbar* (8 February 2020), https://al-akhbar.com/World/284364 accessed 7 April 2021. I thank Patrick Higgins for bringing this article to my attention.

[81]   Kyle Powys Whyte, 'Indigenous Experience, Environmental Justice and Settler Colonialism', https://papers.ssrn.com/abstract=2770058 accessed 7 April 2021 (original emphasis).

[82]   Freedom Mazwi and George T Mudimu, 'Why Are Zimbabwe's Land Reforms Being Reversed?' (2019) 54 *Economic & Political Weekly*, https://www.epw.in/engage/article/why-are-zimbabwes-land -reforms-being-reversed accessed 7 April 2021; Sam Moyo and Paris Yeros, 'Intervention: The Zimbabwe Question and the Two Lefts' (2007) 15 *Historical Materialism* 171.

in cities, slums, and countryside alike.[83] In the North American settler states, Indigenous struggles at Standing Rock and by way of Idle No More have been catalysts for the growth of a much broader consciousness of the national question among non-Indigenous radicals.[84]

It has been among many Indigenous peoples that rights to access and use of the environment are intertwined most closely with rights to land and consequently the 'land back' call. The Anchorage Declaration, which assembled Indigenous representatives from around the world, called for states to 'recognize, respect and implement the fundamental human rights of Indigenous Peoples, including the collective rights to traditional ownership, use, access, occupancy and title to traditional lands, air, forests, waters, oceans, sea ice and sacred sites'.[85] The Anchorage Declaration calls for restitution to 'return and restore lands, territories, waters', as well as 'sacred sites that have been taken from Indigenous Peoples'.[86] To call upon a state to do something demands that decolonisation be a banner for action, including struggle from peoples living in settler-colonial states and demanding that their governments restore land and treaty rights. And since land is the relationship underlying settler-colonial state formation, a relationship created by colonial primitive accumulation, restitution implies revolutionary change in world property structures. Similarly, the International Indigenous Peoples Forum on Climate Change connects such calls to its criticism of Reduce Emissions from Deforestation and Forest Degradation (REDD) and other carbon-offsetting 'Clean Development Mechanism' projects, noting that 'land and resource rights' of Indigenous peoples need to be respected before any consideration of REDD or REDD+ carbon compensation.[87] That is, they recognise that Indigenous peoples need to be able to determine the political paths to decide how to structure their internal socio-ecologies. Along kindred lines, The Red Nation demands that:

> treaty rights and Indigenous rights be applied and upheld both on- and off-reservation and federal trust land. All of North America, the Western Hemisphere, and the Pacific is Indigenous land. Our rights do not begin or end at imposed imperial borders we did not create nor give our consent to.[88]

Furthermore, The Red Nation explicitly draws connections between politics and environmental management, highlighting how national self-determination is elemental and prior to acting ethically as a custodian of nature: 'We must first be afforded dignified lives as Native peoples who are free to perform our purpose as stewards of life if we are to protect and respect our nonhuman relatives—the land, the water, the air, the plants, and the animals.'[89]

---

[83]   Ricardo Jacobs, 'An Urban Proletariat with Peasant Characteristics: Land Occupations and Livestock Raising in South Africa' (2018) 45 *Journal of Peasant Studies* 884.

[84]   Nick Estes, *Our History Is the Future: Standing Rock Versus the Dakota Access Pipeline, and the Long Tradition of Indigenous Resistance* (Verso 2019); Roxanne Dunbar-Ortiz, *An Indigenous Peoples' History of the United States* (Beacon Press 2014).

[85]   Indigenous Peoples' Global Summit on Climate Change, 'The Anchorage Declaration' (24 April 2009), http://unfccc.int/resource/docs/2009/smsn/ngo/168.pdf accessed 7 April 2021.

[86]   'Anchorage Declaration'.

[87]   International Indigenous Peoples Forum on Climate Change, 'Policy Proposals on Climate Change' (27 September 2009), https://www.forestpeoples.org/sites/default/files/publication/2010/08/iipfccpolicysept09eng.pdf accessed 7 April 2021.

[88]   The Red Nation, 'The Red Deal: Indigenous Action to Save Our Earth—Part Three' (2020) 4 (de-emphasised from original), http://therednation.org/wp-content/uploads/2020/04/Red-Deal_Part-III_Heal-Our-Planet.pdf accessed 7 April 2021.

[89]   Red Nation, 'The Red Deal: Indigenous Action to Save Our Earth—Part Three', 8.

DECOLONISATION AND SAFEGUARDING NATURE

In an under-remarked bit of historical poetic justice, biodiversity flourishes to the greatest degree in those parts of the planet inhabited by Indigenous peoples. Rather than the idea that we should protect species by surrounding them with political or legal walls or placing them on preserves only accessible to the monied, non-human nature can be lived in and among.

Globally, Indigenous lands enjoy levels of biodiversity equal to or higher than even many 'protected areas'.[90] As the ecologist Victor Toledo points out, 12 countries—Australia, Brazil, China, Colombia, Ecuador, India, Indonesia, Madagascar, Mexico, Peru, Philippines, and Venezuela—have the highest number of endemic species, including mammals, birds, reptiles, amphibians, freshwater fishes, butterflies, tiger beetles, and flowering plants. Of those 12 countries, nine are on the list of 25 nations with the greatest number of endemic languages. Of the 233 marine, freshwater, and terrestrial bioregions with the greatest diversity of habitats and species, Indigenous peoples live in 136; half the world's 3000 Indigenous groups live in these eco-regions.[91] More recent work on Australia, Brazil, and Canada, three countries that continue to carry out genocide against Indigenous peoples, demonstrates that biodiversity—from grizzly bears to kangaroos, frogs to songbirds—is richest in Indigenous-managed lands.[92]

Protecting and respecting land treaty rights—the 'land back' claim—is the quick route to safeguarding the future. This is not due to some primordial or timeless capacity of Indigenous peoples to live in nature peacefully and harmoniously. It is because Indigenous peoples are often engaged in primary production in the general sense. They have cosmologies based on a humane relationship to the land, and they carry out forms of production, from hunting to husbandry to horticulture, based on ancestral knowledge about how to live in, on, and with the land. They also know how to work with and gently remould ecological cycles, rather than wrenching them through genetic tinkering or chemical saturation.[93] This does not mean that primary production should be the eternal lot of Indigenous peoples. As with all other peoples, Indigenous peoples have rights of sovereignty, and that includes the right to under-take industrialisation or select another path of their choosing. It does, however, mean that Indigenous land-management is generally superior to settler land-management. Defence of Indigenous treaty rights, and the restoration or restitution of land, creates a safer world for all of humanity.[94] In western Canada, for example, the members of the West Moberly and Saulteau First Nations are working to restore the caribou, a lesson in the merits of Indigenous landscape-management and biodiversity-conservation.[95]

---

[90]   Richard Schuster et al, 'Vertebrate Biodiversity on Indigenous-Managed Lands in Australia, Brazil, and Canada Equals That in Protected Areas' (2019) 101 *Environmental Science & Policy* 1.

[91]   Víctor Toledo, 'Indigenous Peoples and Biodiversity' in Simon Avner Levin (ed), *Encyclopedia of Biodiversity*, vol 3 (Academic Press 2001) 451.

[92]   Schuster et al, 'Vertebrate Biodiversity'.

[93]   Toledo, 'Indigenous Peoples and Biodiversity'.

[94]   Monica Evans, 'Respect for Indigenous Land Rights Key in Fight against Climate Change' *CIFOR Forests News* (25 September 2020), https://forestsnews.cifor.org/67515/respect-for-indigenous-land -rights-key-in-fight-against-climate-change?fnl=en accessed 7 April 2021.

[95]   David Moskowitz, 'Saving Caribou and Preserving Food Traditions Among Canada's First Nations' Civil Eats (29 October 2020), https://civileats.com/2020/10/29/saving-caribou-and-preserving -food-traditions-among-canadas-first-nations/ accessed 7 April 2021.

In a bit of historical justice, I write these words as apocalyptic wildfires have dyed the skies of the US west coast a hazy orange. Indigenous techniques of land-management included controlled burns based on a holistic method of living in nature, rather than above or in control of it. Indigenous peoples used fire to maintain 'basketry materials, medicinal plants, acorn trees and hunting grounds', says Elizabeth Azzuz, a member of the Yurok Tribe.[96] Before the settler invasion, large and frequent burns immolated fuel, which ensured that unintentional fires spread slowly, having no fuel on which to feed. The settler-capitalist invasion banned burning and built monoculture timber plantations in lieu of a tapestry of grasslands and agro-forestry. In northwestern California's Klamath Basin, members of the Karuk and Yurok tribes have continued to carry out controlled burns, retaining their knowledge of fire science and transmitting that knowledge between generations. Jackie Fielder, a candidate for the California State Senate and an Indigenous socialist, recently praised the Karuk efforts.[97] A new revolutionary land-tenure regime, decolonisation, and swift changes in land-management practices drawing on Indigenous technical knowledge could avoid the next conflagration. 'Land back' is neither surrender nor sacrifice, but the shift which makes the world big enough for all of us.

CONCLUSION

Recent years have seen an explosion in debates about shifting the human relationship with the environment. The idea of a GND has occupied the greatest attention. But it has emerged alongside an array of other plans. Many are significantly more radical, but there are also conservative plans for financialising nature, dispossessing smallholders and pastoralists, and building a new and more ecologically sustainable world-system (that is just as hierarchical as the present one, if not more so). This chapter has considered the necessary elements for a green anti-imperialism and a green strategy for South-North convergence. First is the foundational question of politics: peoples controlling their own fate. Second is the matter of making good on colonial and neocolonial debts, depredations, enclosures, and dispossessions: the ecological debt and specifically the climate debt. Third is the specific role of Indigenous peoples in biodiversity management. Fourth is the struggle for demilitarisation. Each of these ambitions is closely related to classical concerns about the national question, including the burden of anti-imperialist transformation and its role in the North. Each is necessary for just transition on a world scale. And each must be on the agenda for a shift to a sustainable and egalitarian world system.

---

[96]   Tony Marks-Block, 'Indigenous Solutions to California's Capitalist Conflagrations' *Monthly Review Online* (23 October 2020), https://mronline.org/2020/10/23/indigenous-solutions-to-californias-capitalist-conflagrations/ accessed 7 April 2021.
[97]   Marks-Block, 'Indigenous Solutions'.

24. Ideology, narrative, and law: 'Operation Car Wash' in Brazil

Enzo Bello, Gustavo Capela, and Rene José Keller

INTRODUCTION

This chapter focuses on 'Operation Car Wash' (OCW), a criminal investigation in Brazil launched in 2014 by the Federal Police and the Federal Public Ministry of Brazil, and headed by the public prosecutor Deltan Martinazzo Dallagnol and the Federal Judge Sergio Fernando Moro. On the surface, OCW could be understood as a judicial operation, since it unfolded within the domain of the judiciary. In this chapter, however, we argue that OCW is better understood as an enterprise, a kind of ideological joint venture, between the legal and mass media apparatuses. We focus on the ideological crisis, a part of the political crisis,[1] in order to expose the actual frailty of any given hegemonic bloc, and to capture the forms by which the divergence and imbalance between the forces that make up a momentary hegemony can lead to attacks from the ideological state apparatuses (ISAs). Our argument is that the OCW episode demonstrates that the state cannot be understood either as a mere instrument of a class or as a subject, but should instead be understood as a fragile, yet powerful, crystallisation of class struggle.

We attempt to grasp the ideological effects of OCW by examining its capacity to construct and build upon existing narratives. We explain how, in the case of OCW, the structural relationship between the judiciary and the press worked on the narrative plane. We examine narrative by undertaking a discussion of form and structure. The methodology we adopt is similar to Althusser's conception of ideology as that which sets the stage or produces the framework for a given life theatre.[2] We analyse OCW through its narrative effect, or the narrative form and function it produces, in an effort to examine what Jameson called the 'ideology of form'.[3] We argue that ideology has a specific structure, producing modes of understanding and engagement. OCW built narratives about Brazilian politics and became an additional vector in the process that led to the general crisis that is ongoing today. We examine the structure of narrativity used and produced by OCW, and we do so by displacing it—that is, by showing its taken-for-granted connections. We do so not so much in the interest of 'dialectically developing' the official narrative offered by the press and judiciary—a narrative that advances their preferred rules, methods, and forms—but to present the official narrative with a different structure, trying to 'destroy this intangible image, to set in motion the immobile'.[4]

---

[1]   Nicos Poulantzas, 'The Political Crisis and the Crisis of the State' [1976] in Nicos Poulantzas, *The Poulantzas Reader* (James Martin ed, Verso 2008) 294, 314.

[2]   Louis Althusser, *For Marx* (first published 1965, Ben Brewster tr, Verso 2005) 151.

[3]   Fredric Jameson, *The Political Unconscious: Narrative as a Socially Symbolic Act* (Cornell University Press 1981).

[4]   Althusser, *For Marx*, 151.

The chapter contextualises OCW, analysing how it transformed from an investigation into money laundering into an ideologically powerful force that simultaneously disorganised and attempted to reorganise the Brazilian state and the hegemonic bloc that ruled it. We examine the images produced through law and the press in order to understand their possible ideological effects, beginning by first explaining how we understand ideology and clarifying why narrative (as a form) is fundamental to understanding law, its intersection with Marxism, and the nature of OCW. From the perspective we adopt here, a law-and-Marxism perspective as it has been developed in Brazil in recent years,[5] we argue that the country has undergone and continues to live through a general crisis. Specifically, we argue that there has been: (a) an intensification of class and related social struggles, and the concomitant politicisation of every element of society (i.e., political crisis); (b) a worldwide reduction in rates of profit, accompanied by a reorganisation of relations of production, the structural difficulties of value valorisation, and, specific to Brazil, a specific conjectural economic crisis since 2014; and, finally, (c) the general consensus, or the 'cement' that unites state apparatuses, has been put into question by repeated scandals, political processes, and a serious ideological crisis.[6] The election of Jair Bolsonaro as president is part of the reorganisation of this hegemonic bloc, itself always an 'unstable equilibrium of compromises'.[7] Given the general crisis, this has propelled different sectors of society to positions of power. Following Marx's analysis of the 1848 Revolution in France,[8] we attempt to understand why in moments like these, when divisions and contradictions are intensified, certain class fractions and their representatives appear as solutions, or at least appeasements, to the continuation of the general logics of capitalist exploitation, domination, and profit.

LAW, IDEOLOGY, AND NARRATIVE

When we think of stories—in movies, literature, or any other cultural product—it hardly seems that they have a fundamental role in exploitation. However, as Althusser argued, in order to comprehend how capitalism is able to maintain structures of exploitation and domination, we must understand the modes of constructing consent, acceptance, and agreement, even more than the repressive forces by which they are imposed.[9] Ideology, then, plays a fundamental

---

[5] See e.g., Márcio Bilharinho Naves, *Em Marxismo e direito: um estudo sobre Pachukanis* (Boitempo 2000); Alysson Mascaro, *Estado e forma política* (Boitempo 2013); Martonio Mont'Alverne Barreto Lima, *Direito e Marxismo: tempos de regresso e a contribuição marxiana para a Teoria Constitucional e Política* (Lumen Juris 2019); Ricardo Prestes Pazello and Moisés Alves Soares, 'Stutchka e as contribuições para a cultura jurídica soviética revolucionária' (2020) 7 *Revista Culturas Jurídicas* 1.

[6] On the economic, political, and ideological crises in capitalism and their connections to the state, see esp. Nicos Poulantzas, *The Poulantzas Reader* (James Martin ed, Verso 2008). For crises in Brazil's contemporary conjuncture see Virgínia Fontes, 'Crise do coronavírus ou crise do capitalismo?' *TV Boitempo* (São Paulo, 3 July 2020), https://www.youtube.com/watch?v=YvwS9oAyhUU accessed 7 April 2021.

[7] Poulantzas, 'The Political Crisis', 309.

[8] Karl Marx, *O 18 de Brumário de Luís Bonaparte* (first published 1852, Nélio Schneider tr, Boitempo 2011) 64.

[9] Louis Althusser, *On the Reproduction of Capitalism: Ideology and Ideological State Apparatuses* (first published 1995, GM Goshgarian tr, Verso 2014) 241.

role in the reproduction of the basic conditions of capitalism. Further, ideologies sometimes function as, with, or by way of stories. Stories do not just tell us something; they do not simply 'pollute' or 'colonise' minds with the images they 'give us'. They are also practiced in the very way people's lives are organised. There is a story-like structure to the way people are made not only to think, but also to live their lives.

Ideology is first and foremost an effect of actual practices of the mode of production from which it emerges. As Althusser puts it, ideology emerges from the 'social classes at grips in the class struggle'.[10] An explicit example is offered by Marx's description of the industrial reserve army, as a function of the necessity of producing surplus value through wage-suppression as well as a mode of disciplining the workforce by reminding it of what must be done in order to be 'integrated' into the system.[11] This is a process through which the logic of economic violence is naturalised by the myth, in Barthes' sense,[12] that people who do not work are outcasts through no fault but their own. The actual unemployment and real-life difficulties, then, serve as elements of a story, one in which repression and violence, both symbolic and material, serve ideological functions.

As Saidiya Hartman explains, the scene of violent acts not only produces familiarity through repetition but also calls upon people, interpellating them as witnesses, as voyeurs in the 'terror of the mundane'.[13] Ideology is precisely this process by which, on the one hand, relations of production, relations of domination, the necessary conditions for the functioning of a given social formation, are taken for granted, are naturalised; and, on the other hand, people are called upon to witness, to view the world as it is, and to enjoy it, relish it, agree with it. Otherwise disagreeing with the Althusserian notion of ideology, Paul Ricoeur argues that the 'real surplus value' is the excessive demand for this reckoning—for the agreement with, and belief in, the theatre that is the exercise of power in the relation of domination.[14]

This demand, this call by the ideological process to recognise oneself, is part of Althusser's best-known and (for us) most important thesis. For Althusser, ideology interpellates, hails, calls upon concrete individuals as subjects.[15] Interpellation is what calls us to recognise ourselves as part of a given world, in which we hold a specific place and willingly, in the exercise of our freedom, accept things 'the way they are'. This notion of a subject constituted by processes, by a call, and not as substance, as a fixed existence prior to history, is an attempt to move away from Hegel,[16] from the logic that ultimately signals nothing but the actualisation and return to a single, higher, all-empowered subject: God, duty, justice, or some other higher organising principle.[17] For Althusser, subjects are constituted by the history of class struggle,

---

[10]   Louis Althusser, *Lenin and Philosophy, and Other Essays* (first published 1971, Ben Brewster tr, Monthly Review Press 2001) 126.

[11]   Karl Marx, *O Capital*, vol 1 (first published 1867, Rubens Enderle tr, Boitempo 2013) 707.

[12]   Roland Barthes, *Mythologies* (first published 1957, Richard Howard and Annette Lavers tr, Hill and Wang 2012) 250.

[13]   Saidiya V Hartman, *Scenes of Subjection: Terror, Slavery, and Self-Making in Nineteenth-Century America* (OUP 1997) 4, 6.

[14]   Paul Ricoeur, *Hermeneutics and the Human Sciences: Essays on Language, Action and Interpretation* (John B Thompson ed and tr, CUP 1981).

[15]   Althusser, *On the Reproduction of Capitalism*, 188.

[16]   Georg Wilhelm Friedrich Hegel, *The Logic of Hegel, Translated from the Encyclopaedia of the Philosophical Sciences* (first published 1817, William Wallace tr, OUP 1892).

[17]   Althusser, *On the Reproduction of Capitalism*, 196.

by ideological processes, and therefore move within it, not outside it. Ideology constitutes roles and social functions, and recruits people to fill them by reminding them of their duty, their responsibility or 'need to work in order to survive'.[18]

There are multiple examples that demonstrate interpellation as a phenomenon which constitutes 'subjects', be they in the form of ethnic groups,[19] professional classes,[20] or, in Frantz Fanon's sense, the racialised subject itself.[21] As Fanon puts it, '[b]eneath the body schema I had created a historical-racial schema. The data I used were provided not by "remnants of feelings and notions of the tactile, vestibular, kinesthetic, or visual nature" but by the Other, the white man, who had woven me out of a thousand details, anecdotes, and stories.'[22] Importantly, we can also apply Althusser's theses to the Brazilian judiciary, in order to understand how the interpellation of people as individualised and individuated subjects functions, and, in turn, how it propagates ideology.

Much has already been written about the marks and labels that are attached to persons and that constitute them as specific types of people—as specific subjects of law and capitalism.[23] These people are, thus, interpellated as criminals. But there are other effects as well. Perhaps most clearly, the signifier 'criminal' goes beyond the person who commits the crime. It is a signifier that utilises the body and specific characteristics of specific people, themselves already marked and classified according to other social processes, as Stuart Hall argues,[24] in order to reaffirm prevailing social norms and feed 'moral panics' that justify criminal persecution.[25] Much like the commodity, whose value is only determined through its relations with other commodities,[26] the image of a criminal needs a body, an embodied image, to reveal itself and gain social value. The judicial process produces such images that feed off already existing social realities and characterisations—the fruit of social processes such as racialisation—and also fix and instantiate others. It functions through and with interpellation.

Likewise, judges are also interpellated subjects. However much they manifest state and capitalist power, they are themselves constituted by such power. They are transmitters and reinforcers of such power, not its ultimate sources of origin. Ideology constitutes subjects insofar as it develops, moulds, and attaches social imagery to people, who are then called upon

---

[18]   Louis Althusser, *Essays in Self-Criticism* (first published 1974, Grahame Lock tr, New Left Books 1976) 94.

[19]   Jean-François Bayart, *The State in Africa: The Politics of the Belly* (2nd edn, Mary Harper et al tr, Polity Press 2009).

[20]   Silvio Luiz de Almeida, *Racismo estrutural* (Pólen Livros 2019).

[21]   Importantly, here, we do not mean that 'race' is the product of ideological processes. As convincingly shown by scholars such as Denise Ferreira da Silva, 'race' is a constitutive part of the apparatuses of knowledge that attempt to make sense of the world. It is thus a product of science just as much as it is a product of history. Our point is that processes such as racialisation then serve as points of articulation for interpellation of the subject as racial subject. Denise Ferreira da Silva, *Toward a Global Idea of Race* (University of Minnesota Press 2007)

[22]   Frantz Fanon, *Black Skin, White Masks* (first published 1952, Richard Philcox tr, Grove Press 2008) 91.

[23]   See e.g., Erving Goffman, *Stigma: Notes on the Management of Spoiled Identity* (Simon & Schuster 2009); Howard S Becker, *Outsiders: estudos de sociologia do desvio* (J Zahar 2009).

[24]   Stuart Hall, *The Fateful Triangle: Race, Ethnicity, Nation* (Harvard University Press 2017) 46.

[25]   Stuart Hall et al, *Policing the Crisis: Mugging, the State, and Law and Order* (2nd edn, Macmillan 2013) 219.

[26]   Marx, *O Capital*, vol 1, 134–35.

to confirm what is expected. A judge is a judge because they are formed—produced, really— through years of education, both formal and informal, by selection processes and interpersonal relations, all of which ensure that they are in a position to speak authoritatively as a judge. The judge is spoken to as a judge, and spoken for as a judge, through ideological processes. A subject, after all, is spoken of, and spoken to, before they ever speak.[27] When called upon to manifest themselves as a judge, they respond as such. They are interpellated, called upon, as a judge and not by, say, their proper name, because the interpellation demands a certain mode of response.

Whether they are understood as social roles, transmitters, or interpellated subjects, judges enjoy no more than relative autonomy. This does not mean that they only do as they are told, or that they have no real possibility to 'act as they please'. In fact, ethnographic studies of judges in Brazil indicate that many judges usually choose what they want to do before considering any relevant law, literally 'doing as they please'.[28] Nevertheless, our argument is that their acts and autonomy are still relative, since they are themselves—as people and as judges—products of other, more complex social processes.

When we speak of narrativity and its attachment to ideology, then, it is to make evident the fact that although reality as such exists, people's meaningful representations, their theories and conceptions, are based not only upon images that are continuously constructed by social processes but also upon an explanatory cloak that attempts to integrate and render intelligible the contingent aspects of life in a string of determinations.[29] This explanatory cloak, this narrative, is the effect of processes such as OCW, in which the images, connections, and information developed make themselves present in everyday life through a mass media apparatus, which offers a vocabulary enveloped in the commodity news form and thus sets the terms in which people discuss what is deemed to be 'everyday life'.[30] In the capitalist mode of production, relations of production are also relations of exploitation, making the stories that are told, that are produced, that are the effects of these relations, stories that give us meaning and make readable, or understandable, actual exploitation as if it were 'just the way things are'.

The narratives and images that are constructed should not be understood as false per se. Rather, they should be understood as painting a picture, one that presents a perspective on society which is meant to delimit how we can understand it. Ideology as a narrative, a material narrative, offers closure, in the sense of establishing limits and boundaries on what 'counts', and even on what is 'real'.[31] The idea that people need to take care of their 'real' lives instead of struggling politically, for example, plays on that sense. The 'real' here means 'working to pay bills', 'studying to get a diploma', or everything that 'counts' in 'reality'. Ideology is not—and should not be understood as—a product of an explicit conspiracy between the classes, organisations, and institutions that dominate the contemporary global order, but as an effect of existing relations of power in and through which struggle offers people a view of how things 'really are'.

---

[27]   Michel Pêcheux, *Language, Semantics and Ideology: Stating the Obvious* (first published 1975, Harbas Nagpal tr, Macmillan 1982) 106.
[28]   Eduardo Cravo Junior, *Ser humano ou ser juiz: etnografia da persuasão racional* (2011), https:// repositorio.unb.br/bitstream/10482/11092/1/2011_EduardoCravoJunior.pdf accessed 7 April 2021.
[29]   Althusser, *On the Reproduction of Capitalism*, 198.
[30]   Hall et al, *Policing the Crisis*, 64.
[31]   Hall et al, *Policing the Crisis*, 67.

THE CARWASH OPERATION

The importance of Marx for understanding concrete developments like OCW can be approached through what Althusser regards as his 'theory of history',[32] or what Jameson calls its 'narrative capacity'.[33] Marx's theory, which Althusser and others hold to be a 'scientific theory of history',[34] seeks to understand social formations in their complex totality. In order to understand law, for example, one must consider the social relations that both determine it and are in turn determined by it. As a 'level' of a social formation that is 'structured in dominance',[35] law has its own (relative) autonomy. Law's relatively autonomous sphere is determined not only by its structural relationship to the base but also by its relation to processes of class struggle. Dialectics, then, as movement, as the 'soul of all knowledge which is truly scientific', as a theoretical engagement that understands that 'wherever there is life, wherever anything is carried into effect in the actual world, there Dialectic is at work',[36] pushes us to think about processes instead of just the crystallised effects they eventually produce. Although Althusser criticises the use of Hegelian dialectics by Marxists,[37] he does not do so because he is opposed to the idea of movement, or the logic of a process that is ever producing variation. On the contrary, Althusser's point is that the 'whole', the social totality, as understood by Marx, involved multiple levels, structures, and even temporalities that were changing continuously, but that were still held together by a specific mode of production.[38] In order to understand OCW, therefore, we first offer a glimpse into some of the processes that led to it, produced it, or shaped it in some way or another. This then enables us to explain it more fully.

The Context that Produces the Carwash Operation

When we speak of the contexts and processes into which OCW inserts itself, we understand them to be the product of concrete, real history, in Althusser's sense, but also as forces which conjoin facts and events in order to enact a discourse that is attuned to structures of power. There are multiple contexts and processes from which one can select, but we will present synthetically some that we consider indispensable to understand OCW, given that they shape the historical and conjunctural elements that conditioned its possibility in the first place. First among these processes is Brazil's colonial history. On the one hand, this history influenced, and still influences, Brazil's integration into the global division of labour.[39] On the other, it connects Brazil's current institutions to the legacy of slavery. Latin American—and, more

---

[32] Louis Althusser et al, *Reading* Capital: *The Complete Edition* (first published 1965, Ben Brewster and David Fernbach trs, Verso 2015) 267.

[33] Jameson, *The Political Unconscious.*

[34] Althusser et al, *Reading* Capital, 359.

[35] Nicos Poulantzas, 'Towards a Marxist Theory' [1966] Poulantzas, *The Poulantzas Reader*, 139, 152.

[36] Hegel, *Encyclopedia*, 148.

[37] Althusser, *For Marx*, 99.

[38] Althusser et al, *Reading* Capital, 240; Karl Marx, 'A Contribution to the Critique of Political Economy' [1859] in Karl Marx and Frederick Engels, *Collected Works*, vol 29 (Lawrence & Wishart 1987) 257.

[39] Florestan Fernandes, *Capitalismo dependente e classes sociais na América Latina* (2nd edn, Zahar 1975).

specifically, Brazilian—social scientists have emphasised the persistence of this legacy in the 'structural racism' that pervades the Brazilian social formation.[40] One indication of such structural racism is the fact that 65 per cent of Brazil's incarcerated population is currently 'coloured'.[41] A recent study has also suggested that OCW itself reproduced familial and colonial logics in its judicial practices and ideological narratives.[42]

Another important aspect of Brazil's history is that it has had two dictatorships and today lives with some of the by-products of these dictatorships: the military police, special courts, and treatment for military personnel, and the highest rate of police killings in the world.[43] Added to that, OCW rode a wave of legal reform that hardened the rules of the Penal Code and permitted the use of 'lawfare'.[44] Laws such as the Anti-Money Laundering Statute in 1998,[45] and the Criminal Organisations Law from 2013,[46] were instrumental for the OCW investigation. The latter, for example, introduced the 'plea bargain' as a possibility for defendants. Without this possibility, OCW would not have happened as it did. OCW is also part of a larger movement within Brazilian society that started demanding 'moralising action' against corruption specifically caused by the Workers' Party (Partido dos Trabalhadores, or PT) since 2006.

The so-called 'fight against corruption' has historically been a part of Brazilian politics, but its resurgence and attachment to the PT[47] is connected to a largely mediatised and publicly scrutinised political scandal that led to the condemnation and imprisonment of many of the PT top officials.[48] OCW is also embedded in a larger process of an economic crisis dating back to 2008, but that only really hit Brazil in 2014, the year OCW began officially. When the finan-

---

[40]   Aníbal Quijano, 'Colonialidad del Poder y Clasificación Social' (2000) 11 *Journal of World-Systems Research* 342, https://jwsr.pitt.edu/ojs/index.php/jwsr/article/view/228 accessed 7 April 2021; Clóvis Moura, *Sociologia do negro brasileiro* (Ática 1988); Florestan Fernandes, *Capitalismo dependente e classes sociais na América Latina* (2nd edn, Zahar 1975); Sidney Chalhoub, 'The Legacy of Slavery: Tales of Gender and Racial Violence in Machado de Assis' in Lamonte Aidoo and Daniel F Silva (eds), *Emerging Dialogues on Machado de Assis* (Palgrave Macmillan 2016) 55.

[41]   Infopen, *Levantamento nacional de informações penitenciárias* (Ministério da Justiça e Segurança Pública / Departamento Penitenciário Nacional 2017).

[42]   Ricardo Costa de Oliveira, José Monteiro, Mônica Goulart, and Ana Vanali, 'Prosopografia familiar da Operação "Lava-Jato" e do Ministério Temer' (2017) 3 *Revista NEP—Núcleo de Estudos Paranaenses da UFPR* 1, https://revistas.ufpr.br/nep/article/view/55093 accessed 7 April 2021.

[43]   Azam Ahmed, 'Where the Police Wear Masks, and the Bodies Pile Up Fast' *New York Times* (20 December 2019).

[44]   Orde F Kittrie, *Lawfare: Law as Weapon of War* (OUP 2016); Silvina M Romano (ed), *Lawfare: guerra judicial y neoliberalismo en América Latina* (Mármol-Izquierdo 2019).

[45]   Federal Statute n. 9.613/1998.

[46]   Federal Statute n. 12.850/2013.

[47]   As we have argued elsewhere 'this Party (the PT) represented the hope of many Brazilians after the military dictatorship [Brazil was ruled by a US-backed military dictatorial regime from 1964 to 1985] due to its message and its mechanisms of participation. The corruption scandals attacked not only the politicians of the PT but also the dreams of many Brazilians.'

Enzo Bello, Gustavo Capela, and Rene José Keller, 'Breaking Routines Towards Conservatism? The 2013 Protests in Brazil' in Judith Bessant, Analicia Mejia Mesinas, and Sarah Pickard (eds), *When Students Protest: Universities in the Global South* (Rowman & Littlefield 2021) 19, 21.

[48]   In 2006, judges invoked the 'dominion over the fact theory' (*teoria do domínio do fato*)—developed by the German criminal law scholar, Claus Roxin—to condemn the defendants. In 2012, the Court held some of the defendants guilty because of their position in government. Claus Roxin and his pupils considered the theory was wrongly used by STF. Luís Greco and Alaor Leite, 'Fatos e mitos sobre a teoria do domínio do fato' *Folha de São Paulo* (São Paulo, 18 October 2013), https://m.folha.uol.com

cial markets in the United States collapsed, Brazil was initially able to withstand the blow, for multiple reasons.[49] But starting in 2014, Brazil entered a recession that would eventually lead to retractions of 3.55 and 3.28 per cent in 2015 and 2016, respectively. This contributed to reduced growth in the gross domestic product (GDP) even before its historical downturn in 2020 with the coronavirus pandemic.[50]

Lastly, OCW also hinges on the massive urban protests of 2013, which marked a moment of wide-ranging criticism of the whole political establishment and called for extensive social reforms. However, what began as protests against police brutality, in favour of greater and stronger public services, as well as disapproval of the Brazilian state's immense expenditure on stadiums for the 2014 FIFA World Cup, ended up questioning the political establishment as a whole, rehashing some of the rhetoric of widespread corruption. During these protests, agents of the Federal Police, as well as Federal Prosecutors, spent large sums of money to advocate for an increase in their investigative powers, with each insisting their office was the only one capable of ending corruption.[51]

When OCW came onto the scene, it attached itself to processes that were already in play. The connections between OCW and these processes is what allowed it and its actors to feel empowered to challenge the political establishment, and, most importantly, the hegemonic bloc that had been built since the PT victory in 2002. It is the multiplicity and connectivity of these large and complex processes that pushed Brazil's political crisis forward as a whole. It would be a mistake to suppose, for example, that the judiciary was the sole 'subject' or culprit of the crisis. What allowed it to strengthen and further these processes was the judiciary's special connection to all these processes, its privileged access to information (criminal cases and investigations), and, finally, its ability to produce a narrative that mobilised social and state forces in the name of the morally 'good'.

The Narrative of the Carwash Operation as Structure (and Its Elements)

We understand OCW as a process, one that produced a narrative in an attempt to reorganise, by disarticulating, the hegemonic bloc that was in place and that prioritised the PT. Using Poulantzas' rendering of different class fractions, and their struggles within the apparatuses,[52] we argue that while the hegemonic bloc was stable for a certain period of time, the world eco-

.br/opiniao/2013/10/1358310-luis-greco-e-alaor-leite-fatos-e-mitos-sobre-a-teoria-do-dominio-do-fato.shtml accessed 7 April 2021.

[49] André M Biancarelli, 'A Era Lula e sua questão econômica principal: crescimento, mercado interno e distribuição de renda' (2014) 58 *Revista do Instituto de Estudos Brasileiros* 263, https://www.scielo.br/scielo.php?pid=S0020-38742014000100012&script=sci_abstract&tlng=pt accessed 7 April 2021; João Sicsú, 'Brasil: é uma depressão, não foi apenas uma recessão' (2019) 23 *Revista de Economia Contemporânea* 1, https://www.scielo.br/pdf/rec/v23n1/1980-5527-rec-23-01-e192312.pdf accessed 7 April 2021.

[50] Reuters Staff, 'IMF Raises Brazil 2020 GDP Forecast to -5.8% From -9.1%' *Reuters* (5 October 2020), https://www.reuters.com/article/brazil-economy-imf/imf-raises-brazil-2020-gdp-forecast-to-5-8-from-9-1-idUKL1N2GW200 accessed 7 April 2021.

[51] 'Megaoperação contra corrupção coincide com campanha contra PEC' *Correio Braziliense* (10 April 2013), https://www.correiobraziliense.com.br/app/noticia/brasil/2013/04/10/interna-brasil,359673/megaoperacao-contra-corrupcao-coincide-com-campanha-contra-pec.shtml accessed 7 April 2021.

[52] Poulantzas, 'Political Crisis', 309.

nomic crisis, Brazil's own political crisis, and the reconfiguration of relations of production due to technological advances all disrupted the always unstable compromise that had allowed Brazil to become, for a while, an 'emerging economy'. This disruption was expressed, and given voice, by acts of class fractions that held specific state apparatuses such as the judiciary, represented here by Sergio Moro and Deltan Dallagnol. In this context, OCW is best understood as a symptom, an effect and representation of a crisis, as well as an attempt to reorganise the Brazilian social formation.

Fredric Jameson argues that one of the symptoms of crisis, at least in the political and ideological domain, is a loss of narrativity.[53] Like Poulantzas,[54] for whom ideology serves as a 'cement' to unify state apparatuses, Jameson understands that ideology unites, sets the terms, and lays the groundwork for other explanations. For Jameson, narration has a structure, a form, that allows for such 'cementing' or 'uniting'. This 'universally translatable form', which makes sense of the world by presenting us with certain paths, images, and characters, is able to make the way we live seem 'natural'—or, if not natural, at least insurmountable and fully functional: 'the way *it has to be*', as Althusser observes.[55] Narrative, then, as a form, allows us to understand how the '(imaginary) relation to the relations of production' takes hold,[56] how practices tell stories, and how these stories are united, formally, materially, and around a structure that is ultimately produced and reproduced by relations of force, class struggle, and relations of production.

According to Hayden White,[57] narrative is a device of form, a 'form-giving device' which links events, images, and characters in a chain that seems necessary, that seems to be the immediate, or mediate, cause of our present world. With that in mind, it becomes clear that one of the fundamental aspects of the narrative, more so than the elements it conjoins as its contents, is the story itself—the plot, or emplotment, as White understands it. It is through the plot that fragments and contradictions, processes and critical occurrences, come to be ordered, that what is and what is not relevant, what counts and what does not count, are distinguished—all while 'making sense' of the otherwise chaotic conditions of social reality. In fact, narrativity not only represents but justifies, since, as we learn from Hegel,[58] the distinctions between the normative and the factual are not as clear-cut as many empiricists would have us believe. For White, those who deem the fact, the immediately present, to be completely separate from processes of justification tend to forget that their certainty is predicated on normative affirmations, or at least on other processes of mediation, which allow the present to be understood as 'not absent'. The distinction itself is alive, and necessarily so, in any form of affirmative understanding.

According to Jameson, one of narrative's main functions is to select—or, in Hegel's sense, to mediate—relevant facts of the past and articulate different images, figures, and characters in order to produce an understanding of the present, as well as to project possible futures.[59]

[53] Jameson, *The Political Unconscious*.
[54] Nicos Poulantzas, 'Marxist Political Theory in Britain' [1967] in Poulantzas, *The Poulantzas Reader*, 120, 131.
[55] Althusser, *On Reproduction,* 198 (original emphasis).
[56] Althusser, *On Reproduction,* 183.
[57] Hayden White, *The Content of the Form: Narrative Discourse and Historical Representation* (Johns Hopkins University Press 1990).
[58] Hegel, *Encyclopedia*.
[59] Jameson, *The Political Unconscious*.

Narrativity can thus work to reselect and impose new readings, which allow for alternative modes of understanding and thus different discursive underpinnings for political action. Again, the narrative produced by OCW—the practices and discourses that both the press and OCW participants contributed to producing—is not false or 'unrealistic'. These discourses are simultaneously realistic and ideological, which is precisely how they produce a plausible narrative. They apprehend and give expression to existing contradictions within Brazilian society, specifically the PT's real incapacity to counter unequal structures and produce new relations of production within the Brazilian social formation, and, at the same time, 'live their misery within the arguments [narratives] of a religious and moral conscience'.[60]

While such discourses work with elements that are indeed 'real', they point to a clear-cut problem: despite the disenchantment for Brazilians who believed in the realisation of past promises, the narrative displaces such contradictions and their resolution. Ideology here works much like fetishism, insofar as it replaces the actual social forces in question (i.e., class struggle) with relatively superficial political conflicts (e.g., the conflict between Luiz Inácio Lula da Silva, or Lula, and Sergio Moro), due to 'a symbolic connection of thought, of which the person concerned is usually not conscious'.[61] It then presents a solution based on these latter conflicts, instead of the former: imprison Luiz, elect Bolsonaro. Such a solution refers us back to Jameson, since he understands that narratives acquire specific styles and create specific characters to explain the world according to conditions of possibility produced by the (capitalist) narrative itself. This is achieved by an operation that translates certain oppositions into other, ideological, ones.[62] Notably, this dialectic between changes in relations of force (i.e., changes in class struggle) and changes that occur in the structural relationship between culture, ideology, and relations of production produces 'styles' of narrative, such as romanticism, realism, and naturalism. For Jameson, while romanticism represents the first apprehension of capitalism's contradictions, realism affirms such a reality as objective and naturalism represses such contradictions, cultivating the 'resentment' typical of the modernist novel.[63]

What is important here is that Jameson's depiction of the modern novel's standard solution to social grievances is in many ways similar to the political solutions presented by the OCW narrative: on the one hand, a discourse of rapid and necessary modernisation; on the other hand, an attachment to an idyllic past, which, in Brazil's case, harkens back to the epoch of settler colonialism. The similarity could be attributed to the fact that reality imitates fiction, in the sense that our depiction of reality has the same structure as fiction, but it could also be understood by the fact that this narrative was built in unison with apparatuses like Brazil's large media conglomerates. The function of these conglomerates is not only to produce and reproduce the news but also to entertain, in part through *novelas* (soap operas) that are nothing but televised modern novels.

The 'whole story' of OCW's development is immense, with multiple twists and turns. We cannot really do it full justice here, but we will try to give a general outline with in-depth explications of specific events we believe marked the operation. OCW began as a task force that included the Federal Police, Federal Prosecutors, and, as we have come to find out, Federal

---

[60] Althusser, *For Marx*, 139.
[61] Sigmund Freud, *Three Essays on the Theory of Sexuality* (first published 1905, James Strachey ed and tr, Basic Books 1967) 21.
[62] White, *Content of the Form*, 159.
[63] White, *Content of the Form*, 161.

Judges. It started as an investigation into money laundering connected to a congressman from the State of Paraná, and eventually it explored the misconduct of multiple high-profile politicians and businessmen in connection with the state-owned oil company Petrobrás, one of the largest such companies in the world.

The operation as a whole had multiple 'phases', marked by the capture and imprisonment of important people: either politicians or CEOs of some of Brazil's largest companies. The targets of these phases were usually signalled by the names given to them by police and prosecutors. The names were creative: 'Dolce Vita', 'Casablanca', 'Final Judgment', 'Radioactivity', among others. Each name was typically the subject of explanations by police officers and prosecutors, who allowed the press to cover the operation as it happened and also held extensive press conferences afterwards. They would then explain what they had found, what they hoped to understand, and, in what became a symbol of the operation, who they believed to be the 'boss' of the whole scheme—Lula.

The PT had been the main political force in Brazil since 2002, with Lula and later Dilma Rousseff having been elected president. Their connections to the state-owned Petrobrás, as well as to other branches of large business in Brazil, were therefore inevitable, given the structures of Brazil's capitalist state. A scandal in 2006 had already indicated corruption within the PT, but the investigation was never able to reach Lula, who went on to become the most popular president in the country's history. Importantly, Lula was the first ever blue-collar factory worker to be elected president. He had been the face of the PT and of its creation during the 1980s, mostly due to his role in helping to organise large strikes during the military dictatorship. OCW would eventually lead to Lula's imprisonment, in a judicial back and forth that was highly televised and discussed by news channels, political pundits, and on the streets. It was the main political topic for more than a year, and, importantly, one that would lead to Rousseff's impeachment in 2016 and Bolsonaro's election in 2018.

It is important to note that OCW's power cannot be reduced to one moment; its entire narrative is what stands out. However, one specific moment illustrates OCW's capacity as well as the way it functioned in conjunction with the media. On 16 March 2016, Judge Moro gave Brazil's largest media conglomerate, Globo, access to wiretapped phone calls between then-president Rousseff and Lula. During the call, she offered Lula a position in her government. Dilma was already undergoing an impeachment process, in part due to the scandals of OCW, which included Lula. In order to garner help, and to help Lula himself, she invited him to become her chief of staff. In Brazil, ministers (the chief of staff is categorised as one) enjoy 'executive immunity', which means that they can be prosecuted and judged only at the Supreme Court level. This prerogative was one of the issues against which OCW's narrative rallied. OCW invoked the logic—the narrative logic—that everyone should be judged in the same way, by the same courts, because privileges such as these 'immunities' benefit the powerful. The narrative, thus, attached to its judgment, to its rendering of justice, a formal notion of equality: 'equal treatment before the law'. As explained by Marx, this formal rendition of equality is at the very basis of bourgeois law, which uses the signifier 'equality' to conceal the material inequality on which it is based.[64]

---

[64]   Karl Marx, *Critique of the Gotha Programme: A Contribution to the Critique of the Social-Democratic Draft Programme of 1891* (first published 1891, Foreign Languages Publishing House 1959) 9.

By handing the tape of the call to the press, which played it over and over for days, Moro reinforced connections between the operation and the media. First, the very organisation of the media, particularly news production, allows it to obtain information from actors like judges who are in a position (or simply want) to divulge information. Such authorities are usually considered reliable sources because they have access to information to which very few others are privy. Their access to sensitive details makes them people who could reveal new, exciting, and otherwise unavailable information. The media's interest is structurally attached to the judiciary's desire to present such information in a manner that makes it scandalous, so that it can be consumed as a spectacle.[65] The fact that it involved famous politicians increases 'newsworthiness'; it draws an audience. The media, like any other capitalist enterprise, works under constraints of capital, not only in the sense of 'having to reproduce a dominant ideology', but also in its own pursuit of profit.[66] In other words, the story the media tells people about the 'reality' of life needs to be functional in the ideological sense, but it also needs to be a spectacle in order to compete and be more valuable than other possible stories.

In Brazil, the production of images and stories is a typical function of the main news organisations, both when it pertains to 'real facts' and when it pertains to 'fiction'. Globo, Record, Band, SBT, and Rede TV! (the Brazilian entrepreneurial media oligopoly) all make money from their extremely popular *novelas*, in which they sell narratives of what is portrayed as Brazil's past and present. Perhaps for that reason, OCW functioned much like a soap opera. The culmination of its main plot occurred on 7 April 2018, when Judge Moro finally jailed Lula, six months before the presidential election. Lula was leading in the polls at the time, ahead of Bolsonaro, who was eventually elected. Bolsonaro invited Moro to be his minister of justice months before the election took place.[67] Moro's acceptance of this offer fuelled speculation that both men saw the entire operation as a conspiracy against the PT, or as a way of demonstrating the dedication of two political heroes (Moro and Bolsonaro) who take it upon themselves to 'cleanse' Brazilian society.

OCW deployed images of a society that needed to be normalised, cleansed, and cured, as their main protagonists themselves constantly stated.[68] Moro, Dallagnol, and other representatives of the judiciary would affirm, during the operation, the importance not only of punishing powerful people but also of sending a message to the whole of Brazilian society.

> Corruption, as an isolated crime, exists everywhere in the world, but the *systematic corruption*, the payment of bribe as rule of the game, it is not so common, representing a severe degeneration of public and private customs ... The government has the main responsibility for creating a political and economic environment free of *systematic corruption*. With larger visibility and power, *it teaches through example. Corrupted agents must be expelled from public life* ... It is necessary to consider that *systematic corruption* is the product of an *institutional and cultural weakness*.[69]

---

[65] Hall et al, *Policing the Crisis*, 59.

[66] Cesar Bolanos, *Indústria Cultural, Informação e Capitalismo* (Hucitec/Polis 2000) 50.

[67] Today this fact is public knowledge in Brazil; see Gabriel Sabóia and Igor Mello, 'Moro relatou convite de Bolsonaro antes da eleição, diz jornalista' *UOL* (10 June 2019), https://noticias.uol.com.br/politica/ultimas-noticias/2019/06/10/moro-relatou-convite-de-bolsonaro-antes-da-eleicao-diz-jornalista .htm accessed 7 April 2021.

[68] Moro, 'Sergio Moro explica sua visão da Justiça' *Revista Exame* (20 May 2016); Luís Roberto Barroso, 'Ministro Barroso disserta sobre combate à corrupção e refundação do Brasil' *Migalhas* (1 April 2019).

[69] Moro, 'Sergio Moro explica sua visão da Justiça' (emphases added).

In other words, they thought they needed to educate people in order to change the national culture. Put in moral, or even moralistic, terms, they sought to overcome a dark past of corruption and patrimonialism and found Brazil anew through a process of modernisation.

Reminding us of Barthes' claim that 'the bourgeoisie is defined as *the social class which does not want to be named*',[70] a justice of the Brazilian Supreme Court, Luís Roberto Barroso, affirmed OCW as a 'non-ideological' process:

> My faith in a moment of the country's refoundation is not connected to the recent elections or this or that government—it is independent of ideologies. It is grounded on the opposite, in the changes occurring in civil society, which does not accept the unacceptable anymore, and has developed a huge demand for integrity, idealism and patriotism.[71]

Although there are a range of other developments that are both interesting and relevant to understand OCW, what seems most important is, first, the operation's destabilisation of Brazil's political landscape, tilting it towards the segment led by Bolsonaro, and, second, its connection with the press, particularly in regard to fostering an imagery, discourse, and narrative that would foment a specific view—a 'worldview', in Althusser's sense—about Brazilian society.

CONCLUSION

OCW inserts itself into multiple and variable narratives, ideological processes, and historical developments. It is not only affected by them, but also produces its own narrative, ideological process, and historical developments. Following Jameson, we understand narrative as a socially symbolic act, inasmuch as it both augments and restricts reality by the logics it imposes in order to produce a plot, tell a story, and unite events, thereby making sense of them as an integrated 'whole'. OCW produced—and worked within the structures of—a narrative. It conveyed messages, constituted subjects and characters, and delineated a plot. And it did so effectively because of the structure of ideology and its material enactments, such as the imprisonment of Lula.

As explained by Althusser[72] and Pashukanis,[73] law plays an important role in this regard. It ensures both the functioning and the reproduction of relations of production, the former through the '*legal system*, the basic elements of which are the *law of property* and the *law of contract*',[74] the latter in people's consciousness through legal-moral ideology.[75] This reveals the relevance not only of acts themselves, but also of the discourse invoked by acts of prosecutors, judges, and the mass media in connection with OCW. Their acts, and not just their words, presented OCW as an institutional player in the fight against corruption and as a solution to the problems of Brazilian politics. It invoked the idea of the state as subject, able to be the neutral

---

[70]   Barthes, *Mythologies*, 250 (original emphasis).
[71]   Barroso, 'Ministro Barroso disserta sobre combate à corrupção e refundação do Brasil'.
[72]   Althusser, *On the Reproduction of Capitalism*, 168.
[73]   Evguiéni B Pachukanis, *Teoria geral do direito e marxismo* (first published 1924, Paula Vaz de Almeida tr, Boitempo 2017).
[74]   Althusser et al, *Reading* Capital, 393 (original emphases).
[75]   Althusser, *On the Reproduction of Capitalism*, 203.

arbiter of social conflicts.[76] And it created, or interpellated, 'heroes' capable of reorganising, seemingly by themselves, what were presented as long-standing structural problems.

OCW played with the idea of 'cleansing', which reveals the colonial and racist logics that were at work in the project.[77] These racist elements, or 'fragments' of discourse, are part and parcel of the functioning of ideology as the imaginary relation of the actual relations of production in Brazilian society. As Hall and others argued, the constitution of the criminal as the problematic figure, as an evil character, conjures, on the one hand, the image of stable, integrated, and pacified society, and, on the other, that which does not belong, that which is outside its necessary and natural place.[78] The moral panic of the bourgeoise is the manifestation, or the symptom, of a fear produced by the visibility of other worlds that seem to be rising against their own, prompting the ISAs to produce new (yet old) images to represent the 'error', the 'evil', the 'anti-social'. The workings of the ISAs, in conjunction with their repressive counterparts, is to reintegrate and reorganise a given social formation by linking fragments, using 'old' enemies and antagonists, and then representing the image of the society that is desired. It should come as no surprise, then, that Bolsonaro's politics speaks the language of racism openly: it is directly related to the process of criminalisation that presented itself as a solution to Brazil's political issues and the narratives built around it.

[76] Friedrich Engels, *A origem da família, da propriedade privada e do Estado* (first published 1884, Nélio Schneider tr, Boitempo 2019).

[77] Frantz Fanon, *The Wretched of the Earth* (first published 1961, Constance Farrington tr, Penguin 1967) 29.

[78] Hall et al, *Policing the Crisis*, 153.

25. The poetry of the future: Law, Marxism, and social change

Paul O'Connell

While it is well known that Marx, and his long-time collaborator Engels, never developed a fully articulated theory of law, state, and rights,[1] it is clear that subsequent generations of Marxists have more than made up for this. From Lenin and Gramsci,[2] Neumann and Kirchheimer,[3] Pashukanis and Renner,[4] through to Althusser,[5] Thompson, and Poulantzas,[6] a large number of Marxists have set themselves the task of applying Marx's method to the study of law. The ideas developed by these thinkers have, in turn, been picked over by subsequent generations, whether in the state debates of the 1970s and 1980s,[7] the neo-Gramscian revival that began in the mid to late 1990s,[8] or the resurgence of interest in Pashukanis, in particular among international lawyers, from the early 2000s onwards.[9] Taken together, these debates and analyses have done much to develop and enhance distinctive Marxist accounts of law—accounts which break with simple instrumentalism or mechanical readings of the base-superstructure metaphor, elucidate the relative autonomy of law and the state, and unmask the myriad ideological functions of law.[10] In this regard, existing Marxist accounts of law have gone a long way to help us interpret and understand the place of law, rights, and the

---

[1]   As Perry Anderson puts it, 'Marx left behind a comprehensive theory of the political economy of capitalism, but no comparable political theory of the bourgeois State, or of the strategy and tactics of revolutionary socialist struggle by a working-class party for its overthrow'. Perry Anderson, *Considerations on Western Marxism* (Verso 1979) 4.

[2]   VI Lenin, *The State and Revolution* (first published 1917, Robert Service tr, Penguin 1992); Antonio Gramsci, *Selections from the Prison Notebooks* (Quintin Hoare and Geoffrey N Smith eds and tr, International Publishers 2005).

[3]   Franz Neumann, *The Democratic and the Authoritarian State: Essays in Political and Legal Theory* (Herbert Marcuse ed, Free Press 1964); William E Scheuerman (ed), *The Rule of Law Under Siege: Selected Essays of Franz L. Neumann and Otto Kirchheimer* (University of California Press 1996).

[4]   Evgeny Pashukanis, *Law and Marxism: A General Theory* (Pluto Press 1978); Karl Renner, *The Institutions of Private Law and Their Social Function* (Routledge & Kegan Paul 1949).

[5]   Louis Althusser, *On the Reproduction of Capitalism: Ideology and Ideological State Apparatuses* (first published 1995, GM Goshgarian tr, Verso 2014).

[6]   EP Thompson, *Whigs and Hunters: The Origin of the Black Act* (Pantheon Books 1975); Nicos Poulantzas, *State, Power, Socialism* (first published 1978, Patrick Camiller tr, Verso 1980).

[7]   Simon Clarke, 'The State Debate' in Simon Clarke (ed), *The State Debate* (Macmillan 1991) 1.

[8]   A Claire Cutler, 'Gramsci, Law and the Culture of Global Capitalism' (2005) 8 *Critical Review of International Social and Political Philosophy* 527.

[9]   See esp. China Miéville, *Between Equal Rights: A Marxist Theory of International Law* (Brill 2005).

[10]   Alan Hunt, 'Marxist Theory of Law' in Dennis Patterson (ed), *A Companion to Philosophy of Law and Legal Theory* (2nd edn, Blackwell 2010) 350; Sonja Buckel, *Subjectivation and Cohesion: Towards the Reconstruction of a Materialist Theory of Law* (first published 2007, Monika Vykoukal tr, Brill 2020) 68–210.

state in reproducing the world we see around us. They tend to say less, however, about how we might change it.

The argument here, put simply, is that the main currents in Marxist accounts of law, rights, and the state are too often indifferent to the transformative, revolutionary character of Marxism. In line with Marxist theorists in other fields,[11] Marxist critics of law have lost sight of the crucial principle at the heart of Marxism: when it comes to comprehending capitalist society, the point is to change it, not just elucidate the ways in which it cages us. While fully accepting that there are and should be many Marxisms,[12] I nonetheless argue that we gain a richer appreciation of the nature of law, rights, and the state, and of their relationship with movements for fundamental social change, when we foreground this fundamental principle of Marxism, namely that the point is to change the extant social order. In effect, then, this chapter is an exercise in methodological orientation.

To elucidate this argument, I first set out a couple of key strands in different Marxist approaches to law, rights, and the state. In particular, I consider the commodity-form theory of law developed by Pashukanis, and the closely related idea of the 'withering away' of legal and state forms. I also touch on the structuralist-functionalist accounts associated with Althusser and Poulantzas. My aim is to show that while each of these approaches performs an important role in unmasking aspects of the role that law and state power play in capitalist societies, they lack a positive element. In other words, while they do a good job of identifying the malady, they say little or nothing about how we move towards the cure. This is a fundamental shortcoming for any theory which seeks to situate itself in the Marxist tradition. The reason for this is that Marxism is a theory of and for revolutionary practice and working-class self-emancipation.[13] It is not a dispassionate social science, even less so a contemplative school of philosophy. It is—or at least should be—the set of ideas corresponding to the living movement to abolish the present order of things.[14]

For a variety of reasons, not least the defeats of the historical left and many workers' movements, this central aspect of Marxism has been sidelined in recent decades. As such, it is necessary here to explain and justify the assertion that this is the beating heart of the Marxist tradition. The argument here is developed as follows. In the first section, I set out some of the key elements of leading Marxist accounts of law. In the second section, I restate and defend an understanding of Marxism as a theory for radical politics and social change. In the third section, I apply this methodological orientation to two concrete problems. Specifically, I take up the question of how Marxists should engage with human rights and with institutional and

---

[11] Ellen Meiksins Wood, *Democracy Against Capitalism: Renewing Historical Materialism* (CUP 1995) 19.

[12] Marshall Berman, *Adventures in Marxism* (Verso 1999) 19; André Tosel, 'The Development of Marxism: From the End of Marxism-Leninism to a Thousand Marxisms—France-Italy, 1975–2005' in Jacques Bidet and Stathis Kouvelakis (eds), *Critical Companion to Contemporary Marxism* (Brill 2008) 39.

[13] As Engels put it: 'Marx was before all else a revolutionist. His real mission in life was to contribute, in one way or another, to the overthrow of capitalist society and of the state institutions which it had brought into being, to contribute to the liberation of the modern proletariat, which he was the first to make conscious of its own position and its needs, conscious of the conditions of its emancipation.' Frederick Engels, 'Karl Marx's Funeral' [1883] in Karl Marx and Frederick Engels, *Collected Works*, vol 24 (Lawrence & Wishart 1989) 467, 468.

[14] Daniel Bensaïd, *Marx For Our Times: Adventures and Misadventures of a Critique* (first published 1995, Gregory Elliott tr, Verso 2002) xv.

constitutional reform, giving substance to both the Marxist critique of the capitalist mode of production and the obligation to transform the extant order.

WHAT YOU SEE IS WHAT YOU GET

As a preliminary point in developing the argument here, it is necessary to say something about the trajectory of Marxism over the last 100 years. This account is necessarily partial and limited, but it should suffice to situate the rest of the discussion in this chapter. Marxism emerged, in the mid to late nineteenth century, as the leading theory of proletarian revolution. It was a set of ideas articulated, in the first instance by Marx and Engels, to equip the working class with the theoretical weapons they would need to win their own emancipation and over-throw the capitalist mode of production. This core principle is emblazoned in the rules of the First International, which Marx wrote,[15] and constitutes what Hal Draper calls 'the heart of Marxism'.[16] This Marxism contributed to the emergence of mass parties of the working class (particularly in western Europe), the development of more militant, disciplined trade unions, and ultimately a set of radical transformations of the social, political, and cultural landscapes of countless countries.[17]

At the dawn of the twentieth century, and in the midst of two world wars, Marxism also inspired the 1917 Russian Revolution, as well as the failed 1918–19 German Revolution. Both of these experiences were pivotal, setting the trend for the subsequent development of Marxism and Marxist ideas and establishing a pattern with which we still have to reckon today. In an important analysis of the impact of these two experiences, Perry Anderson notes that both, in different ways, led to fundamental ruptures in the Marxist tradition. In eastern Europe, following the failure of the Russian Revolution, Marxism was institutionalised as dogma, and exported around the world through the Comintern. In western Europe the defeat of the German Revolution, and the murder of Rosa Luxemburg and its other leading figures, led to the retreat of many Marxists from transformative politics. As Anderson put it, what emerged and came to be known as 'Western Marxism' is marked, first and foremost, by the 'structural divorce of this Marxism from political practice'.[18]

The broad tradition of Marxist and Marxisant thought which developed under the banner of Western Marxism has since, in various forms, become dominant in the post-Soviet era, and is characterised by defeatism and pessimism—by a rejection of the central conviction of classical Marxism that society could be fundamentally transformed through the self-activity of the working class. This represents the rise within Marxism of what Walter Benjamin termed

---

[15]   Karl Marx, 'Provisional Rules of the Association' [1864] in Karl Marx and Frederick Engels, *Collected Works*, vol 20 (Lawrence & Wishart 1985) 14; Marcello Musto, 'Introduction' in Marcello Musto (ed), *Workers Unite! The International 150 Years Later* (Bloomsbury 2014) 1.

[16]   Hal Draper, *Socialism from Below* (first published 1966, Center for Socialist History 2001) 8.

[17]   Geoff Eley, *Forging Democracy: The History of the Left in Europe, 1850–2000* (OUP 2002) 33–84; Edmund Wilson, *To the Finland Station: A Study in the Writing and Acting of History* (Farrar, Straus and Giroux 1972) 131–209; Donald Sassoon, *One Hundred Years of Socialism: The West European Left in the Twentieth Century* (IB Tauris & Co 2014) 5–26.

[18]   Anderson, *Considerations on Western Marxism*, 29; Tom Bottomore, *The Frankfurt School and Its Critics* (2nd edn, Routledge 1995).

'left-wing melancholy',[19] an 'attitude to which there is no longer in general any corresponding political action. It is to the left not of this or that tendency, but simply to the left of what is in general possible. For from the beginning all it has in mind is to enjoy itself in a negativistic quiet.'[20] At its worst, and all too often, what this perspective leads to is a hollowing out of the emancipatory element of Marxism. As John Holloway argues:

> [w]hat we see first ... is the dominant moment of the antagonistic unity. And something awful happens. Our critique degenerates into a theory of domination. Marxism becomes a theory of capitalist domination. Reactionary claptrap, in other words—a theory that encloses us in the enclosure that it pretends to criticise. A theory of Cassandra, a theory that separates the analysis of capitalism from the movement of struggle, a theory that understands Marxism as the analysis of the *framework* within which class struggle develops.[21]

In this way, a crucial element of what constitutes Marxism is sundered from analysis. Marxist critiques become accounts of domination, increasingly abstruse and recondite variations on the theme of how capitalism reproduces itself, with no exit in sight.[22]

In different but ultimately complementary ways, the legal form analysis pioneered by Pashukanis and the structuralist-functionalist accounts developed by Althusser and Poulantzas reproduce versions of this one-sidedness. Pashukanis' work is foundational for all subsequent debates in Marxist analyses of law.[23] Pashukanis' attempt to map a theory of the legal form onto Marx's analysis of the commodity form in *Capital* still arguably marks his work out as 'both truer to Marx and theoretically more sophisticated' than most other attempts to conceptualise law from within the Marxist tradition.[24] For present purposes, what is most important about Pashukanis' work is that it was concerned less with this or that specific legal measure than with elaborating 'a materialist interpretation of legal regulation as a specific historical form'.[25] With this in mind, Pashukanis argues that the legal form is a specifically bourgeois form, and plays a cognate role in concealing and facilitating interaction between individuals to that of the commodity form. In short, in the same way in which the commodity form creates abstract relations of equality between qualitatively different commodities, the legal form constitutes real, unequal individuals as abstract, equal juridical subjects.[26]

Marx identified commodity production and exchange, and the commodity form, as crystallising a complex set of social relations of exploitation and unequal exchange which develop

---

[19]   Walter Benjamin, 'Left-Wing Melancholy (On Erich Kästner's New Book of Poems)' (1974) 15 *Screen* 28.

[20]   Benjamin, 'Left-Wing Melancholy', 30.

[21]   John Holloway, 'Crisis and Critique' (2012) 36 *Capital & Class* 515, 516 (original emphasis).

[22]   Simon Clarke, 'Marxism, Sociology and Poulantzas' Theory of the State' (1977) 1 *Capital & Class* 1, 20.

[23]   For more thorough engagement with Pashukanis, see Matthew Dimick's chapter in this volume.

[24]   David Greenberg and Nancy Anderson, 'Recent Marxisant Books on Law: A Review Essay' (1981) 5 *Contemporary Crises* 293, 295. For trenchant Marxist critiques of Pashukanis' approach see Bob Fine, *Democracy and the Rule of Law: Marx's Critique of the Legal Form* (Blackburn Press 1984) 157–62; and also 'An Assessment by Karl Korsch' in Evgeny Pashukanis, *Law and Marxism: A General Theory* (Barbara Einhorn tr, Pluto Press 1978) 189.

[25]   Pashukanis, *Law and Marxism*, 54.

[26]   Pashukanis, *Law and Marxism*, 63–64.

'behind the backs of the producers of commodities'.[27] Pashukanis holds that the legal form plays a complementary role, as 'the mystified form of a specific social relation'.[28] The commodity form and legal form are linked, as necessary forms of appearance and social regulation in the capitalist mode of production. The legal fetishism characteristic of bourgeois societies thus 'complements commodity fetishism'.[29] Law, then, is a historically specific form of social regulation that attains its distinctiveness and import only with the ascendancy of the capitalist mode of production, and the system of generalised commodity production and exchange for profit. As such, the transition to a higher form of society, communism, will (following Pashukanis' reading of Marx, Engels, and Lenin) lead to the 'withering away of the categories of bourgeois law', which will 'mean the withering away of law altogether, that is to say the disappearance of the juridical factor from social relations'.[30]

The great virtue of Pashukanis' theory is that it departs from a narrow focus on this or that law or legal regime, focusing instead on the systemic character of law and the integral role it plays in reproducing capitalist relations of production. However, the implications of his theory for political practice are problematic. The framing of law as an ultimately superstructural phenomenon that will wither away with the advent of 'a society in which the contradiction between individual and social interests has been broken down',[31] makes it possible to defer the question of how specific movements for fundamental social change should, concretely, engage with the legal form and with the content of legal norms and institutions. As Bob Fine argues, 'Pashukanis offered an abstract negation of bourgeois jurisprudence, simply reversing its portrayal of law, highlighting its dark side over its light side'. For Fine, this departs from Marx's dialectical approach, and as such fails to appreciate law's multi-facetedness.[32] Indeed, Isaac Balbus, an exemplary advocate of the legal form approach, argues that the logical consequence of this analysis of the specifically bourgeois character of law and its role in reproducing capitalism is that it demonstrates clearly 'the incompatibility of legalism and socialism'.[33]

Thus, Pashukanis' approach, which Sonja Buckel criticises for its 'one-dimensional determining logic',[34] allows for questions of legal strategy, or engagement with rights and legal reforms, to be deferred and also denigrated. On the latter point, Balbus is unequivocal when he argues that:

> the legal form is a specifically 'bourgeois' form; those who would simultaneously uphold this form and condemn the capitalist mode of production which 'perverts' it simply fail to grasp that part they uphold is inextricably tied to the very system they condemn … It follows, therefore, that the legal form cannot be the basis for a fully developed, genuine socialist or communist society.[35]

---

[27]   Karl Marx, *Capital: A Critique of Political Economy*, vol 1 (first published 1867, Ben Fowkes tr, Penguin 1990) 201.

[28]   Pashukanis, *Law and Marxism*, 79.

[29]   Pashukanis, *Law and Marxism*, 117.

[30]   Pashukanis, *Law and Marxism*, 61.

[31]   Pashukanis, *Law and Marxism*, 104.

[32]   Fine, *Democracy and the Rule of Law*, 159.

[33]   Isaac D Balbus, 'Commodity Form and Legal Form: An Essay on the "Relative Autonomy" of the Law' (1977) 11 *Law & Society Review* 571, 580.

[34]   Buckel, *Subjectivation and Cohesion*, 102.

[35]   Balbus, 'Commodity Form and Legal Form', 580.

The recognition that the legal form is intrinsic to the capitalist mode of production quickly becomes the basis for relegating engagement with questions of the legal form, and the substance of legal norms and institutions is dismissed as a secondary consideration. If the legal form is homologous with the commodity form, and arises on the material substratum of the relations of commodity production, the focus should be on the abolition of this material basis, with a politics focused, among other things, on human needs.[36]

This view complements Pashukanis' rejection of the need to develop any concept of 'proletarian law', and his insistence that the focus should be on building the political and social forces necessary to abolish the 'particular historical conditions which had helped bring [the legal form] to full fruition'.[37] While Pashukanis accepted that, in the short term, the 'proletariat may well have to utilise [the legal form,] ... that in no way implies that [this form] could be developed further or be penetrated by a socialist content'.[38] The crucial point is that any such engagement must be limited and informed by an understanding of the legal form, stripped of all ideological illusions.[39] In this respect, Pashukanis' account of law, of its specificity and deep imbrication in the reproduction of capitalist social relations, performs an important job in clearing away bourgeois, liberal, and formalist illusions about the nature of law. But in the end, his approach offers little in the way of guidance on how law should be engaged in situations that are a long way away from involving the abolition of the value relation and commodity form. As such, Pashukanis' critical account is both valuable and fundamentally disempowering. The exposure of the specific character of the legal form brings out an important aspect of the ideology of liberal legalism, but the reification and ossification of the form concept in Pashukanis' analysis renders it static, and of only secondary importance in concrete political struggles.

While Pashukanis' work remains a key reference point for all subsequent Marxist analyses of law, the 'crisis of Marxism' that began in the late 1950s saw new theoretical approaches emerge. Chief among them were the structuralist-functionalist theories elaborated by Althusser and Poulantzas.[40] In the context of thinking through the nature and place of law in capitalist societies, Althusser's principal contribution was to stress the centrality of ideological and repressive state apparatuses in the reproduction of capitalist relations of production.[41] Crucially for Althusser, these distinct but overlapping apparatuses, or structures, are autonomous from the immediate relations of production and direct interests of specific classes, serving ultimately to sustain and reproduce the extant order, with the economic base being the ultimately determining factor. With respect to law, Althusser stresses its distinctiveness as 'a *system* which, by its nature, aspires to internal consistency and comprehensiveness'.[42]

Because of Althusser's fidelity to a very particular variation on the traditional base-superstructure metaphor,[43] the law ultimately remains epiphenomenal on his account. That is to say,

[36] Balbus, 'Commodity Form and Legal Form', 580–81.
[37] Pashukanis, *Law and Marxism*, 61.
[38] Pashukanis, *Law and Marxism*, 160.
[39] Pashukanis, *Law and Marxism*, 160.
[40] For more thorough engagement with these theories, see the chapters by Bob Jessop, Rafael Khachaturian, and Enzo Bello, Gustavo Capela, and Rene José Keller in this volume.
[41] Althusser, *On the Reproduction of Capitalism*, 1–2.
[42] Althusser, *On the Reproduction of Capitalism*, 58 (original emphasis).
[43] Robert Fine and Sol Picciotto, 'On Marxist Critiques of Law' in Ian Grigg-Spall and Paddy Ireland (eds), *The Critical Lawyers' Handbook* (Pluto Press 1992) 15, 17.

while Althusser conceives law as a formal and abstract system of rules and norms that take on a degree of relative autonomy, so that it applies to and can be invoked by all juridical persons,[44] it ultimately 'only exists as a function of the existing relations of production'.[45] The way in which this circle is squared is that while law is a reflection of existing relations of production, and serves to reproduce those relations, it does so by occluding the reality of those relations of inequality and exploitation. As Althusser puts it, law 'has the form of law … only on condition *that the relations of production* as a function of which it exists *are completely absent from law itself*'.[46] Law as a system of formal, abstract rules rests on legal ideology, supplemented with moral ideology and the background threat of the repressive state apparatus (police, courts, prisons, etc).[47] As such, it plays an integral role in ensuring the smooth functioning and reproduction of capitalist relations of production.[48]

While Althusser stresses that law, as the ideological state apparatus par excellence, is relatively autonomous, he also insists that it is necessarily repressive,[49] and, crucially, that 'all law is by essence … inegalitarian and bourgeois'.[50] For Althusser, then, law plays a crucial role in ideologically obscuring and legitimating the extant relations of production. It arises as a reflex of the material relationships embedded in these relations. And as a system of abstract, formal norms striving for internal coherence, it also operates autonomously, to a degree, from the dominant classes in capitalist society.[51] Despite such relative autonomy, the extant relations of production remain determinate in the final instance,[52] with the law playing a fundamental role in their reproduction. As such, Althusser, echoing Pashukanis, insists that the demands and aspirations of socialist and communist movements cannot be captured by or articulated through law.[53] Notwithstanding a rhetorically radical position that purports to foreground 'a proletarian class viewpoint in philosophy'[54] and stresses the centrality of class struggle to understanding law,[55] this leads Althusser to an ultimately one-sided understanding of law as intrinsic to capitalist reproduction, without any real understanding of how, short of a wholesale transformation of the mode of production, movements for fundamental social change can or should engage with law, rights, and the state.

Poulantzas, in turn, built on and elaborated the system developed by Althusser. With respect to law specifically, Poulantzas' thinking went through three broad stages of development, moving gradually from placing greater to lesser emphasis on the significance of law, eventually opting instead to foreground the role of the state.[56] Even so, in his later work, Poulantzas

---

[44]   Althusser, *On the Reproduction of Capitalism*, 59.

[45]   Althusser, *On the Reproduction of Capitalism*, 59.

[46]   Althusser, *On the Reproduction of Capitalism*, 59 (original emphases).

[47]   Althusser, *On the Reproduction of Capitalism*, 67–68.

[48]   Althusser, *On the Reproduction of Capitalism*, 169.

[49]   Althusser, *On the Reproduction of Capitalism*, 65.

[50]   Althusser, *On the Reproduction of Capitalism*, 61.

[51]   Althusser's assessment mirrors, in part, Engels' view on the relative autonomy of law. See Frederick Engels, 'Engels to Conrad Schmidt, in Berlin, 27 October 1890' in Karl Marx and Frederick Engels, *Collected Works*, vol 49 (Lawrence & Wishart 2010) 57, 60–61.

[52]   Althusser, *On the Reproduction of Capitalism*, 237–38.

[53]   Althusser, *On the Reproduction of Capitalism*, 61.

[54]   Althusser, *On the Reproduction of Capitalism*, 4.

[55]   Althusser, *On the Reproduction of Capitalism*, 8.

[56]   Buckel, *Subjectivation and Cohesion*, 138; James Martin, 'Poulantzas: From Law to the State' in Jean-Numa Ducange and Razmig Keucheyan (eds), *The End of the Democratic State: Nicos Poulantzas, a Marxism for the 21st Century* (Palgrave Macmillan 2019) 123.

still recognised the role of law as 'an important factor in organising the consent of the dominated classes'.[57] Like Althusser, Poulantzas also insisted on the inherently violent nature of law and legal regulation within capitalist society,[58] understanding capitalist law as 'an axiomatic system, comprising a set of *abstract, general, formal and strictly regulated norms*'.[59] Distancing himself from the tradition associated with Pashukanis, Poulantzas insisted that the key to understanding capitalist law cannot be found in the system of commodity exchange, but must instead be 'sought in the social division of labour and the relations of production'.[60]

In this regard, Poulantzas, in line with his broader understanding of the relative autonomy of the state,[61] insists that while law serves to obscure 'politico-economic realities',[62] and plays a central role in 'expanding the *real submission* of Labour to Capital',[63] it also reflects the real contradictions and class antagonisms ingrained within the extant relations of production.[64] As a result, the law can play its specific role in 'organizing the consent of the dominated classes'[65] only because it also inscribes within its own, relatively autonomous system concessions extracted by the working class from the ruling classes. As Poulantzas puts it:

[l]aw does not only deceive and conceal, and nor does it merely repress people by compelling or forbidding them to act. It also organizes and sanctions certain *real rights* of the dominated classes (even though, of course, these rights are invested in the dominant ideology and are far from corresponding in practice to their juridical form); and it has inscribed within it the material concessions imposed on the dominant classes by popular struggle.[66]

The law, then, is no mere sham concealing the interests and machinations of a homogeneous ruling class, but rather a relatively autonomous site of struggle which reflects and in turn shapes the real class antagonisms and struggles characteristic of capitalist relations of production.

Crucially for Poulantzas, the specificity of capitalist law, and its relative autonomy as a terrain of class struggle, are, in the final analysis, limited and circumscribed by what he understood as the pre-existing economic base of capitalist society.[67] As he puts it, 'in the capitalist mode of production, the specific relations of production assign to the economic a role that is at once determining and dominant'.[68] This introduces a crucial antagonism, and limitation, into Poulantzas' understanding of the role of law in capitalism. For while he insists on the specificity and relative autonomy of law, he nonetheless regards law 'as, in essence, a subordinate body of ideas and values whose very form supported capitalist economic relations of production through the implicit threat of violence, supplied legitimacy to the power bloc, or obscured the state's capitalist nature with a veil of impartiality'.[69] As a consequence,

---

57   Poulantzas, *State, Power, Socialism*, 83.
58   Poulantzas, *State, Power, Socialism*, 76–77.
59   Poulantzas, *State, Power, Socialism*, 86 (original emphasis).
60   Poulantzas, *State, Power, Socialism*, 86.
61   Poulantzas, *State, Power, Socialism*, 17–18.
62   Poulantzas, *State, Power, Socialism*, 83.
63   Poulantzas, *State, Power, Socialism*, 90 (original emphasis).
64   Poulantzas, *State, Power, Socialism*, 83.
65   Poulantzas, *State, Power, Socialism*, 83.
66   Poulantzas, *State, Power, Socialism*, 84 (original emphasis).
67   Clarke, 'Marxism, Sociology and Poulantzas' Theory of the State', 13–16.
68   Poulantzas, *State, Power, Socialism*, 88.
69   Martin, 'Poulantzas', 132.

Poulantzas' own understanding of the relationship between the economic base (the mode of production) and superstructure (relations of production) results in the former fundamentally limiting the latter, ultimately negating the very autonomy and focus on class struggle that he sought to emphasise.

Poulantzas then ends up arriving at the same destination as Pashukanis and Althusser before him, albeit through a somewhat different route. Like them, he stresses the specificity of capitalist law, its inherently violent and repressive character, and the central role it plays in obscuring and mystifying the reality of capitalist social relations. But also like them, he ultimately cannot contemplate a meaningful way of engaging with law as part of broader struggles to transcend the existing social order. As Martin puts it, 'while Poulantzas gave us some idea about how we might understand legal systems in the capitalist state, he never says enough to help us see the way law is a site of political struggle'.[70] Notwithstanding Poulantzas' attempts to introduce greater nuance and complexity into the debate, and to emphasise the importance of social struggles in shaping the law, in his analysis the law 'was still perceived as, fundamentally, an oppressive apparatus serving dominant economic classes'.[71] Pashukanis, Althusser, and Poulantzas, then, have all made vitally important contributions to helping us understand one side of the equation in regard to law's role in capitalist societies. They all fall short, however, when it comes to grasping the other side of the equation—that is, 'the crucial question of law's emancipatory potential'.[72] The remainder of this chapter is dedicated to redressing that balance.

'THE POINT IS TO CHANGE IT'

The central problem with the Marxist accounts considered thus far is that they are locked into the sort of one-sided criticism lamented by Holloway.[73] As such, these ostensibly radical critiques can lead to quite disempowering and reactionary conclusions. As Simon Clarke argues with particular reference to Althusser and Poulantzas, because such theorists treat production and distribution as distinct, rather than a complex totality, their focus shifts to the role of social structures in reproducing capitalist relations of distribution, leaving the technical realm of production untouched or undertheorised.[74] As such, there is no real sense in which the dominant mode of production, capitalism as such, can be transcended on this theoretical approach, which leads invariably down the road of reformism and political quietism.[75] Within this schema, in which political and ideological forms are given primacy but in the end determined by an unyielding economic base:

> [e]very event becomes a victory for the system, another demonstration of the eternal character of bourgeois relations of production. The struggle of the working class against those relations of pro-

---

[70]   Martin, 'Poulantzas', 129.
[71]   Martin, 'Poulantzas', 130.
[72]   Buckel, *Subjectivation and Cohesion*, 214.
[73]   Holloway, 'Crisis and Critique', 516.
[74]   Clarke, 'Marxism, Sociology and Poulantzas' Theory of the State', 8–10.
[75]   Clarke, 'Marxism, Sociology and Poulantzas' Theory of the State', 9.

duction is devalued, its achievements becoming simply bonds which tie the working class ever more tightly into the system, its substantive defeats having a retrospective inevitability.[76]

For Clarke this approach should be rejected because it is fundamentally at variance with Marx's understanding of the complex totality of all social relations within capitalism.[77] It is also politically reactionary because it serves as a justificatory theory to 'postpone the revolution into an indefinite future, and to explain the necessary failure of any political initiatives in the present'.[78]

A similarly scathing assessment of such one-sided analyses is offered by István Mészáros, who argues that these approaches:

> [manage] to combine a mechanical conception of determination and 'homology' with a complete depreciation of the subject of socio-historical action … Such vulgar-Marxist reflections of the temporarily prevailing social immobility separate theory and practice from, and oppose them to, one another in a fatalistic/voluntaristic vision of historical determination.[79]

For Mészáros, such approaches break with Marx's understanding of the dialectic of base and superstructure and 'the irrepressible dynamism implicit in it'.[80] A more consistently Marxist approach, he argues, should 'account for the "active side" through which history is constantly being made, and not merely given as a brute conglomeration and fatalistic conjuncture of self-propelling material forces'.[81] This latter point is echoed by Ellen Meiksins Wood, who argues that various post- and neo-Marxisms born of the defeats of the twentieth century coalesce around the view that primacy should be accorded to dominating, even inescapable, ideas and structures, while displacing the central role of class struggle in transforming society. This, she argues, is a fundamental break with Marxism.[82]

There is much merit to these criticisms and claims. While Marx produced an immense body of work, covering political economy, philosophy, history, and other contemporary disciplines, perhaps nothing sums up better the purpose, drive, and import of his oeuvre than his 11th thesis on Feuerbach, in which he famously states that the 'philosophers have only *interpreted* the world, in various ways; the point is to *change* it'.[83] This maxim has been described as 'the most famous and most integral to Marx's emancipatory project',[84] and it informs and underpins every subsequent step in his theoretical and practical political development. As Karl Korsch argues, Marx 'devoted his whole life to transforming socialism from a theoretical ideology

[76]   Clarke, 'Marxism, Sociology and Poulantzas' Theory of the State', 20.
[77]   Clarke, 'Marxism, Sociology and Poulantzas' Theory of the State', 10.
[78]   Clarke, 'Marxism, Sociology and Poulantzas' Theory of the State', 25.
[79]   István Mészáros, *Social Structures and Forms of Consciousness*, vol 2 (Monthly Review Press 2011) 34.
[80]   Mészáros, *Social Structures and Forms of Consciousness*, 34.
[81]   Mészáros, *Social Structures and Forms of Consciousness*, 35.
[82]   Ellen Meiksins Wood, *The Retreat From Class: A New 'True' Socialism* (Verso 1986) 1–48.
[83]   Karl Marx, 'Theses on Feuerbach' [1845] in Karl Marx and Frederick Engels, *Collected Works*, vol 5 (Lawrence & Wishart 1976) 3, 5 (original emphases).
[84]   Paul Prew et al, 'The Enduring Relevance of Karl Marx' in Paul Prew et al (eds), *The Oxford Handbook of Karl Marx* (OUP 2019) 3, 9.

and practical utopia into a realistic and material science of practice'.[85] In a similar vein, Wood argues that the objective of Marx's theoretical and political project was to 'provide a theoretical foundation for interpreting the world in order to change it ... to provide a mode of analysis especially well equipped to explore the terrain on which political action must take place'.[86]

The essential characteristic of Marx's work was an effort to elaborate a theory of the capitalist mode of production and its attendant relations of exploitation, and to support the '*real movement*' to abolish and transcend that system.[87] As Mészáros puts it:

> [t]he deepest meaning of the Marxian conception is the passionate advocacy of *structural change* to be accomplished in a *global epochal sense* directly affecting the whole of humanity. Without focusing on this dimension of Marx's work neither the central message nor the animating spirit of his approach is comprehensible.[88]

Marx's critical work, then, was never simply or primarily about the exploration or 'balancing of concepts', but rather about the 'grasping of real relations',[89] with a view to developing a theory that could become a material force in the struggle of the working class to overthrow the capitalist order.[90]

One consequence of this central animating aspect of Marx's work is that while Marx never purported to write recipes for the cook-shops of the future,[91] his critical work always entailed a positive element. In an introduction to Marx's 'Critique of the Gotha Programme', Korsch expands on this key idea, noting that:

> Marx was a *positive dialectician and revolutionary* ... he never allows his critical work to become a mere *negation* of the errors and superficialities analysed in his letter. He always goes on to expound or briefly indicate the *positive* ... concepts which should replace the error and illusion he criticises. He is not content to criticise and refute the parts of the Programme which are the results of a false and superficial principle. This refutation always yields a positive development of conclusions drawn from the deeper ... materialist position which he advances in its place. It is through this *positive* development that the process comes to an end in a way that the 'materialist dialectician' finds really satisfying.[92]

Marxism is 'not a doctrinal system, but a ... theory of social struggle and the transformation of the world'.[93] Grasping this essential link between Marx's theoretical and political work and commitments is fundamental to understanding his project, and to thinking about how we can and should build on it today. As Peter Hudis argues, pursuing the link between theory and

---

[85]   Karl Korsch, *Marxism and Philosophy* (first published 1923, Fred Halliday tr, New Left Books 1970) 157.

[86]   Wood, *Democracy Against Capitalism*, 19.

[87]   Karl Marx and Frederick Engels, 'The German Ideology' [1846] in Karl Marx and Frederick Engels, *Collected Works*, vol 5 (Lawrence & Wishart 1976) 19, 49 (original emphasis).

[88]   Mészáros, *Social Structures and Forms of Consciousness*, 15 (original emphases).

[89]   Karl Marx, *Grundrisse: Foundations of the Critique of Political Economy* (first published 1939, Martin Nicolaus tr, Penguin 1993) 90.

[90]   Karl Marx, 'Contribution to the Critique of Hegel's Philosophy of Law. Introduction' [1844] in Karl Marx and Frederick Engels, *Collected Works*, vol 3 (Lawrence & Wishart 1975) 175, 182–87.

[91]   Marx, *Capital*, 99.

[92]   Korsch, *Marxism and Philosophy*, 140 (original emphases).

[93]   Bensaïd, *Marx For Our Times*, 4.

practice was central to Marx's work 'from the inception of his intellectual project, and we hardly do justice to the internal coherence of his project' if we sunder this decisive link.[94]

In contrast to theories of law, rights, and the state that overemphasise the ways in which social forms and structures necessarily contribute to the reproduction of capitalist relations of production, and the capitalist mode of production generally, a more thorough Marxist account should also look, to paraphrase Leonard Cohen, for the cracks that let the light in. In an important sense, a central aspect of Marx's understanding of society and social change is captured in his well-known statement that people make their own history, though 'they do not make it under circumstances chosen by themselves, but under circumstances directly encountered, given and transmitted from the past'.[95] Among the circumstances that are 'directly encountered' and that condition political practice are the social forms (including the legal form) and existing institutional and ideological arrangements that structure and reproduce capitalist relations of production. While these forms and relations impose definite constraints on what is politically possible, there remains an obligation to articulate a Marxist approach to law that can provide a basis for thinking about how movements for fundamental social change can engage with law, rights, and the state.

MARXISM, HUMAN RIGHTS, AND INSTITUTIONAL REFORM

In 'The Eighteenth Brumaire of Louis Bonaparte', Marx argued that the social revolutionaries of the nineteenth century could not draw their 'poetry from the past, but only from the future'.[96] This challenge remains for us today—particularly, as I argued above, since one of the main failings of much contemporary Marxist theory and socialist politics is that we have 'lost sight of an alternative' to the extant social order.[97] With respect to law, rights, and the state, this means grappling concretely with the inherent limitations of law and the legal form in ways that might contribute to building alternatives to the status quo—in order to find the seeds of an alternative future in the shell of the old. In his caustic dismissal of 'lawyer's socialism', Engels (with Kautsky) made it clear that 'the working class cannot adequately express its condition in terms of the legal illusion of the bourgeoisie'.[98] At the same time, he acknowledged that:

> [a]n active socialist party is impossible without such demands, like any political party. The demands that derive from the common interests of a class can only be put into effect by this class taking over political power and securing universal validity for its demands by making them law. Every class in struggle must therefore set forth its demands in the form of *legal demands* in a programme.[99]

---

[94]   Peter Hudis, 'Political Organization' in Marcello Musto (ed), *The Marx Revival: Key Concepts and Key Interventions* (CUP 2020) 108, 123.

[95]   Karl Marx, 'The Eighteenth Brumaire of Louis Bonaparte' [1852] in Karl Marx and Frederick Engels, *Collected Works*, vol 11 (Lawrence & Wishart 1979) 99, 103.

[96]   Marx, 'Eighteenth Brumaire', 106.

[97]   Michael A Lebowitz, *Build It Now: Socialism for the Twenty-First Century* (Monthly Review 2006) 43.

[98]   Frederick Engels and Karl Kautsky, 'Lawyer's Socialism' [1886] in Karl Marx and Frederick Engels, *Collected Works*, vol 26 (Lawrence & Wishart 1990) 597, 599.

[99]   Engels and Kautsky, 'Lawyer's Socialism', 615 (original emphasis).

This 'double character' of law and the legal form, as both a 'structural obstacle to social emancipation' and a limited form of emancipation and protection that must be engaged in some way, 'constitutes its complexity, which cannot be theoretically resolved in one way'.[100] Such real contradictions, inherent in the contradictory unity of capitalist social relations and law's role in reproducing them,[101] can only be addressed through concrete practice and in particular through class struggle.

In a global context of persistent capitalist crises,[102] with the attendant 'authoritarian, anti-democratic, money-saturated and carceral drift of capitalist state policies almost everywhere',[103] the erosion of the 'legal and democratic achievements of social struggles',[104] and the structural undermining of rights and living standards,[105] two areas of struggle and contestation merit consideration: the vexed question of human rights and the issue of new institutional forms. In the remainder of this chapter, I will sketch some of the implications of the methodological reorientation urged above for how Marxists should understand and engage with struggles around these two broad areas. With respect to law and the legal form, my approach is informed by an appreciation of the centrality of working class self-activity for challenging and transforming the existing social order, and also by a rejection of the iron formalism and structuralism implicit in Pashukanis, Althusser, Poulantzas, and others. Rather than understanding the legal form as a category that is fixed and distinct from its content, or the law as merely ancillary to the material base of capitalist production, this approach is informed by the view that 'form and content are integrated in a contradictory unity',[106] and that the challenge for a Marxist approach is to 'socialise and democratise both the form and content of law'.[107]

Human Rights

There is a wealth of literature on human rights, from defenders of the mainstream discourse and institutional practice,[108] through left-liberal critiques,[109] and more comprehensive critical accounts.[110] With their emergence as the secular faith of a putatively post-ideological age,

---

[100] Buckel, *Subjectivation and Cohesion*, 268.

[101] Marx, *Grundrisse*, 100–1; Clarke, 'Marxism, Sociology and Poulantzas' Theory of the State', 21; Fine, *Democracy and the Rule of Law*, 209.

[102] Greg Albo, Sam Gindin, and Leo Panitch, *In and Out of Crisis: The Global Financial Meltdown and Left Alternatives* (PM Press 2010); Bill Dunn, *The Political Economy of Global Capitalism and Crisis* (Routledge 2014); Andreas Bieler and Adam David Morton, *Global Capitalism, Global War, Global Crisis* (CUP 2018).

[103] David Harvey, *The Enigma of Capital and the Crises of Capitalism* (OUP 2011) 240.

[104] Buckel, *Subjectivation and Cohesion*, xi.

[105] William I Robinson and Yousef K Baker, 'Savage Inequalities: Capitalist Crises and Surplus Humanity' (2019) 9 *International Critical Thought* 376.

[106] Clarke, 'Marxism, Sociology and Poulantzas' Theory of the State', 77.

[107] Fine and Picciotto, 'On Marxist Critiques of Law', 19.

[108] Kathryn Sikkink, *Evidence for Hope: Making Human Rights Work in the 21st Century* (Princeton University Press 2017).

[109] Stephen Hopgood, *The Endtimes of Human Rights* (Cornell University Press 2013); Samuel Moyn, *Not Enough: Human Rights in an Unequal World* (Harvard University Press 2018).

[110] Gary Teeple, *The Riddle of Human Rights* (Merlin Press 2005); Radha D'Souza, *What's Wrong With Rights? Social Movements, Law and Liberal Imaginations* (Pluto Press 2018).

human rights' 'success' has also fuelled a minor cottage industry of human rights critiques.[111] There is an important strand of human rights scholarship that argues, largely on the back of Marx's early writings, that Marxism is incompatible with support for human rights.[112] Human rights, like the legal form in general, simply serve to obscure and legitimate the extant social order, and as such cannot and should not form part of any movement or project for emancipatory social change.[113] While there is some basis for this position in Marx's critique of the formal, abstract, and limited freedom secured by bourgeois rights in the context of the unfreedom of capitalist relations of production, the Marxist tradition as such ultimately leaves the issue unresolved.[114]

The challenge, then, is to think through the role of human rights in the contemporary global order and their relevance to movements for fundamental social change—that is to say, movements and organisations whose politics is geared towards undermining and transcending capitalism, rather than merely ameliorating some perceived excesses or shortcomings. Commenting on the various constitutional drafts that emerged during the political and social upheavals in France following the abortive revolutions of 1848, Marx makes a comment which is instructive in this regard:

> The right to work is, in the bourgeois sense, an absurdity, a miserable, pious wish. But behind the right to work stands the power over capital; behind the power over capital, the appropriation of the means of production, their subjection to the associated working class and, therefore, the abolition of wage labour, of capital and of their mutual relations. Behind the '*right to work*' stood the June insurrection.[115]

Marx makes a similar point with respect to the Ten Hours Act, the 'modest Magna Carta' of the working class,[116] which he saw as an important practical victory for workers, but also, and more importantly, as the 'first time that in broad daylight the political economy of the middle class succumbed to the political economy of the working class'.[117] In both instances Marx shows a clear-eyed understanding of the dialectic of form and content. While he is unequivocal about the inherent limitations of bourgeois right, he is equally clear that these forms of appearance, bourgeois right, should not be mistaken for the 'essential relation' that lies hidden behind it.[118]

In general, the language and practice of human rights undoubtedly plays a role in occluding the reality of capitalist social relations, but struggles over human rights, and the institutionalised protection of human rights, can also provide space for movements to build opposition to the extant order. On this point, Buckel notes that:

---

[111] Stefan-Ludwig Hoffmann, 'Introduction: Genealogies of Human Rights' in Stefan-Ludwig Hoffmann (ed), *Human Rights in the Twentieth Century* (CUP 2011) 1.

[112] Steven Lukes, 'Can a Marxist Believe in Human Rights?' (1981) 4 *Praxis International* 334.

[113] Balbus, 'Commodity Form and Legal Form', 580; Slavoj Žižek, 'Against Human Rights' (2005) 34 *New Left Review* 115.

[114] Paul O'Connell, 'On the Human Rights Question' (2018) 40 *Human Rights Quarterly* 962.

[115] Karl Marx, 'The Class Struggles in France' [1850] in Karl Marx and Frederik Engels, *Collected Works*, vol 10 (Lawrence & Wishart 1978) 45, 78 (original emphasis).

[116] Marx, *Capital*, 416.

[117] Karl Marx, 'Inaugural Address of the Working Men's International Association' [1864] in Karl Marx and Frederik Engels, *Collected Works*, vol 20 (Lawrence & Wishart 1985) 5, 11.

[118] Marx, *Capital*, 682.

[a]s an independent technique of consensus, the legal form thus provides for the functioning of hegemony a lever to generalise interests. In consequence, weaker forces can also always draw upon the legal form. Social relations of forces therefore inscribe themselves in the legal form in a *relational manner* only to the extent that a certain norm can become hegemonic. The rights that are realised and materialised in the legal form, in particular due to their independent existence, cannot simply be circumvented; they therefore do indeed constitute 'weapons' in social conflicts—ones that are also available to the weaker positions.[119]

At a time when the rights to protest, organise, undertake strike action, and engage in free speech are being undermined around the world,[120] a process that will no doubt be accelerated by the expansion of executive power during the Covid-19 pandemic,[121] defending basic democratic rights is integral to building and supporting movements for more fundamental social change. Engels understood this when he stressed the importance of such rights, notwithstanding their limitations, for providing the conditions for the working class to 'win everything else'.[122] The defence of such rights is necessary to facilitate the development of self-activity and political organisations that can struggle to move us beyond the extant order, but also to institutionalise democratic norms that would be essential in any future revolutionary or transitional period.[123]

Alongside the defence of democratic rights, struggles for social and economic rights (water, food, housing, health care, etc) can provide the basis for introducing 'a dialectics of subversion of the logics of capital'.[124] Such rights provide:

a certain respite for the working classes from the terror of an unmitigated labour market and the dictates of the workplace *and* because they create 'spheres' in civil society (in education, health, social security) that are not directly subject to so-called market principles and the unmitigated pursuit of private profit. From the point of view of transnational capital, however, all social rights present barriers to capital accumulation.[125]

By positing certain goods and services as essential human needs and placing their production and distribution under a modicum of democratic control, such rights challenge one of the core

---

[119]   Buckel, *Subjectivation and Cohesion*, 268 (original emphasis). See also Eugene Genovese, *Roll, Jordan, Roll* (Vintage Books 1976) 25–27.

[120]   Will Bordell and Jon Robbins, '"A Crisis in Human Rights": New Index Reveals Global Fall in Basic Justice' *The Guardian* (31 January 2018); World Justice Project, *Rule of Law Index 2017–2018* (World Justice Project 2018).

[121]   Keith Ewing, 'Covid-19: Government By Decree' (2020) 31 *King's Law Journal* 1.

[122]   Frederick Engels, 'The Prussian Military Question and the German Workers' Party' [1865] in Karl Marx and Frederick Engels, *Collected Works*, vol 20 (Lawrence & Wishart 1985) 37, 77. The 'everything else' to which Engels refers is the capture of state power and the building of industrial power through trade unions, resulting in the overthrow of the bourgeois order. Engels believed that to achieve this end, the workers' movement had to push the democratic rights of liberalism as far as possible, in order 'to establish the environment necessary for its existence, for the air it needs to breathe' as a fighting, revolutionary movement (78). Lenin makes a similar point about the necessity and inherent limitation of democratic rights; see VI Lenin, 'The Proletarian Revolution and the Renegade Kautsky' [1918] in VI Lenin, *Collected Works*, vol 28 (Progress Publishers 1974) 104, 108.

[123]   Ellen Meiksins Wood, 'C.B. Macpherson: Liberalism, and the Task of Socialist Political Theory' (1978) 15 *Socialist Register* 215, 228–37.

[124]   Prabhat Patnaik, 'A Left Approach to Development' (2010) 45 *Economic & Political Weekly* 33, 35.

[125]   Gary Teeple, 'Honoured in the Breach: Human Rights as Principles of a Past Age' (2007) 1 *Studies in Social Justice* 136, 141–42 (original emphasis).

impulses of the capitalist mode of production: the commodification of every aspect of the life course. It is in part for this reason that Leo Panitch and Sam Gindin argue that we must make 'the public goods and services required to meet workers' collective needs the central objective of class struggle'.[126]

As it stands, such struggles are already commonplace. Quite distinct from the human rights industry that dominates mainstream human rights practice (encompassing the main UN treaty bodies, major NGOs, and most academics and academic institutions that engage with human rights), social movements around the world have mobilised the language of human rights alongside other emancipatory discourses in broad political and social campaigns to access, control, and decommodify water, food, housing, and more.[127] Such struggles play an important role in advancing immediate material demands, in introducing practices of decommodification,[128] and in developing the capacities of working class and marginalised peoples. All of these are important, but the latter point, in particular, is crucial for advancing forms of socialist politics. As Lebowitz argues:

> [s]truggles for tenant rights, free public transit, support for public and co-op housing, increasing citywide minimum wages, initiating community gardens, climate action at the neighbourhood and community level, immigrant support, and opposition to racial profiling and police oppression—all have the potential for people to develop their capacities and a sense of strength.[129]

It follows that while a Marxist analysis must always be attentive to the ideological role of law and human rights, and the limited forms of freedom and equality attainable through these forms, the struggle over their content, and the power relations the form represents, must still be a central concern for transformative socialist politics. The challenge, as always, is to engage with human rights in ways that do not foster or reproduce the ideological illusions of liberal legalism and mainstream human rights practice. But this is the inescapable practical challenge of socialist politics and not, as Marx noted, something that can be resolved through critical theory alone.[130]

New Institutional Forms, or 'Socialist Constitutionalism'

Engaging with law today in order to advance struggles of fundamental social change that might prefigure a different future also raises the question of the institutionalisation of radically new forms of collective empowerment and decision-making. This, in turn, raises the question of the state—of state power and the possibility of new institutional forms in the place of law. On this point, Lebowitz argues that 'to construct a socialist society in reality, one step in every particular path is critical—control and transformation of the state'.[131] In a similar vein,

---

[126]   Leo Panitch and Sam Gindin, 'Marxist Theory and Strategy: Getting Somewhere Better' (2015) 23 *Historical Materialism* 3, 17 (de-emphasised from original).

[127]   William T Armaline, Davita Silfen Glasberg, and Bandana Purkayastha, *The Human Rights Enterprise: Political Sociology, State Power, and Social Movements* (Polity Press 2015); Paul O'Connell, 'Human Rights: Contesting the Displacement Thesis' (2018) 69 *Northern Ireland Legal Quarterly* 19.

[128]   O'Connell, 'On the Human Rights Question', 986–88; Gøsta Esping-Andersen, 'Multi-Dimensional Decommodification: A Reply to Graham Room' (2000) 28 *Policy and Politics* 353.

[129]   Michael A Lebowitz, *Between Capitalism and Community* (Monthly Review 2021) 166.

[130]   Marx, 'Contribution to the Critique of Hegel's Philosophy of Law. Introduction', 182–83.

[131]   Lebowitz, *Build It Now*, 68.

David Harvey notes that 'there is no way that an anti-capitalist social order can be constructed without seizing state power, radically transforming it and reworking the constitutional and institutional framework that currently supports private property, the market system and endless capital accumulation'.[132]

One of the central antagonisms in capitalist society is that the state and its laws and formal institutional arrangements curtail and delimit meaningful forms of democracy, in ways that mirror and complement the despotism of the relations of production at the heart of the capitalist mode of production.[133] For this reason 'democracy is the core of the problem for transcending capitalism',[134] and a Marxist orientation towards questions of state power and new institutional forms will not be preoccupied with insular debates around parliamentary reform or judicial power (though these may, in specific circumstances, have some salience). Instead, they will be focused on apprehending and supporting the development of new institutional forms that instantiate more substantive forms of democracy. The characteristics of such forms are sketched out by Lebowitz, who argues that they can and should include:

[d]emocratic decision making within the workplace (instead of capitalist direction and supervision), democratic direction by the community of the goals of activity (in place of direction by capitalists), production for the purpose of satisfying needs (rather than for the purpose of exchange), common ownership of the means of production (rather than private or group ownership), a democratic, participatory, and protagonistic form of governance (rather than a state over and above society), solidarity based upon recognition of our common humanity (rather than self-orientation), and the focus upon development of human potential (rather than upon the production of things)—all these are limbs of a new organic system, the truly human society.[135]

All of this entails a break with liberal constitutional notions of the division between the public and private spheres, or between state and civil society. Instead, the focus would be on developing democratic control in all spheres of life.

As with struggles over rights, examples of what these new forms might look like are already available. Whether it is participatory budgeting,[136] community wealth-building,[137] worker co-operatives, or, from historical experience, workers' councils.[138] Whatever the specific form, any such innovations will, in the short to medium term, require some form of legal articulation. In this context, 'what matters is to develop procedures that make subjects not only the authors of their own laws, but of the network of political conditions that surround them'.[139] A form of 'socialist constitutionalism' (for want of a much better term) would entail developing practices and new institutional forms which can empower people and begin to prefigure alternative

[132]   Harvey, *The Enigma of Capital*, 256.
[133]   Marx, *Capital*, 477.
[134]   Erik Olin Wright, *Envisioning Real Utopias* (Verso 2009) vi.
[135]   Lebowitz, *Build It Now*, 66–67.
[136]   Gianpaolo Baiocchi, 'Participation, Activism, and Politics: The Porto Alegre Experiment' in Archon Fung and Erik Olin Wright (eds), *Deepening Democracy: Institutional Innovations in Empowered Participatory Governance* (Verso 2003) 45.
[137]   Joe Guinan and Martin O'Neill, 'From Community Wealth-Building to System Change' (2019) 25 *IPPR Progressive Review* 383.
[138]   James Muldoon, 'Council Democracy: Towards a Democratic Socialist Politics' in James Muldoon (ed), *Council Democracy: Towards a Democratic Socialist Politics* (Routledge 2018) 1.
[139]   Buckel, *Subjectivation and Cohesion*, 270.

institutions for a more democratic and egalitarian future. Isabelle Garo elaborates on this point, noting that:

> [w]e can achieve democracy if genuinely democratic organisations are maintained and expanded, anticipating in the present the true democracy to come, going beyond but not rejecting the crisis-ridden parliamentary forms. It is only if there is a collective intellectual elaboration that a Marxism of today can accost and bring about, to at least sketch out, the social and political commons that alone can put an end to the reign of the capitalist law of value.[140]

In an historical period in which we are some distance from the 'higher phase' of communist society that will render legal regulation superfluous and dispensable,[141] there remains an urgent need to transform public 'institutional forms, purposes and capacities',[142] in ways that expand popular and substantive democratic control and help develop alternatives to the extant relations of production 'within and in opposition to the existing society'.[143] All of which will entail engaging with law and legal institutions in ways that rupture the depoliticising, reifying tendency of law in capitalist societies, striving, in this sense, to tear 'the imaginary flowers from the chain not so that man shall wear the unadorned, bleak chain but so that he will shake off the chain and pluck the living flower'.[144]

Such initiatives and novel institutional formations will inevitably run up against—and be constrained by—the existing legal forms and institutional arrangements of state power. This is unavoidable, and something that can be overcome not by dismissing the one-sided domination of the legal form but only through concrete political interventions. It is crucial here to insist again that forms of law and state are 'determined not by the will of the rulers alone but by the real relations between and within the classes which comprise bourgeois society'.[145] Law in capitalist society has system-preserving tendencies. But these tendencies are not iron laws; they are 'received conditions', but there is still scope to act and 'make history', even within these constraints. In this regard, only 'class struggle is capable of reorienting the course of history and of engaging the long and difficult task of the democratic and co-ordinated abolition of capitalism'.[146]

CONCLUSION

An aphorism attributed to Gustav Mahler holds that tradition is 'not the worship of ashes, but the preservation of fire'. When it comes to the Marxist tradition, the white-hot heart of that fire is the endeavour to understand capitalist society, so as to change and transcend it. Following almost two centuries of growth, political victories, defeat, and contraction, certain aspects of this tradition have fallen out of favour. Across the broad Marxist tradition, the

---

[140] Isabelle Garo, 'For a Strategic Marxism' in Daniel Bensaïd, *Recorded Fragments: Twelve Reflections on the 20th Century* (IIRE and Resistance Books 2020) 109, 116.

[141] Karl Marx, 'Critique of the Gotha Programme' [1875] in Karl Marx and Frederick Engels, *Collected Works*, vol 24 (Lawrence & Wishart 1989) 75, 87.

[142] Panitch and Gindin, 'Marxist Theory and Strategy', 18.

[143] Lebowitz, *Build It Now*, 63.

[144] Marx, 'Contribution to the Critique of Hegel's Philosophy of Law. Introduction', 176.

[145] Fine, *Democracy and the Rule of Law*, 94.

[146] Garo, 'For a Strategic Marxism', 113.

critical aspect remains acute and incisive, pointing to the various ways in which capitalism produces inequality, unfreedom, and degradation. However, a sustained period of defeat and isolation, notwithstanding recurrent crises of the capitalist system, has resulted in the emancipatory aspect of the Marxist tradition being sidelined by the laments of 'poets of negation',[147] producing versions of Marxist and Marxisant critical theory that articulate a closed system dominated by the law of value, accompanied by a left-wing melancholia that cannot imagine anything beyond capital.

With respect to law, the state, and rights, a rich tradition of scholarship has emerged over the last 100 years, building on the method and insights provided by Marx's work. However, as with trends in the wider Marxist field, these theories, notwithstanding their differences, have also tended to coalesce around a one-sided articulation of the role of law in capitalist society, stressing its place in the architecture of domination and exploitation. This misapprehends the actual role and place of law, but more importantly also feeds a potentially debilitating political quietism masked by rhetorical radicalism.[148] This approach breaks with the crucial transformative core of the Marxist tradition. Since engagement with law and the legal form cannot be avoided,[149] the challenge going forward is to elaborate a Marxist theory of law, state, and rights that recognises law's role in preserving and reproducing the extant social order, but also points to the ways in which legal form and content can be engaged with to locate and nurture the kernel of the future in the contradictions and stubborn reality of the present.[150]

---

[147]   Michael A Lebowitz, *The Socialist Imperative: From Gotha to Now* (Monthly Review 2015) 177.
[148]   Clarke, 'Marxism, Sociology and Poulantzas' Theory of the State', 9.
[149]   Fine and Picciotto, 'On Marxist Critiques of Law', 20.
[150]   Karl Marx, 'Letters From the *Deutsch-Französische Jahrbücher*' [1843] in Karl Marx and Frederick Engels, *Collected Works,* vol 3 (Lawrence & Wishart 1975) 133, 142.

26. Nomocratic social change: Reassessing the transformative potential of law in neoliberal times

Honor Brabazon

INTRODUCTION

This chapter revisits the long-standing debate in critical legal and political theory about the transformative potential of law in light of the neoliberal context, in which law-based tactics seem increasingly unavoidable for social movements. I offer a theoretical analysis that points, at a high level of abstraction, to several pitfalls and possibilities for this debate as it grapples with the specificities of the neoliberal conjuncture. More precisely, I call for greater attention to Marxist analysis of the legal form as a way to prevent constraints that are in many ways particular to the current moment from unduly narrowing engagement with the question at the heart of this debate—that is, the question of whether social movements can use law and other tools of the systems they are struggling against in their efforts to dismantle those systems.

Given the constraints facing social movement organising in the neoliberal context, particularly increased pressure on movements to engage with law, there is a temptation to evaluate the transformative potential of law from a position of tacit acceptance of the inevitability of law-based tactics and either to ignore Marxist analysis of the limitations that the legal form poses for anti-capitalist struggle or to trust that a movement's radical goals will somehow mitigate these limitations. This chapter argues that grounding evaluation of law's transformative potential more firmly in Marxist analysis of the legal form—including appreciation of the necessity of dismantling the legal form and of examining the role the legal form plays in different conjunctures—allows for a richer understanding of the challenges and possibilities of law-based social movement tactics in the neoliberal period. It also argues that such analysis helps to develop a more robust conceptualisation of law's transformative potential, one which can help to move the debate forward.

I first identify the core tension in Marxist thought concerning the question of law's transformative potential. I then proceed to demonstrate the advantages of greater attention to the legal form for understanding the limitations and possibilities of law's transformative potential. To do so, I acknowledge the appeal for Marxists during the neoliberal period of accepting the use of law for transformative change. However, I further demonstrate how concerted analysis of the neoliberal conjuncture, focusing on the particular role of the legal form in shaping and cohering the neoliberal political sphere, provides a fuller account of the specificities of the neoliberal moment and the difficulties for movements that try to avoid law-based tactics.

The chapter then goes on to illustrate how such an analysis simultaneously highlights certain vulnerabilities inherent in neoliberal social relations, which social movements can take advantage of through subversive engagements with law that actively challenge the legal form. I highlight how such subversive engagements with the legal form are missed in this debate, which tends to focus on movements' radical or reformist goals rather than on the role of the legal form in the way movements actually engage with law, regardless of their broader goals (for instance, whether movements try to subvert the legal form or merely use law as reformist movements would, taking advantage of law's content and legitimacy for short-term gains). I argue that a 'law for/as politics' framework better captures these subversive engagements with the legal form—and their enhanced transformative potential in the neoliberal context.

The chapter ultimately puts forth the 'law for/as politics' framework as a way of taking this debate further by reconceptualising law's transformative potential—as dependent not just upon the long-term goals of the movement or its immediate contextual considerations, but also upon the relationship between the extent to which the movement engages subversively with the legal form and the role of the legal form in the broader political conjuncture. My central point is that attention to the legal form need not be deterministic, but may instead capture an important register of agency and contingency that is not typically considered.

THE MARXIST'S DILEMMA

Marxist interventions in the debate about whether law can be used in the pursuit of revolutionary, emancipatory, or transformative change have tended to be framed in terms of two approaches.[1] The first maintains that law cannot be used to challenge capitalist social relations as it is constitutive of them. Consequently, other and often more militant tactics must be employed. The second considers the transformative potential of law to be structurally limited but still realisable. Such realisation may, for instance, be achieved through the adoption of laws to assist subversive struggles or the harnessing of existing laws for counter-hegemonic pursuits.

The stakes of this debate for Marxists can be illustrated by counterposing understandings of law in Marxist legal scholarship with the common conceptions of law in mainstream legal scholarship and in the popular imagination, which are typically liberal and formalist but which tend to seep into Marxist thinking about law's transformative potential nonetheless. Liberal legalism is an extensive and varied scholarly tradition, as is legal formalism, but it is sketched in broad strokes here in order to illustrate the loose ideas about law that underpin common understandings of social change and to offset the relative difficulty for Marxists of assessing law's transformative potential.

In general terms, liberal and formalist conceptions of law typically present law as a fixed, politically neutral, and self-sustaining order that operates and can be understood independently of the historical context out of which it arose. While law might be seen as a site in which social contestation plays out, legal decisions are not understood to be shaped by such contestation or relations of politico-economic power. Rather, law tends to be understood as a determinate

---

[1]   Note that this is not meant to suggest an overly reified distinction between 'using law' and 'not using law', as though movements can simply decide whether to include or exclude law from their struggles. Rather, juridical relations characterise so much of social life that social movements are shaped by law and face legal consequences even if they do not deliberately invoke the law. Still, in order to focus the discussion provided in this chapter, it is the movement's explicit decisions to use the tools provided by the prevailing formal legal system (e.g., engaging in court challenges) that are the subject of my analysis.

set of rules that exists in an autonomous social field, independent of the political, economic, and other spheres, and in many ways from the broader social forces that shape the emergence and development of laws and that influence their interpretation. Power relations, and the substantive inequalities they produce, are consequently viewed as separate from the nature of law, which is seen as equally capable of protecting the vulnerable from domination and exploitation through the formal equality embodied in central principles of liberal legalism such as the rule of law—loosely, the notion that the law applies equally to all.[2]

On this view, it is not difficult to see how it is possible for law to be used by social movements[3] to further social change. Because the enforcement and adjudication of law are considered to operate independently from power and historical contestation, law itself is seen as a neutral framework or 'empty vessel' through which any number of interests can be expressed and furthered. That is, progressive interests can be pursued merely by making the content of law more progressive or by using the courts to ensure that progressive laws and legal principles are enforced.

However, on this understanding of law, the form of law is taken as a given: as natural or socially inevitable, rather than as the product of—and as productive of—the particular set of historically specific political and economic relations that characterise capitalism, as Marxist legal scholars have argued. The recent renewal of Marxist legal thought has continued to push Marxist analysis of law beyond a simplistic base-superstructure formulation, underscoring the importance of the legal form not exclusively as part of an ideological or extra-economic superstructure but as an expression of capitalist social relations of production that is as integral and essential as the economic.[4]

This shift owes much to Evgeny Pashukanis' analysis of the particular legal form that social regulation takes under capitalism.[5] Pashukanis argued that the legal form emerged as a supposedly apolitical arbiter between formal equals, structuring the relationship between

---

[2]   See e.g., Philippe Sands, *Lawless World: Making and Breaking Global Rules* (Penguin 2006); Geoffrey Robertson, *Crimes Against Humanity* (Penguin 2006); Alon Harel, *Why Law Matters* (OUP 2014). Robert Knox outlines this difference in 'Strategy and Tactics' (2010) 21 *Finnish Yearbook of International Law* 193, 203, 219, and Umut Özsu provides useful background in 'The Necessity of Contingency: Method and Marxism in International Law' in Ingo Venzke and Kevin Jon Heller (eds), *Contingency in International Law: On the Possibility of Different Legal Histories* (OUP 2021) 60. Many have written on this separation of spheres in liberal thought, from Karl Polanyi, *The Great Transformation: The Political and Economic Origins of Our Time* (Beacon Press 1944) to Ellen Meiksins Wood, *The Origin of Capitalism: A Longer View* (Verso 2002) and A Claire Cutler, *Private Power and Global Authority: Transnational Merchant Law in the Global Political Economy* (CUP 2003).
[3]   I refer to 'movements' and 'social movements' in this chapter, but this debate is also relevant to individual activists, lawyers, and formal or informal groups involved in activism, whether or not they are part of a collectively oriented movement. For discussion of the role of international lawyers in this context, see Grietje Baars, *The Corporation, Law and Capitalism: A Radical Perspective on the Role of Law in the Global Political Economy* (Brill 2019); also Knox, 'Strategy and Tactics'.
[4]   Bob Fine, *Democracy and the Rule of Law: Liberal Ideals and Marxist Critiques* (Pluto Press 1984) 207; also China Miéville, *Between Equal Rights: A Marxist Theory of International Law* (Brill 2005). See, among others, Raymond Williams, 'Base and Superstructure in Marxist Cultural Theory' (1973) 82 *New Left Review* 3, for a critique of simplistic understandings of base and superstructure more generally. See Özsu, 'The Necessity of Contingency', for the limited extent to which this framework was part of Marx and Engels' analysis.
[5]   Evgeny B Pashukanis, *Law and Marxism: A General Theory* (first published 1924, Barbara Einhorn tr, Ink Links Ltd 1978).

individuals in capitalist society as parties to, and participants in, commodity exchange, and in doing so positioning substantively unequal individuals as abstract formal equals.[6] Pashukanis thus argued that the logic of the legal form is homologous to the logic of the commodity form: it is through the legal form that qualitatively different commodities come to be related in abstraction from differences in the labour that produced them, so that they can be measured and exchanged for profit on the basis of some degree of quantitative equivalence.[7]

On this view, law is not merely a set of rules; the legal form mediates and organises capitalist social relations. Like the commodity form, the legal form is co-constitutive of capitalist social relations. On this basis, Marxists have argued that, while individual legal decisions may at times bring short-term gains, law's potential to dismantle capitalism is limited, and using law to advance anti-capitalist struggles may ultimately legitimise and reinforce the capitalist system.[8] Likewise, critical legal scholarship more broadly has demonstrated numerous ways in which law is indeterminate, exhibits 'structural bias', and is constitutive of relationships of power and domination rather than an apolitical antidote to them.[9] That is, while law is not always and exclusively an agent of oppression, it structures and legitimises such relationships, and it shapes the conditions in which they develop, operate, and are challenged in ways that limit its potential to dismantle these relationships.

Given these critiques of law, in contrast with liberals, those who seek to problematise and challenge capitalist social relations are (or should be) far more ambivalent about the effectiveness of using legal avenues to change the systems and relationships that the legal form constitutes, legitimates, and reproduces. However, this has not always been the case, and when faced in the neoliberal period with the seeming foreclosure of tactical options that do not engage law directly (along with a diminished number of successful revolutions from which to draw insights), tension has grown in this debate around the question of what radical movements can or should do when more militant tactics that ignore or defy the law are less politically feasible.

Thus far, the general tendency has been to avoid addressing this tension directly. There has been very little work in the neoliberal period that directly traces the implications of the critical understandings of law outlined above for the pursuit of transformative change. There has certainly been much writing on the general topic of law, capitalism, and social change, which has underscored that the presence of progressive laws and legal principles does not

---

[6]   Pashukanis, *Law and Marxism*; Miéville, *Between Equal Rights*; Isaac D Balbus, 'Commodity Form and Legal Form: An Essay on the "Relative Autonomy" of the Law' (1977) 11 *Law & Society Review* 571. Note that individuals remain substantively unequal; the legal form merely abstracts from their social contexts and the power differentials between them.

[7]   Pashukanis, *Law and Marxism*; Balbus, 'Commodity Form and Legal Form'.

[8]   Miéville, *Between Equal Rights*, is the quintessential recent example.

[9]   This is essentially Knox's concise formulation in 'Strategy and Tactics', esp 201–3. See Martti Koskenniemi, 'By Their Acts You Shall Know Them (and Not by Their Legal Theories)' (2005) 15 *European Journal of International Law* 839; Martti Koskenniemi, *From Apology to Utopia: The Structure of International Legal Argument* (rev edn, first published 1989, CUP 2005); Lawrence Solum, 'On the Indeterminacy Thesis: Critiquing Legal Dogma' (1987) 54 *University of Chicago Law Review* 462; David Kennedy, *Of War and Law* (Princeton University Press 2006); Duncan Kennedy, 'A Left Phenomenological Critique of the Hart/Kelsen Theory of Legal Interpretation' (2007) 40 *Kritische Justiz* 296; Peter Gabel and Paul Harris, 'Building Power and Breaking Images: Critical Legal Theory and the Practice of Law' (1982) 11 *New York University Review of Law and Social Change* 369; Roberto Unger, 'The Critical Legal Studies Movement' (1983) 96 *Harvard Law Review* 561.

necessarily yield progressive outcomes, as liberal law reformers would suggest.[10] But does this mean that the efforts of social movements to pass or invoke progressive laws are detrimental to progressive outcomes, or just that they are ineffective or insufficient? Furthermore, if law is constitutive of relations of power and domination, and it systematically favours the interests of power and domination, can law ever be used to counteract systems of power and domination? And does this possibility change in different political conjunctures? These questions have not yet been sufficiently addressed. Attempts to do so during the neoliberal period have tended to point to examples in which law has been used by movements with radical aims for short-term gains without grappling with the specificities of the neoliberal conjuncture or with how the limitations posed by the legal form for the long-term pursuit of systemic change were or could be mitigated in those cases.[11]

The move away from analysis of the legal form where questions of 'practice' are concerned is unsurprising given efforts by Marxist scholars in recent decades to nuance or even bracket structural analysis as a way of avoiding charges of determinism.[12] It is also unsurprising given the challenges that social movements have faced in the neoliberal period, including the seeming inability of movements to avoid tactics that engage law directly and the unabated urgency of systemic change. However, it would be a mistake to allow the perceived necessity of using law-based tactics in a given conjuncture to unduly (and even, I suspect, unconsciously) shape conclusions in the debate more broadly. Instead, a concerted analysis of the specificities of the neoliberal conjuncture which centres the role of the legal form can provide a more robust account of the constraints on radical movements' decisions about using law, one that points not to a deterministic account but toward more diverse engagements with law that might now have greater transformative potential.

NEOLIBERALISM AND THE NOMOCRATIC POLITICAL SPHERE

Marxist analysis of neoliberalism has tended to focus on the financialisation of capital and the severe attacks on labour that have characterised the neoliberal moment.[13] The work of

---

[10]   See e.g., David Kennedy, 'The International Human Rights Movement: Part of the Problem?' (2002) 15 *Harvard Human Rights Law Journal* 101; Lucie E White and Jeremy Perelman (eds), *Stones of Hope: How African Activists Reclaim Human Rights to Challenge Global Poverty* (Stanford University Press 2010); Harry Arthurs, 'Governing the Canadian State: The Constitution in an Era of Globalization, Neo-Liberalism, Populism, Decentralization and Judicial Activism' (2003) 13 *Constitutional Forum* 1, 16–23.

[11]   Critical legal scholars, Marxists included, have been wont to defer to the legitimacy of law in their critiques of law—for instance, pointing out the illegality of certain foreign policies, or suggesting more or better laws in response to international law's failures. See Balakrishnan Rajagopal, *International Law from Below: Development, Social Movements and Third World Resistance* (CUP 2003); Antony Anghie, *Imperialism, Sovereignty and the Making of International Law* (CUP 2004); Boaventura de Sousa Santos and César A Rodríguez-Garavito (eds), *Law and Globalization from Below: Towards a Cosmopolitan Legality* (CUP 2005).

[12]   See Knox, 'Strategy and Tactics', for discussion of the mistaken divide between theory and practice in questions of strategy and tactics.

[13]   Alfredo Saad-Filho, 'Crisis *in* Neoliberalism or Crisis *of* Neoliberalism?' (2011) 47 *Socialist Register* 242; John O'Connor, 'Marxism and the Three Movements of Neoliberalism' (2010) 36 *Critical Sociology* 691; Costas Lapavitsas, *Profiting without Producing: How Finance Exploits Us All* (Verso

scholars like Gérard Duménil and Dominique Lévy, for instance, has illustrated how the neoliberal project sought to reconfigure post-Second World War class arrangements to restore the economic and political power of the top fractions of the capitalist classes, which had been weakened by the formal and informal tripartite agreements between the state, capital, and labour that characterised the post-war period in many countries.[14] Marxist scholarship on labour and social movements has documented the challenges that working class and other subaltern movements have faced as this reconfiguration has foreclosed avenues of struggle previously available.

Very few texts, however, have evaluated the role of law in these processes as more than just the vehicle through which these changes have been brought about—that is, not just how the *content* of law has become neoliberal, but also how the legal *form* has shaped both the 'nomocratic' conception of democratic governance and other neoliberal ideas and policies that constrain and control dissent.[15] As the following analysis will show, explicitly addressing the effects of a conjuncture on the transformative potential of law, including investigating the role played by the legal form within that configuration of capitalist social relations, provides a richer understanding of the shifting transformative potential of law in a given period. This includes not only the constraints this configuration imposes but also its vulnerabilities and contradictions, in which possibilities for advancing transformative change may lie.

'Neoliberalism' is a highly contested and often poorly defined shorthand that is used to describe the dominant politico-economic ideology from the 1980s onward. The role of the legal form in neoliberal thought and policy becomes more clear when neoliberalism is understood not only as a class-based political project but also as a utopian-epistemological intellectual current.[16] Neoliberal thought originated in the 1920s and 1930s as a marginal intellectual project that attempted to articulate the ideal configuration of social relations for the realisation of a very particular notion of freedom—freedom as the ability to pursue individual self-interest through autonomous, competitive market transactions.[17] The utopian society

---

2013); Leo Panitch and Sam Gindin, *The Making of Global Capitalism: The Political Economy of American Empire* (Verso 2012).

[14]   Gérard Duménil and Dominique Lévy, *The Crisis of Neoliberalism* (Harvard University Press 2011). See also Gøsta Esping-Andersen, *The Three Worlds of Welfare Capitalism* (Polity Press 1990).

[15]   Exceptions include Robert Knox, 'Law, Neoliberalism and the Constitution of Political Subjectivity: The Case of Organised Labour' in Honor Brabazon (ed), *Neoliberal Legality: Understanding the Role of Law in the Neoliberal Project* (Routledge 2017) 92; Ntina Tzouvala, 'Continuity and Rupture in Restraining the Right to Strike' in Brabazon (ed), *Neoliberal Legality*, 119; Honor Brabazon, 'Dissent in a Juridified Political Sphere' in Brabazon (ed), *Neoliberal Legality*, 167. While there is Marxist scholarship on law and neoliberalism (e.g., Honor Brabazon (ed), *Neoliberal Legality*; Akbar Rasulov et al, 'World Trade Law After Neo-Liberalism' (2014) 23 *Social & Legal Studies* 403–56), and on the limitations posed by neoliberalism for previous means of pursuing social change (e.g., James Petras, *Social Movements in Latin America: Neoliberalism and Popular Resistance* (Palgrave Macmillan 2011)), I am speaking here of scholarship that considers the limitations posed by neoliberalism for the transformative potential of law (i.e., scholarship evaluating the extent to which it is possible to use law in the pursuit of transformative social change given the specificities of the neoliberal juridico-political context).

[16]   Honor Brabazon, 'Introduction: Understanding Neoliberal Legality' in Honor Brabazon (ed), *Neoliberal Legality: Understanding the Role of Law in the Neoliberal Project* (Routledge 2017) 1.

[17]   See e.g., Milton Friedman, *Capitalism and Freedom* (University of Chicago Press 1962). See also Philip Mirowski, *Never Let a Serious Crisis Go to Waste: How Neoliberalism Survived the Financial Meltdown* (Verso 2014) 437; Quinn Slobodian, *Globalists: The End of Empire and the Birth of Neoliberalism* (Harvard University Press 2018).

these thinkers imagined included new types of subjectivity and social relations,[18] which I have argued elsewhere are modelled on the legal form and ideas about law that support it in ways that are specifically oriented toward containing and controlling dissent.[19]

Of particular interest to neoliberal thinkers is the capacity of the legal form to, in a sense, depoliticise the social relations that law mediates. The Marxist analysis of the shift to a legal form of social regulation during the transition to capitalism in England that is outlined below usefully highlights the depoliticising mechanisms inherent in the legal form. As Pashukanis demonstrated, as capitalist systems of commodity exchange developed over time, the formal rules governing social interaction needed to be abstracted from specific contexts. This process of abstraction marked a shift from rules which enforced the unequal status of different groups of people, and which were dependent upon the parties' unequal positions within a feudal hierarchy, to a way of governing relations between all potential buyers and sellers, who thereby came to be viewed as equals before the law. [20] Social regulation was no more neutral than it had been under feudalism, but its legitimacy now depended upon the concealment of its political character and its appearance as an apolitical arbiter. During this transition, power and authority came to be understood not as things that were inflicted by one person on another, but as the mutual subordination of both parties to an independent rational authority: the law.[21] This depoliticising capacity of the legal form—including its ability to abstract legal subjects from their social context and power differentials, to present its rules as universal and fixed, and to portray its adjudication as a technical matter of interpreting universal and fixed legal texts—has been central to commodity exchange, and has shaped the conception of law as a system of generalised rules that are interpreted through reason and applied equally to everyone following rational procedural formalities without consideration of political concerns or outcomes.[22]

The depoliticising logic of the legal form—its abstraction from, and mystification of, power relations and political struggle—lies at the root of the neoliberal interest in 'nomocracy' and the restrictions it poses for social movement tactics. Moreover, as I have argued, the capacity of the legal form to 'depoliticise' politics effectively permeates the neoliberal worldview far more deeply than just its mode of formal governance, which further alters the terrain on which movements' engagements with law play out.[23]

Neoliberal theorists like Friedrich Hayek advocated for nomocracy as a system of rule explicitly due to its ability to restrain political actors and minimise political engagement. A nomocracy is described in neoliberal writing as a society governed by abstract, end-independent rules that apply equally to all—in short, a society governed by the rule of law.[24] That is, whereas

---

[18] Pierre Dardot and Christian Laval, *The Way of the World: On Neoliberal Society* (first published 2009, Gregory Elliott tr, Verso 2013).

[19] Brabazon, 'Dissent'.

[20] Fine, *Democracy and the Rule of Law*; Michael E Tigar with Madeleine R Levy, *Law and the Rise of Capitalism* (Monthly Review Press 1977); Ellen Meiksins Wood, 'Peasants and the Market Imperative: The Origins of Capitalism' in A Haroon Akram-Lodhi and Cristóbal Kay (eds), *Peasants and Globalization: Political Economy, Rural Transformation and the Agrarian Question* (Routledge 2009) 37; Karl Marx, 'On the Jewish Question' [1844] in Robert C Tucker (ed), *The Marx-Engels Reader* (WW Norton & Co 1978) 26.

[21] Fine, *Democracy and the Rule of Law*; Tigar, *Law and the Rise of Capitalism*.

[22] Karl Klare, 'Law-Making as Praxis' (1979) 40 *Telos* 123.

[23] Brabazon, 'Dissent'.

[24] FA Hayek, *New Studies in Philosophy, Politics, Economics, and the History of Ideas* (first published 1978, Routledge 1990); FA Hayek, *The Road to Serfdom* (Routledge 1944) 32; FA Hayek, *The*

a welfare-statist 'teleocracy', as Hayek refers to it, is a system of governance organised around the pursuit of particular ends, or outcomes, such as universal access to health care or broad participation in public life, a nomocracy is organised around ensuring particular procedures and ways of interacting.[25] For instance, in a welfare-statist teleocracy, the end goal is a just outcome; in a nomocracy, the outcome is just if a just procedure was followed to arrive there.

Neoliberal thinkers have advocated nomocratic governance based on the premise that governments cannot use policy to achieve outcomes that advance values deemed to be in the public interest (such as racial equality or universal access to health care) because nobody can truly know the interests of others.[26] This means that any claim to direct policy in the public interest would only be a coercive and undemocratic attempt to impose one group's conception of justice, or one group's conception of another group's needs, onto others.[27] Instead, governments should merely establish end-independent legal frameworks that ensure that each individual can pursue their own self-interested goals through their decisions in the market.[28] On this view, the aggregate of everyone's freely made market decisions represents the only true picture of the public interest. (Although, curiously, neoliberal thinkers do still presume to know that their conception of freedom as the ability to make such market decisions is in the interest of everyone.)

Of course, both teleocracy and nomocracy employ law. And notably, neither is *laissez-faire*. But in a teleocracy law is understood to be primarily 'directional' and instrumental—a means to particular ends—while in a nomocracy it is primarily 'relational'—a set of mainly universal, general, abstract rules that are prohibitive, not directive, and that govern interaction independent of any broader goal.[29] For neoliberal thinkers like Hayek, a relational use of law is 'correct' as it provides a framework of constraints within which democracy must operate—a framework which applies equally to all citizens and protects them from elected leaders who claim to know the unknowable: what is in the common interest.[30]

Constitution of Liberty (first published 1960, Routledge 1977) 18; Michael Oakeshott, *Rationalism in Politics and Other Essays* (Methuen 1962); Stefano Moroni, 'Rethinking the Theory and Practice of Land-Use Regulation: Towards Nomocracy' (2010) 9 *Planning Theory* 137. Marx described capitalism similarly as government of laws, not of people; for discussion, see Fine, *Democracy and the Rule of Law*, 100. As noted below, it would be a mistake to expect all features of neoliberal thought and policy to be entirely new, as neoliberalism is not distinct from capitalism more generally.

[25]   FA Hayek, *Law, Legislation and Liberty: A New Statement of the Liberal Principles of Justice and Political Economy*, 3 vols in 1 (Routledge 1982); ER Alexander, Luigi Mazza, and Stefano Moroni, 'Planning Without Plans? Nomocracy or Teleocracy for Social-Spatial Ordering' (2012) 77 *Progress in Planning* 37, 52 (discussing TP Roth and VJ Vanberg).

[26]   Hayek, *The Road to Serfdom*; Alexander, Mazza, and Moroni, 'Planning Without Plans?', 46–59; Herbert A Simon, *Reason in Human Affairs* (Stanford University Press 1983); Nicholas Rescher, *Ignorance* (University of Pittsburgh Press 2009); Oakeshott, *Rationalism*; Hans-Hermann Hoppe, *Economic Science and the Austrian Method* (first published 1995, Ludwig von Mises Institute 2007); Karl Popper, *In Search of a Better World: Lectures and Essays from Thirty Years* (first published 1984, Routledge 1994).

[27]   Hayek, *The Road to Serfdom*, 62–63.

[28]   RE Barnett, *The Structure of Liberty: Justice and the Rule of Law* (Clarendon Press 1998); Mirowski, *Never Let a Serious Crisis Go to Waste*; cf Alexander, Mazza, and Moroni, 'Planning Without Plans?', 51.

[29]   Alexander, Mazza, and Moroni, 'Planning Without Plans?', 39, 53; Moroni, 'Rethinking', 146, 148.

[30]   Alexander, Mazza, and Moroni, 'Planning Without Plans?', 57–58.

Nomocracy is portrayed in neoliberal thought as a means of ensuring the rule of law, but it also fundamentally presupposes that everyone in a given society is always and already (sufficiently) equal in their ability to engage in market transactions, in the power of their market decisions relative to those of others, and in the ability of such decisions to reflect their interests fully.[31] That is, the formal equality on which nomocracy centres allows it to paper over, and effectively accept, substantive inequalities. The legal form is so attractive to neoliberal thinkers not only for its ability to constrain governments but also for its capacity to depoliticise social relations by obscuring such substantive inequalities and the power differentials that produce and are produced by them, which makes redistributive claims more difficult to articulate and advance. As I will demonstrate, analysis of the neoliberal political sphere more broadly that centres the legal form illustrates how this depoliticising capacity has been mobilised by neoliberal thinkers in areas beyond the formal system of nomocratic rule as well, which has restricted the tactics available to social movements in even more insidious ways.

BEYOND NOMOCRACY: THE INCREASING JURIDIFICATION OF THE POLITICAL SPHERE

While nomocracy is advanced by Hayek and others explicitly in order to constrain the power of democratically elected governments, the parameters and logic of the political sphere have come increasingly to mirror the logic of the legal form during the neoliberal period in ways that also restrict how democratic debate unfolds and how political dissent is articulated. It is for this reason that I have argued that neoliberalism should be understood as a juridical project, in addition to a political and economic one.[32] I have identified elsewhere four broad ways in which the political sphere has been reimagined and reconfigured around the logic of the legal form. These include different ways in which claims that law is politically neutral, abstract, rational, and fixed shape the neoliberal conception of political interaction, helping to naturalise current power configurations and make subaltern, collective, and redistributive claims more difficult to articulate and advance.[33] These shifts, which I will only summarise briefly below, deepen the impression that law-based tactics are unavoidable even for radical movements. But they also highlight vulnerabilities in neoliberal social relations and suggest possibilities for more subversive engagements with law than the debate about law's transformative potential has considered.

The first shift involves a reframing of the state as a neutral arbiter between equal individuals, mirroring the logic of the legal form. The welfare state, in its many variations, has generally been viewed as an active agent that intervened in society and the market in the public interest. This public interest was understood to include social goals of egalitarianism and redistribution.[34] By contrast, neoliberal theorists conceive the state as an agent for actively facilitating,

---

[31]   Among many other unspoken assumptions. It is also notably limited in its account of who is to decide upon the procedural laws that constrain democracy and structure market transactions, and how they are to do so.

[32]   Brabazon, 'Introduction'.

[33]   Brabazon, 'Dissent'. More detailed analysis of these four shifts can be found here.

[34]   The welfare state and the neoliberal state have varied greatly in their implementation. The post-war state-centred model and the neoliberal model are discussed here as ideal types; there are, of course, many variations on the ground. It could rightly be argued that law and the state have always

rather than tempering, the operation of competitive markets, including the construction of the social relations best suited to them. Since the public interest is determined through individual market transactions in neoliberal thought, the state is considered to be a 'manager' of competing claims between self-interested individuals.[35] Much like the image of law as a neutral arbiter between legal subjects, this conception of the state naturalises current power configurations.[36]

The second shift involves a reframing of political subjects and democratic engagement around the formal equality embodied in the 'rule of law'. In fact, neoliberal democracy is essentially politics as rule of law. In the post-war period, substantive inequality was recognised by many states and efforts were made to amplify the voices of traditionally disadvantaged groups as a prerequisite for an inclusive public sphere, with varying degrees of commitment and success. Likewise, labour unions were regarded as partners in a shared social project in corporatist and other welfare state models. In the neoliberal vision of the political sphere, these groups are either reconceptualised as 'stakeholders', with interests of equal value to other (often more powerful) 'stakeholders', or relegated to 'special interests' subordinate to the interests of 'business' and the market.[37] Political subjects are modelled on legal subjects: competitive, self-interested individuals who are abstracted from political or historical inequalities and who are instead seen and judged as formal equals. This has further obscured power differentials and concealed the relevance of class and other social hierarchies, which hinders redistributive claims.[38] Neoliberal democracy is largely procedural, limited to free market decisions and elections in which ostensibly equal citizens express their own interests through their vote. Collective action is increasingly discouraged as the attempt of a well-organised

---

fulfilled these roles, and that social life has always been juridified under capitalism, but what is discussed here is mainly a marked change in degree, through which these roles have been expanded and intensified. The differences are not highlighted here to romanticise the welfare state or to overstate the uniqueness of neoliberalism, but simply to point out that important differences exist and that labelling all of them 'capitalist' without appreciating such nuances conceals important dynamics of capitalism—dynamics revealed as capitalism is formulated and reformulated in different conjunctures. Furthermore, transitions from the welfare state model to the neoliberal model have not followed a single path, nor have they been uni-directional, uniform, or complete. See Brabazon, 'Introduction'.

[35]   Philip Mirowski, 'Postface: Defining Neoliberalism' in Philip Mirowski and Dieter Plehwe (eds), *The Road from Mont Pèlerin: The Making of the Neoliberal Thought Collective* (Harvard University Press 2009) 417; Bob Jessop et al, *Thatcherism: A Tale of Two Nations* (Polity Press 1988); Nikolas Rose, 'Governing "Advanced" Liberal Democracies' in Andrew Barry, Thomas Osborne, and Nikolas Rose (eds), *Foucault and Political Reason: Liberalism, Neo-Liberalism and Rationalities of Government* (University of Chicago Press 1997) 37; Engin Isin, 'Governing Toronto without Government: Liberalism and Neoliberalism' (1998) 56 *Studies in Political Economy* 169.

[36]   Naturally, all states are 'framed' in law, as law is intrinsic to the power and authority of the state form. However, the neoliberal state is not only framed in law but also modelled more directly on the private law notion of a strict enforcer of the 'rule of law' and a manager of competing interests—on the model of the legal form.

[37]   Dardot and Laval, *The Way of the World*, 226; Leo Panitch and Donald Swartz, *The Assault on Trade Union Freedoms: From Wage Controls to Social Contract* (Garamond Press 1993) 47, 60, 63.

[38]   The neoliberal subject resembles and draws from the classical liberal subject. However, differences include a heightened competitive imperative between individuals in neoliberal thought and an acceptance that some people 'losing' (i.e., socio-economic inequality) is not an unfortunate aberration but a natural characteristic of a well-functioning system. See Dardot and Laval, *The Way of the World*; Mirowski, 'Postface', 438, for an elaboration of differences between the liberal and neoliberal subject.

minority to acquire more political influence than they would otherwise have as equal individuals through their vote—essentially as a violation of the rule of law.[39]

The third shift involves a reframing of social concerns themselves around the legal form. For instance, as development issues have been incorporated into neoliberal policy, development has been reframed from a political project to a 'legal/institutional reform' project.[40] Likewise, as the universalising language of rights increasingly has come to form the only legitimate discourse of resistance, communities have reframed their articulation of social concerns and their pursuit of social change to be compatible with this framework, further crowding out and colonising non-Western, often more collective, approaches.[41] This process is furthered through the articulation of new rights as individual rights, or, in the case of Indigenous peoples, as individual rights that entrench colonial worldviews/ontologies.[42]

The fourth and final shift involves a reframing of the relationship between policymakers and the law. In the welfare state model, dissent was considered, at least in theory, to be part of the fabric of a rich democracy, and progressive social change was enacted even by conservative governments because the legitimacy of the government depended to some extent upon its ability to maintain political stability and also engage, if not address, the views of historically disadvantaged political minorities. In contrast, the legitimacy of the neoliberal state rests on its appearance of neutrality with respect to different groups' interests: on its ability to enforce the rule of law. In practice, this means that collective advocacy is often portrayed by government officials not as a quintessential feature of the democratic process but as bullying or intimidation that circumvents it.[43] Neoliberal governments also seem to have a greater tendency to

---

[39]   Brabazon, 'Dissent', 175. Collective action is not, however, discouraged when it takes the form of 'enterprise monopolies' (Tzouvala, 'Continuity and Rupture'). This is not to say that the welfare state model was not wedded ideologically to the rule of law, but rather that, in this model, political subjectivity and interaction are not themselves modelled on the rule of law to the extent that they are in the neoliberal period. This shift is part of an explicit and conscious effort on the part of neoliberal thinkers. Hayek and other neoliberals claimed not only that the rule of law required this kind of state and subjectivity, but that this kind of state and subjectivity themselves embody the rule of law. Likewise, competitive, self-interested individuals abstracted from political or historical inequalities always have been part and parcel of capitalist social relations; see Marx, 'On the Jewish Question'. Neoliberalism is, after all, not separate from capitalism but a phase or version of capitalism in which certain traits and patterns of capitalist social relations are emphasised, intensified, and made central. Neoliberalism, again, is thus not distinct from capitalism. Rather, the degree of abstraction, and the extent to which competitiveness permeates the neoliberal subject, are characteristic of neoliberalism, as is the extent to which democratic engagement (the political sphere) is modelled on the formal equality between these subjects. See Dardot and Laval, *The Way of the World*; Mirowski, *Never Let a Serious Crisis Go to Waste*; Slobodian, *Globalists*.
[40]   Kerry Rittich, 'The Future of Law and Development: Second-Generation Reforms and the Incorporation of the Social' in David Trubek and Alvaro Santos (eds) *The New Law and Economic Development: A Critical Appraisal* (CUP 2006) 203, 205, 232.
[41]   Susan Marks, 'Human Rights and Root Causes' (2011) 74 *Modern Law Review* 57; Kennedy, 'International Human Rights Movement'; Jessica Whyte, *The Morals of the Market: Human Rights and the Rise of Neoliberalism* (Verso 2019); White and Perelman (eds), *Stones of Hope*; Rajagopal, *International Law from Below*.
[42]   Panitch and Swartz, *Assault on Trade Union Freedoms*, 47, 60; Kristin Ciupa, 'The Promise of Rights: International Indigenous Rights in the Neoliberal Era' in Honor Brabazon (ed), *Neoliberal Legality: Understanding the Role of Law in the Neoliberal Project* (Routledge 2017) 140.
[43]   Stephen D'Arcy, *Languages of the Unheard: Why Militant Protest Is Good for Democracy* (Between the Lines 2014). See e.g., Peter Dominiczak, Steven Swinford, and Ben Riley-Smith, 'Theresa

mobilise a formalist understanding of laws and their enforcement as automatic, technocratic, and apolitical in order to minimise political opposition while not enforcing laws they dislike. For instance, they pass laws that are never intended to be enforced;[44] explicitly suspend existing laws, such as civil liberties, by invoking 'exceptional' or 'emergency' circumstances;[45] or simply do not enforce existing laws they do not wish to enforce.[46] This is possible because the image of the state as a neutral arbiter of the rule of law eclipses law's indeterminacy and the role of political will, not just in the enactment of laws but also in their enforcement.

IMPLICATIONS FOR DISSENT

Attention to the role of the legal form in shaping neoliberal thought and policy reveals how deeply the terrain on which social movements make tactical decisions about whether to engage law is being altered. The shifts outlined above have combined with nomocratic governance to strengthen barriers to political debate and resistance, contributing to the impression that legal avenues have become the only viable route for pursuing social change.

In the neoliberal political sphere, legitimate dissent is dissent expressed through voting or litigation, in which parties are positioned as abstract, formally equal stakeholders. While social movement activists have long used law as a tool in their struggle, law is now often the primary mechanism through which their actions are interpreted and made intelligible. Whereas previously law identified only the outermost boundaries of protest, law now regulates seemingly every aspect of protest, from the language, attire, and location of protestors to the way protest is framed and interpreted by politicians and reporters.[47] In this increasingly juridified

May to Dare Parliament to "Defy the Will of the People" If She Loses Article 50 Court Battle' *The Telegraph* (3 December 2016).

[44]   See Charles Hale's analysis of 'neoliberal multiculturalism': Charles R Hale, 'Does Multiculturalism Menace? Governance, Cultural Rights and the Politics of Identity in Guatemala' (2002) 34 *Journal of Latin American Studies* 485; Charles R Hale, 'Rethinking Indigenous Politics in the Era of the "Indio Permitido"' (2004) 38 *NACLA Report on the Americas* 16.

[45]   Examples include immigration detention policies, counter-terrorism laws, and crowd-control tactics at protests that suspend established legal principles and civil liberties. See Ronald J Daniels, Patrick Macklem, and Kent Roach (eds), *The Security of Freedom: Essays on Canada's Anti-Terrorism Bill* (University of Toronto Press 2001); Amnesty International, Canadian Council for Refugees, Canadian Tamil Congress, and International Civil Liberties Monitoring Group, 'Rights Advocates Decry Detention of Refugee Claimants From MV Sun Sea' press release (10 February 2011), https://web.archive.org/web/20120603071700/http://www.amnesty.ca/media2010.php?DocID=247 accessed 7 April 2021; National Union of Public and General Employees and Canadian Civil Liberties Association, *Breach of the Peace—G20 Summit: Accountability in Policing and Governance* (2011), https://www.securitepublique.gc.ca/cnt/cntrng-crm/plcng/cnmcs-plcng/rsrch-prtl/dtls-en.aspx?d=PS&i=85440775 accessed 7 April 2021.

[46]   Examples include governments delaying and obstructing access to information requests, not complying with their obligations pursuant to Indigenous treaties, and starving the budgets of state agencies to which they are opposed. See Alasdair Roberts, 'Structural Pluralism and the Right to Information' (2001) 51 *University of Toronto Law Journal* 243; Ken Rubin and Kirsten Kozolanka, 'Managing Information: Too Much Publicity, Not Enough Public Exposure' in Kirsten Kozolanka (ed), *Publicity and the Canadian State* (University of Toronto Press 2014) 195.

[47]   AK Thompson, *Black Bloc, White Riot: Anti-Globalization and the Genealogy of Dissent* (AK Press 2010) 67. See e.g., Craig Forcese and Kent Roach, *False Security: The Radicalization of Canadian Anti-Terrorism* (Irwin Law 2015); Ligue des droits et libertés, *Manifestations et repressions* (Ligue des

climate, tactics that ignore or defy the law may not have the same resonance, while the deeper generalisation of formal equality makes structural inequalities more difficult to articulate and advance.[48] Mainstream politicians and journalists are quicker to portray tactics that ignore or refuse to consider the law—such as wildcat strikes, occupations, institutional interruptions, and other direct action tactics—as less legitimate, which facilitates their repression and dismissal.[49]

Those who wish to pursue these tactics regardless are forced to grapple with the question of the extent to which militant tactics retain legitimacy during this period of heightened juridification. In a context in which the logic and language of the legal form increasingly permeate ever larger areas of social and political life, shaping our political consciousness and channelling dissent toward legal avenues, can radical movements avoid actively engaging the law? And if radical movements must engage the law, what distinguishes their use of law from those of reformist movements?[50]

WHY NOT JUST USE LAW?

If the only options available to movements are seen to be ignoring or breaking the law and using the law as reformist movements do—that is, taking advantage of the content of law and the legitimacy of the legal form to advance their short-term aims—then using law as reformist movements do increasingly appears to be the only viable option left to radical movements today. Indeed, finding ways to justify radical movements' leveraging of the content and legitimacy of law has been the orientation of much recent Marxist legal scholarship on the transformative potential of law. However, the concerns raised by Pashukanis and others about the limitations of the legal form remain largely unaddressed in these interventions. Moreover, there are more subversive possibilities within the law that these interventions miss. For instance, if the logic of the legal form is so fundamental to neoliberal policy and the worldview

---

droits et libertés 2015). And protest that does not conform to this hyper-regulation is seen as 'bullying' or as criminal and 'violent'. Brabazon, 'Dissent'; Jordan T Camp, *Incarcerating the Crisis: Freedom Struggles and the Rise of the Neoliberal State* (University of California Press 2016); Cemal Burak Tansel (ed), *States of Discipline: Authoritarian Neoliberalism and the Contested Reproduction of Capitalist Order* (Rowman & Littlefield 2017). A notable exception is the right-wing protest sometimes encouraged by neoliberal leaders, such as former US President Donald Trump. However, this kind of protest is encouraged as a means of countering various obstructions to the rule of law for which left-wing protestors and liberal politicians are blamed. Moreover, that protest is encouraged by neoliberal leaders does not necessarily mean that protest is encouraged in the neoliberal worldview; rather, it can be understood as one of many layovers from previous periods. See Honor Brabazon, 'Yelling "Fire" in a Crowded Occupation: Cynical Fire Hazard Claims and the Technocratic Containment of Dissent' (2020) 29 *Social & Legal Studies* 549.

[48]   Honor Brabazon, 'Juridifying Agrarian Reform: The Role of Law in the Reconstitution of Neoliberalism in Bolivia' (2021) *Canadian Journal of Development Studies,* https://www.tandfonline.com/doi/abs/10.1080/02255189.2021.1945551 accessed 24 August 2021.

[49]   D'Arcy, *Languages of the Unheard.*

[50]   The content of the terms 'reformist' or 'radical'/'revolutionary' can be spelled out in a number of different ways. My broader point is that the very terms of the debate are unhelpfully crude in that they do not capture the well-populated terrain occupied by movements with transformative goals that engage with law without outwardly questioning the legal form. This prevents the debate from distinguishing 'radical' from 'reformist' engagements with law.

that underpins it, is there increased subversive potential in tactics that go beyond reformist uses of law and instead seek to challenge and subvert the legal form on which neoliberal social relations are based?

As Marxist theorisation of the transformative potential of law has been rejuvenated over the past 15 years,[51] there has been growing attention to the legal form. However, the extent and implications of the limitations posed by the legal form for the pursuit of transformative change through law remain undertheorised. Instead, there is a tendency within this literature to assume implicitly that the radical goals of a movement can override these limitations. This slippage seems to be facilitated by the general tendency in this debate to focus on a movement's radical or reformist goals as a means of determining what differentiates a radical from a reformist use of law, rather than on the movement's actual engagement with law. This tendency is rooted in a valuable attempt to avoid determinism, but the inadvertent suggestion that the radical intentions of a movement alone can mitigate the limitations of the legal form seems to deviate from a materialist analysis.

China Miéville initiated this recent iteration of the debate over law's transformative potential in Marxist legal thought by drawing from Pashukanis to underscore the limitations of the legal form. Miéville argued against the common position amongst critical legal scholars that—despite the structural limitations of law—international law offered radical movements a resonant language of critique and useful tools with which to make incremental advances until systemic change was possible.[52] Instead, he argued that invoking international law actually legitimises the current legal order and hinders transformative change. He demonstrated how, through recourse to law, critical scholars ignore or set aside the deeper, systemic restrictions of the legal form, which constrain—if not eliminate—the possibility of effecting transformative change through international law.

As subsequent work has made important attempts to develop and nuance this argument, it has largely insisted upon the possibility that radical movements can still employ law-based tactics by focusing on the potential advantages of the content of law in the short term without addressing how the significant limitations of the underlying legal form can be avoided.[53] There is much excellent work, for instance, on law's relative autonomy, law's contradictions, and the origin of certain laws in subaltern struggle. This work has provided fruitful explanations of why law produces important short-term advantages for movements in some cases but has

---

[51] See e.g., Susan Marks (ed), *International Law on the Left: Revisiting Marxist Legacies* (CUP 2008); Knox, 'Strategy and Tactics'; Miéville, *Between Equal Rights*; Bill Bowring, *The Degradation of the International Legal Order? The Rehabilitation of Law and the Possibility of Politics* (Routledge-Cavendish 2008); Paul O'Connell, *Vindicating Socio-Economic Rights: International Standards and Comparative Experiences* (Routledge 2012); Akbar Rasulov, '"The Nameless Rupture of the Struggle": Towards a Marxist Class-Theoretic Approach to International Law' (2008) 19 *Finnish Yearbook of International Law* 243; Umut Özsu, 'Grabbing Land Legally—A Marxist Analysis' 32 (2019) *Leiden Journal of International Law* 215.

[52] China Miéville, 'The Commodity-Form Theory of Inernational Law: An Introduction' (2004) 17 *Leiden Journal of International Law* 271; Miéville, *Between Equal Rights*.

[53] Marks (ed), *International Law on the Left*; Knox, 'Strategy and Tactics'; Miéville, *Between Equal Rights*; Bowring, *Degradation of the International Legal Order?*; Rasulov, '"The Nameless Rupture of the Struggle"'; Özsu, 'Grabbing Land Legally'; Anthony Carty, 'Marxist International Law Theory as Hegelianism' (2010) 10 *International Studies Review* 122; Mike Macnair, 'Law and State as Holes in Marxist Theory' (2006) 34 *Critique* 211; Honor Brabazon, 'Occupying Legality: The Subversive Use of Law in Latin American Occupation Movements' (2017) 36 *Bulletin for Latin American Research* 21.

not yet countered the claim of law's overall structural bias.[54] After all, Miéville and others who have argued against law's transformative potential do not argue that law may never be useful for radical movements. Instead, they explain why the pursuit of transformative change through law can only get movements so far, and that the long-term disadvantages of using law outweigh these short-term victories.

The few recent interventions in Marxist legal scholarship that have asked how the disadvantages of the legal form can be mitigated have tended to emphasise the context of a movement's engagement with law,[55] understood as the configuration of a movement's use of law within the movement's long-term political strategy. For instance, these interventions argue that movements can mitigate some of law's detrimental effects by using it in a limited and self-aware way, and by combining it with extra-legal (e.g., political) tactics. This attention to the place and role of law within a movement's broader strategy is essential, as I too have argued,[56] but it is still unclear how precisely a particular configuration of law within that broader strategy would avoid or minimise the costs of engaging the law identified by Marxist analysis of the legal form. If a movement does not rely exclusively on law, the movement may not contribute to the continuous public legitimation of the legal form implicit in any use of law to the degree that it would if it embraced the pursuit of specifically legal change wholeheartedly as its focus.[57] Moreover, a movement can use its engagements with law for short-term goals as opportunities to mobilise for broader change (such as using a trial to publicise a movement's political aims or using a loophole in legislation to obtain greater resources for impoverished communities and build their mobilisational capacities in the process).[58]

Yet while these are undoubtedly advantageous, the difference between a radical movement's use of law and a reformist use of law lies in the centrality of law to the movement's strategy—that is, the fact that the radical movement is simultaneously pursuing broader transformative goals, and that this use of law might advance some such goals. In other words, the actual use of law by a radical movement that consciously seeks to configure law in a specific way as part of its broader strategy still mobilises the content and legitimacy of law, leaving the legal form intact, as reformist movements do, regardless of the movement's intentions beyond the moment in which it uses law or where its use of law fits within its broader political strategy.

---

[54]　See e.g., Bowring, *Degradation of the International Legal Order?*; Marks (ed), *International Law on the Left*.

[55]　Robert Knox, review of Bowring, *The Degradation of the International Legal Order?* (2010) 18 *Historical Materialism* 193; Knox, 'Strategy and Tactics', 225; Brabazon, 'Occupying Legality'; White and Perelman (eds), *Stones of Hope* (2010). See also the early classics: Rosa Luxemburg, *The Essential Rosa Luxemburg: Revolution or Reform and The Mass Strike* (first published 1898/1906, Helen Scott ed, Integer and Patrick Lavin tr, 2008); Georg Lukács, *Tactics and Ethics, 1919–1929: The Questions of Parliamentarianism and Other Essays* (first published 1968, Michael McColgan tr, New Left Books 1972).

[56]　Brabazon, 'Occupying Legality'.

[57]　A limitation of the task of assessing the transformative potential of law in general, is that legitimation is central to analysis of law's constitutive role in capitalist social relations—and thus in the barriers to using the legal form for transformative change. But legitimation is, of course, very difficult to measure, as is delegitimation.

[58]　Brabazon, 'Occupying Legality'; Knox, 'Strategy and Tactics', 225, 212; Kirsten Kozolanka, 'Unworthy Citizens, Poverty, and the Media: A Study in Marginalized Voices and Oppositional Communication' (2010) 86 *Studies in Political Economy* 55.

Radical movements that attempt to maximise the subversiveness of their use of law by situating it within long-term transformative goals still effectively seek to use law's legitimacy to delegitimise the broader politico-economic system. They make no effort to delegitimise the legal system that constitutes and enables that broader politico-economic system. Presumably, the legal form itself might be challenged at a later time, when circumstances allow for it, but it is not clear how such circumstances might be brought about. In fact, by using the legitimacy of law to their advantage, movements using this approach arguably make such a broader challenge to the legal system in the future more difficult.[59] That is, if the argument made by Pashukanis and others—that the legal form is as fundamental to capitalist social relations as the commodity form—is to be taken seriously, and not papered over due to the constraints of the current conjuncture, it means that dismantling the legal form is as essential to the process of challenging and replacing capitalism as dismantling the commodity form, and that challenging one while bolstering the legitimacy and institutional power of the other would be counter-productive. In contrast, as the following section demonstrates, the 'law for/as politics' framework accounts for the possibility that law can be used in other ways that might actively challenge the legitimacy of the legal form, thereby hastening its demise. It is here that movements might be able to take advantage of the vulnerabilities of increased dependence on the legitimacy of the legal form in the neoliberal period.

'LAW FOR/AS POLITICS', AND THE VARIABILITY OF LAW'S TRANSFORMATIVE POTENTIAL

The focus on the legal form in the 'law for/as politics' framework sheds light on alternative ways of engaging law, and on their varying transformative potential in different conjunctures.[60] Instead of focusing on ways that movements with radical goals use the legal avenues open to them (asking 'how can, or how do, radical movements use law?'), this framework begins with an examination of law itself—with Marxist analysis of the legal form and the limitations it poses for transformative change in general and within specific conjunctures in particular. It asks how these barriers might be mitigated and how the legal form might be subverted and eventually dismantled (asking 'how and when can law be engaged radically?'). This approach opens space for assessing the transformative potential not only of different ways of using the content of law for short-term gains, but also of tactics that *actively challenge* the legal form (rather than setting aside a critique of the legal form in order to take advantage of the content of law). In this formulation, when law is used *for* politics, law is used as a tool or vehicle for a (subversive) political pursuit. When, by contrast, law is used *as* politics, the use of law itself is a (subversive) political pursuit as well. Law is still used as a tool for a political pursuit here, but this substantive political pursuit (such as a favourable court decision) is subordinate to the procedural political pursuit of using the law in a subversive way to achieve it.[61]

---

[59]   Knox highlights some of these concerns in his opposition to the claim that critical legal scholars can make political interventions in liberal legal terms depending upon the context. Knox, 'Strategy and Tactics', 208.

[60]   Brabazon, 'Occupying Legality'.

[61]   Brabazon, 'Occupying Legality'.

The use of law *as* politics is based on an awareness that both the substantive content of law and the very process of engaging the law are inherently political, and it seeks to mobilise this political terrain to its advantage. That is, while the substantive pursuit of legal change alone involves using the content of law without questioning or subverting the form of law, the procedural pursuit involves using the content of law to question and subvert the form of law. In cases of law *for* politics, law is used in a way that takes advantage of the legal form, using law's liberal image to legitimate and institutionalise the substantive political goal being sought. By contrast, in cases of law *as* politics, law is used not to enjoy but to exploit the legal form in order to expose the contradictions and limitations of law's liberal image and to challenge its legitimising and institutionalising characteristics.[62]

Tactics that use law *as* politics embody a recognition that the legitimacy of the legal form is dependent upon certain shared social assumptions about its nature as impartial, apolitical, and independent of historical context, and also about the equality of legal subjects (such as employers and workers or peasants and landowners). As distinct from uses of law *for* politics, this fragility of the law is used as leverage in uses of law *as* politics. For instance, tactics that use law *as* politics can force the state to choose between two undesirable options by creating a situation that reveals the friction between the ideals of the legal form and the concrete processes used to maintain neoliberal social relations, while pointing out the absurdity of these myths in the first place and encouraging a broader questioning and challenging of law's legitimacy. Whereas, in uses of law *for* politics, questioning the legitimacy of the prevailing legal order in the future would delegitimise the substantive gains won using the law, in the case of law *as* politics, questioning (or suspending belief in) the legitimacy of the prevailing legal order is an integral part of the tactic itself. These uses of law are not inconsistent with subsequent questioning and challenging of the capitalist system as a whole, and in fact are designed to hasten it.[63]

Importantly, law *as* politics not only encourages questioning of the legal order in practice by highlighting cases where law fails to live up to its image as an apolitical, rational, and self-referential system—questioning that could lead to reforms that ensure better compliance with the existing legal order. To take Balbus' example, tactics that aim to draw attention to cases in which the rich receive more lenient sentences than the poor are typically underpinned by an implicit affirmation that legal equality is a principle that can and should govern social relations. Such tactics thus uphold the legitimacy of the legal order rather than questioning whether substantive inequality is something this order can ever address adequately.[64]

Consistent with Balbus' argument,[65] tactics that use law *as* politics highlight the absurdity of law's legitimating claims, whether or not these claims are upheld in practice. In other words, unlike tactics that seek to shame the law into conforming with its own standards, the impudent element of a use of law *as* politics ensures that it is not the outcome of a legal decision that will determine whether that decision will reinforce or challenge the legal order.[66] Rather, the very manner in which the movement uses law itself contains an implicit challenge to the legal order. Movements using law *as* politics choose particular cases and aspects of law that

---

[62] Brabazon, 'Occupying Legality'.
[63] Brabazon, 'Occupying Legality'.
[64] Balbus, 'Commodity Form and Legal Form', 582.
[65] Balbus, 'Commodity Form and Legal Form', 582.
[66] Brabazon, 'Occupying Legality'.

expose the contradictions and limitations of the legal form, regardless of whether the ultimate legal decision appears to uphold law's legitimating ideals. Instead, movements use tactics through which the very fact that a legal decision must be made, between the available options and given the relevant principles, contributes to the delegitimisation of the legal order. This not only reduces the legitimisation of law that occurs through law's use, as might tactics that situate law within a broader political strategy, but it actively delegitimises the very principles underlying the legal form.[67]

This framework illustrates that engagements with law can hold more or less transformative potential, not depending upon the (radical or reformist) goals of the movement that deploys them but upon the very way in which that movement uses the law—upon, that is, the degree to which it actively challenges the form of law and does not merely take advantage of its content. Moreover, while many interventions acknowledge that law does not always have the same effect regardless of micro-level political circumstances, this framework demonstrates how the transformative potential of law can be altered by the specificities of the neoliberal period and other capitalist conjunctures. For instance, if law plays a particularly fundamental role in shaping the subjectivities and social relations of the juridified and nomocratic neoliberal political sphere, a delegitimisation of the legal form, such as one pursued through a use of law *as* politics, might have far-reaching effects on the legitimacy of all social relations that law mediates during the neoliberal period, and within capitalism more generally.

However, uses of law *as* politics are not always effective or resonant. Nor is law *as* politics alone sufficient to delegitimise the legal form and capitalism as a whole.[68] Moreover, this is not to suggest that using law *as* politics is the only way that radical movements can or should use law. Rather, my point is the opposite: there are multiple ways of engaging law which can be more or less subversive, depending upon how that type of engagement with law interacts with the role of the legal form in that political conjuncture. Importantly, this framework shows that while movements with radical goals make assessments of the kind of change that is politically feasible in a given conjuncture, this does not necessarily mean they have to use the tools or tactics on offer as they are intended.

The distinction between uses of law *for* politics and law *as* politics distinguishes not only between movements with reformist or radical goals, and not even only between movements with reformist and radical understandings of law (or between those who retain faith in the liberal legal order but seek to perfect it and those who are fundamentally sceptical as to its ability to deliver justice). In addition, the 'law for/as politics' framework distinguishes those who are sceptical of the possibility of effecting transformative change through law but who nonetheless take advantage of its content and legitimacy as the best available option or as an interim measure,[69] from those who also use this short-term pursuit as an opportunity to ques-

---

[67]   This approach has roots in theories of revolutionary reformism; see Brabazon, 'Occupying Legality'.

[68]   This is particularly the case when the approach is used in opposition to more left-wing governments; see e.g., Brabazon, 'Occupying Legality'.

[69]   Again, it is certainly possible to understand that systemic politico-economic change cannot occur without systemic juridical change and still set aside that critique of the legal form in order to take advantage of the content of law. Indeed, that approach is quite common. However, it has not been demonstrated how this approach would be effective at advancing systemic change—how, despite the short-term advantages the law may provide, it does not merely hinder systemic juridical change, and, by extension, systemic political-economic change.

tion and challenge the form of law itself, thereby contributing to future systemic change. This framework includes the use of law by movements that are not secretly sceptical about law's legitimising claims and transformative potential, waiting to openly challenge the legal system until later (but without specifying how these 'later' circumstances will be created). Instead, they express their scepticism about law in the very way in which they use law. The importance of incorporating an active challenge to the legal form rests on understanding that systemic politico-economic change cannot occur without systemic juridical change.

CONCLUSION

Focusing on the neoliberal context, this chapter argued that renewed attention to the legal form can provide a richer picture of both its limitations and possibilities for transformative social change. First, I showed how analysing the neoliberal conjuncture in a way that is attentive to the role of the legal form highlights how the logic and language of law have come increasingly to shape political life, such that spaces, languages, and opportunities for dissent have become increasingly circumscribed. This process has reduced the extent to which militant tactics alone can defy the law without losing legitimacy and facing repression. And it has meant that avoiding concerted uses of legal channels is less and less feasible for radical movements. Second, however, the chapter argued that increased reliance on the legal form has also created certain vulnerabilities that movements can exploit. The chapter demonstrated that focus on the legal form, within the 'law for/as politics' framework, highlights such subversive potential in the law. In particular, it illustrates how, in the current conjuncture, the use of law *as* politics in order to expose, challenge, and even mock the law may have greater potential to delegitimise the neoliberal model—and capitalist social relations more generally—which the legal form shapes so fundamentally. The chapter has shown how this focus on the legal form reframes the debate about law's transformative potential. The transformative potential of law, on this account, is variable and contingent, and must be understood in the context of the social relations of specific capitalist conjunctures. Rather than sidestepping or ignoring the tension between Marxist analysis of the limitations of the legal form (and the apparent inevitability of tactics that engage law in the way that reformist movements do), this chapter has argued that centring the legal form can help to confront the question directly and move the debate forward. In doing so, it also shows that allowing for agency and contingency in Marxist analysis does not necessarily involve diminishing or suspending critique of the force of structural constraints. Instead, it can involve locating vulnerabilities within the logics of those structures, which can then allow us to begin the process of dismantling them.

27. Beyond fetishism and instrumentalism: Rethinking Marxism and law under neoliberalism

Igor Shoikhedbrod

INTRODUCTION

The aim of this chapter is to rethink Marxism's relationship to law by considering the extent to which law can serve as a vehicle for progressive change in the era of neoliberalism. Reflections on law among Marxists have generally ranged from reasoned suspicion to outright contempt. In 1975, EP Thompson, the eminent Marxist historian, caused controversy on the left when he concluded his account of the eighteenth-century Black Act with a resolute defence of the rule of law. Thompson's unqualified endorsement of the rule of law had the regrettable consequence of detracting Marxist critics from engaging constructively with his valuable insights concerning historical struggles over law and rights. After exploring the theoretical context for Thompson's views, I examine Marx's parallel reflections on the struggle for a legally limited working day, and explain why Marx and Engels valued legal struggles, even as they welcomed the revolutionary supersession of capitalist property relations. The chapter then considers legal efforts to expand the negatively circumscribed right of personal security to include a socio-economic right to housing in Canada. Although these experiences reaffirm the view that transformative change is to be sought through political mobilisation and contestation, law offers a medium by which oppressed classes can resist further encroachments by states and multinational corporations while advancing a democratic socialist alternative to financialised capitalism that is in keeping with the Marxist quest for human emancipation.

CLASS-BOUND LAWS AND THE ANTINOMY OF EQUAL RIGHTS: MARX AND EP THOMPSON

Karl Marx's intellectual journey from rational law to a historically grounded conception of right developed in confrontation with the openly classist and autocratic laws of the Prussian state—the wood theft law, censorship legislation, and criminal proceedings against democratic forces in the aftermath of the 1848 Revolution, in Prussia.[1] Although Marx identified the ways in which positive law typically serves ruling class interests, he did not conflate class domination with law as such. Nowhere was Marx's support for legality more evident than during the reactionary period that followed the defeat of the March Revolution of 1848. At the time, Marx

---

[1]   For a more elaborate treatment of Marx's conception of justice, legality, and rights, see Igor Shoikhedbrod, *Revisiting Marx's Critique of Liberalism: Rethinking Justice, Legality and Rights* (Palgrave Macmillan 2019).

issued a fierce condemnation of the Prussian Press Bill that sought to undermine what he took to be a critical bulwark against arbitrary authority, namely the power of a free press. Marx's reflections are well worth revisiting today because they betray his otherwise overlooked concern with basic principles of legality. Marx warned:

> From the day when this Bill becomes law, officials may with impunity carry out any arbitrary act, any tyrannical and any unlawful act. They may calmly administer beatings or order them, arrest and detain people without a hearing; the press, the only effective control, has been rendered ineffective. On the day when this Bill becomes law, the bureaucracy may celebrate a festival: it will have become mightier, less restrained and stronger than it was in the pre-March period.[2]

The parallel between Marx's formative reflections on the Prussian wood theft law[3] and EP Thompson's critical rendition of the Black Act is more than a passing coincidence, since it raises the issue of classist laws in connection with the formal equality that underpins liberal legality. Thompson leaves readers with little doubt concerning the classist character of the notorious Black Act of 1723, which carried the death penalty for rebellious peasants caught stealing deer, cutting trees, and burning property.[4] In Thompson's words, the Black Act was 'a bad law, drawn by bad legislators, and enlarged by the interpretations of bad judges'; and '[n]o defence, in terms of natural justice, can be offered for anything in the history of the Black Act'.[5] However, rather than depicting the Black Act as a ready-made piece of class legislation against the propertyless, Thompson observes that the process of enclosure introduced new property rights while dismantling the customary use rights that were previously enjoyed by hunters and cottagers in the commons. In this way, Thompson portrays law in eighteenth-century Britain as a battleground over competing conceptions of law and rights. Thompson is clear on this point:

> What was often at issue was not property, supported by law, against no-property; it was alternative definitions of property-rights: for the landowner, enclosure—for the cottager, common rights; for the forest officialdom, 'preserved grounds' for the deer; for the foresters, the right to take turfs. For as long as it remained possible, the ruled—if they could find a purse and a lawyer—would actually fight for their rights by means of law.[6]

While *Whigs and Hunters* chronicles recurring cases of legal manipulation in favour of ruling class interests, Thompson frames his critical assessment of the notorious Black Act with the qualification that legal mediation is never exhausted by ruling class interests alone. Thompson argues that 'if we say that existent class relations were mediated by the law, this is not same thing as saying that the law was no more than those relations translated into other terms, which masked or mystified the reality'.[7] Thompson thereby paves a middle ground between

---

[2]   Karl Marx, 'The Prussian Press Bill' [1848] in Karl Marx and Frederick Engels, *Collected Works*, vol 7 (International Publishers 1977) 250, 251.

[3]   See Karl Marx, 'Proceedings of the Sixth Rhine Province Assembly. Third Article—Debates on the Law on Thefts of Wood' [1842] in Karl Marx and Frederick Engels, *Collected Works*, vol 1 (International Publishers 1975) 224.

[4]   EP Thompson, *Whigs and Hunters: The Origin of the Black Act* (Allen Lane 1975) 267.

[5]   Thompson, *Whigs and Hunters*, 267.

[6]   Thompson, *Whigs and Hunters*, 261.

[7]   Thompson, *Whigs and Hunters*, 262.

the traditional standpoints of legal formalism and class instrumentalism. Legal formalism sets off from the most rudimentary nuclei of legal relations and seeks to demonstrate law's insularity, neutrality, and internal coherence. Among Marxists, the formalist position was best captured by Engels and Karl Kautsky in their critique of Anton Menger's 'juridical socialism', which sought to construct a comprehensive socialist philosophy of law in abstraction from the material conditions of life and the science of political economy.[8] The formalist outlook has a tendency to fetishise law by endowing it with its own purpose and justification. Whereas the formalist outlook exaggerates law's autonomy, the class instrumentalist account is more reductionist in character, seeing in law only the content of class domination.[9] It is important to note that class instrumentalists do not simply regard law as an instrument of class politics; they are committed to the additional thesis that law everywhere and always benefits the ruling class at the expense of subordinate classes.

Writing in the historical aftermath of Stalinism and Nazism, Thompson opposes the unflinching attitude of some Marxists, who treat class-bound laws and law as such as twin instances of class domination.[10] Reflecting on law in eighteenth-century Britain, Thompson submits:

> We reach, then, not a simple conclusion (law = class power) but a complex and contradictory one. On the one hand, it is true that the law did mediate existent class relations to the advantage of the rulers; not only is this so, but as the century advanced the law became a superb instrument by which these rulers were able to impose new definitions of property to their even greater advantage.[11]

Nevertheless, Thompson ultimately rejects instrumentalist accounts that present law only as a tool for class domination, noting that even the notorious Black Act set limits on state power by holding the rising Whig oligarchy to its own juridical standards. These juridical standards were eventually appropriated by subordinate classes, who took up the incontrovertible right of the 'free-born Englishman' to privacy, *habeas corpus,* and equality before the law.[12]

Beyond offering a critique of class instrumentalism, Thompson argues that the law cannot fulfil its legitimising function as an ideology without appealing to a general and impersonal standard that is free of direct and arbitrary manipulation by a ruling class.[13] Before

---

[8]   Frederick Engels and Karl Kautsky, 'Lawyer's Socialism' [1887] in Karl Marx and Frederick Engels, *Collected Works*, vol 26 (International Publishers 1990) 597, 600–1.

[9]   Pierre Bourdieu's essay on the legal field provides a helpful classification of both formalist and instrumentalist accounts of law, including their respective shortcomings. See Pierre Bourdieu, 'The Force of Law: Toward a Sociology of the Juridical Field' (1987) 38 *Hastings Law Journal* 814. For a good overview of the class instrumentalist position, see Hugh Collins, *Marxism and Law* (OUP 1982) 16–34.

[10]   Thompson, *Whigs and Hunters*, 266. Thompson likely has in mind the structural Marxism of Louis Althusser. Thompson's critical remarks do not always do justice to the complexities of Althusser's structuralism and ignore potential areas of theoretical convergence. In this respect, Christopher Tomlins is correct in critiquing Thompson's caricatured polemic against Marxist structuralists, whose most sophisticated representatives (e.g., Nicos Poulantzas) emphasised law's 'relative autonomy' in ways that occasionally mirror Thompson's own account of law. See Christopher Tomlins, 'Marxist Legal History' in Markus D Dubber and Christopher Tomlins (eds), *The Oxford Handbook of Legal History* (OUP 2018) 515, 526.

[11]   Thompson, *Whigs and Hunters*, 264.

[12]   Thompson, *Whigs and Hunters*, 264.

[13]   Thompson, *Whigs and Hunters*, 263.

Thompson's concerns are brushed off as liberal heresy, it pays to briefly compare them with how Marx and Engels understood the background presuppositions of modern bourgeois law. In *Capital*, Marx writes:

> It is in the interest of the ruling section of society to sanction the existing order as law and to legally establish its limits given through usage and tradition. Apart from all else, this, by the way, comes about of itself as soon as the constant reproduction of the basis of the existing order and its funda-mental relations assumes a regulated and orderly form in the course of time. And such regulation and order are themselves indispensable elements of any mode of production, if it is to assume social stability and independence from mere chance and arbitrariness. These are precisely the form of its social stability and therefore its relative freedom from mere arbitrariness and mere chance.[14]

Similarly, in a letter to Conrad Schmidt, Engels writes as follows:

> In a modern state not only must the law correspond to the general economic situation and be its expression, it must *of itself* constitute a *coherent* expression that does not, by reason of internal con-tradictions, give itself the lie ... All the more so for the rarity with which a statute book is the harsh, unmitigated, unadulterated expression of the domination of one class: this of itself would be contrary to the 'concept of law.'[15]

Consequently, Thompson is generally in agreement with Marx and Engels that modern law is rarely the direct expression of unmitigated class domination and arbitrariness.

After distinguishing his view that law is mediated by class struggle from the instrumentalist charge that law is synonymous with direct class domination, Thompson argues that law's universality—the idea that laws should apply equally to rich and poor, rulers and ruled— imposes definite constraints on ruling class power and provides a medium for contestation. Whereas the 'rule of law' offers a benchmark for assessing and criticising overtly classist and authoritarian pieces of legislation, the only medium for contestation in an autocratic regime is force itself.[16] Thompson also grants that the idea of equality before the law remains a sham as long as class inequalities are not only maintained but transplanted globally.[17] Despite these preliminary qualifications, Thompson arrives at the bold and unyielding conclusion that the rule of law is 'an unqualified human good' insofar as it constrains arbitrary exercises of power by the state and elites.[18]

Not surprisingly, Marxist scholars of law have been inclined to dismiss Thompson's championing of the rule of law as a naïve capitulation to liberal jurisprudence. The irony of detailing repeated instances of legal manipulation by the British ruling class before concluding with a roundabout defence of the rule of law as an 'unqualified human good' is suspect and problematic. Even if one were to grant Thompson's claim that the rule of law inhibits the exer-

---

[14] Karl Marx, *Capital: A Critique of Political Economy*, vol 3 (first published 1894, International Publishers 1967) 793.

[15] Frederick Engels, 'Engels to Conrad Schmidt, in Berlin, 27 October 1890' in Karl Marx and Frederick Engels, *Collected Works,* vol 49 (International Publishers 1975) 57, 60–61 (original emphases).

[16] For a more extensive treatment of the rule of law and its ideal, including an engagement with rule of law critics, see Christine Sypnowich, 'Utopia and the Rule of Law' in David Dyzenhaus (ed), *Recrafting the Rule of Law: The Limits of Legal Order* (Hart 1999) 178. See also Christine Sypnowich's chapter in the present volume.

[17] Thompson, *Whigs and Hunters*, 266.

[18] Thompson, *Whigs and Hunters*, 266.

cise of arbitrary state power, it does not follow that the rule of law is therefore an 'unqualified human good'.[19] The most charitable interpretation for Thompson's reasoning in this context is that the political legacy of the Stalinist disdain for legality among some Marxists led him to insist emphatically on the decisive difference between a state that is constrained by law and one that is characterised by arbitrary exercises of power. For Thompson, dispensing with the rule of law and the legal rights afforded by it 'encourages us to give up the struggle against bad laws and class-bound procedures, and to disarm ourselves before power'.[20] The trouble is that Thompson's unqualified defence of the rule of law in the closing pages of *Whigs and Hunters* ended up disarming the critical side of his analysis of law, eclipsing his otherwise valuable insights concerning the battles that were waged over law and rights by contending classes in eighteenth-century Britain.

Bob Fine has presciently observed that Thompson's unqualified endorsement of the rule of law was a case of bending the stick too far, such that the critique of Stalinism was accompanied by an altogether uncritical approach to the rule of law.[21] Be that as it may, contemporary legal formalists will not be any more content than class instrumentalists with Thompson's rendition of the rule of law. Ernest Weinrib, a leading contemporary exponent of legal formalism, has argued that 'in the richest understanding of the Rule of Law, law is intelligible from within and is thus conceptually sealed off from the interplay of extrinsic purposes emanating from the political realm'.[22] Nothing could be further from the truth for Thompson, for whom law penetrated the political and economic realms and was itself penetrated by these realms:

> I found that law did not keep politely to a 'level' but was at *every* bloody level; it was imbricated within the mode of production and productive relations themselves (as property-rights, definitions of agrarian practice) ... it contributed to the self-identity both of rulers and of ruled; above all, it afforded an arena for class struggle, within which alternative notions of law were fought out.[23]

Unfortunately, justified critique of Thompson's uncritical embrace of the rule of law among Marxists has come at the expense of a more constructive engagement with his insights concerning the value of legal struggles in class-based societies.[24] Christopher Tomlins, who has offered the most elaborate critique of Thompson in recent years, has implored Marxist legal historians to 'shun the four horsemen—dogma, sectarianism, excessive abstraction, and political correctness'.[25] It would have been instructive for Tomlins to extend his teachings about

---

[19]   For critiques of Thompson along these lines, see Morton Horowitz, 'The Rule of Law: An Unqualified Human Good?' (1977) 86 *Yale Law Journal* 561; Michael Mandel, 'Marxism and the Rule of Law' (1986) 35 *University of New Brunswick Law Journal* 7.

[20]   Thompson, *Whigs and Hunters*, 266.

[21]   Bob Fine, *Democracy and the Rule of Law: Liberal Ideas and Marxist Critiques* (Pluto Press 1984) 175.

[22]   Ernest Weinrib, 'The Intelligibility of the Rule of Law' in Allan C Hutchinson and Patrick Monahan (eds), *The Rule of Law: Ideal or Ideology* (Carswell 1987) 81. Weinrib's Kantian-inspired and naturalist account of formalism, with its special emphasis on private law, is by no means exhaustive of the formalist tradition. For a discussion of earlier versions of formalism that give greater attention to public law, see Rob Hunter's chapter in this volume.

[23]   EP Thompson, 'The Poverty of Theory or An Orrery of Errors' [1978] in EP Thompson, *The Poverty of Theory and Other Essays* (Monthly Review 2008) 1, 96 (original emphasis).

[24]   A good example of this one-sided stance is Adrian Merritt, 'The Nature of Law: A Criticism of E. P. Thompson's *Whigs and Hunters*' (1980) 7 *British Journal of Law and Society* 194, 206.

[25]   Tomlins, 'Marxist Legal History', 538.

intellectual generosity, plurality, and imaginative thinking to his critique of Thompson.[26] A forceful critique of Thompson's 'mystical shell' (i.e., his uncritical defence of the rule of law) should not detract Marxists from engaging thoughtfully with his 'rational kernel' concerning the value of legal struggles. In the spirit of such thinking, it helps to compare Thompson's contributions about legal contestation with Marx's reflections on the struggle to limit the length of the working day. While Marx does not regard the idea of the rule of law as an *unqualified* human good, especially against a background of class domination, his outlook on the contestable nature of law shares more in common with Thompson than it does with his class instrumentalist detractors. This is best evidenced by Marx's incisive reflections on the 'working day', where class struggle and law assume an unlikely partnership in historical efforts to establish what counts as a 'normal working day'.

LAW AND THE STRUGGLE TO ESTABLISH A 'NORMAL WORKING DAY'

Capital is often read as Marx's attempt to unearth the immanent logic or 'laws of motion' governing capitalist production and exchange, as well as its dissolution. Those who read *Capital* primarily through the lens of the law of the tendency of the rate of profit to fall are bound to overlook the significance that Marx ascribes to the legal victories that had been achieved by the working class through class struggle. While legal enactments do not eliminate capitalism's tendency for crisis and the prospects of revolution, Marx recognised that progressive legislation could shape the course of this tumultuous process for the better. In the preface to *Capital,* Marx writes:

> Apart from higher motives, therefore, their own most important interests dictate to the classes that are for the nonce the ruling ones, the removal of all legally removable hindrances to the free development of the working class. For this reason, as well as others, I have given so large a space in this volume to the history, the details, and the results of English factory legislation. One nation can and should learn from others. And even when a society has got upon the right track for the discovery of the natural laws of its movement ... it can neither clear by bold leaps, nor remove by legal enactments, the obstacles offered by the successive phases of its normal development. *But it can shorten and lessen the birth-pangs.*[27]

Notwithstanding his eager anticipation of communist revolution, Marx did not regard factory legislation as a *fait accompli* by the ruling class. It must be kept in mind that Marx was describing the capitalist mode of production as it was unfolding during the course of the Industrial Revolution, which was marked by deplorable working and living conditions for the children, women, and men whose only commodity for sale in the market was labour-power. Marx describes the English Factory Acts as oscillating between deference to capital's drive for limitless exploitation and the introduction of countervailing legal measures against the wholesale subordination of labour to capital. Marx writes:

---

[26] Tomlins, 'Marxist Legal History', 538.
[27] Karl Marx, *Capital: A Critique of Political Economy,* vol 1 (first published 1867, International Publishers 1967) 9–10 (emphasis added).

> What strikes us, then, in the English legislation of 1867, is, on the one hand, the necessity imposed on the parliament of the ruling classes, of adopting in principle measures so extraordinary, and on so great a scale, against the excesses of capitalistic exploitation; and on the other hand, the hesitation, the repugnance, and the bad faith, with which it lent itself to the task of carrying those measures into practice.[28]

Despite his trenchant criticism, Marx does not conclude from the above passage that the struggle for a legally limited working day was somehow a futile endeavour on the part of the working class. Instead, he reiterates that the length of the working day is set out by law, the content of which is shaped by a broader class struggle between capital and labour. Marx affirms that:

> [t]he creation of a normal working-day is, therefore, a product of a protracted civil war, more or less dissembled, between the capitalist class and the working-class. As the contest takes place in the arena of modern industry, it first breaks out in the home of that modern industry—England.[29]

Marx assumes in his discussion of the working day that capitalists and labourers possess equal legal rights, and that legality prevails in capitalist democracies, notwithstanding the persistence of exploitation in the sphere of production. While this view still resonates with a modified instrumentalist charge that legality serves a mystifying function in capitalist democracies, instrumentalists have difficulty explaining why Marx of all thinkers would concern himself with the progressive results of factory legislation if law is merely an ideological veneer for class domination. A more accurate and productive reading of Marx's reflections on the working day offers clues as to why he recognises the value of legality while remaining committed to the supersession of capitalist property relations. After all, capitalist property relations do not exhaust all possible forms of property, just as bourgeois law does not exhaust law as such. Marx's characterisation of the antinomy of rights is especially instructive in this context. While capitalists invoke a legal right to extend the working day as much as possible, workers invoke a countervailing legal right to set protective limits against further encroachment on their health and bodily integrity. Marx writes:

> The capitalist maintains his rights as a purchaser when he tries to make the working-day as long as possible … On the other hand, … the labourer maintains his right as seller when he wishes to reduce the working-day to one of definite normal duration. There is here, therefore, an antinomy, right against right, both equally bearing the seal of the law of exchanges. Between equal rights force decides. Hence is it that in the history of capitalist production, the determination of what is a working-day, presents itself as the result of a struggle, a struggle between collective capital, *i.e.,* the class of capitalists, and collective labour, *i.e.,* the working-class.[30]

The antinomy of rights about which Marx writes in this passage is inconceivable without an impersonal system of law in the background, understood here as a system of legal rules that confers equal *formal* protections on all rights-bearers. To avoid misunderstanding, Marx's point here is not that liberal rights are equal in their exercise or effects (they are not). Rather, the *form* of law in capitalist societies presupposes juridical equality as a precondition for

---

[28]   Marx, *Capital*, vol 1, 494.
[29]   Marx, *Capital*, vol 1, 299.
[30]   Marx, *Capital*, vol 1, 234–35.

contract. In the absence of such legal rules, no legislation could prevent capitalists from uni-laterally extending the working day as long as possible, as was indeed the case in the earliest phases of industrial capitalism. Against this background, Marx affirms that:

> the revolution effected by machinery in the juridical relations between the buyer and the seller of labour-power, causing the transaction as a whole to lose the appearance of a contract between free persons, afforded the English Parliament an excuse, founded on juridical principles, for the interference of the state with factories.[31]

Marx's reference to the decisive role of 'force' as between equal rights is meant to highlight that the length of the working day is not fixed in advance by the capitalist class, as would have to be assumed on the class instrumentalist view. Instead, the length of the working day and the status of factory legislation are shaped by a broader class struggle in which the working class plays an active and decisive role. Not unlike Thompson, Marx sees the legal sphere as an arena for contestation between labour and capital, each endowed with equal rights on the basis of bourgeois law.

Holding true to his preface in the first volume of *Capital*, Marx's chapter on the working day also offers a comparative assessment of factory legislation in Britain, France, and America. In each case, Marx brings to bear the important legal victories that had been achieved by the working class. For example, Marx notes that while France's 12-hour working day lagged behind England's Ten Hours Act, it had the advantage of setting stricter limits on the length of the working day in all factories: 'French law proclaims as a principle that which in England was only won in the name of children, minors, and women, and has been only recently for the first time claimed as a general right.'[32] Marx then turns his attention to America, where the abolition of legally sanctioned slavery was accompanied by a demand for an eight-hour working day:

> In the United States of North America, every independent movement of the workers was paralyzed so long as slavery disfigured a part of the Republic. Labour cannot emancipate itself in the white skin where in the black it is branded. But out of the death of slavery a new life at once arose. The first fruit of the Civil War was the eight hours' agitation, that ran with the seven-leagued boots of the locomotive from the Atlantic to the Pacific, from New England to California.[33]

To be sure, Marx's chapter on the working day also closes with a dialectical reversal. The relation between capital and labour, which was originally premised on a voluntary exchange between equals, culminates in exploitation and class domination. Yet the formal equality that undergirds liberal legality also supplies the working class with tools for resisting capitalist exploitation and pressuring parliament and the courts to implement limits on the length of the working day. Marx affirms this point in his characteristically satirical style:

> For 'protection' against the 'serpent of their agonies,' the labourers must put their heads together, and, as a class, compel the passing of a law, an all-powerful social barrier that shall prevent the very workers from selling, by voluntary contract with capital, themselves and their families into slavery and death. In place of the pompous catalogue of the 'inalienable rights of man' comes the modest

---

[31]   Marx, *Capital*, vol 1, 397.
[32]   Marx, *Capital*, vol 1, 300.
[33]   Marx, *Capital*, vol 1, 301.

> Magna Charta of a legally limited working-day, which shall make clear 'when the time which the worker sells is ended, and when his own begins.'[34]

Lest there be doubt about the sincerity of Marx's pronouncements, this is not the only occasion where he suggests that the law should be deployed as a safeguard against unbridled exploitation. In his 1866 commentary for the Geneva Congress of the International Workingmen's Association, Marx stresses the urgency of protecting children and young workers against the destructive effects of capitalist production by means of collective legal action:

> They [the working class] know that, before everything else, the children and juvenile workers must be saved from the crushing effects of the present system. This can only be effected by converting *social reason* into *social force,* and, under given circumstances, there exists no other method of doing so, than through *general laws,* enforced by the power of the state. In enforcing such laws, the working class do not fortify governmental power. *On the contrary, they transform that power, now used against them, into their own agency.* They effect by a general act what they would vainly attempt by a multitude of isolated individual efforts.[35]

Far from bolstering the power of the state, workers have collective recourse to law in order to protect themselves and their families from further encroachments by capital.[36]

Class instrumentalists will point out that Marx's discussion of the working day is hardly a ringing endorsement of legislative reform, since improvements in factory legislation did not abolish capitalist property relations or bring an end to exploitative relations of production. While this cannot be denied, the fact that property relations were not radically altered in Britain, France, or the United States did not prevent Marx from acknowledging the important legal victories won by the working class, however limited they may appear to twenty-first-century observers in the global North. In contrast to class instrumentalists, Marx sees law as a constraint on state power and a means of contestation against unbridled capitalist exploitation. To be sure, acknowledging that the law offers a medium of contestation for oppressed classes is not the same as arguing that recourse to legal strategies will result in a revolutionary transformation of existing property relations. The latter position appears to have been advanced by Thomas Hodgskin, whom Marx cites in *Capital* as inquiring into legislation that contributed to the transformation of feudal property into capitalist private property in England. Marx's pithy response to Hodgskin is that '[t]he author should have remembered that revolutions are not made by laws'.[37] As far as Marx was concerned, a radical transformation in property relations would require nothing short of a revolutionary change in the material conditions of life. Such a transformation would usher in a different standard of right and legislation reflecting changed needs. Incidentally, Engels and Kautsky arrived at a similar conclusion after critiquing the misguided assumptions of 'juridical socialism'. Although Marxist socialists do not conceive of law as a neutral and self-referential sphere in the fetishistic manner of legal formalists:

---

[34]   Marx, *Capital*, vol 1, 302.

[35]   Karl Marx, 'Instructions for the Delegates' [1866] in Karl Marx and Frederick Engels, *Collected Works*, vol 20 (International Publishers 1985) 189 (emphasis added).

[36]   Marx's remarks here lend support to the views of commentators who argue against the unavoidable displacement of political struggles by legal struggles. For a critique of the 'displacement thesis', see Paul O'Connell, 'Human Rights: Contesting the Displacement Thesis' (2018) 69 *Northern Ireland Legal Quarterly* 19.

[37]   Marx, *Capital*, vol 1, 751.

[t]his does not mean to say, of course, that the socialists will refrain from making *specific legal demands*. An active socialist party is impossible without such demands, like any political party. The demands that derive from the common interests of a class can only be put into effect by this class taking over political power and securing universal validity for its demands by making them law ... Every class in struggle must therefore set forth its demands in the form of *legal demands* in a programme. But the demands of every class change in the course of social and political transformations, they differ from country to country according to the country's distinctive features and level of social development.[38]

In the present conjuncture, Marxists are still confronted with existing laws and juridical norms, and it is within this terrain that struggles against regressive laws are waged in capitalist democracies. Since capitalist democracies are characterised by an antinomy of equal rights, giving up on legal struggles would mean abandoning an important arena in which oppressed classes can resist encroachments by the state and transnational capital. A contemporary Marxist approach to law cannot limit itself to a choice between an instrumentalist paradigm that reduces law to class domination and a formalist paradigm that makes a fetish out of law while abstracting from background asymmetries of class power. By drawing on Thompson's view of law as a medium of social contestation and Marx's reflections on the struggle for a legally limited working day, contemporary Marxists have sufficient resources for revaluing legally based struggles in the era of neoliberalism.

The present politico-economic climate in most capitalist democracies is one in which laws regulating labour and social security are informed by a neoliberal policy framework that extolls privatisation, deregulation, and fiscal austerity. The last 40 years of neoliberal ideological hegemony have been accompanied by increased marketisation, wealth inequality, economic precariousness, and the historic weakness of organised labour, particularly in North America and much of western Europe.[39] The next section draws on recent legal strategies that have been pursued by anti-poverty activists and progressive lawyers in Canada against the background of neoliberal hegemony.

LEGAL STRATEGIES FOR PROGRESSIVE CHANGE IN AN ERA OF NEOLIBERALISM: HOUSING AND ITS CRISES

Canadian courts have seen an increase in constitutional-based challenges in light of severe housing crises across the country. The most recent legal development in this arena took place in the case of *Tanudjaja v AG (Canada)*,[40] where a group of self-identified homeless individuals joined housing advocacy groups to challenge the province of Ontario and the federal government for failing to develop a national housing strategy. The challenge was launched on the ground that government inaction on homelessness violated sections 7 ('life, liberty and security of the person') and 15 ('equal protection and equal benefit of the law without discrimination') of Canada's federal bill of rights, the Charter of Rights and Freedoms. The

---

[38]   Engels and Kautsky, 'Lawyer's Socialism', 615–16 (original emphases).
[39]   For a well-researched political history of neoliberalism along Marxist lines, see David Harvey, *A Brief History of Neoliberalism* (OUP 2005). Like Harvey, I interpret neoliberalism here as a class-based ideological project that manifests itself most clearly under financialised capitalism.
[40]   *Tanudjaja v Canada* [2014] ONCA 852.

claimants maintained that successive governments did not adjust social assistance rates in keeping with the rising costs of rent, initiate the construction of more affordable housing units, or implement responsible rent controls in ways that could alleviate issues of homelessness and poverty in Canada.

Tanudjaja broached the principle of the separation of powers and the role of courts in vindicating the rights of disadvantaged social groups. The classical liberal rights to life, liberty, and security of the person have traditionally been famed as negative rights, that is to say, as legal protections against state intrusion. *Tanudjaja* was a unique challenge in that it sought to expand the negatively circumscribed right of personal security to include a positive right to housing. Citing evidence that the debilitating consequences of homelessness disproportionately target Indigenous people, single mothers, people with physical disabilities, and individuals who rely on social assistance, the claimants maintained that homelessness constituted an analogous ground for discrimination that deprived economically marginalised individuals of their constitutional rights to equality and personal security. The case eventually made its way to the Ontario Court of Appeal, where a majority upheld an earlier decision to dismiss the application on the basis that it was not justiciable, with the rationale being that the Charter of Rights and Freedoms does not place positive obligations on the government to provide access to adequate housing.

The reference to non-justiciability in this case was anchored in the view that homelessness and poverty are public policy issues that are best left to legislatures, and are not matters that can or should be addressed by courts. It is worth noting that the claimants in *Tanudjaja* did not question the constitutionality of federal or provincial legislation. Instead, they argued that the neoliberal policy choices of successive governments contributed to the exacerbation of homelessness and poverty in ways that undermined constitutional rights to equality and personal security.[41] Liberal jurisprudence typically regards civil and political rights as justiciable because they involve negative constraints on state action, whereas socio-economic rights place positive obligations on states to provide access to resources that entail definite distributive costs. To be sure, not all legal scholars accept the stark contrast between negative and positive rights. For example, Martha Jackman and Bruce Porter argue that the relegation of socio-economic rights to legislatures undercuts their status as rights and reduces positive claims to a debate about competing political interests that are never equal.[42] The extrication of socio-economic rights from judicial oversight also prevents marginalised groups from challenging neoliberal policies on legal grounds, which progressive legal advocates regard as a betrayal of the rule of law.[43]

Although Canada's Supreme Court has not ruled out the possibility that the right to personal security could someday include positive entitlements, it has maintained a narrow interpretation of rights that continues to be at odds with the International Covenant on Economic, Social, and Cultural Rights, as well as more progressive constitutions that recognise rights to food, shelter

---

[41]   Tracy Heffernan, Fay Faraday, and Peter Rosenthal, 'Fighting for the Right to Housing in Canada' (2015) 24 *Journal of Law and Social Policy* 10.

[42]   Martha Jackman and Bruce Porter, 'Introduction: Advancing Social Rights in Canada' in Martha Jackman and Bruce Porter (eds), *Advancing Social Rights in Canada* (Irwin Law 2014) 1, 14–15.

[43]   Martha Jackman and Bruce Porter, 'Rights-Based Strategies to Address Homelessness and Poverty in Canada: The *Charter* Framework' in Martha Jackman and Bruce Porter (eds), *Advancing Social Rights in Canada* (Irwin Law 2014) 65, 105–6.

and education. Even in cases where a socio-economic right to housing was ostensibly recognised, as in *Abbotsford (City) v Shantz*,[44] Canadian courts have ruled that municipalities cannot forcefully prevent homeless people from temporarily erecting tents in public parks because doing so would violate rights to liberty and security of the person. Once again, the scope of one's right to liberty and security of the person is confined to negative constraints against state intrusion and does not entail a positive right to the material conditions necessary for realising a minimal level of security or liberty. In other words, homeless people cannot be prevented from setting up makeshift shelters in public parks, but their rights to liberty and security of the person do not obligate the state to provide access to housing. Such judgments, even as they tacitly acknowledge the crisis of homelessness in Canada, give renewed meaning to Anatole France's quip concerning the 'majestic equality of the law',[45] except this time the rich and poor alike *are* allowed to sleep in public parks, if only for temporary periods.

The problem of implementing socio-economic rights in practice extends beyond the Canadian context and reflects the broader challenge of pursuing redistributive changes through courts in the era of neoliberalism. The egalitarian thrust of socio-economic rights confronts an ideological framework that extols privatisation and market imperatives while decrying the public provision of goods. While socio-economic rights aim to broaden access to essential public goods, neoliberal policies push in the opposite direction by reinforcing existing wealth disparities and thwarting legally based efforts at achieving progressive social change.[46] The tension between socio-economic rights and neoliberal ideology has been well documented by legal scholars. Paul O'Connell argues that recent judicial decisions in Canada, India, and South Africa evidence convergence around a formal and atomistic conception of rights that caters to neoliberal policy directives. Absent structural changes in the global capitalist system, O'Connell anticipates that the predominance of a 'market-friendly' interpretation of rights by courts will undermine the pursuit and advancement of socio-economic rights globally.[47] Samuel Moyn contends that the historical links between neoliberalism and human rights suggest that human rights discourse is largely a powerless companion in the battle against economic inequality.[48] Cécile Fabre grants the relevance of structural barriers to the implementation of social rights but criticises 'left-wing radicals' who dismiss efforts to constitutionalise socio-economic rights. For Fabre, '[t]o reject social rights and their constitutionalization on the grounds that one should in fact concentrate on tearing capitalism asunder or at the very least on profoundly reforming it amounts to holding the poor hostage to these governments' goodwill, or lack thereof'.[49] Fabre's cautionary remarks against rejecting the struggle for socio-economic

---

[44]   *Abbotsford (City) v Shantz* [2015] BCSC 1909.

[45]   Anatole France, *The Red Lily* (Winfred Stevens tr, Mead & Co 1995) 91.

[46]   For a good selection of essays that critically examine the relationship between law and neoliberalism, see Honor Brabazon (ed), *Neoliberal Legality: Understanding the Role of Law in the Neoliberal Project* (Routledge 2017).

[47]   Paul O'Connell, 'The Death of Socio-Economic Rights' (2011) 74 *Modern Law Review* 554.

[48]   See Samuel Moyn, *Not Enough: Human Rights in an Unequal World* (Harvard University Press 2018).

[49]   Cécile Fabre, *Social Rights Under the Constitution: Government and the Decent Life* (OUP 2000) 186.

rights harkens back to a much older, though still lively, debate among Marxists,[50] about the choice between pursuing reform or revolution.

The discussion about attempts to advance a socio-economic right to housing in Canada demonstrate the challenges as well as the limitations of legal strategies in the service of progressive change. Legal strategies offer oppressed groups tools for resisting arbitrary laws and safeguarding existing rights against encroachment by states and elites. However, legality cannot be relied upon to counteract, let alone abolish, class antagonisms that are generated by the imperatives of capital accumulation. With respect to the housing crisis, Engels' critical reflections on the underlying 'solution' to the housing question is as prescient as ever: 'it is not that the solution of the housing question simultaneously solves the social question, but that only by the solution of the social question, that is, by the abolition of the capitalist mode of production, is the solution of the housing question made possible'.[51] For present purposes, this means that even the most robust versions of legality, which grant the importance of socio-economic rights relative to civil and political rights, are forced to confront the unruly elephant in the room, namely that of hyper-financialised capitalism. Where, then, does this leave Marxism and law today?

LAW'S LIMITS AND THE RENEWED URGENCY OF TRANSFORMATIVE POLITICS

Law has had a critical reception among Marxists, typically being dismissed as an ideological veneer for class domination. At the same time, Marx and Engels made a point of differentiating between a law-governed state (*Rechtsstaat*) and outright class domination, recognising that legality represents an important advance over absolutism and the regime of ascribed status and feudal privilege. Moreover, although they wrote at different historical junctures and assessed different laws, Marx and Thompson both viewed the legal sphere as an arena of contestation that could yield important victories for oppressed classes. Such critical ambivalence towards law has led Hugh Collins to suggest that '[t]here is an unresolved contradiction in the Marxist position in so far as it includes a blanket concern for legality and liberty as well as an attack on the Rule of Law'.[52] However, this seeming contradiction can be resolved once the object of critique is made clear and law's place is recast in the context of Marxism's broader commitment to realising the goal of human emancipation.[53]

The core of the Marxist project is concerned with achieving social conditions that are free of class domination. To this end, the target of Marxist critique is not legality per se, nor the

---

[50]   Robert Knox, 'Marxism, International Law and Political Strategy' (2009) 22 *Leiden Journal of International Law* 413. Knox argues that contemporary Marxists should engage in 'principled opportunism', that is, deploying the law for political aims whenever it is advantageous from a strategic point of view.

[51]   Frederick Engels, 'On the Housing Question' [1872] in Karl Marx and Frederick Engels, *Collected Works*, vol 23 (International Publishers 1988) 317, 347–48. For a recent perspective on the housing crisis that draws on Engels' account, see David Madden and Peter Marcuse, *In Defense of Housing: The Politics of Crisis* (Verso 2016).

[52]   Collins, *Marxism and Law*, 146.

[53]   Karl Marx, 'On the Jewish Question' [1844] in Karl Marx and Frederick Engels, *Collected Works*, vol 3 (International Publishers 1975) 146.

presupposition of legal equality, but the material conditions that generate class domination. Formal equality conceals and even legitimates substantive material inequalities between individuals, but it is not the source of domination on the Marxist view. What Collins has identified as an unresolved contradiction in the Marxist account reflects a deeper tension between the idea of equal rights that animates liberal legality and the empirical reality of class domination. Viewed from this angle, the Marxist critique points to the impossibility of actuating equal rights in practice under capitalist conditions of production and exchange.

Notwithstanding his criticisms of the formality of bourgeois law, Marx did not adopt a purely dismissive approach to law either in his capacity as a philosopher or revolutionary activist, and neither should those who remain committed to the goal of emancipatory transformation today.[54] A contemporary Marxist approach to jurisprudence should reclaim the protections associated with the law, not least because these protections secure a minimal level of freedom and provide a forum for contesting neoliberal policies at a time when wealth is concentrated in fewer hands and democratic sovereignty is being undermined by the unsurpassed power of transnational capital.[55] As has been demonstrated, there are limits to how far legal strategy can be taken within a Marxist framework that aims to realise a democratic socialist alternative to financialised capitalism, one in which co-operative ownership and principles of worker control are extended to the sphere of production. However, the latter is a political project that extends beyond the bounds of legality and calls upon grassroots social movements (certainly including but not strictly limited to those of the working class) that are actively mobilised against neoliberal hegemony and the prevailing system of financialised capitalism.

Writing in the mid-nineteenth century, Marx was convinced that capitalism would succumb to the weight of built-in contradictions between socialised production and the private appropriation of surplus value, and he placed his faith in an organised working-class movement that would revolt against exploitative production and create the material conditions for communism. While Marx's insights into the global dynamics of capital accumulation remain indispensable, the working class that he imbued with transformative potential is more fragmented and politically divided than the transnational capitalist class with which it must now contend. What is worse is that existing trends of wealth concentration and corporate dominance appear to be giving way to a neoliberal-style authoritarianism that is increasingly averse to democratic dissent and that risks curtailing the scope of existing rights.[56] The fate of legal struggles therefore assumes a more heightened significance in the present political context, where a weakened left is also confronted by the steadfast ascendance of right-wing nationalist movements, particularly in the United States and Europe, that are directing frustration with austerity and economic precariousness into open hostility towards migrant workers, refugees, and racialised minorities. The prospects for democratic socialist renewal will depend on popular support for social movements that are mobilised against capitalism. However, these movements also rely

---

[54] August Nimtz Jr demonstrates in his recent book that Marx and Engels were more practically committed to the democratic breakthrough and the defence of civil liberties than avowed liberals like Alexis de Tocqueville and John Stuart Mill. August Nimtz Jr, *Marxism versus Liberalism: Comparative Real-Time Political Analysis* (Palgrave Macmillan 2019).

[55] Sheldon Wolin, *Democracy Incorporated and the Specter of Inverted Totalitarianism* (Princeton University Press 2008); Wendy Brown, *Undoing the Demos: Neoliberalism's Stealth Revolution* (MIT Press 2015).

[56] See Ian Bruff, 'Neoliberalism and Authoritarianism' in Simon Springer, Kean Birch, and Julie MacLeavy (eds), *The Handbook of Neoliberalism* (Routledge 2016) 107, 115.

on legal levers against arbitrary power, and this expands the space in which an anti-capitalist politics may be waged. Marx and Engels understood the significance of this insight in their lifelong battles against Prussian authoritarianism, as well as in their revolutionary commitments to superseding capitalism.

CONCLUSION

Rethinking Marxism and law under neoliberalism means approaching Marx's formative distinction between political and human emancipation in dialectical rather than purely oppositional terms. By political emancipation, Marx had in mind a liberal state that is governed by law and committed to protecting the rights of individuals against an empirical background of material inequality and class domination. The chief defect of political emancipation is that it does not liberate human beings from exploitative production and class domination; they are relegated instead to the private sphere and concealed by the formalism of liberal law. Despite its shortcomings, political emancipation represents a progressive advance and marks the highest form of emancipation that can be achieved within the prevailing capitalist social order.[57] Moreover, the basic presuppositions of political emancipation—legality and equality before the law—are necessary but insufficient conditions for realising the more complete form of emancipation that Marx associated with the communist society of the future. If we are to revive and extend Marx's insights into the twenty-first century, then the pursuit of a democratic socialist alternative to financialised capitalism also warrants rethinking law's role in furthering human emancipation.[58]

To be sure, rethinking law's role in furthering human emancipation does not mean subscribing to the misguided formalist view that law possesses an untapped capacity for transcending deep-seated material contradictions, which Marxism must deny. If anything, the contradictions of financialised capitalism bear the limits of the law and highlight the renewed urgency of transformative politics. Marxists can appreciate that legality and legal struggles constrain arbitrary power while remaining committed to superseding capitalist property relations and the narrow horizon of liberal justice. This would be the mark of a vibrant and critical Marxism that is conscious of its history and still speaks to the needs and challenges of our time.

---

[57]   Marx, 'On the Jewish Question', 155.
[58]   Alan Hunt, 'Marxist Theory of Law' in Dennis Patterson (ed), *A Companion to Philosophy of Law and Legal Theory* (Blackwell 2010) 355, 359.

28. Law and the socialist ideal

Christine Sypnowich

INTRODUCTION

The relation between the socialist ideal and a just legal order has been a fraught question in the history of Marxism since the Bolshevik Revolution more than 100 years ago. I addressed this question in my early work, arguing that an ideal socialist society would need legal institutions such as rights and the rule of law.[1] The purpose of this chapter is to bring those views into dialogue with my recent research on 'egalitarian flourishing' for a broader audience, demonstrating that a just legal order is an essential prerequisite for the socialist project of furthering equal human well-being. I had the opportunity to consider these issues on two recent visits, one to Prague, on the 30th anniversary of the Prague Spring, an effort at socialist transformation which was crushed by Soviet bloc tanks, the other to Havana, the capital of arguably the only surviving 'really existing' socialist society. 'Socialism with a human face' was the rallying cry of the Prague Spring activists who challenged the contempt for law in Soviet bloc societies,[2] presaging those societies' collapse 20 years later. In contrast, Cuba, also associated with the Bolshevik tradition, recently celebrated the 60th anniversary of its revolution with a new constitution, in a mood of both triumph and reform. It seems timely, therefore, to reflect on the socialist ideal and the legal and political philosophy it entails.

At the heart of the left's disappointment with Soviet bloc societies has been a paradox of individuality. On the one hand, communist states have intruded on individual life, violated human rights, and were arbitrary in their decrees and interventions—they have been overly, and arbitrarily, involved in citizens' lives.[3] On the other hand, communist states showed a callous disregard for human well-being, failing to provide the necessary constituents of a flourishing life—in this way, they have been insufficiently or inadequately involved in indi-

---

[1] See *The Concept of Socialist Law* (Clarendon 1990); 'The Future of Socialist Legality: A Reply to Hunt' (1992) 193 *New Left Review* 16; 'Proceduralism and Democracy' (1999) 19 *Oxford Journal of Legal Studies* 649; 'Socialist Law' in Christopher Gray (ed), *The Philosophy of Law: An Encyclopaedia* (Garland 1999) 539; 'Utopia and the Rule of Law' in David Dyzenhaus (ed), *Recrafting the Rule of Law: The Limits of Legal Order* (Hart 1999) 178; 'The Civility of Law: Between Public and Private' in Maurizio Passerin d'Entrèves and Ursula Vogel (eds), *Public and Private: Legal, Political and Philosophical Perspectives* (Routledge 2000) 93; 'The Left and Wrongs: Marxism, Law and Torts' in Michael Lobban and Julia Moses (eds), *The Impact of Ideas on Legal Development* (CUP 2012) 150; 'Law and Ideology', *Stanford Encyclopaedia of Philosophy* (2005, last revised 2019).

[2] Galia Golan notes the focus on 'the return of the rule of law for the protection of the rights and liberties' of Czech citizens as a key prong of any effort at de-Stalinisation. See Galia Golan, *The Czechoslovak Reform Movement: Communism in Crisis 1962–1968* (CUP 1971) 210–22.

[3] There is considerable literature on the legal failings of the former USSR. For some classic writings see Harold Berman, *Justice in the USSR* (Harvard University Press 1963); Roy Medvedev, *Let History Judge* (Spokesman 1976); FJM Feldbrugge and William B Simons (eds), *Perspectives on Soviet Law in the 1980s* (Martinus Nijhoff 1962).

viduals' lives.[4] In our post-Soviet world, where the market is king, this critique also applies to capitalist societies, of course: income inequality means a flourishing life is only unevenly realised,[5] and the rule of law, though understood as an achievement of Western liberalism, is undermined by egregious examples of arbitrary power, typically in the name of 'security', be it national or domestic.[6]

I argue that the problem of individuality requires a conception of law that takes a dualistic strategy in pursuit of the equal society. On the one hand, equality before the law requires procedural guarantees whereby the political community's aims, however valuable, cannot be achieved through arbitrary interference in individual freedom. On the other hand, equality with respect to how people live requires a legal order that provides the constituents of human flourishing, thus going beyond private rights, fostering what the Prague philosopher and activist Karel Kosík called 'the universally developed individual'.[7] In this chapter, I explore the role of procedural justice in socialist theory and practice, the problem of value and utopia, and how a socialist legal order must focus on human flourishing in the pursuit of equality. I aim to show how socialist law should both affirm the juridical yet go beyond it in order to inspire an invigorated socialist ideal worthy of the legacy of Prague 1968.

PROCEDURAL JUSTICE AND INDIVIDUAL FREEDOM

Most Western critics of 'really existing socialism' focused on issues of legality, and the need for rights and procedures to protect individual freedom. That is not surprising, given that Western liberalism's central contribution to political theory can probably be said to be the idea that the individual should be protected from the intrusions of the state by means of law. Furthermore, the events of the Prague Spring centred on resisting the arbitrary power of the state.

The rule of law involves the idea that law must meet certain procedural standards, that it be open, transparent, clear, and accessible. Law cannot be retroactive, arbitrary, or incoherent. These procedural standards enable the individual to understand what the law requires, so as to be in a position to adjust plans and act accordingly. There is considerable debate on whether the rule of law determines what may count as the content of law, with defenders of the market like Friedrich Hayek contending that the rule of law, in its protection of individual liberty against unaccountable state power, is wedded to the policies of a market economy, a view

---

[4]   Perhaps the most dramatic example of disregard for the well-being of its people is Moscow's utilisation of Soviet citizens as cannon fodder for the Battle of Stalingrad. See Antony Beevor, *Stalingrad: The Fateful Siege, 1942–1943* (Penguin 1999). In peacetime the Soviet Union was behind other developed countries when it came to the health status of its population, though there were also periods of improvement (e.g., Soviet children reached the 50th percentile of the United States in the late 1960s, compared to the 20th percentile in the beginning of the twentieth century, though a period of stagnation followed). Elizabeth Brainerd, 'Reassessing the Standard of Living in the Soviet Union: An Analysis Using Archival and Anthropometric Data' (2010) 70 *Journal of Economic History* 83.

[5]   For an influential recent treatment see Thomas Piketty, *Capital in the Twenty-First Century* (Arthur Goldhammer tr, Harvard University Press 2014).

[6]   See David Dyzenhaus (ed), *Civil Rights and Security* (Routledge 2016).

[7]   Karel Kosik, 'The Individual and History' in Nicholas Lobkowicz (ed), *Marx and the Western World* (University of Notre Dame Press 1967) 177, 178–79.

shared by some socialists as a basis for rejecting law, as we shall see.[8] Moreover, among liberal legal theorists there is disagreement about the moral content of the rule of law, with Joseph Raz contending that a belief in the rule of law is not needed to believe that 'the good should triumph', a riposte to the more substantive moral conception of the rule of law offered by thinkers such as Lon Fuller.[9] Nonetheless, it seems reasonable to make the more modest claim that, in requiring that the state govern by rules rather than arbitrary decrees, the rule of law provides a measure of consistency in the state's actions, and that this is of moral import. An unpredictable, arbitrary political order, whatever its purposes, undermines the ability of the individual to choose how to live. Thus, perhaps paradoxically, freedom to act involves knowing which actions are not permitted, since in order to be able to conduct oneself without fear of violating the norms of the political community, one must have a clear understanding of the parameters set by those norms as they are encapsulated in law.

The communist ideal in eastern Europe, however, carried with it a legal nihilism with deep roots in the Marxist tradition whereby, in an ideal socialist society, law will 'wither away'.[10] Marxism's view of the relation between law and capitalism is complex, but can be grouped into three themes: law is a vehicle of egoism; law is an instrument of class rule; and law is a form of ideology.[11] Marx defines law as a means of expressing the distorted, selfish interests of capitalist agents in his early writings, where he argues that law arose with the division of society into the spheres of civil society and state, whereby the latter serves the former, providing rights that are no more than 'the rights of the egoistic man, separated from his fellow men and from the community'.[12] This understanding of law as a vehicle for egoism was developed into a systematic jurisprudence by the Soviet legal theorist Evgeny Pashukanis. Pashukanis went beyond the content of law to focus on the legal form itself, arguing that law is inherently capitalistic and mediates the relations between market egoists,[13] offering an incisive analysis that has proven highly influential among thinkers on the left outside of the Soviet Union.[14]

The second theme, that law is a kind of ideology, is related to the egoism view, since ideology provides a cultural representation of legal institutions such as rights and contracts, which, in their claim to provide a measure of impartiality, equality, and freedom, serve in fact

---

[8]   FA Hayek, *The Road to Serfdom* (first published 1944, Routledge & Kegan Paul 1971) 57–59.

[9]   Joseph Raz, *The Authority of Law: Essays on Law and Morality* (Clarendon 1979) 211; Lon L Fuller, *The Morality of Law* (Yale University Press 1969).

[10]   Friedrich Engels, 'Socialism: Utopian and Scientific' [1880] in Robert C Tucker (ed), *The Marx-Engels Reader* (2nd edn, WW Norton & Co 1978) 683, 713.

[11]   Here I am drawing on Sypnowich, *Concept of Socialist Law*, ch 1.

[12]   Karl Marx, 'On the Jewish Question' [1842] in Robert C Tucker (ed), *The Marx-Engels Reader* (2nd edn, WW Norton & Co 1978) 26, 43.

[13]   Evgeny Pashukanis, 'The General Theory of Law and Marxism' [1924] in Evgeny Pashukanis, *Selected Writings on Marxism and Law* (Piers Beirne and Robert Sharlet eds, Peter B Maggs tr, Academic Press 1980) 76–81. The law of torts, in which self-interested behaviour causes harm that is typically righted by financial compensation, seems to be particularly at odds with the socialist ideal. See Sypnowich, 'The Left and Wrongs'.

[14]   See e.g., Isaac Balbus, 'Commodity Form and Legal Form: An Essay on the "Relative Autonomy" of the Law' (1977) 11 *Law & Society Review* 571, and less explicitly Duncan Kennedy, 'Form and Substance in Private Law Adjudication' (1976) 89 *Harvard Law Review* 1685. A stimulating Marxist theory of international law draws on Pashukanis' analysis of how the legal form is predicated on commodity exchange; see China Miéville, 'The Commodity-Form Theory of International Law' in Susan Marks (ed), *International Law on the Left: Re-examining Marxist Legacies* (CUP 2009) 92.

to mystify the substantive unfairness, inequality, and alienation inherent in capitalist relations. Marx and Engels' metaphor in 'The German Ideology' is illuminating: ideology is depicted as akin to a *camera obscura*, where the image within the camera is upside down but is otherwise an accurate reflection of the object being projected.[15] Thus, ideology wins compliance through deception, but in order to do so, its guarantees cannot be total fiction; legal institutions, then, must have some genuine efficacy. As Engels noted, the determining character of the material sphere 'does not preclude the ideological spheres from reacting upon it in their turn', and this autonomy in the realm of ideology enables law to mitigate the negative impact of capitalist relations of production. For Engels, it would 'offend the "conception of right"' for law to be mere domination.[16] EP Thompson thus concluded that intrinsic to the ideological force of law is its capacity to impose inhibitions on economic power. As he put it, '[i]f the law is evidently partial and unjust, it will mask nothing, legitimise nothing, contribute nothing to any class's hegemony'.[17] As ideology, therefore, law is illusory, but also to a significant degree efficacious, in its promise of freedom.

If legal ideology provides an embellished story about the fairness of capitalism by mitigating the 'harsher effects of class structures',[18] this raises the third theme, which bears on law's relation to social class. The view of law as ideology considers the mystifying role performed by law to serve not just the egoistic relations of market actors, but also the economically most powerful social class. Unlike the egoism view, though, the definition of law as class rule stresses the brute hierarchical relations at work in capitalist social forces. It is this conception, as elaborated by Lenin rather than Pashukanis, which generally came to dominate the Moscow academies after Lenin's death.[19] It might seem surprising that the least attractive Marxist conception of law, which reduces legal institutions to the expression of brute power, would be the one that prevailed in a socialist society. But the view of law as a club wielded by the dominant class to subdue other classes suited the Stalinist order; it was, of course, this view that underlay the decision to send tanks through the streets of Prague. Law was used as an instrument of tyranny, but with the rationale that it was a regrettable necessity in the transitional period between capitalism and fully fledged communism, when classes—and class conflict—would disappear.

The case of Cuba provides a more complex picture. In his revolutionary Sierra Maestra Manifesto of 1957, Fidel Castro made a passionate plea for constitutional government, free and impartial elections, freedom of information, and individual and political rights (a theme

[15]   Karl Marx and Frederick Engels, 'The German Ideology' [1846] in Robert C Tucker (ed), *The Marx-Engels Reader* (2nd edn, WW Norton & Co 1978) 146, 154.
[16]   Frederick Engels, 'Engels to C. Schmidt, in Berlin, 5 August 1890' and 'Engels to C. Schmidt, Berlin, 27 October 1890' in Karl Marx and Frederick Engels, *Selected Works*, vol 3 (Progress 1976) 483 and 489 (at 483–84 and 492). See also Antonio Gramsci, *Selections from the Prison Notebooks* (Quintin Hoare and Geoffrey Nowell Smith ed and tr, International Publishers 1971) 246; Colin Sumner, 'The Rule of Law and Civil Rights in Contemporary Marxist Theory' (1981) 9 *Kapitalistate* 63.
[17]   EP Thompson, *Whigs and Hunters: The Origin of the Black Act* (Allen Lane 1975) 263.
[18]   Colin Sumner, *Reading Ideologies: An Investigation into the Marxist Theory of Ideology and Law* (Academic Press 1979) 274–75.
[19]   AY Vyshinsky, 'Fundamental Tasks of the Science of Soviet Law' [1938] in John Hazard (ed), *Soviet Legal Philosophy* (Harvard University Press 1951) 303. See also Sypnowich, *Concept of Socialist Law*, 17–23.

also prominent in Che Guevara's revolutionary writings of the early 1960s).[20] Of course, Cuba's record on human rights has long been criticised.[21] However, the country has a new constitution which was approved by a nation-wide referendum in February 2019, after an extensive and inclusive consultation process (though again with reports of efforts to repress dissent) that actually resulted in changes to the final document.[22] Among the distinctive features of the new constitution are limits to the terms and maximum age of the president, the presumption of innocence, and rights of *habeas corpus*, as well as protections for women from gender violence, the prohibition of discrimination on the basis of sexual orientation, and the elimination of the reference to marriage as being between a man and a woman (this was the compromise solution after controversy among Catholics and evangelicals thwarted a radical provision in the draft document that specified marriage as being between 'two people').

The arrival of the global coronavirus pandemic in March 2020 has made progress on constitutional matters difficult. A small country facing enormous economic challenges, largely due to the grinding hardship imposed by the decades-long American blockade, Cuba's response to Covid-19 was in many ways impressive. Its long record of achievement in public health was evident once again as missions of medical personnel were sent abroad to hot spots like Italy, and the country's biotech sector innovated and produced vaccines that it shared with other countries in the global South.[23] Yet by July 2021, Cuba had gone from having one of the world's lowest infection rates to one of the Western hemisphere's highest, with a lack of medical supplies crippling the country's response.[24] That, and the dire economic situation (worsened due to the pandemic's impact on the integral tourism sector), prompted Cubans to demonstrate in significant numbers throughout the country. Security forces responded with arrests, beating, and pepper-spraying, as well as tightening up the internet access which had facilitated the protests.[25] The government, however, has also responded with measures to improve the standard of living for Cubans, such as removing duties on supplies brought

---

[20]   Ernesto Che Guevara, 'Episodes of the Revolutionary War' [1963] in Ernesto Che Guevara, *Che Guevara Reader* (2nd edn, David Deutschmann ed, Ocean Press 1997) 34.

[21]   Human Rights Watch declared that '[t]he Cuban government continues to repress and punish dissent and public criticism. The number of short-term arbitrary arrests of human rights defenders, independent journalists, and others was lower in 2019 than in 2018, but remained high'. See Human Rights Watch, *Cuba 2019*, https://www.hrw.org/world-report/2020/country-chapters/cuba accessed 7 April 2021.

[22]   The 2019 Cuban Constitution is available at https://www.constituteproject.org/constitution/Cuba_2019.pdf?lang=en accessed 7 April 2021. For information about efforts to repress dissent, see HRW, *Cuba 2019*. For valuable commentary see Geoff Thale and Teresa García Castro, 'Cuba's New Constitution, Explained', WOLA—Advocacy for Human Rights in the Americas (10 April 2019), https://www.wola.org/analysis/cubas-new-constitution-explained/ accessed 7 April 2021.

[23]   See Nelson Acosta, 'Cuban Doctors Head to Italy to Battle Coronavirus' *Reuters* (22 March 2020) https://www.reuters.com/article/us-health-coronavirus-cuba-idUSKBN219051; and also Helen Yaffe, 'Cuba's Five COVID-19 Vaccines' LSE Blog (31 March 2021), https://blogs.lse.ac.uk/latamcaribbean/2021/03/31/cubas-five-covid-19-vaccines-the-full-story-on-soberana-01-02-plus-abdala-and-mambisa/ accessed 24 August 2021.

[24]   Ed Augustin and Daniel Montero, 'Cuba's Health System Buckles Under Strain of Overwhelming Covid Surge' *The Guardian* (22 August 2021), https://www.theguardian.com/world/2021/aug/22/cuba-coronavirus-vaccines-health-system accessed 24 August 2021.

[25]   Marc Frank and Sarah Marsh, 'Cuba Sees Biggest Protests For Decades as Pandemic Adds to Woes' *Reuters* (12 July 2021), https://www.reuters.com/world/americas/street-protests-break-out-cuba-2021-07-11/ accessed 24 August 2021.

in by travellers, and allowing more small businesses.[26] The country has been knocked again, however, by additional sanctions from US President Biden, which are certain to worsen an already desperate situation.[27] One hopes that post-pandemic, the most recent chapter in Cuban constitutionalism will eventually prove to be the beginning of a process of building a socialist society that can realise its liberatory ideals and truly eschew the 'law as weapon' view that characterised the Batista dictatorship and the repression of dissent in many communist countries, including Cuba itself, more in line with Castro's 1950s theme of a 'beautiful ideal of a free, democratic, and just Cuba'.[28]

By contrast, all three conceptions of law on the orthodox Marxist view take legal institutions to be necessary only in a defective society. Selfish interests in private property, injustice camouflaged in order to exact compliance, and class conflict where the dominant class rules by force—all are reasons for law that would be abhorred by socialists. Blatant disregard for legality was evident in the events of 1968, when the state was made to rule by arbitrary decree and untrammelled force, part of a long history of pseudo-legal phenomena that include show trials, in which dissenters have been prosecuted in sham proceedings; parasite laws, according to which citizens are prosecuted for laziness, poor reputation, or social stigma; and comrades' courts, tribunals notorious for their lack of procedure and where rumour and gossip passed for evidence.[29]

The need to respect the human rights of citizens of even the most communitarian of societies was vividly appreciated in 1968, both as an abstract ideal and as an urgent practical necessity, once the full power of the state was brought to bear on individuals seeking to exercise the fundamental freedom to express their political views. If we are to respect the integrity of the individual, we must ensure that individuals can take responsibility for their actions by providing a stable and predictable legal context, with rights and procedures. Although no Czech advocate for 'socialism with a human face' had in mind the perpetuation of ideology, the complex nature of ideology, in which some measure of emancipation must be delivered to serve the purpose of legitimation, revealed the value of legality and how it could be used to resist the 'law as club' approach. The dismissive attitude to legal institutions under capitalism that distinguished some Western leftist arguments of the early 1960s, such as Herbert Marcuse's likening of liberal institutions to fascism, was an indulgence that could no longer be sustained.[30]

In our post-Soviet era, it is apparent that legality would be an essential feature of any truly emancipatory society. The Soviet Union's short-lived *glasnost* phase raised hopes for a revival of socialist ideals, and the possibility that they might be imbued with a new spirit of democracy. These hopes were dashed with the collapse of communism, but that cataclysmic event also posed the necessity for Marxist revisionism. That is, it seemed imperative to re-conceive socialist values once the example, and burden, of 'really existing socialism' had gone, bringing

[26]   'Cuba Protests: Tax on Food and Medicine Imports Lifted' BBC News (15 July 2021), https://www.bbc.com/news/world-latin-america-57844864 accessed 24 August 2021.

[27]   Sabrina Rodriguez and Marc Caputo, 'White House Sticks with Hardline Approach to Cuba' *Politico* (19 August 2021), https://www.politico.com/news/2021/08/19/cuban-americans-biden-administration-adds-cuba-sanctions-506319 accessed 24 August 2021.

[28]   Fidel Castro, *Sierra Maestra Manifesto* (12 July 1957), http://www.latinamericanstudies.org/cuban-rebels/manifesto.htm accessed 7 April 2021.

[29]   Sypnowich, *Concept of Socialist Law*, 46–55.

[30]   Herbert Marcuse, *One-Dimensional Man: Studies in the Ideology of Advanced Industrial Society* (Beacon Press 1964).

greater exposure of the injustice, tyranny, and unfreedom of Stalinist societies, and the need for individual rights, legal procedures, and the rule of law.[31] Thompson paved the way in 1975 when he controversially applauded the rule of law as an 'unqualified human good' which would persist after the overthrow of capitalism.[32]

What, then, are the kernels of morality that lurk beneath their ideological expression in capitalist law? On the orthodox view, insofar as individuals lose their character as egoistic monads and owners of commodities with the achievement of socialism, they no longer behave in ways that require legal regulation. However, the claim about interpersonal conflict over-looks the possibility that even on the assumptions of a transformed set of human relations, of a 'communist man' imbued with empathy, fellow-feeling, and a spirit of co-operation, law might be necessary to mediate disagreement. Marx admitted that in the transition period between capitalism and full-blown communism, certain forms of law would persist.[33] But such a view about the temporary persistence of egoism nonetheless tends to assume the 'withering away' thesis, where interpersonal disputes are a contingent, remediable aspect of social life. Fully educated to live by socialist norms of behaviour, we would live in harmony with our fellows, co-operating in collective projects almost instinctively, without external compulsion. As Marx proclaimed in the 'Critique of the Gotha Programme', once socialism had secured the 'all-round development of the individual' and 'all the springs of common wealth flow more abundantly', 'the narrow horizon of bourgeois right' would be surpassed.[34] The orthodox view meant that Soviet-style societies tended to regard anti-social behaviour as qualitatively distinct from criminal activities under capitalism, even relegating them to a form of mental illness in need of medical treatment rather than judicial regulation. However, even the most committed socialist citizens could, for instance, disagree about the best way to mobilise and distribute resources—self-interest need not be selfish; if non-egoistic differences among individuals are possible, then conflict would outlive capitalism, and law would continue to be necessary to mediate socially useful conflicts about how best to achieve socialist ideals.

Moreover, law is also necessary to set out the principles of the socialist society: equality, liberty, and how they are to be instantiated in individuals' relations with each other and with public institutions. Perhaps the most important liberty to be protected by law is freedom of expression. Censorship is at odds with the principle of legality, which seeks to prevent arbitrary power that undermines individuals' agency and liberty. The idea that individuals should be permitted to articulate their views, in speeches, newspapers, or books, was an important theme among the Prague activists. Freedom of the press in fact dated back to 1867, when it was guaranteed in the December Constitution. As one commentator put it, 'someone with a fine sense of irony' must have fixed the date for the passing of the new Czechoslovak press law exactly 100 years later, with the ushering in of severe restrictions on newspapers and publishing in 1967.[35] The unpredictability with which the state enforced this edict hampered the simple running of newspapers and became, as Ivan Klíma noted, 'an obstacle to social

[31] Sypnowich, 'The Future of Socialist Legality'. For a recent argument for a Marxist conception of law and rights see Igor Shoikhedbrod, *Revisiting Marx's Critique of Liberalism: Rethinking Justice, Legality and Rights* (Palgrave Macmillan 2019), and also Igor Shoikhedbrod's chapter in this volume.
[32] Thompson, *Whigs and Hunters,* 265.
[33] Karl Marx, 'Critique of the Gotha Programme' [1875] in Karl Marx and Frederick Engels, *Collected Works*, vol 24 (Lawrence & Wishart 1989) 75, 86–87.
[34] Marx, 'Critique of the Gotha Programme', 87.
[35] ZAB Zeman, *Prague Spring: A Report on Czechoslovakia 1968* (Penguin 1969) 46–47.

progress'.[36] The Czechoslovaks were cognisant of the social implications of freedom of expression, as John Stuart Mill famously argued when he made his utilitarian case for allowing a range of views to be expressed, so that '[w]rong opinions and practices gradually yield to fact and argument', to the benefit of society and humankind.[37] Noteworthy, in our era of Trump and fake news, is how the Czech critics were also aware that formal guarantees of freedom of expression are no match for political machinations bent on the repression and distortion of information.[38]

At the fourth Czechoslovak Writers' Congress in June 1967, Milan Kundera's famous speech focused on the opportunity for creative expression as central to the very identity of a nation, without which its civilisation, he said quoting the Slovak poet Ján Kollár, becomes 'a mean and sick thing; it does not live, but only survives, it does not flower but only vegetates, it does not produce trees, only shrubs'. Those who 'get hay fever' the moment freedom is mentioned, and talk about limits to freedom of expression, simply legitimise tyranny. No truly progressive society has 'tried to fix its own limitations', yet in Czechoslovakia, Kundera said, 'the guarding of frontiers is still regarded as a greater virtue than crossing them'.[39] Other writers emphasised that freedom of expression should be limited only by the criminal law, and noted that government cannot produce good policy if its officials lack guarantees of personal freedom. In this, the Prague group remind us of the inherently precarious nature of civil liberties and due process, and of how national security, law and order, can often mean heavy-handed repression which denies individuals their civil rights.

There are other values at stake in freedom of expression that point to the second prong of 'socialism with a human face'. That is, the legal framework for human emancipation should provide not just equality before the law and the guarantee of fundamental liberties, but also substantive equality, so that all may enjoy the full development of their individuality. The Prague writers were particularly concerned with how human well-being depends on the liberty to express oneself. Kosík emphasised integrity, or being true to oneself, as essential to human freedom, and his words were doubtless coloured by a context where civic engagement meant informing on one's neighbours, and where one was expected to stifle curiosity, avoid criticism, and be quiet and conform. Autonomy, in contrast, he said, 'means ... to not be on one's knees ... to show one's own face and not to hide behind a borrowed mask ... to portray courage, not cowardice'.[40] The idea of 'showing one's face' is particularly evocative, given the 'human face' theme of socialist renewal in Prague 1968. And in Slavic languages, there are etymological connections between the word 'face' and a rich understanding of personhood, further underscoring the contrast between authenticity and personality on the one hand, and the Stalinist order, with its 'faceless' bureaucrats, an anonymous 'they' who censor and repress to maintain a 'soulless' society, on the other hand. In contrast to fascism, the tragedy of Stalinism, Kundera argued, was that it was the 'heir to a great humanist movement' that it betrayed. As he put it, 'to watch such a humanist movement being perverted into something opposite, removing every human virtue, transforming love for humanity into cruelty to people,

[36]   Quoted in Zeman, *Prague Spring*, 47.
[37]   John Stuart Mill, 'On Liberty' [1859] in John Stuart Mill, *A Selection of His Works* (John M Robson ed, Macmillan 1966) 1, 27.
[38]   Zeman, *Prague Spring*, ch 1.
[39]   Quoted in Zeman, *Prague Spring*, 57–59.
[40]   Kosik, 'The Individual and History', 190.

love for truth into denunciation, opens up tremendous insights into the very foundations of human values and virtues'.[41]

SOCIALISM AND VALUE

A reckoning with the prospects for socialism after the fall of Stalinist societies was undertaken by the analytical Marxist, GA Cohen, whose political commitments and philosophical views were deeply influenced by the problems of communism. For Cohen, the disappointment of many progressives in the Soviet experiment was by no means allayed by that system's collapse. He evocatively captured the complicated feelings of loss at the time:

> It is true that I was heavily critical of the Soviet Union, but the angry little boy who pummels his father's chest will not be glad if the old man collapses. As long as the Soviet Union seemed safe, it felt safe for me to be anti-Soviet. Now that it begins, disobligingly, to crumble, I feel impotently protective towards it.[42]

Cohen observed how the complex grief experienced by the left with the fall of the socialist states of eastern Europe was often accompanied by fatalism about the very idea of socialism. In this regard, he shared Fredric Jameson's complaint that emboldened defenders of the status quo in the post-Soviet era insist that 'the system (now grasped as the free market) is part of human nature; that any attempt to change it will be accompanied by violence; and that efforts to maintain the changes (against human nature) will require dictatorship'.[43] Arguably much of Cohen's subsequent work on justice, equality, and normativity sought to counter this fatalism.

Unlike the sharp contrast that Marx and Engels sought to draw between the 'utopian' and the 'scientific', Cohen called for a scientific approach to socialist argument, using the tools of analytical philosophy, in order to better defend utopian ideals.[44] He stressed the idea of justice, countering commentators who contended that Marx's historical materialism rules out not just the idea of socialist law, but also the possibility of assessing a social order with putatively objective normative criteria such as justice.[45] Cohen expressed a salutary impatience with such scholastic preoccupations: 'while Marx believed that capitalism was unjust, and that communism was just, he did not always realize that he had those beliefs'.[46] Cohen argued that exploitation, as a result of which the worker is 'robbed' of their product, must be understood as a species of injustice for Marx.[47] Indeed, what else could be at issue in the dispute between Marxists and defenders of capitalism if not justice?

Cohen deployed the idea of justice to counter the post-Soviet malaise among many progressives. He criticised the tendency to favour actively a bad option (e.g., market inequality)

[41] Quoted in Zeman, *Prague Spring*, 59.
[42] GA Cohen, *Self-Ownership, Freedom and Equality* (CUP 1995) 250.
[43] Fredric Jameson, 'The Politics of Utopia' (2004) 25 *New Left Review* 35, 35.
[44] Christine Sypnowich, 'G. A. Cohen's Socialism: Scientific But Also Utopian' (2012) 8 *Socialist Studies* 19, 20–34.
[45] Robert Tucker, *Philosophy and Myth in Karl Marx* (CUP 1964) 20; Allen Wood, *Karl Marx* (2nd edn, Routledge 2004) 127–42. See also Steven Lukes, *Marxism and Morality* (OUP 1985).
[46] Cohen, *Self-Ownership, Freedom and Equality*, 139. See also Norman Geras, *Marx and Human Nature: Refutation of a Legend* (Verso 1983).
[47] GA Cohen, *History, Labour and Freedom: Themes From Marx* (CUP 1995) 212.

after having concluded that no alternative (e.g., socialism) is available.[48] He diagnosed the rationalisation of political pessimism as the fallacy of adaptive preference formation, where, in confronting the failure to achieve the ideal, the ideal is recast as the inferior; the fox in Aesop's fable decides that the unattainable grapes are probably sour. Hence, the collapse of Soviet communism prompted the conclusion among many commentators that socialism was not just difficult to achieve, but undesirable.[49]

Cohen continued this 'admonition against surrender to the pull of conventional thinking'[50] in a second way, in his critique of John Rawls. Cohen targeted how Rawls models principles of justice on assumptions about human behaviour. According to Cohen, a theory of justice, properly understood, should not be held hostage to empirical claims about human nature or social organisation. Rawls contended that if it turned out to be the case that incentives are needed to induce the talented to produce extra resources to mitigate the position of the worst off, then they should be permitted.[51] Cohen countered that the just society forgoes the idea that distribution should be based on market success; the incursion of market calculation, whatever its match to the propensities in human behaviour, renders such a society less just. Community is at the heart of justice, expressed in the 'antimarket principle according to which I serve you not because of what I can get in return by doing so but because you need or want my service'.[52]

Moreover, justice involves not just this general idea of fellow-feeling, but also more specifically 'justificatory community', that is, where there is a set of people among whom there prevails a norm according to which everyone must justify their behaviour. Justice involves an 'interpersonal test' whereby deviations from the norm must be justified by those who will profit from the deviation to those who will not.[53] If a community is committed to the principle of equality, the talented cannot turn around and demand higher pay. To do so is to put such 'high-fliers', as Cohen says, 'outside the community'.[54] Rawls' theory thus fails by its own lights, since the idea of justice depends on community in order to override the logic of the market and justify the redistribution of wealth.

Indeed, we can adduce a third consideration here, one relating to how Cohen understands the broader philosophical consequences of taking the feasible to be the ideal. Cohen contends that the incentives argument licenses an insufficiently egalitarian position, and as such reneges on the project of a theory of justice. Ultimately, Rawls proffers mere 'rules of regulation', not principles of justice.[55] Cohen's critique of Rawls generated an additional research project—the elaboration of a theory of metaethics according to which normative principles are ultimately fact-independent. For Cohen, any moral or political principle that seems to be grounded in factual considerations can actually be traced to a more basic, fact-independent principle.[56]

---

[48]   GA Cohen, 'On the Currency of Egalitarian Justice' (1989) 99 *Ethics* 906, 917; Cohen, *Self-Ownership, Freedom and Equality*, 253–55.

[49]   Cohen, *Self-Ownership, Freedom and Equality*, 256.

[50]   Cohen, *Self-Ownership, Freedom and Equality*, 265.

[51]   John Rawls, *A Theory of Justice* (Harvard University Press 1971) 78. In later work, Rawls refers in passing to the 'need' for inequalities in light of their role as incentives. John Rawls, *Justice as Fairness: A Restatement* (Harvard University Press 2001) 68.

[52]   GA Cohen, *Why Not Socialism?* (Princeton University Press 2009) 39.

[53]   Cohen, *Why Not Socialism?*, 42–45.

[54]   GA Cohen, *Rescuing Justice and Equality* (Harvard University Press 2008) 32.

[55]   Cohen, *Rescuing Justice and Equality*, 284–85.

[56]   Cohen, *Rescuing Justice and Equality*, 229.

There is considerable critical literature about the extent to which this move advances our understanding of the nature of inferences about morality.[57] Of particular interest here, however, is how Cohen's conception of the fact-independence of normative claims might be related to the politically salient question of their value, objectivity, and connection to the socialist ideal.

David Miller has rejected Cohen's effort to rescue justice from facts, arguing that a political philosophy 'for earthlings' must be thoroughly action-guiding, so that we 'allow the unavoidable limitations of the earthly city to shape our understandings of justice' in order to 'mark out a road down which we might travel'.[58] Otherwise we are left, he claims, with 'political philosophy as lamentation', which 'places justice so far out of the reach of human beings that nothing we can practically achieve will bring us significantly closer to the cherished goal'.[59] Thus, whereas Cohen warns against concessions, Miller finds radicals risk resignation, their ambitious ideals finding no purchase in a real world that is hopelessly 'contaminated'.[60] However, arguably it is also a kind of resignation to rein in the ambit of one's political ideals, to insist that the feasible rule the roost. Political philosophers will inevitably be alive to questions of feasibility, so that their analyses may perform what Adam Swift calls 'a crucial practical-evaluative role'.[61] Political philosophers do not scorn issues of application, but rather strive to understand when the exigencies of application call for a degree of moral sacrifice, in the knowledge that the ideals are still worth struggling for.

Resignation is thus the peril of the political philosophy whose moral compass is derived solely from questions of implementation. If we nurture an idea of utopia as a goal, as aspirational, we may avoid what David Estlund terms 'utopophobia',[62] without dispensing with a clear-eyed understanding of the shortcomings of the real world and how they might be ameliorated. The concept of socialist law must shake off the unfortunate view of law as a merely coercive apparatus functional for capitalism, required only insofar as selfishness, or what Hume called the 'circumstances of justice', are in play.[63] There is no question that the disappointments of history can teach us valuable lessons about the significant obstacles to our ideals. And perhaps those obstacles are such that we might have to settle for aims that fall short, at least for a certain period of time. In the 1990s, for example, Cohen contended that '[a]s far as immediate political programmes are concerned, market socialism is probably a good idea', though it was an inferior form of socialism.[64] Insofar as market socialism retained

---

[57] See e.g., Thomas Pogge, 'Cohen to the Rescue!' (2008) 4 *Ratio* 454; Kyle Johannsen, 'Explanation and Justification: Understanding the Functions of Fact-Insensitive Principles' (2016) 11 *Socialist Studies* 174.

[58] David Miller, *Justice for Earthlings: Essays in Political Philosophy* (CUP 2013) 248–49.

[59] Miller, *Justice for Earthlings*, 230, 232. See also Ingrid Roebyns, 'Ideal Theory in Theory and Practice' (2008) 34 *Social Theory and Practice* 341.

[60] Miller, *Justice for Earthlings*, 2.

[61] Adam Swift, 'The Value of Philosophy in Nonideal Circumstances' (2008) 34 *Social Theory and Practice* 363, 364.

[62] David M Estlund, *Democratic Authority: A Philosophical Framework* (Princeton University Press 2008) ch 14. See also David Estlund, 'Human Nature and the Limits (If Any) of Political Philosophy' (2011) 39 *Philosophy and Public Affairs* 207.

[63] David Hume, 'An Enquiry Concerning the Principles of Morals' [1751] in David Hume, *Enquiries Concerning Human Understanding and Concerning the Principles of Morals* (3rd edn, LA Selby-Bigge and PH Nidditch ed, Clarendon 1978) 169, 184–85.

[64] GA Cohen, 'The Future of a Disillusion' (1991) 190 *New Left Review* 5, 15.

the competitiveness and inequality of capitalist transactions, it could not be understood as the best realisation of the goals of justice inherent in the socialist project.

Cohen was reluctant to draw further conclusions about morality, such as the fate of the fact-value distinction, or the question of realism in ethics, i.e., whether there are objective moral 'facts'. For Cohen, his claim was about the structure of belief, regardless of whether a person's affirmations of fact-insensitive principles 'are to be understood as claims about a timeless normative reality, or as expressions of taste, or as emotional commitments, or as universally prescribed imperatives'.[65] However, this caveat seems disingenuous. Cohen's idea of values being independent of facts certainly appears to be at odds with the positivistic distinction between facts and values, whereby values are understood as having none of the properties of facts. If we consider the motivations for Cohen's thinking on these issues, it was precisely in order to maintain the objective reality of norms of justice, in the face of the potentially undermining force of the world of empirical facts, that prompted his trajectory into the world of metaethics.

Indeed, the main political message here is that radical thinkers must not be hemmed in by anti-realist conceptions of normativity, such as the orthodox Marxist insistence that ideas can only emanate from material conditions, and that law exists only to serve the flawed social order of capitalism.[66] The ideals of equality and community are subjects about which there can be truths, and that have validity and authority, whatever people's opinions, inclinations, or behaviour. Appreciating the role of legality in protecting individuals from state power points to the normative character of legality, which serves as a corrective to the inadequacies of the actual practices of law in any society. In order for the law's moral ideals to be realised fully, law must function as action-guiding rules and show respect for people's agency. Socialist law, in both its form and content, must therefore be understood in a normatively rich way.

INDIVIDUALITY AND FLOURISHING

The socialist ideal can be hampered by legal proceduralism for reasons other than antipathy to law among certain sections of the left. Legal proceduralism has had considerable influence on political philosophy, particularly liberalism. I have noted how, in his critique of the welfare state, Hayek argued that law's procedural rules required a *laissez-faire* economy in which the state provides a framework for private initiatives.[67] By contrast, left-liberal theorists like Rawls and Ronald Dworkin insist that the state properly plays a role in remedying economic disadvantage. Rawls in particular endorsed a 'property-owning democracy' as an 'alternative to capitalism',[68] picking up on the idea that Marx's view of 'freely associated producers' involves a 'democratic economic plan'.[69] Rawls was also concerned that citizens enjoy the genuine 'worth' or 'fair value' of equal political liberties.[70]

---

[65]   Cohen, *Rescuing Justice and Equality*, 257.

[66]   Kai Neilsen invokes this in his critique of Cohen as a 'Marxist in Platonic Robes' in his 'Rescuing Political Theory from Fact-Insensitivity' (2012) 8 *Socialist Studies* 216.

[67]   Hayek, *The Road to Serfdom*, 56–59; FA Hayek, *The Constitution of Liberty* (Routledge & Kegan Paul 1960) 214–16.

[68]   Rawls, *Justice as Fairness*, 135–36.

[69]   Rawls, *Justice as Fairness*, 372.

[70]   Rawls, *Justice as Fairness*, 148–49.

Nonetheless, Rawls' political liberalism does not reject Hayek's counsel altogether, retaining a preoccupation with keeping the state at bay. Here we have a second sense, besides the fatalism about human behaviour diagnosed by Cohen, in which Rawls' egalitarianism is limited in scope. The legal ideal of impartiality plays a complex role. Rawls contends that 'the basic institutions and public policies of justice' should be understood as 'neutral with respect to comprehensive doctrines and their associated conceptions of the good'.[71] Rawls' 'neutrality of aim' reflects what Raz characterises as an 'epistemic withdrawal from the fray',[72] which dictates that the scope of the political be constrained by formal procedures: the decision process of the original position; the tenets of public reason; or political liberalism's explicit exclusion of considerations about the good life. Indeed, Rawls' proceduralist ethic became especially prominent in his later work, where the focus on constitutional questions over the remedy of economic disadvantage attracted much critical comment.[73]

It should be noted that Rawls put much store by 'the good' of a 'well-ordered' political society,[74] and admitted that perfectionist views about valuable ways of living might play a role in legislative decisions about 'suitably circumscribed questions' like the protection of habitat for wildlife.[75] Yet he retained a traditional view of perfectionism as in principle inegalitarian, involving the idea that 'some people have special claims because their greater gifts enable them to engage in the higher activities that realise perfectionist values'.[76] I have argued in recent work, however, that it is possible to articulate an 'egalitarian perfectionism', according to which it is human flourishing that we seek to make more equal in our theories of justice. On this view, concern for impartiality in the law should not be allowed to have 'imperialistic designs' on all political questions, so that the community forfeits its responsibility to foster equal human well-being.[77]

Although they called for an emancipation that Western commentators tended to reduce to formal rights and liberties, the Prague thinkers had in mind a substantive understanding of freedom as essential to the project of a humanising socialism. Whereas liberal egalitarians insist that individual freedom is at issue only in the context of state regulation, the social critics of Prague were mindful of the twin threats—the state and the market—to human self-realisation. At the Writers' Congress Antonín Liehm noted how liberalism produces a 'democratization of culture' that 'fills us with envy', but that artists should be wary of ideal-ising the capitalist alternative. For in the West, the cultural market in a consumer society promotes both the worthy and the worthless with equal zest. Moreover, the marketplace can also produce a culture 'distorted by uniformity'. A truly socialist society, in contrast, frees culture from the 'double pressure' of political power and market power, from both the authoritarian

---

[71]   Rawls, *Justice as Fairness,* 153 n.

[72]   Joseph Raz, *Ethics in the Public Domain* (Clarendon Press 1994) 46.

[73]   Brian Barry, 'John Rawls and the Search for Stability' (1995) 105 *Ethics* 874; Susan Moller Okin, '*Political Liberalism,* by John Rawls' (1993) 87 *American Political Science Review* 1010; Bernard Williams, 'A Fair State' *London Review of Books* (13 May 1993).

[74]   Rawls, *Justice as Fairness,* 98–99.

[75]   Rawls, *Justice as Fairness,* 152 n.

[76]   Rawls, *Justice as Fairness,* 152.

[77]   Christine Sypnowich, *Equality Renewed: Justice, Flourishing and the Egalitarian Ideal* (Routledge 2017) 85–87. See also Christine Sypnowich, 'A New Approach to Equality' in Roberto Merrill and Daniel Weinstock (ed), *Political Neutrality: A Re-evaluation* (Palgrave Macmillan 2014) 178.

repression of culture and the debased homogenisation that comes with market forces,[78] a theme that presciently anticipates our era of mass marketing, algorithms that induce online purchases, love via Tinder, unparalleled levels of obesity, Facebook friends, and presidential tweets.

Marx's concept of exploitation focused on a mode of production in which capitalists appropriate the surplus value produced by workers. But the argument about exploitation also focused on the effect of alienation, pointing to what an unjust social order does to people, how it affects their ability to live well. This theme was prominent among the Prague dissidents, who discussed how Kafka, the critic of the alienating forces of the capitalist Czech society of his time, might be read in conjunction with the undeniably Kafkaesque tendencies of the Stalinist regime.[79] 'Socialism with a human face' would restore to us our free, creative activity, making possible, as noted above, what Marx calls the 'all-round development of the individual'.[80]

For this to be possible, Liehm argued, the state must support artists without seeking to censor or control them. The Prague writers' sense of the fragility of culture contrasts sharply with Western liberal philosophers' confidence that equality is best served when individuals are left alone to 'choose the good' without the involvement of the political community. Liberal egalitarians tend to insist that treating people as equals means respecting their choices of how to live, no matter how ignoble and degrading those choices may be. Mill's 'marketplace of ideas' is thought to entail what has been called a 'cultural marketplace' in which individuals may pursue their projects largely unfettered. Dworkin, for example, insists that the state should be neutral about the good in order to treat people as equals. As he puts it, the 'beer-drinking, television-watching' citizen's plan of life should not count any less than the plans of life of the intellectual or the aesthete. 'A liberal theory of equality rules out … appeal to the inherent value of one theory of what is good in life'.[81] In this regard, the concern for arbitrary state interference in individual liberty that underlies the rule of law ideal is exported to the domain of politics more generally, so that the state plays no role in individuals' decisions about how to live.

In contrast to the neutralism of contemporary liberal egalitarianism, the egalitarian tradition that provided the philosophical groundwork for the emergence of the welfare state was unabashed about linking the redistribution of wealth to questions of the good life. For the British political economist William Beveridge, for example, at issue was not just disparities of wealth but problems of 'idleness' and 'squalor'—that is, defects in ways of living.[82] And the socialists RH Tawney and Harold Laski also assumed that the remedy of inequality would involve a 'high level of general culture' and the conviction that civilisation is 'a common enterprise which is the concern of all', enabling people to 'lead a life of dignity'.[83] Even Mill, famous

---

[78]   Quoted in Zeman, *Prague Spring*, 60.
[79]   Vladimir Kusin, *The Intellectual Origins of the Prague Spring: The Development of Reformist Ideas in Czechoslovakia 1956–1967* (CUP 1971) 66.
[80]   Marx, 'Critique of the Gotha Programme', 87.
[81]   Ronald Dworkin, 'Liberalism' in Stuart Hampshire (ed), *Public and Private Morality* (CUP 1978) 113, 132.
[82]   William H Beveridge, *The Pillars of Security* (MacMillan 1943) 16.
[83]   RH Tawney, *Equality* (George Allen & Unwin 1931) 108; Harold Laski, *Democracy in Crisis* (George Allen & Unwin 1933) 265. See also Sypnowich, 'A New Approach to Equality'; Sypnowich, *Equality Renewed,* 136–37; and also Christine Sypnowich, 'Liberalism, Marxism, Equality and Living Well' in Jan Kandiyali (ed), *Reassessing Marx's Social and Political Philosophy: Freedom. Recognition and Human Flourishing* (Routledge 2018) 187.

for his warnings against state interference in individual liberty, took the view that the aim of a political community is to enable its members to realise their potential and live well, and that individuality is a central element of well-being.[84]

The Stalinist experience shaped the Prague visionaries' ideas about the complex nature of human flourishing as both vulnerable to state repression and in need of nurture and support. In his speech at the 1967 congress, Ludvík Vaculík spoke of how power 'chooses' people, but not just the obvious candidates who desire power, but also 'people obedient by nature, people with bad consciences, people whose desire for comfort, advantage and gain knows no moral conditions'.[85] The stunting of character, the effacement of virtue, and the narrowing of horizons and ideals are all deleterious consequences of the unfree society that undermine people's well-being. Ideas about the cultural constituents of human flourishing are found in Marx's critique of bourgeois society and his arguments for the overcoming of alienation. Capitalism, Marx argued, is an affront to the 'nobility of man', makes people 'stupid and one-sided', and leads to 'the general distorting of *individualities*'. [86] Communism, therefore, involves creative labour and community as well as the satisfaction of basic needs.[87]

Marx contended that capitalist inequality means that work, which should be the source of human fulfilment, becomes an alien activity, a mere means to satisfy external needs. In contemporary Cuba, economic deprivation means the satisfaction of basic needs remains an everyday preoccupation, however transformed the mode of production, difficult to reconcile with how the Cuban Revolution had within its sights not just productivity for sustaining human life but also individual fulfilment in work, so that it is 'part of the good life ... something associated with life's happiest moments, not its burdens'.[88] This ideal of socialism was one in which work is 'the reconquering of one's true nature through liberated labor', the achievement of 'culture and art', nothing short of 'full freedom'.[89]

For Marx, economic inequality is to be condemned not just because of the material impoverishment with which it is associated, but also because human beings cannot realise their distinctively human and creative capacities. What he termed our 'species-being' means that as human beings we participate in 'conscious life activity', in which our productive powers, our 'work upon the objective world', are capable of shaping our environment, at least to some degree, 'in accordance with the laws of beauty'.[90] Essential human characteristics include consciousness, intentionality, language, co-operation, the fashioning and use of tools, and creative intelligence, what Marx contended distinguished the 'worst architect' from the 'best of bees'.[91] As he put it, in labour we duplicate ourselves, 'intellectually, but also actively', and therefore contemplate ourselves in the world we have created.[92]

---

[84]   Mill, 'On Liberty', 72.

[85]   Quoted in Zeman, *Prague Spring*, 63.

[86]   Karl Marx, 'Economic and Philosophic Manuscripts of 1844' in Karl Marx and Frederick Engels, *Collected Works*, vol 3 (Lawrence & Wishart 1975) 229, 300, 313, 325 (original emphasis).

[87]   David Leopold, *The Young Karl Marx* (CUP 2007) 225, 278.

[88]   Ernesto Che Guevara, 'A New Culture of Work' [1962] in Ernesto Che Guevara, *Che Guevara Reader* (David Deutschmann ed, Ocean Press 1997) 116, 150.

[89]   Ernesto Che Guevara, 'Socialism and Man in Cuba' [1965] in Ernesto Che Guevara, *Che Guevara Reader* (David Deutschmann ed, Ocean Press 1997) 212, 220, 225.

[90]   Marx, 'Economic and Philosophic Manuscripts', 276–77.

[91]   Leopold, *The Young Karl Marx*, 225.

[92]   Marx, 'Economic and Philosophic Manuscripts', 277.

It is worth noting that Marx's critique of capitalism had a deep influence on the Victorian designer William Morris, who was radicalised when he found that his aesthetic ideals were thwarted by market forces. Morris was no stranger to the problem of overweening state power and the importance of individuals having rights against the coercive state. In 1887 the London chief of police banned public meetings in Trafalgar Square, which Morris protested in a letter to the editor, pointing to the practicality of the space for open air meetings. Three days later, on 13 November, the square was the setting for what one historian has described as 'the most ruthless display of establishment power that London has ever seen': 10 000 marchers, including Morris, carrying flags and banners, playing music, and singing, were attacked by police on horseback, wielding truncheons, as if, Morris recalled, they were 'soldiers attacking an enemy'.[93] Not quite the half-million Warsaw Pact troops and tanks that occupied Prague for eight months, but a sober reminder of the dangerous potential of state power bent on stamping out political expression.

Yet Morris, unlike today's egalitarian liberals, did not conclude from the example of state-led repression that the just legal order should reduce its scope, and be barred from addressing how people should live. Morris was adamant that the equal society should marshal its political resources so that all could live well: a 'decent life' would involve 'a beautiful world to live in', a 'new and higher life' for people. And it was this focus on objective value—in contrast to the supposed neutralism of contemporary liberals—that was the impetus for Morris' socialism.[94] Morris' activism began with efforts to conserve historic architecture, which he saw as essential to the flourishing of a city's inhabitants—a principle that is famously exemplified in the streets of Prague, and which is being attempted, with some success, in Havana.[95] Morris went on to link the aesthetic with the political in his idea of craftsmanship, a source of well-being for both the creator and consumer of well-made artefacts. For Morris, productive relations under capitalism meant not only that workers' standard of living is inadequate, but also that work stunts their capacities for creative expression. Morris lamented 'the dead weight of sordid, unrelieved anxiety, the anxiety for the daily earning of a wretched pittance by labour degrading at once to body and mind' as the true 'foe to art'. There will be, he declared, 'no share in art' or 'beauty in our lives' until capitalist society gave way to 'real society' in which people live as equals.[96]

Intrinsic to the pursuit of social justice, therefore, is a conception of how to live. The Prague visionaries, for all their critique of Soviet-style central planning, had in mind, as one historian put it, 'a highly cultured form of human society', a 'socialist democracy', that would make state power more accountable to 'civic society' while enabling human beings to enjoy culture, to be creative, critical, and self-determining. The truly socialist state, they argued, would be a cultural state, one that fosters human well-being.[97] Anti-Stalinism and the pursuit of legal guarantees against state domination did not necessarily mean the abandonment of the socialist ideal. On the contrary, law should secure a framework in which the cultivation of human flourishing under conditions of equality is possible.

---

[93]   Fiona McCarthy, *William Morris: A Life for Our Time* (Faber & Faber 1994) 566–70.
[94]   William Morris, *News from Nowhere and Selected Writings and Designs* (Penguin 1978) 173.
[95]   See Nigel Toft, 'Old Havana as an Exemplary Case of World Heritage Protection' (2011) 3 *International Journal of Cuban Studies* 32.
[96]   Morris, *News from Nowhere*, 142–43.
[97]   Kusin, *Intellectual Origins*, 57, 101, 116.

CONCLUSION

Che Guevara complained that Cuba's critics assumed that socialism is 'characterised by the abolition of the individual for the sake of the state'.[98] Such easy dismissals of the socialist ideal persist today. With the tumultuous events of 1968 and the collapse of the Soviet Union behind us, and ongoing concerns about the situation in Cuba, it may be suggested that we live in a post-socialist age. However, I have tried to make a case for the socialist ideal in which law would play a central part in protecting the individual from arbitrary power, and in providing a framework for enabling the flourishing that is the measure of equality. As I noted at the outset, these are times in which the rights and freedoms that many take for granted as the inheritance of liberal legalism are threatened by new powers of state surveillance, be they anti-social behaviour edicts, arbitrary measures against immigrants, or broad police powers in the service of anti-terrorist policy. The citizens of prosperous societies remain unequal in wealth, well-being, and the opportunity to make meaningful contributions to their communities. A 'human' socialism, one that is vigilant in its protection of the individual against state power but also rejects a juridicalisation of politics that leaves individuals exposed to the alienating and inegalitarian market, is as important as ever.

---

[98]   Guevara, 'Socialism and Man in Cuba', 212.

29. Marx on law and method

Natalia Delgado

INTRODUCTION

Methodology is central to all social science. However, legal scholarship too often focuses on the analysis of its objects—specific cases, policies, or pieces of legislation—without sustained engagement with questions of method, beyond the preliminary choice of relevant literature or theoretical framework. This applies to much of what has been produced in the vein of critical legal studies, law and economics, socio-legal studies, and a variety of other schools and traditions. It also applies to much Marxist legal scholarship.[1] For example, many works in the Marxist tradition of legal theory follow Evgeny Pashukanis' commodity-form theory of law, but often fail to engage with the methodological questions that underlie his own work.[2] By contrast, Marx's methodological commitments have been examined closely in other disciplines, such as philosophy and political economy. This is important since an understanding of the methodological frameworks in Marx's writings has important theoretical as well as practical implications for the study and critique of capitalism.

This chapter engages with questions concerning the objects and methods of legal research, drawing upon close readings of Marx and Engels' writings. It also discusses secondary literature on Marx with respect to law, as well as on Marx's general method. First, the chapter discusses Marx and Engels' principal observations about law as an object of research. Second, it focuses on the method of Marx's critique of political economy in *Capital* and other writings. As is well known, Marx himself did not develop a systematic account of law or legal theory.[3] Legal structures were not central to his thought. However, they have a place in his writings, and this is often dismissed or overlooked, partly because his statements on law are scattered across an enormous, unfinished body of work, and partly because they are also sometimes inconsistent or insufficiently elaborated. This chapter does not adopt a reductionist approach to Marx's writings, seeking to deduce his views on law from his analysis of commodities and value. Nor does it embrace a particular Marxist theory of law, such as Pashukanis' theory of the legal form as strictly homologous to the commodity form. If *Capital*, after 150 years, is

---

[1]   See e.g., Maïa Pal, 'On the Methodological Limits of the Commodity Form Theory of Law in *The Corporation, Law and Capitalism*' (2020) 8 *London Review of International Law* 191. On Marx, law, and method, see e.g., Paul O'Connell, 'Law, Marxism and Method' (2018) 16 *tripleC: Communication, Capitalism and Critique* 647; Robert Knox, 'A Marxist Approach to *R.M.T. v the United Kingdom*' in Damian Gonzalez-Salzberg and Loveday Hodson (eds), *Research Methodologies for International Human Rights Law: Beyond the Traditional Paradigm* (Routledge 2019) 13.

[2]   Evgeny Pashukanis, *Law and Marxism: A General Theory* (first published 1924, Barbara Einhorn tr, Ink Links 1978) 65. On this problem see Vinicius Casalino, 'Karl Marx's Dialectics and the Marxist Criticism of Law' (2018) 9 *Direito e Praxis* 2267, 2270.

[3]   For useful discussion see Andrew Vincent, 'Marx and Law' (1993) 20 *Journal of Law and Society* 371. For a recent collection of articles on Marx and law, see (2019) 10 *Droit & Philosophie: Annuaire de l'Institut Michel Villey*.

still relevant to understanding the politico-economic system within which we continue to live, Marx and Engels' interventions in specifically legal debates are similarly relevant, since capitalism is still maintained by legal structures. As such, this chapter argues that some elements of Marx's method for the critique of classical political economy can be applied to the analysis of law.

MARX'S OBJECT

Marx first studied jurisprudence at the University of Bonn, before transferring to Berlin in 1836. During those years he studied modules on 'The Encyclopaedia of Jurisprudence', 'Institutions', 'History of Roman Law', 'History of German Law', 'European International Law', 'Natural Right', 'Pandects', 'Criminal Law', 'Ecclesiastical Law', and 'Common German Civil Procedure'. He did so with influential jurists such as Frederick Carl von Savigny and Eduard Gans.[4] According to Marx, German positive law represented 'the metaphysics of law', and was ultimately a legacy of Kant's transcendental idealism.[5] Several scholars agree that legal studies had a significant impact on Marx's thought throughout his life.[6] For example, Marx maintained a lifelong interest in Roman law, particularly concerning issues of possession and real (i.e., land) property, because it preceded bourgeois law and legal institutions.[7] Even in Marx's more historical writings, such as 'The Civil War in France', we find analyses of courts and legislation.[8]

In Berlin Marx's thought was influenced by a variety of contemporaneous debates in philosophy and the social sciences.[9] Throughout Germany as a whole, the 'Historical School of Jurisprudence', which held that law is best understood as an expression of the social customs, practices, and experiences of a given people, had emerged and gained significant influence. Its main representatives, Gustav Hugo and Savigny himself, were opposed to much of the legal heritage of the French Revolution, and codification efforts more generally.[10] A partisan of Roman law and exponent of legal positivism, Savigny was a loyal defender of the feudal

---

[4]   Michael Heinrich, *Karl Marx and the Birth of Modern Society*, vol 1 (Monthly Review Press 2019) 126, 160, 170.

[5]   Donald R Kelley, 'The Metaphysics of Law: An Essay on the Very Young Marx' (1978) 83 *American Historical Review* 350, 354.

[6]   See Hermann Klenner, *Vom Recht der Natur zur Natur des Rechts* (Akademie Verlag 1984) 68–67; Kelley, 'Metaphysics of Law', 350–51; Heinrich, *Karl Marx*, 66. As Heinrich notes, Heinrich Marx—Karl Marx's father—was a noted lawyer in Trier.

[7]   Kevin B Anderson, *Marx at the Margins: On Nationalism, Ethnicity, and Non-Western Societies* (rev edn, University of Chicago Press 2016) ix–xi.

[8]   Regarding the changes introduced by the Paris Commune, for instance, Marx wrote that: '[t]he judicial functionaries were to be divested of that sham independence which had but served to mask their abject subserviency to all succeeding governments to which, in turn, they had taken, and broken, the oaths of allegiance. Like the rest of public servants, magistrates and judges were to be elective, responsible, and revocable.'

Karl Marx, 'The Civil War in France' [1871] in Karl Marx and Frederick Engels, *Collected Works*, vol 22 (Lawrence & Wishart 1975) 307, 332.

[9]   Bruce Brown, 'The French Revolution and the Rise of Social Theory' (1966) 30 *Science & Society* 385.

[10]   Hermann Klenner, 'Savigny's Research Program of the Historical School of Law and Its Intellectual Impact in 19th Century Berlin' (1989) 37 *American Journal of Comparative Law* 67.

nobility's privileges, and played a key role in debates about legal codification efforts, opposing the Code Napoléon and similar codes in Prussia and Austria.[11] For most members of the 'Historical School', including Savigny, history was self-justifying, and rights were rooted in and derived from historical facts. Savigny sought to validate property rights, for instance, on the basis of existing social relations of possession.[12] Among those who were hostile to many elements in the 'Historical School' was Hegel, who in 1818 was instated as a professor of philosophy in Berlin, where he published his first book on the philosophy of law.[13] Hegel shared Savigny's opposition to natural law theory, but disagreed with him and other exponents of the 'Historical School' on the grounds that they defended a traditional legal system which he believed did not 'allow the full deployment of freedom of property or of the person'.[14]

Marx and Engels developed their principal views with respect to law in this social and intellectual context and largely against the background of their engagement with Savigny and Hegel. Their most significant views on law relate to: (a) the sources of law; (b) the rejection of artificial divisions in law; (c) the identification of the contradictions between the law's form and its material content; and (d) the temporal primacy of facts over legal forms. Each of these points is worth considering closely.

First, as part of his broader critique of idealism, Marx rejected the view that sources of law arise purely from within the sphere of law itself. Instead, he argued that the historical development of societies was the principal driver behind the creation, maintenance, and modification of sources of law.[15] Marx also rejected any ideal source of law: God,[16] natural law,[17] reason, or any other force or abstraction or postulate supposedly standing above social relations. He argued against the tendency to emphasise the ideal appearance of the 'self-determining concept' at the expense of its concrete social foundations, including the people who actually embody

---

[11]   Klenner, 'Savigny's Research Program', 68, 79.
[12]   Klenner, 'Savigny's Research Program', 358.
[13]   Klenner, 'Savigny's Research Program', 76. For Hegel's work see Georg WF Hegel, *Elements of the Philosophy of Right* (first published 1821, Allen W Wood ed, HB Nisbet tr, CUP 1991).
[14]   Klenner, 'Savigny's Research Program', 77.
[15]   Klenner, 'Savigny's Research Program', 75; Norman Levine, *Marx's Discourse with Hegel* (Springer 2012) 155. Marx criticised the work of Hugo and the 'Historical School' strongly in 'The Philosophical Manifesto of the Historical School of Law' [1842] in Karl Marx and Frederick Engels, *Collected Works*, vol 1 (Lawrence & Wishart 1975) 203.
[16]   'To be radical is to grasp the root of the matter. But for man the root is man himself. The evident proof of the radicalism of German theory, and hence of its practical energy, is that it proceeds from a resolute *positive* abolition of religion. The criticism of religion ends with the teaching that *man is the highest being for man*, hence with the *categorical imperative to overthrow all relations* in which man is a debased, enslaved, forsaken, despicable being.'
Karl Marx, 'Contribution to the Critique of Hegel's Philosophy of Law. Introduction' [1844] in Karl Marx and Frederick Engels, *Collected Works*, vol 3 (Lawrence & Wishart 1988) 175, 182 (original emphases).
[17]   'I do not intend discussing here all the arguments put forward by the advocates of private property in land, by jurists, philosophers and political economists, but shall confine myself firstly to state that they have tried hard to disguise the primitive fact of conquest under the cloak of '*Natural Right*'. If conquest constituted a natural right on the part of the few, the many have only to gather sufficient strength in order to acquire the natural right of reconquering what has been taken from them.'
Karl Marx, 'The Nationalization of the Land' [1872] in Karl Marx and Frederick Engels, *Collected Works*, vol 23 (Lawrence & Wishart 1988) 131, 131 (original emphasis).

the 'concept' in real history: ideologists, philosophers, theoreticians, and others.[18] He observed that the 'real subject' of politico-economic analysis, namely society, 'remains outside the mind and independent of it ... so long as the mind adopts a purely speculative, purely theoretical attitude. Hence the subject, society, must always be envisaged as the premise of conception even when the theoretical method is employed.'[19] More famously, Marx also claimed that the ruling class presents 'its interest as the common interest of all the members of society, that is, expressed in ideal form: it has to give its ideas the form of universality, and present them as the only rational, universally valid ones'.[20]

Marx developed this critique of idealism in opposition to Pierre-Joseph Proudhon and Ludwig Feuerbach. The critique highlighted Marx's increasing disenchantment with the philosophical tradition of Kant, Fichte, Hegel, and Schelling, a tradition that dominated much of the human sciences in the early to mid-nineteenth century.[21] Marx deplored Hegel's tendency to idealise empirical reality, and thus to turn (his own particular conception of) the state into an embodiment of the universal.[22] In the 1844 'Economic and Philosophical Manuscripts', for instance, Marx disagreed with Hegel in the following terms:

> When, for instance, wealth, state power, etc., are understood by Hegel as entities estranged from the *human* being, this only happens in their form as thoughts ... They are thought-entities, and therefore merely an estrangement of *pure*, i.e., abstract, philosophical thinking. The whole process therefore ends with absolute knowledge. It is precisely abstract thought from which these objects are estranged and which they confront with their presumption of reality.[23]

As a consequence of this theoretical position, Marx also attacked the theory of free will and the juridical illusion that reduces law to an expression of abstract will. The concept of free human will is the foundation of private law, and presents the human as an abstract individual, a pure relation of the 'I' to the world.[24] In 'The German Ideology', written in 1838 but never published during their lifetimes, Marx and Engels criticised 'the illusion that law is based on the will, and indeed on the will divorced from its real basis—on *free* will'.[25] They did so because they subscribed to the view that the material conditions of life do not derive from individual wills, but instead from social relations of production.[26] In the same work, they criticised the 'fortuitous' fantasy of lawyers that persons establish legal relations between and among each other in accordance with their free will (e.g., workers entering into employment contracts).[27]

---

[18] Karl Marx and Frederick Engels, 'The German Ideology' [1846] in Karl Marx and Frederick Engels, *Collected Works*, vol 5 (Lawrence & Wishart 1975) 19, 62.

[19] Karl Marx, 'Economic Manuscripts of 1857–1858 (First Version of *Capital*)' in Karl Marx and Frederick Engels, *Collected Works*, vol 28 (Lawrence & Wishart 1986) 1, 38–39 (hereinafter 'Economic Manuscripts of 1857–1858 I').

[20] Marx and Engels, 'The German Ideology', 60.

[21] Hugo Sinzheimer, 'De jonge Marx en de sociologie van het recht' (1937) 22 *De socialistische Gids* 1.

[22] See e.g., Karl Marx, 'Contribution to the Critique of Hegel's Philosophy of Law' [1843] in Karl Marx and Frederick Engels, *Collected Works*, vol 3 (Lawrence & Wishart 1988) 3.

[23] Karl Marx, 'Economic and Philosophic Manuscripts of 1844' in Karl Marx and Frederick Engels, *Collected Works*, vol 3 (Lawrence & Wishart 1975) 229, 331 (original emphases).

[24] Sinzheimer, 'De jonge Marx'.

[25] Marx and Engels, 'The German Ideology', 90 (original emphasis).

[26] Marx and Engels, 'The German Ideology'.

[27] Marx and Engels, 'The German Ideology', 91.

In an article on capital punishment, Marx emphasised that 'Hegel, instead of looking upon the criminal as the mere object, the slave of justice, elevates him to the position of a free and self-determined being'.[28] For Marx, the actions of human beings and the satisfaction of their basic needs depend not only on their will, but also, and ultimately more importantly, on the economic conditions that dominate social life. Law presupposes these conditions, though for the most part silently.[29]

Second, Marx argued that law's social and historical development needs to be investigated directly and closely. '[A]rbitrary divisions must not be introduced', he wrote in an early letter to his father, noting that 'the rational character of the object itself must develop as something imbued with contradictions in itself and find its unity in itself'.[30] In order to understand this process, Engels added, it was necessary to observe legal principles as materialisations of economic conditions.[31] Marx and Engels repeatedly highlighted the contradictions between a legal superstructure—a form of ideology—and its social material base.[32] For example, Marx pointed out as early as 1853 that 'robbery of commons, fraudulent transformation accompanied by murder, of feudal and patriarchal property into private property—these are the titles of British aristocrats to their possessions'.[33] Furthermore, in 1881, he explained in a letter to the Russian revolutionary Vera Zasulich that the basis for any capitalist private property in western Europe (with its numerous legal protections) was the producer's separation from the means of production, particularly the direct producer's dispossession and expropriation.[34]

Third, Marx theorised the opposition in capitalism between social content and legal form. The social content is the defining factor—the essence, the hidden, the invisible, the disappeared—of the legal form.[35] It comprises the social relations of production—the relations between classes.[36] The legal form, on the other hand, is the defined factor—the appearance, the

---

[28]   Karl Marx, 'Capital Punishment.—Mr. Cobden's Pamphlet.—Regulations of the Bank of England' [1853] in Karl Marx and Frederick Engels, *Collected Works*, vol 11 (Lawrence & Wishart 1979) 495, 496.

[29]   Sinzheimer, 'De jonge Marx'.

[30]   Karl Marx, 'Letter from Marx to His Father in Trier' [1837] in Karl Marx and Frederick Engels, *Collected Works*, vol 1 (Lawrence & Wishart 1975) 10, 12.

[31]   Frederick Engels, 'Engels to Conrad Schmidt, in Berlin, 27 October 1890' [1890] in Karl Marx and Frederick Engels, *Collected Works*, vol 49 (Lawrence & Wishart 2001) 57.

[32]   Bob Fine, *Democracy and the Rule of Law* (Blackburn Press 1984) 33. On the concept of superstructure see esp. Frederick Engels, 'Engels to Joseph Bloch, in Königsberg, 21[-22] September 1890' in Karl Marx and Frederick Engels, *Collected Works*, vol 49 (Lawrence & Wishart 2001) 33.

[33]   Karl Marx, 'Elections.—Financial Clouds.—The Duchess of Sutherland and Slavery' [1853] in Karl Marx and Frederick Engels, *Collected Works*, vol 11 (Lawrence & Wishart 1979) 486, 493.

[34]   Karl Marx, 'Marx to Vera Zasulich, in Geneva, 8 March 1881' in Karl Marx and Frederick Engels, *Collected Works*, vol 46 (Lawrence & Wishart 1992) 71.

[35]   Imre Szabó, 'The Notion of Law' in Csaba Varga (ed), *Marxian Legal Theory* (Dartmouth Publishing Co Ltd 1993) 261.

[36]   Pashukanis writes as follows: '[T]he matter really consists of showing the role and character of law as form in specific and concrete branches of law and concrete historical conditions with a relation to concrete content. Only in this manner can the real relation of form and content be established and can one be convinced that it is far from identical in different instances. Often legal form hides economic content directly contrary to it (thus in the period when we conducted the policy of restricting the kulak, the leasing of a horse or tools by a poor peasant to a rich one often hid the sale of the first's labour power to the second).'

mystification, the phenomenon, what is visible, immediate, even superficial.[37] The legal form is subject to change arising from modifications to social content.[38] Indeed, it is the expression of a specific social content. Crucially, Marx also used the term 'form' in reference to some of the principal categories of *Capital*: commodity form, value form, and money form. According to Isaak Illich Rubin, Marx's position is that form grows within and out of content, such that there is an internal relation between the two.[39] Similarly, Gastón Caligaris and Guido Starosta argue that Marx's mode of reasoning begins with form, because form is what is immediate to us, and then moves on to content, which is less immediately apparent.[40]

However, Marx also recognised that the legal form is itself concrete and material.[41] Engels observed that the legal form, like the '[p]olitical, … philosophical, religious, literary, artistic, etc.' , does not have 'mere[ly] passive effect, but rather that there is reciprocal action based, *in the final analysis*, on economic necessity which invariably prevails'.[42] Between the form of the law and its content are mediating structures and institutions like contracts.[43] These mediating structures and institutions express the interconnection of social life in its totality.[44] Marx wrote as follows:

> The legal forms in which these economic transactions appear as *voluntary actions* of the participants, as the expressions of their *common will* and as contracts that can be enforced on the individual parties by the power of the state, are mere forms that cannot themselves determine this content. They simply express it. The content is *just* when it corresponds to the mode of production and is adequate to it. It is *unjust* as soon as it contradicts it. Slavery, for example, is *unjust* on the basis of the capitalist mode of production; so is cheating on the quality of commodities, etc.[45]

Fourth, Marx argued that the content of law enjoys temporal priority over its form.[46] Social facts, for Marx, precede legal forms and representations.[47] New relationships emerge within social reality, and are only subsequently encased in corresponding legal forms. This is illus-

---

Evgeny Pashukanis, 'The Marxist Theory of State and Law' [1932] in Evgeny Pashukanis, *Selected Writings on Marxism and Law* (Piers Beirne and Robert Sharlet eds, Peter Maggs tr, Academic Press 1980) 273, 298.

[37]   Szabó, 'The Notion of Law'.

[38]   Kálmán Kulcsár, 'Ideological Changes and the Legal Structure: A Discussion of Socialist Experience' in Csaba Varga (ed), *Marxian Legal Theory* (Dartmouth Publishing Co Ltd 1993) 419.

[39]   Isaak Ilich Rubin, *Essays on Marx's Theory of Value* (first published 1923, Miloš Samardžija and Fredy Perlman tr, Black Rose Books 1973) 117.

[40]   Gastón Caligaris and Guido Starosta, 'Which "Rational Kernel"? Which "Mystical Shell"? A Contribution to the Debate on the Connection Between Hegel's *Logic* and Marx's *Capital*' in Fred Moseley and Tony Smith (eds), *Marx's* Capital *and Hegel's* Logic (Brill 2014) 89, 101–2.

[41]   Fine, *Democracy,* 44. See also Szabó, 'The Notion of Law'.

[42]   Frederick Engels, 'Engels to W. Borgius, in Breslau, 25 January 1894' in Karl Marx and Frederick Engels, *Collected Works*, vol 50 (Lawrence & Wishart 2004) 264, 265 (original emphasis).

[43]   Fine, *Democracy,* 43.

[44]   Roman Rosdolsky, *The Making of Marx's* Capital (Pete Burgess tr, Pluto Press 1977) 565.

[45]   Fred Moseley (ed), *Marx's Economic Manuscript of 1864–1865* (Ben Fowkes tr, Brill 2015) 445 (original emphases).

[46]   Caligaris and Starosta, 'Which "Rational Kernel"?, 101.

[47]   See e.g., Karl Marx, 'Marx to Ferdinand Lassalle, in Berlin, 22 July 1861' in Karl Marx and Frederick Engels, *Collected Works*, vol 41 (Lawrence & Wishart 1985) 316.

trated in chapter 28 of the first volume of *Capital*, concerning 'primitive accumulation', and also Marx's defence speech in his own 1849 trial.[48] In that speech Marx argued that:

> society is not founded upon the law; that is a legal fiction. On the contrary, the law must be founded upon society, it must express the common interests and needs of society—as distinct from the caprice of the individuals—which arise from the material mode of production prevailing at the given time. This *Code Napoléon*, which I am holding in my hand, has not created modern bourgeois society. On the contrary, bourgeois society ... merely finds its legal expression in this Code. As soon as it ceases to fit the social relations, it becomes simply a bundle of paper.[49]

Marx reiterated this point in the 1877 'Notes on Adolph Wagner', stating that:

> [t]his *actual* relation, which only arises through and in the exchange, is later given *legal form* in the contract, etc.; but this form neither creates its content, the exchange, nor the *relationship between the persons inherent in it*, but vice versa.[50]

Marx insisted on this argument with respect to several bourgeois legal institutions. For example, private property was in his view a basic *factum*. Only subsequently was the legal determination of—and right to—private property formalised in law.[51] In his articles in the *Rheinische Zeitung* intervening in debates on the law on the theft of wood, Marx examined how the poor's customary rights to collect wood from forests were dismantled in order to protect the private property of the capitalist class, raising forest regulations to the level of criminal law.[52] In 'The German Ideology', he and Engels emphasised the disintegration of the natural community and the expansion of trade and commerce as facts that allowed Roman civil law to develop a 'juridical illusion', which linked mere will to private property, conceding the *jus utendi et abutendi* over a thing.[53] Finally, in regard to landed property, Marx wrote as follows:

> What makes a *colony* a colony is not just the amount of fertile land to be found in its natural condition. It is rather the circumstance that this land has *not been appropriated*, it has *not* been subsumed under *landed property*. This makes all the difference between the old countries and the colonies as far as land is concerned: the legal or factual *non-existence of landed property*.[54]

---

[48]   Karl Marx, 'Trial of the Rhenish District Committee of Democrats' [1849] in Karl Marx and Frederick Engels, *Collected Works*, vol 8 (Lawrence & Wishart 1977) 323.

[49]   Marx, 'Trial of the Rhenish District Committee of Democrats'.

[50]   Karl Marx, 'Marginal Notes on Adolph Wagner's *Lehrbuch der politischen Oekonomie*' [1881] in Karl Marx and Frederick Engels, *Collected Works*, vol 24 (Lawrence & Wishart 1989) 531, 553–54 (original emphases).

[51]   Marx, 'Contribution to the Critique of Hegel's Philosophy of Law'.

[52]   Against the naturalisation of the property rights by the new legislation Marx wrote: 'We demand for the poor a *customary right*, and indeed one which is not of a local character but is a customary right of the poor in all countries. We go still further and maintain that a customary right by its very nature can *only* be a right of this lowest, propertyless and elemental mass.'
Karl Marx, 'Proceedings of the Sixth Rhine Province Assembly. Third Article—Debates on the Law on Thefts of Wood' [1842] in Karl Marx and Frederick Engels, *Collected Works*, vol 1 (Lawrence & Wishart 1975) 224, 230 (original emphases). See further Alan Hunt and Maureen Cain, *Marx and Engels on Law* (Academic Press 1979) 22–25.

[53]   Marx and Engels, 'The German Ideology', 91.

[54]   Moseley (ed), *Marx's Economic Manuscript of 1864–1865*, 744 (original emphases).

In relation to the right of inheritance, he wrote that:

> [w]hat we have to grapple with, is the cause and not the effect, the economical basis—not its juridical superstructure. … It was one of the great errors committed about 40 years since by the disciples of St. Simon, to treat the *right of inheritance*, not as the *legal effect*, but as the economical cause of the present social organisation. … To proclaim the abolition of the *right of inheritance* as the *starting-point* of the social revolution, would only tend to lead the working class away from the true point of attack against present society. It would be as absurd a thing as to abolish the laws of contract between buyer and seller, while continuing the present state of exchange of commodities.[55]

In summary, Marx and Engels advanced four fundamental arguments with respect to the law. First, they roundly rejected any source of law based upon idealism, or justifications that are not rooted in concrete social relations. Second, they argued that the law should be studied in its totality, and with an eye to its social and historical development. Third, they understood the form and content of the law to be closely intertwined. Fourth and finally, they regarded social reality as having temporal primacy over the form of law.

MARX'S METHOD

In *Capital*, among other writings, Marx offered a range of insights into his method for undertaking a critique of classical political economy. In a series of letters in 1859, Marx insisted that Engels write a review of his work and method.[56] Engels did so, and his review is of particular significance for understanding Marx's methodology.[57] In this section, I argue that it is useful to consider Engels' discussion of Marx's method alongside the observations Marx himself makes in his own work.

Marx distinguished his method of inquiry from his method of presentation.[58] These two methods are both rooted in seventeenth-century scientific thought.[59] One offers analysis, deconstructing the object of research. The other offers synthesis, presenting the results of that

---

[55]   Karl Marx, 'Report of the General Council on the Right of Inheritance' [1869] in Karl Marx and Frederick Engels, *Collected Works*, vol 21 (Lawrence & Wishart 1985) 65, 65–66 (original emphases).

[56]   Karl Marx, 'Marx to Engels, in Manchester, 19 July 1859' in Karl Marx and Frederick Engels, *Collected Works*, vol 40 (Lawrence & Wishart 1983) 469, 471 (original emphases): 'Biskamp wanted to write a short review of my *Critique of Political Economy*, etc. I dissuaded him, for he knows nothing about the subject. But since he has undertaken (in the *Volk*) to say something about it, I should like you to do it for him (say next week, but not this). Briefly on the method and what is new in the content.'

See also Karl Marx, 'Marx to Engels, in Manchester, 22 July 1859' in Karl Marx and Frederick Engels, *Collected Works*, vol 40 (Lawrence & Wishart 1983) 472, 473 (original emphases): 'Should you write something, don't forget, 1. that it extirpates Proudhonism root and branch, 2. that the *specifically* social, by no means *absolute*, character of bourgeois production is analysed straight away in its simplest form, that of the *commodity*'. See further Frederick Engels, 'Engels to Marx, in London, 3 August 1859' in Karl Marx and Frederick Engels, *Collected Works*, vol 40 (Lawrence & Wishart 1983) 478.

[57]   What follows is drawn from Frederick Engels, 'Karl Marx, "A Contribution to the Critique of Political Economy"' [1859] in Karl Marx and Frederick Engels, *Collected Works*, vol 16 (Lawrence & Wishart 1980) 465.

[58]   See generally Karl Marx, 'Postface to the Second Edition' [1873] in *Capital: A Critique of Political Economy*, vol 1 (Ben Fowkes tr, Penguin 1990) 94.

[59]   See e.g., Vesa Oittinen, 'Marx's Method: A Kantian Moment' in Pablo Sánchez León (ed), *Karl Marx y la crítica de la economia politica: Contribuciones a una tradición* (Pamiela 2019) 99.

research in an orderly, methodical sequence.[60] For Marx, the method of inquiry rested upon tracing internal connections between the material under analysis. In particular, Marx's method of inquiry was characterised by extensive reading. He would engage heavily with multiple works by the same author, and would systematically go about filling notebooks with excerpts and comments, to which he would then refer when composing his own writings.[61] This method is distinct from the theoretical presentation of material. In Engels' view, the presentation could be organised either logically or historically.[62] Engels stated that the task of exposing all strata of the historical process of capitalism could never be completed in full in a single work.[63] As a result, Marx chose to present the material in question logically rather than historically.[64] For example, Marx often brought different sources and scholars—from classical political economy, political theory, and German philosophy, among others—into conversation with each other, generating a kind of dialogue from which he was then able to develop his own critique.[65]

The first methodological element arising from Marx's writings is the dialectical form of his presentation. In many of his published works and correspondence, Marx recognised himself as a disciple of Hegel.[66] In *The Poverty of Philosophy*, he supported Hegel's dialectics against Proudhon, and positioned dialectics in contradistinction to most economists' understanding of bourgeois society as organised by natural laws and customs.[67] As Marx famously put it, the dialectical method:

> it includes in its positive understanding of what exists a simultaneous recognition of its negation, its inevitable destruction; because it regards every historically developed form as being in a fluid state, in motion, and therefore grasps its transient aspect as well; and because it does not let itself be impressed by anything, being in its very essence critical and revolutionary.[68]

This is not a minor point. The radical dimensions of Hegelian dialectics may be understood through a genealogy of its rejection within Marx's work, beginning with the German social

---

[60]   Oittinen, 'Marx's Method'.

[61]   Rob Beamish, *Marx, Method, and the Division of Labor* (University of Illinois Press 1992) 16, 37, 94.

[62]   Engels, 'Marx's "A Contribution"', 475.

[63]   Engels, 'Marx's "A Contribution"', 470.

[64]   Michael Heinrich has recently criticised Engels' review of Marx's 'A Contribution', focusing on Engels' argument about a logical rather than historical presentation of the material. See Michael Heinrich, 'Comment faire la critique de l'économie politique? Relire Engels (et Marx)' *Contretemps* (22 December 2020), http://www.contretemps.eu/engels-marx-methode-economie-politique-heinrich/?fbclid=IwAR3h-i2ZIesiFsMiyAKNi0tr0fOVaxTb29zUnA7nuRN_os1VyuD2PrMvw1M accessed 7 April 2021.

[65]   Beamish, *Marx*, 93.

[66]   See e.g., Karl Marx, 'Marx to Engels, in Manchester, 1 February 1858' in Karl Marx and Frederick Engels, *Collected Works*, vol 40 (Lawrence & Wishart 1983) 258. But see also Karl Marx, 'Marx to Ludwig Kugelmann, in Hanover, 6 March 1868' in Karl Marx and Frederick Engels, *Collected Works*, vol 42 (Lawrence & Wishart 1987) 543, 544 (original emphases): 'He knows full well that my method of exposition is *not* Hegelian, since I am a materialist, and Hegel an idealist. Hegel's dialectic is the basic form of all dialectic, but only *after* being stripped of its mystical form, and it is precisely this which distinguishes *my* method.'

[67]   Karl Marx, 'The Poverty of Philosophy' [1847] in Karl Marx and Frederick Engels, *Collected Works*, vol 6 (Lawrence & Wishart 1976) 105.

[68]   See Marx, 'Postface', 103.

democrat Eduard Bernstein[69] and culminating in the Frankfurt School and the work of late twentieth-century philosophers like Louis Althusser and Jacques Derrida.[70] However, such a rejection of the Hegelian Marx is far from representative of the totality of Marx's own views. Marx's writings consistently highlight the relevance of Hegel's *Science of Logic* to his own thought.[71] Dialectics accorded with Marx's understanding that all social phenomena are transitory,[72] and that capitalism is an historical phenomenon,[73] making it possible for him to foresee a revolution and a new historical epoch beyond capitalism.[74] It also agreed with his theory of capitalism's general laws of motion,[75] a process of movement, in both space and time, in which capital (like value, commodities, money, and workers) flows and circulates. Engels reminded his readers that dialectics allowed Marx to overcome the static opposition of thesis and antithesis that is so foundational to metaphysics (the binaries of true and false, good and evil, what is and what ought to be, and so on).[76]

This being said, it is also true that Marx made a point of distancing himself from the 'mystification which the dialectic suffers in Hegel's hands'.[77] Marx alerted his readers to the dangers of a method that begins with cognition, on the ideational rather than material level, writing that in his case 'the reverse is true: the ideal is nothing but the material world reflected in the mind of man, and translated into forms of thought'.[78] The 'dialectical form of presentation', he

---

[69]   Eduard Bernstein, *The Preconditions of Socialism* (first published 1899, Henry Tudor ed, CUP 1993) ch 2.

[70]   See generally Raya Dunayevskaya, *The Power of Negativity: Selected Writings on the Dialectic in Hegel and Marx* (Peter Hudis and Kevin B Anderson ed, Lexington 2002) xvi. See also Néstor Kohan and Belén Gopegui, *Nuestro Marx* (Oveja Roja 2013).

[71]   Marx noted the relevance of Hegel's *Science of Logic* for his own method on a number of occasions. See e.g., Karl Marx, 'Marx to Engels, in Manchester, 16 January 1858' in Karl Marx and Frederick Engels, *Collected Works*, vol 40 (Lawrence & Wishart 1983) 248, 249 (original emphases): 'What was of great use to me as regards *method* of treatment was Hegel's *Logic*, ... I should very much like to write 2 or 3 sheets making accessible to the common reader the *rational* aspect of the method which Hegel not only discovered but also mystified.'

[72]   Against dialectics stands the understanding of bourgeois society as eternal. Marx criticised this as follows: 'When the economists say that present-day relations—the relations of bourgeois production— are natural, they imply that these are the relations in which wealth is created and productive forces developed in conformity with the laws of nature. These relations therefore are themselves natural laws independent of the influence of time. They are eternal laws which must always govern society. Thus there has been history, but there is no longer any. There has been history, since there were the institutions of feudalism, and in these institutions of feudalism we find quite different relations of production from those of bourgeois society, which the economists try to pass off as natural and as such, eternal.'
Marx, 'The Poverty of Philosophy', 174. On Marx's critique of this separation between theory and history see Lucia Pradella, *Globalization and the Critique of Political Economy: New Insights from Marx's Writings* (Routledge 2015) 166.

[73]   Georg Lukács, *The Young Hegel: Studies in the Relations between Dialectics and Economics* (first published 1948, Rodney Livingstone tr, Merlin Press 1975).

[74]   See the various writings collected in VI Lenin, *Collected Works*, vol 38 (International Publishers 1945).

[75]   Frederick Engels, 'Ludwig Feuerbach and the End of Classical German Philosophy' [1886] in Karl Marx and Frederick Engels, *Collected Works*, vol 26 (Lawrence & Wishart 1990) 353.

[76]   Engels, 'Ludwig Feuerbach'.

[77]   Marx, 'Postface', 103.

[78]   Marx, 'Postface', 102.

wrote, 'is right only when it knows its own limits'.[79] Marx examined those limits of exposition in a number of his own writings. In the *Grundrisse*, for instance, he explained the transformation of money into capital, and stressed that the foundations of bourgeois society came about through a 'lengthy historical process'.[80] Or to take another example, consider the following passage from *Capital*:

> The historical conditions of its [capital's] existence are by no means given with the mere circulation of money and commodities. It arises only when the owner of the means of production and subsistence finds the free worker available, on the market, as the seller of his own labour-power. And this one historical pre-condition comprises a world's history. Capital, therefore, announces from the outset a new epoch in the process of social production.[81]

Historical materialism is the second decisive element in Marx's method.[82] Historical materialism, in Marx's hands, is the systematic critique of the dualism between idealism and abstract materialism.[83] Marx argued that no legal or political relation is capable of being understood fully in isolation, or purely in abstract thought. Instead, it may be understood comprehensively only in the context of 'the material conditions of life'.[84] Consequently, he insisted that his analytical method did not begin with 'concepts' as such, but rather with the 'simplest social form' that presents itself to experience.[85] In other words, Marx's starting-point was the 'present', the highest stage of maturity and historical development of the object of study.[86] 'The anatomy of man is a key to the anatomy of the ape', and not the other way around.[87] The origins of capitalism cannot be outlined without first asking what capital is.[88] Conversely, abstract historicism, in order to understand a phenomenon, observes the 'natural' order or sequence of events

---

[79] Karl Marx, 'Economic Manuscripts of 1857–1858 (First Version of *Capital*)' in Karl Marx and Frederick Engels, *Collected Works*, vol 29 (Lawrence & Wishart 1987) 3, 505 (hereinafter 'Economic Manuscripts of 1857–1858 II').

[80] Marx, 'Economic Manuscripts of 1857–1858 II', 505.

[81] Marx, *Capital*, 274.

[82] Marx did not use the expression 'historical materialism'; it was introduced by Engels in a letter to Conrad Schmidt in 1890. Frederick Engels, 'Engels to Conrad Schmidt, in Berlin, 27 October 1890' in Karl Marx and Frederick Engels, *Collected Works*, vol 49 (Lawrence & Wishart 2001) 57.

[83] Patrick Murray, *Marx's Theory of Scientific Knowledge* (Humanities Press 1988) 69.

[84] See Karl Marx, 'A Contribution to the Critique of Political Economy' [1859] in Karl Marx and Frederick Engels, *Collected Works*, vol 29 (Lawrence & Wishart 1987) 257, 262.

[85] Marx, 'Notes on Adolph Wagner's *Lehrbuch*', 544. On this point Marx wrote: 'Even a history of religion that is written in abstraction from this material basis is uncritical. It is, in reality, much easier to discover by analysis the earthly kernel of the misty creations of religion than to do the opposite, i.e. to develop from the actual, given relations of life the forms in which these have been apotheosized. The latter method is the only materialist, and therefore the only scientific one. The weaknesses of the abstract materialism of natural science, a materialism which excludes the historical process, are immediately evident from the abstract and ideological conceptions expressed by its spokesmen whenever they venture beyond the bounds of their own speciality.'
See Marx, *Capital*, fn 4 on 493, 494.

[86] Evald Ilyenkov, 'The Logical and the Historical' [1960] in Evald Ilyenkov, *Intelligent Materialism: Essays on Hegel and Dialectics* (Evgeni Pavlov ed and tr, Brill 2018) 182, 200.

[87] Marx, 'Economic Manuscripts of 1857–1958 I', 42; Ilyenkov, 'The Logical and the Historical', 189.

[88] Ilyenkov, 'The Logical and the Historical', 195.

in time.[89] For Marx the 'logical' understanding of the 'present' is the key to the theoretical understanding of the 'past'.[90] Engels confirmed this starting-point and elaborated on Marx's method as follows:

> Using this method we begin with the first and simplest relation which is historically, actually available, thus in this context with the first economic relation to be found. We analyse this relation. The fact that it is a *relation* already implies that it has two aspects which are *related to each other*. Each of these aspects is examined separately; this reveals the nature of their attitude to one another, their reciprocal action. Contradictions will emerge which require a solution. But since we are not examining here an abstract mental process that takes place solely in our mind, but an actual event which really took place at some time or other, or is still taking place, these contradictions, too, will have arisen in practice and have probably been solved. We shall trace the mode of this solution and find that it has been effected by establishing a new relation, whose two contradictory aspects we shall then have to set forth, and so on.[91]

As this passage explains, Marx focused on relationships, interconnections, transformations, metamorphoses, and processes between categories, such as commodity and money.[92] He did not focus on isolated units of analysis. Even as early as his correspondence with his father, for instance, we find him writing that:

> [a] triangle gives the mathematician scope for construction and proof, it remains a mere abstract conception in space and does not develop into anything further. It has to be put alongside something else, then it assumes other positions, and this diversity added to it gives it different relationships and truths.[93]

Following Engels, then, a social relation should be studied in the first place as a process of unfolding whereby at least two constituent elements come to the fore. Marx initially introduced the category of the commodity in its two principal aspects: the commodity as bearer of use-value, and the commodity as bearer of exchange-value. Once these aspects have been examined, the social relation in question should itself be examined with a view to understanding how they interact and affect each other. Again, following Engels, contradictions will appear within the relation under analysis, and these contradictions will themselves need to be examined closely, particularly in light of concrete social practices in which they manifest.

---

[89]   Ilyenkov, 'The Logical and the Historical', 198.

[90]   Ilyenkov, 'The Logical and the Historical', 190, 200. Marx wrote: 'In order to develop the laws of bourgeois economy, therefore, it is not necessary to write the *real history of the relations of production*. But the correct observation and deduction of these laws, as having themselves become in history, always leads to primary equations ... which point towards a past lying behind this system. These indications, together with a correct grasp of the present, then also offer the key to the understanding of the past.' Marx, *Grundrisse*, 460–61 (original emphasis).

[91]   Engels, 'Marx's "A Contribution"', 475–76 (original emphases). Engels also develops this method in Frederick Engels, 'Socialism: Utopian and Scientific' [1880] in Karl Marx and Frederick Engels, *Collected Works*, vol 24 (Lawrence & Wishart 1987) 281.

[92]   Michael Heinrich, *Die Wissenschaft vom Wert: Die Marxsche Kritik der politischen Ökonomie zwischen wissenschaftlicher Revolution und klassischer Tradition* (Verlag Westfälisches Dampfboot 2017) 171; Bertell Ollman, *Dance of the Dialectic: Steps in Marx's Method* (University of Illinois Press 2003) 36–38.

[93]   Marx, 'Letter from Marx to His Father in Trier', 12.

Marx emphasised the immanent, internal contradictions of social relations, refusing to fetishise external causes.[94] As Evald Ilyenkov observed, when a contradiction emerges in the theoretical exposition of a given social reality, the metaphysician typically responds by attempting to clarify the contradiction by narrowing concepts, offering rigorous definitions of relevant terms, or insisting that the contradiction is external rather than internal to the reality.[95] The metaphysician thereby seeks to displace that part of the reality in which the contradiction has materialised.[96] By contrast, Marx proceeded from the assumption that a contradiction in a definition is objectively unresolved.[97] In his view, the contradiction is not resolved simply by declaring in theory that the phenomenon in question is not in fact contradictory.[98] Contradictions reflect tensions inherent within relations, up to the point of their imminent dissolution.[99]

As illustrated by the passage reproduced above, Engels believed that the next methodological step involved tracing the solution of the unresolved internal contradiction in the form of a new social relation. This, in turn, returns us to our initial starting-point, inviting us to analyse the new social relation, disintegrate it into its constituent elements, and trace its own solution in the form of still another social relations.[100] Michael Heinrich has described this process of interrelation as one in which 'categories are *unfolded* from one another', showing 'how one category necessitates the existence of another'.[101] For his part, David Harvey has offered a diagram to demonstrate how those categories unfold in *Capital* from commodity (use-value, exchange-value) to value (concrete labour, abstract labour), and then to forms of exchange-value (equivalent form, relative form), to the money form (social relations between things, material relations between persons), and so on.[102]

In the *Grundrisse*, Marx explained the sequence in which categories such as commodity, money, and capital present themselves in accordance with the method of rising from the abstract to the concrete.[103] For Marx, these categories should not follow their historical order of appearance, or their appearance in the world of ideas. Indeed, he wrote, '[t]heir order of succession ... is determined rather by their mutual relation in modern bourgeois society'.[104] In formal logic, the concrete has traditionally been associated with the definitions of things (e.g., books, trees, houses), while the abstract has conventionally been associated with the

---

[94]   The concept of contradiction, derived from Hegel's *Science of Logic,* provided the opportunity for Marx to further develop the idea of antagonism between classes already present in David Ricardo's work. See e.g., Karl Marx, 'Marx to Engels, in Manchester, 10 October 1868' in Karl Marx and Frederick Engels, *Collected Works,* vol 43 (Lawrence & Wishart 1988) 127.

[95]   Evald Ilyenkov, *The Dialectics of the Abstract and the Concrete in Marx's* Capital (first published 1960, Sergei Syrovatkin tr, Aakar Books 2008) 262.

[96]   Ilyenkov, *Dialectics,* 262.

[97]   Ilyenkov, *Dialectics,* 265–66.

[98]   Ilyenkov, *Dialectics,* 267.

[99]   Frederick Engels, 'Anti-Dühring' [1878] in Karl Marx and Frederick Engels, *Collected Works,* vol 25 (Lawrence & Wishart 1987) 1, 23, 34.

[100]   Engels, 'Marx's "A Contribution"', 476.

[101]   Michael Heinrich, *An Introduction to the Three Volumes of Karl Marx's* Capital (first published 2004, Alexander Locascio tr, Monthly Review Press 2012) 37.

[102]   See David Harvey, *A Companion to Marx's* Capital: *The Complete Edition* (Verso 2018) 111.

[103]   Beamish suggests that Marx follows the order from Hegel's *Logic,* marking 'a progression from the simple and immediate to the complex and mediate'. Beamish, *Marx,* 175.

[104]   Marx, 'Economic Manuscripts of 1857–1958 I', 44.

properties of things (e.g., qualities like virtue, courage, value) or the relationships into which they enter.[105] As Ilyenkov explained, Marx departed from such approaches, regarding the abstract as the 'simple, the one-sided, the fragmentary' understanding of a given relation, and the concrete as 'the unity of diverse aspects' of that relation.[106] When seeking to understand the complexity of capitalism, we commence from the starting-point of a largely fragmentary understanding of the social relations that present themselves before us. Our efforts should then be focused on seeking to comprehend the unity of these relations—the concreteness of *what is*—as a totality.[107] And this has implications for specifically legal matters. Pashukanis, for one, argued that Marx's methodological observations are transposable to a general theory of law in which 'the State is a point of arrival and not of departure'.[108]

Finally, Marx's logical method of presentation drew on historical illustrations, particularly for 'continuous contact with reality'.[109] In the early 1860s, for instance, he wrote as follows:

> On the other hand—and this is much more important—our method indicates the points at which historical analysis must be introduced, or at which the bourgeois economy as a mere historical form of the production process points beyond itself towards earlier historical modes of production. To present the laws of the bourgeois economy, it is not necessary therefore to write the *real history ...* of the *production relations*. But the correct analysis and deduction of these relations always leads to *primary equations*, which point to a past lying behind this system. If, on the one hand, the *pre-bourgeois phases* appear as *merely historical*, i.e. as *presuppositions which have been superseded*, the present conditions of production [on the other hand] appear as *superseding themselves* and therefore as positing themselves as *historical presuppositions* for a future society.[110]

In Marx's work, the theoretical is constantly confronted with the historical and empirical. The converse also holds true. According to Heinrich, Marx skilfully introduced historical elements into his work, and he did so in three ways. First, he did so as a precondition for understanding the existing state of affairs. This is illustrated by the fact that the theoretical exposition that typically dominates Marx's method of presentation in works like *Capital* is often followed by a historical exposition. For instance, the chapters on 'the so-called primitive accumulation' appear only at the end of the first volume of *Capital*.[111] Second, and closely related to this first point, Marx turned to historical exposition when the explanatory scope of his theoretical exposition had reached a limit. Thus, historical exposition dominated Marx's discussion of workers' struggles over the length of the working day in chapter ten of the first volume of *Capital*, a crucial hinge from discussions of absolute surplus value to relative surplus value

---

[105]   Ilyenkov, *Dialectics,* 10.

[106]   Ilyenkov, *Dialectics,* 32, 34.

[107]   Ilyenkov, *Dialectics,* 37. See also the introduction in Karl Marx, *Grundrisse* (first published 1939, Martin Nicolaus tr, Penguin 1993); Heinrich, *Die Wissenschaft,* 171; also Enrique Dussel, *Kategorie* (UAM-Iz 2006), https://marxismocritico.com/2011/10/20/kategorie/ accessed 7 April 2021.

[108]   Casalino, 'Karl Marx's Dialectics', 2270; Pashukanis, *Selected Writings,* 66.

[109]   Engels, 'Marx's "A Contribution"', 477. See also Beamish, *Marx,* 167. On historical research see e.g., Karl Marx, 'B. Bauer's Pamphlets on the Collision with Russia' [1857] in Karl Marx and Frederick Engels, *Collected Works,* vol 15 (Lawrence & Wishart 1986) 181.

[110]   Karl Marx, 'Economic Manuscript of 1861–1863' in Karl Marx and Frederick Engels, *Collected Works,* vol 34 (Lawrence & Wishart 1989) 1, 236 (original emphases).

[111]   Heinrich, *Die Wissenschaft,* 171.

in the book's later chapters.[112] Third, for Marx, historical examples served to illustrate points made at a high level of abstract generality.[113]

To conclude, this part has examined the key methodological elements in Marx's work: Hegelian dialectical logic and historical materialism. Following Engels, Marx's method begins with an actual social relation. Applying Marx's method to a legal object of research—a legal relationship—requires that this relation be decomposed into at least two elements, and that their interaction be understood. The next step involves identification of the contradictions inherent within the relation, as well as the processes whereby these antagonisms are resolved through a new relation. As a final step, the form of the legal relation must be unmasked so that its material content may be discerned. This necessitates consideration of both the form and the content of each aspect of the legal relation in question.

CONCLUSION

This chapter has discussed Marx and Engels' engagement with a range of questions pertaining to different areas of law, such as property, contract, family, and labour law. Law does not disappear from Marx's work after he completed the 'Contribution to the Critique of Hegel's Philosophy of Law' in 1843. While Marx clearly subordinated juridical problems to problems of political economy, I have argued that juridical concerns were of abiding relevance throughout his work as a whole. Based on Marx and Engels' own writings, I have proposed an approach to the study of law. Marx's methodological insights were the result of a series of path-breaking theoretical developments that allowed him and others to comprehend the revolutionary nature of surplus value production and accumulation under capitalism. Yet the methodological questions in Marxist analyses of law have remained rather underdeveloped. A clearer framework for the analysis of the core legal structures of capitalism promises to enable critical legal scholarship to address the urgent problems of our time more effectively. The analytical tools and different elements of Marx's method are significant, not least because they encourage us to think differently about legal research and how to build legal theories and arguments today.

---

[112] Heinrich, *Die Wissenschaft,* 171; Alex Callinicos, *Deciphering Capital: Marx's Capital and Its Destiny* (Bookmarks 2014) 153; Beamish, *Marx,* 164.

[113] Heinrich, *Die Wissenschaft,* 171. For example, in order to explain the division of labour, Marx discussed the social histories of various forms of machinery and technology.

30. Principles for a dialectical-materialist analysis of law and the state

Dimitrios Kivotidis

INTRODUCTION

In this chapter I attempt to outline the fundamental principles of a dialectical-materialist analysis of law and the state. For the purposes of my analysis, 'law' is here defined as the system of state-sanctioned and enforceable rules that reflect the dominant mode of production and its corresponding social relations, thereby ensuring their reproduction and consolidating the power of the ruling class.[1] Similarly, 'the state', understood as a product of class conflicts and contradictions, is here defined as the set of mechanisms and institutions that ensure, through a combination of repressive and ideological means, the reproduction of capitalist social relations, the consolidation of the rule of the dominant class, and the continued exploitation and subordination of the exploited class.[2] Finally, I understand 'dialectics' as a mode of conceiving reality in its multi-faceted and contradictory movements.

---

[1] The 'classics' of Marxism do not offer an authoritative definition of law. Nevertheless, there are several passages and fragments that may be used to construct a working definition. In *The Communist Manifesto*, for instance, Marx and Engels refer to the bourgeois class and its 'jurisprudence', which 'is but the will of your class made into a law for all, a will, whose essential character and direction are determined by the economical conditions of existence of your class'; see Karl Marx and Frederick Engels, 'Manifesto of the Communist Party' [1848] in Karl Marx and Frederick Engels, *Collected Works*, vol 6 (Lawrence & Wishart 1976) 477, 501. During the first decades of socialist construction in the Soviet Union there was intense debate among legal and political theorists around the question of socialist law. Evgeny Pashukanis, perhaps the best-known Soviet legal theorist, argued in his 1924 *General Theory of Law and Marxism* that the legal form reaches full development, as the basic form of commodity exchange, only under capitalism. See Evgeny Pashukanis, 'The General Theory of Law and Marxism' [1924] in Evgeny Pashukanis, *Selected Writings on Marxism and Law* (Piers Beirne and Robert Sharlet eds, Peter Maggs tr, Academic Press 1980) 37, 79. The working definition provided here guards against the problematic elements of Pashukanis' approach by focusing on the mode of production as a whole rather than only a specific aspect of it (i.e., exchange relations).

[2] This follows Engels' definition of the state as 'a product of society at a certain stage of development', a society that 'has become entangled in an insoluble contradiction with itself, that ... has split into irreconcilable opposites which it is powerless to dispel'. This 'power seemingly standing above society which would alleviate the conflict and keep it within the bounds of "order"; and this power, having arisen out of society but placing itself above it, and alienating itself more and more from it, is the state'. Frederick Engels, 'The Origin of the Family, Private Property and the State' [1884] in Karl Marx and Frederick Engels, *Collected Works*, vol 26 (Lawrence & Wishart 1990) 129, 269. Emphasis on the historical and class nature of the state is necessary to guard against theories that position the state as a neutral entity, developed not only by mainstream bourgeois thinkers such as John Rawls (John Rawls, *A Theory of Justice* (Harvard University Press 2005)) and Robert Dahl (Robert A Dahl and Bruce Stinebrickner, *Modern Political Analysis* (Pearson 2002)), or critical bourgeois thinkers such as Axel Honneth (Axel Honneth, *The Idea of Socialism: Towards a Renewal* (first published 2015, Joseph Gamahl tr, Polity

For the purposes of this chapter, dialectics consists of three elements. The first such element is many-sidedness. Dialectical analysis is concerned with the interconnectedness of social processes. A dialectical analysis of the legal form must therefore take into account the intricate relations between legal, political, and socio-economic processes. This stands opposed to the kind of examination of isolated and fragmented social phenomena one finds in much traditional positivist social science. The second element is movement. A dialectical analysis is an analysis of social processes. Dialectical materialism assesses juridico-political phenomena in their process of development. Additionally, social, political, and juridical processes are viewed as historical processes. Capitalism is not eternal, and neither are law and the state. Instead, they are historical phenomena. Hence, any examination of the legal form must grapple with real historical movements.[3] The third and final element is contradiction. The historical movement of juridico-political and socio-economic processes develops on the basis of struggles and contradictions. Contradiction appears in economic forms (in the form of the contradiction between use-value and exchange-value, between concrete labour and abstract labour, or between necessary labour and surplus labour). It also appears in social forms (in the contradiction between the socialised labour process and the private ownership of the means of production, or in the class struggle as a motor of history).

In what follows, I discuss the interconnected questions of the welfare state form, labour legislation, and the right to strike. Examining these questions together is crucial for understanding capitalist law and the capitalist state. For instance, in order to understand why in 2018 a supposedly 'left-wing' government in Greece adopted legislation that restricted the right to strike,[4] one must understand the role of the welfare state form in reproducing contradictory social relations under capitalism, the role of labour law in mediating relations between capitalists and workers, and the historical development of class struggle (the working-class struggle that secured legal protection of social rights, as well as the bourgeois struggle that played a key role in limiting and sometimes even abolishing these rights).

THEORY AND PRACTICE

As already noted, dialectics is associated with a demand for many-sidedness—a commitment to understanding social phenomena in their totality, rather than as isolated and unrelated fragments. Marx refers to the concept of totality throughout his work, perhaps most memorably in the preface to 'A Contribution to the Critique of Political Economy'. There he writes that:

> neither legal relations nor political forms could be comprehended whether by themselves or on the basis of a so-called general development of the human mind, but ... on the contrary they originate

---

Press 2018)), but also by certain figures within the Marxist tradition, especially Poulantzas (Nicos Poulantzas, *State, Power, Socialism* (first published 1978, Patrick Camiller tr, Verso 2000)).

[3]   See e.g., Anthony Chase, *Law and History: The Evolution of the American Legal System* (New Press 1999).

[4]   See esp. art 211 of Act 4512/2018, which limits the exercise of the right to strike by requiring a 50 per cent turnout of union-registered members.

in the material conditions of life, the totality of which Hegel, following the example of English and French thinkers of the eighteenth century, embraces within the term 'civil society'.[5]

It is important to explain the concepts of the abstract and the concrete, as they are used in Marx's dialectical logic. The concepts of abstract and concrete in Marx's dialectical logic have different meanings from the meanings associated with the terms 'abstract' and 'concrete' in ordinary language. When Marxists speak of the 'concrete' in the context of dialectics, they do not mean a concrete 'thing' that presents itself to our senses, at least not exclusively. Similarly, when they speak of the 'abstract', they do not mean something that exists solely in the realm of cognition or phenomenological experience. For Marx abstract labour is objectively real, in the form of value.[6]

In Marx's dialectical logic, the abstract and the concrete are epistemological categories that help one to comprehend reality in its movement and interconnectedness. The concrete here is a unity of diverse elements. For its part, abstraction corresponds to one-sidedness, the initial point of analysis. At the beginning of an analytical process, the abstract is merely one part or aspect of the whole. At the end of this process, the abstract becomes an expression of the concrete totality, because it has been analysed in relation to other aspects of the whole. In this respect, dialectical analysis 'is a continuous process of transition from one definition into the other'.[7] It demands many-sided analysis of an object: an object must be examined in its development, its self-motion, its connections to other objects, and the appearance and resolution of its internal contradictions. Some scholars have thus argued that the method Marx employs in *Capital* involves an 'ascension from the abstract to the concrete'.[8]

A dialectical analysis of law and the state makes use of certain categories, such as the 'unity of form and content', the 'reproduction of relations of production', and the 'relative autonomy of law and state'. First, law and the state are abstracted from the specific material conditions from which they emerge and to which they ultimately refer. Second, law and the state perform a distinct class function, reproducing dominant relations of production as well as the rule of the dominant class. Third, law and the state perform this function by virtue of their 'relative autonomy'.[9]

These categories are not immutable truths, but rather epistemological maxims for scientific analysis. Engels stresses that the laws of dialectics are abstracted from the history of nature

---

[5]   Karl Marx, 'A Contribution to the Critique of Political Economy' [1859] in Karl Marx and Frederick Engels, *Collected Works*, vol 29 (Lawrence & Wishart 1987) 257, 262.

[6]   Evald Ilyenkov, *The Dialectics of the Abstract and the Concrete in Marx's* Capital (first published 1960, Sergei Syrovatkin tr, Aakar Books 2008).

[7]   Georg Lukács, 'What is Orthodox Marxism?' in Georg Lukács, *History and Class Consciousness: Studies in Marxist Dialectics* (first published 1923, Rodney Livingstone tr, MIT Press 1972) 3.

[8]   For a comprehensive exposition of the views of these scholars see Periklis Pavlidis, 'Towards the Understanding of the Method of Ascent from the Abstract to the Concrete in Marx's *Capital*: The Contribution of MM. Rozental', E. V. Ilyenkov and V. A. Vazyulin' (2010), https://www .academia.edu/41586500/Towards_the_understanding_of_the_Method_of_Ascent_from_the_Abstract _to_the_Concrete_in_Marx_s_Capital_The_contribution_of_MM_Rozental_E_V_Ilyenkov_and_V_A _Vazyulin accessed 7 April 2021. See also Natalia Delgado's chapter in this volume.

[9]   Frederick Engels, 'Engels to Conrad Schmidt, in Berlin, 27 October 1890' in Karl Marx and Frederick Engels, *Collected Works*, vol 49 (Lawrence & Wishart 2010) 57, 60–61.

and human society, not the other way around.[10] So does Lenin in his attempt to read Hegel materialistically:

> Logic is the science not of external forms of thought, but of the laws of development 'of all material, natural and spiritual things,' i.e., of the development of the entire concrete content of the world and of its cognition, i.e., the sum-total, the conclusion of the *History* of knowledge of the world.[11]

Dialectical materialism is concerned not with the application of infallible principles to the examination of natural and social phenomena, but with praxis and the verification of principles in or by reference to objective social reality. Ideas for understanding the world help shape the world—to the extent allowed by the development of productive forces and relations. This means that objective social reality is the ultimate test of the accuracy of scientific theories.

This brings me to another point: the relationship between the scientific and the ideological aspects of Marxist analysis. Since Marx's 11th thesis on Feuerbach,[12] these seemingly opposed elements have been conjoined in Marxist analyses of the contradictions of capitalism. The struggle for scientific understanding of social processes is united with the struggle to overcome exploitation and inequality. Marxist explanations of this unity are based in part on the materialist theory of ideology.[13] Ideas are not products of pure intellectual processes; they are produced during the course of human activity. With the development of capitalist society and the exacerbation of the division of labour, abstract ideas are used to elaborate more or less systematic views, theories, and doctrines.

General views and ways of thinking, or systems of abstract ideas, become established as characteristic of the outlook of an entire society, or of a significant portion thereof.[14] These views and ways of thinking are called 'ideologies'. In class-divided societies, ideologies take on a class character. Class divisions give rise to different class interests, based on different relationships to the means of production, different roles in the social organisation of labour, and different ways of securing a share of the social wealth. It is on the basis of these interests that class ideologies are developed. Despite the class nature of ideology, though, ideological developments have their own distinct characteristics, their own internal laws.

---

[10]   Frederick Engels, 'Dialectics of Nature' [1883] in Karl Marx and Frederick Engels, *Collected Works*, vol 25 (Lawrence & Wishart 1987) 311, 356.

[11]   VI Lenin, 'Conspectus of Hegel's Book *The Science of Logic*' [1914] in VI Lenin, *Collected Works,* vol 38 (Progress Publishers 1976) 85, 92–93 (original emphasis).

[12]   'The philosophers have only *interpreted* the world in various ways; the point, however, is to *change* it.' Karl Marx, 'Theses on Feuerbach' [1845] in Karl Marx and Frederick Engels, *Collected Works*, vol 5 (Lawrence & Wishart 1976) 3, 8 (original emphases).

[13]   This is set out in *The German Ideology*: 'The ideas which these individuals [individuals who enter into definite social and political relations] form are ideas either about their relation to nature or about their mutual relations or about their own nature. It is evident that in all these cases their ideas are the conscious expression—real or illusory—of their real relations and activities, of their production, of their intercourse, of their social and political conduct. ... If the conscious expression of the real relations of these individuals is illusory, if in their imagination they turn reality upside-down, then this in its turn is the result of their limited material mode of activity and their limited social relations arising from it.'

See Karl Marx and Friedrich Engels, *The German Ideology* (first published 1932, Prometheus Books 1998) 41.

[14]   Maurice Cornforth, *Dialectical Materialism: An Introduction*, vol 3 (first published 1954, Lawrence & Wishart 1976) 66.

A dialectical-materialist analysis of law and the state unites political intervention and scientific analysis. The struggle for scientific analysis, in opposition to idealist and metaphysical approaches, is simultaneously a political struggle against bourgeois conceptions of law and the state. Scientific analysis is an essential prerequisite for political struggle and is itself a form of political struggle. For instance, analysis of the state as an instrument of oppression, which is necessary for the consolidation and social reproduction of class power and the reproduction of capitalist social relations, contributes to the scientific understanding of the state, against metaphysical conceptions of the state as a set of natural, necessary, or even immutable structures or institutions.[15] It also helps to rebut the reformist belief that the bourgeois state can be used to 'build the road to socialism'.[16]

FORM AND CONTENT

Let me now turn to the first principle, namely the principle that law and the state abstract from and correspond to specific socio-economic contents. I will begin with the example of property as a social and legal relation in order to illustrate how the categories of 'form' and 'content' shed light on the role of law in the social totality. To begin with, property relations are of fundamental importance for the capitalist mode of production, since the capitalist ownership of the means of production—as reflected in private law and safeguarded by the legal order organised as public law—results in capitalist ownership of the final product, enabling the extraction of surplus value and the accumulation of capital. In addition, individual property must be alienable in the market. A modern property regime is a set of social relations based on exclusive possession and enjoyment of a thing or resource. This regime is in need of an organised system of violence that sanctions and preserves the social relations that sustain it. What is more, modern capitalist property relations are structurally different from the relations of subjugation specific to feudal society. The system of violence upholding feudal property relations was significantly less centralised, corresponding to a different mode of extracting surplus product through extra-economic means.[17] The relation between a property regime and

---

[15]   Such metaphysical conceptions of the state, characteristic of the bourgeois worldview, are found in the work of diverse thinkers, from Hobbes and Locke to conservative 'counter-revolutionaries' like Juan Donoso Cortés and Joseph de Maistre, especially their views about the 'absolute sinfulness and depravity of human nature' (Carl Schmitt, *Political Theology: Four Chapters on the Concept of Sovereignty* (first published 1922, George Schwab tr, University of Chicago Press 2005) 57), and to Deleuze's metaphysical image of the *Urstaat*, the primordial state, which detaches form from content and elevates it to the status of an eternal structure (Gilles Deleuze and Félix Guattari, *Anti-Oedipus: Capitalism and Schizophrenia* (first published 1972, Robert Hurley, Mark Seem, and Helen R Lane tr, Continuum 2004) 237–38).

[16]   See, for instance, Poulantzas' views on the state, which heavily influenced the Eurocommunism of the 1970s; see Poulantzas, *State, Power, Socialism*. On Poulantzas see further the chapters by Bob Jessop and Rafael Khachaturian in this volume.

[17]   For Marxist debates on the transition from feudalism to capitalism, see especially Paul Sweezy et al, *The Transition from Feudalism to Capitalism* (Verso 1978). This debate focuses on the factors at work in the transition to capitalism, particularly the question whether these were internal or external to feudalism. On the role of class struggle and the development of capitalist relations through market dependence in the English countryside, captured by the concept of 'agrarian capitalism', see TH Aston and CHE Philpin (eds), *The Brenner Debate: Agrarian Class Structure and Economic Development in*

a system of violence is the point at which law relates to the state (and private law relates to public law). Last but not least, the modern legal form of property presupposes the idea of the 'legal subject'.

Consider now how 'form-and-content' dialectics explains the property relation. Marx's theory of value reveals how social relations between individual labourers are concealed in the commodity form. Here, too, the legal form is a one-sided relation between a person and thing. The common-sense notion of property refers to a 'thing' (e.g., a car, a house). 'This is my property', says someone to exclude everyone else from the enjoyment of this thing or resource. But the substantive content is a social relation expressed in the form of a 'thing'. Behind the form of the 'thing', or object, lies a system of social relations, not only between a subject and the object but also between different subjects.

For a many-sided analysis of the form of property, one must consider the form in tandem with the simple commodity relations of capitalist society. First and foremost, it is the demands of commodity production and exchange that necessitate the form of the 'free and equal legal subject'. In particular, the sale and purchase of labour-power as a commodity is the foundation of capitalist social relations. The worker, who neither owns nor wields control over the means of production, must sell their labour-power as a commodity. They must become a 'legal subject', an owner of labour-power, free to exchange this labour-power in return for a wage as a nominally equal party with the capitalist, the owner of the means of production.[18]

The 'legal subject' is a 'mask' in which socio-economic relations are personified. Behind the 'legal subject' as a possessive individual, one finds the possessor of commodities, the possessor of capital, the possessor of labour-power, and the possessor of land. Property and contract, the two most rudimentary forms of legal relation, presuppose the 'legal subject' as a free and possessive individual. But the process of consuming the commodity of labour-power, bought in an abstract process of exchange like any other commodity, takes place in the depths of the production process. The central function of the legal form—a form of historically specific socio-economic relations, characterised by principles of equality, freedom, and voluntariness—is the obfuscation of the exploitation intrinsic to this production process.

The public legal form—that is, the state form—must be considered together with the socio-economic content of law, the reproduction of which it facilitates. The 'unity of form and content' means that socio-economic changes account for changes in the form of public power. The public legal form plays a crucial role in the reproduction of capitalist relations of production. Ascribing a central role to 'popular sovereignty' and 'the public interest', the public legal form abstracts from the contradictory nature of these relations. Such juridical concepts obfuscate the reality of a class-divided society, contributing to its legitimation and reproduction. Moreover, changes in the public legal form are contingent upon the intensification of socio-economic contradictions. For instance, the welfare state was initially established in response to capital's need for a state that was capable of playing an active role in both the management of economic activity and the reproduction of capitalist society. However, this 'Keynesian compromise' provided 'no means of securing the sustained accumulation

---

Pre-Industrial Europe (CUP 1985); Ellen Meiksins Wood, *The Origin of Capitalism: A Longer View* (Verso 2002).

[18]   See Pashukanis, 'General Theory', 76–81, together with Karl Marx, 'Capital: A Critique of Political Economy—Volume One' [1867] in Karl Marx and Frederick Engels, *Collected Works*, vol 35 (Lawrence & Wishart 1996) 1, 177–186.

of capital', soon becoming 'a barrier to capital' as full employment and rising wages could not counter the tendency of the rate of profit to fall.[19] It was therefore gradually replaced by more 'neoliberal' forms once it could no longer accommodate the relations it had first arisen to reproduce. This development is evidence of the historicity of the state form, which is contingent upon class struggles and socio-economic contradictions. This demonstrates that many-sided analysis of the legal form involves examination of law in its unity with the state and other elements of the superstructure, as well as elements of the socio-economic base. This analysis must be bi-directional, as the legal form develops its own historicity while shaping and being shaped by socio-economic developments.

The legal form and its socio-economic content do not, of course, exist in 'pure' separation in social reality. Only in the field of scientific abstraction can the legal form be separated from its content.[20] In the case of the employment contract, for instance, the legal form (in this case, the contract whereby one party agrees to sell their labour-power to the other in exchange for wages) cannot be separated from the socio-economic content of real exploitative relations. However, distinguishing between form and content at the level of abstract scientific analysis is essential for grasping the role of law (and its emphasis on abstract formalism, as expressed in basic principles of freedom, equality, and property) in reproducing the socio-economic content. The dialectics of legal form and socio-economic content presupposes their internal unity, in the actual relations of capitalist commodity production. Only in the context of such a unity can substantive content give birth to and determine its form.[21]

RELATIVE AUTONOMY

The concept of relative autonomy is crucial for grasping the role of law and the state in a social formation, as well as the relation between class on the one hand and law and the state on the other. The class character and relative autonomy of the state and its laws are intrinsically linked. Relative autonomy is necessary for the state to act as a factor of cohesion and consolidation of class power (the intra-class aspect), as well as for the effective exercise of class rule (the class aspect). As EP Thompson argues in regard to the latter, the essential precondition for the effectiveness of law, in its function as ideology, is that it display an independence from gross manipulation and appear to be just. If the law is obviously unjust or evidently partial, it conceals and legitimises nothing, and therefore contributes nothing to the hegemony of a given class.[22] Further, relative autonomy characterises both the capitalist state (which 'best serves the interests of the capitalist class only when the members of this class do not participate directly in the state apparatus, that is to say when the *ruling class* is not the *politically governing class*')[23] and the law under capitalism (which, according to Engels, must correspond to general

---

[19]   Simon Clarke, *Keynesianism, Monetarism and the Crisis of the State* (Edward Elgar 1988) 354.

[20]   Valentina Lapayeva, *Zitimata Dikaiou sto Kefalaio tou Marx [Issues of Law in Marx's* Capital] (Synchroni Epochi 1982) 55.

[21]   Lapayeva, *Zitimata Dikaiou.*

[22]   EP Thompson, *Whigs and Hunters: The Origin of the Black Act* (first published 1975, Penguin 1990) 263.

[23]   Nicos Poulantzas, 'The Problem of the Capitalist State' [1969] in James Martin (ed), *The Poulantzas Reader: Marxism, Law, and the State* (Verso 2008) 172, 179 (original emphases).

economic conditions and give expression to them in a way that is to some degree internally coherent).[24]

The concept of relative autonomy also preempts any characterisation of the dialectical conception of law and the state as straightforwardly instrumentalist. As I have already argued, classes are not metaphysical subjects producing superstructural objects. The relation between class on the one hand and law and the state on the other is not one of unilateral action of subject upon object. The state and its laws *objectively* function to reproduce the relations of production for the benefit of the capitalist class. This constitutes their class character. It also means that changes to relations of production and class struggle processes—that is, the intensification of socio-economic contradictions—may lead to modifications of the state and its legal order. These processes can only be understood through the relative autonomy of state and law from socio-economic contradictions. Relative autonomy allows the state and law to be responsive to the intensification of socio-economic contradictions and to fulfil their function in a social formation more effectively.

It would be wrong to assume that the function of the state is a purely 'negative' one, as if it were restricted solely to reflecting bourgeois interests in their immediate appearance. The state 'also acts in a positive fashion, *creating, transforming and making* reality'.[25] In other words, law 'does not only deceive and conceal, and nor does it merely repress people by compelling or forbidding them to act. It also organises and sanctions certain *real rights* of the dominated classes ... and it has inscribed within it the material concessions imposed on the dominant classes by popular struggle'.[26] The problem of the state and law's 'positive' function (in the form of labour legislation, the welfare state's social programmes, or even court decisions upholding the rights and interests of members of the dominated classes) has been an especially challenging problem for Marxist analysis of law and the state. The crucial question is whether the state loses its class character when it, say, regulates the working day through legislation. Is it justifiable to claim that such laws, which in their immediate appearance seem to serve the interests of the working class, also respond to the need—perhaps not immediately evident, but more vital still on that account—to reproduce a class-divided society?

Legal protection of social rights for the toiling classes is proof of the relatively autonomous nature of bourgeois law. However, the protection of such rights can be explained by the contradictory nature of capitalist society. Rights that until recently were taken for granted in many jurisdictions (e.g., the eight-hour working day, decent working conditions, rights of collective bargaining) were won through hard-fought battles, organised struggles, and co-ordinated strikes and protests. These struggles were gradually reflected in bourgeois law. Indeed, even strike action, the chief weapon of working-class struggle, came to be protected through legislation (and in certain jurisdictions even in constitutional instruments). Strike action, born as a means for workers to struggle for the improvement of their working and living conditions, was criminalised in many jurisdictions during the nineteenth century. In Greece, strike actions were declassified as a criminal offence in 1920.[27] Under pressure from the popular struggle

---

[24]   Engels to Schmidt, 60–61.
[25]   Poulantzas, *State, Power, Socialism*, 30 (original emphasis).
[26]   Poulantzas, *State, Power, Socialism*, 84 (original emphasis).
[27]   See Law No. 211/1920. See further C Sevastidis, *To Dikaioma Apergias kai o Dikastikos Elenchos Askisis tou* [*The Right to Strike and the Judicial Review of its Exercise*] (Sakkoulas 2015) 7;

that overthrew the military dictatorship in 1974, the right to strike was recognised in the 1975 Greek Constitution.

Notwithstanding the limitations that always accompany the enshrinement of social rights in a constitutional text,[28] it is undeniable that the bourgeois state and its laws may under certain conditions reflect the interests of the working class. However, this does not mean that the state is thereby cleansed of its class character, since a state may reflect the immediate interests of the working class to a certain degree while still reflecting the general and overriding strategic interests of the ruling class. For instance, it is safe to argue that the lengthening of the working day (for the production of absolute surplus value) and the rise in intensity of labour exploitation (for the production of relative surplus value) are in the immediate interest of the capitalist class. However, as Marx showed in his analysis of the English Factory Acts in *Capital*, restricting the length of the working day so as not to exhaust the worker, and thereby securing the conditions for the reproduction of their labour-power, is also in the interest of capital, in a broader strategic sense. For Marx the English Factory Acts are not only 'positive', in the sense of introducing significant improvements in working conditions, but also 'negative', in the sense of expressing capital's 'greed for surplus labour' and 'blind eagerness for plunder'.[29]

The same point can be made, *mutatis mutandis*, about labour law, and the welfare state in general. The welfare state was in the strategic interests of capital, helping to reproduce capitalism by absorbing socialist and social-democratic pressures and facilitating sustained capital accumulation after the Second World War. Welfarism also proved to be a useful weapon in the political and ideological battle to contain the advance of international working-class movements. The state's relatively autonomous character is what enables it to perform its class function effectively, promoting the strategic interests of capital even when it appears to concede certain rights to the dominated classes. One could also argue that Poulantzas' engagement with the problem of the state's 'positive' measures is what leads him to define the state as 'a relation, or more precisely as the condensate of a relation of power between struggling classes'.[30] Rejecting the instrumentalist conception of the state as a mere tool of capital, Poulantzas concludes that the state should, 'like capital', be understood as 'a relationship of forces, or more precisely the material condensation of such a relationship among classes and class fractions'.[31] This view of the state, characteristic of the Eurocommunist current that runs counter to the Marxist-Leninist view of the state, has been influential in the abandonment of revolutionary commitments by western European communist parties. Ultimately, Poulantzas' view of the state reproduces the same bourgeois-instrumentalist views against which structuralists have

---

Ntina Tzouvala, 'Continuity and Rupture in Restraining the Right to Strike' in Honor Brabazon (ed), *Neoliberal Legality: Understanding the Role of Law in the Neoliberal Project* (Routledge 2017) 119.

[28] As Marx notes with regard to the 1848 French Constitution, each of the freedoms it recognised was protected as an inalienable right of French citizens, but 'always with the marginal note that it is unlimited so far as it is not limited by the '*equal rights of others and the public safety*''. See Karl Marx, 'The Eighteenth Brumaire of Louis Napoleon' [1852] in Karl Marx and Frederick Engels, *Collected Works*, vol 11 (Lawrence & Wishart 1979) 99, 114 (original emphasis). For instance, the constitutional protection of the right to strike in the current Constitution of Turkey is subject to the restriction that it not be exercised 'in a manner contrary to the rules of goodwill, to the detriment of society, and in a manner damaging national wealth' (art 54).

[29] Marx, 'Capital', 247.

[30] Nicos Poulantzas, 'The Capitalist State: A Reply to Miliband and Laclau' [1976] in James Martin (ed), *The Poulantzas Reader: Marxism, Law and the State* (Verso 2008) 270, 283.

[31] Poulantzas, *State, Power, Socialism*, 128 (de-emphasised from original).

warned.[32] This is a position that distorts the category of relative autonomy, effectively merging it with the idea that the state is 'class-neutral'. The relative autonomy of law and the state may thus be utilised by theorists of reformist persuasion to promote a false perception of law and the state as 'class-neutral' mechanisms.

In response, the inadequacies of defining the state simply as a 'material condensation of the relationship between classes' need to be noted. The crucial question here is as follows: If the state is the condensate of a shifting relation of social forces, does this mean that the state is indifferent to the struggle between these forces? Is it neutral with respect to this struggle? This question has been answered in a way that qualifies Poulantzas' definition:

> Any correlation of forces contains, with the exception of transitional historical periods, a *dominant component*. It ultimately contains the socio-economic and political component which holds the *monopoly of power at both economic and political levels*. As a result, any reflection of the correlation of forces on the legal superstructure finds its *absolute limit* in this: it cannot supersede the fundamental component, i.e. the ruling class, its state, and its legal system. Any integrated legislative conquests of the subordinate classes are always secondary.[33]

As erroneous as it is to assume that law and the state are mere reflections of ruling-class interests, it is equally erroneous to conclude that either shed their class character upon assuming a liberal or democratic form, or with the adoption of 'positive' measures on behalf of the working class. The state assumes different forms based upon the concrete level of intensification of socio-economic contradictions (i.e., class struggle and intra-class conflict). Nevertheless, these forms accommodate the vital role of the state in reproducing class rule and the conditions of capital accumulation. More sharply, to argue that the state is the material condensation of class struggle is accurate only insofar as the state is first understood as a *class state*, one that contributes to the reproduction of the capitalist mode of production. Such a class state is not designed to reflect the interests of the dominated classes, at least not fully. This would undermine its role in reproducing capitalist social relations.

Similarly, to argue that adherence to the 'rule of law' may cleanse the law of its class content is to disregard, among other things, the availability of ample emergency provisions in actually existing constitutional systems, as well as the intimate relation between constitutional norms and their various exceptions. The principle of the 'rule of law' captures a form of public power different from the arbitrary decision-making of absolute monarchies and dictatorial governments. However, the fact that constitutional-democratic states exercise their public power in the name of the 'rule of law' does not negate the fact that '[t]he State often transgresses law-rules of its own making by acting without reference to the law, but also by acting directly against it'.[34]

Celebrations of the 'rule of law', such as Thompson's claim that it represents 'a cultural achievement of universal significance',[35] need to be avoided in favour of concrete analyses

---

[32]   Ellen Meiksins Wood, *The Retreat from Class: A New 'True' Socialism* (Verso 1986); Colin Barker, 'A "New" Reformism? A Critique of the Political Theory of Nicos Poulantzas' (1979) 2 *International Socialism*, https://www.marxists.org/history/etol/writers/barker-c/1979/xx/poulantzas.htm accessed 7 April 2021.

[33]   Dimitrios Kaltsonis, *Dikaio, Koinonia, Takseis* [*State, Society, Classes*] (Synchroni Epochi 2005) 31 (original emphases).

[34]   Poulantzas, *State, Power, Socialism*, 84.

[35]   Thompson, *Whigs and Hunters*, 265.

that approach the juridical and the political as forms within a larger social totality. If the law and the state are relatively autonomous on account of their class character, it follows that the more formal, general, and codified a juridical state structure happens to be, the more effectively it will fulfil its class function, 'by virtue of the formal, abstract liberty and equality that it crystallizes and the calculability that is grafted onto them'.[36] In other words, the more abstract and relatively autonomous a juridical state structure is, the more likely it is that it will be able to accommodate the intensification of socio-economic contradictions.

CLASS FUNCTION

Thus far I have argued that the state's relatively autonomous character is essential to its class function, as its contribution to the reproduction of capitalism objectively promotes the interests of the dominant class. The category of 'reproduction' is central to understanding the dialectic between the socio-economic base and the juridico-political superstructure. Base and superstructure are distinct elements of a unity in which the superstructure helps to establish and maintain the conditions under which capitalist exploitation is carried out and relations of production are reproduced.[37] Consequently, a social formation dominated by the capitalist mode of production endures so long as the conditions of capitalist production endure; the conditions of capitalist production endure so long as capitalist relations of production continue to be reproduced; and, finally, capitalist relations of production continue to be reproduced so long as the juridico-political superstructure continues to facilitate their reproduction. In order for this 'topographical representation' not to be rendered as a formalistic schema, law, the state, and ideology must be understood as distinct aspects of a larger social unity. These aspects cannot exist in a pure state, nor can they be separated in actuality. The interdependence of legal, political, and ideological phenomena must be analysed.

Althusser argued that law's function is not simply to ensure the reproduction of capitalist relations of production, but also, and more directly, to ensure the *operation* of capitalist relations of production.[38] In performing this function, law may be understood to exhibit three characteristics. The first such characteristic is systematicity: law takes on the form of a system that aspires to internal consistency, so that contradictions may be minimised or concealed, as well as comprehensiveness, so that it may cover a wide range of different cases. The second characteristic is formalism: law's formalism abstracts from the content of what is exchanged. The third is the repressive nature of law: law always and necessarily presupposes the existence of an effective system of disciplinary power. This implies not merely the existence of penal law but also of public law, a codified system of relations between different institutions regulating the creation, application, and interpretation of legal rules and instruments. This framework is central to Althusser's analysis of capitalist society. Althusser warns against subjectivist interpretations of the relation between law and class power. He claims that 'certain Marxists,

---

[36]   Nicos Poulantzas, 'Marxist Examination of the Contemporary State and Law and the Question of the "Alternative"' [1964] in James Martin (ed), *The Poulantzas Reader: Marxism, Law and the State* (Verso 2008) 25, 40.

[37]   Louis Althusser, *On the Reproduction of Capitalism: Ideology and Ideological State Apparatuses* (firs published 1995, GM Goshgarian tr, Verso 2014) 93.

[38]   Althusser, *On the Reproduction of Capitalism*, 169.

and by no means the least of them, have "fallen" to the wrong side of the path on the ridge by presenting the state as a *mere instrument* of domination and repression in the service of *objectives*, that is, of the dominant class's *conscious will*'.[39] This, he writes, reflects 'a bourgeois, instrumentalist-idealist conception of the state reinforced by a bourgeois idealist (humanist) conception of social classes as "subjects"'.[40]

Althusser is correct in rejecting a metaphysical conception of the state as a mere instrument of domination. And social classes should not be understood in a metaphysical sense, as unified subjects, not least because dialectical-materialist analysis of the relation between class power and state authority must explain the presence of conflicting tendencies within the same class. However, since they occupy specific places within the larger system of relations of production, classes have objective interests on the basis of which they are capable of acting as agents of production. It is precisely these interests that are protected through law and the state.

This has certain implications. On the one hand, class and intra-class contradictions need to be examined closely through concrete analyses of concrete situations. The state's role in capitalist society, specifically its role in reproducing relations of production, cannot be fulfilled unless it is relatively autonomous and gives expression to the class struggle. On the other hand, the economic power of the capitalist class, the class that owns the means of production and appropriates surplus value for the purpose of accumulating capital, is consolidated and expressed in the form of the state. Consequently, law is best understood as *class law*, and the state as *class state*. Yet (class) law and the (class) state reflect class struggle, as is evident, for instance, in the different forms with which the ruling class exercises its power under different socio-historical conditions. The different forms of state power showcase the state's relative autonomy, demonstrating that it reflects the class struggle and the degree of intensity of social contradictions.

A related claim that has been made against the dialectical-materialist analysis of law and the state is that there is no necessary link between class interest on the one hand and legislation and judicial interpretation on the other. Such claims overemphasise the relatively autonomous character of law in order to sever the objective relation between law and class power. This relation is not automatic or unmediated. The class origins of a judge or a state official are not, for instance, absolutely determinant of a decision they make or a rule they choose to apply. Instead, the relation between law and class power is objective and dialectical.[41] In order to illustrate this point, let me return to the example of the right to strike. The class function of law manifests in a number of different ways. It first manifests in the form of legislation that restricts the exercise of a right of vital importance for the working class. In the aftermath of the 2007–08 global financial crisis, the right to strike was restricted through legislation across Europe, following the European Union's 'best practice' legal principles. In Greece, Article 211 of Act 4512/2018 limits the exercise of the right to strike by setting a requirement for a 50 per cent turnout of union-registered members. This measure follows the 'best practice' already

---

[39]   Althusser, *On the Reproduction of Capitalism*, 72 (original emphases).
[40]   Althusser, *On the Reproduction of Capitalism*, 72.
[41]   This point is made well by Poulantzas, who argues that the relation between the bourgeois class and the state is an objective relation, and that while different members of the state apparatus have different class origins, these origins recede into the background in relation to their class position within the apparatus. This means that their objective function is the actualisation of the power of the capitalist class. Nicos Poulantzas, 'The Problem of the Capitalist State' [1969] in James Martin (ed), *The Poulantzas Reader: Marxism, Law and the State* (Verso 2008) 172, 178–79.

applied in the United Kingdom. According to section 2 of the UK Trade Union Act 2016, a 50 per cent turnout of those entitled to vote is required for a decision to undertake industrial action to be legally valid.

The class function of law may also manifest in an interpretation of the law that actually restricts the exercise of the right in question. For instance, the Greek courts, based on a *contra legem* interpretation that finds exercise of the right to strike legitimate only if it is the measure of last resort, have displaced the relevant constitutional provision, and thus rendered it ineffective.[42] As a result, from 2009 to 2014, out of 300 judicial decisions on the legality of strike actions, 88 per cent were declared illegal and only 8 per cent legal.[43] Last but not least, the class function of judicial interpretation might operate in more subtle ways. The European Court of Human Rights' conception of the right to strike has been criticised on the grounds that it disempowers trade union movements, depoliticising their activity and encouraging members to understand the right to strike 'in ways that are ultimately compatible with the maintenance of capitalist social relations'.[44] In part, this is the result of viewing trade union activity through the individualising lens of 'freedom of association'.[45]

From a different angle, 'post-Marxist' theorists have critiqued Marxist analyses of the relation between class power and law and the state. Classes, they argue, are not to be found readymade and already in existence, but instead need 'to be produced through political activities'.[46] This view, exemplified by Ernesto Laclau and Chantal Mouffe's *Hegemony and Socialist Strategy*, is 'grounded in privileging the moment of *political* articulation'.[47] A class is 'created' by the consciousness and political practices of its members. From a dialectical standpoint, Laclau and Mouffe conflate two different processes. The first is the process of developing relations of production, which results in the development of different class positions for different groups—a process manifested, for instance, in the proletarianisation of previously self-employed social strata. The second is the process of achieving class consciousness. These two processes are intertwined, and the relation between them is similar to the one between *dynamis* and *energeia* (in Aristotelian terms) or between the 'in itself' and the 'for itself' (in Hegelian terms). As a result, Laclau and Mouffe's 'anti-essentialism' is intelligible only if understood to mean that classes are not predetermined metaphysical subjects. The issue of class consciousness is related dialectically to this point, but such consciousness is not constitutive of a given class' relation to the means of production. On the contrary, for Laclau and Mouffe, any connections between different social groups need to be 'politically articulated'. Beyond this 'articulatory practice', there are no social interconnections. This is arguably an idealist position.[48]

---

[42]   Sevastidis, *To Dikaioma Apergias*, 131–33.

[43]   Sevastidis, *To Dikaioma Apergias,* 9.

[44]   Robert Knox, 'A Marxist Approach to *R.M.T. v the United Kingdom*' in Damian Gonzalez-Salzberg, and Loveday Hodson (eds), *Research Methodologies for International Human Rights Law: Beyond the Traditional Paradigm* (Routledge 2019) 13, 26–27.

[45]   See esp. art 11 of the European Convention of Human Rights.

[46]   Robert Bocock, *Hegemony* (Routledge 1987) 103.

[47]   Ernesto Laclau and Chantal Mouffe, *Hegemony and Socialist Strategy: Towards a Radical Democratic Politics* (Verso 1986) x (original emphasis).

[48]   For a critical reading, according to which Laclau and Mouffe reduce Marxism to a few dogmatic absolutes by presenting it on the basis of absolute distinctions, see Norman Geras, 'Post-Marxism?' (1987) 163 *New Left Review* 40.

Marxist approaches accept that classes exist independent of consciousness, and that they are not unified subjects but instead replete with intra-class contradictions. From a Marxist standpoint, class struggle in a capitalist society, at a high level of abstraction, is carried out between two principal classes: capitalists and workers. However, a comprehensive class analysis must take into account not just the two main classes, but also intermediate strata as well as different fractions within these classes. The concept of class struggle is an essential element of the dialectical analysis of law and the state. The intense class struggle around the legislation on the length of the working day reveals the clash of antagonistic classes beneath the 'voluntary' legal relations into which 'free' and 'equal' individuals enter. As Marx famously put it, '[b]etween equal rights force decides'.[49]

Intensification of class struggle may result in the inability of specific state forms to accommodate the reproduction of contradictory capitalist relations. This may mean that 'normal', or 'liberal', forms of decision-making may be replaced by exceptional or authoritarian forms. As specific social forms, a given 'norm' and its 'exceptions' correspond to different historical conditions and different levels of intensification of social contradictions. Both 'norm' and 'exception' serve the purpose of reproducing property and productive relations, albeit with different means and in difference circumstances, the specificity of which has to be examined for the change in form to be explained.

Viewed in this light, class struggle consists of two elements: contradictions between the dominant and dominated classes; and contradictions between different fractions of each class, particularly the dominant class. The state and its laws depend on both class and intra-class struggles. The state consolidates bourgeois rule and ensures its reproduction by unifying the different fractions of the dominant class, against both its common enemies and centrifugal tendencies.

CONCLUSION

Returning to the question posed at the outset of this chapter, how is one to understand the fact that in January 2018 a 'left-wing' government in Greece pushed through laws restricting the right to strike? First, the contradiction between formal equality and material inequality needs to be borne in mind. Labour law under capitalism is a set of rules and mechanisms that purport to ameliorate material inequalities and rectify power imbalances between employer and employee. Second, social rights, like all rights, both mediate and reflect social struggles. The right to strike, as a right, was secured through bloody and protracted class struggles. The working class and associated popular forces must fight for the right to strike, as they have done for decades, since it is an essential tool in the struggle for better working conditions. Third, Marxist analysis helps to explain the limits of rights-oriented struggles under capitalism, particularly the limited protection afforded by the capitalist state to the working class. So long as capitalist relations of production are reproduced, the rights of the toiling classes are subject to arbitrary suspension or even outright elimination, because of capital's need to ensure profitability and respond to crises.

---

[49]   Marx, 'Capital', 243.

The Greek labour movement has for many years, and especially in recent years, used the slogan, 'the worker's justice is the law'. How should one understand this normative statement, and how is real effect to be given to it? Based on the analysis I have provided in this chapter, it could be argued that the normative content of 'worker's justice' can never find expression in bourgeois law. The bourgeois state may regulate the working day. It may also recognise positive legal rights and freedoms for the exploited classes, such as the right to strike. But the capitalist state, as the condensation of a relation of forces, is neither indifferent to nor neutral concerning the struggle of those forces. Attesting to this is the fact that between 2009 and 2014, years of intensified class struggle in Greece, 249 out of the 285 strikes that were scrutinised by the courts for their legality were held to be illegal and abusive. It is precisely in this sense that Marxist theory may contribute to the supersession of capitalism, playing a meaningful role as a theory of praxis in the class-conscious movement that gives effect to the normative statement, 'the worker's justice *must be* the law'.

Index

Germany, in 55–7
United States, in 38, 54–6
emancipatory potential, limitations on 237
liberal democracy, conflicts with 41, 59
private property, conflicts with 35–6, 38–40
slavery abolition, and 54
universities 338
disciplinary fetishism 338–40
use-value 285
utopia
neoliberalism, and 482–3
Russian Revolution, and 78–9
utopophobia 521
utopian socialism 482–3, 519–20

Vaculik, Ludvik 525
vagabondage 25, 91, 301–2
value
abstract value 118–20
capitalist social relations, role in 193–4
commodities, use-value of 118–20, 461–2
exchange-value 285
labour-power, of 23, 25, 193, 285–6
Marxist theory of 275–6
money as universal measure of 118, 193–4
surplus value 23–5
unwaged labour 285–6
use-value 285
value form 1, 115, 122, 125, 255, 533
Venezuela 431, 433
Versailles Peace Conference 312
Vietnam 348
violence
economic violence 446
political tactics, role in 6, 8–9, 14–20
property regime, relationship with 547–8
riots 244–5
Vitalpolitik 278–9
Vogel, Lise 287
voluntarism 28–9, 159, 175–6
voluntarist theory of law 29–30, 159
Vyshinsky, Andrey 96

wages
conflicts of interest 23
gender wage gap 293
unwaged labour 283–8, 291–3, 297–8
wage contracts 149, 404–5, 409–10
wage dependence 31–2
wage stagnation 423
wage suppression 446
Wages for Housework 283
war 39, 431
demilitarisation, and 436–8
Paris Commune 235–9, 340

US Civil War 52–4, 58–9, 302, 314, 503
war of manoeuvre 146
war of position 144, 146, 148
wealth, distribution of 362–3, 371–2, 425, 520, 524
Weber, Max 12, 176, 185, 303, 319, 321
Weeks, Kathi 417, 419
Weinrib, Ernest 500
Weir, Stan 413–14
welfare state
employment benefits 316–17, 551
historical development 316–17
housing 505–7
neoliberal approaches 483–4, 487–8, 505–8
nomocracy *vs.* teleocracy in 483–4
pregnancy and maternity benefits 316
public interest, role of 485–6
welfarism
capitalism, relationship between 316–17, 351, 551
West Bank 99–100
Western Europe
Greece 394, 397, 544, 551, 554–7
Italy 16, 140–41, 286, 329, 381, 394
revolutionary trends 551–2
see also France; Germany
western hemisphere
labour inequalities 295
social reproduction theory 295
Western Marxism
Bauer 99, 106
development, influences on 336, 460–61
international law, on 342–3
Kautsky 7–8, 15, 77, 498, 504
Luxemburg 7, 15, 32, 460
see also Frankfurt School; Gramsci, Antonio
White, Hayden 452
White Terror 92–3
Whyte, David 143
Wilson, Woodrow 102, 109, 354
Winstanley, Gerard 39
Wisconsin 256–9
'withering away' thesis
bourgeois state, of 77–8, 82–3, 461–2, 513
commodity-form theory of law 126–7, 133–7, 461–2, 513
women
Bolshevik emancipation of 85–6, 314
care work, gender inequality 283, 287–8, 291–6
economic empowerment 291–2, 298
labour exploitation of 295–7, 314
labour inequality 283
marriage, rights under 84–5
#MeToo movement 147